INTRODUCTION TO
SOCIAL
PSYCHOLOGY

INTRODUCTION TO SOCIAL PSYCHOLOGY

Richard A. Lippa

California State University, Fullerton

Brooks/Cole Publishing Company
Pacific Grove, California

I**T**P ™ The trademark ITP is used under license.

Brooks/Cole Publishing Company
A Division of Wadsworth, Inc.

Printed in the United States of America
10 9 8 7 6 5 4 3 2

Library of Congress Cataloging-in-Publication Data
Lippa, Richard A.
    Introduction to social psychology / Richard A. Lippa. — 2nd ed.
        p.   cm.
    Includes bibliographical references and index.
    ISBN 0-534-17388-8
    1. Social psychology.   I. Title.
HM251.L49   1994
302—dc20   93-35816
                                                                 CIP

Sponsoring Editor: *Marianne Taflinger*
Project Development Editors: *John Bergez and Eileen Murphy*
Marketing Representative: *JoAnn Ludovici*
Editorial Assistant: *Virge Perelli-Minetti*
Production Editor: *Penelope Sky*
Production Service: *Bookman Productions*
Manuscript Editor: *Anne Montague*
Permissions Editor: *May Clark*
Interior Design: *Paula Goldstein*
Cover Design: *E. Kelly Shoemaker*
Cover Illustration: *Diana Ong/SuperStock*
Interior Illustration: *Judith Ogus*
Photo Researcher: *Gail Meese/Meese Photo Research*
Indexer: *James Minkin*
Typesetting: *Graphic World, Inc.*
Cover Printing: *Phoenix Color Corporation*
Printing and Binding: *R.R. Donnelley & Sons Company/Crawfordsville*

To all students of social psychology

BRIEF CONTENTS

CONTENTS

3 PERSONALITY AND THE SELF   65

4 PERCEIVING OTHERS   115

5   THINKING ABOUT OTHERS   157

6   ATTITUDES AND ATTITUDE CHANGE   210

7 PREJUDICE   270

10 AGGRESSION: HURTING OTHERS   428

14 SOCIAL PSYCHOLOGY AND HEALTH   642

15 SOCIAL PSYCHOLOGY AND THE ENVIRONMENT   685

16   SOCIAL PSYCHOLOGY AND THE LAW   731

PREFACE

Here is the credo that guided my work on the second edition of *Introduction to Social Psychology.*

1. I take social psychology seriously and so I have written a book that takes social psychology seriously and encourages students to do the same.
2. I think social psychology is a fascinating and exciting field and so I have written a book that invites students to share my fascination and excitement.
3. I think social psychology is highly relevant to everyday life and so I have written a book that continually links the two.

As I noted in the preface to the first edition, social psychology is very engaging, yet it is a difficult field to survey in an introductory text. Its central topics—social perception, attitudes and attitude change, prejudice, attraction, aggression, prosocial behavior, influence, and group behavior—are the stuff of daily headlines and of great interest to students. Social psychology also includes a sometimes bewildering collection of topics, theories, and informationally dense empirical studies. The ideal social psychology text must be well-organized, cohesive, comprehensive, clear, and engrossing. In addition, it must speak directly to students, inform them about their everyday social behavior, and help them understand the turbulent, ever-changing, multicultural world in which they live.

THE SECOND EDITION

Some topics treated in separate chapters in the first edition have been combined. For example, because social cognition and attribution are so intertwined we combined them in one chapter, "Thinking about Others"; similarly, "Beliefs and Attitudes" and "Persuasion and Attitude Change" are combined as "Attitudes and Attitude Change." To emphasize the relevance of social psychology to daily life, we added two new chapters, "Social Psychology and the Environment" and "Social Psychology and the Law," which significantly expand the applied content of the text. Including Chapter 14, "Social Psychology and Health," the final chapters illuminate the process of applying social psychology to specific areas of research; readers will also appreciate the many substantive findings in health, environmental, and legal psychology.

Research

The second edition preserves the links between current research and the history of social psychology as a field and the history of the world at large. A good mix of classic and contemporary studies is woven into the narrative flow so the reader understands *why* social psychologists study certain topics and *how* research evolves. This emphasis helps students understand current trends in social psychological research. For example, in Chapter 4, "Perceiving Others," I trace the development of research into the accuracy of person perception; in Chapter 6, "Attitudes and Attitude Change," classic and contemporary work on the functions of attitudes are discussed; Chapter 7, "Prejudice," includes research on the authoritarian personality and contemporary critiques of that research; Sherif's classic contributions to conformity research are presented in Chapter 12, "Conformity, Compliance, and Obedience"; and Chapter 13, "Groups," covers classic early work on dimensions of group behavior and styles of leadership.

Theory and Methodology

Chapter 1, "What Is Social Psychology?" contains a brief account of four major theoretical perspectives in social psychology that are developed in full in later chapters. Both Chapter 1 and Chapter 2, "Answering Questions about Social Behavior," cover the role of theory in social psychological research. Chapter 2 includes a number of topics not usually found in introductory texts: meta-analysis, internal and external validity in experiments, quasi-experimental designs, and a nontechnical discussion of the statistical significance of research findings.

Nonmethodological issues introduced in Chapter 2 also reappear in later chapters. For example, in Chapter 3, "Personality and the Self," and Chapter 6, "Attitudes and Attitude Change," the concepts of reliability and validity are developed. In later chapters, the distinction between correlational and experimental studies is reinforced with substantive research examples. Chapter 8, "Gender and Social Behavior," includes the meta-analytic techniques used in research on sex differences, a substantive example of a topic that is first discussed in Chapter 2.

Special Features

Accounts of *dramatic current events* replace the literary examples used as chapter openers in the first edition, demonstrating the daily relevance of social psychology. Chapter 4, "Perceiving Others," begins with a brief account of the Senate hearings that pitted Clarence Thomas against Anita Hill. This example naturally generates questions about the nature and accuracy of person perception. Chapter 5,

"Thinking about Others," begins with Magic Johnson's revelation that he was infected with the HIV virus, a story that serves as an entree to such broader questions as "How does new information affect our impressions of others?" and "How do we process information about other people?" Chapter 6, "Attitudes and Attitude Change," begins with excerpts from Adfolf Hitler's *Mein Kampf* and traces his legacy in statements made by modern neo-Nazis. The stage is thus set for the basic questions, "What are attitudes, and what roles do they play in everyday life?" Chapter 11, "Helping Others," begins with the rescue of truck driver Reginald Denny by bystanders during the Los Angeles riots of 1992; Chapter 16, "Social Psychology and the Law," uses as its central example the trial of four Los Angeles police officers for the beating of Rodney King. Because these examples are so gripping, they serve not only to engage student readers but to stimulate many passionate classroom discussions as well.

Special sections that are part of the ongoing narrative flow increase readers' involvement. *Multicultural Perspectives* examine cross-cultural findings in social psychology. For example, in Chapter 3, "Personality and the Self," this section is about the ways in which the contents of the self vary across cultures. In Chapter 5, "Thinking about Others," the feature is concerned with whether the fundamental attribution error occurs in all cultures. In Chapter 7, "Prejudice," the similarities and differences between authoritarianism in the United States and in Russia are examined; in Chapter 8, "Gender and Social Behavior," we consider how gender differences in self-esteem vary across cultures; and in Chapter 15, "Social Psychology and the Environment," the section is about how members of various cultures differ in their use of personal space. In the matching feature, *Social Psychology in Everyday Life*, research findings are applied to the real world. For example, in Chapter 4, "Perceiving Others,"this section is concerned with how accurately such professionals as police officers can detect deception; in Chapter 5, "Thinking about Others," it covers misattribution theories for depression and text anxiety; and in Chapter 13, "Groups," the effectiveness of brainstorming groups is considered.

Additional Pedagogical Features

Chapter outlines are keyed to *chapter summaries*, and complete *chapter glossaries* are included as well. Special *summary tables* for each chapter contain research findings, presenting an overview of a particular area. The summary tables reiterate important terms and concepts, organize material conceptually, and serve as convenient study aids. They also familiarize students with the numerous technical terms used by social psychologists. For example, in Chapter 5, "Thinking about Others," the table reinforces various concepts in attribution theory: correspondent inferences, Kelly's cube model, the discounting principle, the fundamental attribution error, correspondence bias, the actor—observor effect, misattribution, and so on. Numerous *graphs* clearly illustrate experimental results.

Acknowledgments

The revision of *Introduction to Social Psychology* reflects a huge amount of work by many individuals. This edition took shape under the direction of Wadsworth editor Ken King and was guided to completion by Marianne Taflinger at Brooks/Cole. John Bergez provided early astute developmental assistance before handing the reins to Eileen Murphy. Anne Montague was a copy editor par excellence: her sharp mind and verbal legerdemain improved every chapter. Robin Lockwood amazingly maintained her cheer as she directed production through a blizzard of express mail, faxes, and phone calls. Faith Stoddard coordinated the revision of ancillary material, and May Clark worked good humoredly and efficiently to obtain permissions for all sorts of printed materials.

In the preface to the first edition I acknowledged my two dogs, Seymour (a dachshund) and Puccini (a collie), who in their doggish simplicity provided some perspective to a grinding writing schedule. Puccini passed away last year, but Seymour is still ready to clown around when pressing deadlines draw near. Perhaps book revisions are a bit like life in general: some things pass on, some things live on, and through it all one hopes that the general thrust of evolution is toward improvement.

Richard A. Lippa

REVIEWERS

The quality of any textbook depends on the quality of its reviewers. Mine were among the best, and their ideas and suggestions are incorporated throughout. To each of the following reviewers, thanks. You are, in a very real sense, coauthors.

Robert Bechtel, University of Arizona
Frank Bernieri, Oregon State University
Percy Black, Pace University
Nyla Branscombe, University of Kansas
Jonathan Brown, University of Washington
Richard I. Contrada, Rutgers University
Eric Cooley, Western Oregon State University
Valerie Hans, University of Delaware
Kathleen A. Hoyt, Boise State University
Grace Galliano, Kennesaw State College
Mary Kite, Ball State University
Jon Krosnick, Ohio State University
Richard Leavy, Ohio Wesleyan University
Chris Leone, University of North Florida
Marsha Liss, California State University, San Bernardino
Frank McAndrew, Knox College
Gregory Neidert, Arizona State University
James Newton, San Francisco State University
David Roskos-Ewoldsen, Corr University of Alabama
Kathryn Ryan, Lycoming College
Delia Saenz, Arizona State University
R. Lance Shotlund, Pennsylvania State University
Stephen Slane, Cleveland State University
Vaida Thompson, University of North Carolina
Alan Tomkins, University of Nebraska
Bernard Whitley, Ball State University

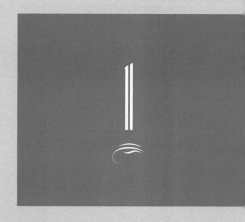

WHAT IS SOCIAL PSYCHOLOGY?

The agony of Yugoslavia keeps replaying itself with new bombardments, massacres, rapes, and "ethnic cleansings." At each horrifying recurrence, world opinion is outraged and opinion leaders call for an end to the barbarism.

. . . The war is about religious differences as well as territory and politics; it involves Serbian Orthodox, Bosnian Muslims and Croat Catholics. Serb militias now occupy 70% of Bosnia and Herzegovina, leaving only Sarajevo and isolated pockets in the hands of Bosnia's mainly Muslim government. Among the most desperate are the besieged Muslim towns in eastern Bosnia, near the frontier with Serbia.

—*Time,* March 15, 1993

A United Nations convoy transports Muslim refugees from a besieged town in Bosnia.

The Cold War is over, and American leaders have spoken of "a new world order." But the agony of Yugoslavia has proved beyond a doubt that the world is still a very troubled place. The brutal fighting among Serbs, Croats, and Bosnians has deep and complex origins: The passing of Yugoslav communist leader Marshal Tito in 1980 and the fall of the Soviet empire in 1989 took the lid off ethnic and religious tensions that had been seething for hundreds of years. At first, leaders of the Yugoslav republics attempted to negotiate with one another, but fighting started despite all their efforts to reach a diplomatic solution. As the armed conflict escalated to greater and greater levels of brutality, hope for a quick resolution faded. The outside world has been watching the growing carnage in dismay and trying to decide how, or even whether, to intervene.

SOCIAL BEHAVIOR AND THE YUGOSLAV CONFLICT

The situation in Yugoslavia is a tragic drama involving ethnic pride and prejudice, politics, economics, and military strategy. It is also a drama in which people constantly interact with other people. Indeed, the Yugoslav conflict prompts many questions about human interactions and the complexities of social behavior:

Question: Why do people behave aggressively?

The fighting in Yugoslavia has been savage beyond belief. What motivates seemingly decent people to brutally murder their former countrymen? More

The grim face of war: A civilian cycles past U.N. peace-keeping forces in Bosnia.

generally, why are people so aggressive? What leads to war, and are there ways to make people less violent?

Question: Why do people help others?

The United States and other nations have tried to provide aid to the suffering civilians of Yugoslavia. The United Nations has been delivering humanitarian aid such as food and medical supplies to the war victims. Why is this aid being sent? Is it the result of compassion and altruism, or are there more practical and calculated reasons for offering help?

Questions: What is the nature of public opinion? Where do attitudes come from, and what changes them?

The excerpt from *Time* magazine that starts this chapter notes that with each new reported atrocity in Yugoslavia, world opinion was "outraged" and opinion leaders called for "an end to the barbarism." But what is "world opinion," and how does it influence the behavior of nations and their citizens? On a more personal level, how do our attitudes and opinions influence our individual actions?

Chances are, several years ago you did not have strong attitudes toward "Serbs" and "Croatians." Today, it's much more likely that you do. Where did your attitudes come from?

Questions: When do people obey their leaders? When don't they?

Serbs, under the leadership of Slobodan Milosevic, have carried out brutal atrocities. Some commentators have even compared Serbia under Milosevic to Nazi

Germany under Adolf Hitler. By following a brutal leader, the Serbian population has seemed to succumb to a "mass psychosis" fed by prejudice and xenophobia. How did Milosovic come to be so powerful? Why do Serbs follow him?

And as the Yugoslav conflict has grown, Western leaders' attempts to intervene and stop the conflict often have seemed ineffectual. Why has there been such a lack of firm leadership in the West?

More broadly, what is the nature of leadership? When is it effective, and when is it ineffective?

Questions: What causes ethnic prejudice? How can ethnic tensions be reduced?

Yugoslavia is a boiling cauldron of ethnic and religious hatreds. Serbs, Croatians, and Bosnians hold negative stereotypes about each other and nurse bitter grudges that go back centuries into the past. The brutal actions taken by Serbs against other ethnic groups introduced a terrible new term into the vocabulary of the 20th century: "ethnic cleansing." The conflict in Yugoslavia poses perennial questions about human relations: What is the nature of prejudice? Why is it so common? What can be done to reduce it? Is it possible for the different groups in Yugoslavia ever to live together peacefully?

These questions seem to arise almost automatically when we think about the fighting in Yugoslavia. They are exactly the kinds of questions posed by the field of social psychology: How do people affect other people? What is the nature of social influence, helping, attraction, aggression, prejudice, and group behavior? Social psychology is a field that gathers facts and develops theories about just such questions.

DEFINING SOCIAL PSYCHOLOGY

Social psychology, according to one classic definition, represents "an attempt to understand and explain how the thought, feeling, and behavior of individuals are influenced by the actual, imagined, or implied presence of others" (Allport, 1985). The core of this definition is that social psychology studies how people influence people. The topics of conformity, obedience, persuasion and attitude change, and group processes are all clearly related to interpersonal influence. Many of the questions we posed about the Yugoslav conflict focused on various kinds of social influence.

Social psychologists study not only how people influence one another, but also other factors that affect social behavior. For example, anxiety-provoking events like those in Yugoslavia can lead people to seek out others—such as threatened civilians in Yugoslavia who try to be with their family members (see Chapter 9). Our physical environment can affect our friendships (for example, we're more likely to be friends with someone who lives near us; see Chapter 9) and our level of aggression (we're more likely to be aggressive when we're confined in a hot, noisy room; see Chapter

10). Note that these findings lie in the realm of social psychology because they study influences on *social* behavior, even though these influences do not necessarily come from other people.

Explanations of Social Behavior

There is yet another way to define social psychology: through the kinds of explanations it offers for various types of social behavior. Figure 1.1 visually presents the factors that a social scientist might use to explain human behavior, including broad group-level explanations (such as evolutionary and cultural factors), individual-level explanations (such as childhood experiences and family history), and mediating variables—internal factors such as personality traits and attitudes. Social psychologists tend to emphasize some of these explanations more than others.

To illustrate, let's consider a particular kind of social behavior: aggression. What leads people to be aggressive? More specifically, what led to the brutal fighting among Serbs, Croatians, and Bosnians in Yugoslavia? Let's begin to provide possible answers to these questions by looking first at the top level of Figure 1.1, group-level explanations. To understand human aggression, it may be useful to examine the *biological groups* to which we belong: mammals, primates, and, of course, our species, *Homo sapiens*. Clearly, Siamese fighting fish and laboratory rats show patterns of aggression different from those of human beings; some of these differences are biologically based. Organized warfare, for example, seems to be a uniquely human activity. Do you think the tensions and resulting aggression in Yugoslavia (and in most other countries as well) could be due in part to evolutionary factors? For example, is it possible that people have evolved with a tendency to be more aggressive to "outsiders" than to their "own kind"?

Human aggression is also influenced by *cultural and social groups*. Some societies, like that of the Arapesh of New Guinea, are reported to be quite peaceful and cooperative, whereas others, like that of the Mundugumor (also of New Guinea), are reported to be dominating and aggressive (Mead, 1935). Although most societies show some degree of violence and aggression, absolute levels can vary dramatically across different cultures. In the late 1980s the United States reported 8.5 homicides per 100,000 people, Canada reported 1.9, and Great Britain reported only .6 (*Demographic Yearbook of the United Nations*, 1991; see Chapter 10). Why these differences? It seems likely that cultural and sociological factors, not biology, are responsible. To return to our example of aggression in Yugoslavia, it might be attributable in part to cultural attitudes toward violence.

Each individual's unique *heredity and physiology* may affect aggression. For example, there is evidence that males, perhaps in part because of the effects of testosterone (a male hormone), are on average more aggressive than females (Eagly & Steffen, 1986b; Maccoby & Jacklin, 1974). Furthermore, men with high levels of testosterone tend to be more aggressive than men with lower levels (Dabbs & Morris, 1990). The warring forces in Yugoslavia (and their leaders) are largely composed of men. (See Chapter 8 for a more detailed discussion of sex differences in social behavior.)

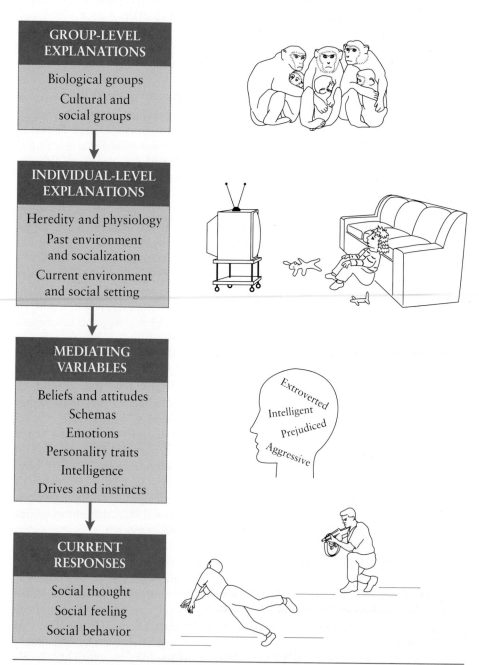

GROUP-LEVEL EXPLANATIONS

Biological groups

Cultural and
social groups

INDIVIDUAL-LEVEL EXPLANATIONS

Heredity and physiology

Past environment
and socialization

Current environment
and social setting

MEDIATING VARIABLES

Beliefs and attitudes
Schemas
Emotions
Personality traits
Intelligence
Drives and instincts

Extroverted
Intelligent
Prejudiced
Aggressive

CURRENT RESPONSES

Social thought
Social feeling
Social behavior

FIGURE 1.1 Levels of explanation of social behavior.

An individual's *past environment* can strongly influence social behavior. For example, child-rearing practices and early learning may affect a person's aggressiveness later in life. One explanation for the observed tendency for women to be less aggressive than men is that girls and women are consistently taught by family members, peers, and the mass media to be less aggressive. And undoubtedly, the past environments of Serbs, Croatians, and Bosnians shaped their aggressiveness through the prejudices they learned from their families and friends while growing up.

A person's *current situation* can also exert a potent influence on behavior. Indeed, this type of explanation is particularly emphasized in social psychology. For example, one famous theory holds that frustration inevitably leads to aggression (Dollard, Doob, Miller, Mowrer, & Sears, 1939). In a classic study, Hovland and Sears (1940) found a significant correlation between the health of the economy and the lynching of blacks in the Old South. Presumably, as whites were frustrated by economic bad times, they vented their resulting hostility on "safe" targets, namely blacks. According to the frustration-aggression hypothesis, factors in the current situation—specifically, anything that thwarts achievement of a desired goal—lead to aggression. Economic frustrations may have helped trigger the civil war in Yugoslavia: some republics felt they were supporting the overall Yugoslav economy more than others. Also, minorities in various parts of Yugoslavia undoubtedly felt frustrated by their lack of job opportunities due to prejudice.

Many other everyday situational factors can also trigger aggression. Consider the ever-present influence of media violence. Do you think that viewing violent T.V. shows and movies leads to aggressive behavior in some individuals? Research evidence on this important topic is discussed in Chapters 2 and 10. Here we'll simply note that this question focuses on how the past environment (watching *Miami Vice* reruns over the past year) and the current environment (watching a video of *The Terminator* right now) may affect a person's level of aggressiveness.

Many topics central to social psychology deal with the effect of current situational pressures on individuals' behavior. For example, research on conformity investigates how pressures from groups of people induce individuals to shift their stated attitudes and beliefs; research on attitude change examines how persuasive messages can change people's opinions; and research on group processes probes how being in a group affects individuals' performance and decision making.

When we consider the third level of boxes in Figure 1.1, *mediating variables*, we seem to slip inside the skin of the individual. Such explanatory variables cannot be directly observed; rather, they must be inferred from a person's behavior. For example, many commentators have explained the violence in Yugoslavia in terms of people's attitudes—the strong prejudices held by various ethnic and religious groups there. Most of us believe that attitudes exist, but they are not "things" that can be directly observed.

Social psychologists tend to study some mediating variables more than others. *Beliefs and attitudes* have traditionally been a favorite kind of mediating variable for social psychologists to study (Allport, 1935; McGuire, 1985). Beliefs comprise the cognitive information individuals hold about various people and things. Attitudes are evaluative responses (that is, feelings of liking or disliking) to people and things. Beliefs and attitudes have always intrigued social psychologists, because they seem closely linked to a host of important social behaviors, including discrimination, attraction, aggression, and altruism (see Chapters 7, 9, 10, and 11).

In recent years, social psychologists have also studied a number of cognitive mediating variables; such variables focus on people's thought processes and ways of assimilating information (see Chapter 5). For example, the concept of cognitive *schemas* (Fiske & Taylor, 1991; Hastie, 1981; Taylor & Crocker, 1981) is at the forefront of current social psychological theory and research. A schema—a kind of mental model or theory that people hold—contains the information we have about social groups and social settings, and even about ourselves. For example, many Serbs undoubtedly hold negative schemas about Bosnians; Bosnians, in return, hold negative schemas about Serbs.

Social psychologists have frequently studied two additional kinds of mediating variables: *emotional states* and *personality traits*. Emotions are transient states of arousal and cognition that motivate and direct behavior, particularly in novel situations demanding quick action (Mandler, 1975). Examples are anger, fear, and elation. Social psychologists particularly study emotions that relate to social behavior. Love and attraction, for example, are eminently social forms of emotion (see Chapter 9).

Personality traits are stable dispositions that influence broad domains of a person's behavior. The personality traits most studied by social psychologists are those that affect our relationships and social behavior (see Chapter 6). For example, social psychologists have studied such varied traits as locus of control (Rotter, 1966; see Chapter 14)—individuals' perception of whether their behaviors are controlled by themselves rather than by external factors; authoritarianism (Adorno, Frenkel-Brunswick, Levinson, & Sanford, 1950; see Chapter 7)—the degree to which an individual possesses a prejudiced, defensive personality; and self-monitoring (Snyder, 1979; see Chapter 3)—the degree to which individuals look to their inner feelings and attitudes or to others to decide how to behave.

Levels of Explanation

In Figure 1.1 the three main levels of explanation are connected by arrows, which represent cause–effect relations among different kinds of explanations. Thus, biological groups we belong to influence the heredity and physiology of each of us, the culture we belong to influences the way our parents reared us (our past environment), and so on. When viewed as interlocking levels of explanation, Figure 1.1 points to an important fact about social behavior: A single level of explanation is rarely sufficient to account for most interesting kinds of social behavior. Thus, a question such as "What is the cause of human aggression?" is overly simplistic because it ignores the complexity of human behavior and the multiple levels of explanation that inevitably apply.

Similarly, there are no single answers to such commonsense questions as "What is the cause of obedience?" or "What is the cause of prejudiced attitudes?" or "What is the cause of romantic love?" When more precisely and specifically framed, however, such questions are worth asking, and indeed, most of this book will be devoted to answering such questions. Figure 1.1 tells us that social scientists can apply many kinds of explanations in their attempts to understand social behavior. By emphasizing some of these explanations more than others, social psychology sheds its unique light on our social thoughts, feelings, and behaviors.

Responses to Be Explained

At the bottom of Figure 1.1 are the *responses* that social psychologists hope to explain: our thoughts, feelings, and observable behaviors. Of course, those of greatest interest to social psychologists are social thoughts, social feelings, and social behaviors. Research on social cognition (see Chapter 5) examines how we process information about other people. Research on attraction investigates why people like and love others (see Chapter 9). And the observable behaviors of greatest interest to social psychologists are interpersonal forms of behavior, such as aggression (when people hurt others; see Chapter 10), altruism (when people help others; Chapter 11), group behavior and processes (how individuals act in concert with others; Chapter 13), and how people influence one another—through persuasion (Chapter 6) and through pressures to conform, comply, and obey (Chapter 12). Note the common social thread tying all these diverse topics together: They all deal with people interacting with other people.

The Self in Social Psychology

In recent years, social psychology has devoted considerable attention to the self (see Chapter 3). The self comprises our current thoughts, feelings, and behavior, as well as a number of mediating variables (see Figure 1.1).

Many psychologists since the time of William James (1890) have considered the self to have two aspects: James called them the "me" and the "I." The "me," or the self as an object of knowledge and contemplation, consists of all the information each of us has about himself or herself. This is why schemas, beliefs, and attitudes are considered part of the self. The "I," or the self as an active agent, is the "execuive" inside us who makes decisions and choices; it is also our ongoing stream of conciousness. In keeping with recent social psychology theories (for example, Carver & Scheier, 1981; see Chapter 3), the active self is conceptualized here, at least in part, as some kind of decision-making process that has the interesting ability to go back and influence the other levels of explanation we've already discussed, a quality represented in Figure 1.2 by the arrows labeled "feedback processes of the self."

To return to the example of aggression, suppose you note one day that you are so frustrated at work, you are about to explode, and as a result you decide to take a week's vacation and go on a cruise to unwind. In other words, you consciously decide to change your environment in order to avoid an outburst of aggression. In such ways, the self monitors behavior and inner states, evaluates them, and then alters them by influencing other levels in the chain of explanations depicted in Figure 1.1.

The self is an important topic in social psychology because there are many essential links between the self and social behavior. The knowledge we have about

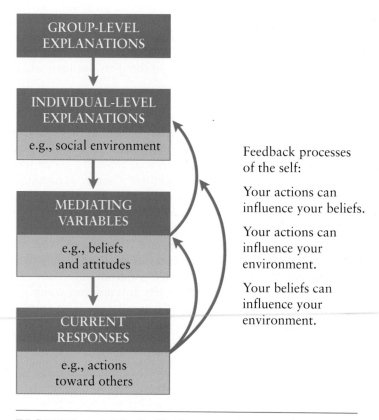

FIGURE 1.2 The feedback processes of the self.

ourselves often comes from other people. Social psychologists study self-perception (how we know our own feelings, attitudes, and emotions) and the self-concept (the organized knowledge and beliefs we have about ourselves). Social psychologists also study self-presentation (the managed images of ourselves that we display to others). Finally, social psychologists are interested in how our self-concept serves to guide our behavior with others.

Differences between Social Psychology and Related Fields

Many disciplines other than social psychology study social behavior, among them anthropology, sociology, political science, and economics. What makes social psychology a distinct field? For one thing, social psychology has its own preferred set of theoretical explanations that differ somewhat from those of other fields. For example, an anthropologist would focus more on culture (a "group-level explanation" in Figures 1.1 and 1.2) as a cause of behavior. Sociology deals with such group-level concepts as social classes and strata. Social psychology, in contrast, generally offers explanations that focus on the *individual* as its unit of analysis—for example, the individual's beliefs, attitudes, and social setting.

SUMMARY TABLE 1.1 An Overview of Social Psychology		
	Characteristic Emphases	*Examples*
Subject matter	Social behaviors and social influences on behavior	Does aggression elicit reciprocal aggression? Do aggressive parents produce aggressive children?
		What effect does punishment have on aggression?
Preferred level of explanation	Individual, situational, with certain mediating variables such as beliefs and attitudes	Focus on the social setting (e.g., aggressive models) as a cause of individuals' aggression
Preferred type of research strategy	Experimental, but also correlational and quasi-experimental	Manipulating amount of TV violence seen by children and observing effects on aggression
Applications	Applying theories to practical issues	Do learning theories predict that TV influences aggression? How?
	Answering important social questions	Does TV violence influence aggression?
	Designing social programs	How can children's programming best be developed to encourage helpful behavior and discourage aggressive behavior?

Social psychology also differs from related fields in its research methods, a topic we'll consider in greater detail in Chapter 2. It is sufficient to note here that social psychologists often prefer to conduct controlled experiments using precise, quantified measures. Contrast this preference with that of classical anthropologists, who use the technique of naturalistic observation—watching people in their daily settings and recording their behaviors, often anecdotally. Summary Table 1.1 highlights the main features that characterize social psychology as a discipline and distinguish it from related fields.

THEORIES IN SOCIAL PSYCHOLOGY

Before social psychology developed as a well-defined field of scientific research in the 20th century, many social theorists and philosophers speculated about the causes of social behavior. They proposed simple, all-encompassing principles that they hoped would explain virtually all aspects of society and social interaction (see Allport, 1985). Different philosophers, for example, invoked each of the following as universal principles: hedonism (people seek to gain pleasure and avoid pain in their dealings with others), imitation (people, from childhood on, look to others to guide their social behavior; they model their behavior on others'), and instincts (people behave in accordance with innate, biologically determined social motives for gregariousness, sex, aggression, and so on).

The Functions of Social Psychology Theories

In general, modern social psychology has avoided overly simplistic "grand principles" and broad unitary theories of social behavior in favor of middle-range theories designed to explain and predict limited aspects of social behavior (Jones, 1985). In essence, social psychologists have said, "Let's tackle smaller, more reasonable problems first before we try to explain the whole world with one theory." Why do social psychologists formulate these middle-range theories, and what are their main functions?

Theories Explain Social Behavior

First, social psychology theories provide systematic ways of explaining and predicting social behavior. A useful theory provides a relatively cohesive set of basic concepts and principles that allows us to make specific predictions about a particular kind of social behavior.

Theories Organize Research Findings

Not only do theories help explain and predict social behavior, they also serve to organize and give meaning to the many varied empirical findings of social psychology research. For example, research on attraction (see Chapter 9) provides many well-documented findings: People tend to like others more when they hold attitudes similar to theirs; people are more likely to be friends or lovers of people who live nearby; and people typically like those who are physically attractive more than those who are unattractive. How are we to understand such findings? Theories help social psychologists organize and conceptualize large bodies of research findings.

Theories Focus and Direct Research

Finally, theories not only explain behavior and organize research findings, they suggest new research hypotheses and directions. Social psychologists can study a virtually infinite number of processes and variables; theories help focus empirical research on specific questions. Whether they are eventually supported or refuted, theories help set the research agendas of social psychologists (Shaw & Costanzo, 1970).

Four Theoretical Perspectives

Social psychology theories come in many varieties, but this book will refer repeatedly to the following kinds: (1) learning theories, (2) cognitive consistency theories, (3) information-processing theories, and (4) equity and exchange theories. Each fulfills the three functions of a good social psychology theory: explaining and predicting social behavior, organizing large bodies of data, and guiding significant programs of research.

SUMMARY TABLE 1.2   Theoretical Perspectives in Social Psychology

Theoretical Approach	Basic Assumptions	Image of Human Social Behavior	Topics in Social Psychology to Which Theories Apply
Learning theories	Human social behavior can be explained by applying research and theory on basic learning processes such as classical and operant conditioning.	People are seen as conditioned organisms under the influence of environmental contingencies; animal learning experiments used as models.	Attitudes and attitude change Group influences Aggression Prosocial behavior Prejudice Attraction
Cognitive consistency theories	People strive for consistency among their beliefs and feelings.	People strive for mental peace and quiet; mental inconsistency is uncomfortable, and people strive to reduce it.	Attitudes and attitude change Attraction Prejudice
Information-processing theories	People strive to understand the world around them.	People are seen as social computers, noticing, encoding, and organizing social information.	Social perception Attitudes Prejudice Prosocial behavior Aggression Group decision making
Equity and exchange theories	Human interactions are governed by their costs, rewards, and profits. People strive for fair or equitable exchanges in social interaction.	Economic model of social relations; includes elements of learning theories, consistency theories, and cognitive theories.	Attraction Prejudice and group conflict Bargaining and negotiation Organizational and industrial behavior

Let's examine a thumbnail sketch of these theoretical approaches (see Summary Table 1.2 for an overview). It is important to recognize that these four theoretical perspectives are not necessarily mutually exclusive. They all may have valid, and somewhat overlapping, applications to the complexity of human social behavior. To make these perspectives a bit clearer and more concrete, let's apply each to the following question: Why do people sometimes behave aggressively?

Learning Theories

Social psychology has borrowed from a long and rich tradition of research on learning processes (Lott & Lott, 1985) such as classical conditioning, operant conditioning, and observational learning, which can be applied to social behavior. For example, aggression is perhaps in part a function of rewards and punishments. People who are rewarded (or at least not punished) for their aggressive acts are more likely to lash out in the future, whereas those who are punished are less likely.

Note that learning theories are in a sense "content-free." They describe basic processes that occur in all people (and animals too), and these processes can apply to many different kinds of social behavior. Variations of learning and conditioning theories have been used in social psychology to analyze attitude formation and change, aspects of attraction, the effects of groups on individual performance, and aggressive behavior (Lott & Lott, 1985).

Cognitive Consistency Theories

Social psychology has long studied people's thought processes. In the 1950s a number of theories were developed that propose people strive for consistency in their thoughts, feelings, and behavior. Perhaps the two most famous consistency theories are Festinger's (1957) theory of cognitive dissonance and Heider's (1946, 1958) balance theory, which was elaborated by Newcomb (1953).

Dissonance theory postulates that when people hold inconsistent beliefs, they experience an unpleasant state that can, in certain circumstances, motivate an attitude change (see Chapter 6). For example, if you believe that cigarettes are terribly unhealthy and also acknowledge that you smoke two packs a day, this uncomfortable and inconsistent knowledge may lead you to change your attitude toward cigarettes—maybe they're *not* so bad for you after all. Dissonance theory is also relevant to aggression: it makes the sad prediction that if we behave aggressively toward someone, our attitude toward our victim becomes more negative. Since it would be inconsistent for us to believe that we hurt a nice person, we shift our attitude and decide the person we hurt is bad and deserved to be hurt.

Balance theory focuses on the consistency or inconsistency of our likes and dislikes. It argues that some patterns of likes and dislikes are cognitively consistent (or "balanced," to use the language of balance theory) and some are not. For example, if you are a Bosnian, and you learn that the United States is taking action to censure Serbia, you will probably like the United States as a result. That is a balanced pattern of likes and dislikes. Balance theory is consistent with the old proverb "My enemy's enemy is my friend." We try to hold patterns of likes and dislikes that are logically and emotionally consistent with one another.

Information-Processing Theories

Simple learning theories and cognitive consistency theories don't fully address the complexity of much everyday social thought and behavior. In our relations with others, we are not "lab rats" molded by past rewards and punishments, nor do we merely strive single-mindedly for mental peace and quiet (that is, consistency). We actively process information and attempt to understand the causes of our own and others' actions. For example, when most of us learn about the Yugoslav civil war, we try to understand *why* people are doing what they do. Why is Serbian president Milosevic continuing the war? Is he insane? Is he trying to gain new territory before a forced cease-fire? Why are political leaders in the West so timid about intervening? Is it because of political pressures at home? Or are they simply wimps?

Attribution theories (Heider, 1958; Jones & Davis, 1965; Kelley, 1967, 1972) focus on the thought processes that people use to figure out the causes of others' behavior. This theoretical perspective sees people as actively thinking information gatherers who sift through the facts of the social world around them and try to understand what those facts mean.

Cognitive theories (attribution theory is just one example) have played a dominant role in social psychology in recent years (Fiske, 1993; Markus & Zajonc, 1985; see Chapter 5), as researchers have tried to understand how people notice, encode (that is, represent in their memory), process, and retrieve (recover from memory) social information. According to this theoretical perspective, each of us is a kind of "social computer."

Cognitive theories have been applied most directly to the study of social perception—how we take in and remember information about other people. Cognitive theories have also been used to study the nature of prejudice, aggression, altruism, and even such clinical disorders as depression.

Equity and Exchange Theories

Learning theories, cognitive consistency theories, and information-processing theories all largely seek to explain the *individual's* social thoughts and behavior. Social psychology, however, is devoted to linking the individual to a broader social context. It is not enough to account for just one person's behavior; we must also describe how the person relates to others.

Equity and exchange theories (for example, Adams, 1965; Homans, 1974; Thibaut & Kelley, 1959; Walster, Walster, & Berscheid, 1978) are economic

Sallie and Charlie Brown illustrate exchange theory.

theories of social behavior that attempt to explain relationships in terms of each partner's "costs," "rewards," and "profits" and the perceived fairness of the exchange. Such give-and-take is a commonplace feature of international negotiations, for example—if one country gives aid to another (the United States gives aid to Bosnia), it very likely may expect a favor in return (Bosnia should agree to the U.S. peace plan).

In a sense, equity and exchange theories extend certain concepts from learning theories to the social domain: People are seen as pursuing rewards and avoiding punishments in their relations with others. But equity and exchange theories are more complex than simple learning theories. For example, they allow for the existence of cognitive processes that can tally up the rewards and costs in a relationship over an extended period of time. In deciding whether or not a marriage is equitable, a person may consider what he or she gave and got over many years. Furthermore, equity and exchange theories, in contrast to simple learning theories, acknowledge the existence of social rules or norms. The *norm of reciprocity* (Gouldner, 1960), for example, holds that we should give as we get from others. If someone does us a favor, we should be willing to do a favor in return.

Equity and exchange theories are also cognitive, in the sense that they emphasize how people think about the rewards, costs, and transactions of social life. And finally, they borrow some aspects of consistency theories in arguing that people strive for reciprocity or equity in their relations. Indeed, a major goal of these theories is to predict precisely when social exchanges are seen as fair and when they are not. Equity and exchange theories have been used productively by social psychologists who study attraction, perceptions of social justice and injustice, competition and bargaining, behavior in industrial and organizational settings, prosocial behavior and altruism, and international relations.

APPLYING SOCIAL PSYCHOLOGY

This chapter has cited the situation in Yugoslavia to illustrate concepts of social psychology. Using a real-life example like this is appropriate, for throughout its history, social psychology has always had intimate ties to the larger political and cultural spheres (Gergen, 1973; Jones, 1985; Sampson, 1977). The horrors of the Germans' extermination of Jews during World War II, for example, stimulated research on the nature of prejudice. The U.S. government's interest in issues of propaganda and persuasion led social psychologists to begin modern research on attitude change in the 1940s and 1950s. The civil rights movement of the 1950s and 1960s led social psychologists to study anew prejudice, stereotypes, and social conflict. Violence and higher crime rates in the 1960s and 1970s inspired new research on aggression and its causes. In the 1980s and 1990s, skyrocketing health care costs and growing awareness of behaviors that contribute to disease led to new research on social psychology factors in health.

Social psychology has addressed in the past and continues to address socially important questions: Does media violence contribute to aggression in our society?

Throughout its history, social psychology has been concerned with topics of social and political relevance. Far left: *The horrors of World War II: survivors of Oswiechim concentration camp—Poland, 1945.* Left: *Convicted of a brutal 1969 mass murder, Charles Manson appears at a parole hearing in 1986.* Below: *The civil rights movement of the 1950s and 1960s.*

What are the best ways for hostile groups to negotiate nonviolent solutions to their conflicts? Does pornography lead to aggression and foster prejudice against women? Do social factors such as the support of friends and family members influence our susceptibility to disease?

The Two Faces of Applied Social Psychology

The chapters that follow will weave together the "pure science" of social psychology with applied research topics. Social psychology research applies to real life in two obvious ways. In some cases the theories, principles, and research findings of social psychology apply to real-life situations, even if they were not initially motivated by real-life applications. Thus, for example, research on attitude change and persuasion (see Chapter 6) has obvious connections to marketing methods and consumer behavior. In other cases, social psychologists purposefully tailor their theoretical principles and research methods to real-life topics with the specific intent of providing answers to pressing social questions. Thus, for example, social psychology research on school integration looks at whether integration is an effective technique to reduce students' prejudice and whether some kinds of integrated classrooms work better than others to reduce prejudice (see Chapter 7).

These two aspects of applied social psychology—theory and research that can be linked to real-life events and research that intentionally seeks to answer questions about social issues—are both integral to this book. As you will see, almost every chapter starts with a real-life example. For instance, Chapter 4 ("Perceiving Others") describes the Anita Hill–Clarence Thomas hearings, and poses the question "How do we know what we know about others?" Chapter 8 ("Gender and Social Behavior") starts with a controversial social question—"What role should women play in the military?"—and takes off from this question to explore social psychology research on gender stereotypes and sex differences. Chapter 16 ("Social Psychology and the Law") uses the 1992 trial of the Los Angeles police officers who beat motorist Rodney King to pose questions about social psychology factors that affect jury decisions. Through these examples, all the chapters link social psychology research and theories to compelling real-life events.

Our discussion of "real life" brings us back to the example we used to start this chapter, the Yugoslav conflict. We noted earlier that the tragedy in Yugoslavia suggests many social psychology questions: What causes aggression? When do people help others? What leads to intergroup conflict? What is the nature of prejudice? To a scientist, each of these questions is interesting in its own right. Answering these questions, however, carries a practical as well as a scientific reward: By understanding the nature of helping, we may be able to induce people to be more helpful. By understanding the causes of aggression, we may be able to reduce it. And by understanding the dynamics of group conflict, we may more successfully negotiate peaceful settlements between antagonistic groups.

THE PROFESSION OF SOCIAL PSYCHOLOGY

What is it like to be a social psychologist? Where do social psychologists work, and what do they do? As shown in Figure 1.3, 75% of social psychologists with Ph.D.s work at colleges or universities; a significant minority (17%), however, find employment in business and government settings (Stapp & Fulcher, 1981). Social psychologists with master's degrees enjoy greater job diversity: 12% work at four-year colleges; 44% work in other, nonuniversity academic settings; 20% work in business and government; and an additional 24% work in human services fields (for example, clinics, public health agencies, probation departments).

It seems likely that in the near future, new areas of applied research in social psychology will lead to new kinds of employment for social psychologists. For example, the recent increase in research on health psychology (see Chapter 14), environmental psychology (Chapter 15), on the social psychology of the legal system (Chapter 16), and on social psychological factors in clinical disorders such as depression (see Chapter 5) promises employment for social psychologists in medicine, environmental studies and regulation, law, and clinical psychology.

The skills of a good social psychologist can be exercised in many kinds of work: market research, opinion polling, evaluation research in business and government (that is, research that assesses the effects of new programs), and statistical analysis of behavioral data.

Many of the social psychologists who work in academic settings divide their time among teaching, staying abreast of new research, and conducting research.

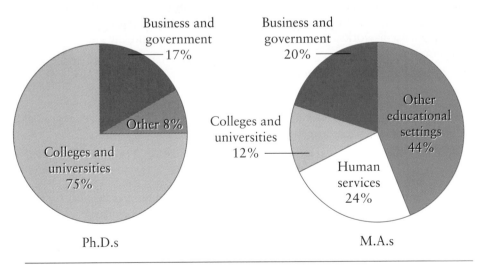

FIGURE 1.3 Where do social psychologists work?

The focus of all this teaching, study, and research is, of course, the subject that social psychologists consider one of the most fascinating in the world: human social behavior.

SOCIAL PSYCHOLOGY IN PERSPECTIVE

Complex real-life events like the religious strife in Yugoslavia pose many questions that are central to social psychology: Why and when are people aggressive? What is the nature of prejudice? When do people help one another? What is the nature of leadership? How do our beliefs and attitudes influence our behavior? Social psychology is a field that tries to answer these and many other questions about social behavior.

The kinds of explanation that have been offered for our social behavior include group-level explanations (the biological and social groups we belong to), individual-level explanations (our past and current environments), and mediating variables (internal factors such as our beliefs, attitudes, schemas, traits, and intelligence).

Social psychologists use theories to explain social behavior, organize research findings, and direct research. Four useful theoretical perspectives in social psychology are learning theories, cognitive consistency theories, information-processing theories, and equity and exchange theories.

Social psychology embraces both pure and applied science. Its theories and research findings often pertain to real-life issues. Some research directly addresses real-life questions ("Does viewing media violence lead to aggressive behavior?") and tries to solve real-life problems ("How can we reduce prejudice?"). The theory and research methods of social psychology have been used to gain important knowledge about a number of applied topics, including social factors in health, how our legal system works, and the link between the environment and our social behavior.

KEY POINTS   Defining Social Psychology

Social psychology studies how people influence other people. It investigates social behavior and factors that affect social behavior.

Social Psychology Explains Social Behavior

Social scientists offer several different kinds of explanations for social behavior: group-level explanations, individual-level explanations, and mediating variables. Social psychologists emphasize the power of our current social setting to influence our behavior. Social psychologists also study the effect of mediating variables such as beliefs, attitudes, schemas, emotional states, and personality traits on our behavior.

Social psychology examines the self as both a cause and an effect of social behavior. The self comprises beliefs we hold about ourselves and internal decision processes that guide our behavior.

Differences between Social Psychology and Related Fields

Social psychology differs from related fields in its explanations of social behavior, its focus on the individual as the unit of analysis, and its research methods.

Theories in Social Psychology

The Functions of Social Psychology Theories

Social psychologists develop theories to explain and predict social behavior, to organize research findings, and to guide future research.

Four Theoretical Perspectives

Four important theoretical approaches in social psychology are (1) learning theories, (2) cognitive consistency theories, (3) information-processing theories, and (4) equity and exchange theories.

Applying Social Psychology

The Two Faces of Applied Social Psychology

Social psychology combines a strong interest in both pure and applied science. Applied social psychology addresses important real-life questions (for example, "Does media violence lead to aggression?") and tries to solve problems ("What are effective ways to reduce prejudice in classroom settings?").

The Profession of Social Psychology

Most social psychologists work in academic settings, but a significant minority have jobs in business, government, and human services organizations. In the future, greater numbers of social psychologists will work in applied fields such as health psychology, environmental psychology, and legal psychology.

KEY TERMS

Applied social psychology: Social psychology theory and research used to answer practical questions or to design and implement programs in real-life settings.

Attitude: An evaluative response (a like or a dislike) directed at an object; a mediating variable studied in social psychology.

Attribution theories: Theories about the thought processes people use to explain the causes of others' behavior.

Belief: Cognitive knowledge about an object; a mediating variable studied in social psychology.

Cognitive consistency theories: Theories that suggest people strive for consistency in their thoughts and feelings; dissonance theory and balance theory are the most famous examples.

Cognitive theories: Theories that emphasize human information processing and its effects on social behavior.

Emotion: A transient state of arousal and cognition that motivates and directs behavior, particularly in novel settings that demand quick action; a mediating variable studied in social psychology.

Equity and exchange theories: Economic theories of social interaction that maintain people monitor the costs, rewards, and profits of their social relations and strive for fair or equitable exchanges of social "goods."

Group-level explanation: An explanation of social behavior that focuses on the individual's membership in social or biological groups.

Individual-level explanation: An explanation of social behavior that focuses on factors unique to the individual (such as heredity and physiology), on the individual's past environment, and on the individual's current environment.

Learning theories: Theories that use principles of learning (such as those supported by research on classical and operant conditioning) to explain aspects of social behavior.

Mediating variable: A hypothetical internal variable that cannot be directly observed and that is used to explain an individual's behavior; examples are attitudes, personality traits, and schemas.

Personality trait: A stable disposition that influences broad domains of an individual's behavior; a mediating variable studied in social psychology.

Schema: A cognitive model or theory that an individual holds about people, groups, events, or things; a mediating variable studied in social psychology.

Social psychology: The scientific study of social behavior and social influences on behavior; it focuses on the individual as its unit of analysis and emphasizes situational variables and certain mediating variables as explanations of social behavior.

Unitary theories: Theories that offer simple encompassing principles (for example, hedonism) to explain a broad range of human social behavior.

ANSWERING QUESTIONS
ABOUT SOCIAL BEHAVIOR

Eichmann told me he could show me this order in writing if it would soothe my conscience . . . . The Führer had ordered the final solution of the Jewish question . . . . It was perfectly clear to me that this order spelled death to millions of people. I said to Eichmann, "God grant that our enemies never have the opportunity of doing the same to the German people." In reply to which Eichmann told me not to be sentimental; it was an order of the Führer and would have to be carried out.

—*Dieter Wisliceny*, a witness at the Nuremburg war crimes trials

(Conot, 1983, pp. 257–58)

Why did so many Germans obey their leaders' inhuman commands during World War II—commands that led directly to the extermination of millions of innocent people? Disturbed by this question, social psychologist Stanley Milgram decided to conduct a series of experiments on obedience in the early 1960s. Like most researchers, Milgram began with a tentative idea, or hypothesis: that the Germans' seemingly blind obedience during World War II resulted from some aspect of the "German character." Milgram intended to study obedience in Germany, but before doing so he needed a way to test and measure obedience. The procedure he devised was relatively straightforward: In the guise of conducting a learning experiment, an experimenter would order subjects to deliver increasingly intense electrical shocks—up to 450 volts—to an innocent victim. The subjects' level of obedience would be defined as the highest level of shock they delivered upon command from the experimenter.

"I'll tell you quite frankly," Milgram stated in one interview (Meyer, 1970), "before I began this experiment . . . I thought that most people would break off. . . . You would get only a very small proportion of people going . . . to the end [to 450 volts], and they would constitute a pathological fringe." To his dismay, Milgram discovered that each subject obeyed completely. His "pathological fringe" turned out to include everyone. Astonished that all his subjects obeyed so readily, Milgram modified and elaborated his procedure to create additional pressures to disobey. Because his ultimate goal was to discover the factors that lead

The defendants in these trials—German government officials and military officers—were charged with horrifying crimes of obedience.

people to obey and disobey, it was necessary to design an experimental situation in which subjects disobeyed as well as obeyed.

Imagine you are a subject in this modified study. You come to a laboratory at Yale University, and the experimenter—a stern-looking man in a white coat—informs you that he is conducting research on the effects of punishment on learning. The experimenter describes the procedure: You will be a "teacher" who reads lists of words to another subject, a pleasant-looking, middle-aged man. You will then test the learner to see whether he correctly remembers the words. Every time he makes a mistake, you are to punish him with an electric shock.

Before the trials begin, the learner tells the experimenter in your presence that he's a bit afraid to receive electric shocks because he's been diagnosed as having a slight heart condition. The experimenter assures the learner that although the shocks may be painful, they will not harm him. While you watch, the experimenter takes the learner to the next room, where he is strapped into an apparatus that looks like an electric chair. The experimenter returns to the main room and seats you at a console that appears to be a shock generator. The machine has a row of levers marked in 15-volt increments, from 15 volts to 450 volts. The voltage levels also have labels ranging from "slight shock" through "strong shock," "intense shock," and "danger: severe shock," followed by "X X X" beyond 435 volts. Your instructions are to read the lists of words over a microphone to the learner in the next room. Periodically you will test his recall of these words. Every time the learner remembers a word incorrectly, you are to deliver a shock as punishment. And with each successive incorrect response, you are to increase the level of shock one step (that is, 15 volts).

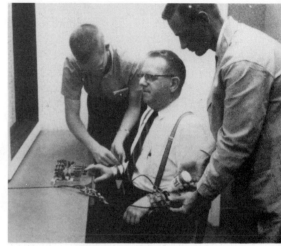

Milgram's experiment on obedience: Top: *the shock generator used in his study.* Bottom: *the "learner" is strapped into a chair and a shock electrode is attached to his arm.*

The experiment begins uneventfully. You read lists of words and then test the learner periodically. Occasionally he makes a mistake, and you deliver his punishment. When you reach the lever marked 75 volts, you hear the learner begin to grunt in pain with each shock. At 120 volts, the learner starts to complain verbally. As you progress to higher levels of shock, the victim shouts out, "I can't stand the pain. Let me out of here! . . . My heart's bothering me. Let me out!" At still higher levels of shock, the learner screams in agony and desperately pleads for his release. Finally, at the highest levels of shock, approaching 450 volts, the learner stops responding entirely. You hear nothing from the next room. For all you know, your victim is sprawled out unconscious in the electric chair.

How far do you think you would obey the experimenter in this version of Milgram's study? Would you continue administering shocks all the way to 450 volts? If you are like the typical subject in Milgram's experiment, the chances are that you would continue to obey the experimenter to the very end. In fact, 62% of Milgram's subjects—a clear majority—proceeded all the way to 450 volts and delivered what they thought were excruciatingly painful electric shocks to the learner upon command from the experimenter.

It should be emphasized that Milgram's subjects did not enjoy inflicting pain on their victim. Indeed, most subjects were horribly distressed and agitated; they stopped periodically and virtually begged the experimenter to check in on the learner. But the experimenter always responded with prompts like, "Please continue. The experiment requires that you continue." Most subjects, despite feeling disturbed and upset, followed the experimenter's orders to the end.

Of course, no learner in the Milgram study was actually shocked. The "learner" was in fact a confederate in the experiment, not a real subject, and the screams from the next room were tape recordings. But to the subjects, the situation was distressingly real.

Clearly, Milgram's initial conjecture was wrong. Destructive obedience doesn't occur just in certain countries, or among a "pathological fringe." When placed in the proper situation, average Americans displayed startling levels of obedience. These results prompted Milgram to alter his research program in an effort to discover the social factors that lead normal people to obey grossly unethical commands. What followed was a series of influential experiments that raised a host of disturbing issues and challenged psychologists to come to grips with the question of when and why people obey those in authority.

Milgram's landmark experiments illustrate a number of points about research in social psychology. Recall that Milgram started with a question about people's real-world behavior: Why were the Germans so obedient during World War II? Milgram's research, like all studies in social psychology, was an attempt to answer his question in a way that was both objective and reliable. Rather than settle for a plausible-sounding intuitive explanation, Milgram strove to gather evidence that would confirm or cast doubt on his initial guess. To do so, he needed to pose precise questions about obedience that could be answered by carefully controlled research. His experiments were designed to isolate and define the behaviors he wished to study as well as their possible causes. For example, the technique of using varying levels of shock gave him an exact measure of subjects' degree of obedience. Milgram wanted to be confident that nothing in his experimental design biased or obscured the meaning of his results. In sum, to answer his questions about obedience, Milgram had to think carefully about *how* he would gather data relevant to those questions.

As the example of Milgram's studies shows, generating objective answers to questions about social behavior is a complex enterprise that often calls for considerable ingenuity and skill. To understand the findings of social psychology, you need some understanding of the procedures researchers use and the reasons for them. You also need to know how research results are reported and what they mean. As we proceed, you may find yourself wondering about the ethics of some research, especially controversial studies like Milgram's. Toward the end of this chapter, we shall consider ethical questions raised by social psychology research. In sum, this chapter introduces the basic concepts you need to understand the logic of research, to evaluate research findings intelligently, and to appreciate the ethical questions posed by some studies.

Every research study you will encounter in this book entails the general stages just outlined: framing a precise and meaningful question, devising ways to define and measure the factors the researcher wants to examine, and designing a study that can provide clear and unambiguous answers to the initial question. Let's look at each of these stages in more detail.

POSING QUESTIONS TO STUDY

Where do research questions come from? Sometimes researchers' questions are based on their intuitions about social behavior, but more often, social psychologists ask questions suggested by theories about social behavior. As noted in Chapter 1, social psychology theories are sets of propositions that are used to organize, explain, and predict empirical (that is, measured) observations (Shaw & Costanzo, 1970). For example, various social psychology theories have been put forward to explain why people change their attitudes, begin and end intimate relationships, and obey authority figures.

Chapter 1 sketched out four main theoretical approaches in social psychology: learning theories, cognitive consistency theories, information-processing theories, and equity and exchange theories. Many of the theories within these approaches are designed to be general enough to apply to a broad range of social behaviors. For example, equity theory—a set of propositions about costs and rewards in social relationships—has been used to understand relationships between employees and bosses, close friends, spouses, and even nations.

Precisely because they are relatively broad, theories are usually impossible to test completely in a single study. Instead, theories are used to generate a host of *hypotheses*—propositions derived from the theory that are specific and capable of being tested. Thus, equity theory might suggest the hypotheses that workers who feel they are not receiving pay commensurate with their efforts will either demand more pay or work less, or that a wife who believes she invests more in her marriage than she receives from her husband will try to get more rewards from her husband, create more costs for him, or end the relationship. In this way, theories help focus researchers' attention on crucial variables, and they help suggest hypotheses that can be tested by objective research.

Useful scientific theories typically are logically consistent and relatively simple. Furthermore, scientific theories are capable of being disproved. In other words, if we don't know what evidence would count against the theory, we have no way of evaluating whether it is correct. Although objective observations may prove that a theory is incorrect (when hypotheses derived from the theory are refuted), observations that support a theory never really *prove* that the theory is *correct*. Rather, confirming data increase the *likelihood* that hypotheses and the theories from which they are derived are correct.

Think back to Milgram's obedience research. Suppose Milgram had begun his research by traveling to Germany and had found that German subjects showed high levels of obedience. This evidence would have provided data consistent with his hypothesis that obedience in Germans resulted from their "national character." Such data would not prove the hypothesis, however. In fact, we know from the data Milgram collected in the United States that his hypothesis about a unique link between German national character and obedience probably was not correct. High levels of destructive obedience can occur in the United States as well as in Germany.

The Milgram example illustrates an important point. Although it may be gratifying when a study seems to lend perfect support to a theory, some of the most important advances in science have resulted from jarring contradictions between the hypotheses generated from a theory and the data collected to test them. Milgram's data did not support his initial hypothesis. Surprised by his own findings, Milgram was spurred to look in new directions for the factors that contributed to obedience. As we will see later, he proceeded to systematically examine *situational* influences on people's willingness to obey. As a result, our understanding of obedience advanced.

In general, the development of theories proceeds hand in hand with the gathering of empirical data. While theories can suggest what data to gather, data often suggest new theoretical generalizations (see Figure 2.1). Often theories must be modified or elaborated as findings emerge that are inconsistent with them.

Measuring Social Behavior: Operational Definitions

Like other scientists, social psychologists want to test their theories in a way that will produce clear, precise results. To do so, they must devise methods to define and measure the variables (that is, the concepts) they wish to study. An operational definition is a description of a concept (such as obedience, conformity, love, or aggression) in terms of the procedures used to measure it. By defining concepts operationally, researchers ensure that other scientists know exactly what the variable means in the context of the study and that others can repeat the measurement if desired. Otherwise, two researchers who were both interested in obedience, for example, might get inconsistent results simply because they used different definitions of obedience.

Sometimes researchers find it difficult to agree on operational definitions, especially for such elusive concepts as conformity, attitudes, anxiety, or romantic love. How can such concepts be reduced to unambiguous operational definitions?

Social psychologists typically use two different kinds of operational definitions: subjective reports and behavioral measures (Aronson, Brewer, & Carlsmith, 1985; Aronson, Ellsworth, Carlsmith, & Gonzales, 1990). In *subjective reports,* people are asked to verbally convey their own experiences, sometimes through direct questioning but more commonly through questionnaires and rating scales. *Behavioral measures,* on the other hand, are direct observations of behavior that are not filtered through the individual's subjective experience.

Suppose, for example, that a researcher wants to operationally define *anxiety* in order to study the effects of anxiety on problem solving in groups. Using

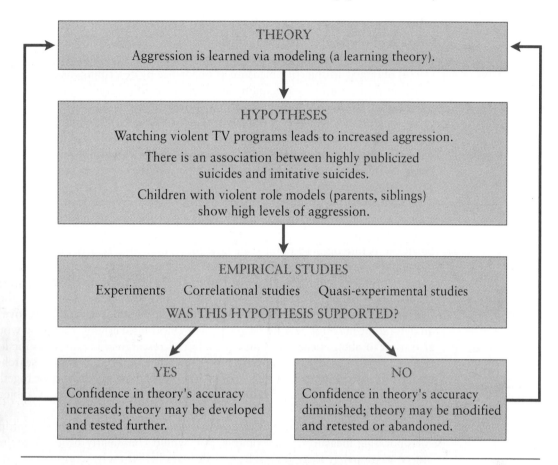

FIGURE 2.1 The reciprocal relationship between theory and research.

subjective measures, the researcher could ask participants to rate themselves on a scale from "1—totally calm, relaxed, and free of anxiety" to "10—nervous, tense, and anxious." Or the researcher could administer a standard anxiety questionnaire—for example, the Taylor Manifest Anxiety Scale (Taylor, 1953), which includes such true-false items as "I worry over money and business," "I have diarrhea once a month or more," "I have had periods in which I lost sleep over worry," and "Life is a strain for me much of the time." In each case, the instrument used to get people to report on their subjective level of anxiety would constitute the operational definition of anxiety in that study.

To obtain behavioral measures of anxiety, the researcher could measure subjects' heart rate, breathing, and galvanic skin response (a measure of electrical skin conductivity and, indirectly, of perspiration). Presumably, anxious people show more physiological arousal than calmer people do. The researcher could also observe and measure anxious mannerisms such as twitching, fidgeting, and speech errors such as stutters, "ahs," and "ums." Such behavioral measures would serve as additional operational definitions of anxiety.

In most of his obedience experiments, Stanley Milgram used a behavioral measure of obedience: a subject's obedience was defined as the highest level of shock he or she used in punishing the learner. In one study, however, Milgram (1974) obtained a subjective measure of obedience by describing his experimental situation to a group of participants and asking them to predict how much they would obey in that hypothetical setting. Interestingly, none of the participants predicted that they would proceed all the way to 450 volts. This finding shows that subjective measures don't always yield the same results as behavioral measures. Take a moment to think of reasons why most people would not predict the high levels of obedience they would in fact display if they were actually placed in Milgram's experimental setting.

Consider now another, very different concept: romantic love. Suppose you wanted to explore some of the factors that lead people to fall in love. How might you operationally define love? To obtain subjective reports, you could have participants rate on a 10-point scale how much they love a particular person. Or you could have them complete "love scales" developed by rigorous principles of test construction—for example, those of Rubin (1970) and Hendrick and Hendrick (1986; see Chapter 9). But can you always rely on what people say about themselves? Some individuals may lie about such personal emotions as love or anxiety; some may not be fully aware of their emotions. Perhaps, then, you would also want to obtain behavioral measures. In one research study on romantic love (Rubin, 1970), dating couples were placed together in a room while researchers unobtrusively measured their degree of mutual eye contact and how close together they sat on a couch. In some studies, researchers even measure directly subjects' levels of sexual arousal.

Social psychologists can be most sure of their findings if they obtain multiple, corroborating measures. For example, you would confidently believe that John indeed passionately loves Joan if he says he loves her strongly, scores very high on various love scales, constantly gazes into her eyes, sits right next to her on the couch, and displays measurable sexual arousal when he is near her. In general, such agreement between different measures of the same concept increases researchers' confidence in the validity of their measurements.

If different measures produce inconsistent results, however, researchers may suspect that the measures are not all measuring the same thing, and they may need to reexamine their operational definitions (Campbell & Fiske, 1959). For example, if different measures of John's "love" for Joan disagree significantly, you might reasonably doubt that they are all truly measuring love. Maybe sexual arousal in fact measures lust, eye contact measures friendliness, and questionnaire scales of love assess idealized romantic love. Clearly, the way concepts are operationally defined greatly affects the meaning of research results.

You may be tempted to conclude from this discussion that behavioral measures are less biased and more scientific than subjective measures. This may be true sometimes, but subjective measures are still important and worth obtaining in many studies. In some cases they are the best measures available, and in others they can corroborate behavioral measures. Furthermore, social psychologists are often interested in studying subjective thought processes in their own right. For example, social psychologists studying attitudes and people's ways of thinking about other people often use subjective measures.

Reliability and Validity of Measures

Whether social psychologists employ subjective or behavioral measures, their measures are useful only if they are shown to have two important properties: reliability and validity. A *reliable* measure is repeatable and consistently obtained. A *valid* measure assesses what it is supposed to. For example, an attitude scale is reliable if it yields highly consistent scores for given subjects when administered at two or more different times. (This kind of reliability, called *test–retest reliability,* is one of several different varieties of reliability.) An attitude scale is valid if it truly measures the attitude it is designed to measure and if it predicts relevant criteria. An attitude scale designed to measure a person's attitude toward abortion, for instance, should distinguish members of "pro-life" groups from members of "pro-choice" groups. If it doesn't, we can reasonably question whether it is a valid measure of individuals' attitudes toward abortion.

Reliability is a necessary but not sufficient condition for validity. That is, a measure cannot validly assess a variable if it is not measuring *something* consistently. But reliability alone does not establish that a measure is valid. We might, for example, get consistent results on a love scale when what we are really measuring is sexual attraction.

Kinds of Social Psychology Research

To answer questions about social behavior, social psychologists must carefully choose the particular kind of study they will conduct and the specific features of that study. These studies come in two main forms: experiments and correlational studies. Each type answers somewhat different kinds of questions about social behavior. In brief, *experiments* are designed to answer cause-effect questions, such as: Does viewing violent pornography lead men to behave more aggressively against women? In contrast, *correlational studies* tell us only that two variables are related, but not whether one causes another. For example, is there an association in different societies between the availability of pornography and the frequency of rape? (See Chapter 10 for a discussion of actual research on these topics.)

To interpret research intelligently, you need to know how experiments and correlational studies differ and the relative advantages and disadvantages of each type of study in answering questions about social behavior. For example, suppose you read a story in the newspaper about a study showing that children exposed to a great deal of television violence are significantly more aggressive than other children. Should you conclude that watching violent TV *causes* children to be more aggressive? As we shall see, the answer depends on what type of study was conducted and how it was designed. Let's look at the defining characteristics of experimental and correlational studies and at the conclusions we can draw from each.

Does TV violence encourage aggression in young viewers?

Experiments: Demonstrating Cause–Effect Relationships

The purpose of an experiment is to demonstrate that one variable has a direct causal influence on another. In an experiment, the researcher manipulates (that is, intentionally alters) a variable, termed the independent variable (IV), and observes its influence on a second variable, termed the dependent variable (DV). For example, suppose you wanted to conduct an experiment testing the effects of television violence on children's aggressiveness. You might show one group of children a violent show and another group a nonviolent show and then observe whether the two kinds of programs have any effect on the children's aggressiveness. In this case, the violence of the show would constitute the independent variable, and the children's observed aggressiveness would be the dependent variable.

Although this procedure sounds straightforward, we have not yet answered a fundamental question: How does the experimenter decide which children see the violent TV show and which children see the nonviolent show? One possibility would be to seek volunteers for the two conditions—ask children whether they would prefer to see the violent or nonviolent TV show. This, by the way, would be a very bad way to conduct the experiment, for variables other than the manipulated independent variable (TV viewing) could then account for any observed difference in aggressiveness between the two groups. For instance, children who volunteer to view aggressive shows might tend to be "bad" children, whereas children who volunteer to view nonaggressive shows might tend to be "nice" children. If you observed that the children who watched the violent TV shows were more aggressive than those who watched the nonviolent shows, you wouldn't know if this difference occurred because of the program they watched or because of their preexisting "badness."

How can researchers rule out this kind of possibility? To guarantee that the independent variable is the *only* variable systematically influencing the dependent variable, experimenters assign subjects randomly to experimental conditions. *Random assignment* is an essential element of any experiment. It occurs when any subject has an equal probability of being chosen for any experimental condition. In an experiment on TV violence and aggression, randomly assigning the subjects would require deciding by a procedure such as the flip of a coin whether a particular child watches a violent TV show or a nonviolent TV show (see Figure 2.2).

How does random assignment clarify the effects of the independent variable? To understand better the logic of experiments, let's consider an actual study on TV violence and aggression conducted by Liebert and Baron (1972). One hundred thirty-six children individually came to a "waiting room" and watched TV programming controlled by the experimenters. Half the children were randomly assigned to see a segment from the old cops-and-robbers show *The Untouchables* that contained two fistfights, two shootings, and a knifing. The remaining children viewed a part of a track meet with lots of activity, but no violence. Viewing or not viewing the violent TV segment constituted the independent variable in this experiment.

Stated a bit differently, one group of subjects was exposed to the experimental treatment (watching violent TV), whereas the other group—the *control group*—was not. The purpose of having a control group is to provide a baseline measure of the dependent variable (in this case, children's aggressiveness) to compare with the measure obtained from the subjects in the experimental (violent TV) group. In this way, researchers can get a precise idea of the effects of the independent variable. In general, a control group in an experiment is a group that does not receive the experimental treatment.

After watching television for a few minutes, the children in Liebert and Baron's experiment participated in a "game" in which they thought they could either help or hurt another child in an adjacent room by pressing buttons on a machine. Finally, the children were allowed to play in a room that contained both aggressive and nonaggressive toys—guns and knives versus a Slinky, a space station, and dolls. The children's aggressiveness in the game and in play served as the dependent measures. Liebert and Baron found that the children who had watched the violent TV segment—boys and girls alike—hurt other children more

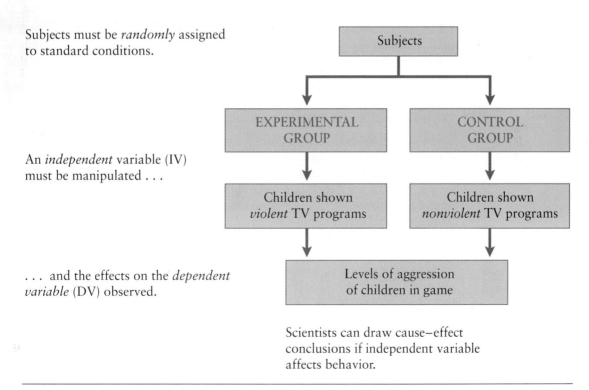

FIGURE 2.2 Schematic diagram of an experiment.

in their game and played more aggressively than the children who had watched the sports segment.

As noted previously, the major strength of experiments is that they allow researchers to infer cause-effect relationships between independent and dependent variables (Aronson, Ellsworth, Carlsmith, & Gonzales, 1990). From their results, Liebert and Baron could conclude that watching the violent TV segment *caused* children to behave more aggressively in their experiment. Why are such inferences possible? The key lies in the random assignment of subjects, which essentially rules out the possibility that something other than the experimental manipulation itself caused the observed difference in aggressiveness.

Let's describe in more detail how this worked in Liebert and Baron's experiment. Many variables can influence children's aggressiveness, among them personality traits (perhaps extroverts are more aggressive than introverts), social class (perhaps lower-class children are more aggressive than middle-class children), religion, ethnic background, and so on. If one group or the other had a disproportionate share of children who were aggressive for any of these reasons, then *extraneous variables* would contaminate the results. But because subjects were *randomly assigned* to the two conditions, all extraneous variables should have balanced out; that is, on average there were as many introverts, middle-class children, and so on in the experimental group as in the control group. Thus, any difference in the aggressiveness of the children in the two groups must have been due to the manipulation of the independent variable—that is, to viewing a violent TV segment versus viewing a track event—not to other factors. Figure 2.3 summarizes the procedures used in this study, which is a good example of a simple experimental design, similar to many experiments you will be reading about in this book.

Correlational Studies: Demonstrating When Two Variables Are Related

Whereas an experiment can establish a cause-effect relationship between variables, a correlational study answers a more general question: Is one variable related to another variable? By "related to," we mean simply that differences in one variable tend to be associated with differences in the other—for example, that children's level of exposure to TV violence seems to go along with their level of aggressiveness. Notice that "related to" is not the same as "causes." In a correlational study, the researcher does not attempt to manipulate one variable in order to observe its effects on the other. Instead, the researcher measures variables as they naturally occur in some setting and observes whether and to what extent they are related to one another (see Figure 2.4). In other words, the researcher assesses the *correlation* that exists between the two variables.

To see how correlational studies can provide insights into the link between naturally occurring variables, let's consider two more studies on TV violence and aggression. McLeod, Atkin, and Chaffee (1972a, 1972b) measured the TV-watching habits and aggressiveness of 473 teenagers in Maryland and 151 teenagers in Wisconsin. Specifically, they asked the teenagers to rate how often they watched 65 different prime-time TV shows that had been independently rated on

Arrange conditions to
isolate the effects of the IV.

Manipulate *only* the IV.

Measure the DV for both groups.

Compare the two groups.
Any differences in the DV
should be caused by the
difference in the IV.

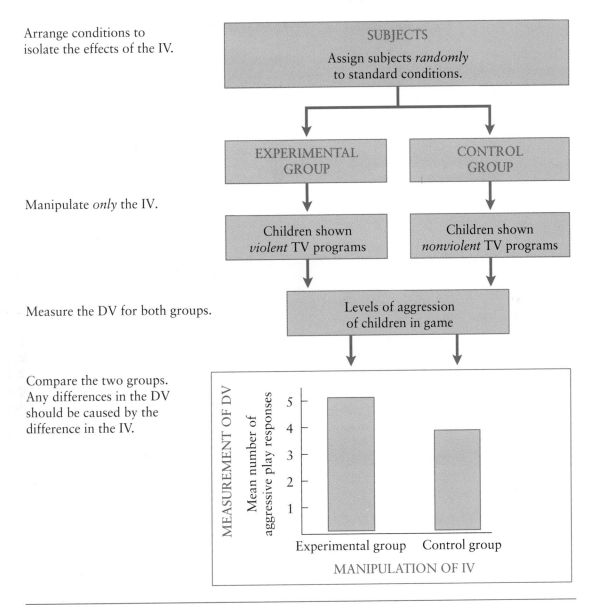

FIGURE 2.3 Liebert and Baron's (1972) experimental question: whether watching violent television programs causes heightened aggression in children.

their degree of violent content. The teens also completed various questionnaires that had them rate their own levels of aggressiveness and delinquency. In the Wisconsin study (1972b), the researchers also asked the teenagers' mothers and peers to rate them on aggressiveness. The question these researchers wished to answer was whether the two variables—reported aggressiveness and amount of time spent watching violence on TV—showed any relationship. The result? The

EXPERIMENTAL STUDY

Is there a causal
relationship?

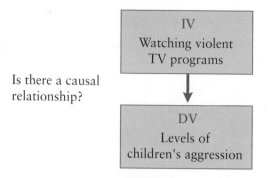

CORRELATIONAL STUDY

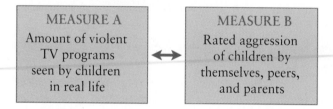

Is there a relationship between these variables?

FIGURE 2.4 Comparing experimental and
correlational studies.

teenagers who watched more violent TV shows in this study tended to describe
themselves as more aggressive, and their parents and friends tended to rate them as
more aggressive as well.

Although the results are consistent with those obtained in Liebert and Baron's
experiment, there is a major difference between the studies. Unlike Liebert and
Baron's experiment, the correlational studies do not allow us to draw any
cause–effect conclusions about TV watching and aggressiveness. Psychologists and
statisticians are fond of noting that *correlation does not equal causation*—it's true,
and worth remembering.

McLeod, Atkin, and Chaffee's correlational studies indicate that viewing
violent TV goes along with real-life aggressiveness. Why is this not the same as
saying that watching violent TV *causes* aggression? The answer: because other
interpretations of the observed relationship are possible (see Figure 2.5). For
example, perhaps innately aggressive children prefer violent TV programs—that is,
it is aggressiveness that causes the TV watching, not the other way around. Or
perhaps some third variable accounts for the observed relationship between
watching violent TV and aggression. Suppose the real cause of aggression in
children is parental aggressiveness—that hostile, aggressive parents produce
hostile, aggressive children. Such parents might also have a preference for violent
TV programs, which of course their children watch too because they live in the same

house. In this case, more-aggressive children would tend to watch more-violent TV, but television viewing would not be the cause of their aggressiveness. None of these alternate interpretations can be ruled out in a correlational study.

If correlational studies do not show causation, why would researchers choose this type of design over an experiment? A key reason is that correlational studies sometimes address more realistic kinds of variables than experiments do. Recall that Liebert and Baron's experiment used a very brief and perhaps somewhat unnatural manipulation of TV violence. In real life, after all, children don't watch shows for just a few minutes, but rather for hours and hours. Similarly, the "game" that allowed the subjects to "hurt" or "help" another child seems to be a somewhat contrived and artificial measure of aggression. In contrast, the correlational study measured TV viewing and aggression as they occur spontaneously in a real-life setting.

A second reason why researchers conduct correlational studies is that a true experiment is sometimes not possible for practical or ethical reasons. For example, researchers could in theory design an experiment in which they would randomly assign some children to watch many violent TV programs every day over a

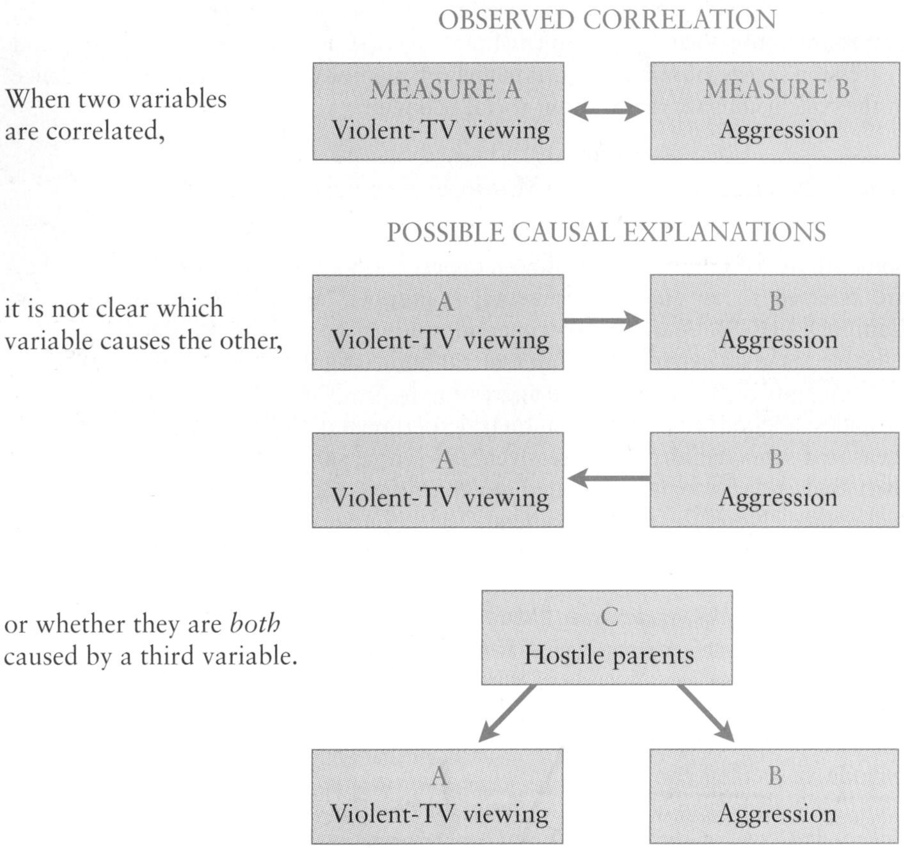

OBSERVED CORRELATION

When two variables
are correlated,

MEASURE A Violent-TV viewing	⟷	MEASURE B Aggression

POSSIBLE CAUSAL EXPLANATIONS

it is not clear which
variable causes the other,

A Violent-TV viewing	→	B Aggression

A Violent-TV viewing	←	B Aggression

or whether they are *both*
caused by a third variable.

C
Hostile parents

A Violent-TV viewing		B Aggression

FIGURE 2.5 Possible causal relationships among correlated variables.

three-year period while other children—those in the control group—would watch no violent TV. Clearly, such a study would be impractical: No one, including parents, can consistently dictate what TV shows children are to watch over a long period of time. Moreover, the study would also be unethical. If you were a parent, would you want your child to be exposed to three years of violent TV programming?

Finally, it is important to note that some variables simply cannot be experimentally manipulated. A good example is biological sex. You cannot randomly assign an individual to be male or female. Therefore, research that studies sex differences (see Chapter 8) is necessarily correlational research.

In summary, experimental studies have the advantages of allowing precise control over the conditions of the study and of establishing causal relationships between variables. But these advantages come at a price: Experiments may not be entirely realistic, and in some cases this method of studying social behavior is impractical or unethical. Correlational studies, on the other hand, may suggest but cannot prove cause–effect relationships and thus may not answer crucial questions. They are often more realistic than experiments, however, and can be carried out in many circumstances where a true experiment would be impossible or unethical. Both types of studies can provide useful information about behavior, and in an important sense they are complementary. As the example of TV viewing and aggression shows, obtaining results from both methods can increase our confidence in the conclusions we draw about social behavior.

Quasi-Experimental Designs: Manipulating Variables without Random Assignment

Some studies combine features of both experiments and correlational studies; they are referred to as quasi-experimental (Campbell & Stanley, 1966; Cook & Campbell, 1979). A quasi-experimental study involves the manipulation of a variable (as in an experiment), but true random assignment of subjects is lacking.

A study on TV viewing and aggression by Joy, Kimball, and Zabrack (1986) provides a good example of a quasi-experimental design. These researchers measured schoolchildren's aggressiveness in three similar Canadian towns. Why these particular towns? One had no television reception until 1974 (it was nicknamed "Notel" by the researchers). The second town received broadcasts only from the Canadian Broadcasting Company (nickname: "Unitel"). And the third town received both CBC broadcasts and those from the three commercial U.S. television networks (nickname: "Multitel"). The researchers measured the mean increase in children's aggressiveness in all three towns during the same time period: just after TV was introduced to Notel. The results of the study indicated that children in Notel showed larger increases in their mean levels of aggressiveness than children in the other two towns, presumably because TV had suddenly been introduced to their community.

This study was not a true experiment because children were not randomly assigned to experimental conditions. Clearly, no researcher has the power to assign children to live in different towns. Nor could the researchers directly manipulate the

SUMMARY TABLE 2.1	*Experimental*	*Correlational*	*Quasi-Experimental*
Type of question addressed	Is there a causal relationship between the variables?	Are the variables related? To what degree?	Does a manipulation that the researcher does not control seem to affect the dependent variable?
Independent variable manipulated?	Yes.	No.	Yes, but it is not under the researcher's control.
Establish causation?	Yes.	No.	No, but may suggest causation.
Advantages	Control. Ability to demonstrate causation.	Can study realistic variables; useful when experiments would be impractical or unethical.	Useful for study of real-life interventions over which the researcher has no control.
Disadvantages	May be artificial; some questions not amenable to experimental study.	Cannot demonstrate cause-effect relations.	Lacks control; does not permit strong causal inferences.
Examples	Liebert and Baron experiment on TV viewing and aggression in children.	McLeod et al. study of TV viewing and aggression in teenagers.	Joy et al. study of the effects on children's aggression when TV was introduced to a Canadian town.

SUMMARY TABLE 2.1   Research Methods in Social Psychology

amount of TV the children watched. There was a "manipulation" of sorts, however: the start of TV broadcasting in Notel. By taking advantage of this naturally occurring change in a key variable, the researchers could indirectly study the effects of this manipulation. As this study makes clear, quasi-experimental designs are quite useful in studying the effects of changes in social policy—interventions over which researchers have no control, but which create "experimental" and "control" groups. Quasi-experimental studies thus combine some of the precision of experiments with the realism of correlational studies. For an overview of experimental, correlational, and quasi-experimental studies, see Summary Table 2.1.

FROM RESEARCH TO THE REAL WORLD: THE ISSUE OF GENERALIZABILITY

Although research in social psychology can sometimes seem far removed from real-life social behavior, ultimately researchers are trying to cast light on the way people act in natural settings. But do Stanley Milgram's obedience experiments really tell us how people respond to authority in everyday situations? And can

By studying people in real-life settings, field research avoids the artificiality of some laboratory studies.

studies of those towns in Canada inform us about the effects of televised violence on children in the U.S., Japan, and Argentina? In other words, how do we know whether the findings of any particular study *generalize* to broader populations and to real-life settings?

The generalizability of research findings depends in part on where a study is conducted—for example, in the laboratory or in the field. Generalizability also depends on how well the study was conducted. As noted previously, correlational and quasi-experimental studies sometimes seem more "true to life" than experiments; as we shall see, however, correlational, quasi-experimental, and experimental studies all have the potential of adding to our understanding of actual behavior. Regardless of research design, bias or errors in research methods can call into question the results of any kind of study. The generalizability of research results is in part a statistical issue: The raw data produced by a study become meaningful only when they are interpreted, often with the aid of statistical techniques. Finally, results are more likely to generalize when they are supported by a preponderance of research evidence. Rarely does a single study establish any important claim. Results generalize when the findings of many different studies accumulate and all point to the same conclusion. Let's consider in more detail the many sides to the issue of generalizability.

Laboratory versus Field Studies

Laboratory studies are conducted, predictably enough, in laboratories, often in university settings with college students as subjects. *Field studies,* on the other hand, are carried out in real-life settings, and thus their results must apply to at least one real-life setting. For this reason, field research, although more difficult to control and standardize than laboratory research, effectively complements laboratory studies.

As you might expect, laboratory research is more likely to be experimental and field research is more likely to be correlational, but both experimental and correlational studies can in theory be conducted in either the field or the laboratory. A good illustration is provided by research on helping in emergencies. In one famous laboratory experiment, Darley and Latané (1968) studied how the presence of other people during an emergency affects helping behavior. The question they posed was: If other bystanders are present, are individuals more likely or less likely to help a victim than if they are alone? To answer this question, Darley and Latané had college subjects talk to another student in a nearby cubicle via a microphone and earphones. Partway through the conversation, the other student seemed to suffer an epileptic seizure. The results of this experiment showed that a given subject was *less* likely to help the victim when other subjects were present than when he or she was alone (this phenomenon is discussed further in Chapter 11).

Helping in emergencies was also the subject of a field study by Piliavin, Rodin, and Piliavin (1969), in which the researchers investigated factors that led New York subway passengers to aid fellow passengers who collapsed in the aisles of subway cars. This study showed, for instance, that people who collapsed (actually experimental confederates) and who seemed to be drunk were helped less often than people who appeared to be disabled.

Although the seizure study was conducted in the laboratory and the subway study was conducted in the field, both were experiments. Each manipulated an independent variable (the number of bystanders present or the apparent drunkenness of the victim) and randomly assigned subjects to experimental conditions. Thus, studies conducted outside the laboratory can fulfill the requirements of an experiment.

Because field studies involve natural settings, they are especially appropriate when social psychologists want to answer questions that directly involve real-life situations and actual social policies (for example, "Does the presence of others affect whether people help victims of medical emergencies in public places?" or "What effect does forced school integration have on students' racial attitudes?").

At the same time, field studies are contaminated by the messiness of real life, with many variables interacting in extremely complex ways. Because data obtained

Piliavin, Rodin, and Piliavin (1969) conducted a field experiment on bystander intervention in New York City subway cars.

in the field are often influenced by variables that are irrelevant to the study, they can be very difficult to interpret. For example, whether or not subjects helped the "victim" in the subway experiment could depend on a host of uncontrollable variables: the number of people in the subway, the ethnic mix, the temperature, the subway's dirtiness, and so on. Laboratory studies, on the other hand, permit researchers to standardize conditions (that is, make them all the same except for the manipulated independent variable) and to control extraneous variables. In Milgram's laboratory experiment on obedience, for instance, all subjects received exactly the same instructions and heard exactly the same tape-recorded screams from the same apparent victim, in exactly the same environment. Thus, the results of laboratory studies like Milgram's are often less ambiguous than those of field studies, for it is possible in laboratory studies to see the effects of one variable with all other variables held constant. Whereas field studies may apply more readily to real-life settings, laboratory studies can often produce clearer and cleaner results. This is one reason both kinds of studies are useful in testing claims about social behavior.

Generalizing from the Results of Experiments

Stanley Milgram chose laboratory experiments as the best means to investigate factors that influence obedience to authority. Milgram's choice is typical of the field of social psychology, which traditionally has emphasized laboratory experiments (Higbee, Millard, & Folkman, 1982). For this reason, it is important to look closely at the power of laboratory experiments to give us helpful information about real-life social behavior. There are some good reasons to question the applicability of laboratory results to everyday situations and behavior: Sometimes laboratory experiments are artificial and contrived (Gergen, 1978; Gilmore & Duck, 1980), and their subject populations are frequently quite limited, often consisting of college students (Sears, 1986).

Laboratory experiments do tell us something useful when they *test a theory* that can be applied to real-life settings or behaviors. For experimental results to generalize to broader populations and milieus, the experiments must be well designed. Finally, results most strongly point to general conclusions when the findings of many different experiments all seem to support one another. Precisely because the laboratory experiment is so dominant in social psychology, it is worth looking at each of these issues more closely.

Must Experiments Duplicate Real Life?

Were Milgram's obedience experiments like real life? In some important ways, no. Most of us, in the course of our daily routine, are not asked to deliver excruciatingly painful electric shocks to innocent victims. Still, Milgram's experiments give us significant data about the nature of obedience. They tell us, for example, that average people (his subjects were a broad sample of New Haven residents) are capable of very high levels of destructive obedience and that such obedience is not necessarily a function of any particular "national character."

Although some social psychology experiments try to mirror real life, many do not. Generally, social psychologists are more concerned that subjects take the experimental situation seriously (as Milgram's subjects certainly did) and less concerned that subjects experience experimental situations that exactly duplicate natural settings (Aronson & Carlsmith, 1968). There is one obvious reason why social psychologists *do not* want to duplicate real life exactly in their experiments: Real life is complex. Precisely because experiments can create a kind of artificial simplicity, social psychologists can isolate specific factors that influence our behavior and thus carefully and systematically examine their effects in a way that would be impossible in real life. In this way, laboratory experiments give us valuable information about processes that occur outside the laboratory.

Furthermore, not every social psychology experiment is primarily intended to establish generalizations about real-world settings and behaviors. Like all scientists, social psychologists often design experiments to test theories and to support or refute the hypotheses derived from those theories (Mook, 1983). A theory that is supported by many laboratory experiments may help explain real-life behavior even if the experiments themselves are not exactly like real life.

Obedience in everyday life: Cult leader David Koresh at the site of his future compound near Waco, Texas. The compound would eventually go up in flames when Koresh ordered his followers to commit mass suicide. Why do people obey charismatic cult leaders like Koresh?

Only Well-Designed Experiments Generalize

For their results to be meaningful and generalize to broader settings and populations, experiments must be well designed. Good experiments show two important characteristics: internal and external validity (Campbell & Stanley, 1963; Cook & Campbell, 1979; Crano & Brewer, 1986).

An experiment possesses *internal validity* if the independent variable manipulates what it's supposed to and only what it's supposed to, if the observed experimental effects are truly caused by the independent variable, and if the dependent variable measures what it's supposed to. For example, Liebert and Baron's experiment on TV and aggression possessed internal validity if it truly manipulated the "amount of violence" in the TV segments, if this manipulation was indeed the cause of the observed differences in the children's aggressiveness, and if the dependent measures—pressing buttons on a machine and playing with aggressive toys—truly represented subjects' levels of aggressiveness.

An experiment possesses *external validity* when its findings apply to populations or settings outside the experiment itself. Liebert and Baron's experiment possesses external validity if its results apply to children other than those in the experiment, to different kinds of violent TV, to children playing at home, and so on. Internal validity is a necessary but not sufficient precondition for external validity; in other words, experimental findings cannot be generalized to broader populations if the variables were not manipulated and measured properly in the first place.

The internal and external validity of an experiment are threatened whenever the independent variable is confounded with another variable. Two variables are said to be *confounded* when they occur together and when it then becomes impossible to tell which variable is causing the effect. For example, in Liebert and Baron's experiment, what caused the differences in aggression between the experimental and control groups? Was it the difference between a violent and a nonviolent TV segment, or was it perhaps instead the difference between a sports and a nonsports TV segment? Notice that in this experiment, these variables were perfectly confounded.

Replication: Accumulating Research Findings

This chapter began with an account of a single provocative study, the Milgram obedience experiment. Often such isolated studies—whether in psychology, medicine, physics, or other sciences—are the subject of dramatic reports in the mass media. As we have seen, however, all studies and research designs have limitations, and it is rare for an important scientific question to be resolved by a single experiment or study. How, then, can we increase our confidence in the reliability and generalizability of research findings from a particular study?

One way is by replicating (or repeating) the study and showing that the replications produce similar results. For example, to assure themselves that Liebert and Baron's experimental findings on TV and aggression were "for real" and not the result of confounded variables or simply chance, other researchers could conduct the same study with different subjects. Successful replications produce the same or similar results each time, adding to the credibility of the research findings. This, by the way, is true of Milgram's findings, which have been replicated in many different studies (Blass, 1992; Miller, 1986).

Furthermore, replications sometimes manipulate and measure variables differently from the initial study. If they still yield the same results, we can be more confident that the results are genuine and not attributable to confounded variables. Such replications help to establish the external validity and generalizability of experimental results. For example, one study measured obedience by having a doctor call 22 nurses and order each of them to administer an obviously dangerous overdose of a drug to a patient (Hofling, Brotzman, Dalrymple, Graves, & Pierce, 1966). All but one of the nurses immediately proceeded to deliver the deadly dose. (The nurses were stopped before they could carry out their orders.) Just as in Milgram's research, the conceptual focus of this study was destructive obedience, but clearly, obedience was elicited and measured quite differently in this study.

Meta-Analysis: Combining the Results of Many Studies

As we have seen, evidence related to significant scientific questions is cumulative, and the results of many research reports need to be brought to bear on an issue

Studying obedience in everyday life. Can you think of reasons why a nurse would obey a doctor's order to deliver seemingly dangerous doses of medication to a patient?

before we can be confident of what the results mean. If, for example, social psychologists want to know whether TV violence leads to aggression in viewers (or more subtly, to identify the circumstances under which TV violence leads to aggression in some viewers), they must consider all research connected to this question. Furthermore, they must devise a systematic way to tally up research findings, particularly when the results of different studies seem to be in conflict.

A recently developed statistical technique called meta-analysis allows researchers to quantitatively combine the results of many studies and decide objectively which findings are reliable and which are not. Meta-analysis also allows researchers to assess the overall magnitude of the findings (Glass, McGraw, & Smith, 1981; Rosenthal, 1984). For example, a meta-analysis of 230 studies on the link between TV viewing and children's aggression found that when the results of all these studies were statistically combined, there was consistent evidence for a moderately large link (Hearold, 1986).

Meta-analysis is useful not only because it helps establish that a finding is reliable, but because it can identify factors that influence when a finding does and does not occur. For example, Hearold's meta-analysis showed that the effects of TV on aggression tend to increase with age for boys, but decrease with age for girls. Furthermore, it found that TV violence encourages aggression in children particularly when the TV violence is portrayed as justified and when the viewing children are frustrated or aroused. We will see additional examples of the usefulness of meta-analysis in Chapter 8 in the discussion of findings on sex differences in social behavior.

Statistics and Social Psychology Research

How do we know whether the results of a particular study are strong enough to be meaningful? In Liebert and Baron's experiment, for example, how much would the measured aggressiveness of children in the violent-TV group have to differ from that of the children in the control group for us to be sure that a true difference between the groups existed? And in correlational studies of children's TV-viewing habits and aggressiveness, how strong does the link between TV viewing and aggressiveness have to be before we believe that it's "for real"? Answering questions of this sort is one of the main topics of *inferential statistics,* the branch of statistics that deals with drawing conclusions from data and testing hypotheses. Although a detailed discussion of statistical analysis is beyond the scope of this book, a few basic principles will help you assess the research you'll read about in subsequent chapters.

Significance Levels

The next time you're at your school library, take a look at some academic journals that publish social psychology research. (Two prominent journals in the field are the *Journal of Personality and Social Psychology* and the *Journal of Experimental Social Psychology.*) Generally, when articles in these journals present an empirical result, they also present a significance level, in the form of a probability. For example, in Liebert and Baron's experiment, the children who viewed violent TV played more aggressively than the children who viewed the televised track meet, and this difference was reported to be statistically significant at the level $p < .01$.

Significance levels indicate how likely it is that results of a given magnitude are attributable to chance factors—that they are a statistical fluke rather than a real finding. In the case of the Liebert and Baron study, the expression $p < .01$ means the probability is less than 1 in 100 that observed differences of the magnitude found in this study were due to chance alone. In general, a low value for p means it is likely the results show true effects and unlikely that they reflect the chance fluctuations that occur in all measurements. Such results are said to be *statistically significant.*

How small must the probability level be to qualify as "significant"? In psychology, a probability level less than .05 is generally regarded as significant. Obviously, we cannot put much faith in results that may be due simply to chance. Note that a "significant" effect is not necessarily a large effect; it is simply an effect that is unlikely to occur through chance alone. Generally, the results reported in this book are significant in the sense just described.

Correlation Coefficients

Correlational studies typically make use of a statistical measure called the correlation coefficient, which indicates how much two variables "go together" (for an additional explanation of correlation, see Figure 2.6). This statistic can range from −1 (a perfect negative, or inverse, correlation) through zero (no correlation) up to +1 (a perfect positive correlation). If the correlation coefficient is zero, no

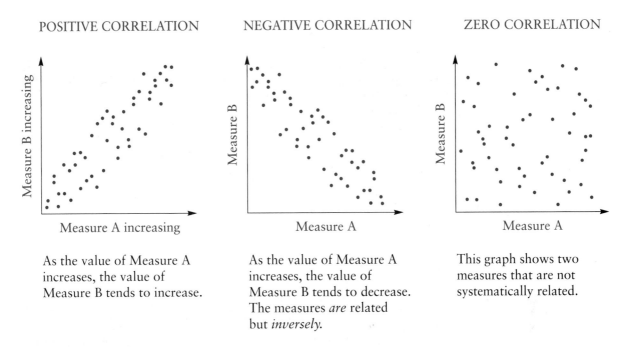

POSITIVE CORRELATION

NEGATIVE CORRELATION

ZERO CORRELATION

As the value of Measure A increases, the value of Measure B tends to increase.

As the value of Measure A increases, the value of Measure B tends to decrease. The measures *are* related but *inversely.*

This graph shows two measures that are not systematically related.

Each point on the graphs above represents a pairing of two measures (such as level of aggression and hours of violent-TV viewing per week) for a given subject. The point is plotted where the two values intersect on the graph.

Can you think of variables that you would expect to be positively correlated? Negatively correlated? Uncorrelated?

FIGURE 2.6 Types of correlation.

correlation exists between the variables. For example, there is very likely no correlation between people's nose length and their intelligence. The value of one variable (nose length) implies nothing about the value of the other variable (how intelligent or unintelligent the person is).

If the correlation coefficient is computed to be a *positive* value, then as the value of one variable increases (or decreases), the value of the other also increases (or decreases). For instance, in most groups of people, height and weight tend to be positively correlated: The taller a person is, the more he or she tends to weigh. Positive correlations range from any value greater than zero to a maximum of +1, which indicates a perfect straight-line relationship between the two variables (see Figure 2.7). Values between zero and +1 indicate varying degrees of positive correlation; for example, a value of .7 indicates a stronger positive correlation than .3.

Variables can also be correlated *negatively,* or *inversely.* That is, they show a relationship, but as the value of one variable increases, the other decreases, and vice versa. For example, grades in school tend to be negatively correlated with absences from class. The greater the number of absences, the lower students' grades tend to be. A perfect negative correlation is denoted by −1; values between zero and −1 indicate varying degrees of negative correlation.

Let's return to our example of TV viewing and aggression to illustrate different kinds of correlations. One representative study found a correlation of .31 between the amount of violent TV boys watched in third grade and their level of aggressiveness ten years later (Lefkowitz et al., 1972). This means there was a positive, but by no means perfect, relationship between the boys' TV viewing and their future aggressiveness.

Suppose the correlation coefficient had turned out to be a different value. (See Figure 2.7 for graphic illustrations of different correlation coefficients.) If the correlation were, say, −.7, then this would indicate a negative, or inverse, relation between watching violent TV and aggression—that is, as the boys viewed *more* violent TV they tended to be *less* aggressive (certainly, this would be an unexpected finding). If the correlation coefficient were 0, then the study would show *no systematic relationship* between viewing violent TV and aggressiveness. Finally, if the correlation coefficient were −1.0 or +1.0 (which almost never occurs in real research data), then the study would show a perfect linear (that is, straight line) relationship between viewing TV violence and aggression.

Why do perfect negative (−1) and positive (+1) correlations almost never occur in research studies? Consider again the example of TV viewing and aggression. Clearly, in real life many factors influence aggression: personality traits, social class, parental practices, and so on. Since TV viewing is just one variable among many that influence aggression, it is unrealistic to expect it to predict people's aggressiveness perfectly. Furthermore, even if TV viewing *were* the only variable to influence aggressiveness, researchers would not be able to measure with absolute reliability either TV viewing or aggression. All operational definitions and measures are subject to some error (that is, they are never absolutely reliable), and such errors alone would prevent measures from showing a perfect correlation.

Correlations need not be perfect to provide useful information about how variables are related. Correlations, like other kinds of statistical results, can be tested for statistical significance. A correlation is statistically significant if the correlation coefficient is sufficiently large (that is, different from zero either in a positive or negative direction) and this difference is unlikely to be the result of chance alone. In general, the correlations reported in this book are significant in the sense just described.

BIAS IN SOCIAL PSYCHOLOGY RESEARCH

Despite procedures intended to promote objectivity, all science is a human enterprise, and it is always possible for bias to enter into the way studies are conducted and interpreted. In addition, social psychologists face certain research problems that physicists and chemists, for example, do not. A physicist designing an experiment on elementary particles does not worry about what the particles are

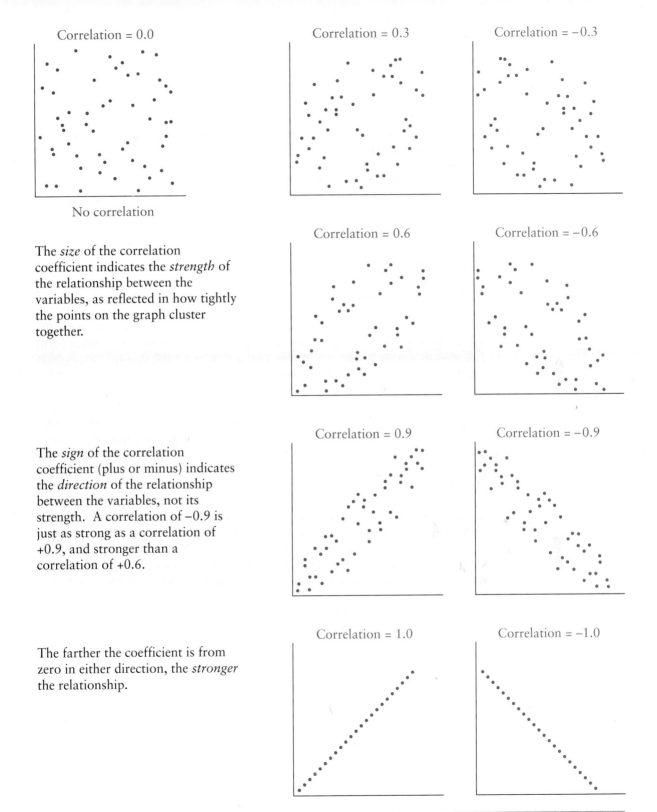

Correlation = 0.0

No correlation

Correlation = 0.3

Correlation = −0.3

Correlation = 0.6

Correlation = −0.6

Correlation = 0.9

Correlation = −0.9

Correlation = 1.0

Correlation = −1.0

The *size* of the correlation coefficient indicates the *strength* of the relationship between the variables, as reflected in how tightly the points on the graph cluster together.

The *sign* of the correlation coefficient (plus or minus) indicates the *direction* of the relationship between the variables, not its strength. A correlation of −0.9 is just as strong as a correlation of +0.9, and stronger than a correlation of +0.6.

The farther the coefficient is from zero in either direction, the *stronger* the relationship.

FIGURE 2.7 Correlation coefficients show the degree of relationship between two variables.

thinking or whether his or her expectations will influence their behavior. The subjects in social psychology studies, however, perceive, feel, and think. They may try to discover the purpose of the experiment or may pick up subtle cues that cause them to alter their behavior. Consequently, social psychologists *must* concern themselves with what human subjects are thinking during the course of an experiment. Experimenters who communicate their expectations to subjects, or subjects who on their own develop hypotheses about the experiment, can bias experimental results. Either kind of bias can alter our interpretation of research results.

Experimenter Bias

Experimenters can sometimes subtly influence their subjects' behavior. In one early study on this effect, Rosenthal and Fode (1963) had student experimenters instruct their subjects to rate photographed faces on a scale ranging from −10 (failure) to +10 (success) as to whether the people in the photographs were experiencing success or failure at the time the photograph was taken. Rosenthal and Fode led half the student experimenters to believe that subjects tended to rate the faces as showing success, and led the other half to believe the opposite: that subjects tended to rate the faces as showing failure. Thus, the independent variable in this study was the expectations of the student experimenters.

Each of the student experimenters was told to read standard instructions informing their subjects how to carry out the rating task. The results showed a clear experimenter-bias effect: Those subjects instructed by student experimenters who *expected* them to rate the faces as showing success did indeed rate the faces as successful, and the subjects whose experimenters expected them to rate the faces as showing failure tended to do so. Somehow, despite the standardized instructions, the experimenters communicated their hypotheses and expectations to their subjects. Rosenthal (1966) has documented many other cases in which experimenters inadvertently biased the results of their experiments.

On the surface, it would seem that experimenter bias should make us skeptical about all social psychology research. How can experiments produce objective results if researchers can so easily influence subjects' behavior?

Experimenter bias is a serious but not hopeless problem. Careful researchers can reduce and often eliminate the possibility of such bias (Aronson, Ellsworth, Carlsmith, & Gonzales, 1990). One solution is to standardize the experiment as much as possible, including the experimenter's words and behavior. The experimenter must try to treat all subjects the same, using the same language and demeanor with each of them. The Milgram obedience experiment provides a good example of standardization: The experimenter always gave the same instructions to all subjects, subjects sat at the same shock machine and heard exactly the same tape-recorded screams, and so on. Such standardization reduced the possibility that the experimenter treated different subjects differently. Mechanization is perhaps the ultimate guarantee of a totally standardized experiment. If a videotape or computer gives the instructions to the subject, there can be no experimenter bias because no human experimenter is present.

Of course, it is neither possible nor desirable to mechanize all social psychology experiments. Another way to eliminate experimenter bias is to design a *blind experiment,* one in which the experimenter does not know which experimental condition the subject is in. For example, in a blind experiment on TV viewing and aggression in children, the experimenter observing the children's aggressiveness would not know whether any particular child had seen a violent or nonviolent TV segment. How could the experimenter be kept blind in this experiment? One possibility is that the experimenter could create two unlabeled videotapes, one containing the violent TV segment, the other containing the nonviolent segment. After leaving the room where the child watches TV, the experimenter would insert one of the tapes in a VCR, show the recorded segment to the child, then return to observe the child's aggressiveness. After a particular child is observed, the experimenter would note which tape had been played and record that fact.

In some social psychology experiments, the experimenter cannot help knowing the status of a subject after the experimental manipulation takes place. Consider Liebert and Baron's experiment, for example: As the experimenter showed a given child one of the TV segments (violent or sports), she watched the child from behind a one-way mirror, and thus she knew the experimental condition the child was in. One way to avoid experimenter bias in this study would be to switch experimenters after the manipulation was completed. A different experimenter—one who had no idea which TV segment the child had just viewed—would then observe and record the child's level of aggressiveness. With careful forethought, it is usually possible to greatly reduce or even eliminate experimenter bias in studies.

Subject Bias

Subject bias occurs when subjects' hypotheses about a study and its purpose systematically influence their behavior. Subjects often try to figure out a study, and once they have determined its apparent purpose, they can choose to be cooperative or uncooperative. Suppose you were in an experiment in which a researcher showed you a violent movie and then asked you to deliver shocks to another subject. Do you think you might guess that the purpose of the study was to determine the relationship between viewing media violence and behaving aggressively? If you did correctly guess the purpose of the study, how would that affect your behavior? You might simply refuse to behave aggressively because you realize that your behavior is being scrutinized, and you know that aggressive behavior is generally seen as bad. If you are cooperative, you might behave more aggressively after viewing the violent movie in order to "help out" the experimenter. Or, if you are uncooperative, you might behave unaggressively simply to defy the experimenter and demonstrate that you cannot be influenced by so transparent a manipulation. Regardless of whether you try to help or hinder the experimenter, if you have correctly perceived the purpose of the study and altered your behavior as a result, the study is hopelessly biased.

Subject bias occurs particularly when a study possesses strong *demand characteristics*—that is, salient cues that inappropriately suggest how the subject should behave (Orne, 1962). What's the difference between experimenter bias and subject bias resulting from demand characteristics? Experimenter bias occurs when the experimenter inadvertently provides cues to the subject about how to behave; demand characteristics refer to inappropriate cues *in the experimental setting itself* that may lead the subject to behave consistently with the experimenter's hypotheses.

To illustrate: Some studies have investigated whether the mere presence of a weapon sometimes leads people to behave more aggressively. (This phenomenon is discussed further in Chapter 10.) In one demonstration of this effect, subjects delivered retaliatory shocks to a peer who had earlier shocked them. In easy view on a nearby table was either a gun or a badminton racket. The main result: Subjects delivered stronger shocks when in the presence of the gun (Berkowitz & LePage, 1967). Suppose you were a subject in this study. If you were in the "gun" condition, do you think you would be suspicious that a gun just happened to be lying on a nearby table? If you correctly guessed that the purpose of the study was to investigate whether the presence of guns influences aggression, then the study would clearly suffer from demand characteristics.

There are several ways to avoid subject bias. One common solution is to deceive subjects so they don't know the true purpose of the study. In Milgram's obedience research, subjects thought they were participating in a learning experiment (a lie—it was really a study on obedience). They believed the middle-aged learner to be another subject (a lie—he was really a confederate). They believed the learner was receiving excruciating electric shocks (a lie—he actually received none), and so on. To the extent the subjects believed all these deceptions, the possibility for subject bias was reduced.

The Milgram study was so well disguised that subjects probably had very little chance to discover its true purpose. Even if subjects could have discovered it, the experiment was so emotionally gripping that they had scant time or attention to devote to anything other than the painful dilemma they faced. Could the Milgram study have been carried out without deception? Probably not. If subjects had known at the start that they were participating in a study on obedience, they probably would not have shown high levels of obedience. Deception, although it entails potential ethical problems, seems to be methodologically essential to this study.

Milgram's experiment used repeated, profound deceptions that led to considerable distress in his subjects. Although most social psychology experiments don't use deception as extreme as that in Milgram's work, many entail some deception, such as "cover stories" designed to mislead subjects about the true purpose of the study (Adair, Dushenko, & Lindsay, 1985; Christensen, 1988; Gross & Fleming, 1982; Sharpe, Adair, & Roese, 1992).

A second solution to subject bias is to measure subjects without their awareness—in other words, to use *nonreactive measures* (sometimes also referred to as *unobtrusive measures*). Subjects who don't realize they are being studied cannot systematically bias results. Nonreactive measures can take many forms: archival data (for example, marriage licenses or singles ads in the newspaper), trace data (for example, how worn particular books are in a library), audio and video recordings of subjects without their knowledge, and so on (Webb, Campbell, Schwartz, Sechrest, & Grove, 1981).

Nonreactive measures can give a "Candid Camera" flavor to social psychology research. To illustrate, suppose you wanted to conduct a survey on alcohol consumption in your community. You could walk door to door, interviewing local residents, but many of your subjects might not answer your questions honestly. You might measure alcohol consumption more accurately by visiting residential streets on trash collection day, searching through garbage cans and counting the number of beer cans, whiskey bottles, and so on. Nutrition studies sometimes use trash-can data as a means of assessing what people really eat. Each of us could be a subject in such a research study without ever knowing it.

ETHICS IN SOCIAL PSYCHOLOGY RESEARCH

Many social psychology studies are straightforward and benign. Research that uses deception and causes distress (as Milgram's studies did) or invades someone's privacy (as trash-can studies may), however, can create a conflict for social psychologists—a dilemma between conducting methodologically sound, unbiased research and treating subjects ethically. How can social psychologists conduct research that is both ethical and scientifically rigorous?

Ethical Problems

The use of nonreactive measures points to one important ethical issue in some social psychology studies: They constitute an *invasion of privacy*. What right do social psychologists have to measure subjects without their awareness? Isn't it wrong to observe people without their consent?

Other studies create *physical and psychological discomfort* in subjects. Milgram's studies, for example, made many of the subjects tense and upset. Imagine you were one of Milgram's subjects. Even if you had eventually disobeyed, you would probably have experienced a great deal of distress. How would *you* feel if you were delivering shocks to a person who shrieked in pain in the next room? And suppose you were one of the majority of subjects who obeyed fully. Wouldn't you emerge from this experience with some very disturbing conclusions about yourself, including "I am willing to inflict horrible pain on another human being merely because someone ordered me to do so"? Does an experimenter have the right to cause this kind of discomfort in subjects?

Deception constitutes yet another ethical dilemma in social psychology research. As we noted earlier, many studies use varying degrees of deception in order to reduce subject bias. But isn't it unethical to lie to people, even in the name of advancing scientific knowledge?

Reducing Ethical Problems: APA Guidelines

The ethical dilemmas that can arise in social psychology research have no absolute solutions. To some extent, each researcher must decide what is ethically acceptable and what is not. Today, studies tend to be much more carefully monitored for potential ethical problems than when Milgram conducted his in the 1960s. The controversy that such studies provoked led psychologists to develop procedures to monitor the ethical propriety of research, and it prompted the federal government to require that each university receiving federal research funds review its research for possible ethical lapses. Further, the excesses of some research pointed to the necessity of institutional control. As a result, the American Psychological Association (APA, 1982) has set forth rigorous guidelines for research on human subjects (see Figure 2.8).

Peer Review

Typically, a proposed study is reviewed by members of a psychology department or a university committee. If the study is judged by the researcher's peers to be at all ethically questionable, it may be rejected, or the researcher may be asked to alter certain procedures or to provide greater safeguards to ensure subjects' well-being.

1. The researcher has the personal responsibility to make a careful ethical evaluation of his or her research.
2. The researcher must determine if subjects are placed at any physical or psychological risk.
3. The researcher is responsible for the treatment of subjects by employees, research assistants, and student researchers.
4. The researcher must establish a clear and fair agreement with subjects before the study (principle of informed consent).
5. Deception is to be employed only when absolutely necessary and when adequate debriefing is provided.
6. Subjects always have the right to decline to participate in a study and to withdraw from a study at any time.
7. The researcher must protect the subject from physical or psychological harm. This includes informing the subject of risk ahead of time, and providing means by which the subject can contact the researcher after the study is over.
8. Whenever possible, research results and hypotheses should be explained to subjects after they participate in a study.
9. The researcher has the responsibility to detect and remove any lasting negative effects of a study on subjects.
10. Information about a subject obtained in a study is confidential. Subjects should be informed who will see data and how the confidentiality of data will be protected.

FIGURE 2.8 Ethical principles for research on humans established by the American Psychological Association.

For example, an ethics committee reviewing a proposal for Milgram's study today might ask the researcher to tone down the experimental procedures, provide subjects with a guaranteed right to quit the study at any time, and have a clinical psychologist on duty at all times to deal with potential emotional problems. Today, many ethics committees would simply reject a proposal for a Milgram-type study. Because of peer review, researchers generally try to minimize deception, discomfort, and invasion of privacy in their studies.

Informed Consent

It is impossible to eliminate deceptive or uncomfortable procedures from all research studies, however. For any study that does involve an activity capable of producing distress or discomfort in subjects, it is essential that researchers obtain each subject's informed consent. Basically, this means each subject is told, at least in rough terms, what the experimental procedure will entail, and furthermore, that he or she may decide to cease participation in the study at any time without penalty. Subjects need not necessarily be given the full details or hypotheses of the study at the start, but they should be filled in on important procedures. If subjects are to receive painful electric shocks, for example, they should be warned of that in advance. Clearly, for subjects who are minors, the notion of consent includes obtaining permission from each child's parents or guardian.

Although clear-cut in theory, the notion of informed consent is somewhat fuzzy in practice. Sometimes it is necessary to conduct certain procedures without the subject's awareness. How complete must a description be to satisfy ethical concerns, yet avoid biasing the study? If you were conducting the Milgram experiment, how much would you tell the subjects at the start?

In studies using nonreactive measures, obtaining informed consent prior to collecting data is impossible. One solution is to obtain such consent after data collection. For example, a researcher who videotapes subjects without their knowledge could inform them after it's over and give them the choice of permitting the use of the videotapes or having them erased.

Debriefing

Informed consent focuses on providing information to subjects *before* they participate in a study. *After* the study is completed, the experimenter must also provide information in the form of a debriefing, or postexperiment interview. Debriefing is an essential part of any carefully conducted social psychology experiment. At this time the experimenter carefully explains any deception that occurred and determines whether the subject was upset by any procedure. Debriefings also serve an important methodological purpose: The experimenter learns what subjects were thinking during the experiment, whether or not they saw through the study, and whether experimental manipulations worked as planned.

Of course, in any study that causes distress in subjects, the researchers should conduct a particularly careful and thorough debriefing. The researchers may even employ clinical psychologists or psychiatrists to interview subjects after the study

Research on animals has been the subject of much recent debate. Research on human subjects can also pose serious ethical questions.

"ACCORDING TO THE AGENDA, TODAY WE START NEGOTIATING WITH THE GUINEA PIGS' LAWYER."

is completed. Ideally, a subject should leave an experiment in a positive mood, unaltered in any lasting way by the experimental procedures.

Some social psychology experiments intentionally give subjects false information about *themselves* as part of the experimental manipulation. In a study on the effects of self-esteem on romantic attraction, Walster (1965) first gave female college students a fake personality test and then falsely told some of the women that they had well-adjusted personalities and others that they had poorly-adjusted personalities. (This experiment, by the way, found that the women with falsely lowered self-esteem were more romantically attracted to a handsome male confederate than were the women with falsely elevated self-esteem.) As part of the debriefing in this experiment, the researcher had to inform the subjects that the personality test results they received were faked.

The debriefing of the women with lowered self-esteem required particular care, because a number of research studies suggest that subjects often continue to believe false information about themselves presented in experiments, even after being informed of the deception (Jennings, Lepper, & Ross, 1981; Ross, Lepper, & Hubbard, 1975). Thus, the women who had been told that they were poorly adjusted might have continued to experience lowered self-esteem even after being assured that the negative feedback was not true. Apparently, subjects often convince themselves during the course of an experiment that false information is really true. (We will consider the perseverance of false beliefs more fully in Chapter

5.) The ethical implication for social psychology research is clear: Any study that provides subjects with false information about themselves must include especially careful and thorough debriefing procedures.

Please note that we have discussed several dramatic studies to illustrate ethical issues in social psychology research. Although some studies raise serious ethical questions, many others use little or no deception, invade no one's privacy, and create no discomfort.

Were the Milgram Experiments Ethical?

In a large number of cases the degree of tension reached extremes that are rarely seen in sociopsychological laboratory studies. Subjects were observed to sweat, tremble, stutter, bite their lips, groan, and dig their fingernails into their flesh. These were characteristic rather than exceptional responses to the experiment.

One sign of tension was the regular occurrence of nervous laughing fits. Fourteen of the 40 subjects showed definite signs of nervous laughing and smiling. The laughter seemed entirely out of place, even bizarre. Full-blown, uncontrollable seizures were observed for 3 subjects. On one occasion we observed a seizure so violently convulsive that it was necessary to call a halt to the experiment.

(Milgram, 1963, p. 375)

Stanley Milgram's obedience experiments created a storm of controversy that has continued to the present (Blass, 1992; Miller, 1986). Is it ethical to expose subjects to pain, distress, and possible long-term psychological changes in order to carry out scientific research? After Milgram published reports of his first obedience experiments, Diana Baumrind (1964) severely criticized the ethics of his research on several levels. She noted:

- Milgram's procedures created unacceptable levels of stress in subjects, as his own descriptions showed.
- Milgram's study could have lasting negative effects on subjects. When the hoax was revealed at the end of the study, they would feel foolish and used. Obedient subjects would have to live with the realization that they *would have* shocked the victim if the procedure had been for real.
- More generally, the embarrassing experience of being duped might leave subjects alienated and suspicious of psychologists and of legitimate authorities in general.
- Whereas a procedure that was somewhat traumatic to subjects might be justified if the studies yielded insights about real-life obedience, obedience in the laboratory is unlike obedience in real life. Subjects have a dependent, trusting relationship with an experimenter that they do not necessarily have with real-life authority figures. Also, the laboratory is an unfamiliar and ambiguous setting that can render subjects more vulnerable to influence.

In responding to Baumrind's criticisms, Milgram (1964) noted that no one could have predicted the ethical dilemmas created by his research before it was actually conducted. The subjects' extreme levels of obedience and their accompanying distress became apparent only after the first studies were run.

At that point, Milgram had to choose whether or not to continue his experiments.

He decided that although his procedures created "momentary excitement," they did not produce long-term negative effects in the vast majority of subjects. He based this conclusion partly on questionnaires that subjects completed after participating in his experiments. In general, subjects reported that they were glad to have participated in the obedience experiment; in addition, about three-fourths stated that they had learned important things about themselves. A small minority of subjects (about 1%) reported that they were "sorry" or "very sorry" to have been in the experiment.

Milgram conducted careful debriefings of his subjects, and a year after his initial experiment, he asked a psychiatrist to interview 40 of his subjects to determine whether his study had had "possible injurious effects." This follow-up revealed no indications of long-term distress or traumatic reactions.

Did Milgram's experiments lead subjects to be less trusting of authorities? Milgram reversed Baumrind's argument: "The experimenter is not just any authority: He is an authority who tells the subject to act harshly and inhumanely against another man. I would consider it of the highest value if participation in the experiment could . . . inculcate a skepticism of this kind of authority" (p. 852).

In response to Baumrind's criticism that subjects in psychology experiments are particularly prone to being influenced by the experimenter, Milgram pointed out that about a third of his subjects successfully rebelled against the experimenter's inhumane commands. He argued that a "person who comes to the laboratory is an active, choosing adult, capable of accepting or rejecting the prescriptions for action addressed to him" (p. 852). Many social psychologists, however, have viewed Milgram's research as a classic demonstration of the power of social settings to overwhelm an individual's freedom of choice and inner values (Blass, 1992; Miller, 1986). It is thus ironic that Milgram justified his experiments by appealing to the subjects' "free will."

As this discussion shows, ethical issues in research are not always clear-cut. Were Milgram's studies ethical? You must be the final judge.

The Social Relevance of Social Psychology Research

In weighing the ethics of social psychology research, it is important to consider the contributions such research makes to science and to society. Research on TV viewing and aggression, for example, obviously has great significance to parents, educators, and society at large. And while Milgram's research extends our theoretical understanding of the factors that influence obedience, it also relates to a pressing real-life issue: Under what circumstances will people obey malevolent authority and commit atrocities against other human beings? Milgram was motivated by a terrible real-life example: Nazis who were "just following orders" when they murdered millions of innocent people during World War II. The implications of Milgram's findings extend well beyond the initial motivating example, however. Perhaps one reason so many people have been so dismayed by Milgram's results is that they provide disturbing evidence that "it *could* happen here."

Certainly, we cannot justify treating subjects unethically to gain valuable knowledge, but in evaluating the ethical pluses and minuses of social psychology research, we should acknowledge as a definite plus the potential of research to help us understand social problems, and design solutions to them. Since its beginnings in the early part of this century, social psychology has probed such important topics as the causes of aggression, the nature of prejudice, the dynamics of propaganda and persuasion, and the good and bad ways groups influence individuals. Recently, social psychology has turned to other applied topics as well, including health psychology, the social psychology of the legal system, and environmental psychology (Rodin, 1985; see Chapters 14, 15, and 16). To the extent it addresses both socially relevant issues and basic theoretical questions about social behavior, social psychology will continue to challenge the ingenuity of its best researchers and the ethics of its best moral thinkers.

RESEARCH METHODS IN PERSPECTIVE

While it is easy to pose many fascinating questions about social behavior, it is not so easy to answer these questions unambiguously with sound scientific studies. Social psychologists attempt to understand social behavior through the application of the scientific method, and over the years they have developed careful, objective procedures for answering questions about social behavior.

Theories of social behavior help social psychologists generate specific testable propositions, or hypotheses. To test their hypotheses, social psychologists observe and measure social behavior. Like all scientists, social psychologists use operational definitions that describe concepts in terms of concrete measurement procedures.

Social psychologists conduct experiments to show cause-effect relationships and correlational studies to demonstrate that two variables are related. Both kinds of study provide useful information. No single study ever conclusively answers a question about social behavior, however. Scientific generalizations in social psychology depend on the cumulative results of many studies.

Social psychology studies are sometimes vulnerable to kinds of bias not found in the natural sciences. Social psychologists have met this challenge by developing procedures and techniques that help guarantee the objectivity of their studies.

Social psychology experiments sometimes create ethical dilemmas. Consequently, researchers have developed careful procedures to safeguard subjects' rights. The challenge of social psychology research is to answer the innumerable questions that we all have about social behavior with studies that are both ethically and scientifically sound.

Posing Questions to Study

KEY POINTS

The scientific method requires that empirical measurements be used to test hypotheses and the theories from which they are derived. Theories are sets of propositions that help explain, predict, and organize empirical data.

Measuring Social Behavior: Operational Definitions

Operational definitions describe concepts in terms of the procedures used to measure them. Subjective reports and behavioral measures are two types of operational definitions used in social psychology.

Reliability and Validity of Measures

Scientific measures should be both reliable and valid. A reliable measure is consistent and repeatable; a valid measure assesses what it is supposed to and relates to real-life criteria.

Kinds of Social Psychology Research

Social psychologists conduct experiments, correlational studies, and quasi-experimental studies.

Experiments demonstrate cause–effect relationships. In experiments, researchers manipulate independent variables and observe their effects on dependent variables, and they randomly assign subjects to experimental conditions in order to minimize the effects of extraneous variables.

In correlational studies, researchers observe naturally occurring relationships between variables. Such studies cannot prove that one variable causes effects in another.

In quasi-experimental studies, a variable is manipulated, but subjects are not randomly assigned to conditions. Quasi-experimental designs are often used to study social interventions over which researchers have no direct control.

From Research to the Real World: The Issue of Generalizability

A fundamental question in social psychology research is: When do the results of a study apply to broader populations and settings?

Laboratory versus Field Studies

Laboratory studies are conducted in controlled, laboratory environments, whereas field studies are conducted in natural settings. Either type of study can be an experiment or a correlational study. Field studies necessarily generalize to a real-life setting.

Generalizing from the Results of Experiments

Because real life is complex and messy, experiments tend to study the effects of a small number of variables in simplified and controlled settings. Even when they don't duplicate real-life conditions, experiments and their results may apply to real life by supporting theories that apply to real life.

Well-designed experiments possess internal and external validity. An experiment possesses internal validity when its variables are measured and manipulated properly, and it possesses external validity when its results can be generalized to broader settings and populations. The confounding, or simultaneous occurrence, of variables can be a threat to internal and external validity.

Replication: Accumulating Research Findings. Our confidence in scientific results is increased by replication (exact or modified repetitions of a study).

Meta-Analysis: Combining the Results of Many Studies. Meta-analysis is a statistical technique that combines the results of many studies to determine the reliability of those results, the average size of results, and whether results depend on other variables.

Statistics and Social Psychology Research

Statistical analysis is necessary to describe data and to test whether findings are legitimate or attributable to chance. Research results are considered statistically significant when "p-levels" are less than .05, and are thus unlikely to be the result of chance.

The correlation coefficient—a statistical measure that can range from -1 to 1—gauges the degree of association between two variables.

Bias in Social Psychology Research

Social psychology research is subject to biases not found in natural science research.

Experimenter Bias

Experimenter bias occurs when experimenters inadvertently communicate their hypotheses to subjects. Blind experiments, standardization, and mechanization of experiments are methods used to reduce or eliminate experimenter bias.

Subject Bias

Subject bias occurs when participants figure out the purpose of a study or respond to demand characteristics (revealing cues in the experimental setting). Deception and nonreactive (unobtrusive) measures can be used to reduce or eliminate subject bias.

Ethics in Social Psychology Research

Social psychology research sometimes raises ethical questions and requires ethical safeguards.

Ethical Problems

The subjects in social psychology experiments sometimes suffer pain, psychological discomfort, deception, and invasion of privacy.

Reducing Ethical Problems: APA Guidelines

Professional guidelines, institutional peer review, informed consent, and careful debriefing help guarantee that researchers treat subjects in ethically acceptable ways.

Most proposed social psychology studies are reviewed by committees that screen them for potential ethical problems before they are carried out.

Informed consent means that research subjects are told of procedures they will be exposed to in a study and assured that they have the right to withdraw from the study at any time without penalty.

Subjects in social psychology research typically participate in a postexperiment interview called a debriefing, in which they describe their reactions to the study and are informed of the study's purpose and of any deception that occurred.

Were the Milgram Experiments Ethical?

Subjects in Milgram's obedience experiments experienced considerable distress. Many of them learned unpleasant facts about themselves, and may have come to distrust legitimate authorities. Milgram argued that despite subjects' discomfort, his experiment was ethical.

The Social Relevance of Social Psychology Research

Social psychology research often addresses socially important topics and so makes a positive contribution to society.

KEY TERMS

Behavioral measures: Direct observations or measurements of subjects' behavior that do not rely on subjects' reports about themselves.

Blind experiments: Experiments in which the experimenters do not know what conditions subjects are in; in *double-blind* experiments, neither subjects nor experimenters know what conditions subjects are in.

Confounded variables: Variables are said to be confounded in a study when they occur simultaneously, and thus it is impossible to tell which variable accounts for the observed effects.

Control group: A group of subjects in an experiment that is not exposed to the experimental treatment and serves as a comparison group.

Correlation coefficient: A statistical measure of the degree of linear relationship between two variables; can range from −1 to 1.

Correlational study: A study in which the relation between naturally occurring variables is observed; no variables are manipulated, and subjects are not randomly assigned to conditions.

Debriefing: A postexperiment interview between experimenter and subject in which the experimenter learns about the subject's reactions to the experiment, reveals any deception, and explains the purpose of the study.

Demand characteristics: Cues in experimental settings that inappropriately influence subjects' behavior and thus bias results.

Dependent variable: The variable that is influenced by the independent variable in an experiment.

Experiment: A study in which an independent variable is manipulated so that its effect on the dependent variable can be observed, and subjects are randomly assigned to experimental conditions. Experiments permit cause-effect conclusions.

Experimenter bias: Contamination of research results that occurs when experimenters inappropriately communicate their hypotheses and expectations to their subjects.

External validity: The degree to which the results of an experiment generalize to broader settings and populations.

Extraneous variables: In an experiment, variables other than the independent variable that may influence the dependent variable. The effect of extraneous variables is minimized by random assignment of subjects.

Field study: A study conducted in a natural environment outside the laboratory.

Independent variable: The variable that the researcher controls and manipulates in an experiment to determine whether it influences the dependent variable.

Inferential statistics: The branch of statistics that deals with drawing conclusions from data and testing hypotheses.

Informed consent: The process of telling subjects about the general procedures used in a study and obtaining their consent to participate as subjects.

Internal validity: A property possessed by an experiment when variables are measured and manipulated properly and when variables are not confounded with other variables.

Laboratory study: A study (usually carefully controlled and standardized) that is carried out in a laboratory environment.

Meta-analysis: A statistical technique used to quantitatively combine the findings of many studies on the same topic in order to determine whether findings are reliable, the overall magnitude of findings, and whether findings depend on other variables.

Nonreactive measures: Measures of subjects' behavior obtained without their knowledge. Also known as *unobtrusive measures.*

Operational definition: A definition of a concept in terms of the specific procedures or methods used to measure it.

Quasi-experimental study: A study in which a variable is manipulated, but subjects are not randomly assigned to conditions.

Random assignment: Occurs when a subject has an equal probability of being assigned to experimental conditions. An essential requirement for an experiment.

Reliability: The repeatability and consistency of a measure.

Replication: Repeating a study, exactly or with some variations, to show that its results are reliable.

Statistical significance: The probability that research findings are attributable to chance. In psychology, results are considered statistically significant if the probability is less than .05 that the results are attributable to chance.

Subject bias: Contamination of research results that occurs when subjects pick up cues from the experimental setting or figure out the purpose of the study.

Subjective reports: Data that consist of subjects' statements about their own behavior or mental states; typically collected via rating scales, questionnaires, or interviews.

Validity: The ability of a measure to predict real-life criteria; a measure is valid when it measures what it is supposed to measure.

Variable: A measured social psychology concept.

PERSONALITY AND THE SELF

In published interviews, the rock star Madonna has acknowledged she is an exhibitionist and that she likes to make outrageous statements: "It's not something I sit around and think about. It's rather unconscious. I just sort of naturally say things to shock, not necessarily to offend" (*Rolling Stone*, October 15, 1992, p. 178). In addition, Madonna has stated that while she is comfortable with nudity, she doesn't like everything about her body: "I look in the mirror and go, 'ugh'. . . I find all kind of flaws. It's like, 'Oh God, why couldn't I be taller?'" (*Newsweek*, November 2, 1992, p. 103). Finally, Madonna has admitted that she's sometimes sick of being Madonna and that she would like to go out in public once in a while and not be recognized.

Y̦ou now know a little bit about what Madonna thinks about herself—her personality traits, her physical self, and her role as an entertainer. The purpose of this information is not to focus on Madonna, however. Rather, it is to get you to think about the two concepts that are central to this chapter: personality and the self. So, enough about Madonna. Let's turn to a more interesting topic: namely, you.

Who are you?

Since I can't interview you, I'd like you to interview yourself by completing the following exercise. Take a sheet of paper and write the following sentence ten times: "I am _____ ." Fill in the blank with a new answer each time. List what you think are the ten most salient characteristics that describe who you are.

Finished? How did you describe yourself? Perhaps you listed your personality traits ("I am shy"), your abilities ("I am intelligent"), your physical traits ("I am fit"), and your membership in social or ethnic groups ("I am Hispanic"). Maybe you used other kinds of self-descriptions as well.

In this simple exercise, you have just described aspects of your personality and your self. Do you think the characteristics you listed significantly influence your behavior? If you are like most people, your answer is probably yes. Indeed, the self and the personality constitute two of the most intuitively appealing explanations we can offer for our own and others' behavior. Perhaps you explain your reluctance to talk to strangers at parties as arising from your shyness (a personality trait), for example, and your volunteer charity work by noting that you see yourself as a helpful person (that is, being helpful is part of your self-concept).

As these examples illustrate, the concepts of personality and the self refer to processes *within* individuals that are believed to influence their behavior. Although social psychology has traditionally emphasized *situational* factors that affect how we behave with others, in recent years many social psychologists have turned their attention to the effects of personality and the self on social behavior (Markus & Wurf, 1987; Snyder & Ickes, 1985; Suls & Greenwald, 1986).

The many faces of Madonna. Right: *On stage.* Far right: *Off stage, attending a basketball game.*

Social psychologists have studied certain personality traits because they relate directly to specific social behaviors, such as discriminating against others, helping others, hurting others, and affiliating with others. The traits of introversion and shyness, for example, may affect the degree to which people affiliate with others and form friendships. Social psychologists have studied other traits because they influence when people behave consistently with other personality characteristics or, in contrast, when they respond primarily to social pressures. As we shall see later in this chapter, some kinds of people (termed low-self-monitoring individuals) are influenced relatively more by their inner traits, attitudes, and values, and consequently tend to behave more consistently across situations. Others (high-self-monitoring individuals) are influenced more by their social setting and consequently may behave quite differently in different circumstances.

From a conceptual point of view, the self is an important topic in social psychology because it links the individual, social influences, and social behavior (Greenwald, 1982; Schlenker, 1985). The self contains the internalized rules and standards of society. Because these standards become part of the self, they can lead us to behave—at least at times—in socially approved ways. For example, do you believe you are honest? If your answer is yes, do you usually act in accordance with that view of yourself? How did you acquire *honesty* as part of your self-concept?

In addition to examining how the self affects social behavior, social psychologists also explore how social influences affect the self. Paradoxically, the self—perhaps the most private and individual aspect of each of us—has social origins and social consequences. You'll probably agree that your self-concept depends a great deal on feedback you have received from your family, your friends, your teachers, and so on. Could you know that you are "honest," "intelligent," "attractive," or "unathletic" without feedback from other people or without comparing yourself with others?

Viewing personality and the self in social terms leads social psychologists to pose some fundamental questions about who we are as individuals. Do we each possess consistent, unitary selves, or do we have many selves? Do most of us have stable personality traits that make us behave consistently across many settings and over time, or are we to some extent chameleons, "different people" in different situations and at various times. For example, would you describe yourself as shy, outgoing, or something in between? However you think of yourself, aren't there times when you act more shy and other times you act less shy? Perhaps you are most shy with new acquaintances but the life of the party with close friends, or outgoing with peers but quiet around groups of older people. If in fact our behavior varies across situations, can we really say we have fixed "traits" that determine how we act? To what degree can we alter what we think of as our personalities?

Social psychologists have posed many questions about social influences on personality and the self: Do we change our self-concept and the way we present ourselves to others depending on who we're with? (Do you think the way Madonna acts in front of an audience is different from the way she acts when alone at home?) How do we arrive at our social identities—the beliefs we share with others about who we are? (How does Madonna know she is an "exhibitionist"? Do you agree that she is? Why?)

As we follow the thread of such questions, we soon find that personality and the self, and their relationship to behavior, are more complex than most of us would imagine. The concepts of personality and the self address the intricate interplay between our inner world (our traits and beliefs about ourselves) and our outer world of social relationships and roles (our friends and the feedback they provide us and roles as students, family members, and so on).

This chapter begins by examining the concept of personality. We start with two major theoretical approaches to understanding personality—trait theories and social learning theories—and then describe research generated by these two approaches. Next, we consider the related topic of the self. A discussion of classic theories of the self will lead us to a number of basic empirical questions: How does the self develop? How is knowledge about the self stored in our memory, and how does this knowledge influence the way we think about ourselves and others? How does our self-concept regulate our behavior? Do we have different public and private selves—one we show to others and one we reveal only to ourselves? Applying what we learn about the self, we will turn finally to a practical question: How is the self-concept related to mental health?

As we discuss these questions, you may want to return to the ten characteristics you listed to describe yourself. Consider the research findings we review in terms of this list: What are the ways you characteristically describe yourself? How did you learn these self-descriptions? Are your traits and characteristics consistent or contradictory? And what effects do your personality and self-concept have on your behavior?

PERSONALITY AND SOCIAL BEHAVIOR

Characters in a play typically have distinctive and consistent traits. Shakespeare's Macbeth, for example, possessed unprincipled ambition; Othello, uncontrollable jealousy; and Hamlet, chronic melancholy and indecisiveness. Do real people show such consistent traits?

The term *personality* traditionally has referred to the distinctive, internal, and consistent qualities and outward behaviors that seem to make one individual unlike the next. Personality psychologists generally study the ways people *differ* from one another. For example, some individuals (like Madonna) are exhibitionistic and outgoing, others are shy and reserved; some are dominant, others submissive; some are anxious and nervous, others calm and relaxed. Personality theories try to explain and understand such individual differences in terms of a variety of *internal* processes that influence our behavior, such as our traits, interpersonal needs, expectations, and knowledge.

Implicit in the traditional concept of personality is the idea that people show behavioral *consistency,* both across settings and over time (Allport, 1937; Mischel, 1968; Mischel & Peake, 1983). For example, if Madonna is an "extroverted" person, she presumably displays extroverted behaviors frequently and in many situations: she has many friends, she talks readily with other people wherever she is, and she often seeks out parties and other ways of being with people. Furthermore, if she is an extroverted person today, she is likely to continue to be extroverted a year from now, or ten years from now.

These central themes of personality psychology—individual differences, internal causes of behavior, and the consistency of behavior—have been addressed by two distinct theoretical approaches: trait theories and social learning theories. Although other approaches to personality exist, such as psychoanalytic and humanistic theories (see Liebert & Spiegler, 1987; Maddi, 1976), trait and social learning theories have generated the most empirical research in contemporary social psychology. Furthermore, these approaches address a fundamental question that is central to social psychology: How much is our behavior determined by stable internal traits, and how much is it determined by situational factors?

Mel Gibson as Hamlet. Do people have consistent traits, like characters in a play?

Trait Theories: Personality as Stable Internal Dispositions

Do you think people show consistent behavior across time and settings? Do you often explain how someone acts by saying "That's just how he is" or "She has that type of personality"?

If you answered yes to these questions, you most likely subscribe to a trait theory of personality. Trait theories are based on the premise that people possess internal dispositions (such as extroversion, shyness, and honesty) that have a general influence on their behavior. Consequently, these theories assume that people tend to show consistent behavior across time and settings, and that their behavior is directly related to an underlying trait. Notable trait theories include those formulated by Gordon Allport (1937, 1961), Raymond Cattell (1965), and Hans Eysenck (1952).

Most of us, as amateur personality psychologists, are trait theorists. Indeed, traits often constitute the largest single category of terms we use to describe other people and ourselves (Park, 1986). (Return to the ten characteristics you listed at the start of this chapter to describe yourself and count how many of them are personality traits.) But everyday notions of personality traits must be made more exact to be scientifically useful. Two key tasks for trait theorists are *identifying* and *measuring* personality traits.

Identifying Personality Traits

A major challenge for trait theories is cataloging how many basic traits there are in human personality. In a monumental compilation, Allport and Odbert (1936) identified some 18,000 trait words used in the English language. Clearly, to arrive

at useful generalizations, trait theories must focus on considerably fewer fundamental traits. Fortunately, studies in which subjects are asked to rate themselves on
large numbers of traits disclose considerable redundancy in trait words. For
example, the traits *introverted, reserved,* and *outgoing* may all describe pretty much
the same dimensions of personality—*outgoing,* of course, is simply the reverse of
the first two. Indeed, statistical analyses using a technique called factor analysis
show that subjects' ratings of themselves often boil down to just a small number of
underlying factors, or cohesive trait dimensions.

Five broad and fundamental trait dimensions (often referred to as the "Big
Five") are repeatedly found in personality research: *extroversion, agreeableness,
conscientiousness, emotional stability,* and *openness/culturedness* (Digman, 1990;
Hogan, 1983; John, 1991; McCrae & Costa, 1987). Traits related to the Big Five
are shown in Figure 3.1. Personality researchers often find these Big Five personality

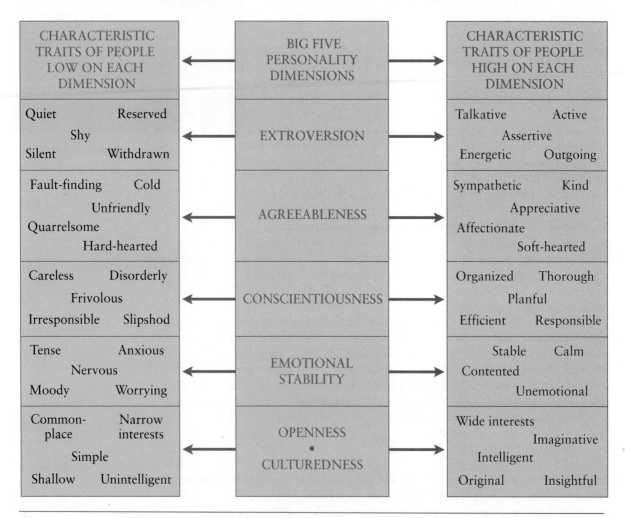

FIGURE 3.1 The "Big Five" dimensions of personality. *Source:* Adapted from John, in Pervin (1990).

traits in studies on people from other countries and cultures as well as in studies on residents of the United States and Canada (Church & Katigbak, 1989; Digman, 1990; Goldberg, 1993; John, 1990; Paunonen, Jackson, Trzebinski, & Forsterling, 1992). The Big Five constitute very general "superfactors" of personality. Numerous more-specific traits can be measured as well—for example, extroversion might be broken down into more-specific subtraits such as sociability, impulsiveness, and assertiveness.

Measuring Personality Traits

Psychologists often measure traits with standardized personality questionnaires that ask subjects to rate themselves on specific traits (such as *aggressive* or *extroverted*) or to answer trait-related questions (such as "I enjoy going to parties often") either by choosing a fixed response ("Yes/No" or "True/False") or by checking a scale (for example, a 5-point scale ranging from "Strongly agree" to "Strongly disagree"). A good personality test is carefully crafted; its questions or items are selected by rigorous statistical analysis and test-development procedures (Anastase, 1976; Cronbach, 1984). Generally, proposed test items are administered to large groups of people, and only those items that successfully discriminate among people with respect to the trait under examination are used in the final test. For example, only those questions that on average are answered differently by people who have independently been identified as anxious and nonanxious people (for example, by clinical psychologists) will be used in an anxiety scale.

A good personality test demonstrates two important properties we discussed in Chapter 2: *reliability* and *validity*. A reliable test measures a trait consistently. A valid personality test truly measures the trait it's intended to measure and predicts real-life behaviors relevant to the trait. Figure 3.2 describes several different kinds of reliability and validity in personality tests.

Shyness as a Trait

Are you shy? If so, you're in good company. More than 80% of college students report that they have been shy at some point in their lives, and about 40% describe themselves as chronically and consistently shy (Zimbardo, 1986). Extreme shyness has the power to disrupt normal social relationships and can show itself in physical symptoms such as blushing, sweating, and nervous butterflies in the stomach. Shyness also shows itself in characteristic thought processes such as painful self-consciousness and self-criticism in social settings, and in social behaviors such as keeping quiet in groups, avoiding eye contact with others, and awkward body language (Cheek & Melchior, 1990).

Researchers investigating shyness have found that it can be conceptualized as a personality trait, and they have developed a number of scales to measure it (Briggs, Cheek, & Jones, 1986). Shyness, as measured by such scales, correlates positively with measures of fearfulness and anxiety (that is, the shyer you are, the more fearful you are), and negatively with measures of self-esteem,

Kinds of Reliability	
Internal reliability	All items of the personality scale (for example, a shyness scale) measure the same trait.
Temporal (test-retest) reliability	Measure is reliable over time. For example, if people fill in a shyness scale two times, a month apart, their scores are quite similar each time.
Reliability across measures	Different measures of same trait correlate with one another. For example, two different shyness scales correlate strongly.
Kinds of Validity	
Concurrent validity	The measure correlates with currently related behaviors. For example, people's scores on a shyness scale correlate with their current degree of participation in a group discussion.
Predictive validity	The measure predicts related future behavior. For example, scores on a shyness scale predict the number of new friends people make during the coming year.
Discriminant validity	The measure predicts related behaviors better than other measures. For example, a shyness scale predicts better than an anxiety scale people's physiological arousal when talking to a new person.
Construct validity	The measure shows patterns of correlations with other variables that make theoretical sense. For example, shyness scales correlate positively with measures of fearfulness and anxiety and negatively with measures of self-esteem and extroversion.

FIGURE 3.2 Kinds of reliability and validity.

assertiveness, and extroversion (the shyer you are, the less self-esteem you have). Shy behaviors are relatively stable over time and settings (Briggs, Cheek, & Jones, 1986), and studies show that genetic factors have a substantial impact on individuals' degree of shyness (Plomin & Daniels, 1986).

Although shyness has a hereditary component, shy people *can* learn to modify and reduce their shyness when it creates problems in their lives (Scholing & Emmelkamp, 1990). For example, they can learn relaxation exercises and social skills to make them more comfortable in social settings (Alden & Cappe, 1986), and they can learn to open up in groups that have rules encouraging everyone to speak and participate (Zimbardo, 1986).

One effective treatment program for shy people used a uniquely social psychological approach (Haemmerlie & Montgomery, 1986). As you know, social psychology emphasizes the power of the social setting to influence behavior. A number of social psychology theories have followed up on this insight by suggesting that one way to change people's self-concept ("I am shy") is to first place them in a setting that leads them to change their behavior—for example, by putting them in a situation where they will talk successfully with others. (Note that this is just the opposite of the assumption of many psychotherapies—that first you must change a person's self-concept through counseling, and then behavioral changes will follow.)

In one study, Haemmerlie and Montgomery (1982) identified a group of college men who were particularly shy with women and who consequently didn't date much. The researchers asked the men, in the context of participating in a psychology experiment, to engage in 10- to 12-minute conversations with college women who were instructed to be as friendly as possible. The men did not know they were being "treated" for their shyness; they simply thought they were subjects in a study on "dyadic interaction processes." Most of the men showed a long-term reduction in their shyness as a result of this simple procedure. A second study found the same results for a group of shy college women; having pleasant and successful conversations with friendly college men significantly reduced their shyness (Haemmerlie, 1983).

Such research makes an important point: Although personality traits like shyness sometimes have a strong impact on our behavior, we are still capable of learning to modify our behavior. If you feel uncomfortably shy in some settings, first remember that you are not alone. The next new person you talk to at a party may be just as shy as you. Experiment with new behaviors designed to reduce your shyness. For example, any time you're in a group of people, experiment with talking to a new person, if only for a minute or so. And remember, if you feel unable to overcome your shyness by yourself, you can seek out the help of knowledgeable counselors and clinical psychologists who can work with you at developing effective strategies to reduce your shyness.

Shyness can lead to discomfort and isolation in social settings.

Social Learning Theories: Personality as Learned Behavior

So far, we have considered viewpoints that see personality in terms of traits. But are traits really the whole story? For example, do you think *masculinity* and *femininity* are fixed traits? Are some men highly masculine (for example, Ralph loves to watch football and race cars, and he wants to be an Army officer), whereas other men are consistently not masculine (Henry loves to watch ballet and to paint, and he wants to be an interior decorator)? The trait approach to masculinity and femininity tends to assume that people have a fixed degree of masculinity and femininity and, furthermore, that people tend to behave in ways that are consistent with their traits across situations. For example, if Juanita is highly feminine, then she should be feminine at home, at school, on dates, and at work. (See Chapter 8 for a detailed discussion of masculinity and femininity).

Proponents of social learning theories tend to disagree with the assumptions we just listed about masculinity and femininity; they view masculine and feminine behaviors as *learned* rather than as the surface manifestation of fixed traits. More generally, social learning theories (for example, those of Bandura, 1977, 1986; Miller & Dollard, 1941; Mischel, 1973; Rotter, 1954) consider the environment, not internal traits, to be the source of many of the individual differences we call personality. A basic assumption of social learning theories is that individual differences in behavior are learned through such processes as classical conditioning, operant conditioning, and observational learning.

Another assumption is that behavior is *not* necessarily consistent across settings and over time. For example, Ralph may be masculine when he's around his "macho" friends who reward masculinity, but he may behave in less masculine ways when he's with his family. And Juanita might be extroverted with her close friends, who always respond warmly to her, but introverted at the Ritz Country Club, where people tend to snub her. Think about your own behavior. Are you consistently shy, anxious, masculine, or feminine in all situations, or do you behave quite differently depending on who you are with and where you are?

Research based on social learning theories relies more on actual observation of behavior and on individuals' subjective reports of their own behavior than on standardized personality tests. For example, a social learning researcher who wanted to study Juanita's anxiety might measure her heart rate in different situations or ask her to keep a diary of her anxious feelings at different times and places throughout the day. The idea behind such research is to study the environments that elicit specific kinds of behavior (Mischel, 1982). According to social learning theories, the individuality of our personalities is not the product of a unique pattern of traits; instead, it resides in a person's unique *pattern of behavior and learning history*. In other words, what makes Juanita unique is not traits of shyness, anxiety, femininity, and so on, but the highly individualized array of situations in which she has learned to be shy, or anxious, or feminine.

What, then, do social learning theories say about the three central tenets of trait theory: the existence of general internal causes of behavior, stable individual differences, and behavioral consistency? As you probably have already surmised, social learning theories question all three assumptions. First, behavior is seen not as a function of internal traits, but as the product of environmental factors. Second, individual differences are not considered to be always stable; people can learn to behave in new ways. Third, behavior is not deemed to be always consistent across settings; rather, different environments often elicit different behaviors. Behavior may show consistency *over time in the same setting*, however, because the same environmental factors are present (Mischel & Peake, 1983; Wright & Mischel, 1987). Thus, for example, your level of shyness may vary with the situation, but you are *always* shy at cocktail parties when you don't know anyone present.

Traits or Social Learning? Testing the Assumptions of Personality Theories

Clearly, trait theories and social learning theory make different assumptions and correspondingly different predictions about behavior. Notice, though, that these predictions can be tested. That is, if we want to know which approach is right, we can make specific predictions based on each set of assumptions and then see which predictions are borne out. This is precisely the *empirical* approach that characterizes a scientific investigation of such questions as whether men and women show stable levels of masculine and feminine behavior, and whether people vary in their level of shyness across situations. Let's turn to some empirical research that investigates the utility and limits of trait theories and social learning theories.

Testing the Assumptions of Trait Theories

Do measured personality traits in fact strongly predict people's behavior? Several major reviews of personality research in the 1960s (Mischel, 1968; Peterson, 1968; Vernon, 1964) suggested that traits are *not* particularly good predictors of behavior. In an influential book, *Personality and Assessment,* Walter Mischel (1968) noted that the correlations between trait measures of personality and behavioral criteria typically were quite small, rarely exceeding .3. (Recall from Chapter 2 that zero represents no correlation, and 1 is a perfect correlation.)

How has trait theory's major prediction that behavior is consistent across situations fared in research studies? Personality psychologists have studied the cross-situational consistency of behavior for over half a century. In one classic study, Hartshorne and May (1928, 1929; Hartshorne, May, & Shuttleworth, 1930) measured the "morality" of schoolchildren in a number of different settings. For example, they recorded how much the children cheated on tests, stole party favors, broke rules in athletic contests, and so on. Surprisingly, they found little consistency in the children's moral behavior; a given child might cheat on tests, for example, but never steal. Such findings clearly contradict the hypothesis that children possess a general trait of "morality" or "immorality." Other studies have shown that people are frequently inconsistent with respect to degrees of extroversion, punctuality, and conscientiousness (Dudycha, 1936; Mischel & Peake, 1982, 1983; Newcomb, 1929).

Does this evidence suggest that trait theory, although intuitively appealing, is simply wrong? Not necessarily. Some personality theorists have argued that early researchers' inability to demonstrate consistencies among behaviors, and between traits and behaviors, was in part attributable to flawed research methodology. For example, Epstein (1980, 1983) argued that in order to measure behavior *reliably,* researchers must "aggregate" behaviors—that is, obtain a sum of many measures of behavior—rather than assess single behaviors. Reliability is a prerequisite to validity. In order for trait measures to predict behavior and for behavior to show consistency, both behavior and traits must be measured reliably.

In research that provided support for this point, Jaccard (1974) reported a correlation of only .1 between a trait measure of dominance and subjects' self-reports of single dominant behaviors (such as "controlling conversations"); the correlation coefficient increased dramatically to .6, however, when trait scores were used to predict a summed measure of 40 *different* dominant behaviors. Similarly, Epstein and O'Brien (1985) reported that when classic studies such as Hartshorne and May's research on morality in children are reanalyzed using *summed* measures of behavior, behavior proves to be much more "traitlike" and consistent.

Bem (1983; Bem & Allen, 1974) offered another remedy for the poor performance of trait measures in early research attempts to predict behavior. He argued that specific traits may be useful predictors of behavior for only some people; to predict a person's behavior from his or her traits, we must first determine whether the trait is even relevant to that individual. Indeed, Bem and Allen (1974) found that people who rated themselves as consistent on a trait showed more consistent, traitlike behavior. These findings have been replicated in other studies as well (see, for example, Kenrick & Stringfield, 1980; Zuckerman, et al., 1988).

Similarly, Mischel and Peake (1982; also see Buss & Craik, 1980) noted that people may show traitlike consistency among some behaviors but not others. In particular, behaviors that people themselves view as *prototypical* of a trait (that is, an ideal example) will be more likely to reflect their trait scores and to show consistency. For instance, if you think that "turning in assignments on time" is a good example of your conscientiousness but that "dressing neatly" is not, then a trait measure of conscientiousness should predict your punctuality about assignments better than it will predict personal neatness.

In sum, to increase the ability of trait measures to predict behavior, researchers must ask several questions: Has the behavior under study been measured reliably? Are only some subjects consistent on the trait in question? What behaviors do subjects themselves perceive to be relevant to the trait? When traits are measured and conceptualized properly, they can lead to significant predictions of related behaviors (Funder, 1991; Kenrick & Funder, 1988).

Traits and Situations Together

Even when researchers use optimal methodologies and proper assessment of traits, people may still behave inconsistently across settings (Mischel & Peake, 1983). To social psychologists, this inconsistency is not necessarily surprising, for social psychology has long assumed that the social setting has a profound impact on individuals' behavior (Ross & Nisbett, 1991). As we shall see in Chapter 5, some social psychologists have argued that most of us have a perceptual bias when it comes to explaining behavior: We tend to overemphasize the internal causes of behavior (such as personality traits) and underemphasize the external causes of behavior (situational pressures). In other words, social psychologists have proposed that personality traits may often be more in the eye of the beholder than in people's actual behavior. This tendency may partially explain why most of us are trait theorists in everyday life.

Research teaches us it is simplistic to believe that behavior results *solely* from external factors such as social pressures or internal factors such as traits. In fact, the most plausible view is that behavior is determined by the complex interactions of traits and situations (Endler, 1981, 1983; Lewin, 1935, 1936; Mischel, 1977; Snyder & Ickes, 1985).

Suppose I asked three people—Juan, Jin, and Jane—to report about their anxiety in three different settings: while taking an exam, while going out on a date, and while eating in a fancy restaurant. Would their anxiety depend most on their traits (Juan is never anxious, but Jane is always anxious), on the situation (everyone is anxious taking a test, but no one is anxious eating in a restaurant), or on idiosyncratic interactions between the individuals and the situations (Jane, who is extremely shy, is most anxious on dates; Jin, a dunce, is most anxious taking exams)? In a series of studies on self-reports of anxiety, Endler and Hunt (1966, 1969) found that the evidence lent greatest support to the third possibility. They found that interactions between people's traits and the situations were typically more than twice as important in accounting for self-reported anxiety than either traits or situations alone. This finding, which has been replicated in many other studies (Bowers, 1973), provides evidence that people vary in anxiety across situations, each in his or her own idiosyncratic way.

In studying the link between people's traits and the situations they are in, researchers should note that in real life, people are not just passively exposed to situations, they often *choose* them (Emmons, Diener, & Larsen, 1986; Snyder & Ickes, 1985). For example, shy people may decide to avoid social gatherings, whereas outgoing extroverts may seek them out. Thus, our personality traits may in part determine what settings we inhabit and in this way indirectly as well as directly influence our behavior. In other words, traits and situations may not be as separate and independent as past thinking would have it.

Strong and Weak Situations as a Moderator Variable

Why do people sometimes behave consistently with their personality traits and sometimes not? Are some people more "traitlike" in their behavior than others? Some researchers have used the concept of moderator variables to answer these questions. A *moderator variable* is a go-between kind of variable that determines when one variable (for example, a personality trait) has an effect on another variable (behavior). Researchers using this approach try to find moderator variables that identify situations as powerful or weak in influencing behavior and that distinguish "traitlike" people from "nontraitlike" people (Snyder & Ickes, 1985.)

Let's consider situational moderator variables first. Some situations are powerful, compelling, and unambiguously interpreted by most people. Behavior at church, for example, is highly scripted—that is, it is guided by rigid social conventions and cultural rules. It is a *strong situation*. Thus, at church Jennifer and Louise both tend to be quiet, sober, and reserved, they wear "proper" clothes, and they generally do not yell, tell off-color jokes, or giggle. *Weak situations* are less scripted and so permit more variability in people's behavior. When Jennifer and Louise go to the park, they can choose to talk with other people or to be alone. They can wear pants, skirts, or gym shorts. They can choose to sleep under a tree or to jog. Because their behavior is not as strictly constrained as when they are at church, they may differ more in how they act. While Jennifer (an extrovert) chats with passersby or joins a softball game, Louise (an introvert) finds a quiet spot to read. Thus, a situation's strength or weakness may moderate the influence of personality traits on behavior (Mischel, 1977).

Monson, Hesley, and Chernick (1981) demonstrated the moderating effects of strong and weak situations by studying the relationship between subjects' self-reported extroversion and the actual extroversion they displayed in a conversation with two experimental confederates. These researchers created one weak situation and two strong situations. In the weak situation, the confederates engaged in natural, unconstrained conversation with the subjects. In the two strong situations, the confederates either encouraged extroverted behaviors by constantly asking questions of the subjects or encouraged introverted behaviors by ignoring the subjects. The correlation between the subjects' self-reported trait extroversion and their behavioral extroversion was much higher in the weak situation (a correlation of .63) than in the strong situations (correlations of .25 and .36, respectively). Furthermore, the subjects' *degree* of extroversion was more varied in the weak situation than in the strong situations. In short, the subjects' behavior reflected their personality traits more in the weak situation than in the strong situations.

Findings like these point to a significant difference between social psychological and personality research. Social psychologists often create strong situations in their experiments. That is, the independent variables in many social psychology experiments are powerful situational manipulations (recall Milgram's obedience studies, described in Chapter 2). Because social psychologists tend to study strong situations such as those that produce obedience, conformity, and aggression in large numbers of people, they may inadvertently ensure that personality traits have little influence on the behaviors they study. In contrast, personality psychologists tend to be interested in the ways people differ from one another when they are in situations that do not strongly constrain their behavior.

Self-Monitoring as a Moderator Variable

Do some people behave more consistently with their personality traits than others? Snyder (1979, 1987) maintains that this is true—and that the explanation lies in the degree to which people monitor their behavior to be consistent with either their traits or the demands of the situation. According to Snyder, low-self-monitoring individuals act in a manner consistent with their internal traits, whereas high-self-monitoring individuals act more in accordance with the demands of their social setting.

Snyder (1987) suggests that low-self-monitoring individuals have a *principled* concept of the self—they define themselves in terms of their inner values, beliefs, and traits ("I am liberal, free-thinking, honest, reserved . . . "). In contrast, high-self-monitoring individuals have a *pragmatic* concept of the self—they define themselves in terms of their roles and behaviors in different social settings ("I am treasurer of my sorority, a social organizer at family gatherings, the second violin in the university orchestra . . . ").

Snyder (1974) developed the Self-Monitoring Scale to measure individual differences in self-monitoring (see Figure 3.3). This scale has been shown to

To rate yourself on self-monitoring, complete the following scale. If a statement is true or mostly true as it applies to you, check the space in the "T" column. If a statement is false or not usually true as it applies to you, check the space in the "F" column.

T F

☐ ☐ 1. I find it hard to imitate the behavior of other people.

☐ ☐ 2. At parties and social gatherings, I do not attempt to do or say things that others will like.

☐ ☐ 3. I can only argue for ideas that I already believe.

☐ ☐ 4. I can make impromptu speeches even on topics about which I have almost no information.

☐ ☐ 5. I guess I put on a show to impress or entertain others.

☐ ☐ 6. I would probably make a good actor.

☐ ☐ 7. In a group of people I am rarely the center of attention.

☐ ☐ 8. In different situations and with different people, I often act like very different persons.

☐ ☐ 9. I am not particularly good at making other people like me.

☐ ☐ 10. I'm not always the person I appear to be.

☐ ☐ 11. I would not change my opinions (or the way I do things) in order to please someone or win their favor.

☐ ☐ 12. I have considered being an entertainer.

☐ ☐ 13. I have never been good at games like charades or improvisational acting.

☐ ☐ 14. I have trouble changing my behavior to suit different people and different situations.

☐ ☐ 15. At a party I let others keep the jokes and stories going.

☐ ☐ 16. I feel a bit awkward in company and do not come across quite as well as I should.

☐ ☐ 17. I can look anyone in the eye and tell a lie with a straight face (if for the right end).

☐ ☐ 18. I may deceive people by being friendly when I really dislike them.

The answer key is printed below. If your answer matches the key's answer, give yourself one point for that item. Otherwise, give yourself no points. Add up your points over all 18 items.

1(F); 2(F); 3(F); 4(T); 5(T); 6(T); 7(F); 8(T); 9(F); 10(T); 11(F); 12(T); 13(F); 14(F); 15(F); 16(F); 17(T); 18(T).

Snyder (1987) reports that college students with scores of 11 or greater tend to be high self-monitoring individuals, whereas students with scores of 10 or lower tend to be low self-monitoring individuals. A score of 13 or greater places you among the upper 25 percent of college students on self-monitoring, whereas a score of 7 or lower places you among the lowest 25%.

FIGURE 3.3 Are you a high self-monitoring person or a low self-monitoring person? *Source:* Adapted from Snyder (1987).

Madonna imitating Marilyn Monroe. Madonna's chameleon-like ability to change her appearance suggests that she is a high self-monitoring individual.

comprise three factors or components (Briggs, Cheek, & Buss, 1980): extroversion, other-directedness (looking to others as a guide to one's own behavior), and acting ability.

Research shows that high-self-monitoring people are indeed more sensitive to situational demands than low-self-monitoring people are, and that their behavior is more variable across situations (Snyder & Monson, 1975). High-self-monitoring people seem to be social chameleons who can change their behavior to suit their audience and to fit the norms of the situation (Danheiser & Graziano, 1982; Lippa, 1976, 1978). In contrast, low-self-monitoring people are more "true to themselves" and behave across situations in a manner that is more consistent with their inner traits, attitudes, and beliefs (Snyder & Swann, 1976; Snyder & Tanke, 1976; Tunnell, 1980). Self-monitoring thus appears to be an *internal* moderator variable that affects how much traits determine behavior.

SOCIAL PSYCHOLOGY IN EVERYDAY LIFE

 ### The Effects of Self-Monitoring

Can the effects of self-monitoring be seen in real life? Recent research suggests that the answer is yes. High- and low-self-monitoring individuals, for example, show interesting differences in consumer behavior. A low-self-monitoring consumer is more likely to buy a car because it's reliable, fuel-efficient, and durable, whereas a high-self-monitoring consumer is more likely to buy a car because it's stylish, "sexy," and has a high-status image (Snyder, 1987; Snyder & DeBono, 1985, 1987). Put another way, low-self-monitoring consumers seem attracted to a product because of its intrinsic quality and its capacity to express their personal values; high-self-monitoring consumers are more attracted to a product because it conveys the right image to a social audience.

Similarly, low-self-monitoring individuals are attracted to *other people* more on the basis of inner characteristics such as attitudes, values, traits, whereas high-self-monitoring individuals are attracted to others more on the basis of appearances (Snyder, Berscheid, & Glick, 1985; Snyder, Berscheid, & Matwychuk, 1988). In romantic relationships, low-self-monitoring people tend to be more committed and to strive to find one partner to satisfy all their needs, whereas high-self-monitoring people tend to be less committed and to seek varied partners (Snyder & Simpson, 1984). In friendships as well, low-self-monitoring individuals seek close, committed friends with whom they share basic attitudes, values, and interests. In contrast, high-self-monitoring individuals tend to have many "special purpose" friends and acquaintances with whom they share specific activities—a tennis-playing friend, a theater-going friend, and so on (Jamieson, Lydon, & Zanna, 1987; Snyder, Gangestad, & Simpson, 1983).

Even the personal problems of low- and high-self-monitoring individuals show some interesting differences. Low-self-monitoring people report being more depressed by events that injure their sense of who they are—for instance, being accused of hypocrisy. High-self-monitoring people, on the other hand, report being more depressed by events that injure their public image or sense of social skill—for instance, failing to impress people at a party or on a job interview. Once they are depressed, low- and high-self-monitoring individuals report different strategies for coping with their blues. Low-self-monitoring people are more likely to seek out friends and vent their feelings, whereas high-self-monitoring people are more likely to change their setting and "act" in a better mood (Snyder, 1987).

In sum, the traitlike behaviors of low-self-monitoring people and the more situationally variable behaviors of high-self-monitoring people show up in everyday life as well as in the social psychology laboratory. Notice that self-monitoring provides a new angle on the traits-versus-situation debate. Not only do traits interact with situations to produce behavior, but some people behave more in accordance with traits, others more in accordance with situations. Notice, too, how the insights of two contrasting views of personality—a trait explanation and a situational explanation—ultimately led to a more complex understanding of personality and behavior in which the assumptions of both approaches have a place.

Summary Table 3.1 provides an overview of some of the factors we have discussed (including self-monitoring) that influence the relationship between traits and behavior.

SUMMARY TABLE 3.1   Factors That Moderate the Relationship between Traits and Behavior

Moderator Variable	Example	General Principle
Behaviors being predicted	Aggregated behaviors	Trait measures predict aggregated behaviors better than single behaviors.
	Prototypical behaviors	Behaviors that are prototypical of a trait are better predicted by trait measures.
Situational factors	Strong versus weak situations	Strong situations overwhelm the influence of traits; weak situations allow traits to express themselves.
Person variables	Self-reported consistency	Some people are consistent on some traits; to predict behavior, the researcher must determine whether the trait is relevant to an individual.
	Self-monitoring	Low-self-monitoring individuals behave more consistently with their traits; high-self-monitoring individuals respond more to the social setting and thus are more variable.

THE SELF

I am a free man, an American, a United States Senator and a Democrat, in that order. I am also a liberal, a conservative, a Texan, a taxpayer, a rancher, a businessman, a consumer, a parent, a voter, and not as young as I used to be nor as old as I expect to be—and I am all those things in no fixed order.

—Lyndon Johnson, who later became the 35th president of the United States (cited in Gordon, 1968, p. 123)

I don't type, file or spell well. It's hard to type when you can't spell and it's hard to file when everything you've typed looks like alphabet soup.

I'd do better at something creative, and I feel I *am* somewhat creative, but *somehow* I *lack* talent to go with it, and *being* creative without talent is a bit like being a perfectionist and not being able to do anything right.

All my life I've wanted to *be* somebody. But I see now that I should have been more specific.

—Chrissy, in *The Search for Signs of Intelligent Life in the Universe* (Wagner, 1986, p. 35)

Research on self-monitoring suggests that whereas one person will look more to the social setting when deciding how to behave, another will look more to his or her "inner self"—but what is the self? Is it different from personality? And how does the self develop?

Before tackling these challenging questions about people's selves, let's first pose a possibly simpler question: Does a dog have a self? Dogs can have personality traits—stable, internal dispositions that lead to consistent behaviors different from those of other dogs. The neighbor's pit bull is very aggressive, regularly attacking other dogs and people; the collie down the street is sweet and friendly. But does either dog have a self? Probably not. The concept of self implies both a conscious, aware "actor within" that initiates behavior and knowledge about one's feelings, traits, thoughts, and behaviors, both present and past. Look at the quotes that start this section. Both Lyndon Johnson and Chrissy reflected on their characteristics and accomplishments. To have a self, an organism must be conscious and self-reflective (Gergen, 1971).

Can chimpanzees recognize themselves in reflected images?

Some clever research has investigated the degree to which various animals possess a sense of self (Gallup & Suarez, 1986). In one experiment, Gallup (1977) let a number of chimpanzees observe themselves in mirrors. He then anesthetized the chimps and dyed one eyebrow and one ear of each chimp bright red. After regaining consciousness, the chimps were again allowed to observe themselves in a mirror. Interestingly, many of them began touching their newly scarlet ears and eyebrows, a clear indication that they recognized themselves and were curious about their altered appearance. Human infants begin to show similar self-recognition in mirrors at about 2 years of age (Bertenthal & Fisher, 1978; Lewis, 1986; Lewis & Brooks, 1978). Orangutans show self-recognition in mirrors (again using the dye test method), but lower primates (such as rhesus monkeys and macaques) and lower mammals (dogs, rats) do not and thus seem to lack even a primitive sense of their physical self.

Classic Views of the Self

Gallup's experiments with chimps yielded another fascinating result: Chimps reared in social isolation did not learn to recognize themselves in mirrors, whereas those whose rearing included social interaction with other chimps did. This finding is particularly interesting because several noted theorists have argued that the self develops in humans because of social feedback and participation in social roles.

The Self and Social Feedback

William James (1890), the preeminent American psychologist of the late 19th century, was perhaps the first great modern "self" theorist. James argued that our sense of self embraces not just our inner values, interests, and traits, but also our friends, intimate relationships, and even our possessions. The social nature of the self was further emphasized by Charles Horton Cooley (1902) and George Herbert Mead (1934), both of whom argued that people develop selves only by incorporating the perspectives of other people. Cooley invoked the metaphor of a social mirror, which he called "the looking-glass self." This refers to the vision of the self that is reflected to us when we communicate with other people. Mead offered his related concept of "the generalized other"—the "organized community or group which gives to the individual his unity of self" (p. 154). James, Cooley, and Mead all argued that the self is a social creation; a person growing up alone on a desert island could not develop a self, for a self requires social experience and feedback.

The "I" versus the "Me"

William James introduced another important idea that was to have a lasting impact on later theory when he argued that the self has two quite different aspects: the "I" and the "me." The "I" is the active self, the ongoing stream of consciousness; the "me" is the self as an object of thought and includes all the knowledge and beliefs one holds about one's self. "I" am writing this paragraph right now, but when I stop and think about my work, I start thinking about "me"—about my writing skills, my past writing, and my feelings of fatigue.

For Mead (1934), the distinction between the "I" and the "me" was partly a matter of memory: "The 'I' of this moment is present in the 'me' of the next moment" (p. 174). In other words, the "I" is the spontaneous actor of the current instant, whereas the "me" is the remembered self, the content of our self-reflective knowledge.

Social psychology research on self-concepts, self-knowledge, and self-schemas (which we will discuss shortly) has focused primarily on the "me" rather than the "I," in part because the "me" is more easily studied (Kihlstrom & Cantor, 1984). It is easy to ask people to report beliefs they have about themselves (the contents of the "me"); it is considerably harder to measure the internal processes responsible for choosing people's actions from second to second.

If the self is a social creation, then it must be learned rather than inborn. And in fact, both Sigmund Freud ([1930] 1961a), the founder of psychoanalytic theory, and Jean Piaget ([1924] 1966), one of the most influential developmental psychologists of the 20th century, held that we do not possess selves when we are born. Freud speculated that the mystical oneness with the universe that we sometimes feel as adults (for example, during some religious experiences) represents a return to our infantile state of selflessness, when we literally did not know that we were separate from our mother (or indeed from the rest of the universe). We are born unconscious, and what Freud called the ego (that is, the conscious self) does not develop until later. Similarly, in his landmark descriptions of cognitive development, Piaget argued that young children do not fully realize the distinction between private experiences and other people's experiences. For example, a 4-year-old child may expect his parents to know about a dream he had the previous night.

At what ages do human beings recognize themselves in reflected images?

Duval and Wicklund (1972) later argued that awareness of self develops largely as a result of social conflicts. For example, young Billy becomes aware of his "aggressiveness" when his mother scolds him for hitting his little brother so often. Even as adults, we may become conscious of new aspects of ourselves through social conflict and disagreement. When you first visit a foreign country with different customs, for instance, you may suddenly become aware of behaviors you had never thought about before. When all the people around you hold their forks in their left hands for both cutting and eating a piece of food, you suddenly become aware that in the same situation you switch the fork to your right hand. And when in conversation everybody stands 8 inches away from you, you painfully realize that you really prefer a distance of 18 inches.

Duval and Wicklund's argument implies that people will be more aware of, and more likely to describe themselves in terms of, characteristics that distinguish them from others. This hypothesis has been supported by empirical research. McGuire and his colleagues found that schoolchildren were more likely to describe themselves using traits, physical characteristics, or demographic information that distinguished them from others (McGuire & McGuire, 1982, 1988; McGuire, McGuire, Child, & Fujioka, 1978; McGuire & Padawer-Singer, 1976). Thus, red-haired children were more likely to mention their hair color in self-descriptions, black children in a mostly white school were more likely to list their race, and so on.

As children grow older, their self-descriptions become more abstract and sophisticated. A number of studies have asked children of different ages to answer the question "Who am I?" (Livesly & Bromly, 1973; Montemayor & Eisen, 1977). Young children describe themselves in concrete, physical terms, whereas older children are more likely to include abstract traits, values, and interests in their self-descriptions. To illustrate, here's a self-description from a fourth-grade boy:

> My name is Bruce C. I have brown eyes. I have brown hair. I have brown eyebrows. I'm nine years old. I LOVE sports! I have seven people in my family. I have great! eye site [sic]. I have lots! of friends. I live on 1923 Pinecrest Drive. I'm going on 10 in September. I'm a boy. I have an uncle that is almost 7 feet tall. My school is Pinecrest. My teacher is Mrs. V. I play Hockey! I am almost the smartest boy in the class. I LOVE! food. I love fresh air. I LOVE school. (Montemayor & Eisen, 1977, p. 317)

Contrast Bruce's self-portrait with that of a 17-year-old girl in the 12th grade:

> I am a human being. I am a girl. I am an individual. I don't know who I am. I am a Pisces. I am a moody person. I am an indecisive person. I am an ambitious person.

The self-schema comprises a complex mix of beliefs, aspirations, and fantasies.

I am a very curious person. I am not an individual. I am a loner. I am an American (God help me), I am a Democrat. I am a liberal person. I am a radical, I am a conservative. I am a pseudoliberal. I am an atheist. I am not a classifiable person (i.e., I don't want to be). (Montemayor & Eisen, 1977, p. 318)

Clearly, as individuals progress from childhood to adulthood, they develop a "me" that is complex, subtle, elaborated, abstract, and even contradictory.

Hart and Damon (1986) describe four fundamental aspects of a child's self-concept: the *physical* self ("I am tall"), the *active* or behaving self ("I am good at baseball"), the *social* self ("I am friendly to others"), and the *psychological* self ("I believe in world peace"). These researchers propose that as children progress from early to late childhood, the emphasis on these four aspects of self shifts more toward the social and psychological aspects. However, recent research suggests that children as young as 3 years of age have the ability to describe some of their simple psychological characteristics (Eder, Gerlach, & Perlmutter, 1987).

Knowing Thy Self: The Self as a Schema

The concept of self implies that people possess knowledge about themselves. Recently, social psychologists have measured how our knowledge about ourselves is stored in memory and what effect that knowledge has on our behavior. In an important set of studies, Hazel Markus (1977) argued that the "me" can be conceptualized as a *schema*—that is, an organized set of knowledge that exists in memory. This *self-schema* includes the beliefs one holds about oneself, and it influences how a person perceives social events, remembers information, and infers new facts. (We will return to the general topic of cognitive schemas in Chapter 5.)

The Self-Schema and Information about the Self

In a series of experiments, Markus (1977) examined how self-schemas affect the ways people process information about themselves. In one study, she identified groups of college women who rated themselves highly on the traits of *independence* or *dependence* and who also deemed these traits very important to their self-descriptions. These women were assumed to be *schematic* on the respective traits—that is, they possessed rich and well-developed self-schemas related to either independence or dependence. Markus also identified another group of women who were *aschematic* on independence and dependence—that is, they neither rated themselves highly on these traits nor viewed these traits to be very important to their self-description.

All subjects then participated in an experiment in which a series of adjectives were displayed on a screen. The subjects were asked to press one of two buttons to indicate whether a given adjective did or did not describe them. Measuring the speed with which subjects responded, Markus found that subjects who were schematic on independence responded much more quickly to adjectives relating to independence *(individualistic, outspoken)* than to adjectives related to dependence *(timid, submissive)*. Subjects who described themselves as schematic on dependence showed just the opposite pattern, and aschematic subjects showed no difference in response speed between the two kinds of adjectives (see Figure 3.4).

In addition, schematic subjects were better able to list examples of behavior relevant to their schemas than aschematics were; for example, a woman who was schematic on independence could list many ways that she was independent. Schematic subjects also resisted more strongly the information from a bogus personality inventory that contradicted their self-schemas. Markus, Crane, Bernstein, and Siladi (1982) reported similar effects for self-schemas related to masculinity and femininity. Thus, the self-schema influences how quickly we can answer questions about ourselves, how readily we remember our behaviors, and how we know what is true or not true about ourselves.

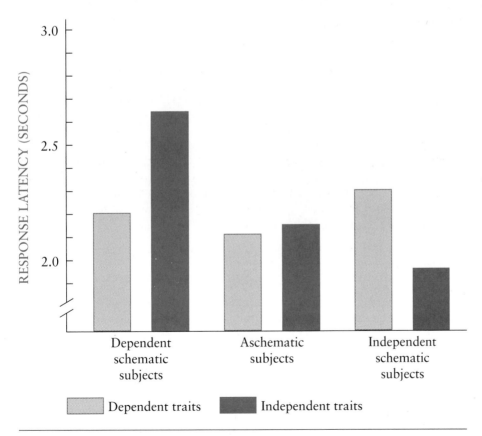

FIGURE 3.4 Do self-schemas affect how quickly we process information about ourselves? *Source:* Data from Markus (1977).

The Self-Schema and Information about Others

Do self-schemas also influence the way we describe *other people's* behavior? Markus, Smith, and Moreland (1985) hypothesized that people who are strongly schematic on a given dimension (such as *independence* or *masculinity*) are "experts" about that particular domain of their behavior. They further hypothesized that because of their expertise, schematic people "chunk" the behaviors of others into higher-order units when those behaviors are relevant to their own self-schemas. For example, if you see a man drive up on a motorcycle, smoke a cigarette, and play basketball, you could see these as three separate behaviors, or you could chunk the behaviors into a higher-order unit to you—they're all masculine behaviors. Markus, Smith, and Moreland hypothesized that you're more likely to chunk the behaviors in this way if you yourself are schematic on masculinity.

To test this idea, Markus and her colleagues used the same methods as those in the "independence" study to identify men who were schematic or aschematic on masculinity. The subjects viewed two films, one depicting a man engaged in stereotypically masculine activities such as lifting weights and watching a baseball game and another depicting a man engaged in activities irrelevant to masculinity such as playing records and eating an apple. The subjects were asked to press a button whenever they saw what they considered to be a "meaningful unit of action."

The results were consistent with the hypothesis that subjects who were schematic on masculinity were experts in the domain of masculinity. When they viewed stereotypically masculine behaviors, the schematic men chunked behavior into larger units than schematic men did, thus producing fewer total units. When viewing behavior that was irrelevant to masculinity, however, men who were schematic and aschematic on masculinity did not differ in the number of units they produced (see Figure 3.5).

Self-schemas, then, can influence how we process information not only about ourselves but about others as well. One reason two people may see the same behaviors differently is that they have different self-schemas.

MULTICULTURAL PERSPECTIVE

Are the Contents of the Self the Same Across Cultures?

There are few things we take more for granted than our sense of self. Yet if the self is a social creation, then what we think of as the self might vary considerably in different cultures. And in fact, research bears this out.

How does our culture influence our sense of self? Most cultures in North America and Europe tend to emphasize the *individuality* of the self. Members of these cultures generally define themselves in terms of their inner traits, feelings, goals, and abilities. In contrast, many cultures in Asia, Latin America, and Africa emphasize the *connectedness of the self with other people*. Members of these cultures define themselves more in terms of their social relationships and their roles in social groups (Markus & Kitayama, 1991). Figure 3.6 contrasts these two different cultural perspectives on the self.

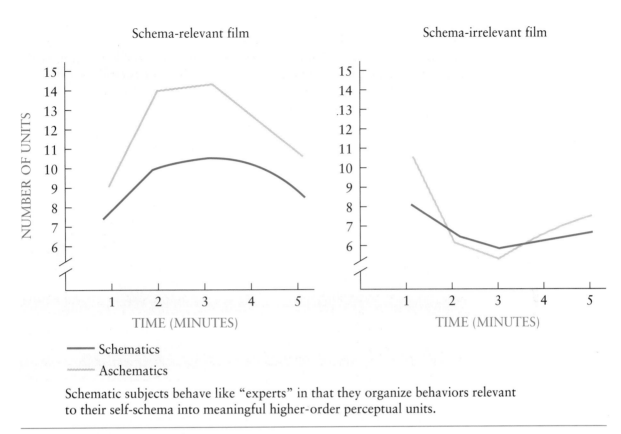

Schematic subjects behave like "experts" in that they organize behaviors relevant to their self-schema into meaningful higher-order perceptual units.

FIGURE 3.5 Do self-schemas affect how we process information about others? *Source:* Adapted from Markus, Smith, and Moreland (1985).

One simple way to demonstrate these two cultural perspectives is to ask members of different cultures to describe themselves with 20 sentences that start "I am . . . " (Kuhn & McPartland, 1954). Subjects' responses are then coded as describing either private aspects of the self (that is, internal, individual traits, such as "I am assertive," "I am friendly," "I am emotional") or collective, social aspects of the self (for example, "I am a mother," "I am Filipino," "I am a college student," "I am Roman Catholic"). Recent research shows that in Asian countries, typically 20% to 52% of subjects' self-descriptions refer to aspects of the collective self, whereas in Europe and North America, only 15% to 19% of subjects' self-descriptions do (Triandis, 1989). Conversely, Europeans and North Americans are significantly more likely than Asians to describe themselves in terms of internal traits that generalize across social settings (Cousins, 1989; Trafimow, Triandis, & Goto, 1991).

The very words used to describe the self vary across cultures. *Jibun,* the Japanese word for self, is defined as "one's share of the shared life space," and in Japan, the self is viewed not as a fixed set of traits, but rather as something that changes in different relationships (Hamaguchi, 1985).

Chinese people practicing Tai Chi. This form of exercise emphasizes harmony and coordination with others and thus illustrates an interconnected sense of self. In contrast, the forms of exercise chosen by many Americans—such as jogging and competitive sports—illustrate a more individualistic sense of self.

These profound differences in cultural conceptions of the self may influence the motivations people bring to their work and other everyday activities. Americans may be motivated to achieve in academic and work settings so they can express their inner abilities, compare favorably with others, and exert personal control and influence, whereas Asians may achieve more to satisfy their families and teachers and fulfill interpersonal obligations (Bond, 1986; Yu, 1974). Because of their collective view of achievement, Japanese workers prefer managers who are demanding, fatherlike, and concerned about the workers' personal affairs even when they are unrelated to work (Hayashi, 1988). Americans, in contrast, often feel more comfortable with task-oriented leaders who separate personal matters from work (Markus & Kitayama, 1991).

Other differences in values and behavior are also rooted in cultural views of the self. For people who grow up in cultures with an individualistic conception of the self, self-esteem (a person's general sense of worth) often depends on being a unique individual, expressing one's inner traits and abilities. Such individuals are generally expected to promote themselves—for example, in job interviews. In contrast, people who grow up in cultures with a more collective sense of self achieve self-satisfaction more from relating smoothly with others, belonging to appropriate social groups, and displaying modesty and the ability to fit in (Markus & Kitayama, 1991).

Feature of Self Compared	*Cultural Conception of Self*	
	Independent	Interdependent
Definition of self	Separate from social context	Connected with social context
Structure of self	Bounded, unitary, stable	Flexible, variable
Important features of self	Internal, private (abilities, thoughts, feelings)	External, public (statuses, roles, relationships)
Tasks of self	Be unique Express self Realize internal attributes Promote own goals Be direct; "say what's on your mind"	Belong, fit in Occupy one's proper place Engage in appropriate action Promote others' goals Be indirect; "read other's mind"
Role of others	*Self-evaluation:* others important for social comparison, reflected appraisal	*Self-definition:* relationships with others in specific contexts define the self
Basis of self-esteem	Ability to express self, validate internal attributes	Ability to adjust, restrain self, maintain harmony with social context

FIGURE 3.6 Key differences between an independent and an interdependent construal of self. *Source:* Markus and Kitayama (1991).

Appreciating such cultural differences is becoming more and more important in an increasingly interdependent world. Probing what is and is not universally true of the self across cultures is only one way social psychology can help us interact more successfully with our neighbors in the global village.

Differences between Self-Knowledge and Other Knowledge

We have knowledge about many people and things—the president of the United States, the Catholic church, our friends, and, of course, ourselves. Is the knowledge we have about ourselves different from other kinds of knowledge? The answer is almost certainly yes. The information stored in the self-schema typically differs from other kinds of knowledge in its complexity and in the degree to which it is highly defended. And self-knowledge typically has stronger emotional consequences than other kinds of knowledge. Learning a negative fact about yourself has the power to make you feel much worse than learning the same fact about the president of the United States, for example. What are some of the psychological consequences of these differences between self-knowledge and other kinds of knowledge?

The Complexity of Self-Knowledge and Its Effect on Memory

As we just noted, the self-schema is complex, in part because we simply have a lot more information about ourselves than we do about almost anything else (Kihlstrom et al., 1988). Except perhaps for the respite of sleep—and even dreams offer a kind of information about the self—we are constantly awash in our thoughts, feelings, and behaviors. Also, unlike other sorts of knowledge, self-knowledge possesses a narrative continuity, an unbroken thread of observation through time (Cantor & Kihlstrom, 1987; Gergen & Gergen, 1983, 1988). We each try to make sense of our own life histories, and we constantly interpret and reinterpret the self (Linton, 1978). To make matters even more complicated, we not only possess information about our past and current selves, we also have images of future selves (Markus & Nurius, 1986) and can imagine ourselves acting in different ways and interacting with different people (Hermans, Kempen, & van Loon, 1992). Clearly, the self is a complex mix of memories, interpretations, fantasies, and aspirations.

The complexity of self-knowledge has been demonstrated indirectly through its effect on memory: People remember information that is related to the self better than they remember other kinds of information. In one study, Rogers, Kuiper, and Kirker (1977) showed subjects 40 adjectives, one at a time, and asked them to make one of four kinds of judgments about each adjective: (1) Was it printed in big letters? (2) Did it rhyme with another word? (3) Did it mean the same thing as another word? or (4) Did the adjective describe the subject? For example, if the adjective was "NEAT," subjects would be asked one of the following questions: "Is it printed in big letters?" or "Does it rhyme with 'heat'?" or "Does it mean the same as 'clean'?" or "Are you neat?" Each kind of judgment was made for 10 of the 40 adjectives. Note that the self-schema was involved only when a subject was asked whether the adjective applied to the self.

After they had judged the adjectives, and without prior warning, the subjects were asked to recall as many of the 40 adjectives as they could. The results showed a pronounced *self-reference effect*: The subjects' recall was much superior for adjectives that had been judged in relation to the self. This effect was most marked for adjectives that subjects said did in fact describe them (see Figure 3.7).

In general, the self-reference effect proves to be quite robust (Brown, Keenan, & Potts, 1986), and researchers continue to explore why and when it occurs (Greenwald & Banaji, 1989; Kihlstrom et al., 1988; Klein & Loftus, 1988). Their current consensus is that words processed for self-reference are remembered better in part because they become associated with the rich knowledge contained in the self-schema. The more that new knowledge is related to prior knowledge, the better we tend to remember it. The intricately elaborated self-schema provides more paths that lead into memory, allowing us to locate information (Keenan & Baillet, 1980).

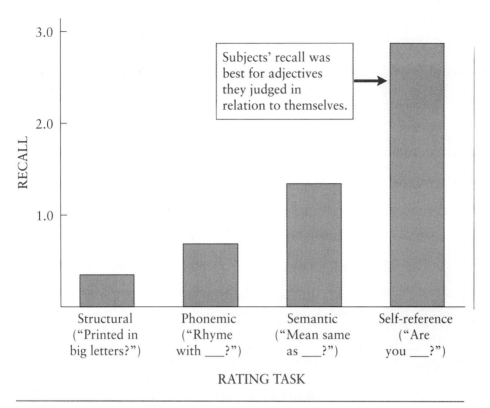

Subjects' recall was best for adjectives they judged in relation to themselves.

FIGURE 3.7 Do we remember information better when it has been processed for self-reference? *Source:* Data from Rogers, Kuiper, and Kirker (1977).

Resistance of the Self to Change

In addition to aiding memory for self-relevant facts, the complexity of the self-schema may also make the self resistant to change. The huge self-schema has a lot of inertia to it. As Thoreau wrote in his *Journal* (1840), "For an impenetrable shield, stand inside yourself."

The self-conserving nature of the self can undoubtedly be attributed to more than simply the sheer amount of information in the self-schema, however. We frequently maintain the integrity of our selves through active effort and, sometimes, defensiveness. Indeed, the self has been compared to a totalitarian dictator that needs to control information and revise history for his or her personal benefit (Greenwald, 1980). According to this point of view, the self—an organization of knowledge and beliefs—is conservative and does not change easily or lightly. In fact, the self will at times distort or forget facts in order to preserve itself. This enforced stability may be quite useful, for if the self readily changed with each new piece of information, life would become chaotic; our sense of the unity of our personality and behavior would quickly be shattered.

How does the self maintain itself and convince itself that self-knowledge is "true" knowledge? Swann and Read (1981) argue that we often seek *self-*

Self-verification: Sometimes people behave in ways that make their self-concept absolutely clear to others. This woman's appearance sends a strong message to other people that she is rebellious and non-conforming. (Photo © Ken Miller, 1993.)

verification; that is, we engage in behaviors and thoughts that serve to prove the validity of our self-concepts. We can verify our self-concepts in three specific ways: (1) by selectively soliciting feedback from others that confirms our self-concepts; (2) by selectively remembering feedback that confirms our self-concepts; and (3) by actively trying to prove to others the truth of our self-concepts.

Swann and Read found evidence for all three processes. In one experiment, female subjects rated themselves as either likable or unlikable and then reviewed statements made about them by another person. Some subjects were led to believe that the other person probably liked them; others were led to believe that the person probably disliked them. Subjects who thought themselves to be unlikable spent more time looking at the statements when they thought the other person disliked them, whereas subjects who thought themselves likable spent more time looking at the statements when they thought the other person liked them. In other words, subjects attended more to information that seemed likely to confirm their self-concept.

These results are particularly intriguing because they indicate that the "unlikable" subjects actually attended more to potentially painful information—that is, information verifying their unlikability. In a related experiment, Swann and Read found that subjects recalled more statements made by another person when they believed that person confirmed their self-concept. Thus, not only do we pay more attention to self-verifying information, we remember it better as well.

How do people respond when others threaten their self-concept? To answer this question, Swann and Read extended their experimental procedure a step further. College men who had rated themselves as either likable or unlikable engaged in a nine-minute conversation with a college woman. The men were told ahead of time either that the woman was apt to like them or apt to dislike them. After the conversation, the women were asked to rate how much in fact they liked their conversation partners. As Figure 3.8 indicates, men who regarded themselves as unlikable were particularly unlikable when they thought their partner would like them! And men who regarded themselves as likable were particularly likable when they thought their partner would dislike them. Apparently, when their partner seemed about to challenge their self-concept, the men tried harder to prove the accuracy of their self-concept.

Recent research adds another dimension to the resistance of the self-concept to change by suggesting that when events challenge our self-concept, we experience stress—even when the events themselves are positive! In two separate studies, Brown and McGill (1989) asked subjects with low and high self-esteem to report positive life events that had occurred over the previous 12 months (for example, getting a new boyfriend or girlfriend). The researchers also obtained measures of subjects' health (self-reported illnesses in one study, and subjects' number of visits to the university health center in the second). In both studies, the occurrence of many positive events led subjects who had high self-esteem to be healthier, but those with low self-esteem to be less healthy. The surprising findings, of course, were those for low-self-esteem subjects. But these findings make sense from the vantage point of self-verification research. Apparently, positive life events posed a painful challenge to the self-concepts of those with low self-esteem and led them to experience significant stress and upset.

Self-Awareness and Behavior

So far, we have discussed the nature of the self-schema and how it affects our memory and the way we present our selves to others. But ultimately, the self-schema is of interest to social psychologists because it influences everyday social behavior. Do we generally act consistently with our self-schemas? When do we, and when don't we?

Shelly Duval and Robert Wicklund (1972) proposed a theory of self-awareness that suggests the contents of the self (the knowledge and standards stored in the self-schema) are more likely to influence our behavior when we are *paying attention* to the self. According to this theory, conscious attention can be directed either toward the self or toward the external environment. When attention is self-focused, we think consciously about who we are—about our beliefs, values,

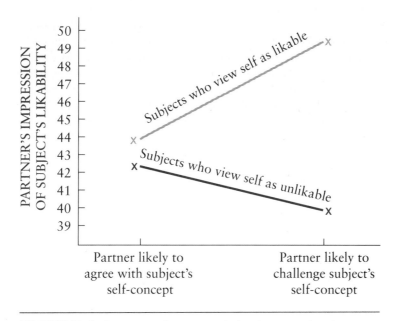

FIGURE 3.8 Do we change our behavior to maintain our self-concepts? *Source:* Data from Swann and Read (1981).

and traits. When attention is externally focused (for example, on a football game), we are not consciously in touch with our selves.

In everyday life, self-awareness can be triggered by the scrutiny of others or by eye contact, or by explicit requests from others to think about ourselves and our behavior (Wicklund, 1982). When a father stares at his son, who has just broken a vase, and says, "What do you have to say about this, young man?", the boy is very likely pushed into a state of self-directed attention.

In research studies, self-awareness is triggered by a number of simple methods, including placing subjects in front of a mirror, tape-recording and videotaping them, and having others watch and evaluate them. All of these techniques make people "self-conscious" in the sense that they start paying attention to themselves. Researchers have used these techniques to explore what happens when people are more or less self-aware. Let's see what they have discovered.

The Consequences of Self-Directed Attention

According to Duval and Wicklund, when people direct their attention to them-selves, they begin to compare their behavior to internal standards (which may have been internalized from society). For example, when you take a social psychology test and you start thinking consciously about yourself, you'll probably wonder whether you're performing as well as you would like. If you don't match your internal standards, you become uncomfortable (for instance, if you seem to be getting enough questions wrong to earn you a "C" on your test rather than your hoped-for "A").

Self-awareness theory predicts that when you notice a discrepancy between your actual behavior and your internal standards, you have two ways of reducing the resulting discomfort: You can change your behavior to be more consistent with your internal standards ("I'm going to study twice as hard for the next test and get an 'A'!"), or, if meeting your standards is unrealistic (when the tests are simply too difficult), you can try to avoid self-awareness ("I'm going to a movie to take my mind off things" or "I'm going to get drunk and forget all about my grades").

Many studies have provided support for the basic propositions of self-awareness theory. For example, Duval, Wicklund, and Fine (described in Duval & Wicklund, 1972) demonstrated that people do in fact avoid self-awareness after irredeemable failure. In their experiment, college women took a bogus IQ test and were informed that they had performed either quite well or quite poorly. The subjects were then sent to another experiment with these instructions: "If the experimenter doesn't show up within five minutes, you can leave." Sometimes the room in which the subjects waited contained a mirror and a TV camera pointing at them; sometimes it did not. The researchers assumed, of course, that those who waited in the room with the mirror and camera would be more self-aware.

The researchers hypothesized that subjects who had failed to do well on the IQ test and who were also self-aware would be most uncomfortable and therefore would spend less time in the waiting room before deciding to leave. (Would you have wanted to hang around looking at yourself in a mirror after having "failed"

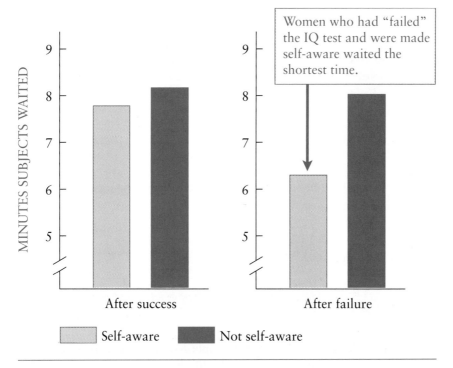

FIGURE 3.9 Do we avoid self-awareness after failure? *Source:* Adapted from Duval and Wicklund (1972).

the test?) And indeed these subjects waited a significantly shorter time in the room than did others (see Figure 3.9).

Another interesting effect of self-awareness relates to people's moral behavior. Most college students report that they are honest, but most will also cheat on a timed IQ test (by working past the time limit) if given the opportunity (Diener & Wallbom, 1976). When do people behave in a manner that is consistent with their internal morals, and when don't they? One possible answer is that people behave in a particularly moral way when they are in a state of self-focused attention. Beaman, Klentz, Diener, and Svanum (1979) demonstrated this in a clever experiment that showed children trick-or-treating on Halloween were less likely to steal extra candy from an unattended bowl when a big mirror was placed behind it.

Other studies in which subjects were placed in the presence of a mirror (that is, in a state of self-awareness) showed that self-aware subjects delivered what they thought were electric shocks to victims to a degree that was more consistent with their attitudes toward aggression (Carver, 1975); that subjects responded to pornography in a manner that was more consistent with their self-reported attitudes (via a questionnaire) toward it (Gibbons, 1978); and finally, that subjects' sociability in a conversation better reflected their self-reported sociability (Pryor, Gibbons, Wicklund, Fazio, & Hood, 1977). Thus, self-awareness serves as a

Rate yourself on each item on a 5-point scale that ranges from 1—extremely characteristic of you to 5—extremely uncharacteristic of you.

1. I'm always trying to figure myself out.
2.* Generally, I'm not very aware of myself.
3. I reflect about myself a lot.
4. I'm often the subject of my own fantasies.
5.* I never scrutinize myself.
6. I'm generally attentive to my inner feelings.
7. I'm constantly examining my motives.
8. I sometimes have the feeling that I'm off somewhere watching myself.
9. I'm alert to changes in my mood.
10. I'm aware of the way my mind works when I work through a problem.

*Reversed items

FIGURE 3.10 The private self-consciousness scale. *Source:* Fenigstein, Scheier, and Buss (1975).

moderator variable that influences when people do and do not behave in ways that are consistent with their personalities and attitudes.

In addition, research suggests that by heightening awareness of internal arousal and inner feelings, self-focused attention intensifies a person's current mood or emotion (Gibbons, 1990; Scheier & Carver, 1977; Scheier, Carver, & Gibbons, 1979, 1981). If you're happy, focusing attention on yourself will make you feel happier; if you're sad, it will make you feel sadder.

Some people are more likely to engage in self-focused attention than others. For them, self-awareness can be viewed as a personality trait. Fenigstein, Scheier, and Buss (1975) developed a scale of *private self-consciousness* that measures how much people focus on their inner thoughts and feelings and internal states (see Figure 3.10). Many studies indicate that people who have a high degree of private self-consciousness behave in ways that are more consistent with their inner traits, attitudes, and values (Gibbons, 1990). In one study, Scheier, Buss, and Buss (1978) found that subjects with high degrees of private self-consciousness behaved in ways that were more consistent with their self-described level of aggressiveness than did people low on private self-consciousness. Thus, private self-consciousness also serves as a moderator variable that helps to predict when people do and do not engage in behaviors that are consistent with their personality traits.

A Control Model of the Self

According to self-awareness theory, the self is, at least in part, a process that attempts to match behavior to standards stored in the self and to modify behavior when it doesn't meet these standards. Carver and Scheier (1981; Scheier & Carver, 1988) have elaborated some of the insights of self-awareness theory into a general theory based on cybernetics, or control theory (Miller, Galanter, & Pribram, 1960; Wiener, 1948).

Control theory describes how a system (such as a heater with a thermostat) exerts control to maintain some desired state (a constant temperature). The basic

Thermostat control system

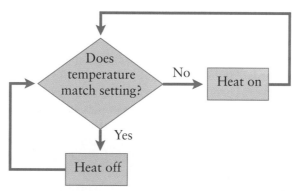

Carver and Scheier's Control Model of the Self

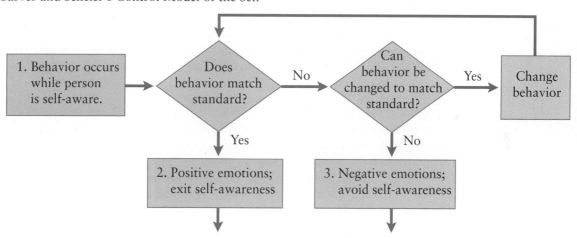

According to the model presented here, the self differs from a thermostat control system in three important ways:
1. The control system of the self operates only when the individual is in a state of self-awareness.
2. The control processes of the self have emotional and motivational consequences (such as happiness, upset, or guilt).
3. When behavior cannot be matched to standards, the self may try to avoid the pain of self-awareness and exit from the control "loop." (In contrast, a thermostat controlling a heater that is inadequate for the task will not become "upset" and decide to "give up"!)

FIGURE 3.11 Can the self be conceptualized as a control system? *Source:* Adapted from Carver and Scheier (1981).

ontrol system is a *feedback loop* (see Figure 3.11), in which the control
ts current conditions or input against some standard. For example, a
t tests current room temperature against the setting of the thermostat. If
rd is met ("It's warm enough in the house"), the furnace is turned off or
f the standard is not met ("It's too cold!"), the control system initiates a
rning on the furnace) that will produce some change in the system so that
rd is matched. Thus, the control system acts whenever its standard is not
keeps checking current conditions and acting until the standard is met.
nalogy, Carver and Scheier suggest when the self is in a state of
ness, it acts as a control system (again, see Figure 3.11). When you think
r grades, the control system that is your self asks, "Am I meeting my
standards?" If the answer is yes (you're a 4.00 student), you feel happy, and you do
not have to change your behavior. You can "exit" self-awareness now—that is, stop
consciously thinking about your grades and turn your attention to other matters.
If you are not meeting your standards (you're a 1.50 student), then the control
system poses another question: "Can I change my behavior to match my
standards?" If the answer is yes, then you will study harder to try for better grades.
If you're studying as hard as you can, however, and you still don't get the grades you
desire, then you're in a quandary. You probably feel guilty, ashamed, and upset, so
you strive to exit self-awareness by avoiding thinking about yourself.

This mental avoidance can take different forms: You can distract yourself
(shift your attention to external events, by watching TV, for example) or blur your
self-awareness with drugs or alcohol (Hull, 1981; Hull, Young, & Jouriles, 1986).
In sum, self-awareness triggers a control process that guides us to behave as we
"should," and if this fails, we try not to be self-aware.

Action Identification Theory

To match our behavior to a standard, we first have to decide what our behavior is.
But the same behavior can be categorized in different ways. For example, right now
you are reading your book. How do you describe your current behavior? Some
possibilities are: "I'm flipping pages." "I'm underlining important parts of the
chapters." "I'm reading social psychology." "I'm working to get an 'A' in my class."
"I'm striving for a good undergraduate record so I can go to medical school."

According to Wegner and Vallacher's (1986) action identification theory, we
can classify our actions at many levels of abstraction. Generally, we prefer to identify our behavior in terms of higher-level goals, standards, and purposes ("I'm
working to get an 'A' in my class"), but when behavior is difficult, unfamiliar, or
complex, we often move to lower-level descriptions ("I'm underlining important
parts of the chapter"). People may also move to less abstract descriptions when they
learn they are failing at a task. You might say, "I'm holding my racquet wrong"
rather than "I'm playing tennis badly." Some people in general prefer to describe
their behavior at higher levels of abstraction than others (Vallacher & Wegner,
1989).

Action identification theory suggests yet another way people can avoid
painful self-awareness: They can focus on their behaviors as specific, unrelated,

concrete acts rather than as meaningful acts in the pursuit (or nonpursuit) of higher goals. For example, a dieter who goes on an eating binge may avoid painful self-awareness by describing her behavior as "I'm eating cheesecake" rather than "I'm breaking my diet" (Heatherton & Baumeister, 1991). Similarly, suicidal people may avoid painful awareness of their behavior (and thereby make their suicide easier to carry out) by describing their acts in limited, concrete ways ("I am buying a gun") rather than in terms of higher-order purposes or meanings ("I am violating my personal religious standards and threatening my chances for a satisfying future") (Baumeister, 1990).

Self-Discrepancy

Self-awareness theories suggest that the self regulates behavior—or adjusts awareness of behavior—by assessing the discrepancy between overt actions and internal standards. But we all have many possible standards of behavior available at any given time. For example, when you talk with your parents, do you adjust your conversation to display your internal standards of intelligence, morality, or niceness? Why do we choose to attend to one standard and not another? In their original formulation, Duval and Wicklund (1972) argued that some standards are particularly salient in a given situation. When taking a test, for example, your standard of behavior will be intellectual excellence, whereas at a party it may be physical attractiveness and personal charm.

More recently, Tory Higgins (1987) argued that people hold various kinds of inner standards. Standards can either be your own ("I want to be a straight-A student") or those of other people ("My mother wants me to be a straight-A student"). Furthermore, standards can represent either your ideals and personal goals ("I want to be a concert pianist") or your duties and obligations (a kind of moral conscience, as in "I must not cheat"). Thus, according to Higgins, you can experience four main kinds of discrepancy between yourself and your standards: (1) You may not match your own ideals. (2) You may not match another's ideals. (3) You may not match your own moral "oughts." (4) You may not match another's moral "oughts."

Higgins's research shows that different kinds of self-discrepancy produce different kinds of negative emotions (Higgins, 1989; Higgins, Klein, & Strauman, 1985; Strauman & Higgins, 1987). If you don't meet your own ideals, you feel disappointment and dissatisfaction ("All my life I wanted to be a concert pianist, but I'm not going to make it—drat!"). If you don't meet another's ideals, you feel shame or embarrassment ("All my life Mother wanted me to be a concert pianist . . ."). If you don't live up to your own moral conscience, you feel guilt and self-contempt ("I cheated on my test . . ."). If you don't live up to another's moral standards, you feel agitated, threatened, and perhaps even fearful ("If Mother finds out I cheated, she'll kill me!").

Why do we focus on a particular kind of self-discrepancy at a given moment? Higgins (1987, 1989) argues that it depends in part on how recently and frequently we have been aware of such discrepancies in the past. For example, if we've been dwelling on ways we've violated our moral standards in the past, then we are likely to evaluate new behaviors in that way. Some kinds of self-discrepancies are "primed," ready to be applied to new situations.

We began our discussion of self-awareness with a question: When are we most likely to behave consistently with our self-schemas? Self-awareness theory replies: When we consciously pay attention to ourselves. Self-awareness induces us to behave in accordance with our internal standards, or, if this fails, to exit self-awareness through mental distraction, drugs, or reclassification of our behavior. When we fail to meet the standards stored in our self-schema, we experience various kinds of negative emotions.

Public and Private Selves

So far, we have discussed the self as something internal and private, though we indicated earlier its social origins. The self has a public face as well—or rather, many public faces. Think for a moment of all the different selves you are, depending on who you are with. Do you display the same characteristics to your mother, your lover, your friends, and your professor? Do you change the self you present to others in subtle or dramatic ways?

A number of psychologists have emphasized that the self is in part a collection of roles and public performances (Baumeister, 1986; Schlenker, 1980). William James noted this aspect of the self in his pioneering work:

> [W]e may practically say that [a man] has as many different social selves as there are distinct groups of persons about whose opinions he cares. He generally shows a different side of himself to each of these different groups. Many a youth who is demure enough before his parents and teachers swears and swaggers like a pirate among his "tough" young friends. We do not show ourselves to our children as to our club companions, to our masters and employers as to our intimate friends. (1890, vol. 1, p. 294)

The Self as an Actor

The most extreme view of the public self is that it is a facade. Sociologist Erving Goffman argued this point by using a theater metaphor: In interacting with others, we play roles just like actors on a stage. To stay in character, we speak the right lines, display convincing nonverbal behaviors, and use appropriate props. It's not good enough, for example, that a minister be a brilliant theologian; he must also preach in an inspiring tone of voice, fold his hands in a pious manner, and wear a clerical collar. In *The Presentation of Self in Everyday Life* (1959), Goffman argued that con artists, used-car dealers, and professional actors are not the only ones who manage their appearances. Everyone does!

Goffman described social life in general as theater, with onstage and offstage areas and well-defined scripts for different settings. Most jobs, for example, require some degree of *impression management*—that is, control of the appearances we present to others (Leary & Kowalski, 1990). Imagine that you wait on tables in a restaurant. While serving your customers, you are onstage; you must smile, maintain your posture, and carry and serve food with care. When you walk through

Public and private selves: Senator Bob Packwood of Oregon publicly was a strong supporter of women's rights, but he is alleged to have sexually harassed numbers of women.

the swinging doors into the kitchen, however, you are offstage—out of view of your audience. There you can slouch, or yawn, or complain to the cook about how much your feet hurt. We literally become different people with different audiences.

Self-Presentation

Social psychologists have documented many strategies that people use to create favorable or powerful images of themselves in the eyes of others (Jones & Pittman, 1982; Jones & Wortman, 1973). Among these strategies are *ingratiation* (saying or doing things to be liked), *intimidation* (presenting an image of power or competence to increase influence over others), and *self-promotion* (saying positive things about oneself, often in order to be viewed as competent). Generally, we engage in such self-presentational strategies to gain rewards and power and to avoid costs in social relationships.

One common self-presentational strategy is simply telling others what they want to hear. In a clever study, Zanna and Pack (1975) led female undergraduates at Princeton University to believe that they would interact either with a very desirable man (a tall Princeton man who was looking for a girlfriend) or a not-so-desirable man (a very short non-Princeton man who already had a girlfriend). These women were also told either that the man liked very traditional women (women who were "emotional," "passive," and "soft") or nontraditional women (women who were "independent," "competitive," and "dominant"). The women then completed an attitude questionnaire and a so-called intelligence test.

The subjects' responses to the questionnaires betrayed the effects of self-presentational calculation. Women who believed they would interact with the highly desirable man molded their responses to the man's preferences. Those who thought that the man liked traditional women described themselves in more traditional terms; those who thought the man liked nontraditional women described themselves as relatively more nontraditional. Interestingly, the women who thought they would interact with the less desirable man did not change their self-presentation in either direction—apparently he was not worth the effort. Perhaps the most startling finding of this experiment, however, was that the women who expected to interact with a desirable man who liked traditional women also performed significantly *worse* on their "intelligence tests" than other women did. In other words, in hopes of appearing traditional and feminine, the women played dumb. Such is the power of impression management!

Basking in Reflected Glory

People make themselves look better in others' eyes not merely by saying what others want to hear, but also by associating themselves with "winners" and disassociating themselves from "losers" (Schlenker, 1980; Tesser & Rosen, 1975). Have you ever noticed that when the local football team wins, everyone says that "we" won, but when the team loses, it becomes "they" lost? Similarly, college students are more likely to wear shirts, jackets, and buttons that identify their school after their football team wins than after a loss (Cialdini, Borden, et al., 1976). Apparently, one way we enhance our image is by basking in the reflected glory of others.

There's a paradox, however, to this strategy. Suppose everyone at your school is a great athlete. By associating yourself with their success, you should feel good about yourself. But if you are a poor athlete, you have reason to feel bad about yourself, too—in comparison to your group, your performance is inferior. When do we bask in the reflected glory of people we're associated with, and when do we directly compare ourselves with those people? Tesser (1986; Tesser & Moore, 1986) argues that people seek reflected glory in matters that are not highly relevant to their own self-concepts and for which they don't have high aspirations. If being an athlete isn't vital to your self-concept, then you can readily bask in your friends' reflected glory if they are great athletes. People do compare themselves, however, with closely associated others in highly self-relevant areas. If you aspire to be a great scholar, for example, you're likely to compare your scholastic performance with that of your friends (and to feel bad about yourself if they all score higher on a big test than you do).

Tesser, Campbell, and Smith (1984) found evidence for these hypotheses in a study that asked 270 fifth- and sixth-grade students to list the activities (for example, academics, sports, art, or music) that were most and least important to them. The children also rated their own and other students' performances in these activities. The results indicated that children tended to choose friends who were superior to them in irrelevant activities (presumably to bask in reflected glory) but inferior to them in highly relevant activities (presumably to yield favorable comparison).

In sum, the public self is a somewhat changeable mask we present to other people. We get what we want from others by sometimes ingratiating ourselves, saying what they want to hear, and by sometimes basking in the reflected glory of successful friends and associates.

The Self and Mental Health

SOCIAL PSYCHOLOGY IN EVERYDAY LIFE

Like all scientists, social psychologists study the self (and other topics) for the thrill of discovery. What could be more fascinating than gaining an understanding of who we are and who we think we are? Sometimes scientific research carries the additional bonus of providing new perspectives on practical problems. Research on the self is no exception. It has yielded insights into mental disorders such as depression and, as a result, it has suggested new kinds of treatment and therapy.

It may come as no surprise to you that our sense of self is related to our mental health in many complex and subtle ways. Perhaps the most dramatic example of a pathological self is the multiple personality syndrome, in which an individual possesses several seemingly separate personalities (American Psychiatric Association, 1987; Osgood, Luria, Jeans, & Smith, 1976). Multiple personalities, although dramatic, are also quite rare. A more common mental disorder involving the self is depression. Social psychologists have been using research on the self to understand and help alleviate this common problem. Let's examine some of the links between the self and depression.

Self-Awareness and Depression Pyszczynski and Greenberg (1987; see also Lewinsohn, Hoberman, Teri, & Hautziner, 1985) argue that depression is intimately tied to self-awareness. Certain kinds of depression, known as *reactive depressions,* are most likely to occur after a major loss, such as the death of a loved one or the end of a romantic relationship or a job. For most people, having intimate relationships and doing meaningful work are two of life's most important goals. Recall that according to self-awareness theory, if you do not meet your goal, then you try to change your behavior to achieve a better match. If that is impossible, you give up the goal and try to avoid self-awareness.

Most of us find it possible to give up small goals such as getting an "A" in a class, but suffering a major loss such as the death of a loved one prevents us from achieving a goal that is difficult to relinquish. If you are confronted with having to relinquish a treasured goal, self-directed attention is triggered—you focus a lot on yourself and your misery. The discrepancy between your goal (having a relationship with your deceased loved one) and your current situation (a horrible loss) is impossible to remedy. In addition to feeling the anguish of this discrepancy, your state of self-focused attention makes you even more aware of your pain. You are in a "control loop" from which you cannot exit—you can't resolve the discrepancy between your current state and a major goal, and the goal is simply too important to let go of emotionally.

This conflict is the beginning of depression. Because depressed people are self-focused, they begin to explain events in terms of the self, so the self seems to be the cause of the misery (Abramson, Seligman, & Teasdale, 1978). These explanations in turn contribute to a depressive self-schema that characterizes the self as worthless and responsible for these negative events.

Paradoxically, once a depressive self-schema is established, depressed persons begin to maintain their misery. (You may be acquainted with depressed people who actually seem to prefer misery to doing something that would cheer them up.) This behavior is an example of a self-verification process. As we noted earlier, people act to verify their self-concepts even when such actions make them unhappy (Swann & Read, 1981). Although painful, a depressive self-schema at least makes the world understandable and predictable to the depressed person ("Bad things happen to me because I am worthless and deserve them"), and it helps the depressed person avoid being burned again by painful losses in the future—after all, a person who feels worthless and deserving of bad things will not seek out a new satisfying relationship or job (Pyszczynski, 1982). Figure 3.12 schematically summarizes the link between self-awareness and depression.

This analysis of a link between depression and self-awareness has suggested some new ideas for research. For example, depressed people do in fact prove to be highly self-focused (Ingram & Smith, 1984; Smith, Ingram, & Roth, 1985), and clinical descriptions of depressed people note their chronic preoccupation with themselves (Beck, 1976; Brown & Harris, 1978). Not only do depressed people show higher self-awareness in general, they show the particularly self-defeating pattern of seeking self-awareness after negative events. Experimental studies indicate that depressed people, unlike nondepressed people, prefer sitting in front of a mirror (that is, being in a self-focused state) after failure and actually dislike self-focused attention after success (Pyszczynski & Greenberg, 1985). When depressed people are in a self-focused state, they are more likely to recall negative information about themselves (Pyszczynski, Hamilton, Herring, & Greenberg, 1989).

If heightened self-awareness is one component of depression, then one goal of therapy should be to teach depressed people to lessen their focus on themselves, especially after negative events (just as when we are mildly depressed it helps to take our minds off ourselves by going out with friends or to a movie). One researcher has noted that insight therapies, in which subjects focus on themselves, tend to be less effective in treating depression than cognitive or behavioral therapies, which focus more on rechanneling the depressed person's thought processes or behavior (Schmitt, 1983). The last thing depressed people may need is therapy that induces them to contemplate their pain and loss in yet more agonizing detail.

If inappropriate self-focus is a component of depression—for example, choosing self-focus after failures but not after successes—then another goal of therapy should be to train depressed people to pay more attention to their

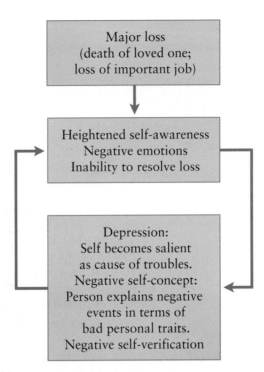

According to Pyszczynski and Greenberg (1987), depression often begins when a person suffers a profound loss that triggers negative emotions and heightened self-awareness. Self-awareness makes the self salient as a cause for the individual's misery. As the vicious cycle progresses, the depressed person develops a negative self-concept and explains misfortunes as attributable to bad personal traits. Self-verification leads the depressed person to elicit negative responses from his or her social environment, which leads to more negative emotions and heightened self-awareness, and the cycle continues.

FIGURE 3.12 Self-awareness and the vicious cycle of depression.

successes and positive experiences and less attention to their failures and negative experiences.

Complexity of the Self-Concept and Depression Another way to help people deal with profound losses is to encourage new and different ways of seeing themselves. Recent research suggests that people who have varied self-concepts are more resistant to depression than those whose entire identities are linked to one relationship (for example, with a spouse) or to one role (for example, success at school). Apparently, to avoid depression you shouldn't "put all your eggs in one cognitive basket."

To evaluate this hypothesis, Patricia Linville (1985) assessed 59 college men on the complexity of their self-concepts. Specifically, she asked them to sort 33 traits, each typed on a separate card, into any number of groups that

SUMMARY TABLE 3.2 Research on the Self		
	Topic of Research	*Processes Studied*
The "me"	Self-schemas	Ease of processing self-relevant information; schematic individuals as experts; self-reference effect—information processed for self-reference is remembered better.
	Self-verification	How people act to prove the validity of their self-concept: For people with low self-esteem, self-verification may conflict with self-enhancement (trying to gain positive information about the self).
Self-directed attention (aspects of the "I")	Self-awareness theory	Self-directed attention leads to comparison of behavior with standards. Behavior is changed when possible to match standards; otherwise, self-directed attention is avoided.
	Control model of self	The self as a cybernetic feedback loop; an elaboration of self-awareness theory.
The public self	Self-presentational strategies	Ingratiation; intimidation; self-promotion; basking in reflected glory.
Applied topics	Self-awareness and depression	Reactive depression as a feedback loop without an exit; the vicious cycle of depression.
	Self-complexity	People with complex self-concepts tend to be less emotionally volatile and less susceptible to depression.

described aspects of themselves. A subject might sort *relaxed, reflective, lazy,* and *quiet* into a pile reflecting the "classroom self," and *lazy, impulsive, unorganized,* and *not studious* into a pile representing the "bad self." The more groupings subjects produced, the more complex their self-concept was considered to be. Subjects were also rated higher on self-complexity when traits tended not to be placed in more than one pile.

After completing the trait-sorting task, subjects took a bogus test of "analytical ability." Half the men were told they had performed very well on the test; the other half were informed that they had done poorly. After receiving this feedback, the men rated their mood and how "creative" they felt. The men with less complex self-concepts were more affected by feedback—that is, they felt worse after failure and more elated after success. The implication of this experiment is that people with relatively simple self-concepts may find themselves more depressed than those with more complex self-concepts when confronted by the inevitable negative events that occur in everyone's life.

Correlational studies looking at real-life mood swings have also provided evidence for a link between self-complexity and depression. For example, Linville (1985) found that college women with simpler self-concepts experienced wider mood swings over a two-week period than did women with more complex self-concepts. By implication, people who are low on self-complexity are more likely to become depressed after receiving negative information about themselves.

In research that directly tested the hypothesis that self-complexity buffers people against depression, Linville (1987) measured the self-complexity of 106 college students and also obtained measures of their stress levels, physical symptoms of stress (colds, stomach pains, headaches), and psychological symptoms (depression, perceived stress). These data provided clear evidence that high levels of stress lead to more severe physical and psychological symptoms in subjects low in self-complexity than in subjects with greater self-complexity.

Taken as a whole, Linville's research suggests that people who are prone to depression may need to be taught to see themselves in many different ways, for people with varied self-concepts seem less susceptible to a loss in any given realm of life.

Summary Table 3.2 lists the various research findings on the self that we've discussed. ⬟

PERSONALITY AND THE SELF IN PERSPECTIVE

Who are you? The answer to this question turns out to be surprisingly complex. One thing that makes you who you are is your personality—the distinctive internal qualities and outward behaviors that characterize you as an individual and that make you different from other people. *Trait theories* view your personality in terms of the unique and consistent traits you possess, whereas *social learning theories* conceptualize personality as the unique ways you have learned to behave in the various settings of your life.

Both trait and social learning theories address a question that is central to social psychology: How much is our social behavior determined by who we are, and how much is it determined by the situation we are in? As this chapter demonstrates, personality characteristics and situations both can have a powerful impact on our behavior. To gain a full understanding of social behavior, social psychologists must therefore study both personality and situational factors.

Who you are also depends on your multifaceted self. Social psychologists study the self because it provides a conceptual link between the individual and the social world. The self guides our behavior, helps us respond to our social setting, and it frequently incorporates the feedback we receive from others and contains the rules we learn from our society. While seemingly private and internal, the self in fact has social origins and social consequences.

Sometimes we tend to behave consistently with our self-concepts (for example, when the situation leads us to focus our attention on ourselves), and sometimes we don't (for example, when the situation draws our attention away from ourselves). Thus, research on the self, like research on personality, shows that both internal and situational factors work together to guide our behavior.

Both our personality and self have many real-life consequences. Personality traits (such as shyness) can influence our comfort in social settings and the number of friends we have. Whether we are low or high on self-monitoring influences not only whether we behave consistently with our traits or change depending on the situation we're in, but also the kind of work we do, the kinds of products we buy, and the nature of our friendships and intimate relationships. Our multifaceted self has the power to guide our everyday social behavior. It can influence when we pursue our internal standards (for example, to earn high grades) or when instead we try to take our minds off ourselves (for example, through entertainment, drink, or drugs). It can even influence our mental health.

It is no wonder, then, that social psychologists continue to be fascinated by the complex nature and consequences of each individual's personality and self.

KEY POINTS   Both *personality* and *the self* refer to processes within individuals that influence their social behavior.

Personality and Social Behavior

Personality research examines internal causes of behavior, individual differences in behavior, and the consistency of behavior over time and settings.

Trait Theories: Personality as Stable Internal Dispositions

Trait theories of personality argue for the existence within people of stable internal dispositions that lead to consistent behavior across settings and over time.

Personality traits are often measured by standardized tests. Such tests must display both reliability and validity. Five broad dimensions of personality found in many studies are extroversion, agreeableness, conscientiousness, emotional stability, and openness/culturedness.

Shyness is a stable trait related to physical symptoms, self-consciousness, and avoidant behaviors in social settings. A number of effective techniques can reduce painful degrees of shyness.

Social Learning Theories: Personality as Learned Behavior

Social learning theories argue that behavior is learned and often varies across situations. Consequently, social learning researchers often study the environments that elicit behavior.

Traits or Social Learning? Testing the Assumptions of Personality Theories

To test the assumptions of trait and social learning theories, personality researchers have studied how well personality test scores predict related behaviors and how consistent trait-related behaviors are across situations.

Reviews published in the 1960s argued that trait measures often do not correlate strongly with related behaviors, and early research, like Hartshorne and May's work on morality in children, suggested that behavior is often quite inconsistent across settings.

More-recent research indicates that aggregated behaviors often show traitlike consistency, whereas single behaviors do not. People may show traitlike consistency in some domains of behavior but not others. Finally, traits best predict behaviors that are prototypical of the trait.

Traits, situations, and their interactions all influence behavior. Research on *moderator variables* seeks to identify factors that determine when behavior is and is not influenced by situations and when it is and is not influenced by traits.

People in *strong situations* behave more as the situation dictates, whereas people in *weak situations* behave in ways that are more consistent with their traits.

Low self-monitoring individuals behave more consistently with their inner traits, attitudes, and values, whereas high self-monitoring individuals are more responsive to their social settings.

The Self

The concept of *self* implies that people have conscious, self-reflective knowledge. Research using mirrors suggests that only higher primates show self-recognition.

Classic Views of the Self

The classic self theories of James, Cooley, and Mead emphasize the social origins of the self.

People are not born with selves. Rather, the self develops as a result of feedback from a social environment. Distinctive characteristics are often salient in our self-descriptions. The self-concept grows more complex and abstract with age.

According to William James and George Herbert Mead, the "I" is the active, choosing self, and the "me" is self-reflective knowledge stored in memory.

Knowing Thy Self: The Self as a Schema

The self-schema comprises the organized knowledge people have about themselves.

People who are schematic on a given trait possess an elaborate self-schema concerning behavior relevant to that trait. Schematic people respond quickly when asked whether they possess schema-relevant traits.

People who are schematic on given traits behave like "experts" in that they group other people's behavior into large, meaningful units when it is relevant to their own schematic traits.

The conception of self in Western cultures tends to be individualistic, focusing on inner traits, abilities, and goals, whereas the conception of self in many Asian, South American, and African cultures is more collectivistic, focusing on interpersonal relationships and roles.

Differences between Self-Knowledge and Other Knowledge

Self-knowledge differs from other kinds of knowledge in that it is complex, highly defended, and emotionally involving.

People often remember information better that is judged in terms of its relevance to the self. This self-reference effect occurs because self-relevant information gets associated with the complex and multifaceted information stored in the self-schema.

Self-knowledge is often highly defended. Research on self-verification shows that people try to prove the validity of their self-concepts by selectively seeking and remembering information that is consistent with them, and through their behavior.

Self-Awareness and Behavior

According to Duval and Wicklund, people can direct their attention either toward themselves or toward external events.

People are most likely to behave consistently with their self-concepts—their traits, attitudes, and values—when they are focusing their attention on themselves, and they also experience emotions more intensely at those times. Self-awareness is in part a function of situational factors and in part of the personality trait of private self-consciousness.

In terms of *control theory,* the self can be conceived as a control system that strives to match behavior to internal standards when the self is in a state of self-directed attention. When the system cannot match its behavior to standards, it seeks to "exit" from self-awareness.

Action identification theory proposes that people can describe their behavior at different levels of abstraction. People generally prefer to classify behavior at higher levels of abstraction, but when behavior is difficult and unfamiliar and when people receive failure feedback, they often choose lower levels of abstraction.

People can hold four kinds of inner standards: their own ideals, others' ideals, their own moral "oughts," and others' moral "oughts." Discrepancy between behavior and these four kinds of standards leads to negative emotions—respectively, dissatisfaction, shame, guilt, and agitation.

Public and Private Selves

The public self can be conceptualized as a collection of varied roles.

Erving Goffman offered a theater metaphor for the public self: Everyone is an actor who plays different roles depending on the social setting. Research demonstrates that people often display themselves differently to different social audiences.

People employ many strategies to make themselves look good to others, including ingratiation and saying what others want to hear. Another way people may boost their public image is by basking in reflected glory—that is, by publicly associating themselves with successful others. People are most likely to bask in reflected glory on dimensions that are not very important to them and are most likely to compare themselves directly to others on important dimensions.

Social Psychology in Everyday Life: The Self and Mental Health

Research on the self has been applied to understanding and treating mental disorders.

Self-awareness theory has been used to understand the causes of depression. When a person suffers a major loss, self-directed attention is triggered and cannot readily be stopped. Incessant self-directed attention leads to self-blame, negative self-descriptions, and destructive self-verification processes.

People with simple self-concepts are more emotionally responsive to information about their successes or failures, are more emotionally volatile, and suffer more depression in response to real-life stress than people with complex self-concepts do.

KEY TERMS

Action identification theory: Wegner and Vallacher's theory that people can describe their behavior at different levels of abstraction. The theory holds that people generally prefer to classify behavior at higher levels of abstraction, but when behavior is difficult and unfamiliar or when people receive failure feedback, they often choose lower levels of abstraction.

Control theory: Also known as cybernetic theory; describes how systems (such as thermostats) regulate themselves to maintain some state of equilibrium. The basic mechanism of a control system is a feedback loop, in which the system tests to see whether some standard is met, and when it is not, it institutes corrective action. The self in a state of self-awareness acts as a control system.

Impression management: Controlling the appearances we present to others to create a desired image.

Moderator variables: Factors that influence when two other variables are related; in personality research, situational moderator variables (such as weak versus strong situations) specify in what situations traits are and are not likely to influence behavior; personality moderator variables (such as self-monitoring) identify people who tend to behave in a manner that is consistent with their traits and those who tend to behave more according to situational pressures.

Personality: Traditionally, this term refers to the consistent, stable, distinctive internal qualities and outward behaviors that characterize individuals and make them different from one another; see *trait theories* and *social learning theories* for two different approaches to personality.

Private self-consciousness: A trait that assesses the degree to which people engage in self-focused attention.

Reflected glory: The self-enhancement we seek by associating with successful, competent, or attractive people.

Reliability: Possessed by a personality test when it measures some trait consistently.

Self: According to different theories, the self is (1) the organized, self-reflective knowledge we hold about ourselves, (2) the active agent that monitors and chooses behavior, and (3) a collection of social roles and self-presentational strategies.

Self-awareness theory: A theory that proposes people can focus attention either on themselves or on the external environment. When attention is self-focused, people think about their internal standards and try to match their behavior to these standards; if it is not possible to meet the standards, self-awareness is painful and people strive to avoid it.

Self-complexity: The degree to which people have varied and independent facets to their self-concept; less-complex self-concepts are related to emotional volatility and susceptibility to depression.

Self-discrepancy: Occurs when we do not behave in a manner that is consistent with internal standards. Higgins describes four kinds of self-discrepancy: violations of one's own ideals, of others' ideals, of one's own moral "oughts," and of others' moral "oughts". Each kind of violation leads to different negative emotions.

Self-monitoring: A personality trait that assesses the degree to which an individual behaves consistently with inner traits, attitudes, and values or with the demands of the social setting; self-monitoring serves as a moderator variable in personality research.

Self-reference effect: The tendency for people to remember information better that is judged in terms of its relevance to the self.

Self-schema: The organized knowledge we have about ourselves; the self-schema can influence perception, memory, and inference about ourselves and others.

Self-verification: The tendency for people to engage in behaviors and thoughts that serve to prove the validity of their self-concept.

Social learning theories: Personality theories that propose individual differences in behavior are learned through classical conditioning, operant conditioning, and observational learning; such theories hold that behavior is not necessarily consistent across situations.

Test-retest reliability: Possessed by a personality test when respondents' scores remain relatively stable over time.

Trait theories: Theories of personality that assume people possess consistent internal dispositions (such as extroversion or shyness) that exert a broad influence on their behavior; such theories predict behavior should be relatively consistent across situations.

Validity: Possessed by a personality test when it measures the trait it is supposed to measure.

PERCEIVING OTHERS

Who to believe—the judge or the professor?

Clarence Thomas and Anita Hill sat under the same hot white lights at the United States Senate, a damaged man and an injured woman demanding justice. Two parallel lives that had looked exemplary suddenly collided over an ugly story of sexual harassment. Poised and intelligent, Hill said that when she had worked for Thomas a decade earlier, he harassed her with barnyard talk of porn flicks, group sex, bestiality and his own sexual prowess. Jaw taut with outrage, Thomas categorically denied all of it, arguing that a mob from the sewer was out to lynch him. One witness was telling the truth, the other was lying; one was a victim, the other a hypocrite. But which was which?

—*Newsweek,* October 21, 1991

Left: *Clarence Thomas and his wife listen to testimony during Senate hearings.* Right: *Law professor Anita Hill appears before the Senate Judiciary Committee.*

It was Supreme Court nominee Clarence Thomas's word against Anita Hill's, and no piece of evidence in the televised hearings proved conclusively who was lying and who was telling the truth. Despite the uncertainty, the United States Senate had to reach a decision—to confirm or reject Clarence Thomas's nomination to the Supreme Court. On Tuesday, October 15, 1991, the Senate voted to confirm Thomas by a vote of 52 to 48, and that vote reflected the public's judgment of Clarence Thomas and his accuser, law professor Anita Hill. According to one poll, 39% of Americans thought Clarence Thomas was telling the truth, 22% thought Anita Hill was telling the truth, and 39% weren't sure (*Newsweek,* October 21, 1991).

THE NATURE OF PERSON PERCEPTION

Like many Americans, you may have formed an impression of Clarence Thomas and Anita Hill, and perhaps you even felt you knew who was lying and who was telling the truth. Try to imagine a world in which you *do not* form impressions of the people you see. It's a bit like imagining a world in which your heart doesn't beat. Person perception—the process by which we judge the traits and characteristics of others—is an integral part of everyday life. From Senate hearings to job interviews to our most routine interactions with others, it influences how we feel about others and how we act toward them. We constantly observe our friends, family members, romantic partners, teachers, and coworkers, and try to figure them out. Research on person perception poses the fundamental question: How do we know what we know about other people?

Perceiving People versus Perceiving Objects

To understand how we perceive people, it helps to think first about how we perceive inanimate objects. The goal of both object and person perception is to discern stable qualities from often inconsistent sensory information. After viewing a table, for example, you may try to judge such stable features as its shape and size. Similarly, after observing a woman, you may try to judge her honesty, friendliness, intelligence, age, and so on. Although we receive varied and often inconsistent information about people, we still generally perceive them to possess traits—that is, stable internal dispositions. In one study, college students were asked to describe other students in their seminar class (Park, 1986). Sixty-five percent of all their statements contained what could be classified as traits.

Pause for a moment to consider how remarkable this abstraction of unobservable traits from observations of others' behavior really is. Which of the following is harder: judging the intelligence of a friend or judging the shape of a car? Identifying a coworker's emotions or identifying the color of a house? Deciding whether one politician is more honest than another or deciding whether one book is larger than another? You'll probably agree that judging people's traits and emotions is typically more complicated than judging the shapes, colors, and sizes of inanimate objects.

Person perception, more than object perception, may be subject to a host of *errors and biases*. Let's return to the Clarence Thomas confirmation hearings for one example: Polls indicated that more women than men believed Anita Hill was telling the truth when she charged Thomas with sexual harassment. What do you think accounted for this difference, and who do you think was more biased in their perceptions of Anita Hill—men or women?

Person perception may at times suffer from bias because of our emotional involvement in the process. For example, do you always accurately perceive someone you're in love with? Person perception may also be biased by strong personal and cultural preconceptions. The study of stereotypes, for example, demonstrates that we sometimes judge people on the basis of our preconceptions about the groups they belong to rather than on the basis of their individual characteristics. (See Chapter 7 for more on stereotypes.)

Person perception is also more complex than object perception because we generally perceive people, but not objects, as *causal agents*—that is, as conscious, self-directing beings possessing wishes, motives, and intentions. In judging Anita Hill and Clarence Thomas, many observers speculated on what *motivated* their behavior. To decide whether Hill was being honest or dishonest, for example, observers wanted to understand *why* she had said what she said.

Another difference between person and object perception is that people, unlike objects, may try to deceive us or mislead us with *false information*. This, of course, was a central issue in the Clarence Thomas hearings. A critical task for the senators (and for the American public) was to decide who was telling the truth and who was lying. More generally, one common goal of person perception is to break through possibly deceptive surface information to uncover the real truth about a person.

A final, and rather subtle, difference between person perception and object perception is that our perception of a person can sometimes change that person's behavior. One notable study demonstrated this effect in the classroom (Rosenthal & Jacobson, 1968). Teachers were led to believe by fake IQ-test results that some of their elementary school students were bright "late bloomers" whereas others were not. Later those children who had been labeled bright did indeed perform better on an achievement test than control children did. Numerous studies have replicated these findings (Babad, Inbar, & Rosenthal, 1982; Harris, 1991). Apparently, when teachers *perceive* students to be bright, they may start treating those students differently and thereby ultimately encourage them to be "brighter" than other children.

Similarly, if you perceive a person to be cold and distant, perhaps you'll treat the person accordingly, which will have the net effect of proving you right: The other person will in fact be cold and distant in response to your own aloofness (Curtis & Miller, 1986). In other words, person perception can sometimes have a *self-fulfilling* quality that object perception does not (Jussim, 1991). This last point suggests one reason social psychologists take a strong interest in person perception. How we perceive others certainly affects our behavior toward them—and it may affect their behavior toward us as well. Thus, if we want to understand social behavior, we need to inquire how people arrive at their judgments of others.

Approaches to the Study of Person Perception

Do you think we generally perceive the truth about other people, or do we often see in them only what we want to see? Person perception has been conceptualized in several different ways (Brewer, 1988; Fiske & Neuberg, 1990; Zebrowitz, 1990). One view holds that person perception is *data-driven,* or determined by the various pieces of information we have about others. A second view holds that person perception is *theory-driven,* or determined by our preconceptions about people. A third view (known as the *ecological perspective*) contends that person perception uses both data and preconceptions in functionally adaptive ways. Let's briefly elaborate on each of these perspectives.

Person Perception as Data-Driven, Or, "Seeing Is Believing"

According to this perspective, there are objective truths to be known about people (for example, Ralph is lying), and there are pieces of sensory evidence that can inform us of the truth. For example, you might judge whether Ralph is lying by observing the degree to which he maintains eye contact, stutters and stammers, and fidgets when he talks. Assuming these are valid indicators of lying, you could mentally add up the information to come to a reasonably accurate overall judgment of Ralph's truthfulness.

Person Perception as Theory-Driven, Or, "Believing Is Seeing"

Sometimes person perception depends on our prior knowledge and preconceptions as well as on objective information. Stated a bit differently, our judgments of others are not always truths based on facts, but are sometimes constructed interpretations based on what we *expect* to see.

Recall that more women than men believed Anita Hill's charges of sexual harassment against Clarence Thomas. Apparently, women and men observed the same "facts," yet frequently came to different conclusions. Why? Perhaps women and men possessed different views about the nature of sexual harassment and held different beliefs about how common sexual harassment is in the workplace, and these preconceptions led them to construct different interpretations of the same evidence.

The Ecological Approach, Or, "Seeing Is for Doing"

The ecological perspective (Baron, 1988; McArthur & Baron, 1983) acknowledges that person perception is based on both observation of others and mental preconceptions. More than the data-driven and theory-driven approaches, however, the ecological approach emphasizes the functional purposes of person perception and the ways it has evolved over time to serve adaptive ends.

For example, it clearly is useful for people to be able to perceive when someone is angry so that they can defuse or avoid a threatening situation. According to the ecological perspective, other people send out signals (such as their facial expressions) that give us useful and valid information about their emotions, if we pay attention to it. In the case of facial expressions, we may be particularly attuned to reading others' emotions, and especially emotions like anger, because of biological evolution. In support of this idea, research shows that facial expressions seem to be perceived almost at once, without much thought or reflection (Baron, 1988). Further research suggests that we recognize anger more quickly in faces than happiness, perhaps because it is particularly important to recognize (and avoid) people displaying this emotion in everyday life (Hansen & Hansen, 1988).

Note that both the data-driven and theory-driven approaches view person perception as requiring considerable thought—you must add up facts about people and come to a final conclusion, or you must apply your preconceptions to assimilate and understand newly acquired information. The ecological approach, on the other hand, acknowledges the possibility that some kinds of perceptions reflect almost immediate judgments that occur because they have helped us (or our ancestors) to survive in the past.

The ecological perspective suggests a distinction between rapid, automatic judgments we make about other people versus more time-consuming and "thoughtful" judgments. This chapter focuses primarily on quick kinds of judgments we make about others—for example, perceiving emotions from facial expressions and judging a person's personality from immediately available cues such as physical appearance and nonverbal behaviors. Chapter 5 focuses on the more "thoughtful" kinds of judgments emphasized by the data-driven and theory-driven approaches.

FIRST IMPRESSIONS

Think of the first day you were in your social psychology class and saw your new teacher. What were your immediate impressions, and what were they based on? Probably your impressions were strongly influenced by your teacher's appearance and nonverbal mannerisms. Folk wisdom advises us not to judge a book by its cover, but in our everyday dealings with people, it's difficult not to. How do we arrive at our first impressions of others—and how do people judge us? Let's consider some of the main factors that influence first impressions.

Physical Characteristics

Most of us judge people's traits at least in part from their facial and bodily features. Common beliefs in our society are that people with high foreheads and clear eyes are intelligent, that highly muscular men are gregarious but stupid, and that blondes do indeed have more fun. Surveys indicate that college students believe a person's character and personality can be read from his or her face (Ligett, 1974; McArthur, 1982), and many research studies document specific relationships that people perceive between physical and psychological traits (Bradshaw, 1969; Dibiase & Hjelle, 1968; Secord, Dukes, & Bevan, 1954; Zebrowitz, 1990). Let's focus on two particularly important aspects of physical appearance that prove to have a large influence on our impressions of others: facial babyishness and physical attractiveness.

Facial Babyishness

Why do you think the face of child star Shirley Temple was found to be so attractive in movies of the 1930s, and what makes Macaulay Culkin's face so appealing in movies of the 1990s? One answer may be that both actors' faces have babyish features that tend to be perceived as cute and appealing. Faces that are perceived as babyish are round and have relatively large foreheads and eyes and relatively small eyebrows, noses, and chins (Zebrowitz, 1990; Zebrowitz, Brownlow, & Olson, 1992).

Perceptions of "baby faces" differ in a number of important ways from perceptions of more mature faces. Berry and McArthur (1986) found that adults with babyish facial features are perceived to be more submissive, honest, and naive than other adults, and these perceptions are shared by people of different ages and from different racial backgrounds (Keating, 1985; McArthur & Berry, 1987; Montepare & Zebrowitz-McArthur, 1989).

The impressions created by babyish facial features can have important real-life consequences. Judges in simulated jury trials find baby-faced men more likely to be guilty of crimes of negligence, whereas men with mature-looking faces were more likely to be found guilty of intentional crimes (Berry & Zebrowitz-McArthur, 1988). Parents perceive baby-faced children as less responsible for their bad behavior; they expect less maturity of them and assign them less demanding

One of these faces has more babyish features than the other. Does this lead you to judge one individual to have different personality traits than the other?

responsibilities, even when they are thought to be the same age as more mature-looking children (Zebrowitz, 1990), and adults generally tend to use "baby talk" more with children possessing baby faces than with those possessing more mature faces, even if the children are the same age (Zebrowitz, Brownlow, & Olson, 1992). Finally, facial babyishness may contribute to gender stereotypes. On average, women have more babyish facial features than men do. This may contribute to common stereotypes about women—that they are "immature," "passive," and "incompetent" (Friedman & Zebrowitz, 1992).

Because facial babyishness has been shown to influence the perceptions of people of all ages in different cultures, it seems reasonable to assume that reactions to this physical characteristic are either biologically innate or universally learned from contact with babies. Undoubtedly, universal reactions to creatures with babyish features (such as feelings of tenderness and nurturance) are biologically useful in that they lead adults to take care of young and helpless members of their species. Both biological evolution and personal life experience may have led most of us to be responsive to facial babyishness in others. Note that this argument fits in well with the ecological perspective on person perception, which proposes that some rapid, automatic processes of person perception develop because they are highly adaptive.

Physical Attractiveness

In movies, good characters are often physically attractive, and bad characters are often unattractive. Do you think this is accidental?

Our judgments of people in real life often parallel our judgments of movie characters. Many people seem to perceive attractive people to be "better" than unattractive people (Feingold, 1992b; Hatfield & Sprecher, 1986). This is an example of a *halo effect* in person perception—when a person is perceived as good on one dimension ("he's handsome," "she's beautiful"), he or she tends to be perceived as good on other dimensions as well ("he's friendly," "she's intelligent"). In one of the first studies on this topic, Dion, Berscheid, and Walster (1972) found clear evidence for the "halo" created by physical attractiveness. They noted that subjects judged attractive people in photographs to be more "sensitive, kind, interesting, poised, modest, and sociable" than unattractive people, even though the only information the subjects had about the people was how they looked. Subjects also predicted that attractive people would have better jobs and happier marriages than unattractive people. Apparently, in the minds of many, "what is beautiful is good" (Berscheid & Walster, 1974b). See Chapter 9 for a broader discussion of how physical attractiveness affects our liking for others.

Some of the predictions subjects made for attractive and unattractive people may have a degree of accuracy. An analysis of data from national surveys conducted at the University of Michigan found, for example, that the annual income of good-looking men was on average almost $2,000 higher than that of homely men, and that of good-looking women was more than $1,200 higher than that of homely women (Quinn, 1978). These survey data also documented that attractive men and women held both more prestigious and better-paying jobs. A more recent study yielded similar results when it looked at the effects of facial attractiveness on the career success of over 700 male and female MBAs (Frieze, Olson, & Russell, 1991). In this study, each subject was rated on a 5-point scale of attractiveness. The main findings: Men on average earned an additional $2,600 a year and women an additional $2,150 for each point higher they were rated on physical attractiveness.

To add insult to injury, the work of attractive people is sometimes judged to be of higher quality than equivalent work performed by less attractive people. For example, Landy and Sigall (1974) asked subjects to evaluate an essay that had apparently been written by either a beautiful woman or a homely woman. Some subjects read a well-written essay, others a poorly written essay. The results showed that subjects rated the essay more positively when they thought it had been written by an attractive woman, and bias in favor of the attractive woman was particularly strong when the essay was of low quality. In other words, if you do outstanding work, you don't have to be beautiful for your work to be appreciated, but if your work is of marginal quality, good looks will help compensate for it.

Evaluations made by children may sometimes be biased by physical attractiveness as well. By the time they are in nursery school, attractive children are already more popular with their playmates than less attractive children (Dion & Berscheid, 1972, 1974), and even infants seem to prefer attractive to unattractive faces (Langlois, Roggman, & Rieser-Danner, 1990).

Teachers' evaluations of their students can be biased by their students' appearance. Clifford and Walster (1973) asked 300 fifth-grade teachers in Missouri to evaluate educational transcripts that included a small photograph of the child. These teachers rated attractive children as more intelligent and socially adjusted than unattractive children, even though the transcripts for the attractive and unattractive children were the same. Similarly, Martinek (1981) found that gym teachers expected attractive children to perform better at physical activities.

Attractive people are less likely to get caught and reported as criminals than unattractive people are; if caught, they are treated more leniently in the courtroom by juries and judges (Deseran & Chung, 1979; Efran, 1974; Mace, 1972; Steffensmeier & Terry, 1973). Attractiveness may be a disadvantage to one kind of defendant, however: a person who is alleged to have used his or her looks for unethical ends, such as the suave, handsome con man who bilks elderly women of their pensions (Sigall & Ostrove, 1975).

In most research studies on physical attractiveness, people or photographs of people are rated on their attractiveness, and thus, a person is defined to be attractive when a group of raters agrees that the person is attractive. The question may have occurred to you: What specific physical characteristics make one person attractive and another unattractive? Recent research provides some answers. Faces with regular features that are typical of the population they are drawn from are perceived to be more attractive than faces with irregular or extreme features (Langlois & Roggman, 1990). Similarly, bodies tend to be perceived as attractive when they are not extreme. For example, women prefer men with slightly larger than average chests more than highly developed "muscle men" (Beck, Ward-Hull, & McLear, 1976), and they tend to find medium-height men more attractive than tall or short men (Graziano, Brothen, & Berscheid, 1978).

Adult facial attractiveness seems to be a function of features that signal youth, sexual maturity, and friendliness. Women's faces that are found to be attractive possess the youthful characteristics of large eyes and small noses, the sexually mature features of high cheekbones and narrow cheeks, and the friendly features of a large smile, highly set eyebrows, and dilated pupils (Cunningham, 1986). (Highly set eyebrows and dilated pupils may show friendliness indirectly by signaling interest and attention.) Similarly, men's faces that are rated as attractive show the youthful features of large eyes and relatively small noses, the sexually mature features of large chins, prominent cheekbones, and relatively thick eyebrows, and the friendly feature of a wide smile (Cunningham, Barbee, & Pike, 1990).

Group Stereotypes Based on Physical Appearance

When you meet a person for the first time, what are the first things you judge about him or her? Three characteristics that most people notice virtually instantaneously are gender, age, and ethnic background (Brewer & Lui, 1989; Fiske, 1993; Stangor, Lynch, Duan, & Glass, 1992). Our perceptions of these characteristics can influence other impressions in many ways by calling into play our preconceptions concerning *groups* of people (such as "men," "old folks," or "whites").

Once we classify a person as male or female, for example, we immediately make inferences about many other characteristics. An early study found that college students tend to think that women are relatively more "talkative, tactful, and gentle," whereas men are more "aggressive, independent, and competitive" (Broverman, Vogel, & Broverman, 1972). See Chapter 8 for a more detailed discussion of gender and gender stereotypes.

Age, like gender, may be a fundamental attribute that we use to quickly judge and classify virtually all people (Brewer & Lui, 1989; Perdue & Gurtman, 1990). For example, a 40-year-old man may be perceived as more stable and emotionally mature than an 18-year-old; the 18-year-old may be perceived as more impulsive, fun-loving, and reckless. Research suggests that many people hold negative stereotypes about the elderly—for example, that they are "crotchety, set in their ways, and forgetful" (Levin & Levin, 1980; McTavish, 1971). These negative views may be partially offset, however, when people distinguish among different kinds of old people—"grandmotherly types," "elder statesmen," "senior citizens," and so on (Brewer, Dull, & Lui, 1981).

Finally, most of us judge others' racial and ethnic backgrounds based on physical characteristics such as skin color and facial appearance. Once we make such judgments, a host of inferences typically follow. One early study on ethnic stereotypes found that Princeton students in the 1930s thought that Italians were "artistic, impulsive, and passionate"; the English were "sportsmanlike, intelligent, and conventional." Blacks were thought by these white college males to be "superstitious, lazy, and happy-go-lucky," whereas Turks were "cruel, very religious, and treacherous" (Katz & Braly, 1933). Many studies indicate that in our society, people with dark skin are often judged to have fewer desirable traits than those with lighter skin (Brigham, 1971). Clearly, such inferences from ethnicity are generally baseless and very often wrong. Once we've judged people's ethnicity, however, we *think* we know other information about them as well. (Chapter 7 presents a more detailed discussion of stereotypes and prejudice.)

In sum, physical characteristics such as facial appearance, physical attractiveness, and skin color strongly influence our first impressions of others. Such physical characteristics lead us to make quick, sometimes automatic, judgments about others' gender, age, and ethnic background, and these judgments in turn lead us to infer others' characteristics based on social stereotypes.

Nonverbal Behaviors

After viewing Clarence Thomas's testimony, many commentators noted that he seemed passionately outraged by the accusations against him. Anita Hill, on the other hand, seemed relatively unemotional and controlled during her testimony. Clearly, viewers were not just listening to what Clarence Thomas and Anita Hill said, but they were attending also to how they said it and how they appeared.

In forming impressions of other people, most of us pay attention not only to the relatively static cues such as appearance and attractiveness, but also to the more dynamic, stylistic aspects of a person's behavior. We may notice whether a person's gestures are expansive or constricted, nervous or relaxed. Or we may notice whether a person talks slowly or quickly. Considerable research suggests that we readily infer personality traits from stylistic, nonverbal cues (Ambady & Rosenthal, 1993; Lippa, 1983; Riggio, Lippa, & Salinas, 1990). For instance, we may decide that someone with expansive gestures and a loud voice is extroverted, whereas a person who fidgets, twitches, and stutters is neurotic.

The Significance of Nonverbal Information

How important are nonverbal behaviors in creating first impressions? Suppose you meet someone who says he's coolheaded and calm, but as he speaks, his hands tremble, and his voice cracks with nervous tremors. Which information would influence your impression more—his words or his nonverbal behaviors? Many studies that ask subjects to judge conflicting verbal and nonverbal cues have found that people weight nonverbal information more heavily (Mehrabian & Wiener, 1967). Apparently, we often assume that nonverbal information is more honest and less controlled than verbal information. Notice that these studies do not imply nonverbal behaviors carry more information than verbal behavior, but rather that when verbal and nonverbal behaviors are inconsistent, we are more likely to *believe* the nonverbal message.

Winston Churchill flashes an emblem—his famous "V-for-victory" sign—at sailors during World War II.

Kinds of Nonverbal Behavior

Nonverbal behavior includes qualities of voice such as pitch, volume, rate, and tone; facial expressions; and physical movements such as hand gestures and touching. It might seem to you a relatively easy task for researchers to compile a "dictionary" of the meanings of different nonverbal behaviors—for example, a smile means happiness, a clenched fist means anger, and so on. Actually, nothing could be further from the truth. The reason is that nonverbal behaviors come in many different varieties and serve many different purposes, and thus their meanings are frequently ambiguous.

Let's illustrate this variability by looking at one kind of nonverbal behavior: physical movements of some part of the body. In an effort to analyze such nonverbal behaviors, Ekman and Friesen (1969b) identified five main classes of body movement: emblems, affect displays, illustrators, regulators, and adaptors.

Emblems are fixed, culturally learned and defined gestures for which dictionary definitions could be given within a specific culture. For example, in our society the "V-for-victory" sign, the "A-okay" sign, and "the finger" are all emblems. By definition, emblems can vary across cultures. Whereas we form a circle with a thumb and forefinger to say "Okay," in other societies this same gesture, particularly if lowered a bit, is considered obscene.

Affect displays are emotional expressions. Facial expressions of anger, sadness, or happiness are all affect displays. Later in this chapter we'll discuss research on how accurately people can judge emotions from such expressions.

Illustrators, as the term suggests, nonverbally illustrate physical events or thought processes. Think of illustrators as nonverbal pictures, metaphors, or analogies. For example, I might hold my hands two feet apart when I tell you about the fish that just got away.

Regulators help lend structure to social interactions. In a sense, they are the nonverbal oil that lubricates the flow of social life. For example, as I talk to you, I nod my head, we establish eye contact, my eyebrows move up and down, and I gesture to emphasize points and to take turns in the conversation. Such nonverbal cues serve to signal attention and to help segment and emphasize the verbal flow. Often we are unconscious of regulators in ourselves and others, but try watching from a distance as two people engage in a conversation. Chances are that without hearing the words, you'll be able to sense the flow of the conversation simply by paying attention to the nonverbal behavior.

Adaptors are self-directed gestures that occur when a person is not paying attention to himself or herself, or when a person is in conflict or distracted. When you glance around the classroom during a test, you may see one student twirling a piece of hair with her finger, another pulling at his beard, and a third rubbing her hand on her thigh. All three movements are adaptors. Such gestures have sometimes been interpreted by clinicians to be reflections of the individual's personality. For example, Mahl (1968) interviewed a woman who constantly slipped her wedding ring off and on her finger during the interview. Mahl interpreted this adaptor as expressing the woman's ambivalence about her husband and marriage.

Ekman and Friesen's classification shows that nonverbal behaviors come in many different varieties. Some nonverbal behaviors may be at least partly biologically innate (for example, affect displays, which tend to be similar across cultures), whereas others clearly are not (for example, illustrators). Some are learned (for example, emblems), whereas others are not (some affect displays). Some represent conscious, intentional communications (for example, an emblem like "the finger"), whereas others are largely unconscious (for example, many adaptors and regulators). Given their diversity, it is amazing that we form impressions so quickly and readily from nonverbal behaviors. See Figure 4.1 for Ekman and Friesen's classification of nonverbal communication and body movement.

Nonverbal Behavior, Power, and Preference

Despite the diversity of nonverbal behaviors, we often use them to infer two main characteristics of people and social relations: power and preference. Power refers to status and dominance in social life; preference refers to our degree of liking for or intimacy with others. Perhaps these themes occur so often in nonverbal communication because they are basic to social life itself (Foa, 1961; Leary, 1957; Triandis, 1977). Consistent with the ecological perspective, it makes sense that human beings have evolved to notice cues of status and liking in other people; the

Affect displays: The facial expressions of these two Guatemalan women show their intense grief as they mourn over the remains of their murdered husbands.

This vulgar emblem has a definite meaning for most Americans.

The man on the left uses an illustrator to demonstrate how to assemble mechanical parts.

ability to judge others' status and liking for us can be seen as a survival skill. Let's look at the themes of power and preference in action, through three specific nonverbal behaviors: eye contact, personal space, and touching.

Movement	Description	Example
Emblems	Fixed, culturally learned and defined gestures for which dictionary definitions could be given within a specific culture	
Affect displays	Displays of emotion, often through facial expressions	
Illustrators	Nonverbal pictures, metaphors, or analogies	
Regulators	Nonverbal cues that signal attention and help segment and emphasize the verbal flow	
Adaptors	Self-directed gestures that occur when a person is not paying attention to himself or herself or when a person is in conflict or distracted	

FIGURE 4.1 Nonverbal communication and body movement. *Source:* Ekman and Friesen (1969b).

Eye contact frequently signals either intimacy or dominance (Exline, 1972). Research indicates, for example, that the more in love couples report themselves to be, the more time they spend gazing into each other's eyes (Rubin, 1970). In competitive settings, on the other hand, eye contact is often seen as challenging and aggressive. Low-status people typically engage in less eye contact than high-status people, and furthermore, highly competitive people increase eye contact in competitive settings (Exline, 1972). The total context of a particular setting probably determines whether eye contact signals power or preference (Ellsworth & Carlsmith, 1968). Thus, eye contact with your date means something very different from eye contact with a potential mugger.

Personal space, like eye contact, often conveys information about intimacy and dominance. Americans act as if they have an 18-inch bubble of personal space around them that marks the boundary of "intimate distance" (Hall, 1966; see Chapter 15). Generally, close friends, family, or romantic partners may venture within our 18-inch bubble, but others tend to stay outside.

Not only do we maintain our personal space with others on the basis of intimacy, we also pay careful attention to such distances in judging others' relationships. If you saw a couple standing an inch apart while they talked together in the cafeteria, for example, you would probably assume they had a relationship very different from that of another couple standing two feet apart.

Like eye contact, personal space can signal power as well as intimacy. Imagine, for example, that you are called to your boss's office. You enter and stand in front of the desk, probably at a respectful distance. Now reverse the situation. When your boss comes to your desk, he or she will probably feel comfortable stepping right up beside your chair. Low-status people tend to respect the personal space of high-status people; the reverse is not true. Theodore White described a dramatic example of this in *The Making of the President, 1960*: Once it became clear late on election night that John Kennedy was the next president of the United States, his associates and friends stood farther away from him than they had before.

Touching is a third nonverbal behavior that signals intimacy and power in social life (Frank, 1957; Goffman, 1967; Jourard & Rubin, 1968). We tend to touch those we like and those we're intimate with more than those we dislike. Furthermore, we touch those of lower status more than those of higher status. A boss, for example, might ask an assistant to retrieve a file and might touch the

The use of personal space, eye contact, and touching can signal both status . . .

. . . and intimacy.

assistant's shoulder at the same time. When the assistant returns with the file, however, it is quite unlikely that the assistant will touch the boss in return.

The research on eye contact, personal space, and touching suggests that we use these nonverbal cues to signal and regulate emotional and social relations. In particular, nonverbal cues can provide important information about how we view intimacy, power, and status in our social relationships.

JUDGING PERSONALITY

So far we've talked about the raw material of first impressions—our observations of others' physical appearance and nonverbal behaviors. But what do we judge from such observations? Typically, we try to judge others' personality traits (their long-term, consistent patterns of behavior), their emotions (short-term feelings in response to the setting), and their authenticity (whether they are lying). For example, viewers of the Clarence Thomas hearings tried to assess his personality ("Does he have moral integrity?") and his emotions ("Is he angry and outraged at this moment?"). They also tried to decide whether his testimony was truthful. Perhaps the most basic question we can ask about judgments of personality, emotion, and deception is: How accurate are they? First we will examine the accuracy of our judgments of personality traits, and later we will examine the accuracy of our judgments of emotional states and deception.

The Accuracy of Personality Judgments

Could you tell whether Clarence Thomas possessed moral integrity? How about Anita Hill? More generally, can you tell moral people from immoral people, introverts from extroverts, neurotics from stable individuals, or assertive people from passive people? Put simply, can you accurately judge another's personality? Studies that attempt to answer such questions face two important methodological problems.

First, what *criteria of accuracy* should be used? Different studies have used personality test scores, ratings by intimates and peers, and even the judgments of clinical psychologists, but each of these criteria has potential problems. Personality tests are not always valid (Mischel, 1968; see Chapter 3). Intimates and peers may provide biased ratings or possess incomplete knowledge. Nor is clinical judgment always accurate—sometimes clinicians don't agree with one another in assessing clients (Crow & Hammond, 1957). In this regard, it's worth comparing person perception to object perception again. If I want to determine how accurately a person perceives color or brightness, I can objectively measure these attributes and compare the measurements to the person's perceptions, but if I want to determine how accurately a person perceives another's personality, no absolute objective criteria exist.

A second significant methodological problem relates to the *kinds of behavior* on which subjects base their judgments. Should subjects judge others after watching them in a brief film? Should they talk to people for half an hour before judging them? Should they judge only friends they've known for years? Subjects' accuracy in judging strangers after a few minutes may reflect their skill at interpreting physical characteristics and nonverbal cues, whereas accuracy in judgments about long-term acquaintances might reflect their ability to mentally process complex social information.

Early Research and the Statistical Measure of Accuracy

Early research on personality judgment focused on quick impressions of others based on brief exposure to limited information. Dymond (1949, 1950) devised a particularly clever technique to sidestep the criteria problems we have noted. As a part of her procedure, she asked subjects to use a 5-point scale to rate themselves on six traits: *superior–inferior, friendly–unfriendly, leader–follower, shy–self-assured, sympathetic–unsympathetic,* and *secure–insecure.* After briefly interacting with these subjects, judges were then asked to predict how the subjects had rated themselves on the six traits. Note that in this study the judges did not evaluate a subject's "true" personality, but rather put themselves in the subjects' place and filled in rating scales as they thought the subjects had in rating themselves.

Dymond believed she had devised a technique to measure empathy—the ability to take the role of someone else. She found that some judges were more accurate at predicting subjects' self-ratings than others and that judges' accuracy correlated with their degree of general intelligence, extroversion, and warmth. By 1955, 50 similar studies had been published (Taft, 1955). The evidence on whether accuracy is a general trait that correlates with other personality and intelligence measures turned out to be inconclusive, however.

To understand why, we must look a little more carefully at the kinds of measures of accuracy these researchers used. Their basic technique was to find the difference between a judge's prediction for a subject and the subject's self-rating. For example, if I judge that Alice rated herself 5 on a 7-point scale of friendliness, and Alice in fact rated herself 3, then my accuracy for that trait is off by 2 points. The degree a judge was off in his or her predictions was added over the different traits being predicted and over the different people being judged. The result was an overall index of accuracy for each judge. The larger the index (or score), the farther off were the judge's estimated ratings from the subjects' self-ratings; the closer to zero the score, the more accurate were the judge's estimated ratings—that is, the closer they were to subjects' self-ratings.

This overall accuracy score provided a simple, comprehensive measure, but it was obtained at the cost of considerable underlying complexity. A detailed mathematical analysis of such accuracy scores, Cronbach (1955) showed that these seemingly simple measures contained many different components. In addition, they were influenced by judges' *response sets*—their habitual ways of filling in rating scales. Without presenting the mathematical detail, let's describe in simple terms some of the problems Cronbach uncovered.

One common response set occurs when we assume that others answer questions similarly to the way we do. Indeed, most people frequently assume that others' opinions and behavioral choices are more similar to their own than they actually are (Campbell, 1986; Marks, & Miller, 1987; Mullen et al., 1985; Ross, Greene, & House, 1977). For example, people who consider themselves shy are likely to overestimate the number of other people who also describe themselves as shy. This tendency is known as the *false consensus effect*.

How does this relate to our accuracy in judging other people? Apparently, some of us are fairly accurate in judging other people simply because we are similar to the people we are rating, and thus we are helped by the false consensus effect—that is, by judging others to be like ourselves. This kind of accuracy does not reflect true perceptiveness but rather a coincidental similarity between judges and the people they are judging.

Even if we could eliminate the accuracy that results from false consensus, Cronbach showed that accuracy scores still include several different components. Two that are particularly important for our discussion are stereotype accuracy and differential accuracy. *Stereotype accuracy* is that resulting from the rater's sense of how groups of people in general fill in their rating scales. This kind of accuracy does not reflect the rater's ability to perceive true personality differences among subjects. For example, you may feel that college students generally rate themselves as low on anxiety and high on honesty. If you're right, this assumption will help your accuracy in rating a group of college students, not because you're sensitive to each person's personality traits, but rather because you're knowledgeable about how college students on average rate themselves. *Differential accuracy,* on the other hand, refers to a rater's ability to predict how individual people rate themselves (for example, Mary rates herself as more extroverted than Carlos and less anxious than Seymour). Differential accuracy is probably what the original researchers on the accuracy of personality judgments wished to study.

New Directions in Accuracy Research

Because of the statistical complexities revealed by Cronbach's analysis, many researchers stopped conducting studies on the accuracy of personality judgments after the 1950s. After decades of neglect, however, interest in the question has clearly revived in recent years (Ambady & Rosenthal, 1992; DePaulo, Kenny, Hoover, Webb, & Oliver, 1987; Funder, 1987; Jussim, 1991; Kenny, 1991; Kenny & Albright, 1987; Kruglanski, 1989).

Researchers have proposed new statistical techniques for measuring accuracy. For example, the *social relations model* holds that when people judge others, their evaluations are determined partly by themselves, partly by the people they're judging, and partly by the unique relationship between the two (Kenny & Albright, 1987; Kenny & La Voie, 1984). To distinguish these factors, the model provides a mathematical technique for breaking accuracy scores into their different parts. To give a commonsense illustration, if everyone in your family rated everyone else on a scale of "likability," these ratings would in part be determined by the particular rater—perhaps your mother is a Pollyanna who tends to rate everyone as being quite likable. The ratings would be determined in part by characteristics of the people being rated—perhaps everyone tends to agree that your sister is unlikable.

Finally, ratings would be determined in part by unique relationships between people—you might rate your favorite brother as likable, although no one else does.

The social relations model eliminates some of the statistical shortcomings of previous methods. Furthermore, it acknowledges that perceived traits have reality only within the context of particular social relationships. A person's social characteristics (such as "friendliness") are not objective quantities like the height of a tree, but rather qualities that change to some degree depending on who the person is with at the time.

We can further refine our understanding of the accuracy of personality judgments by noting that not all personality traits are equal—some are evidently easier to judge accurately than others. Albright, Kenny, and Malloy (1988) used the social relations model in a study that asked small groups of unacquainted college students to rate one another on five traits: *sociable, good-natured, responsible, calm,* and *intellectual* (these are different names for the "Big Five" personality traits discussed in Chapter 3). Interestingly, students showed moderately good agreement in their ratings of two of the traits, *sociable* and *responsible,* suggesting that there are reliable physical cues from which these two traits may be inferred. Furthermore, judges agreed moderately well with subjects' self-ratings on these traits, suggesting some degree of accuracy in their first impressions. Judges did not show such good agreement and accuracy when judging how good-natured, calm, and intellectual subjects were. Other studies add to this evidence that we can judge extroversion more readily and accurately than other traits (Funder & Dobruth, 1987; Kenny, Horner, Kashy, & Chu, 1992; Park & Judd, 1989).

It should come as no surprise to you that people in general agree more in their judgments of others' traits the better acquainted they are with the people they're judging (Colvin & Funder, 1991; Funder & Colvin, 1988; Paunonen, 1989). But people can also show significant degrees of accuracy judging strangers they have viewed only very briefly (Ambady & Rosenthal, 1992; Kenny, Horner, Kashy, & Chu, 1992).

Finally, we may be most accurate in judging others when we judge their characteristics in a particular setting with which we are familiar (Swann, 1984). For example, how "friendly" do you think your social psychology teacher is in general? This may be too broad a question for you to answer accurately. After all, you probably don't see your teacher at parties, or in stores, or with his or her family members. However, you are in a good position to judge how "friendly" your teacher is during class and with students during office hours. In fact, such circumscribed accuracy is probably more important to you than being able to judge your teacher's overall friendliness. After all, *you* must interact with your teacher during class and office hours, and that's when his or her level of friendliness will make a difference in your life.

As you can probably tell from the last example, accuracy researchers are beginning to emphasize the accuracy of person perception in specific real-life settings. To understand how perception of personality really works, it's not sufficient to assess people's accuracy in judging others solely by having them make global ratings on trait scales. We must also determine whether they can accurately predict real-life outcomes and behaviors. For example, can people reliably foresee whether others will make good friends, roommates, or employees?

We began this section with a fascinating question: How accurately can people judge others' personality traits? The answer turns out to be complicated, in part depending on the criterion of accuracy and the statistical methods used to measure accuracy. Still, recent research shows that people can under certain circumstances show fairly good accuracy in judging others' personality traits.

SOCIAL PSYCHOLOGY IN EVERYDAY LIFE

 ### Accuracy and Students' Evaluations of Their Teachers

If you are like students at many colleges and universities, there's a good chance that you are asked to evaluate your teachers and professors at the end of a course. How do you make these ratings? "The answer's obvious," you may be saying to yourself at this point. "After sitting in a class for months, I simply know from direct experience the degree to which my teacher is 'organized,' 'knowledgeable,' 'stimulating,' and 'an overall good teacher.'"

Recent research by Nalini Ambady and Robert Rosenthal (1993) may force you to rethink a bit this "obvious" answer, however. In one study, Ambady and Rosenthal asked nine college women to rate 13 different college teachers on a number of traits (such as *active, confident, dominant, enthusiastic, optimistic,* and *warm*) after viewing very brief, 10-second videotapes of the teachers as they taught. Intriguingly, the women agreed substantially with one another in most of their ratings. But the real surprise of this study was that the women's ratings based on the 10-second video clips correlated very strongly with actual student ratings of the teachers' effectiveness.

In essence, Ambady and Rosenthal found they could accurately predict college students' ratings of their professors simply by measuring other students' reactions to 10-second video clips of the professors. Ambady and Rosenthal got quite similar results in a second study of 13 high school teachers, and, even more startling, they found that judges who viewed 5-second and even 2-second video clips of the high-school and college teachers made trait judgments that significantly predicted actual student ratings of these same teachers.

What are we to make of these results? One possibility is that students' evaluations of their teachers may be influenced more by their teachers' nonverbal style (and less by the actual organization and content of the course) than students realize. If we take students' evaluations of their teachers to be reasonably accurate measures of "teaching ability," however, then we are left with the remarkable conclusion that people can judge teaching ability quite accurately after viewing only a very brief videotape of teachers in action.

Although surprising, this conclusion makes sense in a certain way, related to our earlier discussion of the accuracy of personality judgments. Note that in Ambady and Rosenthal's research, the criterion of accuracy was not a global rating of personality. Rather, it was a kind of real-life criterion—*teaching ability* as rated by actual students. Thus, their research demonstrated that people can show startling degrees of accuracy *when their judgments of real-life behaviors are used to predict real-life characteristics in a particular, limited situation.* This research is a good example of how social psychologists have tried in recent years to focus on real-life settings when they study the accuracy of personality judgments and first impressions. ⌒

What Traits Do We Use to Describe Others?

In real life, nobody gives us a scale and asks us to rate another person on extroversion or insecurity. Rather, we judge and categorize people in ways that seem meaningful and relevant to us. Do you think each person has unique ways of categorizing and evaluating others, or do all people judge others on pretty much the same attributes? In other words, are the traits and categories we use to perceive others dictated more by who *we* are or more by the qualities of the person we are judging? It would seem that for our perceptions to be accurate, they must be determined by the actual qualities of the person we are judging.

Are the Categories of Person Perception in the Eye of the Beholder?

In an early study addressing this question, Dornbusch and his colleagues (1965) asked children at summer camp to describe their tentmates. Each description was coded as falling into one of 69 categories that described kinds of attributes possessed by other children, such as humor, interpersonal skill, physical ability. In general, the categories children used in describing their camp mates seemed to be more a function of who was doing the describing than of the person being described. Thus, a child might choose to describe others in terms of their sense of humor because that category was important to the child, rather than because it was an obvious trait of the children being judged.

Bernadette Park (1986) conducted a similar study on seven college students who were all in the same seminar class. Each week for seven weeks these students wrote a detailed description of every other student in the class. Like the summer camp study, this one found that the attributes students used to describe one another (for example, degree of intelligence, friendliness, physical appearance) were more a function of the student doing the describing than of the students being described. Again, the categories of person perception seemed to be *projected* by the perceiver more than they were dictated by the perceived person.

Initially, Park observed whether a given category, such as intelligence, was used in various students' descriptions of one another. In a second analysis, however, she also looked at the positivity or negativity of the description. (Thus, for example, "Jane is intelligent" and "Jennie is stupid" are both descriptions about the same attribute, intelligence, but they are opposite in positivity.) In this second analysis, Park rated an attribute as occurring in two descriptions if it was mentioned in both *and* it was equally positive or negative in both. In this analysis she found that students' descriptions were now more a function of who was being judged than of who was doing the judging. The implication is that we can't see just whatever we want to in other people. While the dimensions and categories we use to perceive others may be a function of who we are, our perceptions of where someone falls on these dimensions are still often determined by real characteristics of the person we are judging.

Sometimes we may apply very idiosyncratic categories and dimensions when we evaluate other people. In particular, we sometimes classify other people in terms of how similar they are to important people in our lives (Anderson & Cole, 1990). For example, have you ever disliked someone because he or she reminded you of your despised "ex"? Or maybe you like your new teacher because she reminds you of your favorite aunt. Clearly, these are ways of classifying and perceiving people that are unique to you.

Dimensions of Perceived Personality

The categories of person perception considered so far include all the attributes an individual may have (for example, height, intelligence, sports ability, sense of humor). Suppose we limit people to describing others using just personality traits. Do all people use the same standard personality trait dimensions in judging others?

To answer this question, Rosenburg, Nelson, and Vivekanathan (1968) provided subjects with a list of 60 traits (*serious, shrewd, boring, submissive, honest,* and so on) and asked them to group those traits that "go together" in actual people. The data from this grouping task were analyzed by a statistical technique called *multidimensional scaling,* which plots the traits in geometric space. Traits that subjects tend to group together are close to one another in space, whereas traits that are rarely grouped together are far apart.

Using multidimensional scaling, Rosenburg and his colleagues identified two basic underlying dimensions along which subjects grouped traits: good versus bad intellectual traits and good versus bad social traits (see Figure 4.2).

Other researchers have used a statistical technique called *factor analysis* to identify additional dimensions of person perception (Conley, 1985; Goldberg, 1981; McCrae & Costa, 1985; Norman, 1963). Such studies regularly find five main dimensions of personality in subjects' ratings of other people's traits: (1) extroversion, (2) agreeableness, (3) conscientiousness, (4) emotional stability, and (5) intelligence-culturedness. Factors 1, 2, and 4 seem to represent what Rosenburg and his colleagues called "good and bad social traits," factors 3 and 5 "good and bad intellectual traits." In other words, this five-factor model is a finer-grained analysis of the dimensions of perceived personality than the two-dimension model.

Do these five basic trait dimensions reflect the true underlying dimensions of personality, or do they simply exist in the eye of the beholder? Psychologists have argued both positions (see Block, Weiss, & Thorne, 1979; Passini & Norman, 1966; Powell & Juhnke, 1983; Shweder, 1982). You may recall from Chapter 3 that when people rate their *own* traits (as opposed to the traits of other people), these same Big Five trait dimensions emerge. This would suggest that the Big Five are real dimensions of personality, and people tend to perceive others along these dimensions because they are perceiving what's really there. McCrae and Costa (1987) found that subjects' self-ratings on the five basic dimensions of personality

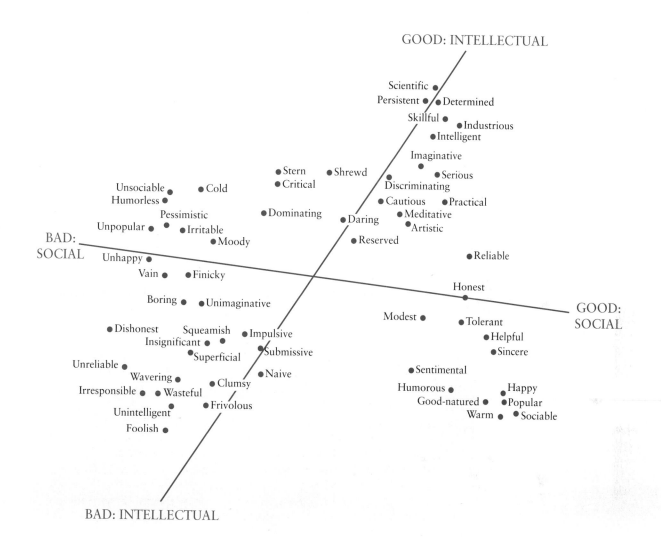

FIGURE 4.2 Two main dimensions underlie our impressions of others. *Source:* Rosenburg, Nelson, and Vivekanathan (1968).

correlated quite strongly with peers' ratings of them on the same dimensions, and they argue for the psychological reality of the five dimensions.

Studies on the categories and traits used to perceive others add a new twist to the question: How accurately can we perceive others' personalities? Sometimes we may categorize others and judge their traits in ways that are unique to us. Notice that in such cases, it may not even make sense to compare the accuracy of your judgments with another person's, for it's not the same judgments being made.

Despite the idiosyncratic nature of some judgments we make about others, research suggests there are broad personality dimensions that many people use in common to evaluate others. Multidimensional scaling studies point to two overarching dimensions of person perception: good versus bad intellectual traits and good versus bad social traits. Factor analysis studies find five main personality dimensions used to perceive others. It seems likely that agreement with others and accuracy in our judgments are most likely to be found for these broad dimensions of personality.

JUDGING EMOTIONS

Who was angrier during their testimony before the Senate Judiciary Committee, Clarence Thomas or Anita Hill? Who was more nervous? These questions lead us naturally to the second main accuracy question we mentioned earlier: How accurately can people judge emotions in others? Modern research on the judgment of

*Based on their facial expressions, what are these people looking at? **Answer:** They are looking at photographs of their village and family members taken years earlier. As this photo illustrates, emotional expressions in real-life settings may sometimes be complex, ambiguous, and hard to interpret.*

emotion is generally traced to the work of the man whose name has become synonymous with biological evolution, Charles Darwin.

Darwin's Legacy

Most famous for his monumental *Origin of Species* (1859), Darwin is also well known to psychologists for a seminal work titled *The Expression of the Emotions in Man and Animals* (1872), in which he sought to uncover the evolutionary origins of emotional expression. Darwin argued that emotional expressions evolved because of their survival value. For example, members of a species who can communicate fear to one another have a better chance of escaping from predators.

Darwin attempted to explain how emotional expressions evolved in the first place. His "principle of serviceable associated habits" held that evolution borrowed already existing behaviors for the new purpose of emotional expression. To illustrate this principle: Consider how people often show disgust by wrinkling their noses and pulling back their upper lips. According to Darwin, this expression evolved from a more primitive vomit response. A second principle, "antithesis," held that once an emotional expression is established, the opposite emotion will be signaled by the opposite expression or body position. So, for example, if people display angry dominance by staring, showing their teeth, hunching their shoulders forward, and clenching their fists, then they should show docile submission with the opposite expressions: averted gaze, closed mouth, slumped shoulders, and open hands.

Darwin's evolutionary theory suggested that emotional expression is innate and therefore cross-culturally universal. If emotional expressions are biologically "wired in," as Darwin suggested, then we should see a definite correspondence between emotions and expressions throughout the world, and people should be fairly good at identifying emotions from expressions. Thus, Darwin's writings led to several testable hypotheses.

Early research on Darwin's theories was relatively unsophisticated (Ekman, Friesen, & Ellsworth, 1972). For example, in one early set of studies, Landis (1924, 1929) attempted to determine how well subjects could match facial expressions with the situations that elicited them. He photographed subjects' faces while they listened to a Wagner opera, looked at erotic pictures, and—believe it or not—watched a rat being decapitated. Each activity was intended to evoke a different emotion. Next, Landis showed the photos to judges and in essence asked them, "In which of these photos do you think the subject is listening to an opera? Or looking at erotic pictures? Or watching someone decapitate a rat?" Landis found that judges were not very good at such matching, and later researchers concluded from his findings that people cannot accurately recognize emotions from facial expressions.

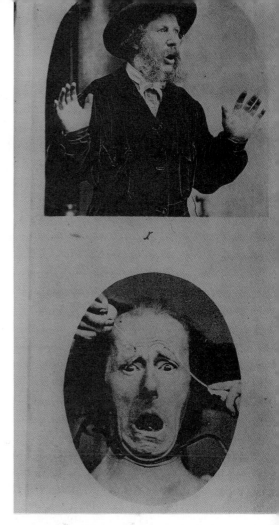

Photographs from Darwin's The Expression of Emotion in Man and Animals. *What emotions do you think are being expressed here?*

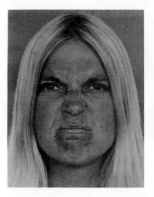   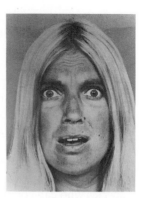

FIGURE 4.3 Photographic examples of four primary emotions. Which emotion do you think is being portrayed in each photograph? *Source:* Ekman and Friesen (1975).

Answers from left: disgust, anger, happiness, fear.

This conclusion was premature, however, for Landis's study suffered from a number of serious flaws. First, it's not clear what emotions Landis evoked in his subjects—a prude might be disgusted by erotic pictures, whereas a libertine might be delighted. Second, the judges in Landis's study were not really asked to identify emotions from facial expressions; rather, they were asked to match situations with expressions. Finally, Landis's subjects were aware that they were being photographed, so they may well have been controlling their expressions.

Given all these methodological problems, it's not surprising that Landis's findings have been superseded by more carefully conducted research, which indicates that subjects are able to recognize six *primary* emotions from posed facial expressions: happiness, sadness, surprise, fear, anger, and disgust (Ekman, Friesen, & Ellsworth, 1982b). (See Figure 4.3 for photographic examples.) Outside the laboratory, judging people's emotions from their expressions is undoubtedly more complex, for in everyday life we try to judge more complex emotions, such as love and jealousy. Furthermore, in real life, emotional expressions occur in intricate mixtures and shift rapidly over time. Finally, in everyday situations, people often control their emotional expressions to varying degrees for both personal and cultural reasons.

Ekman and Friesen (1969b) use the term *display rules* to refer to cultural norms that govern emotional expressions. An average American woman who is feeling happy may display a full, toothy smile. In contrast, a traditional Japanese woman may show only a tiny, inhibited smile. Various groups within a culture may also have different display rules. In our society, for example, it is more acceptable for women to show grief openly than it is for men. The basic display of grief is probably the same for men and women, but men have learned to inhibit that display more. Conversely, women in our society seem to control their displays of hostility and aggression more than men do.

MULTICULTURAL PERSPECTIVE

Facial Expressions across Cultures

Despite the presence of display rules, recent research suggests that the display and recognition of primary facial emotions is universal across cultures (Ekman, Friesen, & Ellsworth, 1982b); that is, people the world over seem to show and recognize the six basic emotions in the same ways. This finding supports Darwin's hypothesis that emotional expressions are to some degree biologically innate.

Studies by Dickey and Knower (1941), Ekman and his colleagues (Ekman, Friesen, & Ellsworth, 1982a; Ekman, Friesen, O'Sullivan et al., 1987), and Izard (1969) all indicate that members of various literate cultures (for example, Japan, the United States, France, and Brazil) substantially agree on the emotions displayed in facial photographs. Although this evidence does not prove conclusively that people the world over *display* emotions with the same expressions, it does suggest that various cultures *interpret* facial expressions in the

Is this expression of emotion universal across cultures?

Do people from different cultural groups display emotions with the same kinds of facial expressions?

same way. Of course, the cultures included in these studies all have considerable exposure to one another. Perhaps cultural contamination explains why these cultures share conventions about facial expressions; maybe the Japanese have seen so many *I Love Lucy* and *Dynasty* reruns that they have learned to recognize and interpret our most common facial expressions.

Ekman and Friesen (1971) attempted to circumvent the problem of cultural contamination by studying a preliterate tribe in New Guinea that had had no contact with Western civilization. In one study, they told tribe members stories that depicted a specific emotion—for example, "A man's child died and he felt sad." Then they showed the New Guinea subjects a set of photographs, which were similar to those in Figure 4.3, and asked the natives to choose the photograph that best represented the emotion in the story. Interestingly, the New Guinea tribe members generally picked the same photographs that Westerners did. In other words, the two groups agreed that certain conventional facial expressions represented certain emotions.

Ekman and Friesen (cited in Ekman, 1972) also photographed posed New Guinea subjects expressing various emotions. The researchers again told them stories (for example, "You are standing in the forest, and suddenly you see a wild boar about to attack you. You are afraid") and asked them to make an appropriate facial expression. Study participants in the United States later judged which of the six primary emotions the person in the photograph intended to express. In general, these U.S. participants were able to categorize correctly the intended emotions of the New Guinea subjects (see Figure 4.4).

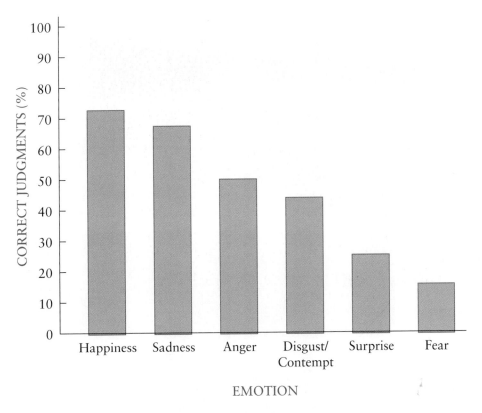

EMOTION

Clearly, U.S. subjects were better at identifying some emotions (for example, happiness and sadness) than others (surprise and fear). New Guinea natives tended to confuse expressions of surprise and fear more than Americans, perhaps because in their lives the two tend to go together. Maybe this explains why their posed expressions of surprise and fear were judged rather poorly.

FIGURE 4.4 U.S. subjects' recognition of posed facial expressions of New Guinea subjects. *Source:* Based on Ekman and Friesen (1971), in Ekman (1972).

Measuring Facial Emotions and Expressions

The research just summarized indicates that people can accurately judge primary emotions from facial expressions and that such judgments are fairly consistent across many cultures, but it doesn't tell us *how* people judge emotions from facial expressions. What expressions display each of the six primary emotions? In order to study more precisely the relation between facial expressions and emotions, researchers have developed objective facial scoring systems.

For example, Ekman and Friesen (1976, 1978, 1982) have developed a microscopic approach to measuring facial movements—the *Facial Action Coding System* (FACS). This system codes very specific facial movements like "raising the

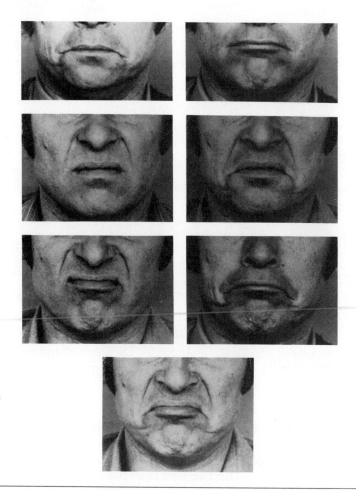

FIGURE 4.5 These are photographic examples of facial movements from the Facial Action Coding System (FACS). This system allows researchers to measure specific facial movements, often resulting from the movement of single muscles. *Source:* Ekman (1976).

inner brow," "raising the outer brow," and "lowering the brows." Often, a single muscle controls these movements. FACS is intended to measure any kind of facial movement, not just emotional expressions. See Figure 4.5 for some photographic examples of downward mouth movements coded in the FACS system. A number of studies suggest that the FACS system may be capable of validly identifying different emotions in the face (Ekman, Friesen, & Ancoli, 1980; Ekman & Friesen, 1982; Ekman, Hagar, & Friesen, 1981). Thus research that started with global judgments of emotion based on facial expressions has progressed in recent years to very precise and specific measurement of facial movement. Such precise measurements may lead to a better understanding of the relation between emotion and facial expression.

Besides measuring facial expressions more precisely, social psychologists have also begun to measure people's ability to accurately perceive emotional expressions. The Profile of Nonverbal Sensitivity, or PONS test, presents videotaped samples of emotional expressions for subjects to identify (Rosenthal, Hall, DiMatteo, Rogers, & Archer, 1979). The PONS test is analogous to an intelligence test; both kinds of test try to reliably assess individual differences, one in how nonverbally perceptive people are, the other in how smart people are. Research using the PONS test suggests that perceiving emotions may indeed be a general ability (Funder & Harris, 1986; Rosenthal et al., 1979). One reliable finding emerging from research on the PONS test is that women on average are superior to men in judging emotional expressions (Hall, 1984).

DETECTING DECEPTION

After hearing the conflicting testimony of Clarence Thomas and Anita Hill, the Senate had to decide: Who was lying and who was telling the truth? Being able to detect deception is an important skill in everyday life, one that we make use of all the time, in evaluating friends, business contacts . . . and witnesses at Senate hearings.

The study of deception and its detection has focused on several important questions: How well can people catch deceptions in others? Are some people better at identifying liars than others? What cues, if any, give liars away? And what cues do people *think* (whether correctly or not) give liars away (DePaulo, Stone, & Lassiter, 1985; Ekman, 1985; Zuckerman, DePaulo, & Rosenthal, 1981)?

Can People Spot a Liar?

Studies investigating how well we detect deception have taken many forms. In one series of experiments, after nurses viewed either a pleasant or a disturbing film, they were asked to convince an interviewer that they had just viewed the pleasant film (Ekman & Friesen, 1974; Ekman, Friesen, O'Sullivan, & Scherer, 1980). Judges looking at videotapes of the nurses then tried to determine when the nurses were lying and when they were not. Other studies have asked subjects to pretend to like someone they in fact dislike and then see how well judges can detect this deception (DePaulo, Lassiter, & Stone, 1982; DePaulo & Rosenthal, 1979).

How successful are people at spotting such deceptions? In general, slightly better than chance, but not by much (DePaulo, 1992; DePaulo, Stone, & Lassiter, 1985). For example, suppose you see videotapes of 20 people, 10 of whom are lying and 10 of whom are telling the truth. If you randomly guess who is lying and who is telling the truth, then by chance alone you should be correct about 50% of the time. In studies of this kind, the overall accuracy of subjects who are trying to detect deception ranges from 45% to 60%—that is, just slightly above the accuracy level subjects would be expected to achieve by chance alone (Kraut, 1980).

Cues That Give Liars Away

If you watched the Clarence Thomas hearings, what did you attend to when you tried to figure out who was lying? Did you listen carefully to the verbal testimony? Did you focus primarily on nonverbal cues—facial expressions, body movements, tone of voice? Do you think some kinds of nonverbal cues reveal deception more accurately than others?

The Face versus the Body

Most of us are more inclined to believe nonverbal cues than verbal statements when the two are in conflict. But are some nonverbal cues more revealing than others? Ekman and Friesen (1969a, 1974) hypothesized that in general the body (the limbs and torso) provides more valid nonverbal cues to deception than the face does. This

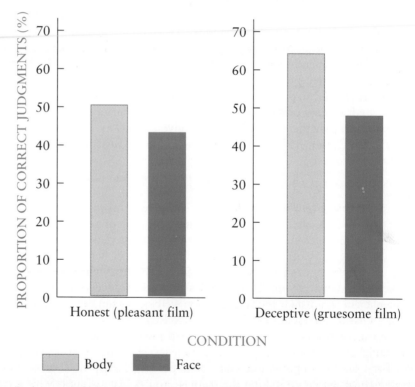

Judges were more accurate detecting honesty and deception when viewing bodies rather than faces. Note, however, that even when attending to body cues, judges did not achieve high levels of accuracy.

FIGURE 4.6 Which provides better cues for deception, the face or the body? *Source:* Based on Ekman and Friesen (1974).

might be so for two reasons: First, the face plays a central role in displaying emotions, and because others pay so much attention to it, we may devote considerable effort to controlling facial expressions. Second, physiological evidence suggests that we have finer muscular control over our faces than over other parts of the body.

When the face does give itself away, it is often with very rapid *micro-expressions* (telltale expressions that can appear and disappear in under a tenth of a second), and many perceivers are insensitive to such rapid, transient expressions (Ekman & Friesen, 1969a; Ekman & O'Sullivan, 1991). Micro-expressions may occur precisely because we generally have such good control of our faces—when an unwanted expression starts to "leak through" onto our face, we are often quick to squelch it, thereby producing a micro-expression.

A number of studies support the proposition that the body leaks more usable information about deception than the face. In one of these studies, Ekman and Friesen (1969a) had subjects watch a filmed psychiatric interview. The woman in the film pretended to be happy and feeling fine, when in fact she was quite distressed and had been recently hospitalized with schizophrenic symptoms. How well could judges see through the woman's facade? Interestingly, judges seemed to perceive the woman's tension and distress more accurately when they viewed films of her body alone; those who viewed only the woman's face were more taken in by her attempt to appear healthy.

In another carefully controlled study, Ekman and Friesen (1974) showed student nurses either a pleasant film or a gruesome one (for example, an amputation operation) and asked them to act in all cases as if they were seeing something pleasant. The nurses were videotaped while watching the films. Clearly, the nurses who viewed the upsetting film were engaging in deception by pretending that the film was pleasant. Later, judges viewed tapes of either the nurses' faces or bodies and tried to determine when the nurses were lying. Again, judges detected deception more accurately from the nurses' bodies, which showed rigidness and inhibition, than from their faces (see Figure 4.6).

Deceptive Smiles

Because people have relatively good control over their faces, broad expressions such as smiles seem to have no consistent relationship to deception (DePaulo, Stone, & Lassiter, 1985; Zuckerman, DePaulo, & Rosenthal, 1981). On average, people do not seem to smile more or less when they are lying. However, Ekman, Friesen, and O'Sullivan (1988) have proposed that when researchers analyze smiles more carefully, they can demonstrate a difference between the smiles of truth tellers and those of liars. Specifically, the "masking smiles" of liars (smiles used to hide other expressions) may be held too long and may be mixed with traces of other facial expressions that reveal a liar's true feelings.

Ekman, Friesen, and O'Sullivan provided some evidence for their claim by analyzing videotapes in which student nurses were interviewed as they viewed either pleasant or upsetting films (those used in the earlier study by Ekman and Friesen). This time, however, the researchers zeroed in on the nurses' smiles. A student nurse was rated as showing an honest smile when she smiled without

Photographs of real and masking smiles. The top left photograph shows a real happy smile. The other photographs show deceptive masking smiles (the subject was trying to appear happy while viewing disgusting or upsetting films). How are these smiles different?

The face with the real smile contains no hints of other emotions. In the lower left and upper right photos of masking smiles, a hint of disgust is displayed by the slightly raised upper lip. In the lower right photo, a hint of sadness is displayed by slightly pulled down lip corners.

showing other facial movements characteristic of negative emotions (such as sadness or disgust), and was rated as showing a masking smile when her smile was accompanied by these other facial movements (see the accompanying photographic illustrations).

Although the student nurses did not show any differences in their overall degree of smiling during honest and deceptive interviews, they did show different *kinds* of smiling. Specifically, when they lied, they showed fewer honest smiles and more masking smiles.

Honest smiles that signal true happiness and enjoyment are called *Duchenne smiles* (in honor of Duchenne de Boulogne, the 19th-century French anatomist who first described them). A Duchenne smile involves characteristic movements of the mouth (caused by contractions of muscles in the cheek) *and* contraction of muscles around the eyes that leads to happy-looking crinkling of the skin around the eyes. Thus, to tell an honest smile from a deceitful smile, look to the eyes, not just to the mouth. Duchenne smiles correlate strongly with self-reported amusement and happiness, whereas other kinds of smiles do not (Ekman, Davidson, & Friesen, 1990).

Vocal Cues of Deception

So far we have focused on nonverbal face and body cues, but other cues may also provide information about deception. A person's spoken words contain both verbal information and *paralinguistic* cues (nonverbal qualities of speech such as tone of voice, speech nonfluencies, and pauses). Paralinguistic cues may offer ways to detect deception. For example, voice pitch seems to be reliably associated with deception: When people lie, their voice tends to go up in pitch.

Many studies have investigated how well people can detect deception from

Kind of Cue	Are Cues Associated with *Perceived* Deception?	Are Cues Associated with *Actual* Deception?
VOCAL		
Speech hesitations	YES	YES: Liars hesitate more.
Voice pitch	YES	YES: Liars speak with higher pitch.
Speech errors (stutters, stammers)	YES	YES: Liars make more errors.
Speech latency (pause before starting to speak or answer)	YES: People think liars pause more.	NO
Speech rate	YES: People think liars talk slower.	NO
Response length	NO	YES: Liars give shorter answers.
VISUAL		
Pupil dilation	(No research data)	YES: Liars show more dilation.
Adaptors (self-directed gestures)	NO	YES: Liars touch themselves more.
Blinking	(No research data)	YES: Liars blink more.
Postural shifts	YES: People think liars shift more.	NO
Smiling	YES: People think liars smile less.	NO, for overall smiling but liars show different kinds of smiles than truth tellers.
Gaze (eye contact)	YES: People think liars engage in less eye contact.	NO

FIGURE 4.7 Nonverbal cues and deception. *Source:* Adapted from DePaulo, Stone, and Lassiter (1985).

verbal content and voice quality, alone and combined with other kinds of information. A review of more than 30 such studies (DePaulo, Stone, & Lassiter, 1985) confirms that people detect deception from body or voice cues more accurately than from facial cues. (See Figure 4.7.) As Ekman and Friesen had found earlier, when subjects view just the face, they detect deception at only chance levels. Furthermore, subjects detect deception more accurately from the combination of body and voice cues than from the combination of body, voice, and face cues. Apparently, facial cues are *misleading*.

Another perhaps surprising conclusion is that the words people speak, even independent of tone of voice, convey accurate information about deception. Although you might think that people could control quite well the verbal content of their lies, this does not always seem to be the case. Liars may give themselves away through the brevity of their answers or through the noncommittal content of their responses, for example.

Actual versus Perceived Cues of Deception

Many people think that "shifty eyes" and "stuttering" are valid signs of lying, but are they in fact? More generally, how reliable are the cues we *think* give people away? A number of studies suggest that the following are in fact valid indicators of deception: speech hesitations, higher voice pitch, pupil dilation, and adaptors (self-directed gestures). Alas, as Figure 4.7 shows, these cues are not necessarily the cues we use in practice when judging whether someone is lying (DePaulo, Stone, & Lassiter, 1985). For example, judges attend to speech hesitations and voice pitch as cues to deception (which are valid), but not to pupil dilation and adaptors (also valid). At the same time, judges mistakenly attend to irrelevant cues such as speech rate, posture shifts, and amount of eye contact.

SOCIAL
PSYCHOLOGY
IN EVERYDAY
LIFE

 ### Detecting Deception in Real Situations

For some people, detecting deception is a professional duty. Customs inspectors and narcotics investigators must pick out and interview suspicious-looking characters, and they must decide whether their suspects are answering their questions honestly. Have such professionals honed their skills at detecting deception so that they are significantly superior to laypeople?

In one study designed to answer this question, Kraut and Poe (1980) asked airline passengers to try smuggling contraband (small packages of white powder that looked like illegal drugs) past a real U.S. Customs inspector at an airport. The "smugglers" of course lied when questioned, whereas other passengers (not smuggling contraband) told the truth when they went through Customs. Both the lying smugglers and the truthful subjects were videotaped during the Customs interview, and the videotapes were then shown to both experienced Customs inspectors and to laypeople, who were asked to decide which video-taped subjects should be physically inspected and which should not. The viewers were informed that about half the videotaped subjects were attempting to smuggle contraband.

Were the judges accurate in identifying the smugglers? No. In fact, the smugglers were chosen slightly *less* often for inspection than the nonsmugglers! Were Customs officers better than laypeople? No, the two groups were equally poor. Interestingly, while neither Customs officers nor lay judges were very good at identifying smugglers, they generally agreed about who the guilty-*looking* people were. In particular, people with shifty nonverbal comportment (including nervous mannerisms, poor eye contact, and speech hesitations) were more likely to be chosen for inspection, as were younger people and people of lower socio-economic status. This research provides further evidence that the cues we use to perceive deception in others are not necessarily valid ones.

Research by DePaulo and Pfeifer (1986) offers additional evidence that not all presumed "experts" in detecting lies are in fact especially adept at it. Two groups—experienced federal law enforcement officers and undergraduates—were asked to detect deception in videotaped subjects who answered questions about their attitudes on various topics; they lied in half their answers and told the truth in the other half. The officers were no better than the students at detecting lies; in fact, they were slightly worse. Students showed a mean accuracy of 54.3% correct identifications, whereas the officers showed a mean of 52.3%. For both groups, the results were just slightly above the level that could be expected to occur by chance alone (50%).

Although the officers were no better than the students at spotting the lies, they expressed more confidence in their judgments than the students did. Furthermore, they showed increasing confidence in their judgment as the trials progressed, whereas students did not. But clearly, the officers' confidence was unwarranted—they were no more accurate than the students, and they showed no increase in accuracy over time. DePaulo and Pfeifer suggest that the officers were deluded about their level of skill in part because they had never received adequate feedback about their successes and failures at detecting deception in their professional work.

In an intriguing recent study, Ekman and O'Sullivan (1991) identified one professional group that possessed superior abilities at picking out liars. The researchers asked groups of U.S. Secret Service agents, polygraph administrators from the CIA and FBI, municipal and superior court judges, police officers, psychiatrists, and college students to view videotaped interviews of ten student nurses, five who were lying and five who were telling the truth.

Can you guess the group that stood out as the best guessers? It was the Secret Service agents. Ekman and O'Sullivan hypothesize that because they must continually scan crowds to guard government officials from attack, Secret Service personnel have learned to be especially sensitive to suspicious nonverbal cues. In contrast, the other professional groups represented in the study (such as police officers and judges) make relatively more use of verbal evidence in trying to detect deception.

Ekman and O'Sullivan also found that, in general, subjects who tended to be accurate in detecting deception (regardless of what group they were in) were more likely to focus on nonverbal as opposed to verbal cues, and tended to be adept at recognizing facial micro-expressions.

In sum, research suggests that many professional "lie detectors," like laypeople, are not terribly good at detecting deception. The findings about Secret Service agents, however, alert us to the fact that there may be certain groups who are particularly skilled at detecting deception from nonverbal cues. Can people be trained to be better detectors of deception? Yes, at least to a degree. In order to improve people's accuracy, it may be necessary to both tell them explicitly what cues they should attend to and give them experience in detecting deception as well as frequent and immediate feedback about their accuracy. For example, DePaulo, Lassiter, and Stone (1982) told some subjects to pay particular attention to tone of voice (a valid cue of deception) in order to judge whether videotaped people were lying. Subjects who received these instructions were more accurate than a control group given no special hints. Apparently, with proper instruction, we may be able to profit from social psychology research and become better detectors of deception. Such research may ultimately suggest ways to improve the skills of such people as Customs inspectors and law enforcement officers. ⌒

PERCEIVING OTHERS IN PERSPECTIVE

The Clarence Thomas–Anita Hill hearings remind us that it is not always easy to judge others accurately. Still, everyday life requires that we continually try to assess others' personality traits and emotions and decide whether people are lying to us. Such judgments are complex, determined in part by our observations of others' appearances and behavior and in part by our preconceptions. Sometimes we judge others rapidly and automatically (for example, when we gauge anger from facial expressions), and such automatic judgments may have evolved because they are highly adaptive.

Our perceptions of people are more complicated than our perceptions of inanimate objects. For example, they depend more on inferences, are frequently biased by personal and cultural preconceptions, and are complicated by the fact that people sometimes try to deceive us. All of these factors are likely to decrease the accuracy of our judgments.

Despite such complexities, people show fairly good ability to judge others' personality traits and emotions. They can make reasonably accurate judgments of others' personality traits, sometimes based on very limited information, and they can discern the six primary emotions in facial expressions.

Judgments of deception seem to be more difficult—indeed, people's accuracy in detecting deception is generally only slightly better than what would be expected by chance. Perhaps this is to be expected. After all, when we try to figure out when someone is lying, we typically face an opponent who is actively trying to mislead us. This is not generally the case when we assess someone's personality characteristics or emotions.

Still, as we have seen, even liars sometimes give themselves away—if we know what to look for. Social psychology research helps inform us what to look for when we try to detect others' deceptions, and more broadly, it helps us understand the complexity of our judgments of other people's personalities and emotions.

KEY POINTS   The Nature of Person Perception

Research on person perception investigates how people judge the characteristics of others, the accuracy of those judgments, and the ways people form stable impressions of others from varied information.

Perceiving People versus Perceiving Objects

Person perception differs from object perception in five ways: Person perception relies more heavily on inferences; person perception is more subject to errors and biases; people are perceived as causal agents; people sometimes attempt to deceive us; and people may change their behavior as a result of the way they are perceived.

Approaches to the Study of Person Perception

Social psychologists have described three main approaches to the study of person perception.

The *data-driven* approach says we perceive truths about others by observing relevant pieces of information and combining them.

The *theory-driven* approach says we often construct perceived reality based on our prior expectations.

The *ecological approach* says we use both sensory data and prior expectations to make rapid judgments that are functionally adaptive in guiding our actions.

First Impressions

Our first impressions of others are frequently based on their physical appearance and nonverbal behaviors.

Physical Characteristics

Two important physical characteristics that determine our impressions of others are *facial babyishness* and *physical attractiveness.*

People with babyish faces are judged to have childlike traits and are seen as less responsible than people with mature faces.

Physically attractive people are often perceived more favorably than unattractive people, and this "halo" has consequences in educational, work, and legal settings.

Three important characteristics judged from physical appearance are gender, age, and ethnic background, all of which may activate group stereotypes and thus influence our perceptions of others.

Nonverbal Behaviors

People consider nonverbal behaviors in forming impressions of others.

People tend to regard nonverbal information as more honest than verbal information when the two are in conflict.

Five important kinds of body movements are emblems, illustrators, affect displays, regulators, and adaptors.

Nonverbal behaviors such as eye contact, the use of personal space, and touching frequently provide information about power and intimacy.

Judging Personality

People often try to assess the stable, long-term personality characteristics of others.

The Accuracy of Personality Judgments

The accuracy of personality judgments depends on the criteria of accuracy used, the behavior observed by judges, and the statistical measure of accuracy used.

Early research on the accuracy of personality judgments asked judges to predict others' self-ratings on various personality traits. Judges' accuracy at such a task was influenced by a number of factors, including (1) the degree to which they assumed others had traits similar to theirs; (2) how well judges estimated how groups of people rated themsel   .erage (stereotype accuracy); and (3) how well judges estimated actual differences among people's self-ratings (differential accuracy).

The *social relations model* provides a new way of statistically measuring accuracy. It holds that accuracy depends on the perceiver, the person being judged, and the unique relationship between the two.

Recent research on the accuracy of personality judgments finds that people can judge some traits accurately (such as extroversion), and it focuses more on accuracy in real-life judgments and in limited settings.

Trait ratings made after viewing very brief videotapes of teachers as they teach predict actual student evaluations of their teachers accurately.

What Traits Do We Use to Describe Others?

In everyday life, people are free to choose the categories and dimensions they use to judge others.

When people freely choose how to describe others, the categories they use are often determined more by the people making the descriptions than by the people being described.

Most people tend to perceive others' personalities as varying along a few main dimensions. Multidimensional scaling studies show two broad dimensions of perceived personality: good versus bad social traits and good versus bad intellectual traits. Factor analysis studies show five dimensions of perceived personality: extroversion, agreeableness, conscientiousness, emotional stability, and intelligence-culturedness.

Judging Emotions

People frequently try to judge others' emotions—transient, short-term feelings people experience in reaction to the setting they are in.

Darwin's Legacy

Charles Darwin argued that emotional expressions are products of biological evolution, and thus such expressions are biologically innate and cross-culturally universal. Darwin proposed principles for how emotional expression originally evolved.

Research shows that people can accurately recognize six primary emotions from facial expressions: happiness, sadness, surprise, fear, anger, and disgust.

Multicultural Perspectives: Facial Expressions across Cultures

People in different cultures tend to show agreement in displaying and recognizing primary emotions.

Measuring Facial Expressions and Emotions

The Facial Action Coding System (FACS) allows researchers to measure specific facial movements, often resulting from the movement of single muscles.

Detecting Deception

Detecting deception is a useful skill in everyday social life.

Can People Spot a Liar?

In experimental studies, people are able to detect deception in others at levels only slightly better than chance.

Cues That Give Liars Away

Social psychology research provides information about the cues that are related to lying and the cues people *think* are related to lying.

People can detect deception better from body cues than from facial expressions. Micro-expressions, very rapid facial movements, sometimes indicate deception; they are relatively hard to detect, however.

Overall, smiling bears no relation to deception. Liars tend to show kinds of smiles different from those of truth tellers, however. Honestly felt smiles, called Duchenne smiles, involve muscles around the eyes as well as mouth movements. Smiles associated with deception often do not involve muscles around the eyes and may occur with traces of other expressions.

People can detect deception at levels better than chance from paralinguistic cues (nonverbal qualities of speech such as raised voice pitch) and the verbal content of speech.

The cues that actually relate to deception are not always the ones people attend to in trying to detect deception.

Social Psychology in Everyday Life: Detecting Deception in Real Situations

Many law enforcement officials (with the possible exception of Secret Service agents) prove to be no better than laypeople at detecting deception from nonverbal cues. Research may provide ways to train people to be better at detecting deception.

KEY TERMS

Adaptors: Nonverbal behaviors consisting of self-directed movements and gestures.

Affect displays: Nonverbal expressions of emotion.

Differential accuracy: The ability of judges to ascertain differences in others' personality traits; one component of accuracy in judging personality.

Display rules: Cultural norms that regulate the display of emotions.

Emblems: Nonverbal behaviors (like the "okay" sign) that are learned, cultural conventions and thus can be assigned specific meanings.

Facial Action Coding System (FACS): A system for measuring small facial movements that often result from the movement of single muscles.

Facial babyishness: A complex of facial characteristics (large forehead and eyes, small chin and nose) that has a significant impact on impressions.

False consensus effect: The tendency for individuals to assume that other people behave more similarly to them than they do in fact.

Illustrators: Nonverbal gestures, such as showing the size of an object, that physically illustrate a concept.

Micro-expressions: Very brief facial expressions that may indicate deception.

Nonverbal behavior: Behavior other than linguistic speech that often conveys information about people; examples include gestures, eye contact, use of personal space, and touching.

Paralinguistic cues: Cues in speech other than the linguistic content (such as tone of voice) that may provide information about the speaker.

Person perception: The process by which people judge the traits and characteristics of others.

Primary emotions: The basic emotions that can be accurately judged from facial expressions—happiness, sadness, surprise, fear, anger, and disgust.

Profile of Nonverbal Sensitivity (PONS test): A test designed to measure people's ability to judge emotional expressions accurately.

Regulators: Nonverbal behaviors, such as gestures accompanying conversations, that serve to structure social interactions.

Social relations model: A statistical approach to assessing the accuracy of judgments about others that assumes judgments are a function of the rater, the person being judged, and the unique relationship between the two.

Stereotype accuracy: Accuracy in judging others' self-ratings that is attributable to the judge's knowledge of how groups of people in general rate themselves.

5

THINKING ABOUT OTHERS

He told us about his problem at the dinner table. . . . He pushed back his chair and stood in front of us, and at first we thought he was going to make some kind of joke or tell some kind of happy story. He always has been good at that, making us smile. That has been part of his charm.

" . . . I will have to retire from the Lakers. . . ." Magic Johnson told us.

"What?" we said.

"I don't have the AIDS disease," he said. "But I do have the HIV virus. . . ."

The news was so dramatic, so incredible, that we didn't even allow it into our heads the first time he spoke the words. HIV-positive? Must be a mistake. Magic? Nonsense. When he continued and the idea took hold, a chill went through us all, a personal chill reserved for only the most dire of family pronouncements.

—*Sports Illustrated*, November 18, 1991

On November 7, 1991, basketball superstar Earvin "Magic" Johnson stunned the world when he announced that he was retiring from the Los Angeles Lakers because he had tested positive for HIV, the AIDS virus. In the days that followed his announcement, millions of fans throughout the world thought about Magic Johnson and his revelation. Print and broadcast journalists covered the story closely, and they as well as the public at large analyzed Johnson's behavior and character. Some said Magic was courageous for discussing his condition so frankly. Some noted his grace and cheerfulness under great stress. Many wondered how the public's knowledge that Johnson was infected with the AIDS virus would change their impressions and perceptions of the sports hero.

If you were like most people, you too probably thought a lot about Magic Johnson when you learned he was infected with the AIDS virus. Maybe you wondered how he came to be infected and asked yourself whether he was responsible for his condition. You probably tried to analyze your thoughts and feelings toward Johnson and figure out how they were changed by this dramatic new piece of information.

We all spend a lot of time thinking about others. We notice and remember facts about others—for example, "Magic Johnson is rich, a great athlete, African-American, and he's infected with the AIDS virus." We organize the facts and form overall impressions: "Whatever's true, I still think Magic Johnson's a great guy." We speculate about the causes of people's behavior: "I think Magic made his announcement because he's a really gutsy and poised person." And we make inferences that go beyond the given facts: "Gee, if this could happen to Magic Johnson, it could happen to anyone. It could even happen to me."

The varied ways we think about others is the central topic of this chapter. In discussing the many ways people remember information and think about other people, we will focus on four main topics: (1) *attribution,* which deals with how we judge the causes of other people's behavior; (2) *impression formation,* the processes we use to add together data to form total impressions of people; (3) our preconceptions, called *schemas,* and how they affect the way we think about other people; (4) *social inference*—ways we go beyond the given facts to try to figure out new things about people based on limited information. Throughout our discussion, we will return again and again to a fundamental question: How good are we at processing information and reaching conclusions about other people?

ATTRIBUTION: ASSIGNING CAUSES TO BEHAVIOR

Why do you think Magic Johnson announced his HIV status to the world one day after he himself learned he was infected? Was it something about Magic's personal traits? For example, did he do it because he was a courageous, forthright, and honest person? Or do you think he *had to* make the announcement, given the situation he was in? If Magic had simply quit professional basketball, members of the press would undoubtedly have dug until they found the reason for his premature retirement. Perhaps, then, Magic made his announcement less because of his personal characteristics than because of situational factors—he knew the truth would come out sooner or later.

We are concerned here not so much with what really motivated Magic's announcement as *what determines how we arrive at our explanations of his and others' behavior.* Social psychologists call our causal explanations of behavior *attributions,* and how we arrive at these explanations is the subject of *attribution theories.* Such theories seek to identify the thought processes we use when we explain our own and others' behavior.

The process of attribution is significant in everyday life, because all of us respond to people on the basis of how we perceive the causes of their behavior. For example, you may admire Magic Johnson more if you think he announced his infection because of his personal courage rather than because a reporter threatened to leak the story to the press. In fact, we constantly seek to understand why people do what they do. What factors influence our attributions? Are most of us prone to making certain kinds of errors when we try to figure out the causes of behavior?

Basketball superstar Magic Johnson.

Attribution Processes: Internal versus External Causes

A basic question we always have to answer about another's behavior is whether it is internally or externally caused (Heider, 1958). An *internal* explanation for Magic's behavior ("He's courageous") focuses on his personal traits or characteristics. An *external* explanation ("He was pressured to do so by the situation") places the cause of his behavior in the environment or social setting.

We may also try to answer other important questions about the causes of people's behavior (Anderson, 1991; Ross & Fletcher, 1985; Weiner et al., 1972; Wimer & Kelley, 1982). For example, we often want to know whether behavior results from *stable* or *unstable* causes. Stable causes are those perceived to be permanent and enduring; unstable causes are temporary and fluctuating. Some causes are perceived to be both internal and stable ("Jim flunked because he is stupid"). Such stable, internal causes are often referred to as *dispositional* causes. Other causes may be perceived to be internal but unstable (for example, a person's effort: "Jim didn't study hard for the last test, but he may for the next one"). Similarly, some causes are perceived to be external and stable (for example, task difficulty: "Social psychology is a very difficult class, and that's why Jim did poorly on the test"), whereas others are perceived to be external and unstable (for example, transient situational factors: "The student sitting next to him during his exam kept sneezing, which distracted him").

Does Peppermint Patty's teacher explain her behavior internally or externally?

The distinction between perceived internal and external explanations has been particularly important to attribution theories and research. Attribution theories often make the assumption, which probably matches your own common sense, that for most of us, there is a mental trade-off between perceived internal and external causes. That is, the more you think a behavior was internally caused, the less you think it was externally caused, and vice versa (Jones, 1990). So, for example, the more you think Magic Johnson announced his HIV status because he was "gutsy and courageous," the less likely you are to think he did it because "he was forced to."

All things being equal, we often seem to prefer internal over external explanations of others' behavior (Heider, 1958; Jones, 1990; Ross, 1977). So, all things being equal, we are probably more likely to explain Magic Johnson's announcement in terms of his inner traits ("He's courageous") than in terms of situational pressures ("The press forced him to do it"). And on average, I may be more likely to explain my student's poor test performance in internal terms ("He's not very smart") than in external terms ("He was distracted during the test by the sneezing of the student who sat next to him").

Theories of Attribution

Regardless of whether you believe Magic Johnson made his announcement because of the kind of person he was (internal causes) or because of situational pressures (external causes), how did you arrive at your conclusion? What evidence influenced you? These are the kinds of questions addressed by attribution theories. Two particularly influential theories of attribution emerged in the 1960s: Jones and Davis's (1965) theory of correspondent inferences, and Kelley's (1967) cube model of attribution.

Jones and Davis's Theory of Correspondent Inferences

Suppose you observe Susan donate $1,000 to the American Cancer Society. Will you infer an internal trait from this behavior—for example, that Susan is generous? If you indeed decide Susan is generous, you are making a *correspondent inference*— the inference that her behavior corresponds to an underlying internal trait.

Jones and Davis identified a number of logical rules of thumb that people use to infer dispositions from behavior. These rules help explain how we make the leap from observing behavior to inferring underlying traits and dispositions. One rule is the principle of *social desirability*. Jones and Davis argue that when we try to infer dispositions from behavior, we tend to consider socially undesirable behavior to be more informative about a person's traits and attitudes than socially desirable behavior. (In this context, "socially desirable" means "normative" or "expected in this situation.") For example, we typically expect people to be somber at funerals, friendly and talkative at parties, and studious and attentive in classrooms. Such behavior is socially desirable. Thus, we consider a smile at a funeral to be more informative about a person's traits than a smile at a party. One study showed that we believe job applicants' statements about themselves more when they don't fit the job (that is, when they're socially undesirable) than when they do (Jones, Davis, & Gergen, 1961). So, for example, if a woman applying for the position of librarian said she was "quiet" and "organized," you might not be sure whether she really was—she might just be saying what's expected to get the job. But if she said she was "noisy" and "disorganized," you would probably believe her.

Let's return to Magic Johnson for another example of the principle of social desirability. You may have reasoned to yourself, "AIDS is such a dread disease and there is so much stigma attached to it that not many people would be willing to publicly state they were infected with the AIDS virus. The fact that Magic Johnson did announce his infection therefore says something about his unique traits—he's courageous."

The principle of social desirability. Does this woman's strange and unexpected appearance lead you to strongly attribute internal traits to her?

According to Jones and Davis, not only do we observe the social desirability of behaviors, we also analyze their consequences or *effects*. Then we try to infer something about the person's dispositions by working backward. For example, the effect of recycling cans, lowering the thermostat in winter to 65 degrees, and riding a bike to work is to protect the environment. If you observe Martha engage in these behaviors, you may then use the effects they all have in common to infer something about Martha's traits—she's a dedicated environmentalist.

When different behaviors (for example, reading books and going to school) have the same effects (they educate you), they are said to have *common effects*. When different behaviors (reading books and going to parties) have different effects (one educates you, the other improves your social life), they have *noncommon effects*. Jones and Davis propose that behavioral choices with unique noncommon effects lead us to make stronger inferences about a person's dispositions than behaviors with common effects do.

Suppose your friend Joe is shopping for a new car. He has been looking at models made by Toyota, Volkswagen, and Mercedes. Some effects are common to the purchase of any of these cars—for example, whichever he buys, Joe will probably get a reliable car, and he will definitely get a foreign car. Only one of these three makes, however, is a high-status car. Getting a high-status car, then, is a unique noncommon effect that occurs only if Joe buys a Mercedes. If Joe chooses a Mercedes, you may say to yourself, "Ah-hah, Joe is a status-seeker." In drawing this

Did Magic Johnson announce he was infected with the AIDS virus because of his internal traits or because of the pressures of the situation?

conclusion, you used the unique noncommon effect of Joe's chosen behavior to infer a personality trait. Research studies show that people do use noncommon effects to infer others' traits (for example, Newtson, 1974).

Kelley's Cube Model of Attribution

Jones and Davis's principles of attribution apply to *single* observations of behavior (you observe Magic Johnson announce he's HIV-positive; you observe Joe buy a Mercedes). In everyday life, however, we often observe repeated instances of people's behavior at different times and in different places. For example, your explanations of the causes of your mother's behavior are probably based on many observations of your mother. Similarly, your notions about the personality of Magic Johnson and the president of the United States are based on repeated observations. A model of attribution developed by Harold Kelley helps us analyze how people mentally process multiple observations of behavior.

Kelley argues that three kinds of information are crucial in determining our attributions: consistency, consensus, and distinctiveness information. *Consistency* refers to the extent to which a person's behavior varies across related situations and over time. *Consensus* refers to how the person's behavior compares with other people's behavior. And *distinctiveness* refers to the extent to which the person's behavior varies across targets—whomever or whatever the behavior is directed at.

Let's make these concepts clearer with a concrete example. Suppose you observe Seymour try to pick up Muriel in a local bar. How do you decide why Seymour behaved as he did? Did Seymour make a pass because of his internal traits (for instance, he's lecherous) or because of external factors (because Muriel is irresistible, or because all men act that way in bars)? According to Kelley's model, to answer this question you must consider consistency, consensus, and distinctiveness information.

To obtain consistency information about Seymour's behavior, you could observe it over time—for example, by noting whether he had come on to Muriel the last three times he was in the bar. For consensus information, you could compare Seymour's behavior with that of other men in the bar—for example, the behavior of Tom, Dick, and Harry. Finally, for distinctiveness information, you could note how Seymour behaves with several different "targets" (in this case, other women in the bar)—let's say Amy, Tricia, and Marcie.

How do you use these three kinds of information in deciding what "caused" Seymour's behavior? According to Kelley's *covariation principle,* you attribute a behavior to the cause with which it covaries over time. (Variables "covary" when they are correlated with each other.) Thus, if Seymour's pickup behavior varies over time or across settings, you'll conclude that the attempt you just observed him make was caused by the particular setting. If Seymour tried to pick up Muriel today, for example, but he had never done so in the past, then it seems reasonable to conclude that his behavior is due to something in the current situation or circumstance— perhaps he drank too much today. If the pickup behavior varies over men, you'll conclude it's because of the men's traits. For example, if Seymour comes on to Muriel, but Tom, Dick, and Harry do not, then it seems likely that Seymour's behavior is due to some unique trait of his. And finally, if Seymour's behavior varies over women, you'll conclude that it's due to the particular woman he's with; if Seymour makes passes at Muriel, but never at Amy, Tricia, and Marcie, then his behavior is probably evoked by something about Muriel or his special feelings for her (see Figure 5.1).

Kelley argued that certain patterns of consistency, consensus, and distinctiveness information, in combination, lead us to make internal attributions, whereas other patterns lead us to make external attributions. For example, high consistency, low consensus, and low distinctiveness lead to internal attributions. To return to our example, suppose you learn that (1) Seymour is always trying to pick up Muriel in the bar; (2) Seymour tries, but Tom, Dick, and Harry do not; and (3) it doesn't matter who the woman is—Seymour makes passes at Amy, Tricia, Marcie, *and* Muriel. On the basis of this information, you are very likely to attribute Seymour's behavior to a strong internal cause: for example, Seymour is a lecherous person.

Other patterns of information lead us to make external attributions. For example, high consistency (Seymour always comes on to Muriel when he's at the bar), high consensus (Tom, Dick, and Harry also come on to Muriel), and high distinctiveness (Seymour comes on to Muriel, but not to Amy, Marcie, and Tricia) point to an external attribution—Seymour acted for an "external" reason: because Muriel is irresistible.

Can people actually engage in the elaborate thought processes suggested by Kelley's model? And when given specific patterns of consistency, consensus, and distinctiveness information, do they arrive at attributions like those predicted by the model? Leslie McArthur (1972) attempted to answer these questions by

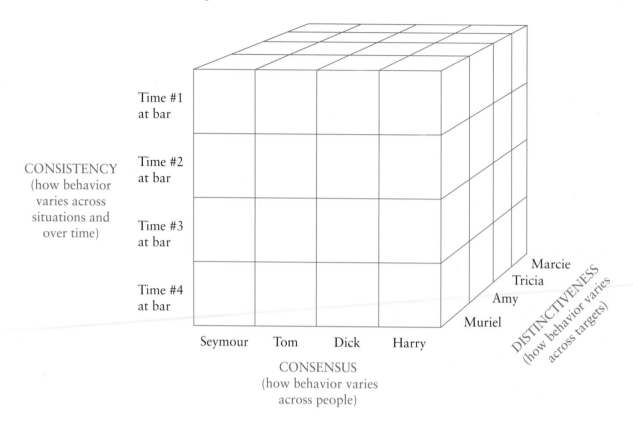

High consistency = Behavior is the same across situations and over time.
Low consistency = Behavior varies across situations and over time.

High consensus = All people show the same behavior.
Low consensus = Behavior varies across people.

High distinctiveness = Behavior varies across targets.
Low distinctiveness = Behavior is the same across targets.

FIGURE 5.1 Consistency, consensus, and distinctiveness information in Kelley's model.

presenting subjects with stories in which consistency, consensus, and distinctiveness information were varied systematically. First a subject was given a brief description of a behavior: "John laughed at the comedian." Then the subject received consistency, consensus, and distinctiveness information: "John has almost always laughed at this comedian" (high consistency), "Other people also laugh at this comedian" (high consensus), and "John also laughs a lot at other comedians" (low distinctiveness).

Various subjects received all the possible combinations of low and high consistency, consensus, and distinctiveness information, and then they were asked to explain why John laughed at the comedian. The results of McArthur's study suggest several interesting conclusions. First, over all possible combinations of information, subjects tended to prefer internal attributions (John's laughter was due to some trait of John's). These were followed in overall frequency by unstable external attributions (that is, John's laughter resulted from some unique occurrence, such as "John was drunk"), and finally by external, stimulus attributions ("John's laughter was caused by the comedian, who was hilarious"). This preference for internal attributions lends research support to the suggestion that people tend overall to prefer internal explanations of behavior to external ones.

McArthur's data also showed that people can process information (at least in the context of this limited experimental situation) in the way Kelley's model suggests. But McArthur's data also pointed to important ways subjects' attributions differed from the model's predictions. For example, Kelley's model seems to assume that subjects consider consistency, consensus, and distinctiveness information equally in arriving at their attributions. But McArthur's data indicate that subjects use consensus information *less* than consistency and distinctiveness information. In our example, this means that in trying to figure out why Seymour tried to pick up Muriel, you pay attention to how Seymour behaves over time and with various women, but you don't care as much about how Tom, Dick, or Harry behaves. Other studies have tended to confirm McArthur's findings (Karaz & Perlman, 1975; Ruble & Feldman, 1976; Zuckerman, 1978).

In recent years, a number of theorists have extended and refined Kelley's model in various ways; however, the basic outlines of Kelley's model seem to be correct (Forsterling, 1989; Lipe, 1991; Medcof, 1990). One new perspective on Kelley's model has been to view it in terms of counterfactual thinking, which we consider next.

Attribution and Counterfactual Thinking

The most direct way to determine the "cause" of a behavior is to observe whether the behavior occurs when the "cause" is present but not when the "cause" is absent. This, in fact, is the logic behind scientific experiments (see Chapter 2). So, for example, if you want to know whether your studying hard "causes" you to get good grades, you could do an experiment: study hard for two of your upcoming tests and don't study hard for another two, and see whether your grades differ in the "study hard" and "don't study hard" conditions.

When we figure out the "causes" of people's behavior in real life, we usually don't have the luxury of conducting experiments. Instead, we typically observe our own or another's behavior (for example, I got an "A" on the social psychology test; Jean flunked it) and try as best we can to figure out the apparent causes of these behaviors based on available information. But even if we cannot perform real experiments, we can perform "thought experiments." This is the basic idea behind *counterfactual thinking*—in essence, people try to imagine whether a given behavior would have occurred if the presumed cause were not present (Lipe, 1991; Wells & Gavanski, 1989).

For example, if you learn that Jean flunked her social psychology test, you might entertain the explanation that it was because she was out late partying the night before. You could mentally test this hypothesis by posing a counterfactual question: Would Jean have flunked if she *had not* been out partying the night before? Note that you can never really know the answer to a counterfactual question like this one. After all, Jean did go out partying, so you will never know what would have happened if she had not.

In a sense, consistency information (as described in Kelley's model) provides "proxy" information that can stand in for the counterfactual question (Lipe, 1991). Although you'll never know what would have happened if Jean had not gone out partying the night before her last test, you can observe that the three times this semester that she partied the night before a test, she flunked, whereas whenever she didn't party the night before a test, she passed. In other words, partying or not partying covaries with Jean's passing tests, and therefore you assume (for the particular flunked test you're interested in explaining) that Jean would *not* have flunked if she had been wise enough to stay home the night before. That is, you decide that her flunking had an external, situational cause.

Different kinds of information (for example, consistency, consensus, and distinctiveness information) lead us to *pose* different kinds of counterfactual questions (Wells & Gavanski, 1989). For example, if I provide you with the consistency information "Jean flunked the three times she partied the night before a test, but she never flunked when she stayed home the night before a test," this leads you to pose the counterfactual question "If Jean had not gone to the party, would she have flunked her latest test?", which leads you to consider a situational explanation. On the other hand, if I provide you with the consensus information "Jean flunked, but everyone else in the class passed," this leads you to pose the counterfactual question "If it were not Jean who took the test, would she have flunked?", which leads you to consider an internal explanation.

Note that viewing attribution in terms of counterfactual questions does not contradict Kelley's theory. Rather, it helps flesh out his theory by specifying how different kinds of information lead us naturally to pose different kinds of counterfactual questions, which focus our attention on different attributional possibilities and, ultimately, lead us to arrive at different attributions about people's behavior.

Mental Shortcuts in Attribution

In figuring out the causes of others' behavior, we do not always ponder consistency, consensus, and distinctiveness information in detail or simulate counterfactual mental scenarios. Sometimes we use mental shortcuts instead—simple cognitive models of causality that allow us to make attributions without fully analyzing all the data available to us (Kelley, 1972).

The Discounting Principle

One pervasive mental shortcut is the discounting principle, which holds that we assign less weight to one cause of a behavior if a second plausible cause is also present (Kelley, 1972). We anticipated this principle when we mentioned the presumed trade-off between internal and external causes. The more you think someone behaved for external reasons, the less you tend to think it was done for internal reasons.

Many studies have provided evidence that people discount internal explanations when strong external explanations are available (for example, Kruglanski, 1970; Thibaut & Rieken, 1955). In one classic experiment, supervisors perceived a worker to be more internally motivated the less frequently they were assigned to supervise the worker (Strickland, 1958). This finding can readily be interpreted in terms of Kelley's discounting principle: Because supervisors had strong evidence of an external cause for the highly supervised worker's performance ("He did it because I was looking over his shoulder all the time"), they discounted internal causes ("He did it because he's a highly motivated worker"). Of course, the person being supervised might be genuinely hardworking. As is always the case with attributions, what we are discussing is not the real cause of people's behavior, but the cause we are apt to assign to it. Beyond its demonstration of the discounting principle, the Strickland study points to an important and unfortunate practical fact: The more you supervise a person, the less you may view the person as highly motivated.

Reward and Intrinsic Motivation.   The discounting principle applies to attributions we make about ourselves as well as to attributions we make about others. Imagine, for instance, that you have been working for some years at a job that is not very stimulating but pays a high salary. You might reasonably decide that you are working hard not because of any real interest, but rather for the money. In other words, you may *discount* your internal interest and motivation (often called "intrinsic motivation") because of an obvious, strong external cause.

In fact, rewards do sometimes undermine our intrinsic motivation in tasks— a tendency called the *overjustification effect*. Lepper, Greene, and Nisbett (1973) demonstrated the overjustification effect in a study in which nursery school children were allowed to draw with markers on blank sheets of paper, an activity the children found fun and interesting. Some children were informed ahead of time that they would receive a reward for playing with the markers, others unexpectedly received a reward after playing, and a third (control) group received no rewards. When the children were given an opportunity to play freely with the markers a week or so later, children who had received expected rewards played *less* than either of the other two groups (see Figure 5.2). Apparently, the expectation of rewards undermined the children's intrinsic motivation to do the task.

The same undermining effect of expected rewards (such as money) has been demonstrated for adult subjects as well (Deci, 1975; Deci & Ryan, 1980, 1985; Lepper & Greene, 1978; Wilson, Hull, & Johnson, 1981). These results are particularly intriguing because they seem to contradict a basic principle of operant conditioning—that rewards following a response *increase* the probability that the response will occur again.

External rewards seem to undermine intrinsic motivation particularly when the rewards are automatic and not related to competence or performance (Deci &

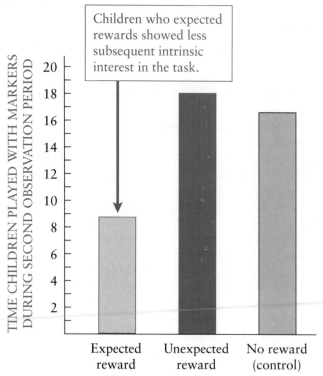

Rewards can undermine intrinsic motivation, particularly when they are expected and when they do not signal competence.

FIGURE 5.2 Effects of expected and unexpected rewards on children's play. *Source:* Data from Lepper, Greene, and Nisbett (1973).

Ryan, 1985). This finding poses a question that may be highly relevant to you: Do *grades* (a kind of reward) ever undermine your intrinsic motivation in your schoolwork? If you view grades as indicating your competence and knowledge, then they need not erode your interest in the subject matter. If, however, you regard grades as "commodities" that don't really show your competence ("I've got to get 40 passing grades and then, thank God, I'll be able to graduate and get a job"), they may undermine your intrinsic interest; you become a student who completes course work because you want to pass rather than because you're interested in the material.

Our Failure to Completely Discount Internal Causes

People often fail to discount internal causes of a person's behavior completely even when strong external causes are apparent. A good real-life example of this phenomenon occurs when we assume that TV and movie actors actually have traits like those of the characters they portray. For example, is Leonard Nimoy, the actor who played Mr. Spock in *Star Trek,* cold, logical, and unemotional in real life? Many of us falsely assume so. Somehow, we irrationally believe that Nimoy's behavior in an acting role is internally caused and thus tells us something about his true personality. Even though we know that Nimoy's behavior is strongly determined by external factors (he's playing a role), we still fail to adequately discount the internal explanation for his behavior (that he's a cold, logical person).

Jones and Harris (1967) demonstrated this "Mr. Spock effect" in an influential experiment in which they asked college students to read another student's speech that either praised or criticized Cuba's communist leader, Fidel Castro. The subjects' task was to guess the writer's *real* attitude toward Castro. Without any other information, subjects could reasonably assume that someone who wrote a speech in favor of Castro was indeed pro-Castro, whereas someone who wrote a speech against Castro was indeed anti-Castro.

The researchers, however, added a complicating factor: Some subjects were told that the writer *freely chose* a pro- or anti-Castro essay, whereas other subjects were told that the speech topic was assigned—that the writer had no choice of topic. Now it made sense for subjects to assume that the student's speech reflected his or her real attitude only if the student freely chose the speech's topic.

Figure 5.3 shows the findings of Jones and Harris's study. Note that discounting did indeed take place. In the "no choice" condition, subjects were less likely to assume that the speech strongly reflected the writer's real attitude. But—and this is the surprising finding—the discounting was not complete. Even in the "no choice" condition, subjects still perceived a significant difference between the attitudes of the writers of pro- and anti-Castro speeches. That is, even with a strong external explanation for the speech-writer's behavior ("He was forced to write on this topic"), subjects still assumed that the writers' attitudes to some degree matched their speeches. This failure to discount internal causes completely in the face of obvious external causes is a highly reliable finding that has been replicated in many different studies (Jones, 1979, 1990).

Apparently, in many situations, we take others' behavior at face value (Jones, 1990). If you see someone write an essay in favor of Fidel Castro, you assume the person must favor Fidel Castro, even if there is evidence that the behavior had an external cause. Realizing that behavior should not always be taken at face value requires a bit of mental work—a cognitive correction process (Gilbert, 1991). Thus, we're particularly likely to fail to discount internal causes adequately despite strong external causes in the following conditions: when we are mentally busy, interrupted, preoccupied, or distracted (Gilbert & Osborne, 1989; Gilbert, Pelham, & Krull, 1988).

Attribution Errors and Biases

We have discussed a number of attribution theories and attributional principles and have noted repeatedly that attributions are the *perceived* causes of behavior, not necessarily real ones. Attribution research provides interesting insights into the possibility for errors in social perception. What kinds of errors are we most likely

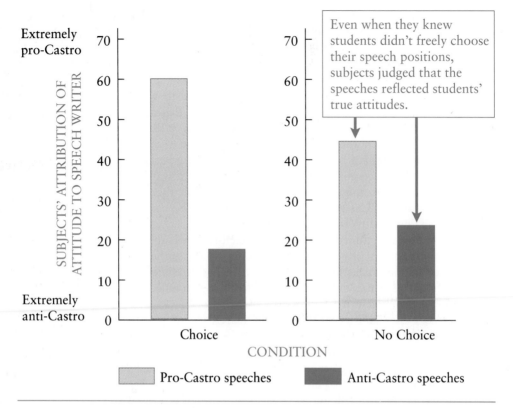

FIGURE 5.3 Subjects' attribution of attitudes from speeches that were either freely chosen or assigned. *Source:* Based on Jones and Harris (1967).

to make when we try to explain the causes of our own and others' behavior? And why do they occur?

The Fundamental Attribution Error

We've already discussed one important attribution error—that people seem to prefer internal, dispositional explanations of behavior over external, situational explanations. As the pro- and anti-Castro speech study demonstrated, people may hold tenaciously to their preferred internal explanations despite the presence of strong and obvious external causes. This tendency to overemphasize internal causes and underemphasize external causes has been labeled the *fundamental attribution error* (Ross, 1977). The related tendency to take behavior at face value and assume that it necessarily reflects underlying internal traits has been called *correspondence bias* (Jones, 1990).

As you will see throughout this book, social settings and social roles often influence people's behavior strongly—but observers often fail to fully appreciate such influences. Ross, Amabile, and Steinmetz (1977) conducted a clever experiment that clearly demonstrates how people may ignore the power of social roles and, as a result, overestimate the importance of internal traits. Pairs of college students played a quiz game in which one student was randomly chosen to be the "quiz master" who asked questions and the other was the "contestant" who answered questions. Quiz masters generated "challenging but not impossible" questions on topics they were familiar with (for example, sports, music, science, and so on). Each quiz master posed ten questions, which were in fact fairly difficult.

After the game was over, subjects rated their own and their partners' level of general knowledge on a 100-point scale. Intriguingly, contestants viewed quiz masters as being considerably more knowledgeable than themselves, whereas quiz masters viewed both themselves and the contestants to be about equally knowledgeable. In other words, contestants attributed both their own behavior ("I didn't get many answers right") and the quiz master's behavior ("She sure asked some tough questions") to internal traits, whereas quiz masters did not. Were quiz masters in fact more knowledgeable than contestants? No—the researchers administered a general knowledge test to all subjects, and it showed no difference between the two groups. Thus, the contestants were in error when they assumed themselves to be less knowledgeable than the quiz masters.

What caused the contestants' mistaken perception? Clearly, subjects' experimentally assigned roles were biased in favor of the quiz masters, who could generate questions in their own areas of expertise. The quiz masters thus ended up appearing knowledgeable, and the contestants less so. Because they were aware of how they selectively generated their questions, the quiz masters realized the hidden advantage conferred by their privileged role and thus did not attribute their difficult questions or contestants' often incorrect answers to internal traits.

The failure of observers to appreciate the power of social settings and roles may partly account for how negative stereotypes develop about disadvantaged groups (Pettigrew, 1979). People often explain the behavior of such groups in terms of members' traits ("They're stupid and lazy") rather than in terms of members' environments and constrained roles ("Poverty, poor medical care, and malnutrition limit their opportunities"). Here again we see a preference for internal over external explanations of people's behavior; furthermore, we see how it can have important real-life consequences.

MULTICULTURAL PERSPECTIVE

Do People in All Cultures Commit the Fundamental Attribution Error?

The United States tends to be an individualistic culture in which people are seen as separate from others, independent, and responsible for their own actions and accomplishments. Many non-Western nations have more collectivist cultures in which people are seen as related to and dependent on others, and behavior is perceived as resulting from the social context and setting a person is in (Markus & Kitayama, 1991; Triandis, 1989; Zebrowitz-McArthur, 1988). Perhaps, then, what social psychologists have called the fundamental attribution error is more common in Western cultures than in non-Western cultures.

Joan Miller (1984) gathered data that showed Hindus in India explain behaviors differently from Americans. In her study, Miller asked Indian and American subjects to explain why someone they knew had performed various "good" and "bad" actions—for example, "Why did your friend help the stranded motorist?" Miller coded the answers as being either dispositional ("Because he's helpful") or situational ("Because there was no one else there to help, and it was dark"). In general, Indian subjects offered internal explanations less than half as frequently as Americans, and external explanations about twice as frequently.

Clearly, in this study, Indian subjects seemed less apt to make the fundamental attribution error than Americans. This may be because people in various cultures *perceive* the causes of behavior somewhat differently. It's also possible, of course, that a person's behavior in Hindu India (a culture with rigid castes and social roles) is *in fact* more influenced by social setting and context than an American's is (Ross & Nisbett, 1991). Whatever the correct explanations for these observed cultural differences, Miller's research provides a clear message: Before announcing the existence of universal errors in attribution, social psychologists must first check whether these errors occur in all countries and cultures. ⇜

The Actor–Observer Effect

The tendency to overemphasize internal causes of behavior seems to be stronger when we explain *others'* behavior than when we explain *our own* behavior. Jones and Nisbett (1972) labeled this phenomenon the actor–observer effect: When we are the actor who performs the behavior, we explain our own behavior more in situational terms, but when we are an observer watching others' behavior, we explain their actions more in internal terms.

Nisbett and his colleagues (1973) found evidence for the actor–observer effect in several studies. In one, subjects were asked to rate themselves, a friend, their father, and TV newscaster Walter Cronkite on a number of traits. They could check one of three alternatives: (1) that the person possessed a given trait (for example, *lenient*), (2) that the person possessed the opposite trait *(firm),* or (3) that the subject didn't have either trait, but rather "it depends on the situation." Subjects checked "depends on the situation" most when rating themselves, less often for their friend and father, and least when rating Walter Cronkite—the person they actually knew least well. These findings support the basic hypothesis of the actor–observer effect; that is, subjects explained themselves more in situational terms and others more in dispositional terms, including a person whose "dispositions" they knew only from seeing him play a very restricted role on TV (see Figure 5.4).

Actor–observer differences have been found in other studies as well (for example, Goldberg, 1978; West, Gunn, & Chernicky, 1975 see Watson, 1982). In

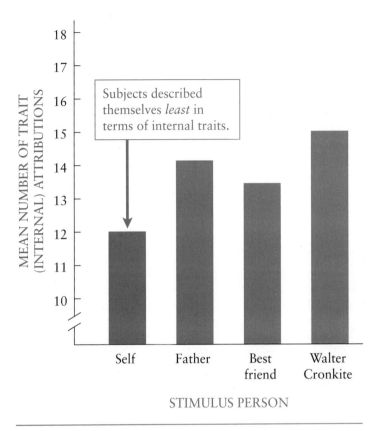

Subjects described themselves *least* in terms of internal traits.

FIGURE 5.4 Trait versus situational attributions for self and others. *Source:* Based on Nisbett et al. (1973).

general, these studies *do not* find that we *never* make dispositional attributions about ourselves; rather, they suggest that we make relatively *more* dispositional attributions about others than about ourselves.

Why should we explain our own behavior differently from the behavior of others? Jones and Nisbett (1972) proposed two possible explanations. First, we generally possess more information about ourselves than about others. For example, you know that you vary in how friendly you are in different situations and with different people, and thus you realize your friendliness "depends on the situation." On the other hand, you've seen a TV personality (like Walter Cronkite or Leonard Nimoy) only in a limited, role-constrained situation. In a sense, you overgeneralize from the person's TV behavior and assume that the behavior reflects a trait.

Second, because of the structure of our perceptual systems, we focus on different things when explaining ourselves and when explaining others. Our sensory systems point outward. For example, you are generally not an object in your own visual field (unless you're watching yourself in a mirror or on a videotape). Thus, when we consider our own behavior, our perceptual systems are focused on the external environment. Other people, though, *are* objects in our perceptual field. We see them as salient, behaving objects, and thus we are more likely to attribute behavior to their inner dispositions.

Is there any evidence for this perceptual explanation of the actor–observer effect? Yes. In one study, two subjects were videotaped as they engaged in a "get acquainted" conversation. Subjects showed the actor–observer effect—they stated that their own remarks were influenced more by the situation and that the other person's remarks were influenced more by his or her personality. Later, the researcher showed some of the subjects videotapes of their own conversations. This video feedback undid the actor–observer effect. After seeing themselves the way other people would, they attributed their own behavior more to internal, dispositional causes (Storms, 1973).

Salience Effects in Attribution

The perceptual explanation of the actor–observer effect is an example of a more general point: People and behavior that are perceptually *salient* (colorful, loud, novel, or distinctive in some way) are seen to be more causally central and influential in general (Taylor & Fiske, 1978).

The effects of perceptual salience on causal attributions were demonstrated particularly clearly in a study by Taylor and Fiske (1975). Two actors engaged in a conversation while subjects sat around them in different positions, observing them. Some of these observers faced the front of one actor and the back of the

Salience effects in attribution. Which person is the most influential member of this group? Why do you think so?

Seating arrangement

Results

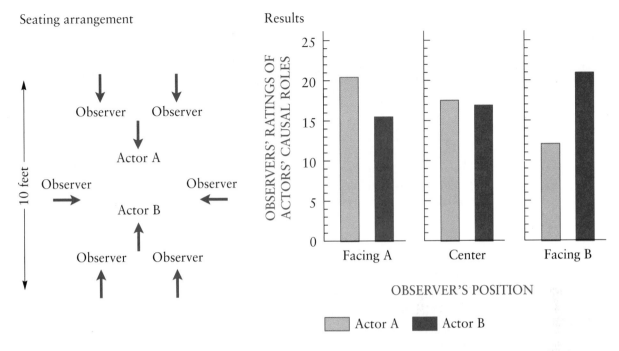

Seating arrangement for actors and observers, with arrows indicating visual orientation

How the subjects rated the actors' causal role

People who are perceptually salient are often perceived to be more causally influential. Imagine that a baseball comes crashing through your window. One of the children playing ball outside has dyed red hair and the rest don't. Who do you think will catch your attention first? Will your first impression be that the child with the dyed hair is likely to be responsible for the misdeed?

FIGURE 5.5 The seating arrangement and results of the Taylor and Fiske (1975) study. *Source:* Adapted from Taylor and Fiske (1975).

second. Other observers could see the faces of both actors. Figure 5.5 shows the subjects' seating arrangement in this study.

After observing the conversation, the subjects were asked how much each actor had set the tone and guided the course of the conversation. The results were quite clear: Observers to the front and back of actors generally perceived the speaker they faced to be more influential than the one they didn't face, whereas observers who could see both actors' faces perceived them to be about equally influential. Other studies extend these findings and show that a person who stands out in a group in any fashion—for example, a woman in an all-male group or a black in an all-white group—is also seen by outside observers as more influential in guiding group discussions and decisions (Taylor, 1981a; Taylor & Fiske, 1978).

Self-Serving Biases in Attribution

There's another route to errors in attribution. Sometimes we may distort the attributions we make about our own behavior in order to protect or enhance our self-esteem. These self-serving biases seem to be fairly common. For example, you'll probably agree that your self-esteem is boosted if you attribute your successes to internal causes ("I received an 'A' because I'm smart") and your failures to external causes ("I flunked the test because my dog kept me up the night before").

A number of studies have found evidence for such self-serving biases in attributions (Carver, DeGregorio, & Gillis, 1980; Van Der Pligt & Eiser, 1983). Interestingly, people seem more willing to inflate their responsibility for successes than to deny their responsibility for failures (Miller & Ross, 1975). Perhaps it would make more sense for us to be more realistic about our failures, for then we could take corrective action. If you receive a low test score and blame it on bad luck (when the real cause was inadequate study), you will only set yourself up for future failure.

Self-serving attributions serve two purposes: They make us feel better about ourselves and they also make us look better to others (Miller, 1978). Greenberg, Pyszczynski, and Solomon (1982) tried to distinguish between these two explanations by asking subjects to explain their successes and failures on an experimental task in two different conditions: when only they knew how they had performed and when an outside observer also knew how they had performed. Interestingly, subjects made self-serving attributions even when they alone knew their level of performance. This result clearly suggests that self-serving attributions are motivated in part by a desire to look good to ourselves as well as to manage appearances for others.

Another way we may protect ourselves from painful attributions is through *self-handicapping strategies,* whereby we devise new apparent causes of our behavior, usually to protect us from other explanations that threaten our self-esteem. For example, imagine that tomorrow you are to take a chemistry test, and deep down you doubt that you'll do well. Tonight your roommate asks if you want to drive with him to visit some friends in the next town. You accept the invitation, and don't get back till 4 in the morning. When you take the exam and do poorly, you can now attribute your bad performance to your lack of sleep rather than to your lack of ability in chemistry. Stated more abstractly, you may seek to create powerful and salient external causes for poor performance so you can avoid attributing your failure to unflattering internal causes. A number of studies have provided evidence that people do in fact engage in self-handicapping attributions (Arkin & Baumgardner, 1985; Berglas & Jones, 1978; Jones & Berglas, 1978).

Misattribution

There is yet another way we can err in our attributions. We can mistakenly attribute our behavior (for example, our emotional arousal) to the wrong cause. Research on misattribution began with a classic study on emotion by Stanley Schachter and

Jerome Singer (1962), who argued that to feel an emotion, two things must occur: (1) You must experience physiological arousal (such as increased heart rate, perspiration, or trembling) and (2) you must label the arousal as being the result of an emotion.

Schachter and Singer conducted an experiment in which they attempted to manipulate separately subjects' physiological arousal and their emotional attributions. On the pretext of studying the effects of a new vitamin on vision, the researchers administered injections to subjects. Some subjects received epinephrine (also known as adrenaline), a stimulant. Control subjects received injections of saline solution. The subjects receiving epinephrine were either correctly informed of the side effects of the drug ("Your hands will start to shake; your heart will start to pound") or were misinformed ("Your feet will feel numb; you will have an itching sensation over parts of your body"). Schachter and Singer hypothesized that subjects with unexplained arousal (the misinformed subjects) would be particularly likely to experience strong emotions, for they would falsely attribute their drug-induced arousal to their emotions.

After administering the injections, the researchers manipulated subjects' perceptions of their own emotions by placing them either in a setting designed to elicit anger or in one designed to elicit euphoria. In the anger-eliciting condition, subjects sat in a room with another subject (actually a confederate) and both completed annoying questionnaires which asked subjects, among other things, to nominate members of their family who "need psychiatric care" and "do not bathe or wash regularly." As he filled in his questionnaire, the confederate became increasingly angry and finally ripped up his questionnaire and stomped out. In the euphoria-eliciting condition, subjects waited with a confederate in a messy room containing papers, folders, and a hula hoop. The confederate shot paper wads at the wastebasket, then made and threw paper airplanes, built towers out of manila folders, and finally twirled the hula hoop. In other words, he acted silly and happy.

In the anger-eliciting condition, misinformed subjects showed a tendency to report feeling more angry and to show more angry behaviors than informed subjects did. In the euphoria-eliciting condition, misinformed subjects tended to report being happier and to show more playful behaviors than informed subjects. Thus, the data provided some support for the hypothesis that unexplained arousal (in this case caused by injected epinephrine) can intensify the experience of emotions because of misattribution.

It's also possible to use misattribution to make people less anxious in anxiety-provoking situations. For example, Olson (1988) asked Canadian college students to deliver a speech before a video camera. Some subjects were told that during their speech they would be exposed to subliminal noise that "makes a person feel unpleasantly aroused." Thus, these subjects could attribute whatever anxiety they felt while speaking to the (nonexistent) subliminal noise. After videotaping subjects' speeches, researchers counted their nervous speech errors (stutters, stammers, "ahs"). Subjects who had been led to misattribute their arousal to the "subliminal noise" showed fewer anxious errors in the speeches.

Attributions and Academic Performance

As the example of speech anxiety suggests, sometimes misattribution can serve therapeutic ends (Forsterling, 1985; Reisenzein, 1983). Some research indicates that college students who suffer from anxiety about their school performance can benefit from "attributional retraining" based on misattribution research. Imagine, for example, that you just completed your freshman year with a 2.5 grade point average, considerably lower than you had hoped. You could attribute your disappointing performance to internal causes ("I'm not very intelligent") or to external causes ("My first year away from home was very disruptive, and the freshman dorm was distracting").

The internal attribution is more likely to impede your future academic performance. If you think you're stupid, you will probably experience anxiety in future academic settings; that is, your negative attributions will trigger additional negative expectations and emotions. On the other hand, if you decide your lackluster freshman record is attributable to external and temporary circumstances, you can start your sophomore year with a clean slate—now you're used to living away from home, and you can move out of the freshman dorm.

To determine whether students' attributions do in fact influence academic performance, Wilson and Linville (1982, 1985) conducted several clever studies. First they identified (via questionnaires) college freshmen whose grade point averages were relatively low and who worried a lot about their academic performance. Next, they gave these subjects information designed to affect their attributions about their academic performance: Half the subjects were informed that students' grades are typically low in their freshman year and improve thereafter; the other half—the control subjects—were given no information about freshman grades. Thus, subjects in the first group were given reassurance that allowed them to attribute their relatively poor grades to transient circumstances rather than to their internal ability.

This simple attributional manipulation affected students' later performance in two measurable ways. First, subjects who were provided with external attributions performed better than control subjects on a scholastic aptitude test administered soon after the study; second, and even more significant, they tended to get higher grades than control subjects during the following semester. Clearly, attributions influence many aspects of our lives. Summary Table 5.1 reviews the multifaceted phenomenon of attribution.

IMPRESSION FORMATION: PUTTING INFORMATION TOGETHER

Information about other people can come from many sources. Sometimes you infer others' traits through attribution processes. Sometimes you simply hear about them from others, or you read about them. To illustrate: You probably

	Concept	Object of Attribution	Factors Affecting Attribution	Comment
GENERAL	Correspondent inference theory	Behavior of others (usually single instances)	Social desirability Common and noncommon effects	The theory tries to explain when we make dispositional attributions.
	Kelley cube model	Behavior of others (multiple observations)	Covariation of consistency, consensus, and distinctiveness information with behavior	The theory tries to specifiy when we make internal or external attributions. According to recent perspectives, the different kinds of information in Kelley's model lead us to pose different kinds of counterfactual questions—that is, questions that ask what would happen if a given cause were *not* present.
ATTRIBUTIONAL SHORTCUTS	Discounting	Behavior of self and others	Presence of one salient cause leads us to discount other causes.	The overjustification effect is an example: Rewards (the salient external cause) can undermine intrinsic motivation.
ATTRIBUTIONAL ERRORS AND BIASES	Fundamental attribution error	Behavior of self and others	Salience of behavior Lack of complete information about the situation	We tend to prefer internal over external attributions. We tend to see behavior as reflecting internal dispositions.
	Actor-observer effect	Behavior of self versus behavior of others	Greater information about self Greater perceptual salience of others' behavior	We tend to explain our own behavior more in external terms, and others' behavior more in terms of dispositions.
	Salience effects	Behavior of others	Perceptual distinctiveness or vividness	Perceptually salient others are seen as more causally influential.
	Self-serving biases	Behavior of self	Degree to which attribution is flattering or unflattering	We tend to attribute our successes to stable, internal factors and our failures to temporary, external factors.
	Self-handicapping	Behavior of self	Anticipated failure and lowered self-esteem	When we anticipate failure, we may provide a "decoy" external explanation to avoid a painful internal attribution.
	Misattribution	Behavior of self	Internal arousal, and possible external causes	People may misattribute their arousal to plausible external causes; this can be used to therapeutic ends.

possess several pieces of information about Magic Johnson—he has a winning smile, he's a great athlete, he's rich . . . and he's infected with the AIDS virus. How do you combine these facts to arrive at an overall impression of Magic Johnson?

Asch's Gestalt Model

To answer this sort of question, Solomon Asch (1946) conducted a classic study on impression formation in which he presented subjects with a list of traits describing a person (for example, "Jim is intelligent, skillful, industrious, warm, determined, practical, and cautious"). Subjects then wrote a brief description of Jim and indicated whether he also possessed other specified traits (whether, for example, Jim is "generous," "wise," or "happy").

How did subjects form their overall impressions from the initial trait list? Asch saw two possibilities: They could use either "algebraic" or "Gestalt" processes in combining information. To illustrate the difference between these two possibilities, let's focus on a specific judgment a subject might make: How "likable" is Jim? According to the algebraic approach, the subject in some sense assigns a degree of likability to each trait and then mentally adds or averages these individual pieces of information; the whole impression is simply the sum (or average) of its parts. In deciding how likable Magic Johnson is, for example, perhaps you assign a degree of likability to each fact you know about Magic ("He's rich," "He's African-American," and so on) and average them all together.

According to Gestalt theory, however, more-complex integration processes occur—the whole may be greater than the sum of its parts. For example, Asch suggested that the meanings of certain traits might literally change depending on other traits occurring with them. Thus, the fact that Magic Johnson is infected with the AIDS virus may color every other fact you know about him. Asch argued that our impression of another person is not formed algebraically, but rather it emerges from the total pattern of information. Asch further hypothesized that certain pieces of information, which he termed *central traits,* are more important than others in influencing the total impression. Certainly, Magic

How do we combine information to form impressions of others?

Asch (1946) presented subjects with the following list of traits:

intelligent, skillful, industrious, _____, determined, practical, cautious

The blank was filled with the words *warm, cold, polite,* or *blunt* to see whether each word was a central trait—that is, whether each strongly influenced the subjects' perceptions of *other* traits the described person might have. The following table shows the percentages of subjects who thought the person described by the list of traits also possessed certain additional traits:

	Traits Inserted into List			
Additional Traits	*"Warm"*	*"Cold"*	*"Polite"*	*"Blunt"*
Generous	91%	8%	56%	58%
Wise	65	25	30	50
Happy	90	34	75	65
Good-natured	94	17	87	56
Reliable	94	99	95	100

FIGURE 5.6 Asch's study of central traits.

Johnson's HIV status has now become a central piece of information about him.

In his research studies, Asch suggested that *warm* and *cold* are central traits that dramatically influence how the remaining traits in the list are interpreted. When Asch substituted *cold* for *warm* in his list of stimulus traits, subjects' impressions were drastically altered; however, using *blunt* and *polite* in the initial list instead of either *warm* or *cold* had very little effect on subjects' impressions (see Figure 5.6).

A number of subsequent researchers have criticized Asch's Gestalt approach to impression formation. Wishner (1960), for example, argued that *warm* and *cold* were central traits in Asch's study simply because these traits were quite different in meaning from the other traits in the list. Zanna and Hamilton (1972) furthered this argument, noting that the traits in Asch's initial list—*intelligent, skillful, industrious, determined, practical,* and *cautious*—all tend to be intellectual traits, not social traits. On the other hand, *warm* (or *cold*) is a social trait and thus carries distinctly different information. Thus, *warm* (or *cold*) may be central traits in Asch's experiment because of the nature of the surrounding list. Despite these and other criticisms of his study, Asch's notion of "central traits" was quite influential, as we shall see, in leading to more-recent research on schemas.

Anderson's Weighted Averaging Model

Since Asch's research, social psychologists have carefully investigated algebraic as well as Gestalt models of impression formation. One of the most influential of the algebraic models was the weighted averaging model, developed by Norman Anderson. In Anderson's research (1974), a typical subject might be asked to judge how likable an "intelligent, neurotic, loyal, and proud" person was. Anderson found that each subject's overall impression of the person's likability seemed to be a *weighted average* of the likability of the individual traits and an "initial impression" factor reflecting a subject's general tendency to rate people either positively or negatively. The weighting of information implies that some traits have a greater effect on impressions than others, and the totaling-up of weighted items to form an overall impression implies that each trait's effect is additive (that is, it does not shift the meanings of other traits). See Figure 5.7 for an illustration of Anderson's weighted averaging model.

What determines how information is weighted? Many studies find evidence for a *primacy effect*—that early information is weighted more heavily than later information (Jones, 1990; Jones et al., 1990; Luchins, 1957). In both Asch's and Anderson's research, subjects' impressions were influenced more by the first traits in lists than by later traits. This seems to result from at least two different processes: Early traits influence how subjects interpret later traits, and subjects simply pay more attention to early traits than to later traits (Anderson & Hubert, 1963; Belmore, 1987; Jones & Goethals, 1972; Zanna & Hamilton, 1977).

Suppose you are told that Magic Johnson is a "gifted athlete" and "HIV-positive." How does Anderson's weighted averaging model explain your overall impression of Magic Johnson?

The full equation is as follows:

$$\text{Overall evaluation} = \frac{w_0 I_0 + w_1 I_1 + w_2 I_2 + \dots}{w_0 + w_1 + w_2 + \dots}$$

where: I_0 = your initial impression
w_0 = how much you weight your initial impression
I_1 = your evaluation of trait #1
w_1 = how much you weight the first trait
I_2 = your evaluation of trait #2, and so on

Let's assume that on a 100-point scale of "likability," your initial impression of Magic (I_0) is neutral—that is, "50" on the scale—and that you rate the likability of "gifted athlete" to be "80" and "HIV-positive" to be "10." Now suppose that you weight the trait "HIV-positive" .5—twice as much as you weight "gifted athlete" and your initial impression (both weighted .25).

Then your overall impression of Magic's likability is:

$$\frac{(.25 \times 50) - (.25 \times 80) \div (.5 \times 10)}{.25 + .25 + .5} = 37.5$$

FIGURE 5.7 How do people combine trait information according to Anderson's weighted averaging model?

A second factor in forming an impression of likability is that subjects often weight *negative* information more heavily than positive information (Kanouse & Hanson, 1972). Thus, in forming an impression of Magic Johnson, you might tend to assign more weight to the fact that he's infected with the AIDS virus (a highly negative piece of information) than to other pieces of information. And in forming impressions of presidential candidates, Americans assign more weight to candidates' character weaknesses than to their strengths (Klein, 1991). A third and final factor that influences how we weight information is the *extremity* of the information; extreme information usually carries more weight in impression formation (Skowronski & Carlston, 1987). So the fact that Magic Johnson is one of the greatest basketball players in the world (an extreme piece of information) may influence your impression of him more than the fact that he attended Michigan State (not so extreme a piece of information).

In a way, Anderson's averaging model allows for a kind of "central trait"—a trait that is weighted very heavily in forming an overall impression. However—and this is the crucial point—Anderson's analysis of why a particular trait is central is quite different from Asch's. Anderson simply considers the "central trait" to be a particularly heavily weighted or salient piece of information, whereas Asch argued that a "central trait" literally shifts the meanings of surrounding traits and reorganizes the way we perceive the entire body of information.

Both Gestalt and algebraic models may be valid accounts of certain kinds of impression formation. Anderson's weighted averaging model has typically been applied to relatively simple one-dimensional judgments: "How likable is a person with these traits?" However, the averaging model is more a description of such judgments than it is an explanation of them; it does not tell us much about the thought processes people use in making their judgments.

We are more likely to use Gestalt processes to form impressions of others when we have strong preconceptions about them (what we shall call *schemas* in the next section) and consequently try to "fit in" new information with our preconceptions; we are more likely to use algebraic processes to form impressions of others when we don't hold strong preconceptions and so must start from scratch (Fiske & Neuberg, 1990). For example, if you learn that your new roommate is British, this piece of information may serve as a "central trait" and color other facts you learn about your roommate; however, if you learn your roommate is Liechtensteinian, you probably will have to form your impressions algebraically (add together pieces of information from scratch) because you don't hold any strong preconceptions about Liechtensteinians.

SCHEMAS: THE EFFECTS OF PRIOR INFORMATION ON SOCIAL THOUGHT

When you learned that Magic Johnson was infected with the AIDS virus, your reaction was undoubtedly influenced by more than your immediate experience of

Magic Johnson at that moment. As we noted in the previous section, perceiving a person is not simply a matter of adding up all the current pieces of information; it consists also of relating the information to your prior knowledge and beliefs—for example, the prior knowledge you had of Magic Johnson, of AIDS, and of male athletes. That is, our impressions of others are affected by *cognitive schemas,* the organized beliefs and knowledge we hold, consciously or unconsciously, about different topics and kinds of people (for example, about African-Americans, librarians, college professors). Schemas significantly influence how we perceive, organize, and remember information about others (Fiske, 1993; Fiske & Taylor, 1984, 1991).

Schemas are mental categories, presumably based on experience, that we use to perceive and remember new information. This new information can either be consistent with a schema (for example, you learn that your professor likes classical music, which is probably consistent with your schema for professors), or inconsistent with a schema (your professor is a member of a heavy-metal band), or irrelevant to a schema (your professor is left-handed). A schema leads you to expect certain kinds of information but not others (Hastie, 1981). Schemas that apply to groups of people are related to the notion of a "stereotype" (see Chapter 7), but "cognitive schemas" refer to a broader concept—we can hold schemas about groups of people (African-Americans), particular people (Princess Diana), ourselves (self-schemas are discussed in Chapter 3), and even about social activities (for example, schemas about "going on a date" or "visiting a professor during office hours").

Research on schemas points to various ways our preconceptions influence our social judgments and behavior. We will examine how schemas (1) color our perception of social events, (2) influence our memory, (3) affect the inferences we make, and (4) may guide and channel our social behavior. Finally, in addition to considering the effects schemas have on our thought and behavior, we will examine what triggers us to use certain schemas and how difficult it can be to change schemas once they are established.

Schemas and Perception

A study by Allport and Postman (1965 [1947]) dramatically demonstrates how our preconceptions (that is, schemas) can influence our perception of events. As part of a study on how rumors get transmitted, Allport and Postman asked white subjects to look at a drawing of a scene in a New York subway and then to describe the scene to other subjects, who in turn described what they heard to yet other subjects. The original drawing (see Figure 5.8) portrayed two standing men, one black, the other white, engaged in conversation. The black man held both hands open during the conversation. The white man held an open straight razor in his left hand.

When the subjects passed the information along to others, their descriptions often shifted the razor to the black man's hand. In other words, subjects' preconceptions—their schemas about blacks and whites—influenced what they perceived and later described. Many subjects did not accurately describe reality; rather, they described what they expected to see.

FIGURE 5.8 Illustration used in Allport and Postman's (1947/1965) study on rumor transmission. *Source:* Allport and Postman (1947).

A more recent study by Duncan (1976) shows a similar effect of race schemas on the immediate perception of social events. Duncan asked 104 white college students in California to watch a videotape of two students in discussion. At one point the discussion became rather heated and one student shoved the other. One group of subjects saw a black student shove a white student; another group saw a white student shove a black student (see Figure 5.9).

How did the subjects perceive the shove? Interestingly, when a black student shoved a white student, 75% of the subjects rated this behavior as "violent." However, when a white student shoved a black student, only 17% rated the same behavior as "violent." Instead, 42% of the subjects perceived the white student's shove as "playing around" or "dramatizing"; only 6% described the black's shove that way. A later study showed similar effects in grade school students' perceptions of drawings that portrayed interactions between black and white students. For example, one student bumping into a second student was perceived as more threatening and aggressive when the first student was black (Sagar & Schofield, 1980). In these studies, reality didn't change—but people's perception of reality did.

Subjects' coding of a shove was markedly different depending on whether it was the black or white student who did the shoving.

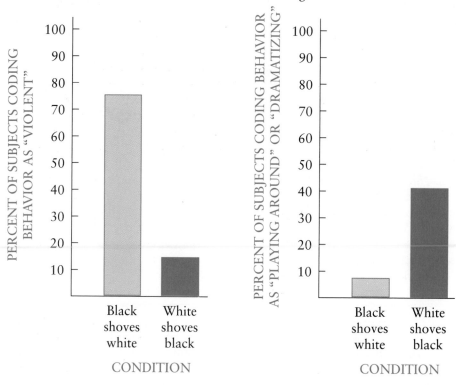

FIGURE 5.9 Do schemas affect our perception of social events? *Source:* Based on Duncan (1976).

In general, when are schemas most likely to influence our perceptions? Schematic thinking is often "lazy" thinking, and schemas tend to influence our perceptions particularly when our information is ambiguous, fleeting, or rushed (Kruglanski & Freund, 1983; Lord, Ross, & Lepper, 1979; White & Carlston, 1983). Stated in reverse, the less "real" information we have to go on and the less time we have to think about that information, the more we will rely on our preconceptions in interpreting social data. For instance, if you become roommates with a student of another race, wouldn't your race schemas influence your impression of your roommate more the first day you move in together than after six months of interaction? In other words, you apply your schemas as a first quick attempt to understand a person. If the person's behavior clearly doesn't match your schema, you may try the more demanding and time-consuming process of actually "adding" or "averaging" raw pieces of information about him or her (Fiske & Neuberg, 1990).

Schemas and Memory

Considerable evidence indicates that schemas help us remember information that is consistent with the schemas (Fiske & Taylor, 1990; Stangor & McMillan, 1992). For example, Claudia Cohen (1981) investigated the effects of role schemas on memory by asking subjects to view a videotape of a woman celebrating her birthday by having dinner with her husband. One group of subjects was informed that the woman was a waitress; a second group was told she was a librarian.

Cohen's videotape portrayed many behaviors considered stereotypically true of each occupation. For example, the videotaped woman wore glasses, liked classical music, had spent the day reading, and had traveled in Europe—all stereotypical "librarian" behaviors. However, she also drank beer, liked pop music, owned a bowling ball, and was openly affectionate with her husband—all "waitress" behaviors.

All subjects viewed the same videotape, which contained an equal number of "waitress" and "librarian" behaviors. Yet subjects were more likely to remember accurately facts that were consistent with the occupational labels they had been given. In a questionnaire that measured memory (sample question: "Did the woman drink beer or did she drink wine?"), subjects showed 88% accuracy in remembering schema-consistent facts, but only 78% accuracy for schema-inconsistent facts. In other words, it's easier to remember that a waitress "drinks beer" than that she "likes classical music," even if both are true. The first fact fits our expectations; the second does not.

Social psychologists have offered various explanations for why studies like Cohen's show that subjects remember schema-consistent information well (Stangor & McClellan, 1992). One simple explanation is that when subjects are unsure of their memories, they *guess* in a way that is consistent with their schemas. For example, if you didn't remember whether the woman in the videotape drank beer or wine, you might *guess* that she drank wine if you knew she was a librarian. Another explanation is that we often incorporate new information into our schemas, and then the schema provides "paths" in memory that help us get at the information.

Many studies show that schemas can improve our memory for schema-consistent facts, but what effects do schemas have on our memory for *schema-inconsistent* information? For instance, suppose you read a news story about Sister Felicia Philanthropy, a nun who rises daily at 5:30 A.M., ministers to the poor in a local soup kitchen, and prays one or two hours daily, but who also occasionally drinks whiskey and tells off-color jokes. The research we have discussed so far suggests that your schema for nuns should help you remember that Sister Felicia ministers to the poor and prays one or two hours daily. But what about the information that she drinks whiskey?

Interestingly, we may sometimes show good memory for schema-inconsistent information (Fiske, Kinder, & Larter, 1983; Graesser, Woll, Kowalski, & Smith, 1980; Judd & Kulik, 1980; Stangor & McMillan, 1992). Hastie (1981) has suggested that if people have enough time and motivation, they ponder schema-inconsistent information and try to fit it into their preexisting schemas. This extra mental work may help explain why some studies find enhanced memory for schema-inconsistent information. Perhaps when you first read that Sister Felicia drinks whiskey, this unexpected information led you to search for an explanation, such as "Well, she must be exposed to so many depressing cases in the soup kitchen that she needs to drink as a release." Such heightened attention and extra cognitive work occurs only for truly inconsistent information, not for irrelevant information (such as "Sister Felicia likes chocolate ice cream"), which we tend to forget easily.

Another factor that can influence when we remember schema-inconsistent information is the strength of the schema (Stangor & Ruble, 1989). A schema that is strong and well-established (for example, a rigid racial stereotype developed throughout your life) tends to dominate your perception and memory—you perceive facts to be consistent with your schema and remember information best when it's consistent with your schema. On the other hand, a schema that is weak or in the process of being formed (for example, your schema of members of Theta Beta Omega, a new campus fraternity) is less likely to bias your perceptions, and you have a better chance of noticing and remembering schema-inconsistent information.

Schemas and Social Inference

Schemas may also influence how we move beyond given facts to make social judgments and evaluations. For example, Linville (1982a, 1982b) offers evidence that the more complex our schemas about groups are, the less extreme our evaluations of people in those groups are. In one study, Linville and Jones (1980) asked white college students to evaluate a law school candidate whose application was either quite strong (graduated magna cum laude, received an Outstanding Senior Thesis Award, participated in impressive extracurricular activities, and had glowing letters of recommendation) or rather weak (only minor honors and extracurricular activities). The applicant was also described as being either black or white. Interestingly, this experiment indicated that a weak black applicant was evaluated more negatively than a weak white applicant, but a strong black applicant was evaluated *more positively* than a strong white applicant. Note that these results do not show a simple pattern of direct prejudice against minority groups—the white applicant was not always evaluated more highly than the black applicant. Some of the findings from this study are presented in Figure 5.10.

Linville and Jones suggest that white subjects' evaluations of black applicants were more *extreme* (positively or negatively) than their judgments of white applicants because schemas for out-groups tend to be less complex than schemas for in-groups. That is, schemas for groups to which we belong are richer and have more features and cognitive dimensions than schemas for groups to which we do not belong. Consequently, the effect of a new piece of information about a member of an in-group is tempered by all the preexisting information. When we judge a member of an out-group, however, the new piece of information is added to a few stereotypic beliefs.

Perhaps an analogy will illuminate Linville's hypothesis that complex schemas lead to less extreme judgments. Imagine that I asked you to rate the

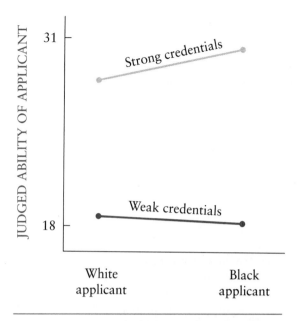

FIGURE 5.10 Evaluations of weak and strong, white and black applicants to law school. *Source:* Adapted from Linville & Jones (1980).

intelligence of two people: your best friend and a stranger who sits near you in class. In one experimental condition I tell you that the stranger (or your friend) just got an "A+" on an exam, whereas in another condition I tell you that she received a "D." Wouldn't your rating of your friend be less influenced by the grade information than your rating of the stranger? After all, you have a rich schema about your friend—you have lots of information and previous experience with her—and it tempers the effect of a single new piece of information. However, the grade—"A+" or "D"—may be the only thing you know about the stranger; as a result, that information will influence your rating of her intelligence disproportionately.

Schemas and Behavior

Can schemas affect our actions as well as our perceptions, memories, and inferences? Several kinds of research suggest that schemas do indeed influence our behavior. Remember, schemas are mental classifications that lead us to expect certain things to be true—for example, that professors will be "smart," that librarians will be "quiet," that the elderly will be "absentminded," and so on. It is perhaps a small step from expecting behavior in others to actually *eliciting* that behavior from them through our actions (Snyder, 1992).

The sociologist Robert Merton (1948) coined the phrase *self-fulfilling prophecy* to refer to the process by which people's expectations become reality. A well-known study by Rosenthal and Jacobson (1968) showed that a teacher's expectations can influence students' behavior: If a teacher thinks a child is a bright "late bloomer" who will soon show a burst of academic achievement, then the child may actually perform somewhat better in school as the year progresses—*because the teacher encourages him to*. Similarly, Rosenthal demonstrated that experimenters' expectations could affect the behavior of their subjects (Rosenthal, 1966; see Chapter 2). Clearly, people can communicate their expectations in ways that can shape others' behavior. And, of course, our expectations are often derived from our schemas.

A clever study by Snyder, Tanke, and Berscheid (1977) showed how college students' schemas about physical attractiveness influence not only how they treat other students, but ultimately how the other students behave in return. In this study, male subjects talked by telephone to females who they were led to believe were either attractive or unattractive. (The women's actual attractiveness was unrelated to what the men were told, and of course the women weren't informed about how the researchers had labeled them.)

Predictably, the men spoke in a warmer and friendlier manner to women they thought were attractive. More surprisingly, the women who had been labeled attractive were in fact warmer, more poised, and more humorous in their conversations; that is, the way men treated the women influenced their behavior. Are attractive people really warmer, friendlier, and more poised? If so, it may partly result from the fact that we create what we expect in others.

Do our expectations about others *always* lead to self-fulfilling prophecies? Not necessarily. Mark Snyder (1992) argues that we are particularly likely to create self-fulfilling prophecies in our interactions with others when our goal is to "diagnose" or "learn what's true" about the other person and less likely when our goal is to "get along" or "have a smooth interaction." This hypothesis was supported by a recent telephone-conversation experiment; this time, college men spoke with college women who they believed to be either obese or normal weight (Snyder & Haugen, 1990). Did the men's generally negative expectations about obese women (for example, that they are "lazy," "boring," and "sexually cold") influence their behavior toward women labeled as obese, and, ultimately, the women's behavior in return? Yes, but only when the men were given the experimental goal of "finding out the kind of person the woman was" during their phone conversation. In contrast, when their goal was "to get along well" in conversation, no self-fulfilling prophecy occurred.

Apparently, when we try to find out "the kind of person someone is" during an interaction, we often initiate a self-fulfilling prophecy by selectively seeking out (and even creating) information that is consistent with our schemas. Apparently, people often ask questions that tend to confirm their expectations (Snyder, 1981, 1992; Snyder & Campbell, 1980; Snyder & Swann, 1978). For example, Snyder and Swann (1978) assigned college women the task of interviewing a partner about her personality. For some subjects, the goal of the interview was to determine whether the partner was an extrovert; for others the goal was to determine whether she was an introvert. Subjects chose their interview questions from a prepared list that included questions about extroverted behaviors ("What would you do if you wanted to liven things up at a party?"), questions about introverted behaviors ("What factors make it difficult for you to really open up to people?"), and neutral questions ("What kinds of charities do you like to contribute to?").

Subjects trying to diagnose their partners' extroversion asked more "extroverted" questions; subjects trying to diagnose introversion asked more "introverted" questions. Their partners' answers were tape-recorded, and judges then rated how extroverted or introverted partners seemed from their responses. Intriguingly, the partners of women trying to diagnose extroversion were in fact judged to be more extroverted from their interview responses; the partners of women diagnosing introversion were judged to be more introverted. By attempting to diagnose a trait, subjects unknowingly asked leading questions and thus encouraged answers consistent with the trait.

Do professional questioners do the same? For example, in examining patients suspected to have specific kinds of mental illness, do psychologists and psychiatrists tend to ask questions that will confirm their hunches? If so, they may be guilty of creating the evidence on which they base their diagnoses.

Activating Schemas: Priming Effects

Suppose you start talking with a woman sitting next to you in class. What schema will you use to organize information you learn about her? Do you perceive new facts in terms of, say, her gender, her ethnic background, or her age? One possibility is that you will classify her on the *most salient* dimension, the one that sticks out in this situation (McGuire et al., 1978; McGuire & Padawer-Singer, 1976). If she is the only woman in an engineering class, you are likely to use a gender schema. If she is the only elderly person in a class of 20-year-olds, then you may apply an age schema.

What schema will you use to organize your perceptions of this woman? One answer is that you'll classify her on the dimension that "sticks out" in this situation. Thus, you are more likely to apply an age schema than a gender or "student" schema.

Another possibility is that a schema you have used in the recent past may "prime" you (that is, make you more likely) to use that schema for new information. One study (Higgins, Rholes, & Jones, 1977) demonstrated such a *priming effect* by first having subjects read a list of either positive or negative traits (for example, *adventurous* versus *reckless*). Later, in a seemingly unrelated study, these same subjects read about a man named Donald who engaged in a number of risk-taking activities like skydiving and racing. Subjects rated Donald's high-risk behavior more negatively when they had earlier been primed with negative traits like *reckless*. A more recent study found a similar priming effect: College students who had been primed with the names of aggressive sports (such as boxing) later described a person they read about as being significantly more hostile and aggressive than students who had been primed with names of nonaggressive sports (golf) (Wann & Branscombe, 1990).

Apparently, a schema that has been used recently is more readily available for subsequent use. An early study by Murray (1933) demonstrated this effect in a different context. Schoolgirls were asked to play a scary game called "Murder" in which all the girls but one scattered throughout a darkened house and hid while the remaining girl—the "murderer"—searched for them and "murdered" them by sneaking up and tagging them in their hiding places. Before and after the game, the girls were asked to rate people in photographs on various characteristics. In general, they perceived the people in the photographs to be more cruel, malicious, and evil after playing the game. Put another way, after the game, girls applied a "Murder" schema to their perceptions of people. Perhaps you've experienced a similar effect after a threatening experience—did strangers on the street suddenly take on frightening characteristics?

The more frequently a schema has been activated in the past, the more likely it is to be applied to new situations (Higgins & King, 1981; Wyer & Srull, 1980). In a sense, a much-used schema may become permanently primed. So police officers, for example, may be permanently primed to interpret other people's behavior in terms of criminality; they may possess a chronically primed "Murder" schema.

The Persistence of Schemas

Clearly, our schemas may be more or less accurate and sometimes positively misleading. Are we perpetual prisoners of our schemas once we have developed them, or do schemas ever change?

If we receive enough contradictory evidence, we may alter a schema, particularly if the contradictory information observed is spread out among many members of the group rather than concentrated in a small number of very deviant members (Crocker & Weber, 1983; Weber & Crocker, 1983). For example, many people seem to think that waitresses like pop music, drink beer, go bowling, and read only romantic novels. Suppose I introduce you to five waitresses. One of them likes classical music, another drinks fine French wines, and yet another reads complex Russian novels in her spare time. Meeting these three waitresses is more likely to change your schema for waitresses than would meeting one waitress who likes classical music, drinks French wines, and reads Russian novels. One very deviant case is less damaging to your schema than many less extreme exceptions because it is easier to explain away: "She's not a *real* waitress; she's actually a graduate student temporarily earning some extra money as a waitress."

Although change is possible, schemas are often remarkably stable. We have already provided some reasons why this is so: People often perceive ambiguous data in ways that are consistent with their schemas; they tend to remember better those facts that are consistent with their schemas; and they often induce others to behave in ways that are consistent with their schemas. In short, schemas can be self-perpetuating.

There is yet another reason for the inertia of schemas: They often lead us to generate thoughts and causal explanations that help us to continue to believe in them, even in the face of subsequent contradictory evidence (Anderson, 1983; Anderson, Lepper, & Ross, 1980). For example, suppose you learn that little Simon was accused of stealing money from other children's lockers at school. You might say to yourself, "Well, of course—Simon's parents are divorced, and his mother's an alcoholic. He's a latch-key kid left alone all day. No wonder he's gotten in with a bad crowd." Based on one accusation, you've constructed an elaborate "bad boy" schema complete with causal explanations. Now suppose you subsequently learn that Simon didn't really steal the money—another student confessed to the crime. Do you totally revise your opinion of Simon's criminality? No. You've spent so much cognitive work explaining and justifying Simon's crime that you've convinced yourself of his criminal tendencies, even though the original evidence has evaporated. If I asked you to rate the likelihood that Simon would steal something, you'd probably rate it higher than you should.

Such a *perseverance effect*—the maintenance of beliefs in the face of discrediting evidence—has been demonstrated in many experiments. In one of these, Ross, Lepper, and Hubbard (1975) falsely informed subjects that a new personality test indicated they were extremely socially sensitive and good at judging other people's traits. Later the subjects were informed that the personality test was invalid and completely worthless in assessing their social sensitivity. Subjects were then asked to rate their actual social sensitivity and perceptiveness. Those who had been told they were sensitive rated themselves as being significantly more sensitive than control subjects did, even though the experimental subjects knew the initial information to be bogus. Apparently, once these subjects were (falsely) informed that they were socially sensitive, they constructed explanations for this "fact" that remained compelling even when the "fact" was invalidated (Anderson, Lepper, & Ross, 1980).

Schemas and Illusory Correlations

Central to many social schemas is the assumption that certain traits or characteristics are associated with a particular category of people—for example, an interest in classical music is perceived to be more associated with being a librarian than with being a waitress. How do we judge that one variable is correlated with another? For example, how do we decide that criminality is correlated with certain ethnic groups or that personality is associated with hair color?

An important set of studies by Chapman and Chapman (1967, 1969, 1982) demonstrated that people may falsely see correlations between variables because of their preconceptions, not because of real occurrences. In one study, Chapman and Chapman (1969) asked subjects to examine clinical information about "psychological patients" with various problems. In particular, the subjects looked at human figures supposedly drawn by patients and read a list of the corresponding patients' psychological symptoms. Subjects were asked to discern whether any features in the drawings (for example, big eyes) were correlated with specific psychological disorders (for example, paranoid thoughts). Some drawings and symptoms similar to those used in this study are presented in Figure 5.11.

In fact, *no correlation* existed between any of the drawings' features and patients' symptoms; the pictures and the lists of symptoms were constructed by the researchers, who randomly paired picture features with psychological

PICTURE DRAWN BY PATIENT	PATIENT'S SYMPTOMS

Patient A

Paranoid thoughts

Depression

Suicidal thoughts

Patient B

Manic-depressive tendencies

Depression

Compulsive behaviors

Patient C

Psychological withdrawal

Suicidal thoughts

Paranoid thoughts

Question to subjects: "Are any features of the pictures correlated with specific disorders?"

FIGURE 5.11 Material similar to that used in Chapman and Chapman's (1969) study of illusory correlations.

conditions. Nonetheless, subjects perceived correlations that confirmed their preconceptions. For example, subjects felt there was a correlation between "big eyes" in drawings and "paranoia" and between "missing hands" and "psychological withdrawal."

Results like these may help explain why some clinical psychologists believe in the value of certain tests, even when research suggests they are invalid. For example, many clinical psychologists use the Rorschach inkblot test to assess personality, despite considerable research that casts doubt on this test's reliability and validity (Chapman & Chapman, 1982). Clinicians often argue that they know "from clinical experience" that such tests are valid, but the Chapman and Chapman research indicates that we must be very careful in accepting the validity of intuitive correlations without more rigorous, scientific evidence.

Summary Table 5.2 (page 200) reviews the many ways schemas affect our thought and behavior.

SOCIAL INFERENCE: GOING BEYOND THE GIVEN FACTS

In discussing schemas, we touched on the topic of social inference: going beyond the given facts to make new judgments about a person or groups of people. Linville's research, for instance, analyzed how in-group and out-group schemas affected subjects' inferences about law school applicants. We now address the topic of social inference more broadly.

Let's start with a concrete example. Take a few seconds and give your best estimates for the following: the probability that the average professional basketball player in the United States is infected with the AIDS virus, the probability that the average African-American is infected with the AIDS virus, the probability that the average white American is infected with the AIDS virus, the probability that *you* are infected with the AIDS virus or will be during the next year.

Where did you get the information you used to make these estimates? Some of your estimates may be based on facts (you read scientific estimates of infection rates in an article), whereas others are based on inferences. Do you think your estimate for "professional basketball players" was affected by the Magic Johnson story? That is, would you have given a different estimate for pro basketball players before you heard the news about Magic? If so, why should information about a single person influence your judgments about a much larger group? All of these questions relate to the following basic issues: How do we make inferences about the social world around us based on the limited information at our disposal? And what errors are we most prone to make?

Sampling Errors

The first stage in making an inference is getting the information. For example, if you want to decide whether Asian students are more industrious than Caucasian students, you must somehow observe some Asian students or retrieve memories of Asian students.

One common error people make in estimating the occurrence of social events is to place too much reliance on small samples (Nisbett & Ross, 1980; Tversky & Kahneman, 1974). For example, you might say, "Yes, the Chinese woman in my class always scores near the top. Asian students *are* more industrious." If the Magic Johnson story affected your estimate of the number of professional basketball players infected with the AIDS virus, your estimate is being influenced by an equally small sample: one person.

Statistical sampling theory shows that small samples are highly unreliable. Would you believe that men are more intelligent than women if I told you I carried out a study in which two men proved to have higher IQ scores than two women? Although concluding anything on the basis of such a limited sample seems ludicrous, we are apparently willing to make everyday inferences on the basis of equally limited samples.

Not only are people inordinately influenced by small samples, they fail to realize that their samples are often quite biased (Nisbett & Ross, 1980). If I asked you whether college students these days are generally liberal or conservative, how would you decide on an answer? You might think of all the college students you know—for example, your friends—and count up how many of them are liberal and how many are conservative. The problem with this process, of course, is that your friends and your school provide far from a random sample of college students. Students at Oral Roberts University might answer my question quite differently from students at San Francisco State.

Even when given clear information about how typical and representative a sample is, subjects often seem to ignore this information. In one study, subjects saw a videotaped interview of a prison guard, who was described as being either quite typical of most guards or quite atypical. In one version of the tape, the guard appeared cruel and inhumane, whereas in another version he seemed quite compassionate. After viewing one of the tapes, subjects were asked to rate how positive they felt about prison guards in general (Hamill, Wilson, & Nisbett, 1980).

The only significant result was that after viewing the compassionate guard, subjects rated guards in general more positively, whereas after viewing the cruel guard, they rated guards in general more negatively. Although subjects' ratings were slightly less extreme when they thought the videotaped guard to be "atypical," this effect was not statistically significant. Notice that subjects were willing to draw conclusions about prison guards in general on the basis of the smallest possible sample—a sample of one! Moreover, they drew these conclusions regardless of whether they were told that the sample was "typical" or "atypical" of guards in general.

The Underuse of Base-Rate Information

In the prison guard study, subjects' judgments were influenced too much by one concrete instance. They didn't seem much influenced by *base-rate information* (broad, often statistical information about how groups or categories behave in general). Base-rate information in this case was that guards in general either were or were not like the one the subjects observed.

The underutilization of base-rate information is quite common. Suppose you want to buy a popular new Italian sports car, a Primavera Tortellini. All the consumer and automobile magazines say the Tortellini is a superb machine with admirable performance and repair records. Then your best friend says to you, "No, don't buy a Tortellini! My mother bought one and it's been the biggest lemon— carburetor problems, a faulty steering column . . . " What will influence you more, the highly positive statistical base-rate information or the one concrete, vivid example from your friend?

Numerous research studies (for example, Bar-Hillel & Fischoff, 1981; Ginossar & Trope, 1980; Nisbett & Ross, 1980; Taylor & Thompson, 1982) suggest that people tend to pay more attention to a single concrete instance than to valid base-rate information (which, because it represents a much better sample, is much more reliable). Perhaps people give more credence to a concrete instance because it is vivid and salient and thus more compelling (Nisbett & Ross, 1980). Whatever the explanation, people often fail to weight base-rate information as heavily as they should.

Heuristics: Shortcuts to Social Inference

Everyday social life entails an extraordinary amount of cognitive "work." We must figure out the causes of people's behavior; we must perceive, store, and retrieve information and fit it into our preexisting knowledge; and we must form organized impressions of others, integrate information, and somehow arrive at adaptive decisions and judgments.

With our mental "computer" so loaded with various duties, it is no wonder that we sometimes use shortcuts to answer certain questions. Instead of exhaustively analyzing a particular problem, we may often apply less time-consuming strategies to give us "quick and dirty" answers to pressing questions. Kahneman and Tversky (1973; Tversky & Kahneman, 1973, 1982) have described several such cognitive *heuristics,* or shortcut thought processes, that yield quick estimates or answers. We will focus on two particularly important ones: the availability heuristic and the representativeness heuristic.

The Availability Heuristic

In considering how serious a social problem drunk driving is, you might recall as many drunk-driving accidents as you can. The more cases you can recall, the more likely you are to judge the problem to be serious. Kahneman and Tversky (1973) call this process of estimating the frequency of some event by the ease with which you can bring instances to mind the availability heuristic.

Although cognitive availability seems like a fairly reasonable process, it can sometimes lead to consequential errors. For example, we may overestimate the frequency of events that are easy to remember (Slovic, Fischoff, & Lichtenstein, 1977). Research suggests that people tend to overestimate the frequency of violent deaths caused by fire, murder, and accident and tend to underestimate the frequency of death from heart disease, strokes, and cancer. Apparently, violent deaths are easier to recall (probably because of media coverage of them), and thus people overestimate their frequency.

Let's return again to the example of AIDS infection. How serious a social problem do you think AIDS infection is? According to the availability heuristic, one way you might try to answer the question is to think of all the people you personally know who have been infected with the AIDS virus. Can you think of any problems

How dangerous do you think air travel is today? One way to estimate the frequency of events (for example, airplane accidents) is to use the availability heuristic: recall as many instances as you can. Because the mass media highly publicize air disasters and because such disasters are vivid and memorable, we probably tend to remember many instances and thus overestimate their frequency.

At Least 19 Killed in Crash at Snowy La Guardia

Pool photo/Richard Harbus

Firefighters working near the wreckage of a jet that crashed last night at La Guardia Airport.

with this approach to estimating the seriousness and prevalence of AIDS infection? Does the availability heuristic explain why people in New York and San Francisco might see AIDS as more of a crisis than people in, say, Coffeyville, Kansas?

The Representativeness Heuristic

How do we decide whether a person is likely to be a member of a group when we have suggestive but inconclusive evidence? For example, suppose I say that Jill is conservative, moralistic, against abortion, and in favor of prayer in the schools. How likely is she to be a fundamentalist Christian? Or suppose I say that Jack is sensitive, artistic, and interested in interior design. How likely is it that Jack is gay?

One statistically correct but quite laborious approach to answering these questions would be to determine the probability that each trait is diagnostic of group memberships, and then mathematically combine the probabilities. For our question about Jill, we could estimate the probability that a fundamentalist Christian is conservative, moralistic, and so on, and then mathematically combine the probabilities to reach a conclusion.

In everyday life, we generally opt for a much simpler thought process: We simply see how well the information matches some imagined average or typical person in the group, and the closer the match is, the more likely we are to judge this person to be a group member. Because Jill's traits seem to match those of the "typical" fundamentalist Christian, we are likely to judge that she is a fundamentalist Christian. Similarly, because Jack's traits match those of the "typical" gay man, we are very likely to judge him to be gay.

Kahneman and Tversky (1973) label this thought process the representativeness heuristic—we decide the likelihood that a person belongs to a certain group by assessing how similar the person's characteristics are to those of the "typical" group member. Like the availability heuristic, this seems like a quick and reasonable (if somewhat rough) way of making such judgments. But the representativeness heuristic can also produce biased judgments.

Using the representativeness heuristic can be particularly misleading if base-rate information is also available. For example, if we learn that Jill is moralistic, conservative, against abortion, in favor of prayer in schools, *and* lives in the Crown Heights section of Brooklyn, it probably would not be wise for us to decide that Jill is a fundamentalist Christian, because Crown Heights is inhabited largely by Orthodox Jews. Regardless of how well other concrete "facts" fit our stereotype of a fundamentalist Christian, in this case the baseline odds are not very good that our judgment is in fact correct.

The representativeness heuristic may also lead us astray when nondiagnostic and diagnostic information are mixed together. Suppose we learn that Jack drives a Toyota, is sensitive, lives in a house, is artistic, works as a lawyer, is interested in interior design, and plays tennis. Are we more or less likely to judge him to be gay now? In experimental tasks like this, most subjects judge Jack as *less* likely to be gay, even though the added "facts" are truly irrelevant to being gay. (The earlier facts may be irrelevant, too, but they reflect typical stereotypes about gays. Whereas many people believe that being "interested in interior design" is diagnostic of being gay, almost everyone would agree that "driving a Toyota" is unrelated to being gay.)

This finding—that nondiagnostic information mixed in with diagnostic information leads to more cautious inferences—is called the *dilution effect* (Nisbett, Zuckier, & Lemley, 1981; Zuckier, 1982). The representativeness heuristic provides one explanation for why the dilution effect occurs. When we learn that a person has a number of characteristics that are unrelated to our image of the "typical" member of some group, we see the total list of characteristics to be less representative of the group. The logical error, of course, results from assuming that nondiagnostic information says anything at all about group membership. Summary Table 5.2 reviews the dilution effect and other principles we have discussed about the nature of social judgments and inferences.

Framing Effects in Decision Making

The way a question is posed (or "framed") can have significant effects on social judgments and decisions. Social psychologists have extensively studied *framing effects* in social judgments and decisions, particularly those involving elements of risk (Tversky & Kahneman, 1984). Such studies often present subjects with a choice between two risk-taking alternatives. For example, imagine that a new strain

SUMMARY TABLE 5.2 Social Thought Research		
Topics and Processes Studied	*Examples*	*Research Findings*
Impression formation (How do people combine information about others?)	Gestalt models	Effects of central traits.
	Algebraic models	Early, negative, and extreme information is weighted heavily in judgments of likability.
Schematic processing of information (Effects of prior knowledge)	Effects on perception	Schematic biases in perception.
	Effects on memory	Better memory for schema-consistent information; mixed results for schema-inconsistent information.
	Effects on inferences	Out-groups evaluated more extremely than in-groups because schemas for out-groups are less complex than schemas for in-groups.
	Effects on behavior	Self-fulfilling prophecies; confirming schemas through selective questioning.
	Priming effects	Evoked schemas affect later judgments.
	Belief perseverance	Schemas resistant to change even in the face of disconfirming information.
	Illusory correlations	Schemas lead people to perceive correlations between variables when none exist.
Social judgment and inference (How do people "go beyond" given information?)	Sampling errors	People base inferences too much on small and biased samples.
	Underutilization of base-rate information	People attend too much to concrete examples and too little to reliable statistical information.
	Cognitive heuristics	
	Availability	People judge an event's frequency by the ease with which they can bring examples to mind.
	Representativeness	People judge likelihood of group membership by comparing features of particular case to prototype.
	Dilution effect	Nondiagnostic information mixed in with diagnostic information leads to more cautious inferences.
	Framing effects	The way questions are framed influences decisions.
	Prospect theory	Perceived aversiveness of a negative event is greater than the perceived value of an equivalent positive event.

of flu has appeared, and medical researchers have developed two new vaccines to combat it. Because of financial limitations, only one vaccine can be used for mass public inoculations. Medical experts have estimated that if vaccine A is chosen, 200 people will be saved; if vaccine B is chosen, there is a ⅓ probability that 600 people will be saved and a ⅔ probability that no people will be saved. Which vaccine would you choose if you were in charge of vaccinating the public? If you are like a majority of subjects, you would opt for vaccine A (Tversky & Kahneman, 1981).

Now consider this second scenario concerning flu vaccinations: If vaccine C is chosen, 400 people will die. If vaccine D is chosen, there is a ⅓ probability that nobody will die and a ⅔ probability that 600 will die. Which vaccine would you pick now? If you are like most subjects, it would be vaccine D. These results are intriguing because the first scenario is logically identical to the second one; all that differs is that the first describes the decision's consequences in terms of lives saved, whereas the second describes consequences in terms of deaths. For example, the chance that 600 people will be saved in the first scenario is logically identical to the chance that nobody will die in the second.

In general, framing studies show that people are more likely to avoid risks and opt instead for a sure thing when decisions are framed in positive terms ("lives saved") and more likely to take risks when decisions are framed in negative terms ("deaths"). Thus, in the first scenario the "sure thing" of saving 200 lives seems better than the "riskier" alternative that entails the possibility of no lives being saved; in the second scenario, the "sure thing" of 400 deaths seems worse than the "riskier" alternative that entails the possibility that no deaths will result.

The way a choice is framed affects decisions in part because the frame provides a standard of reference to use in interpreting information. In one study, subjects were informed that a new cancer treatment had either a "50% success rate" or a "50% failure rate." Though logically equivalent, these two different frames led to quite different evaluations. Subjects in the "50% success" group judged the treatment to be significantly more effective and stated that they would be more likely to advise a close family member with cancer to seek the treatment (Levin, Schnittjer, & Thee, 1988). Clearly, "success" conjures up more positive connotations than "failure" does, and it leads subjects to compare 50% success with *less* successful treatment rates.

More fundamentally, the way a choice is framed affects decisions because people psychologically assign *value* to positive events to a *lesser* extent than they assign *costs* to negative events. Kahneman and Tversky's (1979) *prospect theory* describes this phenomenon. In commonsense terms, prospect theory implies that a given positive occurrence (say, receiving $5) is less psychologically rewarding than a negative occurrence of equal magnitude (losing $5) is punishing. Graphically, prospect theory is described by a curve in which the slope of perceived costs of increasingly negative events is steeper than the slope of perceived values of increasingly positive events (see Figure 5.12). Thus, because people perceive positive outcomes differently from negative outcomes, they tend to take risks when faced with a choice that includes a negative "sure thing" and avoid risks when faced with a choice that includes a positive "sure thing."

Framing can affect many kinds of social decisions. For example, the ways situations are framed can influence how people negotiate in business relationships. One study asked students at Boston University and at the University of Arizona to be "buyers" for retail stores and "sellers" for refrigerator manufacturers in simulated business negotiations (Bazerman, Magliozzi, & Neale, 1985). Many buyers and sellers simultaneously tried to arrive at agreements that would maximize profits

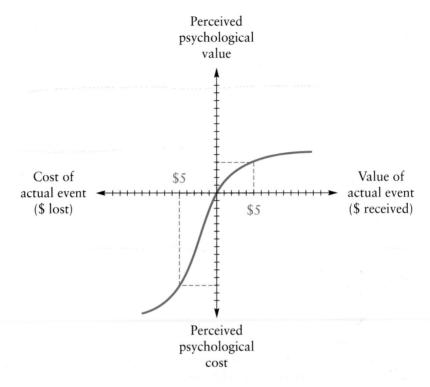

The way a choice is framed affects decisions because people perceive positive outcomes differently than they perceive negative outcomes.

FIGURE 5.12 Prospect theory: The perceived value received from a given positive event is less than the perceived cost incurred by a negative event of the same magnitude. *Source:* Adapted from Kahneman and Tversky (1979).

and minimize expenses for their companies. Subjects' negotiations were "framed" in memos that emphasized one of two goals: that negotiators not exceed a certain level of costs in a deal or that they not accept less than a certain level of profit. Interestingly, subjects whose negotiations were framed in terms of profits rather than costs tended to complete more deals. Thus, the outcomes of negotiations may depend in part on how negotiation goals are framed ahead of time.

SOCIAL THOUGHT IN PERSPECTIVE

How good are we at processing information and reaching conclusions about other people? Studies on attribution and social cognition illustrate the many ways we think about others, and they document a host of errors and biases we sometimes fall prey to.

For example, when we assign causes to other people's behavior, we often commit the fundamental attribution error, emphasizing internal causes too much and situational causes too little, and sometimes we show self-serving biases that protect our egos from threatening attributions about our own behavior.

In forming impressions of others, we logically combine various pieces of information, but sometimes central traits dominate our impressions, and we emphasize early, negative, and extreme pieces of information more than others. The preconceptions contained in our schemas can distort our impressions, bias our perceptions and memories, and, ultimately, influence our behavior toward others and their behavior in return.

And the inferences we make about others are sometimes simplistic and subject to error. For instance, we frequently come to conclusions about groups of people based on small and biased samples, and we often underuse base-rate information. Sometimes, when we are lazy, we use mental shortcuts or heuristics, and while such shortcuts yield useful "quick and dirty" estimates about the social world, they sometimes can lead to serious errors. Finally, our social judgments may be biased by the way questions and situations are framed.

Should all these findings lead us to be disillusioned with the human "computer"? Clearly, the answer is no. Despite the many errors in social thought documented in this chapter, most of us process social information well enough to be reasonably successful in everyday life. In order to achieve more rational thought and better decision making, we must understand how our thought processes work and how they sometimes go wrong. This is the goal of research on social thought.

KEY POINTS

Research on social thought looks at how people deduce the causes of their own and others' behavior, how people combine information about others, how prior knowledge (contained in our schemas) affects how we remember and process information about others, and how we infer social facts from limited information.

Attribution: Assigning Causes to Behavior

Attributions are causal explanations of behavior; attribution theories describe the thought processes people use to arrive at these explanations.

Attribution Processes: Internal versus External Causes

One main goal of attribution is to decide whether others' behavior is internally or externally caused. People often seem to prefer internal over external explanations of behavior.

Theories of Attribution

Social psychologists have developed a number of models of how people arrive at attributions.

Jones and Davis's *theory of correspondent inferences* describes the mental "rules of thumb" people use to infer dispositions from observed behavior. Two of these are the principle of social desirability and the principle of common and noncommon effects.

Kelley's *cube model* of attribution was formulated to explain how people infer internal or external causes from multiple observations of behavior. Kelley's model argues that people observe consistency, consensus, and distinctiveness information and use this information to infer the causes of behavior.

People sometimes try to assign causes to an event by posing *counterfactual* questions that ask whether the event would have occurred if the presumed cause were not present. Consistency, consensus, and distinctiveness information lead us to pose different kinds of counterfactual questions.

Mental Shortcuts in Attribution

Sometimes people do not conscientiously consider all available information and instead opt for simple thought processes to arrive at attribution.

The *discounting principle* is a mental shortcut by which people assign less weight to one cause when another plausible cause is present.

The *overjustification effect* occurs when people discount their internal interest in a task after receiving an expected external reward for performing the task.

Jones and Harris's pro- and anti-Castro experiment shows that people will sometimes explain behavior internally even when obvious external causes are present.

Attribution Errors and Biases

People are subject to a number of attribution errors and biases.

The *fundamental attribution error* occurs when people overemphasize internal explanations and underemphasize external explanations. Members of individualistic cultures seem to commit the fundamental attribution error more than members of collectivist cultures.

The *actor-observer effect* occurs when people attribute their own behavior relatively more to situational causes and others' behavior more to internal, dispositional causes.

People and behavior that are perceptually *salient* tend to be perceived as more causally influential.

Self-serving biases occur in attribution when people too strongly explain their successes internally and their failures externally. People engage in *self-handicapping strategies* when they create apparent external causes of failures to protect themselves from internal attributions that threaten their self-esteem.

Misattribution occurs when people attribute their own arousal to a false cause. The Schachter and Singer experiment on the two-component theory of emotion, the first of many misattribution studies, showed that unexplained arousal from a shot of epinephrine could intensify subjects' feelings of anger and euphoria.

Other research shows that people can sometimes be induced to misattribute actual emotional arousal to external causes. Students' academic anxiety can be reduced if they are led to misattribute their academic failures to external causes.

Impression Formation: Putting Information Together

Impression formation is the process by which people combine information about others to make overall judgments.

Asch's Gestalt Model

Solomon Asch proposed a Gestalt model of impression formation and argued that central traits can both exert a strong influence on total impressions and shift the meanings of other traits.

Anderson's Weighted Averaging Model

Norman Anderson developed a weighted averaging model of impression formation. Research on impression formation shows that early, negative, and extreme information tends to be weighted heavily.

Gestalt processes of impression formation are more likely to occur when we hold strong preconceptions about people, whereas algebraic processes are more likely to occur when we "start from scratch" in forming impressions of others.

Schemas: The Effects of Prior Information on Social Thought

Schemas represent our organized knowledge about people and things.

Schemas and Perception

People often perceive social information in ways that are consistent with their schemas. Such effects are strongest when information is ambiguous and judgments are rushed.

Schemas and Memory

People remember information well when it is consistent with their schemas. Information that is inconsistent with schemas may be remembered well if people have time to think about it and relate it to their schemas and when schemas are weak and not well developed.

Schemas and Social Inference

Schemas for in-groups are often more complex than schemas for out-groups. This leads people to evaluate members of out-groups more extremely than they evaluate members of in-groups based on equivalent information.

Schemas and Behavior

People often elicit in others behavior that confirms their expectations. Schemas thus may lead to self-fulfilling prophecies. Self-fulfilling prophecies are most likely to occur in interactions with others when our goal is "to learn the truth" about others rather than "to get along smoothly" with them.

Activating Schemas: Priming Effects

Once schemas are triggered, or primed, they often influence subsequent perceptions and judgments.

The Persistence of Schemas

Schemas are often resistant to change. The perseverance effect occurs when people maintain false beliefs in the face of discrediting evidence.

Schemas and Illusory Correlations

Illusory correlations occur when people's expectations lead them to perceive a correlation between variables when none exists.

Social Inference: Going Beyond the Given Facts

Social inference occurs when we make assumptions about the social world based on limited information.

Sampling Errors

People often base social judgments on samples that are too small and biased.

The Underuse of Base-Rate Information

People often underutilize broad, reliable statistical information—that is, base-rate information—when making judgments and decisions.

Heuristics: Shortcuts to Social Inference

Heuristics are shortcut cognitive processes that yield quick, rough estimates or answers.

The *availability heuristic* refers to estimating the frequency of an event on the basis of the ease with which we can call instances to mind.

The *representativeness heuristic* refers to estimating the likelihood that a person is a member of a social group by assessing how well his or her traits match the "typical" group member's. The *dilution effect* (making more cautious inferences when nondiagnostic information is mixed in with diagnostic information) may result from the representativeness heuristic.

Framing Effects in Decision Making

Framing effects occur when social judgments and decisions are influenced by the wording used to describe the situation. In general, when decision outcomes are framed in terms of positive consequences, people tend to avoid risk; when outcomes are framed in negative terms, people tend to take risks. Kahneman and Tversky's *prospect theory* helps explain such framing effects.

KEY TERMS

Actor-observer effect: The tendency for people to attribute their own behavior relatively more to external, situational causes and others' behavior more to internal, dispositional causes.

Attribution: The processes by which people assign causes to their own and others' behavior.

Attribution theories: Social psychology theories that attempt to define the thought processes people use to explain their own and others' behavior.

Availability heuristic: The practice of estimating the frequency of an event according to the ease with which instances of the event can be brought to mind.

Base-rate information: Broad, often statistical information about groups or categories of objects; people often underutilize such information in making judgments and decisions.

Causal schemas: Mental models of causality and of how causes combine to influence behavior; an example is the discounting principle.

Central traits: According to Asch's Gestalt model of impression formation, central traits are highly important pieces of information that serve to organize a total impression and that influence the meanings of other traits.

Common and noncommon effects: Different behaviors have common effects when they have the same effects and noncommon effects when they have different effects; correspondent inference theory holds that behaviors with unique noncommon effects lead to stronger dispositional attributions.

Consensus information: The degree to which behavior varies among different people who engage in the behavior; an important dimension of information in Kelley's cube model of attribution.

Consistency information: The degree to which behavior varies over time or across settings; an important dimension of information in Kelley's model of attribution.

Correspondence bias: The tendency for people to assume that behavior reflects internal dispositions.

Correspondent inference: An inference of a disposition from a behavior.

Counterfactual question: An attempt to figure out the cause of an event by asking what would happen if the cause were absent.

Covariation principle: Behavior is attributed to the cause with which it systematically varies over time; the basic principle of Kelley's cube model of attribution.

Dilution effect: The phenomenon whereby people are more cautious about making inferences when undiagnostic information is mixed in with diagnostic information.

Discounting principle: The attributional principle that we assign less weight to a given cause of behavior if another plausible cause is also present; an example of a causal schema.

Distinctiveness information: The degree to which behavior varies as a function of its object or target; an important dimension of information in Kelley's cube model of attribution.

External explanations: Causal explanations of behavior that place the cause outside the person—in the setting or in the environment.

Framing effects: Occur when decisions are influenced by the wording of the decision outcomes.

Fundamental attribution error: The tendency found in many studies for people to overemphasize internal explanations of behavior and underemphasize external explanations.

Heuristics: Shortcut cognitive processes that yield quick estimates or answers.

Illusory correlations: Perceived correlations between uncorrelated events; when people expect events to be correlated, they are likely to perceive illusory correlations.

Impression formation: How people combine information about others to make overall judgments or evaluations of them.

Internal explanations: Explanations of behavior that place the cause inside the person—for example, the behavior is attributable to the person's traits or abilities.

Kelley's cube model of attribution: People observe consistency, consensus, and distinctiveness information, then attribute behavior to the cause with which it systematically varies over time.

Misattribution: Occurs when a person attributes arousal to a source that is not the true source.

Overjustification effect: The undermining effect of expected rewards on intrinsic motivation.

Perseverance effect: The tendency for false beliefs to be maintained in the face of discrediting evidence.

Priming: Occurs when a schema activated in one setting affects judgments made in another setting.

Prospect theory: A theory developed by Kahneman and Tversky that explains framing effects in decision making. It holds that because people tend to perceive negative events (for example, losing $5) more extremely than positive events of equivalent magnitude (gaining $5), they tend to seek risks when decision outcomes are framed in terms of negative "sure things" but to avoid risks when outcomes are framed in terms of positive "sure things."

Representativeness heuristic: The practice of gauging the probability that a person belongs to a particular social group by assessing how similar the person's characteristics are to the "typical" group member's.

Salience effect: The tendency for perceptually salient people and behavior to be perceived as more causally influential.

Schachter–Singer theory of emotion: The subjective experience of emotion depends on two factors: physiological arousal and the cognitive labeling of the arousal.

Schema: Organized knowledge about people and things.

Self-fulfilling prophecy: The process whereby people's expectations become reality through their own actions.

Self-handicapping strategies: Occur when people create salient external "causes" of their failures to avoid making internal attributions that threaten their self-esteem.

Self-serving bias: The attributional tendency for people unrealistically to explain their successes internally and their failures externally.

Social desirability principle: A primary tenet of correspondent inference theory that maintains people are more likely to attribute dispositions from behavior that is socially undesirable (that is, unexpected or nonnormative).

Weighted averaging model: Norman Anderson's algebraic model of impression formation; it holds that a person's impression of someone's likability is determined by a weighted average of the likability of individual traits, plus an "initial impression" factor reflecting the judge's tendency to rate people positively or negatively in general.

ATTITUDES AND ATTITUDE CHANGE

I was repelled by the conglomeration of races . . . by this whole mixture of Czechs, Poles, Hungarians, Ruthenians, Serbs, Croats, and everywhere, the eternal mushroom of humanity—Jews and more Jews.

—Adolf Hitler, *Mein Kampf*, p. 123

[David] Duke says that his Nazi ties were a youthful indiscretion. But in 1989 he was photographed shaking hands with the vice chairman of the American Nazi Party. During a debate . . . last week, Duke renounced his racist past. But as late as 1989 he sold racist music tapes with titles like "Niggers Never Die."

—*Newsweek*, November 18, 1991

The press calls him a "Yuppie fascist." Bronzed, handsome and eloquent, Jorg Haider, 42, heads the Freedom Party of Austria, a fast-growing right-wing movement that plays on the country's fears of being swamped by immigrants from Eastern Europe. "We talk about things that citizens don't have the courage to express openly and honestly," Haider tells a gathering of businessmen at a Vienna hotel. . . . In less polished moments, Haider's vocabulary might as well be drawn from Goebbel's dictionary. Political problems should be given a "final solution." His opponents face "total war."

—*Newsweek*, April 27, 1992

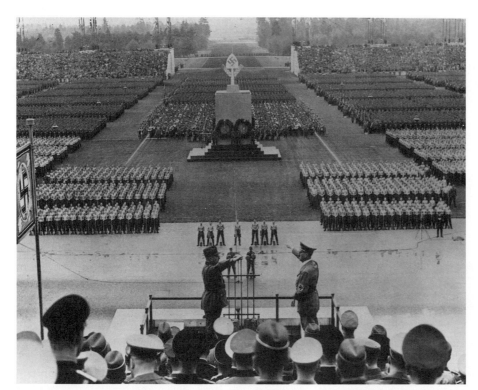

Millions of Germans idolized Adolf Hitler despite his virulently prejudiced attitudes.

Adolf Hitler expressed his attitudes quite openly. He hated Jews and other "non-Aryan" minorities; he detested Bolsheviks (Communists) and labor unionists; he despised the French and Russians; he coveted the territory of other nations. The political attitudes Hitler stated so clearly in *Mein Kampf* instigated the bloodiest war in world history, and his racial attitudes led directly to the horrors of the Nazi Holocaust.

Although Hitler died in 1945, his attitudes lived on, adopted and modified by others. In 1991 a former American Nazi, David Duke, ran as a candidate for governor of Louisiana, appealing to white voters' racial fears and prejudices. Although Duke lost the election, he rallied considerable support throughout the United States and received a majority of white votes in Louisiana. While Duke waged his divisive campaign in the United States, extreme right-wing leaders and political parties gained strength throughout Western Europe as well. In reunified Germany, neo-Nazi skinheads revived terrible images from the past as they marched in torchlight rallies and staged brutal attacks against ethnic minorities (*Newsweek*, April 27, 1992).

While repugnant to most of us, the attitudes of Nazis and neo-Nazis illustrate something quite commonplace: We all have attitudes, and these attitudes influence our behavior in many complex ways. Our attitudes help us evaluate the people, places, and things we encounter each day, and they affect almost

Young David Duke dressed in Ku Klux Klan garb.

David Duke ran for governor of Louisiana in 1991 and made a bid for the U.S. Presidency in 1992.

everything we do. Sometimes attitudes even have the power to start wars and motivate mass murder.

Consider some of your own attitudes—toward other ethnic groups, nations, social issues, political leaders, and historical figures. Let's be even more specific. What are your attitudes toward Japan, Iraq, Serbia, legalized abortion, Bill Clinton, Adolf Hitler? Where do you think your attitudes come from, and how do you use them to guide your behavior? How likely is it that your attitudes will change, either through your own efforts (for example, when you seek out new information by reading the newspaper) or through others' efforts (when they try to persuade you)?

These are exactly the questions we shall address in this chapter: What are attitudes? How are they formed? How (and how much) do they guide our behavior? Can they be changed, and, if so, how? The answers to these questions are important, because attitudes are important. Just ponder Adolf Hitler's attitudes and their terrible consequences.

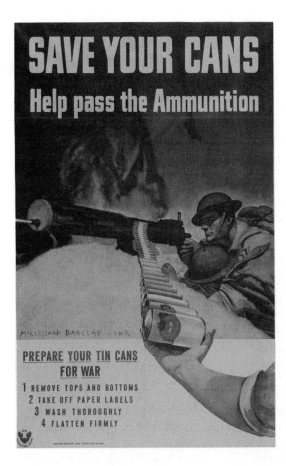

SAVE YOUR CANS
Help pass the Ammunition

PREPARE YOUR TIN CANS
FOR WAR
1 REMOVE TOPS AND BOTTOMS
2 TAKE OFF PAPER LABELS
3 WASH THOROUGHLY
4 FLATTEN FIRMLY

The U.S. government's concern about propaganda and persuasion during World War II stimulated social psychological research on attitude change.

⌒ WHAT ARE ATTITUDES?

The people in their overwhelming majority are so feminine by nature and attitude that sober reasoning determines their thoughts and actions far less than emotion and feeling.

And this sentiment is not complicated, but very simple and all of a piece. It does not have multiple shading; it has a positive and a negative; love or hate, right or wrong, truth or lie, never half this way and half that way.

—*Mein Kampf,* p. 183

Hitler had his own view of the nature of attitudes. You probably do as well. What exactly are attitudes? Although it may seem obvious to you that everyone has them, it is not so obvious what constitutes a good scientific definition of attitudes and which operational definitions provide reliable ways of measuring them.

Characteristics of Attitudes

Here is a working definition of *attitude* that can serve as a starting point: An attitude is a learned evaluative response, directed at specific objects, which is relatively enduring and influences and motivates our behavior toward these objects (Eagly & Chaiken, 1993; Olson & Zanna, 1993; Petty & Cacioppo, 1981). Let's briefly consider each of the key characteristics listed in this definition.

First, according to most modern theorists, an attitude is *evaluative* (Bem, 1970; Eagly & Chaiken, 1993; Fishbein & Ajzen, 1975; Oskamp, 1977); it involves a like or a dislike. For example, Adolf Hitler hated France, labor unions, and Jews. Second, unlike a mood or emotion, an attitude is necessarily *directed at some target*. You can be generally happy, sad, or anxious, but you hold attitudes *toward* things: the president of the United States, your college, abortion, and so on.

Third, an attitude is relatively *enduring*. Emotions can come and go in seconds, but attitudes are more stable; in this sense, attitudes are like personality traits (Ajzen, 1987; see Chapter 2). If you are fiercely opposed to capital punishment today, chances are you will still be so a week from now.

Fourth, most of us believe that attitudes *influence and motivate our behavior*. This seemingly obvious assumption has not always been easy to demonstrate in research studies; nevertheless, attitude theorists have generally maintained that attitudes somehow mediate behavioral responses (Ostrom, 1989). For example, prejudiced attitudes lead to discrimination; positive attitudes toward political candidates lead us to vote for them; negative attitudes toward some brands of breakfast cereals lead us not to buy them, and so on.

Attitudes are assumed to be more generally motivating than simple habits or reflexes. That is, an attitude does not lead to a single, rigid response, but instead is reflected in many different behaviors. Hitler's prejudiced attitudes certainly motivated many of his brutal decisions and actions during the 1930s and 1940s.

Finally, attitudes are *learned;* that is, they come from experience. Recently a number of social psychologists have proposed that some of our attitudes may be influenced by genetic factors (Eaves, Eysenck, & Martin, 1989; Tesser, 1993). For example, attitudes toward music may develop partly because of genetically influenced temperamental factors—perhaps people who tend to like peace and quiet prefer classical music, whereas people who like lots of stimulation prefer jazz and rock.

Still, most attitude researchers assume that most socially significant attitudes are learned. This probably matches your common sense as well: As an infant, you were blissfully unconcerned with the decay of inner cities, pollution, abortion, capital punishment, but by now you probably have attitudes about all of these topics. How did you acquire these attitudes? We shall address this question of attitude formation shortly.

Learning prejudiced attitudes in Nazi Germany. An official anti-Semitic exhibition in Berlin, 1938.

The Functional Approach to Attitudes

One way to gain a deeper understanding of attitudes is to ask why people hold them at all. What purposes do attitudes serve in our lives?

A number of theorists have argued that attitudes can fulfill various psychological functions (Katz, 1960; Pratkanis & Greenwald, 1989; Shavitt, 1989; Smith, Bruner, & White, 1956). Among these are (1) the *instrumental* function of helping us gain rewards and avoid punishments, (2) the *ego-defensive* function of protecting our self-esteem and helping us avoid personality conflicts and anxiety, (3) the *knowledge* function of helping us order and assimilate complex information, (4) the *value-expressive* function of reflecting deeper values and ideals, and (5) the *social-adjustment* function of establishing our social identity and fostering smooth relations with friends and peers.

Herek (1986, 1987) used a functional analysis to understand attitudes toward homosexuals. In one study, he asked college students in California to write essays explaining why they held generally positive or negative attitudes toward homosexuals. Statistical analyses of the coded content of these essays indicated that students' attitudes served three different functions: ego-defensive, value-expressive, and a combination instrumental/knowledge function based on their actual experiences with gay people (see Figure 6.1 for excerpts from actual essays). Sixty-four percent of students' essays contained a single attitude function; 36% combined two

Function Served	
Knowledge/ instrumental	[I have generally positive attitudes because] I have come to know some of these people and find them no different from any other people. This has not always been the case. In junior high and high school I didn't condemn so to speak but I held strong opinions against them. This was an attitude formed without any knowledge of homosexuality or homosexuals. When I first came to [college] I still had some of the same attitudes. Little did I know that the guy in the next room was gay. We became good friends and did things together all the time. Eventually he told me and it was then that I realized that homosexuals only differ in sexual preference.
Ego-defensive	[I have generally negative attitudes because] I feel homosexuality is not a normal lifestyle. I do, however, feel more comfortable with a male homosexual than with a lesbian. Male homosexuals may have a different lifestyle but they are not physically dangerous to me as a woman, and I feel casual friendships between myself and male homosexuals are less tense. Lesbianism, however, is disgusting to me.
Value-expressive	[I have generally positive attitudes because] I don't think sexual preferences are a basis of judgment of someone's character or personality. Sexual preferences are a personal matter, and as long as a homosexual doesn't offend anyone or force his/her temptations on someone who is unwilling, there is no reason to condemn him/her. Homosexual tendencies aren't a deficit in someone's upbringing. I have these attitudes because of my own upbringing to be open-minded and nonstereotypical or nonjudgmental.

[I have generally negative attitudes because] in the Bible it clearly states that homosexuality is a SIN. I believe that no one can be a Christian if he/she is a homosexual. I believe the Bible is correct, and I follow its beliefs word for word. I am a Christian. |

FIGURE 6.1 College students explain why they hold their attitudes toward homosexuals. *Source*: Herek (1987).

or more functions in the same essay. Thus, a given attitude may serve more than one function simultaneously.

Some attitudes tend to serve predominantly one function for most people (Shavitt, 1990). For example, our attitudes toward consumer products such as air conditioners and coffee tend to serve an instrumental function—we generally like or dislike such products for the features they possess and the pleasures or costs they bring. Other attitudes, like those we hold toward our own appearance and personality, are more likely to serve an ego-defensive function, for they are strongly associated with our self-esteem and feelings of adequacy. Still other attitudes, such as those we hold toward the American flag or toward our university sweatshirt, tend to serve a social-adjustment function—they help establish our social identity. We shall link the functional approach to attitudes to research on persuasion later in this chapter.

Attitude Measurement

"I respect Jewish people," [David] Duke told an interviewer last week. But as recently as the mid-'80s he said, "[Jews] probably deserve to go into the ash bin of history."

—*Newsweek*, November 18, 1991

What are David Duke's *real* attitudes? Attitudes cannot be seen, touched, or weighed, yet we all think they exist and are important. But if attitudes cannot be directly observed, how can they be measured?

Beginning in the 1920s and 1930s, social psychologists developed various kinds of scales to measure people's attitudes. Two kinds of scales that are often used today to measure attitudes are Likert scales and semantic differential scales.

Likert Scales

Likert scales, or *summated rating scales,* are probably the attitude scales most commonly used today (Likert, 1932; McNemar, 1946; Murphy & Likert, 1938; Poppleton & Pilkington, 1964). You have probably filled out many of these scales in your life.

Likert scales list a number of attitude statements and ask you to rate how much you agree or disagree with each. Your score on the scale is simply the sum of your numeric responses on all the items—hence the name "summated rating scale." Figure 6.2 presents a Likert scale for measuring attitudes toward homosexuals (Kite & Deaux, 1986). The items of a good Likert scale are developed and selected according to rigorous statistical principles of scale development.

Semantic Differential Scales

Semantic differential scales focus on the meanings people associate with various concepts (for example, "Iraq," "Mother Teresa," "AIDS," "Social Security"). Researchers using this approach ask people to rate concepts on dimensions of perceived meaning such as *good–bad, smooth–rough, beautiful–ugly, fast–slow* (Osgood, Suci, & Tannenbaum, 1957). Such research consistently supports the idea that evaluative scales (such as *good–bad, beautiful–ugly,* and *worthy–unworthy*) account for most of the variation in people's ratings of various concepts. Scales like these seem to be ideally suited to measure attitudes. Subjects reveal their attitude toward, say, the president of the United States by rating him on a number of

Likert scales are commonly used in attitude research. Subjects rate the degree to which they agree or disagree with items that have been selected to be clear and to measure the same attitude. A subject's score on a Likert scale is the sum of his or her responses—thus the term *summated rating scale*.

Please indicate your level of agreement with the items below using the following scale:

1	2	3	4	5
Strongly agree		*Neutral*		*Strongly disagree*

1. I would not mind having homosexual friends.
2. Finding out that an artist was gay would have no effect on my appreciation of his/her work.
3. I won't associate with known homosexuals if I can help it.
4. I would look for a new place to live if I found out my roommate was gay.
5. Homosexuality is a mental illness.
6. I would not be afraid for my child to have a homosexual teacher.
7. Gays dislike members of the opposite sex.
8. I do not really find the thought of homosexual acts disgusting.
9. Homosexuals are more likely to commit deviant sexual acts, such as child molestation, rape, and voyeurism (Peeping Toms), than are heterosexuals.
10. Homosexuals should be kept separate from the rest of society (i.e., separate housing, restricted employment).
11. Two individuals of the same sex holding hands or displaying affection in public is revolting.
12. The love between two males or two females is quite different from the love between two persons of the opposite sex.
13. I see the gay movement as a positive thing.
14. Homosexuality, as far as I'm concerned, is not sinful.
15. I would not mind being employed by a homosexual.
16. Homosexuals should be forced to have psychological treatment.
17. The increasing acceptance of homosexuality in our society is aiding in the deterioration of morals.
18. I would not decline membership in an organization just because it had homosexual members.
19. I would vote for a homosexual in an election for public office.
20. If I knew someone were gay, I would still go ahead and form a friendship with that individual.
21. If I were a parent, I could accept my son or daughter being gay.

Note: Items 1, 2, 6, 8, 13, 14, 15, 18, 19, 20, and 21 are reverse-scored.

FIGURE 6.2 A Likert scale for assessing attitudes toward homosexuals. *Source*: Adapted from Kite and Deaux (1986).

evaluative semantic differential scales; each subject's mean rating is considered to be a measure of his or her attitude (Ajzen & Fishbein, 1980; Fishbein & Ajzen, 1975).

The Validity of Attitude Scales

Traditional attitude scaling techniques assume that people are willing and able to report honestly on their attitudes. This assumption may not always be warranted, however. People who respond to an attitude scale can usually figure out what attitude the scale is designed to measure, and they may sometimes distort their responses to make themselves look good to others or to please the researcher (recall the discussion of subject bias in Chapter 2). For example, many prejudiced people are unlikely to report their attitudes with complete honesty because they feel that such attitudes are considered by many to be undesirable or that the researcher might disapprove of them.

Adolf Hitler apparently was an exception, for he quite freely expressed his virulent prejudices in *Mein Kampf*. It seems safe to assume that he would have expressed his prejudices on an attitude scale as well. On the other hand, former Nazi David Duke tended to disguise his attitudes somewhat to make them more acceptable to members of mainstream society.

How can social psychologists get around such problems in order to detect and measure people's real attitudes? Researchers have devised some clever techniques for inducing subjects to respond honestly to attitude scales. For example, in the *bogus pipeline method* (Jones & Sigall, 1971), subjects are led to believe that the researcher can accurately measure their attitudes physiologically (for instance, by recording from electrodes attached to the arm). One study demonstrated that white subjects expressed more negative attitudes toward blacks when attached to the "bogus pipeline" than when not (Sigall & Page, 1971). Presumably, these subjects answered more honestly—by expressing a greater degree of bigotry in their questionnaire responses—when they thought the researchers already knew the truth about their prejudices from their physiological responses.

Behavioral Measures of Attitude

The bogus pipeline is a fake physiological measure used to induce people to tell the truth when filling out attitude scales. But are there physiological measures that do yield valid information about people's attitudes? Some researchers have tried to use relatively subtle changes in physiological arousal as indexes of attitudes. For example, physiological arousal as assessed by the galvanic skin response (a measure of skin conductivity related to perspiration) may be associated with prejudice. One study indicated that subjects who were prejudiced against blacks tended to show a greater galvanic skin response when touched by a black research assistant than nonprejudiced subjects did (Porier & Lott, 1967). Pupil dilation may also be an unobtrusive physiological measure of attitude (Hess, 1975). When exposed to people or things that evoke strong attitudes, subjects often show pupil dilation.

Unfortunately, such physiological measures can indicate only the *presence* of some attitude (or more precisely, an emotional response to an object), not its direction (whether the subject likes or dislikes the object). Furthermore, physiological measures have frequently been found less reliable than self-report measures, and self-report measures are simply easier to obtain. For these reasons, social psychologists have commonly relied on scales rather than physiological measures to operationally define attitudes.

Newly developed physiological measures may overcome some of these problems, though. Some recent studies have attempted to measure attitudes by recording the electrical activity in facial muscles that are responsible for the display of emotion in humans (Cacioppo & Petty, 1987; Cacioppo & Tassinary, 1990). Electrodes are attached to various locations on subjects' faces so that electrical activity can be measured, even when no facial movement is visible. Such methods hold the promise of both reliably measuring subtle emotional responses and assessing the *kind* of emotional reaction by identifying the specific pattern of muscle responses.

ATTITUDE FORMATION

Today it is difficult, if not impossible, for me to say when the word "Jew" first gave me ground for special thoughts.

. . . Not until my fourteenth or fifteenth year did I begin to come across the word "Jew" with any frequency, partly in connection with political discussions. This filled me with a mild distaste, and I could not rid myself of an unpleasant feeling that always came over me whenever religious quarrels occurred in my presence. . . .

As in all such cases, I now began to try to relieve my doubts by books. For a few hellers I bought the first anti-Semitic pamphlets of my life.

—*Mein Kampf,* pp. 51–56

Where do our attitudes come from? There are three general kinds of answers to this question: We learn attitudes through conditioning and modeling; we form attitudes to serve needs in our personality; and we think through our attitudes logically, developing them from related beliefs and attitudes or inferring them from our behavior. Each of these answers provides part of the truth about attitude formation.

Learning Theories and Attitude Formation

Psychologists have long studied three basic kinds of learning: classical conditioning, operant conditioning, and observational learning (also known as modeling). Each of these plays a significant role in attitude formation.

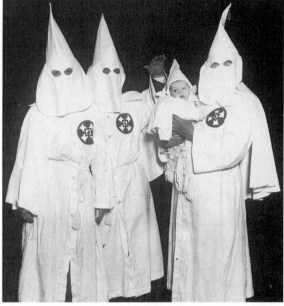

Learning attitudes through modeling and conditioning: Left: *The indoctrination of young Germans in a Hitler youth camp.* Above: *A Klansman in training.*

Classical Conditioning

In *Mein Kampf,* Adolf Hitler seems to suggest that he underwent a process of classical conditioning in associating the word *Jew* with religious quarrels that were unpleasant. The basic principle of classical conditioning is one of association: When a formerly neutral stimulus (for example, a bell) is paired with a stimulus that automatically produces a physical reaction in you (tasty food, which makes you salivate), eventually the neutral stimulus will come to evoke the same physical reaction. That is, if the bell is paired with food many times, eventually the bell by itself will lead you to salivate.

Generally, classical conditioning occurs for involuntary responses such as salivation. Other involuntary responses that can be classically conditioned include changes in heart rate, perspiration, narrowing of blood vessels, and alterations in digestive processes. How do these involuntary responses relate to attitudes? Remember that an *emotional response* to some object is central to the notion of an attitude. Emotional responses are often characterized by physiological arousal (increased heart rate, blood pressure, perspiration), and it is exactly these kinds of responses that can be classically conditioned. Thus, some attitudes can be viewed as classically conditioned emotional responses to specific objects.

In an early study demonstrating the classical conditioning of attitudes, Staats and Staats (1958) asked subjects to remember words paired with various nation-

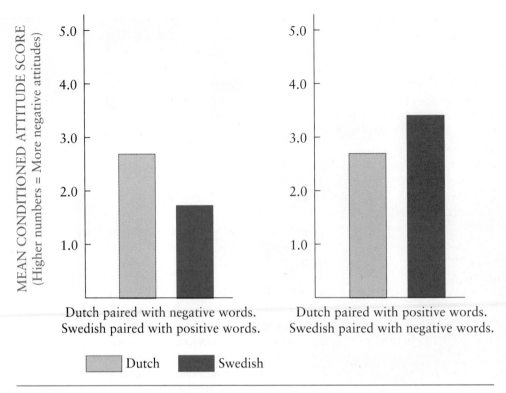

MEAN CONDITIONED ATTITUDE SCORE
(Higher numbers = More negative attitudes)

Dutch paired with negative words.
Swedish paired with positive words.

Dutch paired with positive words.
Swedish paired with negative words.

Dutch   Swedish

FIGURE 6.3 Can attitudes be classically conditioned in the laboratory?

ality names, such as *French–blue, Dutch–gift, German–table, Swedish–pain.* One target nationality, Dutch, was always paired with words having pleasant emotional connotations (such as *gift, beauty, romance*), whereas a second target nationality, Swedish, was always paired with negative words *(pain, ugly, bitter)*.

When toward the end of the study subjects were asked to rate how they actually felt about the various nationality groups, their attitudes toward the Dutch had become a bit more positive and their attitudes toward Swedes a bit more negative. In a separate group of subjects, the target nationalities were reversed: Dutch was paired with negative words and Swedish with positive words. These subjects later reported a more negative attitude toward the Dutch and a more positive attitude toward Swedes. (Figure 6.3 presents the results of this study.)

In another, more recent experiment, subjects developed negative attitudes to words *(mother, lawyer)* and to nonwords *(thomer, sartil)* when these stimuli were paired with uncomfortable electric shocks (Cacioppo, Marshall-Goodell, Tassinary, & Petty, 1992). One interesting finding from this study was that the conditioned negative attitudes were stronger for the nonwords than for the words. This suggests that classical conditioning may be particularly potent in forming attitudes toward things (words, people) when we don't have a lot a prior knowledge about them or preexisting mental associations with them.

Can classical conditioning lead us to form attitudes in real life as well as in experiments? Might we acquire prejudices this way, for example? The answer is undoubtedly yes. You can probably think of many possible examples of classically conditioned attitudes in real life: If newspaper stories and TV programs frequently tend to associate members of certain minority groups with violent crimes, then we may come to show conditioned fear whenever we see members of these groups. Perhaps Adolf Hitler underwent classical conditioning when he read his first anti-Semitic pamphlets and when the word *Jew* was associated with negative emotions during conversations early in his life.

Furthermore, attitudes that are classically conditioned to specific objects can generalize to related objects. For example, if a woman is abused by three specific men (that is, these men are associated in her life with pain and emotional distress), she may develop negative attitudes toward men in general. And people sometimes show classically conditioned responses not only to a specific stimulus (such as a bell or a man), but also to *semantically related* words and concepts (for example, the words *bell* and *man*). This process is known as *semantic generalization* (Bem, 1970; Zanna, Kiesler, & Pilkonis, 1970).

The occurrence of semantic generalization indicates that *language* is important in the conditioning of human attitudes. We sometimes hold strong prejudices against groups with which we've had no actual contact. Semantic generalization provides one explanation for how such prejudices can develop. If you read newspaper articles that associate the word *Serb*, for example, with unpleasant events, conditioned negative emotions to the word *Serb* could easily develop and generalize to the people referred to by the word. You come to hold strong negative attitudes toward Serbs, where none existed before.

One reason bigoted labels such as "kike," "nigger," and "faggot" help create and sustain prejudice is that they associate groups of people with negative emotions, and the feelings we acquire toward these words can generalize to the people referred to by the words.

Operant Conditioning

Operant conditioning occurs when rewards and punishments influence *voluntary* behaviors. This kind of learning is closely identified with Harvard psychologist B. F. Skinner, who conducted important research on the effects of *positive reinforcements* (rewards) on behavior (for example, Skinner, 1953).

A basic principle of operant conditioning is that when a voluntary response is followed by a reinforcer, the probability of future occurrences of that response is increased. From this perspective, attitudes can be viewed as voluntary responses that shift depending on our history of reinforcement. Certainly any verbal statements that express attitudes can be viewed as *operant responses* subject to conditioning.

Chester Insko (1965) demonstrated that attitude statements can be operantly conditioned in a study surveying the attitudes of University of Hawaii students toward "Aloha Week," the campus homecoming week. In a telephone survey, students were subtly conditioned with verbal reinforcers. Whenever students in one experimental condition said anything favorable about Aloha Week, the experimenter responded with "Good"; other subjects were verbally reinforced whenever they made *unfavorable* comments about Aloha Week. About a week later, the subjects completed another, apparently unrelated, questionnaire assessing their attitudes toward Aloha Week. Subjects who had earlier been reinforced for positive statements expressed more positive attitudes toward Aloha Week than students reinforced for negative comments did.

Undoubtedly, operant conditioning can help establish important real-life attitudes as well. As you grew up, did your parents reward you for expressing "proper" religious and political attitudes? Do you think therefore that some of your current religious and political attitudes were influenced by operant conditioning?

Modeling and Observational Learning

Certain forms of learning can take place just by watching others, without classical conditioning or direct reinforcement (Bandura, 1977). For example, children may learn to be aggressive merely by observing their friends fight or by watching violent television shows. In addition to learning aggression, children who watch media violence may develop more tolerant attitudes toward aggression (see Chapter 10). Similarly, children may learn to help others and develop prosocial attitudes by observing positive models (Chapter 11).

It seems likely that Germans in Hitler's Germany learned horribly prejudiced attitudes toward Jewish people and other groups through all the processes of learning we just sketched out: In propaganda, the Jewish population was associated with corruption and immorality (classical conditioning); Germans who expressed their prejudice openly were rewarded, for example with positions of power in the Nazi party (operant conditioning); and Germans modeled the rampant intolerance displayed by many of their fellow citizens (observational learning).

Implications of Learning Theories

What do learning theories imply about the formation of attitudes? First, attitudes need not be logical or rational. According to classical conditioning theory, an attitude can at times be something like a phobic response, blindly conditioned by past associations, sometimes without our conscious awareness (Krosnick, Betz, Jussim, Lynn, & Stephens, 1992). Thus, we can acquire attitudes that, rationally, we might wish not to have; we can sometimes feel prejudice even when we believe it is not right or ethical.

Second, conditioned attitudes need not necessarily be consistent with one another. As we shall see later, personality theories and inference theories of attitude formation assume that people do show considerable consistency among their attitudes. But learning theories imply that attitudes can be acquired helter-skelter, depending on our history of conditioning and reinforcement and the models we happen to have been exposed to.

On a more positive note, learning theories of attitude formation are fairly optimistic about the possibility of changing people's attitudes. After all, whatever is learned can be altered through new learning.

Personality and Attitude Formation

If we do not lift the youth out of the morass of their present-day environment, they will drown in it. . . . This cleansing of our culture must be extended to nearly all fields. Theater, art, literature, cinema, press, posters, and window displays must be cleansed of all manifestations of our rotting world and placed in the service of a moral, political, and cultural idea. Public life must be freed from the stifling perfume of our modern eroticism, just as it must be freed from all unmanly, prudish hypocrisy. . . . The right of personal freedom recedes before the duty to preserve the race.

—Mein Kampf, p. 255

[David Duke's] hating began early in life . . . [his] adolescence was lonely and difficult. His older sister . . . married as a teenager and left home when Duke was 12 . . . when Duke was 16 his father moved out. . . . The departures left Duke alone with an alcoholic mother who was shuttled in and out of hospitals. [A] housekeeper . . . says Maxine Duke's drinking so frustrated [David] that he once threatened to douse her with hair spray and set her on fire. . . . As Duke's home life unraveled, he began to drift into racist politics.

—Newsweek, November 18, 1991

Do you think that the extreme attitudes held by people like Adolf Hitler and David Duke sometimes fulfill conscious or unconscious needs in their personalities? For example, perhaps Hitler's virulent prejudices compensated for feelings of inferiority he felt because of his humble origins, or perhaps his obsessive concerns with sex reflected insecurities about his own masculinity. And perhaps David Duke's prejudices stemmed in part from an unhappy childhood and the boiling rage he felt toward his parents.

Is there any research evidence that our personalities can influence attitudes we develop? Prominent research on the *authoritarian personality* shows that highly prejudiced people sometimes use their bigoted attitudes to express repressed anger toward punitive parents and to guard against feelings of inadequacy and insecurity (Adorno, Frenkel-Brunswick, Levinson, & Sanford, 1950; see Chapter 7 for a more detailed discussion). Furthermore, such people often conform rigidly to conventional morality and sex roles. Research on the authoritarian personality helps explain why some people are strongly and consistently prejudiced against many different minorities; it is because their prejudice results from their upbringing and their resulting personality dynamics. (Adolf Hitler and David Duke certainly seem to provide plausible examples of a link between personality and extreme prejudice.)

Child-rearing practices and the personality traits that result from them can affect our broader political attitudes as well. For example, Tomkins (1965, 1987) suggests that children reared by parents who value their uniqueness and right to express themselves are likely to grow up to hold liberal political attitudes, whereas children reared by parents who emphasize obedience and compliance with social rules are likely to develop conservative political attitudes.

Furthermore, the different childhood experiences of liberals and conservatives lead them to develop different dominant emotions in adult life—for example, shame and joy are more characteristic emotions for liberals, whereas anger and excitement are more characteristic for conservatives (Tomkins, 1987). Consistent with this hypothesized link between political attitudes and emotions, Carlson and Brincka (1987) found that Americans could more readily imagine conservative Republicans (Ronald Reagan and George Bush) as characters in TV plots involving anger and retribution (for example, fighting invaders in a historical drama) and liberal Democrats (Walter Mondale and Geraldine Ferraro) in TV plots involving joy and human affiliation (for example, a family reunion). Apparently, laypeople as well as social psychologists see some link between political attitudes and personality.

Recent research on the functions of attitudes toward homosexuals offers additional evidence that personality may play a part in attitude formation. Herek (1987) found that subjects with negative ego-defensive attitudes toward gay people were more likely to have generally defensive personalities and show high conformity to conventional sex roles. By implication, negative attitudes toward homosexuals may stem in part from defensiveness, anxiety, and worry about sex roles.

Religious attitudes may also serve needs in individuals' personalities. Batson and Ventis (1982) noted that people who profess strong devotion to orthodox religious beliefs report relative freedom from worry and guilt. Although they do not prove a cause-effect relationship, these findings suggest that some people may adopt strong religious beliefs to reduce their anxieties.

Logical Inference and Attitude Formation

So far, we have considered nonrational ways that attitudes are formed. It may be reassuring to know that sometimes we do use more logical processes to think our attitudes through. There are two ways logical thought processes can lead to new attitudes. First, once attitudes exist for whatever reason, they become the raw material from which we build new attitudes. Second, and more subtly, when we're not sure of our attitudes, we sometimes infer them from our behavior.

Inferring Attitudes from Other Beliefs and Attitudes

How do you decide whom to vote for in a presidential election? If you are thoughtful, you probably evaluate the candidates' positions on a number of issues that are important to you and then mentally add up how much their positions agree or disagree with yours. Your overall attitude toward each candidate then reflects this tally. In other words, you gather information about the candidates and logically combine it to form your overall attitudes toward them.

Social psychologists have developed a number of mathematical models of how we combine beliefs and attitudes from other, broader attitudes. One of these, Martin Fishbein's *value-expectancy model,* provides a relatively simple explanation of how general attitudes are formed out of related smaller pieces of information (Fishbein, 1963; Fishbein & Ajzen, 1975). It proposes that we build our attitudes toward, say, a presidential candidate from relevant beliefs about the candidate and from our evaluations of those beliefs.

To illustrate: Suppose you read a magazine article about Senator Porkbarrel, a candidate for president of the United States, which indicates that he is against legalized abortion, in favor of increased defense spending, and against restricting lumber harvests to protect endangered species. These are your *beliefs* about Porkbarrel. In Fishbein's model, to determine your overall attitude toward the candidate we must know how you *feel* about each belief that you hold about him. That is, how do you feel about people who oppose legalized abortion, and so on?

According to the value-expectancy model, your overall attitude toward Porkbarrel is a sum of each belief you have about him ("How sure am I that he's against legalized abortion?") multiplied by how deeply you care about that belief ("I strongly support candidates who oppose abortion"). The value-expectancy model is one of many that tries to state in formal mathematical terms how we build up broad overall attitudes from related beliefs and attitudes. Such models apply most readily to rational attitudes that we develop by consciously considering relevant information (Fazio, 1989, 1990).

Inferring Attitudes from Behavior: Self-Perception Theory

Logical thought processes may lead to attitude formation in another way. Sometimes when we are not sure of our attitudes, we may infer them from our behavior (Bem, 1965, 1972).

This notion may seem counterintuitive to you at first. Don't we automatically *know* what our attitudes are? Most of us assume that while it may be difficult at times to figure out *other* people's attitudes, we surely know our own.

In some cases, however, our attitudes are weak, ambiguous, or even nonexistent. Bem's *self-perception theory* proposes that in these circumstances, we infer our attitudes from our behavior. For example, suppose you are asked your attitude toward red meat. Unless you have consciously reflected on this question (perhaps for health reasons or because you're a vegetarian), chances are you aren't sure off the top of your head just what your attitude is. In this circumstance, you might recall instances of your own behavior: "This past week I ate hamburgers for lunch on five days, and I ate two steaks, roast beef, and lamb chops for dinner." From these observations, you would *infer* your attitude: "Gee, I guess I must really like red meat."

According to Bem, then, when our attitudes are ill-defined, we function like an outside observer—that is, we note our behavior and the situation in which it occurs and then use this information to infer our attitudes. We typically infer our attitudes more from behavior that is freely chosen than from behavior that is coerced. If you freely choose to read *War and Peace,* for example, you'll probably

SUMMARY TABLE 6.1 Processes of Attitude Formation		
Process	*Description*	*Example*
Learning Processes		
Classical conditioning	Emotional reactions to object learned when object is paired with a stimulus that elicits these reactions.	Staats and Staats (1958) study: Attitudes conditioned to nationality name by being paired with positive or negative words. Semantic generalization.
Operant conditioning	Verbal expressions of attitude strengthened by rewards.	Insko (1965) "Aloha Week" study: Students conditioned to have more or less favorable attitudes toward homecoming week through verbal reinforcement.
Observational learning	Beliefs and attitudes learned by watching others behave.	Learning attitudes toward aggressive behavior by watching aggressive models in violent TV shows.
Personality		
Personality processes	Attitudes develop to defend individual against anxiety or feelings of insecurity.	Research on authoritarian personality showing that some people vent repressed feelings of anger and insecurity via prejudice against minority groups.
Logical Thought		
Logical-inference processes	Attitudes logically inferred from relevant beliefs and attitudes.	Fishbein's (1963) value-expectancy model: Attitudes may be based on relevant beliefs and evaluations of those beliefs.
Self-perception	Attitudes logically inferred from behavior and its situational context.	Chaiken and Baldwin (1981) study: People with weak ecological attitudes inferred their attitudes from their questionnaire responses.

conclude that you like this long Russian novel, but if your literature professor "forces" you to read it for a class assignment, you won't necessarily conclude that you love *War and Peace*.

Consistent with Bem's theory, other research shows that people infer their attitudes from their behavior particularly when they haven't already given much thought to the topic—that is, when such attitudes are weak or even nonexistent (Fazio, 1987). Chaiken and Baldwin (1981) demonstrated this in an experiment that manipulated subjects' ecological attitudes by inducing them to endorse either relatively pro-ecology or relatively anti-ecology behavioral statements (such as "I litter," "I carpool," or "I pick up garbage") on a questionnaire. They did this through a clever linguistic device: they inserted either the word *frequently* or *occasionally* into the statements. When the pro-ecology statements contained *occasionally* ("I occasionally pick up garbage"), subjects were more likely to endorse them, but when they contained *frequently* ("I frequently carpool"), subjects were less likely to endorse them.

Subjects induced to endorse many pro-ecology statements later rated their attitude as more pro-ecology, whereas subjects induced to endorse many anti-ecology statements later rated their attitude as more anti-ecology. This self-perception effect was particularly strong for subjects whose initial environmental attitudes were weak and inconsistent. Most of us assume we say what we believe, but this study suggests that instead, we sometimes believe what we say.

Our discussion so far indicates that attitudes may be formed via a number of processes. Summary Table 6.1 reviews the three main routes to attitude formation we have discussed: learning processes, personality processes, and logical thought.

ATTITUDES AND BEHAVIOR

Was there any form of filth or profligacy . . . without at least one Jew involved in it?

If you cut even cautiously into such an abscess, you found, like a maggot in a rotting body, often dazzled by the sudden light—a kike! (p. 57)

The demand for restoration of the [German borders] of 1914 is a political absurdity of such proportions and consequences as to make it seem a crime. . . . They were not the result of a considered political action, but momentary frontiers in a political struggle that was by no means concluded. (p. 649)

—Mein Kampf

Reading *Mein Kampf* is a chilling experience, in part because the book predicts so clearly the horrors to come during the 1930s and 1940s, when Hitler set out to eliminate the Jewish people of Europe and greatly expand German territory through military invasions. In *Mein Kampf*, Hitler presented the world with the detailed manifesto of a ruthless madman several years before he gained power in Germany. His attitudes would prove to motivate his behavior to the bitter end, with tragic consequences for the entire world.

Was Hitler a typical case? In general, if you know an individual's attitudes, can you predict his or her behavior? Despite the compelling anecdotal example of Hitler's attitudes in *Mein Kampf*, research studies have not always shown a strong relationship between attitudes and behavior.

Putting the Attitude-Behavior Question in Context

A classic study by Richard LaPiere (1934) was one of the first to question how well attitudes predict behavior. LaPiere investigated the correspondence between people's prejudiced attitudes (as assessed by a questionnaire) and prejudiced actions. To test whether words match deeds, LaPiere accompanied a Chinese graduate student couple in their travels across the United States; they sought accommodation at 251 restaurants, hotels, and other public establishments. (At this time in U.S. history, prejudice against Asians was much more overt than it is today.) The Chinese couple was refused service only once.

Six months later, LaPiere mailed a questionnaire to each establishment. Included in it was the question "Will you accept members of the Chinese race as guests at your establishment?" Out of 128 responses, over 90% answered "No." Thus, there seemed to be very little correspondence between the attitudes of establishment operators, as measured by questionnaires, and actual behavior.

After reviewing 42 studies that examined how well attitudes predict behavior, Wicker (1969) concluded that "it is considerably more likely that attitudes will be unrelated or only slightly related to overt behaviors than that attitudes will be closely related to actions." While this conclusion may surprise you, other attitude experts have frequently echoed it (Abelson, 1972; McGuire, 1985).

Are our attitudes largely unrelated to our behavior? Note that this is not just an academic question. Real-life professionals such as market researchers, political consultants, and public health officials study attitudes because they assume that attitudes affect our behavior. For example, market researchers assume that our attitudes toward products affect our purchases; political consultants assume that our attitudes toward candidates affect which candidate we vote for; and public health officials assume our attitudes toward diseases and health-related behaviors (for example, toward AIDS and toward using condoms) affect our actions (our sexual behaviors). For many kinds of real-life applications, it is important to understand the relationship between people's attitudes and their behavior.

Over the past 20 years, researchers have developed better methods to demonstrate links between attitudes and behavior, and they have proposed theoretical models that specify how our attitudes, in concert with other factors, influence our behavior (Eagly & Chaiken, 1993; Pratkanis, Breckler, & Greenwald, 1989). To demonstrate links between attitudes and behavior, research has increasingly turned to more qualified questions: One set of questions focuses on methodology (What are the *best ways to measure* attitudes and behavior?) and how attitudes combine with other factors to influence behavior (What *other variables* work in concert with our attitudes to guide our behavior?) A second set of questions focuses on attitudes themselves: What *kinds of attitudes* most influence our behavior? A third set focuses on personal variables: What *kinds of people* are most likely to show consistency between their attitudes and actions? A final set focuses on situational factors: What *kinds of settings* lead people to act consistently with their attitudes? Let's summarize some of the research evidence on these questions.

Measuring Attitudes and Behavior Properly

To predict behavior successfully, attitude measures must be fine-tuned to match the behaviors they are to predict (Fishbein & Ajzen, 1975). For example, if a researcher's goal is to predict housing discrimination against Hispanics, she should measure home sellers' attitudes toward *selling or leasing homes to Hispanics* rather than, say, attitudes toward Hispanics or attitudes toward minorities in general. However, if her goal is to predict more general behaviors (say, discriminatory behaviors against all minorities), then a general prejudice scale may be appropriate. The guiding principle is that to assess the relationship between attitudes and behavior correctly, both must be measured at the same level of generality or specificity.

Furthermore, when researchers wish to investigate the influence of attitudes on broad, general behaviors (for example, individuals' overall religiosity), they must make sure they measure more than one behavior. Martin Fishbein and Icek Ajzen (1975; Ajzen & Fishbein, 1980) argue that some behaviors, by definition, are not single acts, but rather *classes of behavior*. To measure such classes of behavior reliably, researchers must assess many behaviors and pool these measurements together.

To demonstrate this point, Fishbein and Ajzen (1974) examined how well religious attitudes predict religious behaviors. In addition to having subjects complete questionnaires on their attitudes toward religion, Fishbein and Ajzen also asked them to indicate how frequently they engaged in 70 different kinds of religious behavior. For example, subjects were asked whether they pray before or

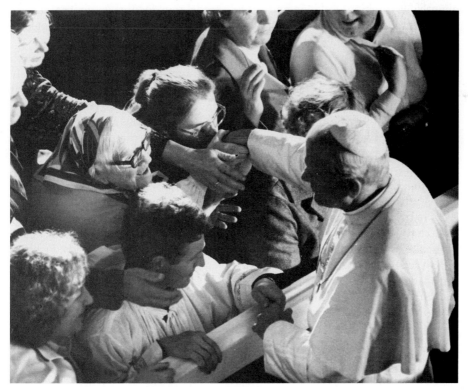

Do religious attitudes predict religious behaviors? As the text notes, attitudes often predict aggregated behaviors better than they predict single behaviors.

after meals, donate money to religious institutions, take classes or courses in religion, attend religious services, and so on.

Fishbein and Ajzen found that religious attitudes correlated quite poorly *with single religious behaviors* such as "attend religious services." In fact, the average correlation between attitudes and single behaviors was only .15. When the 70 behaviors were summed to form a composite measure of religious behaviors, however, the correlation between attitudes and religious behaviors rose dramatically (to .71). Clearly, then, attitudes can strongly predict *aggregates* of behavior.

Fishbein and Ajzen's Theory of Reasoned Action

It is naive to think that our attitudes are the only factors influencing our behavior. So the critical question becomes: What factors *in addition to attitudes* are important in shaping our behavior? Fishbein and Ajzen (1975; Ajzen & Fishbein, 1980) offered one well-known answer to this question. Their *theory of reasoned action* proposes two main factors that influence our voluntary actions: attitudes and subjective norms. *Attitudes* refer to our evaluative feelings about a behavior; *subjective norms* refer to our beliefs about the way significant others wish us to behave. So, for example, your attitude toward smoking consists of your positive or negative feelings about smoking, whereas your subjective norms consist of your beliefs about what important people (such as your mother and best friend) think about your smoking. Fishbein and Ajzen's model thus focuses on internal factors (our attitudes) and external factors (normative social pressures, as represented in our beliefs) that together affect our behavior.

In Fishbein and Ajzen's model, attitudes and subjective norms combine to influence our *behavioral intention,* which is our subjective estimate of how likely we are to engage in a given behavior. For example, what's the probability that you will smoke during the coming month? Your estimate is your behavioral intention to smoke. Ultimately, it's your behavioral intentions that determine your behavior (whether you do in fact smoke). The results of many studies using Fishbein and Ajzen's model suggest that, on average, people's attitudes predict their behavioral intentions more strongly than subjective norms do (Farley, Lehmann, & Ryan, 1981; Van den Putte, 1991). Figure 6.4 summarizes Fishbein and Ajzen's model.

In the theory of reasoned action, the relative power of people's attitudes and subjective norms to influence their intentions and behaviors varies depending on the particular attitudes and people being studied. To illustrate: In one study, Fishbein (1966; see Fishbein & Ajzen, 1975) attempted to predict whether college students intended to engage in premarital sexual intercourse during a particular semester. He found that for male students, subjective norms were more important than attitudes in predicting intentions, whereas for female students the reverse was true.

Fishbein and Ajzen named their model a "theory of reasoned action" because it holds that attitudes and subjective norms influence behavior primarily when behavior is conscious and voluntary, and thus "reasoned." Voting is a good example of behavior that can be successfully predicted by the model because voting is a

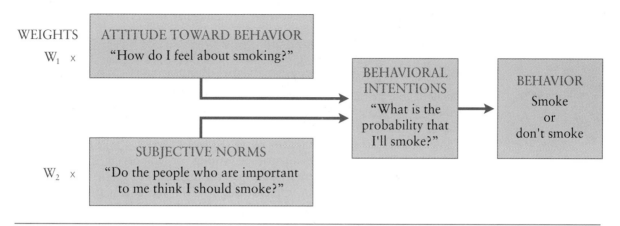

WEIGHTS

$W_1 \times$ ATTITUDE TOWARD BEHAVIOR
"How do I feel about smoking?"

$W_2 \times$ SUBJECTIVE NORMS
"Do the people who are important to me think I should smoke?"

BEHAVIORAL INTENTIONS
"What is the probability that I'll smoke?"

BEHAVIOR
Smoke
or
don't smoke

FIGURE 6.4 What is the relation between attitudes and behavior according to Fishbein and Ajzen's theory of reasoned action?

voluntary behavior (at least in this country) and because most of us consciously think about our political beliefs and choices.

The theory of reasoned action is less successful in predicting behavior that is not completely voluntary—behavior, for example, that requires special abilities or is unthinking and habitual (Fazio, 1990; Ronis, Yates, & Kirscht, 1989). To illustrate this point, Ajzen and Madden (1986) attempted to predict whether a group of upper-division college students would receive "A's" in their classes based on their attitudes toward getting "A's" and their subjective norms. Note that receiving "A's" may not be totally under some students' volitional control; no matter how much students value getting "A's" (attitude) and no matter how much students believe their parents and friends want them to get "A's" (subjective norms), if students lack ability, they may not get "A's." Indeed, Ajzen and Madden found that a weighted combination of attitudes and subjective norms correlated only moderately well with students' grades (correlation coefficient = .39).

To increase the ability to predict behavior that is not entirely under volitional control, Ajzen (1987, 1989, 1991) recommends adding a third variable—perceived behavioral control—to the theory of reasoned action. That is, social psychologists should measure subjects' attitudes, subjective norms, and their perceived ability to carry out the behavior of interest. Other researchers recommend adding another variable, a measure of "habit"—that is, how much a person has engaged in the particular behavior in the past (Bentler & Speckart, 1979).

Fishbein and Ajzen's model has been used successfully to predict many important kinds of real-life behaviors, including women's choices to work or be homemakers (Sperber, Fishbein, & Ajzen, 1980), family planning decisions (Crawford & Boyer, 1985; Fishbein, Ajzen, & McArdle, 1980), consumer behavior (Fishbein & Ajzen, 1980), and safe and unsafe sexual practices in the age of AIDS (Fishbein et al., 1992). One study found that high school students' attitudes and subjective norms toward going to college, as assessed from survey data collected in

1955, predicted their level of educational attainment 15 years later moderately well (Harrison, Thompson, & Rodgers, 1985).

What Kinds of Attitudes Best Predict Behavior?

Do all of your attitudes influence your behavior equally? Common sense probably tells you that some of your attitudes are stronger or more important than others, and it is these attitudes that are most influential in guiding your behavior. Contemporary attitude researchers agree (Krosnick, 1988, 1989; Petty & Krosnick, 1992). But what makes an attitude "strong" or "important"?

One answer is that attitudes formed through direct experience tend to be stronger and, as a result, they influence our behavior more than attitudes formed through secondhand information (Fazio, 1990; Fazio & Zanna, 1981). For example, what do you think influences your attitude more toward a particular make of car—the experiences you had as an owner of that kind of car or the information you receive in TV ads?

One reason attitudes formed through direct experience have a powerful impact on our behavior is that they tend to be highly *accessible*—that is, they are strongly associated with the attitude object, and they come swiftly and automatically to mind (Fazio, 1986, 1989). To illustrate: Do you think your attitudes toward cockroaches are highly accessible? For most of us, cockroaches are strongly associated with negative feelings, and these feelings occur swiftly and automatically whenever we see a cockroach. Thus, our attitudes toward cockroaches are highly accessible. Furthermore, it seems likely that our attitudes toward cockroaches strongly guide our behavior—when most of us see a cockroach, we either run away or smash the roach.

How do researchers measure the accessibility of people's attitudes? One way is to see how quickly people can answer questions about their attitudes. In a study of attitudes toward then-President Ronald Reagan, Russell Fazio and Carol Williams (1986) asked people in a shopping mall to respond to a number of attitude statements about Reagan by pressing one of five buttons labeled "Strongly agree" to "Strongly disagree." The speed with which people pressed the buttons served as a measure of attitude accessibility: Quick responses implied that attitudes were accessible; slow responses indicated they were relatively nonaccessible.

Fazio and Williams contacted their subjects again after they had viewed two televised debates between Reagan and his Democratic opponent, Walter Mondale, and asked the subjects to rate how impressive they found Reagan to have been in the debates. Subjects with highly accessible attitudes showed a stronger link between their attitudes and their perceptions of Reagan in the TV debates (a correlation of .74) than did subjects with nonaccessible attitudes (a .40 correlation). Furthermore, when subjects were contacted again after the 1984 presidential election, those with highly accessible attitudes showed a much stronger link between their attitudes and voting behavior than did voters with nonaccessible attitudes (a correlation of .89 versus .66). The message of this research is clear: Strong, accessible attitudes are those that are most likely to influence our behavior.

What Kinds of People Behave Consistently with Their Attitudes?

Are some people more likely than others to behave in a manner consistent with their attitudes? You may recall from Chapter 3 that people who are low on the trait of self-monitoring tend to act according to their inner feelings, characteristics, and attitudes, whereas people who are high on self-monitoring tend to act more as the situation dictates (Snyder, 1979, 1987). Not surprisingly, a number of studies suggest that low-self-monitoring individuals tend to show greater correspondence between their attitudes and their behavior, whereas high-self-monitoring individuals show less correspondence (Snyder, 1982, 1987). Self-monitoring may affect the link between attitudes and behavior in part because it influences the accessibility of attitudes (Kardes, Sanbonmatsu, Voss, & Fazio, 1986). That is, low-self-monitoring people can call their attitudes to mind more easily than high-self-monitoring people can, whereas high-self-monitoring people can call to mind the norms and rules of social situations more easily than low-self-monitoring people can (Jamieson & Zanna, 1989).

Another personality trait that can affect the link between attitudes and behavior is private self-consciousness—the degree to which people chronically focus attention on themselves and think about their thoughts and feelings (see Chapter 3). In general, people who are highly self-conscious tend to show more consistency between their attitudes and behavior than people who are less self-conscious. For example, highly self-conscious people showed a stronger link between their attitudes toward aggression and their actual aggressiveness in an experiment than less self-conscious subjects did (Scheier, Buss, & Buss, 1978). In sum, attitudes influence behavior in some kinds of people more than others.

What Kinds of Situations Lead People to Behave Consistently with Their Attitudes?

As we just noted, people who are highly self-conscious are particularly likely to act consistently with their attitudes. But self-consciousness doesn't just depend on the kind of person we are; it can also be triggered by the situation we are in. As noted in Chapter 3, we often become self-conscious when we see a video camera pointed at us, when we view our reflection in a mirror, or when we see someone watching and evaluating us. A number of studies suggest that when people are placed in settings like these, their attitudes predict their behavior reasonably well, but in settings that pull their attention away from themselves, attitudes do not predict behavior so well (Carver & Scheier, 1981). In essence, our attitudes are most likely to influence our behavior when we pay attention to ourselves and contemplate our attitudes.

Surprisingly, when people are asked to think about the *reasons* for their attitudes, their attitudes become less predictive of their behavior (Wilson, Dunn, Kraft, & Lisle, 1989). (Note that thinking about your attitudes is *not* the same thing as thinking about the *reasons* for your attitudes. If I ask you to think about your attitude toward Coca-Cola, you'll probably contemplate whether you like it or not. But if I ask you for the *reasons* you hold your attitude toward Coca-Cola, you might start thinking about possible factors such as its taste, its caffeine content, and so on.)

SUMMARY TABLE 6.2   Factors That Influence When Attitudes Predict Behavior

Measurement Factors

Attitudes and behaviors should be measured at same level of generality or specificity if they are to be related to one another.

In many applications, summed rather than single measures of behavior should be used for attitudes to predict behavior.

Kinds of Attitudes

Attitudes formed through direct experience are more likely to predict behavior.
Accessible attitudes are more likely to predict behavior.

Kinds of People

Low-self-monitoring individuals are more likely than high-self-monitoring individuals to behave consistently with their attitudes.

People who are highly self-conscious are more likely to behave consistently with their attitudes than are people who are less self-conscious.

Kinds of Situations

Settings that induce self-awareness lead people to behave consistently with their attitudes.

When people are asked to provide the reasons *why* they hold their attitudes, consistency between attitudes and behavior is reduced.

Why does thinking about the reasons for our attitudes lead us to be *less* likely to behave consistently with them? Apparently, when we consciously think about why we hold our attitudes, we often come up with limited, biased, and sometimes just plain wrong explanations and thus lose touch with our original gut feeling. This finding has practical implications for consumer research: Researchers should always measure consumers' preferences for products *before* asking them why they hold their preferences; otherwise, their preferences may not predict their purchases very well.

Summary Table 6.2 lists the many factors that determine when attitudes are most likely to influence related behaviors.

SOCIAL
PSYCHOLOGY
IN EVERYDAY
LIFE

   Attitudes and Smoking

Let's conclude our discussion of the link between attitudes and behavior by considering a couple of important real-life questions: Do people's attitudes toward smoking influence whether they smoke, and can changing these attitudes alter their smoking behavior? These questions are not just of theoretical interest—they are a matter of life and death, for almost 400,000 people die prematurely each year in the United States as a direct result of smoking cigarettes (U.S. Department of Health and Human Services, 1989).

Strong circumstantial evidence indicates that public attitudes toward smoking are linked to cigarette consumption. As data have accumulated about the health dangers of smoking, leading to more negative public attitudes toward smoking, the percentage of cigarette smokers has decreased in the United States—from 53% of adults in 1955 to 28% by the early 1990s (U.S. Department of Health and Human Services, 1981; *New York Times,* November 9, 1991).

Research into the effects on smoking of anti-smoking ads points even more strongly to a link between attitudes and smoking (see Chapter 14 for an additional discussion). Since the mid-1960s, government health agencies and organizations such as the American Cancer Society and the American Heart Association have worked hard to inform the public that smoking is dangerous. Their message seems to have gotten through: Surveys and polls show that a huge majority of people now know that smoking is unhealthy, and a majority of smokers want to stop smoking (Gallup, 1981a, 1981b; Leventhal & Cleary, 1980). This, of course, is one factor leading to a reduction in smoking.

Unfortunately, while informational ads about the long-term health risks of smoking help change adults' attitudes and behavior, they are less effective for teenagers, whose attitudes toward smoking are more influenced by peer pressure and the desire to project a sophisticated image (Murray, Johnson, Luepker, & Mittelmark, 1984). This may help explain why the percentage of teenagers who smoke has not declined in recent years (*Wall Street Journal,* September 13, 1991; *Washington Post,* November 19, 1991).

Aware of the nature of teens' attitudes toward smoking, the tobacco companies have developed ad campaigns specifically for young people. Some of these ads link smoking to a "cool" image—for example, the Joe Camel and Kool Penguin ad campaigns (*Wall Street Journal,* February 20, March 13, 1992). Other ads target teenage girls by associating smoking with slimness—even the names selected for cigarette brands, such as "Superslims" and "Ultra Lights," have this intent *(Washington Post).* (Can you conceptualize these advertising strategies in terms of the functional and classical conditioning approaches to attitudes discussed earlier?)

The Joe Camel cigarette ad campaign appeals to teenagers' concern with their social images.

Do attitudes influence smoking? The answer seems to be yes. Obviously, advertisers try to change public attitudes toward smoking because they ultimately want to influence their smoking behavior. This leads us naturally to the question we consider next: How does persuasion work?

PERSUASION: WHEN OTHERS CHANGE OUR ATTITUDES

... by turns glib and menacing, Haider [head of Austria's right-wing Freedom Party] epitomizes Europe's new breed of upscale, far-right politicians. Compared with the bullies of the past . . . [they] tend to be articulate and relatively presentable. Their message is authoritarian and sometimes racist. But they speak for great numbers of Europeans who have lost faith in more moderate political parties, who are disoriented by post-communist upheavals and who fear interlopers from other countries and cultures.

In recent months, far-right parties have scored striking advances in city and regional elections in Germany, France, Italy, Austria, Belgium and Denmark. Moderate politicians don't know how to respond effectively.

—*Newsweek,* April 27, 1992

We live in a world of persuasion. Politicians give speeches to persuade us to vote for them. Companies mount print, radio, and TV advertising campaigns to persuade us to buy their products: In the United States, advertisers currently spend over $132 billion a year to influence consumer attitudes (Schoell & Guiltinan, 1992). Public health organizations run public service messages to persuade us to wear seat belts, eat less fat, avoid cigarettes, practice safe sex. Given our society's obsession with persuasion, it is not surprising that social psychologists have conducted a huge amount of research on this ever-relevant topic.

Studies on persuasion and attitude change began with some relatively simple and straightforward questions: Are there some kinds of people who are more persuasive than others? Are there some kinds of messages that are particularly persuasive? Are there some kinds of people who are most readily persuaded? As research on persuasion developed, however, social psychologists began to pose more subtle kinds of questions: What kinds of thought processes lead to persuasion?

A Communication Model of Persuasion: The Yale Research

Perhaps the most direct approach to persuasion is to view it as a communication process (Lasswell, 1948; Smith, Lasswell, & Casey, 1946). This was the approach taken during and after World War II by a group of researchers at Yale University who studied persuasion. Stimulated by the United States government's interest in gaining factual information about wartime propaganda and persuasion, these

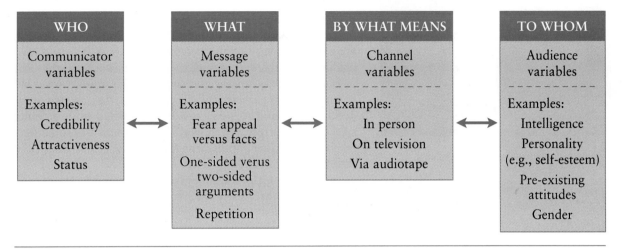

WHO	WHAT	BY WHAT MEANS	TO WHOM
Communicator variables	Message variables	Channel variables	Audience variables
Examples: Credibility Attractiveness Status	Examples: Fear appeal versus facts One-sided verus two-sided arguments Repetition	Examples: In person On television Via audiotape	Examples: Intelligence Personality (e.g., self-esteem) Pre-existing attitudes Gender

FIGURE 6.5 Four factors in the communication process that influence persuasion.

social psychologists carried out the first large-scale, comprehensive studies on attitude change by focusing on four broad factors involved in persuasion: (1) communicator variables, (2) message variables, (3) channel variables, and (4) target or audience variables (see Figure 6.5). In short, the Yale researchers studied *who* says *what* by *what means* to *whom*.

Communicator Variables

Duke is attempting to run from his past by repackaging himself as a populist. His affable, game-show-host looks and just-folks manner have been insidiously successful in blunting the impact of a past pocked with racism, Jew-hating and revisionism.

—*Newsweek,* November 18, 1991

You probably do not find Adolf Hitler a very credible communicator. How about David Duke? In order to gain greater credibility, Duke dissociated himself from fringe organizations he previously had embraced (such as the American Nazi Party and the Ku Klux Klan), adopted mainstream political rhetoric, and even underwent cosmetic surgery to achieve a more pleasing appearance.

Does a communicator's credibility in fact influence his or her persuasiveness, and what makes a communicator credible or noncredible? In a classic study, Carl Hovland and Walter Weiss (1951) studied the effects of the communicator's credibility on attitude change. Subjects read an article arguing for the practicality of building nuclear-powered submarines. (This was before such submarines actually existed.) One group of subjects was told the article was by J. Robert Oppenheimer, a famous and respected physicist; another group was told the article came from the Soviet newspaper *Pravda.* The researchers presumed, of course, that Oppenheimer was a high-credibility source and *Pravda* a low-credibility source.

The 1992 Presidential candidates. Their debate illustrates a number of factors that influence persuasion, such as speaker attractiveness and credibility and the use of emotional appeals and one-sided versus two-sided messages.

It probably comes as no surprise that the high-credibility source produced more attitude change as measured immediately after delivery of the persuasive message than the low-credibility source, even though the actual message was the same in both cases. Taken together with similar studies on other communicator characteristics (such as expertness, trustworthiness, prestige, and attractiveness, all of which seem to enhance credibility), this research shows that persuasion may sometimes result from speaker appeal rather than the logic, believability, or rationality of the message itself.

Communicator variables (such as credibility, status, and attractiveness) are often used to good effect in advertising. When a "hidden camera" shows "real people" endorsing a product, advertisers are hoping we will view the speakers as unbiased and credible. And, of course, celebrities—frequently highly attractive ones—deliver persuasive messages in commercials as well. Sometimes the expertise, credibility, and attractiveness of the spokesperson (as in the famous TV ad campaign in which football star Joe Namath sold panty hose) have very little to do with the product itself. Recent research supports advertisers' intuitions that speakers perceived to be attractive, credible, expert, trustworthy, and unbiased are indeed more persuasive (Andreoli & Worchel, 1978; Bochner & Insko, 1966; Chaiken, 1979; Craig & McCann, 1978; Petty & Cacioppo, 1981). The effects of such speaker variables on persuasion are greatest, however, when the targeted attitudes are not very important to the recipient, and they tend to fade quickly (Chaiken, 1987).

Message Variables

[Duke's] coded distillations of white economic and racial resentment are by now the most thoroughly decoded in American politics. They include "crime in the streets" (black-on-white crime), "welfare illegitimacy" (black unwed mothers), "affirmative action" (black economic advancement) and "heritage" (whites first).

—*Newsweek,* November 18, 1991

Even allowing for communicator variables such as credibility and attractiveness, some messages are more persuasive than others, regardless of their source. Three message characteristics that have been shown to influence persuasion are: (1) the degree to which the message evokes fear, (2) whether the message uses one-sided or two-sided arguments, and (3) message repetition. Let's briefly review the findings about each of these factors.

Is fear an effective way to change people's attitudes? Leventhal (1970) found that high-fear messages work under certain conditions. First, the message must arouse substantial fear (for example, you must convince a person who engages in unsafe sexual practices that they are in fact dangerous). Second, the recipient of the message must be convinced that if the recommendation in the message (to practice safe sex) is not followed, fearful outcomes (disease, death) are quite likely to occur.

And finally, the recipient must be convinced that heeding the message's recommendations will indeed eliminate the fearful outcomes (engaging in safe sex very much reduces the risk of contracting sexually transmitted diseases such as AIDS). If a persuasive message frightens without providing an easy way to reduce fear, however, it may be ignored, rejected, or denied by the recipient (Jepson & Chaiken, 1986).

To be effective, should persuasive messages be one-sided or two-sided? Hitler cynically wrote in *Mein Kampf* that "all effective propaganda must be limited to a very few points and must harp on these in slogans until the last member of the public understands. . . . As soon as you sacrifice this slogan and try to be many-sided, the effect will piddle away." (p. 181). Was he correct?

Hovland, Lumsdaine, and Sheffield (1949) addressed this question in a study during World War II that presented American soldiers with a message arguing that the Pacific war might continue for a long time. Some soldiers heard a one-sided message that stressed only Japan's resources and strengths, whereas other soldiers heard a two-sided message that also provided, and refuted, several arguments for Japan's weakness. This research found no *overall* differences in how much soldiers in the two groups were persuaded. However, soldiers who initially agreed that the Pacific war would be long were more persuaded by one-sided arguments supporting that position, whereas soldiers who initially disagreed with the message were more persuaded by the two-sided arguments. The general principle seems to be: Use one-sided arguments with people who already tend to agree with you, but use two-sided arguments with people who disagree with you.

Two-sided messages have yet another advantage over one-sided messages: They make people more resistant to later arguments against the original message (Lumsdaine & Janis, 1953). This finding led William McGuire (1964) to propose that people can be "inoculated" against persuasive messages. To become resistant to strong persuasive messages, McGuire argued, people should first be exposed to messages that weakly attack their beliefs and attitudes. Note that this relates to one-sided versus two-sided messages in the following way: To make people resistant to later persuasion, it is not sufficient to give them only "pro" arguments supporting their beliefs and attitudes; we must also give them "con" arguments that attack their beliefs, so they can build up their defenses against such arguments.

McGuire and Papageorgis (1961) demonstrated the effectiveness of inoculation in a study that attacked people's common cultural beliefs (for example, "You should brush your teeth after every meal"). Two days before hearing a strong attack on their beliefs, one group of subjects heard arguments affirming their beliefs, whereas another (inoculation) group heard both attacks on their beliefs and refutations of these attacks (a kind of two-sided message). The inoculated subjects proved to be much more resistant to the subsequent strong attack than subjects exposed only to supportive arguments. Inoculation techniques have subsequently been used to help children think critically about unscrupulous TV ads (Feshbach, 1980) and to resist peer and media pressure to smoke (Evans, Smith, & Raines, 1984; Flay et al., 1985; McAlister et al., 1980). Inoculation has also been used to reduce the impact of negative political ads—that is, when voters view "inoculation" ads that refute the content of attack ads, they are less likely to change their attitudes when they view later attack ads (Pfau & Bergoon, 1988).

Message repetition is the final message variable we shall consider. Advertisers seem convinced that the more they repeat a message, the better, and politicians' media consultants seem to agree. How many times have you heard that "Coke is it" or that phoning a far-off friend or relative is the way to "reach out and touch someone," and how many times have you heard political candidates repeat the same themes on TV during the week before Election Day? Does repetition enhance persuasion? Two lines of evidence answer this question with a qualified yes.

First, many studies show that simply being exposed repeatedly to a stimulus, on average, increases our liking for that stimulus (Bornstein, 1989; Zajonc, 1968). This *mere exposure effect* occurs for sounds, abstract symbols, words, and even people. How does this relate to attitude change? If you hear the jingle for Coke and see pictures of Coke cans thousands of times during your life, your attitude toward Coke may become more positive, and you may be more likely to buy it than a competing brand.

If you feel personally immune to the mere exposure effect in advertising, tally up the number of name-brand products you purchase. Although consumer magazines tell us that generic products are often as good, many of us feel safer and more comfortable buying name brands, even though they are considerably more expensive. This may be attributable in part to mere exposure.

Research on mere exposure effects typically studies how repeated exposure to stimuli (brand names, people, pictures, songs) affects our "gut-liking" for them. Other studies have investigated how repetition of an assertion or argument affects comprehension and subsequent persuasion. Recent research suggests that the more times you hear or read an assertion, the more likely you are to believe it is true (Arkes, Boehm, & Xu, 1991), and research on repeating messages suggests that *some* repetition can be a good thing. Wilson and Miller (1968), for example, found that presenting legal arguments in a jury trial three times was more effective than a single presentation; such repetition led subjects to remember the arguments better and to agree with them more strongly. Moderate repetition may make messages more persuasive by helping us comprehend and retain them.

Sometimes repetition can be overdone. Whereas many repetitions foster retention of arguments, they can also lead to *reduced* attitude change (Cacioppo & Petty, 1979, 1980; Gorn & Goldberg, 1980). Perhaps people become irritated and bored by too much repetition (Bornstein, Kale, & Cornell, 1990). Advertisers try to avoid these negative effects of repetition by using the technique of "repetition with variation"—that is, they repeat the same message in different ways in different kinds of ads. Apparently, repetition with variation works, for when ads are varied, people tend to adopt more favorable attitudes toward advertised products with increased exposure to ads, particularly when they don't think carefully about the ads (Schumann, Petty, & Clemons, 1990).

Channel Variables

The Louisiana Democratic Party began airing ads focusing on Duke's neo-Nazi roots ("Vote for Duke. Create a Fuehrer," says one tag line).

—*Newsweek,* November 18, 1991

Persuasive messages come to us via many channels: newspapers, magazines, radio, television, videos, movies, computerized mail. Which channel of communication is most persuasive? If you answered, "It depends," then you agree with research findings on this question. There is no single best channel of persuasion; rather, each is suited to different goals and purposes.

Face-to-face persuasion often proves to have more impact than persuasion through the mass media (Berelson, Lazarsfeld, & McPhee, 1954; Katz & Lazarsfeld, 1955). This phenomenon is probably the result of several factors. Face-to-face communicators are more attention-grabbing, and thus they often stimulate more thought and commitment to their messages. It is easier to mentally turn off a written or mass-media message.

The mass media have a major advantage, however, over face-to-face communication: They can readily reach huge numbers of people. Print media (newspapers, magazines, written briefs) possess the additional advantage that they are better comprehended, particularly when the persuasive message is complex. When messages are simple and relatively easy to comprehend, people seem to yield more to audio or audiovisual messages (Chaiken & Eagly, 1976), perhaps because people think more critically about written material than they do about other kinds of persuasive messages (Maier & Thurber, 1968). At the very least, written material allows the reader to go back and reread information that is missed or misunderstood the first time around.

Because written messages seem to generate more thought, they may be affected less by such "superficial" communicator variables as attractiveness, likability, and credibility. Audio and audiovisual messages tend to focus more attention on the speaker and thus heighten the impact of these superficial variables.

An experiment by Chaiken and Eagly (1983) provides a good example. Psychology students at the University of Toronto received a persuasive message prepared by a "college administrator" arguing for higher tuition and reduced student grants. Written, tape-recorded, or videotaped versions of the message were presented to different groups of students. The administrator's likability was varied independently of the channel of communication, by reporting that he had made comments that were either flattering or unflattering about University of Toronto students. After receiving the persuasive message, subjects rated their attitudes about higher tuition and reduced student grants and wrote down all their thoughts about both the speaker and the message.

Chaiken and Eagly found that the speaker's persuasiveness depended on both his likability and the channel of communication (see Figure 6.6). When the communicator was likable, he was more persuasive in audiotapes and videotapes, but when he was unlikable, he was more persuasive in a written message. Furthermore, subjects exposed to the audiotapes and videotapes listed more thoughts *about the speaker* than did subjects who read the written message. These thoughts tended to be negative when the speaker was unlikable and positive when he was likable. In other words, audio and visual media tended to pull recipients' thoughts away from the message and focus them more on the speaker and his attributes.

The practical implication of this research is that an attractive, likable, and charismatic speaker is often more persuasive in audio or audiovisual messages, whereas a speaker who is not attractive (but who may be logically convincing) is

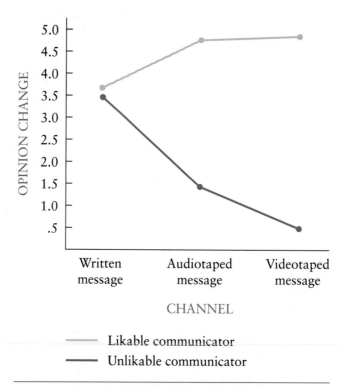

FIGURE 6.6 Do "superficial" communicator variables have more persuasive an effect in some channels of communication than in others? *Source:* Data from Chaiken and Eagly (1983).

more persuasive in print messages. A famous political example provides a case in point: Before the first presidential debate of 1960, John Kennedy was the underdog and Richard Nixon the clear front-runner. During the first debate, Kennedy—tanned, relaxed, and charismatic—was generally perceived to be more persuasive than the pale, wooden, perspiring Nixon (Kraus, 1962; White, 1961). However, many of those who read transcripts of the debate or heard it on radio perceived Nixon to be the winner. Television—a medium that highlights speaker variables and reduces attention to message content—favored Kennedy, who went on to win a very narrow victory over Nixon in the election.

Target or Audience Variables

While Duke has clearly energized a significant anti-black constituency, it's a mistake to write off all his supporters as racists. A moribund economy and anti-incumbent anger have strengthened his hand, causing increasing numbers of Louisianans to discount his radical roots and focus on his no-tax, less-government message.

—*Newsweek,* November 4, 1991

The final factor in the communication model of persuasion is the target or audience. David Duke clearly tailored his speeches to his audiences. He toned down the radical, racist speech of his past and focused instead on racial "code words" and mainstream political issues. To be truly effective, must persuasive messages be tailored to specific audiences, and are there audience variables that have a consistent effect on persuasion?

Research in the Yale tradition investigated a number of audience variables, including intelligence, personality traits (for example, self-esteem), and gender. The results of this research are fairly complex and inconsistent, perhaps because such variables may have opposing effects at different stages of persuasion (McGuire, 1968a, 1968b; Petty & Cacioppo, 1981; Rhodes & Wood, 1992). Intelligence, for example, may *increase* people's comprehension of a persuasive message but *decrease* the degree to which they yield to the message (presumably because an intelligent person can understand arguments better but also can evaluate those arguments more critically). Consistent with this analysis, research shows that a high intelligence enhances persuasion when the message is complex and sound, but decreases persuasion when the message is simple and flawed (Eagly & Warren, 1976).

Like intelligence, self-esteem may increase people's comprehension of a message (people with high self-esteem are less distracted and withdrawn than those with low self-esteem) but decrease yielding (high-self-esteem people have confidence in their own opinions and so are less likely to yield to persuasion). Because of the opposing impact of self-esteem on comprehension and yielding, studies find on average that people possessing *moderate* levels of self-esteem are more readily persuaded than people possessing either low or high levels (Rhodes & Wood, 1992). Apparently, people with moderate self-esteem have high enough self-esteem that they pay attention to the message, but not so high that they are unwilling to budge from their preexisting positions.

A person's tendency to think about arguments in persuasive messages is yet another trait that can influence persuadability. Cacioppo and Petty (1982) developed a scale to measure an individual's "need for cognition" (see Figure 6.7); people with high scores on this scale like to think and actively strive to understand information, whereas people with low scores use mental shortcuts whenever possible and think only as much as is necessary.

People who differ in their need for cognition show quite different responses to persuasive messages (Petty & Cacioppo, 1986). In one study, undergraduate women measured on need for cognition read a proposal arguing that tuition be raised at their university (Cacioppo, Petty, & Morris, 1983). One group of women read a proposal with weak arguments; another read one with strong arguments. The results showed that women with a high need for cognition were more influenced by argument quality than women with a low need for cognition; because they thought a lot about the arguments, women with a high need for cognition were more likely to see the weaknesses of the weak arguments and the strengths of the strong arguments.

Summary Table 6.3 presents the main findings we have examined about the effects of communicator, message, channel, and audience variables on persuasion.

Subjects are asked to respond to the items on scales indicating their "agreement" or "disagreement," or to rate the extent to which the statements are "characteristic" or "uncharacteristic" of them.

1. I would prefer complex to simple problems.
2. I like to have the responsibility of handling a situation that requires a lot of thinking.
3. Thinking is not my idea of fun.
4. I would rather do something that requires little thought than something that is sure to challenge my thinking abilities.
5. I try to anticipate and avoid situations where there is a likely chance I will have to think in depth about something.
6. I find satisfaction in deliberating hard and for long hours.
7. I think only as hard as I have to.
8. I prefer to think about small, daily projects rather than long-term ones.
9. I like tasks that require little thought once I've learned them.
10. The idea of relying on thought to make my way to the top appeals to me.
11. I really enjoy a task that involves coming up with new solutions to problems.
12. Learning new ways to think doesn't excite me very much.
13. I prefer my life to be filled with puzzles that I must solve.
14. The notion of thinking abstractly is appealing to me.
15. I would prefer a task that is intellectual, difficult, and important to one that is somewhat important but does not require much thought.
16. I feel relief rather than satisfaction after completing a task that required a lot of mental effort.
17. It's enough for me that something gets the job done; I don't care how or why it works.
18. I usually end up deliberating about issues even when they do not affect me personally.

Note: Items 3, 4, 5, 7, 8, 9, 12, 16, and 17 are reverse-scored.

FIGURE 6.7 Items from the "Need for Cognition Scale." *Source:* Adapted from Cacioppo and Petty (1982).

The Cognitive Approach to Persuasion

If David Duke gets beaten for governor of Louisiana, the key factor won't be his record as a Klansman and a neo-Nazi. He will lose because the businessmen of Louisiana convinced the state's voters that Duke in the statehouse would be an economic disaster. In apocalyptic chorus, leaders of business and industry

SUMMARY TABLE 6.3 The Communication Model of Persuasion—Findings on Communicator, Message, Channel, and Audience Variables

Communicator Variables

Communicators who are perceived to be credible, trustworthy, expert, and attractive are more persuasive. However, the effects of such variables tend to be short-lived.

Fear-producing messages can be persuasive if they don't arouse too much fear and when they present concrete advice on how to avoid or prevent fearful outcome.

Message Variables

One-sided messages are more effective with people who already agree with the message, whereas two-sided messages are more effective with those who disagree.

Two-sided messages are more effective than one-sided messages in making people resistant to later "counter-propaganda." This finding stimulated research on inoculation—exposing people to attacks on their beliefs and attitudes to make them more resistant to later attacks.

Message repetition can enhance persuasion because of mere exposure effects and increased message comprehension and retention. But too much repetition can lead to reduced attitude change.

Channel Variables

Face-to-face persuasion is on-average more effective than persuasion via mass media, but mass media can reach much larger numbers of people.

Audio-visual channels tend to focus people's attention more on superficial communicator characteristics (such as attractiveness) whereas print media tend to focus attention more on the quality of message arguments and contents.

Audience Variables

Highly intelligent people are more likely than less intelligent people to be persuaded by complex and cogent arguments.

People with moderate self-esteem are more easily persuaded than are people with low or high self-esteem.

People with a high need for cognition think more carefully than people with a low need for cognition, and as a result, may respond more to the quality of arguments.

were warning last week that Duke's election would mean huge losses of income and jobs from tourism, conventions, investment funds and national sporting events.

—*Newsweek,* November 18, 1991

The voters of Louisiana were the targets of a barrage of persuasive messages. Ultimately, they had to *think* about the contents of all these messages. Whereas the Yale research focused on stages of communication during persuasion, recent cognitive approaches have focused more on the *thought processes* people engage in as the targets of persuasion (Greenwald, 1968; Petty & Cacioppo, 1981). This cognitive perspective has led to important new ways of conceptualizing persuasion.

Lazy versus Thoughtful Processing of Persuasive Messages

Much recent evidence suggests that some kinds of persuasion succeed because of quick and "lazy" thought processes on the part of the target, whereas other kinds result from more careful and conscientious thought (Chaiken, 1980, 1987; Eagly & Chaiken, 1984, 1993; Petty & Cacioppo, 1986). Two important models of persuasion, the elaboration likelihood model and the heuristic model, have emphasized this distinction.

According to the *elaboration likelihood model* of Petty and Cacioppo (1981, 1986), persuasion critically depends on the degree to which people elaborate (that is, actively think about) the contents of a persuasive message. The *central route* to persuasion is the "thoughtful" route that involves active thought; the *peripheral route* is the "lazy" route that does not. People follow the central route when they consciously deliberate on the merit, content, and logic of the persuasive message; they follow the peripheral route when they do not carefully reflect on the content of the message but instead rely on simple, superficial cues (such as who's delivering the message) to accept or reject the message. People typically follow the central route to persuasion when the message is personally relevant and important to them; they follow the peripheral route when they do not care much about the message.

The *heuristic model of persuasion* makes a similar distinction between lazy and thoughtful processing of persuasive messages (Chaiken, 1980, 1987). You may recall from Chapter 5 that a heuristic is a simple mental rule of thumb we use to arrive at quick answers or estimates. Chaiken (1980, 1987) argues that when people are *not* personally involved with the topic of a persuasive message, they change their attitudes according to simple heuristics (for example, "Educated people are generally right" or "The more arguments, the more persuaded I am"). When people *are* personally involved with the topic of persuasion, they engage in a more careful, thoughtful analysis of the message and its contents.

The distinction between thoughtful and lazy processing of a persuasive message has a number of important implications. First, many studies find that thoughtful processing leads to more lasting attitudes and attitude change than lazy processing does (Chaiken, 1980, 1987; Cialdini, Levy, Herman, Kozlowski, & Petty, 1976; Petty & Cacioppo, 1986). Because it involves time-consuming consideration of information, thoughtful processing results in attitudes that are highly accessible and easily remembered (Fazio, 1990). Lazy processing, because it is based on transient and superficial cues (such as the sheer number of arguments), results in attitudes that are often temporary and easily forgotten. Not surprisingly, attitudes resulting from thoughtful kinds of processing predict behavior better than attitudes resulting from lazy kinds do (Fazio, 1990; Pallak, Murroni, & Koch, 1983; Petty, Cacioppo, & Schumann, 1983).

Many studies in the Yale tradition can be interpreted in terms of thoughtful versus lazy processing. For example, research on communicator variables such as credibility and attractiveness tend to focus on lazy kinds of processing that are quite transient. The repetition of logically compelling arguments enhances persuasion to the extent it induces people to understand and think about the arguments. Some channels of persuasion (for example, TV) seem to encourage lazy processing based on superficial cues, whereas others (print media) encourage more active and critical thought. Finally, audience variables such as intelligence and need for cognition influence persuasion partly through their influence on active, critical thought. See Summary Table 6.4 for a brief description of lazy versus thoughtful kinds of processing of persuasive messages and research findings relevant to each.

Forewarning and Active Thought

As we just noted, the cognitive perspective holds that thoughtful processing involves active awareness in which people think about persuasive messages, mull them over, generate counterarguments, and so on. Consistent with this perspective, several lines of research show that our *cognitive responses* (that is, our internal arguments for or against a persuasive message) have a large effect on persuasion (Greenwald, 1968; Petty & Cacioppo, 1981).

One piece of evidence for the role of active thought in persuasion is provided by the *forewarning effect*: Merely warning people ahead of time that they will be the target of attempted persuasion makes them more resistant to it. Like inoculation effects, this occurs because forewarned people mentally argue against the (in this case, anticipated) persuasive message.

In one study on the forewarning effect, college students heard a "guest lecturer" advocate that all college freshmen and sophomores be required to live in college dorms—a topic highly relevant to the subjects (Petty & Cacioppo, 1977). Some subjects were told about the topic a few minutes before the lecture, whereas others were simply informed that they would hear a lecture by a counseling-center psychologist. The students were asked to list their thoughts in general before hearing the lecture, and afterward they completed questionnaires that assessed how persuaded they were by the speaker. Subjects who were forewarned generated more arguments against the message and ultimately disagreed with it to a greater extent than did subjects who were not forewarned.

Mood and Active Thought

Do you think that people tend to be more persuaded when they are happy or when they are sad? You might guess that people in good moods generally are easier to persuade than people in bad moods. However, the cognitive approach to persuasion offers a more complex (and perhaps surprising) answer to this question: People in good moods are more likely to engage in lazy processing of persuasive messages, whereas people in bad moods are more likely to engage in thoughtful processing. Because of this, people in bad moods are more responsive to the quality of arguments in a persuasive message than people in good moods are (Mackie & Worth, 1989; Schwarz, Bless, & Bohner, 1991).

One experiment demonstrated this principle by first creating either good or bad moods in a group of German university women by asking them to describe either a pleasant or unpleasant event in their lives. The researchers then presented

SUMMARY TABLE 6.4 Lazy versus Thoughtful Processing of Persuasive Messages

Description	Associated Research Findings	Implications for Resulting Attitudes
Lazy Processing Termed "the peripheral route to persuasion" in the elaboration likelihood model and "persuasion based on heuristics" in the heuristic model of persuasion. The person receiving the persuasive message relies on superficial cues and simple mental rules of thumb rather than actively thinking about the contents of the message.	Occurs when people find message irrelevant and not personally involving More likely when message contents are not related to attitude's function More likely with messages presented via audio-visual channels Stimulated by superficial communicator variables More likely with people who are low in need for cognition More likely when people are in good moods	Attitudes are weak, short-lived, and do not predict behavior strongly
Thoughtful Processing Termed "the central route to persuasion" in the elaboration likelihood model. The person receiving the persuasive message thinks carefully and actively about the contents of the message.	Occurs when people find message relevant and personally involving More likely when message contents are related to the attitude's function More likely with messages presented via print media Stimulated by forewarning More likely with people who are high in need for cognition More likely when people are in bad moods	Attitudes are strong, long-lasting, and strongly predict behavior

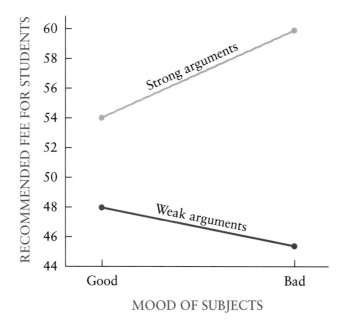

Subjects in a bad mood respond more to argument quality than do subjects in a good mood.

FIGURE 6.8 Attitude change as a function of mood and argument quality. *Source:* Bless, Bohner, Schwarz, and Strack (1990).

the women with a tape-recorded speech that contained either weak or strong arguments in favor of raising student fees (Bless, Bohner, Schwarz, & Strack, 1990). The results showed that women in a bad mood were highly sensitive to the quality of arguments—they were much more persuaded by strong arguments than weak arguments—whereas women in a good mood did not respond as much to the quality of arguments (see Figure 6.8).

You might be wondering why people in a bad mood think more carefully about persuasive messages. One possibility is that negative emotions typically signal "things are not okay." Thus, negative emotions alert us to problems, which we must pay attention to and think carefully about. Good moods signal "everything's all right," and when we are in a good mood, we are more likely to go on blissful "automatic pilot" and not think carefully about what we hear.

Attitude Functions and Active Thought

There is another important factor that determines when we are likely to think carefully about a persuasive message—namely, whether the persuasive message contains arguments that are relevant to the function the target attitude serves in us (Shavitt, 1989, 1990; Snyder & Debono, 1989). As noted earlier, some attitudes (such as those toward brands of coffee) generally serve an instrumental function. That is, they help bring us rewards and avoid costs. Other attitudes (for example, toward brands of perfume) serve a social identity function—they signal the kind of person we are.

To show the effect of attitude functions on persuasion, Sharon Shavitt (1990) developed ads for consumer products (such as coffee and perfume) that focused on either the instrumental qualities of the product (for example, "The delicious, hearty flavor and aroma of Sterling Blend Coffee come from a blend of the freshest coffee beans") or on the social identity of people who buy the product ("The coffee you drink says something about the type of person you are. It can reveal your rare, discriminating taste").

Shavitt found that ads were most persuasive when they addressed the functions served by their target attitudes. Coffee ads that focused on product quality were more persuasive than those focusing on the consumer's social identity, but the reverse was true for perfume ads. Presumably, consumers think more about advertising messages when they address topics relevant to the function served by the attitude. Should ads then in general focus on the product's characteristics or on the consumer's social identity? Shavitt's research shows that the answer depends on the kind of product you are trying to sell.

The answer also depends on the personality of the consumer. Specifically, recent research shows (as we noted in Chapter 3) that low-self-monitoring consumers tend to be more persuaded by ads that address the product's quality (for example, this car is safe, reliable, and fuel-efficient), whereas high-self-monitoring consumers tend to be more persuaded by ads that address the consumer's social identity (this car is "sexy" and has a high-status image) (Snyder & DeBono, 1989).

We have covered a lot of territory in our discussion of persuasion. We started by looking at persuasion as a communication process, examining the effects of communicator, message, target, and channel variables. Then we considered the kinds of thought processes that are triggered by persuasive messages. In one way or another, all the research on persuasion that we've discussed so far addresses one core issue: When are persuasive messages effective in changing our attitudes?

We conclude our discussion of attitude change with a different, and perhaps counterintuitive, perspective—that sometimes we change our own attitudes when we behave in ways that contradict them. This is the central message of research on cognitive dissonance.

COGNITIVE DISSONANCE: WHEN OUR BEHAVIOR LEADS US TO CHANGE OUR ATTITUDES

"I used to be a white-power skinhead," says 14-year-old David Michael Alexander. . . . In the summer of 1990, as he was about to enter seventh grade, Dave's white-power involvement began with the shaving of his head. He became a self-made neo-Nazi skinhead. . . . He grew bolder, putting swastikas in his locker, flaunting his "Heil Hitler" salute, making racist comments, fighting with classmates. . . . Dave is still a skinhead. But now he's vice president of the Detroit chapter of Skin Heads Against Racial Prejudice [SHARP]. . . . Dave gives credit for his transformation to a young black man named Keith, who worked at a record store. Dave ducked into the store one afternoon to escape a group of Albanian kids he'd been taunting. Keith started telling him about SHARP. "At first I thought, oh, man, go to hell," Dave says. "But then I started listening to him." The two went to a few concerts, and Dave thought, "Hey, this guy is cool, and he's black."

—Knight-Ridder News Service, May 23, 1992

What led Dave to change his racist attitudes? Perhaps Dave was directly persuaded by Keith. But there is another possibility as well: When Dave went to concerts with his new black acquaintance, he was behaving in ways that were grossly inconsistent with his neo-Nazi attitudes. Perhaps this inconsistency was uncomfortable and motivated him to change his attitudes. This is the sequence of events predicted by Leon Festinger's theory of cognitive dissonance.

Cognitive Dissonance Theory

Dissonance theory proposes that when people behave inconsistently with their attitudes (and thus hold inconsistent beliefs about what they think and how they act), they experience an unpleasant state of arousal called *cognitive dissonance*. Festinger suggested two main ways people can reduce dissonance: They can change their behavior, or they can change their beliefs and attitudes. Thus, when Dave goes to a concert with his new black acquaintance, he experiences dissonance, which is unpleasant. He can reduce his dissonance by not seeing his friend again (changing his behavior) or by becoming less prejudiced toward blacks (changing his attitudes).

Demonstrating Dissonance in the Laboratory

Dissonance theory has led to many clever research studies. We shall focus on three main kinds: studies on insufficient justification, justification of effort, and derogation of the victim.

Insufficient Justification: When Small Incentives Lead to Large Attitude Shifts

In which of the following two cases do you think Dave would feel more dissonance? (1) He goes to concerts with a new black acquaintance "for no good reason." (2) He goes to concerts with a new black acquaintance because his probation officer ordered him to do so as part of the terms of his probation.

Dissonance theorists would argue that Dave should experience more dissonance in the first case, because he would have behaved in a manner highly inconsistent with his attitudes, but he would have had little justification for

Cigarette smokers may experience dissonance when they try to reconcile negative facts about smoking with their behavior. One way they reduce dissonance is to change their beliefs.

his inconsistency. If Dave's probation officer had forced him to interact with a black acquaintance, however, Dave could "explain away" his behavior as resulting from external pressure and thus not feel upset over his inconsistent actions.

The general principle of *insufficient justification* is this: When we engage in attitude-discrepant behavior for small external incentives, we are more likely to experience dissonance and change our attitudes. In a classic experiment demonstrating this principle, Leon Festinger and J. Merrill Carlsmith (1959) paid Stanford subjects either $1 or $20 to convince another student that two boring experimental tasks they had just performed were in fact fun and interesting. Afterward, the subjects who had lied were asked to rate how fun and interesting they actually had found the boring tasks to be. Which group do you think would be more likely to change their attitude toward the boring task—those who were paid $1 to lie about how interesting the task was, or those who received $20?

Dissonance theory predicts that subjects who got $1 to lie would show more attitude change than those who were paid $20. After all, they had little justification for lying—only one measly dollar—whereas the subjects who received $20 had considerable external incentive to behave inconsistently with their true attitudes. As dissonance theory predicts, the $1 subjects did in fact tend to rate the boring task favorably, whereas $20 subjects as well as control subjects (who simply performed the boring task and then rated it without having to lie to others about it) rated it as boring. See Figure 6.9 for the results of this study.

Cohen (1962) obtained similar findings when he asked students at Yale University to write counterattitudinal essays for varying amounts of money. Specifically, Cohen asked his subjects to write essays *in favor of* the New Haven police. Because the police had recently been accused of behaving brutally during a student demonstration, student opinion was generally against the police. As in the Festinger and Carlsmith study, subjects were offered different amounts of money to behave inconsistently with their attitudes—in this case, either 50 cents, $1, $5, or $10 to write their essay in favor of the police.

After writing their essays, subjects were asked to rate their actual attitudes toward the New Haven police. Consistent with dissonance theory, the subjects who were paid 50 cents shifted their attitudes most (in a direction more favorable to the police), whereas the subjects paid $10 showed no attitude change; they were still

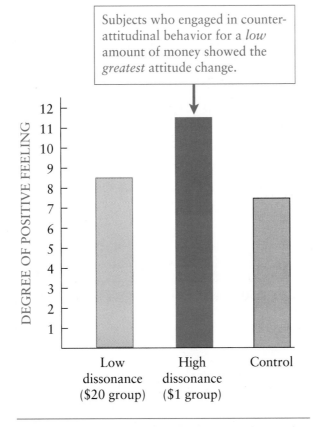

FIGURE 6.9 Cognitive dissonance and attitude change: The results of the Festinger and Carlsmith study. *Source:* Data from Festinger and Carlsmith (1959).

against the police, as were the members of a control group who wrote no essays at all. The subjects who were paid $1 and $5 showed intermediate amounts of attitude change (see Figure 6.10).

Justification of Effort: When We Come to Like What We Suffer for

Why do you think fraternities commonly put prospective members through unpleasant hazings or embarrassing initiation rites? Dissonance theory offers the following analysis: A pledge who is accepted into a fraternity after undergoing a humiliating hazing will experience considerable dissonance if he then decides the fraternity is a "loser." To reduce his dissonance, the pledge comes to like the fraternity *more* after his hazing—in essence to justify his painful experience.

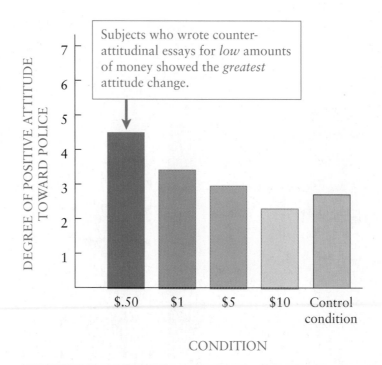

FIGURE 6.10 Insufficient justification and attitude change: Results of the Cohen (1962) study. *Source:* Adapted from Cohen (1962).

In other words, dissonance theory predicts that we sometimes come to like things that we suffer for. Research on *justification of effort* (sometimes called *severity of initiation*) provides support for this principle (Gerard & Mathewson, 1966). In one experiment, college women were invited to participate in a group discussion on the topic of sex, but first they had to take a "screening test" (Aronson & Mills, 1959). Some subjects were given a rather mild "test," which consisted of their reading a list of relatively nonthreatening words with sexual meanings, such as *petting* and *prostitute*. Other subjects underwent a much more embarrassing test that required them to read lists of obscenities and passages from explicit, erotic novels.

After their test, subjects listened over earphones to what they believed was an ongoing group discussion of sex. In reality, the subjects heard a tape-recorded discussion that had been constructed by the researchers to be dull and pointless. The subjects were then asked to rate how interesting they found the group discussion to be. The results: Subjects who had taken the highly embarrassing screening test decided that the discussion group was interesting and worthwhile, whereas those who had taken the mild screening test rated the discussion group to be uninteresting, as did a control group that had had no initiation ("test") at all.

A dangerous fraternity initiation rite. The funnel and tube were used to force large amounts of alcohol into the mouths of unwilling initiates. Do fraternity pledges like their fraternity more after participating in such unpleasant and embarassing rites?

Derogation of the Victim: When Bad Behavior Leads to Negative Attitudes

Dissonance theory makes the unsettling prediction that if we behave badly toward another person, particularly with little justification, we will shift our beliefs and attitudes to justify our bad behavior—that is, we will come to think of our victim negatively. The application of dissonance theory to this derogation of the victim is fairly straightforward. Most of us consider ourselves to be decent, moral people who would not inflict harm on innocent victims. Thus, in a situation where we have harmed an innocent victim, dissonance is aroused. If we can't take back the harmful behavior, the only way to reduce dissonance may be to decide that the victim was "bad" and really deserved ill-treatment. Research studies provide convincing evidence that victim derogation actually occurs (for example, Davis & Jones, 1960; Glass, 1964).

Qualifications to Dissonance Theory

Dissonance is not always aroused when we behave inconsistently with our attitudes. Rather, certain special conditions must be met for attitude-discrepant behavior to arouse dissonance and induce attitude change. First, people must feel that their attitude-discrepant behavior is *freely chosen* and that they are personally responsible for it. Second, they must feel that their attitude-discrepant behavior is *firmly committed and irrevocable*. Third, they must believe their behavior has important *consequences* for others. Finally, dissonance is aroused particularly when people behave inconsistently with attitudes that are *central to their self-concept and related to their basic sense of worthiness* (see Figure 6.11).

Perceived Choice

Linder, Cooper, and Jones (1967) demonstrated the importance of perceived choice in a study that asked subjects to write counterattitudinal essays advocating that controversial speakers be barred from their university. Some subjects were virtually ordered to write their essays, whereas others were *asked* to write their essays and informed that the decision to write the essays was their own. As in many dissonance experiments, subjects were offered either small or large amounts of money to write their counterattitudinal essays. The expected results—that smaller amounts of money produce larger attitude shifts—occurred only among subjects who chose to write their essays. Subjects given no choice actually displayed incentive effects—that is, the larger amount of money produced *greater* attitude change.

Commitment and Irrevocability

Dissonance occurs particularly when our attitude-discrepant behavior is firmly committed and irrevocable. Keith Davis and Edward Jones (1960) demonstrated this clearly in an experiment on victim derogation. They asked subjects to deliver negative evaluations directly to another "innocent" subject (actually a confederate). This set the stage for subjects to derogate their victim—to decide that the reason they had said mean things to the other subject was that she really *was* unlikable.

Davis and Jones added two other factors to their experiment: subjects' perceived choice and the irrevocability of their behavior. The researchers ordered some subjects to deliver their nasty evaluations but asked others to do so voluntarily. Furthermore, the experimenter told some subjects that they would be able to meet their "victim" after the experiment and "take back" the bad things they had said; other subjects were told that they would not meet their victim again and that she would continue to believe the subjects' nasty comments.

Davis and Jones predicted that subjects in the *irrevocable-choice* condition would experience the most dissonance because they would feel responsible for their bad behavior and powerless to correct it. Indeed, the most derogation of the victim (and presumably the highest dissonance arousal) occurred for subjects in this condition.

Consequences of Behavior

Suppose I ask you to write an essay advocating higher tuition at your college (which is probably a counterattitudinal essay for you). Further, imagine the following different consequences of writing this essay: I rip up your essay immediately after

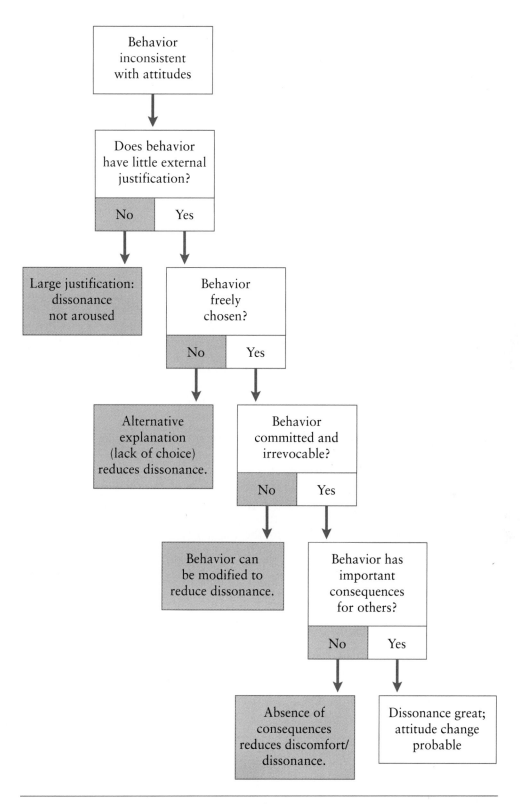

FIGURE 6.11 Qualifying conditions affecting the impact of dissonance on attitude change.

you write it and say it was just an exercise; I inform you that I will use your essay in an attitude-change study that seeks to change other students' attitudes about raising tuition; or I inform you that I will use your essay in a statewide publicity campaign to raise college tuition. Wouldn't you experience more dissonance over writing your essay in the final circumstance? The more you perceive your counterattitudinal behavior to have real-life consequences, the more uncomfortable you will feel and thus the more motivated you will be to shift your attitudes to resolve dissonance. Several studies support this general proposition (for example, Collins & Hoyt, 1972; Cooper & Worchel, 1970).

Dissonance and the Self-Concept

Aronson (1969) proposed that counterattitudinal behavior leads to dissonance particularly for those attitudes that are important or central to one's self-concept. In a related vein, Steele (1988) argued that we experience dissonance particularly when we behave in ways that make us feel bad or worthless and that threaten our self-esteem. Note that in many of the dissonance experiments we have described, subjects don't simply behave in ways that are inconsistent with their attitudes; they lie, they say nasty things to innocent victims—that is, they behave in ways that threaten their basic self-concept as decent, honest, worthy people.

Is It Inconsistency That Leads to Dissonance?

A number of alternate explanations have been offered for the findings of dissonance experiments. Some of these alternate approaches pose the question: Why do people feel aroused in dissonance experiments? As we just noted, one answer is that people feel particularly aroused when they behave in counterattitudinal ways that threaten their self-esteem and sense of personal worth (Steele, 1988; Steele & Liu, 1983). Another answer is that people experience dissonance particularly when their behavior leads to negative outcomes for themselves or others, regardless of whether their behavior is consistent with their attitudes (Cooper & Scher, 1992; Scher & Cooper, 1989). And still another answer is that people feel dissonance particularly when their public image suffers because they *appear* inconsistent to others (Tedeschi, Schlenker, & Bonoma, 1971). Note that all of these perspectives agree that people feel aroused in dissonance experiments and sometimes shift their attitudes as a result. They disagree, however, about what the *causes* of the arousal are.

SOCIAL PSYCHOLOGY IN EVERYDAY LIFE

Can Dissonance Theory Be Used to Reduce Racial Prejudice?

We began our discussion of cognitive dissonance with a real example: A neo-Nazi skinhead changed his attitudes after interacting with a black person. Is there a general principle here for reducing racial prejudice? Dissonance theory suggests that if we can get prejudiced people to behave in nonprejudiced ways,

Dissonance and desegregation. Can dissonance theory help explain when school desegregation proceeds peacefully and when it instead leads to violence?

they may experience dissonance, which will then motivate them to become less prejudiced. Survey research offers some support for this principle: After Americans were induced to *behave* in less prejudiced ways in the 1950s and 1960s (because of court rulings and civil rights legislation), their attitudes became less prejudiced as well (Taylor, Sheatsley, & Greeley, 1978). Thus, attitudes sometimes follow behavior, rather than the other way around.

There are qualifications, however, to using dissonance to reduce prejudice. As noted earlier, for dissonance to be aroused, people must believe that their counterattitudinal behavior was freely chosen, firmly committed, and irrevocable. For example, when prejudiced parents believe they are sending their children to integrated schools of their own free will (because, for example, they have the option of sending them to segregated private schools instead) and when they view integration as firmly committed and irrevocable (because of court rulings and resolute public officials), they will be most likely to change their attitudes. Consistent with this analysis, studies indicate that desegregation of U.S. schools in the 1950s proceeded most smoothly and was most likely to be accepted by communities when it was firmly implemented and portrayed as inevitable and irrevocable by public officials (Pettigrew, 1961). Sometimes, then, when prejudiced people are induced to behave in nonprejudiced ways, they become less prejudiced as a result. Dissonance theory provides one explanation for why such attitude change occurs.

ATTITUDES AND ATTITUDE CHANGE IN PERSPECTIVE

The Nazi example demonstrates that attitudes sometimes have the power to trigger wars and motivate mass murder. Attitudes affect commonplace behaviors as well. For example, they influence which products we buy, what candidates we vote for, and whether we engage in healthy or unhealthy activities such as smoking.

Starting in the 1920s, social psychologists developed ways to measure attitudes, and since then, a huge amount of research has studied how attitudes are formed, how they influence our behavior, and how they can be changed. One overriding message of this research is that not all attitudes are created equal. Attitudes can be formed in different ways, and they can serve various functions in our lives.

Whereas early research indicated that attitudes frequently do not predict behavior very well, recent research emphasizes that some attitudes (for example, accessible attitudes formed through direct experience) tend to predict our behavior more strongly than others. The link between attitudes and behavior is also influenced by how attitudes and behaviors are measured, by characteristics of the situation (for example, does the setting trigger self-awareness?), and by characteristics of the person (is the person highly self-conscious?).

Like attitudes, persuasion comes in different varieties. In particular, there is an important distinction between lazy and thoughtful routes to persuasion. People follow the lazy route when they do not care about the contents of a persuasive message, and the attitudes formed as a result of such persuasion tend to be transient and not strongly related to behavior. People follow the thoughtful route when they find persuasive messages personally relevant and involving, and the attitudes that result from such persuasion tend to be lasting and highly related to behavior. When people engage in lazy processing of persuasive messages, they respond to superficial cues (such as speaker attractiveness and the number of arguments); when they engage in thoughtful processing, they think more about the quality of message arguments.

While most of us assume that our attitudes influence our behavior, dissonance theory argues that our behavior sometimes influences our attitudes. In particular, after behaving in ways that contradict our attitudes, we sometimes shift our attitudes to be more consistent with our behavior. Such attitude shifts occur particularly when we believe our attitude-discrepant behavior is freely chosen, irrevocable, and carries important real-life consequences and when the relevant attitude is strongly linked to our self-concept.

We started this chapter with simple questions: What are attitudes? How are they formed? How do they influence behavior? And how are they changed? A great achievement of social psychology research over the past 60 years is that we now know that meaningful answers to these questions require a subtle understanding of the kinds of attitudes, behaviors, people, and situations we wish to study.

What Are Attitudes?

Characteristics of Attitudes

Attitudes are learned evaluative responses, directed at specific objects, which are relatively enduring and influence behavior in a generally motivating way.

The Functional Approach to Attitudes

Attitudes may serve various psychological functions; these include instrumental, ego-defensive, knowledge, value-expressive, and social-adjustment functions.

Attitude Measurement

Likert scales and semantic differential ratings are two techniques for measuring attitudes through self-report questionnaires.

    The "bogus pipeline" encourages subjects to respond honestly to self-report attitude scales by informing them (falsely) that their attitudes are being physiologically measured.

    Attitudes are sometimes assessed with physiological measures such as the galvanic skin response, pupil dilation, and electrical recordings from facial muscles.

Attitude Formation

There are three main routes to acquiring attitudes: We learn attitudes; we form attitudes to serve needs in our personalities; and we infer our attitudes from related beliefs, attitudes, and behaviors.

Learning Theories and Attitude Formation

Learning theories of attitude formation hold that attitudes are acquired through the processes of classical conditioning, operant conditioning, and modeling.

Personality and Attitude Formation

Personality theories of attitude formation hold that attitudes may develop to serve needs in an individual's personality such as bolstering self-esteem or defending against feelings of insecurity and anxiety.

Logical Inference and Attitude Formation

Logical inference theories hold that attitudes may be derived from other beliefs and attitudes. The value-expectancy model describes how some broad attitudes are inferred from related subbeliefs and attitudes.

    Bem's self-perception theory argues that people infer their attitudes from their behavior and its setting, particularly when preexisting attitudes are weak or even nonexistent.

Attitudes and Behavior

Putting the Attitude-Behavior Question in Context

Early studies often found that attitudes do not predict behavior very well. Recent research finds that under some circumstances, attitudes strongly predict behavior.

Measuring Attitudes and Behavior Properly

To be related, attitudes and behaviors must both be measured at the same level of specificity or generality. Single actions are often unreliable measures of behavior; summed measures of behavior often show a stronger link to attitudes than single behaviors do.

Fishbein and Ajzen's Theory of Reasoned Action

This theory holds that a weighted combination of attitudes (evaluative responses to a target) and subjective norms (beliefs about the way significant others think we should behave) influences behavioral intentions, which ultimately determine behavior. This model has proved useful in predicting many different kinds of voluntary behaviors.

What Kinds of Attitudes Best Predict Behavior?

Attitudes formed through direct experience predict behavior better than attitudes formed through indirect information. Accessible attitudes (which are highly associated with the attitude object and are thus called quickly to mind) predict behavior better than nonaccessible attitudes.

What Kinds of People Behave Consistently with Their Attitudes?

Low-self-monitoring individuals are more likely than high-self-monitoring individuals to behave consistently with their attitudes. People who are highly self-conscious are more likely than less self-conscious people to behave consistently with their attitudes.

What Kinds of Situations Lead People to Behave Consistently with Their Attitudes?

Situations that induce people to pay attention to themselves increase the link between their attitudes and their behavior. When people are asked to provide reasons for their attitudes, they tend to show a weaker relationship between their attitudes and behavior.

Social Psychology in Everyday Life: Attitudes and Smoking

Attitudes toward smoking are linked to smoking behavior. As attitudes toward smoking have become more negative in the United States over the past 30 years, smoking has decreased substantially.

Persuasion: When Others Change Our Attitudes

Research on persuasion looks at how and when persuasive messages change our attitudes.

A Communication Model of Persuasion: The Yale Research

The Yale research used a communication model of persuasion that focused on the effects of communicator, message, channel, and audience variables.

Highly credible communicators persuade more than noncredible communicators, but this effect fades quickly over time.

Fear appeals can lead to attitude change if they successfully create fear and include clear recommendations about how recipients can avoid fearful outcomes.

A one-sided message is more persuasive to people who already agree with the message, whereas a two-sided message is more persuasive to people who already disagree with the message. A two-sided message leads recipients to resist subsequent "counterpropaganda" better than a one-sided message does.

Inoculation studies show that messages that weakly attack as well as support attitudes can make people more resistant to subsequent messages that strongly attack the same attitudes.

Message repetition can enhance persuasion, in part because of the *mere exposure effect,* which occurs when people show increased liking for frequently occurring stimuli. Message repetition may also lead recipients to better comprehend and remember persuasive arguments.

Face-to-face persuasion is often more effective than media persuasion; however, the mass media can reach a much larger audience. Print media encourage more thoughtful processing of persuasive arguments, whereas audio and audiovisual media shift attention from message content to such speaker attributes as attractiveness and likability.

Audience variables such as personality and intelligence have complex effects on persuasion because they may differentially affect comprehension and yielding. Highly intelligent people are most persuaded by persuasive messages that are sound and complex. Because they both attend to the message and are willing to yield, people with moderate self-esteem are more readily persuaded than people with low or high self-esteem. Individuals with a high need for cognition are more influenced by message logic and quality than are people with a low need for cognition.

The Cognitive Approach to Persuasion

The cognitive approach to persuasion holds that persuasion is an active process in which people think about persuasive messages and mentally argue and counterargue with message contents.

Lazy versus Thoughtful Processing of Persuasive Messages. Some kinds of persuasion succeed because of quick and lazy mental processes, whereas other kinds require more careful and conscientious thought.

In Petty and Cacioppo's *elaboration likelihood model,* the *central route* to persuasion is the thoughtful route that involves active cognition; the *peripheral route* is the lazy route that does not. People follow the central route when the persuasive message is personally relevant and important to them; they follow the peripheral route when the message is not relevant to them.

Chaiken's *heuristic model* argues that when people are not personally involved with the topic of a persuasive message, they change their attitudes according to heuristics (simple mental rules of thumb, such as "The more arguments, the more persuaded I am"); when people are personally involved with the topic of persuasion, they engage in a more careful, thoughtful analysis of the message and its contents.

Forewarning and Active Thought. People's cognitive responses (their mental arguments for or against a persuasive message) have a large impact on persuasion. People who are forewarned that they will be the target of a persuasive message tend to argue mentally against it and are thus less persuaded than people who are not forewarned.

Mood and Active Thought. People in bad moods are more likely than people in good moods to think actively and carefully about the contents of a persuasive message. As a result, they are more responsive to the quality of arguments in a message.

Attitude Functions and Active Thought. People tend to be most persuaded by a message that contains information that addresses the function served by the attitude. Such messages tend to stimulate more active thought in the recipient.

Cognitive Dissonance: When Our Behavior Leads Us to Change Our Attitudes

Cognitive Dissonance Theory

Festinger's theory of cognitive dissonance proposes that when people behave inconsistently with their attitudes, they experience a negative state of arousal, called dissonance, which can motivate attitude change.

Demonstrating Dissonance in the Laboratory

Research on *insufficient justification* shows that people who behave in attitude-discrepant ways for small incentives are more likely to shift their attitudes to be consistent with their behavior than are people who behave in attitude-discrepant ways for large incentives. Research on *severity of initiation* shows that people come to like groups or activities for which they must suffer. Research on *derogation of the victim* shows that people who harm others for little justification often develop negative attitudes toward their victims. All of these findings are consistent with dissonance theory.

Qualifications to Dissonance Theory

Counterattitudinal behavior leads to dissonance, particularly when such behavior is perceived to be freely chosen, firmly committed, irrevocable, and of consequence in real life. Furthermore, dissonance is particularly aroused when people engage in behaviors that threaten their self-esteem and their sense of personal worthiness. People may sometimes feel aroused in dissonance studies because their behavior leads to negative outcomes or because they worry about the image they present to others, not because they behave inconsistently with their attitudes.

Social Psychology in Everyday Life: Can Dissonance Theory Be Used to Reduce Racial Prejudice?

When prejudiced people are induced to behave in nonprejudiced ways, they sometimes become less prejudiced. This is particularly likely to occur if the prejudiced people believe that their attitude-discrepant behavior is voluntary and firmly committed.

KEY TERMS

Accessibility: The degree to which attitudes are associated with the attitude object and come quickly and automatically to mind.

Attitude: A learned evaluative response, directed at specific objects, that is relatively enduring and influences behavior in a general motivating way.

Audience variables: Characteristics of the audience or target of persuasion; examples include intelligence and personality traits.

Behavioral intention: In Fishbein and Ajzen's theory of reasoned action, an individual's subjective probability of engaging in a behavior.

Bogus pipeline: A technique to induce subjects to answer attitude questionnaires more honestly by leading them to believe (falsely) that their attitudes are also being measured physiologically.

Central route to persuasion: In the elaboration likelihood model of persuasion, the route followed when subjects consciously deliberate on the merit, content, and logic of information in a persuasive message.

Channel variables: The medium through which a persuasive message is delivered; examples are face-to-face communication, print media, radio, and television.

Classical conditioning: The kind of learning that occurs when a person learns an involuntary response (such as salivation or increased heart rate) to a new stimulus (such as a bell); some attitudes may be classically conditioned emotional responses.

Cognitive dissonance: An unpleasant state of arousal that occurs when people behave inconsistently with their attitudes; according to Festinger's theory, dissonance can motivate attitude change.

Cognitive responses: Internal, self-generated arguments for or against a persuasive message.

Communicator variables: Characteristics of the person delivering a persuasive message; examples are speaker credibility and attractiveness.

Ego-defensive function: Attitudes serve this function when they help us protect our self-esteem and avoid personality conflicts and anxiety.

Elaboration likelihood model: Petty and Cacioppo's model that proposes persuasion depends on the degree to which people actively cognitively process the contents of a persuasive message.

Heuristic model of persuasion: Chaiken's model which proposes that when people find a persuasive message personally involving, they consider the contents of the message carefully, but when they find a message uninvolving, they change their attitudes according to heuristics—simple mental rules of thumb.

Inoculation: Increasing resistance to persuasive messages by exposing relevant beliefs to earlier weak attacks as well as supportive information.

Instrumental function: Attitudes serve this function when they help bring us rewards or avoid costs.

Knowledge function: Attitudes serve this function when they help us order and assimilate information.

Likert scales: The most commonly used attitude-testing technique. They ask subjects to rate how much they agree or disagree with a number of statements relevant to the attitude; subjects' responses over all the items are then summed.

Mere exposure effect: The tendency to like stimuli more the more frequently we are exposed to them.

Message variables: Characteristics of the content of a persuasive message; examples are the presence or absence of fear appeals and the use of one-sided or two-sided arguments.

Modeling: The kind of learning that occurs when people observe another's behavior and imitate it; attitudes may be learned through modeling.

Operant conditioning: The kind of learning that occurs when voluntary responses are rewarded; attitudes and their verbal expression may sometimes be operantly conditioned responses.

Peripheral route to persuasion: In the elaboration likelihood model of persuasion, the route followed when subjects do not carefully reflect on the content of a persuasive message but rather attend to superficial cues, such as speaker credibility or the number of arguments presented.

Self-perception theory: Bem's theory holds that particularly when attitudes are weak or ambiguous, people sometimes infer their attitudes from their behavior and the setting in which it occurs.

Semantic differential scales: Scales of evaluative meaning (such as *good-bad, worthy-unworthy*) used to measure attitudes; subjects rate the attitude object on these scales and their responses are summed.

Semantic generalization: Occurs in human classical conditioning when people show a conditioned response not only to a specific stimulus but also to semantically related words and objects.

Social-adjustment function: Attitudes serve this function when they help us present a desired image of ourselves to a social audience (for example, to our friends and peers).

Subjective norms: In Fishbein and Ajzen's theory of reasoned action, our beliefs about the way significant others think we should behave.

Theory of reasoned action: Fishbein and Ajzen's theory that a weighted combination of attitudes and subjective norms predict behavioral intentions, which in turn predict voluntary behavior.

Value-expectancy model: A model of attitude formation that proposes an attitude is formed by combining salient beliefs about the attitude object multiplied by evaluations of those beliefs.

Value-expressive function: Attitudes serve this function when they express deeper values.

7

PREJUDICE

At the Book Garden, a women's bookstore in downtown Denver, it began with a series of anonymous phone threats. "You queer dyke bitches!" one caller screamed. At a bookstore across town, another angry voice called in a bomb threat: "You got too many fags and queers working there." And when a staffer picked up the phone at the Denver Gay and Lesbian Community Center, she heard: "We're going to blow up your f—————building."

Anti-gay threats and slurs are hardly new—in Denver or anywhere else. But in Colorado the voices of hate have taken on a new edge. On Nov. 3, state voters approved—by a margin of 53 to 47 percent—a measure designed to strip away legal protections for gays.

—*Newsweek,* November 23, 1992

*Rally opposing
Amendment 2, an
anti-gay initiative
passed by Colorado
voters in 1992.*

This has been a century marked by horrible episodes of prejudice. Perhaps the most ghastly example is the Nazis' "final solution" in Europe, in which 6 million innocent men, women, and children were systematically exterminated simply because they were Jewish. Hitler looked to the mass murder of Armenians by Turks at the beginning of the century as a kind of model for his attempted genocide against the Jews. And while the world vowed "never again" after witnessing the Holocaust, the last decade of the 20th century has been marked by new atrocities spawned again by cruel prejudices: fire bombings of immigrant minorities in Germany, "ethnic cleansing" by Serbs in Bosnia, brutal repression of the Kurds in Iraq . . . the list goes on.

And lest we forget, the opening excerpt reminds us that prejudice still exists in the United States as well. In all eras and in all countries, it seems, bigotry rears its ugly head and disturbs the peaceful conduct of human affairs. Precisely for this reason, it is essential that we understand prejudice. In his classic analysis, *The Nature of Prejudice*, Gordon Allport (1954) noted that "it required years of labor and billions of dollars to gain the secret of the atom. It will take a still greater investment to gain the secrets of man's irrational nature. It is easier, someone has said, to smash an atom than a prejudice." Despite the difficulty of the task, social psychologists have worked doggedly to understand the nature of prejudice and to mitigate its destructive consequences. Their research has addressed some fundamental questions about prejudice: What is its nature? How can it be measured? What are its causes? And how can it be reduced?

✐ STUDYING PREJUDICE

In the early morning hours last Feb. 2 [in Portland, Maine], Benjamin Kowalsky, a 33-year-old community-development worker suffering from AIDS, was chased down and attacked by three rock-throwing youths who yelled, "Hey faggot, we're going to get you." Ten days later another gay man was severely beaten by a gang of 10 men. This time police collared some of the assailants, but the victim declined to press charges for fear of losing his job.

—*Newsweek*, September 14, 1992

We often know prejudice when we see it—it is obvious, blatant, and ugly. But prejudice is displayed in more covert ways too—through a cold tone of voice or physical distance. What is prejudice, and how do social psychologists define it?

Defining Prejudice

Prejudice refers to a negative attitude that is based on another person's membership in a social group. We may hold prejudices about lesbians and gay men, African-Americans, women, Jewish people, Puerto Ricans, actors, disabled people, fraternity members, football players. Such attitudes are often overgeneralized—we apply them inflexibly to a group or to individual members of a group based on limited or insufficient information.

Like most attitudes, a prejudice can be considered to have affective (emotional), cognitive (belief), and behavioral (overt action) components (Bagozzi, 1978; Hilgard, 1980; Stangor, Sullivan, & Ford, 1991). As noted in Chapter 6, the concept of attitude has often been defined primarily in terms of its *affective*, or emotional, component. Prejudice is clearly characterized by a host of negative feelings. The excerpt that starts this chapter contains quotes that express strong negative emotions about lesbians and gay men, including disgust, revulsion, and hatred.

The cognitive component of prejudice embraces the *beliefs* or *stereotypes* we hold about the targets of prejudice. Many people's attitudes toward gay men and lesbians, for example, are not just evaluative; they also include beliefs—that gay men are "artistic" and "feminine" and lesbians "athletic" and "masculine" (Herek, 1991). In many cases, the beliefs that go with prejudiced attitudes are elaborate and complex. In fact, prejudiced attitudes and their accompanying stereotypes may have much in common with cognitive *schemas;* that is, they are organized mental categories that contain information about various groups and people (Ashmore & Del Boca, 1981; see Chapter 5). Later in this chapter we'll describe the nature and measurement of prejudiced beliefs and stereotypes in greater detail.

The third component of a prejudiced attitude is behavioral. The term *discrimination* refers to overt acts that treat members of certain groups unfairly. Discriminatory behavior can be as subtle as certain nonverbal behaviors (for example, standing apart, not smiling) or as blatant as unfair housing practices,

Before passage of the *Civil Rights Act of 1964, many public facilities in the United States were legally segregated.*

preferential hiring, and unjustified firing. As these examples suggest, sometimes discrimination is practiced by individuals, sometimes by groups and social institutions (companies, colleges, government agencies), and sometimes by entire societies (South Africa, the Old South).

Prejudiced people and groups often express their negative attitudes through segregation—physical separation from disliked people and groups. The United States legally maintained the highly discriminatory doctrine of "separate but equal" in relations between blacks and whites until the 1950s. Although it is beginning to dismantle apartheid, the institutionalized and legally sanctioned separation of the races, South Africa is still a society that is almost totally segregated.

At its most extreme, prejudice can lead to physical harm. As the quotes that open this chapter illustrate, gay people in the United States sometimes experience vandalism, physical assaults, and bombings because of others' prejudice against their sexual orientation. Allport (1954) described how hostile statements progressed to genocide in one of the most brutal expressions of prejudice in history: Hitler's propaganda "led Germans to avoid their Jewish neighbors and erstwhile friends. This preparation made it easier to enact the Nurnberg laws of discrimination which, in turn, made the subsequent burning of synagogues and street attacks upon Jews seem natural. The final step in the macabre progression was the ovens at Auschwitz" (p. 15).

Analyzing Prejudice

Prejudice can be analyzed at many levels. In an early discussion, Gordon Allport (1954) formulated six levels of analysis, which begin with the broad social causes of prejudice and progress to the more specific individual causes. Figure 7.1 illustrates these levels. The top of the figure shows the broadest factors: historical causes and sociocultural factors that influence prejudice. The lower parts of the figure present more specific elements in individuals' lives that foster prejudice: the social situations people find themselves in, their personality traits and dynamics, and their phenomenology—their beliefs and stereotypes about groups. At the bottom of Figure 7.1 is the target of prejudice—the "stimulus object."

A concrete example will make these levels of analysis clearer. Let's analyze prejudice against African-Americans—an example that is particularly appropriate for two reasons: First, racial prejudice has been an extremely important social and political issue in the United States throughout its history. Second, as a result, racial prejudice has been the subject of an enormous amount of research in American social psychology.

Historical Analysis

To understand prejudice against blacks, it helps to understand its historical origins and development. This form of prejudice has a long history in the United States, beginning with the institution of slavery in colonial America. The agricultural economy of the South depended more on slavery than the industrial economy of the North did, and these economic differences and growing moral outrage against

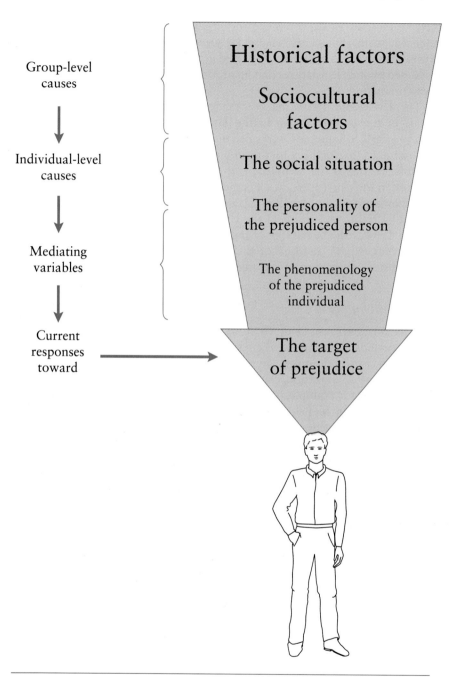

FIGURE 7.1 Levels of analysis in the study of prejudice.

slavery in the mid-1800s combined to trigger the Civil War in 1861. In 1863, President Lincoln's Emancipation Proclamation ended slavery in the United States; however, during the Reconstruction period in the postwar South, "Jim Crow laws" were passed by state legislatures that institutionalized various forms of segregation and discrimination.

The 1940s and 1950s marked the beginning of the modern era of race relations in the United States. In the famous 1954 case *Brown v. Board of Education,* the U.S. Supreme Court ruled that the "separate but equal" doctrine that had maintained segregation in the public schools since 1896 was no longer acceptable. So began the turbulent and as yet unfinished efforts to implement integration in the classroom. (We'll consider the success of these efforts from the vantage point of social psychology research toward the end of this chapter.) The modern civil rights movement in the United States achieved a major legislative success in 1964 with the passage of the Civil Rights Act banning discrimination based on color, religion, national origin, race, and sex. (See Jones, 1972, for a more complete historical account of prejudice against blacks in the United States.)

Sociocultural Factors

The historical approach tends to study specific kinds of prejudice in specific historical periods. In contrast, the sociocultural approach (the second level in Figure 7.1) focuses on the links between prejudice in general and broad sociological concepts, such as urbanization, class mobility, and population shifts and density. In the United States, for example, prejudice has often been directed against immigrant urban populations by higher-class, less urban, and more established residents. As blacks and other minorities (Italians, Poles, Irish, Eastern European Jews) flocked to America's big cities in the early 20th century, providing cheap labor to fuel the economy, they often became the targets of cruel stereotypes and prejudice.

The Social Situation

Both the historical and sociocultural approaches focus on "group-level explanations"—broad social forces and factors that lead to prejudice. Allport's third level of analysis enters the traditional realm of social psychology by focusing on the individual's immediate social situation as a cause of prejudice. For example, prejudice and discrimination against blacks in the Old South was for many simply a matter of *conforming* to group norms and behavior (Pettigrew, 1958, 1980). If you grow up in a bigoted family and society, you are likely to adopt their bigotry through standard processes of social learning and influence. Social psychology has devoted considerable attention to the situational level of analysis, and we'll examine research on situational influences on prejudice throughout this chapter.

Personality and Prejudice

Personality analysis, the fourth level in Allport's diagram, focuses on the traits and character of the individual as a cause of prejudice. Research on the *au-*

thoritarian personality (Adorno, Frenkel-Brunswick, Levinson, & Sanford, 1950), which we'll discuss in greater detail later, suggests that some people may be extremely prejudiced because they were reared by punitive, status-anxious parents and as a result developed defensive, angry personalities. Some Freudian psychologists have argued that prejudiced people often project onto out-group members their own bad traits (Ackerman & Jahoda, 1950; Bettelheim & Janowitz, 1950). Thus, a white person with repressed feelings of aggression might consider blacks to be "violent."

The Phenomenology of Prejudiced Individuals

Social psychologists often try to understand prejudice from the point of view of the prejudiced person. Social psychology research on stereotypes, for example, documents people's prejudiced beliefs and attempts to understand how they develop. In one of the first studies to measure stereotypes, Daniel Katz and Kenneth Braly (1933) found that a majority of 100 white Princeton students believed blacks to be "superstitious" and "lazy." The study of stereotypes often documents what people *believe* to be true of other groups, even though the evidence for these beliefs may be weak or lacking. Social psychologists study how stereotypes are formed and sustained, sometimes in the face of nonexistent or contradictory evidence.

The Stimulus Object

Allport's final level of analysis deals with the "stimulus object." Prejudices and intergroup hostilities may be based at times on real characteristics of groups; this idea has sometimes been called the *earned reputation theory.*

Typically, social psychologists have not been interested in documenting actual group differences. (One interesting exception, discussed in Chapter 8, is research on sex differences.) Although differences among groups exist, social psychologists have generally assumed that prejudices and stereotyped beliefs about group differences are typically more abundant and more extreme than the objective evidence can support. As we'll see later, people may sometimes form stereotypes based on no supporting evidence, simply as a result of normal thought processes.

The levels of explanation shown in Figure 7.1 are helpful in thinking about social psychology research on prejudice. We'll begin our examination of prejudice with a description of the phenomenology of prejudiced individuals: What is the nature of stereotypes and prejudiced beliefs? How are they best measured? How do they develop? And what are their consequences in everyday social life? Then we'll turn to the social causes of prejudice: socialization (child-rearing practices and the personality traits they lead to), social ideologies (for example, political and religious beliefs we learn from those around us), group membership, and intergroup competition. Finally, we'll consider ways of reducing prejudice. Our analysis will focus on situational factors—for example, does contact between members of different groups sometimes reduce prejudice?

STEREOTYPES: PREJUDICED BELIEFS

A petition drive by the Oregon Citizens Alliance (OCA) has produced Ballot Measure 9, which would void portions of the state's hate-crimes law and invalidate the phrase "sexual orientation" in any statute where it now appears. It also requires educators to set curriculum standards equating homosexuality with pedophilia, sadism and masochism as behaviors "to be discouraged and avoided." Despite new scientific evidence that homosexuality may have genetic origins, OCA members talk openly of "curing" gays.

—*Newsweek*, September 14, 1992

Ballot Measure 9 went down to defeat in the general election of November 1992, but the stereotypes it expressed undoubtedly live on. *Stereotype* (originally a printing term) was first used in its modern sense by the journalist Walter Lippmann (1922). Instead of dealing with the complexity of the real world around us, Lippmann argued, we create cognitive simplifications—stereotypes—to guide how we perceive people around us and how we process social information. What are stereotypes, and how can they be measured? What impact do they have on our thoughts and behavior toward other groups?

Measuring Stereotypes

The first attempts to measure stereotypes were relatively simple. The classic study by Katz and Braly cited earlier set the tone for much subsequent research. One hundred Princeton undergraduates were asked to indicate which of 84 traits they felt were "typical" of various groups, including Americans, Japanese, Jews, British, Negroes, and Turks. Most of these subjects agreed that just a few traits characterized each group, and thus each group seemed to possess a strong and relatively simplistic stereotype (see Figure 7.2).

Stereotypes as Percentage Estimates

Katz and Braly's method asked subjects to indicate whether all members of a group either possessed or did not possess a given trait. When asked to make such ratings about various groups in later studies, college students have sometimes objected to this all-or-none approach, stating that they don't subscribe to the notion that all people in a certain group possess given traits (Karlins, Coffman, & Walters, 1969). Although you might believe, for example, that *on average,* Americans are more "materialistic" than people in many other countries, you probably wouldn't agree that *all* Americans are materialistic or that *all* citizens of other countries are nonmaterialistic. For these and other reasons, social psychologists have developed ways to measure stereotypes beyond Katz and Braly's all-or-none approach.

For example, Brigham (1971) proposed that researchers ask subjects *what percentage* of people in a given group possess various traits. Thus, to assess your

Group	Trait	Princeton Subjects Associating Trait with Group (%)
Americans	Industrious	48
	Intelligent	47
	Materialistic	33
	Ambitious	33
	Progressive	27
Jews	Shrewd	79
	Mercenary	49
	Industrious	48
	Grasping	34
	Intelligent	29
Negroes	Superstitious	84
	Lazy	75
	Happy-go-lucky	38
	Ignorant	38
	Musical	26

FIGURE 7.2 Results of early stereotype measurement study. *Source:* Data from Katz and Braly (1933).

stereotypes about Americans, I might ask you to estimate what percentage of Americans you think are materialistic. But even this strategy has flaws. If you think that 75% of all Americans are materialistic, does this mean you hold a strong stereotype about Americans? We can't be sure until we know how materialistic you think people generally are. If you think 75% of *all* people are materialistic, then clearly your view of Americans is no different from your view of anyone else.

The Diagnostic Ratio Approach

Clark McCauley and Christopher Stitt (1978; McCauley, Stitt, & Segal, 1980) offer a remedy to the flaws of stereotype measurement that is probably the most satisfactory to date. They suggest that besides asking what percentage of a group possesses a given trait, researchers must also ask subjects what percentage of *people in general* possess the trait. From these numbers, researchers can then compute the *diagnostic ratio* for a given subject by dividing the subject's estimate for the target group by his or her estimate of the percentage of people in general who possess the same trait.

For example, if you think that 75% of Americans are materialistic but only 50% of people in general are materialistic, then your diagnostic ratio for this trait would be 75/50 = 1.5. Clearly, if the diagnostic ratio is greater than 1, then you believe that Americans possess the trait more than people in general do. If the diagnostic ratio equals 1, then you see no difference between Americans and people in general on the trait. And if the diagnostic ratio is less than 1, then you consider Americans to possess the trait less than people in general do.

In one of the first studies to use the diagnostic ratio approach, McCauley and Stitt (1978) asked 69 junior college students to estimate the percentage of Germans they felt possessed various traits. Figure 7.3 lists the students' estimates as well as their estimates of the percentages of people in general who possess these traits, and finally, it presents the computed diagnostic ratios. Note that diagnostic ratios sometimes yielded information quite different from the raw percentage ratings. If you looked only at the percentage ratings, you would conclude that the two traits most stereotypically associated with Germans were *pleasure-loving* and *industrious*. However, the diagnostic ratios indicate that whereas subjects considered the trait *industrious* to be more characteristic of Germans than of people in general (diagnostic ratio = 1.14), they considered the trait *pleasure-loving* to be *less* characteristic of Germans than of people in general (ratio = 0.89). The high estimated percentage of "pleasure-loving" Germans is misleading because an even higher percentage of people in general were estimated to possess this trait.

Trait	Percentage of People in General Judged to Have Trait	Percentage of Germans Judged to Have Trait	Diagnostic Ratio
Efficient	49.8	63.4	1.27
Extremely nationalistic	35.4	56.3	**1.59**
Ignorant	34.0	29.2	.66
Impulsive	51.7	41.1	.79
Industrious	59.8	68.2	1.14
Pleasure-loving	82.2	72.8	.89
Scientifically minded	32.6	43.1	**1.32**
Superstitious	42.1	30.4	.72
Tradition-loving	62.4	57.2	.91

The percentage ratings in the middle column seem to suggest that the two traits most associated with Germans are *pleasure-loving* and *industrious*. But the diagnostic ratios show that the two traits perceived to most distinguish Germans from people in general are *extremely nationalistic* and *scientifically minded*.

FIGURE 7.3 Junior college students' judgments of the percentages of Germans possessing various traits, with computed diagnostic ratios. *Source:* Data from McCauley and Stitt (1978).

Are Stereotypes Wrong?

We have just discussed some of the most common ways stereotypes are measured, and in the process, you have learned some commonly held stereotypes about Americans, blacks, Jews, and Germans. Do you think such stereotypes are wrong? Even if you think that some stereotypes are based on a "kernel of truth," might they nonetheless often be gross exaggerations?

Social psychologists have long speculated that stereotypes can lead to a number of errors in our perceptions of others (Allport, 1954; Campbell, 1967; Judd & Park, 1993). For example, stereotypes may often unjustly portray out-groups more negatively than in-groups, they may exaggerate differences between groups, and they can lead people to underestimate (and even ignore) differences among people within other groups. What is the evidence for these hypotheses?

Research does often find that stereotypes about out-groups are more negative than those about in-groups. In Katz and Braly's (1933) classic study, for example, the traits attributed by white Anglo-Saxon Princeton students to Americans (who, of course, constituted an in-group) were generally positive, whereas those attributed to out-groups (Jews, Chinese, Italians, Negroes, and Turks) were consistently more negative (see Figure 7.4). *Ethnocentrism*—the belief that our own group is superior to other groups—is frequently embedded in our stereotypes.

Recent research documents a more subtle error fostered by stereotypes: They lead us to view in-groups as more complex and varied than out-groups. The perception of out-groups as uniform, homogeneous, and undifferentiated is

Nationality or Group	Mean Desirability of Traits
Americans	6.77
English	6.26
Germans	6.02
Japanese	5.89
Irish	5.42
Jews	4.96
Chinese	4.52
Italians	4.40
Negroes	3.55
Turks	3.05

FIGURE 7.4 The ethnocentrism of stereotypes. Katz and Braly (1933) computed the mean desirability of each of the traits that 100 Princeton students ascribed to ten nationalities or groups. (Desirability ratings were made on a scale from 1 to 10, with higher ratings indicating greater desirability.) *Source:* Data from Katz and Braly (1933).

expressed by the classic prejudiced statement "They all look the same to me." There is some literal truth to this statement—facial identification studies show that people tend to remember and identify other people's faces better when they are members of their own racial and ethnic groups (Shapiro & Penrod, 1986; see Chapter 16).

Not only do we think members of out-groups look the same, we often judge them to have uniform traits and attitudes as well. One recent study asked University of Colorado business and engineering majors to rate students in each major on two characteristics: their traits (How extroverted are business/engineering majors?) and on their attitudes and interests (How much does a business/engineering major enjoy solving brainteasers such as Rubik's Cube?). Subjects were also asked to list as many "sorts or types" of business majors (or engineering majors) as came to mind. The results showed that students in each major rated students in the other major more stereotypically than those in their own, and furthermore, they listed more subtypes for their own major than for the other major (Park, Ryan, & Judd, 1992).

It is not surprising that we often possess more complex knowledge of in-groups than of out-groups; after all, we generally interact with members of our own group more, and thus we've learned more about them. But the perception that in-groups are more complex and varied than out-groups holds even for an "out-group" that we deal with on a daily basis: the opposite sex. Park and Rothbart (1982) asked male and female college students to rate what percentages of men and women would endorse various statements, some of which were stereotypically feminine (for example, "I would like to care for a small baby as a way to express my love") and some of which were stereotypically masculine ("I often seek out competitive challenges—whether intellectual or athletic"). Women rated men as endorsing more stereotypically masculine statements than men themselves did, and men rated women as endorsing more stereotypically feminine statements than women themselves did.

Furthermore, Park and Rothbart's data imply that this illusion of uniformity in the out-group did *not* result because subjects were trying to make their own group look good at the expense of the other group. Regardless of whether the stereotypical statements were positive or negative, subjects tended to view the out-group more stereotypically. These findings are particularly interesting because men and women typically have a great deal of contact with members of the other sex. If the illusion of uniformity exists in the stereotypes we hold about out-groups we know well and interact with daily, then how much stronger must it be for out-groups we don't know well and interact with infrequently?

SOCIAL
PSYCHOLOGY
IN EVERYDAY
LIFE

Have Stereotypes and Prejudice Weakened in Recent Years?

The most simple and direct answer to this question is yes. Katz and Braly's famous 1933 stereotype study has been replicated four times: in 1951, 1967, 1982, and 1988 (Dovidio & Gaertner, 1991). Figure 7.5 presents data from all five studies on stereotypes about blacks. In general, these studies show a steady decline in Americans' willingness to express simplistic, negative stereotypes

Percent of Subjects Selecting a Trait to Describe Black Americans (Formerly "Negroes") in 1933, 1951, 1967, 1982, and 1988

	1933	1951	1967	1982	1988
Superstitious	84	41	13	6	2
Lazy	75	31	26	13	6
Happy-go-lucky	38	17	27	15	4
Ignorant	38	24	11	10	6
Musical	26	33	47	29	13
Ostentatious	26	11	25	5	0
Very religious	24	17	8	23	20
Stupid	22	10	4	1	1
Physically dirty	17	—	3	0	1
Naive	14	—	4	4	2
Slovenly	13	—	5	2	1
Unreliable	12	—	6	2	1
Pleasure loving	—	19	26	20	14
Sensitive	—	—	17	13	15
Gregarious	—	—	17	4	6
Talkative	—	—	14	5	5
Imitative	—	—	13	9	4
Aggressive	—	—	—	19	16
Materialistic	—	—	—	16	10
Loyal to family	—	—	—	39	49
Arrogant	—	—	—	14	7
Ambitious	—	—	—	13	23
Tradition loving	—	—	—	13	22
Individualistic	—	—	—	—	24
Passionate	—	—	—	—	14
Nationalistic	—	—	—	—	13
Straightforward	—	—	—	—	12

FIGURE 7.5 Changes in racial stereotypes across time. *Source:* Karlins, Coffman, and Walters (1969).

about various ethnic and racial minorities. Similarly, surveys that ask white Americans about their racial attitudes (for example, do they believe in school integration, and how would they feel about bringing a black friend home for dinner) show steadily increasing racial tolerance over the past 30 years.

Does this mean that ethnic stereotypes and prejudice are no longer problems in the United States? Hardly. Many different surveys of racial attitudes show that about 20% of white Americans still express strong and direct racial prejudice, and while this is a minority, it is still a sizable portion of the population (Dovidio & Gaertner, 1991). Furthermore, among the 80% of "non-prejudiced" whites, many still harbor subtle forms of prejudice. The theory of *aversive racism* proposes that many white Americans hold mixed feelings toward blacks: On the one hand, they espouse the American ideals of freedom, fairness, and equality, but on the other, they have also learned from society feelings of superiority toward blacks and feelings of discomfort toward minorities (Gaertner & Dovidio, 1986). The aversive racist will behave in a nonbigoted fashion when in public settings and when consciously aware of social norms of fairness but will also show more negative feelings toward minorities when he or she can get away with it.

Recent research has distinguished between "old-fashioned" or "redneck" racism, which is crude, direct, and unambiguous, and "modern" or "symbolic" racism, which is more subtle and beneath the surface (Kinder & Sears, 1981; McConahay, 1986). Rather than expressing open prejudice and negative stereotypes about African-Americans, whites who have a high degree of symbolic racism maintain that "blacks have received more economically than they deserve" and "blacks are getting too demanding in their push for equal rights."

Thus, research on the course of prejudice and stereotypes in the United States presents both good news and bad news. The good news is that overt prejudice and racism have decreased. The bad news is that more subtle and symbolic forms of prejudice are still flourishing.

The Formation of Stereotypes

How do people acquire the generalized and sometimes inaccurate beliefs that make up stereotypes? One answer is that people form relatively accurate stereotypes by attending to traits and characteristics that best distinguish various social groups (Ford & Stangor, 1992). As we have already seen, however, stereotypes can often be inaccurate. This inaccuracy is not always attributable to malice; sometimes it results from the unavoidable ways we all attend to and remember social information. Social psychologists have recently gained considerable insight into the normal thought processes that can help create and sustain stereotypic beliefs about social groups. Let's examine three such cognitive factors: sampling errors, memory overload, and illusory correlations.

Sampling Errors and Stereotypes

All of us strive to categorize the world, to make it more predictable and controllable. Gordon Allport (1954) was one of the first of many social psychologists to note that stereotyping is closely related to other kinds of categorization. If you believe that dogs bite strangers, for example, you will know not to approach strange dogs. Similarly, if you believe that certain groups of people are dishonest, you will not do business with them. But how do we form these generalizations in the first place? And why do we reach negative conclusions about some groups but not others?

As noted in Chapter 5, we often reach conclusions about various groups based on only samples of information, and, unfortunately, our samples are often biased. Rothbart (1981) compiled a number of sampling biases that can lead people to develop stereotyped beliefs. To understand these biases, let's use as an illustration the common (and certainly false) stereotype that women are bad drivers. How might you develop such a stereotype in the first place? Unless you simply learn it, you would have to reach this conclusion after observing the driving habits of many men and women. Figure 7.6 presents some hypothetical data on the numbers of good and bad drivers you've observed and whether they were women or men. Notice that the proportion of bad female drivers is exactly the same as the proportion of bad male drivers. Still, people can reach the wrong conclusions from such "valid" data in a number of ways.

For example, a number of studies (Kanouse & Hanson, 1972; Pratto & John, 1991; see Chapter 5) suggest that people disproportionately attend to *negative* information in reaching conclusions. Thus, we are likely to focus our attention on the data in the "bad drivers" column of the table, and we may conclude from it that there are twice as many bad female drivers as there are bad male drivers.

Memory Limitations and Stereotypes

In everyday life, we rarely (if ever) have an objective tally before us (such as the data in Figure 7.6) when we reach an abstract conclusion about a group of people. Rather, we must retrieve facts from memory, and our memories are often biased by our preconceptions (see Chapter 5). If you believe that women are bad drivers, you'll probably find it easier to remember information that is consistent with those beliefs.

Furthermore, Figure 7.6 glosses over the thorny question of how you classify a person's driving as being either "bad" or "good" in the first place. For example, women pay lower auto insurance premiums than men, so if the criterion for "good"

The table shows a hypothetical sample of observed good and bad drivers of both genders. The proportion of bad drivers is the same for both genders, but because we tend to notice bad drivers more than good drivers, we may mistakenly conclude that women are poorer drivers than men. Our error lies in sampling data on "bad drivers" only and ignoring data on "good drivers."

Sex	Bad Drivers	Good Drivers	Proportion of Bad Drivers
Women	40	80	33%
Men	20	40	33%

FIGURE 7.6 How might sampling biases contribute to the formation of stereotypes?

or "bad" is insurance statistics, women are *better* drivers than men. Yet, as Chapter 5 documented, social judgments are often quite ambiguous, and preexisting schemas can dramatically influence our perceptions and interpretations of observed behaviors. Thus, what reckless male drivers classify as "bad" driving in some women may in fact be sensibly cautious driving.

The discussion of Figure 7.6 assumes that we remember specific instances of people's driving, categorize them as good or bad, and then associate each instance of driving with the driver's sex. When exposed to large amounts of redundant information, however, people may treat repeated instances of a behavior from a single person as independent instances of group behavior (Rothbart, Fulero, Jensen, Howard, & Birrell, 1978).

An examination of Figure 7.7 should make this point clearer. Note that sometimes we observe more than one instance of bad driving in a specific woman ("Betty was in a car accident" and "Betty received numerous traffic tickets"). But overall, the figure shows more good than bad female drivers. If people organize information in their memories with individual women as the units remembered, they will correctly recall that there are more good women drivers than bad women drivers. But if they remember behaviors, they will incorrectly perceive that women show more instances of bad driving behavior than good driving behavior.

In this example, if we organized information by *people*, we would remember that there were more "good" women drivers than "bad" women drivers. But if we organized information by *behaviors*, we would remember that women displayed more instances of bad driving than instances of good driving.

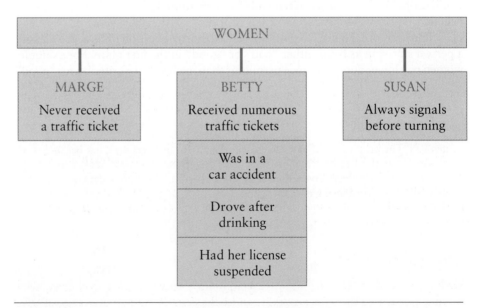

FIGURE 7.7 Stereotypes and memory organization.

Experiments by Rothbart and his colleagues (1978) demonstrated that when subjects' memories were loaded with too much information (64 pairings of people with traits), they lost track of repeated information for specific individuals. On the other hand, when they were not overloaded with information (16 pieces of information about people), subjects could accurately keep track of repetitious information and could organize that information with people as the basic units. Unfortunately, Rothbart's overloaded-memory condition is more likely to reflect reality. In the complex social environments of everyday life, we are exposed to a flood of information that competes for limited attention and memory resources. This can lead us to develop unrealistically negative stereotypes about an entire group if a few noticeable members of the group display lots of bad behaviors.

Stereotypes as Illusory Correlations

In Chapter 5 we noted that preexisting associations between pairs of facts or events can lead people falsely to perceive a correlation between those events. Thus, if you think women are more likely than men to be bad drivers, you may perceive a correlation between gender and driving aptitude after observing a number of drivers on the road, even when none exists.

We may also perceive an illusory correlation when two events or facts share some distinctive feature, such as occurring very infrequently or being very attention-grabbing. In a study demonstrating this effect, Hamilton and Gifford (1976) asked college students to read statements about both a minority group ("Group B") and a majority group ("Group A"). Twice as many statements described majority group members as described minority group members, and for each group, about twice as many statements were positive as were negative (see Figure 7.8).

Although no correlation between group membership and descriptions existed, subjects perceived such a correlation, overestimating the number of negative statements associated with members of the minority group. According to Hamilton and Gifford's interpretation, events that shared the characteristic of being infrequent (negative descriptions and minority-group membership) became associated in subjects' minds; that is, the shared distinctiveness of the events led to an illusory correlation between them.

These findings are quite disturbing; in real life, very negative traits (for example, being dishonest) and very negative acts (such as murder) tend to be rare, and, almost by definition, observations of minority members are rarer than observations of majority members. Thus, the cognitive mechanisms that lead to illusory correlations may inevitably place minorities at a disadvantage in terms of how they are portrayed in our stereotypes.

Consequences of Stereotypes

We have looked at some of the ways we *form* stereotypes. Once they exist, how do they affect our thought processes and behavior? Recent studies suggest that stereotypes may serve as schemas that influence how we process information

In Hamilton and Gifford's (1976) study, subjects read positive and negative behaviors shown by members of arbitrarily defined "majority" and "minority" groups. The following table illustrates the experimental design.

DESCRIPTIONS	Group A (Majority)	Group B (Minority)
Positive	18 Descriptions e.g., "John tells the truth" and "John's in Group A"	9 Descriptions e.g., "Steve shows up on time for work" and "Steve's in Group B"
Negative	8 Descriptions e.g., "Mike tells lies" and "Mike's in Group A"	4 Descriptions e.g., "Tom shows up late for work" and "Tom's in Group B"

As the following results show, subjects attributed positive behaviors more to the majority group and negative behaviors more to the minority group, even though the proportion of positive and negative behaviors was the same for both groups. The key factor seems to be that negative descriptions and minority descriptions shared the characterisitc of being *less frequent* and therefore more distinctive, which led subjects to associate them.

Probability that subjects attribute positive and negative behavior to members of Group A and Group B

	Group A (Majority)	Group B (Minority)
Positive behaviors	.65	.35
Negative behaviors	.48	.52

FIGURE 7.8 Illusory correlations and stereotypes.

about members of other groups, how we treat them, and, ultimately, how they respond to us.

Effects on How We Think about Others

One effect negative racial schemas may have is to bias our perceptions of people's performances and abilities in everyday life. In an experiment demonstrating this point, Jeff Greenburg and Tom Pyszczynski (1985) showed that an ethnic slur can trigger a destructive chain of schematic processing in those who overhear it. Subjects observed a staged debate between a black confederate and a white confederate on the value of nuclear energy. (The black debater argued in favor of nuclear energy; the white debater argued against nuclear energy.) In some experimental conditions the black debater presented clearly superior arguments; in other conditions the white debater presented the superior arguments.

After the debaters left the room, subjects were asked to evaluate each debater's skill and to rate on a scale which debater had won. Before making these ratings, subjects were exposed to the crucial manipulation of the study: A subject (actually a confederate in the experiment) was overheard making either a racist or a nonracist comment about the black debater. The nonracist confederate said, "There's no way the pro debater won the debate." The racist confederate said, "There's no way that nigger won the debate."

How did this ethnic slur affect the evaluations? Subjects who overheard the ethnic slur rated the black debater significantly lower, particularly when his arguments were of low quality (see Figure 7.9). Greenberg and Pyszczynski suggest that overhearing derogatory ethnic comments primed a nega-

Stereotypes as illusory correlations: A suspect in the 1993 bombing of the World Trade Center in New York. Did the constant barrage of publicity implicating a small number of radical Moslems in the bombing create a strong belief in many Americans that "Moslems are fanatics?"

tive racial schema which subjects then used when interpreting and evaluating the debaters. In the researchers' words, "Noxious labels for out-groupers . . . are not merely the symptoms of prejudice but carriers of the disease as well."

Stereotypes Can Automatically Lead to Prejudice

Do you know common stereotypes about lesbians and gay men? About blacks? About Japanese people? Chances are you do, even if you consider yourself a nonprejudiced person. In one study, Patricia Devine (1989) asked white University of Wisconsin students who were either low or high on prejudice toward blacks to list common cultural stereotypes about the characteristics of blacks. Both nonprejudiced and prejudiced groups produced quite similar lists, thus showing equal knowledge of racial stereotypes.

Given that almost all of us are familiar with common cultural stereotypes, does this acquaintance sometimes lead us automatically and inadvertently to display prejudiced thoughts and actions? Perhaps. In a second study, Devine (1989) found that after white college students were briefly exposed to words stereotypically related to blacks (for example, *ghetto, Africa, plantation*), they later judged a person described in a paragraph more negatively. This effect was automatic and unconscious—the stereotypical words were presented so quickly to the subjects that they could not accurately identify what words they had seen. Still, the subliminal perception of stereotypic words was enough to prime, or activate, negative thoughts and associations.

Are we then prisoners of the automatic prejudice triggered by negative social

Note: Ratings could range from 1 ("very poor") to 21 ("excellent")

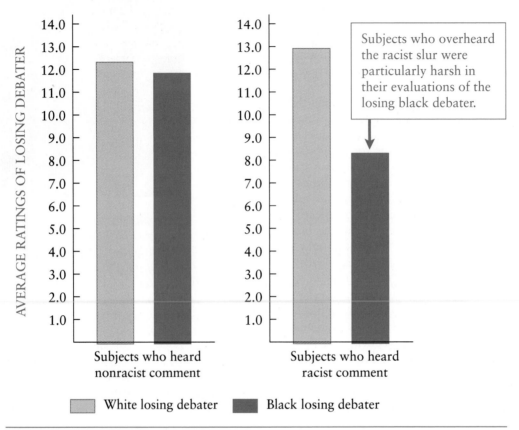

FIGURE 7.9 The effect of an overheard racist slur on cognitive processes.
Source: Data from Greenberg and Pyszczynski (1985).

stereotypes? Must we succumb to prejudice even when we wish otherwise? The answer seems to be no, at least when we can consciously think about our beliefs and feelings (Devine, 1989; Devine et al., 1991). One study found that when white college students *consciously* listed their thoughts and beliefs about African-Americans, prejudiced students listed significantly more negative thoughts than nonprejudiced students (Devine, 1989). Thus, when we consciously think about our racial attitudes, we can decide what is fair and unfair, right and wrong, and act accordingly.

The Self-Perpetuating Nature of Stereotypes

Stereotypes are formed and maintained not only by our thoughts but also by our actions toward others. Stereotypes sometimes have the unfortunate effect of leading us to behave in ways that perpetuate them.

The self-perpetuating nature of gender stereotypes was demonstrated convincingly in a clever experiment by Berna Skrypnek and Mark Snyder (1982). Pairs of college students, each consisting of a man and a woman, had to decide how to divide pairs of experimental tasks between themselves. Sometimes, one of the tasks was stereotypically feminine (for example, icing and decorating a cake) and the other was stereotypically masculine (for example, fixing a light switch). Subjects could not see each other as they negotiated; they sat in different rooms and communicated their task preferences electronically. This arrangement allowed the researchers to mislead some of the men about the gender of their partners: Specifically, some men were correctly told that their partner was a woman, some were given no information about the gender of their partner, and some were falsely told that their partner was another man.

Each pair of subjects had three trials in which to signal their task preferences to one another and reach agreement on their task divisions. On the first trial, the partners signaled their preferences simultaneously. If they didn't agree, they then moved on to second and third trials, in which the man signaled his preference first, and his partner responded with her preference.

Skrypnek and Snyder computed an index of how stereotypically masculine or feminine the tasks the women finally agreed to perform were. When the women had been labeled as females to their male partners, they ended up "choosing" significantly more feminine tasks than when they had been unlabeled or labeled as male. This "preference" for more feminine tasks remained even in a second stage of the experiment in which the woman, rather than her male partner, initiated negotiations during trials 2 and 3. In other words, once a woman labeled as female accepted her role, she tended to persevere in this division of labor, even when she could negotiate otherwise.

In sum, this study provides evidence that our stereotypical expectations can influence not only our own behavior toward members of other groups, but their behavior as well. Others may behave in ways that are consistent with our stereotypes because *we induce them to.* If a man expects a woman to perform certain "feminine" tasks, he may influence her in both subtle and not-so-subtle ways to meet his expectations.

This study yielded an additional disturbing finding: When subjects disagreed in the early stages of negotiation, the males were significantly more likely to compromise—to give in to their partner's preferences—when they were led to believe she was male. Apparently, not only did the men expect the women to accept their stereotypical roles; they also expected them to be more submissive in negotiations as well.

Effects on the Self-Esteem of Targets

What is it like being the victim of hostile, negative stereotypes? As Gordon Allport (1954) noted, "One's reputation, whether false or true, cannot be hammered, hammered, hammered, into one's head without doing something to one's character" (p. 142). Allport compiled a list of reactions people sometimes show to negative stereotypes and prejudice: They may deny membership in the disparaged group and try to "pass" as a majority member; they may withdraw and passively submit to prejudice; they may engage in protective joking and clowning; and sometimes they may attack their persecutors either through sly subterfuge or militant action.

Perhaps the most obvious prediction psychologists can make about people who are the targets of negative stereotypes and prejudice is that they will suffer from lowered self-esteem. Intriguingly, this "obvious" prediction is frequently *not* supported by research (Crocker & Major, 1989). For example, many studies suggest that in general, African-Americans and Hispanics do not have lower self-esteem than whites (Hoelter, 1983; Jensen, White, & Galliher, 1982), women do not have lower overall self-esteem than men (Wylie, 1979; see Chapter 8); homosexuals do not consistently have lower self-esteem than heterosexuals (LaTorre & Wendenburg, 1983), and so on.

How do victims of stereotypes and prejudice manage to protect and maintain their self-esteem? There are several answers to this question (Crocker & Major, 1989). First, the victims of stereotypes may "explain away" negative feedback from others as attributable to prejudice. Second, in judging their worth and success, they may compare themselves to people in their own group rather than to more advantaged majority-group members. And finally, victims of prejudice may base their self-esteem on characteristics in which their group excels.

Research evidence exists for all three of these processes, but let's focus on the first, that people who are the targets of prejudice can use it to "explain away" negative feedback. In one recent study, the subjects, who were black and white college students, were individually evaluated by another white student based on their answers to a self-descriptive questionnaire. Some subjects received positive evaluations and others negative evaluations. In addition, some subjects believed the white evaluator could see them; others believed the evaluator did not see them and thus was unaware of their race. The results: When they believed their race was known to the evaluator, black subjects attributed both negative and positive feedback more to prejudice than whites did, but these differing attributions did not occur when subjects thought the evaluator was unaware of their race (Crocker, Voelkl, Testa, & Major, 1991).

These findings show that one way blacks (and other victims of negative stereotypes) may protect their self-esteem from negative feedback is to attribute it to prejudice ("She didn't like me because she's prejudiced, not because of anything about me.") The downside, unfortunately, is that this pattern of attribution sometimes occurs for positive feedback as well ("Maybe she said nice things about me because I'm black and she's trying to compensate"). Thus, people who are the targets of negative stereotypes and prejudice are often unclear about others' motives, and they try to carefully weigh the reasons why others treat them as they do; they often pay more careful attention to the details and nuances of social interactions than nonstereotyped people do (Frable, Blackstone, & Scherbaum, 1990).

The victims of stereotypes and prejudice may be particularly likely to suffer from lower self-esteem when they hold *themselves* responsible and blameworthy for their flaws. Obesity provides a good example. There is considerable prejudice against overweight people in our society, and furthermore, obesity is judged by many to be controllable; thus, overweight people are seen as being responsible for their condition (Millman, 1980). One recent study found that while overweight women tended to attribute a man's unfriendliness to their weight, they did not blame the man for his prejudice. Rather, they blamed themselves (Crocker, Cornwell, & Major, 1993). Perhaps because of this self-blame, overweight people often suffer from lower self-esteem than normal-weight people (Wadden, Foster, Brownell, & Finley, 1984).

⌒ SOCIAL CAUSES OF PREJUDICE

For many gays, a symbolic low point came during the Republican National Convention in Houston last month, where repeated attacks on "the homosexual lifestyle" evoked images of moral decay and unraveling family life. Conservative Doberman Pat Buchanan told delegates that gay rights have no place "in a nation we still call God's country."

The blatant rhetoric only turned off most Americans, and Republican campaign strategists quickly backed President George Bush and his surrogates away from overt gay-bashing.

—*Newsweek*, September 14, 1992

Up to this point we have focused on stereotyped beliefs, their causes and consequences. However, as we noted earlier in this chapter, this focus constitutes only one level of analysis. Let's turn now to the broader individual and social causes of prejudice. In particular, let's examine socialization and personality, social ideologies, and the organization of people into social groups as causes of prejudice.

The Authoritarian Personality

Are certain kinds of people particularly likely to be prejudiced against many different groups? If so, why are they so prejudiced? Influential research on the authoritarian personality, conducted in the 1940s at the University of California, Berkeley, attempted to answer just these questions (Adorno et al., 1950).

As a first step, the researchers developed two questionnaire measures of prejudice: an Anti-Semitism Scale, which assessed attitudes toward Jewish people, and an Ethnocentrism Scale, which assessed attitudes toward many different minorities (see Figure 7.10 for sample items). Looking to Nazism as an example, the researchers assumed that prejudice was particularly associated with the political right, and accordingly they developed a scale of economic and political conservatism. Finally, based on the assumption that prejudiced people tend to have defensive personalities, the researchers developed the "F Scale," a test designed to assess fascist (that is, right-wing, totalitarian) personality tendencies (again, see Figure 7.10 for sample items).

Items from the Anti-Semitism Scale

The trouble with letting Jews into a nice neighborhood is that they gradually give it a typical Jewish atmosphere.

I can hardly imagine myself marrying a Jew.

No matter how Americanized a Jew may seem to be, there is always something different and strange, something basically Jewish underneath.

Items from the Ethnocentrism Scale

Negroes have their rights, but it is best to keep them in their own districts and schools, and to prevent too much contact with whites.

Zootsuiters prove that when people of their type have too much money and freedom, they just take advantage and cause trouble.

America may not be perfect, but the American Way has brought us about as close as human beings can get to a perfect society.

Items from the Political and Economic Conservatism Scale

The best way to solve social problems is to stick close to the middle of the road, to move slowly, and to avoid extremes.

The only way to provide adequate medical care for the entire population is through some program of socialized medicine.

In general, full economic security is harmful; most men wouldn't work if they didn't need the money for eating and living.

Items from the F Scale

Obedience and respect for authority are the most important virtues children should learn.

When a person has a worry or problem, it is best for him not to think about it, but to keep busy with more cheerful things.

People can be divided into two distinct classes: the weak and the strong.

The wild sex life of the old Greeks and Romans was tame compared to some of the goings-on in this country, even in places where people might least expect it.

FIGURE 7.10 Sample items from the four scales developed in research on the authoritarian personality. Subjects were asked to rate how much they agreed with each item on a six-point scale ranging from 1 ("strongly disagree") to 6 ("strongly agree"). *Source:* Adapted from Adorno et al. (1950).

After administering the four questionnaires to large numbers of volunteers (solicited from groups such as labor unions, community clubs, and teachers' organizations) and analyzing their responses, the researchers concluded that prejudiced attitudes are relatively consistent; that is, some people tended to be generally prejudiced against many minority groups, whereas others tended to be generally nonprejudiced. Furthermore, prejudiced people did tend to be politically and economically more conservative than nonprejudiced people, and prejudiced people showed more fascist personality characteristics as well.

The researchers next turned to their second question: How does prejudice develop? To obtain an answer, they intensively interviewed 40 prejudiced and 40 nonprejudiced subjects. These interviews pointed to a number of significant differences between the two groups. Prejudiced people generally engaged in more rigid, black-and-white kinds of thought than nonprejudiced people. Highly prejudiced subjects tended to focus more on dominance and power in their lives than on warmth and intimacy; they seemed to be concerned with status and success. Nonprejudiced subjects expressed more concern about personal relationships and helping others.

Prejudiced subjects tended to describe themselves in positive, glowing terms, whereas nonprejudiced subjects gave comparatively mixed self-portraits. The researchers interpreted this difference to mean that prejudiced people engaged in unrealistic self-glorification, whereas nonprejudiced people had a more accurate and balanced sense of their strengths and weaknesses.

Finally, prejudiced subjects would say nothing overtly negative about their parents. This finding was particularly interesting and ironic because prejudiced subjects consistently described their parents as strict and punitive disciplinarians, whereas nonprejudiced subjects described their parents as

Zootsuiter: Mexican Americans who wore clothes like these were the targets of prejudice in the 1940s. An item of the Ethnocentrism Scale (See Figure 7.10) addressed this particular form of prejudice.

loving and tolerant. Although prejudiced subjects would not openly criticize their parents, their interviews often revealed deep underlying hostility. The parents of prejudiced subjects, more than those of nonprejudiced subjects, seemed to hold unrealistically high expectations for their children. Their children *had* to be successful.

From their results, the researchers wove a portrait of the childhood development and resultant personality of the prejudiced person. They used Freudian concepts to explain a syndrome known as the "authoritarian personality," which accounts for certain prejudice by seeing its roots in status-anxious, dominating parents who use considerable physical discipline and little love in raising their children. Such children experience feelings of inadequacy in addition to hostility toward their parents. Because their parents are punitive, however, these children can't express this hostility, and because their parents expect them to "make it" and be "perfect," the children can't express their insecurities openly, either. Instead, they repress their aggression and feelings of inadequacy. Ultimately, such children develop into adults who vent their repressed hostilities and anxieties through prejudice toward various minority groups.

Criticisms of the Research

To this day, the Berkeley research on the authoritarian personality remains the largest single effort aimed at understanding prejudice in terms of child-rearing practices and personality dynamics. Although acknowledged as classic, this research has been criticized on a number of grounds (for example, Altemeyer, 1988; Christie & Jahoda, 1954; Snyder & Ickes, 1985). Some of this criticism addresses methodological matters. For example, critics have noted flaws in the way questionnaires were developed and in the methods used to conduct and code interviews. Despite these valid concerns, most subsequent research has supported many of the main conclusions of the original studies on the authoritarian personality—most notably that prejudiced attitudes, submission to authority, anger toward unconventional out-groups, and conservative religious and political attitudes are all linked (Altemeyer, 1981, 1988; Bierly, 1985; Christie, 1978; Christie & Cook, 1958; Kirscht & Dillehay, 1967; Weigel & Howes, 1985).

Because the original authoritarian-personality research and subsequent studies have revealed significant correlations between prejudice and factors such as social class, education, and IQ (Christie, 1991; Hyman & Sheatsley, 1954; Kornhauser, Sheppard, & Mayer, 1956), some social psychologists have argued that lack of education, low social class, and low intelligence—not personality—best account for prejudice. According to this analysis, parents who are authoritarian and strict disciplinarians (often because of their class background, education, and so on) generally produce children who are the same because of social learning and modeling (Altemeyer, 1988).

Recent research indicates that general levels of authoritarianism vary with social and economic conditions—for example, American culture shows more authoritarianism in economically stressed than in nonstressed periods (Doty, Peterson, & Winter, 1991). This finding again points to the importance of demographic rather than personality factors as explaining authoritarianism. In sum, many critics have held that the original research on the authoritarian personality focused *too exclusively* on personality as a cause of authoritarianism and prejudice.

MULTICULTURAL PERSPECTIVE

Is Authoritarianism the Same in Russia and the United States?

As we noted earlier, some research findings about authoritarianism have stood the test of time. But are they true in other countries and cultures as well? One early criticism of research on the authoritarian personality was that it focused too much on "right wing" authoritarianism and did not acknowledge that there are also "left wing" (for example, Communist) authoritarians (Shils, 1954). In Western democracies, research evidence shows a tendency for authoritarianism to be more associated with the political right wing than left wing (Altemeyer, 1988).

Although the concept of authoritarianism was developed to account for "fascist" tendencies in people, the core characteristics of authoritarian people—conventionality, submission to authority, and angry, self-righteous aggression toward out-groups—are not directly defined by political attitudes. Thus, the specific political attitudes authoritarian people hold may vary from country to country. A recent study demonstrated just this point when it compared authoritarian attitudes among Russians (surveyed in 1991) and Americans (McFarland, Ageyev, & Abalakina-Paap, 1992). Russians who were highly authoritarian tended to oppose laissez-faire individualism but supported equality (for example, free and equal medical care for everybody), whereas highly authoritarian Americans showed just the opposite pattern.

What are we to make of these differences? The most likely explanation is that both Russian and American authoritarians displayed their core characteristics of being conventional and submitting to authority. In Russia, this means (or at least it meant until recently) adhering to the doctrines of the Communist Party (equality, favoring a command economy), whereas in the United States, it means supporting free-market capitalism. Despite these differences between Russian and American authoritarians, there is one way they are quite likely to be similar: Both will tend to be nationalistic (strongly supportive of their respective in-groups) and prejudiced against out-groups and minorities in their respective countries.

Social Ideologies and Prejudice

Prejudice is often linked to broader social ideologies (organized systems of values, beliefs, and attitudes). Research has focused particularly on two ideological domains: political beliefs and religious beliefs.

Political Beliefs and Prejudice

As we've already noted, the Berkeley researchers who first investigated the authoritarian personality assumed that prejudice was associated with the political right. To test this hypothesis, they developed a political and economic conservatism scale based on a traditional view of the political spectrum: Conservatism (the political right) advocates personal initiative, free enterprise, and minimal government intervention, whereas liberalism (the political left) advocates social welfare programs and government regulation of business and supports labor unions. The research on the authoritarian personality found a moderately strong correlation between conservatism and prejudice. More recent research also has detected links among political conservatism, authoritarian beliefs, and prejudice (Altemeyer, 1988; Eisenman, 1991; Sears, Lau, Tyler, & Allen, 1980; Sniderman & Hagen, 1985). In one survey, for example, conservatives tended to oppose racial integration more than liberals did (Kinder & Sears, 1985).

However, a correlation does not necessarily indicate a cause-effect relationship (see Chapter 2). The correlation between political conservatism and prejudice may be attributable to other variables that are linked to conservatism, such as age, education, and religious beliefs. A number of researchers have noted that an essential component of conservative political ideology is a strong belief in personal responsibility and initiative (Katz & Hass, 1988; Sniderman & Hagen, 1985). To the extent that conservatives believe "We are what we make of ourselves," they may see disadvantaged people as responsible for their own plight.

Religious Beliefs and Prejudice

Most religions espouse a version of the Golden Rule: Do unto others as you would have them do unto you. Christian denominations frequently emphasize that all of us are "God's children." Thus, religious ideology would seem well suited to reducing prejudice.

Are church members in fact less prejudiced than nonmembers? Unfortunately, systematic research shows that the answer is no. One review categorized 34 studies as showing a positive correlation between church membership and prejudice, but only 2 as showing a negative correlation. The authors concluded that "at least for white, middle-class Christians in the United States, religion is [associated not] with increased love and acceptance but with increased intolerance, prejudice, and bigotry" (Batson & Ventis, 1982, p. 257).

Similar findings come from a recent nationwide survey of 1,799 people in the Netherlands (Eisinga, Felling, & Peters, 1990). In general, people who did not belong to churches (about 44% of the population) expressed significantly less prejudice toward ethnic minorities such as Turks, Gypsies, and Moroccans than church members did. Furthermore, the more strongly respondents endorsed traditional Christian beliefs (such as "There is a God whom we can know through Jesus Christ" and "There is a God whose kingdom will come"), the more prejudice they tended to express. Consistent with this finding, other research shows that authoritarian people are more likely than nonauthoritarian people to be religious "true believers" who accept conventional, orthodox religious doctrines (Altemeyer, 1988).

Extending earlier work by Gordon Allport (1959; Allport & Ross, 1967), Batson and Ventis (1982) argue that there are different kinds of religiousness, and each relates differently to prejudice. Some individuals are intrinsically religious; they view their religion as a central, necessary part of their identity. Others are extrinsically religious; they view religion as a means to other ends (pleasing parents, access to social and business contacts). And finally, some individuals view religion as an existential quest in which they wrestle with the basic questions of life without necessarily arriving at final, clear-cut answers.

Frequency of church attendance has sometimes been taken as a rough indicator of the intrinsic versus extrinsic orientation; regular churchgoers are assumed to be more intrinsically religious (Gorsuch & Aleshire, 1974). Among church members, the relatively inactive majority (those who attend church events on average less than once a week) tend to be more prejudiced than the more active minority (Batson & Ventis, 1982), which may imply that intrinsically religious people are less prejudiced than extrinsically religious people.

However, one study found that although intrinsically religious people *express* less prejudice than extrinsically religious people on questionnaires, they prove to be equally prejudiced when prejudice is measured behaviorally (Batson, Naifeh, & Pate, 1978). The only people with both nonprejudiced attitudes and actions are those with a high degree of quest orientation. Thus, the lower prejudice expressed by the intrinsically religious may be more a matter of social desirability than of genuine feeling (Batson & Flory, 1990). Furthermore, intrinsically religious people may be especially prejudiced against groups who are stigmatized by religious doctrines. Herek (1987b) found, for example, that extrinsically religious college students tended to be prejudiced against both gay people and blacks; the intrinsically religious, however, tended to show higher prejudice toward gay people than toward blacks—perhaps because of their religious ideologies supporting anti-gay attitudes. Similarly, McFarland (1989) found that intrinsically religious people were particularly prejudiced against gay people and Communists.

In sum, although some religious beliefs can reduce prejudice, church membership and strong religious beliefs tend to be associated with prejudice. These correlations do not prove a cause-effect relationship, however; the connection between religiousness and prejudice may be mediated by such other variables as age, social class, and education level (Simpson & Yinger, 1985). And like political beliefs, religious ideologies in part influence prejudice indirectly through their implicit assumptions about free will, personal initiative, and divine providence (Sniderman & Hagen, 1985).

Social Groups and Prejudice

So far, we have considered various social factors that lead us to learn prejudice: the way our parents treat us early in life and the political and religious ideologies we adopt throughout life. Let's turn now to a more immediate social cause of prejudice: group membership.

As we noted earlier, when we're a member of a group, we often believe that our own group (the in-group) is superior to other groups (out-groups). You can probably think of many reasons for our bias favoring in-groups. We are typically more similar to in-group members than to out-group members, and considerable research suggests that we like similar people more than we like dissimilar people (Byrne, 1971; see Chapter 9). We typically have more rewarding interactions with in-group members than with out-group members. Finally, we are simply exposed more to people in our own group than to people in other groups, and mere exposure often leads to liking (Zajonc, 1968; see Chapters 6 and 9).

Research on the Minimal Group

What would happen if we eliminated all these reasons for ethnocentrism? Suppose we place you in a room with nine strangers and arbitrarily—by the flip of a

Does the division of the world into in-groups and out-groups necessarily lead to prejudice?

coin—divide you into two groups. Your group has no history of past interaction; it shares no common goals or aspirations. Will you like your group more than you like the other group in this minimal-group situation? Many recent studies suggest that yes, you will like your group more, even if its creation was totally arbitrary.

Henri Tajfel (1978, 1982) and his colleagues conducted many studies investigating this effect. For example, Tajfel, Billig, Bundy, and Flament (1971) asked teenage British schoolboys to participate in a study that purported to deal with visual perception. The boys were shown slides that contained a large number of dots and were asked to quickly estimate the number of dots in each slide. The experimenter told them that some people are "overestimators" who consistently estimate more dots than there really are, whereas others are "underestimators." After the boys had completed the task, the experimenter randomly informed half of them that they were overestimators and half that they were underestimators. Next, the boys played a game in which they assigned points to other boys—points that later could be traded in for money. The main finding: The boys allocated points so that members of their in-group were rewarded more than members of the out-group. In other words, an overestimator rewarded other overestimators more in the experimental game, and underestimators rewarded other underestimators more.

In some sense, the groups created in this study may not have been totally arbitrary—perhaps the boys in a particular group felt that sharing a perceptual trait created a kind of similarity. To eliminate this possibility, later studies (such as Billig & Tajfel, 1973; Locksley, Ortiz, & Hepburn, 1980) devised truly arbitrary minimal groups. Subjects were assigned to groups in an openly random fashion—for example, by the flip of a coin. Yet even when subjects knew that their group had been formed totally by chance, they still showed in-group favoritism.

Tajfel's original study (Tajfel et al., 1971) demonstrated that subjects reward members of their in-group more than they reward members of the out-group. Other research extends this finding by showing that subjects in minimal-group situations also rate members of their group as being more attractive and likable (for example,

Brewer & Silver, 1978; Locksley, Ortiz, & Hepburn , 1980; Turner, 1978). Such subjects rate work produced by their group as being of higher quality than work produced by the other group (Ferguson & Kelley, 1964), and they also show attributional and memory biases that favor the in-group (Howard & Rothbart, 1980); for example, they remember in-group members' good behaviors better than they remember their bad behaviors. Finally, people in minimal groups tend to be more competitive toward the out-group than they would be as individuals (McCullum et al., 1985). In sum, these results suggest that the simple perception of being a group member leads us to like our group better, to treat other groups worse, and to behave competitively toward other groups.

Social Identity Theory

Why should mere membership in a group lead to consistent in-group favoritism? Tajfel and his colleagues (Tajfel, 1981, 1982; Tajfel & Turner, 1979) proposed a theory of social identity that attempts to answer this question.

In essence, the theory argues that a person's identity or self-image has two parts, one personal and the other social. Your personal identity contains specific facts about you as an individual: "I'm a straight-A student," "I'm a poor dancer," "I give money to the American Cancer Society." Your social identity derives from the groups you belong to: "I'm a student at State U," "I'm Catholic," "I'm Italian." Your self-esteem can be affected by both your personal identity and your social identity. For example, self-esteem related to your personal identity is probably boosted by being a straight-A student and diminished by being a poor dancer. But self-esteem related to your social identities depends on how you evaluate the groups to which you belong. For example, being Italian will boost your self-esteem if you feel positively about Italians; being a student at State U will lower your self-esteem if you consider it to be a lackluster academic institution. (See Chapter 3 for further discussion of self-concept.)

According to social identity theory, people are motivated to overvalue their own groups because doing so boosts their self-esteem. An experiment by Oakes and Turner (1980) supports this hypothesis. Subjects were arbitrarily divided into two groups on the supposed basis of their preference for the paintings of one of two modern artists. (This experimental design is quite similar to that of the "overestimators-underestimators" study described earlier.) As typically occurs in these studies, subjects rewarded members of their in-group more than they rewarded members of the out-group. But these researchers took the study a step further: Subjects completed a self-esteem scale, and the researchers found that subjects who showed in-group favoritism actually reported higher self-esteem than control subjects did.

Meindl and Lerner (1985) demonstrated the connection between self-esteem and group membership in yet another way. They reasoned that subjects whose self-esteem had been artificially lowered might "put down" the out-group to bolster their own damaged self-image. These researchers induced English-speaking Canadian subjects to suffer the embarrassment of accidentally dropping the experimenter's "important" deck of computer cards on the floor. These subjects were then asked to rate French-speaking Canadians on various traits. Subjects who had suffered this insult to their self-esteem were harsher in their ratings of the out-group than control subjects were.

Using quite different methods, a more recent study found additional evidence that information threatening to our self-esteem and sense of personal security can lead to prejudice toward out-groups. In this experiment, some Christian students were asked to think in detail about their own deaths, whereas others did not engage in this upsetting exercise. Then all the subjects were asked to evaluate two other students based on their responses to a questionnaire; one of these students was clearly Christian (a member of the in-group), the other Jewish (an out-group member). Subjects who had contemplated their own mortality showed greater prejudice toward the Jewish student but more positive attitudes toward the Christian one, demonstrating a link between insecurity about oneself and the tendency to stigmatize out-groups (Greenberg et al., 1990).

In sum, Tajfel's social identity theory points to a fundamental psychological process that leads us to perceive our own groups in the best possible light, sometimes at the expense of other groups. We do this for the most selfish of reasons: to make us feel better about ourselves.

Intergroup Competition and Prejudice

Group membership may lead to prejudice in yet another way. When people are split into groups in real life, they often must compete for limited resources. In two innovative field studies, Muzafer Sherif (Sherif, Harvey, White, Hood, & Sherif, 1961; Sherif & Sherif, 1953) investigated how group competition leads to the development of prejudice and intergroup hostilities.

Creating Prejudice through Group Competition

In Sherif's first study, 24 white, lower-middle-class boys from New Haven, Connecticut, were sent to an isolated summer camp. On the fourth day of camp, the boys were divided randomly into two groups, the Red Devils and the Bull Dogs. For the next five days, the two groups lived separately, ate at separate tables, and engaged in camp recreational activities separately. Each group established secret hideaways and camping spots and developed its own leaders, social structure, and group norms.

After strong in-group feelings had developed, the staff announced that a series of competitions would take place between the Bull Dogs and the Red Devils. Each group would be awarded points for its performance in various sports events (a daily tug-of-war contest, touch football games, and softball), as well as for their performance in carrying out camp duties such as cleaning their cabins. Each member of the winning group would receive an expensive camping knife, a highly desired prize.

Intergroup competition. Japanese-Americans in Manzanar "relocation camp," 1942. Whereas Japanese-Americans were perceived as a security threat during World War II, German-Americans were not. Why do you think this was so?

Anti-Japanese prejudice resurfaces in 1992, this time because of economic competition.

The competitions marked the beginning of hostilities between the groups. The Bull Dogs won the overall sports contest and received the coveted camping knives. The Red Devils responded by calling them "dirty players" and "cheats." On the evening of the Bull Dogs' victory, the staff held a party for all the boys, but arranged for the Red Devils to arrive first so that they could take the best ice cream and cake. The Bull Dogs retaliated for receiving the inferior remains by calling the Red Devils "low, rotten pigs," "dirty pigs," and worse.

Hostilities continued even after the games were over. One group purposely made messes to increase the work of the other group on K.P. duty. Staff members had to break up food fights that were about to lead to physical violence, and the two groups waged a "war" with green apples that resulted in two broken windows. This third stage of conflict bore all the hallmarks of prejudice and intergroup hostility: The boys showed a preference for the in-group and put down the out-group, they developed stereotypes of the out-group, and they competed—at times violently—for desirable goods. The mere establishment of groups led the boys to identify with their respective groups; injecting competition produced prejudice and intergroup violence.

Why did competition lead so readily to prejudice and conflict in Sherif's field experiment? First, note that when placed in distinct, separate groups, the boys developed a strong identification with their group. Minimal-group research suggests that even an arbitrary division into groups leads people to prefer their in-group and to reward it preferentially. When this in-group preference was combined with competition for desirable, limited resources (camping knives, party food), the boys seemed to head to an inevitable conflict.

Equity theory (Adams, 1965; Hatfield, Walster, & Berscheid, 1978; see Chapters 1 and 9) proposes that people strive for a "fair" allocation of resources in social life. For example, if you work for a company, you want to be paid in proportion to the work you do. But what would be an equitable allocation of resources for the Bull Dogs and Red Devils? The researchers arranged the contest so that it was "winner take all," necessarily leaving the other group feeling deprived, even cheated; however, even splitting the prizes and rewards equally between the two groups might not have been enough. After all, if your group is "better," doesn't it deserve greater rewards? One unfortunate consequence of group membership is that we often overestimate the goods due our group and underestimate what's due other groups.

Defusing Intergroup Hostility: The Pursuit of Common Goals

Does competition between social groups inevitably lead to intergroup hatred, prejudice, and violence? Sherif was interested not only in tracing the development of intergroup conflict, but also in uncovering techniques to reduce it. About ten years after his Bull Dog/Red Devil study, he conducted an ambitious replication that went a step further (Sherif, 1966). The subjects this time were 22 white, middle-class boys from Oklahoma City, and the location was an isolated summer camp at Robber's Cave State Park, Oklahoma. These boys were divided into two groups from the very start. For the first week, the two groups, who labeled themselves the Rattlers and the Eagles, were totally segregated, learning of the other's existence only toward the end of the week.

As in the earlier study, the staff set up a series of competitions between the groups. Again there were desirable rewards for winning: an impressive trophy, medals, and fancy camping knives. Again, as the games progressed, hostilities broke out. After the Rattlers won the first baseball game, the Eagles, eager for revenge, found and burned the Rattlers' banner. Various assaults and counterassaults followed.

Part of Sherif's purpose in this new research was to test the hypothesis that intergroup conflict can be reduced by providing equal-status, noncompetitive contact between the hostile groups in their pursuit of a superordinate goal—a higher-order goal that the groups must work together to achieve and that brings rewards to both groups (Allport, 1954; Amir, 1969, 1976; Deutsch, 1949).

So the researchers at Robber's Cave created artificial "emergencies" that could be resolved only if the two groups cooperated. When the camp lost its water supply because of a leak in a mile-long pipe, the boys broke into teams composed of both Eagles and Rattlers to inspect the pipe. And when a truck that would carry the boys to a much-desired campout got stuck in mud, they all combined forces to pull it out. Pursuing such superordinate goals and introducing non-competitive activities that included *all* the boys reduced the conflict between the Eagles and Rattlers. By the end of the study, the two groups were working and playing together. Furthermore, boys started to choose friends from both the out-group and in-group. In this limited setting, then, with the help of benevolent authorities, groups that had been separated by competition and prejudice learned to live together peacefully.

Sherif's studies add intergroup competition to the many factors contributing to prejudice already discussed in this chapter. See Summary Table 7.1 for a review. These factors are clearly interdependent. For example, social ideologies may lead to certain child-rearing practices, which in turn may lead individuals to develop certain personality traits and attitudes. The many sources of prejudice listed in Summary Table 7.1 help explain why prejudice remains a stubborn social problem.

Factors Related to Prejudice against Lesbians and Gay Men

SOCIAL
PSYCHOLOGY
IN EVERYDAY
LIFE

As we noted at the beginning of this chapter, a huge amount of social psychology research has focused on racial prejudice. However, this should not blind us to the fact that many other socially significant kinds of prejudice exist. One that has recently received increased public, media, and political attention is prejudice toward lesbians and gay men. Social psychologists have begun to explore this specific kind of prejudice, and in many ways this research confirms the importance of several of the factors we've already discussed.

SUMMARY TABLE 7.1 Sources of Prejudice			
Kind of Explanation	*Levels of Analysis*		*Example*
Group-level ↓	Sociocultural factors	Cultural and social groups	Cultural and social ideologies, political and religious doctrines
Individual-level	The social situation	The past environment The current environment and setting	Authoritarian personality research on child-rearing practices
		Groups	Minimal group research: Mere existence of in-groups and out-groups leads to preferential treatment of the in-group
			Sherif's studies: Intergroup competition leads to prejudice
		Situational cues	Overhearing ethnic slur can trigger prejudiced thoughts
Mediating variables	The personality of the prejudiced person	Personality	Authoritarianism
	The phenomenology of the prejudiced individual	Beliefs, attitudes	Prejudiced beliefs and attitudes learned in many possible ways
			Religious and political beliefs and attitudes
		Stereotypes, schemas, and cognitive processes	Learned by observing and remembering social information; can be influenced by sampling errors, memory overload, and illusory correlations
Current responses toward ⟶	The target of prejudice	Prejudiced thoughts Prejudiced feelings Prejudiced behaviors	Our behaviors may induce others to behave consistently with our stereotypes

Are some kinds of people more likely than others to hold negative attitudes toward gay people? The answer provided by a number of studies is yes. One consistent finding is that men on average are more prejudiced than women toward gay people (Herek, 1984; Kunkel & Temple, 1992). Why is this so? One reason may be that men often affirm their masculinity by putting down feminine traits and characteristics, and since male homosexuality is seen by many men to be "feminine," it is derogated. And because lesbians are often perceived to be "dominant," "powerful," "strong," and "independent of men," men may often see them as a threat to their male power, status, and sexual prerogatives, with the net result that they dislike lesbians as well (Herek, 1991).

People who endorse traditional sex roles—for example, who believe that husbands should work and control finances and that wives should rear children and take care of the home—tend to be more prejudiced toward homosexuals, perhaps because they view them as a threat to traditional sex roles (Herek, 1984). People who are religious, politically conservative, and who live in rural areas also are more likely to be prejudiced toward them (Bouton et al., 1989; Herek, 1984, 1991). These findings are consistent with research we discussed earlier, and they indicate that political and religious ideologies play an important role in prejudice against gay people. In the United States, residents of the South and Midwest tend to be more prejudiced against homosexuals than people in other regions are (Herek, 1984). These regional variations suggest that prejudice toward gay people may develop in part as a kind of conformity to local norms.

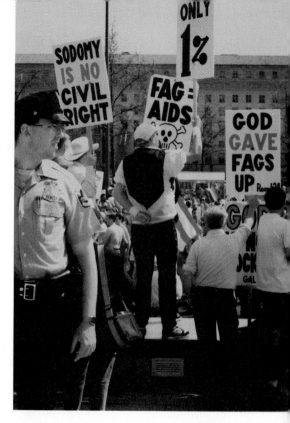

Is there a link between religious beliefs and prejudice towards gay people?

Authoritarianism is consistently correlated with prejudice against gay people (Herek, 1988, 1991). Indeed, negative attitudes toward gay people seem to be a defining feature of authoritarianism in recent years (Altemeyer, 1988). You'll recall that early research on the authoritarian personality found that people who are prejudiced against one minority tend to be prejudiced against other minorities as well. This finding holds for prejudice against homosexuals—people who are prejudiced against them are more likely to express racial prejudice as well (Bierly, 1985).

Not surprisingly, real-life contact with homosexuals makes a difference in people's attitudes—people who have openly gay friends and associates tend to be less prejudiced toward gay people in general (Gentry, 1987). Furthermore, people's attitudes toward homosexuals tend to become more positive as they acquire more education and information about them. Thus, when people attend human sexuality classes, human relations workshops that address gay and lesbian concerns, or hear gay speakers, they often become less prejudiced as a result (Anderson, 1981; Cerny & Polyson, 1984; Lance, 1987).

In general, prejudice against gay people has declined in the United States over the past ten years or so, and an increasingly large number of Americans (now a majority) support civil rights for them (Sniderman, Brody, & Tetlock, 1991). Why have public attitudes changed? One reason may be that increasing numbers of people in the United States know openly gay people or, at least, they have seen some in the mass media. These findings show that prejudiced attitudes can change, and they lead us naturally to the final topic of this chapter: What are effective ways of reducing prejudice? ⤳

REDUCING PREJUDICE

In his memoir "Coming Out Conservative," the conservative activist Marvin Liebman recalls Ronald Reagan's distress when his son wanted to become a dancer. "Aren't dancers sort of . . . funny?" he asked. Mr. Reagan was soothed when Mr. Liebman invoked the names of Baryshnikov and Fred Astaire. But Mr. Liebman was ashamed.

He writes: "I had stood quietly and achingly a gay man in the closet, competent to deal with Ronald Reagan's open fears about his son, unable to deal openly with the facts of my own life. I had failed to tell him that many of us were 'funny' and that there would be nothing degrading about it if 'unfunny' people, like him, did not make it so."

—*New York Times*, October 28, 1992

As we just noted, people tend to be less prejudiced against gay people when they have contact with gay friends and acquaintances. Does this finding hold for other groups as well? For example, would blacks and whites get along better if they had more contact with one another? As the Robber's Cave study showed, one way to reduce intergroup prejudices is to bring people from antagonistic groups together, particularly in pursuit of a common goal. After all, people cannot learn that their stereotypes are wrong and that members of other groups are just people like themselves unless they interact with them.

Intergroup contact does not always breed goodwill, however. When contact is between privileged majority children and underprivileged minority children, for example, contact may increase tensions and reinforce stereotypes. What conditions must be met in order for intergroup contact to reduce prejudice? Drawing on the work of others (see Miller & Brewer, 1984), Gordon Allport first strongly focused social psychologists' attention on the hypothesis that certain kinds of intergroup contact are necessary to produce beneficial results. Allport concluded that

> prejudice . . . may be reduced by equal status contact between majority and minority groups in the pursuit of common goals. The effect is greatly enhanced if this contact is sanctioned by institutional supports (i.e., by law, custom or local atmosphere), and provided it is of a sort that leads to the perception of common interests and common humanity between members of the two groups. (1954, p. 281)

Many studies have examined the validity of Allport's intergroup-contact hypothesis over the past 30 years (see, for example, Amir, 1969, 1976; Harding, Proshansky, Kutner, & Chein, 1969; Katz, 1970; Miller & Brewer, 1984). One focus of this research has been to determine *when* intergroup contact leads to greater harmony and reduced prejudice. Besides the qualifying conditions suggested by Allport, others have suggested that intergroup contact is most effective when it's intimate rather than casual, when it's pleasant and noncompetitive, and when it occurs between groups that already possess somewhat favorable attitudes toward each other before contact takes place (Amir, 1969).

Contact between Groups in Schools

Can we design programs that produce healing contact between real-life social groups who dislike one another—programs that are analogous to the final stages of the Robber's Cave study? Beginning in 1954 with the Supreme Court decision of *Brown v. Board of Education* that threw out the "separate but equal" doctrine, the United States embarked on a dramatic experiment in social change when it began to desegregate the public schools. Suppose your job was to implement school desegregation. What would be the most effective way to reduce prejudice and foster racial harmony?

Does intergroup contact reduce prejudice? Assistant Secretary of Housing and Urban Development Roberta Achtenberg—an open lesbian—works with her secretary.

The list of factors provided by Allport and Amir offers guidance, but it also gives some reasons for pessimism. How can we arrange equal-status, intimate, pleasant contact in the pursuit of common goals between groups that are initially hostile to each other and often come from very different socioeconomic backgrounds? Research suggests that the more affluent a community is, the less it welcomes bused-in minority children to its schools (Miller, 1990). And while busing disadvantaged urban minority children to a white suburban middle-class school may physically intersperse the children in classrooms and school activities, it does not produce "equal-status" contact between white children and minority children—the white children will most likely continue to have a cultural and educational edge over the minority children. Can schools foster friendly, intimate contact between such different groups? And what common goals can children pursue in school that will promote racial harmony?

Recent summaries of research on school integration have documented mixed results. Since the mid-1950s, as integration has been partially implemented in the United States, educational achievement has declined somewhat for both blacks and whites (Gerard, 1983; Miller & Brewer, 1984). Of course, declining scholastic performance may not necessarily be attributable to integration. And while integrated schooling may increase interracial friendships, minority students still often remain at an educational disadvantage that translates to lower status and power in the classroom compared to their majority classmates (Cohen, 1984), and integration typically does not lead to increased self-esteem in African-American schoolchildren (Stephan, 1991).

Still, integration does have a number of long-term advantages for minority students (Stephan, 1991). For example, blacks who attend integrated high schools are less likely to drop out and more likely to attend and complete college. Furthermore, they tend to get better jobs and earn more money than blacks who attended segregated schools. Finally, they are more likely to form interracial friendships, and both blacks and whites who attend integrated schools are more likely to live in integrated housing as adults.

When is school integration most likely to be effective? One thing is clear: Simply placing students of different races and ethnic groups together in the classroom is not enough to produce high-quality integrated education. Because the typical North American classroom values individual achievement and competition among students, members of disadvantaged minority groups often compare poorly with majority students, and as a result, they frequently fall behind in school and are labeled "stupid" by the majority group. One solution suggested by social psychologists is to introduce cooperative learning procedures into the classroom (Aronson, 1978; Chasnoff, 1978; Lyons, 1980; Roy, 1982; Singh, 1991).

In one study, Weigel, Wiser, and Cook (1975) compared the effects of cooperative and traditional teaching techniques in newly desegregated schools. Subjects were junior high and senior high school students who were new to these integrated schools. Approximately 60% of the students were white, 20% were African-American, and 20% were Hispanic. In the traditional classrooms, students worked as individuals in whole classes of students; in the cooperative classes, students worked in racially mixed teams of four to six students and cooperated as a group on all assignments. The teachers in this study were ethnically varied, and each teacher taught both traditional and cooperative classes.

The results of this study suggest that cooperative ethnic contact indeed has positive effects. Students in the cooperative classes showed significantly less

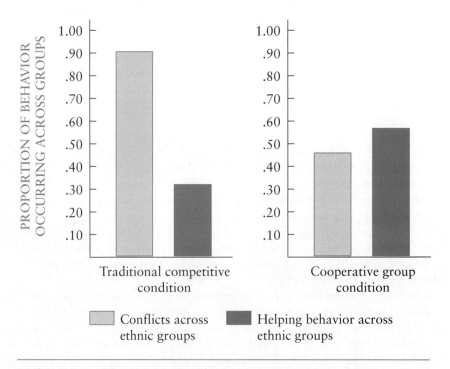

FIGURE 7.11 Effects of cooperative teaching techniques in newly desegregated schools. *Source:* Data from Weigel, Wiser, and Cook (1975).

interracial conflict and were significantly more likely to help students of other races (see Figure 7.11). Furthermore, white students in cooperative classrooms were less likely to say that white students possess more desirable traits than minorities do and were more likely to choose nonwhite students as partners in various activities. But even though cooperative classrooms clearly led to greater harmony between groups *in the classroom,* students in these classrooms showed no *general* shifts in their attitudes toward minorities or toward integration and segregation. Other research has produced similar results (Cook, 1984).

The Effect of Contact on Intergroup Attitudes

Sometimes, making friends with a person from a different racial or ethnic group does not lead to changed attitudes toward the group. Why should this be the case? One possibility is that though we come to like individuals we know from other groups, we don't view these friends as representative or typical of the larger group.

An experiment by David Wilder (1984) attempted to determine when pleasant contact between members of different (and somewhat hostile) groups leads to better feelings between the groups and reduces stereotypes about the out-group. Specifically, Wilder had women students from Rutgers or Douglas College (both part of the State University of New Jersey) work on various problems (for example, anagrams or riddles) with a female confederate who pretended to be a student from the other college. Earlier testing had shown that women from each college had fairly strong, somewhat negative stereotypes about women from the other college. Rutgers women tended to view Douglas women as conservative, too concerned with their appearance, and overly interested in good grades; Douglas women described Rutgers women as apathetic toward scholarship, as "party animals" interested only in having a good time, and as too liberal.

Will this male officer change his attitudes about women officers after working with one?

Some of Wilder's confederates reinforced the stereotype of their supposed school. For example, one confederate labeled as a Douglas student dressed nicely and wore makeup, said she was a home economics major, talked about her conservative political club, and mentioned that she hoped the experiment would be brief because she had a lot of studying to do. Other confederates did not reinforce the stereotypes associated with their supposed school. Wilder manipulated another variable in this experiment: The confederate was pleasant and helpful to some subjects, and unpleasant and denigrating to others.

In this experiment, contact with the confederate most influenced subjects' evaluations of the out-group (that is, the other college) when the interaction was pleasant and the confederate was perceived as *typical* of her college—that is, when she matched subjects' stereotypes (see Figure 7.12). Although subjects' liking for the out-group was increased by contact, their stereotypes about the out-group remained much the same.

This study points to an important bind in which minority group members sometimes find themselves. If they cultivate liking from majority group members, this liking will be generalized to their group only if they are perceived as typical of their group (that is, when they show stereotypical traits and characteristics). But that just serves to reinforce those stereotypes, including unflattering ones.

In general, contact with out-group members is most likely to lead us to develop more favorable attitudes toward out-groups when our interactions are structured enough to ensure that the contact is positive in tone (Desforges et al., 1991) and when contact leads us to view ourselves as members of one large group rather than in terms of in-groups and out-groups (Gaertner, Mann, Dovidio, Murrell, & Pomare, 1990). Thus, for example, if your school runs human relations workshops to bring together students from different racial and ethnic backgrounds, it should design them to have two characteristics: (1) The workshops should be structured enough to ensure that participants have positive and constructive interactions (they should avoid, for example, free-for-all rap sessions, which run the risk of degenerating into hostile exchanges). (2) They should develop a common group identity ("We are all students at this university with common interests and goals") rather than focus on identities based solely on race or ethnicity ("I am African-American," "I am white," "I am Hispanic," "I am Asian"). Note that Sherif's Robber's Cave study achieved both these goals: By creating "problems" that the boys could solve only through specific, engrossing activities and by introducing superordinate goals, Sherif fostered structured positive interactions among the boys that led them to think of themselves as one group (campers at Robber's Cave) rather than two (Eagles or Rattlers).

Residential Contact

Over the past 40 years, the United States has had great success in racially integrating public facilities and the workplace, some success in integrating schools, and less success in integrating neighborhoods (Hamilton, Carpenter, & Bishop, 1984; Schnare, 1980; Van Valey, Roof, & Wilcox, 1977). One reason for residential segregation may simply be that people prefer to live with "their own kind"; certainly

Note: Higher numbers represent more positive ratings of women's colleges.

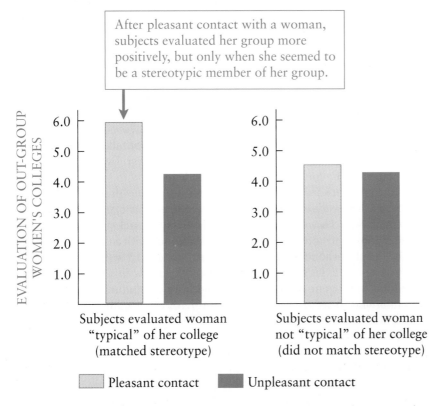

After pleasant contact with a woman, subjects evaluated her group more positively, but only when she seemed to be a stereotypic member of her group.

Pleasant contact   Unpleasant contact

The Wilder study helps explain why positive interaction with one member of a minority group may not change our attitudes toward the group. If we view the individual as an "exception" (that is, he or she doesn't match our stereotype of the group), then we won't modify our stereotypes and attitudes about the group as a whole.

FIGURE 7.12 Evaluating a group after interacting with one member of the group. *Source:* Data from Wilder (1984).

there is a lot of social psychology evidence suggesting that similarity leads to attraction (as we shall see in Chapter 9), and people of similar races, ethnic and religious backgrounds, and socioeconomic levels often do choose to live together in the same neighborhoods.

The generally lower economic status of certain minorities—African-Americans, for example—may contribute to segregation; minorities simply are less able to afford "mainstream" housing. But this is at best a partial explanation, because blacks and whites of the same socioeconomic status still tend to live in segregated settings (Bianchi, Farley, & Spain, 1982; Wilson & Taeuber, 1978).

Survey research and opinion polls point clearly to prejudice as a major cause of residential segregation. Although whites have become more tolerant of integration in housing over the past several decades, many still hold reservations. Whites strongly prefer to live in all-white neighborhoods, whereas blacks have a much stronger preference for integrated housing (Farley, Schuman, Bianchi, Colasanto, & Hatchett, 1978; Lake, 1981).

In an early and still often cited study, Deutsch and Collins (1951) investigated the effects of equal-status interracial contact in government housing projects in New York City. Although many psychologists interpret that research to be supportive of the contact hypothesis, others (for example, Cagle, 1973) have argued that enforced residential mixing leads to few actual social contacts between the races. You can live next door to someone and still not talk to him or her.

But is talking really necessary to change attitudes? David Hamilton and George Bishop (1976) conducted an ambitious field study to see what happens to white residents' attitudes when blacks move into their previously segregated neighborhood. These researchers identified eight middle-class, white neighborhoods around New Haven, Connecticut, in which a black family had recently purchased a home and compared these neighborhoods with a control group of ten comparable neighborhoods into which a white family had just moved.

As you might expect, the arrival of a black family in a formerly all-white neighborhood was quite noteworthy. Neighbors continued to describe it to research interviewers as a "change in the nature of the neighborhood" for a year afterward, whereas the arrivals of white families in control neighborhoods were soon forgotten. Also not surprisingly, the initial comments made by whites about their new black neighbors tended to be negative.

Even though whites did not interact much with their new black neighbors, their attitudes nevertheless became less prejudiced and less racist during the following year. Hamilton and Bishop suggest that the whites probably held negative stereotypes about blacks ("They don't take care of their houses") and negative expectations about what would happen to their neighborhood ("Property values will go down"). When their dreaded expectations were not realized after a year of integration, whites' attitudes changed.

Hamilton and Bishop's study implies that contact need not necessarily be intimate, or social, or face to face to produce positive results. Particularly if, through their actions and appearances, minority members contradict stereotypes commonly held by the majority, then the majority's attitudes and beliefs may be altered simply by passive contact—by observing, if not relating to, the minority members. This research suggests that, under certain circumstances, residential integration can help reduce prejudice.

Vicarious Contact through the Mass Media

Sometimes we do not have to encounter members of another group physically to be "in contact" with that group. For years, the mass media have at times intentionally and at times inadvertently fostered stereotypes and prejudice. A study during World War II analyzed how "stock" minority characters were portrayed in the media (Writers' War Board, 1945). Generally, heroes and "good" characters were

Left: *The cast of "Sesame Street": Does the favorable portrayal of different ethnic groups on TV shows reduce prejudice?*
Below: *The white actors who played "Amos & Andy" portrayed a highly stereotyped image of African-Americans.*

Anglo-Saxon, whereas menials, servants, and criminals were likely to be minorities. According to this study, the portrayals provided by popular fiction "could easily be used to 'prove' that Negroes are lazy, the Jews wily, the Irish superstitious, and the Italians criminal." This analysis from the 1940s focused considerable attention on radio, the dominant mass medium of the day:

> The broadcasting fraternity has been arguing for years as to whether "Amos 'n' Andy" helps or hurts the Negro race. Some Negroes do, some don't, object to the series. Another continuing argument revolves around "Rochester" on the Jack Benny program. This presentation is good-natured and pictures "Rochester" as quick-witted and wise, yet it is stereotyped on all the usual accounts—addiction to drink, dice, wenching, and razors. (quoted in Allport, 1954, p. 201)

Today, stereotyping in the media is less extreme than it was 40 years ago. For example, in 1949–50, blacks appeared in less than 1% of all magazine ads; this increased to 2% in 1967–68, and, most dramatically, to 9% by 1982. And over the past 20 years, more and more series on prime-time TV have featured black characters, including the hugely popular *Cosby Show* (Dovidio & Gaertner, 1991). Despite these changes, research evidence still accumulates about negative portrayals of various minorities and of women. Furthermore, it's important to note that while African-Americans appear in TV shows roughly in proportion to their numbers in American society, Asian and Hispanic Americans do not—they are clearly underrepresented. And until quite recently, some minorities—lesbians and gay men, for example—rarely appeared at all in the mass media. When they did, they were portrayed in extremely negative and stereotypic ways.

The mass media have undoubtedly contributed to prejudice and stereotyping in our society. Can they contribute to its reduction as well? The answer seems to be a tentative yes. For example, children who watched integrated social interactions on the show *Sesame Street* developed more positive attitudes toward blacks and Hispanics (Bogatz & Ball, 1971). A Canadian replication of this study introduced content into *Sesame Street* that was directly relevant to Canadian minorities: Asians, Indians, and French-Canadians (Gorn, Goldberg, & Kanungo, 1976); again, sympathetic media portrayals led to reduced prejudice. The Canadian preschoolers who viewed *Sesame Street* were more likely to pick nonwhite children as potential playmates than control children were.

An extensive review of research on the effects of TV on racial and ethnic attitudes concludes that positive attitude change is possible, particularly with extensive viewing (Graves, 1980). "You've got to be taught to hate," states a well-known song lyric from the musical *South Pacific*. Fortunately, with the help of enlightened media programming, people can be taught not to hate as well.

PREJUDICE IN PERSPECTIVE

This chapter has focused primarily on racial prejudice and prejudice toward lesbians and gay men. There are many other kinds of prejudice throughout the world, however, that create misery for millions of people. Social psychologists have studied prejudice in its various forms for well over half a century, and in the process, they have measured its course, analyzed its causes, and studied ways to reduce it. This research indicates that prejudice is a perennial but not hopeless problem.

Stereotypes are the cognitive side of prejudice; they embody all the beliefs we hold about social groups. While stereotypes have much in common with other kinds of mental categories, they can at times seriously distort our perception of social reality. Stereotypes often describe out-groups more negatively than in-groups and portray them as being more extreme and uniform than they actually are. Inaccurate stereotypes can sometimes be formed through normal mental processes—for example, through sampling errors and memory overload—and they may sometimes represent illusory correlations. The negative stereotypes we hold about some groups can have serious consequences in everyday life—they can bias the ways we judge members of out-groups, they can guide our behavior in ways that lead out-group members to behave consistently with our stereotypes, and they can undermine the self-esteem of their targets and make them unsure of the reasons for our actions.

Prejudice is a social phenomenon, and thus it has many social causes. Among these are child-rearing practices, social learning, and the authoritarian personality traits and attitudes they sometimes lead to; political and religious ideologies; the division of our social world into groups; and the competition that often occurs between these groups.

While prejudice has many causes, it is not inevitable, and when it occurs, it can be reduced. Social psychologists have intensively studied how positive contact between groups can reduce prejudice and increase intergroup harmony. Cooperative classrooms can help develop positive racial attitudes in integrated schools; residential integration can reduce prejudice; and positive images of various groups in movies and TV can teach us all not to hate.

For more than 50 years, social psychologists have pursued a simple but important idea: To overcome prejudice, we must first understand it.

Studying Prejudice

Defining Prejudice

A prejudice is a negative attitude toward a group or toward an individual member of a group. Prejudiced attitudes comprise emotions, beliefs, and behaviors.

Analyzing Prejudice

Prejudice can be analyzed in terms of historical, sociocultural, situational, personality, and phenomenological factors.

Stereotypes: Prejudiced Beliefs

Measuring Stereotypes

Stereotypes are overgeneralized and often inaccurate beliefs we hold about groups or group members. Several different methods have been developed to measure

KEY POINTS

stereotypes, including having people identify in an all-or-none fashion traits that characterize groups, having people rate the percentage of group members who show traits, and computing a diagnostic ratio—that is, dividing people's estimates of the percentage of group members who show traits by their estimates of the percentage of people in general who show the same traits.

Are Stereotypes Wrong?

Stereotypes frequently portray out-groups more negatively than in-groups, and they lead people to underestimate the variability of people in out-groups.

Social Psychology in Everyday Life: Have Stereotypes and Prejudice Weakened in Recent Years?

While people have not expressed in recent years ethnic and racial stereotypes that are as negative and simplistic as those expressed in earlier times, prejudice still remains in more disguised and symbolic forms.

The Formation of Stereotypes

Stereotypes can result from biased sampling of social information, the processing of complex social information with limited memory resources, and illusory correlations.

Consequences of Stereotypes

Stereotypes can influence how people process social information and how people evaluate members of other groups. Stereotypes often lead to behavior that induces out-group members to behave consistently with the stereotypes. The targets of negative stereotypes may protect their self-esteem by attributing negative feedback to prejudice.

Social Causes of Prejudice

The Authoritarian Personality

Research on the authoritarian personality shows that some individuals are consistently prejudiced against many minority groups. Such people report having punitive, status-anxious parents and tend to describe themselves and their parents in an unrealistically positive manner and minorities in an unrealistically negative manner. Authoritarian people show submission to authority, conventionality, and hostility toward out-groups. Whereas earlier research on authoritarianism explained it in terms of Freudian personality dynamics, modern research tends to explain it more in terms of social learning.

Authoritarianism in Russia is linked to opposition to laissez-faire free enterprise and support for equality; just the opposite is true in the United States.

Social Ideologies and Prejudice

Both political conservatism and religiousness are correlated with prejudice. The causes of these correlations are complex.

Social Groups and Prejudice

Minimal-group research shows that when people are arbitrarily divided into groups, they show bias in favor of their in-group. Tajfel's *social identity theory* argues that this bias results from people's motivation to boost their self-esteem through a positive social identity.

Intergroup Competition and Prejudice

Competition among groups for scarce resources can lead to prejudice. In two classic studies of schoolboys at summer camps, Muzafer Sherif found that group competition inevitably led to conflict, prejudice, and stereotypes in the two competing groups. The creation of superordinate goals helped reduce conflict and prejudice in the second study.

Social Psychology in Everyday Life: Factors Related to Prejudice against Lesbians and Gay Men

Prejudice toward gay men and lesbians is associated with being male, religious, conservative, and supportive of traditional sex roles. It is more common in rural areas and in certain regions of the United States than others. Individuals tend to be less prejudiced toward gay people the more acquaintance they have with them.

Reducing Prejudice

The intergroup contact hypothesis holds that certain kinds of contact between groups (for example, contact that is socially supported, equal-status, and in pursuit of common goals) lead to a reduction of prejudice.

Contact between Groups in Schools

Competitive classrooms may amplify social inequities when unequal-status students from different groups are integrated. Cooperative classrooms, which have students work together on projects, are more effective in increasing interaction between students from different groups.

The Effect of Contact on Intergroup Attitudes

Although intergroup contact can lead to more positive interactions among members of different groups, it does not necessarily lead to changed attitudes toward out-groups. Positive experiences with an out-group member is most likely to lead to changed attitudes toward the out-group when the member is seen as typical of his or her group.

Residential Contact

Prejudice is a significant cause of residential segregation. Housing integration can be effective in reducing stereotypes and prejudice.

Vicarious Contact through the Mass Media

Although the mass media have often perpetuated negative stereotypes and prejudice, they can also reduce prejudice through favorable depictions both of minority groups and of interactions among different groups.

KEY TERMS

Authoritarian personality: A personality syndrome hypothesized to lead to consistently prejudiced beliefs and attitudes; research suggests that authoritarian people tend to have been reared by punitive, status-anxious parents, and as a result they hold rigid and conventional beliefs, submit readily to authority, and show hostility to out-groups.

Aversive racism: A hypothesized variety of subtle and indirect racism; the aversive racist is conflicted—he or she believes in equality and fairness but still has learned from society negative feelings toward racial minorities.

Diagnostic ratio: A method of measuring stereotypes in which subjects are asked to estimate what percentage of people in a group possess a trait and also what percentage of people in general possess the same trait; the diagnostic ratio is the ratio of these two percentage estimates.

Discrimination: Overt acts that express prejudice and treat members of a group unfairly compared to members of other groups.

Ethnocentrism: The belief that one's own group is superior to other groups.

Minimal group: An arbitrary group with no social history that is created in the laboratory; research on minimal groups shows that people evaluate in-groups more positively than out-groups, even in such arbitrary groups.

Prejudice: A negative prejudgment of a group or group member that is often unwarranted and based on limited, insufficient information; a prejudice can be conceptualized as a negative attitude comprising emotional, cognitive, and behavioral components.

Social identity theory: Tajfel's theory that people have both personal and social identities; people are motivated to evaluate in-groups more positively than out-groups in order to enhance their social identities and increase self-esteem.

Superordinate goal: A higher-order goal that can be achieved only if groups cooperate with one another; Sherif argued that intergroup contact in the pursuit of superordinate goals can help reduce intergroup conflict and prejudice.

GENDER AND SOCIAL BEHAVIOR

Exposure to danger is not combat. Being shot at, even being killed, is not combat. Combat is finding . . . closing with . . . and killing or capturing the enemy. It's *killing*. And it's done in an environment that is often as difficult as you can possibly imagine. Extremes of climate. Brutality. Death. Dying. It's . . . uncivilized! And women *can't do it!* Nor should they even be thought of as doing it. The requirements for strength and endurance render them *unable* to do it. And I may be old-fashioned, but I think the very nature of women disqualifies them from doing it. Women give life. Sustain life. Nurture life. They don't *take* it.

—*General Robert H. Barrow,* former commandant of the
Marine Corps, in testimony to the Senate Armed Services Committee
concerning the role of women in the military (*New York Times,* July 21, 1991)

New roles for women in the 1990s. Women participating in Army combat training.

Do you think women should serve in the military? Why or why not? In fact, many women do serve in the armed forces of the United States and other countries as well. Broken down by service, women make up 5% of the U.S. Marine Corps, 9% of the Navy, 11% of the Army, and 14% of the Air Force—overall representing about 11% of the 2.1 million Americans in uniform. The percentage of women serving as officers in each branch of the military is roughly comparable to the percentages just listed; however, the highest-ranked officers still tend to be disproportionately male: About 16% of lieutenants are women, 13% of captains and majors, 5% of lieutenant colonels and colonels, and under 1% of generals and admirals (*Los Angeles Times,* February 14, 1991).

Clearly, many women serve with distinction in the military. But military women still do not have the same opportunities as men. In the Navy, women are not allowed on carriers, battleships, or destroyers, and in the Army, women are not allowed in the infantry or in commando units. (Some of these prohibitions seem likely to change between the time I write these words and the time you read them.)

Should women perform the same duties as men? For example, should women serve as combat soldiers? As of the early 1990s, the American public was quite divided on this issue. A 1992 Roper poll found that 47% of Americans opposed the government's policy of banning women from front-line combat duties; 44% supported the policy. A large majority of Americans (58% to 69%)

believed that women should be permitted to work in warships, combat aircraft, and tank and artillery crews; only a minority (about 40%), however, felt that women should participate in Marine landings and hand-to-hand combat. While most Americans agreed that women should have the *right* to serve in combat roles, they also felt that such participation should be voluntary, which is not always the case for men.

The debate over women's roles in the military reflects a larger debate about the social roles of women and men in general. Should women and men have equal opportunities in education, work, and public life, and equal participation in all aspects of private life as well? Does our society treat women and men differently, and if so, is this different treatment unfair? Do social stereotypes portray women and men as different, and are such stereotypes limiting and destructive to both men and women? Are women and men in fact different? If so, how and how much?

The debate about women's role in the military touches on all these questions, and it is exactly these important and at times politically charged questions we shall address in this chapter.

Police woman training for riot control.

THE CHANGING ROLES OF MEN AND WOMEN

To understand social psychology research on gender, it helps first to consider briefly the recent history of women and men, and their changing roles in society. (For a succinct chronology of the role of women in the U.S. military, see Figure 8.1). Throughout much of recorded history, the relationship between men and women has been one of clear inequality. As recently as the 19th century, scientists generally maintained that women were intellectually inferior to men, and some suggested that if women even attempted to think and work like men, they would lose their reproductive capacity (Cole, 1979; Ehrenreich & English, 1979; Shields, 1975; Spence, Deaux, & Helmreich, 1985). Women in the United States could not vote, sit on juries, or manage their own financial affairs. They could not even demand legal custody of their children. By law, women were chattel—property—of men.

Barred from most forms of higher education a century ago, women now make up almost 55% of U.S. college students (U.S. Department of Education, 1992). The education that women pursue often differs from that pursued by men, however. In recent years, women have earned a majority of the bachelor's degrees awarded in some fields—for example, 90% of B.A.s in home economics, 78% in education,

1901: Army establishes auxiliary of nurses. In 1908, Navy installs similar auxiliary.

World War I: Navy and Marines enlist women to fill clerical positions. After war, women are demobilized.

World War II: Army's WAC (Women's Army Corps), Navy's WAVES (Women Accepted for Voluntary Emergency Service), and parallel organizations established in other branches. Some women serve in war zones, but away from front. Overall, women make up 2.3% of military.

1948: Legislation is enacted banning women from combat. Ceiling of 2% placed on number of women in each branch. Army gives WAC permanent status.

1950: Congress temporarily lifts 2% limit during Korean War.

1967: 2% limit permanently removed, along with many restrictions on grades to which female officers could rise. Percentage of women in the military is still less than 1%.

1968: First major increase in number of women in services since 1953. About 7,500 women serve in Vietnam, but none in combat assignments.

1970: Two women promoted to rank of general, first time in U.S. history.

1972: Five-year program established to increase number of women in nonmedical fields.

1975: Military academies ordered to open their doors to women.

1978: Women's Army Corps is dismantled, integrates its personnel into regular Army.

1983: Female pilots fly support helicopters during Grenada invasion.

1986: Four women co-pilot noncombat planes during Libyan mission.

1989: Army Capt. Linda Bray, leading 30 military police, engages in combat in Panama.

1990: Army rejects Pentagon advisory group's suggestion that women be allowed combat assignments on experimental basis.

1991: 30,000 women make up 6% of U.S. forces in Gulf War.

FIGURE 8.1 Chronology of the role of women in the U.S. military. *Source: Los Angeles Times,* February 14, 1991.

73% in foreign languages, and 67% in fine arts—but a minority in other fields—31% of B.A.s in physical sciences, 26% in architecture, 14% in engineering, and under 1% in military science (U.S. Department of Education, 1992).

Apart from their abilities, women and men often have quite different levels of interest in various educational fields and careers (Eccles, Adler, & Meese, 1984; Lubinski & Benbrow, 1992). For example, men tend to be more interested in "thing-oriented" topics like engineering and the physical sciences, whereas women tend to be relatively more interested in "people-oriented" fields like social sciences and the humanities.

Right and bottom left: *"Rosie the Riveter" did "men's work" during World War II . . . but during the 1950s she returned to the home.* Bottom right: *The women's movement of the 1970s and 1980s has led to broader job opportunities for women today.*

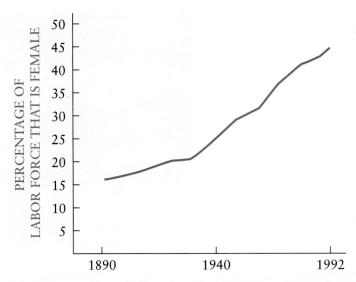

Since 1890—and especially since World War II—the percentage of U.S. workers who are female has increased dramatically.

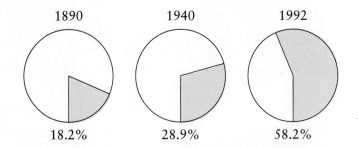

PERCENTAGE OF U.S. WOMEN WHO WORK

And by the early 1990's, a sizable majority of U.S. women worked.

FIGURE 8.2 Women in the civilian labor force—1890–1992.

Employment discrimination based on sex is now illegal in the United States under the Civil Rights Act of 1964, yet women still face discrimination in the workplace. Over the last century, the percentage of women in the U.S. labor force has grown steadily (see Figure 8.2), and while increasingly more women work as high-status professionals, women still on average hold lower-status jobs than men, receive lower wages than men, and have fewer opportunities for advancement (Tavris & Wade, 1984; Touhey, 1974).

As of the early 1990s, the ratio of the median income of working women to that of men was about .72—that is, the median income of women was 72% of men's

(*New York Times,* October 18, 1992). This ratio varies somewhat depending on the kind of work—for example, it is .94 for high school teachers, .82 for doctors, .76 for bus drivers, and .74 for billing clerks (Hartmann & Spalter-Roth, 1991). According to some observers, the discrepancy results from the fact that women haven't yet "worked their way up," in some cases because of childbearing. There are marked differences even in the pay of female and male service workers who have the same levels of education, skills, and work history. Perhaps because these disparities are so entrenched, many women have come to expect and accept lower pay and less advancement in their jobs than men do (Major & Konar, 1984).

As women have become increasingly active in the work world, they have also tended to retain primary responsibility for child care and housekeeping in the United States (Biernat & Wortman, 1991; Gunter & Gunter, 1990; Heiss, 1986). Even though attitudes toward sex roles have been changing in recent years, many men have not substantially increased their contributions to housework (Hochschild, 1989; Pleck, 1979; Walker & Woods, 1976).

In sum, despite marked changes in the roles of women and men throughout the 20th century, gender still has a profound effect on social organization and on individuals' behavior, especially in the areas of work and family.

PSYCHOLOGICAL RESEARCH ON SEX AND GENDER

Some psychologists use the word *sex* to refer to the biological status of being male or female and *gender* to refer to social definitions of male and female, including all the nonbiological characteristics that society uses to differentiate men and women (Deaux, 1985; Kessler & McKenna, 1978; Unger, 1979). For most of us, sex is defined primarily by the genitalia—women have vaginas, and men penises. Gender, however, is displayed and defined by a host of cues and behaviors, including styles of dress, nonverbal mannerisms, hobbies and interests, occupations, personality traits, and roles in family life.

Social psychology research on sex and gender has traditionally focused on two main topics: how people perceive men and women, and the existence or nonexistence of sex differences (Deaux, 1985; Unger, 1979). The first kind of research often investigates the stereotypes people hold about men and women, and how people evaluate men and women differently. (For example, are women perceived to be more emotional and less logical than men? Do managers judge equivalent work of women and men differently?) Sex-difference research attempts to document the ways men and women actually are alike and different in their behavior. (For example, are men on average more aggressive than women? Are women more nonverbally sensitive than men? Do men engage more in task-oriented behaviors in groups, and women more in emotional, friendly behaviors?) We shall consider both of these topics in this chapter.

The topic of behavioral sex differences will lead us naturally to theories of how sex (genes and genitalia) develops into gender (different behaviors and roles for women and men). Finally, we'll turn to the topic of gender and individuality. In particular, we'll discuss links between gender and self-esteem and the nature of masculine and feminine personality traits.

STEREOTYPES ABOUT MEN AND WOMEN

ABOARD THE USS JASON

Seaman Sonya Snowden wears the dungarees and light-blue work shirt of enlisted crew. She is in uniform. She *is* uniform. Another blue crest in a toiling sea of men.

The Navy ship is 40 miles off San Diego. But for this emergency drill, the vessel is steaming the Strait of Hormuz dodging mines.

A voice surges over the intercom:

IRANIANS CARRYING AIR-LAUNCHED ANTI-SHIP MISSILES

Like the other 175 women and 815 men on board, Snowden buckles a life preserver around her back, snaps a gas mask to her hip. She pulls on a flash hood and chemically impervious gloves. Her curves and curls disappear under layers of gear. All signs of femininity are leveled.

But not erased. Snowden is the only woman in her division. Guys tell the petite 23-year-old "Nice butt" and "I'd like to run you up." They wag their tongues at her. . . .

"Men feel like we're invading," [Snowden] says, but then adds proudly, flexing a bone-hard biceps, "The guys call *me* he-woman."

Three years in the Navy, this sailor is ship-wise: ready, willing and able . . . to conform with the macho culture.

—*Washington Post*, September 22, 1992

Does this excerpt about Sonya Snowden support or challenge your stereotypes about women? Your stereotypes about men? What *are* your stereotypes about women and men—that is, what traits do you think women and men possess, and how do they differ from one another? Do you agree with the following? "Women are weaker than men. Men are more mechanically inclined than women. Women are more emotionally sensitive and supportive than men. Men are sexually cruder than women." Research on stereotypes about women and men probes these and other common beliefs about the sexes.

Personality Stereotypes

Strong stereotypes exist about the personality traits possessed by men and women. (See Chapter 7 for a discussion of the definition and measurement of stereotypes.)

One well-known early study asked 80 college women and 74 college men to rate how much "an adult woman" or "an adult man" possessed each of 122 different personality characteristics. The data showed that subjects believed many traits to be more characteristic of one sex or the other (Rosenkrantz, Vogel, Bee, Broverman, & Broverman, 1968; see Figure 8.3).

Furthermore, statistical analyses of subjects' ratings indicated the existence of two *clusters* of traits that subjects thought differentiated women and men (again, see Figure 8.3). One cluster of traits, seen as more typical of men, related to instrumental, goal-oriented characteristics, such as *competitive, logical, skilled in business, self-confident*. The second cluster, seen as more typical of women, dealt with nurturing and expressive characteristics, such as *gentle, aware of the feelings of others, easily expresses tender feelings*.

These stereotypes—that men possess instrumental traits and women expressive traits—have been documented in many different studies (Ashmore, Del Boca, & Wohlers, 1986). They are held by people of varying ages (including children as young as 5 or 6), by single and married people, and by educated and uneducated people (Biernat, 1991; Broverman, Vogel, Broverman, Clarkson, & Rosenkrantz, 1972; Kohlberg, 1966; Ruble, 1983). These stereotypes are relatively consistent across cultures (Williams & Best, 1982), and they show themselves in men's and women's ratings of themselves as well as in their ratings of others (Stake, 1992; Williams & Best, 1990). And despite changes in women's and men's social roles, these stereotypes remain largely unchanged in recent years (Bergen & Williams, 1991; Martin, 1987; Ruble, 1983).

Do gender stereotypes portray men and women's personalities as "different but equal"? Not always. People sometimes perceive the "male" end of various trait dimensions to be more desirable than the "female" end (Rosenkrantz et al., 1968). (For example, being *logical* is desirable; being *illogical* is not. *Logical* is sometimes judged to be more characteristic of men and *illogical* more characteristic of women.) Widiger and Settle (1987) have argued that the Rosenkrantz study exaggerated the value people attach to "male" traits simply because their list included more positively valued "male" traits than "female" traits. When Williams and Best (1982) assessed the personality stereotypes about men and women held by people in many different countries, they found that stereotypically "male" traits were judged to be only slightly more positive than "female" traits, a finding consistent with Widiger and Settle's analysis. However, "male" traits were also judged to be more "active" and "strong" than "female" traits, and strength and activity often have positive connotations. Perhaps men and women are perceived as possessing different kinds of good traits—men as more achieving and powerful, but women as generally nicer and more pleasant (Eagly & Mladinic, 1989; Eagly, Mladinic, & Otto, 1991).

Gender stereotypes are not always applied equally to men and women. Eagly and Kite (1987) demonstrated this when they asked 300 male and female students at Purdue University to rate the probability that the people in 28 countries possessed assorted instrumental traits (such as *ambitious, aggressive*) and expressive traits *(kind, understanding)*. One group of students made their ratings for people of different nationalities with their sex unspecified (for example, they rated the probability that the Swiss are honest); other groups rated the men or the women

The table shows the traits associated with each sex by a sample of college men and women in 1968. The traits are grouped in terms of the rated desirability of being "masculine" or "feminine" on a given trait.

STEREOTYPICAL SEX-ROLE ITEMS (responses from 74 college men and 80 college women)

Competency Cluster: Masculine pole is more desirable   *Warmth-Expressive Cluster: Feminine pole is more desirable*

FEMININE	MASCULINE	FEMININE	MASCULINE
Not at all aggressive	Very aggressive	Doesn't use harsh language at all	Uses very harsh language
Not at all independent	Very independent	Very talkative	Not at all talkative
Very emotional	Not at all emotional	Very tactful	Very blunt
Does not hide emotions at all	Almost always hides emotions	Very gentle	Very rough
Very subjective	Very objective	Very aware of feelings of others	Not at all aware of feelings of others
Very easily influenced	Not at all easily influenced	Very religious	Not at all religious
Very submissive	Very dominant	Very interested in own appearance	Not at all interested in own appearance
Dislikes math and science very much	Likes math and science very much	Very neat in habits	Very sloppy in habits
Very excitable in a minor crisis	Not at all excitable in a minor crisis	Very quiet	Very loud
Very passive	Very active	Very strong need for security	Very little need for security
Not at all competitive	Very competitive	Enjoys art and literature	Does not enjoy art and literature at all
Very illogical	Very logical	Easily expresses tender feelings	Does not express tender feelings at all easily
Very home-oriented	Very worldly		
Not at all skilled in business	Very skilled in business		
Very sneaky	Very direct		
Does not know the way of the world	Knows the way of the world		
Feelings easily hurt	Feelings not easily hurt		
Not at all adventurous	Very adventurous		
Has difficulty making decisions	Can make decisions easily		
Cries very easily	Never cries		
Almost never acts as a leader	Almost always acts as a leader		
Not at all self-confident	Very self-confident		
Very uncomfortable about being aggressive	Not at all uncomfortable about being aggressive		
Not at all ambitious	Very ambitious		
Unable to separate feelings from ideas	Easily able to separate feelings from ideas		
Very dependent	Not at all dependent		
Very conceited about appearance	Never conceited about appearance		
Thinks women are always superior to men	Thinks men are always superior to women		
Does not talk freely about sex with men	Talks freely about sex with men		

Traits stereotypically perceived to be related to gender fell into two clusters: instrumental traits (such as *dominant, competitive,* or *adventurous*), perceived to be more typical of males, and expressive traits (such as *tactful, gentle,* or *expresses tender feelings*), perceived to be more typical of females.

FIGURE 8.3 Gender stereotypical traits. *Source:* Rosenkrantz et al. (1968).

of a given nationality (they rated the probability that Swiss men or Swiss women are honest).

Two interesting findings emerged. First, stereotypes of nationality groups in general resembled stereotypes of their men more than those of their women. Second, the ratings of instrumental and expressive traits for the men of different countries were quite variable; by contrast, women were given low ratings on instrumental traits and high ratings on expressive traits regardless of their nationality (see Figure 8.4). In other words, women of different nationalities tended to be judged more in terms of their gender, whereas men were judged more in terms of their nationality.

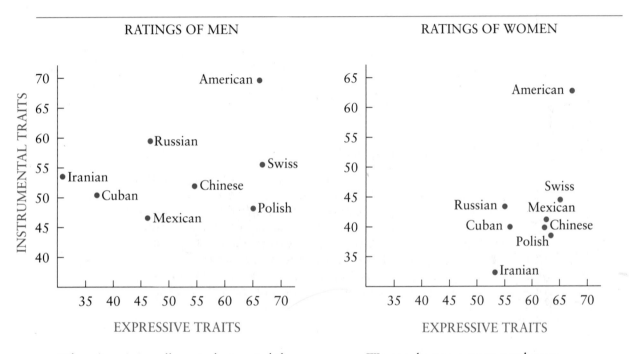

When American college students rated the men and women of various countries on a number of instrumental and expressive traits, the males were rated quite variably. For example, Iranian males were perceived to be low on expressive traits (not *kind* or *understanding*) and moderate on instrumental traits (*dominant, ambitious*), whereas Polish males were perceived to be high on expressive traits but relatively low on instrumental traits.

Women, however, were rated more uniformly. Except for American women, women from various countries were uniformly perceived to be high on expressive traits but low on instrumental traits. In other words, women tended to be perceived in terms of gender stereotypes, whereas men were perceived in terms of nationality stereotypes.

FIGURE 8.4 Stereotypes of men and women of different countries. *Source:* Adapted from Eagly & Kite (1987).

The researchers explained their findings in terms of the social roles of men and women in most countries:

> Because women have considerably less power and status than men do, no doubt their behavior is observed relatively little by foreigners, and the behavior that is observed consists largely of domestic activities and, for some countries, work carried out in low-status, poorly paid occupations. As a result, stereotypes of nationalities are more similar to stereotypes of their men than of their women.
>
> (Eagly & Kite, 1987, p. 461).

This study found that American women were rated less in terms of gender stereotypes than women of other countries (again, see Figure 8.4). Why was this so? The American college student subjects in the study undoubtedly had observed American women in more varied roles than women of other countries, and thus they did not form such strong stereotypes about American women. Furthermore, they showed ethnocentrism—as Americans, they rated Americans (including American women) as generally having better traits than people of other countries.

Broader Stereotypes about Gender

Gender stereotypes embrace more than personality traits. To assess people's everyday conceptions of gender, Myers and Gonda (1982) asked 200 Canadian college students to define the words *masculine* and *feminine*, and then they grouped these responses into different categories. In order of frequency, students most often defined masculinity and femininity in terms of physical appearance and characteristics (for example, "muscular," "wears makeup," or "has a deep voice"), social or biological roles ("bears children," "sexually attractive to men [or women]," "gay" or "not gay"), and biological sex. Personality characteristics were fourth in frequency, accounting for only about 14% of subjects' total responses. A subsequent study asked a group of married men and women in Austin, Texas, to describe masculinity and femininity and to describe what defined their own manhood or womanhood. Again, physical characteristics and social and family roles seemed to define subjects' commonsense notions of gender more than personality traits did (Spence & Sawin, 1985).

Kay Deaux (1984; Deaux & Lewis, 1983, 1984) provided additional evidence that gender stereotypes have many components. In one study, she asked subjects to rate the probability that men and women display various characteristics; for example, what's the probability that a woman "cooks meals" or is "warm" or is "muscular"? Some of the results of this study are presented in Figure 8.5.

Notice that the differences between the subjects' probability judgments for women and for men tend to be larger for physical characteristics and role behaviors than for personality traits. Deaux's research also demonstrated that the different components of gender stereotypes are rather loosely linked; that is, her data showed relatively weak correlations among probability estimates of "male" or "female" physical characteristics, roles, personality traits, and sex (being biologically male or female). Thus, people believe that certain behaviors and

Probability Judgments of Traits*			Probability Judgments of Role Behaviors*			Probability Judgments of Physical Characteristics*		
Charac-teristic	For Men	For Women	Charac-teristic	For Men	For Women	Charac-teristic	For Men	For Women
Independent	.78	.58	Financial provider	.83	.47	Muscular	.64	.36
Competitive	.82	.64	Takes initiative with opposite sex	.82	.54	Deep voice	.73	.30
Warm	.66	.77	Takes care of children	.50	.85	Graceful	.45	.68
Emotional	.56	.84	Cooks meals	.42	.83	Small-boned	.39	.62

Note: The larger the difference in the estimates for men and women on a given item, the more that characteristic was stereotypically perceived to differentiate the two sexes.

*Subjects' estimates of the probability that the average person of either sex would possess a characteristic.

Subjects' stereotypes tended to be stronger for role behaviors and physical characteristics than for personality traits.

FIGURE 8.5 Components of stereotypes about men and women. *Source:* Based on Deaux and Lewis (1983).

characteristics tend to correspond with being either male or female, but they do not hold these stereotypes in an all-or-nothing fashion. These stereotypes can have important real-life consequences, however, as we shall see in the following sections.

Gender Stereotypes and the Perception of Ability

The lieutenant squints mascaraed lashes at the sun on the horizon. She rises onto her toes. The windows on the bridge are too high for most women, but Deann Van Wormer refuses to stand on a box, because "it says I need something extra as a woman to stand my watch—and I don't."

If Van Wormer were a man, her colleagues say, the star lieutenant would be chief engineer on a battleship. Instead she's stuck on a repair ship with mediocre male officers.

—*Washington Post*, September 22, 1992

Has Deann Van Wormer's career advancement been blocked because she was a woman? Despite her excellence, has Van Wormer been judged less competent than male peers simply because of her sex? More generally, are women sometimes perceived to be less able than men because of their gender and not because of the quality of their work?

Gender and Perceptions of Competence

An early experiment addressing such questions had female subjects read essays on "masculine" topics (for example, city planning) and "feminine" topics (for example, elementary school teaching). Some subjects were told the authors of the essays were men; others thought the authors were women. The subjects evaluated articles attributed to male authors more positively than those attributed to female authors, even when the topics addressed were "feminine." Thus, women seemed to be prejudiced against other women (Goldberg, 1968).

A review of more than 100 studies like this one argued that the evidence is quite weak that people in general evaluate men's work more positively than equivalent work performed by women (Swim, Borgida, Maruyama, & Myers, 1989). Furthermore, studies like Goldberg's sometimes suffer from the methodological problem of using male names that are more attractive than the female names used, and the effects of name attractiveness are then confounded with gender bias (Kasof, 1993).

Still, there seem to be particular circumstances in which women are judged to be less competent than men based on equivalent information. One such situation is when women perform "masculine" rather than "feminine" tasks (Pheterson, Kiesler, & Goldberg, 1971; Swim et al., 1989), which is noteworthy because the high-status jobs in most societies are usually considered "masculine." Another scenario is when men and women are evaluated for hiring based on equivalent résumés or job applications (Olian, Schwab, & Haberfeld, 1988). This too is noteworthy because of the everyday importance and real-life consequences of such evaluations.

In addition to sometimes judging women as less competent than men, subjects in experimental studies also sometimes *explain* women's and men's work performance differently. Subjects tend to attribute women's success more to luck or extremely hard work and men's success more to their ability (Deaux & Emswiller, 1974; Nieva & Guteck, 1981). Thus, John gets an "A+" on his chemistry exam because he's smart, but Jane gets an "A+" because she studied hard and had a good day. These differing attributions may result in part from the *assumption* that women are less competent than men.

Can Information about Individuals Overcome Gender Stereotypes?

Do our gender stereotypes always influence our judgments of particular people, and can concrete information about individuals override our reliance on such stereotypes? Ann Locksley and her colleagues conducted an experiment that showed concrete information about specific women and men seems at times to eliminate the effects of general stereotypes (Locksley, Borgida, Brekke, & Hepburn, 1980). Both male and female subjects were asked to read descriptions of a college woman and a college man and to estimate on a scale from zero (never) to 100 (always) how assertive they were. Some subjects received no behavioral information about the woman or man. Other subjects received information that was diagnostic of assertiveness—for example, that in class the student broke into a conversation that was being dominated by another student. A third group of subjects received information that was irrelevant to assertiveness—for example, that the student went to get her (or his) hair cut before class.

When subjects received either no behavioral information or information that was irrelevant to assertiveness, they stereotypically judged the woman to be less assertive than the man. When provided with information that was diagnostic of assertiveness, however, gender stereotypes disappeared, and subjects perceived both the woman and the man as assertive (see Figure 8.6).

Locksley's results, although intriguing, seem to go against common sense. Don't gender stereotypes sometimes influence our judgments of particular men and women, even when we possess concrete information about them? A careful mathematical analysis examined how individual subjects estimate probabilities (for example, the probability that a person is assertive) based on information about the person's group membership (this person is female) and information about the specific individual (this person breaks into conversations). The researchers found that stereotypes do influence people's judgments of individuals, even when information is present about the specific individual that contradicts the stereotype. However, judgments made on the basis of concrete information are less influenced by stereotypes than are judgments based on no concrete information (Rasinski, Crocker, & Hastie, 1985).

	Judged Assertiveness of an Individual Who Was:	
Kind of Information	Male	Female
Sex only	49.4	46.6
Sex and a behavior unrelated to assertiveness	48.7	44.1
Sex and a behavior diagnostic of assertiveness	67.6	67.3

Note: The higher the number in the table, the more assertive the individual was judged to be.

FIGURE 8.6 Subjects' judgments of a woman's or a man's assertiveness based on sex and concrete behavioral information. *Source:* Data from Locksley, Borgida, Brekke, and Hepburn (1980).

Additional evidence that gender stereotypes can influence people's judgments even in the presence of individuating information comes from the important real-life arena of personnel selection. Glick, Zion, and Nelson (1988) asked 200 business professionals in Wisconsin to evaluate a job résumé. Sometimes the applicant's name was "Kate Norriss" and sometimes it was "Ken Norriss." In addition, sometimes the job applicant was described by "feminine" behaviors (for example, the applicant had worked as an aerobics instructor and had been captain of the pep squad) and sometimes by "masculine" behaviors (the applicant had worked in a sporting goods store and had been captain of the varsity basketball team). Subjects were asked to rate the applicant's personality and to judge how qualified the applicant was for each of three jobs: sales manager for a heavy machinery company ("masculine" job), administrative assistant at a bank (gender-neutral job), and dental receptionist/secretary ("feminine" job).

The results indicated that concrete information about specific feminine and masculine behaviors, rather than the applicant's sex, determined personality impressions. However, the businesspeople still rated male applicants as more qualified for the "masculine" job and female applicants as more qualified for the "feminine" job, despite the individuating information. Apparently, these business-people based their judgments *both* on gender stereotypes and on the individual's characteristics and work experience.

SOCIAL
PSYCHOLOGY
IN EVERYDAY
LIFE

Gender Stereotypes and the Chilly Classroom Climate for Women

What I find damaging and disheartening are the underlying attitudes . . . the surprise I see when a woman does well in an exam—the condescending smile when she doesn't.

(*female,* physical sciences, Berkeley)

I have witnessed female students in two lower-division courses treated as ornaments—as if they lacked any semblance of intellectual capacity—both occasions by male instructors.

(*male,* social sciences, Berkeley)

A professor repeatedly cuts off women while in the middle of answering in class. He *rarely* does this to men.

(*female,* Harvard)

—from Sandler and Hall (1982),
"The Classroom Climate: A Chilly One for Women?"

Do gender stereotypes sometimes lead teachers to treat male and female students differently? The distressing answer provided by a number of studies is yes (Sandler & Hall, 1982, 1986). In particular, teachers often interact with their students in ways that reinforce gender stereotypes and that favor males over females. Three specific ways teachers create a "chilly classroom climate" for women are: (1) They sometimes view male students as more intellectually competent than women. (2) They sometimes assign more power and status to male than to female students. (3) They sometimes perceive and evaluate male and female students in different and biased ways. Let's look at some examples of these various kinds of teacher bias.

Teachers may sometimes use common gender stereotypes (for example, that women are "maternal" and "nurturant") to conclude that the academic ambitions of women are not as serious as men's. As one woman recalled, "I told my advisor I wanted to continue working towards a Ph.D. He said, 'A pretty girl like you will certainly get married. Why don't you stop with an M.A.?' " (Sandler & Hall, 1982, p. 10). To appreciate how stereotypic this advisor's comment was, change the sex of the student—imagine an advisor telling his male student, "A good-looking guy like you will certainly get married. Why don't you stop with an M.A.?"

Perhaps because they view males as more likely to achieve academically and pursue careers, teachers often encourage male students more. This differential treatment starts in grade school and continues in junior and senior high school (Vandell & Fishbein, 1989). It shows itself in various ways: Teachers often talk with boys more than girls during classroom interactions (Eccles & Blumenfeld, 1985), and they often pose more complex questions to boys than to

The chilly classroom climate for women. Do teachers treat female and male students differently?

girls and encourage boys' responses more than girls' (Sadker & Sadker, 1982). When students ask questions, teachers often respond more to questions from male students. As one Berkeley student noted, "Women who [ask questions] are not answered, so women have stopped asking questions." (Sandler & Hall, 1982).

Because of gender stereotypes, men often end up having more power in the classroom than women do. They may be chosen more frequently than women as teacher assistants, for example, and they may take better physical locations than women when observing laboratory demonstrations. Sometimes the power differences between male and female students can be quite blatant: "Some women have reported certain professors instruct male medical students to 'scrub' with the faculty but women medical students with nurses. These kinds of arrangements may not only lead women students to doubt their competence, but also prevent women . . . from learning as much as men students" (Sandler & Hall, 1982, p. 7).

Teachers' gender stereotypes sometimes lead them to perceive and evaluate female and male students in quite different ways. Women may be judged more in terms of their physical appearance, and men more in terms of their competence and scholastic achievements. A Harvard woman reported, "I have yet to hear a professor comment on the daily appearance of a male colleague. I have yet to go through a week without some comment pertaining to my appearance" (Sandler & Hall, 1982).

Gender stereotypes may also intrude when faculty negatively evaluate women who are pursuing studies in traditionally "masculine" fields. One female student reported, "I was interested in majoring in crop science in the College of Agriculture and went to see my academic advisor. He encouraged me to change my major instead to horticulture, because it would not be as difficult a major as crop science. He told me that crop science required fieldwork and would be hard for a woman to handle" (Sandler & Hall, 1982, p. 11). As we noted earlier, women are still very much underrepresented in fields such as engineering, physical sciences, and architecture. The chilly climate women find in these traditionally masculine fields may help explain why this is so.

One message of this research is that gender stereotypes have the power to touch *you* in a setting you undoubtedly spend a lot of time in: the college classroom. And while we have emphasized the effects of the classroom climate on women, undoubtedly it affects men as well—for example, it reinforces their gender stereotypes and inhibits their ability to work well with female peers.

Is it possible to make the classroom climate friendlier toward women? The answer is certainly yes. First, teachers and schools must realize that there is a problem that needs to be solved. Second, schools need to implement policies that educate teachers about their gender stereotypes and that offer clear instructions about how to treat women and men equally in the classroom (Sandler & Hall, 1986).

✑ SEX DIFFERENCES IN BEHAVIOR

Opening combat to women . . . raises a thorny civil rights issue. Equal opportunity is not the same in the military as it is in civilian life—where no one actually forces you to, say, take a job or sit at a lunch counter. When pressed, commanders can take any soldier in any specialty, except chaplains and medics, and make him a rifleman. If combat jobs are opened to women officers who want them, courts citing the equal protection doctrine would presumably rule that women who *don't* want them are eligible for transfer too, just as men are.

Two female officers who testified before Senator John Glenn's subcommittee on defense manpower said that risk is part of signing up to defend your country. The two sergeants said many women would think about quitting instead. Recruiters might face a nightmare. The services prize their enlisted women, who have more education, initially get promoted faster, and even when pregnancy is included, take less time off than men, who lose it to sports and auto injuries and drug, alcohol and discipline problems.

Proponents of letting women fill some combat jobs recall the aphorisms that were once used to keep blacks out of them, to wit, that they would run, could not follow orders, and were psychologically unequipped to lead whites. Only through integration under Truman did such notions get refuted. Women, they argue, deserve the same chance.

—*New York Times,* July 21, 1991

The debate about women in the military sometimes focuses on presumed differences between men and women—for example, that men are more aggressive than women and that women are more reliable workers than men. Are these—or any of the other stereotypical beliefs about women and men discussed earlier—based on fact? And even if there are psychological and behavioral differences between women and men, do gender stereotypes nonetheless exaggerate the perceived magnitude of these differences? Let's turn to these intriguing and sometimes hard-to-answer questions.

The Study of Sex Differences

Psychologists have devoted considerable energy to studying and understanding the behavior of men and women (Deaux, 1985; Eagly, 1987; Lips, 1993; Maccoby & Jacklin, 1974). Research on sex differences clearly has great social relevance, particularly at a time when the roles of women and men are rapidly changing, and such research is often controversial and disputed with great emotion. The study of sex differences may fall prey to two opposite biases (Hare-Musten & Marecek, 1988). The first overemphasizes differences, casting females and males as "opposite

Changing images of women in the movies. Mary Pickford, 1920s.

sexes" with mutually exclusive qualities. The second bias, which is in part a response to sexist traditions in society and in psychological research, tends to minimize and even ignore sex differences. The truth of the matter of psychological sex differences probably lies somewhere between these two extreme interpretations of the evidence (Eagly, 1987; Eagly & Wood, 1991). In order to understand the evidence concerning sex differences, it is important to understand some basic statistical concepts and methods first.

The Statistical Assessment of Group Differences

When groups of people (for example, women and men) are measured on some physical or psychological characteristic (for example, height, aggressiveness, IQ, or amount of eye contact during interaction), these measures can be plotted as frequency distributions. Such distributions show the numbers of people displaying different ranges of scores. When plotted as a graph, they often take the approximate form of a bell-shaped theoretical curve called the *normal distribution* (see Figure 8.7). To investigate sex differences, psychologists must compare two distributions, one for women and one for men. Let's illustrate this for a variable that obviously differs between the sexes: height.

Kathryn Hepburn, 1940s.

Susan Sarandon and Geena Davis in "Thelma & Louise," 1991.

Some measures (such as height and IQ) obtained from large samples of people approximate a bell-shaped curve called the normal distribution. The mean of a distribution is the arithmetic average of all observed scores. In a normal distribution, the mean is at the center of the distribution. The standard deviation is a conventional measure of the spread of a distribution. In a normal distribution, about two-thirds of all scores are between one standard deviation below and one standard deviation above the mean.

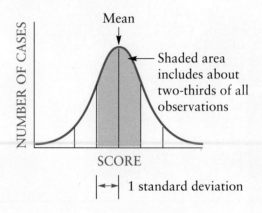

FIGURE 8.7 The normal distribution.

The *mean* of a distribution is the arithmetic average of the scores of all the people plotted in the distribution. According to one study, the mean height of American women is 64 inches (5 feet, 4 inches), and the mean height of American men is 70 inches (5 feet, 10 inches) (Gillis & Avis, 1980). In a normal distribution, the mean is exactly at the middle of the distribution.

The *standard deviation* is a conventional measure of the spread of a distribution (again, see Figure 8.7). You can roughly think of the standard deviation as being the average distance individuals' scores are from the mean. If most people's scores are close to the mean, the standard deviation is small, whereas if most people's scores are spread out far away from the mean, the standard deviation is large. In the Gillis and Avis (1980) data, the standard deviation of height for each sex is 2.3 inches.

In a normal distribution, a little over two-thirds of all scores fall within one standard deviation above or below the mean (again, see Figure 8.7). Because height is approximately normally distributed, about two-thirds of American women have a height between 61.7 inches and 66.3 inches, and about two-thirds of American men have a height between 67.7 and 72.3 inches. Thus, most men are taller than most women.

Figure 8.8 provides a graphic illustration of the distributions of women's and men's heights. As you can see, these distributions are quite distinct; they do not overlap very much. To quantify the degree of difference between the two

As explained in the text, the *d* statistic is a measure of the degree of difference between the means of two normal distributions, expressed in standard deviation units.

Panel (**a**) shows the distribution of women's and men's heights. The computed value of *d* is very large, indicating that men are noticeably taller than women on average and that the two distributions do not overlap much.

(**a**) *d* = 2.6 (very large)

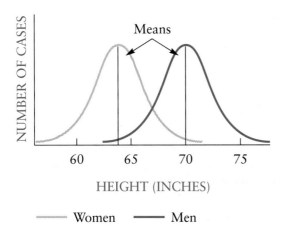

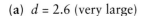 Women ——— Men

d values of 2.6 are very rare in psychological research. For psychological data, Cohen (1977) describes *d* values of .8 as "large," values of .5 as "medium," and values of .2 as "small."

(**b**) *d* = .8 (large) (**c**) *d* = .5 (medium) (**d**) *d* = .2 (small)

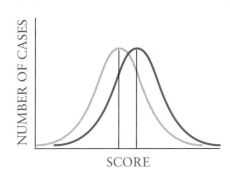 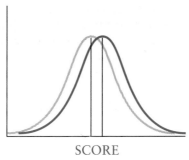 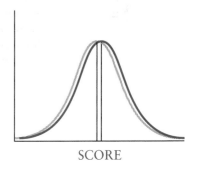

Note: To simplify the discussion, we have assumed that the normal distributions for both men and women have equal standard deviations. This assumption is not always warranted, however. For example, in measures of intellectual abilities, men's scores often have a greater spread (larger standard deviation) than women's scores do—that is, there are more very low-scoring and very high-scoring men than women. However, *d* can still be computed for such distributions.

FIGURE 8.8 Pairs of normal distributions with differing means.   343 distributions, statisticians compute the difference between the mean height of women and the mean height of men and divide the difference by the standard deviation of these distributions. The resulting number is called d, the value of which can be either positive or negative. In our example, d is: $(64 - 70)/2.3 = -2.6$. The value of d tells how far apart the means of two distributions are, in standard deviation units.

As a general rule of thumb for psychology research, Cohen (1977) suggests that a d value of .2 is small, a value of .5 is medium, and a value of .8 is large (enough so to be readily perceived in everyday life). Figure 8.8 shows pairs of distributions with d values of .2, .5, and .8, respectively. By Cohen's guidelines, the difference between the mean heights of women and men is enormous ($d = 2.6$).

Meta-Analysis of Sex Differences

The d statistic allows us to systematically study sex differences. For any study that measures the means and standard deviations of females' and males' scores on a given variable (height, aggression, mathematics ability, and so on), we can compute d. But the existence of a sex difference cannot be proved by a single study alone. (See Chapter 2 for a more complete discussion of this issue.) The solution is to average d values from many studies addressing the same issue—for example, whether there are sex differences in aggression.

This is exactly what the statistical technique of *meta-analysis* does (Eagly & Wood, 1991). In the process, meta-analysis accomplishes three main goals: (1) It tells us when a sex difference is reliably found over many studies. (2) It informs us how large the average sex difference is. (3) It tells us whether sex differences depend on other variables.

For example, in a meta-analysis of 64 studies on gender and aggression, Eagly and Steffen (1986b) computed the average value of d to be .40, with men on average being more aggressive than women. Because this difference was relatively consistent across studies, it was found to be statistically significant—that is, not likely to be due to chance. According to the guidelines we described earlier, the observed sex difference in aggression is best classified as small to medium-sized. Finally, Eagly and Steffen found that across studies, sex differences in aggression were influenced by other variables; for example, d values were higher in studies that measured physical (rather than psychological or verbal) aggression, which implies that men are particularly more *physically* aggressive than women.

The Evidence for Sex Differences

With these basic tools in mind, let's turn our attention to the research findings on sex differences. Figure 8.9 shows the results of many meta-analyses that have estimated the size of sex differences for various social behaviors (nonverbal behaviors, aggression, helping, group conformity, behavior in small groups), cognitive abilities, and physical abilities and characteristics.

You might wonder why we are concerned with cognitive abilities (such as math or verbal skills) and physical abilities (such as grip strength) in a social psychology text. There are two reasons. First, such differences may contribute to

Behavior	Source	Mean Value of d (Positive Values Denote Females Higher)	Number of Studies from Which d Was Computed
SOCIAL BEHAVIORS			
Nonverbal behaviors	Hall (1984)		
Decoding skill		.43	64
Social smiling		.63	15
Amount of gaze		.68	30
Personal space (distance of approach in natural settings)		−.56	17
Expansiveness of movements		−1.04	6
Filled pauses ("ahs" and "ums" in speech)		−1.19	6
Aggression	Hyde (1986)	−.50 (median *d* value)	69
Group conformity	Becker (1986)	.28	35
Helping	Eagly & Crowley (1986)		
Overall		−.34	99
When being watched		−.74	16
When not being watched		.02	41
Behavior in small groups	Carli (1982)		
Positive social-emotional behaviors		.59	17
Task-oriented behaviors		−.59	10
Leadership			
Overall in lab groups	Eagly and Karau (1991)	−.32	74
Task leadership	Eagly and Karau (1991)	−.41	61
Social leadership	Eagly and Karau (1991)	.18	15
Democratic vs. autocratic style	Eagly and Johnson (1990)	.22	23
Self-disclosure	Dindia & Allen (1992)	.18	205
COGNITIVE ABILITIES			
Verbal	Hyde & Linn (1988)	.11	165
Math	Hyde (1986)	−.43	16
Visual-spatial	Hyde (1986)	−.45	10
PHYSICAL ABILITIES AND CHARACTERISTICS	Thomas & French (1985)		
Throw velocity		−2.18	5
Throw distance		−1.98	11
Grip strength		−.66	4
General motor activity	Gillis & Avis (1980)	−.49	127

FIGURE 8.9 Meta-analyses of sex differences. This table shows the results of a number of meta-analyses of studies on sex differences. Listed are the mean values of *d* from all studies that examined a particular variable and the number of studies from which the mean values of *d* were computed.

gender stereotypes and influence the gender roles society creates for women and men. For example, if men are physically stronger than women, this may lead to a stereotype that men are more "forceful" and have "stronger" personalities. Second, the sizes of sex differences in cognitive and physical abilities can be useful in comparing the sizes of sex differences in such social behaviors as aggression, helping behavior, and conformity in groups (Eagly, 1987).

Let's summarize the main findings presented in Figure 8.9. First, the nonverbal behaviors of women and men differ in a number of interesting ways (Hall, 1984). Women on average are superior to men in decoding nonverbal cues, particularly facial expressions (see Chapter 4). Women smile more and engage in more eye contact during social interactions than men do. On the other hand, men maintain greater personal space and are more expansive in their body movements and postures (see Chapter 15). Men make more errors in speech than women do and use more "filled pauses" ("ahs" and "ums") when they talk. As the *d* values in Figure 8.9 indicate, sex differences in nonverbal behaviors are often fairly large.

Smaller sex differences emerge in studies on such social behaviors as aggression, helping, susceptibility to social influence, and self-disclosure. On average, men are more aggressive than women (Eagly & Steffen, 1986b; Hyde, 1986); however, as we noted before, this difference is larger for physical than for psychological aggression. On average, men help more in emergencies than women do (Eagly & Crowley, 1986); this finding is qualified by the fact that men help more particularly when they are being watched and when the victim is female, which suggests that men may be motivated by the opportunity to display their masculine valor to an audience as much as by the need to be helpful. Women on average are more susceptible than men to social influence in attitude change and conformity studies (Becker, 1986; Eagly & Carli, 1981). This sex difference tends to be strongest in group-conformity experiments in which subjects are under the surveillance of other people. Finally, women tend to disclose more about themselves in conversations than men do, particularly when talking to other women (Dindia & Allen, 1992). In sum, women and men show small to medium differences in aggression, helping behavior, susceptibility to influence, and self-disclosure; however, these differences are often moderated by situational factors.

Research on behavior in small groups identifies some moderate to large differences in the behavior of men and women (Carli, 1982). Women on average show more positive social–emotional behaviors (acting friendly, agreeing with others, offering emotional support); men show more task-oriented behaviors (giving and asking for opinions, trying to solve the group task). These differences may indicate that women are more effective than men in group tasks requiring considerable discussion and negotiation, and that men may be more effective in those requiring focused, task-oriented behavior (Wood, 1987).

As leaders, women and men show small to moderate differences. Men are somewhat more likely to emerge as leaders of laboratory groups than women are, and men are particularly more likely to be the task-oriented leaders of groups, and women the social and emotional leaders (Eagly & Karau, 1991). Women in leadership positions are more likely than men to employ democratic as opposed to autocratic methods (Eagly & Johnson, 1990).

Men and women on average display a number of differences in cognitive abilities (Halpern, 1992; Hyde, 1981). For example, men tend to perform better than women on tests of math and visual–spatial ability; these differences seem in general to be growing smaller in recent years, however (Feingold, 1988; Rosenthal & Rubin, 1982). Earlier reviewers noted an overall female superiority in verbal ability (Hyde, 1981; Maccoby & Jacklin, 1974), but the most recent evidence suggests that this difference in general verbal ability no longer exists (Hyde & Linn, 1988); however, there may be sex differences favoring women in certain specific verbal skills such as fluency (Mann, Sasanuma, Sakuma, & Masaki, 1990).

Not surprisingly, women and men display a number of consistent physical differences. Men are stronger than women, particularly at tasks requiring upper body strength (Wardle, Gloss, & Gloss, 1987). Men show higher levels of general motor activity than women do (Eaton & Enns, 1986), and women generally have more flexible joints than men do (Percival & Quinkert, 1987).

The Meaning of Sex Differences

What can we make of these findings? Clearly, women and men display a number of differences in behavior. They are by no means "opposite" sexes, however; the means of the measures of certain characteristics simply differ between the sexes to various degrees. In general, there is considerable overlap between the distributions of women's and men's social behaviors, and thus sex accounts for only a fraction of the total variation in these measures (Hyde, 1981; Tavris & Wade, 1984).

On the other hand, even if the difference between the *means* of two distributions is relatively small, differences can become quite large at the tails of the distributions. For example, although the mean d value for the difference in women's and men's math ability is only .43, sex differences at the extremes of the distributions are much larger. Five times as many males as females score above 600 on the math part of the Scholastic Aptitude Test, and the ratio of males to females who receive scores above 700 is 17 to 1 (Stanley & Benbrow, 1982). Sex differences of the magnitude presented in Figure 8.9 can have practical consequences (Eagly, 1987; Eagly & Wood, 1991; Rosenthal & Rubin, 1982). For example, sex differences in math ability of the magnitude just described could influence the number of men and women who become mathematicians, engineers, and scientists—professions that require math ability in the upper tail of the distribution (Lubinski & Benbrow, 1992).

Some of the sex differences listed in Figure 8.9 provide at least partial support for the gender stereotypes we discussed earlier. For example, the behavior of women and men in small groups is consistent with the stereotype that women are more expressive and men more instrumental. Men *are* somewhat more aggressive than women, as the stereotype holds. But, despite the kernel of truth to some gender stereotypes, it is important to emphasize that stereotypes often exaggerate the extent of sex differences (Maccoby & Jacklin, 1974; Martin, 1987).

A final important point about studies on sex differences: They do not necessarily tell us *why* sex differences exist. Are sex differences biological (that is, genetic and hormonal)? Or are they learned from our culture or from our parents?

Are they imposed on us by the structure of society and by social settings? To understand the research findings on sex differences, we must consider theories that attempt to *explain* both sex differences and the development of gender in individuals.

THEORIES OF GENDER AND SEX-TYPING

ABOARD THE USS JASON

"This is my home," says a cheerful Lisa Hefner. The 22-year-old petty officer bends down to show off her two-inch-thick mattress, the bottom of a gray metal triple-decker bunk. . . .

It's almost 10 p.m. Most of the women are in bed, blue curtains drawn. Hefner is standing in a narrow passage between berths, whispering with Roberta Hirst, 27, who's already tucked under a quilt she brought from home. Hefner wears a "Free Kuwait" nightshirt. Women are asked to sleep in no less than a T-shirt and underwear. Hirst jokes: "In case someone bombs the ship. They don't want girls running around in their panties." . . .

Hefner and Hirst are picturing an all-female ship. "USS PMS," says Hirst. "The whole ship would go on the monthly all at once and we'd go out and destroy the world in a day."

—*Washington Post,* September 22, 1992

Hefner and Hirst joke about a very serious topic, for many societies have oppressed women because of presumed biological differences between women and men. Do sex differences in hormones actually make a difference in men and women's behavior?

More broadly, how do people come to behave like men and women? How does being male or female come to be linked to personality traits, aggressiveness, conformity, nonverbal behaviors, cognitive abilities, hobbies, and occupational interests? A number of theories have addressed these challenging questions. We'll focus on six approaches: biological theories, Freudian theory, social learning theories, cognitive theories, social role theory, and self-presentation theory. These theories are not necessarily mutually exclusive, however; each may shed a bit of light on the complex topic of gender.

Different theories of gender emphasize different kinds of explanations (see Summary Table 8.1). For example, biological theories stress evolution and the individual's physiology as explanations of sex differences. Freudian theory focuses on the individual's past environment, particularly on emotional relations with parents early in life. Social learning theories emphasize conditioning and modeling as the processes responsible for gender-related behaviors. Cognitive theories focus on how we label ourselves as male or female and on the schemas we hold about gender. Social role theory describes the differing status and tasks assigned to men and women in most societies and their psychological consequences. And finally,

SUMMARY TABLE 8.1	Theoretical Perspectives on Sex Differences and Gender
Theory	*Main Focus*
Biological theories	
Evolutionary theories	Evolutionary pressures on prehistoric women and men.
Physiological factors	Hormonal and brain differences between the sexes.
Freudian theory	Early emotional and sexual attachments to parents.
Social learning theories	
Classical conditioning	Labels such as "sissy" acquire strong emotional connotations.
Operant conditioning	Different behaviors rewarded and punished for boys and girls.
Observational learning	Children imitate male and female parents, peers, and media models.
Cognitive theories	
Kohlberg's cognitive–developmental theory	Self-labeling as male or female leads to gender-related behaviors.
Gender schema theory	Gender schemas comprise cultural beliefs about gender; gender schematic individuals monitor their own and others' behavior with respect to masculinity and femininity.
Social role theory	Different social roles occupied by men and women lead to gender stereotypes and different behaviors in men and women.
Self-presentation theory	Gender is a social "performance" that varies depending on gender schemas, the setting, and the social audience.

self-presentation theory holds that we display gender-related behaviors as a kind of impression management—we act in "male" or "female" ways to project a certain image to people around us. Let's describe each of these theoretical approaches in more detail.

Biological Theories

Biological theories argue that innate differences exist between women and men. This is obviously true for certain physical characteristics and physiological processes. Women produce ova and men produce sperm. Women menstruate and experience cyclical patterns of hormonal activity that men do not. Women give birth and lactate; men do not. Women's bodies produce more estrogen (female hormones) and men's bodies produce more androgens (male hormones), although both women and men produce both kinds of hormones.

Edward O. Wilson (1978), the father of modern sociobiology, argues that because women were responsible throughout the evolutionary history of our species for bearing, nursing, and caring for children, they evolved to be more nurturing, and because men were responsible for hunting and fighting, they evolved more aggressiveness and better visual–spatial ability. Furthermore, Wilson suggests, women and men have different optimal reproductive strategies:

Women must guarantee that the relatively few offspring they bear will survive, whereas men, who produce millions of sperm, can father an indefinite number of offspring. As a result, women have evolved to be more sexually coy and desirous of committed relationships that provide stable resources, and men have evolved to be more sexually aggressive and promiscuous. (See Chapter 9 for a broader discussion of evolutionary theories of sexual and romantic attraction.) Not surprisingly, such speculations are highly controversial (Fausto-Sterling, 1985).

When assessing the role of biological factors, researchers ask four main empirical questions (Maccoby & Jacklin, 1974): (1) Do sex differences occur early in development, before considerable learning has a chance to take place? (If so, the case for biological explanations of sex differences is strengthened.) (2) Do sex differences occur consistently across cultures? (Cross-cultural variability would suggest sex differences are learned, whereas cross-cultural universality would be consistent with biological causes.) (3) Do sex differences occur consistently across species, particularly species closely related to human beings (for example, other primates)? (If so, the case for biological causes is strengthened.) (4) Do physiological variables related to gender (such as sex hormones) have an effect on the behaviors in question? (If so, this provides direct evidence that sex-linked biological variables may contribute to behavioral sex differences.)

Using these four kinds of evidence, can we make a convincing case that some sex differences result in part from biological factors? Perhaps the strongest case for biological origins can be made with respect to aggression (Maccoby & Jacklin, 1974, 1980). Boys are more aggressive than girls as early as age 2 or 3; interestingly, recent evidence suggests that sex differences in aggression *decrease* with age (Hyde, 1986). In a large majority of cultures, men are more aggressive than women (D'Andrade, 1966); this difference is reflected in virtually all social indexes of aggression, including participation in warfare, violent crimes, homicides, and suicides. From an early age, male nonhuman primates are more aggressive than females (Moyer, 1976). And finally, there is evidence that sex hormones, particularly testosterone, are related to aggression in humans and animals (Dabbs, 1992; Moyer, 1976; Olweus, 1986; see Chapter 12).

Does this mean that men are more aggressive than women primarily for biological reasons? Not necessarily. It merely means that there very likely are biological underpinnings to observed sex differences in aggressiveness. These biological predispositions may be amplified or dampened by culture and social learning.

The evidence for direct biological causes of sex differences in social behaviors other than aggression (such as nonverbal behaviors, helping behavior, and susceptibility to influence) is considerably weaker. As we've already noted, these differences are often strongly affected by situational factors, which suggests social rather than biological determinants.

Another sex difference that may have a biological foundation is that of visual–spatial ability. One theory holds that this difference results from varying degrees of brain lateralization in women and men. For most people, language skills depend more on the left hemisphere of the brain, whereas visual–spatial skills depend more on the right hemisphere. The lateralization hypothesis assumes the separation of the functions of the two hemispheres is more complete and extreme in men than in women. Even though the evidence for this hypothesis is complex and inconsistent, it seems likely that biological factors *are* responsible to some degree for the frequently observed sex differences in visual–spatial ability (Halpern, 1992). Again, such a conclusion does not preclude the possibility that these differences are also influenced by cultural factors and learning.

Freudian Theory

Until the 20th century, most scholars and laypeople simply assumed that biological differences between women and men explained their behavioral differences. This assumption was radically challenged by Sigmund Freud (1961b, 1961c [1924, 1925]), the father of psychoanalytic theory.

Freud argued that children's early sexual feelings and their emotional ties to their parents lead them to develop masculine or feminine identities. Both boys and girls begin life with their mother as their primary love object. But after age 3, boys' and girls' development diverges sharply. According to Freudian theory, a particularly critical period occurs for the typical boy between the ages of 3 and 6, when he first experiences genital pleasure. At this point, the boy's love for his mother takes on a sexual tinge and he becomes aware that his father is a major competitor for his mother's affection.

At about this same time, the theory continues, the boy notices the genital differences between men and women and learns that women lack penises. Frightened, the boy assumes that women once possessed penises but somehow lost them, which intensifies the boy's fear of his father and of his own sexual desires, for he reasons that his vengeful father may remove his own penis as punishment for his incestuous desires for his mother. This intense *castration anxiety* leads the boy ultimately to give up his sexual wishes for his mother and to identify with his father. It is as though the boy unconsciously reasons: If I act like Daddy, then someday I will have someone like Mommy.

Freud invented the term *Oedipus complex* to refer to the boy's unconscious feelings of sexual attraction to his mother and his rivalry with his father. This term was based on the Greek myth of Oedipus, who unwittingly killed his father and married his mother. According to Freud's theory, the proper resolution of the Oedipus complex occurs when boys identify with their fathers and thus become masculine.

Freud proposed a fundamentally different scenario for girls. They too presumably notice the genital differences between males and females between ages 3 and 6; however, rather than fearing the loss of their genitals, girls unconsciously assume that their penises have already been removed! Freud (1961c) believed that

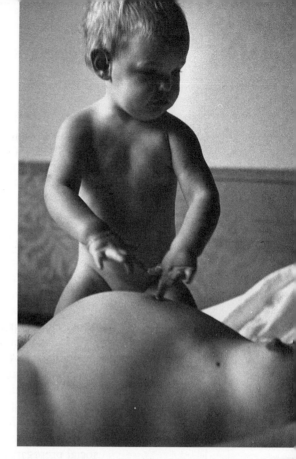

According to psychoanalytic theory, the intense early emotional attachment between mother and infant sets the stage for later sex-typing.

351

girls naturally valued penises more than vaginas because penises are "strikingly visible and of large proportions, at once recognize[d] as the superior counterpart to their own small and inconspicuous organ . . ." (p. 252).

According to classical Freudian theory, girls are unconsciously forlorn because of their genital "inferiority," and *penis envy* is the prime motivation of the feminine personality. Throughout life, women strive to regain their missing penis by having love relations with men and by having children, particularly male children. Thus Freud explained the "feminine" desire for close emotional relationships and for children.

Freud proposed other significant consequences of women's psychosexual development. Because of their genital "inferiority," women often feel contempt for other women, specifically for their own mothers. For this reason, girls give up their mothers as primary love objects, and instead court their fathers, taking on an "appropriate" male love object. The self-disparagement (due to genital "inferiority") and the desire to please their fathers (and indirectly all males) leads women to be masochistic in their love relationships. Finally, Freud theorized that because girls do not experience the wrenching castration anxiety typical of boys, they do not generally resolve their Oedipal stage as decisively as boys do. Thus, women end up being more infantile and possessing weaker moral consciences than men.

As you might well guess, feminist scholars have roundly criticized Freudian theory as sexist. Karen Horney (1973 [1922]), a prominent disciple of Freud, argued that what Freud called "penis envy" was really status envy. Women, particularly in Freud's time, yearned not for men's organs but for their power and social prerogatives.

Although most contemporary developmental and social psychologists reject much of Freud's account of how masculinity and femininity develop in children, Freud deserves credit for advancing gender theory beyond naive biological determinism. Although famous for the phrase "Anatomy is destiny," Freud did not believe that people are *born* psychologically male or female. Rather, he argued that genital differences lead to different experiences early in life and that these early experiences lead people to develop "male" or "female" patterns of behavior.

Social Learning Theories

Whereas biological theories and some aspects of Freudian theory emphasize innate differences between men and women, social learning theories emphasize the learned ones. Walter Mischel (1966, 1970), for one, has argued that differences in women's and men's behavior can be explained by well-understood principles of classical conditioning, operant conditioning, and modeling.

For example, classical conditioning can help explain why "labels like 'sissy,' 'pansy,' 'tough,' or 'sweet' acquire differential value for the sexes" (Mischel, 1966, p. 61). The word *sissy* generally accompanies ridicule in a boy's life and thus becomes a very unpleasant label. A boy will not want to behave like a "sissy" if the very concept is conditioned to arouse feelings of loathing and revulsion.

Operant conditioning, which occurs when girls' and boys' behaviors are rewarded and punished in systematically different ways, can also lead to sex differences: "Boys and girls discover that the consequences for performing . . . behaviors are affected by their sex, and therefore soon perform them with different frequency" (Mischel, 1966, p. 60). Thus, little Joan may receive smiles and praise when she plays with dolls and a toy cooking set, but little John may receive frowns and disapproval for exactly the same behaviors.

Finally, children may acquire sex-typed behaviors through observational learning. Children often learn about "female" and "male" behaviors without being directly rewarded or punished, simply observing their friends, parents, relatives, and the portrayal of various characters in the mass media. Such models are particularly influential when they have a nurturing relationships with the children, are powerful, and control rewards (Bandura & Huston, 1961; Bandura, Ross, & Ross, 1963a; Mischel & Grusec, 1966). Parents, of course, meet all three of these criteria.

Social learning theory makes an important distinction between the acquisition of behaviors and the performance of those behaviors; people can learn behaviors through observation, but they don't necessarily perform them. For example, most women could convincingly go through the motions of shaving their faces and most men could convincingly go through the motions of shaving their legs, even though they don't usually do so. Thus, social learning theory argues that women and men are capable of performing the same behaviors, but they don't because of past conditioning, rewards, punishments, observational learning, and all the situational contingencies that exist in a society that treats women and men differently.

Children learn sex-typed behaviors. Top: This boy learns about "male" activities through the toys he's given to play with. Bottom: This girl learns how to behave "like a woman" by modeling her mother.

A great deal of research supports social learning theory's basic contention that environmental factors help create and sustain sex differences. For example, a number of studies suggest that parents treat girls and boys differently from birth (Block, 1978; Intons-Peterson, 1988; Rubin, Provenzano, & Luria, 1974; Snow, Jacklin, & Maccoby, 1983). Parents provide different toys to their girls and boys (Rheingold & Cook, 1975) and decorate their rooms in dramatically different ways. Parents in essence treat girls as "women-in-training" and boys as "men-in-training." Both parents and peers encourage sex-typed behaviors in children, and they discourage behaviors that are not sex-typed (Fagot, 1977; Pitcher & Schultz, 1983). In one study, when a 3-year-old boy stated that he wanted to cook dinner, a female playmate firmly informed him that "daddies don't cook" (Garvey, 1977). In modern industrial society, the mass media are also quite important in socializing gender. Television, radio, and the print media often portray women and men in stereotypical ways, and children often view media characters as models for behavior (Basow, 1986).

Cognitive theories of sex-typing. Once children label themselves as "boys" and "girls," they are strongly motivated to identify with their sex, and they sometimes derogate the other sex.

Cognitive Approaches to Gender

Social learning theories tend to portray the acquisition of sex-typed behaviors as a rather passive process whereby the child develops in such a manner as conditioning and modeling dictate (Archer & Lloyd, 1985; Maccoby & Jacklin, 1974, 1980). Clearly, however, the development of gender identity and sex differences also involves a cognitive process of self-labeling and self-definition. We are not male or female just through what we are conditioned to do; we are also male or female through what we think about ourselves.

Cognitive–Developmental Theory

In his cognitive–developmental account of sex-typing, Lawrence Kohlberg (1966) proposed that children progress through a number of discrete cognitive stages in becoming psychologically "male" or "female." Drawing on the work of the Swiss developmental psychologist Jean Piaget, Kohlberg argued that children's conceptions of gender develop in step with their more general levels of cognitive growth. For example, most children can correctly identify their sex by age 2 or 3 (Gesell, Halverson, & Amatruda, 1940); this accomplishment requires that they acquire stable gender categories. About the same time, children also acquire other kinds of "object constancy" (the knowledge that objects have stable, enduring qualities). According to Kohlberg's analysis, once children develop a stable gender identity ("I am a girl") and stable gender categories ("All people are either female or male"), they begin to identify with others of their own sex ("I am a girl; therefore, I like other girls, and girls are good").

Although they are aware of gender as a social category, young children do not think about gender as adults do. For instance, they do not realize that "male" and "female" are defined most fundamentally by genitalia; instead, they define gender by its surface manifestations, such as clothing, hair length, and the kinds of games one plays. Three- and 4-year-olds will often state that they could be the other sex if they wanted to—all they would have to do is change their clothing, hairstyle, and toys!

By age 6 or 7, children consistently realize that sex and gender are constant and linked to male and female genital differences. Thus, Kohlberg argued, Freudian accounts of sex-typing, which assume awareness of genital differences between ages 3 and 6, are simply wrong. According to Kohlberg's theory, children older than age

7 continue to develop their concept of gender; for example, they learn diffuse gender stereotypes ("Women are gentler than men") and cultural symbols associated with gender ("The moon is a female symbol").

Kohlberg proposed that the act of gender self-categorization ("I'm a girl" or "I'm a boy") leads the child to develop stereotypically female or male behaviors. In Kohlberg's words, "cognitive theory assumes this sequence: 'I am a boy, therefore I want to do boy things, therefore the opportunity to do boy things . . . is rewarding.' " Social learning theory, on the other hand, argues for a different sequence: "I want rewards, I am rewarded for doing boy things, therefore I want to be a boy" (Kohlberg, 1966, p. 89). It is not rewards that make the boy masculine, Kohlberg argued; rather, it is identifying oneself as male that makes masculine activities rewarding.

Recent research investigating cognitive theories of gender shows that children as young as 3 years of age correctly label their sex and tend to play with gender-consistent toys; however, they do so because of perceived social standards, not because they feel uncomfortable playing with cross-sex toys. By age 4, however, most children start actively evaluating themselves on gender-related behaviors—and they begin to feel extremely uncomfortable engaging in cross-sex activities (Bussey & Bandura, 1992). Thus, there may be some truth to both social learning theories and cognitive theories of gender: Children first come to behave in "male" and "female" ways because of modeling, reinforcement, and social pressures; however, in time they internalize these gender standards and strongly evaluate their own behavior according to these internalized standards.

Discomfort with cross-sex behavior seems to be stronger for boys than girls (Katz, 1986), perhaps because society punishes boys who are "sissies" more than girls who are "tomboys." In one study, 7-year-old boys were videotaped as they served as actors engaging in cross-sex play: changing diapers on a baby doll (Bussey & Bandura, 1992). After the taping, one boy exclaimed, "It's the most awful thing I have ever done." Clearly, children over the age of 4 not only know what is "masculine" and "feminine"; they also strongly evaluate their behavior based on this knowledge.

Gender Schema Theory

Sandra Bem (1981) extended Kohlberg's cognitive analysis of gender to adults. According to her gender schema theory, people learn a complex network of gender-related concepts and symbols from their cultures. For example, "tender" and "petunias" may be seen as feminine, whereas "aggressive" and "jackhammers" are masculine. Once people have acquired gender schemas, they perceive their own and others' behavior through the filter of those schemas. (See Chapters 3 and 5 for a more extensive discussion of how schemas affect self-perception and social perception.)

Bem's theory proposes that people who are strongly gender-schematic tend to perceive the world in terms of "male" and "female," and they try to keep their own behavior consistent with stereotypical standards for their sex. Although there has been considerable debate about the measurement and consequences of gender schemas (Edwards & Spence, 1987; Markus, Crane, Bernstein, & Siladi, 1982;

Payne, Connor, & Colletti, 1987), most researchers accept the general proposal that people's gender schemas can influence their gender-related behaviors and thought processes.

Social Role Theory

In most cultures, women and men occupy quite different roles (Barry, Bacon, & Child, 1957; D'Andrade, 1966). Women are more responsible for child-rearing and domestic duties; men are more responsible for hunting, fighting, and, in modern industrial society, income-producing work (although this has clearly changed substantially in recent years). According to Alice Eagly's (1987) social role analysis of gender, this sex-based division of labor, which occurs in virtually all societies, leads necessarily to sex differences in behavior and to the stereotypical perceptions that women and men are different. Constrained by their social roles to rear children and take care of homes, women show more nurturing behaviors, and people in turn perceive women to be more nurturing. Constrained and guided by their social roles in the competitive world of work, men display more competitive, assertive behaviors, and as a result people perceive men to be more competitive and assertive. However, Eagly contends that these behavioral differences are more a function of roles than of gender.

Eagly's theory does not focus on innate differences between women and men, although it does not deny that such differences may exist. Rather, it stresses the power of social settings to govern social behaviors and affect their perception. Thus, in Eagly's theory, settings that make gender roles particularly salient and that assign different status to women and men should create marked differences in the behavior of women and men, whereas settings that do not make gender roles salient and that assign equal status to women and men should lead them to show similar behaviors.

An experiment by Eagly and Steffen (1986a) provides evidence that social roles, rather than gender per se, lead to stereotypical perceptions of men and women. College-student subjects read descriptions of people (either females or males) engaged in one of three kinds of work: caring for a home and children without outside employment, working part-time outside the home, or working full-time outside the home. In a control condition, subjects received no occupational information. In all conditions, subjects were asked to rate the described person on a number of instrumental and expressive traits (*independent, dominant, kind, warm*).

The results (see Figure 8.10) showed that women and men were judged stereotypically when no occupational information was provided; that is, women were perceived as more expressive and men as more instrumental. But when occupational role information was provided, women and men were evaluated by their role, not by their sex. Thus, full-time employees, whether male or female, were judged more highly on instrumental traits than on expressive traits, and both male and female homemakers were judged more highly on expressive traits than on instrumental traits. These results imply that when more women are employed full-time and more men participate in child care and housekeeping, gender stereotypes may fade.

Sex of Stimulus Person	Attribute Dimension	Occupation of Stimulus Person			
		No Occupational Description	Full-time Employee	Part-time Employee	Homemaker
Female	Expressive	3.82	3.23	3.66	4.20
	Instrumental	3.06	3.60	2.96	2.88
Male	Expressive	2.99	3.28	3.28	4.11
	Instrumental	3.41	3.40	2.58	2.88

Mean Ratings of Stereotypical Attributes of Females and Males

When occupational information was provided, members of both sexes tended to be perceived more in terms of their occupational roles than in terms of their gender.

Note: Higher numbers mean the stimulus person has more of the trait.

FIGURE 8.10 Social roles and gender stereotyping. *Source:* Adapted from Eagly and Steffen (1986a).

Do men and women actually behave differently because of their different social roles? Many sex differences—differences in nonverbal behavior, aggression, helping behavior, and conformity—can be interpreted in terms of women's and men's roles. For example, women, who play the nurturing role in most families, are more sensitive nonverbally, show more affiliative nonverbal behaviors such as smiling, are more expressive, and participate more in the social and emotional dynamics of group interactions. But, Eagly argues, placed in different roles, women may show dramatically different behavior.

Two experiments by John Dovidio and his colleagues (1988) powerfully illustrate how social roles can modify the behavior of men and women. Specifically, these studies measured subjects' patterns of gaze during social interactions. In general, people who possess more power in a relationship gaze at their partner more when they are talking than when they are listening (Ellyson & Dovidio, 1985). Pairs of college men and women were asked to discuss various hobbies, such as basketball, skiing, and swimming. In the first experiment, the researchers selected topics of discussion to create three different conditions: The woman was more expert on the topic of discussion, the man was more expert, or neither subject was more expert. The percentage of the time subjects spent gazing at their partner during their conversations was measured both while subjects were speaking and while they were listening.

Who acted more "powerful" in this experiment, women or men? As Figure 8.11 shows, when neither partner possessed expertise and when men possessed more expertise than women, men displayed more "powerful" patterns of gaze. When women possessed more expertise, however, they displayed more powerful patterns of gaze than men.

In a second, conceptually similar experiment, Dovidio and his colleagues again asked male–female couples to discuss various topics. This time, however, one

Condition		Percentage of Time Spent Looking at Partner	
		While Speaking	*While Listening*
Male has expertise	Males	53	54
	Females	40	74
Female has expertise	Males	30	49
	Females	58	56
Neither subject has expertise (control condition)	Males	47	53
	Females	41	77

Males showed more "powerful" patterns of gaze (that is, they gazed *relatively* more while speaking than while listening) when their expertise was greater than or equal to that of their female partners, but females showed more powerful patterns of gaze when they possessed greater expertise.

FIGURE 8.11 Social roles and patterns of gaze in male-female interactions. *Source:* Data from Dovidio et al. (1988).

subject was given the role of rewarding and evaluating the quality of the other's discussion. In a control condition, neither partner evaluated the other. The results: In the control condition and in the "male evaluates female" condition, men showed more "powerful" patterns of gaze than women did; when women had the power to evaluate and reward their male partners, they displayed the more powerful pattern of gaze.

The results of these experiments fit nicely with Eagly's social role theory. In their usual roles, women and men often show nonverbal differences consistent with their socially dictated differences in status. But when women's roles give them power, sex differences in nonverbal behavior may disappear and even reverse. Many of the sex differences in nonverbal behavior reported earlier (for example, that women smile more and men take up greater personal space) can be interpreted as resulting from status and power differences between women and men (Deutsch, 1990; Henley, 1977).

Self-Presentation Theory

All of the theories we have reviewed so far try to explain how we end up with the characteristic known as gender: Gender is dictated by biology, by early relations with parents, by conditioning and modeling, by cognitive labeling and schemas, and by social roles. Whatever approach you accept, gender in these theories is a real "thing" that people end up possessing in a fairly fixed form.

More radical views hold that gender is a cultural invention, a social construction (Kessler & McKenna, 1978; Unger, 1989), and a self-presentation we enact in certain settings and with certain people. Kay Deaux and Brenda Major (1987) argue that self-presentation research (see Chapter 3) can help us understand gender-related behaviors. We play our roles as men and women depending on our own concepts of gender, others' expectations, and the setting in which we happen to be. For example, the same woman may be a no-nonsense, assertive executive at work but quite "feminine" when on a date. Similarly, as we saw in Chapter 3, college women may describe themselves in more stereotypically feminine terms (and even perform worse on an intelligence test) when they anticipate meeting a very attractive man who prefers "traditional" women (Zanna & Pack, 1975).

A more recent study has demonstrated that women will change the amount of food they eat depending on the man they're with (Mori, Chaiken, & Pliner, 1987). Both women and men stereotypically perceive women who eat small amounts of food to be more "feminine," so when a woman wants to present a feminine image she may eat less. Indeed, the researchers found that when women participated in a discussion with an "attractive" man (that is, a man who was currently available and who had interesting hobbies and high academic ambitions), they tended to eat significantly less of the snack mix that "just happened" to be on the table than when they talked with an "unattractive" man.

Another study documents yet another self-presentational strategy women use to display their femininity: modifying their voices. Montepare and Vega (1988) recorded college women's phone conversations with either intimate or casual male friends. When women spoke to their boyfriends, their speech displayed significantly more "feminine" characteristics: Their voices were higher in pitch, more "baby-like," more pleasant, and more variable in tone. Furthermore, judges rated these women's speech to be significantly more "submissive" and "scatterbrained" when they conversed with their boyfriends. Many of these women were consciously aware of the change; some observed that their voices became more "babylike," "endearing," "girlie," "cutesy," and even "slightly whiny." Clearly, women display different vocal characteristics depending on the social setting and on the image they want to project. Thus, self-presentation theory suggests, gender displays are quite variable across settings and across social audiences.

Men too may change their display of gender-related behaviors depending on the setting and their social audience. In an experiment in which college men interacted with a partner—another man who was described as either heterosexual or homosexual—subjects who thought they were interacting with a homosexual partner discussed their attractions to women more than those who interacted with a heterosexual partner (Kite & Deaux, 1986). By implication, some of the men felt the need to display their masculinity in this situation.

Which Theory Is Right?

Summary Table 8.1 presents the theoretical approaches to gender we have discussed, along with their main assumptions. You may be wondering at this point: Which theory is right?

One way to answer this question is to report which theoretical perspectives are most influential in guiding current social psychology research. In general, cognitive approaches to gender (cognitive–developmental theory and gender schema theory), social role theory, social learning theory, and self-presentation theories have been studied most in recent social psychology research. These approaches fit in with the traditional social psychology assumption that cognitive and situational factors have a large influence on our behavior. In certain research areas (for example, the study of mate selection and human sexuality; see Chapter 9), evolutionary theory plays a larger role in the analysis and study of sex differences, although it is the subject of considerable debate and controversy. The Freudian perspective is the least influential theoretical approach in current research on gender and sex differences.

It's important to reiterate that the various theoretical perspectives we have discussed are not necessarily mutually exclusive. For example, boys may be more physically aggressive than girls in part because of biological factors. These differences may sometimes be amplified by social learning and self-labeling. Male aggressiveness may also at times be a self-presentational strategy—for example, teenage boys may display aggressiveness when trying to impress their "macho" friends. Thus, different theories yield different pieces to the puzzle of gender.

GENDER AND THE INDIVIDUAL

[Paula] Acosta works in an engine repair shop with two other women and eight men. "I like getting all dirty," Acosta says. . . .

Acosta is in charge of supplies. It's desk work, and at first she worried she had been stuck with "a female's job." When she learned the position was rotated among men too, she felt relief.

"The standard we're measured up to here is a male one."

Masculinity is valued. Femininity is not.

—*Washington Post*, September 22, 1992

Paula Acosta seemed to feel bad about the possibility of being "stuck with 'a female's job.'" Do you think that being male or female, masculine or feminine, influences *your* self-esteem? How do you know whether you are masculine or feminine? Must you be either one or the other, or can you be both at once?

In this final section, we turn to questions like these as we explore the topic of gender and individuality and examine how gender is linked to our self-esteem, self-concept, and personality.

Gender and Self-Esteem

Self-esteem refers to our general sense of being worthy or good. It seems consistent with common sense that people who are the butt of prejudice have lower self-esteem, but interestingly, research does not always support this notion (Crocker & Major, 1989; see Chapter 7). As we have seen, women often have lower status than men, and women sometimes are the targets of negative stereotypes compared to men. Does this lead women to have lower self-esteem than men?

Differences in Men's and Women's Self-Esteem

Most early summaries of research found no reliable differences between men's and women's overall self-esteem (Maccoby & Jacklin, 1974; Spence & Helmreich, 1978; Wylie, 1979). More recent studies, however, sometimes note a difference favoring males, particularly during childhood and adolescence (Keltikangas-Jarvinen, 1990; Richards, Gitelson, Petersen, & Hurtig, 1991).

While the overall self-esteem of adult women and men probably does not differ very much, the nature of women's and men's self-esteem and the behaviors on which it is based may differ. One recent study of 898 Canadian college students found that men on average viewed themselves more positively than women on math aptitude, problem-solving ability, and athletic ability, whereas women viewed themselves more positively on verbal ability, honesty, and reliability (Marsh & Byrne, 1991). Another study found that women of all ages have lower self-esteem than men about their physical appearance and weight (Pliner, Chaiken, & Flett, 1990).

Josephs, Markus, and Tafarodi (1992) have argued that women's self-esteem depends more on how they evaluate their relationships with others, whereas men's self-esteem depends more on how they evaluate their individuality, achievement, and power. They demonstrated this difference in a study that delivered bogus test results to college men and women informing them that they lacked either achievement-related abilities or abilities needed for interpersonal sensitivity and nurturance. Men and women with high self-esteem were threatened by this negative feedback, and they compensated for the "bad news" by predicting they would perform significantly better on a future test (see Chapter 3 for related research on self-verification processes). However, subjects of each sex showed this pattern of compensation only when the negative feedback was relevant to their sex. That is, women predicted the most future improvement when their social sensitivity and nurturance were placed in doubt, whereas men predicted the most improvement when their achievement abilities were placed in doubt.

MULTICULTURAL PERSPECTIVE

Gender and Self-Esteem across Cultures

The conclusion that women's and men's overall self-esteem does not differ is based largely on studies carried out in the United States. Is this finding true of women and men in other countries as well? To answer this question, John Williams and Deborah Best (1990) asked groups of college men and women in 14 countries to check which of 300 trait adjectives described themselves.

Malaysia	19.6
India	12.6
Italy	7.7
Japan	7.3
Singapore	3.4
Germany	3.1
Nigeria	.4
Netherlands	–.6
Pakistan	–2.7
United States	–3.2
Canada	–5.4
England	–12.2
Finland	–16.6
Venezuela	–29.4

Note: Positive numbers mean men have higher self-esteem; negative numbers mean women have higher self-esteem.

FIGURE 8.12
Differences in men's and women's self-esteem in fourteen countries. *Source:* Williams and Best (1990).

Each adjective had earlier been rated on how positive or negative it was, and thus Williams and Best could compute how positive each subject's overall self-description was.

Williams and Best found that in some countries (for example, Finland and Venezuela), women tended to describe themselves more positively than men, whereas in other countries (Malaysia and India), men described themselves more positively than women (see Figure 8.12). Their findings for the United States replicated those of previous studies: U.S. women and men did not differ much in their overall self-esteem.

Did societies in which women had higher self-esteem differ from societies in which men had higher self-esteem? Yes. Williams and Best found that, in general, women tended to have high self-esteem relative to men in societies that were higher in economic and social development, that had a higher percentage of Protestants (in comparison to Catholics or Moslems), that had higher percentages of women attending universities and working outside the home, and that were less authoritarian and more liberal in their sex-role ideologies. While interesting in their own right, these findings make an important general point as well: Psychological findings on sex differences exist in a cultural context, and they sometimes vary from society to society. ⬾

Gender and Personality

Whether because of biology, learning, or social roles, many individuals come to possess gender-related personality traits—that is, consistent internal tendencies to behave in culturally defined "feminine" or "masculine" ways (see Chapter 3 for a broader discussion of trait theories of personality). According to this trait approach, on average, women and men show differences in their degrees of masculinity and femininity. Furthermore, meaningful individual differences exist *within each sex* as well, with some women, for example, being relatively more feminine and others relatively more masculine in their behavior.

Early Masculinity–Femininity Scales

The measurement of masculinity–femininity as a personality trait has a long and somewhat controversial history in American psychological research. Lewis Terman (famous for bringing intelligence testing to the United States in the early 20th century) and Catherine Cox Miles (1936) developed one of the first tests to measure masculinity–femininity, and they conducted research to see whether subjects' masculinity–femininity scores were related to other personality and intellectual traits, and to heterosexual and homosexual behavior. Following Terman and Miles's work, many later personality and vocational-interest inventories included masculinity–femininity scales (Campbell, 1966; Gough, 1964; Hathaway & McKinley, 1943; Strong, 1943). Most of these scales were developed specifically to differentiate women and men (or sometimes, homosexuals and heterosexuals). Thus, for example, an item on a personality inventory would be included on the masculinity–femininity scale if groups of women and men answered the question differently on average.

Early masculinity–femininity tests made two fundamental assumptions: that masculine and feminine behaviors, attitudes, and interests are fairly consistent and cohesive within individuals, and that "masculinity" and "femininity" are opposite ends of a single bipolar dimension (Constantinople, 1973). Furthermore, these early tests tended to promote the implicit value that it is good for people to possess masculinity–femininity scores "appropriate" to their sex—that it is desirable for women to be "feminine" and men "masculine."

However, after a half-century of research, many of these early assumptions have proved to be unwarranted (Constantinople, 1973; Reinisch, Rosenblum, & Sanders, 1987). "Masculine" and "feminine" attitudes, interests, and traits are not always cohesive (Spence & Sawin, 1985), and the content of masculinity–femininity tests, like the content of gender stereotypes, proves to be multidimensional (Lunneborg, 1972). And finally, "masculinity" is not necessarily always good for men, nor "femininity" always good for women. For example, Maccoby (1966) and, more recently, Lubinski and Humphreys (1990) have observed that many girls and boys who perform the best intellectually are *not* extremely sex-typed. Girls with high degrees of stereotypical femininity tend not to strive for achievement as much as less stereotypically feminine girls (Stein & Bailey, 1973), and they also tend to suffer from higher anxiety and lower self-esteem (Sears, 1970). On the other hand, boys with high degrees of stereotypic masculinity tend to be impulsive and aggressive (Maccoby, 1966), which can interfere with their academic achievement.

Masculinity and Femininity as Separate Dimensions

With the women's movement of the 1970s came fresh approaches to the measurement of masculinity and femininity. Rejecting the notion that masculinity and femininity constituted opposite ends of a single dimension, a number of psychologists developed tests that measured masculinity and femininity as separate and independent traits (Bem, 1974; Heilbrun, 1976; Spence, Helmreich, & Stapp, 1974). Typically, these newer tests defined masculinity in terms of the instrumental personality traits stereotypically associated with males (for example, *aggressive, dominant, strong*) and femininity in terms of expressive traits associated with women *(compassionate, tender, warm)*. Thus, subjects could score high on one scale and low on the other (for example, high on femininity but low on masculinity). But they could also score high on both the masculinity and femininity scales; such subjects are referred to as "androgynous," from the Greek *andr,* "men," and *gyne,* "women" (see Figure 8.13).

Sandra Bem (1974, 1975; Bem, Martyna, & Watson, 1976), one of the first androgyny researchers, argued that androgyny defined a new standard of mental health and psychological adjustment. Unlike traditionally masculine men and traditionally feminine women, androgynous people are less constrained by limiting sex roles and are more adaptable—they can be warm and nurturing or strong and assertive according to the needs of the situation. In a series of research studies, Bem (1975; Bem et al., 1976) found that androgynous subjects (who typically made up about 20% to 30% of the college populations from which they were drawn) were both independent in the face of pressures to conform and nurturing in offering help to troubled peers. Traditionally masculine men, although independent in the face of pressures to conform, were not nurturing; traditionally feminine women, although nurturing with a troubled peer, "caved in" to group pressure. Bem argued that androgynous people showed both good masculine *and* good feminine behaviors, whereas traditionally masculine and feminine people show competence only in masculine or in feminine domains (Bem & Lenney, 1976).

In traditional tests, masculinity-femininity was conceived as a single bipolar dimension. Thus, you could be either feminine or masculine, but not both. Traditional scales often implied the unstated value that it is good for women to be feminine and for men to be masculine.

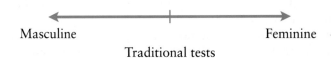

Masculine   Feminine
                     Traditional tests

More recently, psychologists have conceptualized masculinity and femininity as two independent dimensions. Masculinity scales measure the degree to which individuals report possessing positive instrumental traits, and femininity scales measure the degree to which individuals report possessing positive expressive traits. Individuals who have high degrees of both masculinity and femininity are termed "androgynous."

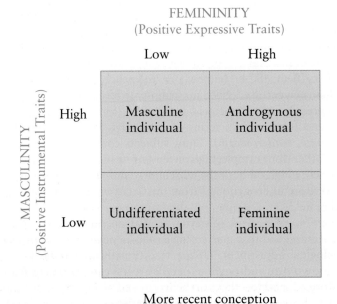

More recent conception

FIGURE 8.13 Traditional and current conceptions of masculinity and femininity.

Since the mid-1970s, hundreds of studies have explored the implications of the new masculinity, femininity, and androgyny tests (Cook, 1985). This research provides a somewhat mixed picture. A comprehensive meta-analysis of studies on masculinity, femininity, and androgyny found that masculinity scores indeed tend to predict instrumental behaviors and that femininity scores indeed tend to predict expressive behaviors (Taylor & Hall, 1982). Although both masculinity and femininity are at times related to indexes of mental health and adjustment, the link between masculinity and psychological adjustment is considerably stronger than that between femininity and adjustment (Bassoff & Glass, 1982; O'Heron & Orlofsky, 1990). Thus, masculine and androgynous people tend to be better adjusted primarily because of their higher masculinity. This finding does not support Bem's hypothesis that the *combination* of high masculinity and high femininity leads to mental health.

Another meta-analysis found that high masculinity and low femininity scores tend to be associated with better performance on math and visual–spatial tests (Signorella & Jamison, 1986). Although these results indicate that masculinity and femininity are related to cognitive performance, clearly they do not indicate that androgyny leads to cognitive superiority, at least in these stereotypically masculine domains. Indeed, a high degree of femininity is associated with *poorer* performance on these cognitive tests.

In what contexts is a high degree of femininity desirable? A number of studies suggest that people who have high degrees of femininity may have more successful and satisfying relationships and marriages (Antill, 1983; Kurdek & Schmitt, 1986). This conclusion makes sense, of course, because highly feminine people are more sensitive, nurturing, and warm; that is, they possess just those characteristics needed to be a good partner in a relationship. Spence and Helmreich (1978, 1980) argue that masculinity and femininity scales are in fact instrumentality and expressiveness scales; for this reason, masculinity scales can predict behaviors such as assertiveness and achievement reasonably well, and femininity scales can predict behaviors such as interpersonal warmth and nurturing reasonably well, but these scales are at best weakly related to other kinds of gender-related behaviors.

Beyond Masculinity, Femininity, and Androgyny

Androgyny clearly was an idea whose time had come in the 1970s, a period when traditional sex roles were changing rapidly. Androgyny research challenged the traditional assumptions that "masculinity" was the opposite of "femininity," and that men necessarily should be masculine and women feminine. But androgyny research still viewed masculinity and femininity as fixed, well-defined traits that people possess to varying degrees. Sandra Bem (1981) acknowledged in her work on gender schema theory that androgyny "is insufficiently radical from a feminist perspective because it continues to presuppose that . . . masculinity and femininity have an independent and palpable reality rather than being themselves cognitive constructs" (p. 363).

Androgyny research suffered from another problem as well: It defined masculinity and femininity in highly restricted ways—specifically, in terms of

Men and women are still negotiating their changing roles.

gender-stereotypic personality traits. When you use the terms "masculine" and "feminine," do you intend them to refer only to instrumental and expressive personality traits? Probably not. For most of us, "masculinity" and "femininity" refer to many additional aspects of behavior such as styles of nonverbal communication, ways of dressing and grooming, choices of occupations and hobbies, and roles in family life.

To complicate matters still further, not only do "masculinity" and "femininity" comprise many different kinds of behaviors, these concepts also vary somewhat across cultures and over time. For example, wearing pants is not viewed as a particularly "masculine" behavior for women in the United States today, but a hundred years ago it was undoubtedly seen as quite masculine for women to wear pants in the United States, and it probably still is today in Saudi Arabia. Similarly, many "masculine" men today wear earrings in the United States, but 30 years ago, no "real man" would have thought of doing so. Clearly, then, the behaviors that define "masculinity" and "femininity" are not fixed in stone, and existing masculinity and femininity scales may have erred in assuming that they could measure these concepts in fixed and universal ways (Lippa, 1991; Lippa & Connelly, 1990).

How then can we measure concepts such as masculinity and femininity that are intrinsically variable over time and across cultures? One answer is that we can define masculinity and femininity only through behaviors that distinguish men from women *in a particular culture at a particular time in history* (Lippa & Connelly, 1990). In the America of the 1990s, for example, "feminine" behaviors might include wearing cosmetics, studying nursing, and cooking for family members, whereas "masculine" behaviors might include wearing ties, studying engineering, and doing home repairs. These are "masculine" and "feminine" behaviors in the following limited sense: Men in our society are currently more likely to show the "masculine" behaviors and women more to show the "feminine" ones. These behaviors may not distinguish men and women in other cultures and in other historical periods, however, and they may not distinguish men and women in our society in the future.

According to this cultural and historical perspective, "masculinity" and "femininity" are real in the sense that they constitute concepts that make sense to us; we use these concepts to think about ourselves and others. But at the same time, "masculinity" and "femininity" should not be regarded as fixed and rigid concepts.

Rather, they are "moving targets," ever changing, and as men's and women's roles continue to evolve in our society, we shall undoubtedly arrive at new and different views of what it means to be "masculine" and "feminine."

GENDER AND SOCIAL BEHAVIOR IN PERSPECTIVE

A central message of this chapter is that we have not yet achieved a completely gender-fair or a gender-neutral society. Gender is still very much with us in many varied and complex ways, and if recent history is any indication, society will continue to grapple with the social and political consequences of gender inequities, gender stereotypes, and changing sex roles for years to come.

Social psychology research helps us understand our preconceptions about gender. As we have seen, many studies document that many people believe women differ from men in their personality traits, abilities, and competence. Social role theory holds that these perceived differences are often due more to the socially defined roles of men and women than to innate differences between the sexes.

While social psychology research shows that the behavior of men and women sometimes differs, these differences are small to moderate in size, and they often vary depending on the social setting. Social psychology research and theory remind us that gender is frequently determined by social beliefs, social roles, and social expectations as much as by biology.

Research on masculinity, femininity, and androgyny challenges many of our preconceptions about the nature of "masculinity" and "femininity," and points to the possibility that both men and women can display varying degrees of masculine and feminine characteristics. A few of the thought-provoking findings we have discussed: Traditional feminine sex roles in women are correlated with poorer adjustment and lower self-esteem; stereotypical masculine traits such as assertiveness and striving for achievement can be healthy for both women and men—for example, they lead to higher self-esteem and better adjustment in all people; and feminine qualities such as compassion and sensitivity are attractive in a friend, romantic partner, or spouse, regardless of whether that person is male or female.

Social psychology research shows us that gender remains one of the most fundamental categories that we apply to ourselves and others and that gender continues to have complex links to our social behavior, self-concept, and personality. Social psychology research documents gender stereotypes, but also suggests ways to transcend those stereotypes; it demonstrates sex differences, but it also emphasizes the social context and causes of many of these differences. It serves a useful social as well as scientific purpose when it leads us to acknowledge the complexity of gender, to appreciate the diversity of human beings, and to accept people for who they are, regardless of their sex or gender.

The Changing Roles of Men and Women

The roles of women and men have changed substantially in recent years. However, women and men still differ on average with respect to the education and work they pursue, the wages they receive, and the roles they carry out in family life.

Psychological Research on Sex and Gender

Sex refers to the biological status of being male or female; *gender* refers to social definitions of being male or female. Social psychology research on sex and gender has traditionally focused on two main topics: how people perceive men and women, and the existence or nonexistence of sex differences.

Stereotypes about Women and Men

Personality Stereotypes

Common stereotypes hold that expressive traits (such as *warmth* and *nurturing*) are more characteristic of women and instrumental traits (such as *competitiveness* and *aggression*) are more characteristic of men.

Traits ascribed to men are sometimes more positive than those ascribed to women. General stereotypes of nationality groups tend to be those that describe men, not women.

Broader Stereotypes about Gender

Gender stereotypes comprise probabilistic beliefs about the physical traits, social and family roles, sexual behavior, and personality traits of women and men.

Gender Stereotypes and the Perception of Ability

Work performed by women is sometimes evaluated more negatively and attributed to different causes than equivalent work performed by men is.

Can Information about Individuals Overcome Gender Stereotypes?

Judgments of individual women and men based on concrete information tends to be influenced less by gender stereotypes than judgments based on gender alone are; however, concrete information does not eliminate the influence of gender stereotypes.

When personnel managers learn both the sex and individuating information about job applicants, their judgments of applicants' personalities are determined by individuating information, but evaluation of applicants' suitability for jobs is influenced by gender stereotypes as well.

Social Psychology in Everyday Life: Gender Stereotypes and the Chilly Classroom Climate for Women

Gender stereotypes contribute to classrooms unfriendly to women in which teachers behave in ways that are biased in favor of male students. Teachers sometimes view male students as being more competent than female students, assign more power and status to male students, and evaluate male and female students differently.

Sex Differences in Behavior

The Study of Sex Differences

Meta-analysis is a statistical procedure that enables researchers to combine results of many studies on sex differences to determine (1) whether sex differences are reliable across studies, (2) the average size of sex differences, and (3) whether sex differences depend on other variables.

The Evidence for Sex Differences

Recent meta-analyses indicate that women and men on average show differences in nonverbal behaviors, aggression, helping behavior, and susceptibility to social influence. Meta-analyses show that in group settings, women engage more in expressive behaviors and men engage more in instrumental behaviors. Men are more likely to emerge as leaders of small groups in laboratory studies, and men and women show somewhat different styles of leadership. Women tend to be somewhat more self-disclosing than men, particularly when speaking to other women.

The Meaning of Sex Differences

Documented sex differences tend to be small to moderate in magnitude, but sometimes they may have real-life consequences. The existence of sex differences does not necessarily inform us about the reasons for these differences.

Theories of Gender and Sex-Typing

Biological Theories

Biological theories attempt to explain sex differences in terms of evolution, heredity, and physiology. Such explanations are plausible if sex differences occur early in development, show consistency across cultures, show consistency across species, and relate to sex-linked physiological variables (such as hormones). Of all documented sex differences in social behavior, the sex difference in aggression has the strongest evidence of a degree of biological cause.

Freudian Theory

Freudian theory argues that early emotional and sexual attachments to parents lead children to develop masculine or feminine identities.

Social Learning Theories

Social learning theories argue that sex differences and gender-related behaviors are learned through processes of classical conditioning, operant conditioning, and observational learning.

Cognitive Approaches to Gender

Kohlberg's cognitive–developmental theory says that after labeling themselves as female or male, children strive to behave consistently with their gender labels.

Bem's gender schema theory argues that people acquire gender schemas that comprise cultural beliefs about gender. Individuals who are gender-schematic hold strong gender schemas and tend to monitor their own and others' behavior in terms of "femininity" and "masculinity."

Social Role Theory

Eagly's social role theory maintains that the differing roles assigned to women and men in all societies lead to stereotypical perceptions of and different behaviors in women and men.

Self-Presentation Theory

Self-presentation theories argue that gender-related behaviors are variably displayed depending on the setting and others' expectations. Both women and men sometimes change their displays of femininity or masculinity depending on their social audience.

Gender and the Individual

Gender and Self-Esteem

Research in the United States shows that men and women do not differ in overall self-esteem. However, women's self-esteem may depend more on their social relations, and men's on their individuality, power, and achievement.

Multicultural Perspectives: Gender and Self-Esteem across Cultures

The relationship between gender and self-esteem varies across cultures. Countries in which women have high self-esteem relative to men tend to be more industrialized, more Protestant, have more women working and attending universities, less authoritarian political systems, and less traditional sex-role ideologies.

Gender and Personality

Early personality tests conceptualized masculinity–femininity as a single bipolar dimension, and early researchers tended to assume that women are best adjusted when they score on these tests as "feminine" and men when they score as "masculine."

More recent conceptions hold that masculinity and femininity are two independent dimensions. Sandra Bem argued that people with high degrees of both masculinity and femininity (androgynous people) may be more adaptable and mentally healthy than traditionally masculine or feminine individuals. Research has not consistently supported this hypothesis.

Masculinity is positively related to various measures of mental health and to performance on mathematics and visual–spatial tests. Femininity is positively related to success in interpersonal relationships.

Recent research has emphasized that "masculinity" and "femininity" are concepts that may vary across cultures and over time.

KEY TERMS

Androgyny: The state of possessing both masculine and feminine traits; in terms of recent masculinity and femininity scales, an individual is androgynous if he or she reports possessing both instrumental and expressive personality traits.

Biological theories: Theories that explain sex differences and gender-related behaviors in terms of evolution, heredity, and physiology.

Cognitive–developmental theory: Kohlberg's theory that an individual's self-labeling as male or female is critical in the development of gender-related behaviors.

Femininity: A personality trait defined in recent scales as the degree to which an individual reports possessing expressive qualities.

Freudian theory: Theory originating with Sigmund Freud that focuses on unconscious mental processes and early sexual and emotional development; it argues that girls become feminine and boys masculine because of their early sexual feelings and their emotional ties to their parents; see *Oedipus complex* and *penis envy*.

Gender: Social definitions of male and female, including all the nonbiological characteristics society uses to differentiate men and women (such as dress, nonverbal behaviors, social roles, occupations, and so on).

Gender schema theory: Bem's theory that people possess schemas comprising cultural information about gender; those possessing strong gender schemas monitor their own and others' behavior in relation to its "masculinity" and "femininity."

Gender stereotypes: Social beliefs about women's and men's personality traits, abilities, social roles, physical characteristics, and sexual behavior.

Masculinity: A personality trait defined in recent scales as the degree to which an individual reports possessing instrumental qualities.

Oedipus complex: According to Freudian theory, a young boy's unconscious feelings of sexual attraction to his mother and rivalry with his father; the resolution of the Oedipus complex leads to sex-typing.

Penis envy: According to Freudian theory, a major motivation in women's lives; because girls believe they have been castrated and because they unconsciously covet the "superior" male organ, they strive to regain their lost penis, often through having relationships with males or through bearing children.

Self-presentation theories: Theories that propose gender-related behaviors are a social performance that varies depending on the setting and the social audience.

Sex: An individual's biological status of being male or female.

Social learning theories: Theories that say sex differences and gender-related behaviors are the results of classical conditioning, operant conditioning, and observational learning.

Social role theory: Eagly's theory that the different roles occupied by women and men lead to differences in the perception of women and men and in their behavior.

9

LIKING AND LOVING OTHERS

And so the Prince finally claimed his Princess, with every dash of clockwork spectacle and storybook splendor at England's matchless command. As the Archbishop of Canterbury declared, last week's marriage of Charles Philip Arthur George, Prince of Wales, 32, and Lady Diana Frances Spencer, 20, was "the stuff of which fairy tales are made." She was a bride of nonpareil luminance, wreathed in ivory tulle and trailing a 25-foot silken train; he was the romantic groom, stalwart in full-dress naval uniform with medals and sword agleam.

—*Newsweek,* August 10, 1981

Prince Charles and Diana Spencer at their wedding. This dream marriage of 1981 ended in a nightmarish separation more than 10 years later.

Close relationships, even those between princes and princesses, have their ups and downs. The marriage of Prince Charles and Lady Diana provides a sad case in point; what started as a fairy tale in 1981 ended as a nightmare in 1993. It is easy to be cynical about this privileged pair, whose marital troubles became front-page news around the world. But of course, the Prince and Princess of Wales are not alone. Currently, about half of all marriages in the United States end in divorce, and more than that are troubled at one time or another. Rather than providing an easy excuse for cynicism, Charles and Diana's storybook romance and messy separation provides us with a highly public example to consider as we examine the factors that influence the development, success, and failures of friendships and close relationships.

One thing is clear: Despite the heartaches they sometimes bring, our relationships—with lovers, spouses, and friends—are as important to most of us as food, drink, and shelter. What would our lives be without love and friendship? Individually and as a culture, we seem obsessed with interpersonal attraction, its causes, its maintenance, and its significance. Perhaps this is one reason for the media's intense scrutiny of Charles and Diana's courtship, marriage, and breakup. Attention from media as varied as scholarly articles, popular newspaper columns like "Dear Abby," and tabloid accounts of celebrity couples shows that attraction is a topic that attracts us all. From birth on, our lives tell the story of relationships between and among people.

THE SCIENTIFIC STUDY OF ATTRACTION

Is it possible to analyze and understand close personal relationships scientifically? Can we dissect friendship and love by conducting experiments and analyzing data?

Although most of us think frequently about our friendships and romances, social psychologists did not devote much research to these topics until the mid-1960s (Berscheid, 1985; Levinger, 1980), perhaps because they viewed "love" as inaccessible to standard scientific methods. The scientific study of attraction, and particularly of love, has probably been inhibited by the common cultural attitude that love is mysterious, indescribable, and beyond empirical study.

Certainly, social psychologists cannot provide the same kind of information about love that poets and novelists give us. But the information they *can* provide is useful and thought-provoking nonetheless. This chapter will present scientific theories and research on why people like and love others. These topics are clearly important; each of our lives started with an act of attraction, and much of our happiness at work, at play, and in family life depends on the quality of our friendships and loves. Even Charles and Diana would probably agree on this point.

374

Attraction is a topic that attracts us all. In this chapter we will examine attraction from many different perspectives.

For both practical and theoretical reasons, social psychology has traditionally brought certain emphases to the study of liking and loving. First, *the current situation* as a cause of attraction has been prominent. As you will see, our account of the early stages of attraction will reflect this emphasis, focusing on *broad, often external, variables,* such as situationally produced anxiety, proximity, mere exposure, similarity, and physical attractiveness.

Early social psychology research on attraction tended to focus more on *initial and early stages of friendships and romantic attractions* than on their long-term development (Berscheid, 1985; Huston & Levinger, 1978). Why? Because it was simply easier to study variables that influence the beginnings of relationships, for beginnings can be created in the laboratory.

Similarly, social psychology traditionally focused on *mild attraction* (liking, and particularly liking after first meetings and based on first impressions) rather than on stronger attractions (committed friendships, passionate and romantic love). Again, this focus was partly due to the logistics of conducting research. Mild attraction can be created quickly and investigated in a laboratory experiment, whereas intense attraction requires time to develop and generally is not open to experimental investigation.

Until relatively recently, social psychologists have perhaps overemphasized the *cognitive processes that lead to attraction,* in part because of social psychology's general emphasis on cognition (Fiskes, 1993; Markus & Zajonc, 1985). According to the cognitive perspective, liking and loving are related to broader research on beliefs and attitudes (Berscheid, 1985): We are attracted to people based on the information we have about them. We strive to create consistency among our likes and dislikes (Heider, 1958; Newcomb, 1953). Equity and exchange theories assume that people rationally compute the costs and rewards of relationships in deciding whether or not to pursue them. Attraction as mental calculation has received considerable attention in social psychology; attraction as raw emotion has received less attention (Berscheid, 1983). Certainly, as common sense probably tells you, we sometimes select our friends and lovers rationally. But do we always? All of us seem to know someone who "fell in love with the wrong person." Sometimes love is blind.

In recent years, social psychologists have expanded their approaches to attraction. They have increasingly studied romantic and passionate love, sometimes by conducting longitudinal studies that follow dating and married couples over extended periods of time to determine what leads to satisfaction and long-term commitment in some relationships and misery and breakups in others (Fincham & Bradbury, 1990; Jones & Perlman, 1991; Kelley et al., 1983).

Theories of attraction have expanded to include more than just broad, situational variables and rational thought processes. For example, the findings and theories of evolutionary biology over the past two decades have led to a new appreciation of biological and evolutionary factors in attraction (Buss, 1987, 1988, 1989; Buss & Schmitt, 1993). Close and intimate relationships, relatively neglected topics in the past, are now the focus of many studies and theories (Jones & Perlman, 1991; Kelley et al., 1983). And researchers are studying with new interest how our emotions and early relations with parents influence our adult romantic attractions (Berscheid, 1983; Hazan & Shaver, 1987). This chapter will describe both traditional and newer approaches to the study of an ever-fascinating topic: why we like and love others.

THE BEGINNINGS OF ATTRACTION

Before we ask why people like and love others, let's consider a more basic question: Why do people simply want to be with others? The word *affiliation* is used by social psychologists to refer to a desire or motivation to be with others, sometimes regardless of one's liking for those others. *Attraction,* on the other hand, refers to a positive attitude or emotion we feel toward others, which presumably leads us to approach them and seek their companionship. You'll probably agree that sometimes you want to affiliate with others even though you are not strongly attracted to them—for example, when you're lonely, bored, or anxious.

Anxiety and Affiliation: The "Dr. Zilstein Experiment"

In the late 1950s, Stanley Schachter (1959) carried out an important set of studies that tested a seemingly simple hypothesis: When people are upset and anxious, they are more likely to affiliate with others. (I recall an event that seems to support this hypothesis. As I walked home from school on the day President John F. Kennedy was assassinated in 1963, I saw people standing in groups on the sidewalk, discussing the day's horrifying events. Neighbors who hadn't spoken to one another in days and sometimes months now needed to be together.)

It is one thing to observe in everyday life that people want to be with others when they're upset, but it is another thing to demonstrate this proposition in the laboratory. As you know from Chapter 2, when social psychologists want to establish a cause–effect relationship between two variables, they conduct experiments. Does anxiety *cause* affiliation? To answer this question, Schachter brought college women to the laboratory, made some of them quite anxious, and then gave them the opportunity to wait alone or with others.

Here's how the experiment worked: The subjects were greeted by Dr. Zilstein, the experimenter, who explained that he was studying the effects of electric shocks on people. He informed half the subjects that the shock they received would not be painful. He informed the remaining subjects that they would receive extremely painful electric shocks.

Both groups of subjects were asked to complete a questionnaire while they waited for the experiment to begin. Casually, Dr. Zilstein informed them that they could fill out the questionnaires while sitting alone in a room or while sitting with other subjects, and he asked them to mark on their form where they would like to wait. The subjects' choice, to be alone or with others, was the dependent measure that interested Schachter, and you may be relieved to know that the subjects were not really shocked in this experiment.

Were the high-anxiety subjects more likely than the low-anxiety subjects to choose to wait with others? The answer was a clear yes (see Figure 9.1).

Reasons for the Anxiety–Affiliation Relationship

Why do anxious people seek out others? You can probably think of several plausible reasons: to gain reassurance and reinforcement, to distract themselves, or perhaps to clarify feelings and compare their reactions to those of others. All of these factors may at times motivate affiliation (Hill, 1987).

This last explanation—that we sometimes seek out others so that we can compare ourselves with them—has a distinguished history in social psychology. Leon Festinger's (1954) *social comparison theory* argues that whereas we can

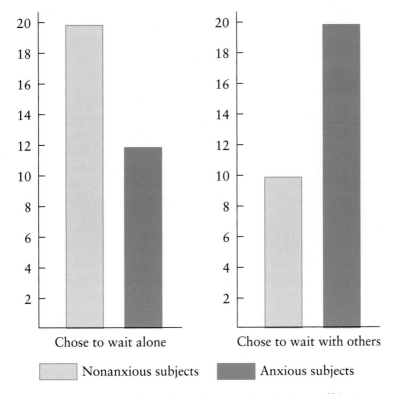

The results supported the hypothesis that anxiety leads to affiliation: Anxious subjects chose to wait with others far more than nonanxious subjects did.

FIGURE 9.1 Results of Schachter's "Dr. Zilstein study" testing whether anxiety leads to affiliation. *Source:* Data from Schachter (1959).

objectively know physical reality (for example, how much we weigh), we cannot directly know social reality (how smart we are). To know social reality, we must compare ourselves with others.

Furthermore, Festinger hypothesized that we generally seek to compare ourselves with *similar* others. For example, if you want to know how "smart" you are, shouldn't you compare yourself with other college students rather than with your 5-year-old cousin or a Nobel laureate physicist? Indeed, a good time to see social comparison processes in operation is when professors return exams and students eagerly compare scores to see how they stack up against their friends and acquaintances.

Schachter (1959) conducted a clever follow-up experiment to determine whether social comparison processes led to affiliation in his Dr. Zilstein study. The new study was similar to the original, with one significant difference: Some of the highly anxious subjects were told they could wait with other subjects in the shock study; others were informed that they could wait with students waiting to talk to their professors.

This new version of the experiment posed an interesting question: Will anxious subjects wait with just anybody, or only with people who share their predicament? If subjects are merely seeking distraction, then anybody should do, but if they are seeking social comparison, then they need to affiliate with fellow subjects facing the threat of painful electric shocks. The results indicated that anxious subjects wanted to wait *only* with other subjects in the shock experiment. Schachter facetiously summarized his results by concluding that whereas his original study supported the old saying that "Misery loves company," the follow-up study amended that to "Misery loves, in particular, miserable company." These results, of course, are consistent with the social comparison explanation for the anxiety–affiliation link. Many subsequent studies have provided additional evidence for the importance of social comparison processes in affiliation (Rofe, 1984; Suls & Wills, 1991).

SOCIAL
PSYCHOLOGY
IN EVERYDAY
LIFE

 Do Anxious People Always Compare Themselves with Similar Others?

Imagine you've just been diagnosed with cancer. You have surgery to remove the tumor, and your doctors tell you the odds are good that you'll recover completely. Whom would you rather talk to at this point—another patient who has just had a surgery quite similar to yours or a former patient who has completely recovered from a surgery like yours?

Festinger and Schachter assumed that a main reason people compare themselves with others is to know the truth about themselves and compare their feelings with others. However, people also compare themselves with others to enhance their view of themselves and to defend themselves from threatening emotions (Taylor & Lobel, 1989; Wills, 1981, 1991). Breast cancer patients often mentally compare themselves with women who are worse off than they are (Wood, Taylor, & Lichtman, 1985)—for example, a woman who has had a lumpectomy might compare herself with a less fortunate woman who has had a complete mastectomy. Such a comparison makes psychological sense, because the patient can feel better about her own situation as a result. Cancer patients often report that they feel they are coping better than other cancer patients, and they often seem to believe they are healthier than other patients with comparable conditions (Taylor, Falke, Shoptaw, & Lichtman, 1986). While these thoughts may be unrealistic, they help patients defend against the anxiety triggered by their life-threatening disease.

While cancer patients often *mentally* compare themselves with others who are worse off, they prefer to *interact* with patients who are coping well with their disease (Taylor & Lobel, 1989). Friends who are long-term, well-adjusted cancer survivors provide "success stories" that seem to inspire cancer patients and make them optimistic and hopeful about their own future. This is one of the purposes of cancer survivor support groups.

What does all this say about social comparison processes? Whom do we seek to be with when we're anxious or threatened? It depends partly on our motivations. If we want accurate information about ourselves, we may seek out similar others who face our predicament; if we want inspiration, advice, and problem-solving skills, we may seek out better-off people who have faced our predicament successfully; and if we want to feel better about ourselves and reduce our anxiety, we may make "downward comparisons" with people who are worse off than we are. The way cancer patients achieve both anxiety reduction and inspiration is by mentally comparing themselves with people who are worse off while actually affiliating with recovered patients who are better off. ✎

✎ FROM AFFILIATION TO ATTRACTION

Often, we seek out others not because we're upset or anxious, but because we're positively attracted. Why do we like some people? What leads us to initiate relationships with some individuals but not with others? Let's seek answers to these questions by turning to several broad variables—proximity, mere exposure, similarity, and physical attractiveness—that influence the early development of friendships and romances.

Proximity: The Architecture of Attraction

. . . Prince Charles has known his future bride virtually all her life . . . she was literally the girl next door, at least for part of each year. Though the Spencers spent most of their time at Althorp, their magnificent 500-year-old home in Northamptonshire, for years they rented a large country home on the royal family's 20,000-acre Sandringham estate. It was there that Charles met Diana as a little girl.

—*Time,* March 9, 1981

To become friends or lovers with someone, you must first meet that someone. One powerful variable that determines whether you meet someone is *proximity*—the physical or architectural distance that separates you.

A classic study by Festinger, Schachter, and Back (1950) demonstrated the power of proximity when it analyzed friendship patterns at Westgate West, a housing project for married graduate students at MIT. Student families were randomly assigned to available apartments, so almost none of the residents knew one another upon moving in. Later, when residents were asked to list their three closest friends in the housing project, about two-thirds of those friends turned out to live in the same building as the subjects who listed them. Furthermore, of the close friends listed in a subject's own building, about two-thirds lived on the same floor as the nominating subject.

There were five apartments on each of two floors in the typical Westgate building (see Figure 9.2). The Westgate study indicated that people who lived in the middle apartments of their floors (apartments 3 and 8 in Figure 9.2) tended to be nominated as friends more than those who lived in the end apartments, and that those who lived in first-floor apartments near the staircases connecting the two floors (apartments 1 and 5) tended to be nominated more than those who lived farther away from the stairs. Note that middle apartments were both centrally located and in close proximity to neighbors on either side. And if you lived near the staircase, you would encounter other residents more often because you would bump into them as they used the stairs.

Similar studies have investigated friendship patterns in college dormitories. In one that measured students' friendships in a large University of Chicago dormitory, neighboring doors were only 8 feet apart. Yet, on average, students were more likely to be friends with a student who lived one door away than with one who lived two doors away, and so on (Priest & Sawyer, 1967). It's not surprising that large distances make a difference in friendships, but in this study, the difference between 8 and 16 feet made a difference as well.

Using somewhat different methods, another study asked college students to name two other students with whom they thought a friendship might develop

Festinger, Schachter, and Back (1950) studied how the architectural proximity of residents in housing units like this one affected their friendships with other residents.

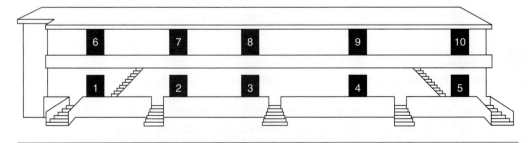

FIGURE 9.2 Schematic diagram of a Westgate West building. *Source:* Adapted from Festinger, Schachter, and Back (1950).

during the school year. Three months later, subjects rated the intensity of these developing friendships. The farther away a potential friend lived, the less likely he or she was to become a friend (Hays, 1985).

Similar results come from studies on noncollege housing projects. In one study, the elderly residents of an urban housing project tended to nominate as their closest friends people who lived in the same building (88% of the nominated friends) and people who lived on the same floor (almost 50% of the nominated friends) (Nahemow & Lawton, 1975).

Proximity affects not only friendships but more intimate relationships as well. An early sociological study that examined 5,000 marriage license applications in Philadelphia and plotted the residences of each applicant on a street map found a clear relationship between proximity and attraction. The proportion of couples getting married "decreased steadily and markedly as the distance between contracting parties increased" (Bossard, 1931). In other words, more couples who lived one block apart got married than couples who lived two blocks apart, and so on. Other studies point to similar conclusions (Katz & Hill, 1958; Kerckhoff, 1974; Ramsoy, 1966).

The research on proximity and attraction makes an important point: To form a relationship with someone, you must first come into contact. Your residential, educational, and work settings can have a decisive influence on who you do and don't meet. Parents who send their children to "the right schools" so they will meet and marry "the right people" implicitly acknowledge the role of proximity in attraction.

Mere Exposure: I've Grown Accustomed to Your Face

The closer people live, work, or sit to us, the more we see them. Research on the *mere exposure effect* (see Chapter 6) shows that, all things being equal, people tend to like stimuli more the more frequently they have been exposed to them (Bornstein, 1989; Zajonc, 1968). Does this phenomenon apply to interpersonal attraction? The answer seems to be yes.

One experiment found that when subjects were shown photographs of men for various numbers of times, on average they indicated that they liked the men more the more frequently they had seen the photographs (Zajonc, 1968). Another study had subjects sit next to other subjects on the pretext of participating in an experiment on taste perception. The researchers arranged for subjects to move around during the course of this experiment, so that they sat next to other subjects varying numbers of times. On average, the more frequently subjects had sat next to other subjects, the more they liked them (Saegert, Swap, & Zajonc, 1973). Thus, these results show evidence for a mere exposure effect when the stimuli are live human beings.

Another study asked police cadets who were assigned to their rooms and classroom seats alphabetically to list their closest friends among other cadets. These subjects were more likely to list someone who was alphabetically similar to them (Segal, 1974). These results again point to the pervasive effects of mere exposure and proximity. Note that in real life these two variables are often confounded:

Does similarity lead to attraction?

When you live, work, or sit near another person, one result is that you simply tend to see that person more frequently.

Similarity: Birds of a Feather

He liked solitude; she needed people. She wanted to dance; he preferred fishing. An observer later described them as a "queeny-bopper with an unhip uncle."

—from an article about Charles and Diana's breakup, *Life*, February 1993

The evidence is clear: We tend to like people more who are similar to us. In general, we associate more with people who are similar to us in age, socioeconomic status, level of education, political affiliation, attitudes and values, personality traits, religion, and even physical dimensions such as attractiveness and height.

Don't believe it? Think of your closest friend. How similar is he or she to you in age? In degree of education? In ethnic background? In values and attitudes? If you are like most people, your best friend is probably a lot more similar to you than not. Researchers at the University of Michigan demonstrated this fact in a survey of 1,000 Detroit-area men who answered questions both about themselves and their three closest friends (Laumann, 1969). Their results showed that friends tended to come from similar social, educational, and religious backgrounds. A more recent study of adult friendships in a Midwestern town shows similar findings: Friends tend to be similar to one another in income, marital status, leisure activities, degree of education, and club memberships (Johnson, 1989).

Intimate relationships also seem to follow the similarity principle. Many studies indicate that people engage in *assortative mating;* that is, they mate in nonrandom ways, and in particular they seem to match themselves on a variety of dimensions. An early study demonstrated that engaged couples tended to be similar in age, social class, ethnicity, and religion (Burgess & Wallin, 1943). More recent research indicates that engaged and married couples also show matching on intelligence, values, degree of smoking and alcohol consumption, and even physical dimensions such as physical attractiveness, height, weight, and—believe it or not—even lung volume and ear lobe length (Buss, 1985; Feingold, 1988; Osborne, Noble, & Wey, 1978; Schafer & Keith, 1990; Vandenberg, 1972). A study of dating couples found that couples who stayed together were more similar in age, intelligence, and physical attractiveness than those who broke up (Hill, Rubin, & Peplau, 1976).

Virtually all the research just surveyed demonstrates that similarity is *correlated* with attraction in everyday life, but it doesn't necessarily prove that similarity *leads to* attraction. A study by Theodore Newcomb (1961) was one of the first to clearly suggest a cause–effect link between similarity and attraction.

Newcomb provided a group of University of Michigan men with free rooms in a local boardinghouse if they would agree to participate in a study on friendship formation. All the students were strangers to one another at the start, and thus Newcomb could observe friendships as they developed and probe the causal factors underlying these friendships. Newcomb's data indicated that attitudinal and value similarity predicted who became friends with whom. For example, one group of five friends shared common liberal political views and interests in intellectual and artistic subjects, whereas another group of three friends were all politically conservative engineering students.

In an interesting variation on his boardinghouse study, Newcomb (1961) intentionally pitted similarity against proximity, by assigning pairs of dissimilar students as roommates. For example, an incoming freshman interested in liberal arts and classical music might be paired with an older student who was enrolling in the business school after having served in the military. Surprisingly, such roommates generally became good friends, even though they were quite different. Apparently, although we often tend to seek out those who are similar to us, we can learn to like dissimilar others if we come in close contact with them.

In a series of experiments, Byrne and his associates have shown a cause–effect link between attitudinal similarity and attraction—that is, when we share similar attitudes with another person, we tend to like him or her more. Typically, in these experiments pairs of subjects filled out attitude questionnaires, and each subject was given false information about the other subject's questionnaire responses. The experimenter could thus directly manipulate how much a subject thought the other person agreed with his or her attitudes. Such studies consistently show a strong linear relationship between subjects' perceptions of the proportion of attitudes they share with another person and their liking for that person (see Figure 9.3). This link between attitudinal similarity and attraction holds across cultures, age groups, and educational and mental health statuses (Byrne, 1971).

Stage Models of Attraction

Clearly, there is abundant evidence that we tend to like people who are similar to us. But do we seek out the same kinds of similarity in the beginning of a relationship as we do later on? A number of social psychologists have suggested that friendships and close relationships pass through a series of stages or "filters," and that we attend to different characteristics in a friend or romantic partner during each stage (Kerckhoff & Davis, 1962; Levinger & Snoek, 1972; Murstein, 1970).

Murstein's (1970) stimulus–value–role model (see Figure 9.4), for example, suggests that an intimate relationship starts at a stimulus stage, during which each party judges the other on such externally apparent characteristics as age, appearance, ethnicity, and gender. Typically, we seek others who are similar to us on these dimensions (with the one notable exception of gender in heterosexual attraction). This initial "cut" of the population based on broad demographic and appearance variables can greatly limit our pool of eligibles—the population from which we select potential friends or lovers. The variable of gender in romantic attraction is an

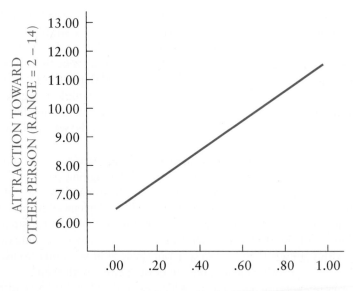

As the graph shows, the greater the proportion of attitudes subjects shared with the stranger, the more subjects liked him.

FIGURE 9.3 The effects of attitude similarity on attraction. *Source:* Byrne and Nelsen (1965).

obvious example; most people reduce their prospects by half on that one criterion alone.

Note that screening people at the stimulus stage does not require actual interaction. You may be able to tell at a glance that someone is "not right" for you, based on his or her age, appearance, or ethnicity. Murstein's second stage, the value stage, does require interaction, however, because now you seek to learn about the other person's attitudes and values. After several dates with an attractive romantic partner, you may start to find out your partner's religious values, political attitudes, opinions about family life, leisure activities, career, and so on. In this stage, the similarity principle seems to predominate again, for in general, people seek others with similar attitudes, values, and interests.

In Murstein's third stage, the role stage, you assess how well your potential partner agrees with the roles you expect each party to take in the relationship. For example, in a marriage, each partner may have expectations about how a husband and wife are supposed to behave. People who believe in traditional sex roles may assume the husband should earn money, mow the lawn, carry out the trash, and physically discipline the children; the wife should decorate and clean the house, prepare food, and provide emotional support for the family. In contrast, people

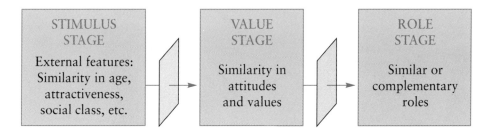

STIMULUS STAGE		VALUE STAGE		ROLE STAGE
External features: Similarity in age, attractiveness, social class, etc.	→	Similarity in attitudes and values	→	Similar or complementary roles

FIGURE 9.4 Murstein's stimulus–value–role model.

who believe in egalitarian relationships may hold that husbands and wives should share tasks equally. If marriage partners don't agree about such divisions of labor, they may be in for considerable conflict.

An earlier stage model of courtship and attraction suggested that in addition to compatible roles, couples seek out complementary personality traits and needs in each other (Kerckhoff & Davis, 1962). For example, a dominant person might be most compatible with a submissive marriage partner. Although this notion that "opposites attract" seems plausible for certain personality traits, it has not generally been supported by research studies (Hill, Rubin, & Peplau, 1976; Levinger, 1983; Murstein, 1976; Winch, 1958).

While it's clear that not all relationships develop in the same predictable way (Levinger, 1983), stage models provide a starting place for understanding the complexity of real relationships and suggest testable hypotheses about the kinds of variables that may affect relationships at different times in their life cycles.

Physical Attractiveness

At long last, Prince Charles, . . . heir to the British throne, was to be married. His betrothed: Lady Diana Spencer, 19, a blushing beauty with an impressive pedigree. . . .

The next Princess of Wales appears to be everything the Prince has been searching for in a wife—tall (5 ft. 9 in., 2 in. shorter than he), slim and long-legged—the type he has said he favors.

—*Time*, March 9, 1981

Although he may have been blind to their future compatibility, Prince Charles apparently was not blind to Diana Spencer's beauty. For many years, however, social psychologists *were* strangely blind to beauty, for they largely ignored its role in attraction. Social psychologists had some seemingly valid reasons for neglecting the topic. After all, when people are surveyed concerning what they look for in dates and mates, physical attractiveness is never at the top of the list (Buss & Barnes, 1986; Hill, 1945; Hudson & Henze, 1969; Hudson & Hoyt, 1981). They typically report that they are more interested in "honesty," "warmth," "dependable character," "emotional stability," and "a sense of humor."

Although physical attractiveness is to some extent "in the eye of the beholder," social psychological research indicates that people tend to show high levels of agreement when rating others' physical attractiveness.

"Do you think I'm attractive?"

But do people practice what they preach? One study attempted to answer this question by setting up "computer dates" for over 700 incoming freshmen at the University of Minnesota (Walster, Aronson, Abrahams, & Rottman, 1966). These students filled out questionnaires, supposedly so they could be matched up with a computer date for a big dance arranged by the researchers. In these questionnaires the researchers assessed subjects' attitudes, personalities, and scholastic aptitudes. They also had student researchers unobtrusively rate each subject's physical attractiveness.

Students were matched randomly with their "computer dates" (with one qualification—the man had to be taller). On the night of the dance, students met their dates and went to the university gymnasium (the site of the dance), where they talked, danced, met other freshmen, and got to know their dates. After a couple of hours, the researchers rounded up all available students during an intermission and asked them to fill out a questionnaire evaluating their dates.

Did scholastic aptitude, attitudes, or personality traits affect students' liking for their dates? Not at all. Did physical attractiveness? Yes. Only one strongly significant finding emerged from this study: The more physically attractive their dates were, the more the students liked them.

These findings unleashed a flood of research on the social implications and consequences of physical attractiveness. A number of replications of the "computer date" study (Brislin & Lewis, 1968; Curran & Lippold, 1975; Tesser & Brodie, 1971), including one conducted on gay men (Sergios & Cody, 1985), have shown quite consistent results: Subjects' perceptions of their dates' attractiveness and their dates' actual physical attractiveness exert a stronger influence on the subjects' attraction to the dates than virtually any other characteristic does. Why does physical attractiveness have such a powerful effect on attraction in these studies? One possibility is that the studies focus on first impressions at the very earliest stages of relationships, and in these kinds of situations, subjects don't have time to assess the "deeper" characteristics of their dates.

In real-life relationships (as opposed to "computer dates"), dating and married couples tend to be matched on attractiveness (Feingold, 1988). In a field study in which researchers observed couples in natural settings (such as bars and theater lobbies) and rated each partner on physical attractiveness, beautiful women, as the similarity principle predicts, were more likely to be with beautiful men, average-looking women with average-looking men, and homely women with homely men (Silverman, 1971).

McKillip and Riedel (1983) observed both opposite-sex and same-sex pairs of people in real-life settings and rated each member of the pair on attractiveness. The researchers then asked the pairs whether they were friends or lovers, and how strong and committed their relationship was. Interestingly, both friends and lovers tended to be matched on physical attractiveness. Furthermore, close and committed relationships tended to show more matching than casual relationships did, and male friends showed matching more than women did. One recent study found that college roommates tend to be more satisfied with each other when they are similar in physical attractiveness (Carli, Ganley, & Pierce-Otay, 1991).

It probably comes as no surprise to you that physically attractive people are more popular. The computer date study found that attractive students had dated more than less attractive students over a six-month period. Another study extended these results by showing that the correlation between attractiveness and popularity was stronger for females than for males (Berscheid, Dion, & Walster, 1971). It would be in keeping with traditional sex-role stereotypes for women's popularity to depend more on appearance and for men's to be related to wealth, intelligence, or athletic ability (Diana and Prince Charles provide an interesting example here!). Studies consistently indicate that men rate the physical attractiveness of a romantic partner to be more important than women do, and this is so in many different countries (Buss & Barnes, 1986; de Raad & Doddema-Winsemius, 1992; Feingold, 1990, 1991; Stroebe, Insko, Thompson, & Layton, 1971). People in general seem to evaluate and judge women more than men on the basis of their physical attractiveness (Jackson, 1992).

Does physical attractiveness confer any advantages other than popularity? Subjects who were asked to rate photographed people on many different traits judged physically attractive people to have more attractive personalities as well. Furthermore, subjects predicted that the attractive people could expect better job prospects and happier marriages (Dion, Berscheid, & Walster, 1972). Apparently, in the minds of many, beautiful is not only popular, it is better as well (Berscheid & Walster, 1974b).

A review of more than 70 studies on stereotypes about physically attractive people concluded that physically attractive people tend to be perceived as superior to unattractive people on some characteristics more than others. Specifically, attractive people are seen as more socially skillful and popular than unattractive people (no surprise here). They are also perceived to be higher on intelligence, psychological adjustment, power, and dominance. However—and this is an important qualification—attractive people are *not* perceived to be more trustworthy, honest, sensitive, or nurturant than unattractive people. Thus, attractive people are not always judged to have better traits than unattractive people. Furthermore, a person's physical attractiveness tends to have less influence on our judgments the more additional information we possess about a person (Eagly, Ashmore,

Makhijani, & Longo, 1991). Thus, looks should bias our judgments of strangers more than our judgments of friends and family members.

Are stereotypes about physically attractive people true? Perhaps not surprisingly, physically attractive people do prove to be more popular, socially skilled, and sexually experienced than unattractive people, and they seem to suffer less from shyness and loneliness (Feingold, 1992b). The broader stereotypes about attractive people seem unjustified, however: Physically attractive people do not differ from less attractive people in their personality traits, self-esteem, or intellectual ability. Perhaps one reason attractiveness does not show strong links to self-esteem is that people tend to be relatively poor judges of their own attractiveness. The average correlation between people's ratings of their own attractiveness and ratings made by others is a low .24, and while people's actual physical attractiveness is unrelated to their self-esteem, their self-rated level of attractiveness is (Feingold, 1992b). Apparently, if you *think* you're attractive, you generally feel good about yourself, regardless of the truth of the matter.

Although physically attractive people tend to be popular, it's worth noting that extreme attractiveness may sometimes have paradoxical effects (Hatfield & Sprecher, 1986). For example, extremely attractive people may have fewer same-sex friends (Krebs & Adinolfi, 1975), and they may be seen as conceited, vain, adulterous, and unsympathetic (Dermer & Thiel, 1975). Finally, very attractive people may suffer from an attributional dilemma: They don't know whether others like them for their looks or "for themselves." Perhaps, then, the best of all possible worlds is to be above average in attractiveness, but not *too* attractive.

THEORIES OF ATTRACTION

Why do proximity, similarity, and physical attractiveness influence attraction? Are there general theories that can help us understand the varied findings we've presented so far? Three kinds of social psychology theories apply directly to the topic of attraction: learning theories, exchange and equity theories, and cognitive consistency theories. We turn to these theories now to gain a deeper understanding of why we like and love some people but not others.

Learning Theories

Here's a simple proposition: We tend to like people more when they are associated with pleasure, and less when they are associated with pain or costs. All things being equal, for example, you will probably like an acquaintance who tells witty stories more than one who continually tells obnoxious jokes. Thus, attraction may be viewed as a kind of classical conditioning (Byrne & Clore, 1970; Lott & Lott, 1974); liking and disliking are in part conditioned emotional responses that occur when people have been associated with positive or negative events in the past (Griffit & Veitch, 1971; Lott & Lott, 1968).

Operant conditioning also plays a role in attraction. In general, behaviors that are rewarded tend to become more frequent, and those that are punished tend to be extinguished. This is certainly true of our interactions with other people. Chances are, if you ask someone out on a date and have a wonderful time, you are likely to ask that person out again. If, however, you suffer through your date's boring conversation and boorish manners, you are unlikely to ask him or her out in the future.

While these principles may seem obvious to you, they are helpful in understanding the effects of proximity, similarity, and physical attractiveness. When we are physically near others, for example, our chances for pleasant interactions and rewarding social exchanges with them increase. When people have similar attitudes and interests to ours, the likelihood for rewarding interaction increases; if cross-country skiing is your passion in life, isn't it rewarding to meet another passionate cross-country skier? Furthermore, people with attitudes similar to our own reward us by validating our opinions and making us feel that we are right (Byrne, 1971). And a good-looking person is reinforcing simply by his or her mere presence—after all, "a thing of beauty is a joy forever."

The learning perspective implies that if you want a friendship or romance to last, you must continue to reward your partner and ensure that the relationship continues to be associated with pleasant things. Relationships may indeed begin to fail when we take them for granted and cease providing rewards (praise, candlelit dinners, fun evenings out, hugs) for our friends and lovers.

Exchange and Equity Theories

Exchange theory and equity theory are in some sense extensions of learning theories. For example, George Homans's (1961, 1974) version of exchange theory applies aspects of B. F. Skinner's theory of operant conditioning to human social relations. Homans uses economics terminology, though: We experience rewards, costs, and profits in our relationships. In a love relationship, sex and companionship may be "rewards," periodic fights and the irritating habits of your lover or spouse may be "costs," and your profits are simply your net rewards minus your net costs.

Exchange Theory: The Economics of Relationships

Exchange theory makes the plausible assumption that we tend to choose those relationships that are most profitable, and furthermore, that relationships tend to be stable when both parties receive approximately equal profits. For example, "computer date" studies on physical attractiveness show that people prefer the most attractive partner possible (that is, they seek out the most reward and profit they can possibly get), but in everyday life they settle for partners with about their own level of attractiveness (for the relationship to endure, both parties must receive about equal profits). When a relationship is unbalanced on one dimension (say, a homely man is married to a beautiful woman), we may automatically assume that the "profits" balance out some other way (perhaps the man is rich).

Thibaut and Kelley (1959) extended the basic assumptions of exchange theory by proposing that in deciding whether to stay in a relationship, we not only assess the costs and rewards of the relationship, we hold these costs and rewards up to a *comparison level*—some standard dictated by social norms and personal expectations. After marrying Prince Charles, for example, Diana undoubtedly expected him to provide her with various expected "rewards," such as tenderness, companionship, and concern for their children. Charles may have expected in return that Diana would provide him with a regal, discreet, and demure consort. In various ways, Charles and Diana did not meet each other's expectations, and instead presented each other with unexpected "costs."

Thibaut and Kelley's version of exchange theory also proposes the notion of a *comparison level for alternatives:* The level of costs and rewards a person will accept in a relationship is compared to the costs and rewards available in alternative relationships. Perhaps Diana grew particularly dissatisfied with her marriage, for example, when it became clear to her that more satisfying alternative relationships were available to her. In essence, Thibaut and Kelley's notion of a comparison level for alternatives suggests that we must consider the costs and rewards of a relationship not in isolation, but in the context of available alternative relationships and *their* potential costs and rewards. Some people remain in bad relationships simply because nothing better is available to them and they would rather receive their current inadequate rewards than none at all (Drigotas & Rusbult, 1992; Simpson, 1987).

Equity Theory: Investing in Love

Equity theories can be viewed as an extension of exchange theories. These theories hold that we focus not only on the costs and rewards of a relationship, but also on the *investments* that we bring to it (see Adams, 1963, 1965; Walster, Walster, & Berscheid, 1978). For example, your current romantic partner may provide you with certain rewards (hugs and companionship) and extract certain costs (work!— you do all the cooking and cleaning). In addition, you may bring certain investments to your relationship ($100,000 in the bank and five years of effort devoted to nurturing the relationship). We can think of costs and rewards as consequences that result from the relationship and investments as inputs or goods brought to the relationship. In intimate relationships, investments differ from costs and rewards in that they cannot be easily removed from the relationship (Rusbult, 1983). For example, if you have spent ten years developing a good understanding of your spouse, shared many important emotional experiences together, and bought and decorated an expensive house that you jointly own, you have created a number of investments that are not easily undone.

The principle of equity holds that each partner should receive profits from a relationship in proportion to his or her investment. This is obvious in economic transactions: If one partner invests $50,000 in a new company and another invests $25,000, the first partner will certainly expect twice as much return on the investment as the second. Similarly, in friendships and romances, we expect "returns" from a relationship in proportion to our investments (whether in money, time, effort, or valued commodities like physical attractiveness). Thus, perhaps your lazy romantic partner believes it's only fair that you do all the housework because he or she is more physically attractive than you and also has a more distinguished family pedigree, thereby bringing more worth to the relationship.

Equity theory also predicts that when a relationship is inequitable—when a partner feels deprived of a "fair share," given his or her investment—the relationship is in trouble. Overbenefited partners tend to feel guilty; underbenefited partners feel angry. (You might think it would be great to get "more than your fair share" in a relationship, but in fact, equity theory predicts this is uncomfortable. Research supports this prediction, although, not surprisingly, people often seem to be *more* upset when they're underbenefited than when they're overbenefited in relationships.) Ultimately, when inequity exists, something's got to give in the relationship.

Both exchange theories and equity theories can help explain research findings on *similarity* in relationships. Almost by definition, a relationship in which people are matched on certain characteristics (socioeconomic status, professional accomplishment, attractiveness, intelligence) is more likely to be a fair trade in which the partners bring equal investments and can provide equal rewards and profits to each other.

Cognitive Consistency Theories

A third perspective on attraction maintains that our likes and dislikes may sometimes result from our attempts to create consistency among our thoughts and feelings. We've already discussed one important consistency theory in Chapter 6: Festinger's theory of cognitive dissonance, which hypothesizes that people strive for *logical consistency* among their beliefs. *Balance theory* focuses more on the consistency of our likes and dislikes (Heider, 1958; Newcomb, 1953).

Figure 9.5 illustrates a simple example, the pattern of likes and dislikes among three people: Prince Charles, Princess Diana, and Queen Elizabeth (Charles's mother). Let's look at this situation from the point of view of Queen Elizabeth. Assume that when Charles and Diana started having marital problems, Queen Elizabeth loved them both. According to balance theory, this pattern of likes and dislikes is unbalanced—that is, a state of tension exists. One way to decide whether a triad of likes and dislikes is balanced or unbalanced is to answer the following question: Would this pattern be comfortable for the people involved? If your answer is yes, the pattern is likely to be balanced. If your answer is no, the pattern is probably unbalanced. A more mechanical way to determine whether a triad is balanced is to multiply the three signs algebraically. If the result is negative—as it is for the top triangle in Figure 9.5—the triad is unbalanced. If the result is positive, a state of balance exists.

Balance theory argues that people will shift their likes and dislikes to restore balance to an unbalanced triad. For example, Queen Elizabeth could restore balance to her cognitions in one of three ways. She could try to patch things up between Charles and Diana. If the link between Charles and Diana becomes

UNBALANCED

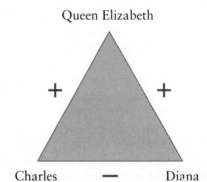

BALANCED

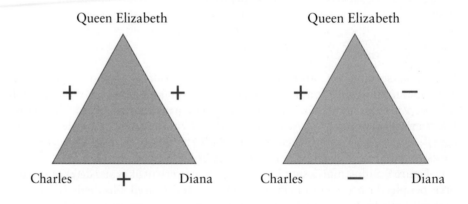

FIGURE 9.5 Balance theory and attraction.

positive (+) then balance is restored—everyone loves everyone. Alternatively, she could reject Diana; if the link between Queen Elizabeth and Diana becomes negative (−), balance is restored. In essence, she could say, "Any wife who makes my son unhappy is despicable." Or Queen Elizabeth could side with Diana against her son; if the Queen likes Diana (+) but dislikes her son (−), this too restores balance. But if Queen Elizabeth becomes disgusted with both Charles and Diana, then all links become negative, and the triad, unfortunately, remains unbalanced (not to mention full of bad feelings).

Balance theory assumes that certain patterns of likes and dislikes are more comfortable than others and that we sometimes shift some of our likes to create mental consistency. In a clever experimental demonstration of just this point, Aronson and Cope (1968) instructed a graduate research assistant to be either nice or obnoxious to individual subjects. Then, in the subject's presence, the graduate student was either praised or chewed out by a professor. As balance theory predicts, subjects tended to either like or dislike the professor so that a balanced triad could result. For example, if the assistant was obnoxious to the subject (a negative relationship) and the professor chewed out this obnoxious assistant (a negative between the assistant and professor), then the subject would tend to like the professor (a positive between subject and professor). Although these results may not seem startling, notice that subjects are basing their like or dislike for the professor only on the professor's relationship with a third party and not on any direct interaction. This experiment and the theory that motivated it provide some support for an old Arabic saying: "My enemy's enemy is my friend."

Balance processes can be seen in real life. Suppose you have a bitter breakup with a spouse or lover. Both of you consider Tom a good friend. Isn't it difficult to remain friends with Tom when he still associates with your ex? You may decide, in keeping with balance theory, that anyone who is a friend of your disgusting ex can't be friends with you. Or you may try to convince Tom that your ex isn't worth knowing. When one major relationship changes in our lives, we often have to shift others to maintain consistency in the total configuration of relationships.

Like learning, exchange, and equity theories, balance theory can help explain empirical data on attraction. For example, balance theory predicts that we will be most comfortable in relationships when we hold attitudes similar to those of our partner. If you and your best friend hold similar, positive attitudes toward the current president of the United States, then your likes are in balance. But if you admire the president and your best friend despises him, then a state of unbalance exists.

Note that we have now provided three different explanations for similarity effects in attraction: (1) Similarity in others is rewarding. (2) Similarity in relationships fosters equity in social relations. (3) Attitudinal similarity with friends and romantic partners leads to cognitive balance. Note that these different theories don't necessarily compete with one another. Each may capture part of the truth of attraction. One reason the similarity principle is so strong and consistent in research on attraction is that a number of different processes undoubtedly lead us to like similar more than dissimilar others.

LOVE

"I love you."

—*Diana,* after Charles proposed

"Whatever love means."

—*Charles*

What *does* "love" mean? How many kinds of love are there? And is this a question science can answer?

We generally take love for granted. We don't necessarily take for granted the love we give and receive in our own lives, but we do take for granted the human need to give and receive love. We simply know intuitively that most people seek out intense emotional attachments with others. Music, art, literature, and drama treat love as a central human experience, and individually, many of us feel some of our deepest emotions in the realm of love.

Love in its various forms—passionate love, romantic love, parental love—is not necessarily just a stronger form of liking. Most of the research findings and theories of attraction we have discussed so far apply to loving as well as liking. Even so, loving may be qualitatively different from liking in several ways. Passionate and parental love very likely have biological underpinnings and evolutionary histories that distinguish them from liking: Passionate love is clearly related to reproduction, and parental love to the survival of offspring. Love may be more "emotional" and less "cognitive" than liking. Berscheid and Walster (1974a) speculate that passionate love may involve more illusion and fantasy than mere liking does. The beloved is idealized, and love may sometimes be a kind of obsession. Finally, the time courses of love and liking may be quite different: Passionate love may resemble a blazing fire that burns bright and then dies quickly, whereas a good friendship may be more of a steady flame.

Because love is complex, we'll look at it from various perspectives. We'll examine the biological evolution of love, then its cultural history and variations, and finally, we'll turn to social psychology research on the measurement of love and various factors that lead it to grow or fade.

Evolutionary Theory and Love

Why do human beings love? Let's pose this question in biological rather than literary or philosophical terms. Perhaps human love evolved from maternal love in birds and mammals (Mellen, 1981). Clearly, such love, as well as the love of offspring for their mothers, serves a biological purpose: The nurturing and protection evoked by such love ensure the survival of the species and the transmission of genes from one generation to the next.

Evolutionary theorists have attempted to explain some of the unique characteristics of human love and sexuality—that is, ways we *differ* from our closest animal relatives. For example, chimpanzees and gorillas do not display the kind of intense pair-bonding that humans do (Mellen, 1981). Jane Goodall (1971), who observed chimpanzees in the wild, reported that chimps are quite promiscuous; a female in heat will mate with many males in succession. Occasionally a male and a female will form a "consort pair" and go off by themselves for a time, but this is typically brief and exceptional behavior. In chimpanzee society, males have little or no involvement in rearing the young, and the period of infant helplessness is considerably shorter than it is for humans.

What event in the evolution of the human species prompted the development of intense emotional bonds between adults? To answer this question, evolutionary theorists look back hundreds of thousands of years to our hominid ancestors (see Buss, 1987; Dawkins, 1976; Mellen, 1981; Symons, 1979). Human evolution was characterized by a huge increase in brain size that enabled our species to develop and use tools, to hunt with foresight, and to invent language and culture.

As human brain size increased, however, childbirth became more difficult because the newborn's head was larger. As an evolutionary adaptation to this phenomenon, human infants were born at a more immature stage of growth (so mothers would not have to bear a fully developed head). These helpless infants had to be cared for over an extended period. The advent of language and culture further extended the time needed to train and socialize the young.

A strong family unit evolved to care for and educate children. According to some evolutionary theories, romantic love and intense pair-bonding serve the evolutionary purpose of binding together family units to nurture helpless infants.

Male–Female Differences in Love and Sexuality

Some evolutionary theorists (such as Buss, 1989; Buss & Schmitt, 1993; Dawkins, 1976; Mellen, 1981; Symons, 1979) argue that men's sexuality differs from women's, in part because of biological evolution. Furthermore, these theorists hypothesize that men and women seek different characteristics in a mate, also because of differing evolutionary pressures on males and females.

According to modern evolutionary theory, the "goal" of natural selection is to maximize the transmission of genes from generation to generation. Women and men may best achieve this goal somewhat differently. Compared with men, women make a huge biological "investment" in their offspring, for they must gestate, give birth to, nurse, and care for their young. And compared with men, women can produce only relatively few offspring. Thus, to ensure that their genes survive, women must guarantee (not in a personal sense, but in evolutionary terms) that their relatively few, "high-cost" offspring survive until they are reproductively mature.

In contrast, men produce abundant sperm (not a single egg each month, as women do), and they are not as constrained by the biological burden of bearing and caring for the young. As a result, they potentially can father an indefinite number

*Varieties of love:
A wedding party in
Zaire, Africa.*

*A lesbian couple with
their son.*

of offspring. Thus, evolutionary theorists argue, men have evolved to be more interested in sex, more promiscuous, and less desirous of emotional commitment and pair-bonding (Buss & Schmitt, 1993). Men can "sow their wild oats" to maximize the transmission of their genes; women cannot.

Indeed, surveys since the time of Alfred Kinsey and his colleagues (1948, 1953) suggest that men are more sexually active and open to casual sex than women

Attachment between pet and pet owner.

Mother and baby.

are. Consistent with survey findings, a recent field study found that college men agreed much more readily than college women to an invitation to casual sex. Specifically, attractive college men and women (who were confederates in the research) approached opposite-sex students and said, "I have been noticing you around campus. I find you very attractive." They then made one of three requests: (1) "Would you go out with me tonight?" (2) "Would you come over to my

The evolutionary perspective on love.

apartment tonight?" or (3) "Would you go to bed with me tonight?" Women and men responded to the first request similarly: 50% agreed to the date. However, there was a large difference in their responses to the second and third requests: Only 6% of the women agreed to go to the confederate's apartment, but 69% of the men did, and no woman agreed to go to bed, but 75% of the men did (Clark & Hatfield, 1989).

According to evolutionary theorists, not only do men and women have different kinds of sexual motivations, they seek somewhat different characteristics in a mate. Because a woman must be young, healthy, and strong to bear and raise children, men have evolved to prefer youth and beauty in a mate more than women do. (Beauty indirectly indicates youth, health, good physical condition, and reproductive fitness.) As we noted previously, survey research suggests that men do in fact give higher priority to beauty in a mate than women do (Buss, 1988; Buss & Barnes, 1986; Jackson, 1992). Men's romantic preference for young, "reproductively fit" women proves to be true for men of all ages and across many cultures; in contrast, women consistently prefer mates who are *similar* to them in age rather than young (Kenrick & Keefe, 1992).

Because of their intense biological commitment to the care of their offspring, women more than men have evolved to seek a mate who can provide continuing resources for those offspring. Indeed, survey research consistently shows that on average, women more than men prefer mates with good earning potential and high educational and occupational status (Berscheid & Walster, 1974a; Buss, 1985; Buss & Schmitt, 1993; Feingold, 1992a). A survey of data from 10,000 men and women in 33 different countries yielded quite consistent cross-cultural evidence that women throughout the world valued earning ability and ambition in a mate more than men did, whereas men valued youth, physical attractiveness, and chastity in a mate more than women did (Buss, 1989).

Why do men value chastity more than women do? This relates to yet another evolutionary hypothesis: Not only do men and women emphasize somewhat different characteristics when choosing a mate, they also respond differently when a chosen mate is unfaithful. In particular, men on average are more upset than women by a mate's sexual infidelity, whereas women are relatively more upset by a mate's emotional infidelity (Buss, Larsen, Westen, & Semmelroth, 1992).

Evolutionary theory has a ready explanation for this difference (Trivers, 1972). Because men can never be as certain of the paternity of their children as women can, men have evolved to be sexually jealous and to drive off sexual competitors. Because women require commitment and investment from a mate for their children to survive and prosper, and because the maternity of their children is never in doubt, they have evolved to be jealous of a mate's possible *emotional* commitments to rivals.

Criticisms of Evolutionary Theory

Evolutionary theory reminds us that love and sex serve biological as well as cultural purposes, and it argues that a complete understanding of human love requires us to look to our biological past as well as to examine the current social setting. It is important to note, however, that evolutionary theory, particularly when used to explain male–female differences in human love and sexuality, has often been the subject of passionate debate (Epstein, 1988).

One common criticism of evolutionary approaches is that they frequently explain behavior after the fact and thus offer post hoc explanations for any and all observed phenomena. Often the "facts" that evolutionary theories attempt to explain (for example, that men evaluate prospective mates more on physical attractiveness than women do) have plausible cultural as well as evolutionary explanations. For example, men may value physical attractiveness in a mate more than women do because they tend to have more wealth, power, and status than women and thus they don't need to marry for economic reasons as much as women do; men can afford to attend more to superficial characteristics such as physical attractiveness. Furthermore, because men initiate romantic relationships more than women in most societies, they get to pick partners more directly on the basis of looks than women do.

Some psychologists object to evolutionary theory because they interpret it to imply that the current social order is, in some sense, biologically fixed and immutable and that certain negative traits are "wired in" to people—for example, that men are biologically destined to be "promiscuous" and women to be "gold diggers." However, modern evolutionary theory *does not* argue that "biology is destiny" in any simple or rigid way. Cultural learning and environmental influences—as well as biological evolution—undoubtedly exert strong influences on human love and sexuality, and contemporary evolutionary theory acknowledges the importance of these influences (Daly & Wilson, 1988; Tooby & Cosmides, 1990). Thus, evolutionary explanations of love are not necessarily incompatible with sociocultural and psychological perspectives. Rather, each approach tends to focus on different levels of explanation (Jackson, 1992).

Let's turn now to the sociocultural and psychological perspectives on love. As we shall see, whatever our evolved biological predispositions may be, romantic love and sexual desire still express themselves in remarkably varied ways across cultures and in different individuals.

MULTICULTURAL PERSPECTIVE

Historical and Cultural Variations in Love

Asked if she feels prepared for the life ahead of her, the future Queen of England responded in the sweet, storybook style that has already endeared her to Britons: "With Prince Charles beside me, I cannot go wrong."

—*Time,* March 9, 1981

Love is in some ways a cultural invention. As evolutionary theory suggests, intense emotional and sexual attractions and pair-bonding between people may well be a nearly universal human experience. But the particular form these attractions take, the ethical and moral context in which they occur, and their relation to romance, marriage, and family vary enormously over historical time and across cultures. (For extended discussions of these and related issues, see Bullough, 1976; D'Emilio & Freedman, 1988; De Riencourt, 1974; Hunt, 1959; Murstein, 1974.) The following brief account of the history of love in Western civilization will give you a sense of how much attitudes toward love have varied over time and across cultures.

Western conceptions of love originated in ancient Greece, which was perhaps the first society to idealize romantic love, to hold it in high ethical esteem, and thus to view love as a noble and greatly desirable goal in life. To this day, we use classical Greek images and mythology (Cupid, the Roman god of love, derives from the earlier Greek god, Eros), and we use Greek terminology to describe kinds of love ("erotic," "platonic").

Honeymooners at Niagara Falls, 1908. Have conceptions of romantic love changed through history?

The kinds of love idealized in ancient Greece were quite different from those idealized in modern America, however. Because women in ancient Greece generally had low status, Greek men often viewed marriage with distaste; to produce legal heirs was a "duty" they fulfilled for the state. Whom, then, did the typical Greek man love? There seem to have been two possibilities: another male in a homosexual relationship or a courtesan, who was typically more educated, elegant, and desirable than his wife. Thus, Greek love, although idealized and socially supported, did not take place in the context of marriage or family.

Women had higher status in imperial Rome than they had in ancient Greece. The Romans idealized love less and practiced sex with more license than the ancient Greeks. In many ways, Roman society was "modern": Divorce, abortion, contraception, and extramarital sex were all quite common. Romantic liaisons in Rome often were not accompanied by emotional commitment or idealization, and love was not necessarily attached to marriage.

Very early Christianity adopted Roman mores and was fairly tolerant of love and sexuality in various forms. However, as the Roman Empire crumbled and the church became the central social and moral institution of Europe, a much sterner attitude toward love and sex emerged. Christianity idealized chastity rather than sexual love. Because of its ties to "original sin," sex was considered to be corrupting. The writings of Saint Augustine in the early fifth century defined the new Christian abhorrence of sex, even in marriage: ". . . marriage and continence are two goods," he wrote, "the second of which is better."

Common attitudes toward love and sexuality did not recover from the blow dealt by Augustine and other early Christian theologians until the period of *courtly love* in Europe during the 12th century. The Hollywood images we have of this period are of daring knights in armor performing valiant deeds for their high-born ladies. Indeed, the art of courtly love (see Capellanus, 1969) prescribed that knights perform difficult deeds to gain even a glimpse of their ladies. Courtly love, however, was a dalliance available only to the nobility; the peasants and serfs of medieval Europe married for practical economic reasons, not for something so frivolous as love. Furthermore, courtly love was conducted outside marriage; the lady was typically of higher status than the knight who admired her. Courtly love was so idealized that it rarely led to physical intimacy, let alone sexual intercourse; the lady was worshiped from afar. Such "romantic love" seems very strange from a modern perspective.

Western civilization since the Renaissance has gone through cycles: Sometimes love and sex are valued and idealized, sometimes not; sometimes love occurs primarily within marriage, sometimes not. The people of some historical periods have taken a cynical and licentious attitude toward love and sex (for example, during the Enlightenment in Europe in the late 1700s), and others have had a more idealized and repressed view (Victorians in the late 1800s). In the United States, popular attitudes toward love and sex have evolved considerably over the past 200 years: In colonial times (the 1700s), love and sex were viewed mainly in terms of procreation; in the 19th century, they were viewed more in terms of emotional intimacy; and in the 20th century, love and sex have been seen relatively more in terms of pleasure and economic commerce—for example, think of how much love and sex are used in today's commercial advertising (D'Emilio & Freedman, 1988). Whatever the reasons for these historical and cultural changes in popular attitudes toward love and sex, they clearly show that such attitudes are both historically and culturally variable.

Sex Ratios and Attitudes toward Love

Marcia Guttentag and Paul Secord (1983) have offered a startlingly simple explanation for some of the cultural and historical variations in attitudes toward love that we have just described. The critical variable, according to these researchers, is the sex ratio: the ratio of men to women in a particular society. Even though we take it for granted that there are about equal numbers of men and women in most societies, this is not always true. Variations in birth rates, death rates, and immigration and emigration patterns for men and women can lead to large inequalities in men and women's relative numbers.

What happens when the sex ratio is high (that is, when men outnumber women)? Guttentag and Secord hypothesize that

> young adult women would be highly valued. The manner in which they would be valued would depend on the society. Most often, single women would be valued for their beauty and glamour, and married women as wives and mothers. Men would want to possess a wife and would be willing to make and keep a commitment to remain with her. But in some societies, this might be carried to an extreme, and scarce women might be valued as chattels and/or possessions. . . . [W]omen would be valued as romantic love objects. (pp. 19–20)

However, when women outnumber men:

> More men and women would remain single or, if they married, would be more apt to get divorced. . . . The divorce rate would be high, but the remarriage rate would be high for men only.
>
> . . . Sexual relationships outside of marriage would be accepted. . . . Women would not expect to have the same man remain with them throughout their childbearing years. Brief liaisons would be usual. . . . [M]en would have opportunities to move successively from woman to woman or to maintain multiple relationships with different women. . . . The outstanding characteristic of times when women were in oversupply would be that men would *not* remain committed to the same woman. . . . The culture would not emphasize love and commitment, and a lower value would be placed on marriage and the family. (pp. 20–21)

To test these hypotheses, Guttentag and Secord analyzed sex ratio data from a number of countries and during different historical periods, including ancient Greece, medieval Europe, and the United States during a number of eras. In general, they found that men outnumbering women was related to the idealization of women, marriage, and romantic love, and women outnumbering men was related to both decreased idealization of women and love and to increased sexual license.

According to Guttentag and Secord, men outnumbered women in the United States until about 1940, but after that, the sex ratio decreased fairly steadily (see

Figure 9.6). Thus, they argue, the dramatic changes in sexual and romantic mores that occurred in the United States after World War II were due in part to changes in the sex ratio.

Recent evidence suggests that the long-term declining trend in sex ratios is changing, particularly for young men and women in the United States. Indeed, men in their 20s now outnumber "marriageable" women (Pederson, 1991). Why is this so? Since the "Baby Boom" period in the United States (roughly from the mid-1940s to 1960), birth rates have been decreasing, with the net result that older cohorts (for example, people aged 25–28) tend to be more numerous than younger cohorts (people aged 23–25). Because men tend to marry younger women, U.S. men in their 20s now outnumber their potential marriage partners. Thus, if Guttentag and Secord's sex-ratio hypothesis is correct, we should expect attitudes toward love and women to shift in our society. Specifically, there should be increased idealization of women and romantic love and lower divorce rates in the years to come.

The Psychology of Love

The evolutionary and cultural/historical perspectives on love complement rather than compete with the perspectives of social psychology. Psychological influences

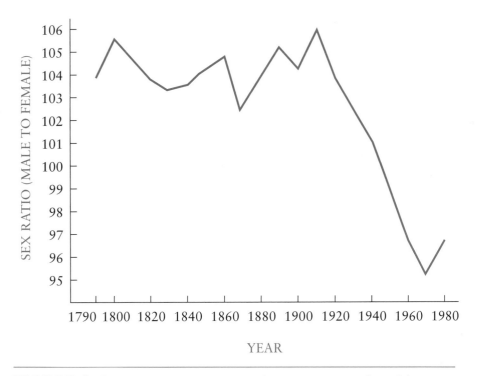

FIGURE 9.6 Sex ratios throughout U.S. history. *Source:* Adapted from Guttentag and Secord (1983).

on love, after all, occur within a broader biological and cultural context. Let's turn now to three uniquely psychological questions: How can we empirically measure love? Does romantic love in adulthood relate to childhood experiences with parents? And how do we know when we're in love?

Three Ways of Defining Love

In a line of poetry so often repeated that it has become a cliché, Elizabeth Barrett Browning asked, "How do I love thee? Let me count the ways." How do social psychologists count the ways of love? Do we have acceptable methods to measure so elusive a concept?

After combing through the philosophical and scientific literature on love, Zick Rubin (1970, 1973, 1974) developed questionnaires to measure liking and loving. In Rubin's conceptualization, liking and loving were related, yet somewhat different, kinds of attraction: Liking for another person entails respecting the person's abilities, judgment, and attitudes, whereas loving entails feelings of intimacy, caring, and preoccupation. Rubin developed two scales to measure different kinds of attraction. The love scale assesses feelings of intimacy, possessiveness, and preoccupation toward another, whereas the liking scale assesses feelings of respect and perceived similarity with another.

In one study, Rubin asked 182 student couples (dating or engaged, but not married) to rate both their partners and a close same-sex friend on his liking and loving scales. The resulting data indicated that subjects' liking and loving scores for their romantic partners were moderately correlated. Not surprisingly, subjects reported that they loved their romantic partners considerably more than they loved their friends. Subjects did not report nearly as great a difference in their liking for friends and romantic partners.

Rubin asked his subjects how probable it was that they would marry their romantic partners. Both liking and loving scores were correlated with this response, but the correlation with loving was stronger. Six months later, Rubin's subjects were mailed questionnaires that asked what had happened in their relationships. The results: Both liking and loving scores somewhat predicted the courses of these romantic relationships (that is, whether the relationships fell apart, got weaker, or intensified); these scores better predicted the relationships of students who described themselves as being "romantic" than those of students who described themselves as "nonromantic."

Rubin developed a single-score measure of romantic love, but more recently, researchers have tried to divide love into parts or types. For example, Sternberg (1986; Sternberg & Grajek, 1984) has characterized love relationships along three dimensions: intimacy (can you talk with and confide in your partner?), passion (do you feel sexually attracted and "in love"?), and commitment (do you intend to remain in your relationship?). (See Figure 9.7.) Rubin's love scale seems to assess intimacy and passion, but not commitment.

Note that different combinations of Sternberg's three components are possible. For example, you can feel intimacy and commitment, but not passion;

this kind of "companionate" love is almost like a good, solid friendship. Or you can feel passion, but neither intimacy nor commitment, in a quick, volatile affair; as the Cole Porter song puts it, "just one of those crazy flings." Some relationships possess commitment, but neither intimacy nor passion; marriages that grow cold and distant but stay intact for financial reasons or "for the children" fit this category. Of course, the ideal romantic relationship is high on all three dimensions, but such "consummate loves" may be difficult to achieve and more difficult still to sustain.

Drawing on the work of sociologist J. A. Lee (1973), Hendrick and Hendrick (1986) have developed questionnaires that assess three primary "styles" of love—Eros (passionate, erotic, intensely felt emotional love), Ludus (game-playing love with little commitment), and Storge (friendship love)—as well as three secondary "styles" of love—Pragma (practical, "shopping-list" love), Mania (obsessive, possessive love), and Agape (altruistic, selfless love). See Figure 9.8 for sample items from Hendrick and Hendrick's scales.

According to Sternberg, love can be analyzed in terms of three components: passion, intimacy, and commitment. Love may contain high degrees of one, two, or all three components.

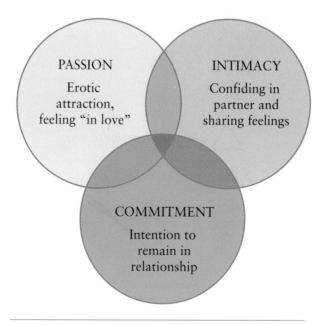

FIGURE 9.7 Sternberg's love components.

A "secondary style" is supposed to combine aspects of the "primary styles" to each side but is also supposed to be qualitatively different from its two neighboring "primary styles."

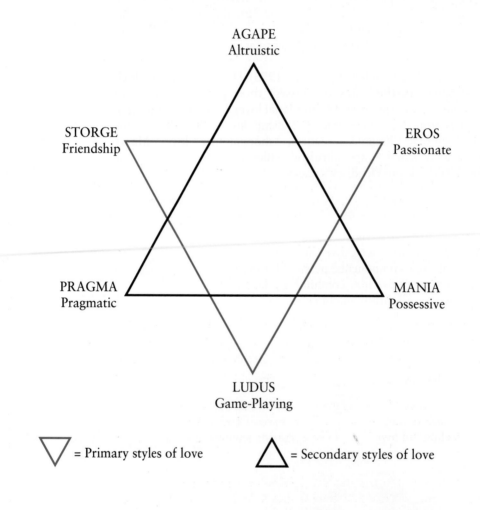

AGAPE
Altruistic

STORGE
Friendship

EROS
Passionate

PRAGMA
Pragmatic

MANIA
Possessive

LUDUS
Game-Playing

▽ = Primary styles of love   △ = Secondary styles of love

FIGURE 9.8 Love style scales. *Source:* Adapted from Lee (1973).

Following are some of Hendrick and Hendrick's scale items that operationally define each of these six styles. Which style or styles do you think characterize you? You might test yourself by thinking of a current or past relationship and rating your agreement or disagreement with each of the items shown. Do you tend to agree most with the items for any particular style?

EROS
1. My lover and I have the right physical "chemistry" between us.
2. Our lovemaking is very intense and satisfying.
3. My lover fits my ideal standards of physical beauty/handsomeness.

LUDUS
4. I try to keep my lover a little uncertain about my commitment to him/her.
5. I have sometimes had to keep two of my lovers from finding out about each other.
6. I enjoy playing the "game of love" with a number of different partners.

STORGE
7. Genuine love first requires *caring* for a while.
8. The best kind of love grows out of a long friendship.
9. Love is really a deep friendship, not a mysterious, mystical emotion.

PRAGMA
10. I consider what a person is going to become in life before I commit myself to him/her.
11. A main consideration in choosing a lover is how he/she reflects on my family.
12. One consideration in choosing a partner is how he/she will reflect on my career.

MANIA
13. Sometimes I get so excited about being in love that I can't sleep.
14. When my lover doesn't pay attention to me, I feel sick all over.
15. If my lover ignores me for a while, I sometimes do stupid things to get his/her attention back.

AGAPE
16. I cannot be happy unless I place my lover's happiness before my own.
17. I am usually willing to sacrifice my own wishes to let my lover achieve his/hers.
18. I would endure all things for the sake of my lover.

FIGURE 9.8 Continued. *Source:* Adapted from Hendrick and Hendrick (1986).

This relationship seems to be high on commitment but low on intimacy and passion.

Clearly, these love styles can be conceptualized, at least in part, in terms of Sternberg's three dimensions. For example, Eros is high on passion; Ludus is low on commitment and intimacy, and perhaps moderately passionate; and Storge has high degrees of commitment and intimacy but not of passion.

Empirical data suggest that on average, men and women differ somewhat in their love styles (Hendrick & Hendrick, 1986). Men take a more playful, uncommitted attitude toward love, whereas women regard love more like friendship and base it more on practical considerations. Note that these findings are consistent with evolutionary hypotheses.

Consistent with the similarity principle, college-student couples in one study tended to be matched on their love styles (Hendrick, Hendrick, & Adler, 1988). By implication, partners whose definitions of romantic love differ from each other's may experience conflict and thus be less likely to maintain their relationships. This study also found that subjects' love styles were related to their satisfaction with their relationship. For both men and women, Eros tended to positively correlate and Ludus to negatively correlate with relationship satisfaction; apparently, erotic attraction helps (and game-playing hurts) the perceived quality of a relationship. For women, Storge (friendship love) was also correlated with satisfaction.

Attachment Theory: The Childhood Origins of Love Styles

William Rees-Mogg, . . . former editor of the *Times* of London . . . has a persuasive notion about why Charles, who often seems obtuse, is so elusive. He places the responsibility largely on gruff Prince Philip, whose military deportment may have terrified the little boy. Philip thought it took a hard education to make a strong prince, and packed the sensitive Charles off to Gordonstoun in Scotland—a place that was as much marine boot camp as school. He hated it. . . .

[Queen Elizabeth] and Prince Philip, both austere and chilly as parents, were able to instill a concept of duty in their children, but not . . . warmth. . . .

—*Time,* November 30, 1992

What leads us to be the kinds of lovers we are? Many psychologists believe that the way we love as adults is strongly linked to the kinds of attachments we formed with our parents early in life.

Developmental psychologists have long noted three different kinds of attachment that infants and toddlers show toward their mothers; these are termed *secure, anxious/ambivalent,* and *avoidant* attachments (Ainsworth, Blehar, Waters, & Wall, 1978). Secure children have confidence that their mothers will respond to their needs, and these children confidently explore their environment in the presence of their mothers. Anxious/ambivalent children are unsure that their mothers will respond to them, and as a result often demand attention and seem anxious when their mothers ignore them or leave the room. Avoidant children seem to expect nonresponsiveness from their mothers and are withdrawn, detached, and don't seek their mothers out.

A clear relationship exists between mothers' behavior toward their children and the attachment styles their children display: Secure children tend to have responsive and supportive mothers; anxious/ambivalent children have inconsistently responsive mothers; and avoidant children have rejecting and nonresponsive mothers. Studies find that on average, 62% of American children are secure in their parental attachments, 15% anxious/ambivalent, and 23% avoidant (Campos, Barrett, Lamb, Goldsmith, & Sternberg, 1983).

Do these attachment styles carry over into adulthood? The answer of many recent studies seems to be yes. Hazan and Shaver (1987) developed a simple method to measure whether adults show secure, avoidant, or anxious/ambivalent styles in their romantic relationships. They created brief paragraphs that described each style, and asked subjects to check which one best fit them. Here are the paragraphs; you can decide which one best describes you:

(Secure) I find it relatively easy to get close to others and am comfortable depending on them and having them depend on me. I don't often worry about being abandoned or about someone getting too close to me.

(Anxious/Ambivalent) I find that others are reluctant to get as close as I would like. I often worry that my partner doesn't really love me or won't want to stay with me. I want to merge completely with another person, and this desire sometimes scares people away.

(Avoidant) I am somewhat uncomfortable being close to others; I find it difficult to trust them completely, difficult to allow myself to depend on them. I am nervous when anyone gets too close, and often, love partners want me to be more intimate than I feel comfortable with.

When Hazan and Shaver studied how 620 Colorado residents classified themselves according to these paragraphs, they found percentages amazingly similar to the results from studies of children: 56% of adults were secure in their romantic attachments, 19% were anxious/ambivalent, and 25% were avoidant. Furthermore, secure subjects reported warmer and more loving relationships with their parents than anxious/ambivalent or avoidant subjects, and romantically avoidant subjects in particular reported their mothers to be cold and rejecting.

Not surprisingly, attachment styles are related to Hendrick and Hendrick's love style scales, which we described earlier. Feeney and Noller (1990) found that secure lovers tend to be relatively high on Eros and Storge; avoidant lovers tend to be low on Eros and Agape; and anxious/ambivalent lovers tend to be particularly high on Mania. Furthermore, compared with avoidant and anxious/ambivalent lovers, secure lovers tend to experience happier romances—they have more commitment, trust, and satisfaction in their relationships (Simpson, 1990).

Whereas Hazan and Shaver (1987) viewed adult attachment styles as fitting into three discrete categories, more recent research suggests there may be two different kinds of avoidant people: those who dismiss the importance of close relationships and strive to be independent and self-sufficient, and those who want close relationships but are fearful of being hurt by untrustworthy partners (Bartholomew & Horowitz, 1991). According to this perspective, attachment styles depend on basic mental models we have of our own worthiness or unworthiness and of others' worthiness or unworthiness (see Figure 9.9). Needless to say, social psychologists are eagerly pursuing research on the causes and consequences of different attachment styles.

ATTITUDE TOWARD SELF

		Negative	Positive
ATTITUDE TOWARD OTHERS	Positive	Anxious/ ambivalent	Secure
	Negative	Avoidant (fearful of intimacy)	Avoidant (dismissing of intimacy)

FIGURE 9.9 Four kinds of attachment styles defined by attitude toward self and general attitude toward others. *Source:* Adapted from Bartholomew and Horowitz (1991).

The effects of extraneous arousal on romantic attraction. Does adrenaline make the heart grow fonder?

How Do You Know You're in Love?

Passionate love is a strong emotion. In Chapter 5 we discussed Schachter and Singer's theory of emotion, which proposes two conditions as being necessary for any intense emotion to be felt: You must experience physiological arousal, and you must label that arousal as being caused by some emotion. The label is often influenced by your situation and by cultural conventions.

Berscheid and Walster (1974a; Walster & Berscheid, 1971) applied this two-component theory of emotion to passionate love. The application is straightforward: To experience passionate love, you must experience physiological arousal and you must label your arousal as being caused by love. According to this theory, if you can unobtrusively increase a person's arousal in the presence of a potential romantic partner, you may increase his or her feelings of love and attraction because the arousal would be misattributed as being caused by love.

In his *Ars Amatoria* ("The Art of Loving"), the canny Roman poet Ovid gave advice on seduction technique that is consistent with the two-component theory: Take your romantic target to the gladiatorial fights to increase the target's passion and attraction to you. Because seeing bloody combat is physically arousing, Ovid seems to suggest that the target may attribute part of this arousal to the person next to him or her (if that person is a culturally appropriate love object). If this suggestion seems improbable to you, note that many of the places people go on dates—amusement parks, horror and adventure movies, rock concerts, and sporting events—have the net effect of arousing them. Indeed, one recent study found that couples who had just viewed a violent suspense thriller were more likely to leave the theater complex talking or touching than couples who had just viewed a nonarousing movie (B. Cohen, Waugh, & Place, 1989).

Many other studies suggest that the "rush" of arousal can sometimes spark romance. For example, the arousal triggered by viewing erotica, performing exercise, or being threatened with painful electric shocks often leads subjects to report more attraction to potential romantic partners in the laboratory (see Carducci, Cozby, & Ward, 1978; Dermer & Pyszczynski, 1978; Stephan, Berscheid, & Walster, 1971; White, Fishbein, & Rutstein, 1981; White & Knight, 1984).

In one clever study, an attractive female experimenter approached men as they crossed either a high, rickety suspension bridge or a low, safe bridge. The woman introduced herself as a psychology researcher and asked the men to make up stories for a psychology study. She then gave the subjects her name and phone number and told them to call her if they wanted more information about the study. The results: The men interviewed on the high, rickety bridge included more sexual imagery in their stories than men interviewed on the low bridge did, and they were significantly more likely to call the woman later (Dutton & Aron, 1974). Apparently, unexplained arousal can heighten attraction. Or, in the words of Walster and Berscheid (1971), "Adrenaline makes the heart grow fonder."

Conversely, if you misattribute the arousal you feel in the presence of a possible romantic partner to other causes, you may feel less attraction. In one recent experiment, college men talked with an attractive college woman (actually a confederate) who was very friendly—she smiled a lot, engaged in frequent eye contact, and leaned toward the men. Earlier, the men had taken a "vitamin pill" (a brewer's yeast tablet); some were told it might make them feel "excited, aroused, and a little flushed." The men who expected to be aroused from the pill tended to be less attracted to the woman (McClanahan, Gold, Lenney, Ryckman, & Kulberg, 1990).

The two-component theory offers insight into a perplexing feature of passionate love: It can sometimes be stimulated by strong negative emotions. Have you ever experienced a heated "lover's quarrel" that then seemed to heighten the passion of "making up"? The arousal of anger can contribute to passion if the situation is right—for example, if hostile glares give way to smoldering glances. This is entirely in keeping with the two-component theory.

Clearly, attraction, liking, and love have been approached at several levels of explanation, ranging from broad biological and social forces to the highly specific individual-level factors in the two-component theory of emotion. Summary Table 9.1 gives an overview of the theory and research we have presented on this endlessly fascinating subject. As the table makes clear, liking and loving are influenced by many different factors.

THE LIFE CYCLE OF CLOSE RELATIONSHIPS

Why then did the fairy-tale romance collapse into a sordid soap opera? There was the numbing royal routine of frozen smiles and banquet chatter. There was

	Theoretical Approaches	Type of Explanation	Variables/Issues Studied
SUMMARY TABLE 9.1 Theories and Research on Attraction and Their Relation to the Explanations of Social Behavior			
Group Level	Historical/cultural approach	Cultural norms Social groups	Comparison of love across cultures and historical periods; sex ratios
	Evolutionary theory	Biological evolution Biological groups	Physiology; species differences and similarities; sex differences
Individual Level	Learning theories	Environmental (past and current environments)	Rewards, punishments, conditioned emotions; can be used to explain effects of proximity, similarity, and physical attractiveness
	Attachment theory	Early relations with parents	Effects on love style, personality, and adult romantic relations
Mediating Variables	Exchange and equity theories	Cognitive tallies of costs and rewards (also social norms)	Give-and-take in relationships; longevity of relationships; satisfaction with relationships; help explain similarity effects
	Social comparison theory	Affiliation resulting from desire to compare self with others	Affiliation resulting from situationally induced anxiety
	Schachter-Singer theory of emotion	Cognitive labeling and physiological arousal	Extraneous arousal intensifies feelings of passionate love
	Balance theory	Cognitive consistency processes	Patterns of likes and dislikes among several people/objects; effect of attitude similarity
	Love styles, components, and scales	Love as an attitude or personality trait	Effects of love styles on relationship satisfaction and duration; the subjective experience of love

Dianamania, a feeding frenzy of the press that devoured the pair's privacy, a madness of crowds that brushed him aside as it lifted her to super-stardom. Above all, there was the incongruity of the couple. She was a vibrant woman longing for closeness and excitement. He was a prematurely aging fussbudget terrified of intimacy. . . . Separated at last, they can begin to repair the damage they have done to the House of Windsor.

—*Life,* February 1993

Relationships have beginnings, middles, and, alas, ends. Recently social psychologists have begun to analyze the life cycle of intimate relationships. Levinger (1980, 1983) has described five possible stages in the development of a close relationship: (1) initial attraction, (2) buildup, (3) continuation and consolidation, (4) deterioration and decline, and (5) ending (see Figure 9.10). Clearly, not all relationships go

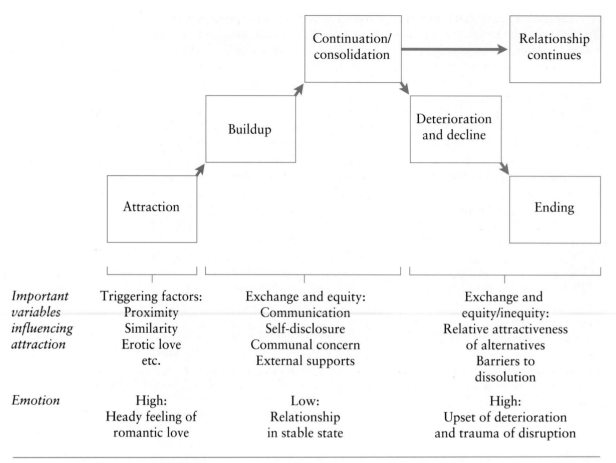

FIGURE 9.10 Levinger's five stages in the life cycle of a close relationship.

through all stages—for example, some relationships may enter the "deterioration" stage but then revive and cycle back to "buildup" or "continuation." To gain a better understanding of the life cycle of relationships, let's briefly consider each of Levinger's stages.

Initial Attraction and Beginnings

As we've already seen, proximity influences the beginnings of many relationships, and we generally seek out others who are similar to us in age, attractiveness, socioeconomic status, and attitudes. Clearly, we tend to respond most to those who seem attracted to us (Huston & Levinger, 1978). Most basic of all, beginnings occur when we are actively seeking a relationship: A happily married person may not necessarily view another person as a potential new romantic partner, but a searching single person probably will.

Erotic and passionate love may provide a strong source of attraction in the beginnings of romantic relationships. Unfortunately, research and theory on the nature of human emotion suggest that these intense feelings are unlikely to persist at their initial peak levels (Berscheid, 1983; Solomon & Corbit, 1974). So feeling "head over heels" in love may be fun while it lasts, but it is unlikely to sustain a relationship over the long haul.

Altman and Taylor's (1973) *social penetration theory* describes the beginning and intensification of a close relationship in terms of increasing levels of self-disclosure (that is, the revealing of important information about oneself) and of social exchange (the exchange of social goods and rewards). The closer your relationship is with another, the more you tend to know about that person. Indeed, research suggests that dating and married couples who confide in each other generally have happier and more lasting relationships (Adams & Shea, 1981). Both close friendships and romantic relationships are fostered by the exchange of intimate information (Hays, 1985).

Self-disclosure, a gradually unfolding process in close relationships, is characterized by mutual and reciprocal exchanges (Cozby, 1973; Taylor, De Soto, & Lieb, 1979). The process is complicated by people's tendencies, particularly early in a relationship, to provide false or limited information about themselves. As Lederer and Jackson (1968) state in *The Mirages of Marriage,* "During the wooing, both people constantly attempt to be as attractive as possible; each tries to exhibit only those parts of himself which will please and capture the other" (p. 246). Even though social penetration theory suggests a definite linear increase in intimacy, real relationships may follow a more variable, cyclical pattern of self-disclosure (Altman, Vinsel, & Brown, 1981).

Building a Relationship

Although physical appearance, demographic characteristics, and the heady excitement of romantic love may provide the initial impetus to close relationships, subsequent progress likely depends more on processes of social exchange (recall our earlier discussion of exchange and equity theories). As noted previously, in close relationships we exchange information about ourselves; we also exchange goods, pleasures, and sometimes unpleasantness.

When 100 students at the University of North Carolina were asked to rate the "rewards" and "costs" of their current or previous romantic relationships, some of the rewards they cited were physical attractiveness of their partner, similarity of attitudes with partner, pleasantness of partner's personality, partner's sense of humor, and sexual satisfaction; some of the costs mentioned were time constraints created by the relationship, monetary costs, embarrassing behaviors of partner, conflict with partner, and partner's lack of faithfulness. Using an exchange theory model, the researcher was able to predict quite well these college students' relationship satisfaction and their commitment to continue their relationships based on these measured rewards and costs. (Rusbult, 1980).

Continuation and Consolidation

Many relationships reach a stable "middle age" in which the partners have worked out a mutually agreed-upon pattern of social exchange and relationship norms. In such mature relationships the partners have meshed their lives together smoothly, with innumerable points of connection. Despite these many close ties, however, the partners may display little overt emotion. In essence, emotion may be dampened by the very success of the relationship (Berscheid, 1983).

According to one theory, emotions (such as elation, fright, upset, and anger) typically accompany a violation of expectations and a disruption of the normal course of life, as occurs, for example, when you learn that your spouse or lover has been unfaithful (Mandler, 1975). Thus, there may be some truth to the notion that people tend to take relationships for granted once they settle into a stable state. The closeness and strong emotional ties of a mature relationship may become apparent only when the relationship breaks up (through death or departure of one member) and when the remaining partner is traumatized by the disruption. The bonds of love that exist in mature relationships may be like the roots of a tree—we can appreciate their true depth only when the love (or tree) is uprooted.

Communication in Relationships

Consistent with popular wisdom, communication between partners helps maintain relationships. Gottman (1979) reports that in successful marriages, spouses listen to each other and often validate each other's points of view. Couples in unsuccessful marriages are more likely to engage in "cross-complaining," venting their ire without really listening to or acknowledging what their spouse is saying. One recent study found that spouses' negativity (for example, criticizing each other and showing boredom, anger, and irritation) was more likely to predict their marital satisfaction than were their levels of sexual interest or activity (Huston & Vangelisti, 1991). Partners in successful marriages may not always be rapturously passionate, but they are likely to talk and constructively listen to each other and tend not to pick at each other.

After coding the conversations of 73 married couples for positive and negative statements, Gottman and Levenson (1992) concluded that happy couples as well as unhappy couples make negative comments, but the *ratio* of positive to negative comments is much higher in the happy couples—indeed, successful couples showed more than five times as many positive as negative comments.

This suggests a "good manners" model of relationship success: To maintain the health of a relationship, it's often more important to squelch negative comments and hurtful behaviors than to increase positive comments and behaviors (Montgomery, 1988; Rusbult, Verette, Whitney, Slovik, & Lipkus, 1991). Caryl Rusbult and her colleagues (1991) found support for this "good manners" model in a series of studies: People were more likely to swallow their anger and irritation and inhibit negative comments when they cared about their partner and their relationship and when they felt no other good relationships were available to them. Some people—for example, those who were empathic and who were more stereotypically feminine—proved more likely than others to squelch negative responses to their partners' bad behavior. Not surprisingly, couples tended to be happiest when *both* partners controlled their negativity and showed "good manners."

Please note that the "good manners" model *does not* advise us simply to avoid discussing problems with our partners in close relationships. Rather, it recommends refraining from responding to our partners' negative comments with retaliatory negative comments. There *are* constructive ways to discuss problems in relationships. Instant retaliation is not one of them. The "good manners" model warns us of the dangers of destructive negative comments that we use to zing our partner in the heat of the moment.

Exchange versus Communal Relationships

Close relationships tend to be different from other kinds of relationships—we expect more emotional sharing in them and less precisely reciprocated quid pro quo. Clark and Mills (1979; Clark, Mills, & Powell, 1986; Mills & Clark, 1982) distinguish between exchange relations and communal relations. *Exchange relations* (such as a business transaction) are characterized by a careful tally of costs and an expectation of constant reciprocity. *Communal relations* (the give-and-take in good marriages) are characterized by concern with your partner's well-being and with giving according to your partner's need, not according to rigid standards of reciprocity. If partners in intimate relationships calculate their exchanges too explicitly, the relationship may be in danger (Levinger, 1980). Nit-picking over what we give and get in a relationship probably means we are unhappy about what we're getting.

External Supports

Not surprisingly, external factors and a positive social environment can help relationships continue. Marriages tend to last longer when there is adequate income and joint property, and supportive family and friends (Levinger, 1976). Low income and unstable jobs contribute to rockier marriages (Jaffe & Kanter, 1976). Love may conquer all, but it still helps to have money in the bank and good friends.

Deterioration and Decline

For all they have been through, Prince Charles and Princess Diana are still recognizably the same people whose kiss lit up screens in 24 time zones. But we know them better now—too well, in fact. Her peevishness, his coldness; her bubble-brained woman's magazine wisdom, his Spenglerian glooming about modern civilization. If we're so tired of them, imagine how they must feel about each other.

—*Newsweek*, December 21, 1992

Not all relationships decline and dissolve; yet it may be unrealistic to expect the rewards and pleasures of a close relationship to continue to grow forever. Research suggests that on average, marital satisfaction tends to decline somewhat over time (Blood & Blood, 1978). Perhaps this is to be expected based on external factors alone. As relationships continue and we get older, we may learn that not all of our youthful ambitions will come true, and the intense passions of romantic love and sexual excitement fade somewhat.

Still, the fading of romantic love into *companionate love*—a love based on intimacy, affection, and mutual interdependence, rather than on intense passion—does not necessarily signal the end of a relationship. Why do some relationships stay warm and caring, whereas others degenerate into bitter acrimony and painful separations?

Alternatives and Barriers

Drawing from exchange theory, Levinger (1976) noted three broad factors that influence the likelihood of a relationship's ending: (1) the attractiveness of the relationship itself, which is positively related to its rewards and negatively related to its costs, (2) the attractiveness of alternative relationships, and (3) the barriers to ending the relationship (for example, costs such as lawyers' fees, alimony payments, family disapproval, emotional upset).

The divorce rate in the United States has increased sharply throughout much of this century: 19% of marriages commencing in 1929 ended in divorce, 27% in 1950, 34% in 1960, and approximately 50% from the mid-1970s to the present (*Newsweek,* January 13, 1992; Weed, 1980). Perhaps this increase can be attributed in part to changing patterns of rewards, costs, and barriers. For example, divorce has become less stigmatized. In the 1960s, Nelson Rockefeller could be discounted as a presidential candidate because of his divorce, but in the 1980s, Ronald Reagan was enthusiastically elected by conservative voters who were apparently unconcerned about his earlier divorce. Furthermore, women have become less economically dependent on marriage (see Chapter 8). Berscheid and Campbell (1981) argue that once the costs and barriers to divorce declined, more people divorced, which added to the pool of people available for alternative relationships, which in turn further encouraged divorce. With fewer social, legal, and economic constraints to stay married, a person today may stay in relationship more because of "the sweetness of its contents" (Berscheid, 1985).

Drigotas and Rusbult (1992) have recently collected data showing that people are particularly likely to stay in relationships when they depend on their partners for satisfaction of important needs (such as needs for intimacy, sex, companionship, intellectual stimulation, security); conversely, people are more likely to end relationships when they are not dependent on their partners for need satisfaction. These researchers note that our dependence on our relationship to fulfill needs results from two things: the degree to which our partner satisfies important needs *and* the availability of alternative relationships that could also satisfy these needs (note the clear link to exchange theories). Alternative relationships don't have to be a single person—for example, you may conclude that your spouse no longer fills your needs very well and realize that you get satisfying intimacy and intellectual stimulation from your best friend, and great support and security from your family members. These multiple alternatives may be so satisfying to you that you decide to end your marriage, which no longer does what it once did for you.

Equity and Inequity in Relationships

Equity theory (see Hatfield, Utne, & Traupman, 1979; Walster, Walster, & Berscheid, 1978) adds another factor to the "economics" of breakups: Partners in close relationships not only analyze their needs and compare rewards and costs to those of alternative relationships, they also attend to their investments. When inequity exists—that is, when the ratios of profits to investments are unequal for the partners—the relationship suffers.

To illustrate: Five hundred college men and women were asked to rate their perceptions of the equity in their romantic relationships. Did they feel they were getting more than their fair share in the relationship, less than their share, or was the give-and-take equitable? Consistent with equity theory, both overbenefited and underbenefited subjects predicted that their relationships were less likely to last than subjects in more equitable relationships did. Also consistent with equity theory, overbenefited subjects felt guilty, whereas underbenefited subjects felt angry. When contacted three months later, students in inequitable relationships were more likely to report that they had broken up (Hatfield, Walster, & Traupman, 1978).

Extending equity theory to the relationships of married couples, these researchers asked 2,000 married men and women to rate the degree to which they felt overbenefited or underbenefited in their relationships. They found that subjects who felt underbenefited engaged sooner and more frequently in extramarital affairs (Hatfield, Traupman, & Walster, 1978). Apparently, when you're not getting what you think you should from your spouse, you are more likely to look outside the relationship for additional rewards. These discontented spouses may also have engaged in extramarital affairs to punish their spouses—that is, to create additional "costs" for them in the marriage. This possibility is also perfectly in keeping with equity theory: To "even the score" (create equity), you may adjust your partner's costs and rewards and your own costs and rewards in the relationship; furthermore, you may adjust these costs and rewards singly or in combination.

Negotiating Bad Times

When problems arise in a relationship, what can be done to rectify them? Rusbult and Zembrodt (1983) asked 50 undergraduates to describe how they dealt with dissatisfactions in their romantic relationships. Sophisticated statistical analyses indicated that virtually all the responses fell into one of four categories: *voice* (actively talking and discussing problems), *loyalty* (passively waiting for things to improve), *neglect* (distancing oneself from the relationship and allowing it to decline), or *exit* (leaving the relationship). These four modes vary on two dimensions: how active–passive they are and how constructive–destructive they are (see Figure 9.11).

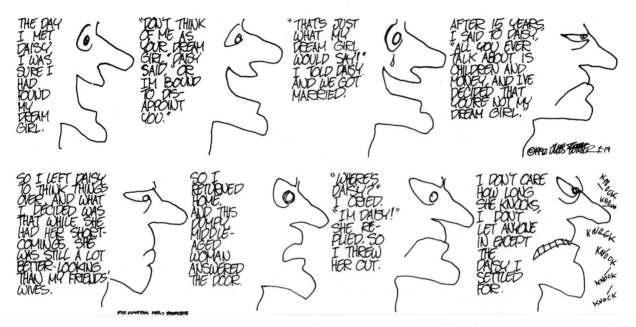

The life cycle of a relationship. Why do some loves fade while others stay warm and caring?

Subsequent research suggests that people's style of dealing with dissatisfaction relates to levels of happiness and distress in their ongoing relationships (Rusbult, Johnson, & Morrow, 1986). For example, subjects who reported being less content with their relationships had partners who engaged in "exit" or "neglect," the two destructive modes.

Endings

. . . Queen [Elizabeth] agreed that Charles and Diana should separate. Diana got custody of the boys and the right to be Queen. The War of the Waleses was over—and so was the fairy tale.

—*Life,* February 1993

Like Charles and Diana, many Americans seem to believe that "exit" is an acceptable response to a troubled marriage. As noted earlier, many polls and social surveys estimate that approximately half of all U.S. marriages that begin today will end in divorce, although there is some evidence that the divorce rate may have declined slightly in the early 1990s (*Newsweek,* January 13, 1992).

Breakups are rarely mutually desired (Burgess & Wallin, 1953), and often one party in a marriage or relationship plans for and emotionally "works through" the breakup more than the other does (Levinger, 1983; Vaughan, 1986). One review of research on this topic concluded that men on average seem to suffer more disruption from breakups than women do (Bloom, White, & Asher, 1979). Rubin, Peplau, and Hill (1981) drew a similar conclusion, and also observed that men in relationships were more insensitive than women to relationship problems and were

There are four common ways of dealing with dissatisfaction in relationships.

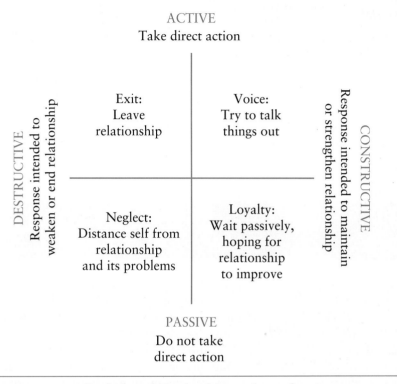

ACTIVE
Take direct action

Exit:
Leave
relationship

Voice:
Try to talk
things out

DESTRUCTIVE
Response intended to
weaken or end relationship

CONSTRUCTIVE
Response intended to maintain
or strengthen relationship

Neglect:
Distance self from
relationship
and its problems

Loyalty:
Wait passively,
hoping for
relationship
to improve

PASSIVE
Do not take
direct action

FIGURE 9.11 Rusbult and Zembrodt's typology of responses to dissatisfaction in relationships.

less likely to foresee a breakup. Perhaps on average, women ponder and evaluate their relationships more than men do, and thus they're more likely to perceive storm clouds approaching on the horizon. Another reason women may suffer less than men from breakups is that they tend to have more varied kinds of social support than men—more friends and confidants to turn to after a breakup (see Chapter 14).

Traditionally, research on the end of marriages tends to be anecdotal and scanty (see Burgess & Wallin, 1953; Waller, 1930; Weiss, 1975). Some recent studies have focused on the explanations people give for their breakups (Bradbury & Fincham, 1990, 1992). While it's clear that negative attributions in marriage are related to negative behaviors and marital distress, it is much less clear whether the attributions are causes or effects of troubled relationships. Because husbands' and wives' verbal accounts and explanations of their breakups may not always be true, we should often take them with a grain of salt (Levinger, 1983). It probably comes as no surprise that ex-spouses frequently offer quite disparate accounts of the same events that led up to their divorce; there is a tendency to see one's own behavior in a much better light than one's ex's (Gray & Silver, 1990). Research on the causes, both real and perceived, of breakups is just in its infancy.

One thing is certain, however: Despite the frequency of breakups, close relationships do survive. Most who divorce eventually remarry. As Woody Allen (who has had his share of relationship problems) states at the end of the movie *Annie Hall*:

> I thought of that old joke: . . . this guy goes to a psychiatrist and says, "Doc, my brother's crazy. He think he's a chicken."
>
> And the doctor says, "Well, why don't you turn him in?"
>
> The guy says, "I would, but I need the eggs."
>
> Well, I guess that's pretty much now how I feel about relationships. They're totally irrational and crazy and absurd, but I guess we keep going through it because most of us need the eggs.

LIKING AND LOVING OTHERS IN PERSPECTIVE

Attraction is a topic that attracts us all. Despite a slow start, social psychology research on attraction has exploded over the past 30 years, and we now have a solid foundation of scientific research on factors that lead people to like and love others.

Research shows that situational factors have a big impact on whom we affiliate with and whom we like. Situationally produced anxiety motivates us to affiliate with others who share our predicament. Architectural arrangements influence whom we befriend. In general, the more frequently we're exposed to people, the more we like them, and we typically like people more who are physically attractive and who are similar to us in various ways.

Social psychology theories remind us that attraction is not mysterious and indescribable. Many of the theories that apply to social behavior in general help us understand liking and loving. Learning theories show that we are attracted to people who are rewarding and who are associated with positive events. Exchange and equity theories tell us that we mentally compute "rewards" and "costs" in our relationships, and strive for a fair give-and-take. Balance theory describes how some patterns of likes and dislikes are more comfortable for us than others and how we strive for emotional consistency in our attractions.

The same theoretical principles that apply to liking also apply to love, but love proves to be more complex than liking in a number of ways and thus requires additional theoretical explanations. Evolutionary theory reminds us that human romantic and sexual love has been molded by biological evolution. Cultural and historical analyses point to the social construction of love and document variations in how love is labeled and linked to morality and family life. Attachment theory shows that our relationships with our parents early in life can influence our adult romantic relationships. And finally, psychologists' attempts to measure love show that love has a number of different components and that people show different styles of romantic love.

Social psychology has begun to study the life cycles of close relationships. We now understand some of the factors that lead people to enter into close relationships, to stay in them, and sometimes to break them off. We also have identified some of the behaviors and communication styles that distinguish people in successful and unsuccessful relationships.

Because most of us experience friendships and close relationships, social psychology research on attraction is relevant to most of us. It can help us to understand our friendships and loves better and to nurture them more successfully in the future.

The Scientific Study of Attraction

Research on attraction has traditionally emphasized external variables, mild forms of attraction, early stages of attraction, and cognitive rather than emotional processes. In recent years, research has also addressed evolutionary theory, emotional factors, and intimate, long-term relationships.

The Beginnings of Attraction

Anxiety and Affiliation: The "Dr. Zilstein Experiment"

People often seek affiliation when they are anxious.

Reasons for the Anxiety–Affiliation Relationship

Anxious people often affiliate with others facing the same predicament so that they can compare feelings with them.

Social Psychology in Everyday Life: Do Anxious People Always Compare Themselves with Similar Others?

Anxious people may compare themselves with worse-off or better-off people, depending on their motivations. Research on cancer patients indicates they mentally compare themselves with those worse off to feel better about themselves, but they actually affiliate with successful cancer survivors to foster hope and optimism.

From Affiliation to Attraction

Proximity: The Architecture of Attraction

We are more likely to become friends and romantic partners with people who live or work near us.

Mere Exposure: I've Grown Accustomed to Your Face

The power of proximity is due in part to the mere exposure effect—we like stimuli the more frequently we're exposed to them.

Similarity: Birds of a Feather

Our friends and romantic partners tend to be similar to us on a host of dimensions. Attitudinal similarity leads to attraction.

Stage Models of Attraction

These specify the variables that most influence attraction in different stages of relationships. Murstein describes three stages in close relationships: a stimulus stage, a value stage, and a role stage.

Physical Attractiveness

Physical attractiveness has a broad impact on attraction. In general, attractive people tend to be judged as more popular, intelligent, and powerful than unattractive people, but they are not judged to be more trustworthy, honest, or nurturant. Men choose romantic partners and friends on the basis of physical attractiveness more than women do.

Theories of Attraction

Learning Theories

Learning theories argue that attraction can be understood in terms of operant and classical conditioning.

Exchange and Equity Theories

Exchange and equity theories offer an economic analysis of attraction in terms of "costs," "rewards," "profits," and "investments." People tend to prefer the most profitable relationships. Stable relationships tend to provide partners with nearly equal profits. People strive for reciprocity or equity in their relationships.

Cognitive Consistency Theories

Balance theory analyzes attraction in terms of our desire to maintain cognitively harmonious patterns of likes and dislikes.

Love

Evolutionary Theory and Love

Evolutionary theory argues that romantic love evolved as a means of binding the human family unit together, thus ensuring care for helpless infants. It hypothesizes that biological evolution has led to a number of male–female differences in human love and sexuality.

Historical and Cultural Variations in Love

Historical analyses of love indicate that different cultures and historical eras vary in the degree to which they idealize romantic love and incorporate romantic love into marriage.

The *sex ratio hypothesis* holds that when men are more numerous than women, women and romantic love are valued, but when women are more numerous than men, women and romantic love are devalued.

The Psychology of Love

Rubin developed liking and loving scales that help predict the course of romantic relationships. Sternberg argued that love consists of varying degrees of three components: intimacy, passion, and commitment. Hendrick and Hendrick developed scales to measure six "styles" of romantic love: Eros, Storge, Ludus, Pragma, Mania, and Agape.

Attachment theory describes three styles of romantic attachment—secure, anxious/ambivalent, and avoidant—and hypothesizes that they develop from the styles of attachment people showed in childhood with their parents.

Schachter and Singer's two-component theory of emotion implies that extraneous arousal can sometimes intensify feelings of passionate attraction, whereas misattribution of arousal to external factors can diminish attraction.

The Life Cycle of Close Relationships

Levinger described five stages in the development of close relationships: initial attraction, buildup, continuation and consolidation, deterioration and decline, and ending.

As described by *social penetration theory,* the first stages of close relationships are characterized by increased self-disclosure and social exchange.

Consistent with exchange theory, rewards and costs in a relationship help predict relationship satisfaction and commitment.

Successful relationships are characterized by a high ratio of positive to negative communications and a conscious effort to squelch overly negative responses to a partner's negativity.

In exchange relationships, partners carefully tally costs and rewards and expect exact reciprocity. In communal relationships, people do not keep score and instead give resources more in response to the partner's needs.

Rewards, costs, and barriers help predict whether relationships will end. People whose needs are not met in their relationships and who perceive alternative relationships that can satisfy these needs are more likely to end their relationships. Equitable relationships are more likely to survive than inequitable relationships.

Rusbult and Zembrodt identified four kinds of behavior that people use to deal with dissatisfaction in relationships: voice, loyalty, neglect, and exit.

KEY TERMS

Affiliation: Choosing to be with others; the desire or motivation to be with others.

Assortative mating: Nonrandom mating, usually occurring because people tend to mate with partners who are similar to them.

Attachment theory: Describes three styles of romantic attachment—secure, anxious/ambivalent, and avoidant—and hypothesizes that they develop from similar styles of attachment children show with their parents.

Attraction: A positive attitude or emotion felt toward another person.

Balance theory: Proposes that people strive for cognitively harmonious patterns in their likes and dislikes.

Communal relationships: Relationships characterized by concern with the partner's well-being, in which costs and rewards are not tallied exactly.

Companionate love: A love based on intimacy, affection, and mutual interdependence, rather than on intense passion.

Comparison level: In Kelley and Thibaut's version of exchange theory, a comparison level is a standard of expected costs and rewards in a relationship; such a standard is dictated by social norms or personal expectations.

Comparison level for alternatives: In Kelley and Thibaut's version of exchange theory, the level of costs and rewards a person will accept in a relationship based on alternative relationships that are available.

Equity theory: An economic theory of relationships that focuses on rewards, costs, profits, and investments; stable relationships tend to be equitable—both partners have the same ratio of profits to investments; equity theory differs from exchange theory in that the former incorporates the concept of "investment."

Exchange relationships: Relationships characterized by a careful tally of rewards and costs; exact reciprocity is expected.

Exchange theory: An economic theory of relationships that focuses on rewards, costs, and profits in relationships; people are hypothesized to prefer maximally profitable relationships, and relationships endure to the extent that both parties receive equal levels of profit.

Learning theories: Theories that explain attraction in terms of operant and classical conditioning.

Mere exposure effect: The tendency to like stimuli more the more frequently we've been exposed to them; partly accounts for proximity effects in attraction.

Proximity: Physical closeness to another person, often determined by architectural and residential arrangements.

Sex ratio: The ratio of men to women in a society; the sex ratio hypothesis holds that high sex ratios (more men than women) lead societies to idealize women and love, whereas low sex ratios lead societies to devalue women and love.

Similarity principle: People are more frequently friends and romantic partners with others who are similar to them in demographic, intellectual, personality, and physical characteristics.

Social comparison theory: Festinger's theory that people desire to compare themselves with similar others in order to know their own social feelings and attributes.

Social penetration theory: Altman and Taylor's theory that describes the development of close relationships in terms of increasing self-disclosure and social exchange.

Stimulus–value–role model: Murstein's model that proposes people in relationships progress through three stages in which they focus respectively on the surface attributes of their partner, shared attitudes and values, and relationship roles.

10

AGGRESSION: HURTING OTHERS

The law has always made room for killers. Soldiers kill the nation's enemies, executioners kill its killers, police officers under fire may fire back. Even a murder is measured in degrees, depending on the mind of the criminal and the character of the crime. And sometime this spring, in a triumph of pity over punishment, the law may just find room for Rita Collins.

. . . Her husband John was a military recruiter, a solid man who had a way with words. "He said I was old, fat, crazy and had no friends that were real friends. He said I needed him and he would take care of me." She says his care included threats with a knife, punches, a kick to the stomach that caused a hemorrhage. Navy doctors treated her for injuries to her neck and arm. "He'd slam me up against doors. He gave me black eyes, bruises. Winter and summer, I'd go to work like a Puritan, with long sleeves. . . ."

She tried to get out. She filed for divorce, got a restraining order, filed an assault-and-battery charge against him. . . . But still, she says, he came, night after night, banging on windows and doors, trying to break the locks.

It wasn't her idea to buy a weapon. "The police did all they could, but they had no control. They felt sorry for me. They told me to get a gun." She still doesn't remember firing it. She says she remembers her husband's face, the glassy eyes, a knife in his hands. "To this day, I don't remember pulling the trigger."

—*Time,* January 18, 1993

JANUARY 18, 1993 $2.95

TIME

FIGHTING BACK

Rita Collins had enough of her husband's beatings, so she killed him. Now, after five years in jail, she's hoping for clemency. Do women who turn against their abusers deserve a special kind of forgiveness?

0 724404 1

The cover story of this 1993 issue of Time *magazine featured battered wife Rita Collins.*

After reading about John and Rita Collins's violent marriage, you are probably left with many unanswered questions: Why was John Collins so vicious and violent? Was it something about his personality? His past? His biochemistry? Did Rita Collins have to kill her husband? What was going on in her mind at the time of the murder? Was her aggression a matter of self-defense? Or was she just "paying back" the brutality she had received from her husband over the years?

Whatever the causes of John and Rita Collins's violence, their story reminds us that aggression intrudes into virtually all human affairs, from intimate family relationships to the dealings of nations. We tend to think of aggression as something "out there"—in "bad" families, on tough urban streets, or in distant wars—but aggression is often as close as the house next door . . . and sometimes the next room in our own home. A major survey of family violence found that 20% of parents hit their children with objects such as sticks, switches, and straps; 3% kicked, bit, or punched their children. Mothers and fathers hit each other as well. The researchers note that "if you are married, the chances are almost one out of three that your

429

husband or wife will hit you" (Straus, Gelles, & Steinmetz, 1980, p. 32). In 4% of the marriages surveyed, spouses reported attacking each other with knives or guns! Spouse-beating occurred in all social classes, religions, and ethnic groups. Apparently, many people interpret a marriage license as a "hitting license" (Straus et al., 1980).

A glance through the daily newspaper should convince you that violence extends well beyond the family. Throughout the 1980s, violent crime (murder, rape, robbery, and aggravated assault) in the United States increased at a faster rate than the general population. Between 1977 and 1990, the number of violent crimes rose from a little over 1 million to a staggering 1,820,130, including more than 23,000 homicides and more than 102,000 forcible rapes each year (*World Almanac*, 1992).

Violence occurs regularly on a much larger scale, too—nations as well as individuals kill and maim others. Ashley Montagu (1976), a noted anthropologist, described one researcher's attempt to tabulate the number of wars in recorded history. The result: Through the early 1960s, there had been 14,531 wars. Since then, the world has seen war in Vietnam, genocide in Cambodia, several wars between Israel and various Arab countries, the Soviet invasion of Afghanistan followed by a bloody guerrilla insurgency, a British skirmish with Argentina over the Falkland Islands, revolutions and guerrilla wars in Central America, prolonged conflict between Iran and Iraq, war in the Persian Gulf, horrible civil wars in Sudan, Somalia, and the former Yugoslavia . . . and the list goes on.

Statistics on family violence, violent crime, and war all point to the fundamental questions we will consider in this chapter: Why are people so aggressive? Is aggression a natural behavior for human beings? Or is it learned—from our culture, from the mass media, and from other people? What conditions lead people to do violence against others, and what conditions reduce violence?

DEFINING AGGRESSION

Although most of us think we know aggression when we see it, a closer analysis shows that our commonsense notions about it are not as clear as we might think. For example, which of the following behaviors do you think are examples of aggression (see Johnson, 1972)?

A cat kills a mouse.

A hunter shoots an animal.

A doctor gives an inoculation to a screaming child.

A tennis player smashes her racket after missing a shot.

A boxer gives his opponent a bloody nose.

A Boy Scout tries to assist an old lady but trips her by mistake.

A husband constantly demeans and criticizes his wife.

A firing squad executes a prisoner.

A woman commits suicide.

The president of the United States asks Congress for permission to go to war.

These examples differ from one another in several ways. Sometimes a living being is harmed (killing a person or animal, punching someone), sometimes not (smashing a tennis racket). Sometimes the harm is intentional (hunting), sometimes not (the accidental tripping). Sometimes the harm is physical (shooting, punching), sometimes psychological (criticizing). Sometimes harm is directed at another (punching someone), sometimes at oneself (suicide). Finally, sometimes harm is done out of emotion or anger (the frustrated tennis player), sometimes for monetary reward (the professional boxer) and because it is "part of the job" (the firing squad). People may even inflict pain (the doctor giving a shot) in the best interests of the person being hurt.

Here's a general working definition (see Baron, 1977; Johnson, 1972; Krebs & Miller, 1985): *Aggression is behavior directed against another living being that is intended to harm or injure.* This definition rules out some of the previous examples as being truly aggressive (such as the doctor administering a shot). Our definition applies primarily to human behavior, because the intentionality of animal behavior is difficult, if not impossible, to determine. And our definition allows for the possibility of psychological as well as physical injury, although we shall focus primarily on physical aggressiveness in this chapter.

Social psychologists distinguish between two main kinds of human aggression: hostile aggression and instrumental aggression (Baron, 1977; Buss, 1961, 1971; Feshbach, 1970; Zillman, 1979). *Hostile aggression* is generally provoked by pain or upset; it is emotional, and its primary purpose is to do harm. For example, a husband punches his wife after she yells at him, "You're a bust, you're a failure, I want you out of here, I can always get men who'll work, good men, not scum like you" (Straus, Gelles, & Steinmetz, 1980, p. 37). It seems likely that this husband was furious when he punched his wife and fully intended to harm her. (This man's anger does not justify his violence, however. Later in this chapter we shall discuss therapeutic techniques designed to help abusive men learn to control their anger and violent behavior. Responsible individuals do not punch their spouses, regardless of how angry they are.)

Anything that increases emotional arousal increases the likelihood of hostile aggression. In addition, hostile impulses are particularly likely to lead to deadly behaviors in the presence of facilitating stimuli (such as weapons). Sometimes "passion killings" occur when a person is furious *and* has easy access to a weapon.

Unlike hostile aggression, *instrumental aggression* is not necessarily caused by anger or emotion. Its goal is to gain some desired rewards, such as money or valuable goods. The Mafia hit man who kills for pay is engaging in instrumental aggression. Some robbers assault their victims to gain money, not to do harm. In the words of one New York mugger, "We ain't into the kill thing. Anybody on that junk is workin' out of the fruit and nuts bag. We just want the money, like anybody else" (Stevens, 1971). Indeed, some muggers refer to committing a robbery as "getting paid." A child who hits another child to obtain a desired toy, or a football player who tackles his opponents with bone-crunching force to win games and a high salary may also be practicing instrumental aggression.

Instrumental aggression is molded by environmental rewards and social learning. A school bully may gradually increase his aggression against peers, for example, if he gains rewards as a result (such as power and others' possessions) and learns that no one punishes his aggression.

Not only are hostile and instrumental aggression triggered by different factors, they also may be reduced in different ways. Hostile aggression can often be reduced if we can somehow distract the person in a passionate rage and give him time to cool off; instrumental aggression is more likely to be reduced by changing the models, rewards, and punishments that influence the aggressive behavior (Dodge, 1991).

MEASURING AGGRESSION

Research studies have measured aggression in many different ways (Baron, 1977; Bertilson, 1983; Krebs & Miller, 1985). Early studies tended to use verbal measures (for example, Davitz, 1952; Doob & Sears, 1939; McClelland & Apicella, 1945). After some sort of provocation, subjects would be asked to rate another person, and if the ratings were negative, subjects were presumed to be showing aggression. But are you really being "aggressive" if you rate another person as being "unattractive" or "unintelligent"? One problem with verbal ratings is that they often have no real consequences for the supposed target of your aggression; they do no real injury.

More-recent studies have tended to use behavioral measures of aggression. One popular laboratory device, the "aggression machine," was developed by Arnold Buss in the early 1960s (Buss, 1961). Under the guise of studying the effects of punishment on learning, subjects in "aggression machine" studies are given the opportunity to deliver supposed electric shocks to a "learner." The number, intensity, and duration of shocks serve as measures of aggression. (This experimental design recalls Milgram's obedience paradigm; see Chapter 2.) Other behavioral measures of aggression include observed violence during play (Bandura, Ross, & Ross, 1963b; Liebert & Baron, 1972) and simulated aggression, such as throwing sponge-rubber bricks and shooting rubber bands at people (Diener, 1976; Diener, Doneen, & Endresen, 1975) or playing war games (Zillman, Johnson, & Day, 1974).

How well do these various laboratory measures of aggression reflect aggression in everyday life (Krebs & Miller, 1985)? Many studies suggest a significant relationship between lab measures of people's aggressiveness and their levels of aggressiveness outside the lab (Berkowitz & Donnerstein, 1982). The real-life validity of aggression research is most obvious in studies that assess real-life kinds of aggression—for example, children's aggressiveness as rated by their parents and teachers; levels of family violence; and homicide rates.

FACTORS THAT INFLUENCE HUMAN AGGRESSION

Counselors have found that men resort to violence because they want to control their partners, and they know they can get away with it—unlike in other relationships. "A lot of people experience low impulse control, fear of abandonment, alcohol and drug addiction, all the characteristics of a batterer," says Ellen Pence, training coordinator for the Domestic Abuse Intervention Project in Duluth. "However, the same guy is not beating up his boss."

Most men come to the program either by order of the courts or as a condition set by their partners. The counselors start with the assumption that battering is learned behavior. Eighty percent of the participants grew up in a home where they saw or were victims of physical, sexual or other abuse.

—*Time,* January 18, 1993

Human aggression is complex behavior shaped by many different factors, and theorists have attempted to explain it at many different levels (see Figure 10.1). At the *group level* of explanation, psychologists study the biological groups (such as species and biological sex) and cultural groups (nations; ethnic and religious groups) that people belong to and how they affect their aggressiveness. At the *individual level,* psychologists study the influences of individuals' heredity and physiology (hormone levels, brain structures), their past environment (did they watch a lot of violent TV shows as children?), and their current environment (are they currently frustrated, in pain, or being physically attacked by others?). At the third level of explanation are *mediating variables*—hypothetical processes within us—that influence aggression, such as instincts, emotions, arousal, attributions, schemas, attitudes, and personality traits.

The levels of explanation shown in Figure 10.1 offer a way of organizing theories and research on aggression. They suggest that there is no single "cause" of human aggression. The various explanations listed in Figure 10.1 are not mutually exclusive; rather, they are intertwined. For example, a person's biological group (being male or female) determines his or her physiology (levels of sex hormones) and can affect his or her environment (treatment by friends and parents), which ultimately influences mediating variables such as personality traits and attitudes. With this complexity in mind, let's consider a number of broad interrelated factors that influence human aggression.

Biological Groups, Instincts, and Aggression

Is aggression instinctive? Sigmund Freud (1961 [1930]) argued that people are often motivated by primitive, biologically based, aggressive impulses. More

GROUP-LEVEL EXPLANATIONS

Biological groups (evolution)

Cultural and social groups

↓

INDIVIDUAL-LEVEL EXPLANATIONS

Heredity and physiology (hormone levels, brain structure)

Past environment (family rearing, TV viewing)

Current setting (current models, painful stimuli, frustrating situations)

↓

MEDIATING VARIABLES

Beliefs and attitudes
Schemas
Emotions
Personality traits
Intelligence
Drives and instincts
Arousal
Attributions

↓

AGGRESSIVE BEHAVIOR

FIGURE 10.1 Levels of explanation applied to aggression.

recently, the European ethologist Konrad Lorenz (1966) also proposed that people, like other animals, possess innate aggressive impulses. Whereas most animals have evolved ways to inhibit aggression among members of their own species, according to Lorenz, people have not, for technological advances have outpaced the evolution of human inhibitions. In Lorenz's words: "The invention of artificial weapons upset the equilibrium of killing potential and social inhibitions; . . . man's position was very nearly that of a dove which, by some unusual trick of nature, has suddenly acquired the beak of a raven" (p. 34). Automatic rifles, hand grenades, missiles, and nuclear warheads are fearsome beaks indeed!

Both Freud and Lorenz believed that aggressive drives build up and must somehow be vented. Freud, particularly toward the end of his life, was quite pessimistic about the possibilities for peace. He felt there would always be wars and conflict. Lorenz, slightly more optimistic, proposed that athletic contests and other kinds of staged aggression could perhaps provide safety valves that would allow people's inevitable aggressive impulses to be expressed in a controlled way.

Aside from being pessimistic, simple instinct theories of human aggression are scientifically unsatisfying because their explanations seem to be circular: Why are people aggressive? Because of their aggressive instincts. How do we know people possess aggressive instincts? Because they are aggressive. When instinct theories are specific enough to provide testable hypotheses, they may simply prove to be wrong. For example, the "catharsis hypothesis"—the notion that by venting their aggressions, people display less aggression later on—follows from the theories of both Freud and Lorenz (and is consistent with many people's commonsense notions as well), yet, as we shall see, it has often been refuted by research evidence.

Instinct theories of aggression seem to suggest that biological factors strictly determine and inevitably lead to aggressive behavior (Montagu, 1976). In fact, however, biological factors create in people and animals a predisposition to be aggressive *in certain situations*. As Edward O. Wilson (1975), the father of modern sociobiology, notes, "Aggression evolves not as a continuous biological process, like the beat of a heart, but as a contingency plan of the animal's endocrine and nervous system, programmed to be summoned up in time of stress" (p. 248). Aggression exists as a potential, but not an inevitable, behavior (Lore & Schultz, 1993).

From an evolutionary perspective, aggressive behavior may sometimes help animals survive and reproduce (Maynard-Smith, 1974). An aggressive animal may get more food by fighting off competitors, mate successfully by fighting off sexual rivals, and guarantee its survival and that of its offspring by fighting off predators. But aggression also has substantial costs. If you fight too much, a rested rival or predator may pounce on you when you're weak and defeat you. Moreover, if you lose a fight (and sometimes even when you win a fight), you may be injured or killed. Because of these potent costs, Maynard-Smith argues, members of many species fight if they must, but bluff or flee if they can. Within social species, aggression is used to compete—not to kill—and to enforce the social "law and order" of dominance hierarchies (Montagu, 1976).

Krebs and Miller (1985) summarize the evolutionary view of aggressive behavior succinctly and suggest a number of testable hypotheses:

Are there genetic influences on aggression?

Because of its potentially high costs, aggressive behavior should be employed mainly in circumstances where other methods of satisfying needs are not available (e.g., in overcrowded situations, when there are insufficient resources) and/or when the potential gains of aggression are great. Because of the potential costs to individuals in most social species of the injury and death of an ingroup cohort, ingroup aggression should be more constrained than outgroup aggression. (p. 10)

Cultural Influences on Aggression

Human aggression varies considerably across cultures. As Montagu (1976) observes, "When aggressive behavior is strongly discouraged, as among the Hutterites and Amish, the Hopi and Zuni Indians, it is practically unknown" (p. 21). Conversely, in cultures that encourage and even glorify violence, aggression is quite common. Irenaus Eibl-Eibesfeldt (1979) describes the horrible atrocities committed by warring Pygmy tribes, the !Kung Bushmen of southwest Africa, and the Aranda tribes of central Australia. Many "advanced" societies, including our own, show high levels of aggressive behavior as well. Indeed, among Western industrialized countries, the United States shows particularly high levels of violence: Homicide rates in the United States are three to seven times those in most European countries (Lore & Schultz, 1993; see Figure 10.2). These figures don't include institutionalized violence, such as killings committed by soldiers and police officers.

What determines whether a particular culture is violent or peaceful? Eibl-Eibesfeldt (1979) believes that one kind of violence, a culture's propensity to go to war, may depend in part on the availability of resources necessary for survival:

Wars are fought for hunting grounds, pasture land, and arable land, and if in earlier times climatic alterations made a group's living area inhospitable, it was actually compelled to find new territory by force of arms. The drying up of the Central Asian steppes set the Mongol peoples in motion, and their warlike expeditions took them all the way to Europe. Their clash with the Teutonic peoples in turn forced the latter to migrate.

. . . War is a means that aids groups to compete for the wealth essential to life (land, mineral resources, etc.).

. . . If one asks whether modern war still performs functions I have described, the answer is yes. (pp. 185–186)

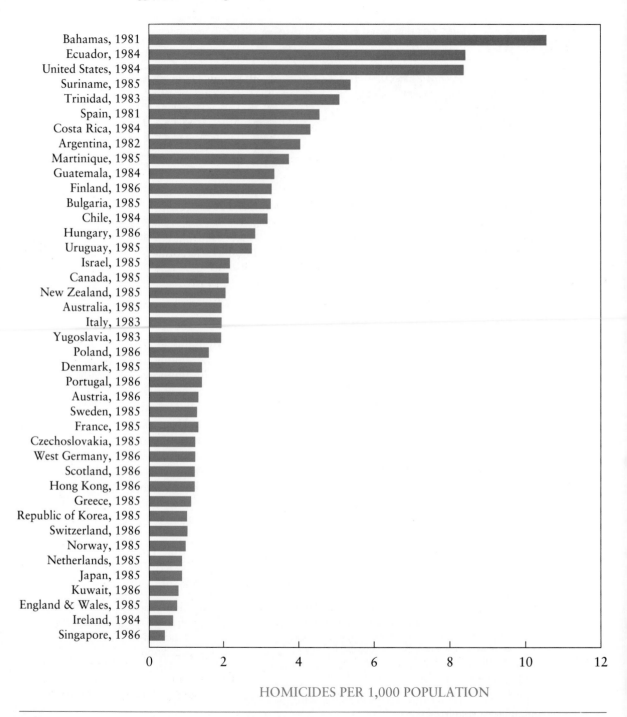

FIGURE 10.2 Crude homicide rates for selected countries. *Source:* Reiss and Roth (1993).

MULTICULTURAL PERSPECTIVE

Wars and the Cycle of Violence

Whatever their causes, wars are horrible, for reasons we all know: They frequently bring injury, devastation, and death to large groups of people over broad geographical areas. But wars may have another, more subtle and lingering destructive effect: They may foster increased domestic violence in societies for years afterward.

To test the hypothesis that wars may lead to increases in the general level of violence in societies, Dane Archer and Rosemary Gartner (1984) studied homicide rates in 29 combatant countries and 15 noncombatant countries in the five years following World Wars I and II. They found that combatant countries tended to show sharply higher homicide rates after both world wars, whereas noncombatant countries did not (see Figure 10.3). To replicate their findings, Archer and Gartner also analyzed homicide rates in combatant and noncombatant countries after "smaller" wars (for example, the Vietnam War, the 1967 Arab–Israeli War, the 1965 conflict between India and Pakistan over the Kashmir region). The results were quite similar: Combatant nations tended to show a

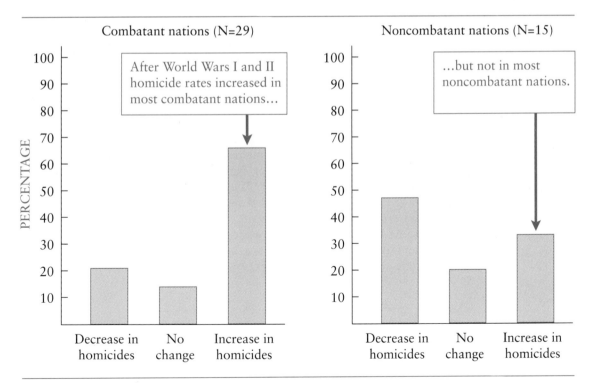

FIGURE 10.3 Changes in homicide rates after World Wars I and II in combatant and noncombatant nations. *Source:* Data from Archer and Gartner (1984).

significant increase in homicide rates during the five years following the war; noncombatant nations, if anything, showed a net decrease.

Why does war tend to be followed by an increase in domestic violence? Archer and Gartner offered a number of possible explanations: Social structures (for example, families, law enforcement agencies) disintegrate during war and this leads to an increase in violence. Economic conditions worsen and stimulate violent crimes. Disturbed war veterans return home and contribute to domestic violence. And finally, war tends to legitimize and glorify violence and provide a model of aggressive behavior for all.

Drawing on the data they collected, Archer and Gartner find the last explanation most plausible. They note that homicide rates tended to increase after wars regardless of whether the fighting nations won or lost and regardless of whether the wars took place at home or abroad. These findings go against the "disintegrating social structure" explanation. Postwar unemployment levels seem unrelated to postwar increases in homicide rates, contrary to the "economic conditions" explanation. And postwar homicide rates increase in all age groups and among both women and men, not only among returning veterans, contrary to the "returning veterans" explanation. The "legitimization of violence" explanation, according to Archer and Gartner, is the one most consistent with their data.

Whatever the cause, we are left with a disturbing finding: To the long list of horrors that war brings, we can add one more—wars may stimulate domestic violence for years after they are over. At the level of cultures and nations, then, violence seems to beget violence. As we shall see later, this may occur at an individual level as well.

Individual Differences in Aggression

Psychologists don't ignore evolutionary and cultural factors that influence aggression, but they tend to be more interested in explaining why people *within* a given society vary in their levels of aggressiveness. Why do some people hit their spouses, whereas others do not? Why are some children aggressive bullies and others gentle? Among the proposed answers: Individuals' levels of aggression vary because of their personality traits, physiological factors (such as brain structures and hormone levels), and what they have learned from their families, friends, and the mass media. Let's examine some of these individual-level explanations and mediating variables.

Aggressiveness as a Trait

Are some people generally more aggressive than others? And is a given individual's overall level of aggressiveness stable over time? In other words, can aggressiveness be viewed as a kind of personality trait?

Research indicates that an individual's level of aggressiveness is indeed relatively consistent and stable over time. Dan Olweus (1979) summarized the results of 16 studies on the temporal consistency of aggression, including classics

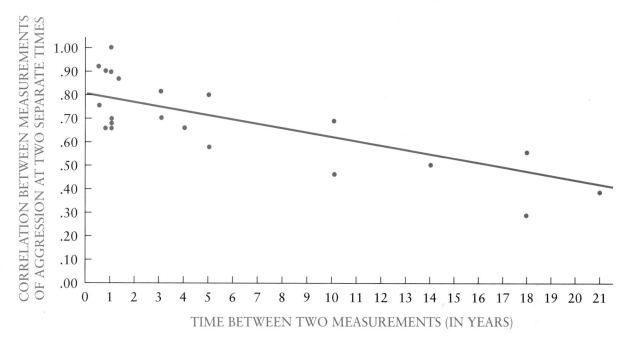

Individuals' measures of aggressiveness correlate significantly even when measures are obtained more than 20 years apart.

FIGURE 10.4 The stability of aggressiveness over time. *Source:* Adapted from Olweus (1979).

by Kagan and Moss (1962) and Block (1971), and found that aggressiveness is almost as stable a characteristic as intelligence (see Figure 10.4). Huesmann, Eron, Lefkowitz, and Walder (1984) found that the aggressiveness of 8-year-old children (as rated by their peers) significantly predicted their levels of aggressiveness and criminal behavior as adults 22 years later. Note that the observed consistency of aggressiveness over time does not mean that people necessarily show the same *kinds* of aggressive behavior at all ages (Caspi, 1987). For example, an aggressive person might bite playmates as a child but verbally abuse his or her spouse as an adult.

Part of the stability of overall aggressiveness may result from genetic and biological factors. Rushton and his colleagues (1986) studied the self-reported aggressiveness of 573 pairs of adult British twins in order to estimate the heritability of aggressiveness. The correlation between the aggressiveness of identical twins was .40, whereas the correlation for fraternal twins was only .04, clearly indicating a genetic component to the trait. Statistical analyses indicated that over 50% of the variability in these subjects' self-reported aggression was due to hereditary factors.

Animal studies also demonstrate the possibility of genetic influences on aggression. Birds, rats, and dogs can be bred for aggressiveness (Moyer, 1976). In one controlled study, Lagerspetz (1964) reared six generations of mice, allowing only the most aggressive and least aggressive males to reproduce each generation.

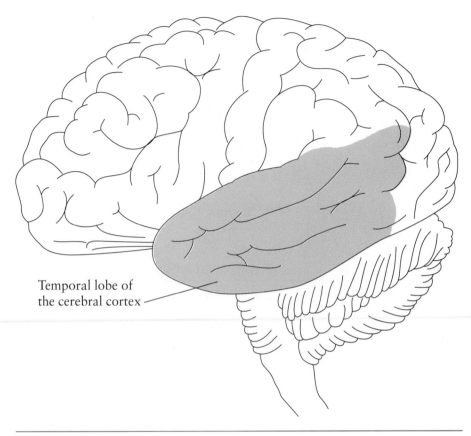

Temporal lobe of
the cerebral cortex

F I G U R E   1 0 . 5   The temporal lobe.

By the sixth generation, the most aggressive of the "peaceful" mice was less aggressive than the least aggressive of the "violent" mice.

Physiology and Aggression

Exactly how are aggressive tendencies linked to heredity and physiology? Research has focused on several distinct biological factors. First, aggression is related to specific structures in the brain: regions of the temporal lobe (the sides of the cortex, or surface, of the brain; see Figure 10.5) and of the limbic system (a crescent-shaped array of structures deep inside the brain; see Figure 10.6). Clinical evidence suggests that tumors or infectious diseases affecting these areas can trigger aggression (Moyer, 1976). Brain injuries before or during birth may also contribute to later aggression and criminal violence (Brennan, Mednick, & Kandel, 1991; Mednick, Brennan, & Kandel, 1988).

One 43-year-old man with a brain tumor in his temporal lobe attempted to kill his wife and daughter with a butcher knife for no apparent reason. And a 29-year-old chemist with a temporal lobe tumor became so abusive toward his wife

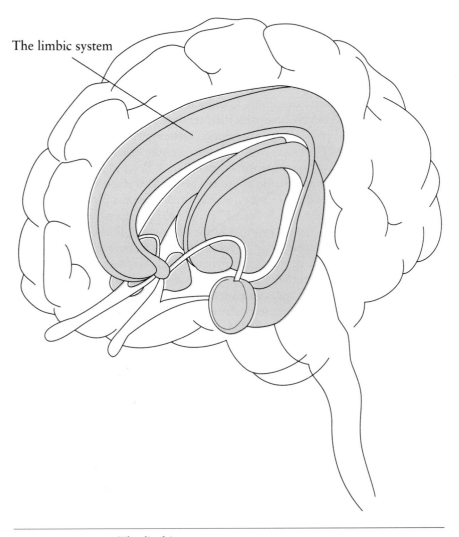

FIGURE 10.6 The limbic system.

that she left him and so irritable on the job that he was fired. In both cases, the men's aggressiveness subsided after their tumors were surgically removed. The highly publicized case of Charles Whitman ended much more tragically. After seeing a psychiatrist and complaining of excruciating headaches and uncontrollable violent impulses in 1966, Whitman shot his wife and mother, climbed atop a tower at the University of Texas, and shot another 38 people, killing 14. Whitman was killed by the police, and an autopsy revealed a malignant tumor the size of a walnut in the temporal lobe of his brain (Sweet, Ervin, & Mark, 1969).

Body chemistry, too, can influence aggression. In particular, some studies suggest a relationship between the sex hormone testosterone and aggression (Dabbs, 1992; Olweus, 1986), which may partly account for the well-documented findings that men and boys are more aggressive than women and girls (Maccoby & Jacklin, 1974, 1980) and that these sex differences occur across cultures and across species of primates. As noted in Chapter 8, men are in particular more *physically* aggressive than women (Eagly & Steffen, 1986b).

Differences in aggression among individuals of the same sex may also be partly a function of testosterone levels. One study found that Swedish teenage boys' testosterone levels were correlated with their tendency to respond to provocations with both verbal and physical aggressiveness (Olweus, 1986), and another study documented that prison inmates with high testosterone levels were more likely to have committed violent crimes (Dabbs, Frady, Carr, & Besch, 1987). Although sex hormones may influence aggression in human beings, it is important to emphasize that physiology *is not* destiny. Hormones may predispose people to aggression in certain situations, but they do not "cause" people to be aggressive (Mazur, 1983).

Like naturally occurring hormones, some drugs can influence human aggression. Research as well as anecdotal evidence suggests that anabolic steroids (which are closely related to testosterone) can increase aggressiveness (Choi, Parrott, & Cowan, 1990). Alcohol, perhaps in part because it tends to reduce inhibitions, increases subjects' aggressiveness in experimental studies (Bushman & Cooper, 1990). Marijuana does not increase, and in certain circumstances may even reduce, aggression (Myerscough & Taylor, 1985; S. Taylor et al., 1976).

Environmental Factors

Biological evolution, cultural norms, and individuals' physiology and heredity all play roles in the complex story of human aggression. However, social psychologists usually concentrate more on environmental and psychological influences. What environmental factors most commonly lead to aggression? And how do their effects work?

Aggression as a Response to Aggression

Perhaps the most obvious environmental cause of aggression is being attacked by someone. This certainly seems to be a major factor in Rita Collins's killing of her husband. Research consistently shows that people respond to attacks with counterattacks, often in a matched, reciprocal fashion (Borden, Bowen, & Taylor, 1971; Dengerink & Myers, 1977; Ohbuchi & Kambara, 1985). The principle that aggression begets aggression is basic to most social psychology experiments on aggression. To elicit aggressive behavior in the laboratory, social psychologists frequently have confederates attack experimental subjects verbally or with electric shocks and then allow the subjects to retaliate against their attackers. (Perhaps an optimistic conclusion to draw here is that most people don't attack others for no good reason. In laboratory studies, aggression must be *elicited* in most people; it doesn't just spontaneously occur.)

The reasons that attacks elicit counterattacks are many: Principles of equity and exchange demand that we "give" as we "get" in social relationships (see Chapters 1, 9, and 11). Furthermore, when we are attacked, we become angry and aroused, and this state generates hostile aggression. And finally, when we are attacked, we are often in pain.

Physical Pain

In bullfighting, men called *banderilleros* thrust decorated barbs, called *banderillas*, into the shoulders and neck of the bull before the matador enters the arena. The bull—bleeding, goaded, and enraged—becomes all the more ferocious. The bullfight makes use of a basic psychological principle: Pain incites aggression.

Ulrich and Azrin (1962) were the first psychologists to systematically study the nature and limits of this phenomenon. Specifically, they observed that when two rats were shocked in a small box with an electrified floor, the animals would rear up on their hind legs and fight with each other by "boxing" and biting. Pain also leads to aggression in many other animals, including monkeys, cats, opossums, raccoons, roosters, alligators, and snakes (Azrin, 1967; Moyer, 1976).

Ulrich and Azrin initially referred to the relationship between pain and aggression as automatic and "reflexive." Even animals that have been raised in total social isolation will attack in response to pain (Hutchinson, 1983), suggesting that the pain–aggression link does not have to be learned. Pain does not *inevitably* lead to aggression, however. Many animals will try to escape rather

The bullfight makes use of the principle that pain incites aggression.

than fight after receiving shocks. Pain incites aggression particularly when the animals are confined to a small space and cannot escape (Azrin, Hutchinson, & Hake, 1966).

Although the basic link between pain and aggression may be "wired in," learning can strongly influence pain-induced aggression. Animals that are low in dominance hierarchies have been found to show little aggression when in pain, perhaps because they have learned to inhibit their aggression when around more dominant animals (Ader, 1975). Furthermore, the effects of pain on aggression critically depend on the animal's history of reinforcement. When pain-induced aggression is rewarded with a decrease in pain, fighting becomes more likely after pain (Azrin, 1967); conversely, when pain-induced aggression is punished with greater pain, fighting becomes less likely.

Hutchinson (1983) posed an interesting question about the "fighting" that follows pain: Is it truly aggressive—that is, intended to injure another animal—or is it "defensive" behavior, an attempt to reduce or escape from pain? The answer may very well be both (Berkowitz, 1983a). Azrin, Hutchinson, and McLaughlin (1965) found that shocked monkeys would actually learn to pull a chain in order to obtain something to attack. In other words, a pained animal finds fighting rewarding.

Can pain can lead to aggression in human beings as well as in animals? (When you are in psychological or physical pain, does it sometimes seem to you that you "look for a fight" with people around you?) Some studies find that exposure to unpleasant stimuli such as bad smells (Rotton, Barry, Frey, & Soler, 1978), cigarette smoke (Jones & Bogat, 1978), and disturbing pornography (White, 1979) leads people to be more aggressive. But "unpleasant" stimuli aren't the same as "painful" stimuli. For obvious ethical reasons, social psychologists cannot expose human subjects to extremely painful electric shocks to see whether they will attack another person.

Berkowitz, Cochran, and Embree (1981) did, however, conduct a somewhat milder experiment. On the pretext of studying the effects of discomfort on performance in a work setting, they asked college women to place their hands in a tank of either comfortably warm or painfully cold water while "supervising" another woman working in a nearby cubicle. These subjects could deliver either rewards (nickels) or punishments (blasts of noise) to the "worker" as part of their supervision. Some subjects were told that the punishments hurt the worker and interfered with her performance; others were told that appropriately delivered punishments would help the worker's performance. The results: The supervisors in pain were least rewarding and most punitive, particularly when they thought their punishments would hurt. Thus, people (like shocked rats and monkeys) seem motivated to hurt others when they're in pain.

Heat

Heat is yet another kind of unpleasant stimulus that can have a pervasive impact on human aggression. Experimental studies suggest that, within limits, people become more aggressive as temperatures rise; this relationship sometimes breaks down when heat becomes so oppressive that people don't have the energy to be aggressive (Baron & Bell, 1975; Bell & Baron, 1976).

Correlational studies also indicate that heat makes people "hot under the collar." Carlsmith and Anderson (1979) reported a significant relationship between temperature and the frequency of riots in the United States during the late 1960s and early 1970s. The number of violent crimes in Chicago and Houston (Anderson & Anderson, 1984) and in Des Moines and Indianapolis (Cotton, 1986) tend to increase with the temperature, and hot cities have higher rates of violent crimes than more temperate cities do (Anderson, 1987). Violent crimes are more related to temperature than nonviolent crimes, which suggests a specific link between heat and *aggressiveness* rather than between heat and crime (Anderson, 1987). Heat is particularly likely to raise crime rates when it is combined with high humidity (Harries & Stadler, 1988). Finally, family violence also tends to increase as temperatures rise (Rotton & Frey, 1985).

Frustration

Clearly, physical pain and discomfort sometimes lead to aggression. Does psychological pain have the same effect? One kind of psychological pain, frustration, has long been studied as a likely cause of aggression. You can probably think of many instances in life when frustration seems to lead to aggression. Some people speculated that the Los Angeles riots of 1992 were motivated in part by economic frustrations. And on February 8, 1993, a patient stormed into a Los Angeles

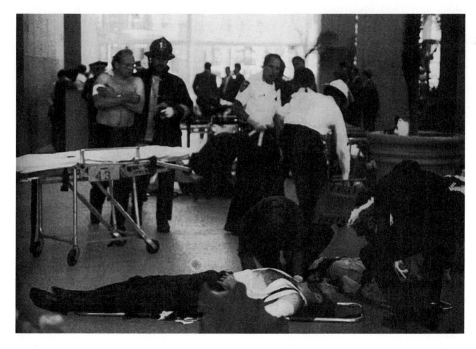

Frustration and aggression: In July 1993, a gunman killed 8 people and wounded 6 more at a San Francisco law office, supposedly because of his frustration over a legal case they were handling.

hospital emergency room and shot three doctors, claiming that he had been frustrated by long waits and poor medical service in the facility.

In their classic book *Frustration and Aggression,* Dollard, Doob, Miller, Mowrer, and Sears (1939) argued for a strong version of the frustration–aggression hypothesis: that frustration *always* leads to aggression, and aggression is *always* caused by frustration. According to their definition, frustration is "interference with the occurrence of [a] . . . goal-response." Thus, if you are very hungry and about to sit down to eat a delicious dinner, the phone call that interrupts you is frustrating. And if you are sexually aroused, whatever prevents sexual activity is frustrating.

Do frustrations in fact lead to aggression? Early research findings suggested that they do, at least at times. In one classic study, Barker, Dembo, and Lewin (1941) put children into a room that contained many desirable toys. Some children were permitted to play with the toys, whereas others were allowed to "look but not touch" and were thus frustrated. In subsequent play, the frustrated children proved to be more aggressive and destructive.

Other early studies linked frustration to prejudice and aggression against out-groups. For example, Hovland and Sears (1940) found a significant correlation between the price of cotton and the lynching of blacks in the South between 1882 and 1930, and this finding has been replicated recently using more sophisticated statistical analyses (Hepworth & West, 1988). Presumably, the frustration of hard economic times led white Southerners to violence against vulnerable blacks. Not only broad societal levels of economic frustration but also more personal kinds of frustration may sometimes lead people to vent their anger, particularly on out-group members. Miller and Bugelski (1948) found that men who were prevented at the last minute from enjoying an entertaining night on the town expressed more negative attitudes toward various minority groups.

Contrary to the original frustration–aggression hypothesis, however, frustration does not *inevitably* lead to aggression. Many studies demonstrate that our thought processes can influence whether or not frustration triggers actual aggression. Baron (1977) argued that arbitrary and strong frustrations in particular goad people to aggression, whereas mild frustrations or frustrations that exist "for a good reason" are less likely to provoke aggression. If you are in a big hurry and are stopped behind a car at an intersection when the light turns green, yet you can't move because the driver in front of you is combing his hair, you will probably feel angry, and perhaps you'll honk in frustration. But if you're stuck at the intersection because the driver in front of you had a heart attack and is being carried off by paramedics, you probably will not feel hostility. You are frustrated, but there is a good reason for the delay.

Kulik and Brown (1979) clearly demonstrated how our thought processes and attributions can affect the relationship between frustration and aggression. They asked 60 Harvard undergraduates to solicit charitable donations by telephone. Some subjects were led to expect success in general (they were told that 60% to 65% of the people called would donate), and others were led to expect little success (that only 10% to 15% of people would donate). Subjects actually spoke to a confederate, who refused their request for money in different ways. In one condition, the confederate refused abruptly and unpleasantly, telling the subject that charities were a "rip-off." In another condition, he told the subject that he was sympathetic to charities but had recently been laid off from work and thus couldn't afford to make a donation now. Thus, in the second condition, the subject was frustrated by a refusal that seemed justified.

Subjects' anger upon completing a call was measured by recording how hard they slammed down the phone. In addition, subjects' verbal aggression during a call and their choice of sending mild or critical follow-up letters to the people they solicited were observed. As you can guess, subjects showed more anger and aggression when their frustration was unexpected and arbitrary. Thus, the effects of frustration depend on our expectations and how reasonable the frustration seems to be (see also Burnstein & Worchel, 1962; Worchel, 1974).

So the original strong version of the frustration–aggression hypothesis turns out to be false: Frustration does not always and inevitably lead to aggression. The converse hypothesis—that aggression always presupposes frustration—is also false. Physical pain as well as frustration can lead to aggression. And as we shall see, pain and frustration are not the sole causes of aggression. Aggression can simply be a learned behavior.

Where does 50 years of research leave the original frustration–aggression hypothesis? Much reduced and qualified, to be sure. Leonard Berkowitz (1978, 1983b, 1988) argues that frustration leads to aggression insofar as it makes people angry, and that frustration incites aggression because it is a kind of pain: psychological pain. A profoundly frustrating experience may be similar to a sharp jolt of electricity: Both can make us mad, and if the occasion is right, we may lash out at a convenient target who happens to be near.

Economic Frustration and Societal Aggression

SOCIAL PSYCHOLOGY IN EVERYDAY LIFE

Can the frustration–aggression hypothesis shed any light on the causes of such societal upheavals as the French Revolution of 1789, the American race riots of the mid- to late 1960s, or the Los Angeles riots of 1992? Perhaps bad economic times or government oppression led to frustration, which then exploded into violence.

Some historians have argued that frustrated optimism, rather than abject pessimism, produces revolutions. The noted French political writer Alexis de Tocqueville (1856) observed in his analysis of the French Revolution that:

> the French found their condition the more unsupportable in proportion to its improvement. . . . Revolutions are not always brought about by a gradual decline from bad to worse. Nations that have endured patiently and almost unconsciously the most overwhelming oppression often burst into rebellion against the yoke the moment it begins to grow lighter. . . . Evils which are patiently endured when they seem inevitable become intolerable when once the idea of escape from them is suggested. (p. 214)

Political scientist James Davies (1972), looking at several historical examples, including the French Revolution, proposed a "J-curve" theory of social revolutions (see Figure 10.7). "Revolutions are most likely to occur when a

*Economic frustration
and violence: The Los
Angeles riots of 1992.*

prolonged period of objective economic and social development is followed by a short period of sharp reversal" (p. 68); that is, social frustration occurs particularly when people have come to expect improved conditions but actually experience worsening conditions. This hypothesis seems to fit the Los Angeles riots of 1992: The affluent 1980s were followed by a severe recession in California in the early 1990s. (Clearly, a number of other factors also helped trigger these riots.)

Do research findings offer any support for Davies's hypothesis? A study of 84 nations found a clear relationship between political instability (strikes, riots, revolts) and economic frustration (Feierabend & Feierabend, 1972). "Frustrated countries" were defined as those that suffered from poor economic conditions (such as low GNP, inadequate food supplies, insufficient numbers of telephones and doctors) but were well acquainted with the higher living standards of industrial, urbanized countries. Furthermore, nations with highly oppressive or nonoppressive governments were found to be more stable than nations with moderately oppressive governments. Thus, de Tocqueville's observation that revolutions are more often born of a "ray of hope" than of absolute hopelessness may be correct.

Both Feierabend and Feierabend's research and Davies's J-curve theory suggest that frustration may be more a function of *relative deprivation*—the gap between expectations and reality—than of absolute levels of deprivation. Poor

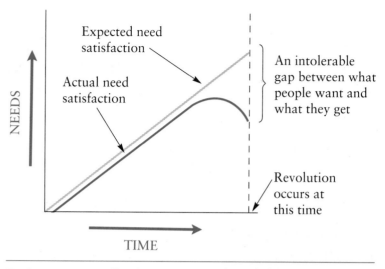

FIGURE 10.7 Davies's "J-curve" theory of violent social revolution. *Source:* Adapted from Davies (1972).

countries exposed to the high standards of living of industrialized nations are more frustrated than poor countries isolated from the modern world. Similarly, deprived people who have experienced some recent progress are more frustrated than people who have experienced only poverty and oppression, and poor people who are aware of others' affluence are more frustrated than poor people aware only of other poor people.

The links between economic frustration and social unrest are highly relevant to today's world. Citizens of former Soviet-bloc countries have recently faced terrible economic deprivation, at a time when their hopes for prosperity had been raised by the collapse of Communism. The coming years will show whether the sharp economic decline experienced by many of these people triggers social violence. ✍

Arousal

How does frustration lead to aggression? One answer is that it simply leads to general arousal, which then "energizes" aggressive behavior, particularly in a person who has already learned to respond in aggressive ways (Bandura, 1973). Classic learning theories suggest that anything which increases general arousal or "drive" increases the probability of dominant responses. If aggressive responses are dominant (that is, well learned), then increased arousal will lead to increased aggression (Berkowitz, 1983b; Zillman, 1988).

Schachter and Singer's (1962) two-component theory of emotion (see Chapter 5 for details) suggests another way increased general arousal can influence aggression. As you'll recall, this theory proposes that a person is more likely to experience a strong emotion when physiologically aroused in a setting that leads the

Is aggression innate or learned?

person to attribute that arousal to an emotion. The implication for human aggression: Anything that increases unexplained physiological arousal may contribute to hostile aggression. For example, fear, sexual excitement, or even physical exercise may facilitate aggression, particularly if the aroused person attributes his or her arousal to anger (Zillman, 1983).

Research has in fact demonstrated that arousal from an unrelated source can increase later angry aggression. One study found that after being insulted by a confederate, subjects were more aggressive if they had just watched a sexually arousing film than if they had watched a nonarousing film (Zillman, 1971). Presumably, subjects mistakenly interpreted their heightened arousal as being hostile rather than sexual. A similar experiment had male subjects read a sexually explicit passage from the novel *Rabbit, Run* by John Updike. While they read, a confederate "distracted" them with electric shocks. Some subjects were told that their arousal was the result of reading the sexual passage, others that it was caused by the shocks, and yet others that it was caused by a pill they had taken. The results: Subjects who attributed their arousal to the shocks were more aggressive when shocking the confederate in retaliation than were subjects who attributed their arousal to the sexual passage or to the pill (Geen, Rokosky, & Pigg, 1972). In other words, sexual arousal may be particularly likely to foster aggression when it is misattributed to anger. A number of other studies have also shown that sexual arousal can contribute to later aggression (Donnerstein, Donnerstein, & Evans, 1975; Zillman, Hoyt, & Day, 1974).

In sum, frustration and situations that produce arousal are two environmental factors that can lead to aggressive behavior. But there is another, even more fundamental environmental influence on aggression: namely, learning, in all its varied forms.

Social learning of aggression: do violent toys foster violent behavior in children?

Social Learning and Aggression

Do people learn to be aggressive? If so, how? In his influential social learning analysis of aggression, Albert Bandura (1973) argued that people may learn to be aggressive (or nonaggressive) through both operant conditioning and observational learning.

The basic principle of operant (also known as instrumental) conditioning is straightforward when applied to aggression: The probability that aggressive behaviors will occur increases when they are rewarded. The effects of instrumental conditioning on aggression have been demonstrated in both animals and people. Peaceful rats can be taught to attack other rats if they are deprived of water and rewarded with a drink for attacking (Ulrich, Johnson, Richardson, & Wolff, 1963). The positive reinforcement of food and the negative reinforcement of terminating painful shocks can also be potent rewards for aggressive behaviors in animals (Hutchinson, 1972; Scott, 1973).

The rewards that mold human aggression are even more numerous, including both primary (unlearned) reinforcers such as food, drink, and sex, and secondary (learned) reinforcers such as money, material goods, and social status. Studies indicate that when aggression brings people candy, material goods, money, or social approval, it is more likely to occur in the future (Buss, 1971; Gaebelein, 1973; Walters & Brown, 1963). A telling field study observed children's attempts to retaliate in response to other children's aggression. When children succeeded (for example, by regaining an expropriated toy), they subsequently tended to be more aggressive. Apparently, if you fight and win, you're more likely to fight again (Patterson, Littman, & Bricker, 1967).

Of course, people do not learn to aggress merely by trying out violent behaviors in a hit-or-miss fashion, hoping for rewards. They often learn by observing others and imitating their behavior. The importance of observational learning is central to Bandura's (1973) analysis: Not only can people become aggressive just by watching others, they can also learn through observation when aggression is rewarded and when it is punished. In addition, aggressive models don't only show us *how* to behave aggressively; they sometimes show us that it is *acceptable* to behave in violent ways in particular settings.

In a classic series of experiments, Bandura, Ross, and Ross (1961, 1963b) demonstrated that children can learn to behave aggressively simply by watching aggressive models. In one experiment, nursery school children were taken to a room containing a number of toys, including a "Bobo doll," a large inflated clown weighted on the bottom so that whenever it was knocked down it popped back upright. Some children observed an adult punch and kick the Bobo doll while yelling statements like, "Sock him in the nose" and "Hit him down." Other children watched the adult play peacefully. Later, the children were allowed to play freely with the toys, and their behavior was recorded by hidden observers. Children who had been exposed to aggressive models were significantly more aggressive, often in ways that exactly imitated the adults. Boys tended to imitate adults' aggression more than girls did, and both boys and girls tended to imitate male models more than female models. Furthermore, the children imitated aggressive models more when the models' aggression was rewarded (by another adult giving them soft drinks, candy, and compliments) and less when it was punished (by another adult scolding them and spanking them with a rolled-up magazine) (Bandura, 1965).

In these Bobo doll studies, children do not always exactly imitate the aggression observed; sometimes they aggress in novel ways. Thus, watching models does not merely teach children specific aggressive behaviors; it may release their inhibitions against aggression in general. Furthermore, children have been observed performing aggressive acts they learned in Bobo doll experiments as much as eight months later (Hicks, 1965, 1968), and their learned behavior is sometimes directed against real people as well (Hanratty, O'Neal, & Sulzer, 1972). This last point is particularly important, for in the case of the original Bobo doll studies, you could argue that children weren't *really* behaving aggressively, for they weren't harming other people.

The Mass Media and Aggression

Bandura's analysis implies that besides learning aggressive behavior by directly observing others, people may learn it by watching violence in TV shows, videos, and movies. It also suggests that people may become less inhibited after viewing media violence.

Imitative violence clearly occurs in real life as well as in Bobo doll experiments. For example, recent research shows that suicide rates increase significantly after highly publicized suicides and that people who attempt an imitative suicide are often similar in some way (for example, in age or gender) to the person described in the publicized suicide (Bollen & Phillips, 1982; Phillips &

Carstensen, 1990). Auto fatalities also increase after publicized suicides (Phillips, 1979), suggesting that some "car accidents" are in fact suicides. In 1987, Southern California experienced an outbreak of "freeway shootings" in which motorists shot and sometimes killed one another. Although initially engendered by frustration at traffic gridlock, these shootings were propagated through media coverage and subsequent imitation. Such "copycat" crimes are more likely to be committed by some people—for example, those with prior criminal records—than others (Surette, 1990).

A careful analysis found evidence for yet another kind of imitative violence: Homicide rates increased by more than 12% on average following heavyweight championship prizefights, and this increase tended to be greater following highly publicized fights (Phillips, 1983). These findings are significant because they suggest that media violence may inspire not only direct imitation, but unrelated kinds of aggression as well.

Media violence influences actual aggressive behavior in other ways as well. Social psychologists speculate that media violence can desensitize viewers so that they become less upset by actual violence. Both children (Cline, Croft, & Courrier, 1973) and adults (Thomas, 1982) who view violent television programming seem to experience less physical arousal when they subsequently behave aggressively. In addition, watching excessive media violence may influence viewers' long-term attitudes and values about aggression and about the general levels of violence in society (Gerbner, Gross, Signorielli, & Morgan, 1980). Compared with people who watch little television, heavy viewers of TV overestimate the prevalence of violence in society, the percentage of people employed in law enforcement, and the possibility that violence will affect them.

Aggressive Cues and the Weapons Effect

Violent TV may instigate aggression in still another way. Drawing on recent research on memory, Leonard Berkowitz (1984) has proposed that viewing TV violence primes aggressive ideas and thoughts, which then facilitate aggressive behaviors. In one experiment, subjects viewed film of either a brutal prizefight or a footrace (Berkowitz, 1965). Later they were given the opportunity to deliver a supposed electric shock to another student, who was described as either a college boxer or a speech major. The results were clear: Subjects who had seen the boxing movie were more aggressive toward the "boxer" than toward the "speech major." Boxing had become a cue (something like a conditioned stimulus) to aggression for these people.

Social psychologists have focused considerable attention on one specific kind of aggressive cue: namely, weapons. Clearly, weapons are directly involved in many kinds of aggression; almost half of all murders in the United States are committed with guns. Do weapons have more subtle effects as well? For example, do they sometimes serve as conditioned cues to aggression? This is a question with important social consequences. In a classic and controversial experiment, Berkowitz and LePage (1967) showed that after receiving shocks from a peer (actually a confederate), subjects gave more shocks back in return when a gun, as opposed to a badminton racket, was lying on a nearby table. Berkowitz (1968) noted, "Guns not only permit violence, they can stimulate it as well. The finger pulls the trigger, but the trigger may also be pulling the finger."

Some studies have failed to replicate this "weapons effect," and some have even found that the presence of a gun *reduces* aggressive behavior in certain situations (Turner & Leyens, 1992). Page and Scheidt (1971) attributed the weapons effect in experiments to *demand characteristics*—that is, they contended that the subjects saw through the purpose of such studies. Demand characteristics are unlikely to provide a complete explanation, however, because weapons effects are sometimes found even in field studies in which subjects don't realize they are subjects (Turner & Leyens, 1992). Indeed, the more naive subjects tend to be in such studies and the less worried they are about being evaluated, the *more* they tend to show the weapons effect (Carlson, Marcus-Newhall, & Miller, 1990).

Other factors also undoubtedly determine the ways guns influence our thoughts and behavior. These include our cultural and personal attitudes toward guns and aggression, whether we fear retaliation in the presence of guns, whether we have had bad personal experiences with guns in the past, and whether guns are associated with other kinds of thoughts (for example, revenge fantasies) (Toch & Lizotte, 1992; Turner & Leyens, 1992).

TV shows and movies may help make weapons "aggressive cues" when they repeatedly associate weapons with vivid portrayals of *justified* violence. TV may further stimulate real-life aggression by constantly providing people with such cues to aggression in the comfort of their living rooms. The learning of novel aggressive cues from violent TV, as well as the power of these cues to trigger real-life aggression, can be seen in a carefully controlled experiment by Wendy Josephson (1987), who showed violent and nonviolent TV programs to 396 second- and third-grade Canadian boys. In the violent program, a SWAT (Special Weapons and Tactics) police team killed or knocked unconscious a group of snipers who had murdered a police officer in cold blood. The SWAT officers communicated throughout the TV segment via walkie-talkies. The nonviolent TV show portrayed a police officer coaching a boys' motorbike racing team.

After viewing the TV shows, the boys played a game of floor hockey in a gymnasium. But before they played, each boy was asked by the experimenter to give a pregame interview "like they do on the radio." The interview was conducted with either a tape recorder and microphone or with a walkie-talkie. Observers then rated the boys' verbal and physical aggression during the hockey game. In this ingenious experiment, Josephson found that boys who had watched the violent TV show were more aggressive, particularly those who were interviewed with a walkie-talkie. The walkie-talkie, which had played a critical role in the violent TV show, served as an aggressive cue.

The Effects of TV Violence on Children

Josephson's experiment is one of many that look at the effects of violent TV programming on children. Children may be particularly susceptible to such

A scene from the TV cartoon show "Speed Racer." Does media violence like this foster aggressive behavior in children?

programming, for they lack a mature understanding of what they see on TV and may be more easily influenced than adults (Liebert & Sprafkin, 1988). Clearly, the effect of TV viewing on children is a topic of great social importance, and both national commissions (National Commission on the Causes and Prevention of Violence, 1969) and Surgeon General's reports (Cisin et al., 1972) have focused on the potentially negative effects of violent TV on children.

Before we assess these effects, let's first examine how violent the content of TV programming actually is. Since the late 1960s, George Gerbner and his colleagues at the University of Pennsylvania have conducted careful content analyses of the violence depicted in prime-time and weekend daytime television (Gerbner, Gross, Signorielli, & Morgan, 1986). Their data show that U.S. TV programming is very violent and that the level of violence has remained relatively constant over the past 20 years (see Figure 10.8). Particularly distressing are the levels of violence in cartoons, which are directed specifically at children. According to Gerbner, the typical TV cartoon portrays an aggressive act once every three minutes, on average.

At the request of *TV Guide* magazine, the Center for Media and Public Affairs taped and analyzed the programming of ten major TV channels in Washington, D.C., for 19 consecutive hours on April 2, 1992. Their results: "A total of 1,846 individual acts of violence; 175 scenes in which violence resulted in one or more fatalities; 389 scenes depicting serious assaults; 362 scenes involving gunplay; 673 depictions of punching, pushing, slapping, dragging, and other physically hostile acts; 226 scenes of menacing threats with weapons" (*TV Guide*, August 22–28, 1992, p. 10).

And children watch this violence. By the mid-1980s, the average U.S. household had a TV set turned on more than seven hours a day (Steinberg, 1985). Infants less than 1 year old are exposed to more than one hour of TV each day

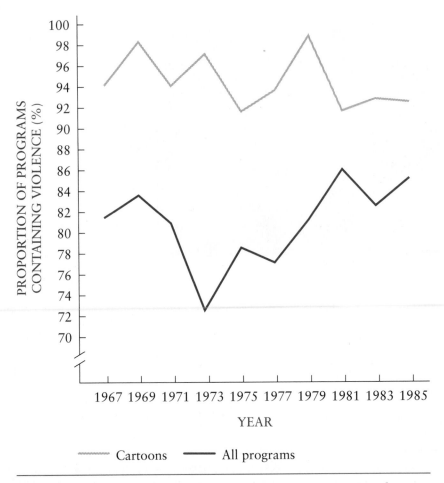

FIGURE 10.8 Percentage of U.S. TV programs containing violence, 1967–1985.

(Hollenbeck & Slaby, 1979); by early adolescence, children view almost four hours daily (Liebert & Sprafkin, 1988). Similar patterns of childhood TV viewing are found in other developed countries as well (Murray, 1980).

Does watching all this TV violence actually influence children's behavior? Many experimental and correlational studies suggest that it does. First, laboratory experiments show that immediately after viewing violent TV shows, children often behave and play more aggressively (Liebert & Baron, 1972; Steuer, Applefield, & Smith, 1971; Wood, Wong, & Chachere, 1991) and choose aggressive solutions to social problems (Leifer & Roberts, 1972).

A set of three carefully conducted field experiments in the United States and Belgium showed that viewing violent films significantly increased the aggressiveness of juvenile delinquents living in minimum-security institutions (Parke,

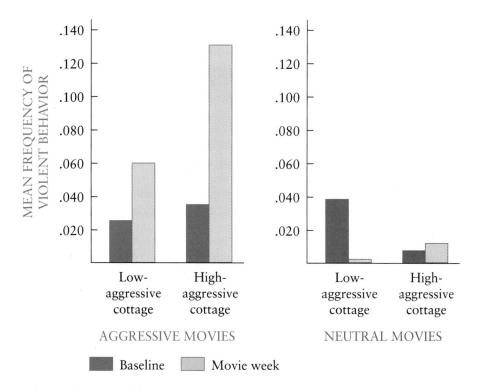

The results showed that boys who viewed violent movies tended to become more aggressive, and this effect was most pronounced for boys who were highly aggressive to start with.

FIGURE 10.9 Violent behaviors of juvenile-delinquent boys after exposure to violent or nonviolent movies. *Source:* Adapted from Parke et al. (1977).

Berkowitz, Leyens, West, & Sebastian, 1977). In the Belgian experiment, boys living in different cottages saw either violent or nonviolent movies each night for a week. Observers periodically rated different aspects of the boys' aggressiveness—for example, their physical threats (fist-waving), physical attacks (hitting, slapping, kicking), verbal aggression (cursing, insulting), and noninterpersonal physical aggression (hitting or breaking an object). These observations were made during a "baseline" period (the week before the boys saw the films) and also during the week of watching the films. Each boy's reputed aggressiveness was also assessed. The results, shown in Figure 10.9, suggest that viewing violent movies particularly increased the physical aggressiveness of the boys who were the most aggressive to start with. This study makes the important point that children are not affected equally by violent entertainment.

Correlational studies also suggest a relationship between TV viewing and aggression in children (Freedman, 1992; Huesmann, Eron, Berkowitz, & Chaffee,

1992). One large-scale research effort studied 1,505 children in the United States, Finland, Poland, and Australia (Eron & Huesmann, 1986; Huesmann, Lagerspetz, & Eron, 1984). All of these related studies found significant correlations—with correlation coefficients generally ranging from .2 to .3—between the amount of violent TV children watch and their aggression as rated by peers. These correlations, although not strong, were quite consistent across studies. Similar findings come from other correlational studies. A meta-analysis of 188 studies on TV viewing and aggression conducted from 1957 to 1990 found an average correlation between TV viewing and aggression of .31 (Comstock & Paik, 1990).

The relationship between TV viewing and aggression seems particularly strong for boys who identify intensely with the violent characters they see on TV, for girls who prefer "masculine" activities, and for children in general who are not socially or intellectually skilled (Eron & Huesmann, 1986). The relationship between TV viewing and aggression may sometimes be reciprocal; that is, violent TV increases aggressiveness, and aggressiveness also leads to increased viewing of violent TV (Huesmann, Lagerspetz, & Eron, 1984). Thus, for some children at least, viewing violence and acting aggressively seem to feed on each other.

Using data collected over a period of 22 years, L. Rowell Huesmann and his colleagues (Huesmann, 1986; Huesmann, Eron, Lefkowitz, & Walder, 1984) found a significant relationship between subjects' viewing of violent TV at age 8 and their aggressiveness and level of criminal behavior at age 30 (see Figure 10.10). An analysis of these same data found a significant correlation of .41 between amount of violent TV viewed at age 8 and a composite index of aggressive behaviors at age 30 (Eron, 1987).

A fascinating quasi-experimental study of TV viewing and aggression found that when TV broadcasting was introduced in 1974 to a town in the Canadian Rockies that had previously been without TV, children's general levels of aggressiveness increased, whereas in two nearby comparison towns that already received TV broadcasts, children's aggressiveness did not increase (Joy, Kimball, & Zabrack, 1986; see Chapter 2).

Dozens of studies have investigated the relationship between TV violence and children's aggressiveness. Virtually no researchers in the area doubt at this point that viewing violent TV is correlated with aggression in children (Freedman, 1992; Huesmann, Eron, Berkowitz, & Chaffee, 1992). Although some social psychologists have questioned whether there is a proven *cause–effect* link between TV viewing and aggression (see Freedman, 1984, 1992), the preponderance of research evidence and expert opinion supports just this conclusion (Dorr & Kovaric, 1980; Friedrich-Cofer & Huston, 1986; Hearold, 1986; Huesmann et al., 1992; Wood et al., 1991).

In a comprehensive meta-analysis of 230 studies, Susan Hearold (1986) found consistent evidence that TV violence is related to children's aggressiveness. In addition, she observed the following trends: The effects of viewing violent TV tend to increase with age for boys but decrease for girls; TV violence encourages real-life violence, particularly when it is realistic and portrayed as justified; and finally, children need not be aroused to be affected by TV violence, but frustration

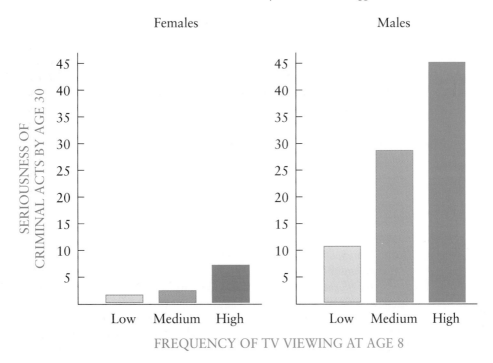

Eron (1987) argued that specific programs viewed in childhood do not directly influence aggression during adulthood. Rather, the effects of watching TV are indirect, changing attitudes and teaching people aggressive behaviors and aggressive styles of social interaction.

FIGURE 10.10 Seriousness of criminal acts before age 30 as a function of frequency of TV viewing at age 8. *Source:* Adapted from Eron (1987).

and arousal can heighten the effects of media violence on children's aggressiveness. Thus, research is moving from the simple question "Is there a link between violent-TV viewing and aggression in children?" to more complex questions such as, "Which children, in what situations, are most likely to be stimulated to violence by viewing violent TV?"

Media Sex and Aggression

The mass media may influence aggression yet another way: through the sexual content of their programming. The effects of media "obscenity" and "pornography" has been the topic of two controversial government reports (Report of the Commission on Obscenity and Pornography, 1970; Attorney General's Commission on Pornography, 1986) and remains a subject of intense debate among both government officials and scholars (Einsiedel, 1988; Koop, 1987; Linz & Donnerstein, 1988; Linz, Donnerstein, & Penrod, 1987; Wilcox, 1987). What does social psychology research tell us about this provocative topic? Might portrayals of sex be linked to aggressive behavior? What kinds of sexual material is most likely to foster aggression? And what kinds of aggression are most stimulated by sexual material?

We've already described some theory and research that addresses these questions. For example, we noted that any kind of arousal can contribute to angry aggression (Zillman, 1983), and sexual excitement is certainly a kind of arousal. In addition, social learning theory suggests that viewers of *violent* pornography may learn new forms of sexual aggression from it (Byrne & Kelley, 1984), that they may become "desensitized" to sexual violence, and that they may (falsely) learn that others frequently derive sexual pleasure from aggression. Finally, the constant combination of sex and aggression in the mass media may lead people to cognitively associate the two and so classically condition sexual arousal to aggressive cues and aggressive behavior to sexual cues (Malamuth, 1984). In simple terms, media combinations of sex and aggression may lead some people to become sexually "turned on" by violence.

Does recent research provide any support for these social psychology perspectives on media sex and aggression? Unfortunately, yes. A number of recent experimental studies suggest that violent pornography can increase aggression, particularly by men against women. In one experiment, 120 male subjects were angered by either a male or a female confederate. Subjects then viewed either an erotic film (a couple having intercourse), an aggressive–erotic film (a man with a gun breaks into a woman's home and forces her to have sexual intercourse), or a neutral film (a talk-show interview). Finally, the subjects participated in a separate "learning experiment" in which they could deliver supposed electric shocks to the confederate who had earlier angered them (Donnerstein, 1980).

The results of this experiment are disturbing: Subjects who had viewed the aggressive–erotic film were most aggressive, particularly against the woman confederate (see Figure 10.11). A related set of experiments found again that aggressive–erotic films increased angered males' aggression against females but not against males. Furthermore, they found that when aggressive–erotic films suggested that the depicted women enjoyed forced sex, even nonangered men increased their aggressiveness against women (Donnerstein & Berkowitz, 1981).

Violent pornography not only may stimulate aggression against women, it may also modify the viewer's long-term beliefs and attitudes as well (Linz, Wilson, & Donnerstein, 1992). In one study, men at the University of Manitoba watched either nonsexual movies or movies in which a man sexually overpowered a woman. A week later, in a seemingly separate study, the men completed a questionnaire that assessed their attitudes toward women and toward rape. The men who had viewed the sexually violent movies expressed a greater tolerance toward rape and greater agreement that women enjoy rape (Malamuth & Check, 1981). A replication found that viewing sexually violent movies increased belief in rape myths, particularly in men who already possessed negative, aggressive attitudes toward women (Malamuth & Check, 1985).

Sexually explicit movies seem most likely to foster rape myths and change sexual attitudes when they combine depictions of aggression and sex (Donnerstein,

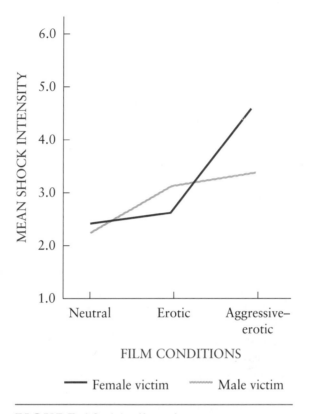

FIGURE 10.11 Effect of aggressive–erotic films on aggression. *Source:* Adapted from Donnerstein (1980.)

1984; Imrich, Mullin, & Linz, 1990). Indeed, the violent content may be more responsible for the antisocial consequences than the sexual content. "Slasher" movies are not terribly graphic sexually; however, they present vivid violence against women in a nonexplicit sexual context. "Slasher" movies, like violent pornography, can make men more tolerant toward sexual violence and rape (Imrich et al., 1990; Linz et al., 1992).

Correlational as well as experimental studies suggest a link between pornography and aggression against women. Although some early studies suggested that liberalized laws against sexually explicit movies and publications had neutral or even positive consequences, more recent evidence tends to find a connection between access to pornography and aggressive crimes (Ben-Veniste, 1971; Byrne & Kelley, 1984; Court, 1984; Kutchinsky, 1973). For example, in recent times the crime of rape has become more common in societies and communities with liberal pornography laws. One study found that when legal restraints were imposed against free access to pornography in the state of Hawaii from 1974 to 1976, rape rates tended to decrease in comparison with the preceding and following years (Court, 1984).

A number of studies have found substantial correlations between sales of sexually explicit men's magazines (such as *Hustler, Oui,* and *Playboy*) and rape rates in various states in the United States (Baron & Straus, 1984, 1985, 1986; Scott & Schwalm, 1988). Of course, correlation does not prove causation. Indeed, sales of "outdoors" and "masculine interest" magazines such as *Field and Stream, Guns and Ammo,* and *The American Hunter* also correlate with rape rates (Scott & Schwalm, 1988). This suggests that consumption of "masculine interest" magazines and rape rates may all be a function of a third variable—for example, "macho" attitudes and sex roles, which vary somewhat from region to region in the United States.

While the cause–effect relations between real-life viewing of sexually explicit materials and aggression are undoubtedly complex, one thing is certain: The production and distribution of such materials have increased in recent decades (Lederer, 1980; McCarthy, 1980; Williams, 1979). As of 1980, in the United States alone the sale of erotically explicit magazines was a business earning $4 billion annually (Lederer, 1980). And although it is difficult to measure trends in the content of pornographic materials precisely, pornography seems to have become more violent in the past two decades, particularly in the late 1970s (Linz et al., 1987). With the advent of home video recorders, erotically explicit films are available to a larger audience than ever before. Finally, it's important to note that today, even standard TV and movie fare contains considerable sexual violence as a matter of course. Recent content analyses of Hollywood movies show that one out of eight films contains depictions of rapes, and popular R-rated movies contain as much sexual violence as "hard-core" X-rated movies (Radecki, 1990; Yang & Linz, 1990).

Sexual Violence

Research on pornography relates to a much larger social issue, the incidence of sexual violence in general. One survey of 500 women in Albuquerque, New Mexico, found that 14% had been victims of attempted rape, and 10% had been victims of actual rape. In general, "invasive" sexual assaults (undesired fondling, attempted rape, and rape) were carried out by acquaintances, friends, and relatives, whereas "noninvasive" assaults (obscene phone calls, offenses by "flashers" and "Peeping Toms") were perpetrated by strangers (DiVasto et al., 1984).

Another study underlines the finding that violence, including sexual violence, frequently occurs in close relationships. More than 500 college students were surveyed to assess violence in their heterosexual relationships. Over half the men and women reported committing some violent act against their partner, such as throwing something, pushing, or slapping. Two questions in the survey assessed sexual violence: How often have you "used strong physical force to try to engage in a sex act against other's will," and how often have you "used violence to try to engage in a sex act against other's will"? Almost 12% of male respondents, and under 2% of female respondents, acknowledged engaging in such coercion (Sigelman, Berry, & Wiles, 1984).

In an attempt to identify potential rapists, Malamuth (1981) asked college men to rate their likelihood of raping a woman if they could be absolutely assured that they would not be apprehended or punished. Disturbingly, 35% admitted to some possibility of committing such a rape, whereas the remaining 65% responded that it "was not at all likely." A separate survey found that 15% of 201 college men surveyed reported "having forced intercourse at least once or twice." The subjects completed a battery of personality and attitude measures, and the sexually coercive men were characterized as irresponsible, lacking in social conscience, and possessing negative and aggressive attitudes toward women (Rapaport & Burkhart, 1984). Malamuth, Check, and Briere (1986) extended these findings. They identified three groups of men: those who reported experiencing no, moderate, or high sexual arousal to the use of force. Men who were aroused by force tended to be more accepting of violence against women and dominance over women; however, the groups did not differ in their sex drive or degree of sexual inhibition.

Feminist analyses of sexual violence against women have sometimes argued that sexual violence and rape are acts of power and dominance rather than sexual acts (Brownmiller, 1975; Dworkin, 1987; Groth & Birnbaum, 1979). While the results of the Malamuth, Check, and Briere study don't necessarily support this strong conclusion, they certainly show that men's motivations to dominate and hurt women play a greater role in sexual violence than people generally think, and their sexual motivations play a weaker role.

Causes of Family Violence

Now that we have examined many different causes of violence, let's analyze how some of these causes come together to produce a problem of enormous social importance: family violence. The topic of family violence came out of the closet and onto the front pages in the late 1980s largely because of one highly publicized story, that of Elizabeth "Lisa" Steinberg, a 6-year-old girl who died after being brutally beaten by her adoptive father (*Newsweek*, November 23, 1987). Both child abuse and spouse abuse are quite common in the United States (Gelles & Cornell, 1990; Keller & Erne, 1983; Sigler, 1989), and both kinds of abuse are almost certainly underreported in "official" statistics.

Is it possible to identify people who are likely to become abusive parents or spouses? A study of 2,000 married couples identified 25 characteristics that predicted wife-beating or husband-beating. Using these 25 items as a checklist, the researchers assigned each couple a score from zero to 25, depending on how many of the 25 characteristics were true of the couple (Straus, Gelles, & Steinmetz, 1980). The checklist and how well it predicted spouse abuse is shown

Lisa Steinberg—one of the many victims of family violence.

in Figure 10.12. The same researchers also developed a similar checklist to predict child abuse. This list of 16 family characteristics and its relation to child abuse is shown Figure 10.13.

The checklists for both spouse abuse and child abuse point to some important contributors to family violence—economic deprivation, large families, drunkenness, stress, and a history of violence in preceding generations—and they serve to remind us that broad social factors can have a powerful influence on family violence. Of course, this is true for violence in general as well (Anderson, 1987).

But if broad social and economic factors help predict and explain family violence, they by no means tell the whole story. Violence occurs in families of all classes, races, religions, occupations, and education levels (Sigler, 1989). What individual characteristics distinguish people who abuse family members? Gender is one: Men are more likely than women to batter their spouses, and this pattern has been true throughout history (Caesar & Hamberger, 1989). Many men who physically abuse women suffer from negative personality characteristics: low self-esteem, feelings of inadequacy, and poor impulse control (Dobash & Dobash, 1977–78; Hershorn & Rosenbaum, 1985; Martin, 1982). Similarly,

CHARACTERISTIC PREDICTORS OF BOTH WIFE-BEATING AND HUSBAND BEATING

1. Husband employed part time or unemployed
2. Family income under $6,000
3. Husband a manual worker
4. Husband very worried about economic security
5. Wife very dissatisfied with standard of living
6. Two or more children
7. Disagreement over children
8. Grew up in family in which father hit mother
9. Married less than ten years
10. Age 30 or under
11. Nonwhite racial group
12. Above-average score on Marital Conflict Index
13. Very high score on Stress Index
14. Wife dominant in family decisions
15. Husband was verbally aggressive to wife
16. Wife was verbally aggressive to husband
17. Gets drunk but is not alcoholic
18. Lived in neighborhood less than two years
19. No participation in organized religion

CHARACTERISTIC PREDICTORS OF WIFE-BEATING

20. Husband dominant in family decisions
21. Wife is full-time housewife
22. Wife very worried about economic security

CHARACTERISTIC PREDICTORS OF HUSBAND BEATING

23. Wife was physically punished at age 13-plus by father
24. Wife grew up in family in which mother hit father
25. Wife a manual worker

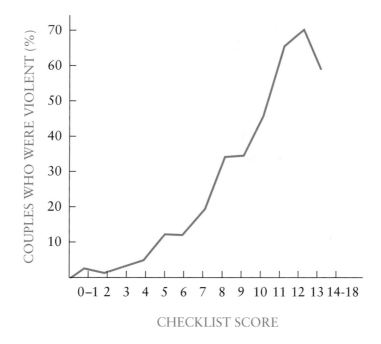

FIGURE 10.12 Factors that predict spouse abuse. *Source:* Adapted from Straus, Gelles, and Steinmetz (1980).

parents who physically abuse their children often show personality and emotional problems: They are socially isolated, emotionally defensive, insecure, and have poor communication skills (Newberger & Bourne, 1985; Shupe, Stacey, & Hazlewood, 1987; Steele, 1975).

Environmental and relationship factors contribute to family violence as well. Many abusive spouses and parents come from abusive families, and thus

465

IMPORTANT FOR CHILD ABUSE BY EITHER PARENT

1. Was verbally aggressive to the child (insulted, smashed things, etc.)
2. Above-average conflict between husband and wife
3. Husband was physically violent to wife

IMPORTANT FOR ABUSE BY MOTHERS

4. Husband was verbally aggressive to wife
5. Husband a manual worker
6. Husband dissatisfied with standard of living
7. Wife a manual worker
8. Wife age 30 or under
9. Wife was physically punished at age 13-plus by father

IMPORTANT FOR ABUSE BY FATHER

10. Two or more children at home
11. Wife is fulltime housewife
12. Married less than ten years
13. Lived in neighborhood less than two years
14. No participation by father in organized groups
15. Husband was physically punished at age 13-plus by mother
16. Grew up in fa nily where mother hit father

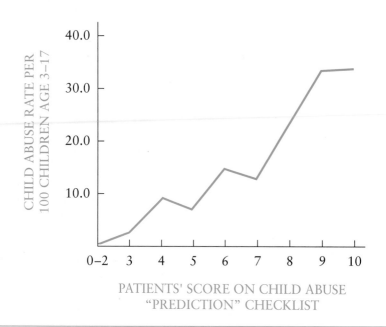

FIGURE 10.13 Factors that predict child abuse. *Source:* Straus, Gelles, and Steinmetz (1980).

they are embedded in a "cycle of violence" (Bakan, 1971; Flammang, 1970; Shupe, Stacey, & Hazlewood, 1987; Stark & Flitcraft, 1987). Not surprisingly, marriages in which one or both partners are abusive are often troubled and unstable; they often suffer from sexual jealousies, and their problems are frequently aggravated by substance abuse (Okun, 1986).

Clearly, family violence is a multifaceted problem with multiple causes. Ferreting out the causes of family violence in particular and aggression in general is an important task for social scientists. Summary Table 10.1 reviews many of the explanations of aggression we have discussed. We turn next to a related and extremely important practical question: How can family violence and aggression in general be reduced?

SUMMARY TABLE 10.1 Explanations of Aggression			
	Level of Explanation	*Theories*	*Variables/Processes Studied*
Group level	Biological group	Instinct theories	Biological evolution
	Social groups	*Biological*	Social norms, cross-cultural variations
	Wars and the legitimization of violence		Effect of war on later domestic violence
Individual level	Heredity and physiology		Brain structures, hormones, sex differences, heritability
	Past environment	Social learning theory	Classical conditioning, operant conditioning, observational learning; media effects
	Current environment	Frustration-aggression hypothesis	Modeling effects; media effects; pain, heat, situationally produced frustration
		Aggressive cues	"Weapons effect"; violent pornography; media effects
Mediating variables	Personality traits		Stability of aggressiveness over time; personality traits of sexually violent men and abusive spouses
	Attitudes		Effects of pornography on attitudes toward women and toward rape; media effects
	Emotional arousal	Schachter-Singer theory	Effects of extraneous arousal, sexual arousal
		Learning theory *B*	Effects of arousal on learned aggressive responses
	Attributions		Attributions about causes of frustrating events; attributions of arousal in situations that lead to anger

REDUCING AGGRESSION

[Abusive men] must be taught to recognize warning signs and redirect their anger. "We don't say, 'Never get angry,' " says Carol Arthur, the Minneapolis [domestic abuse] project's executive director. "Anger is a normal, healthy emotion. What we work with is a way to express it." Men describe to the group their most violent incident. One man told about throwing food in his wife's face at dinner and then beating her to the floor—only to see his two small children huddled terrified under the table. Arthur remembers his self-assessment at that moment: "My God, what must they be thinking about me? I didn't want to be like that."

If the police and the courts crack down on abusers, and programs exist to help change violent behavior, victims will be less likely to take—and less justified in taking—the law into their own hands. And once the cycle of violence winds down in this generation, it is less likely to poison the next. That would be a family value worth fighting for.

—*Time*, January 18, 1993

How can we—both individually and as a society—control and prevent aggression? Many techniques have been proposed (Baron, 1983; Center for Research on Aggression, 1983). Let's focus here on six strategies studied by psychologists: (1) venting aggressive impulses to reduce subsequent aggression (also known as "catharsis"), (2) punishing aggression, (3) providing counseling and social services to aggressive individuals and their victims, (4) creating responses that are incompatible with aggression, (5) providing social restraints to aggression, and (6) using cognitive strategies to deal with aggression.

Catharsis

The concept of catharsis originated with Aristotle (*Poetics*, Book 6), who argued that by viewing powerful emotional events in the theater, people could purge themselves of these emotions. More than 2,000 years later, Sigmund Freud extended the notion of catharsis to aggression. He postulated that aggressive acts could sometimes "drain off" aggressive impulses. But Freud was doubtful, at least in his early writings, whether symbolic aggression could lead to catharsis: "The reaction of an injured person to a trauma has really only . . . a 'cathartic' effect if it is expressed in an adequate reaction like revenge" (Breuer & Freud, 1961 [1893], p. 5).

The notion of catharsis seems consistent with common sense. People often say they need to "let off steam" or "get something off their chest." Numerous studies have looked for catharsis effects, but in general such studies offer little support for the proposition that catharsis can serve as a general technique for controlling aggression (Geen & Quanty, 1977; Quanty, 1976). Let's summarize some of the evidence.

Experimental subjects sometimes show reductions in the physiological arousal caused by anger (for example, raised blood pressure) if given the opportunity to deliver a supposed shock to the person who angered them (Hokanson, 1961; Hokanson & Burgess, 1962; Hokanson & Shetler, 1961). In one study, subjects vented their aggressive feelings toward a tormentor in one of three ways: through physical aggression, verbal aggression, or fantasy aggression (by

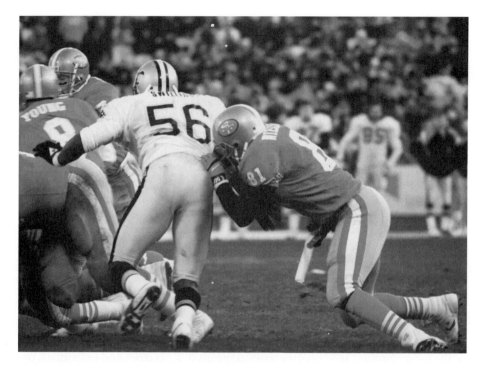

Do athletic contests serve to vent aggressive impulses?

writing aggressive stories) (Hokanson & Burgess, 1962). Only physical aggression successfully reduced physiological arousal (thus providing some support for Breuer and Freud's insight that only true revenge is really satisfying).

Of course, reduced arousal does not necessarily mean reduced aggression. Other studies have investigated the value of catharsis in actually reducing behavioral aggression. In general, this research indicates that physically letting off steam through sports or exercise does not serve the function of catharsis. For example, Patterson (1974) found that, if anything, high school football players were *more* aggressive after a season of football than before it. Apparently, playing football encouraged aggression rather than serving to vent it. Of course, football is a particularly violent contact sport. But a laboratory study on the cathartic value of physical violence that allowed some subjects to pound a rubber mallet before delivering a supposed shock to the confederate who had angered them found that even this relatively benign activity did nothing to vent their aggression.

Verbal catharsis, like general physical activity, does not consistently reduce subsequent physical aggression in experimental studies; it may even increase aggression under certain circumstances (Rothaus & Worchel, 1964; Wheeler & Caggiula, 1966). Focusing on some real-life consequences of verbal catharsis, Straus (1974) found that the verbal venting of hostility seemed to encourage rather than discourage physical aggression between spouses. These findings were replicated in a subsequent study of 2,143 couples that concluded, "For those who engage in little or no verbal aggression, there is little or no physical violence (less than half of 1 percent)." On the other hand, "a clear majority of the top quarter [of married couples] who express conflict through verbal blasts were violent" (Straus, Gelles, & Steinmetz, 1980, p. 169).

Does direct physical aggression serve a cathartic function? A number of experiments suggest that people who are given an opportunity to aggress directly against someone who has angered them may actually become *more* aggressive subsequently and derogate as well as punish their victim (Berkowitz & Geen, 1966, 1967; Buss, 1966; Ebbesen, Duncan, & Konecni, 1975; Geen, 1968; Geen, Stonner, & Shope, 1975). Perhaps the Roman historian Tacitus was right when he wrote, "It is part of human nature to hate the man you have hurt."

This effect—that aggressive behavior leads to further aggression—might be a result of a number of psychological processes. When people aggress against someone, their aggression is "disinhibited." Furthermore, upon aggressing successfully against a tormentor, people learn that their aggression will not be punished and may feel the "positive reinforcement" of revenge. Finally, dissonance theory (see Chapter 6) predicts that after behaving aggressively, people need to justify their bad behavior and may do so by derogating their victim. Derogation may then lead to a vicious cycle of further aggression.

Punishing Aggression

Punishment—delivering an aversive stimulus after an undesired behavior—is one of the most common and commonsensical means that societies and individuals use to control aggression (Blanchard & Blanchard, 1986). Legal systems punish violent criminals by throwing them into jail. Athletic teams punish overly violent players by suspending them. And parents punish aggressive children, sometimes physically (by spanking them) and sometimes more peacefully (giving them "time out").

Sometimes, punishment works. But the noted behaviorist B. F. Skinner (1938) argued that punishment suppresses a behavior only temporarily. For example, a girl who is punished by her father for hitting her little sister may be temporarily deterred by the punishment and desist from hitting, for a while at least. But later, when her fear of punishment dies down, she may return to her violent behavior, particularly if her father is not around.

In general, punishment works best to control instrumental rather than hostile aggression. Someone who commits a "crime of passion" may kill despite threats of

Is punishment an effective deterrent to aggression?

the most terrible punishment (such as the death penalty). And while punishment may sometimes help suppress aggressive behaviors, it does not serve to substitute aggression with more positive or productive kinds of social behavior; at best, then, punishment is a partial solution.

Punishment may be particularly tricky as a method of controlling aggression because punishment is sometimes itself a kind of aggression. As we already know, aggression often instigates anger and counteraggression. Furthermore, an aggressive punisher may serve as a model of aggression. In particular, parental violence and punitiveness often seem to encourage rather than discourage aggression in children (Olweus, 1980; Sears, Maccoby, & Levin, 1957; Stevenson-Hinde, Hinde, & Simpson, 1986). As we mentioned in our discussion of family violence, many studies cite a "cycle of violence": Children who are battered are more likely to be aggressive and to become parents who batter (Dodge, Bates, & Pettit, 1990; Widom, 1989).

It's important to note, however, that abused children are not "predestined" to become abusive parents. A review of a number of studies addressing this question found that only 30% of abused children go on to become abusive parents. The researchers conclude, "Being maltreated as a child puts one at risk for becoming abusive but the path between these two points is far from direct or inevitable" (Kaufman & Zigler, 1987, p. 190).

While punishment may sometimes backfire as a means of controlling aggression, it may nonetheless be a necessary technique to use in concert with other strategies. When is punishment most likely to be effective? Research suggests the following rules of thumb (Baron, 1983): To be effective, punishment should be relatively strong; it should be applied quickly and consistently after the undesired aggressive behavior; and finally (though obvious, it is a principle often violated by parents) punishment should be clearly contingent on the "bad" aggressive behavior. If punishment (or the threat of punishment) is consistent, clear, and strong, it can sometimes be effective in reducing violence.

A specific kind of punishment, arrest, has been studied extensively over the past ten years as a possible means of reducing aggression in men who batter their wives. To appreciate this research, you must realize that the police have traditionally been quite reluctant to intrude into cases of domestic violence (Fields & Fields, 1973; Hirschel & Hutchison, 1992; Langley & Levy, 1977; Roy, 1977), and as a result, spouse abusers often think they won't be caught, arrested, or punished.

Sherman and Berk (1984) conducted an experiment with the participation of the Minneapolis police department to test the effectiveness of three techniques of dealing with domestic violence: (1) counseling both parties involved in the violent episode; (2) separating the combatants for several hours, thus allowing the situation some time to cool off; (3) arresting the violent party. Arrest was most effective in reducing subsequent violence, producing a 10% rate of repeat offenses compared to 19% and 24% in the first two groups.

Because of these findings, a number of police departments across the United States instituted pro-arrest policies for dealing with family violence in the 1980s,

Police officers frequently intervene in cases of domestic violence. Is it effective public policy to arrest husbands who assault their wives?

and the Department of Justice spent $4 million on further studies in six additional U.S. cities to see whether arrest is indeed an effective strategy for handling men who batter their wives (Lerman, 1992). The results of this research place some major qualifications on the original Minneapolis findings: While arrest reduces abusive men's violence in the short run, it does not necessarily do so in the long run. Furthermore, arrest proves to be more effective in reducing the family violence of some men (in particular, those who are employed, married, high school graduates, and white) than others (Sherman, 1992; Sherman et al., 1992). Overall, it seems that abusive men who have some resources and social standing are deterred by the possibility of arrest, whereas those who are most disadvantaged are not—indeed, sometimes arrest backfires for extremely marginal men, and they become even more violent after they have been arrested and released.

SOCIAL
PSYCHOLOGY
IN EVERYDAY
LIFE

Stopping Family Violence

Arrest is at best a partial strategy for dealing with the pervasive problem of family violence. Are there additional methods that can augment it? Goldstein (1983) describes three general kinds of treatment for family violence: Primary prevention techniques are designed to head off family violence before it starts; secondary prevention focuses on early identification of family violence and on trying to nip it in the bud; and tertiary prevention is designed to treat recurring, problematic family violence. Let's outline how each strategy works and provide some examples of each.

Primary prevention relies partly on public education (Gelles, 1982). First, the topic of family violence must be brought into the open. Primary prevention also relies on the enactment of appropriate laws. One proposed legislative re- form is to make spouse abuse a criminal rather than a civil offense, thus simulta- neously increasing legal punishments and social awareness of the problem (Gelles, 1982; Straus, 1980). Another goal of primary prevention is to alleviate some of the broad social and economic causes of family abuse (such as too many children at home, poverty and unemployment, and substance abuse) through adequate day care, family planning resources, drug and alcohol treat- ment facilities, and so on.

Once family violence occurs, secondary prevention becomes important. Family violence must be detected to be stopped. We noted earlier that in 1987, people throughout the United States were shocked by the tragic death of 6-year- old Lisa Steinberg. She "slipped through the cracks" of society. Although some of Lisa's neighbors and teachers reported their suspicions of abuse to social service agencies, the case was not pursued. Secondary prevention is in part a matter of public education. All concerned citizens must learn that domestic vio- lence is their business and that they must report it, insistently and repeatedly if necessary, to the authorities. Police, hospital staffs, private physicians, and the personnel of mental health clinics need to be trained to screen people for evi- dence of family violence.

Tertiary treatment programs deal with ongoing, entrenched patterns of family violence. They involve a complex mix of psychological treatment, legal policy, and social welfare. For example, chronically abused women may be helped by psychotherapy designed to boost self-esteem and alleviate their feelings of helplessness (Hilberman, 1980; Lieberkneckt, 1978). Legal policy can address spouse abuse by clearly defining it as a punishable offense and by instituting "dispute centers" to mediate cases of family violence (Dellapa, 1977). In intractable cases, social welfare systems must exist to al- low victims to escape from abuse. For example, shelters for abused women provide them with an immediate safe haven, as well as with physical, eco- nomic, and psychological support (Goldstein, 1983; Straus, Gelles, & Stein- metz, 1980).

Feminist theorists note that because law enforcement officials have often tacitly condoned wife-beating, laws and law enforcement must be very stern and consistent in their treatment of men who batter women (Adams, 1989; Pence, 1989). Such men must learn that society will not tolerate violence as a way of "solving" family problems. A number of therapeutic programs have been devel- oped to treat men who batter (Caesar & Hamberger, 1989). These involve a number of strategies: They educate abusive men about their (and society's) sex- ist attitudes and assumptions, teach them better communication and conflict- resolution skills, and help them develop more effective techniques for managing their anger and frustrations.

Creating Responses Incompatible with Aggression

Have you ever felt like throttling someone, and then a quick-thinking friend cracked a joke that suddenly eased the tension? Somehow, laughter seemed incompatible with aggression. In general, any response that is incompatible with aggression—for example, humor, empathy, or mild sexual arousal—may serve to reduce aggression (Baron, 1983; Ramirez, Bryant, & Zillman, 1983).

Robert Baron (1976) demonstrated the ability of incompatible responses to defuse hostility in a clever field experiment. Male motorists were frustrated at an intersection when the driver in front of them (actually a confederate) failed to drive on when the traffic light changed from red to green. Hidden observers recorded whether the frustrated drivers honked their horns, made hand gestures, or yelled out angry comments. While the drivers were stopped at the intersection, Baron arranged for three different kinds of distraction to occur: In a "humor" condition, a woman dressed as a clown crossed the street in front of the subject's car; in an "empathy" condition, a woman on crutches crossed the street; and in a "sexual arousal" condition, a scantily clad woman crossed the street. This experiment also included two control conditions: Either no one crossed the street or a "normal," conservatively dressed woman crossed the street. Subjects in the humor, empathy, and sexual arousal conditions all showed less angry reaction than control subjects did.

Providing Social Restraints

Aggression is a social behavior, subject to social influences. We already know that social models can instigate aggression; fortunately, they can also reduce it.

Many experiments suggest that viewing nonaggressive models makes people less aggressive (Baron, 1971; Baron & Kepner, 1970; Donnerstein & Donnerstein, 1976). Nonaggressive people can play more than the positive (but passive) role of being "good examples"; they can also openly censure others' aggressive behavior. Baron (1972) showed that when insulted subjects heard a peer (actually a confederate) criticize the use of high levels of shock, they were much less punitive when they later had the opportunity to deliver a supposed shock to their tormentor. Thus, to reduce individuals' aggression, we should place them among people who disapprove of aggression. More broadly, we must work to create a society that disapproves of, rather than glorifies, violence.

Dan Olweus (1991) showed just how effective social disapproval of violence can be as a real-life strategy for reducing aggressive behavior by developing a program to address the problem of bullying among Norwegian elementary and junior high school students. The impetus for this program was a tragic real-life event: In the early 1980s, three Norwegian schoolboys had committed suicide because they had been so severely abused and tormented by other students. Olweus's program was multifaceted: A 32-page information booklet was developed and sent to all teachers and school personnel in Norway informing them of the bullying problem. Information folders were also sent to parents of school bullies and their victims. Videotapes describing the problem of bullying were produced and shown to schoolchildren throughout Norway. In essence, teachers, parents,

Arnold Schwarzenegger in "The Terminator." In response to public dismay over the high amount of violence in this film, its sequel, "Terminator II," was produced with a significant reduction in violent scenes and gratuitous death.

and students were told, "Bullying is a serious problem, and our society will not tolerate it." The results were dramatic: Reported bullying incidents across Norway decreased more than 50% during the two years after the program was instituted!

Cognitive Strategies

The ability to reason separates humans from other animals. At our best, we can use that ability to help control aggression. Given that we live in a world full of aggressive models, we must somehow "inoculate" people against the abundant cues to aggression that surround them. Huesmann and his colleagues (1983) tried to reduce the impact of violent TV programming on first- and third-grade children by having them write papers about "How television is not like real life," "Why it is bad to imitate TV violence," and "Why it is bad for a kid to watch too much TV." A week after writing their essays, the children were videotaped reading them and answering questions about the same topics in a talk-show format.

This brief procedure turned out to have a lasting effect on the children: It significantly changed their attitudes about TV violence, and, most important, it reduced their levels of aggression two years later! Certainly, this experiment suggests that it is possible to reduce the negative effects of violent TV programming with simple educational exercises. It also provides some suggestions for parents: If they decide to let their children see violent TV shows, they should watch them with

SUMMARY TABLE 10.2 Techniques for Reducing Aggression	
Technique	*When Is It Effective?*
Catharsis (venting aggression through fantasy, exercise, verbal aggression, or physical aggression)	Inconsistently effective; sometimes effective when aggression is targeted directly at tormentor
Punishment (aversive stimulus delivered after an aggressive behavior)	Must be consistent and contingent on aggressive behavior; most effective in reducing instrumental rather than hostile aggression
Social welfare policies and counseling	Requires broad-based societal commitment
Incompatible responses (humor, empathy, or mild sexual arousal)	Documented for aggression in response to mild frustration
Social restraints and modeling (presence of nonaggressive models)	Requires proper social environment; modeling often is strongest when the model is powerful and attractive
Cognitive strategies (analyzing why TV is unrealistic; developing stress-management and communication skills)	Can help to mitigate effects of other variables, such as TV violence and frustration

their children and explain that media violence is "fake" and that while media violence often seems quite painless and harmless, real-life violence is actually painful and deadly. Parents should ask their children to imagine nonviolent solutions to conflicts that are solved violently on TV. Older siblings can be asked to help their parents explain to younger brothers and sisters "how television is not like real life," and in the process, the older children may thereby internalize the message themselves.

Cognitive techniques have been developed recently to help reduce the negative impact of sexually violent films. For example, Margaret Intons-Peterson developed briefing material to present to college men before they viewed sexually violent films. This material described the devastating effects that rape has on its victims, and it presented factual information that debunks common rape myths. After receiving this briefing, college men were less likely to accept rape myths and more sympathetic to a rape victim in a videotaped trial, and this change occurred even after some of the men viewed a "slasher" movie (Intons-Peterson & Roskos-Ewoldsen, 1989; Intons-Peterson, Roskos-Ewoldsen, Thomas, Shirley, & Blut, 1989). Other recent research provides additional evidence that anti-rape information briefings can be effective; furthermore, it suggests that asking men to generate their own arguments against sexual violence and rape myths can be another effective way of blunting the negative impact of sexually violent films (Linz, Arluk, & Donnerstein, 1990).

The message of all this research is clear: There *are* actions we can take to control aggression and to reduce the impact of factors such as violent media that instigate aggression (see Summary Table 10.2 for a review). Perhaps with the aid of social psychology research, we can declare and win a war against aggression itself.

AGGRESSION IN PERSPECTIVE

Aggression is behavior that intentionally harms others. People have behaved aggressively throughout recorded history, and they continue to do so today. Social psychology research attempts to understand the many factors that influence aggressive behavior and studies ways of controlling and reducing aggression.

While we and other animals possess biological predispositions to behave aggressively in certain circumstances, aggression is not inevitable. The low levels of aggression found in some cultures show that it is possible for people to live peacefully. People within a given culture differ in their levels of aggressiveness for many reasons: Aggression is partly a function of the individual's physiology and personality, and environmental factors such as painful stimuli, heat, and frustrating events can incite aggression.

Social psychology has tried to understand how aggressive behavior is learned through classical conditioning, operant conditioning, and modeling. Social psychologists' interest in learning and aggression has led them to study important and controversial real-life topics: Does violent entertainment contribute to aggressive behavior in children? Do sexually violent TV shows and movies incite negative attitudes and violence against women? The answer to both questions seems to be yes.

Research on aggression helps us understand the causes of family violence. While broad social factors such as poverty, unemployment, and substance abuse help predict and explain family violence, other factors are important as well, including sexist attitudes, personality characteristics, and a family history of abuse. Family violence can be treated at many levels: through social welfare programs, legal policy, public education, shelters for abused family members, and therapeutic programs for abusers and victims of abuse.

Aggression is not a hopeless problem. Social psychologists have documented a number of techniques for controlling and reducing it. These include punishment, creating incompatible responses, providing social restraints, and developing cognitive strategies and information that counteract cues to aggression provided by the mass media. Aggression can be reduced if we—as individuals and as a society—wish to do so.

Defining Aggression

KEY POINTS

Aggression is behavior directed against another living being that is intended to harm or injure. Social psychologists distinguish between hostile aggression, which is emotional and provoked by pain or upset, and instrumental aggression, which is unemotional and performed to gain rewards.

Measuring Aggression

Although early research measured verbal aggression, recent research tends to use behavioral measures of aggression.

Factors That Influence Human Aggression

Biological Groups

Freud and Lorenz believed that aggression is an instinct that must be vented. Evolutionary theory suggests that although aggression has survival value, it occurs only under certain circumstances.

Cultural Influences

Aggression is cross-culturally variable. War may occur particularly among groups competing for scarce resources.

Multicultural Perspectives: Wars and the Cycle of Violence

Across cultures, wars tend to increase domestic violence in countries after they are over.

Individual Differences in Aggression

Aggressiveness as a Trait.   Aggressiveness is a trait that is relatively stable over time and is in part due to hereditary factors.

Physiology and Aggression.   Aggression is influenced by specific brain structures and may be affected by testosterone, alcohol, and marijuana.

Environmental Factors

Aggression as a Response to Aggression.   Aggression often elicits counteraggression.

Physical Pain.   Pain frequently incites aggression. Although unlearned, the link between pain and aggression can be influenced by learning.

Heat.   People tend to be more aggressive in hot environments.

Frustration.   The original frustration–aggression hypothesis held that frustration always leads to aggression and that aggression is always the result of frustration. Research suggests that arbitrary, strong frustrations without reasonable explanations particularly incite aggression. Aggression can occur without frustration.

Social Psychology in Everyday Life: Economic Frustration and Societal Aggression.   Frustration can contribute to social upheavals. The *J-curve theory* holds that violent social revolutions are most likely to occur when a prolonged period of economic development is followed by a brief period of economic reversal. Research suggests that economic frustration is more a function of relative deprivation than of absolute deprivation.

Arousal.   Arousal can energize dominant learned aggressive responses; it can heighten anger through misattribution. Arousal created by exercise or by viewing erotica can increase subsequent angry aggression.

Social Learning

Aggression can be learned through operant conditioning and observational learning.

The Mass Media and Aggression.   Experimental and correlational studies document imitative aggression.

Aggressive Cues and the Weapons Effect.   Stimuli (such as weapons) frequently associated with aggression may become learned aggressive cues.

The Effects of TV Violence on Children.   Experimental, quasi-experimental, and correlational studies suggest a causal relationship between children's viewing violent TV and behaving aggressively.

Media Sex and Aggression.   Viewing violent pornography can increase aggression, particularly by males against females, and it can lead men to hold negative attitudes toward women and to endorse rape myths.

Sexual Violence.   Sexual violence is a common and serious problem in the United States.

Social Psychology in Everyday Life: Causes of Family Violence.   Family violence is a serious problem in the United States. Broad social factors (poverty, unemployment, substance abuse), sexism, personality traits, a family history of abuse, and relationship problems all contribute to family violence.

Reducing Aggression
Catharsis

Catharsis—the venting of aggressive impulses through fantasy, physical exercise, verbal aggression, or physical aggression—does not consistently reduce subsequent aggression.

Punishment

Punishment can reduce aggressive behaviors if it is strong, consistently delivered, and contingent on the aggressive response. However, physical punishment may sometimes serve as a model of aggressive behavior for children. Arresting men after they engage in domestic violence is only sometimes effective in reducing their subsequent violence.

Social Psychology in Everyday Life: Reducing Family Violence

Primary, secondary, and tertiary prevention programs can help reduce family violence. Such programs alleviate broad social conditions that foster family violence, educate the public to report family violence to authorities, and provide support and counseling for both abusers and victims of abuse.

Creating Responses Incompatible with Aggression

Incompatible responses such as humor, empathy, or mild sexual arousal can sometimes reduce aggression.

Providing Social Restraints

Nonaggressive models lead observers to be less aggressive.

Cognitive Strategies

Thinking about the bad effects of viewing violent TV can help reduce those effects. Presenting men with information about rape and rape myths can help counteract the negative effects of viewing sexually violent films.

KEY TERMS

Aggression: Behavior directed against another living being that is intended to harm or injure.

Catharsis: The venting of aggressive impulses through fantasy, exercise, verbal aggression, or physical aggression.

Frustration: According to the early research on the frustration–aggression hypothesis, an interference with the occurrence of a goal-response.

Frustration–aggression hypothesis: The theory that frustration leads to aggression and that all aggression is caused by frustration.

Hostile aggression: Emotional, angry aggression often provoked by pain or frustration.

Incompatible responses: Responses such as humor, empathy, or mild sexual arousal that are incompatible with and therefore defuse aggression.

Instrumental aggression: Nonemotional aggression performed to gain a reward.

J-curve theory: Davies's theory that violent social revolutions are most likely to occur when a prolonged period of economic development is followed by a short period of sharp economic reversal.

Relative deprivation: The gap between expectations and reality; frustration may be more a function of relative deprivation rather than of absolute deprivation.

Weapons effect: The effect documented in some experiments that weapons may serve as aggressive cues and thus may increase aggression by their mere presence.

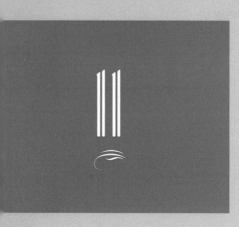

HELPING OTHERS

At every watershed through time, it seems a face emerges to transfix a moment in history. In Vietnam, a naked girl fled napalm. In Tian An Men Square, a single student stared down a line of Chinese tanks. In Los Angeles last year, Rodney G. King lay prone and beaten.

Now, a white gravel truck driver beaten nearly into oblivion in South Los Angeles has become the face on the flip side of the Rodney King coin. . . .

His name is Reginald Oliver Denny. He is 36. He is alive because four strangers who saw him dragged from his truck and beaten nearly to death emerged from the crowd to drive his unwieldy 18-wheeler out of pandemonium to safety.

The rescuers were two women and two men: a young nutrition consultant, a laid-off data control worker, an unemployed aerospace worker and a still-unidentified young man in black whose fellow rescuers first feared was a gang-banger coming to finish Denny off.

—*Los Angeles Times*, May 1, 1992

Lei Yuille, one of the rescuers of Reginald Denny, stated that she knew instantly when she saw Denny being beaten on TV that she had to help him.

Why did four strangers risk their lives to save the life of Reginald Denny? Did they consider the possible dangers of helping a desperately injured man in the middle of a riot? Do you think Denny's rescuers rationally thought through their actions, or did they act impulsively and emotionally? What goaded them into action? Outrage? Compassion? Religious convictions? Were these four individuals average people, or did they have unique personal characteristics that led them to help a wounded man in an extremely dangerous situation?

We may never know the answers to these specific questions. However, the questions just posed, more broadly considered, are exactly those we will try to answer in this chapter as we examine factors that influence when people help one another. One conclusion will be clear to you by the end of this chapter: Helping, like most other kinds of social behavior, is complex. It is influenced both by people's traits and emotions and by the situations they are in. Furthermore, helping can result from a number of motives: In some situations, it is impulsive and emotional, in others it is calculated and thought out, and, sometimes, as we shall see, it may be truly altruistic.

KINDS OF HELPING

Social psychologists use the term *prosocial behavior* to refer to actions people engage in that help others and foster the well-being of others. The dramatic rescue

Emergency intervention. This lineworker gives mouth-to-mouth resuscitation to a colleague shocked unconscious by a live electric wire. Because of his quick action, his coworker lived.

of Reginald Denny illustrates one particular kind of prosocial behavior: *emergency interventions,* quick responses to sudden events that endanger another and that may sometimes place the helper in considerable peril (Latané & Darley, 1970; Piliavin, Dovidio, Gaertner, & Clark, 1981). Helping a man who has been brutally beaten in a riot, rescuing a girl who falls onto subway tracks, rushing into a burning house to save a trapped person, and giving immediate first aid to the bloody victim of an automobile accident are all emergency interventions.

Sharing food and clothing with flood victims, volunteering to be a "buddy" to a person with AIDS, giving money to charities, donating blood regularly to the Red Cross, and lending an ear to a depressed friend are also examples of prosocial behavior. Although they don't require split-second decisions in the heat of a crisis, such generous acts are still very important in everyday life. In fact, such ongoing, long-term forms of prosocial behavior are probably more important to the maintenance of human society than more dramatic but less frequent emergency interventions (Clary & Snyder, 1991).

In the preceding chapter we distinguished between two kinds of aggression: Hostile aggression tends to be impulsive and emotional, whereas instrumental

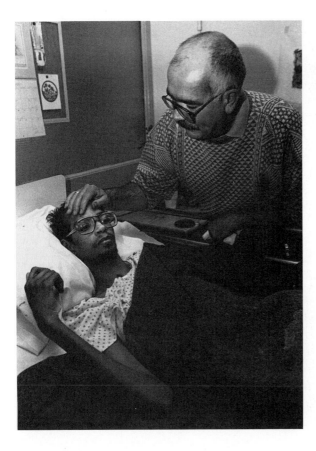

*There are many op-
portunities for pro-
social behavior in
everyday life. Here, a
volunteer worker com-
forts a person with AIDS.*

aggression is influenced by rewards, punishments, and "rational" considerations. Similarly, there are two main kinds of prosocial behavior. One kind of helping is triggered by quick, nonrational, emotional arousal, often in response to emergencies; the other kind is influenced more by the potential helper's analysis of the costs and benefits of helping (Piliavin et al., 1981).

When are people most likely to engage in impulsive rather than calculated helping? Looking at evidence from 26 different studies, Jane Piliavin and her colleagues (1981) concluded that impulsive emergency interventions are most likely to occur when (1) the emergency is quite clear, (2) it occurs in a real-life (as opposed to a laboratory) setting, and (3) the helper has some prior relationship with the victim (for example, the victim needing help is a family member or friend). The rescue of Reginald Denny meets the first two criteria, but not the third: The four rescuers faced an unmistakable real-life emergency, but they had never seen Denny before in their lives.

Denny's rescue may have seemed particularly impressive to you precisely because he was a stranger to the two men and two women who came to his aid. There was "nothing in it for them" to rescue Denny, except great personal danger. The word *altruism* refers to helping another person for no reward, and even at some

A volunteer cares for a baby with AIDS. As the text notes, most kinds of helping are not emergency interventions.

cost to oneself (Batson, 1987; Krebs & Miller, 1985). This definition seems to fit Denny's rescuers.

Philosophers have argued for centuries about whether or not people are ever truly altruistic (Rushton & Sorrentino, 1981). This debate has been subtle and complex, for although people sometimes aid others for no apparent external gain (such as money, rewards, or social esteem), they still may be motivated by internal rewards and punishments (increased self-esteem, or avoidance of guilt or of unpleasant arousal). C. Daniel Batson (1987) has labeled altruism that is motivated by such internal rewards and punishments "pseudoaltruism," because the good acts are actually done to increase the pleasure or reduce the pain of the giver. According to Batson, pure altruism must be motivated by an honest concern for another's well-being, not by any sort of self-reward or by avoidance of self-punishment. Later in this chapter, we'll describe some intriguing recent research that attempts to demonstrate the existence of pure altruism.

Even if pure altruism exists, it is only one of many kinds of prosocial behavior. Peter Blau (1964), a proponent of a cost–reward analysis of why people help others, noted somewhat cynically that people who help others "without a thought of reward and even without expecting gratitude . . . are virtually saints, and saints are rare" (p. 16). Were the rescuers of Reginald Denny saints? Maybe; maybe not. As we noted, we'll never know for sure why these four individuals acted as they did. After reading this chapter, however, you should have a better sense of some of the possible motivations of Denny's rescuers, and you should also have a more complete understanding of some of the factors that make all of us more or less likely to help others.

MEASURING PROSOCIAL BEHAVIOR

Altruism and helping, like aggression, are measured in many different ways. Indeed, operational definitions of prosocial behavior seem to be even more varied than those of aggression (Krebs & Miller, 1985). To list just a few examples, various studies have measured helpfulness by observing whether subjects mail lost letters (Hornstein, Masor, Sole, & Heilman, 1971), give money to people in need (Bickman & Kamzan, 1973; Latané, 1970), contribute to the Salvation Army (Bryan & Test, 1967), donate a kidney to a person suffering from kidney failure (Fellner & Marshall, 1981), aid people who drop their groceries (Tipton & Browning, 1972), stop or call the police to help motorists with flat tires (Bryan & Test, 1967; Penner, Dertke, & Achenbach, 1973), intervene in a fight between a man and a woman (Shotland & Straw, 1976), and help a man who suffers an apparent heart attack (Staub, 1974).

The helping behaviors just listed differ from one another in a number of ways. Sometimes they are in response to emergencies (intervening in a fight), and sometimes not (giving money). Sometimes they entail considerable costs (donating a kidney), and sometimes they don't (mailing a lost letter). Sometimes the beneficiary is aware of being helped (the person who drops groceries), and sometimes not (the motorist the police were called for). Despite their diversity, all the measures of prosocial behavior just listed are behavioral rather than subjective, and this is typical of most research on helping.

MAJOR APPROACHES TO THE STUDY OF HELPING

At least two of the rescuers found themselves lured to the scene by the power of television pictures, broadcast live from helicopters hovering over the intersection of Normandie and Florence Avenues.

"We were watching TV at home," said T. J. Murphy, 30, the aerospace engineer. " 'Somebody's got to get that guy out of there,' we said to each other."

As they got in their car to check out the brewing neighborhood confrontation, they never thought that the rescue would fall to them.

—*Los Angeles Times*, May 1, 1992

GROUP-LEVEL EXPLANATIONS
Biological groups (evolution)
Cultural and social groups

↓

INDIVIDUAL-LEVEL EXPLANATIONS
Heredity and physiology
Past environment (family rearing, TV viewing)
Current setting (number of people in emergency situation)

↓

MEDIATING VARIABLES
Beliefs and attitudes
Emotions
Personality traits
Arousal
Attributions
Internalized social rules and norms
Cognitive calculations of risks and rewards
Empathy

↓

HELPING OR NOT HELPING

FIGURE 11.1 Levels of explanation applied to altruism and prosocial behavior.

Prosocial behavior, like aggression, can be analyzed at many different levels (see Figure 11.1). *Group-level* explanations analyze helping in terms of biological evolution and cultural norms. *Individual-level* explanations focus on the individual's heredity and physiology (Is altruism heritable?), the past environment (Does parental rearing influence children's prosocial behavior? Does TV viewing affect altruism?), and the current environment (Does helping in an emergency depend on the number of other people nearby?). *Mediating variables*, the third level of explanation, include internal psychological states and processes that are presumed to influence helping, such as personality traits, arousal and emotions, guilt, moods, internalized social rules and norms, cognitive calculations of risk and reward, and attributions.

Unlike research on aggression, research on helping has often studied people's mental calculations and decision processes. Perhaps this is because social psychologists have implicitly assumed an "original sin" model of human behavior: Aggression is seen as an innate impulse that is ever present and must always be controlled, whereas altruism is "unnatural"—it is something that must be taught and constantly "hammered in" (Campbell, 1975; Krebs & Miller, 1985). Stated a bit differently, helping others is seen as something we may "reason ourselves into" based on considerations of costs, rewards, and moral principles, but not as something that we do automatically and instinctively.

Figure 11.1 reminds us that there is no single "cause" of helping. In describing research on helping and altruism, we'll begin with group-level explanations and then proceed to individual-level explanations and internal factors such as emotions and personality traits.

Evolutionary Approaches

The evolution of aggressive behaviors is understandable in Darwinian terms, for aggression can help animals survive and reproduce. The evolution of altruism, however, is more problematic. In *The Descent of Man* (1871), Charles Darwin noted a paradox: An animal that behaves in a truly altruistic, self-sacrificing way fosters others' survival at its own expense. But the whole "goal" of Darwinian evolution is survival and reproduction. Altruistic self-sacrifice thus seems to be an evolutionary dead end.

Kin Selection

Modern evolutionary theory partially resolves this paradox through the notion of kin selection (Hamilton, 1964). Whereas classical Darwinian theory focused on individual and species survival, modern evolutionary theory focuses more on gene survival: An animal is evolutionarily successful if it passes its genes on to future generations (Dawkins, 1976; Ridley & Dawkins, 1981). This can occur in two ways: if the animal produces offspring of its own or if its genetic relatives (for example, brothers or sisters) produce offspring. Thus, natural selection should favor animals that show altruism toward genetically related individuals. Pure, self-sacrificing altruism occurs most dramatically in social insects, such as bees.

Worker bees, for example, readily give their lives to protect other bees in their hive (Ridley & Dawkins, 1981).

Reciprocal Altruism

Another kind of helping that can be explained by evolutionary theory is *reciprocal altruism:* behavior that benefits another with the proviso that the other is expected to return the favor. The "cost" of giving up some resources for the benefit of another is more than offset, in terms of evolutionary fitness, by the later reciprocated favor. Biologist Robert Trivers (1971) offers the following as examples of reciprocal altruism in animals: (1) symbiotic cleaning, in which large fish allow certain species of small fish to swim in their mouths without eating them because the small fish clean them of parasites; (2) birds' warning calls that inform other birds of danger but at the same time put the lookout bird at risk by drawing attention to it.

In reciprocal altruism, if one animal helps another but the favor is not returned, then it may not help again. Mathematical modeling studies (for example, Axelrod & Hamilton, 1981) demonstrate that a very simple strategy of reciprocal altruism called "tit for tat" is particularly stable and adaptive. This strategy has just two rules: (1) In a relationship with another, always begin with a cooperative "altruistic" response. (2) In all subsequent interactions, behave as your partner did last—that is, if he was most recently altruistic, be altruistic in return, but if he was selfish, be selfish in return.

The tit-for-tat strategy has several noteworthy features (Trivers, 1983). It is "eternally optimistic," in that it always starts with altruism and returns to altruism whenever the partner does. It has a very "short memory" and is ever-ready to "turn over a new leaf," and thus it is not vindictive—if your partner has cheated in the past and behaved selfishly, you reciprocate altruism as soon as your partner reforms and shows altruism. Finally, this tit-for-tat strategy shows a no-nonsense approach to

Four adult chimpanzees share foliage. In the wild, chimps most often share the meat of freshly captured prey. Is this an example of pure or reciprocal altruism?

cheaters: As soon as your partner is selfish, you are selfish in return. There is no self-sacrificing "turning the other cheek."

Reciprocal altruism is most likely to evolve in species that have the following characteristics (Trivers, 1971, 1983): (1) a long life span; (2) living in close proximity (for example, in social groups) and interacting repeatedly; (3) mutual dependence, whereby survival depends on the help of others; (4) a long period of parental care; and (5) the absence of rigid dominance hierarchies (systems that define "bosses" and subordinates in social groups), which guarantees that altruistic coalitions of individuals confer power to those individuals. Note that complex forms of reciprocal altruism also require that the animal be "smart" enough to keep track of who did and did not help over time. The animals that most possess all these prerequisites for reciprocal altruism are higher mammals, such as dolphins, nonhuman primates, and, of course, human beings.

A number of studies have shown evidence of altruism in nonhuman primates. In a fascinating early demonstration, two hungry chimpanzees were placed in adjacent cages, and one of the chimps was given a small piece of food, which the chimp would often share, sometimes without being "asked" and sometimes after the other chimp begged. In both cases, chimps sacrificed a desired good to help another. Interestingly, more sharing occurred when the chimps were "friends" rather than strangers (Nissen & Crawford, 1936). This makes good biological sense, for acquaintanceship increases the probability of reciprocity.

Helping behaviors have also been observed in whales and dolphins (Conner & Norriss, 1982). According to Trivers (1983),

> This help comes in three forms: standing by, assistance, and support. Standing by occurs when an animal stays with another animal in distress but does not offer obvious aid. Often an individual will remain in a dangerous situation far longer than it would if there were no one in distress. Assistance includes approaching an injured comrade and showing excited behavior, such as swimming between the captor and its prey, biting or attacking capture vessels, and pushing an injured individual away from a would-be captor. . . . Support occurs when one or more animals maintain a distressed animal at the surface of the water—either right-side up or upside-down—and presses upward, leaving this position only long enough to breathe, but keeping the stricken animal at the surface.
>
> . . . There is no doubt that whales and dolphins understand when another cetacean is being captured. They will often bite restraining lines of harpooned animals during capture, propel injured animals away from captors, and even attack the captors. (pp. 53–54)

Higher mammals not only show helpful behaviors, they also show signs of experiencing empathy for others in distress. In a series of controlled experiments, Masserman, Wechkin, and Terris (1964) designed an apparatus in which monkeys could receive food by pulling either of two chains. Both chains delivered food, but one also delivered a shock to another monkey. The monkeys learned to avoid pulling the chain that shocked another monkey, even though this response led to a reward. Apparently, the cries of pain from the other monkey were distressing, and the chain-pulling monkey experienced a kind of empathy for its suffering companion.

You might be wondering whether evolutionary views of altruism are inconsistent with psychological perspectives on altruism and helping. Not necessarily. After all, biological evolution helps mold individuals' psychological traits and characteristics. Thus, altruism toward kin and reciprocal altruism may show themselves in individuals as feelings of "love" and "loyalty" toward family and in-group members and as feelings of friendship toward people who do us favors. In other words, evolutionary principles may complement rather than contradict psychological findings (Rushton, 1988).

In general, evolutionary theories of altruism can account for weak forms of altruism (doing something positive for another when there's "something in it for you"—either fostering your genes' survival or promoting later reciprocity), but they do not predict pure altruism (doing something positive for a stranger in a truly self-sacrificing manner).

Cultural Approaches

Campbell (1975, 1983) has argued that biological evolution cannot explain pure altruism in humans, and even though weak forms of altruism may have evolved in people, selfishness, cheating, and aggression have also evolved as competing behavioral tendencies. Thus, pure, selfless altruism, if it exists, must result from learned cultural rules and moral principles. In Campbell's view, a major function of religious and moral traditions, which teach the virtues of love, kindness, and compassion, is to foster altruism and help control our innate nasty tendencies.

Social Norms

The concept of a norm has been used by anthropologists and sociologists to describe the rules society has developed to guide social conduct. A *norm* is "a statement made by members of a group, not necessarily all of them, that its members ought to behave in a certain way in certain circumstances" (Homans, 1961, p. 40). A norm embodies both a standard of conduct and a cultural belief that people ought to behave according to the standard (Eagly, 1987).

What are the most prominent norms governing prosocial behavior? The nearly universal *norm of reciprocity* prescribes that people help and not hurt those who have helped them (Gouldner, 1960)—stated a bit more informally, "I'll scratch your back if you'll scratch mine." This principle seems to hold for politicians, friends, lovers, and business partners, and social psychology experiments find abundant evidence of its existence. For example, Wilke and Lanzetta (1970) asked subjects to play a "trucking game" in which they had to transport goods across a simulated highway. When a subject's partner (actually a confederate) did a "favor" and helped a subject to transport his goods, the subject tended to reciprocate the favor in a carefully graded way—the bigger the original favor, the bigger the returned favor.

Note the similarity between the norm of reciprocity and the evolutionary concept of reciprocal altruism. Apparently, reciprocity is a highly adaptive behavior that has evolved both biologically and culturally.

Another rule guiding prosocial behavior, the *norm of equity,* is in some sense an elaboration of the norm of reciprocity. It holds that people should receive "goods" from a relationship in proportion to what they invest in the relationship (Walster, Walster, & Berscheid, 1978). Whereas the norm of reciprocity dictates an equal exchange of favors, the norm of equity says that what one gets out of a relationship should be proportional to what one puts into it (see Chapter 9 for a more complete discussion of equity theory). The norm of equity helps define what people perceive to be just and unjust kinds of helping.

Both the norm of reciprocity and the norm of equity regulate the degree to which we engage in prosocial behavior with others, but neither norm promotes pure altruism. Both require that you get something in return for what you give.

The *norm of social responsibility* is a more purely altruistic principle of social behavior that prescribes that a person give aid to people who are dependent and who need assistance (Berkowitz, 1972). The aid should be proportional to the need of the dependent person. Imagine, for example, that a mother wins a lottery and decides to set up trust funds for her two children. One child is handicapped, the other is not. The norm of social responsibility would hold that more money be set aside for the handicapped child, who is more dependent on the parent. Experiments show that people often, but not always, help dependent others in need, even when their aid is anonymous (Berkowitz, 1972; Berkowitz & Daniels, 1963). Sometimes, then, people do perform good deeds without expecting something back from the recipient.

Norms of prosocial behavior, like evolutionary strategies of altruism, presumably developed because they help individuals and groups survive. The norms of reciprocity, equity, and social responsibility lead to stable, mutually rewarding relationships, help guard against cheaters, protect the weakest members of society, and prevent, through agreed-upon rules, the violence unleashed by unbridled self-seeking. Unfortunately, these norms of helping may apply most strongly to relatives and members of in-groups and less to "outsiders" (Krebs & Miller, 1985). Again, we see a convergence between social norms and biological evolution, both of which promote altruism especially toward kin and in-group members—people with whom we repeatedly interact *and* with whom we are likely to share our genes.

Viewed from these perspectives, the rescue of Reginald Denny seems even more remarkable, for Denny was white and his four rescuers were all black. Thus, Denny's rescuers were exposing themselves to considerable danger for an out-group member.

MULTICULTURAL PERSPECTIVE

Do Norms of Helping Differ across Cultures?

Are people in different countries and cultures equally helpful? The answer seems to be no. Anthropologists have documented considerable cross-cultural diversity in altruism and cooperation. An extreme example is the Ik mountain people of Uganda, who are probably among the most selfish people ever studied (Turnbull, 1972). Because of scarce resources and terrible poverty, the Ik culture has evolved to encourage people to be cruel, scheming, and manipulative—hungry sons are reported to steal food even from their sick and dying parents! At the other extreme, cultures such as the Aitutaki of Polynesia and the Arapesh of New Guinea are known for their extreme gentleness and helpfulness (Eisenberg, 1992; Graves & Graves, 1983). Members of these cultures give aid freely to their neighbors, even when it is not requested.

Not only do people in different cultures show different overall levels of helping, they may also view helping in different moral terms. Miller, Bersoff, and Harwood (1990) presented American and Indian Hindu subjects with stories about people who refused to give help to another person. The need for help varied: In some stories, the need was extreme (the person needed mouth-to-mouth resuscitation) and in others it wasn't (the person needed directions to a store). In addition, the relationship between the person needing help and the person refusing to give help varied: In some stories, people refused help to their young children, in others to their best friends, and in others to strangers. After reading the stories, subjects were asked whether the person who refused to give help was morally obliged to help.

The results showed that Americans' judgments of moral obligation were much more influenced than Indians' by the degree of need and by the nature of the relationship between helper and beneficiary. Specifically, Americans believed that people are morally obligated to help when the situation is life-threatening and when they are closely related to the person needing help. In contrast, Indians believed that people are more universally obligated to help. This observed difference may result from the fact that America tends to be an individualistic culture and India a more collectivist culture. Unless there are compelling needs and close personal relationships that warrant helping, Americans tend to believe that individuals are free to "do their own thing." Indian Hindus, on the other hand, view helping as an obligation woven into the social fabric.

Americans may differ from members of other cultures in another way: They tend to view helping more in terms of economic exchange, whereas people in other cultures often view helping more as an integral part of social roles and relationships (Fiske, 1991). Thus, Americans often decide when to help and when not to help based on perceived costs and rewards; members of more collectivist cultures help because it is a natural part of their social roles and interpersonal responsibilities. Help obtained from therapists and counselors provides an interesting example to consider. In America, many people receive emotional support, intimacy, and advice from a kind of paid "friend." Therapy is a commercial enterprise: You receive emotional help for money. Such relationships would be unthinkable in some cultures.

Later we will discuss cost–reward analyses of helping behavior in more detail. Cross-cultural research poses an interesting question: Are such analyses of helping more applicable to Americans than to members of other cultural groups? ⬟

The Limitations of Normative Approaches

Although cultural norms undoubtedly influence prosocial behavior, they rarely lead to exact predictions of helping in specific situations within a given society (Latané & Darley, 1970). Like naive instinct theories, normative theories of prosocial behavior may become circular (Krebs, 1970): Why did Joe give money to the beggar? Because of the norm of social responsibility. How do we know there is a norm of social responsibility? Because people like Joe donate money to dependent people.

Various norms may contradict one another. For example, the norm of reciprocity might suggest that you won't give money to a beggar, who has never done and is unlikely to do anything for you; however, the norm of social responsibility clearly requires you to give, particularly if the beggar is somehow dependent on you. Some people may internalize cultural norms more strongly than others, and thus individual differences may affect when norms are and are not obeyed. Finally, as we shall see in the rest of this chapter, *situational variables* may determine when people do and do not behave consistently with cultural norms. All of this is not to say that the normative approach is false; rather, it is incomplete.

THE PSYCHOLOGY OF HELPING

. . . when they arrived, the police were nowhere to be seen.

Instead, the gravely injured man—his face awash in blood and his eyes swollen shut—had somehow managed to get back behind the wheel and was trying to make his getaway an inch at a time.

Braving hostile onlookers, stalled cars and general chaos, Murphy and his friend joined two others who eventually helped deliver Denny to the door of the Daniel Freeman Memorial Hospital emergency room. Just as the big rig drove up to the door, Denny went into convulsions and started spitting up blood.

"One more minute, just one more minute, and he would have been dead," one of the rescuers said a paramedic told him at the door.

—*Los Angeles Times*, May 1, 1992

Are some people more likely to help than others? Are some settings more likely to trigger helping than others? Let's turn now to these interesting questions and the many psychological factors that influence helping. First, we will describe psychological influences on helping in general, then we'll turn to the fascinating special case of emergency interventions.

Is There an Altruistic Personality?

Chapter 3 discussed a general question: Do people possess stable personality traits that lead them to behave consistently across situations? Let's now pose this

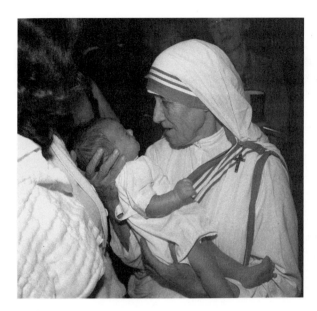

Mother Teresa has devoted much of her life toward improving conditions for the poor in India. Such behavior leads us to ask if there is a prosocial personality.

same question specifically about prosocial behavior: Do people possess a stable trait of altruism that leads them to show consistent levels of helping across situations? Our common sense tells us that at least some people have stable and consistent traits of altruism—think, for example, of Mother Teresa or Albert Schweitzer.

Surprisingly, early research suggested that people show little consistency in their prosocial behaviors. In classic studies, Hartshorne and May (1928, 1929; Hartshorne, May, & Shuttleworth, 1930; see Chapter 3) devised 33 different behavioral measures of altruism, self-control, honesty, and cheating, and administered them to 10,000 elementary and high school students. Measures of altruism included students' votes to divide class money among themselves or to donate it to charity, their decisions to give away items in a gift pencil case to needy children, and their efforts to find stories and pictures to donate to children in hospitals. In general, such single measures of altruism did not correlate strongly with one another (the average intercorrelation coefficient was .23) or with other measures of "morality." Hartshorne and May interpreted these results to mean that altruism and morality are not "unified character traits." Many contemporary researchers have echoed this conclusion (Gergen, Gergen, & Meter, 1972; Krebs, 1978; Mussen & Eisenberg-Berg, 1977).

However, as we noted in Chapter 3, we now know that single measures of behavior tend to be quite unreliable (Epstein, 1979, 1980). When Hartshorne and May's measures of altruism are combined into a composite score, they correlate .61 with measures of the children's reputation for altruism among teachers and classmates (Rushton, 1981b). This clearly suggests a more stable trait of altruism than Hartshorne and May saw in their data. Other, more recent studies have shown evidence for moderate consistency in children's altruism (Eisenberg, 1992; Krebs & Sturrup, 1974; Strayer, Wareing, & Rushton, 1979).

A toddler comforts a friend who is crying after a fall. What leads some children to be more helpful than others?

What are people like who are relatively high on the trait of altruism? Research suggests that altruistic people are empathic, particularly as adults, and able to analyze situations from the emotional and moral perspectives of other people (Batson, Bolen, Cross, & Neuringer-Benefield, 1986; Underwood & Moore, 1982). They possess more strongly internalized norms of prosocial behavior and show more advanced kinds of moral reasoning than less altruistic people—for example, they tend to view what is right or wrong in terms of abstract moral principles rather than in terms of social conventions or moral prescriptions from authority figures (Blasi, 1980; Eisenberg, 1992; Eisenberg-Berg, 1979; Krebs & Rosenwald, 1977; Staub, 1974). Finally, altruistic people tend not to have high degrees of stereotypical masculinity—for example, they report that they are not "dominant" and "aggressive" (Siem & Spence, 1986; Tice & Baumeister, 1985; see Chapter 8).

Christian Rescuers of Jewish Neighbors during World War II

A fascinating real-life example of altruistic people is the Christians in Europe during World War II who saved Jewish people from Nazi extermination by hiding them in their homes and businesses and helping them flee (London, 1970; Oliner & Oliner, 1988). Why did these people risk their lives to aid others? The answers are complex and varied. Some rescuers took small risks initially to help their friends and then gradually got more and more involved in large-scale rescue operations. According to one study, rescuers tended to show three characteristics: They were adventurous risk takers, they strongly identified with at least one parent who was a humanitarian, and many of them had somewhat marginal status in their community—for example, they belonged to a religious or ethnic group that was looked down upon (London, 1970). Note that being a risk taker is probably not a characteristic of altruistic people in general, but it certainly was a necessary characteristic for those attempting to oppose the brutal Nazi regime.

A study of 231 Christians who saved Jewish people in Nazi Europe found that these rescuers were more "other-oriented" and empathic than nonrescuers and believed more strongly in fundamental human values such as justice and caring for one's neighbor (Oliner & Oliner, 1988). Most Christian rescuers during the war acted as individuals, but there is at least one documented case of a whole community working together to save Jewish people: The people who lived in and around Le Chambon, a village in a rural mountainous area of eastern France, are credited with saving thousands of Jews, including large numbers of children, from certain death (Hallie, 1979). They faced great personal danger by hiding Jews in their homes, feeding them, and helping them travel to the Swiss border. Why did they do it? The people of Le Chambon—simple villagers and farmers—saw themselves as living up to their Christian principles; they did not view themselves as being especially heroic. Many of these people were of French Huguenot (that is, Protestant) descent; thus they had a strong cultural memory of being a highly persecuted religious minority themselves and therefore, perhaps, felt a special empathy for the plight of the Jews in Nazi Europe.

The Development of Prosocial Behavior

How do some people come to be more helpful than others? Developmental psychologists have identified a number of factors that lead children to become helpful individuals. The development of empathy and altruism in children is fostered by a loving, caring relationship with a primary caregiver, who may or may not be the child's mother (Sroufe, 1978). This certainly tended to be the case for Christian rescuers during World War II (Oliner & Oliner, 1988). Thus, adult models of altruism contribute to the development of altruism in children (Yarrow, Scott, & Waxler, 1973), and, not surprisingly, what adults *do* is more important than what they *say* in fostering children's altruism (Bryan, 1972).

Rewards and praise can also help mold prosocial behavior in children (Mussen & Eisenberg-Berg, 1977), and children become more helpful when they are placed in the role of helper (Staub, 1975, 1979). This may partly explain cross-cultural differences in helping, for children in some countries (such as Kenya, Mexico, and the Philippines) are more likely than children in others (India, Okinawa, and the United States) to be assigned responsibility for taking care of siblings and other relatives (Whiting & Whiting, 1973).

Finally, general psychological health and security contribute to prosocial behavior: Children who are optimistic, outgoing, and possess good self-esteem tend to behave more helpfully than depressed, reserved, and insecure children (Eisenberg, 1992; Mussen & Eisenberg-Berg, 1977). The short recipe, then, for producing a prosocial child seems to be love, a prosocial environment, and an assignment of responsibility for caring for others (such as siblings, classmates, and pets); and, if you are the child's parent or guardian, be a humanitarian and an altruist yourself!

SOCIAL
PSYCHOLOGY
IN EVERYDAY
LIFE

Does Prosocial Television Programming Lead to Helping in Children?

We know from Chapter 10 that viewing violent television is linked to aggression in children. Can prosocial content in television programs similarly encourage helpful behaviors in children? The answer provided by many research studies seems to be an encouraging yes. For example, after children view videotapes of generous models (such as people who donate their winnings to charity), they are significantly more likely to be generous themselves in similar situations (Bryan, 1975; Elliot & Vasta, 1970; Rushton & Owen, 1975). Television models can also lead children to be more friendly, less prejudiced, and to engage in constructive forms of self-control (Rushton, 1981a).

In a particularly realistic study using real TV shows, children in the experimental group viewed an episode of *Lassie,* a popular TV show from the 1960s about a collie, in which a child risked his life to rescue Lassie's pup from a mine shaft; children in two control groups saw either a "neutral" *Lassie* episode or an episode of the situation comedy *The Brady Bunch* (neither of which contained examples of prosocial behavior). Later, the children were given the choice of earning points for prizes or working to help animals in need. Children who had watched the prosocial episode of *Lassie* were significantly more willing to give up prizes in order to work for the welfare of animals (Sprafkin, Liebert, & Poulos, 1975; see Figure 11.2).

Children's willingness to cooperate with others can also be influenced by television. In one study, second- and third-grade children watched either an episode of *The Waltons* portraying a cooperative solution to a conflict, a control video that did not portray cooperation, or no TV program at all. When they later played with other children in a game, the children who had viewed the cooperative TV show were significantly more cooperative than children in the other two groups (Baran, Chase, & Courtright, 1979).

Some studies have tried to tailor video examples to the prosocial behavior being studied. For example, Moriarity and McCabe (1977) studied 200 Canadian children who participated in team sports (baseball, lacrosse, and ice hockey). Children viewed videotaped examples of their particular sport that illustrated either prosocial behaviors (such as helping others or apologizing for a misdeed), antisocial acts (aggression), or neutral behaviors. Viewing prosocial examples increased the prosocial behavior of most of the children, but intriguingly, aggressive examples had no effect on the children's behavior.

The finding that prosocial television may have a greater impact on behavior than antisocial television is not limited to just the Moriarity and McCabe study. An analysis of almost 200 published tests of the effects of prosocial TV on children's behavior showed that it has a highly significant impact in

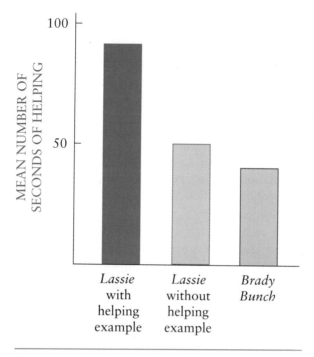

FIGURE 11.2 The effect of prosocial television on children's helping. *Source:* Data from Sprafkin, Liebert, and Poulos (1975).

fostering prosocial behaviors in children and that furthermore, the effect of prosocial TV on prosocial behavior was about twice as large as the effect of TV violence on aggressive behavior. Based on her analysis, Susan Hearold (1986) concluded:

> Many organizations and groups have chosen to work for the removal of sex and violence in televised programs. It is a defensive position: eliminate the negative. Alternatively, I would recommend accentuating the positive: apply money and effort to creating new entertainment programs with prosocial themes, especially for children (to whom the empirical evidence most clearly applies). Although fewer studies exist on prosocial themes, the effect size is so much larger, holds up better under more stringent experimental conditions, and is consistently higher for boys and girls, that the potential for prosocial effects overrides the smaller but persistent effects of antisocial programs. (p. 116)

The Psychology of Emergency Intervention

By the time Murphy, 30, arrived with his friend Tee Barnett, 28, the pair saw no choice but to intervene. "It was just like Rodney King," Murphy said. "They beat, beat and beat him."

But the crowd that appeared uniformly angry and brutal on TV contained people of goodwill, Murphy said. After the cameras cut away, someone must have helped Denny back into his cab.

A young nutrition consultant on her way home from work then hoisted herself onto the side of the truck and was shouting steering instructions to Denny, whose eyes were swollen shut. "To the right," she would yell, "now to the left."

—Los Angeles Times, May 1, 1992

"Ordinary" people often perform quite heroic deeds. The rescue of Reginald Denny provides a dramatic case in point. Lest Denny's rescue make you feel complacent about the strength of human virtue, however, consider in contrast one of the most infamous stories of nonintervention in recent history:

> Kitty Genovese is set upon by a maniac as she returns home from work at 3 a.m. Thirty-eight of her neighbors in Kew Gardens come to their windows when she cries out in terror; none come to her assistance even though her stalker takes over half an hour to murder her. No one even so much as calls the police. She dies. (Latané & Darley, 1970, p. 1)

The behavior of Kitty Genovese's New York City neighbors in 1964 became the subject of impassioned newspaper articles and editorials, magazine stories, an off-Broadway play, religious discourse, innumerable everyday conversations, and a series of famous social psychology experiments (Latané & Darley, 1970). Why were her neighbors so callous and uncaring? Was it the apathy of big-city living? More broadly, why do people sometimes immediately help in emergencies, and sometimes not at all? Before jumping to conclusions about the Kitty Genovese case, let's first analyze the social psychology of emergency situations.

Latané and Darley's Cognitive Model

In their influential book *The Unresponsive Bystander: Why Doesn't He Help?* (1970), Bibb Latané and John Darley portray emergency intervention as a five-stage decision process (see Figure 11.3). To intervene, a potential helper must: (1) notice that something is wrong, (2) decide that it's a true emergency, (3) assume responsibility for the problem, (4) decide how to help, and (5) actually implement the help. Helping can be short-circuited at any of the five stages.

Imagine that you are living in Kitty Genovese's apartment building at the time of the attack. You would first have to hear her screams and become aware of the emergency. If your TV is playing loudly and you live in an apartment far from the attack, you may not reach even this first stage. Suppose you do hear the screams. Then you have to decide whether it is a real emergency. You might decide, for example, that it's "only a lovers' quarrel" in which you shouldn't get involved.

Suppose you actually see the attack and know it's "for real." Now you must take responsibility to help. Perhaps you falsely assume that one of your neighbors has already called the police and thus you fail to act yourself. If you do take responsibility, you now must decide exactly what to do. Should you rush out and try to chase off a dangerous murderer? Should you yell from your window? Should

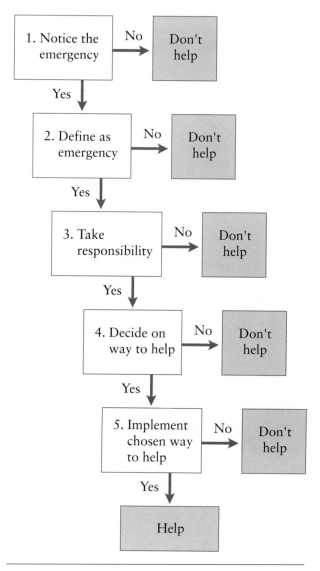

FIGURE 11.3 Latané and Darley's decision
model of emergency intervention (1970).

you call the police? Clearly, some kinds of intervention are riskier than others.
Suppose you decide to go outside and try to rescue Kitty Genovese. Now you must
think about implementing your decision: How should you approach the attacker?
Should you bring a weapon with you?

In an emergency situation, potential helpers must make all these decisions in
a split second. Emergencies are typically events with which we have little
experience. (How many times in your life have you had to intervene in a murder?)
We're often not sure what constitutes correct action. What determines, in such
difficult situations, when people do and do not help?

The bystander effect: Did the presence of many people increase or decrease the chances that this man would receive help?

The Bystander Effect   The murder of Kitty Genovese seemed particularly horrifying and senseless because it took place while 38 neighbors watched. Surely one of them should have helped. After all, there's safety in numbers, right? Maybe not. In a series of ground-breaking experiments, Latané and Darley (1970) demonstrated a surprisingly robust phenomenon termed the *bystander effect:* The presence of other bystanders often *inhibits* people from helping in emergencies.

In one experiment, Latané and Darley (1968) asked some Columbia University students to sit alone in a room and complete a questionnaire on "the problems of urban life." Soon after beginning, each subject suddenly witnessed an "emergency": smoke began pouring into the room from a small vent in the wall. Within four minutes, half the subjects took some action concerning the smoke (for example, reported it to someone), and three-fourths of them took action within six minutes, at which time the experiment ended. In a second experimental condition, groups of three subjects were sitting in the room when smoke began to pour in. Only 1 out of 24 subjects took action within the first four minutes, and only 3 reported the smoke within the entire duration of the

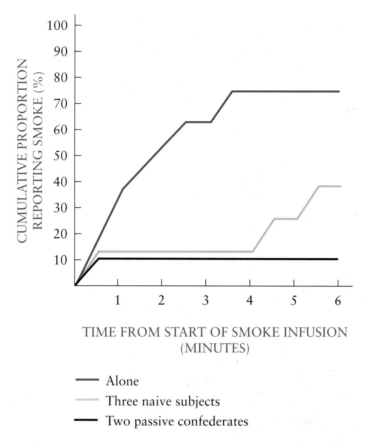

As the graph shows, single subjects were much more likely to seek help, and they responded to the possible emergency more quickly.

FIGURE 11.4 Cumulative percentages of subjects responding in different conditions to smoke pouring into the room. *Source:* Adapted from Latané and Darley (1970).

experiment. In a third condition, two confederates joined the one real subject in the smoke-filled room. The confederates were instructed not to respond to the smoke. If the subject asked them any questions, they said "I dunno" and continued filling in their questionnaires. In this condition, only 1 of 10 subjects reported the smoke (see Figure 11.4).

Why were subjects in a group so much less likely to respond to the smoke? The presence of others seemed to affect the second stage of Latané and Darley's decision process: defining the event as an emergency. These subjects seemed to say to themselves, "If the other people aren't worried, then perhaps it's not really serious."

Indeed, in the group conditions, subjects came up with many ingenious explanations for the smoke: that it was air-conditioning vapor, simulated smog, even "truth gas." Apparently, in an ambiguous emergency situation people look to others to decide how to define the situation and how to respond. Looking to others may sometimes lead to rather unintelligent behavior on everyone's part—a phenomenon labeled *pluralistic ignorance* (Allport, 1924). The fear of embarrassment seems to contribute to such pluralistic ignorance (Miller & McFarland, 1987). In the smoke-filled-room study, for example, subjects in groups didn't want to appear to have lost their cool. The problem, of course, is that if everyone tries to appear calm and composed during an emergency, everyone may be convinced by everyone else's false front that it's "not that serious."

The smoke-filled-room experiment provides intriguing data about some of the dynamics of emergency interventions, but it differs in two crucial ways from the Kitty Genovese incident: The situation was not clearly an emergency, and there was no human victim desperately in need of aid. In an attempt to more closely approach the dynamics of the Kitty Genovese case, Latané and Darley (1970) created a dramatic situation in which subjects believed they were witnessing a student's severe epileptic seizure.

Subjects were told that they would be participating in a discussion of "personal problems faced by normal college students." To ensure anonymity, students would sit in separate rooms and communicate via microphones. Each person would have two minutes to speak; then his microphone would automatically switch off and the next student's would switch on.

In one condition, subjects talked with one other student seated in a nearby room. The student spoke about his difficulties adjusting to college life, and then, with some embarrassment, confided that he sometimes suffered from seizures, particularly when stressed. The conversation switched back and forth, and then, while speaking, the other student actually seemed to have a seizure. He gasped:

> I-er-um-I think I-I need-er-if-if could-er-er-somebody er-er-er-er-er-er-give me a little-er-give me a little help here because-er-I-er-I'm-er-er-h-h-having a-a-a real problem-er-right now and I-er-if somebody could help me out it would-it would-er-er s-s-sure be-sure be good . . . because-er-there-er-er-ag cause I-er-I-uh-I've got a-a one of the-er-sei—er-er-things coming on and-and-and I could really-er-use some help so if somebody would-er-give me a little h-help-uh- er-er-er-er c-ould somebody-er-er-help-er-uh-uh-uh (choking sounds). . . . I'm gonna die-er-er-I'm . . . gonna die-er-help-er-er-seizure-er (chokes, then quiet). (Latané & Darley, 1970, pp. 95–96)

Clearly, the speaker was in trouble and needed immediate help. Did subjects respond? How quickly?

As you may already have suspected, subjects in this experiment were really listening to a tape of a simulated seizure. Latané and Darley systematically varied the size of the discussion groups: In some cases the subject thought that only he and the seizure victim were having a discussion; in some cases the subject thought there was one additional participant; and in some cases the subject thought there were four others, each in separate rooms. Just as in the smoke-filled-room study, the number of other bystanders dramatically affected subjects' helping behavior: The

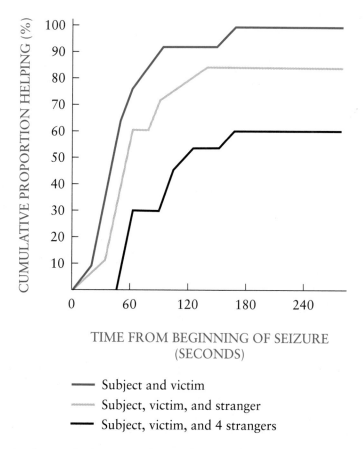

TIME FROM BEGINNING OF SEIZURE
(SECONDS)

——— Subject and victim

········ Subject, victim, and stranger

——— Subject, victim, and 4 strangers

As the graph shows, a subject who was the only person participating in the conversation was more likely to help the victim. All subjects who believed that they were alone when they heard the seizure aided the victim within three minutes; however, not all subjects in the other two conditions aided the victim.

FIGURE 11.5 Cumulative percentages of subjects responding to an epileptic seizure under different conditions. *Source:* Adapted from Latané and Darley (1970).

presence of more people led to less helping (see Figure 11.5, and see Figure 11.6 for a recent newspaper account of a real-life incident that shows a remarkable similarity to the Latané and Darley study).

Because the emergency in the seizure study was unambiguous, the presence of other people could not be influencing subjects' definition of the situation. Indeed, most seemed to grasp the problem immediately. Some subjects gasped to themselves, "My God, he's having a fit!"

No Sympathy at Bar Exam for Rescuers

by RENEE TAWA
TIMES STAFF WRITER

Two law students who stopped taking the State Bar exam this week in Pasadena to help another test-taker who was suffering an epileptic seizure were denied extra time to finish the test, which was completed by about 500 others who seemingly ignored the stricken man.

John Leslie, 28, of North Hollywood, said he was halfway through Tuesday's phase of the grueling, three-day exam at the Pasadena Convention Center when he put down his pencil and rushed to help the man, who was writhing on the floor and turning blue. Another student, Eunice Morgan, a registered nurse in her 40s, also responded.

While test administrators called paramedics, Leslie and Morgan administered cardiopulmonary resuscitation and first aid, trying to keep the 51-year-old victim's head back and jaw forward so he would not choke on his tongue. At one point, the man was unconscious and had stopped breathing, the two law students said.

Afterward, test supervisors refused to let either student make up about 40 minutes that they had spent during the three-hour test session helping the victim. The man was conscious by the time paramedics arrived and was taken to Huntington Memorial Hospital.

Victim Randall L. Carpenter, 51, said it was his 11th attempt to pass the bar exam. Carpenter said the bar should recognize the two good Samaritans—both strangers to him—rather than making them appeal their test scores.

FIGURE 11.6 Do bystanders help the victim of a real-life epileptic seizure?
Source: Los Angeles Times, February 27, 1993.

Latané and Darley argued that under these circumstances the presence of other people influenced the third stage of the decision process: It led to a *diffusion of responsibility,* whereby each person felt less responsible for dealing with the emergency.

Whether they were alone or in groups, subjects in the seizure study *were not* apathetic. Both those who helped and those who failed to help seemed upset. Indeed, subjects who did not intervene often seemed more aroused, showing physical signs of nervousness (trembling hands and sweaty palms). Their inaction can partly be explained by the notion of diffusion of responsibility and partly by subjects' fear of appearing foolish or overly emotional in the eyes of those present.

The seizure study says something potentially quite important about the Kitty Genovese case: People may have been frozen into inaction *because of* their awareness of other bystanders. Kitty's neighbors may have been victims of social influence more than of "bystander apathy." One practical moral of Latané and Darley's research is "Never assume others have responded to an emergency; always act as if you were the only person present."

The bystander effect turns out to be remarkably robust. By the early 1980s, more than 50 studies had investigated the effects of bystanders on helping, and a clear majority showed that people help more when alone than when with others (Latané, Nida, & Wilson, 1981). Thus, the social setting can have a profound effect on individuals' behavior in emergencies.

Emotional Arousal and Perceived Cost as Factors

Latané and Darley's decision model focuses largely on thought processes. Piliavin, Dovidio, Gaertner, and Clark (1981) formulated another model that in some ways extends and complements Latané and Darley's model (see Figure 11.7). One central feature added to this newer, more complex model is bystanders' arousal during an emergency. (We already have some evidence of subjects' distress from the seizure study.) Jane Piliavin and her colleagues argued that there is a strong emotional as well as cognitive component to helping in emergencies.

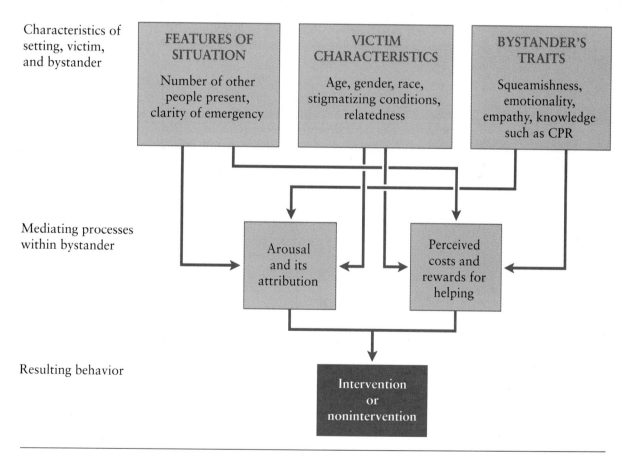

FIGURE 11.7 Piliavin, Dovidio, Gaertner, and Clark's (1981) model of factors that lead to emergency intervention.

Many research studies support the notion that emergencies are physiologically arousing (Dovidio, Piliavin, Gaertner, Schroeder, & Clark, 1991). In one series of studies, subjects watched a woman on closed-circuit TV as she climbed onto a chair to set up a projection screen (Byeff, 1970; Piliavin, Piliavin, & Trudell, 1974; both cited in Piliavin et al., 1981). Suddenly, the woman appeared to fall over, out of the range of the TV camera, and subjects heard a loud crashing sound. Exposure to this emergency increased subjects' heart rates and galvanic skin responses (a measure of skin conductivity and thus of perspiration).

In experiments in which subjects must face an emergency, the subjects' degree of arousal often has a strong correlation with their degree of helping (Dovidio, 1984). In one study, women overheard a female victim scream when a stack of chairs apparently fell on top of her. The correlation between subjects' heart rate increase and the amount of time they waited before intervening was −.58. That is, the more physiologically aroused the women were by the accident, the more quickly they helped the victim (Gaertner & Dovidio, 1977).

Sometimes, though, it is easier for people to *avoid* an emergency situation than it is to help. What determines when arousal leads a person to help and when it leads him or her to flee? According to Piliavin and Piliavin (1972), the answer involves a cost analysis of the situation. Figure 11.8 presents four possible

---

Piliavin and Piliavin (1972) propose that a moderately aroused witness to an emergency assesses the costs of helping and not helping before deciding whether to intervene. The table below predicts what a bystander is most likely to do in an emergency when the costs for helping are low or high and the costs for not helping are low or high.

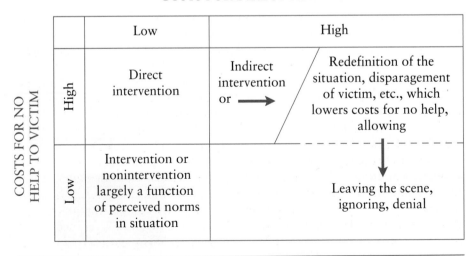

COSTS FOR DIRECT HELP TO VICTIM

		Low	High	
COSTS FOR NO HELP TO VICTIM	High	Direct intervention	Indirect intervention or ⟶	Redefinition of the situation, disparagement of victim, etc., which lowers costs for no help, allowing
	Low	Intervention or nonintervention largely a function of perceived norms in situation		Leaving the scene, ignoring, denial

---

FIGURE 11.8 Piliavin and Piliavin's cost analysis of emergency intervention. *Source:* Adapted from Piliavin and Piliavin (1972).

emergency situations defined by two cost factors: the cost for not helping the victim and the cost for directly helping.

To make this a bit clearer, imagine that you had to decide whether to rescue Reginald Denny. If you knew he was severely injured, then the costs of not helping would be very high: He'd probably die, and you'd experience terrible guilt and the possible disapproval of others if you didn't intervene. If Denny seemed only slightly injured and capable of escaping by himself, the costs of not helping would be much lower. The costs of directly helping may also vary. If you had to face a rioting mob of gang members to rescue Denny, then the costs would be very high indeed: You would have to risk your life. If, on the other hand, the rioters had deserted Denny and moved several blocks away, the costs of aiding Denny would be much lower.

Now look again at the cost analysis presented in Figure 11.8. If the costs of not helping are high (Denny will die) and the costs of helping are low (no rioters are around), you will probably help. If the costs of not helping are low (Denny's not seriously injured) and the costs of helping are also low (no rioters around), your helping will depend on situationally appropriate norms. For example, if Denny is your friend, you might help because of the norms of reciprocity or social responsibility.

If the costs of not helping are high (Denny will die) but the costs of helping are also high (you have to brave rampaging rioters), you face a dilemma. You might choose some "indirect intervention" (for example, calling the police), or you might engage in cognitive defenses that redefine the situation or disparage the victim ("Denny was stupid to get himself into that situation; he doesn't deserve my help"). Finally, if the costs for not helping are low (Denny's not seriously injured) and the costs for helping are high (you have to confront rioters), you may decide simply to leave or avoid the scene. When we think in terms of this kind of cost analysis, we realize that Denny's rescuers in fact behaved quite heroically in a very difficult situation.

A number of studies support the general notion that costs affect helping (and look back to the newspaper story in Figure 11.6 for a real-life example). One experiment, had confederates—men walking with canes—collapse on Philadelphia subways. Sometimes the victim had fake blood trickling from his mouth after falling (which presumably increased the costs of helping, because most people find blood repellent); other times he did not. The unbloodied victim was helped more often and more quickly than the bloody victim. In one trial, two teenage girls saw the victim collapse and got up to help him. Upon seeing the blood, one girl said, "Oh, he's bleeding!" And both girls promptly sat down (Piliavin & Piliavin, 1972).

In another study, subjects witnessed a realistic fight between a man and a woman on an elevator (Shotland & Straw, 1976). In one experimental condition, the woman and man were perceived as strangers (the woman screamed, "Get away from me. I don't know you"); in the other condition, they were portrayed as married ("Get away from me. I don't know why I ever married you"). Thirteen of 20 subjects—well over half—intervened in the "stranger" fight, whereas only 4 of 20 intervened in the "married" fight.

The researchers interpreted this large difference in terms of perceived costs. Indeed, subjects who were shown videotapes of the fights perceived the woman in

A man without legs is ignored by passersby. When will people help others? When won't they?

the "stranger" fight to be in greater danger (thus the cost for not helping was higher), and they also perceived that if they intervened, the combatants were more likely to turn on them in the "married" fight (higher cost for helping) than in the "stranger" fight. Thus, the costs for not helping and the costs for helping were perceived to be quite different for the two kinds of fights. (Note: These perceptions were not necessarily accurate. As you know from Chapter 10, a woman can be in as much danger with her husband as with a stranger.)

The principle that higher costs mean less help applies to all kinds of helping, not just emergency interventions. Allen (1968, cited in Latané & Darley, 1970) illustrated this in a clever experiment in which a bewildered-looking man on a New York subway asked a man reading a body-building magazine whether the subway was going uptown or downtown. (Both men were confederates.) The body-builder then responded with the wrong answer. In this "control" situation, 50% of bystanders on the subway intervened and corrected the mistaken information.

Then Allen modified the experimental conditions to dramatically increase the perceived costs of helping. A minute before the bewildered rider asked for directions, another subway passenger (again, a confederate) stumbled over the body-builder's legs. In one condition, the body-builder shouted threats at the stumbler, and in another, he made embarrassing comments about the stumbler. Would you contradict the body-builder now when he gives incorrect directions to the hapless man? Figure 11.9 shows that few people did.

If the costs of helping are *too* great, people may reduce their arousal by actually fleeing. In one study, residents of Cambridge, Massachusetts, witnessed either an apparent knee injury (a man grabs his knee and falls to the ground) or a heart attack (a man grabs his chest and falls to the ground) as they walked down

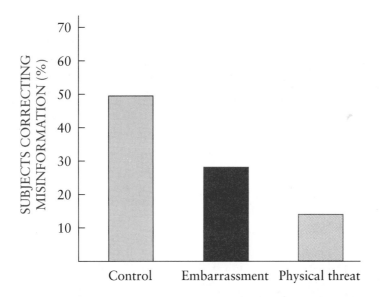

The results clearly showed that the more threatening the confederate had been, the less willing bystanders were to "cross his path" and correct the false information. Thus, the more costly helping seems to be, the less likely we are to offer it.

FIGURE 11.9 Helping a subway rider given wrong information, as a function of costs. *Source:* Latané & Darley (1970).

---

the street. Surprisingly, more subjects helped the knee-injury victim than helped the heart-attack victim (Staub, 1974). Perhaps the costs of dealing with the heart-attack victim were simply too great for many people: "I don't know what to do. He may die while I'm there. What if somebody sues me?" Some people actively tried to avoid or escape the situation by averting their gaze or crossing to the other side of the street. Seeing someone suffer is painful, so if helping is too costly, we may take a "see no evil" stance.

Misattribution of Arousal

There is another way our thoughts can mediate the impact of arousal on helping: through attributions. As we noted in Chapter 5, people sometimes misattribute the causes of their emotional arousal, particularly if the source of their arousal is somewhat ambiguous in the first place (Nisbett & Schachter, 1966).

Gaertner and Dovidio (1977) conducted an experiment in which some subjects were led to misattribute their arousal during an emergency. Subjects were

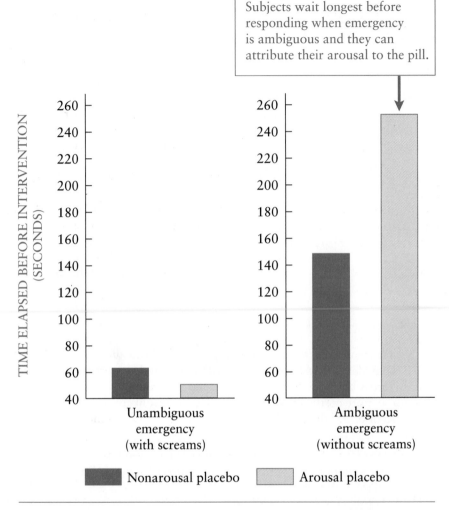

Subjects wait longest before responding when emergency is ambiguous and they can attribute their arousal to the pill.

TIME ELAPSED BEFORE INTERVENTION (SECONDS)

Unambiguous emergency (with screams)

Ambiguous emergency (without screams)

■ Nonarousal placebo　　▢ Arousal placebo

FIGURE 11.10 Misattribution of arousal and speed of helping in ambiguous or unambiguous emergencies. *Source:* Data from Gaertner and Dovidio (1977).

falsely told that they were participating in a study on how ESP is affected by specific drugs. They were then given a pill (actually a placebo) and informed that the drug might have some side effects. Half the subjects were told it might increase their heart rate, whereas the other half were told it might give them a dull headache.

While participating in the "ESP experiment," subjects heard the sounds of a woman moving around in the next room and then what sounded like a stack of chairs falling on her. To vary the ambiguity of this emergency, sometimes the victim screamed and sometimes she did not. The researchers measured how quickly subjects ran to her aid (see Figure 11.10). In the ambiguous emergency (without screams), subjects helped less when they could "explain away" their arousal as being caused by the pill they had taken. This study provides additional evidence that arousal plays a critical role in motivating helping.

Pure Altruism: Fact or Fantasy?

Thus far, our analysis of helping has not included the possibility of pure altruism. People help because they're aroused and upset, and they strive to reduce their arousal. Sometimes they accomplish this by helping others, sometimes by fleeing. In general, people seem to help because it allows them to avoid costs and gain rewards (whether external or internal). And sometimes people help others to display their virtue and heroism to a public audience. But none of this is pure altruism.

Recently, C. Daniel Batson (1987; Batson & Oleson, 1991; also see Hoffman, 1976) has argued that people do sometimes show true altruistic concern for others. In essence, Batson proposes that a person can experience two kinds of upset upon witnessing a suffering victim: *personal distress* (general, unpleasant arousal that the witness wants to reduce however possible) and *empathy* (compassion, sympathetic concern). Personal distress can be reduced by fleeing from a victim, but true empathy will not be satisfied by flight.

This distinction between an uncaring, egocentric arousal and a more caring, loving concern is illustrated well by a disturbing scene in the documentary film *Shoah*, which features interviews of people who participated in and survived the Nazi Holocaust. An elderly German woman recounts her memories of a small Polish town in which Jews were herded together in a church and then forced into vans, where they were gassed with automotive exhaust. She protests that she suffered too; she had to listen to the screams of dying men, women, and children. If she could have escaped from those screams, she implies, everything would have been fine. Clearly, this woman experienced personal distress, but not empathy.

Is it possible to distinguish empathy from personal distress in an experiment? Batson and his colleagues (1981) devised a clever situation to do just that. Female subjects were asked to watch a college woman named Elaine over closed-circuit TV as she received electric shocks in a learning experiment. (Actually, subjects watched a prepared videotape.) As the experiment progressed, Elaine showed increasing distress in response to the shocks. When the experimenter paused to check on her, Elaine explained that as a child she had fallen against an electric fence, which had left her very sensitive to electric shocks. The researcher then proposed a solution: Perhaps the subject watching Elaine over closed-circuit TV would consent to changing places with her. The experimenter then entered the subject's room and asked her whether she would be willing to trade places with Elaine. Subjects who agreed to change places were showing altruism toward Elaine, at some cost to themselves (they would now have to receive the electric shocks).

Batson and his colleagues assumed that all subjects would feel personal distress in this experiment—that is, arousal at witnessing Elaine's discomfort; they experimentally manipulated the degree of "empathy" subjects would feel for Elaine. Some subjects learned that they and Elaine had answered an attitude and

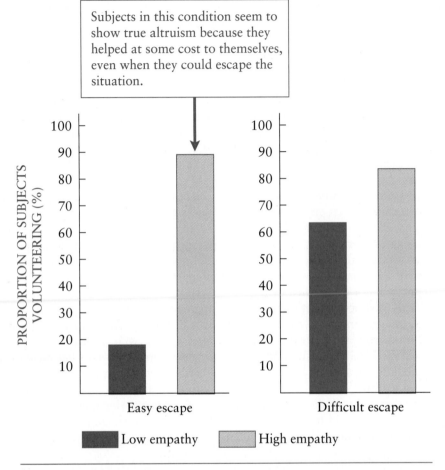

FIGURE 11.11 Willingness to help a suffering victim as a function of empathy and ability to escape. *Source:* Data from Batson et al. (1981).

interest questionnaire quite similarly; this was the "high-empathy" group. Others (the "low-empathy" group) learned that they and Elaine had answered dissimilarly. The ease with which subjects could escape from Elaine's suffering was also manipulated: Some subjects (in the "easy-escape" condition) were told they would have to watch Elaine for only two two-minute learning trials, whereas others (in the "difficult-escape" condition) were told they would have to continue to watch Elaine's suffering for ten trials. (The four experimental conditions are shown in Figure 11.11.)

Subjects who knew they would have to keep watching Elaine should have been motivated to help by personal distress, but subjects who knew they would no longer have to watch did not have that motivation. However, the subjects who felt empathy for Elaine would still have reason to help, for they were honestly concerned with her well-being. Only members of the "easy-escape, low-empathy" group had no motivation to help and thus were not expected to be very altruistic. This is exactly what the data showed (see Figure 11.11).

In a replication of the "Elaine study," Batson and his colleagues (1988) told subjects that before they could receive shocks in Elaine's place, they had to take a qualifying test that assessed their "numeric recall" ability. Intriguingly, highly empathic subjects (as assessed by a self-report questionnaire) earned the highest scores on this test, particularly when they were informed that the score needed to qualify was quite high. Remember, a high score would qualify them to receive shocks in Elaine's place, and they could easily avoid getting these shocks by simply reducing their effort on the test.

Thus, empathic people sometimes help even when they can conveniently escape another's suffering and can come up with a reasonable excuse for not helping. Such people help because they are genuinely concerned about another. Although Batson (1987) believes that people can be motivated by pure altruism, he also notes that such "emotion may be a fragile flower, easily crushed by overriding egoistic concerns" (p. 109).

Guilt, Mood, and Helping

Sometimes people behave "morally" because of external rewards and punishments (such as the threat of a spanking, or the much larger threat of eternal hellfire) and sometimes because of internal emotional states (such as guilt). Let's turn to research on the effects of guilt and other moods and emotions on helping.

Guilt

According to *The American Heritage Dictionary,* guilt is "remorseful awareness of having done something wrong." This definition implies two things: Guilt occurs when we believe we have committed a moral transgression, and it is unpleasant. Equity theory provides one analysis (Walster, Walster, & Berscheid, 1978): Guilt occurs when we "give" too little and "get" too much in a relationship. Imagine, for example, that you are married to an ideal spouse who showers you with love, attention, and material gifts. If you are hostile, indifferent, and stingy in return, you may very well feel guilty. We may also feel guilty when we lie to, unfairly criticize, or accidentally injure others—that is, when we break rules of conventional morality.

Social psychology experiments repeatedly demonstrate that guilt can motivate helping: Once people have been induced to do something wrong (such as break an experimenter's apparatus, cheat on an experimental task, violate a rule, or lie), they are significantly more willing to help the experimenter, and others as well (Carlsmith & Gross, 1969; Katzev, Edelsack, Steinmetz, Walker, & Wright, 1978; McMillen, 1971; Silverman, Rivera, & Tedeschi, 1979; Wallace & Sadalla, 1966).

In one clever experiment, a confederate approached individual women at a shopping center and asked them to take a picture of him with his camera. Unfortunately for these helpful women, the camera was designed to break. In the "guilt" condition of the experiment, the confederate suggested that it was the woman's fault that the camera broke; in the "nonguilt" condition, the confederate reassured the woman that she was not to blame, that the camera frequently "acted up." A little while later, the same women encountered another confederate whose grocery bag had ripped open, scattering candy on the ground. Fifty-five percent of the guilty subjects helped, but only 15% of the nonguilty subjects helped (Regan, Williams, & Sparling, 1972).

In a conceptually similar study, experimenters reprimanded some visitors to the Portland Zoo who, in violation of posted rules, gave food to the bears. To arouse guilt, they scolded, "Hey, don't feed unauthorized food to the animals. Don't you know it could hurt them?" Later, subjects passed a confederate who had dropped his belongings on the ground. Fifty-eight percent of the reprimanded subjects offered help, as compared to under a third of nonreprimanded transgressors (Katzev et al., 1978).

These two studies suggest some important points about guilt and helping. First, people seem to feel particularly guilty about a "bad" act when they are forced to assume responsibility for it: The people who fed the bears but weren't scolded clearly did not feel as guilty as the scolded people. Second, people may relieve their guilt by aiding someone who is not the original victim of their transgression.

Doing good for people who are not the victims of your wrongdoing is somewhat puzzling from the perspective of equity theory, for such helping does not

Do people help because of internal factors such as empathy and guilt or because of external factors such as rewards, costs, and pressures from other people?

"I feel there's a lot of pressure to be good."

"balance the scales" unbalanced by your bad act; it does not right the original wrong or recompense the original victim. Of course, some people believe in divine scales of equity that need to be balanced and believe that God records all our sinful and virtuous deeds, justly rewarding or punishing us in an afterlife (Lerner & Meindl, 1981).

Sadly, it may be impossible for us to make direct amends for our wrongdoings in all cases. Sometimes a bad deed cannot be undone (murdering someone or cheating on a spouse), and sometimes our victims are no longer available to receive compensation (your victim moves to a faraway city or dies). If a transgression is major, even doing good deeds for others may not fully alleviate guilt.

Thus, many societies have devised ways for dealing with unbearable guilt. The ancient Hebrews practiced a ritual whereby people could symbolically lay their sins upon a "scapegoat," an animal which was then released into the wilderness, carrying the community's transgressions with it. Confessions, too, provide a way to vent guilty feelings. Interestingly, experimental studies suggest that confessing a wrongdoing in fact reduces guilt; people who have just confessed help less than those who haven't. One clever field experiment found that Catholics arriving at church during its advertised confessional period made larger donations to the March of Dimes than Catholics leaving church during the same period did, presumably after confession (Harris, Benson, & Hall, 1975).

Bad Moods and Helping

Do negative moods other than guilt affect helping? Suppose you're sad because of a tragic accident you just saw on the nightly news, or depressed because you just failed an exam. Are you more or less likely to be helpful after such an event?

The research evidence is mixed (Carlson & Miller, 1987). In one study, subjects listened to either an uplifting or a depressing news story on the radio and then participated in a game in which they could either cooperate or compete with others (Hornstein, Lakind, Frankel, & Manne, 1975). Subjects exposed to depressing news tended to be more competitive and less cooperative. Further research has suggested that bad news may lead to less helping because it causes subjects to see people in general as bad and undeserving of help (Holloway, Tucker, & Hornstein, 1977; Veitch, DeWood, & Bosko, 1977). Sadness, too, can inhibit helping; studies have found that saddened subjects are less helpful than control subjects (Moore, Underwood, & Rosenhan, 1973; Weyant, 1978).

To complicate the research picture, however, other studies have shown that negative moods can sometimes increase helping. For example, Alice Isen and her colleagues (1973) observed that subjects led to believe that they had failed at an experimental task helped more than control subjects did.

When do negative moods increase helping and when do they decrease it? One possibility is that individuals are more likely to be helpful after negative or embarrassing experiences that are witnessed by others; they then behave in helpful, "altruistic" ways to repair their damaged public image. A study that showed this effect clearly put some schoolchildren in grades 1 through 3 in a bad mood (by asking them to reminisce about a sad experience) and then gave them an opportunity to help other children. In some cases an adult was present and in other cases not. The children in a bad mood were more helpful than control children only when the adult was present. Thus, they seemed to behave helpfully to receive public admiration and reinforcement (Kenrick, Baumann, & Cialdini, 1979).

Adults may differ from children in that they internalize the reward of doing good deeds (Cialdini, Darby, & Vincent, 1973; Cialdini et al., 1987); thus, adults in a negative mood may help specifically to boost their mood (not just to appear good to others). This is a subtly selfish motivation to help. This *negative-mood-relief model* implies that if sad people get a mood boost from another source (such as hearing a funny story or finding some money), then they will have no need to help another person. A number of experiments, alas, support this hypothesis (Cialdini et al., 1973; Cunningham, Steinberg, & Greu, 1980).

Are there other circumstances when negative moods lead to helping? One review of relevant studies found that people in bad moods are particularly likely to help others when they believe they are responsible for having caused negative events (that is, when they feel guilty) and when their attention is focused on another's suffering rather than on themselves (Carlson & Miller, 1987).

Good Moods and Helping

Although the research on bad moods and helping has some subtle twists, the research on good moods and helping is much more clear-cut: "[T]here is joyful consistency to the findings. Happy moods ... consistently motivate helping behavior" (Salovey, Mayer, & Rosenhan, 1991, p. 217). For example, the happiness created when subjects learn they've succeeded at a task (Isen, 1970), receive small gifts of money or food (Isen & Levin, 1972), remember happy events in their lives (Moore et al., 1973), and experience nice weather (Cunningham, 1979) leads to greater helping. In general, happy is helpful (Carlson, Charlin, & Miller, 1988).

Why do positive moods lead to helping? One possibility is that positive moods stimulate positive thoughts in general (Isen, 1987); if other people are seen as "nice," "honest," and "decent," then clearly they deserve to be helped. Another possibility is that happy people are not as self-focused as sad people (see Chapter 3), and the more you direct your attention toward others, the more sensitive you should be to their needs (Carlson, Charlin, & Miller, 1988). Finally, happy people may help others in order to maintain their happy moods (Mayer, Gottlieb, Hernandez, Smith, & Gordis, 1990; Yinon & Landau, 1987). This, by the way, is a subtly selfish reason for helping when you are happy.

Unfortunately, the "warm glow" that leads people to help more after a happy event may be quite transient. In one study by Isen, Clark, and Schwartz (1976), subjects who had just received a free gift (stationery) received a phone call from a confederate, who said that she had reached the wrong number and had just spent her last dime at a pay phone. The confederate asked whether the subject would help her out by making a phone call for her. Subjects experiencing the pleasure of having recently received a free gift were quite helpful: 60% to 100% of subjects in two separate studies made the call when the request came in the first few minutes after the gift did. But this helpfulness faded quickly; when subjects were called 20 minutes after receiving their gift, under 20% complied with the request.

The many explanations of helping behavior that we have discussed so far are reviewed in Summary Table 11.1.

The Flip Side of Helping: Receiving Help

A major factor that can determine whether you help another person is whether the other person *wants* to be helped. It seems commonsensical that people who *need* help *want* to be helped, but a number of social psychology theories suggest this is not always so; receiving help can be a source of pain as well as pleasure.

For example, equity and exchange theories (Adams, 1965; Walster et al., 1978) propose that people want a fair give-and-take in their relationships. Thus, if someone helps you too much, you may feel indebted to him or her, which is clearly uncomfortable. As the Roman historian Tacitus noted, "Benefits are only acceptable so far as they seem capable of being requited; beyond that point, they excite hatred instead of gratitude."

Sometimes people "help" in order to exert control over others. For example, parents may give an allowance so that they can then threaten their disobedient child with cutting it off. And a nation may give economic aid to other nations with the ulterior motive of influencing their policies and extracting favors in return (Gergen & Gergen, 1971). *Reactance theory* states that people are unhappy whenever they believe their freedom of choice is being limited by others (Brehm, 1966; Brehm & Brehm, 1981); thus, if help is seen as an attempt to influence behavior, people may very well shun it.

Finally, receiving aid from others may be unpleasant because it signals some inadequacy on the part of the recipient and thus threatens self-esteem (Fisher, Nadler, & Whitcher-Alagner, 1982). People often believe, for example, that students require help in their studies only when they are hopelessly lost; that workers require help at work only when they are falling far short of the mark; and that people require therapeutic help only when their lives and relationships are a shambles. To some people, accepting help is an admission of failure, particularly if others do not also seem to need such help (Gross, Wallson, & Piliavin, 1979; Tessler & Schwartz, 1972).

In sum, although it might seem consistent with common sense that people would most appreciate help when they are most in need of it, research does not support this "obvious" conclusion (Calhoun, Dawes, & Lewis, 1972; Franklin, 1975; Morse & Gergen, 1971). People may reject sorely needed help for several reasons: It may be viewed as particularly obligating (your helper can later say, "You ingrate—I helped you when you were at rock bottom!"); it may very strongly restrict the recipient's freedom of choice ("I have no choice—I must go on welfare and put up with all their demeaning rules and regulations"); and finally, it may be particularly damaging to self-esteem ("I'm accepting this help because I'm a failure").

SUMMARY TABLE 11.1	Explanations of Helping Behavior		
	Kind of Explanation	*Variables/Processes Studied*	*Research Questions and Topics*
Group-level explanations	Biological groups	Biological evolution	Kin selection, reciprocal altruism
	Cultural groups	Cultural norms	Norms of reciprocity, equity, and social responsibility
Individual-level explanations	Past environment	Modeling, learning	Development of prosocial behavior; media effects
	Current environment	Modeling	Effect of prosocial models; media effects
		Bystander effect	Effect of presence of other bystanders
Mediating variables	Cognitive processes and decision making	Latané and Darley's five-stage model	When will people help in emergencies?
		Piliavin and Piliavin's cost analysis	
	Others	Personality traits	Consistency of altruistic behavior across settings
		Arousal and emotion misattribution	When does emotional arousal lead to helping?
		Empathy	Do people ever show pure altruism?
		Guilt	When and why does guilt motivate helping?
		Bad moods	When and why do bad moods motivate helping?
		Good moods	Why do good moods motivate helping? How long does the effect last?

What kinds of people find aid most threatening? Men often feel less comfortable receiving help than women do (Gourash, 1978; Hoffman, 1972). (Who is more willing to ask for directions when lost, a man or a woman?) In a related vein, "feminine" people are more likely to be comfortable seeking help, whereas "masculine" people are likely to be less comfortable under such circumstances (DePaulo, 1978; see Chapter 8 for a broader discussion of femininity and masculinity).

Cultural rules also play a role in reactions to receiving help. Fisher, DePaulo, and Nadler (1981) noted that "people in Western cultures are taught that independence is a virtue and that dependence is shameful" (p. 418). Communal societies seem to encourage both offering and receiving help more than individualistic societies do. In one illustrative study, people who lived on a kibbutz (an Israeli collective farm) reported that they would be more willing to seek help (for example, in schoolwork) than Israeli city dwellers did. When given an intellectual task, kibbutz dwellers in fact sought more aid when it was presented as a group task, and city dwellers sought more aid when it was an individual task; this pattern was particularly pronounced for male subjects (Nadler, 1986). Thus, situational variables in conjunction with culturally learned rules can influence when people seek help.

In sum, although it may be godly to give, it is often uncomfortable to receive. One final note: Offering help in an emergency is unlikely to trigger resentment. It is help offered in the normal give-and-take of everyday life that is most problematic.

HELPING PEOPLE TO HELP

In the end, Denny's friends and rescuers reached out to find each other—his rescuers in hopes of finding out how Denny had fared, and his family in hopes of thanking them.

"We found out that both Denny and I had 8-year-old daughters," said Barnett [one of Denny's rescuers]. . . .

"Black boys playing with white boys—that's what Dr. King talked about. Working together. Playing together. . . ."

As for the man dressed in black, Murphy and Barnett said they never got his name. He and another man who had helped block traffic for the caravan to the hospital drove the big-rig back to the cement company lot and vanished.

—*Los Angeles Times,* May 1, 1992

As Reginald Denny's rescue proves, people sometimes show amazing heroism, helping others in the most difficult circumstances. But how many of us are willing to follow this and many other shining examples of altruistic acts and people? You'd probably agree that the world would be a much better place if a lot more people were a lot more helpful.

How can people be encouraged to help more? Let's consider four common techniques to increase helping behavior: (1) moral exhortation (verbally urging others to help and to live according to moral and religious principles); (2) providing prosocial models; (3) heightening feelings of responsibility toward people needing help; and (4) personalizing those needing help.

In conclusion, we shall look at recent social psychology research on a very important kind of helping in the 1990s: AIDS volunteer work. This research poses

Blacks and whites work together to clean up after the Los Angeles riots of 1992.

two fundamental questions: What motivates people to do such demanding volunteer work, and how can this and other important kinds of volunteerism be fostered?

Moral and Religious Exhortation

Moralists of all persuasions and leaders of most of the world's major religions have reminded people to show compassion for others and to love their neighbors. Unfortunately, however, simple exhortation—like that found in parents' lectures and religious sermons—is not a particularly powerful way to foster helping and altruism. After all, exhortation is aimed at reminding people of norms of prosocial behavior. But much of the research we have discussed in this chapter shows that helping is often influenced more by features of the social situation (the number of bystanders present, the costs of helping, or the ease of escape from a suffering victim) than by social norms.

A dramatic experiment by John Darley and C. Daniel Batson (1973) powerfully demonstrated how situational pressures can sometimes overwhelm the highest moral principles. Forty students at the Princeton Theological Seminary were subjects in a study that supposedly dealt with "the vocational careers of seminary students." The students were asked to deliver a talk in a nearby university building to assess "how well they could think on their feet." Half the students were asked to speak about "jobs in which seminary students would be most effective." The others were asked to talk about the parable of the Good Samaritan. Here is the parable:

A man was going down from Jerusalem to Jericho, and he fell among robbers, who stripped him and beat him, and departed, leaving him half dead. Now by chance a priest was going down the road; and when he saw him he passed by on the other side. So likewise a Levite, when he came to the place and saw him, passed by on the other side. But a Samaritan, as he journeyed, came to where he was; and when he saw him, he had compassion, and went to him and bound his wounds, pouring on oil and wine; then he set him on his own beast and brought him to an inn, and took care of him. And the next day he took out two dennarii and gave them to the innkeeper, saying, "Take care of him; and whatever more you spend, I will repay you when I come back." Which of these three, do you think proved neighbor to him who fell among the robbers? He said, "The one who showed mercy on him." And Jesus said, . . . "Go and do likewise." (Luke 10: 29–37)

Darley and Batson also manipulated how rushed the subjects were. In the "high-hurry" condition, the students were told, "Oh, you're late. They were expecting you a few minutes ago. You'd better get moving." In the "intermediate-hurry" condition, subjects were told, "The assistant is ready for you, so please go over." In the "low-hurry" condition, subjects were informed, "It'll be a few minutes before they're ready for you, but you might as well head on over."

On the way to the appointment, each seminary student passed an alley in which a confederate was sitting, slumped over, with his eyes closed. The instant the student passed by, the confederate coughed twice, groaned, and kept his head down. Clearly, he needed help!

Were students who had been assigned to talk about the Good Samaritan more likely to help than the others? This result would make sense. After all, these students were preparing to discuss one of the most famous of all biblical injunctions to help a victim in need, so helping should have been highly salient to them. Yet the topic of students' talks did not significantly influence whether or not they helped the man in distress. The hurry manipulation, however, was highly significant: 63% of the low-hurry students, 45% of the intermediate-hurry students, and only 10% of the high-hurry students helped the distressed man. Overall, only 40% of the seminary students offered any kind of aid to the victim.

The irony of these results was not lost on Darley and Batson (1973):

A person not in a hurry may stop and offer help to a person in distress. A person in a hurry is likely to keep going. . . . He is likely to keep going even if he is hurrying to speak on the parable of the Good Samaritan, thus inadvertently confirming the point of the parable. (Indeed, on several occasions, a seminary student going to give his talk on the parable of the Good Samaritan literally stepped over the victim as he hurried on his way!) (p. 107)

It would be easy to view these students as hypocrites who did not practice what they preached, but this interpretation is too simplistic. Some of the hurried subjects did not seem even to notice the victim, because their attention was focused so narrowly on their immediate goal. Those who did notice the victim were placed in a conflict: Whom should they help, the rushed experimenter or the possibly sick victim? Darley and Batson noted, "Conflict, rather than callousness, can explain their failure to stop."

The Good Samaritan study is relevant to a broader finding: People in cities often help less than people in rural areas (Korte, 1981). City dwellers are often more rushed than their rural counterparts, and they also suffer from sensory overload because so many things are happening at once in the city (Milgram, 1970). Thus, people in cities, like Darley and Batson's "high-hurry" subjects, rush to their appointments, narrow the focus of their attention, and are sometimes oblivious to people who need help. (It may also be the case that helping strangers is potentially much more costly—that is, risky—in big cities than in rural areas.)

The Good Samaritan experiment is also relevant to another broad question: Are religious people more altruistic than nonreligious people? In studies using questionnaires, religious people report being significantly more helpful and charitable than nonreligious people, but in studies that look at actual helpful behaviors, there proves to be little relation between religiosity and various kinds of helping (Batson & Ventis, 1982; Batson et al., 1989). In other words, religious people seem to preach (and report) altruism, but they don't necessarily practice what they preach.

You may recall from Chapter 7 that researchers have distinguished among three kinds of religiousness (Allport, 1959; Allport & Ross, 1967; Batson & Ventis, 1982): Intrinsically religious people view religiousness as an end in itself and view religious values as being central to their lives; extrinsically religious people view religion as a means to other ends (social approval, family acceptance, business and social contacts); and finally, people who take a "quest" orientation to religion pursue spiritual questions in an open-minded way, without adhering to rigid theologies.

Not surprisingly, a number of studies suggest that extrinsic religion is not associated with altruism (Batson, 1990; Batson et al., 1989). Intrinsically religious people profess altruism, but don't consistently practice it; furthermore, when intrinsically religious people do offer aid to others, they are often insensitive to whether the recipients want their help or not (Batson & Gray, 1981; Darley & Batson, 1973); it seems that intrinsically religious people often help others to prove to themselves that they are helpful and virtuous, not because they are honestly concerned about the recipient's needs. The quest orientation seems to be the approach to religion that is most consistently associated with both altruistic attitudes *and* deeds (Batson et al., 1989).

The Good Samaritan experiment and other studies on religious beliefs and helping suggest that reminding people of their moral principles may have only limited effects on their helpfulness. If seminary students (who should be exquisitely sensitive to moral issues) do not necessarily help a victim while en route to delivering a talk on the Good Samaritan, how will the rest of us fare under the influence of their sermons?

Modeling

When discussing influences on children's prosocial behavior, we noted that parents' actions may speak louder than their words. Research on TV and prosocial behavior underscores the power that prosocial models can have in influencing children's behavior.

Children learn helpful behaviors by modeling others.

Modeling can foster helping behavior in adults as well. In one experiment, an undergraduate woman stood next to a Ford Mustang with a flat tire in a residential area of Los Angeles. Passing motorists who had seen a man helping another woman change a tire a quarter of a mile back on the road were almost twice as likely to stop and help as motorists who had not previously observed helping. Similarly, more people donate to a Salvation Army solicitor after observing another person (actually a confederate) donate money (Bryan & Test, 1967).

Just as aggression can be discouraged by nonaggressive models, so can helping be encouraged by helpful models. In particular, research suggests that prosocial models who are warm and nurturing and who are perceived as similar to the observer are most effective in fostering imitative helping (Rushton, 1980; Yarrow et al., 1973). On a personal level, when you are helpful, you encourage your family members, friends, and colleagues to be helpful as well.

Assuming Responsibility

How can we encourage people to feel responsible for others' well-being? We already know that the presence of other bystanders during an emergency can lead to a diffusion of responsibility, whereby each individual no longer feels as obligated to intervene. Does the presence of others inevitably decrease helping?

No, not when the other people are friends! Latané and Darley (1970) replicated their seizure study so that some subjects participated in the "group discussion" with a stranger and the seizure victim and others with a friend and the victim. Intriguingly, subjects did not show a diffusion of responsibility when with a friend. This finding has been replicated in more recent studies as well (Rutkowski, Gruder, & Romer, 1983; Yinon, Sharon, Gonen, & Adam, 1982). It's interesting to note that two of the people who rescued Reginald Denny were friends of each other who went to the scene of the melee together. Latané and Darley (1970) speculate that diffusion of responsibility does not occur among friends because they regard themselves as a unit.

Darley, Teger, and Lewis (1973) showed that people sitting face to face respond to emergencies more quickly than people sitting back to back. This implies that nonverbal cues are important in triggering emergency intervention in groups. Friends may be less inhibited in scrutinizing each other's nonverbal cues during an emergency and thus may perceive that their fellow bystander is upset.

Friends can also anticipate discussing the emergency later and thus being accountable to one another for their behavior. You cannot be anonymous in a group of friends; your identity, and your response to the crisis, is known. The effects of bystanders' knowing one another is yet another explanation for the observed differences between city and country dwellers: In small towns, the bystanders to emergencies are likely to be acquaintances; in big cities, they are likely to be strangers.

On a practical level, these research findings suggest that becoming acquainted with the people around you will foster helping. Make it standard practice to meet your neighbors and work colleagues. Not only will you gain friends and acquaintances as a result, you'll increase your chances of helping and being helped during an emergency, for people who know one another tend to take responsibility more readily for one another in emergencies.

Another remarkably easy way to encourage people to be responsible for others is simply to assign them responsibility. In one study, Staub (1970) explicitly told individual kindergarten children that he was leaving them "in charge." When these children heard another person in distress in the next room, they were more likely to intervene. Adults also help more when assigned responsibility. For example, Moriarity (1975) staged thefts of radios and suitcases in public places. Sometimes bystanders had been asked by a confederate to keep an eye on their belongings, sometimes not. When assigned responsibility, subjects intervened in the "theft" in virtually every instance; when not assigned responsibility, only about a third of the bystanders intervened.

Thus, to encourage prosocial behavior in friends, colleagues, workers, students, and children, it helps to assign them the "job" of behaving in helpful ways.

Humanizing the Victim Who Needs Help

In many experiments on bystander intervention, the victim is a nameless person who falls off a chair, or collapses, or suffers a seizure. Certainly, it seems more likely that we would help a friend or a relative than a stranger.

Interestingly, social psychology research shows that even a trivial acquaintance with a victim increases helping behavior. In yet another version of their seizure study, Latané and Darley (1970) had the "victim" meet some subjects in the hallway and strike up a brief conversation before the experiment began. Later, in six-person discussion groups, only 31% of subjects responded to the seizure if they had not previously met the victim; however, 75% responded if they had previously conversed with the victim face to face. Some subjects reported that after meeting the victim they visualized him suffering his seizure, and this spurred them to action. In addition, after talking with the victim, not only did subjects know him, he knew them; thus, subjects may have felt more personally accountable and responsible for his fate.

Subsequent studies have confirmed the finding that a brief interaction which reduces the victim's anonymity can greatly increase the incidence of helping behavior. For example, receiving a warm smile or holding a trivial conversation increases subjects' willingness to help a stranger (Solomon et al., 1981).

All of this research makes an important point: Flesh-and-blood people—people we have seen and talked with—evoke our sympathy more than abstract strangers do. Thus, the ties of acquaintance and friendship facilitate helping in two ways: Bystanders who are friends of one another are more likely to help, and bystanders acquainted with the victims are also more likely to help.

Education about Helping

Now that you've read this chapter, you can use your knowledge to become a more helpful person. For example, because you know that the presence of many bystanders leads to reduced helping, you can consciously decide to help, even when others are present. I had occasion to ponder Latané and Darley's notable research on the bystander effect as I exited from a busy freeway in Southern California and witnessed a tractor-trailer that had toppled off the exit ramp, apparently after driving too fast around a tight curve. My immediate thought was, "Surely someone has already reported this to the police." I thought about the bystander effect and then drove to a pay phone and reported the accident.

Research by Beaman and his colleagues (1978) shows that people like you and me who have learned about the bystander effect are more likely to help in emergencies. In other words, because of our intellectual capacities, we can sometimes "stand above" social influences and act according to our informed social conscience rather than in response to blind social pressures. Thus, our knowledge about helping and altruism can help us to help more often.

AIDS Volunteers and Their Motives

SOCIAL
PSYCHOLOGY
IN EVERYDAY
LIFE

AIDS constitutes an unprecedented medical and social crisis throughout the world. By the time you read these words, there will likely be more than a quarter of a million confirmed cases of AIDS in the United States. Informed estimates are that about 1.5 million Americans are infected with HIV (the virus that causes AIDS), and, barring medical advances, most of these people will eventually develop AIDS (Centers for Disease Control, 1992).

People with AIDS require an enormous amount of help: assistance with cleaning and shopping, finding legal and medical services, and emotional and social support. Much of this help has come from volunteers who willingly take on the daunting task of befriending and assisting people with AIDS, many of whom face acute psychological distress along with their debilitating physical symptoms. Why do these volunteers do it?

To answer this question, social psychologists Mark Snyder and Allen Omoto (1992a, 1992b) developed and administered a questionnaire to measure the motivations of AIDS volunteers in Minneapolis. They identified five main kinds of motives: Some people volunteered to express their basic values (for example, "because of my humanitarian obligation to help others"), some to express their community concerns and solidarity ("to help members of the gay community"), some to help gain knowledge ("to learn about how people cope with AIDS"), some to foster personal growth ("to challenge myself and test my

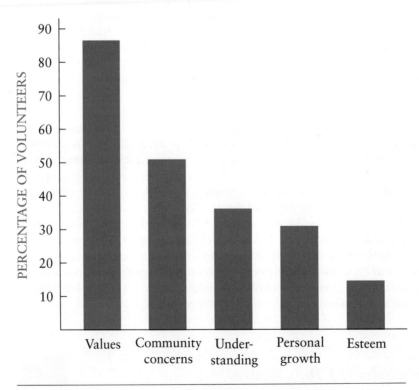

FIGURE 11.12 Percentage of AIDS volunteers choosing each type of reason for volunteering. *Source:* Snyder and Omoto (1992).

skills"), and finally, some volunteered to enhance their self-esteem ("to feel better about myself"). Figure 11.12 shows the percentage of volunteers who offered each kind of reason for their work.

Which of the reasons just listed do you personally find most admirable? It might seem that AIDS volunteers who are pursuing their humanitarian values are those who are most truly praiseworthy. But before we judge these volunteers and their motivations too hastily, consider this: Snyder and Omoto contacted the same AIDS volunteers about a year after they had filled in the initial questionnaire and determined who was still active as a volunteer and who had quit. They found that those most likely to be active a year later were the ones who had volunteered to enhance their self-esteem or to pursue personal growth. Perhaps paradoxically, the volunteers who offered the most seemingly self-serving reasons for pursuing their volunteer work were those who were most likely to stay committed to this highly demanding work.

Of course, the point of this research is not to label some volunteers as "good" and others as "bad." All volunteers deserve our admiration and appreciation. Rather, the goal of this research is to understand *why* people volunteer so that organizations can find volunteers whose motivations match the kinds of jobs that need to be filled. Furthermore, such research can help organizations identify volunteers who are most likely to remain committed to their volunteer work, even when the going gets rough (Snyder, 1993). This research provides a fitting conclusion to this chapter, for it shows once again that helping is complex, and that different people can perform the same helpful acts for quite different reasons. ⬎

HELPING OTHERS IN PERSPECTIVE

Human societies could not exist if people did not help one another. Such helping comes in many forms. Some people offer heroic aid during dangerous emergencies, and some help others in less dramatic ways—through thoughtful acts, charitable contributions, and volunteer work. Some helping is impulsive and emotional, some deliberate and calculated, and some perhaps truly altruistic.

Helping has been explained at many different levels. Biologists have proposed evolutionary theories of helping, which suggest that natural selection can lead to altruism toward kin and to reciprocal altruism but not to pure selfless altruism. Anthropologists and sociologists have studied norms of helping and how they vary across different societies.

Psychologists have tended to focus on two general sorts of questions: (1) Do some people have altruistic personalities, and if so, what are these people like and how did they get to be that way? (2) What kinds of situations lead people to help or not to help?

Altruism proves to be a reasonably consistent personality trait, and altruistic people are likely to be empathic, to have highly developed kinds of moral reasoning, and to have humanitarian values. Children who have altruistic models, loving parents, and an outgoing and adjusted personality are particularly likely to be helpful and to develop into altruistic adults.

Despite the many personal factors that influence altruistic behavior, social psychology research has demonstrated that situational factors also strongly determine when, and indeed, whether we help. Research on the bystander effect shows that the presence of other people can often inhibit helping in emergencies. And while emotional arousal often motivates helping, even aroused people will sometimes fail to help if the costs of helping are too great or if the setting they are in leads them to misattribute their arousal to other factors.

Situationally induced moods can influence when we help. Guilty people are often more likely to help than nonguilty people. People in bad moods are helpful particularly when there is a public audience for the helping, when they see themselves as responsible for negative events, and when they focus their attention on another's suffering. Good moods consistently but temporarily lead to increased helpfulness.

Social psychologists have identified many strategies for helping people to be more helpful, including modeling, assigning responsibility for helping, and humanizing the victim.

Although social psychology research has identified many different "self-serving" factors that influence helping, it has also found that people can sometimes be truly altruistic, helping others because they are genuinely concerned with their well-being. All the helpers of the world—including the rescuers of Reginald Denny, the heroic Christians who saved Jews during World War II, and AIDS volunteers—provide an optimistic model for the rest of us and prove that people can be "Good Samaritans."

KEY POINTS

Kinds of Helping

Prosocial behavior is behavior that intentionally helps or benefits another. Altruism is help offered to another for no external reward, and even at some cost.

Measuring Prosocial Behavior

Studies have employed varied behavioral measures of helping.

Major Approaches to the Study of Helping

Evolutionary Approaches

Evolutionary theories suggest that pure altruism cannot result from natural selection. However, altruism to kin is adaptive because it fosters the survival of one's own genes, and reciprocal altruism is adaptive, particularly in social species, because it fosters indiv idual and group survival.

Cultural Approaches

Norms of prosocial behavior are prescriptive social rules that govern when help should be offered to others. The norms of reciprocity, equity, and social responsibility help enforce and regulate prosocial behavior.

Cultures vary in general levels of helpfulness and in their moral views of helping behavior.

The Psychology of Helping

Is There an Altruistic Personality?

Although Hartshorne and May's early studies suggested that altruistic behaviors in children are not consistent across settings, recent studies show evidence for moderate consistency.

Altruistic people tend to be empathic, to have high levels of moral reasoning, and to hold humanitarian values. The Christian rescuers of Jews during World War II tended to be risk takers, to identify strongly with a humanitarian parent, and to be somewhat marginal members of their communities.

Children who observe prosocial adult models, who are placed in the role of helper, and who are psychologically secure and adjusted are more likely to show helpful behaviors.

Viewing prosocial TV programming increases prosocial behavior in children.

The Psychology of Emergency Intervention

Latané and Darley's Cognitive Model   Latané and Darley describe emergency intervention as a five-stage decision process in which a potential helper must notice the situation requiring intervention, define it as an emergency, assume responsibility, decide how to help, and actually intervene.

Many studies document the *bystander effect,* which occurs when the presence of other bystanders inhibits people from helping in emergencies. This effect results in part from a diffusion of responsibility that occurs when people in groups feel less personally obligated to help than they would if alone. It may also result from pluralistic ignorance, which occurs when people facing emergencies try to appear "in control" in the presence of others, and as a result underestimate how serious the emergency is.

Emotional Arousal and Perceived Costs as Factors   Emergencies are physiologically arousing. Highly aroused bystanders are sometimes more likely to help in an emergency. If the costs of helping are too high, however, they may also flee the scene of the emergency.

Misattribution of Arousal   People who misattribute their arousal during an ambiguous emergency are less likely to help.

Pure Altruism: Fact or Fantasy?

Helping can be motivated both by personal distress (general unpleasant arousal) and by empathy (compassionate concern). Experiments demonstrate the presence of empathy and pure altruism when subjects help a suffering victim even when they could escape from observing the suffering.

Guilt, Mood, and Helping

Guilt—unpleasant feelings of remorse following moral transgressions—motivates prosocial behavior particularly when people assume responsibility for their transgressions. Guilt can motivate an individual to help someone who was not the original victim of the individual's bad deed.

People experiencing negative moods help particularly when they are observed by others, when their helping leads to a more positive mood, when they feel responsible for negative events, and when their attention is focused on another's suffering.

People experiencing good moods are more likely to help, but this helpfulness tends to be short-lived.

The Flip Side of Helping: Receiving Help

Receiving help can be uncomfortable when it makes the recipient feel indebted, restricts freedom, or lowers self-esteem. Gender, personality characteristics, and cultural norms influence an individual's willingness to receive help.

Helping People to Help

Moral and Religious Exhortation

Exhortation has limited effectiveness in encouraging prosocial behavior. The Good Samaritan study shows that seminary students' helping was more influenced by their degree of hurry than by salient moral principles.

Religious people tend to report higher degrees of helpfulness, but they don't always practice what they preach. The quest orientation, but not extrinsic or intrinsic religiousness, tends to be linked with helpful behaviors.

Modeling

Prosocial models foster helping both in children and adults.

Assuming Responsibility

When people assume or are assigned responsibility for helping, they tend to be more helpful.

People are more likely to assume responsibility in emergencies and to help when they are in the presence of friends or acquaintances. The bystander effect is less likely to occur when groups of friends rather than strangers witness an emergency and when people in groups can monitor one another's nonverbal cues.

Humanizing the Victim who Needs Help

People are more likely to help in emergencies when they are acquainted, even trivially, with the victims.

Education about Helping

People can use their knowledge about research on prosocial behavior to be more helpful.

Social Psychology in Everyday Life: AIDS Volunteers and Their Motives

People become AIDS volunteers to express their humanitarian values, to support their community, to gain knowledge, to experience personal growth and challenge, and to boost their self-esteem. AIDS volunteers motivated by the last two reasons are most likely to remain committed to their volunteer work.

KEY TERMS

Altruism: Helping another for no reward, and even at some cost to oneself.

Bystander effect: The tendency for individuals to help less during emergencies when in the presence of others.

Diffusion of responsibility: The tendency for individuals to feel less personally responsible for helping when in the presence of others; one explanation for the bystander effect.

Emergency intervention: Quick helping in response to a sudden event that endangers another and that sometimes puts the helper at risk.

Guilt: A negative emotion that occurs when an individual believes he or she has committed a moral transgression; guilt can motivate helping.

Kin selection: According to modern evolutionary theory, the process by which natural selection favors animals that promote the survival of genetically related individuals; such "altruism" helps ensure that the individual's genes will be propagated to future generations.

Negative-mood-relief model: Proposes that people are more likely to help after experiencing a negative mood if they can boost their mood by helping.

Norm of equity: Prescribes that people should receive goods in a relationship in proportion to their investment.

Norm of reciprocity: Prescribes that people should help and not hurt those who have helped them; that is, people should give as they get in social relationships.

Norm of social responsibility: Prescribes that people give aid to a dependent person in proportion to his or her need.

Pluralistic ignorance: Occurs when people in an ambiguous situation look to others to decide how to define the situation and how to behave. This can lead to unintelligent behavior in emergencies—to avoid embarrassment, everyone tries to appear calm and composed, thereby convincing everyone else that the emergency is not serious.

Prosocial behavior: Behavior that intentionally helps or benefits another person.

Reciprocal altruism: Mutually beneficial behavior between two members of the same or different species; biological evolution can lead to reciprocal altruism because the "cost" of helping another is more than offset by the evolutionary benefits of the reciprocated help.

Tit for tat: A strategy of reciprocal altruism in which a partner in a relationship starts with an altruistic response and in all subsequent interactions reciprocates his or her partner's preceding response (that is, selfishness is matched with selfishness, and altruism with altruism); tit for tat is a highly stable and adaptive strategy of reciprocal altruism.

CONFORMITY, COMPLIANCE, AND OBEDIENCE

ANAHEIM—Like all good Cub Scouts, William and Michael Randall promised to do their best to help other people honor their country and obey the Law of the Pack.

But when it came to pledging a "duty to God," the twin 10-year-olds from Anaheim Hills refused.

"I don't think he's real," Michael said. "Nobody has his signature, nobody has any clothes that he wore, nobody knows if he's dead or something. I just think that he's a fairy-tale."

Said William: "My brother took the words right out of my mouth."

The fourth-graders' stance has put them at loggerheads with Boy Scout officials who say they won't alter the time-honored Scouting pledge for a pair of young atheists.

"The Scout Oath and Pledge have been part of the movement since 1910," said Blake Lewis, national spokesman for the Boy Scouts of America. "You can't pick and choose the parts you want to obey."

—*Los Angeles Times,* November 18, 1991

Michael and William Randall were partners in nonconformity when they refused to say the word "God" in the Cub Scout oath.

William and Michael Randall quickly paid a price for their rebellion against the Boy Scouts of America. Their den leader informed the twins that if they didn't express a belief in God, they would have to drop out of the Cub Scouts. Later, when the case went to court, Boy Scout officials said that William and Michael had not been "expelled" from their den, but they had been informed that they could not advance in rank without satisfying the "religious requirements." Whether threatening expulsion or the inability to advance, the Boy Scouts clearly put the Randall twins under considerable pressure to obey Boy Scout leaders and conform to Boy Scout standards.

Why didn't the Randall twins follow orders and "go along with the crowd," as so many others typically do? Was it due to the strength of their convictions, or was it due perhaps to the fact that they had each other for support? The case of the Randall twins poses a number of questions about the many kinds of social influence that guide our behavior. The Boy Scout code holds obedience to be a cardinal virtue. But is it always desirable to "obey the Law of the Pack"? Do people sometimes show destructive kinds of obedience? In general, when do people obey and conform? Why do they do so? Perhaps the broadest question of all is: How do individuals and groups get us to go along with their beliefs, requests, and commands so frequently?

This chapter is about the nature of social influence, which occurs when our behavior is shaped or altered by other people. Such influence can be subtle—for example, when disapproving looks from others lead us to conform to their standards—and sometimes it can be blatant—as when others make direct requests or issue commands to us.

KINDS OF SOCIAL INFLUENCE

You can probably think of many extreme and dramatic kinds of social influence: People join cults and practice strange rituals because of "peer pressure"; working

Innocuous and dangerous forms of social influence: Left: *A Boy Scout attempting to sell candy.* Bottom: *Nazi youth marching in unison.*

people give away their hard-earned money at the request of smooth-talking salespeople and TV evangelists; servicemen and police officers sometimes kill others at the command of superiors. But as the example of the Randall twins illustrates, social influence operates in more mundane settings as well: in our homes, clubs, classrooms, and workplaces. Indeed, hardly any aspect of life is untouched by social influence.

Social psychologists have extensively studied three main kinds of social influence prevalent in everyday life: *conformity, compliance,* and *obedience.* People *conform* when they maintain or change their behavior to be consistent with group standards; they *comply* when they accede to a request made by another; and they *obey* when they follow a direct command, typically from someone perceived to be a legitimate authority.

Look around, and you will see these three kinds of social influence all about you. You change your style of dress to be more like your friends. (This is conformity.) A neighbor comes to your door and asks you to donate $10 to her school. You refuse. Then she asks you to buy a $2 candy bar instead to support the school. You do (first noncompliance, then compliance). The notorious Nazi war criminal Adolf Eichmann sends hundreds of thousands of innocent men, women, and children to extermination camps after being ordered to do so by his superiors (obedience). You accompany your friend to church for Sunday services; when the whole congregation rises to its feet, you do too, even though you're not sure why everyone is rising (conformity). Your classmate asks for a loan of $5; you reluctantly hand it over (compliance). After waiting in line for half an hour at the Department of Motor Vehicles to register your car, you're told you're in the wrong line and you must go wait in another long line; you go quietly (obedience).

As these examples suggest, social influence can affect matters as trivial as our style of dress and events as profound as the Nazi Holocaust. Social psychologists have strived to answer some basic questions about the nature of social influence: When will people conform, comply, and obey, and when won't they? What psychological processes account for different kinds of social influence? Are individuals always at the mercy of social pressures, or can they sometimes fight back? Just how powerful *is* social influence? Can it totally control our behavior in some settings?

LEVELS OF SOCIAL INFLUENCE

When I agreed to be a cubmaster so that a new pack could form at my son Damian's school, I had to sign an affirmation that I "recognized my obligation to God." I told the district commissioners that I was an atheist, but they weren't concerned as long as I could sign. I signed, saying to myself that I recognize my obligation to God is about the same as my obligation to Santa Claus. My discomfort with this dissimulation was less than the guilt I would feel if I let down the boys in the pack for the sake of my own sanctimonious scruples.

—D. Carroll, *The Humanist,* November–December 1987

Sometimes people go along with others just on the surface, and sometimes they are truly converted to others' beliefs. In an early analysis, Herbert Kelman (1958) identified three different levels of social influence: (1) We may publicly go along with others in order to gain rewards or avoid punishments while refusing to change our private opinions. (2) We may behave like others because we're attracted to them and continue to be influenced as long as our attraction lasts. (3) We may behave like others and adopt others' ideas when we are logically convinced by them. In essence, Kelman argued that some kinds of social influence are shallow and temporary, whereas other kinds are deeper and more enduring.

In the sections that follow, you will discover that the distinction between public and private responses to influence is quite important in recent theory and research. As we discuss research on conformity, compliance, and obedience, ask yourself, "Is it only subjects' public behavior that changes, or their inner beliefs as well?"

CONFORMITY

Twin Anaheim Hills boys who allege that the Boy Scouts of America ousted them because of their refusal to swear an oath to God testified Wednesday that they were members of the organization for nearly three years before their position on religion caused a problem.

"I never said the word 'God' in the Cub Scout Promise," said 10-year-old William Randall. "I just mouthed it. . . . Me and my brother don't believe in God."

—*Los Angeles Times,* November 21, 1991

Although they ultimately rebelled, William and Michael Randall showed a degree of conformity to the Boy Scouts. When he mouthed the word *God,* for example, William Randall conformed to Cub Scout standards, at least in his surface behavior. He must have realized that he would be penalized if he did not conform to some degree.

Like William Randall, we all behave like "the pack" at times, even in situations when we don't believe in what we are doing. We dress like our friends, pray like members of our congregation, and frequently vote for the same political candidates as our family members. We often *conform:* We behave in a manner that is consistent with group standards because of real or implied pressures from the group. What is the nature of conformity, and why and when does it occur?

Classic Research on Conformity

It is one thing to observe conformity in everyday life. It is another thing to scientifically measure it and understand it. Modern scientific research on conformity began with classic experiments by Muzafer Sherif (1935) and Solomon Asch

(1951, 1955, 1956), both of which greatly expanded our knowledge about the nature of conformity. (Please pay careful attention to these two studies, for we will refer to them repeatedly in later sections.)

Sherif and the Autokinetic Effect *Theory.*

Sherif (1935) conducted a series of laboratory studies to document how social pressures influence ambiguous perceptual judgments. In these studies, Sherif made use of a perceptual illusion called the autokinetic effect: When people view a single stationary point of light in the dark, the light appears to move.

In one experiment, Sherif put groups of three subjects in a dark room and asked them to estimate the distance a point of light appeared to move. Each subject initially offered a different estimate—perhaps the first subject reported 8 inches of movement; the second, 2 inches of movement; and the third, 1 inch. Sherif's experiments showed conclusively that when subjects announced their estimates to the group, their judgments tended to converge over successive trials (see Figure 12.1).

When asked, most of Sherif's subjects vehemently denied that they had been influenced by other subjects' judgments, but the data clearly told another story. Sherif theorized that groups create their own norms, or standards; when faced by ambiguous realities, they converge on a reality defined by the group.

Subjects in autokinetic studies seem to experience private conversion to (as well as public compliance with) the group norm; they come to believe the group consensus. For example, subjects who changed their estimates of the amount of light movement after hearing others' judgments continued to be influenced by the group norm as much as a year later, even in the absence of the original group (Rohrer, Baron, Hoffman, & Swander, 1954).

Robert Jacobs and Donald Campbell (1961) extended the autokinetic paradigm a step further by exposing single subjects to three confederates who made extreme judgments (that the light moved 16 inches, in contrast to estimates of 4 inches by control subjects not exposed to confederates). Despite the extremity of the confederates' estimates, the subjects strongly conformed, making judgments almost as extreme as those of the three confederates. Next, Jacobs and Campbell created successive "generations" of four-person groups. They removed one confederate from the group, substituted another naive subject, and again had subjects estimate the movement of the light for 30 trials. Then they removed yet another confederate and added another naive subject. This process continued until the group was composed of naive subjects only. The extreme group norm created by the confederates at the start continued to influence the judgment of successive generations of groups, and that influence subsided only after multiple generations (see Figure 12.2). Do you think this effect occurs outside the laboratory—that we conform to norms that originated in previous times and that have now outlived their usefulness or validity?

Asch's Minority of One against a Unanimous Majority

Sherif's research showed that when asked to make ambiguous perceptual judgments, people conform to emerging social norms. Almost 20 years after Sherif's

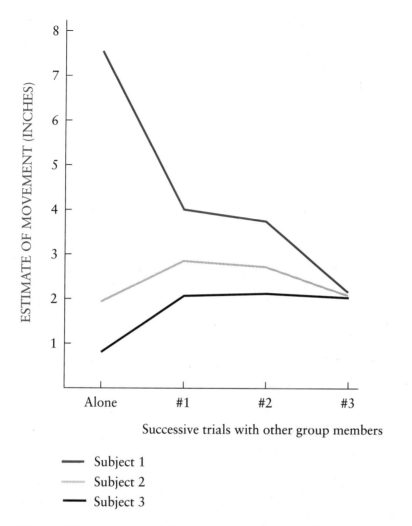

When subjects announced their estimates to one another, their estimates tended to converge over successive trials.

FIGURE 12.1 Results for one group of subjects in Sherif's (1935) autokinetic studies. *Source:* Data from Sherif (1935).

studies, Solomon Asch (1951, 1956) reasoned that if subjects were required to make a more obvious perceptual judgment, they would show less conformity than Sherif's subjects. After all, if you see white, you're not going to say "black" just because everyone else says "black," are you? To test this hypothesis, Asch created an experimental situation that set the standard for most subsequent conformity research.

Imagine that you are the subject in this experiment. You come to a room with seven to nine other subjects (actually confederates, but you don't realize this). The

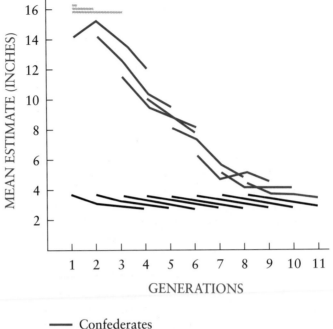

As the graph shows, the extreme norms created by confederates persisted for a number of generations after confederates had been removed from the groups.

FIGURE 12.2 Transmission of an arbitrary norm across "generations" of subjects. *Source:* Jacobs and Campbell (1961).

---

experimenter informs you that this is a study on visual perception. Specifically, your job is to examine three lines of different lengths drawn on a large white card and judge which of the three is equal in length to a standard line drawn on another card. You will make such judgments 18 times during the experiment for different sets of lines. Figure 12.3 shows a sample of the experimental stimuli.

The experiment begins uneventfully, with subjects announcing their answers aloud to the rest of the group. You are the next-to-last person in a row of seated subjects, so most subjects answer before you. The correct answers are quite obvious (again, see Figure 12.3), and on the first two trials all subjects give the correct answers.

On the third trial, however, the first subject gives an obviously incorrect answer. Perhaps you smile to yourself and think, "This guy must have been out partying last night." But then the second subject gives the same incorrect answer. Is

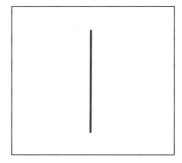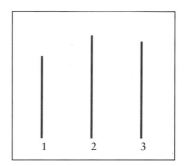

FIGURE 12.3 An example of the stimulus lines used in Asch's classic conformity experiments (1955). Subjects were asked to judge which of the three lines of obviously unequal length (shown in the right panel) were equal in length to the standard line (shown in the left panel). *Source:* Asch (1955).

it possible, two partyers in the same group? The third and fourth subjects also give the same incorrect answer. Now you begin to feel nervous. What's wrong? Why is everyone else seeing the lines differently from you? The correct answer seems obvious, yet the fifth, sixth, and seventh subjects give the same wrong answer. Finally, it's your turn, and you face quite a dilemma: Do you state the answer that your senses tell you is obviously correct, or do you cave in to the unanimous majority that offers what seems to be an incorrect answer?

In Asch's experiment, confederates unanimously gave incorrect answers on 12 of the 18 trials. Of 123 subjects, 94 (that is, 75%) conformed at least once on such a "critical trial." And on average, subjects conformed on more than 4 of the 12 critical trials (that is, more than one-third of the time). Thus, even when the truth was absolutely clear, subjects would often conform to a mistaken but unanimous majority.

Disturbed by his findings, Asch (1955) wrote:

> That we have found the tendency to conformity in our society so strong that reasonably intelligent and well-meaning young people are willing to call white black is a matter of concern. It raises questions about our ways of education and about the values that guide our conduct. (p. 34)

Did Asch's subjects actually come to believe the incorrect answers they stated in conformity with the majority? In general, no. Asch found that if subjects could write their judgments rather than publicly announce them, conformity declined to about a third of the level observed in his original study. (In this variation, Asch arranged for subjects to arrive "late" at the ongoing experiment and told them to join in by writing their judgments rather than by publicly announcing them to the rest of the group.) Thus, subjects' conformity in the original experiment was mostly public compliance.

In subsequent interviews, most of Asch's subjects stated that they did not believe their conforming responses. Why, then, did they go along with an obviously

Adolescents conform when they dress alike.

incorrect majority? One subject answered, "They might think I was peculiar." Another said, "Mob psychology builds up on you." A third noted, "I think a majority is usually right." One subject even offered, "When in Rome, do as the Romans do."

Two themes seem to emerge in the statements made by Asch's subjects. First, they felt pressured by the group; they didn't want to "stick out" and risk ridicule or rejection by the group. Second, they sometimes looked to the group for correct information: "a majority is usually right." Morton Deutsch and Harold Gerard (1955) labeled these two kinds of pressure normative and informational social influence. *Normative social influence* occurs when people conform, often only on the surface, to gain rewards and avoid punishments from the group. *Informational social influence* occurs when people look to the group to gain accurate information. It seems likely that conformity in Sherif's autokinetic studies was due more to informational social influence (subjects looked to the group to define ambiguous reality), whereas conformity in Asch's studies was due more to normative social pressures (subjects didn't want the group to think them "weird," so they caved in even though they didn't really agree with the group). Recent experiments (such as Campbell & Fairey, 1989; Insko, Drenan, Solomon, Smith, & Wade, 1983; Insko, Smith, Alicke, Wade, & Taylor, 1985) offer additional support for the notion that people conform to groups both to be correct (informational social influence) and to be liked and to avoid punishment (normative social influence).

In one variation of his classic experiment, Asch (1952) showed that his subjects had good reason to fear ridicule if they didn't conform to the group. This time he placed one confederate among a group of naive subjects in his line-judgment task. On critical trials, the sole confederate was instructed to give obviously incorrect answers. The majority responded by laughing at this "deviate." Clearly, it's risky to be a nonconformist in a group, for you may indeed be ridiculed. (You might be wondering at this point how Asch's confederates treated subjects in the original critical conformity trials. They were instructed not to stare at subjects or to make any comments. There was no overt ridicule or pressure on Asch's subjects, which makes the high levels of observed conformity even more startling.)

Do groups exert pressures other than ridicule on nonconformists? The answer is clearly yes. Think back to the example of the Randall twins, who were threatened with expulsion from their Cub Scout den if they did not conform to Boy Scout standards. A classic experiment by Stanley Schachter (1951) directly observed the pressures that groups exert on nonconformists. Groups of five to seven college men met to discuss the case of "Johnny Rocco," a juvenile delinquent who was awaiting sentence for a minor crime. The men were asked, in essence, to decide what society should do with Johnny. Should they punish him severely? Send him to reform school? Send him to a foster home? Three confederates were planted in each discussion group. One—the "deviate," or nonconformist—always championed an extreme point of view that differed from that of the rest of the group. The second confederate—the "mode"—always agreed with the majority; he was the "yes-man" of the group. A third confederate—the "slider"—started out disagreeing with the group, but then slid into agreement. Schachter observed how much group members spoke to each confederate, and he measured how much group members liked each of the three confederates.

In general, Schachter's experiment showed that the discussion group liked the mode and the slider, but not the deviate. Furthermore, the group initially spoke (more precisely, argued) with the deviate more than with either the mode or the slider. Apparently, when faced with a nonconformist, the group tried hard to persuade him to agree. When it became clear, however, that he was not going to yield, the group often stopped talking with him, particularly when the group was cohesive (that is, when group members were attracted to one another) and highly involved in the discussion.

The two kinds of normative social influence that occurred in the Johnny Rocco study—direct persuasive communication, followed by rejection—occur in everyday life as well. This sequence seemed to occur with the Randall twins: First Scout leaders tried to persuade them to give in; when that failed, the twins were threatened with expulsion.

A similar example is provided by a small church in Oklahoma that attempted to pressure one of its members to conform to its standards. In 1984, the church discovered that a church member, Marian Guinn, was engaging in extramarital sex. To bring Guinn back into the fold, church elders visited her and tried to persuade her to give up her "sinful" behavior. When she refused, the church publicly announced her sin to the congregation and moved to "withdraw fellowship" from her—that is, to excommunicate her and have all church members shun her (*Newsweek*, February 27, 1984; *Time*, March 26, 1984). Like the groups in Schachter's Johnny Rocco study, this church dealt with a nonconformist first by directly pressuring her and then by rejecting her. Given such pressures, perhaps it is not surprising that people do often conform to standards set by their churches, families, and cliques of friends.

Factors That Influence Conformity

People do not always conform. A significant number of Asch's subjects successfully resisted a unanimous majority. And as we already know, when subjects could record their answers privately rather than announce them publicly, conformity decreased substantially. Thus, conformity must partly be a function of the kind of person you are and partly a function of the setting you are in (see Chapter 3).

Personality

Common sense probably tells you that some people are more likely to conform and others are more likely to be independent in the face of group pressures. Is there in fact a conforming personality? Asch (1956) speculated that people who feel inadequate and who possess low self-worth might be particularly compliant in conformity studies; however, he offered no evidence for this speculation.

Later researchers modified Asch's procedures to examine the role personality plays in conformity. For example, Richard Crutchfield (1955) automated Asch's experimental procedure so that it was unnecessary to use confederates. Subjects made judgments at a control panel, which also supposedly displayed the responses of other subjects. Subjects sat in individual cubicles, and the experimenter controlled the responses that appeared on subjects' control panels. In this streamlined version of the Asch paradigm, Crutchfield found, among other things, that subjects who scored high on intellectual competence and "ego strength" (that is, people with good knowledge of their impulses and good conscious control over them) tended to conform less, whereas subjects who scored high on authoritarianism (see Chapter 7) tended to conform more.

Although specific traits do at times correlate with conformity, these correlations are often weak and vary from study to study. Furthermore, an individual's level of conformity is often quite inconsistent across settings (McGuire, 1968a) and thus doesn't appear very traitlike. To complicate matters further, different personality traits may predict different kinds of conformity.

John McDavid and Frank Sistrunk (1964) gave subjects several personality inventories and then asked them to make perceptual judgments (such as picking which of a pair of projected circles of light was larger) that were either very clear-cut (as in Asch's studies) or quite difficult to judge (as in Sherif's studies). On critical trials, subjects faced a unanimous majority who gave the wrong answer, and the researchers observed how much subjects conformed. Different personality traits were found to correlate with conformity, depending on the sex of the subjects and the ambiguity of their judgments. For example, conformity on clear-cut judgments seemed more related to the subjects' timidity, dominance, and need for approval, whereas conformity on ambiguous judgments was more a function of their degree of trust, degree of suspiciousness and cynicism, and sex-role-related traits. Thus, there probably is no single kind of conforming personality and no small set of traits that consistently predicts all kinds of conformity for all people.

Gender

Crutchfield's (1955) studies were the first of many to show that women on average conform more than men. Recent meta-analyses show that on average, women conform slightly more than men; however, sex differences in conformity vary considerably across studies (Becker, 1986; Eagly, 1987; Eagly & Carli, 1981; see Chapter 8).

Why do women sometimes conform more than men? Sistrunk and McDavid (1971) argue that traditional conformity studies are biased in favor of finding more conformity in women because they often use judgment tasks that are subtly biased in favor of men. Indeed, when Sistrunk and McDavid studied conformity on opinion items, they found that men conformed *more* than women on such "feminine" topics as fashion, home economics, and family care.

Alice Eagly's social role theory of sex differences (1987; see Chapter 8) offers another explanation: Women conform more than men because of the different and often lower-status roles they occupy (for example, secretary rather than boss). Women also frequently occupy nurturing roles (for example, mother, nurse, elementary school teacher), and deference and maintenance of group solidarity are important in such roles. Eagly argues that women should behave consistently with their sex roles particularly in public group settings (when they are being observed by others), and indeed research suggests that sex differences in conformity are strongest when women are in groups and being observed by others (Eagly, 1987; Eagly & Chrvala, 1986). If Eagly's theory is correct, then we should expect sex differences in conformity to decrease as women attain higher social status and as sex roles change.

Group Size

Since Asch's classic studies, social psychologists have tended to focus more attention on situational factors than on personality traits that influence conformity. Perhaps the most obvious situational factor is group size. Doesn't it make intuitive sense that the larger the group that pressures you, the more you will conform?

Commonsense notions are not always supported by data, however. In his original studies, Asch (1955) varied the number of unanimous confederates from 1 to 15 people (see Figure 12.4). Surprisingly, conformity approached its peak level in a group of three or four individuals. Conformity actually seemed to decline

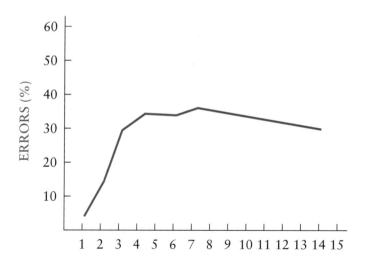

NUMBER OF PEOPLE DISAGREEING WITH SUBJECT

Instead of increasing steadily with group size, conformity reached close to its maximum level when the group consisted of four people.

FIGURE 12.4 Results of Asch's studies of group size and conformity. *Source:* Adapted from Asch (1955).

slightly for the largest groups, a finding that has been replicated by others (for example, Rosenberg, 1961).

One reason that conformity (at least as measured in experiments) may not increase much when pressuring groups are larger than four people is that some subjects may grow suspicious of the unexpected unanimity they observe in the large groups (Insko et al., 1985). Another reason is that subjects often do not consider members of unanimous groups to be independent. They assume that people who announce their judgments after hearing others are being influenced by the previously announced judgments. Indeed, some of Asch's (1956) subjects stated this hypothesis in their interviews: "I thought the mob were following the first man. . . . Yes, people tend to follow the leader."

An experiment by Wilder (1977) clearly demonstrated that a group produces more conformity when its members' judgments are perceived to be independent. After subjects heard tape recordings of four people stating strong opinions about a lawsuit, they were asked to give their own opinions about the suit. Some subjects heard all four people in a single discussion; others heard two separate discussions involving two people each. Although the opinions expressed were the same in each case, the subjects exposed to the two separate groups were influenced more than subjects exposed to one group of four.

In recent years, social psychologists have attempted to construct precise mathematical models to describe the amount of social influence (for example, pressure to conform) that groups of varying sizes exert on target groups of varying sizes (Latané, 1981; Latané & Wolf, 1981; Tanford & Penrod, 1984). Tanford and Penrod's Social Influence Model (1984), for example, holds that a family of curves best depicts the relation between group size and social influence (see Figure 12.5).

There are three important implications of these curves: (1) Initially, social influence increases rapidly with each additional member of the influencing group, but it levels off after a point; in other words, beyond the first few members of the influencing group, each additional member adds less and less to the group's total impact on the target of influence. (The top curve in Figure 12.5 is analogous to Asch's experiments in which one target is influenced by unanimous groups of different sizes. This curve approximates Asch's results very well: Influence increases as groups increase in size to about four people and then levels off.) (2) As the target group gets larger, the curves get flatter; stated another way, adding people to very small groups dramatically increases their power to influence *individuals,* but adding people has less impact on their ability to influence other *groups.* (3) There is a maximum level of social influence that can be exerted by a given group (no curve reaches 1.0 or higher in Figure 12.5); that is, influence does not increase indefinitely as group size increases.

The Social Influence Model proves to be very good at accounting for observed data in many different kinds of studies. For example, Tanford and Penrod (1984) compared predictions made by a computer simulation based on their model with data from classic conformity studies, including Asch's, and their predictions agreed with the results of these studies quite accurately. It is important to note, however, that while the Social Influence Model mathematically describes *how* variables are related, it does not say *why* they are related.

Increasing group size may affect the two kinds of social influence discussed

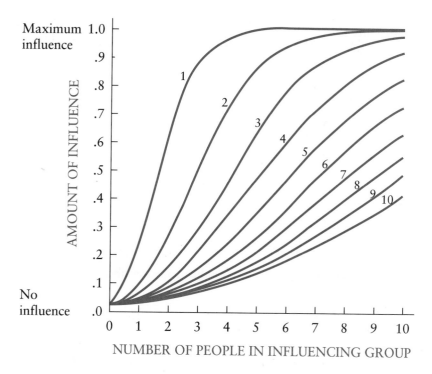

According to Tanford and Penrod's mathematical model, when influencing groups are small, additional members increase the groups' social influence more than when groups are large (the curves rise steeply at first and then "flatten out"). Furthermore, social influence does not increase indefinitely as the size of the influencing group increases (no curve reaches a value greater than 1.0).

FIGURE 12.5 Predictions of the social influence model.
Source: Adapted from Tanford and Penrod (1984).

earlier, informational and normative, differently. Campbell and Fairey (1989) found that changing the size of a pressuring group from one to three people led to big changes in conformity when the judgment task was clear-cut (as in Asch's experiment), but not when the task was ambiguous (as in Sherif's experiment). This suggests that group size has a strong impact on normative social pressure (the kind that was most powerful in Asch's experiment), but less impact on informational social influence (the kind most powerful in Sherif's experiment). More broadly, Campbell and Fairey's study suggests that to fully understand the relationship between group size and social influence, you must understand the kinds of psychological processes that are leading to social influence in a given setting.

Group Attractiveness and Cohesiveness

In general, people conform more to groups they like (Festinger, Schachter, & Back, 1950; Lott & Lott, 1961; Sakurai, 1975). Groups are termed *cohesive* when all members on average are highly attracted to the group, and, not surprisingly, cohesive groups tend to produce greater pressures to conform than noncohesive groups do (Forsyth, 1983; Schachter, 1951).

Theodore Newcomb (1943) conducted a classic study that demonstrated the power of cohesive groups to influence members' opinions. Newcomb's subjects were women attending Bennington College, a small liberal arts school in Vermont; they tended to come from wealthy, politically conservative families. Upon arriving at Bennington, freshmen left their old social groups (families, neighborhoods, and school friends) and came into contact with new groups (upperclassmen, faculty) who were much more politically and economically liberal than the freshmen. Newcomb found that, in general, students' attitudes became more liberal during each succeeding year at Bennington (see Figure 12.6).

Note: Lower scores on the graph indicate greater liberalism.

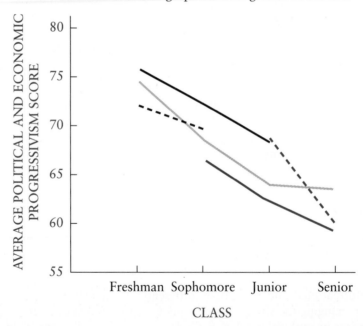

All five classes showed a marked tendency to become more liberal after exposure to the Bennington College environment.

FIGURE 12.6 Results of Newcomb's (1943) study of changes in Bennington students' attitudes. *Source:* Adapted from Newcomb (1957).

Many of Newcomb's subjects experienced a clash between the norms of their old and new groups. One young woman expressed her conflict quite eloquently in an essay she wrote about visiting home:

> . . . I don't want to go home this vacation—there's no one I want to see for more than 5 minutes.
>
> An increasing crescendo of scattered remarks of my friends mounts up in my mind and culminates in a dissonant, minor chord. What is the matter with these dissatisfied, bewildered, cynical girls? It's a simple answer, yet dishearteningly complex. Bennington is their trouble. . . . We went to Bennington, and our friends went to Vassar, Yale, Sarah Lawrence, Harvard, finishing school, St. Paul's-to-broker's-office. They came home changed, a little. A slightly smarter jargon, unerring taste in clothes and Things To Do, and one and all, victrola records of the conventional ideas. We came home, some of us, talking a new language, some cobwebs swept out, a new direction opening up ahead, we were dying to travel. Liberal, we thought we were. "What the hell's happened to You? Become a Parlor Pink [a Communist sympathizer]?" "Well, hardly, ha, ha." It was a little bewildering. (Newcomb, 1943, p. 11)

Presumably, new Bennington freshmen were strongly attracted to the high-status members of their new community—namely, the faculty and upper-classmen—and thus they conformed to the standards of these groups. Students who got most involved in academics, student government, and extracurricular activities tended to show the greatest attitude change, whereas those who did not integrate into the new community and who held on to their old family ties and friends were least likely to change. Moreover, the conformity of many Bennington students to their new community turned out not to be mere public compliance; it developed into permanent attitude change. Interviewing many of his subjects some 20 years later, Newcomb (1963) found that women who had become more liberal during their years at Bennington remained so decades after leaving college.

Status in the Group

The Bennington College study shows that we conform more to groups when we are attracted to them. Do we also conform more to groups that are attracted to us? How does our status in a group influence our conformity to the group?

To answer these questions, James Dittes and Harold Kelley (1956) conducted a two-stage experiment. First, subjects participated in group discussions and were asked to rate the others in the group on their "desirability" and contribution to the group. Subjects were allowed to see how others had rated them (actually they were given fake rating slips filled in by the experimenters). In this way, Dittes and Kelley created four sets of subjects: those who learned that other members of their group had rated them as high, average, low, or very low in desirability.

These subjects then participated in a study similar to Asch's, with this difference: The people who appeared to disagree with them on perceptual judgments were the members of their earlier discussion group. Those subjects who

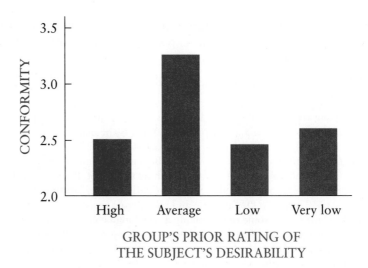

Conformity was greatest among subjects who believed that the group had rated them *average* in desirability.

FIGURE 12.7 Conformity as a function of acceptance by a group. *Source:* Data from Dittes and Kelley (1956).

believed that the pressuring group had earlier rated them as average in desirability tended to conform most (see Figure 12.7).

Dittes and Kelley reasoned that these subjects conformed most because they believed they could improve their status in the group by conforming to group norms. High-status people felt secure in their position and thus not as compelled to conform (Hollander, 1958), whereas low-status people felt already rejected by the group and thus were no longer attracted to it. Perhaps in addition they felt they had nothing to lose by refusing to conform.

Harvey and Consalvi (1960) replicated Dittes and Kelley's findings in a more realistic setting. To investigate the effects of actual status on conformity, they used friendship cliques at a school for delinquent boys in a conformity experiment. The results showed that second-status boys (as measured by the boys' own ratings) conformed more than top-status boys or low-status boys.

Observations from everyday life also suggest that high-status people (such as celebrities) and low-status people (minority out-groups) often conform less to social conventions than average-status people (the middle class) do. Thus, conformity depends not only on how much you like the group, but also on how much the group likes you. Indirectly, it depends on how much you have to gain or lose by not conforming to a group.

In-Groups, Out-Groups, and Conformity

Our perception of a group as an in-group (one that we belong to and share characteristics with) or as an out-group (one we don't belong to and are different from) can have a big effect on whether we conform to the group (Turner, Hogg, Oakes, Reicher, & Wetherell, 1987). The general principle seems to be that we conform more to in-groups than to out-groups. In everyday life, this principle is often confounded with attraction, for we often like in-groups more than out-groups. However, social psychologists have found that even arbitrary assignment to in-groups and out-groups can influence the degree to which subjects conform to groups.

One study demonstrated this point by replicating Sherif's autokinetic study. Groups of six people, consisting of three subjects and three confederates, judged how much they thought a stationary light moved in a darkened room. The confederates were instructed to consistently make judgments larger than the actual subjects' judgments. In some cases the subjects regarded themselves and the confederates to be one uniform group of subjects, and in other cases the three subjects were told they were one group and the three confederates made up another (see Chapter 7 for a discussion of "minimal groups" such as these). The results: When subjects viewed the confederates as a distinct out-group, they conformed less to their judgments in the autokinetic task (Abrams, Wetherell, Cochrane, Hogg, & Turner, 1990).

Similar findings emerged from a replication of Asch's conformity experiment. British psychology students judged the lengths of lines in the presence of three confederates who gave unanimously incorrect judgments on selected trials. Sometimes the confederates were described as other psychology students (that is, as in-group members) and sometimes as history students (out-group members). The results again showed that subjects conformed to an in-group more than to an out-group, and this was particularly so when they had to announce their answers out loud (Abrams et al., 1990).

Social Support: The Presence of Other Nonconformists

Being a subject in Asch's experiment must have been a very lonely experience. Do you think Asch's subjects might have conformed less if just one other group member had broken away from the majority?

Again, we can look back to Asch's (1956) seminal studies for relevant data. In some versions of his experiment, Asch instructed one confederate to give the correct answer and thus dissent from the majority. The effect of this one dissenting opinion on subjects was remarkable: Their conformity dropped to one-fourth the level shown by subjects faced with a unanimous majority. This dramatic reduction was likely due to decreases in both normative and informational social pressure: Subjects observed that nothing terrible happened to the dissenting confederate and thus felt more secure in rebelling against the group themselves; furthermore, they probably became more doubtful about the accuracy of the majority. Subjects reported feeling a bond of attachment to their partner in nonconformity, so they probably experienced social influence emanating from their new "friend" as well as from the disagreeing majority. Think back to the Randall twins. Perhaps they felt more secure in their rebellion against the Boy Scouts because they were partners in nonconformity.

Allies in nonconformity serve to reduce conformity only so long as they continue to rebel against the majority. Asch (1955) found that if the dissenting confederate "returned to the fold" and began agreeing again with the majority, subjects' levels of conformity went up almost to the levels observed in his original experiments.

Does a nonconformist always reduce others' conformity, or are there some limits to this phenomenon? For example, must a dissenting confederate give the *correct* answer to reduce subjects' conformity, or is any disagreeing response sufficient? Asch (1956) found that even when the dissenting confederate gave wrong answers that were worse than the majority's wrong answers, subjects still showed significantly reduced conformity—that is, more of them were emboldened to give the right answer. This finding is accurate for perceptual judgments, but on matters of opinion ("Do you believe there should be government-subsidized health insurance?"), a nonconformist ally was found to reduce conformity only when he or she agreed with the subject's opinion, not when he or she expressed an opinion even more extreme than that of the majority (Allen & Levine, 1968, 1969).

Will a nonconformist reduce your conformity even if you are biased against the nonconformist? Sometimes. Malof and Lott (1962) found that racially prejudiced white subjects showed reduced conformity to an erroneous white majority on perceptual judgments when a nonconformist spoke up, regardless of whether the nonconformist was black or white. Social support from a member of a disliked out-group seems to be less successful in reducing conformity on statements of opinion, however (Boyanowsky & Allen, 1973). Here again we see that in-groups and out-groups make a difference: Not only do we conform more to in-groups than to out-groups, we sometimes attend less to out-group nonconformists as well.

Commitment

The more that people commit themselves to a nonconforming response ahead of time, the more they will stick to it in the face of group pressure. A clever experiment by Deutsch and Gerard (1955) demonstrated this phenomenon clearly. Subjects were asked to write down certain perceptual judgments before seeing confederates' judgments on a control panel. Subjects then made their "official" judgment by pressing a button on their control panel. In one condition, subjects wrote and signed their names to their initial judgments, expecting that they would later hand them in to the experimenter; in a second condition, subjects wrote their judgments on pieces of paper but were not required to turn them in; in a third condition, subjects wrote their initial judgments on a "magic pad" that was erased after each judgment trial; and in a fourth (control) condition, subjects did not write their judgments and thus made no commitment to their initial opinions.

The results: Subjects showed the most conformity in the "no written commitment" condition, intermediate conformity in the "magic pad" condition, and the least conformity in the two "written on paper" conditions (see Figure 12.8). Writing down or publicly expressing our dissent strengthens our subsequent resistance to pressures from a disagreeing majority (Kerr & MacCoun, 1985; Kiesler, 1971).

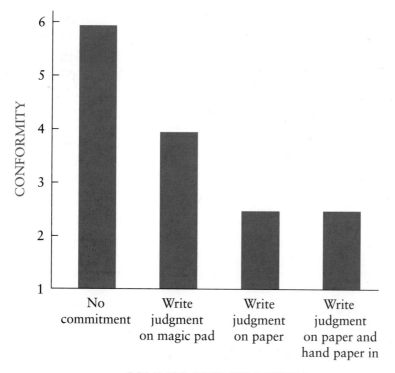

Subjects who had committed themselves by writing down their initial judgments before being exposed to a disagreeing majority showed a greater tendency to "stick to their guns" in the face of group pressure.

FIGURE 12.8 Conformity as a function of commitment to one's own judgment. *Source:* Data from Deutsch and Gerard (1955).

We have now discussed many factors that influence conformity; they are reviewed in Summary Table 12.1. One message of the findings summarized in this table is that social psychologists have tended to focus more on situational factors than on personal traits that influence conformity.

Minority Influence

Traditional conformity research has studied social influence in one direction only: from the group to the individual. Indeed, it could not be otherwise in Asch's studies, for the unanimous group that faced individual subjects was not a real group, but rather a group of confederates instructed to display artificially rigid judgments.

SUMMARY TABLE 12.1	Variables That Affect Conformity	
	Variable	*Effect*
Individual characteristics	Personality traits	May weakly correlate with conformity, but relationships vary depending on type of conformity
	Gender	On average, women conform slightly more than men, but this difference is variable across studies
Situational factors	Public versus private response	Subjects conform more when they must publicly announce responses
	Group size	Increased group size leads to increased conformity as groups increase from one to four members, then conformity levels off; larger groups may lead to greater conformity if group members are perceived to be independent of one another
	Group attractiveness	Subjects conform more to attractive groups than to unattractive groups
	Acceptance by group/ status in group	Average and marginal-status group members conform more than high- or low-status members
	In-group or out-group exerting pressure	In general, subjects conform more to in-groups than to out-groups
	Social support	The presence of a nonconformist in a group reduces conformity
	Commitment	A written commitment to a judgment leads subjects to conform less when faced by an opposing majority

In real groups, however, minorities and majorities interact with and exert mutual influence on each other. Not only did the Boy Scouts of America pressure the Randall twins to conform to their standards, the Randall twins pressured the Boy Scouts of America to change their policies. History is full of examples of dedicated and persuasive minorities, sometimes consisting of single individuals, influencing powerful, entrenched majorities. Scientific geniuses such as Copernicus, Galileo, and Darwin endured scathing attacks from the orthodox majority, but their ideas eventually prevailed. Artistic geniuses such as composer Ludwig van Beethoven, painter Vincent van Gogh, and playwright Anton Chekhov were first scorned as wildly eccentric and untalented, yet later were imitated by the majority. And civil rights activists, from the suffragists to Martin Luther King, Jr., faced vilification by the majority, followed eventually by mainstream acceptance of their ideas.

Do laboratory experiments support the observation that minorities can at times influence a strong majority? Beginning in the late 1960s, the French social psychologist Serge Moscovici (1976) conducted a series of experiments that proved minorities can have a surprisingly potent impact on majority judgments and opinions. In a kind of "reverse-Asch" experiment, Moscovici, Lage, and Naffrechoux (1969) asked groups of subjects to judge whether the color of projected blue slides was blue or green. Each group consisted of two confederates

*When do minorities
succeed in changing
the views of
majorities?*

and four real subjects. The confederates were instructed to label slides consistently as green. The subjects in the majority, faced by a consistently disagreeing minority, labeled the blue slides green more than 8% of the time; furthermore, almost a third of the subjects reported after the trials that they had seen a green slide at least once during the experiment.

Under what conditions is a minority most likely to influence a majority? Studies show that minorities must state their dissenting opinions consistently if they are to budge the majority (Maass & Clark, 1984; Moscovici & Personnaz, 1980; Mugny, 1982). Consistent minorities are perceived to be more confident and committed to their position than inconsistent minorities are (Bray, Johnson, & Chilstrom, 1982; Nemeth & Wachtler, 1973, 1974). At the same time, the minority must not be overly rigid and dogmatically repetitious in stating its dissenting opinion (Nemeth, Swedlund, & Kanki, 1974). Thus, a minority must remain logically and intellectually consistent but vary the way it phrases and negotiates its position (Mugny, 1975).

Minorities may have the greatest influence when their positions reinforce prevailing cultural norms and trends (Maass, Clark, & Haverhorn, 1982; Paicheler, 1976, 1977). For example, civil rights activists of the 1960s were in accord with the prevailing liberal political climate of the time, and leaders of the women's movement during the 1970s voiced opinions reinforced by larger societal changes in women's roles.

Finally, research suggests that *double minorities*—minority groups that differ not only in their opinions but in other obvious ways from the majority—have less impact on majorities than *single minorities* do. For example, Anne Maass and Russell Clark (1982) showed that a minority, believed to be gay, arguing in favor of gay rights was less successful in changing the heterosexual majority's views than a heterosexual minority arguing the same position was. Perhaps double minorities are less persuasive because they are perceived to have less credibility and more of a vested interest in their positions (Maass & Clark, 1984).

Consistent with Schachter's Johnny Rocco study, studies on minority influence often find that dissenting minorities are disliked and even abused (Nemeth & Wachtler, 1974), but intriguingly, such minorities frequently influence the majority nonetheless. How? Majority members often don't want to be associated with the disliked minority and thus will not publicly go along with minority opinions, but privately they are often persuaded—if the minority presents persuasive arguments (Moscovici, 1980; Nemeth & Wachtler, 1973, 1974).

Another experiment by Maass and Clark (1983) demonstrated clearly that minority influence can produce private acceptance while failing to elicit public compliance. Over 400 University of Florida undergraduates read a discussion on gay rights written by five college-age women. In one condition, the majority (four out of five women) was in favor of gay rights, and the minority opposed it. In a second condition, the majority was opposed to gay rights and the minority in favor of it. In a control condition, subjects read no group discussion.

Subjects then expressed their attitudes toward gay rights: Half the subjects were asked to express their attitudes publicly in questionnaires that would be read by other students; the other half expressed their attitudes privately in a questionnaire that would remain anonymous. The results of this study are shown in Figure 12.9. Note that when expressing their attitudes privately, subjects were more influenced by the minority, but when expressing their attitudes publicly, they were more influenced by the majority. (Recall that Asch's data were consistent with these findings, for they showed that majorities pressured subjects into public compliance, but not private acceptance.)

In recent years, social psychologists have debated whether minority influence results from processes different from those that produce majority influence (Campbell & Fairey, 1989; Maass, West, & Cialdini, 1987; Mackie, 1987). Tanford and Penrod's Social Influence Model (see Figure 12.5) describes minority influence with the same kinds of mathematical functions used to describe majority influence, and it predicts that minorities have less impact on groups than majorities do simply because of their numerical inferiority. Undoubtedly, both minorities and majorities can exert normative and informational social influence to varying degrees, although it may be the case that minorities tend to exert relatively more informational influence and majorities relatively more normative influence.

A number of studies suggest that minority influence is sometimes *qualitatively* different from majority influence. As already noted, minority influence often leads more to private conversion, whereas majority influence leads more to public compliance. Group members typically attend more to a lone dissenter than to a unanimous majority and may perceive his or her motives differently from the way they perceive those of a unanimous majority (Maass et al., 1987). For example, a

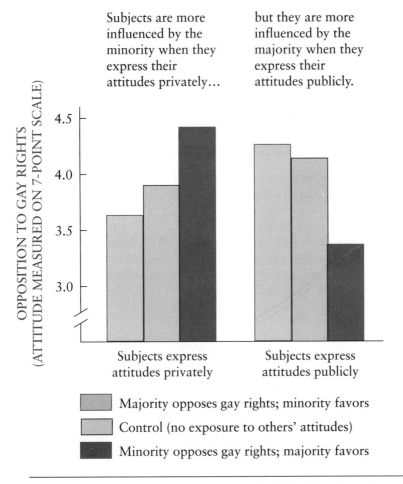

Subjects are more influenced by the minority when they express their attitudes privately... but they are more influenced by the majority when they express their attitudes publicly.

OPPOSITION TO GAY RIGHTS (ATTITUDE MEASURED ON 7-POINT SCALE)

Subjects express attitudes privately

Subjects express attitudes publicly

Majority opposes gay rights; minority favors
Control (no exposure to others' attitudes)
Minority opposes gay rights; majority favors

FIGURE 12.9 Minority influence on public versus private attitudes. *Source:* Data from Maass and Clark (1983).

lone dissenter may be perceived as a courageous and committed (but possibly wrong) individual, whereas a unanimous group may be perceived as conforming "sheep."

Nemeth (1986, 1992) argues that minorities are more likely to produce private conversion in part because a consistent, disagreeing minority leads individuals in the majority to question their pat assumptions and rethink issues. Even when they fail to win the majority over to their side, dissenting minorities sometimes provide the majority with a wider range of acceptable positions. Unanimous majorities, while exerting strong normative social pressure to conform and offering a ready route to consensus, don't necessarily foster careful thought in a group. Nemeth believes that groups facing minority dissent often produce more creative and thoughtful judgments than more uniform and homogeneous groups do. Thus, while they sometimes engender tension and stress, disagreeing minorities may nonetheless enhance the ultimate quality of the group's decisions and judgments.

COMPLIANCE

In an attempt to bully its membership into compliance, many former [Boy Scout] handbooks employed a combination of humiliation ("A boy who doesn't know first aid is of little use when someone is hurt"), commands ("Wherever you go [in the outdoors], you are a guest. Act like one!"), and simple-minded slogans ("Real men hold obedience high!"). But surely, handbook commands such as "Never touch a live tree with your ax—unless you have permission to do so!" may have persuaded more than one 15-year-old to hack away for the first time, simply out of the sheer thrill of rebellion.

—*Mother Earth News*, September–October 1990

Compliance—acceding to a request made by another person—is an everyday occurrence. We comply with friends who ask us for rides, with lovers who ask us to give up our bad habits, with solicitors who ask for charitable donations. Sales staffs, proselytizing religious sects, and self-help therapy groups seeking new, paying members have all developed clever strategies to gain our compliance (Cialdini, 1988, 1993). Why do such strategies work? When do they work? Are they based on valid psychological research? In a world full of requests, it is worthwhile to understand the nature of compliance.

Let's focus on four common strategies used to gain compliance: (1) associating a request with positive situations or moods; (2) playing on the norm of reciprocity—that is, making a request after doing a favor; (3) creating commitment, often by getting a person to agree first either to a smaller initial request or under false conditions; (4) using psychological reactance, or "reverse psychology," to gain compliance.

Positive Moods and Compliance

Are you more likely to be an "easy mark" when you are in a good mood? An early study found that it's easier to gain subjects' compliance and agreement while they are eating (Razran, 1938, 1940). No wonder businesspeople often wine and dine prospective clients (Janis, Kaye, & Kirschner, 1965). Consistent with this early research, recent laboratory experiments show that in general, people tend to accede to requests more when they're in a good mood, and less when they're in a bad mood (Milberg & Clark, 1988).

Perhaps the most direct way to soften someone up before making a request is to say nice things about him or her. Such *ingratiation* is a standard strategy to gain influence with another person. Although you might think people would be suspicious of praise preceding a request, research suggests that we often like people who say nice things about us regardless of their apparent motives (Byrne, Rasche, & Kelley, 1974; Jones, 1964; Jones & Wortman, 1973). Flattery doesn't even have to be true to increase our liking for and subsequent compliance with the flatterer (Drachman, de Carufel, & Insko, 1978).

Robert Cialdini describes a master of ingratiation, Joe Girard, who was named by *The Guinness Book of Records* as "the world's greatest car salesman." What was the secret of his success? In part, it was simply flattering his customers and getting them to like him:

> He did something that, on the face of it, seems foolish and costly. Each month he sent every one of his more than 13,000 former customers a holiday greeting card containing a printed message. The holiday greeting card changed from month to month (Happy New Year, Happy Valentine's Day, Happy Thanksgiving, and so on), but the message printed on the face of the card never varied. It read, "I like you." (Cialdini, 1988, p. 166)

Reciprocity and Compliance

The norm of reciprocity requires us to return favors in social relations (Gouldner, 1960; see Chapters 9 and 11 for additional discussions). Perhaps the success of Joe Girard's greeting cards is partly based on the norm of reciprocity; people want to "repay" the kindness of Joe's cards, so they give him their business.

But wait a minute, you may be thinking; something seems out of balance here: The commission on a car sale is not at all equivalent to the cost of a few cards! Indeed, this is exactly how the clever salesperson or solicitor makes use of the principle of reciprocity to our disadvantage: He does us a small favor and then asks a large favor in return. It seems ridiculous that people should succumb to such a strategy, but the norm of reciprocity is so strong that it often works.

Laboratory research clearly demonstrates that doing a small favor can indeed pave the way to reciprocal compliance. In one study, college-student subjects worked on a task with another student (actually a confederate). During a rest period, the confederate stepped out for a few minutes and then returned either with a cola for the subject or with nothing. Later on, the confederate asked the subject to buy some 25-cent raffle tickets. The results: Subjects who had been given the "free" cola bought an average of two tickets, whereas control subjects (those who had received no cola) bought only one (Regan, 1971). Because colas cost 10 cents when this study was carried out, the sale of one extra 25-cent ticket was a good return on an investment of a dime.

Reciprocity is a strategy of compliance that has been used to good effect by the Hare Krishna sect (Cialdini, 1993). Throughout the 1970s, Hare Krishna members, with their bells, shaved heads, and exotic Eastern garb, approached passersby in airports and other public places, and without a word gave them a "gift," often a flower. If the hapless victim tried to return the flower, the Hare Krishna member would refuse to take back the "gift," and then would ask for a donation. This simple ploy succeeded often because the norm of reciprocity that we

A member of the Hare Krishna sect solicits donations by first giving "free" gifts. This strategy makes use of the norm of reciprocity.

must repay a "gift" with a "gift" is so strong. (Incidentally, most marks immediately threw out their unwanted "gift" flower. The practical Hare Krishnas would collect these discarded flowers to use as "gifts" for their next targets.)

Reciprocity is a commonly used sales strategy. Food companies hire personnel to give away "free samples" in supermarkets, hoping for a purchase in return. Realtors and insurance agents give us "free" bottle openers, pads of paper, and refrigerator magnets, hoping we will keep them in mind when we purchase a home or insurance. And resort developers inform us that we have won "free" appliances—all we have to do is pick them up in person and listen to their sales pitch. Research on reciprocity suggests that "free" gifts are often far from it.

The reciprocity principle helps explain the effectiveness of the *door-in-the-face technique,* which consists of making an outrageously large request that the target is almost certain to reject, then following it with a smaller, more reasonable request. (The technique takes its name from the solicitor who makes an outrageous request, gets the door slammed in his or her face, and then comes back with a more modest request.) A study by Cialdini and his colleagues (1975) provides a dramatic illustration of the phenomenon. College students were asked to commit themselves to spending two hours a week as counselors to juvenile delinquents for at least two years. Not surprisingly, they refused to make this enormous commitment. Then the same students were asked for a smaller favor: Would they then instead help chaperone a group of juvenile delinquents during a day trip to the zoo? Fifty percent of the subjects agreed to this smaller request, compared with 17% of a control group who had not first been approached with the larger request.

Why did so many subjects comply after having turned down the larger initial request? The person making the request made a "concession" by reducing the request, and the norm of reciprocity holds that subjects should "repay" this concession with a concession of their own: compliance with the smaller request. The door-in-the-face technique is a method whereby the solicitor creates a kind of fake debt and then immediately collects on it.

The *that's-not-all technique* also makes use of the norm of reciprocity to induce compliance (Burger, 1986). Here a subject is offered a product (for example, a cupcake at a bake sale) at a high price ($1), and before he or she has time to

The "door-in-the-face" technique: Follow an outrageously large request with one that is more reasonable.

respond, the salesperson sweetens the deal by dropping the price (say, to 75 cents) or by throwing in something extra (say, two cookies). Significantly more subjects will accept this "sweetened" deal than will subjects offered the better deal initially. In part, this effect seems due to subjects' reciprocating the "concession" made by the salesperson. (Note that the door-in-the-face technique differs from the that's-not-all technique in that the subject is given the opportunity to refuse the initial outrageous request in the first method, but he or she is not given time to refuse the initial deal in the second method.)

Commitment and Compliance

Our discussion of conformity noted that committing people to their judgments can help them resist pressures to conform. Commitment has the potential to entrap us as well, however. Two important strategies for gaining compliance rely on committing people (at times unfairly) to a course of action: the foot-in-the-door and the low-ball techniques.

The basic principle of the *foot-in-the-door technique* is simple: Follow a small initial request with a much larger second request. Jonathan Freedman and Scott Fraser (1966) conducted the first study that demonstrated just how powerful the foot-in-the-door technique can be. Posing as representatives of the "Community Committee for Traffic Safety," experimenters asked homeowners in Palo Alto, California, whether they would display in their window a small 3-inch-square sign that read "Be a safe driver." Two weeks later, a different experimenter returned with a much larger request: Would the homeowners allow a large, rather unattractive "Drive carefully" sign to be placed on their front lawn? Surprisingly, 76% of subjects who had earlier agreed to display the window sign complied, compared with 17% of a control group of homeowners who had not been exposed to the initial request. Freedman and Fraser found evidence for the effect even when the topics of the signs were different for the first and second requests (for example, subjects might be asked initially to display a small "Be a safe driver" sign and then a large "Keep California beautiful" sign). Why does complying with a small initial request so increase the likelihood that subjects will comply with a much larger second request?

After complying with a small initial request, people feel committed to their behavior and even come to change their perceptions of themselves (DeJong, 1979; DeJong & Musilli, 1982). For example, after displaying a "Be a safe driver" sign in your window, you might decide that you are committed to the cause of traffic safety, and you might further conclude that you are a helpful, civic-minded person in general. Research shows that a small initial commitment, such as signing a petition (for example, to provide facilities for the mentally handicapped), can significantly increase the probability that you will later donate money to the same cause (Schwarzwald, Bizman, & Raz, 1983).

The *low-ball technique* also uses initial commitment to increase subsequent compliance: The person making the request gets you to comply under very favorable conditions and then reneges on some of these conditions once you commit yourself. For example, a car salesperson may offer you a great deal on your dream car, with lots of options thrown in. You agree to the purchase. Then the salesperson contacts you and says she was mistaken; according to the fine print of the "factory incentive deal," some of the options are not really included in the quoted price. Do you back out of the deal now, or do you grit your teeth and stick to your initial commitment to buy? Surprisingly, many proceed with the deal.

Cialdini and his colleagues (1978) demonstrated the power of the low-ball in a simple study. A woman called up introductory psychology students to schedule them for an experiment. Unfortunately, there was one quite undesirable feature about this experiment: It was scheduled for 7 in the morning. In one experimental condition (the low-ball condition), the woman informed subjects that the experiment was at 7 A.M. *after* they had already agreed to participate. In the control condition, subjects were informed of the 7 A.M. time before they were asked to participate. More subjects agreed to be in the experiment in the low-ball condition (56%) than in the control condition (31%). Furthermore, significantly more of the low-ball subjects (53%) actually showed up, bleary-eyed, to their 7 A.M. appointment than control subjects did (24%).

The foot-in-the-door and low-ball techniques may be particularly potent when used in combination with each other. In a recent random telephone survey, Israeli citizens were particularly likely to agree to answer embarrassing interview questions if (1) subjects had earlier answered a related, very short three-question telephone survey (foot-in-the-door technique) and (2) the surveyor got the subject to commit to participate in the longer survey in the first phone call, and later made this commitment less attractive during the follow-up call by noting that "the university has added some intimate questions to the survey" (low-ball technique). The combined foot-in-the-door and low-ball produced a higher survey response rate (about 80%) than either the foot-in-the-door alone (60%) or the low-ball alone (70%), and all groups exposed to compliance techniques complied more than control subjects (47% response rate) (Hornik, Zaig, & Shadmon, 1991).

The low-ball and the foot-in-the-door can be used for more important purposes than getting college students out of bed early in the morning and persuading people to answer embarrassing questions in surveys. Another study got Iowa residents to conserve energy through a clever application of the low-ball strategy. Specifically, consumers were induced to cut back on their use of natural gas during the winter with the promise that, if they succeeded, their names would be published in a newspaper article praising energy-conserving citizens. Subjects reduced their gas consumption by more than 12%. Then the researchers told the homeowners that the newspaper article would not be published. Once the "reason" for their initial compliance had disappeared, did the homeowners return immediately to their wasteful ways? Not at all. Instead, they reduced gas consumption even more! The low-ball got them to make an initial commitment, but then that commitment took on a life of its own. As a matter of fact, removing the "prop" of their initial reason seemed to induce subjects to justify their acts of conservation with new reasons (for example, "I am a civic-minded, energy-conserving citizen") (Pallak, Cook, & Sullivan, 1980). A more recent study found that simply getting homeowners to actively participate in a home energy audit (foot-in-the-door) and verbally commit themselves to make their house more energy-efficient (for example, to put new weather stripping around doors and windows) greatly increased their compliance with energy-saving recommendations (Aronson & Gonzales, 1990).

Psychological Reactance and Compliance

Are Boy Scouts more likely to hack away at a tree after they are told, "Never touch a live tree with your ax—unless you have permission to do so!"? Sometimes, it does seem that we do things simply because they have been forbidden. And sometimes clever people get us to do something by telling us we cannot or may not be able to do it. A realtor tells an indecisive customer that someone else has just made an offer on a house, and the formerly ambivalent customer immediately makes a higher counteroffer. A salesperson tells a shopper there is "just one left," and the customer snaps it up. A man tells his unwilling-to-make-a-commitment girlfriend that he's found a new girlfriend and wants to end their relationship; she immediately agrees to get married.

Why does taking something away get us to act? The theory of *psychological reactance* says that when people feel their freedom of choice is threatened, they experience unpleasant arousal (that is, reactance), which motivates them to restore their freedom (Brehm, 1966; Brehm & Brehm, 1981). If someone takes away your freedom to buy a house, how can you restore that freedom? Obviously, you must buy the house.

College students seem to react against legal restrictions by desiring to engage in the forbidden activities. For example, underage students find a book more attractive when it is labeled as "restricted to those 21 years and over" (Zellinger, Fromkin, Speller, & Kohm, 1974). Studies like this suggest that censorship may

Susie uses psychological reactance to manipulate Calvin's behavior.

SUMMARY TABLE 12.2	Strategies for Gaining Compliance	
Strategy	Principle	Example
Positive moods	Make request in a setting that creates positive mood in target	Make request during a delicious dinner at a pleasant restaurant
Ingratiation	Say flattering things to target	Praise target's intelligence, appearance, or personality, then make request
Favors	Do small favor for target (makes use of norm of reciprocity)	Buy target a soft drink, then try to sell product
Door-in-the-face	Follow a very large request that the target is likely to refuse with a smaller, more reasonable request (makes use of reciprocity)	Ask target to volunteer for two years of charity work; after he or she refuses, ask target to volunteer to work for one weekend
That's-not-all	Offer a product for a high price, and before target has chance to refuse, lower price slightly or "throw in" something extra (makes use of reciprocity)	Offer to sell a cupcake for $1, then quickly lower price to 75 cents or throw in "extra" cookies
Foot-in-the-door	Follow small initial request with a much larger second request (makes use of commitment and self-perception processes)	Ask target to sign a petition endorsing a charity; come back later and ask for a large donation to the charity
Low-ball	Get target to commit to comply under very favorable terms, then later renege on some of the terms (makes use of commitment)	Car salesperson gets customer to agree to car purchase with many options "thrown in," and then later informs customer that not all options are included
Reactance	Get target to comply by threatening his or her freedom of choice, sometimes by creating an illusion of scarcity	Salesperson informs customer that product is "the last one," and after it's sold the customer will be unable to purchase it

sometimes backfire insofar as it makes the banned material even more attractive to many people (Worchel, 1992). Want to sell a book or a recording? Tell people they *can't* buy it.

Summary Table 12.2 reviews the compliance strategies we have discussed—information you may find highly practical. After all, forewarned is forearmed.

SOCIAL
PSYCHOLOGY
IN EVERYDAY
LIFE

Brainwashing—The Ultimate in Social Influence?

The compliance techniques we have discussed are used by people all the time in everyday life. But stronger kinds of social influence also occur in real-life settings. Two chilling examples are the "brainwashing" techniques used by totalitarian governments on prisoners and the indoctrination techniques used by cults. Of course, no social psychologist could conduct ethically acceptable experiments on brainwashing or cult indoctrination techniques. However, psychologists *have* studied the unfortunate victims of brainwashing and intense indoctrination: for example, political prisoners detained in Nazi concentration camps (Bettelheim, 1943), American soldiers captured by the Communist Chinese during the Korean War (Schein, 1956), and former cult members (Deikman, 1990). What has this research uncovered?

Surprisingly, brainwashing and cult indoctrination often use compliance techniques quite similar to those we have already discussed in this chapter. For example, after capturing American soldiers during the Korean War, the Chinese used the techniques of ingratiation and associating themselves with positive, rewarding events. They reminded Americans how fortunate they were to be captives of the "friendly" Chinese rather than of the "brutal" North Koreans. Although conditions were generally bleak, men who cooperated with the Chinese did receive special favors—small items of clothing, hot tea, fresh fruit. It was made clear, however, that these favors would go only to those who "learned the truth." What was the "truth"? That South Korea had started the war and that the United States was an imperialistic aggressor in a civil war.

Offering rewards to collaborators destroyed solidarity among the soldiers by breaking up groups of friends, removing social supports, and making prisoners suspicious that others were collaborators. Religious cults also use the strategy of breaking up prior relationships, including marriages and families: ". . . powerful cult groups often attack the couple through arranged marriages, the breaking of love relationships by order of the leader or the group, pressure toward group marriage or chastity, sexual relationships with the leader, and/or interfere with the bonds between parents and children" (Deikman, 1990, p. 55).

The treatment prisoners of war and cult members receive in their respective situations is often quite oppressive, and it might seem strange to you that abused people could ever come to identify with their oppressors and be psychologically influenced by them, but this has been documented in numbers of cases. For example, Bruno Bettelheim (1943) noted that inmates in Nazi concentration camps sometimes "identified with the aggressor," even to the point of imitating their SS guards. And cult members have followed seemingly demonic leaders like Jim Jones and David Koresh despite their abusive behavior.

The Chinese made good use of the foot-in-the-door technique in their brainwashing sessions. If a prisoner ever admitted something negative about the United States during one of the grueling, repetitive interviews his captors conducted, he was asked to elaborate on the "errors" of his country, and he was reminded repeatedly of his critical statement in future interrogations. Sometimes prisoners were asked to "copy" innocuous answers provided by the Chinese to interview questions—a seemingly harmless concession. Then these were shown to other soldiers, who believed them to be voluntary collaborations. The prison camps had elaborate sets of rules that were so complex, the prisoners could not help violating some of them. When the inevitable violation occurred, prisoners had to write out confessions of their misdeeds, and this provided an initial foot-in-the-door to extract confessions for larger misdeeds.

The captors also made clever use of the principle of committing people to positions contrary to their beliefs. For example, they offered highly desired prizes, such as cigarettes, for prisoners' essays dealing with certain political top-

Members of the Branch Davidian cult obeyed the orders of their leader, David Koresh, to set their compound on fire. Most died in the resulting inferno.

ics. Writing an essay seemed to prisoners a harmless way to obtain some of the small pleasures of life. But then the "winning" essays—typically selected because they supported some Communist dogma—were published in the camp newspaper. In writing these essays, many prisoners ended up making larger (and more public) commitments than they had bargained on.

The power of both totalitarian prisons and cults to influence people may result in part from the fact that their victims tend to be isolated and dependent. Prisoners of war and cult members are often separated from their friends, family members, normal social groups (such as churches, synagogues, clubs, and schools); they give up their usual everyday roles (employee, homeowner, citizen); and they often lack resources and power (prisoners of war have no possessions or money, and cult members are often required to turn over all their assets to the cult).

Is brainwashing effective? Despite their total control of prisoners' lives and their patient and interminable indoctrination sessions, the Chinese generally seemed not to be highly successful in brainwashing a majority of American prisoners of war (Schein, 1956). We should not necessarily take great satisfaction in this, however, for these attempts at brainwashing suffered from one major limitation: Many of the interrogators lacked a good command of English, and thus the prisoners of war could often rebel with subtle kinds of linguistic sarcasm.

Cults also have a mixed record of success at brainwashing their members. They do sometimes get people to perform seemingly crazy acts. For example, the 900 followers of the Reverend Jim Jones committed mass suicide in their village in Guyana by drinking cyanide-laced Kool-Aid, and the followers of David Koresh did the same by setting fire to their compound in Waco, Texas, and remaining in the resulting inferno. Still, events like these are rare, and people frequently leave cults of their own accord. Such deserters grow disillusioned with the deception and oppression of cult life, and at some point, outside social ties pull them back into everyday reality (Deikman, 1990).

In sum, research on brainwashing and cult indoctrination analyzes powerful influence techniques used in dramatic real-life settings; it provides yet additional evidence that the processes of social influence studied by social psychologists in the laboratory are highly relevant to real life as well. ✍

✍ OBEDIENCE

A Scout is trustworthy, loyal, helpful, friendly, courteous, kind, obedient, cheerful, thrifty, brave, clean and reverent.

—the Boy Scout oath

Right in the middle of the list of virtues identified with Boy Scouts is *obedient*. Certainly, obedience has its good side. You'll probably agree that it is often desirable for children to obey their parents and teachers, for citizens to obey police officers, and for soldiers to obey their commanding officers. Society as we know it could not exist without authority hierarchies in which some people obey others.

But obedience has its evil side as well. During World War II, obedient Germans sent millions of men, women, and children to their deaths in extermination camps. And in 1968, a dramatic and terribly disturbing event occurred in My Lai, Vietnam, that would eventually change many Americans' views of the Vietnam War: American soldiers obeyed commands to kill innocent, unarmed civilians. Mike Wallace of CBS News obtained the following grim testimony from one participant:

Q. Started pushing them off into the ravine?

A. Off into the ravine. . . . And we started shooting them. . . .

Q. Again—men, women, and children?

A. Men, women, and children.

Q. And babies?

A. And babies. And so we started shooting them. . . .

Q. Why did you do it?

A. Why did I do it? Because I felt like I was ordered to do it. (quoted in Milgram, 1974, p. 185)

As noted in the preceding section, over 900 devoted followers of the Reverend Jim Jones obeyed his command to commit mass suicide by drinking cyanide-laced Kool-Aid in 1978, and in 1993, the fanatic followers of David Koresh obeyed his commands first to shoot indiscriminately at federal law enforcement officers, killing

The mass suicide at Jonestown. When are people most likely to obey destructive and immoral commands?

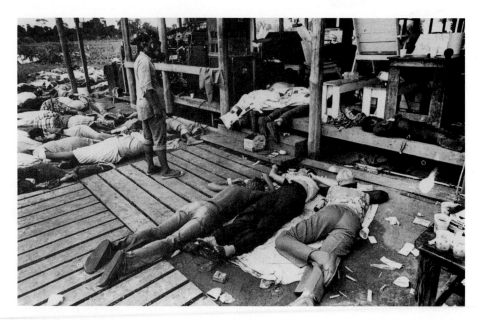

4 and injuring another 15, and then to commit fiery mass suicide, killing about 80 cultists, including 20 children.

All of these examples show that people sometimes do terrible things in the name of obedience. How does obedience differ from the two other varieties of social influence we have discussed, conformity and compliance? For one thing, social pressures to obey are more out in the open, whereas pressures to conform are often beneath the surface. In Asch's studies, for example, confederates exerted no overt pressure on subjects. Pressures to comply are more obvious: Someone makes a direct request. Pressures to obey are most obvious: They occur when someone, typically a legitimate authority, commands us to do something. Obedience also differs from compliance and conformity in that the pressures to obey almost always come from someone who occupies a position of higher status or authority.

Milgram's Obedience Experiments

Why did people obey in Nazi Germany, at My Lai, and at Jonestown and Waco? Could "normal" people obey in such horrible ways, if placed in the right (or rather, wrong) situation? When are people most likely and least likely to obey?

These are exactly the questions addressed by Stanley Milgram (1974) in an extraordinary series of experiments, some of which we examined in Chapter 2. In the guise of conducting a learning experiment, an experimenter asked subjects to deliver increasingly severe and painful electric shocks to an innocent victim strapped into a chair in the next room. The experimenter repeatedly ordered the subject to continue, and as the shocks increased from 15 volts up to the maximum possible of 450 volts, the victim showed increasing evidence of pain; he screamed in anguish and called out repeatedly, "Let me out of here." In one particularly dramatic version of the study, the victim stated that he suffered from a "heart condition." In these versions of the experiment, the "victim" was in fact a confederate, and his highly convincing screams and protests were in fact tape recordings. (See Figure 12.10 for a diagram of the control panel of Milgram's shock machine.)

The basic finding of Milgram's study was that 25 out of 40 subjects (63%) obeyed the experimenter completely and delivered what they thought were shocks of up to 450 volts to the screaming, protesting victim. Milgram (1974) summed up the moral import of his findings succinctly:

> The results . . . are . . . disturbing. They raise the possibility that human nature, or—more specifically—the kind of character produced in American democratic society, cannot be counted on to insulate its citizens from brutality and inhumane treatment at the direction of malevolent authority. A substantial proportion of people do what they are told to do, irrespective of the content of the act and without limitations of conscience, so long as they perceive that the command comes from a legitimate authority. (p. 189)

Proximity to the Victim and to the Authority

Milgram was not satisfied simply to demonstrate obedience in his laboratory; he also wanted to understand the factors that influence obedience. One of these factors was the proximity of the victim: When the victim was in the next room, 63% of the subjects obeyed completely; when the victim sat in the same room as the subject, obedience declined to 40%; and if the subject was required to touch the victim (in order to force his hand down onto the shock plate), obedience declined still more, to 30%. Thus, the farther the subject was from the victim, the more he or she tended to obey the authority.

Similarly, Milgram found in additional experiments that the greater the distance between the subjects and the commanding *authority*, the less they tended to obey. For example, when the experimenter was out of the room and gave his commands by telephone, obedience dropped to 21%.

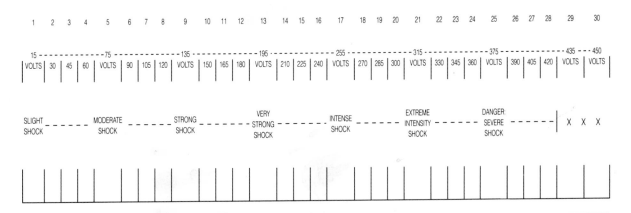

FIGURE 12.10 Diagram of the control panel of Milgram's shock machine. *Source:* Milgram (1974).

In this replication of Milgram's experiment the teacher must force the learner's hand onto the shock plate against his will.

Institutional Setting

Milgram investigated a number of other factors that influence obedience. Among the most important were the institutional setting of the experiment, the presence of peer pressures to obey or rebel, and the roles occupied by the people who gave orders and who were victims. Let's briefly consider each of these variables in turn.

Milgram's initial studies were conducted in a well-equipped laboratory at Yale University. Many of the subjects, who were solicited by newspaper ads from the local community, regarded Yale and its faculty with great respect. Thus, perhaps the obedience of Milgram's subjects was partly a function of the prestige of the institution conducting the research.

To test this possibility, Milgram moved his study to a run-down office building in Bridgeport, Connecticut, a nearby industrial city. The study now seemed to be totally divorced from Yale University; however, the procedures were the same. Did obedience go down markedly? No. It declined just moderately, to 48%.

Conformity and Obedience

In a fascinating set of experimental variations, Milgram combined conformity pressures with pressures to obey. Now the subject was one of three "teachers": One teacher's job was to read the words the victim was to learn, another teacher recorded whether or not the learner gave correct answers, and the third teacher delivered shocks to the learner when he answered incorrectly. In fact, the first two teachers were confederates; the teacher delivering shocks was the real subject. Figure 12.11 presents the layout of this study.

Milgram created two dramatically different situations in this experiment. In the first, the two confederates rebelled against the experimenter; in the second, they complied with orders completely and without protest. In the first

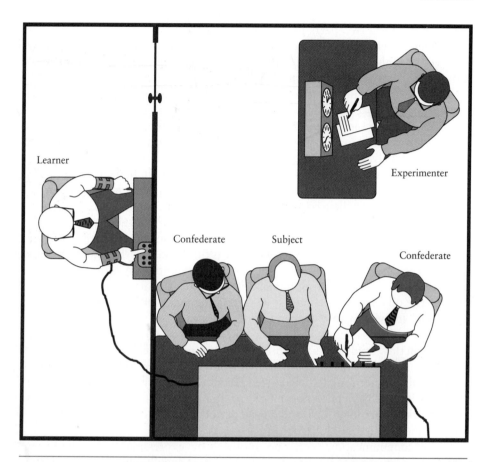

FIGURE 12.11 Adding conformity pressures to the Milgram obedience paradigm: a schematic representation of the experiment's physical setup. In this variation of his obedience studies, Milgram added two more "teachers" (actually confederates) who either obeyed or rebelled against the experimenter. Milgram wanted to see what effect the other teachers' behavior had on subjects' obedience. *Source:* Milgram (1974).

instance, one teacher stopped obeying when shocks reached 150 volts. Despite the experimenter's orders to continue, this teacher left his seat in protest and sat on the other side of the room. The experimenter then ordered the second teacher to take over the first teacher's responsibilities. The experiment continued with just two teachers until shocks reached 210 volts, at which point the second teacher also rebelled. Now the experimenter ordered the third teacher (the actual subject) to take over the responsibilities of the two rebelling teachers.

Upon seeing two peers protest the shock procedures and rebel against the experimenter, what percentage of subjects continued in the study and proceeded to 450 volts? Only 10% obeyed fully. How about in the second version of the experiment, in which the other teachers meekly complied without protest? In that case, 93% of the subjects obeyed fully. Clearly, conformity pressures had an extraordinary impact on subjects' behavior. Indeed, the difference between a 10% and 93% obedience level is virtually the most powerful effect possible. What factor was most successful in influencing obedience? Ironically, another variety of social influence: namely, conformity pressures.

These results suggest that people in groups may at times possess greater resources to resist unjust authority than individuals do, at least when they can look to others to support their rebellion. Additional evidence that social support can foster rebellion comes from an experiment that arranged for groups of subjects to participate in a study on "community standards" (Gamson, Fireman, & Rytina, 1982). Specifically, subjects were videotaped as they discussed their opinions about a court case in which a big oil company was attempting to oust a gas station manager who had spoken out against the company's practice of fixing high oil prices. The oil company claimed it was firing the manager because of his "moral turpitude" in living with a woman out of wedlock.

As the discussions progressed, it became increasingly clear to subjects that their job in this "study" was to express false opinions, which would be videotaped and then used to help the oil company in its court case. Unlike subjects in Milgram's studies, most subjects in this one resisted pressures to comply with the experiment's "authorities." Why were these subjects successful in rebelling? One critical factor was that they were in groups, and during periodic "rest breaks" they could talk to one another.

By communicating with one another—by expressing their distress and defining the situation as unjust—groups of subjects could mobilize their resources. Often, one "trigger person" who was particularly outraged began the rebellion, and then others followed suit. Once some members of the group had rebelled, conformity pressures induced other members to join in. This study and the "peer rebellion" version of the Milgram study demonstrate that there may be safety in numbers when we oppose unjust authority.

The Role of the Person Giving and Receiving Commands

Milgram summarized his many experiments in a book, *Obedience to Authority* (1974). The title makes an important point: We do not obey just any person, but rather someone we perceive to be a legitimate authority. This point is underscored by several intriguing variations of the Milgram study.

In one version, the *learner* (a confederate) ordered the subject to deliver increasingly severe shocks and the *experimenter* received these shocks. How did this strange state of affairs come to be? After the experimenter initially described the study, the learner stated that he was afraid of shocks and reluctant to participate. He then offered a solution: Why didn't the experimenter go through the procedure first as the "learner," and if that worked out, then he would participate? The experimenter agreed and the experiment proceeded, this time with the learner ordering the subject to deliver increasingly severe shocks to the strapped-in experimenter.

As the shock levels increased, the experimenter began to cry out in pain and protest, just as the victim did in other versions of the experiment. He demanded to be released. What happened next? Did the subject obey the confederate goading him on, or did he comply with the experimenter? In fact, no subject completely obeyed the confederate in this version of the study. Indeed, no one exceeded 150 volts, the point at which the experimenter first started protesting.

In another strange permutation of roles, Milgram created a situation in which the *victim* demanded to be shocked while the experimenter suggested terminating the experiment. The experiment began as usual, and when the shocks reached 150 volts, the learner began to cry out in pain. The experimenter stated that this learner's reaction seemed to be more severe than usual and that they should stop the study. The learner, overhearing this comment from the next room, insisted that they continue with the experiment; to stop would be an affront to his manliness. He was certain he could stand the pain.

Did the subject obey the experimenter or the learner in this version of the experiment? Again, no subject proceeded past 150 volts, and thus everyone obeyed the experimenter, not the learner. Although this may not surprise you, there is an important lesson to draw from this variation: The power in Milgram's obedience experiment lay with the experimenter, not with the victim. When the experimenter ordered subjects to deliver shocks, there seemed to be almost nothing the victim could say to get subjects to stop. Conversely, when the experimenter ordered subjects to stop shocking, there was nothing the victim could say to get subjects to continue.

The Milgram Studies in Perspective

Milgram's obedience studies are among the most famous in social psychology. In the words of social psychologist Arthur Miller (1986), "It would not be hyperbole . . . to say that the obedience experiments have sent shock waves throughout the academic world and beyond." Milgram's research has been attacked for the stresses it created in its subjects (Baumrind, 1964), discussed in numerous magazine and newspaper articles, and even dramatized as a television movie (Mixon, 1989). Milgram's studies seem more than just academic investigations of social behavior; they make powerful statements about human nature and the human capacity for evil.

How are we to interpret the high levels of obedience in Milgram's studies? Were his subjects sadists? The answer here seems clearly to be no. Most subjects were extremely upset over their victim's suffering, even to the point of showing such physical symptoms as choking, sweating, and hysterical laughter. And yet they still complied with the experimenter's orders. Milgram conducted one version of his study in which subjects were free to choose their own levels of shock; only two subjects exceeded 150 volts. Thus, although a small minority of sadistic people may exist, sadism is not an adequate explanation for most subjects' behavior.

Milgram (1974) offered several explanations for the high level of obedience in his studies. Consistent with the foot-in-the-door phenomenon, subjects complied first at low levels of shock and then gradually proceeded to higher, more painful levels. Subjects seemed to be restricted by social norms to treat authority figures with politeness and deference. (Think, for example, how you generally talk to such authorities as bosses, clergy, and police officers.) Milgram demonstrated that obedience is not something rare and peculiar; rather, it is part of the fabric of everyday social life. In organized social groups (families, businesses, the military, religions), people occupy positions within authority hierarchies, and they learn to give up their freedom of choice to "legitimate" authorities: parents, bosses, generals, religious leaders. A problem occurs, as Milgram's studies dramatically illustrate, when legitimate authorities ask us to perform immoral acts.

Milgram's findings are dramatic in part because they are so unexpected. Most of us seem to assume subjects' ethics, conscience, and compassion would be stronger—and the influence of the authority figure would be weaker—than demonstrated in Milgram's experiments. Milgram underscored the counterintuitive quality of his findings by asking both naive college students and professional psychiatrists to predict how subjects would behave in his obedience paradigm. Both groups grossly underestimated the actual levels of obedience observed.

Just as some people do not conform in conformity studies, some people do not obey in obedience studies. The existence of the 63% of subjects who obeyed completely in the basic Milgram study should not blind us to the 37% who disobeyed. How were these subjects different? Milgram (1974) investigated the effects on obedience of a number of "person variables" (such as personality, gender, religion, and social class), and in general he did not find strong effects. There was some tendency for people with high degrees of authoritarianism to be more obedient, but the relation between personality traits and obedience typically was weak (Elms & Milgram, 1966). Milgram found that women obeyed as much as men in his paradigm. There was a tendency for Roman Catholics to obey more than Protestants and Jews, and for uneducated and lower-class people to obey more than educated and higher-class people, but again, these effects were weak and inconsistent across studies.

Milgram (1974) concluded that "often, it is not so much the kind of person a man is as the kind of situation in which he finds himself that determines how he will act." According to Milgram, the individual differences that occur in obedience are not well understood.

Replications of Milgram's Findings

Science demands that findings be replicated before they are accepted. A number of replications of Milgram's studies have been published (see Blass, 1991, for a recent review). Some of these document obedience across cultures. For example, Mantell (1971) found that when a group of West German subjects were placed in the Milgram paradigm, 85% obeyed completely. Shanab and Yahya (1977) reported a 63% level of obedience among Jordanian teenage students. (In this study, the experimenter ordering subjects to deliver shocks was a woman.) In a somewhat modified version of the Milgram study, Kilham and Mann (1974) reported high levels of obedience—up to 68%—among Australian subjects.

Other studies have documented destructive obedience in natural settings and in situations that possessed a high degree of realism. For example, one study showed that nurses will deliver dangerous levels of medication if ordered to do so by a doctor (Hofling et al., 1966). And Sheridan and King (1972) conducted a dramatic study in which subjects delivered *real* electric shocks to yelping puppies; their subjects obeyed at even higher levels than Milgram's. In sum, destructive obedience is a real phenomenon occurring in many different places and settings.

Ideological Factors and Obedience

What are the social attitudes and ideologies that lead some people to obey and others not to? Research since Milgram's has begun to address this question.

Religious Attitudes

Earlier we discussed cults, which are quasi-religious groups that demand absolute obedience and compliance from their members. Of course, many mainstream religious groups also require obedience of their members. Perhaps it is not surprising, then, that there is a link between attitudes toward obedience and religious attitudes. As Deikman (1990) notes:

> What is a god if not a supreme authority? In religions the world over, the devout acknowledge their god's divine wisdom, mercy and awesome power; they pray for protection, forgiveness, and benefits. Even in Buddhism, whose founder declared that notions of gods and heavens were illusions, most believers bow to a Buddha idol with all the expectations found in theistic religions. (p. 84)

Is there a relationship between religious attitudes and obedience in Milgram-type experiments? The answer seems to be yes. David Bock (1972) conducted an obedience experiment (similar to Milgram's "voice only" proximity condition) in which he varied the kind of authority the experimenter possessed. Sometimes the experimenter was a scientific authority (a graduate student), sometimes a religious authority (a minister), and sometimes a nonauthority (an unknowledgeable salesman). Bock gave his subjects questionnaires that measured their religiosity and their religious orientations.

Not surprisingly, Bock's subjects obeyed the legitimate authorities (scientist and minister) more than the nonauthority. More interesting was his finding that religious subjects tended to obey the "legitimate" authorities more than nonreligious subjects did. You may recall from Chapters 7 and 11 that social psychologists have studied different kinds of religiousness (Allport & Ross, 1967; Batson & Ventis, 1982). In his study, Bock measured the degree to which his subjects were intrinsically religious (religious for internal reasons—for example, they viewed religion as a central value in their lives), extrinsically religious (religious for external reasons, such as family pressures and social advancement), or antireligious. His results: Intrinsically religious people proved to be most obedient, extrinsically religious people were next, and antireligious people were least obedient. (This study was carried out before scales for the "quest" religious orientation had been developed; see Chapter 7.)

Recall that Milgram-type experiments measure a kind of "immoral" obedience to authority. It is thus ironic that the religious subjects tended to obey most in this kind of situation.

Attitudes toward Responsibility and Obedience

Suppose *you* were a combat soldier during the Vietnam War, and a commanding officer ordered you to shoot innocent civilians, including women and children. Imagine this situation as vividly as you can: You're highly stressed and fatigued; you have recently seen numbers of your buddies killed in action; and you are never quite sure which Vietnamese "civilians" are allies and which are Viet Cong guerrillas. Would you obey the command?

Just this question was posed to almost 1,000 Americans in 1971, three years after the My Lai massacre (Kelman & Hamilton, 1989). A second question was posed as well: What did they think *most people* would do in this situation: shoot or refuse to follow orders? The results of the poll, shown in Figure 12.12, may surprise you: 51% of the respondents said they would follow orders, and 67% said they thought most people would follow orders. Apparently, although laypeople don't predict that they would obey if they were subjects in the Milgram experiment, they clearly recognize the powerful pressures that might lead a person to obey immoral orders from a commanding officer in a combat setting.

In 1971, when Lieutenant William Calley, Jr., was tried for his participation in the 1968 My Lai massacre, a number of opinions polls asked Americans whether

		What Would Most People Do?			All Respondents
		Shoot	Don't Know	Refuse	
What would you do?	Shoot	453	27	9	489 (51%)
	Don't Know	89	57	11	157 (16%)
	Refuse	102	58	161	321 (33%)
All respondents		644 (67%)	142 (15%)	181 (19%)	967 (100%)

FIGURE 12.12 Americans estimate what they and "most people" would do in a situation like the My Lai massacre. *Source:* From Kelman and Hamilton (1989).

they approved or disapproved of bringing Calley to trial (Kelman & Hamilton, 1989). A majority *disapproved:* 59% in one poll and 67% in another. Why? And what distinguished Americans who approved of bringing charges against Calley from those who didn't?

Attitudes about obedience turned out to be critical—in particular, attitudes toward personal responsibility and toward submission to authority. For example, Americans who opposed Calley's trial were much more likely to agree with statements such as: "The trial used Lt. Calley as a scapegoat: one young lieutenant shouldn't be blamed for the failures of his superiors." In contrast, people who approved of Calley's trial were much more likely to agree with statements like the following: "Even a soldier in a combat situation has no right to kill defenseless civilians and anyone who violates this rule must be brought to trial" and "The trial helps put across the important idea that every man must bear responsibility for his own actions."

Kelman and Hamilton (1989) summarize research showing that the tendency to deny or assign responsibility for crimes of obedience is linked to many other attitudes and demographic factors. For example, it is linked to religious attitudes: Nonreligious and Jewish people are more likely to hold someone responsible for crimes of obedience, whereas Christians are more likely to deny personal responsibility. It is also linked to education and social class: Educated people and those of higher socioeconomic status are more likely to assign responsibility than less educated and lower-status people are. In the United States, regional differences in attitudes toward obedience have been found: Residents of the Midwest and South are more likely to deny people's responsibility for crimes of obedience; residents of the Northeast and Pacific Coast states are more likely to assign responsibility.

Overall, people who deny responsibility for crimes of obedience seem to view obedience as a necessary part of social life, whereas people who assign responsibility see obedience more in terms of moral principles and human rights. It would be interesting and informative to find out whether people possessing these two different orientations toward obedience actually showed different levels of obedience in a Milgram-type study. Unfortunately (or fortunately, depending on your perspective), because of the strict ethical guidelines for psychological research that were established after Milgram's landmark experiments, it is next to impossible to do such a study today. The last Milgram-type experiment was published in the United States in the mid-1970s (Blass, 1991).

Obedience research, like the research on conformity and compliance discussed earlier, shows the phenomenal power of social settings to influence our behavior. For a review of the factors that influence obedience and attitudes toward it, see Summary Table 12.3.

RESISTING SOCIAL INFLUENCE

We have just seen that many people agree it would be difficult to disobey an immoral order issued by a commanding officer in a combat setting. Most people

SUMMARY TABLE 12.3	Variables That Affect Obedience
Variable	*Effect*
Proximity to victim	Subjects obey less the closer they are to a suffering victim
Proximity to authority	Subjects obey less the farther away the authority who gives commands is
Institutional setting	Conducting Milgram's obedience experiments in a run-down office building away from Yale University reduced obedience only slightly
Conformity pressures	Obedient peers increase subjects' obedience; rebellious peers greatly reduce obedience
Role of person giving commands	People obey others most when others are perceived to be legitimate authorities; in Milgram's studies, subjects generally obeyed the experimenter but did not obey other subjects
Personality traits	In Milgram's studies, assessed traits correlated weakly with obedience
Gender	Milgram found no difference between men and women in their average levels of obedience
Cultural differences	Cross-cultural replications show some variation across cultures, but obedience in Milgram-type studies tends to be high regardless of culture
Attitudinal and ideological factors	Religious people are more likely to obey in Milgram-type experiments; attitudes toward individual responsibility and toward obedience influence whether people hold individuals responsible for crimes of obedience

acknowledge the intense pressures leading to obedience in such a setting: You might be shot on the spot for insubordination, or you might be court-martialed.

It seems that subjects should have found it easier to disobey in Milgram's experiments, however. Perhaps that is why so many people are so troubled by Milgram's results. Subjects who were clearly distraught over their "immoral" behavior, who were not under any direct, physical duress, and who had no personal animosity toward their victims still could not muster the psychological resources needed to rebel against an unjust authority.

You probably would not want to act like the majority of Milgram's subjects. How can you help ensure that you will not? Perhaps unknowingly you've already taken a first step, for research suggests that people who learn about psychological studies on topics such as obedience may change their behavior in related real-life settings (Sherman, 1980); by implication, knowing about obedience experiments may make you more resistant to unjust authority in real life. Clearly, the first step to resisting unfair social pressures is to think about them, question them, and sometimes challenge them. Obedience should never be blind; it should always be thoughtful.

If you think carefully about the research described in this chapter, you will see many possibilities for resisting social influence. For example, research on both conformity and obedience demonstrates that social support can help us resist social pressures. Let's translate this to a practical example: If you feel you are likely to be susceptible to the sales pitch of a proselytizing self-help group, you might take along a friend who can help you resist the pressure.

Cialdini (1988, 1993) notes that most of the common strategies used to gain compliance suggest corresponding strategies of defense. For example, if you are aware of the "luncheon technique"—that people are more compliant when eating and in good moods—then make it a rule of thumb never to make a major decision at a meal. Tell the person plying you with food and drink that you need to think it over.

Don't be taken in by the low-ball or the foot-in-the-door if you don't want to be. A good strategy here is to ask yourself the explicit question, "Would I agree to do this if I hadn't made my initial commitment?" For example, a car dealer uses the low-ball to induce you to agree to buy a car and then later tells you that some of the options aren't really included. Now ask yourself, "Would I have agreed to purchase this car in the first place if these options had not been included?" If your answer is no, smile politely at the dealer and walk away, regardless of your prior commitment.

If a salesperson uses psychological reactance to corral you, ask yourself, "Is the commodity *really* scarce?" Is your freedom *really* limited? So what if someone has made an offer on this particular house? There are thousands of other houses to be bought. Don't let someone else create illusions of scarcity.

Above all, be aware of the power of social influence. We have seen in this chapter that people will say things they don't believe, agree to give away their hard-earned money, and even torture innocent human beings—all because of pressures from other people. By being informed and constantly aware of the power of social influence, we can better resist it when it is unjust.

CONFORMITY, COMPLIANCE, AND OBEDIENCE IN PERSPECTIVE

Hardly any aspect of life is not affected by social influence. Perhaps this is why social influence is a classic and central topic in social psychology.

Social psychologists have studied three main kinds of social influence: conformity, compliance, and obedience. People conform when they behave in a manner consistent with group standards, usually because of real or imagined pressures from the group. People comply when they accede to another's request, and they obey when they follow a direct command, typically issued by someone perceived to be a legitimate authority.

Research on conformity, compliance, and obedience vividly illustrates a central message of 20th-century social psychology: Our social setting often has an enormous impact on our behavior, and it sometimes even has the power to overwhelm our conscience, self-concept, and personality traits. Conformity pressures can sometimes lead us to publicly deny the evidence of our senses. Requests that make use of clever compliance strategies can get us to donate money, buy expensive products, and answer highly embarrassing questions, even when we don't want to. And commands from legitimate authorities can sometimes lead us to torture and kill innocent human beings despite our moral principles.

Research on social influence is fascinating because it reflects the drama of social life in general. People influence us constantly, every day. Our families, peers, churches, and clubs exert pressure on us to conform. Salespeople, solicitors, evangelists, and political organizations request our time, effort, and money. Parents, police, teachers, officers, and bosses issue commands to us. Probably more than most of us would care to admit, we often do conform, comply, and obey. Social psychology research helps us understand why. Such understanding puts us in a better position to resist social influences when they are manipulative, unfair, or unjust.

KEY POINTS   ## Kinds of Social Influence

Individuals conform when they maintain or change their behavior to be consistent with group standards, comply when they accede to a request made by another, and obey when they follow a direct command, typically from someone perceived to be a legitimate authority.

Levels of Social Influence

Kelman described three levels of social influence: (1) when an individual complies on the surface to gain rewards or avoid punishments, (2) when an individual behaves like others because he or she is attracted to them, and (3) when an individual behaves like others because he or she is rationally persuaded by them.

Conformity

Classic Research on Conformity

Sherif's autokinetic studies showed that subjects who made ambiguous perceptual judgments in a group setting were influenced by other group members' judgments. This influence extended to private beliefs as well as public statements.

Posing a relatively simple task that required subjects to judge the lengths of lines, Solomon Asch found that 75% of his subjects conformed at least once to a unanimous but obviously incorrect majority. Conformity was substantially lower if subjects could privately write rather than publicly announce their answers.

People sometimes conform because of normative social pressures—rewards and punishments delivered by groups to foster conforming behavior and discourage nonconforming behavior. Direct pressure and rejection are two powerful forms of normative social influence exerted by groups. In addition, people sometimes conform because of informational social influence; that is, they look to the group as a source of accurate information.

Factors That Influence Conformity

A number of personality traits correlate weakly with conformity. However, research suggests there is no single kind of conforming personality or set of traits that predicts all kinds of conformity. Women conform slightly more than men, particularly when they are being publicly observed and when sex roles are salient.

Conformity tends to increase as the pressuring groups increase in size to four people, and then remains relatively stable. Larger groups tend to produce greater conformity than smaller groups when group members are perceived to be independent. The Social Influence Model provides a precise mathematical description of the amount of social influence that pressuring groups of varying sizes exert on target groups of varying sizes.

In general, people conform more to groups to which they are attracted. Newcomb's Bennington College study demonstrated that college women changed their attitudes to be more similar to those of attractive upperclassmen and faculty members.

People of average status in a group tend to conform more to the group's standards than high- or low-status people do.

People often conform more to in-groups than to out-groups.

Subjects conform substantially more to a unanimous group than to a group containing one other nonconformist.

The more individuals commit themselves to a response (for example, by writing it down) before announcing it to a disagreeing group, the less likely they are to conform to the group.

Minority Influence

Minority influence occurs when disagreeing minorities influence the behavior of the majority. Minorities are most likely to influence majorities when they argue their position consistently, when their views are in keeping with prevailing cultural trends, and when they are single rather than double minorities.

Minority influence is more likely to produce private conversion, whereas majority influence is more likely to produce public compliance. Furthermore, minority influence sometimes leads groups to think more about the topics of disagreement and arrive at more creative and thoughtful judgments.

Compliance

Positive Moods and Compliance

People are more likely to comply with requests when they are in pleasant moods, which can be triggered by pleasant surroundings or ingratiation.

Reciprocity and Compliance

Doing small favors for people makes them more likely to comply with later requests. This finding is consistent with the norm of reciprocity.

The door-in-the-face technique consists of following a very large request that the target is likely to reject with a smaller, more reasonable request. This technique substantially increases the likelihood that the target will comply with the second request. The that's-not-all technique increases compliance by offering a target a product for a high price and then reducing the price slightly or adding something extra to the deal before the target has time to refuse.

Commitment and Compliance

The foot-in-the-door technique consists of following a small initial request with a much larger second request. This technique substantially increases the likelihood that the target will comply with the second request.

The low-ball technique consists of committing the target to complying with a request that has favorable conditions and then reneging on some of the conditions or adding negative features to the commitment. This technique increases the likelihood that the target will agree to the less favorable terms.

Psychological Reactance and Compliance

People experience psychological reactance—a state of unpleasant arousal—when they believe their freedom of choice is threatened. Consistent with reactance theory, people sometimes can be induced to engage in a behavior by informing them that they cannot.

Social Psychology in Everyday Life: Brainwashing— The Ultimate in Social Influence?

Brainwashing often makes use of standard processes of influence in situations where indoctrinators have complete control over their targets' environment and the targets are isolated and without power or resources.

Obedience

Milgram's Obedience Experiments

Stanley Milgram found that a majority of subjects obeyed an experimenter's command to deliver highly painful electric shocks to an innocent victim.

Obedience declined the closer the victim was to subjects and the farther the experimenter was from subjects.

Obedience in Milgram's study was not strongly influenced by the institutional setting.

Rebellious peers greatly reduced subjects' obedience in Milgram's experiments, whereas compliant peers increased obedience.

Subjects in Milgram's studies obeyed the experimenter but did not obey other "subjects" (confederates). In general, people obey only those they perceive to be legitimate authorities.

Milgram's results are counterintuitive, and they demonstrate the power of social pressures to sometimes overwhelm individual conscience.

Milgram's findings have been replicated in a number of different countries.

Ideological Factors and Obedience

Religious people tend to be more obedient in Milgram-type experiments.

People vary in the degree to which they assign or deny responsibility to individuals charged with crimes of obedience, and attitudes toward obedience are systematically related to religious attitudes, education, and socioeconomic status.

Resisting Social Influence

Knowledge about social influence can help us resist unjust influence in everyday life.

Autokinetic effect: The perceptual illusion that a stationary point of light in a dark room appears to move; Sherif had subjects in groups estimate the movement of such lights as a means to study conformity.

Cohesiveness: The degree to which group members, on average, are attracted to the group; cohesive groups tend to exert more pressure on their members to conform.

Compliance: Acceding to a request made by another.

Conformity: Maintaining or changing behavior to be consistent with group standards.

Door-in-the-face technique: Following a very large request that the target is likely to reject with a smaller, more reasonable request; a strategy to gain compliance.

Foot-in-the-door technique: Following a small initial request with a much larger second request; a strategy to gain compliance.

Informational social influence: Occurs when people look to the group to gain accurate information.

Ingratiation: The strategy of saying pleasant things to another in order to gain compliance.

Low-ball technique: Getting a target to agree to a request under favorable terms and then reneging on some of the terms or adding additional costs once the commitment is made; a strategy to gain compliance.

Minority influence: The influence exerted on majorities by disagreeing minorities.

Normative social influence: Group pressure that causes people to conform to gain rewards or avoid punishments delivered by a group; often leads to public compliance rather than private conversion.

Obedience: Occurs when a person follows a direct command, typically from someone perceived to be a legitimate authority.

Reactance: Negative arousal experienced when people feel their freedom of choice is threatened; reactance can be used as a strategy to gain compliance—people are induced to engage in the desired behavior by informing them that they cannot or may not be able to.

That's-not-all technique: Offering a product at a high price and improving the deal (by lowering the price or adding an additional product) before the target has a chance to refuse; a strategy to gain compliance.

GROUPS

... In a mere quarter-century, the human race has broken its immemorial bond to the life-sustaining surroundings of the home planet. U.S. space pioneers have been able to orbit the globe, walk on the moon, ring the earth with communications satellites and send a machine nearly 1.8 billion miles to inspect the planet Uranus. Such wonders are indeed extraordinary.

Then came *Challenger*. On Jan. 28 the fireball in the blue skies over Florida, after 24 seemingly routine shuttle launches, was seen at first as an inexplicable aberration, akin to an act of God. It was widely assumed that a Government agency with NASA's can-do spirit and engineering wizardry would never permit six crew members and a schoolteacher to perish through some avoidable human error. Surely a mechanical glitch would be found and speedily fixed.

Within days the mechanical problem was located: a joint on one of *Challenger's* two solid rocket boosters had failed. But the root cause of the tragedy ran deeper. A presidential commission, headed by former Secretary of State William Rogers, discovered NASA itself was deeply flawed. Far from representing the best of American know-how, the twelve-member commission found, NASA had become a bureaucracy that had lost its way. Before the first shuttle was launched, the agency had known of the fatal seal problem but had buried it under a blizzard of paper while permitting schedule-conscious managers to keep the orbiters flying.

—*Time*, June 9, 1986

On January 28, 1986, NASA decided to launch the space shuttle *Challenger* despite engineers' serious reservations about the design of its solid rocket boosters. Seventy-three seconds after launch, the flight ended in disaster when the *Challenger* exploded, killing all seven crew members. People throughout the world were stunned by the tragedy. A presidential commission was quickly formed to investigate its causes.

As the story of the *Challenger* unfolded, it became clear that various groups of people had played critical roles in making the decisions that ultimately led to the ill-fated launch. Under intense deadline and financial pressures, management groups at NASA had failed to heed engineers' reports warning of potential problems with the rocket engines. On the day preceding the launch, engineers at the Morton Thiokol Corporation, the company responsible for designing and manufacturing the shuttle's solid rocket boosters, were worried that subfreezing temperatures at Cape Canaveral would interfere with the proper functioning of the O-ring seals in the rocket booster engines. They were overruled by groups of high-level officials at Morton Thiokol who were eager to please impatient NASA

The Challenger *crew on their way to board the space shuttle.*

Lift off . . .

officials. The result of all these poor group decisions was a deadly accident and a national tragedy.

As the *Challenger* accident makes clear, groups sometimes get us into trouble. But it's equally clear that groups can lead us to great achievements as well. The story of the United States space program is, in one sense, a dramatic success story about groups at work. NASA placed men on the moon and launched satellites to explore the far reaches of the solar system by coordinating the effort of many groups of men and women: engineers, computer programmers, medical technicians, metallurgists, test pilots, and so on.

And it's worth noting that a group played a positive role after the accident. The Presidential Commission on the Space Shuttle Challenger Accident was responsible for unraveling the complex factors that led to the tragedy and for making recommendations for improving NASA and its decision-making processes. This group consisted of 12 illustrious members, including former Secretary of State William Rogers, Nobel Prize–winning physicist Richard Feynman, astronaut and physicist Sally Ride, and former astronaut Neil Armstrong. The establishment of the presidential commission was based on a social psychological assumption—that a group of 12 brilliant individuals could pool their collective experience and expertise and thus get to the bottom of the accident better than any single individual could.

In this chapter we shall examine the social psychology of groups so that we can better understand their potential for both good and bad. In the process, we shall

. . . and 73 seconds later, disaster.

pose a number of basic questions about the nature and functioning of groups: How do groups affect individuals' work and thought? Why do some groups (such as the management groups in NASA and Morton Thiokol) make ill-considered, dangerous decisions? What is the nature of leadership, and how do leaders influence the behavior of groups? Why do some groups (such as rioting mobs) behave in uninhibited and brutal ways? And finally, when do groups lead us to behave constructively (to cooperate with others, to conserve natural resources), and when do they lead us to behave destructively (to compete unproductively with others, to ruin collective resources)?

Social psychology theories and research can help us answer these questions, and in the process they can help us understand better how groups of intelligent people made a series of deadly decisions in 1986.

STUDYING GROUPS

Before we answer some of the fundamental questions just posed about group behavior, it helps first to define groups and to consider how social psychologists typically go about studying them.

What Is a Group?

Here are some examples of interesting and consequential groups in everyday life: the board of directors of the Morton Thiokol Corporation, the crew of the space shuttle *Challenger,* an Army platoon, a jury, the United States Senate, a Boston street gang, a class of elementary school students, people attending an Alcoholics Anonymous meeting. What do all of these collections of people have in common? What makes them groups?

Here's a simple definition: A *group* is a collection of individuals who interact and communicate with one another over a period of time. Various theorists have noted the following important characteristics of people in groups: (1) They interact frequently (Lewin, 1948), often face to face (Homans, 1950); (2) they typically share *norms* (prescribed standards of behavior) and occupy agreed-upon, interdependent roles (Newcomb, 1951); and (3) they usually perceive themselves to be part of a collective with the same goals, and they often act similarly to others in the group (Deutsch, 1968; Merton, 1957).

Clearly, the management of NASA and Morton Thiokol possessed all the characteristics just listed. They interacted with one another over extended periods of time. They had agreed-upon roles—for example, the roles of boss, chair, senior engineer, vice president, and so on. They shared norms—for example, the top management of Morton Thiokol probably shared norms of dress; they wore suits and ties to work, not jeans or shorts. And undoubtedly NASA and Morton Thiokol managers perceived themselves as part of a "team" that shared the same goals. While their most immediate and obvious goal was to develop and launch a successful space shuttle, they had broader long-term goals as well. For example,

NASA desired to launch communications satellites and perform commercial, scientific, and military experiments in space. In all probability, the managers at NASA and Morton Thiokol also had still broader goals: to enhance the prestige of their respective organizations and gain continued financial support (congressional funding in the case of NASA, and government contracts in the case of Morton Thiokol).

Research on Group Behavior

How can we study group behavior? The presidential commission on the *Challenger* accident performed a kind of after-the-fact analysis of defective decision making in NASA and Morton Thiokol management groups by studying the written records of their interactions. As you might expect, social psychologists often try to observe groups in action.

Over the years, social scientists have used many different research strategies to study ongoing behavior in groups (Cartwright & Zander, 1968; Forsyth, 1983; Worchel, Wood, & Simpson, 1992). A number of classic studies have observed real-life groups. For example, Whyte (1943) described the social organization of young men who congregated on a street corner in a slum neighborhood of Boston. To study extreme beliefs in cults, Festinger, Schachter, and Back (1950) infiltrated a doomsday sect predicting the imminent end of the world, and Kerckhoff and Back (1968) investigated (after the fact) how and why a group of Southern textile workers succumbed to an outbreak of hysteria-induced illness.

More commonly, social psychologists have studied group processes and group outcomes in the laboratory. *Group processes* refers to the ongoing communications and interactions among group members that lead to group outcomes—for example, who says what to whom over time in a jury and how this communication process results in the final verdict. *Group outcomes* refers to the final products of group activities—for example, the verdict of a jury, the ideas produced by a brainstorming session, or the performance of a relay-race team.

Dimensions of Group Behavior

Many kinds of research point to the existence of a small number of fundamentally important dimensions of group behavior (Schutz, 1958; Triandis, 1978; Wish, Deutsch, & Kaplan, 1976). Beginning in the late 1940s, Harvard social psychologist Robert Bales conducted a well-known series of process studies in which he convened groups of subjects (usually seated around a large conference table) to discuss and resolve human-relations problems. Group members might role-play, for example, that they were engaging in contract negotiations for a company. Based on his observations, Bales (1950, 1970) devised a content-analysis system called Interaction Process Analysis (IPA) that classified each group member's statements and behaviors into one of 12 content categories (see Figure 13.1). Some of the IPA content categories focused on emotional behaviors (for example, "agrees"), whereas others focused on informational, task-oriented behaviors ("asks for information").

General Kinds of Group Behaviors	Specific IPA Content Categories
A. Positive (and mixed) actions	1. Seems friendly 2. Dramatizes 3. Agrees
B. Attempted answers	4. Gives suggestion 5. Gives opinion 6. Gives information
C. Questions	7. Asks for information 8. Asks for opinion 9. Asks for suggestion
D. Negative (and mixed) actions	10. Disagrees 11. Shows tension 12. Seems unfriendly

FIGURE 13.1 The 12 content categories of Interaction Process Analysis. Bales (1970) developed the IPA categories to classify the behavior of participants in groups. *Source:* Adapted from Bales (1970).

Bales quantified each group member's behavior using IPA, and he also asked group members to rate one another on their likability and their contributions to the group. Factor analyses of these data suggested that there was a great deal of redundancy among all these codings and ratings, and in essence, they all seemed to boil down to three main dimensions of group behavior: general activity, likability, and task ability. The *activity* dimension refers to the general quantity of a member's participation in the group. A person who rates high in activity talks a lot and makes numerous suggestions. *Likability* refers to a member's role in the social and emotional life of the group. A person with a high degree of likability engages in many "positive socioemotional behaviors" (that is, he or she praises others, breaks tension, boosts others' morale) and is rated as likable by other members of the group. Finally, *task ability* refers to a member's task-oriented behaviors within the group. A person rated high in task ability contributes to achieving the group's goal (for example, gathers facts, makes suggestions, proposes problem-solving strategies) and is rated as intelligent and productive by other members of the group.

Bales's research pointed to two fundamental functions of groups and group behavior: getting work done and dealing with emotional and social relationships within the group. You can probably think of many obvious examples of the task-oriented functions of groups. Juries piece together evidence and strive to achieve reasoned verdicts, teams of engineers design products such as rocket engines, and legislatures attempt to enact wise and just laws. You can probably also think of many examples of the socioemotional functions of groups. Religious groups provide people with values and a sense of belonging to a larger unit, families nurture and support their members, and therapy groups encourage intimate emotional communication to foster positive changes in members. (Bales, by the way, first started developing his IPA system while attempting to study the dynamics of Alcoholics Anonymous meetings.)

To get work done, groups must often address social and emotional relations within the group. Legislators, for example, frequently argue, debate, and even insult one another, and then mend fences and compromise to pass legislation. And juries typically progress through different stages: Sometimes they are focused on task-oriented work (stating relevant case evidence and points of law) and at other times more on social relationships (attacking others' positions, trying to smooth over hurt feelings in order to reach a unanimous final verdict). See Chapter 16 for a more detailed description of jury deliberations.

⬱ GROUPS AT WORK

In August, 1972, NASA awarded a contract to Rockwell International Corporation's Space Transportation Division for design of the Space Shuttle Orbiter. Martin Marietta Denver Aerospace was assigned development and fabrication of the External Tank, Morton Thiokol Corporation was awarded the contract for the Solid Rocket Boosters, and Rocketdyne, a division of Rockwell, was selected to develop the Orbiter main engines.

NASA divided managerial responsibility for the program among three of its field centers. Johnson Space Center, Houston, Texas, was assigned management of the Orbiter. Marshall Space Flight Center, Huntsville, Alabama, was made responsible for the Orbiter's main engines, the External Tank and the Solid Rocket Boosters. Kennedy Space Center, Merritt Island, Florida, was given the job of assembling the Space Shuttle components, checking them out and conducting launches.

—from the *Report of the Presidential Commission
on the Space Shuttle Challenger Accident*, 1986

People often work in groups. Members of many other animal species do as well. From an evolutionary perspective, these groups make good sense, for they promote collective defense and allow animals to achieve goals that are impossible to achieve as individuals (Forsyth, 1983). A troop of baboons can fight off predators better than an individual can; a pack of wolves can track and hunt prey better than a lone wolf can; and a group of people can build and launch a space shuttle, whereas an individual certainly cannot.

Social psychologists have long been interested in how groups influence individuals' work. Let's turn to two basic questions: Does the mere presence of others influence work performance? And how do groups compare with individuals in the quality of their work?

Social Facilitation

In one of the first social psychology experiments ever published in the United States, Norman Triplett (1897) observed that children, when instructed to wind fishing reels as fast as they could, performed faster in groups than when alone. In other words, Triplett found evidence for a *social facilitation effect*: People perform a task faster or better when they are with others.

After Triplett's research, other experiments demonstrated social facilitation effects in other kinds of performance—for example, when subjects perform simple clerical chores or such simple motor tasks as tracking a moving spot with their finger (Allport, 1920; Dashiell, 1930; Travis, 1925; Zajonc, 1965). Animals, too, often show increased performance when in the presence of other members of their species performing the same behavior. These are called *coaction effects*. Two examples: Ants work harder at building nests in the presence of other working ants (Chen, 1937), and rats eat more heartily when in the presence of other eating rats (Harlow, 1932). This last finding, by the way, seems to hold for people as well: People in groups tend to eat considerably more than people eating alone (de Castro & Brewer, 1992).

Although a number of early studies clearly demonstrated social facilitation, other studies found just the opposite: that the presence of others sometimes slows down or undermines performance. For example, the presence of other people makes it more difficult for subjects to learn the solution to a maze (Husband, 1931; Pessin & Husband, 1933) and to solve complex problems (Allport, 1920). Because the early studies were inconsistent and contradictory, research on social facilitation largely died out by World War II.

After some 30 years of neglect, the topic received renewed attention when social psychologist Robert Zajonc (1965) offered a surprisingly simple and elegant explanation for the contradictions of the earlier studies. Zajonc expressed his explanation in the theoretical language of Hullian learning theory (a stimulus–response theory of animal learning developed in the 1930s and 1940s; for example, see Hull, 1943), but we can state it in more everyday language: The presence of others is arousing, and this arousal facilitates dominant, well-learned habits but inhibits nondominant, poorly learned habits.

To understand the implications of Zajonc's theory of social facilitation better, consider the following question: Does the presence of other people help or hurt the quality of a musical performance—for example, a piano recital? Zajonc's answer: It depends on how well the artist has learned the material. A brilliant virtuoso pianist may be spurred to greater heights of excellence by an audience, whereas a novice may find her fingers twisted by stage fright. Or consider this personally relevant example: When taking an important exam, would you perform better sitting in a classroom full of other students (as is typically the case) or sitting alone? According to Zajonc, if you know the material extremely well, you will probably perform better in the more arousing group setting, but if you know the material only marginally, then you are more likely to perform better in the less arousing, solitary setting (see Figure 13.2).

Social groups occur in many species other *than* Homo Sapiens. *Thus, social groups must contribute to evolutionary fitness.*

Many studies have offered support for Zajonc's theory (Bond & Titus, 1983; Geen, 1991; Guerin, 1986; Zajonc, 1980). The presence of others facilitated college students learning a simple maze but interfered with their learning a complex one (Hunt & Hillery, 1973). Similar effects have even been observed in cockroaches! In a clever experiment, Zajonc, Heingartner, and Herman (1969) had roaches escape from a bright light by running through either an easy maze (in which roaches had to run straight ahead to the goal box) or a difficult maze (roaches had to turn right to get to the goal box; see Figure 13.3). Intriguingly, when cockroaches ran in groups or in the presence of "spectator" cockroaches housed in Plexiglas "audience" boxes, they performed as predicted by Zajonc's theory: Compared with roaches running alone, they ran faster in the easy maze but slower in the difficult maze.

The cockroach study makes an important point. Psychologists and laypeople are tempted to explain social facilitation effects as due solely to competitive feelings or to anxiety about how others are evaluating one's performance. Zajonc's theory holds that the *mere presence* of others is arousing and that this arousal has automatic effects on performance that are independent of competitive feelings or evaluation anxiety. Because it is unlikely that cockroaches possess complex cognitions of any sort, the cockroach experiment suggests that Zajonc's arousal theory is a viable explanation for social facilitation observed in lower animals.

Consistent with Zajonc's theory, the mere presence of others proves at times to be arousing to people as well as cockroaches. In one experiment, Markus (1978) had college students remove their shoes and then put on unfamiliar socks, tennis shoes, and a lab coat that fastened in the back. Later in the same experiment, subjects removed these novel items of clothing and put their own shoes back on. Some subjects were alone while undressing and dressing, others were in the

---

Zajonc's (1965) theory of social facilitation argues that the presence of other people increases arousal, which then facilitates dominant, well-learned habits but inhibits nondominant, poorly learned habits.

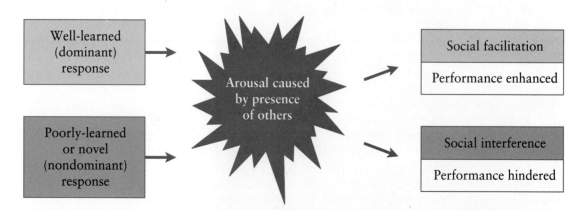

FIGURE 13.2 Zajonc's theory of social facilitation.

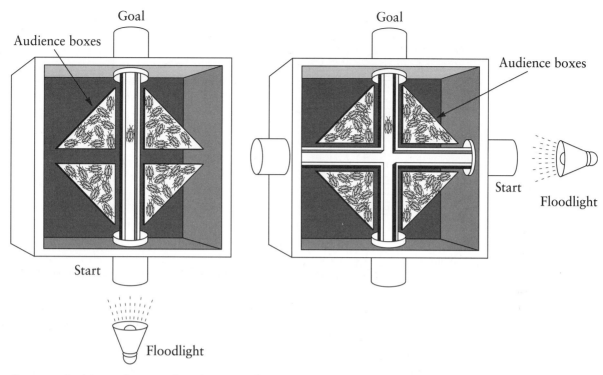

EASY MAZE   DIFFICULT MAZE

Goal   Goal

Audience boxes   Audience boxes

Start   Start

Floodlight   Floodlight

Compared with roaches running alone, roaches running in groups or in the presence of "spectator" roaches ran faster in the easy maze and slower in the difficult maze—a cockroach equivalent of the paradoxical effects of others' presence on human performance.

FIGURE 13.3 Two mazes used in experiments on social facilitation in cockroaches. *Source*: Adapted from Zajonc, Heingartner, and Herman (1969).

presence of someone who watched them, and still others were in the presence of a person who was repairing a machine and had his back to them. Interestingly, the presence of either a watchful or an inattentive person increased the speed of well-learned habits (putting on one's own shoes) but decreased the speed of novel, poorly learned habits (putting on the strange lab coat). Thus, the presence of another person can lead to social facilitation effects even when the other person cannot evaluate (or even see) the behavior of the subject.

In a conceptually similar experiment, Schmitt and his colleagues (1986) asked college students to type their names into a computer either forward (easy task) or backward (difficult, unfamiliar task). Subjects were either alone, in the presence of the observing experimenter, or in the presence of another subject who was wearing a blindfold and earphones. Consistent with Zajonc's theory, being with someone else—even a blindfolded person who could not evaluate them—speeded subjects' performance on the easy task but slowed their performance on the difficult task (see Figure 13.4).

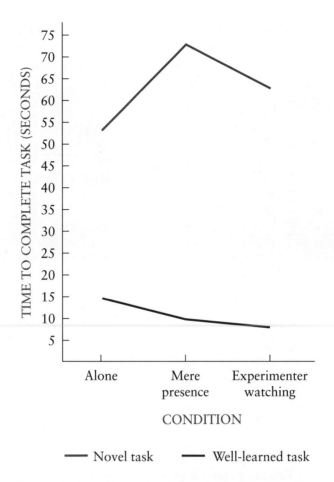

Interestingly, subjects showed social facilitation effects (that is, less time taken on the easy task, more time taken on the difficult task) even when the person present could not see them, which suggests that the mere presence of another person is somewhat arousing.

FIGURE 13.4 Results of a study of mere presence effects in human beings. *Source:* Data from Schmitt et al. (1986).

Why is the mere presence of others arousing? One possibility is that their presence may put us on guard, for we never are quite sure what other people will do (Geen, 1991; Zajonc, 1980). There are other possibilities as well. People, unlike cockroaches, do sometimes experience evaluation anxiety and competitive feelings in the presence of others, particularly when these others are observing us and when there are normative or "right" ways to perform a task (Geen, 1989; Guerin, 1986). Joggers in Santa Barbara, California, were found to run faster when watched by a woman seated on a bench than when they were alone or in the presence of a woman with her back turned to them (Worringham & Messick, 1983). Note that jogging is not simply a well-learned, dominant habit; it is also a behavior that is evaluated according to normative standards: Vigorous jogging is "better" than slothful jogging.

A number of studies show that the presence of others is particularly likely to interfere with our performance on complex tasks when we expect to fail at those tasks, and it's not so likely to interfere when we expect to succeed (Geen, 1979; Sanna & Shotland, 1990). These findings suggest again that it's not always the mere presence of others that leads to arousal and social facilitation effects, but rather, it's the worry that others will evaluate our performance and that we may not come across to others as well as we wish.

Many careful experiments suggest that a number of psychological processes contribute to human social facilitation (Geen, 1991). Zajonc's theory that the mere presence of others is arousing holds, particularly in settings when the other people present are strangers (Guerin, 1986; Zajonc, 1980). As we just noted, people may also experience evaluation anxiety in the presence of others, particularly when there are clear standards of how the behavior should be performed and when they are worried about possible failure (Cottrell, Wack, Seberak, & Rittle, 1968; Geen, 1991; Guerin, 1986). Finally, the presence of others may influence performance because it is cognitively distracting (Baron, 1986). Imagine trying to type a term paper with ten people standing around watching you! Rallying our mental resources in the face of distraction may facilitate easy tasks, but the distraction may be simply too great when we work on difficult tasks requiring complex thought; then the presence of others will interfere with performance.

Note that most theories of social facilitation agree that the presence of other people is arousing; however, their explanations of the nature of the arousal differ. Each theory helps provide a partial explanation for social facilitation effects in people.

Individual versus Group Performance

We noted earlier that the formation of the presidential commission on the *Challenger* accident was based on a seemingly obvious proposition: Twelve experts are more likely than one to successfully unravel the causes of the accident. After all, each member of the commission had special knowledge, perspectives, and experience. Perhaps during their deliberations, one commission member would see something that the others missed, and in group discussions, one member's insights would stimulate new ideas in other members.

You can probably think of many other examples where groups seem to perform better than individuals. It seems obvious, for example, that 20 people can build a house better than one person, that a group of 100 campaign workers can usually generate more votes for their candidate than one campaign worker. Before jumping to the conclusion that groups always outperform individuals, however, consider this example: A head engineer at the Morton Thiokol Corporation wants to develop a new design for the space shuttle rocket boosters. She can assign this task either to a brainstorming group of staff engineers or to a number of individual

*Groups at work:
Farm workers move
a piece of heavy
equipment.*

engineers and then gather their ideas and evaluate them. Which strategy is more likely to produce the most new ideas and the most creative designs?

Here's yet another example: Imagine that your social psychology professor gives your class two test options. Students can take their exams either individually (as you probably do in your current class) or communally—that is, the class as a whole can discuss each question and then vote on the correct answers. Would the average student working alone score better or worse than the class as a whole in the communal version of the test? Here's a more difficult question to answer: Would the *best* student working alone score better or worse than the class as a whole in the communal version of the test?

What is the relationship between a group's performance and the performance of individual members in the group? Social facilitation research investigates how the *mere presence* of others influences performance; in such studies, subjects do not *interact* with the other people present. When people work together on tasks, what happens to individual and group performance? Does interaction in groups help or hinder work? *Are* two heads better than one? Always? Sometimes?

Steiner's Analysis of Group Tasks

Ivan Steiner (1972, 1976) proposed a comprehensive classification of group tasks that helps us analyze work groups and understand the relationship between individual and group performance. Steiner identified four important kinds of group tasks: additive tasks, conjunctive tasks, disjunctive tasks, and divisible tasks (see Figure 13.5).

In an *additive task,* people pool their identical efforts in order to produce a summed group product. A tug-of-war team is a good example: Team members pool their individual tugs to produce a group tug. In general, Steiner argued, additive groups outperform individuals. A team of people usually beats an individual in a

Kind of Task	Description	Examples
Additive	Group members pool or add their efforts	Tug-of-war Crop harvesters
Conjunctive	Group members separately perform same subtask(s)	Relay race Bowling team Mountain-climbing team
Disjunctive	Group members collaborate to arrive at an "either/or," "yes/no" decision	Quiz game team Jury
Divisible	Group members perform subcomponents of task; a true division of labor	Football team Baseball team NASA

FIGURE 13.5 Four kinds of group tasks identified by Steiner (1972, 1976).

tug-of-war. Other examples of additive groups support this conclusion: On average, a group of soldiers will beat an opposing individual soldier, and larger additive groups (1,000 soldiers) will outperform smaller additive groups (100 soldiers).

A *conjunctive task* requires individual members of the group to perform the same subtask, but they don't literally add their efforts together. Examples of conjunctive sports groups are relay-racing, bowling, and mountain-climbing teams. Note that in a relay-racing team, each member separately performs the same subtasks: running as fast as possible and passing the baton smoothly to the next runner. How does individual performance relate to group performance in a conjunctive group? Steiner argued that conjunctive groups generally perform only as well as their *weakest* members. If three members of a relay team run superbly but the fourth runner trips and falls, the team will probably lose. The nature of conjunctive groups is captured by the saying "A chain is only as strong as its weakest link."

The opposite is true of disjunctive groups: Their performance is more a function of their ablest members. A *disjunctive task* involves answering a "yes–no" or "either–or" question based on group deliberation. The communal social psychology test described earlier is a good example. Team quiz games in general are disjunctive tasks. Note that in a quiz game, if one member of the group knows the correct answer, then the group has the possibility of answering the question correctly. Of course, it is also possible that an ignorant majority may vote down the one knowledgeable member in a disjunctive group (Hill, 1982; Nemeth, 1992), and groups sometimes accept the incorrect answers of high-status members over those of lower-status but correct members (Torrance, 1955). There is yet another way groups may fail to pool their knowledge successfully: Although individual members of the group may know accurate pieces of information and correct answers, they don't always express their knowledge in group discussions, and so the group as a whole may lack complete information to come to a correct conclusion (Stasser, 1992).

In a *divisible task,* members perform *different* subcomponents of the task. Baseball, football, and basketball teams are all divisible groups because different players have different positions or roles. Clearly, in our bureaucratic–industrial society, divisible groups are very common and extremely important. Assembly lines are based on a division of labor whereby each worker performs a separate component of the manufacturing task. When corporations execute major projects (such as designing a new rocket engine for NASA, developing a new computer, introducing design changes for the next model-year of cars), they divide the task into pieces and assign these to various groups and group members. The relationship between individual performance and group performance is quite complex in large divisible tasks. Indeed, modern management theory attempts to systematically analyze complicated divisible tasks (such as designing a new rocket engine) in order to uncover the "weakest link" in the task and streamline the group effort.

Social Loafing

Steiner's classification system can help us understand the social psychology of work groups. Let's return to the tug-of-war, a simple additive task. We noted earlier that additive groups generally outperform individuals and that larger additive groups generally outperform smaller additive groups. But is there a literal addition of effort in additive groups? Do four people tend to pull in a tug-of-war four times as hard as the average individual?

The answer to this question is clearly no. In a much-cited early study, the French agricultural engineer Max Ringelmann (1913; see Kravitz & Martin, 1986) first asked male subjects either working alone or in groups of varying sizes to pull on a rope as hard as they could and then measured their effort with a dynamometer (a force meter). Ringelmann found that as the number of workers increased, the average force contributed by each worker decreased (see Figure 13.6). Why? There are two possibilities: Subjects did not coordinate their pulling in an optimal fashion, or subjects showed *social loafing*—that is, they actually exerted less individual effort when in groups (Latané, Williams, & Harkins, 1979).

Experiments have found evidence for both phenomena in additive groups. In one study, college subjects were blindfolded and headphones producing static-like noise were placed over their ears. Subjects were then asked to yell as loudly as they could. Sometimes subjects were alone and sometimes they combined their yells in groups of two or six people. In addition, some subjects were falsely led to believe that they were in groups of two or six people when in fact they were alone. (This deception was possible because subjects wore blindfolds and earphones.) The results of the experiment demonstrated that solo subjects tended to yell louder than individual subjects in groups; furthermore, actual groups showed lower overall performance than the summed performance of "pseudogroups" of solo people (who falsely believed themselves to be in groups) (Latané, Williams, & Harkins, 1979; see Figure 13.7).

What are the implications of these results? The finding that actual groups performed worse than pseudogroups illustrates that group yelling suffered from problems of coordination; apparently, the members of the real groups didn't yell their loudest at the same optimal instant. The finding that individual effort in both

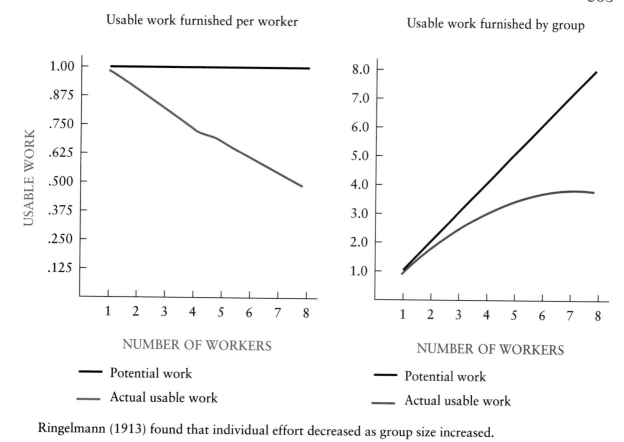

Usable work furnished per worker   Usable work furnished by group

USABLE WORK

NUMBER OF WORKERS   NUMBER OF WORKERS

— Potential work   — Potential work

— Actual usable work   — Actual usable work

Ringelmann (1913) found that individual effort decreased as group size increased.

FIGURE 13.6 The Ringelmann effect. *Source*: Data from Ringelmann (1913).

pseudogroups and actual groups was lower than the individual effort of solo individuals demonstrates social loafing effects: People simply tended to goof off in the real or perceived group situations.

Social loafing is caused by a number of factors. Individuals' efforts are often anonymous in additive group settings; because it is the group's and not the individual's production that is measured, the individual can be a "free rider" with impunity (Harkins, 1987; Sweeney, 1973). Second, people in groups may assume that others will slack off, and so, consistent with exchange and equity theories, they slack off in return (Jackson & Harkins, 1985; see Chapters 1 and 9). Finally, it may be that when people perform in additive groups, they are not as aroused and motivated as people who perform as individuals (Jackson & Williams, 1985).

This last point may seem to contradict social facilitation research. Please note, however, that social loafing studies differ from social facilitation studies in the following crucial respect: Subjects pool their efforts in social loafing studies but not in social facilitation studies. Thus, subjects can "hide in the crowd" in social loafing studies but not in social facilitation studies. The presence of others may *reduce* people's arousal and evaluation apprehension in social loafing studies

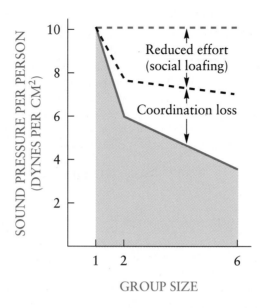

- - - Potential productivity

- - - Sound produced by pseudogroups

——— Sound produced by actual groups

On average, solitary individuals yelled louder than individuals in groups. Furthermore, the efforts of individuals in "pseudogroups" surpassed the average effort per individual in actual groups. Thus, the total performance of additive groups suffers from both "social loafing" and a lack of coordination among individual members.

FIGURE 13.7 Social loafing and loss of coordination in additive groups. *Source*: Adapted from Latané, Williams, and Harkins (1979).

but *heighten* these same variables in social facilitation studies (Harkins, 1987; Harkins & Szymanski, 1987), and this may be particularly true when people expect to fail at the task or are especially worried about others' evaluating them (Sanna, 1992).

Social loafing is clearly a phenomenon that can sap the productivity of real-life additive work groups. One way to reduce social loafing is to inform participants in additive tasks that their individual performances, as well as the entire group's output, are being evaluated. In the galley ships of ancient Rome, slaves worked together in the grueling additive task of pulling the ship's oars. To maintain the slaves' individual efforts, taskmasters constantly monitored their performance and brutally punished slackers. In modern work settings no one would tolerate such a cruel solution to the problem of social loafing; however, managers can periodically evaluate individual workers' performances in group tasks and inform them of the results. Simply having subjects compare their individual outputs to normative standards—that is, to engage in self-evaluation—can sometimes be enough to eliminate social loafing (Szymanski & Harkins, 1987). Thus, individual evaluation—either by oneself or by others—is often an effective way to reduce social loafing. Not surprisingly, social loafing is most likely to be a problem when groups tasks are boring and uninvolving (Williams & Karau, 1991); thus, another way to combat social loafing in real-life work settings is to create jobs that are meaningful and involving to workers.

Are Brainstorming Groups Effective?

SOCIAL PSYCHOLOGY IN EVERYDAY LIFE

Social facilitation research shows that the presence of others may interfere with individuals' performance on complex or unfamiliar tasks, and social loafing research shows that additive groups sometimes foster a loss of individual productivity. Thus, both kinds of research portray groups as sometimes interfering with individual performance. Do groups ever *improve* the quality of individual members' work?

Alex Osborn (1957) argued that groups can foster *creativity* in their members: "The average person can think up twice as many ideas when working with a group than when working alone" (p. 229). Osborn coined the term *brainstorming* to describe what he considered to be the optimal procedure for stimulating creativity in groups. In brainstorming groups, people are instructed to: (1) express any idea that comes to mind, regardless of how strange or ridiculous it seems, (2) refrain from critically evaluating their own or others' ideas at first, (3) generate as many ideas as they can, and (4) build on and extend others' ideas.

Although Osborn's brainstorming technique seems a plausible way to foster creativity in groups, studies generally have shown that brainstorming groups *are not* more creative, either in the quantity or quality of their ideas, than equivalent numbers of separate individuals working on the same task (Diehl & Stroebe, 1987; Lamm & Trommsdorff, 1973). Indeed, the findings of one of the first careful studies of brainstorming were almost exactly opposite to Osborn's prediction: Nominal groups (that is, groups of isolated individuals pooled together for the sake of statistical comparison) produced nearly twice as many ideas as brainstorming groups of an equivalent size (Taylor, Berry, & Block, 1958). Recent studies report similar results (Diehl & Stroebe, 1987; Mullen, Johnson, & Salas, 1991). Despite the lack of research evidence for its effectiveness, brainstorming remains a popular technique for fostering creativity (Ulschak, Nathanson, & Gillan, 1981), and laypeople believe strongly in its effectiveness (Paulus, Dzindolet, Poletes, & Camacho, 1993; Stroebe, Diehl, & Abakoumkin, 1992).

Why didn't the technique of brainstorming live up to early expectations? Diehl and Stroebe (1987) suggested three problems that may reduce creativity

"I like it. It's dumb without trying to be clever."

Brainstorming: Do people in groups produce more and better ideas than individuals?

in brainstorming groups: (1) Members may suffer from social loafing. (2) Despite explicit instructions not to evaluate ideas, group members may still suffer from evaluation anxiety in brainstorming groups. (3) Group settings may sometimes block the production of ideas—for example, one person on the verge of formulating a novel idea may be interrupted by another group member and lose his or her train of thought. In a careful set of experiments, Diehl and Stroebe found some evidence for all three processes in brainstorming groups; however, production blocking seemed to be the most important barrier to creativity.

Research on the limitations of brainstorming suggests some new techniques that may increase creativity in groups. The *nominal group technique* (Delbecq, Van de Ven, & Gustafson, 1975), for example, attempts to combine individual and group creativity into a single process. First, a group discussion leader presents and defines a problem. Second, group members silently generate as many ideas as they can and write them down on paper. Third, each member describes his or her ideas for the group, and the group poses questions but does not criticize or evaluate the ideas. Fourth, members write down and rank what they think are the five best ideas generated by the group. Finally, these votes are then tallied and presented to the group; at this point, another cycle of group discussion may ensue.

Note that because group members work individually during the first stage and because each must present his or her ideas to the group, social loafing is minimized. Because members write down their ideas, production blocking is reduced. Finally, nonevaluative group discussion and anonymous balloting to identify several good ideas help reduce evaluation anxiety and avoid putting individuals on the spot. There may be a price to pay for the nominal group technique, however: It is highly structured, and thus it may not produce the freewheeling discussion of true brainstorming groups.

If you decide to brainstorm in a group setting, recent research provides two additional pieces of advice that may help reduce production blocking: (1) Make sure that the group has plenty of time to do its work, so everyone has a chance to think and talk. (2) Keep the group small (Diehl & Stroebe, 1991).

Decision Making in Groups

The genesis of the Challenger accident—the failure of the joint of the right Solid Rocket Motor—began with decisions made in the design of the joint and in the failure by both Thiokol and NASA's Solid Rocket Booster project office to understand and respond to facts obtained during testing.

The Commission has concluded that neither Thiokol nor NASA responded adequately to internal warnings about the faulty seal design. Furthermore, Thiokol and NASA did not make a timely attempt to develop and verify a new seal after the initial design was shown to be deficient. Neither organization developed a solution to the unexpected occurrences of O-ring erosion and blow-by even though this problem was experienced frequently during the Shuttle flight history. Instead, Thiokol and NASA management came to accept erosion and blow-by as unavoidable and an acceptable flight risk.

—from the *Report of the Presidential Commission on the Space Shuttle Challenger Accident*

Work groups often make decisions: Juries decide who is guilty and who is innocent. The Congress of the United States decides when to declare war on another nation. The Department of Energy decides when a nuclear facility is safe to operate. And NASA decides when to give the go-ahead to manned space launches.

Often groups make wise decisions: Few would argue, for example, with Congress's decision to declare war against the Axis powers in 1941. Unfortunately, groups sometimes arrive at stupid and destructive decisions: Juries condemn innocent people to death. Government agencies place citizens' lives unnecessarily at risk—for example, the Department of Energy operated a uranium-processing plant in Fernald, Ohio, for many years with the clear knowledge that it was contaminating the surrounding countryside with radioactive wastes (*Time*, October 31, 1988). And on a fateful January day in 1986, NASA decided to launch the space shuttle *Challenger* despite engineers' reservations about the design of its solid rocket boosters.

Group Polarization

In order to prevent bad group decisions, we must first understand how groups make decisions. Let's begin with a question that has been the subject of an enormous amount of social psychology research: Do groups tend to make riskier or more conservative decisions than individuals? In the 1950s, the sociological literature suggested that groups exert a stultifying, conservative influence on decision making (see, for example, Whyte, 1956).

But this view was challenged in one of the first laboratory experiments designed to address the issue. MIT graduate student James Stoner (1961) presented subjects with hypothetical "choice dilemmas." Here's a shortened version: Mr. Jones is an engineer who has two job offers—one an average-paying position with a big company offering good benefits and security; the other a highly creative position in a risky new company. If the new company succeeds, Jones will make a fortune; however, there is a significant chance that the new company will fail, and then Jones will be out of a job. How good must the odds be that the risky company will succeed before you would recommend that Jones accept its job offer: 1 in 10, 3 in 10, 5 in 10, . . . 10 in 10?

Stoner first had subjects respond to his choice dilemmas as individuals; then they discussed their responses in a group; and finally, they again responded to the choice dilemmas as individuals. In general, subjects' responses tended more toward riskier choices after group discussion; this phenomenon was soon dubbed "the risky shift." Stoner's finding was replicated by other researchers, even in situations that presented subjects with real rather than hypothetical risks (Bem, Wallach, & Kogan, 1965; Wallach, Kogan, & Bem, 1962).

Although group discussion tended to produce riskier decisions on most choice dilemma items, a small number of items showed more conservative decisions as well (Wallach, Kogan, & Bem, 1962). Indeed, dozens of studies since the early 1960s indicate that the "risky shift" was a misnomer: Group discussion in fact leads to *more extreme* decisions, not necessarily riskier decisions, and today this phenomenon is referred to as *group polarization* (Moscovici & Zavalloni, 1969; Myers, 1982; Myers & Lamm, 1976). What determines the direction of group polarization? The general principle seems to be that after group discussion, members tend to shift in the direction of the average initial position of the group.

In other words, if the group on average responds to a choice dilemma with risky responses, then group discussion will tend to polarize responses to be even riskier, but if the group on average responds initially with conservative responses, then group discussion will polarize responses to be more conservative. One recent study documents a "conservative shift" in an unusual research population: residential burglars. Thirty active burglars were asked to evaluate various Texas homes as burglary sites. In general, when burglars were in groups they tended to be more conservative in their evaluations—that is, they rated homes as less vulnerable and harder to break into successfully (Cromwell, Marks, Olson, & Avary, 1991). Consistent with the group polarization hypothesis, these burglars were relatively conservative in their judgments to start with; thus, they became more conservative after group discussion.

Group polarization applies not only to decisions about risk, but to judgments and attitudes in general. For example, Moscovici and Zavalloni (1969) found that after group discussions, French students expressed more positive attitudes toward General Charles de Gaulle (toward whom they were positive to begin with) but more negative attitudes toward Americans (toward whom they were somewhat negative to begin with). Other research suggests that group discussions may lead relatively unprejudiced people to become even less prejudiced and prejudiced people to become more so (Myers & Bishop, 1970). Group discussion in juries tends to lead members to arrive at more extreme opinions and verdicts after deliberation (Isozaki, 1984; see Chapter 16).

Why does group polarization occur? Research has converged on two processes: informational influence and social comparison processes. *Informational influence* occurs when people learn new information and hear new persuasive arguments during the course of group discussion (Burnstein & Vinokur, 1973, 1977). A nice example comes from the burglar study we just mentioned:

> On one occasion two informants were discussing the rating to be assigned to a [burglary] site: One informant said, "I'd give this place a 7." [The scale ranged from 0 to 10, with 0 a very unattractive target and 10 a very attractive, vulnerable target.] His partner quickly declared, "Hey man, don't you see that dude inside that house [across the street] watching through the curtains? I'm getting out of here. This is a 0." The partner immediately agreed.

On another occasion when three burglars were evaluating sites together, two of them agreed that a site should be given a rating of "6." The third, a female, noted that it was nearly 3:00 PM and that school would soon be out and that children would soon be returning from school and playing nearby. They agreed and lowered the rating to "2." (Cromwell et al., 1991, p. 585)

Clearly, the burglars learned new "facts" from one another during their deliberations, causing the group to shift its judgments.

The second process leading to group polarization, *social comparison,* occurs when people learn the group's consensus during discussion. Experiencing social pressures from the group to conform, members shift in the direction of the perceived group norm. (The informational influence and social comparison explanations of group polarization are clearly linked to the concepts of informational and normative social influence discussed in Chapter 12.)

Laboratory experiments provide abundant evidence that both informational influence and social comparison processes contribute to group polarization (Isenberg, 1986). For example, when people hear novel arguments without learning the specific positions of other members in the group, they still show polarization effects (Burnstein & Vinokur, 1973, 1977); this evidence supports the informational explanation. On the other hand, when people learn others' positions but don't hear their supporting arguments, they also show polarization effects; this evidence supports the social comparison explanation (Goethals & Zanna, 1979; Sanders & Baron, 1977). In real-life groups, informational influence and social comparison processes frequently go hand in hand and may even facilitate each other. Although the effects of informational influence prove to be larger than those for social comparison processes in experimental studies (Isenberg, 1986), this finding may simply indicate that experimental studies do not create social comparison processes that are as powerful as those that can occur in real-life groups, which are often highly cohesive, attractive to members, and engaged in long-term patterns of interaction.

Is group polarization good or bad? As with most things, it depends. On the positive side, group polarization can lead to group consensus, cohesiveness, and group action. On the negative side, it can exaggerate ill-considered judgments and decisions; this may have been the case for the management groups at NASA and Morton Thiokol that made unacceptably risky decisions about remedying flaws in rocket engines and launching space shuttles.

Jury decisions provide an interesting real-life example of group polarization. Often the best predictor of a jury's ultimate verdict is the majority's consensus at the time of the jury's first polling (Kerr, 1981; see Chapter 16). Juries tend to achieve greater consensus over time because the minority often joins the majority (and thus moves in the direction of the average group judgment). Such polarization is most likely to occur in juries when their judgments concern values and opinions (for example, what are fair punitive damages in a libel suit?) rather than factual questions (did the defendant commit the murder?), and juries are more likely to show polarization when they are required to reach unanimous decisions (Kaplan & Miller, 1987).

Group polarization seems to occur most intensely in groups that have strong "in-group" feelings (Mackie, 1986), perhaps because people in such groups falsely perceive opinion in their group to be more consistent and extreme than it really is, and they feel the opinions of group members really "count"; the result is the creation of social comparison processes that forcefully push group members toward polarization. The management groups at NASA and Morton Thiokol probably had such strong "in-group" feelings.

Groupthink

Is group polarization sufficient to explain the poor decisions made by management teams at NASA and Morton Thiokol? Clearly, group discussions of the space shuttle's rocket booster problems did seem to lead to risky decisions. In the words of presidential commission member Richard Feynman, the decision making became

> a kind of Russian roulette. . . . [The shuttle] flies [with O-ring erosion] and nothing happens. Then it is suggested, therefore, that the risk is no longer so high for the next flights. We can lower our standards a little bit because we got away with it last time. . . . You got away with it, but it shouldn't be done over and over again like that. (Report of the Presidential Commission, p. 148)

While it may have contributed to bad management decisions, group polarization is probably not a sufficient explanation for the flawed decision making that led to the *Challenger* accident. What leads groups of intelligent men and women to make obviously foolish and even disastrous decisions sometimes? To answer such questions, Yale social psychologist Irving Janis analyzed a series of famous, ill-fated group decisions, and in the process he discerned a general syndrome of biased decision making in cohesive groups, which he termed *groupthink*:

> I use the term "groupthink" as a quick and easy way to refer to a mode of thinking that people engage in when they are deeply involved in a cohesive in-group, when the members' strivings for unanimity override their motivation to realistically appraise alternative courses of action. "Groupthink" is a term of the same order as the words in the newspeak vocabulary George Orwell presents in his dismaying *1984*—a vocabulary with terms such as "doublethink" and "crimethink." By putting groupthink with those Orwellian words, I realize that groupthink takes on an invidious connotation. The invidiousness is intentional: Groupthink refers to a deterioration of mental efficiency, reality testing, and moral judgment that results from in-group pressures. (1972, p. 9)

We've already mentioned some possible examples of groupthink: trials in which overly zealous jurors sentence innocent defendants to death, the Department of Energy's decision to continue operating an unsafe plant, and, of course, NASA's catastrophic decision to launch the space shuttle *Challenger.*

Janis cites a number of similar episodes from history: In 1938, despite ominous signs of Germany's rapid preparation for war, British Prime Minister Neville Chamberlain and his inner circle of advisors decided to appease Adolf Hitler at Munich, thus setting the stage for World War II and providing Germany with the necessary time to become almost invincible. In 1961, President John F.

This group possesses one of the factors that contribute to group-think: an authoritarian leader who doesn't tolerate dissent.

Kennedy approved his advisors' plan to help a group of Cuban exiles invade Cuba. The result was the Bay of Pigs fiasco, in which all the invaders were captured or killed by Castro's forces and the United States was humiliated. Throughout the mid-1960s, President Lyndon Johnson met regularly with his "Tuesday lunch group" of trusted advisors to discuss the growing U.S. involvement in southeast Asia. Despite discouraging intelligence reports and pleas from war-weary citizens and skeptical allies to disengage, Johnson and his advisors continued to escalate the war, with disastrous consequences for both Vietnam and the United States.

Janis saw commonalities among all these foreign policy blunders: Cohesive, intelligent groups of advisors developed an unrealistic consensus and protected their leaders from any contradictory information. According to Janis (1985), groups are most susceptible to groupthink when they are isolated, cohesive, and homogeneous, and when the leader signals his preferences and discourages debate within the group. Stressful circumstances—recent failures, moral dilemmas, and a seeming lack of viable alternatives—also foster the development of groupthink.

Once groupthink develops, it is characterized by a number of symptoms. The cohesive in-group overestimates its power and moral authority, stereotypes its opposition, rationalizes its poor decisions, and then squelches all dissent by creating an illusion of unanimity. Often the group develops "mindguards," whose job is to protect the group from unwelcome (but realistic) information that might cast

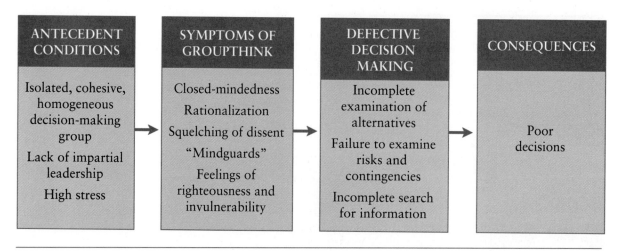

ANTECEDENT CONDITIONS	SYMPTOMS OF GROUPTHINK	DEFECTIVE DECISION MAKING	CONSEQUENCES
Isolated, cohesive, homogeneous decision-making group Lack of impartial leadership High stress	Closed-mindedness Rationalization Squelching of dissent "Mindguards" Feelings of righteousness and invulnerability	Incomplete examination of alternatives Failure to examine risks and contingencies Incomplete search for information	Poor decisions

FIGURE 13.8 The stages of groupthink according to Janis's model.

doubts on its decisions. Figure 13.8 presents an overview of Janis's description of groupthink.

The decisions made by NASA and Morton Thiokol management groups show many of the symptoms of groupthink (Esser & Lindoerfer, 1989; Moorhead, Ference, & Neck, 1991). NASA seemed to have developed an illusion that it was invulnerable to accidents, perhaps because it had not experienced a fatal one since 1967, when a flash fire in a space capsule killed three Apollo astronauts. NASA officials "explained away" troubling data from Morton Thiokol engineers as being inconclusive, and they tended to believe strongly in their moral authority and the virtue of their "mission." For many years, NASA viewed the space program as an intense competition with a despised adversary, the Soviet Union, and NASA's decision making sometimes showed evidence of "mindguarding." For example, some top officials at the Marshall Space Flight Center failed to reveal important engineering data critical of the shuttle rocket casings at key management meetings.

Finally, NASA was highly stressed: It was under severe financial and time constraints. Additional stresses were present before the launch of *Challenger*. In the words of a former NASA safety director:

> There was social pressure: they had thousands of school kids watching for the first school lesson from space. There was media pressure: they feared that if they didn't launch, the press would unfavorably report more delay. And there was commercial pressure: the Ariane [European launcher] was putting objects in space at much lower cost. NASA was also trying to show the Air Force that they could operate on a schedule. (*Time*, June 9, 1986)

The *Challenger* launch had already been postponed once, and the new launch had to occur quickly during a favorable "window" of time, or be substantially postponed again.

Janis saw similar symptoms of groupthink in the foreign policy disasters listed earlier: The advisors of Neville Chamberlain, John Kennedy, and Lyndon Johnson all saw themselves as a moral, righteous elite facing despicable foes (Hitler's Germany, Castro's Cuba, and the Communists in Vietnam). They served leaders who strongly expressed their opinions to the deliberating groups. And finally, all of these advisory groups suffered from a suppression of reasonable dissent. Theodore Sorenson, one of Kennedy's close advisors during the ill-fated Bay of Pigs invasion, noted, "No strong voice of opposition was raised in any of the key meetings, and no realistic alternatives were presented" (Janis, 1972, p. 39). Robert Kennedy, the president's brother, served as a mindguard when he told one dissenter, "The President has made his mind up. Don't push it any further" (p. 42).

How can groups prevent groupthink? Janis (1985) offers a number of prescriptions. The group leader should strive to be impartial and to foster an atmosphere of open inquiry and debate. Group members should be encouraged to express doubts and criticisms as well as support for group plans. "Outside experts" should be brought into the group to challenge it and give it fresh perspectives. Finally, after arriving at a consensus, the group should schedule a "second chance" meeting in which members can voice lingering doubts or reservations.

Janis's original account of groupthink was based on anecdotal historical analysis more than on laboratory experimentation. Janis (1985) argued for the value of a kind of "psychological autopsy" in which the processes leading to bad decisions in real-life groups are dissected after the fact. Experimental evidence for Janis's hypotheses has been mixed (for example, see Callaway, Marriott, & Esser, 1985; Courtright, 1978; Turner, Pratkanis, Probasco, & Leve, 1992).

One direction of recent research has been to extend and refine Janis's original groupthink model. Some researchers have questioned the importance of some of the variables proposed by Janis as leading to groupthink, and others have proposed additional causal variables (McCauley, 1989; 't Hart, 1990; Turner et al., 1992). Among recent suggestions: Group cohesiveness may not be as critical an ingredient as Janis originally thought (McCauley, 1989; 't Hart, 1990). Groupthink may occur particularly when group members' collective self-esteem is threatened and, as a result, they try hard to promote a positive social identity (Turner et al., 1992). Psychological commitment and entrapment may contribute to groupthink; this occurs when groups pledge themselves to costly courses of action (for example, a rocket design), and thus have to swallow their losses to change their course of action (Hart, 1990; Staw & Ross, 1987).

The groupthink concept has now been studied for more than 20 years. It has provided a compelling portrait of bad decision making in stressed groups, and has stimulated a number of studies about the decision process in real-life policymaking groups. The goal of current research is to test the limits of the groupthink concept and try to fit it into broader models of group decision making (Aldag & Fuller, 1993).

☞ LEADERSHIP IN GROUPS

Oldtimers at NASA yearn for a return to the days when Air Force Lieut. General James Abrahamson . . . ran the shuttle program. When he sensed a problem, he awaited no "criticality" rating; he barged into the office of even the lowliest technician to ask how to fix it. Perhaps unfairly, one commissioner insists that "Abe was replaced by wimps."

—*Time,* June 9, 1986

Janis's account of groupthink introduces an important factor into our discussion of groups: namely, leaders. Groupthink, according to Janis, is caused both by characteristics of the group (cohesiveness, homogeneity, stress) and by characteristics of the leader (expression of strong opinions, intolerance of dissent). To understand fully the nature of group processes, we must address the nature of leadership.

What Is Leadership?

Leaders are members of groups who are particularly influential and who act to guide, direct, and motivate the group to achieve its goals (Hollander, 1985). Leadership is in part determined by the leader's characteristics (such as intelligence, experience, skill), the group's thoughts and feelings (the members' attraction to and respect for the leader), the nature of the group (a ballet corps, a jury, a corporate board, a platoon), and the group setting (a highly stressed group versus an unstressed one).

Research on leadership began in earnest during the period immediately following World War II. This early work suggested that leaders engage in two main kinds of behavior: *task-oriented* behaviors that direct the group's work toward achieving the group's goals, and *socioemotional* behaviors that foster positive relations and feelings in the group and that promote group cohesiveness (Bales, 1958; Fleishman, 1973; Halpin & Winer, 1952; Kerr, Schriesheim, Murphy, & Stogdill, 1974). (These two kinds of leadership behavior closely correspond to two of the three main dimensions of group behavior discussed earlier: task ability and likability.) Many studies suggest that both the task-oriented and positive socioemotional behaviors of leaders are correlated with effective job performance of their groups; not surprisingly, workers' overall job satisfaction in work groups seems to depend more on the leaders' positive socioemotional behaviors than on their degree of task-oriented behaviors (Fisher & Edwards, 1988).

A leader who excels at task-oriented but not socioemotional skills is often referred to as a *task specialist* (Bales, 1958), whereas a leader who excels at socioemotional but not task-oriented skills is often referred to as a *socioemotional leader* (Bales, 1958) or a *maintenance specialist* (Thibaut & Kelley, 1959). Great leaders may be those who excel in both areas (Borgatta, Couch, & Bales, 1954).

Theories of Leadership

Social psychologists have taken three different approaches to the study of leadership: (1) the trait approach, which attempts to identify the personal characteristics that distinguish leaders from nonleaders; (2) the situational approach, which examines how social settings foster or inhibit the development of leadership; and (3) the interactional (contingency) approach, which analyzes leadership as a function of both personal and situational factors.

The Trait Approach

The "great man/great woman" theory of leadership holds that leaders are born, not made. The obvious question implied by this approach is: What are the traits that make a person a "natural leader"? Research attempting to answer this question has had a mixed record of success (Bass, 1990).

One of the most consistent research findings is a small but significant relationship between intelligence and leadership (Bass, 1990; Mann, 1959; Stogdill, 1974). Managerial leaders and the heads of small laboratory groups tend to be somewhat more intelligent than the average group member, but intriguingly, they also tend not to be the *most* intelligent member of the group. Apparently, many groups appreciate being led by people who are smarter than they are, but not too much smarter. Gibb (1968) noted that although research consistently indicates that intelligence in fact contributes to leadership skill, "the crowd prefers to be ill-governed by people it can understand" (p. 218). A good example is provided by presidents of the United States. Do you think presidents are the *most* intelligent people in the country?

Specific, task-relevant skills also contribute to leadership (Goldman & Fraas, 1965; Stogdill, 1974). For example, the majority whip of the Senate is a more effective leader if he knows the byzantine procedural rules of the Senate, and the head of an engineering team is more effective when she is an expert at the technical tasks facing her group.

A number of personality and intellectual traits correlate to some degree with leadership. Leaders tend on average to be more energetic, self-confident, and sociable than nonleaders (Bass, 1990; Stogdill, 1974). Leaders also seem to have higher needs for achievement and for affiliation than nonleaders do (Sorrentino & Field, 1986). Physical and demographic characteristics may also correlate with leadership: On average, leaders tend to be taller than nonleaders, but, of course, there are notable exceptions (Napoleon, for example). Leaders in bureaucratic groups (such as business and government organizations) tend to be older than nonleaders, in part because greater knowledge and experience accrue with age but also because leaders must often "work their way up" in most organizations, and this takes time.

The personal characteristics that contribute to leadership may be inherited and ascribed as well as innate. For example, the kings and queens of old Europe were leaders not necessarily because of unusual intelligence or special skills, but by virtue of their hereditary status. Inherited wealth may also confer leadership on some individuals.

Leaders typically possess power, which can derive from a number of different sources. In an influential analysis, French and Raven (1959) described five different kinds of power—reward power, coercive power, legitimate power, referent power, and expert power—and this classification can be applied to the topic of leadership. Leaders possess *reward power* when they control desired goods and resources. For

Pope John Paul II possesses "legitimate power" for many Roman Catholics.

President Bill Clinton. What kind of power does he possess?

example, a boss can use potential pay raises as a means of influencing employees' behavior. *Coercive power* makes use of threats and punishment—a boss threatens to fire an employee who isn't shaping up. Leaders exert *legitimate power* when they are perceived to possess legitimate authority in some domain. For example, Catholics perceive the pope to be a legitimate authority on church doctrine; at work, bosses are often perceived as legitimate authorities. Leaders possess *referent power* when followers are attracted to them. John F. Kennedy was a charismatic president who possessed referent power for many Americans. Finally, leaders have *expert power* by virtue of special knowledge or skills. Albert Einstein possessed clear expert power when he advised President Franklin D. Roosevelt to proceed with the development of the atom bomb.

Figure 13.9 shows scale items designed to measure French and Raven's five bases of power in a work setting (Hinken & Schriesheim, 1989). Research using scales like these finds that workers are usually happiest and most productive when their supervisors use referent and expert power; workers have mixed reactions to supervisors' use of legitimate and reward power, and they have decidedly negative reactions to the use of coercive power (Bass, 1990).

Einstein possessed "expert power" when he advised Franklin D. Roosevelt to proceed with the development of the atom bomb.

The Situational Approach

British Prime Minister Winston Churchill showed little promise in his early career, yet during World War II he emerged as one of the world's great leaders. Was Churchill great because of his personal traits, or did the dire circumstances confronting England during World War II force him to rise to the task?

A number of researchers have noted that strong leaders are more likely to emerge when groups face crisis and stress (Helmreich & Collins, 1967; Mulder & Stemerding, 1963). Churchill took command during England's "darkest hour," and his archenemy, Adolf Hitler, rose to power in a period when Germany suffered from economic disaster and recent military humiliation. Even minor situational factors can foster the development of leadership as well. A series of studies on jury deliberations showed that members who sat at the ends of tables during deliberation were significantly more likely to be selected as jury foremen (Strodtbeck & Hook, 1961; Strodtbeck, James, & Hawkins, 1958).

Several studies suggest that the more frequently people talk and participate in a group, the more likely they are to be perceived as leaders (Bales, 1958; Gintner & Lindskold, 1975; Stein & Heller, 1979). Of course, participation may partly be a function of stable traits such as sociability, but it may also be influenced by situational factors. In one study, when quiet subjects were placed in groups that agreed with them and supported their positions, they began to show more participation and "leadership behaviors" (Pepinsky, Hemphill, & Shevitz, 1958). In

Final Scale Items Responding to the Statement, "My Supervisor Can . . ."

1. *Expert Power*
   Give me good technical suggestions.
   Share with me his/her considerable experience and/or training.
   Provide me with sound job-related advice.
   Provide me with needed technical knowledge.
2. *Referent Power*
   Make me feel valued.
   Make me feel like he/she approves of me.
   Make me feel personally accepted.
   Make me feel important.
3. *Reward Power*
   Increase my pay level.
   Influence my getting a pay raise.
   Provide me with special benefits.
   Influence my getting a promotion.
4. *Coercive Power*
   Give me undesirable job assignments.
   Make my work difficult for me.
   Make things unpleasant here.
   Make being at work distasteful.
5. *Legitimate Power*
   Make me feel that I have commitments to meet.
   Make me feel like I should satisfy my job requirements.
   Give me the feeling I have responsibilities to fulfill.
   Make me recongize that I have tasks to accomplish.

FIGURE 13.9 Scale items that measure French and Raven's five bases of power in a work setting. *Source*: Adapted from Hinken and Schriesheim (1989).

other studies, participants in group discussions watched a light that signaled whenever the experimenter deemed that they had made "good contributions" to the group. Actually, the signal had no relation to the quality of their statements. Not surprisingly, subjects who saw the light go on a lot began to speak more. More surprisingly, these artificially encouraged participants were then more likely to be perceived as leaders by others in the group (Bavelas, Hastorf, Gross, & Kite, 1965; Zdep & Oakes, 1967). Thus, leaders can at times be "manufactured" by situational reinforcements.

A final situational factor that can have a big impact on leadership in groups is communication patterns within the groups. Some groups (for example, corporate and government bureaucracies) have formal, established patterns of communications (described by organizational charts that show who reports to whom and who supervises whom). Figure 13.10 shows several different possible group communication networks; the lines connecting individuals show who can communicate with whom. In general, research suggests that people who occupy central positions in communication networks are more likely to emerge as group leaders than people in more peripheral positions (Cohen, Bennis, & Wolkon, 1961; Shaw, Rothschild, & Strickland, 1957).

Fiedler's Contingency Approach

What makes a leader effective? It probably comes as no surprise to you that leadership effectiveness is in part a function of the leader's characteristics and in part a function of the setting. In his *contingency model of leadership,* Fred Fiedler (1978, 1993; Fiedler & Garcia, 1987) attempted to specify which characteristics of the leader and which characteristics of the situation are critically important in determining leadership effectiveness.

In keeping with earlier research, Fiedler argued that there are two main kinds of leaders: those who are more task-oriented and those who focus more on the emotional relationships in the group. To identify these two kinds of leaders, Fiedler developed a questionnaire called the Least Preferred Coworker Scale, which asks leaders to rate and evaluate the person in their group they like least. According to Fiedler, leaders who describe their least preferred coworker in quite negative terms tend to be task-oriented leaders, whereas those who describe

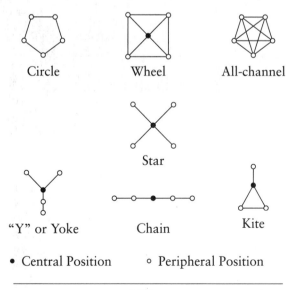

Circle   Wheel   All-channel

Star

"Y" or Yoke   Chain   Kite

● Central Position   ○ Peripheral Position

FIGURE 13.10 Different group networks of communication. *Source*: Shaw (1964).

their least preferred coworker in more positive terms tend to be socioemotional leaders.

Who is the more effective, the task-oriented or the socioemotional leader? According to Fiedler's contingency model, it depends on the nature of the situation. In particular, Fiedler poses three main questions to assess how favorable a given leadership setting is: (1) How good are the leader's relations with group members? (2) How clearly defined are the goals and tasks of the group? (3) How much legitimate authority does the leader possess over the group?

Some situations can be favorable on all three dimensions: The leader has good relations with the group, a clear goal to pursue, and considerable legitimate authority. Some situations are unfavorable on all three dimensions: The leader has poor relations with the group, unclear goals, and little legitimate authority. And, of course, there are intermediate situations, which are moderately favorable or unfavorable. The contingency model proposes that task-oriented leaders are most effective in very favorable or in very unfavorable settings, whereas socioemotional leaders are more effective in intermediate conditions (see Figure 13.11).

According to Fiedler, in very positive situations the leader doesn't have to worry about morale or whether group members will follow instructions, and thus the task-oriented leader need only focus on the task at hand. In very negative situations, morale and group relations are so bad that they may not be easily

In what kinds of situations is it better to be a task-oriented rather than a socioemotional leader?

"No, a question period will not follow!"

According to Fiedler's contingency model of leadership, effectiveness depends both on the leader's style and the favorableness of the leadership setting. Task-oriented leaders tend to be most effective in very favorable or very unfavorable settings, whereas socioemotional leaders tend to be most effective in moderately favorable settings.

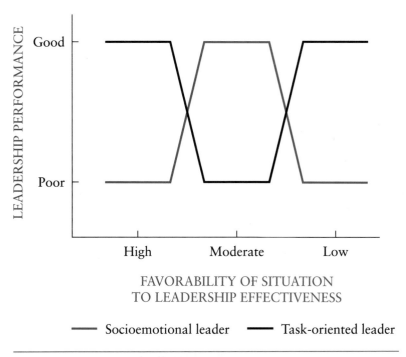

FIGURE 13.11 Fiedler's contingency model of leadership effectiveness. *Source*: Adapted from Fiedler (1978).

improved; again the leader is best served by being task-oriented and by trying to pick up the pieces as best he or she can. In moderately good or bad situations, however, the leader has most to gain by improving morale and personal relations, and thus the socioemotional leader is uniquely effective. Many studies have tested Fiedler's contingency model in both real-life and laboratory settings, and in general they support the general predictions of the model (Fiedler & Garcia, 1987; Peters, Hartke, & Pohlmann, 1985; Strube & Garcia, 1981).

Just as a leader's style (task-oriented or socioemotional) has different consequences in different leadership situations, so does his or her intelligence (Fiedler, 1993). Specifically, leaders' intelligence is often positively correlated with their effectiveness in low-stress leadership settings, but negatively correlated in high-stress settings. Apparently, leaders in low-stress settings have the luxury of thinking through their plans and procedures, and of course, intelligence helps out in such activities. Leaders in high-stress settings, however, are often so pressured that they can't think clearly or adequately, and decisions must be made quickly without the benefit of careful deliberation. In such pressured situations, leaders must often go on "automatic pilot" and make decisions based on previous experience rather than careful thought. So, paradoxically, intelligence contributes little to leadership effectiveness in very high stress situations, when you have to "leap before you think."

GROUPS AND ANTISOCIAL BEHAVIOR

In the now notorious teleconference, four Thiokol vice presidents at first concurred with the fears of their engineers. But when they heard the NASA objections, they decided to take a "management" vote in which the engineers had no voice. Even though Thiokol had taken the seal problem seriously enough to spend more than $2 million seeking a remedy, its top officers involved in shuttle work now ignored the Florida chill and approved the launch. The NASA managers had won the argument. Six astronauts and Schoolteacher Christa McAuliffe lost everything.

—*Time,* June 9, 1986

You'll probably agree that management groups at NASA and Morton Thiokol made a series of terrible decisions that led up to the *Challenger* disaster. Janis's analyses of government policymaking fiascoes provided additional examples of the destructive consequences of groups. Let's turn now to still other ways that groups can create problems.

Some of the questions we shall consider: Are people more likely to behave in evil, antisocial ways in groups? Is behavior more emotional and volatile in group settings? Do group settings encourage the spread of rumors, hysterical emotions, fears, and panic? And finally, do groups tend to encourage unproductive competition among their members and with other groups?

Deindividuation

As we have seen, leaders can sometimes direct group members effectively and motivate them to achieve group goals. There is a darker side to leadership as well, however. Consider Adolf Hitler, Joseph Stalin, Charles Manson, the Reverend Jim Jones, Saddam Hussein, David Koresh. Groups sometimes engage in destructive, irrational activities because of their attachments to their leaders, according to Sigmund Freud (1922). He proposed that the leader is a kind of love object to followers, and that when groups worship and idealize their leaders, they substitute the leader's wishes for their own superego (that is, for their conscience and moral principles). If you substitute the wishes of an Adolf Hitler or a Charles Manson for your own conscience, you are in deep trouble indeed.

Demonstration at an abortion clinic. Is behavior more emotional and volatile in group settings?

Freud drew heavily on an earlier work by Gustave Le Bon titled *The Crowd* (1896), which attempted to analyze processes that lead to mob behavior. In crowds, Le Bon argued, people are more likely to engage in antisocial behaviors because they are anonymous and feel invulnerable. Le Bon wrote that an individual in a crowd "descends several rungs in the ladder of civilization" (p. 36). People in crowds show "impulsiveness, irritability, incapacity to reason," and "exaggeration of sentiments" (p. 40), and they suffer from behavioral contagion and suggestibility comparable to that experienced during hypnosis. Both Freud and Le Bon tended to be quite pessimistic about the effects of crowds on individuals' behavior.

Social psychologists Leon Festinger, Albert Pepitone, and Theodore Newcomb (1952) offered a somewhat different account of the effects of groups on individuals' behavior. They argued that people in groups sometimes experience *deindividuation*—that is, they feel themselves to be "submerged in the group" and lose their personal identities.

Why does such deindividuation occur? Philip Zimbardo (1970) proposed that arousal, feelings of anonymity, and diffusion of responsibility foster deindividuation in group settings. Furthermore, novel environments that produce sensory overload (for example, riots, casinos, Mardi Gras) and drug-induced alterations in consciousness may also contribute to deindividuation. Once in a state of deindividuation, a person shows little self-observation, little consistency with internal standards, and reduced inhibitions. As a result, he or she may engage in repetitive, impulsive, emotional, and at times destructive behaviors.

According to Zimbardo, deindividuation is not a single process; rather, it is an altered subjective state with multiple causes and multiple consequences. Some

Do the crowd settings, anonymity, and costumes typical of Mardi Gras lead to deindividuation?

group settings (those that are arousing, full of distracting stimuli, and in which people cannot be easily identified) are more likely to lead to deindividuation than others. It is interesting to note that in the infamous teleconference in which Thiokol and NASA managers decided to go ahead with the *Challenger* launch, they were somewhat more anonymous than usual by virtue of the fact that participants spoke by phone and thus could not see or personally identify one another.

Research supports the hypotheses that group settings and anonymity affect individuals' willingness to engage in antisocial behaviors. Zimbardo (1970) found that women dressed in white laboratory coats and hoods delivered longer supposed shocks to victims in an experiment than did subjects wearing normal clothes and ID tags displaying their names. Thus, anonymity contributed to uninhibited aggression. (This effect may have also been due in part to the associations white hoods have in our society—for example, to the Ku Klux Klan.) Watson (1973) compiled anthropological data from many cultures across the world and found a strong correlation between the degree to which societies disguise their warriors before they go into battle (for example, by using war paint or masks) and the brutality of their warfare (torturing captives and mutilating victims). These data also suggest a link between anonymity and antisocial behavior.

In a clever experiment, Edward Diener and his colleagues (1976) simultaneously examined the effects of disguise, anonymity, and group membership on antisocial behavior in young trick-or-treaters. The experimenters (women giving out Halloween candy in 27 different homes in Seattle) either identified children, by asking for their names and addresses, or let them remain anonymous. Some

Deindividuated subjects in Zimbardo's (1970) experiment. These subjects delivered longer electric shocks to an innocent victim than did nondisguised subjects wearing name tags.

children naturally arrived in groups; others were alone. Saying they had to "return to work," experimenters left the children standing next to a table with a bowl of candy and a bowl of coins after telling them to take one piece of candy each. A hidden observer recorded whether the children stole extra candy or any coins. The results showed that many children did steal, particularly when they were in groups and were not identified by name (see Figure 13.12).

Deindividuation may be particularly potent in "total institutions," such as mental hospitals, prisons, and concentration camps, which remove people from the moorings of their normal identities and strip them of their individuality. In a simulation of a prison environment, Zimbardo and his colleagues (1972) assigned one group of college men to be prisoners and another group to be guards in a jail constructed in the basement of Stanford University's psychology department. Both prisoners and guards were deindividuated in many ways: The prisoners wore dresslike uniforms and nylon stocking caps (to simulate having their heads shaved), and they were assigned serial numbers to be used in place of their names. Guards wore deindividuating khaki uniforms, billy clubs, and reflective sunglasses that masked their expressions and identities.

Although Zimbardo's prison was to be a "simulation," both prisoners and guards quickly began to act as if the situation were real. The guards created brutal punishments for prisoners who broke the "prison rules." In response, the prisoners staged a "revolt" that was subsequently crushed by the guards. The guards then increased their surveillance and abuse of the prisoners, and within days some prisoners suffered breakdowns and others became docile and apathetic. Many subjects in the prison simulation showed some of the hallmarks of deindividuation: a lowered sense of personal identity, an altered state of subjective consciousness, and a host of disinhibited antisocial behaviors.

One can see parallels between the Zimbardo prison simulation and the deindividuation that occurs in many real-life institutions. For example, the military shaves the heads of new recruits and issues them serial numbers, "dog tags," and standard uniforms. In basic training, soldiers live in groups in a novel environment

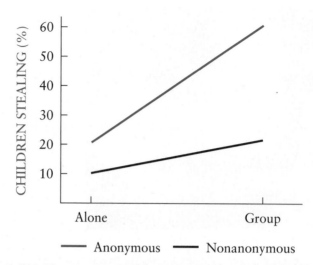

Children were significantly more likely to steal when in groups and when anonymous.

FIGURE 13.12 Effects of group membership and deindividuation on children's likelihood of stealing. *Source*: Based on Diener, Fraser, Beaman, and Kelem (1976).

and are frequently highly stressed and aroused. Separated from their normal social supports, soldiers are drilled to follow commands rather than inner moral standards. The "good soldier" submerges himself in the group and becomes a kind of professional aggression machine.

Deindividuation and Self-Awareness

What is deindividuation like to the person experiencing it? Drawing on recent research on self-awareness, Diener (1980; Diener, Lusk, DeFour, & Flax, 1980) argued that deindividuation is due in part to shifts in individuals' attention. In arousing, overstimulating group settings, people pay attention to the dramatic events around them, not to their inner values, standards, and attitudes. Thus, deindividuated people do not engage in self-directed attention (see Chapter 3), and so are less likely to behave in a manner that is consistent with their internal standards.

To investigate the subjective state of deindividuated people, Steven Prentice-Dunn and Ronald Rogers (1980) asked groups of college men to deliver supposed electric shocks to an innocent victim as part of a "biofeedback" experiment. In a condition designed to create deindividuation, subjects sat in a dimly lit room and heard arousing background noise. Furthermore, these deindividuated subjects were

Recruits are often deindividuated during military training.

not addressed by name, and they were told that the levels of shock they delivered would not be measured. Conditions were just the opposite for individuated subjects: They sat in a brightly lit, quiet room, wore name tags, and learned that the intensities of their shocks would be measured. Consistent with earlier studies, deindividuated subjects delivered more intense shocks to their victims.

Prentice-Dunn and Rogers then asked their subjects to fill out a 19-item questionnaire on their thoughts and experiences during the experiment. A factor analysis of these items indicated that deindividuated subjects differed from control subjects on two main dimensions: altered experience and self-awareness (see Figure 13.13 for examples of each kind of item). Interestingly, both altered experience and degree of self-awareness correlated significantly with the intensity of electric shocks that subjects delivered to their victims. This and other studies (for example, Diener, 1979) suggest that deindividuation is in part a function of reduced self-awareness.

From the perspective of self-awareness theory, deindividuation is neither intrinsically good nor bad; rather, it leads to a relaxation of normal standards, rules, and values. Although most social psychology research has focused on antisocial consequences of deindividuation, there are some exceptions. For example, Spivey and Prentice-Dunn (1990) found that deindividuation led experimental subjects to behave not just more aggressively (delivering shocks to another subject) but also more prosocially (rewarding another subject with money) in the same study. Thus, deindividuation has the potential to remove inhibitions on both good and bad behaviors.

In the study by Prentice-Dunn and Rogers (1980), deindividuated and individuated subjects rated their subjective experiences during the experiment on a number of questionnaire items. Two clusters of questionnaire items distinguished deindividuated subjects from individuated subjects. One assessed "altered experience," the other "self-awareness." The table shows these two kinds of questionnaire items.

Factor 1 (Altered Experience)	Factor 2 (Self-Awareness)
Thinking was somewhat altered	Felt self-conscious
Emotions were different from normal	Heightened sense of individual identity
Felt aroused	Felt inhibited
Responsibility was shared	I had responsiblity for harm doing
Time seemed to go quickly	Concerned with what experimenter
Thoughts were concentrated on the	thought of me
moment	Concerned with what victim thought
Session was enjoyable	of me
Willing to volunteer for similar study	Concerned with what other group
Liked other group members	members thought of me
Feelings of togetherness among group	
members	

FIGURE 13.13 The subjective experience of deindividuation. *Source*: Prentice-Dunn and Rogers (1980).

Gergen, Gergen, and Barton (1973) also demonstrated possible positive effects of deindividuation when they asked groups of college men and women to interact together in an "environmental chamber"—a small padded room. Their instructions were quite vague: "You will be left in the chamber for no more than an hour with some other people. There are no rules . . . as to what you should do together." Subjects were informed that after the experiment, they would not interact with the others any more and that they would depart from the chamber alone.

We've left out a central fact, however: In one experimental condition, the room was brightly lit; in the other, it was dark. Subjects in the dark room were deindividuated because they were anonymous, probably aroused, and in an undefined and somewhat mysterious environment. Half the subjects in the dark room hugged another person, whereas no one hugged in the lit room. Eighty-nine percent of the subjects in the dark room intentionally touched others, whereas none did in the lit room. Subjects in the dark room reported the experience to be fun and sensuous, and many volunteered to return for a repeat experience.

By implication, deindividuation can be freeing when one's inhibitions are painful and limiting. Perhaps this is why we sometimes seek out deindividuating settings, such as the masked, crowded (and fun) chaos of Mardi Gras. Sometimes being somewhat anonymous in a novel setting (for example, being a new student, away from home for the first time, or at a large university) can be a liberating experience.

Groups and Mass Psychogenic Illness

In 1989, 247 high school students became ill in the Santa Monica Civic Center (*Los Angeles Times,* September 4, 1991). The entire building was evacuated; however, no physical cause was ever found for the students' illness. A group of investigating University of California psychiatrists concluded that the students had suffered from *mass psychogenic illness*—an illness of psychological origin that occurs in group settings due to hysterical contagion (Colligan, Pennebaker, & Murphy, 1982).

In one of the first systematic studies of such an illness, Kerckhoff and Back (1968) traveled to a Southern textile factory where a group of female workers had earlier developed a strange malady; the case is well summarized by an early news report:

> Officials of Montana Mills shut down their Strongsville plant this afternoon because of a mysterious illness.
>
> According to a report just in from Strongsville General Hospital, at least ten women and one man were admitted for treatment. Reports describe symptoms as severe nausea and a breaking out over the body.
>
> Indications are that some kind of insect was in a shipment of cloth that arrived from England at the plant today. And at the moment the bug is blamed for the outbreak of sickness. (Kerckhoff, 1982, p. 6)

Over the 11-day course of the "epidemic," 62 factory workers (59 women and 3 men) were treated for the "mysterious illness," but neither doctors nor factory officials could find any infectious agent or diagnose any known disease. The malady disappeared as quickly as it had appeared, and investigators began to suspect psychological rather than physical causes.

Kerckhoff and Back's careful research uncovered some clear patterns to the sickness. The women who fell ill tended to be highly stressed and did not want to continue working at their tedious factory jobs. Furthermore, they tended to deny their stress and were thus more likely to attribute it to an external source, such as some infectious bug. Finally, most of the women who became sick worked during the same shift and in the same area of the plant, and the "disease" typically progressed through social networks. For example, when one woman fell ill, her close friends and work associates were often the next to fall ill.

Since Kerckhoff and Back's seminal study, additional cases of mass psychogenic illness have been reported and analyzed. Colligan and Murphy (1982) reviewed reports of 23 separate instances of hysterical illnesses in work settings involving over 1,000 individuals. Their findings reinforce Kerckhoff and Back's conclusions. Eighty-nine percent of affected individuals were women. In general, people who succumbed to outbreaks of psychogenic illness worked in boring, repetitious, and stressful jobs. (This, by the way, may in part explain why more women than men seem to experience such illness: More women than men may find themselves in boring, dead-end jobs.) Finally, psychogenic illnesses were most likely to occur in work settings characterized by poor management–labor relations.

A number of social psychological processes help to explain mass psychogenic illnesses. The Schachter and Singer two-component theory of emotion (see Chapter 5) holds that both physiological arousal and social comparison processes are important determinants of emotional experience. In general, factory workers who fall prey to mass psychogenic illnesses are highly stressed and aroused, and illness gives them a concrete "reason" for their stress. Furthermore, "sick" people can legitimately leave the stressful setting.

As we already know, anonymous, stressful group settings can foster deindividuation, and this can lead people to behave in uninhibited ways. In addition, people in groups may suffer from behavioral contagion (Wheeler, 1966), which occurs particularly when individuals want to engage in some behavior (such as become sick and leave an unpleasant job) but experience restraining inhibitions. When other people engage in the suppressed behavior, they thereby release observers' inhibitions.

Research on mass psychogenic illness shows that groups can affect not only our work, decision making, and willingness to behave in antisocial ways, but also our health! ⬎

Competition and Cooperation in Groups

Some NASA officials have scrambled to pass off blame for the *Challenger* disaster. The brass at the Marshall Space Flight Center in Huntsville, Ala., have been trying to point the finger at Kennedy Space Center for botching the assembly of the solid rocket booster. Marshall's bureaucrats are accused of ignoring the warnings of engineers at Morton Thiokol, maker of the solid rocket booster, to postpone the launch because the cold weather could have damaged the O rings that sealed the segments of the booster. The evasions and backbiting have shocked members of the presidential panel. "A whole new NASA has got to come out of this mess, not only a new solid rocket booster design," says a commission member.

—Time, March 24, 1986

The story of the space shuttle program and the *Challenger* explosion is a story of competition and cooperation, both within groups and between groups. NASA was competing against European and Soviet space programs. Different space flight centers within NASA competed with one another for prestige, assignments, and funding; at the same time, they cooperated with one another to design, produce, and launch space shuttles. Presidential commission members cooperated with one another to uncover the truth about the *Challenger* accident, and the list goes on.

To better understand the competition and cooperation that go on both within and between groups, social psychologists have turned to mathematical game theory, which analyzes patterns of costs and rewards in different kinds of groups and group tasks (Rapoport, 1960). Experiments have often focused on the smallest groups possible: dyads (two people only). In order to understand competition and cooperation in groups, let's turn to research on two classic experimental situations: the Prisoner's Dilemma and the Commons Dilemma.

The Prisoner's Dilemma

The Prisoner's Dilemma takes its name from the following scenario (Luce & Raiffa, 1957): A district attorney tries to develop a case against two suspects accused of robbing a bank. The suspects are arrested for a minor offense, and the evidence implicating them in the bank robbery is weak. The district attorney therefore devises a devious method to extract a confession from one or both suspects: He takes each suspect to a separate room and tells him that he can either confess or not confess to the bank robbery. If one suspect "turns state's evidence" (that is, informs on his partner) and the other does not, the helpful informer will be freed, whereas his partner in crime will be sentenced to 15 years in jail. If both suspects refuse to confess, each one will receive a one-year sentence for the lesser crime. Finally, if both suspects confess, they will both receive ten years in prison. The reward and cost matrix of this situation is shown in Figure 13.14.

The Prisoner's Dilemma is a dilemma precisely because it sorely tempts each suspect to inform on the other—that is, to compete instead of cooperate. Both can minimize their *combined* time in prison by not confessing. But this strategy requires each to trust the other. If one suspect holds out but the other confesses, then the unfortunate "sucker" goes to jail for 15 years and his devious partner gets off free.

In laboratory experiments, the Prisoner's Dilemma translates to a game in which subjects can choose one of two moves, cooperative or competitive. The combined moves of both players determine each player's rewards or costs. Figure 13.15 illustrates one of many possible Prisoner's Dilemma payoff matrices. Note that for a single trial in the Prisoner's Dilemma, the competitive move is the most rational in the following sense: Your average expected outcome (assuming complete uncertainty as to how your partner will behave) is more positive when you compete than when you cooperate. In Figure 13.14, a suspect's average prison term is five years if he confesses (competes) and eight years if he doesn't, and in Figure 13.15, a player receives on average 25 cents when she competes but loses on average 25 cents when she cooperates.

The picture becomes more complicated, however, when subjects play several trials of the Prisoner's Dilemma game. Then, if a competitive partner victimizes a cooperative player, the cooperative player can switch to a competitive move on her next trial. Research on the Prisoner's Dilemma shows that when one partner behaves competitively, trust is substantially reduced, and the game often degenerates into mutual competition (Brickman, Becker, & Castle, 1979; Deutsch, 1973; Rosenbaum, 1980). Perhaps this occurred in NASA after the *Challenger* accident: When one group blamed another (that is, chose a "move" that brought rewards to itself but led to costs for the other group), the other group returned the "favor."

Conversely, subjects will often reciprocate a partner's cooperative behavior with cooperative choices of their own (Black & Higbee, 1973). Thus, to some degree, cooperation fosters reciprocal cooperation and competition fosters recip-

SUSPECT 2

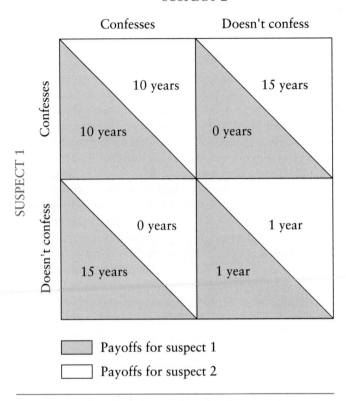

FIGURE 13.14 The original Prisoner's Dilemma: Two suspects are tempted by the cost/reward matrix to confess and inform on each other. *Source*: Based on Luce and Raiffa (1957).

rocal competition (Rubin & Brown, 1975). One important qualification needs to be added to this general finding, however: When one party in the Prisoner's Dilemma behaves in an unconditionally and unilaterally cooperative fashion, the other will often exploit him and choose competitive moves (Reychler, 1979; Shure, Meeker, & Hansford, 1965). The reward structure of the Prisoner's Dilemma tempts subjects paired with overly cooperative partners to earn high rewards by defecting to the competitive response.

Experimental studies have repeatedly found that the simple strategy of "tit for tat" is most consistently effective in getting a partner to cooperate (McClintock & Liebrand, 1988; Rubin & Brown, 1975; see Chapter 11 for a discussion of tit-for-tat behavior in relation to reciprocal altruism). Tit-for-tat behavior consists of starting with cooperation and thereafter consistently responding to your partner's competitive or cooperative move in kind. Why does this strategy lead to cooperation? Axelrod (1984) explains:

What accounts for tit-for-tat's robust success is its combination of being nice, retaliatory, forgiving and clear. Its niceness prevents it from getting into unnecessary trouble. Its retaliation discourages the other side from persisting whenever defection is tried. Its forgiveness helps to restore mutual cooperation. And its clarity makes it intelligible to the other player, thereby eliciting long-term cooperation. (p. 54)

The Prisoner's Dilemma parallels many real-life group situations. For example, the space programs of the United States and other countries can choose either to cooperate (share technical knowledge, perform joint launches) or to compete (try to beat each other in achieving various goals). And in trade relations between, say, the United States and Japan, each country can choose either cooperative policies (low tariffs, a free market for the other country's products) or competitive policies (high tariffs, restricted markets). If both countries cooperate, then both economies may prosper moderately. If one cooperates and the other competes, the competitor has a large economic advantage and the cooperator suffers. If both countries compete, each will suffer economically.

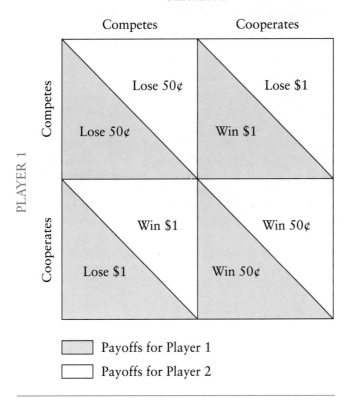

FIGURE 13.15 The Prisoner's Dilemma as an experimental game.

Different players approach the Prisoner's Dilemma and other experimental games with different motives (Knight & Dubro, 1984; McClintock & Van Avermaet, 1982). Some people tend to be *cooperators* who strive to maximize the joint profits of both players. Others are *competitors* who want to maximize the difference between their own profits and those of their partner. And finally, some are *individualists* who strive to maximize their own profits without regard for how their partner is doing. Knight and Dubro (1984) offer some evidence that men are more likely to be competitors and that women are more likely to be cooperators.

Now that you know a bit about the Prisoner's Dilemma, let's return to the topic of groups. Games like the Prisoner's Dilemma can be generalized to include more than two people and so can be played by groups as well as by individuals. Debra McCallum and her colleagues (1985) had college students play the Prisoner's Dilemma either as individuals or as two-person teams. Subjects were significantly less cooperative when playing in groups and were more likely to show motivations typical of competitors—that is, they preferred to maximize the difference in rewards between their group and the other group. Apparently it is more difficult for groups than for individuals to cooperate, perhaps in part because of the tendency for groups to develop ethnocentric attitudes and to derogate out-groups (Insko & Schopler, 1987; see Chapter 7).

The Commons Dilemma

Groups not only have to power to foster competition, they can also lead individuals to exploit limited resources. In a classic paper, Garret Hardin (1968) described what he termed "the tragedy of the commons." Imagine a village with a communal piece of land—the commons—available to all local shepherds. Further, imagine that the commons is large enough to support 50 sheep; more than that will overgraze the commons and reduce it to barren land. If 50 shepherds graze one animal each on the land, all is well. But suppose one shepherd decides to graze two sheep and thus reap more profit from the commons. Not to be outdone, others also graze more sheep. The net result: a barren commons that can support no sheep. By pursuing individual profit, the shepherds instead achieve collective disaster.

The parable of the commons applies to any situation in which a group of people uses a finite resource with a fixed rate of replacement. Some obvious examples are lumber companies deforesting land, nations "harvesting" whales, farmers pumping out underground water for irrigation, and people consuming electricity on a hot summer's day. The tragedy of the commons is that its reward structure creates a *social trap,* a situation in which seemingly rational behavior leading to short-term gains for individuals results ultimately in collective ruin. The individual is always tempted to increase consumption of the communal resource, but if he does, this decision often spurs others to do the same. A downward spiral of group behavior begins and ultimately results in decimation of the resource.

The Commons Dilemma shares a number of features with the Prisoner's Dilemma. Both situations tempt participants to make competitive, exploitive responses. Both constitute what game theorists term "nonzero-sum" games; that is, the profits and losses of all participants *do not* necessarily add up to zero. In the commons, everyone can lose if resources are exploited, whereas everyone can win if resources are conserved wisely. (The game of poker, by contrast, is generally a zero-sum game in which one player's win is necessarily another player's loss.) Finally, in both the Prisoner's Dilemma and the Commons Dilemma, one participant's competition tends to spur others to compete as well, often to everyone's detriment.

The Commons Dilemma, like the Prisoner's Dilemma, can be simulated in laboratory games. One study had college-student subjects gather around a bowl containing ten metal nuts. Students were told that they could remove as many nuts as they wished and that every ten seconds the number of nuts remaining in the bowl would be doubled. The object of the game was for each subject to accumulate as many nuts as possible. Do you think these students devised a fair and rational strategy to "harvest" nuts without depleting them? Unfortunately, no. Most of the groups didn't even make it past the first ten-second replacement period—everyone simply lunged and grabbed as many nuts as he or she could (Edney, 1979).

Some situational factors seem to aggravate the tragedy of the commons. Komorita and Lapworth (1982) found that both the number of people in a group and the number of subgroups in a group were related to exploitation of the commons. Whale hunting provides a good example here. The more people there are who hunt whales and the more subgroups of people (for example, nations) there are who hunt whales, the more we can expect overhunting. Large numbers of people seem more likely to exploit common resources in part because they feel anonymous

Depletion of the Earth's forests. Social psychological research on the Commons Dilemma may help us to manage real-life resources more wisely.

and believe that their individual use makes little difference to the total resource; the existence of subgroups leads to greater exploitation of the commons by fostering feelings of in-group–out-group competition.

The tragedy of the commons *can* be avoided. In some experiments, subjects have resisted the temptation to gobble up resources competitively through rational communication and regulation of consumption (Messick et al., 1983; Samuelson, Messick, Rutte, & Wilke, 1984). Clearly, this is a technique that is sometimes used to conserve real resources. The federal government may carefully regulate the lumber harvest in federal forests, and the electric company may seek volunteers to reduce electricity consumption during peak periods of power use. People are particularly likely to tolerate outside regulation if the allocation of resources is perceived to be fair (Tyler & Lind, 1992).

Brewer and Kramer (1986) reported that subjects show greater restraint in exploiting the commons when they are made to identify with other members of their group. In this age of shrinking forests, fossil-fuel supplies, and basic resources like clean air and water, the challenge we all face in preserving "the commons" for future generations is not simply to identify with our immediate groups, but to identify with our entire planet as well.

⌢ GROUPS IN PERSPECTIVE

The *Challenger* accident illustrates a basic paradox about human groups: They are responsible for some of the greatest human accomplishments, and at the same time, they are responsible for a host of human troubles, including poor decisions, antisocial behavior, and reckless competition and consumption. We began this chapter by considering small groups of managers at NASA and Morton Thiokol who made decisions that eventually led to a tragic accident. We ended by considering a much larger group: humanity on the finite planet Earth. Clearly, human groups are relevant to all human activities, and they hold both considerable promise and peril.

We have seen that groups can profoundly affect our work, our decisions, our morality, our health—and even our future survival on this planet. Among some of the specific findings we have discussed: Groups can facilitate simple kinds of work performance and interfere with more complex kinds of tasks. Groups sometimes lead us to goof off when we perform additive tasks. Groups can lead us to make more extreme decisions and judgments, and when they are stressed and directed by leaders who squelch dissent, groups are capable of making terrible, destructive decisions.

Good leaders motivate and direct groups and help them achieve their goals. Leadership effectiveness depends in part on the leader's traits, in part on the situation, and in part on the match between the leader's style and the setting. Leaders, like groups, sometimes promote good and sometimes evil.

All social behavior, including group behavior, entails the possibility of cooperation and competition. While an individual's choice between cooperation and competition clearly depends on the rewards and costs of each kind of behavior, group settings also have an effect. Specifically, people often become more competitive when they are divided into social groups, and people in large groups and in multiple subgroups are especially likely to exploit communal resources.

This brings us back to the paradox we began with: Human groups are full of possibilities for both good and bad. Groups have sent people to the moon and launched space probes that have roamed across the solar system. They also have made decisions that sent six astronauts and a schoolteacher unnecessarily to their deaths. No one can deny the power of groups to influence our behavior. This is why social psychologists study them so intensely and strive to understand the impact they have on all of us.

Studying Groups

What Is a Group?

A group is a collection of individuals who interact and communicate with one another over time. Group members often share goals and norms.

Research on Group Behavior

Social psychologists study both real-life and laboratory groups. Group research focuses on both group processes and group outcomes.

Dimensions of Group Behavior

Three main dimensions of group behavior are general activity, likability, and task ability.

Groups at Work

Social Facilitation

The mere presence of other people can affect the speed and quality of an individual's task performance. Zajonc's theory of social facilitation holds that the mere presence of others is arousing and that this arousal facilitates dominant, well-learned habits but interferes with nondominant, poorly learned habits. Evaluation anxiety and cognitive distraction also contribute to social facilitation in humans.

Individual versus Group Performance

Group tasks may be additive, conjunctive, disjunctive, or divisible. In additive tasks, group members pool their efforts or production. In conjunctive tasks, all members perform the same subtasks. In disjunctive tasks, groups must make either–or, right–wrong decisions. Divisible tasks are those that can be broken down into different subtasks performed by different group members.

Individuals in additive groups sometimes show social loafing—that is, they exert less individual effort when working in groups than when working alone. Social loafing is reduced when individual performance is evaluated by oneself or by others.

Social Psychology in Everyday Life: Are Brainstorming Groups Effective?

Brainstorming, a technique to encourage the uninhibited expression of creative ideas in group settings, is often ineffective because of social loafing, evaluation anxiety, and production blocking.

Decision Making in Groups

Group polarization occurs when group discussion leads group members to make more extreme decisions or to hold more extreme attitudes. Group polarization results both from informational influence in groups and from social comparison processes.

Groupthink refers to a syndrome of bad decision making that occurs in stressed, cohesive groups directed by leaders who are intolerant of dissent.

Leadership in Groups

What Is Leadership?

Leaders are members of groups who are particularly influential and who act to guide, direct, and motivate the group to achieve its goals. Leaders often engage in task-oriented behaviors (which direct the group's work) and socioemotional behaviors (which foster positive group relations and cohesiveness).

Theories of Leadership

Trait theories study the personal characteristics that are related to leadership. Intelligence and various personality traits are weakly correlated with leadership.

French and Raven described five different kinds of power: reward power, coercive power, legitimate power, referent power, and expert power. Each may contribute to a leader's power and effectiveness. In work settings, workers prefer leaders who use expert and referent power.

Situational theories of leadership focus on characteristics of the leadership setting. Strong leaders are more likely to emerge when groups are stressed, and situational factors such as seating arrangements, reinforcements for individual participation, and communications networks can influence who becomes the leader of a group.

Fiedler's contingency model holds that leadership effectiveness depends both on leadership style and the setting. According to the model, the favorableness of a leadership setting is a function of the positiveness of leader–group relations, the clarity of group goals, and the leader's degree of legitimate power. The contingency model hypothesizes that task-oriented leaders tend to be more effective than socioemotional leaders in very favorable or very unfavorable settings, whereas socioemotional leaders tend to be more effective than task-oriented leaders in moderately favorable settings.

Intelligence tends to contribute to leadership effectiveness in low-stress settings, but it tends to interfere with effectiveness in high-stress settings.

The Good and the Bad of Groups

Deindividuation

People are deindividuated when they lose their personal identity and become submerged in the group. According to Zimbardo, arousal, anonymity, sensory overload, and drug-induced alterations in consciousness can all contribute to deindividuation, which then leads to lowered inhibitions and behavior that is not in keeping with internal standards. Consistent with deindividuation theory, research suggests that anonymity in group settings can foster antisocial behavior.

Deindividuation is due in part to reduced self-awareness. Deindividuated people report experiencing reduced self-awareness and an altered state of consciousness.

Social Psychology in Everyday Life: Groups and Mass Psychogenic Illness

Mass psychogenic illness is an illness of psychological origin that occurs in group settings and is due to hysterical contagion. Such illness occurs most frequently among stressed workers performing tedious jobs, and it seems to result from mislabeled arousal, behavioral contagion, and deindividuation.

Competition and Cooperation in Groups

In the Prisoner's Dilemma, two players simultaneously choose either cooperative or competitive moves. The reward structure tempts each player to choose the competitive response, which rewards the player and simultaneously hurts the other player. Players often reciprocate competitive or cooperative responses tit for tat in repeated trials of the Prisoner's Dilemma game. Groups playing the game tend to be more competitive than individual players.

The Commons Dilemma refers to any situation where a group of people use a finite resource with a fixed rate of replacement. The reward structure of the Commons Dilemma creates a social trap in which seemingly rational individual behavior leads to collective ruin. People tend to exploit the commons more when they are in large groups that are divided into many subgroups. Rational communication and regulation of resources by fair authorities can help prevent the tragedy of the commons.

Activity dimension: A major dimension of group behavior; *activity* refers to the individual's general level of participation in group discussions and activities.

KEY TERMS

Additive task: A task, such as a tug-of-war, in which individuals pool their identical efforts.

Brainstorming: A technique to foster creativity in groups; individuals are asked to express any idea that comes to mind, to refrain from evaluating their own or others' ideas, and to build on one another's ideas.

Coaction effects: Animals or people perform an activity (such as eating) faster or more energetically when in the presence of others also performing the activity.

Commons Dilemma: A situation in which a group of people use a finite resource that has a fixed rate of replacement; in such a situation, individuals are tempted to seek short-term gains that lead to long-term collective ruin; see *social trap*.

Competitors: People who strive to maximize the difference between their own profits and those of their partner in games such as the Prisoner's Dilemma.

Conjunctive task: A task, such as mountain climbing, in which individuals all perform the same subtask; a group engaged in a conjunctive task tends to be only as effective as its weakest members.

Contingency model of leadership: Fiedler's model that holds that leadership effectiveness is a function of the leader's style of leadership and the setting; task-oriented leaders are hypothesized to be more effective in very favorable or very unfavorable settings, whereas socioemotional leaders are more effective in moderately favorable settings.

Cooperators: People who strive to maximize the joint profits of themselves and their partner in games such as the Prisoner's Dilemma.

Deindividuation: A disinhibited state that occurs when people lose their individual identities in group settings; arousal, anonymity, and sensory overload can foster deindividuation; lowered inhibitions and behavior that is inconsistent with internal standards can result from deindividuation.

Disjunctive task: A task, such as a group quiz game, in which the group must arrive at a yes–no, either–or decision or answer; the disjunctive group tends to be as effective as its strongest members.

Divisible task: A task, such as manufacturing an appliance, in which different group members perform different subtasks.

Group: A collection of individuals who interact and communicate with one another over a period of time.

Group polarization: Occurs when group discussion leads group members to make more extreme decisions or to arrive at more extreme judgments.

Groupthink: A syndrome of bad decision making in cohesive groups; according to Janis, groupthink occurs in stressed, cohesive groups directed by leaders who are intolerant of dissent.

Individualists: People who strive to maximize their own profits without regard for how their partner is doing in games such as the Prisoner's Dilemma.

Informational influence: One explanation for group polarization; new information and arguments from a group discussion may make people change their judgments or decisions.

Interaction Process Analysis: A content-analysis system developed by Robert Bales to code behavior in groups; IPA focuses on socioemotional and task-oriented behaviors that are both positive and negative.

Leaders: Members of groups who are particularly influential and who act to guide, direct, and motivate the group to achieve its goals.

Likability dimension: A major dimension of group behavior; it refers to the degree to which an individual engages in positive or negative socioemotional behaviors.

Mass psychogenic illness: An illness of psychological origin that occurs in group settings due to hysterical contagion.

Nominal group technique: A technique to foster both individual and group creativity; individual group members first silently generate ideas and write them down and then discuss them in the group; the group finally selects the best ideas.

Prisoner's Dilemma: A game in which each of two players simultaneously chooses either a competitive or a cooperative response; the reward matrix of the Prisoner's Dilemma is structured so that if both players cooperate, each receives a modest reward; if both compete, each pays a modest penalty; and if one player competes and the other cooperates, the competitor receives a large reward and the cooperator pays a large penalty.

Social comparison processes: Such processes help explain group polarization; social comparison occurs when group discussion leads members to become aware of group norms, and members then shift their decisions or judgments because of this knowledge.

Social facilitation: Occurs when an individual performs a task faster or better in the presence of others than when alone.

Social loafing: Occurs when individuals exert less effort working on a task in a group than when alone; tends to occur in additive tasks in which individual performance is not being monitored.

Social trap: A situation in which seemingly rational behavior leading to short-term gains for individuals results ultimately in collective ruin; see *Commons Dilemma*.

Socioemotional leader: A leader who excels at socioemotional but not task-oriented skills; also known as a maintenance specialist.

Task ability dimension: A major dimension of group behavior; it refers to the degree to which an individual engages in behaviors directed at achieving the group's goal or task.

Task specialist: A leader who excels at task-oriented but not socioemotional skills.

Tit for tat: The strategy that is most successful in eliciting cooperation from a partner in repeated trials of the Prisoner's Dilemma game; tit for tat consists of starting with cooperation and thereafter always responding to your partner's cooperative or competitive move with the same move.

14

SOCIAL PSYCHOLOGY AND HEALTH

That September I was bowling and I broke the same finger a second time. I was surprised because my finger hadn't bothered me that much. But then, without warning, it suddenly snapped. It was terrible. After this, they rebiopsied both my finger and my kneecap and the results were sent to all the same pathologists who had seen the original stuff. It turns out that a tumor had grown on the inside of my finger and had weakened the bone. By Thanksgiving everyone agreed. I had cancer.

—Elizabeth Bonwich, age 16, in Krementz (1989),
How It Feels to Fight for Your Life (pp. 66–67)

Imagine you just learned that you had cancer. What would you think? What would you feel? What would you do?

If you are like most people, you would probably wonder what caused your cancer, and you would almost certainly worry about dying. Perhaps you would try to approach your illness "rationally"—from the perspective of medicine and biology. To understand why you developed cancer, you could read about research on cancer. Scientists certainly have identified many factors that can lead to cancer, including overexposure to sunlight and other environmental hazards (radiation, asbestos, and other toxic chemicals); genetic predispositions; cigarette smoking; excessive alcohol consumption; and diet (too much fat; not enough fruits, vegetables, and dietary roughage). Faced with a diagnosis of cancer, you would probably begin to educate yourself about available treatments such as surgery, chemotherapy, and radiation.

Given all the known physical causes and medical treatments for cancer, you might ask at this point, "What does social psychology have to do with any of this?" The answer is, "Quite a lot." Take another look at the risk factors that lead to cancer. Do you think any of them are susceptible to social influences? For example, does your social environment influence whether you smoke or drink and what you eat? You'll probably agree that it does. And what determines the kind of medical treatment you pursue, or indeed, whether you pursue medical treatment at all? Again, social factors are likely to be important. Women diagnosed with breast cancer, for example, sometimes decide between having a lumpectomy (removal of cancerous tissue and a small amount of surrounding tissue) or undergoing a radical mastectomy (complete removal of a breast) on the basis of social attitudes as much

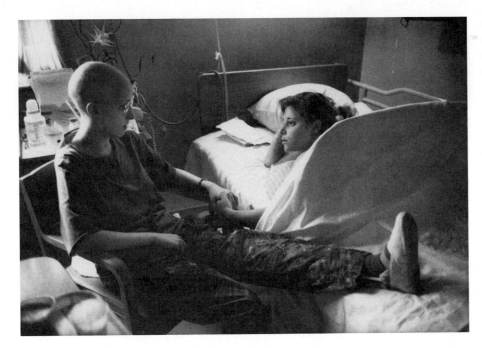

Elizabeth Bonwich, bald from chemotherapy, comforts another cancer patient.

Do social psychological factors such as social support influence people's health and well-being?

as on the basis of medical research evidence. Furthermore, some women may delay seeing a doctor after they notice a lump in their breast because of strong social attitudes that link having breasts with "femininity": These women choose deadly neglect over the slightest possibility of facing a mastectomy.

Social influences on health may be even broader than we've just suggested. Again, imagine that you learn you have cancer. You decide you are going to fight it and get immediate treatment. What factors will determine whether you successfully complete your treatment and whether you are likely to recover fully? Undoubtedly the seriousness of your cancer and the nature of your treatment will make a big difference in your prognosis. But social and psychological factors are likely to play an important role as well. For example, you may be more likely to survive cancer if you have good social support: warm, caring friends and helpful family members. Conversely, you may be more likely to succumb to your cancer if you have stressful relationships and inadequate social support. Social factors may influence how you follow medical advice—whether you take prescribed drugs regularly and complete difficult, time-consuming physical therapy.

Clearly, dividing factors that influence health into the "physical" and the "psychological" is misleading. Psychological factors (such as social support, interpersonal stress, attitudes, and personality traits) can affect physical factors (the risks we expose ourselves to, the healthiness of our lifestyle, the treatments we pursue), and conversely, our physical condition (having cancer) certainly can affect our psychological states and social relationships (levels of stress, anxiety, and optimism, and which people remain our friends). Social life, mental life, and health are intertwined in many complex ways.

This chapter will explore a number of social psychology factors that influence health and illness. Our discussion will focus on three main topics: (1) the effects of stress and social support on health, (2) links between personality and health, and (3) the complex relationships among beliefs, attitudes, and health. Research on these three topics will suggest ways social psychology can join with medical science to help us all lead healthier lives.

STRESS, SOCIAL SUPPORT, AND ILLNESS

When I learned that I was going to lose both my finger and my knee, I was sure that the surgery was going to be the worst part of having cancer. I thought, "I like my fingers. I'm attached to them. I don't want anyone to take one away from me!" But before they could even perform the surgery I had to have chemotherapy to reduce the size of the tumors. As soon as I went to the hospital and saw all the bald people who looked so sick all I could think was, "Is this going to happen to me?" I started dreading the chemo as much as, if not more than, the amputation.

—*Elizabeth Bonwich* (in Krementz p. 67)

There are stresses and there are *stresses*. All of us face minor stresses every day—fights with friends, financial problems, pressing deadlines at work and at school, car trouble—but most of us have not faced the levels of stress that Elizabeth Bonwich endured.

Psychologists have asked a number of basic questions about stress: What exactly is stress, and how can it be measured? Does stress have an impact on our psychological and physical health? If so, how much? Some of us seem to withstand our stresses and stay healthy and optimistic; others succumb to them, grow ill, and despair. Why? Can supportive friends and family members sometimes buffer us against the negative effects of stress?

Stress and Illness

When confronted with threatening physical or emotional stimuli, the body typically responds by mobilizing its resources. The sympathetic nervous system, which prepares the body for emergencies and for quick action, becomes aroused. Heart rate, blood pressure, and respiration increase, and blood is diverted away from the internal, digestive organs to the voluntary skeletal muscles (Selye, 1956, 1976). In such a state of preparedness, the body is ready for either "fight or flight." Although such arousal is frequently just a temporary response to a temporary crisis, it can

Stress is a function of cognitive appraisals as well as of the objective situation.

become chronic if we are exposed to repeated or unrelenting stressors. When the body is constantly mobilized, it begins to exhaust its resources. Continuous arousal can lead to maladies such as ulcers, colitis, asthma, high blood pressure, and reduced immunity to infectious diseases (Selye, 1956, 1976).

Stress depends on our subjective perceptions of events as well as on objective threats; according to one definition, a situation is stressful when it "is appraised by the person as taxing or exceeding his or her resources and endangering his or her well-being" (Lazarus & Folkman, 1984, p. 19). For example, one person may perceive an important job interview as exciting and challenging, whereas another may perceive it as highly threatening and thus regard it as a source of considerable stress.

In an early attempt to measure stress, Thomas Holmes and Richard Rahe (1967) compiled a list of 43 positive and negative events that may require major readjustments in people's lives. Preliminary research suggested that these events tended to precede the onset of disease in a sample of 5,000 patients. Holmes and Rahe asked their subjects to rate how much readjustment each event required. Then, based on these judgments, they assigned a numerical rating of stressfulness to each event. Subjects' overall level of stress was measured by asking them to indicate which of the listed events had occurred during a specified period of time (for example, in the last six months) and then summing the point values of all those events checked by the subjects; the resulting questionnaire was the Schedule of Recent Life Experiences (see Figure 14.1).

Some subsequent researchers have argued for assessing positive and negative life events separately (see Dohrenwend, Krasnoff, Askenasy, & Dohrenwend, 1978, 1982). Others have proposed using individual subjects' ratings of how stressful *they* perceive particular events to be, rather than employing normative ratings made by others (Sarason, Johnson, & Siegel, 1978; Sarason & Sarason, 1984). The basic idea here is that not all "stressful" events are equally stressful to all people.

Furthermore, events that are most likely to be stressful almost certainly vary in different populations. For example, major life stressors may differ a lot among psychiatric patients (sharing a room with an extremely disturbed patient), senior citizens (restricted mobility), parents (having a child with behavior problems), and college students (facing final exams). A specialized stress scale that is probably highly relevant to you is the Undergraduate Stress Questionnaire (Crandall,

Rank	Life Event	Mean Value		Rank	Life Event	Mean Value
1	Death of spouse	100		23	Son or daughter leaving home	29
2	Divorce	73		24	Trouble with in-laws	29
3	Marital separation	65		25	Outstanding personal achievement	28
4	Jail term	63		26	Wife begin or stop work	26
5	Death of close family member	63		27	Begin or end school	26
6	Personal injury or illness	53		28	Change in living conditions	25
7	Marriage	50		29	Revision of personal habits	24
8	Fired at work	47		30	Trouble with boss	23
9	Marital reconciliation	45		31	Change in work hours or conditions	20
10	Retirement	45		32	Change in residence	20
11	Change in health of family member	44		33	Change in schools	20
12	Pregnancy	40		34	Change in recreation	19
13	Sex difficulties	39		35	Change in church activities	19
14	Gain of new family member	39		36	Change in social activities	18
15	Business readjustment	39		37	Mortgage or loan less than $10,000	17
16	Change in financial state	38		38	Change in sleeping habits	16
17	Death of close friend	37		39	Change in number of family get-togethers	15
18	Change to different line of work	36		40	Change in eating habits	15
19	Change in number of arguments with spouse	35		41	Vacation	13
20	Mortgage over $10,000	31		42	Christmas	12
21	Foreclosure of mortgage or loan	30		43	Minor violations of the law	11
22	Change in responsibilities at work	29				

FIGURE 14.1 Holmes and Rahe's Schedule of Recent Life Experiences. *Source:* Holmes and Rahe (1967).

Preisler, & Aussprung, 1992; see Figure 14.2). To get a sense of how stressed you currently are, check all the stressful events listed in Figure 14.2 that happened to you over the past week. A survey of 86 University of Florida undergraduates found that the average student checked about 18 items (Crandall et al., 1992); in very rough terms, then, you can classify yourself as having experienced above-average levels of stress recently if you checked a lot more than 18 items and lower-than-average levels if you checked fewer than 18 items.

The stressful events listed in the Undergraduate Stress Questionnaire are ordered in terms of their perceived severity. In their early attempt to measure stress, Holmes and Rahe assumed that major life changes are more stressful than minor changes. However, researchers have recently noted that minor as well as major

Item	Rated Severity of Stress	Item	Rated Severity of Stress
Death (family member or friend)	3.97	Thought about unfinished work	3.03
Had a lot of tests	3.62	No sleep	3.00
It's finals week	3.62	Sick, injury	3.00
Applying to graduate school	3.59	Had a class presentation	3.00
Victim of a crime	3.59	Applying for a job	3.00
Assignments in all classes due the same day	3.57	Fought with boy-/girlfriend	3.00
Breaking up with boy-/girlfriend	3.45	Working while in school	2.97
Found out boy-/girlfriend cheated on you	3.45	Arguments, conflict of values with friends	2.97
Lots of deadlines to meet	3.41	Bothered by having no social support of family	2.96
Property stolen	3.41	Performed poorly at a task	2.93
You have a hard upcoming week	3.31	Can't finish everything you needed to do	2.90
Went into a test unprepared	3.31	Heard bad news	2.90
Lost something (especially wallet)	3.21	Had confrontation with an authority figure	2.90
Death of a pet	3.21	Maintaining a long-distance boy-/girlfriend	2.86
Did worse than expected on test	3.17	Crammed for a test	2.83
Had an interview	3.17	Feel unorganized	2.83
Had projects, research papers due	3.14	Trying to decide on major	2.79
Did badly on a test	3.14	Feel isolated	2.79
Parents getting divorce	3.10	Parents controlling with money	2.79
Dependent on other people	3.10	Couldn't find a parking space	2.72
Having roommate conflicts	3.10	Noise disturbed you while trying to study	2.69
Car/bike broke down, flat tire, etc.	3.10	Someone borrowed something without permission	2.69
Got a traffic ticket	3.10	Had to ask for money	2.69
Missed your period and waiting	3.08	Ran out of typewriter ribbon while typing	2.66
Coping with addictions	3.07		
Thoughts about future	3.07		
Lack of money	3.07		
Dealt with incompetence at the Registrar's office	3.07		

FIGURE 14.2 Items from the Undergraduate Stress Questionnaire. *Source:* Crandall, Preisler, and Aussprung (1992).

Item	Rated Severity of Stress	Item	Rated Severity of Stress
Erratic schedule	2.62	Problem getting home from bar when drunk	2.24
Can't understand your professor	2.62	Used a fake ID	2.21
Trying to get into your major or college	2.57	No sex in a while	2.21
Registration for classes	2.55	Someone cut ahead of you in line	2.21
Stayed up late writing a paper	2.55	Checkbook didn't balance	2.10
Someone you expected to call did not	2.55	Visit from a relative and entertaining them	2.10
Someone broke a promise	2.55	Decision to have sex on your mind	2.07
Can't concentrate	2.52	Talked with a professor	2.07
Someone did a "pet peeve" of yours	2.52	Change of environment (new doctor, dentist, etc.)	2.00
Living with boy-/girlfriend	2.50	Exposed to upsetting TV show, book, or movie	1.97
Felt need for transportation	2.48		
Bad haircut today	2.45	Got to class late	1.86
Job requirements changed	2.45	Holiday	1.76
No time to eat	2.38	Sat through a boring class	1.66
Felt some peer pressure	2.35	Favorite sporting team lost	1.48
You have a hangover	2.29		
Problems with your computer	2.28		

FIGURE 14.2 *(continued)*

stresses may affect our health (Kohn & Macdonald, 1991). The Hassles Scale lists 117 everyday occurrences that people frequently find to be annoying, irritating, or frustrating, such as "rising prices of common goods," "too many things to do," "taxes," and concerns about "physical appearance" (Kanner, Coyne, Schaefer, & Lazarus, 1981; Lazarus, DeLongis, Folkman, & Gruen, 1985).

Do stresses and everyday hassles affect our health? The answer, distilled from many studies, seems to be a tentative yes: Stress is correlated with both physical and psychological illness. The relationship tends to be relatively weak, however, with correlation coefficients in the range of .2 to .4 (Kobasa, 1982; Kohn, Lafreniere, & Gurevich, 1991; Rabkin & Struening, 1976; Rahe, 1984; Tausig, 1982; Zegans, 1982). The detrimental effects of stress on health tend to subside when the stress subsides; the elevated risk of illness generally does not last more than a year or two after elevated stress levels (Rahe, 1984).

Typically, correlational studies on the connection between stress and illness ask subjects to report the number of stressful events they have experienced recently. *Retrospective studies* ask subjects to report on recent illnesses or symptoms of

Positive as well as negative events may sometimes be stressful. Holmes and Rahe's list of stressful life events includes "change in residence" and "Christmas."

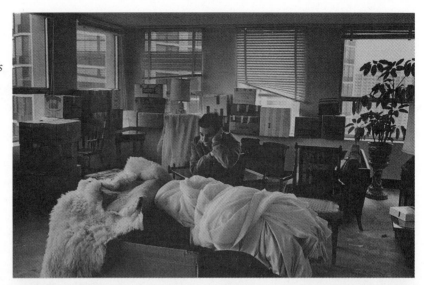

illness at the same time they report their recent history of stress; then the stress score and the illness score are correlated. *Prospective studies* correlate subjects' stress scores with illness assessed at some *later* time to determine whether stress predicts future illness. Retrospective studies may suffer from the problem that current stress levels lead to biased memories and reports of illness. For example, if you are now under great stress you may recall an earlier illness as more severe than it actually was. Moreover, some subjects report high levels of both stress and illness because they have a general tendency to experience negative feelings and report negative experiences (Clark & Watson, 1991; Watson & Pennebaker, 1989).

Despite these and other methodological problems and interpretive ambiguities, many studies suggest that stress is related to many kinds of illness (Cohen & Williamson, 1991; Maddi, Bartone, & Puccetti, 1987). Stress-related diseases include heart disease (Rahe & Lind, 1971), difficulties during pregnancy and birth (Gorsuch & Key, 1974), childhood illnesses (Bedell, Giordani, Amour, Tavormina, & Boll, 1977; Weigel, Wertlieb, & Feldstein, 1989), asthma (Elliott & Eisdorfer, 1982), rheumatoid arthritis (Weiner, 1977), and even the common cold—which is more likely to infect people who are under stress (Cohen, Tyrrell, & Smith, 1993).

Why is stress linked to illness? Experimental studies on animals show that stress suppresses the immune system (Kemeny, Solomon, Morley, & Herbert, 1992; Laudenslager, Ryan, Drugan, Hyson, & Maier, 1983). This helps explain why stress sometimes influences the development of a number of diseases, including cancer- (Justice, 1985). A number of correlational studies on humans also suggest a link between stress and immunity (Kemeny et al., 1992; Kiecolt-Glaser & Glaser, 1992). For example, stressful marriages lead not only to psychological distress in women but also to depressed immune functions (Kiecolt-Glaser et al., 1987). Through its effects on the immune system, stress can activate latent viral diseases such as herpes (Goldmeier & Johnson, 1982). One study demonstrated that the levels of antibodies in college students' saliva were lower during final exam week than they were during either the preceding or following weeks (Jemmott & Magloire, 1988).

Though the correlations between stress and illness found in many studies are relatively weak, this should not be interpreted to mean that stress is unimportant in the development of illness. Clearly, illness is the result of many factors, including genetic predispositions, socioeconomic status, knowledge (do you know the "warning signs" of cancer?), habits (diet, smoking, sexual behavior), exposure to environmental hazards and infectious agents, as well as stress. Even a modest correlation between stress and illness can have social significance when viewed in the context of populations of millions of people.

Social Support and Health

. . . my doctor arranged for me to meet another cancer patient named Özlem. It was great having someone my age to talk to because when you first start going to the hospital you're scared and you don't know what's going on. . . . Özlem had just completed her chemotherapy and she gave me a lot of good advice.

When I go into chemo, I like having someone with me. I need somebody to help me with my bedpan or my throw-up dish, or to raise my feet, or to get me blankets and pillows. My mother is always great about running errands and comforting me. I love having her around when I'm feeling sick, but when I'm feeling better sometimes I feel she stays at the hospital too much. It ruins my social life, because if I'm in a friend's room or I'm cruising around somewhere, she'll always come and get me. At night, if I turn over or shift the blankets, she'll wake right up and ask me, "What's the trouble? What's wrong?" Sometimes I'd rather have my place to myself. It's hard on both of us.

—*Elizabeth Bonwich* (in Krementz, pp. 66–68, 77)

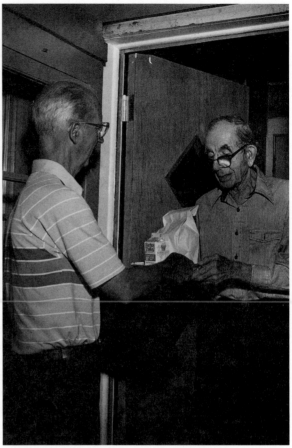

Kinds of social support. Emotional support: The reassurance of love and physical contact.

Tangible support: The "Meals on Wheels" program delivers food to the sick and elderly.

When times are tough, it's important to have the support of other people. Perhaps one reason the connection between stress and health is weak is that other variables influence the strength of the connection or even whether the connection occurs at all. Social support is one such variable that may moderate the effects of stress on illness (Cohen & Syme, 1985a; Coyne & DeLongis, 1986; Schradle & Dougher, 1985; Wallston, Alagna, DeVellis, & DeVellis, 1983). In addition, social support may directly influence the development of illness and subsequent recovery.

Social support has been defined as "the comfort, assistance, and/or information one receives through formal or informal contacts with individuals or groups" (Wallston et al., 1983, p. 369), or even more simply as "resources provided by other people" (Cohen & Syme, 1985b, p. 4). Such resources come in many forms. Cohen and McKay (1984) describe three broad varieties: tangible support, cognitive and informational support, and emotional support.

Informational support: People share their experiences in support groups such as Alcoholics Anonymous, cancer survivors' groups, and grief support groups.

Imagine, for instance, that you contract a severe case of the flu and are bedridden for several days. If your best friend runs errands for you and prepares your meals, she is providing tangible support. If your friend informs you what to expect during the course of your illness ("You'll feel extremely weak for several days and have a high fever"), she is providing informational support. Finally, if your friend tells you that she is concerned about you and that all your friends wish you a speedy recovery, she is offering emotional support. Tangible support reduces your stress by reducing your need to attend to the chores and responsibilities of everyday life. Cognitive support reduces stress by providing clarity and knowledge about your situation. (Often such information takes the form of what social psychologists term social comparison information—see Chapters 9 and 13.) Finally, emotional support fosters your well-being by boosting your self-esteem and informing you that you are loved, valued, and part of a caring social network.

Social support has been measured in many different ways (House & Kahn, 1985). Epidemiological studies (that is, studies of disease patterns in large populations) sometimes rely on self-reports about specific social relationships ("Are you married or single?") as broad measures of social support. Social-network measures assess the number and interconnectedness of social supports ("How many friends do you have? Are they a tightly knit, cohesive group?"). Finally, a number of self-report questionnaires ask respondents about the kinds and degree of social support they receive (Barrera, Sandler, & Ramsay, 1981; Cohen, Mermelstein, Kamarck, & Hoberman, 1984; Sarason, Levine, Basham, & Sarason, 1983; Turner, 1981). Such questionnaires might ask you to list whom you turn to for consolation when you are very upset and to rate how satisfied you feel with the support you receive from each of those people.

Social support may foster health directly; that is, people with high levels of support simply may be healthier on average than people with lower levels of support. Or, more subtly, social support may buffer the effects of stress on health; for example, high levels of social support may have little influence on the health of nonstressed people but may help reduce illness in highly stressed individuals. Research has documented both effects.

Epidemiological studies show that people integrated into social networks show significantly lower mortality rates than more socially isolated people do (Berkman & Breslow, 1983; House, Robbins, & Metzner, 1982; Schradle & Dougher, 1985). In a careful study of 4,725 residents of Alameda County, California, Berkman and Syme (1979) constructed an index of social support from four measures of social contact: marital status, amount of contact with close friends and relatives, church membership, and membership in formal and informal groups. Based on this social network index, subjects were divided into four groups ranging from those with the most numerous social ties to those with the fewest social ties.

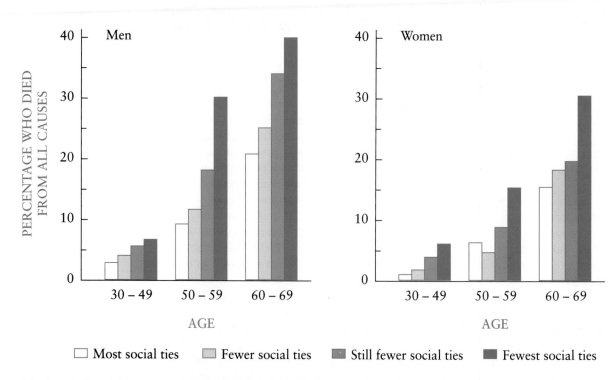

The level of social support was clearly related to death rates for both men and women. Evidently, social isolation is hazardous to your health.

FIGURE 14.3 Social support and mortality in Alameda County, California, 1965–1974. *Source:* Adapted from Berkman and Syme (1979).

Over a nine-year period, Berkman and Syme found that, on average, the people with the fewest social ties died at rates that were two to four times higher than those for people with the most social ties (see Figure 14.3). Furthermore, the degree of social contact was related to deaths from many different causes, including heart disease, stroke, cancer, accident, and suicide (Berkman, 1985).

A meta-analysis of 80 correlational studies on social support, mortality, and illness found overall a relatively weak but significant negative correlation (−.07) between social support and mortality—that is, people with more social support were less likely to die (Schwarzer & Leppin, 1991). Like all correlational studies, epidemiological studies on social support and mortality do not tell us what causes what (see Chapter 2). Why is social support related to death rates? One possibility is that concerned friends and loved ones may lead us to practice preventive and therapeutic health-related behaviors, such as eating and sleeping properly, and to seek medical care (Berkman & Syme, 1979). Social support may help people refrain from unhealthy behaviors, such as drug and alcohol abuse. Lack of social support may lead to psychological states (such as depression) that foster poor health. Finally, both social support and health may be a function of other variables. For example, socially isolated people may tend to be socially unskilled, pessimistic, or maladjusted (Monroe & Steiner, 1986; Newcomb, 1990) or poor and underprivileged (Jenkins, 1982), and such people may lack the resources to develop social supports, even when they need and desire them.

Social psychologists have been extremely interested in the possibility that social support may buffer individuals against the negative effects of stress (Cassel, 1976; Zegans, 1982). In a comprehensive review, Cohen and Wills (1985) noted that such buffering effects are found particularly in studies that measure perceived informational and emotional support; that is, having someone to talk to, boost your morale, and provide you with useful information is particularly valuable when you are highly stressed. Belonging to social networks (families, church groups, friendship networks) has *direct* positive health effects as well. Whether you are stressed or not, your health is likely to be better if you are part of a group that provides you with feelings of well-being and that motivates you to take care of yourself.

Social support may have different effects at different stages of illness (Wallston et al., 1983). For example, the stress-buffering hypothesis holds that social support may protect against the negative effects of stress and hence head off the *development* of illness. Once ill, people with high levels of social support often recover faster and with fewer complications than people with poorer levels of social support do (Wallston et al., 1983). One study found that married men recovered more quickly from coronary bypass surgery and took less pain medication when visited frequently by their wives (Kulik & Mahler, 1989). Social support may persuade chronically ill persons to adhere to medical programs and regimens: taking drugs regularly, watching diet, and seeking regular medical checkups (Caplan, Robinson, French, Caldwell, & Shinn, 1976; Porter, 1969). Thus, social support may reduce decline and neglect in cases of chronic illness.

Our partners in close relationships often provide us with an especially important kind of social support. A number of studies show that married people experience lower mortality rates than single people (Burman & Margolin, 1992).

Of course, the effects of marriage on health depend in part on the *quality* of the relationship (Coyne & Bolger, 1990): Bad ones may be distressing rather than supportive, and thus they may serve to undermine our psychological and physical health (Rook, 1990). Among unmarried people, those who are divorced or widowed experience the worst health and highest mortality rates; these people experience not only social isolation, but stress and loss as well. Men's health often suffers more than women's after a divorce or the death of a spouse (Shumaker & Hill, 1991). Again, we can look to social support for an explanation: Men are more likely than women to have a single "confidante" (often their wife) and few close friends, whereas women are more likely than men to have richer networks of social support. Thus, a man who loses his spouse is likely to lose a larger chunk of his social support than a woman is.

Social support tends to be most helpful when it matches your needs (Cutrona, 1990). For example, if you lose your house, you may need tangible support (a temporary place to live); if you lose your spouse, you may need emotional support (a warm hug and a shoulder to cry on), and if you lose your way, you may need informational support (directions to Elm Street).

Different kinds of social support can foster different kinds of coping. Two main ways people cope with stress are (1) to try to solve their problems and (2) to try to regulate their feelings and emotions (Lazarus & Folkman, 1984). For example, if you learn you have cancer, you could try to actively solve your problem, by reading up on the disease, consulting several specialists, and charting out a treatment plan. You could also work on regulating your feelings and emotions, by practicing meditation to reduce stress, for example, and going to lots of comedy shows and movies. Coping strategies that focus on problem solving are particularly useful when your problems are controllable and solvable (such as car trouble), whereas coping strategies that focus on emotional regulation are particularly useful when your problems are uncontrollable or insoluble (such as untreatable arthritis) (Taylor, 1990).

How does all this relate to social support? If you face controllable and solvable problems, others are likely to be most helpful when they offer you informational and tangible support. For example, if your car breaks down, your friends and family should tell you how to fix your car and offer you a ride home. For problems that are uncontrollable and insoluble, however, others may be most helpful when they offer emotional and tangible support. If you have untreatable arthritis, your friends and family should give you a hug, tell you that you are loved, and help you with errands.

SOCIAL
PSYCHOLOGY
IN EVERYDAY
LIFE

 Are Doctors a Source of Stress or Support?

Finding a doctor you feel is right for you is really important. That relationship is the basis for your whole treatment. Like any relationship, what's right for one person isn't always good for another. If you have cancer, you want to feel close to your oncologist. I ended up switching doctors in the middle of my treatment, right after my surgery and before my long follow-up course of chemo. I didn't feel that I had a particularly good relationship with my first doctor and I thought this would be a good time to change since I had the major part of my chemotherapy left to go. I wanted to work with Dr. Meyers because I had seen him in action. I had also seen a lot of Karen, his nurse-practitioner, and I liked her a lot, too.

—*Elizabeth Bonwich* (in Krementz, pp. 73–74)

As you probably know from real-life experience, doctors can be a source of stress as well as support. Doctors are capable of producing stress when they are cold, abrupt, autocratic, and provide inadequate or incomprehensible information to us. On the other hand, they are supportive when they are warm and empathic, take time to talk with us, and give us complete and understandable information. Social psychology research on doctor–patient communication informs us about the kinds of doctor behaviors that lead to patient satisfaction, and it provides valuable information to doctors about how to improve their medical practices.

One common complaint of patients is that they can't understand their doctors, who too often use confusing technical terms and jargon (DiMatteo & DiNicola, 1982). The following patient describes her misunderstanding vividly:

When my first child was born, the doctor kept coming in every day and asking, "Have you voided?" So I'd say, "No." So in comes the nurse with some paraphernalia that was scary. So I said, "What the devil are you going to do?" And she said, "I'm going to catheterize you, you haven't voided." Well, of course, I knew what catheterization was. I said, ". . . I've peed every day since I've been here." . . . Why didn't he just ask me if I'd peed? I'd have told him. (from Samora, Saunders, & Larson, 1961)

Sometimes doctors simply don't realize that their patients don't understand them, for they frequently overestimate patients' familiarity with medical terms (Segall & Roberts, 1980). Unfortunately, doctors may also sometimes intentionally use complex terms to impress patients and to discourage their participation. In the words of the famous heart surgeon William DeBakey, "Most doctors don't want their patients to understand them! They prefer to keep their work a mystery. If patients don't understand what a doctor is talking about, they won't ask him questions. The doctor won't have to be bothered answering them" (Robinson, 1973).

Another very common complaint of patients is that their doctor doesn't spend enough time with them or offer them enough information (DiMatteo & DiNicola, 1982). A number of studies indicate that most doctors devote less than 10% of their (often brief) interaction time with patients to providing information (Bain, 1976; Waitzkin, 1984, 1985). However, doctors *estimate* that 50% to 75% of their time with patients is spent providing information (Waitzkin & Stoeckle, 1976).

Furthermore, when doctors do provide information, it is often incomplete. Many doctors, for example, prescribe drugs without fully describing their purpose, possible side effects, and how and when to use them (Svarstad, 1976). If anything, doctors should bend over backwards to give complete, detailed, and even repetitive information to patients, who are often anxious and distracted.

Cultural misunderstandings can further contribute to doctor–patient miscommunications. Doctors are highly educated, and many come from relatively privileged socioeconomic backgrounds. As a result, they often lack experience communicating with people of different socioeconomic and ethnic backgrounds (Stoeckle, Zola, & Davidson, 1963).

Most patients want emotional support from their doctor as well as accurate and complete medical information, and they are frequently dissatisfied with their medical care when they perceive their doctor to be cold and unconcerned. Doctors sometimes don't show even basic forms of politeness to their patients, such as saying hello, inquiring "How are you doing?" and maintaining eye contact while talking (DiMatteo & DiNicola, 1982).

Not surprisingly, research shows that patients are most happy with their doctors, and they are most likely to follow their doctors' recommendations, when they feel their doctors are understanding and empathic (Squire, 1990). They are also most likely to seek follow-up care from empathic doctors. While these points may seem obvious, they are often overlooked in medical practice today. Medicine is not just about accurate diagnosis; it is ultimately about getting patients to follow sound medical advice and to continue to seek treatment for ongoing illnesses.

When doctors are detached and uninformative, or worse yet, when they are cold, officious, and provide negative information without emotional support, they can significantly stress their patients. One study found that cardiac patients were more likely to experience heart attacks immediately after being visited by doctors during ward rounds (Jarvinen, 1955). Why would a visit by doctors lead to illness? It might be that the doctors stood around and impersonally discussed aspects of the patients' cases as if they weren't even present. The patient heard upsetting details without receiving desperately needed emotional support, and the resulting stress triggered heart attacks in patients who were marginal to start with.

How can doctors establish better rapport with patients? Step one, of course, is that they must want to. Social psychology research on nonverbal behavior offers some advice to doctors who wish to improve their bedside manner (DiMatteo, 1985, 1991). They should carefully attend to their patients and be sensitive to their nonverbal cues. They should maintain eye contact with patients and reassuringly touch them when it is appropriate (Harrigan, Oxman, & Rosenthal, 1985; Larsen & Smith, 1981). They should try to control their own facial expressions and tone of voice to convey the impressions they want to (DiMatteo, 1985; DiMatteo, Hays, & Prince, 1986; Hall, Roter, & Rand, 1981). It's hard to reassure a patient, for example, when you are frowning and your tone of voice conveys boredom and irritation with the patient's question. See Figure 14.4 for a firsthand account of one patient's dissatisfaction with his doctor's bedside manner.

Despite their best efforts to provide information and understanding, doctors are often unsuccessful in getting patients to comply with their recommendations—to take drugs, change dietary habits, and exercise, for example (DiMatteo &

A Prescription for Healing

by A. STANLEY KRAMER

Hi, Doc! I saw your picture and the article about you in the paper. Didn't recognize you at first. Maybe because you were smiling. I never saw you do that before. It changed your whole appearance. Pretty impressive story. Congratulations! The paper spelled out how you're responsible for providing advanced surgical care from laser surgery to oncology. Wow!

You wouldn't remember my face if you saw it. You did the job on me six months ago. A lot of bladders must have passed under your scalpel in the interim. Actually you didn't seem to recognize me then, until you had my folder in your hand. I remember the file number. So that's who this is from—Bladder #139.

I understand your not recognizing me. No hard feelings. In your office you were always busy running from one examining room to another. Or you were on the phone: to the hospital, another doctor, a lab, another patient. Nurses ran after you with papers. When you did get to me—you were always at least a half hour late—you frowned over your Ben Franklin glasses as though I had made some mistake. I was never a person, just a case. But I was scared, so I asked questions. This seemed to annoy you. My layman's ignorance was so profound, your expression seemed to say, that, really, there was no point in any discussion. I simply wouldn't understand.

You pulled no punches. I guess in becoming a great surgeon you forgot those early courses in doctor/patient relations: that patients tend to panic and imagine the worst; that they need reassurance. You said outright that I had two malignant tumors that must be removed at once. That meant *cancer*. The word scared the hell out of me. I broke out in a sweat. But you didn't seem to notice. You frowned your usual frown and said that radiation or chemotherapy were not options. You gave no explanation and I was too clobbered to ask.

"Speak to my nurse," you said. "She'll arrange the details, tell you what to do and set up the surgery date." Then you were out the door, your white coat flapping, as comforting as an ice-water douche. You were certainly no kindly healer; rather a competent master plumber, assaying a faulty drainage system and prescribing the necessary repairs—to it, not me. There was no compassion in your kit. Maybe you think that's so much mush. Well, it's not. Along with scanners, beepers, lasers, faxes and imaging machines, hope and reassurance can save lives, reduce pain and speed recovery. But that's not your department, is it? That's head stuff, for psychiatrists and psychologists. You deal directly with the biology of life.

Hope *is* biology, Doc. You did nothing to lessen my fears. You didn't reassure me by explaining (as my M.D. brother-in-law did, after it was all over) that my type of tumor was common, easily excised and, if followed by periodic inspection, not likely to shorten my life or impede my functions. A doctor's ability to reassure a patient can help to activate the body's healing system. Positive emotions, like faith, love and determination are biochemical realities. It seems to me, Doc, that you overlooked the mind's power to heal.

Because of you I suffered needlessly, night after night, unable to sleep because of what lay ahead. I barely ate, my mind obsessed. Would you eradicate all the cancer? Had it spread? Was this the beginning of the end? How could my family get along without me?

Good medicine. After the operation I lay worrying, in intermittent pain, three tubes draining, sedating and replenishing me; every movement agony. Would I make it? I asked for you, Doc. The nurse explained you had been in several times while I was unconscious. Couldn't you have managed one visit while I was awake? Just to say that I was doing fine.

I know you're not heartless. You did tell my wife the operation was a success. But that's all. How was I going to be? The nurse explained that you had a very busy schedule, but if anything went wrong she would call you. Like what? Everything was going wrong. One night I got tangled in my tubes when I had a hurry call and couldn't make it to the john. No one told me that this was normal, that the medication frequently did that. I thought I was dying. Somehow you might have found a minute to drop by, to tell me the cancer was gone, how well my recovery was going. But you didn't. Compassion is not mere handholding. It is good medicine. Here's a big word I've just learned: psychoneuroimmunology—the interaction between the brain, the endocrine system and the immune system. In short: the degree to which belief becomes biology.

Your hospital thinks you're super. You've saved many lives and made others more comfortable. You put in grueling days, carry a crushing load, operate in life-or-death crises. Yet, there is no visible indication that you have the slightest feeling for your patients. You are so immersed in the functioning of the organism you are repairing that you seem to forget that each is a person—a thinking creature of hopes and fears, joys and sorrows. And, sometimes, like yourself, a leader in his chosen field.

What should you do about all this, Doc? Possibly nothing. But, couldn't you lighten your caseload? Use some of your precious time to listen to your patients with an unhurried mind and an open heart? Try viewing them as whole people, not merely the containers of malfunctioning parts? Understanding all the factors (including the emotional) leading up to an illness can be as important as the identification of the actual pathology.

Just as a thousand-mile journey begins with one step forward, a step forward for you would be to erase that perpetual frown, that expression of annoyance at uninformed, fearful laymen and replace it with a smile and a few encouraging words. I know you can do it, Doc. Because I have that smiling picture of you from the newspaper.

Kramer, 82, a freelance writer and a former advertising executive, lives in Highland Park, Ill.

IGURE 14.4 One patient's dissatisfaction with his doctor's bedside manner. *Source: Newsweek,* June 7, 1993.

DiNicola, 1982). As you already know, patients with high levels of social support are often more likely to comply with medical advice (Doherty, Schrott, Metcalf, & Iasiello-Vailas, 1983; Sherwood, 1983). Because social influences exert a strong effect on patients' compliance with medical advice, savvy doctors don't treat patients as isolated individuals; when possible, they involve the patient's support system as well. When doctors give information and support to the families and friends of patients, they are often treating the patient as well. Once again, we see important links between social psychology and medicine.

PERSONALITY, HEALTH, AND ILLNESS

I cry a lot at night when I'm alone. My mother is very supportive, but I feel that if I cried to her, she'd get upset and I would feel even worse. Lots of people at the hospital look at me and say, "Wow, she's got a great attitude. She smiles all the time." I think, "Yeah, you should see me at night!" Sometimes I can only sleep during the day when the lights are on and people are around. When everyone is asleep and it's all quiet, I'm wide awake. I listen to the radio for hours, and I can't go to bed without watching David Letterman. I read a lot, too. If you came into my room at two o'clock in the morning, you'd probably see me sitting there with my guide to colleges.

—*Elizabeth Bonwich* (in Krementz, pp. 66–67)

Are some people healthier than others because of their personality characteristics? Popular wisdom holds that some people have a stronger will to live than others do. Even in such overwhelmingly stressful environments as concentration camps, some individuals survive. What distinguishes survivors from nonsurvivors in both everyday life and in highly stressful circumstances? Is psychological and physical health in part a function of personal feelings of worth and control? Of optimism? Of general hardiness?

Feelings of Control

In Chapter 5 we discussed attribution theories, which try to predict when people will make internal and external attributions. The attributions we make about our own behavior depend not just on objective information but also on our personality characteristics and emotional states. For example, depressed people tend to explain their failures as being due to stable, internal causes ("I'm stupid and worthless") and their successes as being due to uncontrollable, unstable, external causes ("I was lucky"). Depressed people also tend to assess the amount of control they have over events more accurately than do nondepressed people, who often harbor the benign illusion that they have more control over events in their lives than they in fact do (Taylor & Brown, 1988).

The tendency to believe that we have control over events versus the tendency to believe that we are victims of circumstance can be conceptualized as a personality trait—a kind of stable attributional style. In 1966, Julian Rotter developed a Locus of Control Scale to assess individuals' perception of the degree to which internal or external factors control events in their lives. Since then, locus of control has become one of the most studied personality traits in social psychology (Strickland, 1989).

Rotter's scale presents respondents with pairs of statements and asks them to check the statement in each pair with which they agree most. Here are three such pairs:

a. It is impossible for me to believe that chance or luck plays an important role in my life.

b. Many times I feel that I have little influence over the things that happen to me.

a. In the long run, people get the respect they deserve in this world.

b. Unfortunately, an individual's worth often passes unrecognized no matter how hard he tries.

a. In my case, getting what I want has little or nothing to do with luck.

b. Many times we might just as well decide what to do by flipping a coin. (Rotter, 1966, pp. 11–12)

People with an internal locus of control (those who explain their behavior as being due to controllable internal factors) tend to choose response *a* on these items, whereas those with an external locus of control (who explain their behavior as being due to uncontrollable external factors) tend to choose response *b*. Individuals with an internal locus of control tend to take more responsibility for their behavior and assume a more active role in planning their actions and changing situations they don't like than people with an external locus of control (Lefcourt, 1984; Phares, 1976; Rotter, 1975).

The Locus of Control Scale has a number of different components (Collins, 1974; Reid & Ware, 1974), so later researchers have developed scales tailored to specific domains, including health-related behaviors (Wallston, Wallston, & DeVellis, 1978; Wallston, Wallston, Kaplan, & Maides, 1976). The Health Locus of Control Scale asks respondents to rate how strongly they agree or disagree with such items as: "If I take care of myself, I can avoid illness," "Good health is largely a matter of good fortune," "People who never get sick are just plain lucky," "I am directly responsible for my health" (Wallston et al., 1976). In other words, the Health Locus of Control Scale asks people to rate how much control they feel over their own health.

Does locus of control correlate with health and health-related behaviors? It seems reasonable to predict that people with an internal locus of control will assume more responsibility for their health, taking action to prevent or remedy illness. Despite the obviousness of this prediction, research suggests a more complex and inconsistent relationship (Wallston & Wallston, 1982). Sometimes individuals with an internal locus of control engage more in preventive behaviors and seek out more health-related information than individuals with an external locus of control do, but sometimes they do not.

When faced with serious illness, however, internal-locus-of-control individuals do seem to cope better (Lefcourt & Davidson-Katz, 1991). For example, women with breast cancer (Taylor, Lichtman, & Wood, 1984) and men and women with various kinds of blood cancer (Marks, Richardson, Graham, & Levine, 1986) who report a more internal locus of control seem to experience better psychological adjustment to their illness (fewer mood problems and less depression). People who feel they have internal control over their recovery tend to recover from both serious and minor illnesses more quickly (Partridge & Johnston, 1989). One study found that elderly people with an internal locus of control experienced better health and even lower mortality rates over a five-year period than those with a more external locus of control did (Reid & Ziegler, 1981).

While a sense of internal control tends in general to contribute to health and adjustment, it may be a liability in some health settings. If an ailing individual with an internal locus of control decides he can "cure himself" and so fails to seek medical attention quickly enough, he may endanger his health. In some situations it may be adaptive to relinquish control, at least temporarily (Taylor, 1979). For example, if you are seriously ill and in an intensive care unit, you might best conserve your strength and mental resources by entrusting your care to competent health professionals rather than worrying about the details of every medical procedure and trying to take charge of your treatment.

Hardiness

A sense of personal control may influence health another way: It may buffer against the bad effects of stress. Suzanne Kobasa (1979, 1982; Kobasa, Maddi, & Kahn, 1982) argued that a sense of personal control is one of three components of what she termed the *hardy personality*. The other two are a sense of commitment (a sense of personal meaning and involvement in life) and a sense of challenge (a desire for growth and change and an openness to new experiences). Hardy individuals negotiate stress well, according to Kobasa, because they believe they have the resources they need to deal with trying events, they do not become helpless and hopeless in the face of adversity, and they thrive on change and challenge. In short, they approach stressful situations with zest rather than dread.

In one early study on hardiness, 259 managers at a large utility company periodically completed questionnaires measuring stress, health, and personality over a five-year period (Kobasa, Maddi, & Kahn, 1982). Personal control was assessed by Rotter's Locus of Control Scale and a scale of powerlessness. Commitment was assessed by an alienation scale (sample item: "Life is empty and has no meaning in it for me"). Challenge was assessed with a need-for-security scale (sample item: "I don't like situations that are uncertain"). Subjects' scores on these three components of hardiness were combined, and subjects were then divided into groups that had high degrees (above the median) or low degrees (below the median) of hardiness. Subjects were independently divided into groups that had high or low degrees of stress.

Managers who were highly stressed and had low degrees of hardiness experienced the most illness (see Figure 14.5). As you might expect, stress also contributed independently to illness, with highly stressed managers reporting more illness than less stressed managers reported. And hardiness independently affected the frequency of illness; hardy subjects on average reported less illness than nonhardy subjects reported.

Some later studies have found that the effects of hardiness depend on other variables and that hardiness effects occur only sometimes (Wiebe & Williams, 1992). One study of college women found that hardiness offered protection against stress only when combined with social support (Ganellen & Blaney, 1984). Similarly, Kobasa and Puccetti (1983) reported that hardy people benefit from social support but that nonhardy people do not. A study of 82 female secretaries failed to find that hardiness buffered the effects of stress on health (Schmied & Lawler, 1986). Perhaps this study did not replicate Kobasa's earlier research because it studied women rather than men. Men (particularly the managers, executives, and lawyers who served as subjects in Kobasa's studies) learn to view control, commitment, and challenge differently from women, particularly in work-related achievement settings. When hardiness studies do find sex differences, they tend to find that men are more likely to show hardiness effects than women are (Williams, Wiebe, & Smith, 1992). Thus, gender may be yet another variable that sometimes moderates hardiness effects.

Still, women sometimes show hardiness effects as well as men. Rhodewalt and Zone (1989) found that hardiness buffered the effects of stress on self-reported illness and depression in 212 women, and furthermore, their data suggested that these effects were due to the tendency of nonhardy women to appraise stressful events much more negatively than hardy women did. Other studies point to the same conclusion (Wiebe, 1991; Wiebe & Williams, 1992; Williams et al., 1992): Hardy people are more likely than nonhardy people to perceive stressful events in nonthreatening ways. Furthermore, when facing stress, hardy people are more likely to cope by seeking support and trying to actively solve their problems, whereas nonhardy people are more likely to cope by avoiding their problems (Williams et al., 1992).

Researchers have recently examined more closely what "hardiness" entails. Some argue that nonhardy people are in fact people who experience negative emotions in general (Allred & Smith, 1989; Funk & Houston, 1987). Furthermore, because hardiness comprises three components, it may be that one, two, or all three components produce hardiness effects and interactions in studies (Carver, 1989; Hull, Van Treuren, & Virnelli, 1987). After reviewing a number of hardiness studies, Hull and his associates (1987) argued that the control and commitment components of hardiness, but not the challenge component, relate significantly to measures of illness and health. More recent research also supports this conclusion (Williams et al., 1992). So, to be hardy, it helps to feel that you have control over events in your life and to see life as meaningful; it may not be as important to seek change and new experiences.

Social Psychology and Health

The numbers displayed in this graph represent tallies of subjects' self-reported illnesses and physical symptoms.

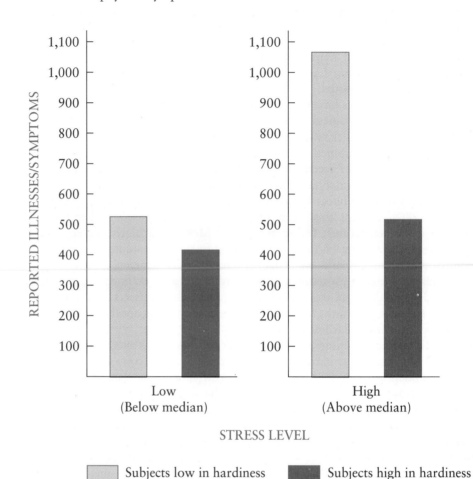

Highly stressed managers reported more illness than less stressed managers, and hardy managers reported less illness than nonhardy managers. Most interesting, however, was the finding that the relationship between stress and illness was much stronger for nonhardy than hardy managers.

FIGURE 14.5 Self-reported illness as a function of hardiness and stress levels. *Source:* Data from Kobasa, Maddi, and Kahn (1982).

Optimism

Having cancer is definitely tough. But I'm learning to deal with it and that's something that's taken a long time—over a year. Now I realize I have to stick it out despite the discomfort, especially when you know people who have finished treatment, successfully. When I started treatment, many of the people I met at the hospital were halfway through treatment. Now most of them are well and I'm halfway there. At first I wasn't sure that I'd make it. Now I believe that if they survived, I can, too!

—*Elizabeth Bonwich* (in Krementz, pp. 80–81)

Social support, a sense of personal control, and hardiness may all have their effects in part because they foster a sense of well-being—a sense of optimism about life. Scheier and Carver (1985) developed a Life Orientation Test that directly assesses optimism: the degree to which individuals generally expect successes and positive events to occur. Some sample items: "In unusual times, I usually expect the best"; "I hardly ever expect things to go my way."

Scheier and Carver note that individuals with high degrees of optimism report less physical illness and greater physical well-being. A number of studies offer support for this hypothesis (Peterson & Bossio, 1991; Scheier & Carver, 1992, 1993). A study of 99 Harvard students selected from the classes of 1942 through 1944 found that the optimism of their questionnaire responses in the 1940s (when subjects were about 25 years old) was significantly correlated with their health 20 to 35 years later (when subjects were 45 to 60 years old) (Peterson, Seligman, & Vaillant, 1988). Optimists and pessimists seem to cope with stress differently (Scheier, Weintraub, & Carver, 1986). Optimists are more likely to try to take action, seek social support, and interpret stressful events as "growth experiences," whereas pessimists are more likely to focus on their feelings of stress and deny or distance themselves from their problems (Scheier & Carver, 1993).

Optimism and pessimism may relate to a broader syndrome of general negative emotionality (Clark & Watson, 1991; Smith, Pope, Rhodewalt, & Poulton, 1989; Watson & Pennebaker, 1989); that is, optimistic people in general do not suffer from negative, anxious feelings, and pessimistic people do. Negative emotionality may correlate with a number of different kinds of illness (Friedman & Booth-Kewley, 1987b).

Clearly, many psychological variables—including personality traits—can influence how people perceive and react to potentially stressful events (see Figure 14.6 for a schematic summary).

Personality and Heart Disease

SOCIAL PSYCHOLOGY IN EVERYDAY LIFE

Coronary heart disease is the leading cause of death in the United States, accounting for over one-third of all deaths each year (U.S. Department of Health and Human Services, 1984). Among the risks that increase the likelihood of heart disease are high cholesterol levels, high blood pressure, a high-fat diet,

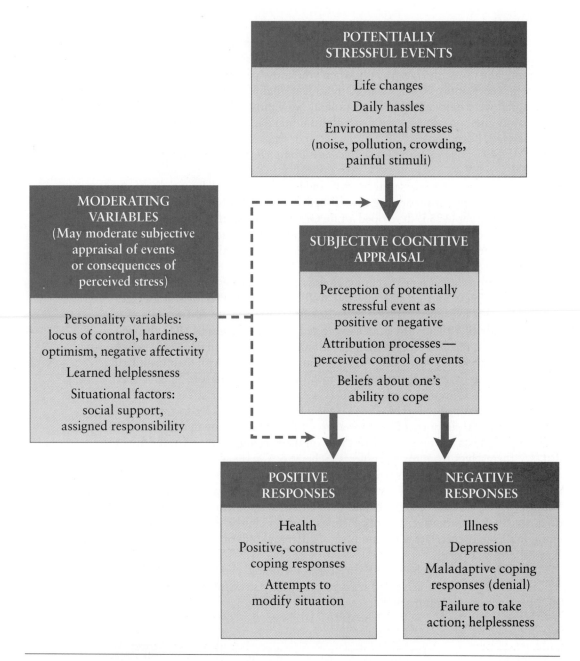

FIGURE 14.6 Social psychological variables, stress, and health.

smoking, and lack of exercise, but these factors are only partially successful in predicting who does and who does not develop heart disease (Keys et al., 1972).

In the 1950s, researchers began to study psychological factors that may contribute to heart disease. Cardiologists Meyer Friedman and Ray Rosenman (1959) described the "Type A" behavior pattern, which, they argued, was conducive to heart disease. Type A behaviors are "characterized by intense ambition, competitive 'drive,' constant preoccupation with occupational 'deadlines' and a sense of time urgency" (p. 1295). People who show Type A behavior are impatient, are often hostile, and frequently try to engage in more than one activity at the same time (for example, eating and working, or driving and talking on the car phone). People who show the contrasting Type B behavior are characterized by lower degrees of urgency, impatience, and incessant goal seeking.

To measure Type A's and Type B's, Friedman, Rosenman, and their colleagues (1968) developed the Structured Interview, a technique in which a trained interviewer asks subjects questions designed to elicit Type A responses and then codes these responses for both verbal and nonverbal content. The 26 questions of the Structured Interview address three main themes: the subject's drive and ambition ("Would you describe yourself as a hard-driving, ambitious type of person in accomplishing the things you want, or would you describe yourself as a relatively relaxed and easy-going person?"); the subject's competitive, aggressive, and hostile feelings ("What irritates you most about your work, or the people with whom you work?"); and the subject's sense of urgency ("Do you have the feeling that time is passing too rapidly for you to accomplish all the things you think you should get done in one day?").

In the Structured Interview, interviewers intentionally interrupt or challenge subjects during their responses to designated questions in order to elicit Type A behaviors. According to Friedman and Rosenman, categorizing people as Type A or Type B depends as much on *how* they answer (for example, are their answers loud and abrupt, and do they interrupt the interviewer?) as on the content of their responses. Indeed, a number of studies suggest that subjects' voice quality alone during the interviews is sufficient to classify subjects as Type A or Type B (Glass, Ross, Isecke, & Rosenman, 1982; Schucker & Jacobs, 1977).

Early research using the Structured Interview indicated that Type A subjects suffered about twice the rate of fatal heart attacks as Type B subjects, an effect that was independent of other risk factors such as smoking, diet, and blood pressure (Brand, Rosenman, Sholtz, & Friedman, 1976; Rosenman, Brand, Sholtz, & Friedman, 1976). These findings have been replicated in other studies (Haynes, Feinleib, & Eaker, 1983). One recent review found that 70% of middle-aged men with heart disease are Type A's, whereas only 46% of healthy middle-aged men are (Miller, Turner, Tindale, Posavac, & Dugoni, 1991).

Because the Structured Interview is a laborious way to classify subjects, questionnaire measures of Type A and Type B behavior have also been developed. Perhaps the best known is the Jenkins Activity Survey, a self-report scale with the same kind of content as the Structured Interview, including items assessing hard-driving competitiveness, speed, and impatience. Many studies show a relation between scores on the Jenkins Activity Survey and heart disease (the average correlation coefficient is approximately .10), but in general, the Structured Interview is a better predictor of heart disease (average correlation of .20; Friedman & Booth-Kewley, 1987a). The Structured Interview and the Jenkins Activity Survey seem to measure somewhat different constructs (Matthews, Krantz, Dembroski, & MacDougall, 1982).

Why does Type A behavior elevate one's risk for heart disease? One possibility is that Type A's possess considerable self-induced stress and respond readily to stressful situations (such as competitive, pressured work settings) with physiological arousal (Krantz, Arabian, Davia, & Parker, 1982; Matthews, 1982). Interestingly, Type A behavior is linked not only to coronary heart disease but also to headaches, gastrointestinal disorders, respiratory disease, and sleep disorders (Woods & Burns, 1984; Woods, Morgan, Day, Jefferson, & Harris, 1984). These findings are consistent with the view that Type A behavior may be associated in general with stress and arousal.

Although Type A behavior has received the greatest share of research attention, other personality traits are also related to heart disease (Friedman & Booth-Kewley, 1987b). Anxiety, depression, and even extroversion show a relation with heart disease that is comparable in magnitude to the relation between Type A behavior and heart disease. One thread that seems to tie all these traits together is their link to stress and autonomic arousal, the physiological arousal that goes along with stress. Rhodewalt and Smith (1991) suggest that hostility is the component of Type A behavior that is most linked to heart disease.

Although Type A people are at greater risk for experiencing a first heart attack, they are not necessarily more likely to experience a recurrence (Matthews, 1988; Ragland & Brand, 1988). Perhaps the hostile, competitive, and urgent emotional style of the Type A person primes the conditions that trigger a heart attack, but after surviving such an attack, Type A's may ambitiously take on the challenge of "reforming" themselves and moderating their Type A behaviors.

Friedman and Ulmer (1984) reported encouraging preliminary findings suggesting that it is possible to teach Type A's who have experienced heart attacks various techniques to modify their urgent, competitive, and emotionally arousing behaviors and thereby reduce their future risk of heart attack. These findings have been replicated in other studies (Gill et al., 1985; Nunes, Frank, & Kornfeld, 1987). Thus, research on Type A behavior has led to useful real-life programs that have already helped save the lives of many people with heart disease.

BELIEFS, ATTITUDES, AND HEALTH

When they told me they thought it was cancer, I went to the library and did a lot of research—the same way I would for a term paper. I started with a book from the American Cancer Society and went on from there. . . . I figured that if I really did have osteogenic sarcoma, I wanted to learn as much as I could while I still had the time and energy and while I was relatively calm and collected. Even now I go and look up procedures so I can better understand what's happening to me. The doctors don't always tell you all that you want to know. I've learned to ask a lot of questions when I talk with them. And to try to find information from other sources, too.

—*Elizabeth Bonwich* (in Krementz, p. 66)

It probably comes as no surprise to you that our beliefs and attitudes can affect our health-related behaviors, and, ultimately, our health. For example, a person's beliefs about the dangers of cigarette smoking can influence whether he or she smokes and, as a result, is susceptible to a host of smoking-related diseases. A person's sexual attitudes can influence whether he or she practices safe sex. And a woman's beliefs about the likelihood and dangers of breast cancer can determine whether she performs monthly self-examinations of her breasts and has regular mammograms (X-rays that provide early diagnoses of breast cancer).

Social psychologists have studied health-related beliefs and attitudes intensively. We shall briefly summarize two models of how beliefs and attitudes influence health-related behaviors: the Health Beliefs Model and the theory of reasoned action. In the process, we will describe how these models have been used to understand and predict two important kinds of health-related behaviors: (1) cigarette smoking and (2) sexual behavior in the age of AIDS.

The Health Beliefs Model

The Health Beliefs Model focuses on four main kinds of beliefs that can influence when we take action to protect our health: beliefs about the costs of taking action, beliefs about the benefits or rewards of taking action, beliefs about our susceptibility to illness, and beliefs about the severity of illness (Becker, 1974; Rosenstock, 1966, 1974, 1988). To illustrate: What kinds of beliefs determine whether a smoker decides to quit? According to the Health Beliefs Model, critical beliefs are those about the costs of quitting ("I'll be really tense and gain weight"), the benefits of quitting ("I'll save a lot of money, won't have stained teeth and smelly clothes, and I won't be likely to get lung cancer"), illness susceptibility ("I'm almost sure to get heart disease or lung cancer if I don't quit"), and illness severity ("Lung cancer is agonizingly painful and usually fatal"). Recent variants of the Health Beliefs Model have also looked at people's beliefs about whether they have the ability (sometimes termed "self-efficacy") to change their behavior (Maddux & Rogers, 1983; Rogers, 1984). Some cigarette smokers, for example, believe that they are addicted, and so they believe they are not likely to be very successful even if they want to quit.

The Health Beliefs Model makes the following important point: Health-related behaviors do not depend solely (or even largely) on having detailed and accurate information about what is healthy and how to engage in healthy behaviors. You probably know the following: Avoid cigarettes, practice safe sex, and wear seat belts. You may even know lots of "how to" details about each—perhaps you have read numerous pamphlets about safe sex and you know the proper ways to use a condom. But do you always practice what you know? Clearly, as the Health Beliefs Model suggests, our health-related behaviors depend also on our beliefs about costs, rewards, and personal susceptibility. For example, although a college student might possess very detailed and correct information about safe sex, he may also believe it is too "costly" ("Wearing condoms reduces the pleasure, and it takes all the spontaneity from sex") and that he is not susceptible to the relevant disease ("AIDS only happens to gays and drug addicts, and I only have sex with 'nice' women").

Many studies have shown that the kinds of beliefs studied in the Health Beliefs Model are strongly related to people's actions to maintain their health, prevent illness, and seek medical care (Janz & Becker, 1984). The Health Beliefs Model may be most effective in predicting the health-related behaviors of educated people with relatively high socioeconomic status—that is, people who are well informed about health risks and health-related behaviors (Wolinsky, 1978). In general, people's beliefs about the costs and barriers to healthy behaviors are most related to their actual behavior, and (perhaps surprisingly) their beliefs about the severity of their potential illness seem to be least related to their actual behavior.

Such findings, when obtained for specific kinds of health-related behaviors, can provide information useful to public health advertising campaigns. If research shows, for example, that college students' beliefs about the "costs" of using a condom are more important in influencing their condom use than are their beliefs about the danger of AIDS or their susceptibility to AIDS, then public health ads and pamphlets should particularly target these beliefs about "costs."

What kind of beliefs influence whether people smoke?

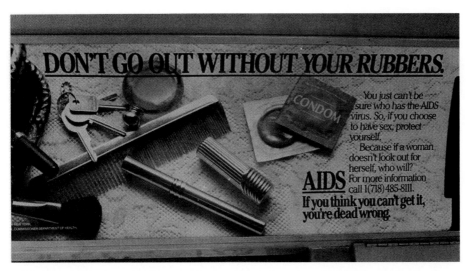

DON'T GO OUT WITHOUT YOUR RUBBERS.

You just can't be sure who has the AIDS virus. So, if you choose to have sex, protect yourself.

Because if a woman doesn't look out for herself, who will?

AIDS For more information call 1(718) 485-8111.

If you think you can't get it, you're dead wrong.

Condom ad in a New York City subway. What kinds of messages are effective in persuading people to engage in safer sexual activities?

Research on factors that lead people to smoke and to quit smoking provides additional support for the Health Beliefs Model. Compared with nonsmokers, smokers have lower estimates of the dangers of cigarette smoking and higher estimates of the costs of quitting (McCoy et al., 1992). Of course, smokers' beliefs may be due in part to rationalization (see the discussion of dissonance theory in Chapter 6). Smokers' beliefs about smoking sometimes show an overly optimistic bias: Smokers believe, for example, that they personally are less at risk for smoking-related illness than the "typical smoker" is (McCoy et al., 1992). Consistent with the Health Beliefs Model, smokers who intend to quit rate the costs of smoking and the rewards of quitting higher than smokers with no intention to quit do, and they perceive a greater likelihood of contracting smoking-related illnesses (Sutton, Marsh, & Matheson, 1990). Again, by assessing people's beliefs about smoking in specific populations, the Health Beliefs Model can help public health workers develop effective advertising and information campaigns to motivate smokers to quit and nonsmokers not to start.

Fishbein and Ajzen's Theory of Reasoned Action

The second model often used to understand health-related beliefs, attitudes, and behaviors is Fishbein and Ajzen's theory of reasoned action, which proposes that two main variables predict people's intentions to engage in healthy (or unhealthy) behaviors: (1) attitudes toward the behaviors and (2) subjective norms (Ajzen & Fishbein, 1980; Fishbein & Ajzen, 1975; see Chapter 6). Attitudes refer to people's evaluation of the relevant behavior, and subjective norms refer to people's beliefs about how others think they should behave. So, according to this model, whether you smoke depends on your attitudes toward smoking and your beliefs about how your friends and family members feel about your smoking.

The concept of subjective norms addresses an important factor not directly addressed by the Health Beliefs Model: namely, our beliefs about how significant people and groups in our life want us to behave. You will probably agree that such beliefs can be very important in influencing health-related behaviors. For example, teenagers may smoke because of perceived peer pressure, and they may engage in unsafe sexual practices because they think their friends believe it's "not cool" to use a condom.

The theory of reasoned action has been called on in recent research to predict condom use among undergraduates (Boyd & Wandersman, 1991) and gay men's intentions to engage in risky and nonrisky sexual behaviors (Cochran, Mays, Ciarletta, Caruso, & Mallon, 1992; Fishbein et al., 1992). Studies using the theory of reasoned action can help measure the relative importance of attitudes and subjective norms in predicting health-related behaviors. For example, Fishbein and his colleagues (1992) found that gay men's attitudes were generally more important than their subjective norms in predicting their intentions to engage in different kinds of sexual behavior. However, subjective norms had a larger impact on gay men's sexual intentions in some cities (Seattle and Denver) than in others (Albany). This finding may have been due to the fact that Seattle and Denver have more active gay communities than Albany, and so gay men in those communities were more exposed to and influenced by other gay men's beliefs. Thus, it seems likely that safe-sex advertising campaigns that focus on normative social pressures (what other gay men are doing, and what the gay community expects individuals to do) would be more effective in cities like Seattle and Denver than in Albany.

USING SOCIAL PSYCHOLOGY TO MAKE PEOPLE HEALTHIER

You now know a lot about how various psychological factors—stress, social support, personality traits, beliefs, and attitudes—can influence people's health. Let's turn in conclusion to research that actively uses social psychological knowledge to improve health.

Helping People Take Control of Their Health

All hospitals should try to set up patient-to-patient discussions. Another way to be in touch with kids is through our newspaper at the hospital school. It's called *Rolling Sloan,* because the place where I have my treatments is called Memorial Sloan-Kettering. This is the third year they've had the paper. There's an advice column in the paper that used to be called "Dear Melissa." Melissa, the girl who initially wrote it, answered serious questions about hospital staff. Her answers were really good; they were very sensitive. When she finished her treatment, I took over the column. Now it's called "Dear Elizabeth." It's great!

Does Charlie Brown suffer from learned helplessness?

I just answered my first letter. The kid who wrote to me wanted to be alone in his room at the hospital, but people would always come in and want to talk to him. His dilemma was that he couldn't tell people that he didn't feel like talking to them without being rude. I gave him three things to try that I use. First, to keep his doors and curtains closed. That's a big deterrent. If that didn't work, I told him to try a "Do Not Disturb" sign. And if all else fails, there's the "heavy eyelid" method. That's where you start opening and closing your eyes as if you're drifting off, but act as though you're fighting to stay awake and listen. Since everyone there is aware of the way medications can make you feel, they'll usually leave you alone so you can have time to yourself.

—Elizabeth Bonwich (in Krementz, pp. 76–77)

Elizabeth Bonwich strove to gain control of her life, even in the difficult setting of a cancer ward. Taking control was an important step in her fight against cancer. Both Rotter's concept of locus of control and Kobasa's construct of hardiness view personal control as a personality characteristic. But control is also a function of situations—for example, it's easier for most people to be in control of their lives when at home than as a patient in a hospital.

Many studies suggest that controllable situations are less stressful than uncontrollable ones. Suls and Mullen (1981) asked subjects to note whether they perceived the stressful events listed in Holmes and Rahe's Schedule of Recent Life Experiences to be controllable or uncontrollable. The researchers found that life changes perceived to be uncontrollable were related to illness, whereas those perceived to be controllable were not. Stern, McCants, and Pettine (1982) reported similar results.

Experiments have shown that noxious stimuli, such as loud noises or electric shocks, are less stressful and easier to tolerate when subjects feel they can control them—for example, by pressing a button to stop them (Glass & Singer, 1972; Kanfer & Seider, 1973; Sherrod, Hage, Halpern, & Moore, 1977). Furthermore, subjects can work better in the presence of unpleasant stimuli when they think they can control their occurrence (Glass & Singer, 1972). Interestingly, in such experiments subjects often do not press the button to terminate the stressful stimulus (usually because the experimenter asks them to try to tolerate the stimulus as much as they can), but the mere knowledge that they *could* "turn off" the unpleasant noise or shocks seems to reduce anxiety and distress.

Research on the stressful effects of crowding also suggests the importance of perceived control. Many studies show that crowding is less stressful when people can exercise some control over it (Baron & Rodin, 1978; Rodin & Baum, 1978; Sherrod, 1974). For example, college students who were randomly assigned to live in dorm rooms on long, crowded corridors and who had to share facilities with many other students were found to be more socially detached, apathetic, and unassertive than students assigned to live in less crowded suites on shorter corridors (Baum & Valins, 1977; see Chapter 15 for additional research on crowding). Being with other people can be unpleasant if you have no control over when and where you interact with them. Patients in a hospital ward clearly know this from personal experience.

People who feel they have no control over important events in their lives may show a maladaptive style of behavior termed *learned helplessness* (Abramson, Garbner, & Seligman, 1980; Seligman, 1975). Martin Seligman (1975) first observed learned helplessness in dogs he trained to jump over a hurdle from one side of a box to the other to avoid painful shocks. In these experiments, an audible tone sounded, and several seconds later, a shock was delivered to the dog's feet through an electric grid on the floor of the box. Dogs readily learned to jump the hurdle to escape such shocks. Indeed, after a number of learning trials, dogs would jump as soon as they heard the signaling tone and thereby entirely avoid receiving shocks.

Some of the dogs in Seligman's experiment, however, had previously been exposed to unavoidable shocks. They had been restrained in a harness, and every time they heard the tone, they received a shock from which they could not escape. Later, when they were unrestrained, these dogs did not learn to jump the hurdle to escape from shocks. Instead, they crouched in their boxes, whining and yelping, without even trying to escape. In essence, the dogs had learned to be helpless.

Learned helplessness applies to people as well as to dogs. In one experiment, Hiroto and Seligman (1975) found that students exposed to uncontrollable noise later failed to discover that they could control the noise by moving a switch in their experimental apparatus. In contrast, students who had been exposed earlier either to no noise or to controllable noise quickly discovered how to control the noise.

Human beings, unlike dogs, reinforce their helplessness with maladaptive thoughts. Abramson, Garbner, and Seligman (1980) described learned helplessness in humans in attributional terms. When people are exposed to uncontrollable aversive events, they develop maladaptive styles of attribution that lead them to generalize their helplessness and attribute it to internal traits. Helpless people tend to consider their inability to control unpleasant circumstances to be due to stable internal factors ("I'm an incapable, incompetent person"). After repeatedly experiencing their inability to control events, helpless people may develop global negative attributions. As you might guess, learned helplessness provides one theoretical model for the development of depression.

Overcoming Helplessness in the Elderly

People living in "total institutions"—mental hospitals, prisons, the military—often experience greatly reduced personal control. Although we don't usually think of hospitals as "total institutions," they too deprive their patients of control (Schulz & Aderman, 1973; Taylor, 1979). When a person checks in to a hospital, his or her status is often reduced from that of a competent, mature adult to that of a passive child who strips upon command, lies in bed, and allows appropriate authorities to poke, prod, and puncture as they see fit. The patient eats whatever the hospital deigns to serve, according to the hospital's schedule. The patient must sleep and awaken according to an institutional regime and is sometimes roused from a deep sleep in order to be subjected to some arbitrary medical procedure. In other words, hospitals intentionally and unintentionally encourage helplessness by taking control away from the patient.

The confiscation of control is perhaps nowhere more apparent than in "homes" for the elderly. Nursing homes often treat their residents with the authoritarian control of medical settings in general. Because of negative stereotypes about the elderly, they often also assume that their clients are incapable of caring for themselves and making reasonable decisions. Thus, patients in nursing homes face a kind of double jeopardy. By assuming complete control, nursing homes frequently encourage the elderly to become helpless, hopeless, and mindless; the elderly person need not actively think, make decisions, or choose rewarding activities. Cognitive and emotional involvement in life fades away (Langer, 1981).

Ellen Langer and Judith Rodin (1976) demonstrated how small degrees of control can dramatically influence the well-being of the institutionalized elderly. Residents on two separate floors of a nursing home in Connecticut were selected to be subjects in an experiment measuring the effects of personal control and responsibility on health. The residents of the two floors were roughly equivalent in physical health and socioeconomic status before the experiment began. The experimental manipulation was relatively simple: The residents of one floor were assigned responsibility for everyday aspects of their lives, whereas the residents of the other floor were informed that the staff would take care of their needs.

Here is what the nursing home administrator told residents who were assigned responsibility:

> I brought you together today to give you some information about Arden House [the nursing home]. I was surprised to learn that many of you don't know about the things that are available to you and more important, that many of you don't realize the influence you have over your own lives here. Take a minute to think of the decisions you can and should be making. For example, you have the responsibility of caring for yourselves, of deciding whether or not you want to make this a home you can be proud of and happy in. You should be deciding how you want your room to be arranged—whether you want it to be as it is or whether you want the staff to help you rearrange the furniture. You should be deciding how you want to spend your time; for example, whether you want to be visiting your friends who live on this floor . . . whether you want to visit in your room or your friend's room, in the lounge, the dining room, etc., or whether you want to be watching television, listening to the radio, writing, reading, or planning social events. In other words, it's your life and you can make of it whatever you want.
>
> This brings me to another point. If you are unsatisfied with anything here, you have the influence to change it. It's your responsibility to make your complaints known, to tell us what you would like to change, to tell us what you would like.
> (pp. 193–194)

After the talk, each resident was given a present from the nursing home, a potted plant, and was informed that the plant was "yours to keep and take care of as you'd like."

Here is what residents on the other floor were told by the administrator:

> I brought you together today to give you some information about Arden House. I was surprised to learn that many of you don't know about the things that are available to you; that many of you don't realize all you're allowed to do here. Take a minute to think of all the options that we've provided you with in order for your life to be fuller and more interesting. For example, you're permitted to visit people on the other floors and to use the lounge on this floor for visiting as well as the dining room or your own rooms. We want your rooms to be as nice as they can be, and we've tried to make them that way for you. We want you to be happy here. We feel that it's our responsibility to make this a home you can be proud of and happy in, and we want to do all we can to help you.
>
> This brings me to another point. If you have any complaints or suggestions about anything, let [nurse's name] know what they are. Let us know how we can best help you. (p. 194)

These patients were also given plants, but they were told that "the nurses will water them and care for them for you."

The results of these instructions were dramatic. During the three weeks that followed the speeches, questionnaires indicated that residents who had been assigned personal responsibility were significantly happier and more active than the other group. Nurses' ratings corroborated these self-reports: Nurses noted that residents who had been assigned responsibility showed greater improvement in their rated well-being and activity. Furthermore, the residents assigned responsibility spent more time visiting each other and talking to staff members; they also participated more in scheduled activities, such as attending movies.

What kind of visits are most likely to make elderly people healthier and happier?

The most dramatic results of the assignment of responsibility were revealed in a follow-up study that assessed residents 18 months later (Rodin & Langer, 1977). Seven of the 47 residents (15%) assigned responsibility had died, whereas 13 of the 44 residents (30%) not assigned responsibility had died, a statistically significant difference. (The death rate for the entire nursing home during the same period was 25%.) Rodin and Langer (1977) noted that assigning personal responsibility to residents may have had a particularly large effect in this nursing home because the staff there was highly responsive to residents' concerns and requests. In other words, residents were reinforced for assuming responsibility for themselves. In nursing homes with less enlightened staffs, however, patients induced to exert control over their lives might learn helplessness and hopelessness instead. A number of nursing homes have responded to research like Langer and Rodin's by assigning more responsibilities to residents (Bowsher & Gerlach, 1990; E. Hall, 1984).

Rodin and Langer's study poses an interesting ethical question, which is highly relevant to health psychology in general: Once research has demonstrated that manipulating perceived control in nursing homes can affect residents' death rates, is it then ethically acceptable to conduct replications to further investigate variables that influence perceived control and health in nursing homes? How would you feel about conducting a study in which some of your subjects might be more likely to die than others because of your experimental manipulations? Few would deny that such research is socially important, but does this importance justify a procedure that literally can mean life or death for some subjects? (See Chapter 2 for a broader discussion of ethical issues in social psychology research.)

The ethical issues in such research are highlighted by another study conducted about the same time as Langer and Rodin's. Richard Schulz (1976) arranged for some Duke University students to individually visit over a period of two months 42 elderly people living in a local church-affiliated retirement home. Students visited according to one of three schedules: Some visited only when the elderly person wanted a visit, and the duration of the visit was determined by the elderly person; some students visited the elderly person at times specified by the student; and some would randomly drop in. Each elderly subject received the same total number of visits. Residents in these three conditions were compared with a group of residents who received no visits at all from students.

Clearly, the subjects had the most control over the visits in the first experimental condition and the least control in the third condition. The subjects were interviewed after the last visits and were rated on their degree of general activity and their physical health. In general, residents were happier and more active when they could control and predict the visits by students, and were less so when students just dropped in (see Figure 14.7). By the way, this research is relevant to our earlier discussion of social support: It suggests that social support may be most beneficial when it is predictable and controllable.

Unfortunately, a follow-up study showed that the residents who had originally most benefited from the students' visits (those in the controllable and predictable visit conditions) experienced the steepest decline in their well-being after the students' visits ceased; they also tended to experience higher mortality

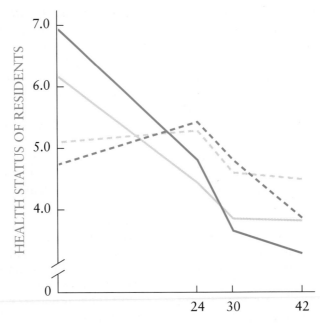

HEALTH STATUS OF RESIDENTS

TIME ELAPSED SINCE END OF VISITS (MONTHS)

——— Controllable visits   - - - No visits
——— Predictable visits   - - - Random drop-in visits

Student visits, particularly those that were controllable and predictable, improved the health status of these elderly people.

FIGURE 14.7 The effect of predictable and unpredictable student visits on the health status of retirement-home residents. *Source:* Adapted from Schulz and Hanusa (1978).

rates (Schulz & Hanusa, 1978; again, see Figure 14.7). Again, these results can be interpreted in terms of perceived control. Unlike subjects in Rodin and Langer's study, who could continue to exercise responsibility and control over their environment throughout the follow-up period, subjects in Schulz's study lost control when the students' visits ceased. Perhaps these elderly people felt heightened sadness and loneliness when they realized that the pleasant (and for some, predictable and controllable) companionship of their student visitors was over.

Studies like these show that relatively minor changes in the routines of homes for the elderly can have a large impact on the quality of residents' lives. In both noninstitutionalized and institutionalized settings, the elderly can benefit from possessing more control in their lives. Kastenbaum (1982) noted that many elderly people voluntarily enter institutions rather than stay at home because they fear being alone if an emergency occurs. Sadly, their anxiety about possibly losing control at home leads them to totally yield control in an institution. One procedure that allows the elderly to remain at home, maintain personal control, and avoid the fear of being alone in an emergency is to provide them with emergency alarms that can be used to signal for help 24 hours a day. Here again, a relatively simple intervention can have dramatic positive effects and can be cost-effective when compared with institutionalization.

The Age of Prevention

Because of my illness, I am seriously considering becoming a doctor. I love science. It's my favorite subject. I especially love dissections. Once, in school, before I got sick, I was working on a sheep heart with two other people, and they said, "You look like you're enjoying yourself. Ugh! You're touching it!" I've always enjoyed that sort of thing, so I'm thinking of becoming a surgeon. One of the requirements for a medical degree should be to have had a serious illness. It makes a big difference in the way you look at things.

—*Elizabeth Bonwich* (in Krementz, p. 76)

Physicians and biologists are not the only scientists who study health. Psychologists do too, as this chapter has documented.

The very success of modern medicine has paradoxically resulted in new medical problems that can be solved only through the joint efforts of psychology and medicine. The conquest of many infectious diseases, improved hygiene, and readily available medical care have led to a steady increase throughout this century in the life span of the average American.

The successes of modern medicine have guaranteed that psychology will play a large role in health care in the future. The Centers for Disease Control (1980) has estimated that in recent years about half of all deaths in the United States can be attributed to "chosen" behaviors: smoking, diet, alcohol and drug abuse, and stressful activities. As much as 80% of deaths from heart disease may be due to such "lifestyle" factors (Hamilton & Rose, 1982), and the two leading causes of fatal cancers are tobacco use (30%) and dietary habits (35%) (Doll & Peto, 1981). Cigarette smoking alone is responsible for about a third of all deaths occurring among middle-aged men (ages 35 to 59) in the United States (Fisher & Rost, 1986; U.S. Department of Health and Human Services, 1989). In other words, many serious illnesses and deaths could be avoided if people would simply change their behavior.

Unfortunately, "simply" isn't so simple. People smoke, eat fatty foods, drink alcoholic beverages, and engage in risky sexual practices because such activities are pleasurable. To practice preventive medicine, individuals must forgo (or at least modify) short-term pleasures in the pursuit of long-term health. Inducing people to engage in preventive behaviors is a complex matter that involves research on beliefs and attitudes (see Chapter 6 as well as earlier sections of this chapter), persuasion (Chapter 6), and social influences on behavior (Chapter 12). In other words, preventive medicine is very much in the domain of social psychology.

In the 1980s and '90s, the world faced a dramatic new health challenge: AIDS (acquired immune deficiency syndrome), a viral disease transmitted primarily through sexual contact and the sharing of contaminated needles during intravenous drug use. In a century marked by the eradication of many infectious diseases, AIDS serves as a reminder that modern medicine is not omnipotent and that health is a function of behavior as well as of medical technology. The battle against AIDS will depend on psychological as well as medical research (Morin, 1988), and social psychologists will contribute their particular expertise about beliefs and attitudes, persuasion, attraction, and social influences on behavior. A cure for AIDS will require new medical discoveries. The prevention of AIDS, however, is attainable with current knowledge—if medical science, social science, and society at large join together to meet the challenge.

SOCIAL PSYCHOLOGY AND HEALTH IN PERSPECTIVE

Our social life, mental life, and physical health are intertwined in many complex ways. This is perhaps the central message of research on social and psychological influences on health.

Research on stress demonstrates how psychological factors can lead to illness. Events are stressful when they are perceived to tax our psychological and physical resources and to endanger our well-being. Major life changes and everyday hassles are frequently perceived to be stressful, and the degree to which people experience such stresses is correlated with their levels of psychological and physical illness.

The impact of stress on health may sometimes be moderated by social support. Research on social support provides evidence that our social relationships— for example, the number and quality of our friendships and family ties—can influence our health. Sometimes this influence is direct—for example, people with good social networks of friends and family members show lower death rates than people with poorer levels of support, and sometimes the influence of social support interacts with other factors—for example, social support may protect against the development of illness in highly stressed people but not in nonstressed people.

A number of personality traits and behavioral styles have the power to influence our health-related behaviors and, ultimately, our health. Among these are locus of control (our perception of how much events in our life are determined by internal, controllable factors versus external, uncontrollable factors), hardiness (our feelings of control, commitment, and challenge in life), optimism (our general expectation of positive outcomes in life), and Type A behavior (the degree to which we show hostile, competitive, and rushed behaviors).

Research on the influence of social factors and personality on health suggests ways we can all lead healthier lives. The following are all reasonable inferences based on the research we have discussed: Stress reduction and stress management are healthy. Positive social support—good friendships, meaningful family ties, and membership in supportive social groups—is healthy. The perception of control, meaning, and joy in life is healthy. Reducing anger, unnecessary competitiveness, and time pressures is healthy.

Often, relatively trivial and low-cost interventions can increase patients' sense of control and social support in medical settings. Research on institutionalized elderly people shows that giving them minor degrees of control in their lives leads to significantly better health and lower mortality. Doctors foster patients' sense of control, support, and optimism when they provide thorough and understandable information and when they show concern and empathy for their patients.

A recurring theme in this chapter has been the concept of personal control. People are happier and healthier when they believe that they are in control of their lives. Perhaps this principle applies to social psychologists who study health as well. By studying social factors in health, social psychology researchers take an active role in discovering new ways to improve health. They hope to learn which personal characteristics and social settings promote health. Such knowledge can help psychologists modify people's behavior and design settings (hospitals, homes for the elderly) so that people can lead healthier lives. Ultimately, research on social and psychological factors in health can help people to take more control of their own health.

Personal control is what preventive medicine is all about. In the age of preventive medicine, social psychology will work in close partnership with medical science to help people behave in ways that keep many illnesses from developing in the first place.

Stress, Social Support, and Illness

Stress and Illness

There is a small but consistent relationship between reported stress and illness. Research studies measure stress by having people complete questionnaires that assess major life changes and everyday hassles.

Social Support and Health

Social support is the comfort, assistance, and/or information one receives from others. Social support may be tangible, informational, or emotional.

People integrated into social networks show significantly lower mortality rates than people who are socially isolated.

Informational and emotional support from others sometimes serves to buffer individuals against the negative effects of stress on health.

Social support is most effective when it matches our needs. Social support can contribute to two important kinds of coping: problem solving and emotional self-regulation.

Social Psychology in Everyday Life: Are Doctors a Source of Stress or Support?

Doctors can be a source of stress when they are abrupt, uninformative, cold, and uncaring. They can be supportive when they communicate thoroughly and in simple language, and when they are warm and empathic. Social psychology research offers advice on how doctors can acquire a better "bedside manner."

Personality, Health, and Illness

Feelings of Control

Rotter's Locus of Control Scale measures individuals' tendency to believe they have control over events in their lives versus the tendency to believe they are the victims of luck or external circumstances. The Health Locus of Control Scale assesses the degree to which people feel in control of their own health.

Locus-of-control measures are related to health behaviors in complex ways. When faced by serious illness, people with an internal locus of control often cope better than people with an external locus of control do.

Hardiness

Kobasa hypothesized that hardy individuals—those who possess a sense of personal control, commitment, and challenge in life—negotiate stress more successfully than nonhardy individuals do. A number of studies suggest that stress leads to less illness in hardy individuals than in nonhardy individuals. The control and commitment components contribute to such hardiness effects more than the challenge component.

Optimism

Optimistic individuals possess a general expectancy that successes and positive events will occur in their lives. Such people report less physical illness, are in fact healthier, and negotiate stress more adaptively than pessimistic individuals. Optimism and pessimism may be related to a broader syndrome of negative emotionality.

Social Psychology in Everyday Life: Personality and Heart Disease

Type A behavior, characterized by intense ambition, competitiveness, impatience, and hostility, is related to coronary heart disease. The Type A behavior pattern is best assessed by the Structured Interview. Programs have been developed that successfully get people to reduce Type A behaviors and so reduce their risk of heart attacks.

Beliefs, Attitudes, and Health

The Health Beliefs Model

The Health Beliefs Model focuses on four main kinds of beliefs that can influence when we take action to protect our health: beliefs about the costs of taking action, beliefs about the benefits or rewards of taking action, beliefs about our susceptibility to illness, and beliefs about the severity of illness. Many studies show that such beliefs do help predict when people act to protect their health.

Fishbein and Ajzen's Theory of Reasoned Action

The theory of reasoned action proposes that people's attitudes and subjective norms influence their intentions to engage in health-related behaviors. Attitudes refer to people's evaluation of the health-related behavior, and subjective norms refer to people's beliefs about how others think they should behave.

The theory of reasoned action has been used to understand factors that influence when undergraduates use condoms and when gay men engage in safe and unsafe sexual practices.

Using Social Psychology to Make People Healthier

Helping People Take Control of Their Health

In general, people perceive uncontrollable life changes to be more stressful than controllable changes. Furthermore, people find noxious stimuli less stressful and are able to work more effectively in their presence when they believe they can exert control over these stimuli.

When animals and people are repeatedly exposed to uncontrollable aversive events, they often show learned helplessness, a behavioral syndrome in which they do not even attempt to escape from aversive stimuli or exert control over their environment. Learned helplessness in humans is reinforced by maladaptive attributions whereby helpless individuals tend to explain negative events in terms of their own stable internal characteristics.

Overcoming Helplessness in the Elderly

Institutions such as hospitals and nursing homes take personal control away from their patients and frequently foster a sense of helplessness. Experiments show that giving the institutionalized elderly responsibility for and control of everyday aspects of their lives enhances their well-being and health.

The Age of Prevention

The triumphs of modern medicine guarantee that social psychology will play an important role in future medical practice and research. The successful practice of preventive medicine requires research on beliefs and attitudes, persuasion, attraction, and social influence.

KEY TERMS

Hardiness: Kobasa's personality construct that comprises three components—a sense of control, commitment, and challenge in life; Kobasa hypothesized that hardiness buffers stressed individuals against illness.

Health Beliefs Model: This model focuses on four main kinds of beliefs that can influence when we take action to protect our health: beliefs about the costs of taking action, beliefs about the benefits or rewards of taking action, beliefs about our susceptibility to illness, and beliefs about the severity of illness.

Health locus of control: The degree to which individuals feel in control of their health.

Learned helplessness: A behavioral syndrome, first described by Seligman, characterized by a failure to avoid aversive stimuli or to try to modify one's environment, that results from repeatedly experiencing uncontrollable aversive events; in humans it is bolstered by maladaptive attributions whereby the helpless individual explains negative events in terms of his or her stable internal traits.

Locus of control: Rotter's construct assessing the degree to which individuals believe they have control over events in their lives versus the degree to which they believe they are victims of luck or external circumstances.

Optimism: The degree to which individuals have a general expectation that successes and positive events will occur; optimism is related to reports of less illness, better health, and to more adaptive coping with stress.

Preventive medicine: Medical practices designed to modify individuals' behavior to head off illness rather than to treat it once it occurs.

Social support: The comfort, assistance, and/or information one receives from others; such support may be tangible, informational, or emotional.

Stress: Threatening external stimuli and the appraisal of such stimuli that lead to chronic arousal of the autonomic nervous system; major life changes and daily hassles are two common sources of stress.

Theory of reasoned action: Fishbein and Ajzen's model proposes that people's attitudes and subjective norms influence their intentions to engage in health-related behaviors. Attitudes refer to people's evaluation of the health-related behavior, and subjective norms refer to people's beliefs about how others think they should behave.

Type A behavior pattern: A style of behavior characterized by extreme ambition, competitiveness, impatience, and hostility; Type A behavior is associated with coronary heart disease.

SOCIAL PSYCHOLOGY AND THE ENVIRONMENT

What kind of planet will our children inherit? Will they have room to roam, air to breathe and food to eat? Will they ever see an eagle flying free or enjoy the solitude of a pristine mountain lake?

Those are among the larger questions on the agenda of an extraordinary meeting of more than 100 world leaders and 30,000 other participants in Rio de Janeiro. . . . Will the countries represented in Rio—notably the U.S.—show the courage and vision and leadership necessary to protect our planet for future generations? The answer is not certain, but there is some hope.

—*Time*, June 1, 1992

On June 3, 1992, representatives of 178 nations gathered for an Earth Summit to discuss a host of serious environmental problems facing our planet, including the thinning of the atmosphere's protective ozone layer, loss of arable land around the world, pollution of oceans and fresh water supplies, the wholesale destruction of tropical rain forests, and the accelerating extinction of thousands of plant and animal species. By the end of the Earth Summit, most participating

Emissions from an electric generating plant in the United States. One sign of our imperiled natural environment.

Al Gore speaks with the leader of the Yanonani Indian tribe during the 1991 Earth Summit in Brazil.

nations had signed a treaty to reduce industrial emissions into the atmosphere and a biological diversity pact to help protect endangered plants, animals, and their habitats.

One broad message that emerged from the Earth Summit was that we can no longer take our multifaceted environment for granted. Built environments such as cities have become extremely complex, and their byproducts (air and water pollution, solid waste) increasingly threaten our natural environments. To design more hospitable built environments (buildings, neighborhoods, cities) and to protect our natural environments (forests, deserts, oceans, rivers), we must understand how our various environments affect us and how we affect them in return. Understanding the intricate relationships between people and their environments is the goal of the relatively new field of *environmental psychology*.

Environmental psychology first developed as a subdiscipline of social psychology, and thus, these two fields have much in common. Both fields assume that our setting has a big impact on our behavior. Social psychology typically studies how *social settings* influence our behavior, whereas environmental psychology focuses relatively more on how *physical environments* influence our behavior. Both social and environmental psychology study how various environmental factors influence social behaviors—for example, how seating arrangements and building designs determine our interactions with others, and how heat, noise, and pollution affect our aggressiveness. And finally, both social and environmental psychology study how *environments composed of other people* influence our behavior—for example, do crowded settings lead us to become aggressive or socially withdrawn?

Our social motives, social behaviors, and social settings are often inextricably linked to our physical environment. Crowding, for example, is a function of both the people around us and the physical spaces we inhabit. Our social motives often determine the way we use physical space—we often maintain fixed distances from others, for example, to regulate our interactions with them, and we create territories (owned spaces such as rooms or study carrels) to defend ourselves against others and to maintain privacy. The seating arrangements we choose at home, work, and in public places are not just for rest and comfort—they also serve to bring us together or keep us apart from others. Even large-scale environments such as neighborhoods and cities are defined by social ties and attitudes as much as by their physical buildings and boundaries. All these examples show that social psychological factors influence our physical environments, and, conversely, our physical environments influence our states of mind and social behaviors.

This chapter will focus on several environmental questions that are linked to social psychology particularly closely: What effect does crowding (a feature of our social environment) have on our behavior? How do we structure our environments by establishing territories and regulating our personal space? How do aspects of our architectural environments (building design, neighborhoods, urban settings) affect our behavior, and how can we use architectural design to foster people's well-being? And finally, how can we use social psychology theory and research to help protect our threatened natural environment?

CROWDING

The United Nations Population Fund has just released new forecasts for population growth, which have been raised sharply. In 1980, the agency projected that the world's population, now at 5.4 billion, would stabilize at 10 billion people roughly 100 years from now, but the new estimates show it surpassing 11.6 billion by the year 2150.

And that prediction may be optimistic, based on the assumption that developing nations can reduce their birthrate . . .

—*Time,* June 1, 1992

We live in a world awash in more and more people, and the population continues to grow exponentially. To get a sense of what this means, consider the following: It took 2 million years for humanity to reach a population of 1 billion (around the year 1800) but only 130 additional years to reach 2 billion. Thirty years later, the population reached 3 billion; 15 years later, 4 billion; and 12 years later, 5 billion. The sixth billion will probably be added after only ten additional years, by the year 1997 (Miller, 1992).

And as the world's population grows relentlessly, it is becoming concentrated in relatively small areas of land in and around major cities. Only 2% of the world's people lived in metropolitan areas larger than 100,000 people in 1850; over 40% do today. By the year 2000, about 50% of the world's people will likely live in urban areas (Miller, 1992). In the United States, over three-quarters of the population already live in major metropolitan areas. One consequence of larger populations and urbanization is that more and more people are living in increasingly crowded settings. What effect does this crowding have on their behavior?

Crowding in Animals

Research on human crowding was stimulated by animal research. In one early study, biologist John Christian (1963; Christian & Davis, 1964) attempted to uncover the causes of a population crash that occurred in a herd of deer living on James Island, off the coast of Maryland in Chesapeake Bay. After many deer died during a particularly severe winter, Christian visited the island to examine dead animals and to investigate the cause of their deaths.

The results of Christian's work were surprising. He found no evidence of starvation (the dead deer had healthy coats of fur and adequate fat stores under their skin), nor was there any sign of infectious diseases. What, then, had caused so many deer to die? Observing abnormalities in the dead animals' endocrine systems (for example, enlarged adrenal glands), Christian argued that as the deer's population increased on James Island, they became more and more crowded. This crowding was stressful, and, according to Christian, the deer died of endocrine shock resulting from the stress.

Soon after Christian's research, other scientists conducted controlled experiments to better understand how crowding affects animal populations. In one such study, John Calhoun (1962) placed a small group of wild Norway rats in an outdoor pen that was a quarter of an acre in size. The rats bred freely in this environment that protected them from predators and provided them with all the food and water they needed.

At first, the rats' numbers increased dramatically, but after about two and a half years, their population stabilized at 150, and at no time in the study did the population exceed 200. Why did the population stabilize? When conditions became too crowded, Calhoun observed that the rats' behavior changed. Dangerous fighting broke out, particularly among male rats, and this fighting disrupted the maternal care that female rats provided to their pups.

In another set of studies, Calhoun (1962, 1970, 1973) housed male and female rats in smaller indoor pens that were divided into four compartments connected by ramps (see Figure 15.1). Food and water hoppers were located in the two "central" compartments—those compartments that were connected by ramps to both their neighboring compartments. At first, the rats' behavior was relatively normal. Male rats staked out territories and set up "harems" of female rats. The females reared pups within the protected territories established by their mates.

But as the population grew, not all males were able to establish territories. Particularly strong and dominant males took over the end compartments and made them their territories by driving off other males. The remaining population became concentrated in the central compartments containing the food and water hoppers. Calhoun coined the term *behavioral sink* to refer to the abnormal and disruptive behaviors that rats showed in these areas.

Some rats in the behavioral sink showed altered sexual habits. Rather than proceed through the courtship behaviors that rats typically engage in before mating, many males attempted to mate without preamble, and rather than mate only with estrous ("in heat") females, many males showed "pansexual" behavior—they attempted to mate with both estrous and nonestrous females, and even with other males. Some males became extremely aggressive and engaged in continual fighting—they were the "street toughs" and "juvenile delinquents" of the behavioral sink. Other males became passive, lethargic, and uninterested in sex. Calhoun termed them "the beautiful ones." Although they appeared healthy and well groomed, they did little but eat and sleep (A number of other animal studies suggest that overcrowding can lead to social withdrawal as well as to aggression and disordered reproductive behavior; see Anderson, Erwin, Flynn, Lewis, & Erwin, 1977.)

The maternal behavior of female rats was disrupted in the behavioral sink. Most mothers ceased to care for their pups adequately, and some even cannibalized their young. Not surprisingly, infant mortality rates were extremely high in crowded pens, generally over 80% and sometimes approaching 100%. In addition to showing disordered maternal behavior, female rats in the behavioral sink showed physiological evidence of stress (such as enlarged adrenal glands) and physical reproductive disorders (such as tumors of the reproductive system and resultant miscarriages).

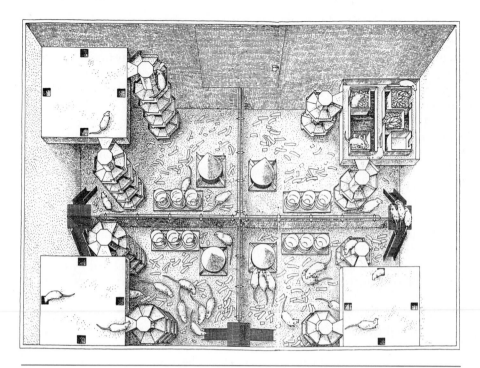

FIGURE 15.1 A rat pen divided into four compartments used in one of Calhoun's studies of crowding in rats. *Source:* Calhoun (1962).

In sum, Calhoun's research and other studies paint a rather dismal picture of the effects of extreme crowding on animal populations. When population density builds up beyond a certain point, animals (such as mice, rats, and monkeys) fight excessively, display abnormal sexual behavior, fail to take care of their young, and show physiological evidence of stress, such as elevated blood pressure and immune suppression, which makes animals more susceptible to infectious diseases (Dubos, 1965; Edwards & Dean, 1977; Henry & Stephens, 1977). As a result, population growth stops, and in some studies, the stresses of extreme population density even lead populations to crash dramatically, sometimes to the point of extinction.

Crowding in People

Do the findings for crowding in animals generalize to people? People living in urban areas often experience quite crowded conditions, as do people in environments such as dormitories and prisons. Are such people at risk for physical and behavioral disorders because of their crowded settings?

Before considering these intriguing questions, let's first look a little more closely at what we mean by "crowding." When studying people, it is important to

A crowded street in New York City. Social psychologists have studied the effects of crowding on work performance, affiliation, and aggression.

distinguish between *population density,* which can be objectively measured as the number of people per unit of space in some setting, and *crowding,* which is the negative subjective experience that sometimes results from high population density (Baum & Paulus, 1987; Stokols, 1972). Density is not identical to crowding. Two people may be guests at the same large party in a small apartment, for example, but their experience may not be the same. The population density is the same for both people; however, one may feel crowded and the other may not.

Density can be further broken down into two basic forms: social density and spatial density (Baum & Paulus, 1987; Baum & Valins, 1977; Paulus, 1980). *Social density* increases when more people occupy in a given space, and it decreases when fewer people occupy the same space. *Spatial density* increases when a given number of people occupy a smaller space, and it decreases when the same number of people occupy a larger space. So if more people arrive at the party, social density increases, but if everyone at the party moves to the larger apartment next door, social density stays the same but spatial density will decrease.

Increased social density does not always have the same effects on people as increased spatial density (Baum & Paulus, 1987). As social density increases, we have to interact with more and more people and structure interactions in larger and larger groups of people in the same area. As spatial density increases, however, we interact with the same number of people, but we are squashed into a smaller space per person. As a result, we may suffer from less privacy and more invasions of our personal space, and even experience physical constraint (as in tightly packed elevators or subway cars). These distinctions will be important in understanding some of the research that follows.

Is Crowding Related to Social Pathology?

Epidemiological studies (that is, investigations of the patterns of diseases and other disorders in large populations) have examined the correlation between population density and measures of social pathology in an attempt to answer the question: Is crowding unhealthy?

A number of studies do find a link between crowding and pathology. In neighborhoods of Honolulu, Hawaii, population density correlated with death rates, incidence of diseases such as tuberculosis, mental hospital admissions, juvenile delinquency, and imprisonment rates (Schmitt, 1966). And in Chicago, population density was linked to mortality rates, mental hospital admissions, and juvenile delinquency (Galle, Gove, & McPherson, 1972). Comparable findings come from studies of other cultures and countries (Booth & Welch, 1974; Levy & Herzog, 1974; Manton & Myers, 1977). An analysis of data collected from 65 countries found that as population density increased, the rates of death, murder, and infant mortality tended to increase and life expectancy tended to decrease (Booth & Welch, 1974).

While studies like those just described often show significant correlations between population density and various kinds of pathology, these correlations sometimes weaken or even disappear when other related variables are statistically controlled for (Baum & Paulus, 1987; Freedman, 1975; Freedman, Heshka, & Levy, 1975). In cities and metropolitan areas of the United States, for example, population density is confounded with such factors as socioeconomic status, educational achievement, and ethnicity. Perhaps people living in densely populated homes and neighborhoods show greater illness and higher crime rates because they tend to be poor and poorly educated, not because they are crowded. Although some studies do show a link between population density and crime even after controlling for factors such as income and education (for example, Booth & Welch, 1973; Schmitt, 1966), the overall evidence is inconsistent. Note that such inconsistencies *do not* mean that crowding is unrelated social pathology; rather, they mean that the cause–effect relationship between crowding and other factors is unclear.

Chronically Crowded Populations: College Students and Prisoners

Another kind of correlational research on crowding focuses on populations known to experience chronic, and sometimes extreme, crowding. Most of this research has focused on two "captive" populations: college students in dormitories and inmates in prisons (Baum & Paulus, 1987).

In one noted study, Andrew Baum and Stuart Valins (1977, 1979) looked at college students in three different kinds of dorms: One kind had long corridors of 20 double-occupancy rooms with shared bath and lounge facilities; a second kind had short corridors of 10 double-occupancy rooms with shared bath and lounge facilities; and a third kind consisted of suites of several double-occupancy rooms, with a bathroom and lounge for each suite. In each dormitory arrangement, a student shared his or her room with one other student, but hallways, bathrooms, and lounges were shared with varying numbers of other students.

Residents of the long-corridor dorms clearly experienced more crowding than residents of the short-corridor or suite dorms did. They complained more of having to endure unwanted contact with other students in their dorm, and they spent more time withdrawn from others in the relative solitude of their rooms. Interestingly, the tendency for long-corridor residents to withdraw from others was even apparent outside the dormitory. When students from long-corridor dorms participated in a laboratory experiment on bargaining, for example, they sat farther away from other students in a waiting room and engaged in less eye contact with them than residents of short-corridor or suite-style dorms did (Baum & Valins, 1977).

You might expect that over time, students in the long-corridor dorms would learn to adapt to their crowded environments. However, Baum and Valins found no evidence for this. In fact, students in long-corridor dorms remained withdrawn from others in laboratory settings throughout the academic year they were studied, and their tendency to "barricade" themselves in their rooms actually increased over time (Baum & Davis, 1980).

It may have occurred to you that long-corridor residents' experience of crowding was more determined by social density than by spatial density. After all, students in all three kinds of dorms had about the same square footage per student to live in, but they differed in the numbers of other residents they had to interact with on a day-to-day basis. What seemed particularly to bother students in long-corridor dorms was that they could not effectively regulate their social interactions with other students.

A recent study of 173 California college students in off-campus apartments provides additional evidence that residential crowding can lead to stress and withdrawal (Lepore, Evans, & Schneider, 1991). The less square footage per person in their apartments, the more psychological stress and anxiety students reported. Perhaps not surprisingly, students who felt they received support and understanding from their roommates tended to report less stress when in crowded apartments than those who did not. However, the phenomenon of good roommates reducing the stress produced by crowding disappeared over time. Why? One possibility is that crowded students withdrew from their roommates, with the sad result that they lost the psychological benefits that come from having supportive roommates. In other words, this study suggests that crowding placed a kind of double whammy on students: It was stressful in its own right, and it led them to withdraw from others and thereby lose social support that would have helped them cope with their stress.

College dorms and apartments, of course, do not come close to creating the extreme levels of crowding found in many prisons. Some prisons house up to 70 inmates in group dormitories containing less than 20 square feet of space per prisoner (Paulus, McCain, & Cox, 1981). You would have to live with about 50 people in a small, 1,000-square-foot house or apartment to achieve a comparable level of crowding. Of course, prisons vary in their degree of crowding and in the kinds of living arrangements they provide to their inmates (group dormitories, single and double cells), and such variations allow researchers to examine whether spatial and social density in prisons correlate with various problems: fights, homicides, health complaints, and mortality rates.

In a study of about 1,500 inmates housed in six federal prisons, two state prisons, and three county jails, Paul Paulus and his colleagues found that, in general, the more inmates had to interact with other inmates because of high social density, the more they complained of negative moods and illnesses (Paulus, 1988; Paulus, McCain, & Cox, 1978, 1981). Furthermore, in the various populations studied, higher prison population densities were associated with dramatically higher rates of suicides, deaths, and psychiatric commitments.

Both prison and dorm studies point to a number of similar conclusions (Baum & Paulus, 1987; Paulus, 1988): First, social density—the number of people you have to interact with in a given setting—is particularly salient in leading to the experience of crowding and to the social and behavioral pathologies that accompany it. Second, architectural arrangements can heighten or reduce the experience of crowding. Suite-style dorms in colleges or sleeping halls with partitions or privacy cubicles in prisons help alleviate the experience of crowding in densely populated settings. Finally, both dorm and prison studies find that people have trouble adapting to extreme levels of uncontrollable crowding. Indeed, people often come to feel worse in crowded settings over time, and they may eventually give up trying to regulate when and how they interact with other people, withdrawing even from supportive relationships.

Crowding in Children

Yet another kind of correlational research focuses on the effects of residential crowding on children. One study found that low-income children from Brooklyn and the Bronx who came from crowded homes tended to show more behavior problems in school and lower scores on reading achievement tests than children from less crowded homes (Saegert, 1982).

Another study found that African-American boys from a low-income housing project were more likely to show learned helplessness in a laboratory task when they came from crowded homes (Rodin, 1976; see Chapter 14 for a discussion of learned helplessness). Specifically, the boys pressed buttons on a machine to receive rewards—either candy or marbles. If a light on the machine was green, the boys got candy, and if it was red, they got marbles. Not surprisingly, the boys preferred candy to marbles, so they pressed the button more rapidly when the light was green. In their first training session, the boys had no control over the light—it simply alternated automatically between red and green every 30 seconds. In a later session, however, the boys could set the light to red or green by pressing a switch. The results: Boys from noncrowded homes were more likely to exercise control and choose the kind of reward they wanted, whereas boys from crowded homes showed a kind of passive fatalism—they were more likely to take whatever rewards they happened to get.

In a second laboratory demonstration of a link between crowding and learned helplessness, Rodin (1976) asked 190 seventh- and eighth-graders from New Haven, Connecticut, to solve a simple intellectual problem. Sometimes the problem was solvable, and sometimes it was unsolvable. Subjects then proceeded to a second solvable problem that was similar to the first. The results: When the first task was solvable, students from crowded and noncrowded homes performed equally well on the second task, but when the first task was unsolvable, students from crowded homes were more likely to perform poorly on the second task (see Figure 15.2). In essence, the students from crowded homes gave up more readily after their initial failure, again showing a kind of learned helplessness.

Experiments on the Effects of Crowding

Correlational studies on chronically crowded people give us important information about the negative feelings and behaviors that are linked to crowding in real-life settings. However, as we've noted many times before, to demonstrate cause–effect relationships social psychologists conduct experiments. Experiments on the effects of crowding have focused on three main questions: What impact does crowding have on people's stress levels and their health? What does crowding do to people's work performance? And how does crowding affect social behaviors such as helping, aggression, competitiveness, and so on?

Like correlational studies, experiments show that crowding often has physiological consequences. Crowded people show evidence of increased arousal. One experiment found that subjects who interacted in a crowded room showed higher blood pressure and heart rates than subjects interacting in a less crowded room (Evans, 1979). Crowding also leads to higher skin conductance and higher levels of stress-related hormones (Baum & Paulus, 1987; Fleming, Baum, & Weiss, 1987; Heshka & Pylypuk, 1975; Singer, Lundberg, & Frankenhaeuser, 1978). Perhaps it is because of their increased stress and arousal that people in extremely

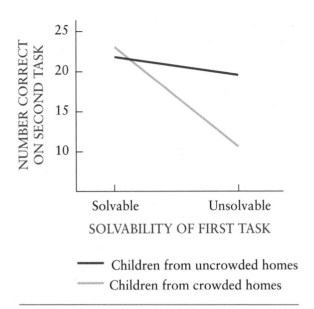

FIGURE 15.2 Performance of children
from crowded and noncrowded homes after
earlier experience with solvable or unsolvable
problems. *Source:* Adapted from Rodin (1976).

crowded real-life settings sometimes experience higher levels of illnesses and even
higher death rates (Cox, Paulus, & McCain, 1984; Epstein, 1982; McCain, Cox,
& Paulus, 1976).

Chapter 13 discussed research on social facilitation, which shows that the
mere presence of just one or a few other people is arousing and that this arousal
influences our work performance. Because crowding is arousing, it makes sense that
it too might influence the quality of our work. Does research support this
prediction? Early experiments found that crowding did not systematically reduce
the quality of people's work on simple clerical tasks (Freedman, Klevansky, &
Ehrlich, 1971; Stokols, Rull, Pinner, & Schopler, 1973). However, later research
(published after 1975) found that crowding can hurt task performance, particularly
when the tasks require complex thought and concentration (Evans, 1979; Klein &
Harris, 1979; Paulus, Annis, Seta, Schkade, & Matthews, 1976).

One experiment asked college students to repeatedly trace their hands
through a maze that was blocked from sight. Groups of either four or eight subjects
worked on the task, in either a large room (about 200 square feet) or a small room
(about 100 square feet). Both social and spatial density affected subjects'
performance: As the number of people went up and the amount of space per person
went down, subjects' error rates increased. Furthermore, studies indicate that
crowding can result in "aftereffects": People have shown less persistence at solving
problems and less tolerance for frustration in experimental tasks after having earlier been exposed to short-term crowding (Baum & Paulus, 1987; Sherrod, 1974).

You'll recall that Calhoun's research on rats focused on their social behaviors: fighting, sexual and maternal functioning, and social withdrawal. Crowding is a social phenomenon, and it seems logical to study the social consequences of crowding. Do experiments show that crowding leads to aggression in humans as well as in rats? The answer seems to be yes, with some qualifications (Aiello, Nicosia, & Thompson, 1979; Ginsburg, Pollman, Wauson, & Hope, 1977; Loo & Kennelly, 1979). Crowding is more likely to lead to aggression in men than in women (Freedman, Levy, Buchanan, & Price, 1972; Stokols et al., 1973) and in situations where people are competing for scarce resources (Rohe & Patterson, 1974). Stated another way, experiments show that crowding is particularly likely to increase aggression in people who already have a tendency to behave aggressively in the first place.

It's important to note that laboratory experiments on crowding and aggression typically create only short-term crowding, and they sometimes measure artificial forms of aggression. Recall that crowding among prison inmates (who suffer long-term, severe, and inescapable crowding) is related to dramatic increases in prisoners' levels of assaults on one another (which is a very realistic measure of aggression) (Cox et al., 1984; Ruback & Carr, 1984). Of course, many prisoners may have strong tendencies toward aggression in the first place. Given that lab experiments can never create crowding as intense and lasting as that found in many prisons, it is interesting that they still find evidence that crowding can increase aggressiveness under certain circumstances.

Like correlational studies, experiments often show that crowded people, when given an opportunity, withdraw from others, both nonverbally—for example, by engaging in less eye contact—and spatially—by moving farther away (Baum & Greenberg, 1975; Baum & Valins, 1977). Crowded people also withdraw emotionally—for example, they are less likely to discuss intimate topics with others (Sundstrom, 1975), and they simply interact less frequently with other people in crowded settings (Baum & Valins, 1977; Hutt & Vaizey, 1966).

Why Does Crowding Have Its Effects?

A number of explanations have been offered for why crowding affects people's work performance and social behavior (Baum & Paulus, 1987; Evans & Lepore, 1992). We've already touched on one explanation: People are frequently physiologically aroused in crowded settings, and such arousal may have negative effects on health and interfere with complex kinds of thought and performance (Evans, 1978; Paulus, 1980; see Chapter 13 for related research on arousal in groups and Chapter 14 for related research on stress and health). Another explanation proposes that crowding can lead to sensory overload: When crowded, we become overstimulated and, as a result, we seek either to mentally "shut down" or withdraw from the setting (Cohen, 1978; Milgram, 1970; Saegert, 1978). Still other theoretical models focus on the behavioral constraints and loss of control produced by crowding: When we live or work in crowded settings, we may not be able to do as we please or interact with people of our own choosing (Baron & Rodin, 1978; Montano & Adamopoulos, 1984; Schmidt & Keating, 1979; Sherrod & Cohen,

Do people lose control of their social interactions in crowded settings?

1979; see Chapter 14 for related research on personal control and health). This loss of control and the sense of helplessness it engenders can be highly stressful and debilitating.

Each of the explanations just listed has implications for designing densely populated settings that make people feel less crowded. The sensory overload and arousal perspective suggests that people will feel more crowded in densely populated settings full of extraneous stimulation than they will in equally dense but less stimulating environments. So, for example, it may be best to decorate crowded waiting rooms with muted colors and subdued artwork and to play calming background music. The loss-of-control perspective argues that crowding becomes more tolerable when is predictable and controllable. According to this point of view, workers can better tolerate crowded environments if they know ahead of time when they will be most crowded and if they believe they can escape from crowding (for example, by taking a work break) whenever they choose (Klein & Harris, 1979).

⌒ SPACE AND TERRITORY

Maurice Strong, secretary-general of the [Earth Summit] conference, wanted [the conference to produce] a short and inspirational document, something that could be hung in a child's bedroom. A Third World delegate responded that most of the children in his part of the world didn't have bedrooms.

—*Newsweek,* June 1, 1992

Can you imagine not having a bedroom of your own? Even if you had access to food, lavatory facilities, and a bed each night, wouldn't it be quite stressful not to have a private, permanent place to call your own? How would you feel if someone entered your bedroom without your permission? Would this upset you? Why?

The questions just posed deal, in one way or another, with the importance of spaces and places in our lives. Most of us feel that certain spaces belong to us, and many of us have special places that are centrally important to our lives, and indeed to our very sense of identity. For example, does your childhood home mean something special to you? Why or why not?

The topic of the previous section, crowding, is linked to the broader topics of how people use space, establish territories, and live and work in various built settings such as houses, offices, and classrooms. What role do personal spaces and physical places play in our social behavior? How do people regulate the space between themselves and others? When and why do people establish territories? And how do architectural arrangements influence our behaviors?

Personal Space

Recall the last time you were at a party talking to a new acquaintance. How far away did you stand while talking? Now recall the last time you sat at a cafeteria table to eat with a friend. Where did you sit—beside or across from her? How far away did you sit? Finally, recall the last time you visited a professor during office hours. How far away did you sit from your professor's desk? What determined your choices in each of these situations? Upon a little reflection, you will probably agree that you adjusted your distance from others, and perhaps your seating position as well, depending on your liking for them, your perception of their power and status, and even your assessment of how much they threatened you.

Personal space refers to a preferred distance or separation that people maintain between themselves and others. Some social scientists have stated that people act as if they have a bubble of space they carry around with them, from which they try to exclude most people except for close friends, lovers, or family members (Hall, 1966; Sommer, 1969). Others have argued that the notion of a "bubble" of personal space is misleading: Although we do maintain distance from others in our social relationships, this distance varies depending on a host of factors such as our personal traits, the setting we are in, and the nature of our relationship with others (Aiello, 1987; Patterson, 1975). There is probably some truth to each of these perspectives, as we shall see as we consider the factors that influence our use of personal space, such as our cultural background, gender, age, and the level of intimacy we wish to have with others.

MULTICULTURAL PERSPECTIVE

Personal Space in Different Cultures and Subcultures

Do people in different cultures use personal space differently? Anthropologist Edward Hall (1963, 1966) argued that the use of personal space constitutes a subtle form of nonverbal communication that varies across cultures.

According to Hall, Americans' personal space tends to be divided into four broad zones, which he labeled intimate distance, personal distance, social distance, and public distance (see Figure 15.3). In Hall's system, an American's bubble of personal space is defined by the boundary between intimate and personal distance, about 18 inches from the body. Unless they are engaging in intimate interactions with family members or romantic partners, Americans try to maintain this distance from other people, and when their 18-inch bubble is violated, they tend to feel anxious and move away from the person who is "not giving them their space."

Hall cited the United States and northern European countries such as England and Germany as examples of *noncontact cultures,* in which people maintain relatively large distances and bubbles of personal space. In contrast, Mediterranean, Arab, and Latin American countries are examples of *contact cultures,* in which people maintain smaller interaction distances and strive for high levels of sensory involvement with others.

Hall's observations have received support from many studies that measure the actual distances at which members of different cultural groups choose to interact (Aiello, 1987; Hayduk, 1983). Studies indicate that Hispanics, French people,

	Kind of Relationship	Possible Kinds of Communication and Interaction
Intimate Distance (0 to 1½ feet)	Romantic partner, close family member; social roles requiring contact (contact sports, physical combat)	Smell, touch, sexual contact, physical aggression; visual and vocal interaction—vision may be distorted
Personal distance (1.5 to 4 feet)	Friends, acquaintances	Primarily visual and vocal; voice at moderate volume; interactions may be personal and not strongly constrained by social roles
Social distance (4 to 12 feet)	Formal relations (business contacts, many teacher–student interactions)	Primarily visual and vocal; louder voice levels; communication is often consistent with social role
Public distance (more than 12 feet)	Public speaking and performances (Politician delivering a speech to a crowd, entertainer performing before an audience)	Primarily vocal; visual detail declines with distance; speakers may use amplification and exaggerated speech intonation and gestures to communicate

FIGURE 15.3 Hall's four-way division of Americans' personal space. *Source:* Adapted from Hall (1963).

Contact and noncontact cultures. Two men talking to one another in Spain . . .

. . . and in America.

Greeks, and Arabs interact at closer distances than Americans do (Little, 1968; 1968; Watson & Graves, 1966). And people from England, Switzerland, and Sweden also tend to maintain relatively large interaction distances (Sommer, 1969).

The use of personal space varies among subcultures within a country as well across countries. Within the United States, for example, whites, Hispanics, and African-Americans use space somewhat differently. Hispanic-Americans tend to interact at closer distances than Anglo-Americans do (Aiello, 1987; Ford & Graves, 1977; Thompson & Baxter, 1973). The interaction distances of African-Americans are more complex in comparison to white Americans, for they change with age. Young African-American children interact at closer distances than white children do, but by age 8 or 9 these differences tend to disappear (Aiello & Jones, 1971; Jones & Aiello, 1973; Severy, Forsyth, & Wagner, 1979), and by the time they are teenagers and young adults, African-Americans often stand farther apart than whites (Aiello & Jones, 1979; Tennis & Dabbs, 1976; Thompson & Baxter, 1973).

When African-Americans and whites interact with one another, they tend to maintain greater interpersonal distances than either African-Americans or whites in same-race interactions do (Booraem, Flowers, Bodner, & Satterfield, 1977; Hendricks & Bootzin, 1976; Rosegrant & McCroskey, 1975). This inter-race distancing tends to grow larger as children grow older—and, perhaps, grow warier of out-group members (Dennis & Powell, 1972).

What are we to make of these cultural and subcultural differences in the use of personal space? One possibility is that they reflect cultural differences in attitudes toward intimacy and autonomy in social relationships (see Chapter 3 for a related discussion of conceptions of the self across cultures). Perhaps people in noncontact cultures emphasize independence and autonomy relatively more than cooperation and intimacy, and the reverse is true in contact cultures. Group differences in personal space may also result from differences in perception of possible threat and aggression in personal relationships—generally we maintain greater distances when we feel more threatened.

Whatever their causes, cross-cultural differences in the use of personal space have the potential to lead to cross-cultural misunderstandings, and a working knowledge of these differences can lead to smoother relations between members of different groups. This was illustrated quite dramatically in a study that asked white university police officers to interview black students while using either the close interaction distance that is typically preferred by adult whites (4½ feet) or the larger distance preferred by adult blacks (6 feet). Afterward, the black students rated their perceptions of the interview and the officers, and their ratings clearly showed that they had much more positive feelings about the police when they used larger interaction distances (Garratt, Baxter, & Rozelle, 1981).

Personal Space and the Regulation of Intimacy

In his anthropological analysis, Edward Hall (1966) emphasized the ways different cultures use space to structure social relationships and to communicate. He noted that personal space not only communicates messages by itself (such as our degree of liking for others and our power and status), it also mediates other kinds of nonverbal communication. When we interact with another person at close distance, we can touch the person, smell the person, and even sexually interact, if we so choose. We can also poke, pinch, and punch the other person.

Consistent with Hall's emphasis on the rich possibilities for communication in physically close interactions, social psychologists have often argued that people regulate their distances from others to maintain some optimum level of intimacy or arousal (Aiello & Thompson, 1980; Argyle & Dean, 1965; Patterson, 1984). According to this perspective, we often prefer an in-between level of intimacy with others—not too much and not too little. Imagine, for example, you go out on a first date. If your date is too intimate with you in one way (too much eye contact and a lot of touching), perhaps you compensate by pulling back some other way—you move farther off. Personal space, then, is one of many behaviors we use to maintain our preferred level of intimacy with others. When our optimal level of intimacy is violated too much (through either too little or too much engagement), we may simply quit the relationship. Thus, if your new acquaintance is either too cool or too warm and touchy on the first date, there may not be a second date.

Psychological theories of how we use personal space and other nonverbal cues try to specify when we reciprocate what our partner does ("If he moves closer, so will I"), when we compensate for what our partner does ("If he moves closer, I'll look away"), and when we simply withdraw from the interaction altogether (Aiello, 1987). One simple formulation is that we reciprocate when we wish to increase intimacy, we compensate when we wish to maintain an optimal in-between level of intimacy, and finally, we withdraw when intimacy is either much higher or much lower than desired and so not easily adjusted to a more acceptable level. The link between intimacy and personal space may partly explain why men and women use personal space somewhat differently—the topic we turn to next.

Gender and Personal Space

On average, men maintain greater distance in their social interactions than women do, particularly when men are interacting with other men (Aiello, 1987). This sex difference begins at a fairly early age and is stable through the teen years (Aiello & Aiello, 1974; see Figure 15.4).

Personal space and gender. Boys on average interact at greater distances than girls.

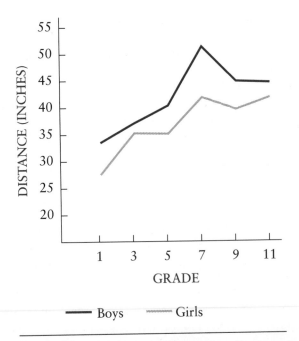

FIGURE 15.4 Mean interaction distances of male and female dyads at six grade levels. *Source:* Aiello and Aiello (1974).

Why do men and women use personal space differently? Perhaps it is because of their different attitudes toward intimacy and independence. In our society, women are often taught to value intimacy more than men are and men are taught to value independence relatively more than women are (see Chapter 8). Another factor leading men to maintain large distances, particularly in their relations with other men, is the stigma attached to male homosexuality in our society (Bell, Fisher, Baum, & Greene, 1990).

Men and women typically interact together at distances in between those maintained by male–male pairs and female–female pairs (Brady & Walker, 1978; Rosegrant & McCroskey, 1975). The one, and perhaps obvious, exception is when the man and woman have a close relationship (boyfriend–girlfriend, husband–wife); such couples tend to interact at very close distances (Baxter, 1970).

A relatively subtle finding is that men and women regulate distance differently in side-by-side and face-to-face seating arrangements. In side-by-side seating arrangements, women sit closer to people they like and farther from people they dislike, whereas men show no differences. In face-to-face seating arrangements, just the opposite is true: Men sit closer to people they like and farther from people they dislike, whereas women show no differences (Byrne, Baskett, & Hodges, 1971). These sex differences may be due to the fact that face-to-face seating is more frequently used in competitive situations and side-by-side seating in friendly relationships (Sommer, 1969). Perhaps men are more sensitive to the nuances of interpersonal distance in potentially competitive interactions, and women in affiliative interactions.

Men's and women's different sensitivity to face-to-face and side-by-side seating also appears in "spatial invasion" studies, which investigate people's reactions to being too closely approached by strangers. In one study, male and female confederates approached college students who were sitting alone at library tables and sat either right next to them or across the table from them (Fisher & Byrne, 1975). After working for a while, the intruders left, and the students were then asked to rate their feelings about the intrusion. Men were particularly upset when the intruder sat across from them, women when the invader sat beside them. These differing reactions were independent of the sex of the intruder.

It probably comes as no surprise to you that we often interact at closer distances with people we like (Sundstrom & Altman, 1976) and that we are more comfortable interacting at close distances with friends than with strangers (Ashton, Shaw, & Worsham, 1980). A bit less obvious is the finding that the relationship between personal space and liking is most often found in mixed-sex and female–female interactions, and less so in male–male interactions (Allgeier & Byrne, 1973; Edwards, 1972; Heshka & Nelson, 1972). Perhaps women more than men regulate their personal space depending on their liking for others, and the reason distance is related to liking in mixed-sex pairs is because of the female members of the pairs.

Most people seem willing to approach women more closely than men (Long, Selby, & Calhoun, 1980), and, in a related vein, men are perceived as more threatening than women when they approach too closely (Ahmed, 1979; Bleda & Bleda, 1978; Krail & Leventhal, 1976). This is probably related to the observation that powerful, high-status people, typically seem to "own" and control more space than less powerful, lower-status people. Men traditionally possess more power than women in most societies, and may show their power by taking up more space than women (Henley, 1977; Sommer, 1969; see Chapter 8). Also, people may maintain greater distance from men than from women because of the realistic assumption that men on average are more physically aggressive than women (see Chapters 8 and 10).

One clever study found that when men and women sit next to one another in airplanes, men used the common armrest between them three times as often as women did, and this difference remained even when men's larger average body size was taken into account (Hai, Khairullah, & Coulmas, 1982). On the ground, pedestrians typically give wider berth to approaching men than women (Dabbs & Stokes, 1975; Silveira, 1972), and when male and female pedestrians approach on the same path, women are much more likely to get out of men's way than vice versa (Silveira, 1972). In general, men seem to experience more upset than women when their space is invaded (Patterson, Mullens, & Romano, 1971), and this may be another reason why people often respect men's personal space more than women's.

Territory and Territoriality

The world is awash in special-interest catastrophes, but the environment is bigger than any of them, because no matter what your cause—Kurdish independence or national health care or the underclass—it won't matter if the environment collapses, taking the world's economy with it. Which is why for the first time in this century, a summit conference will convene . . . in Rio de Janeiro to discuss an issue other than war or the economy, and it will attract leaders of virtually every nation on earth. There are countries without armies, but none without land.

—*Newsweek,* June 1, 1992

We live in a world of territories—national territories, group territories, personal territories. One reason environmental problems present a unique challenge is that they transcend boundaries in a world that is still very much divided into territories. Smokestack emissions from one country produce acid rain in another, and carbon dioxide generated on one side of the world can contribute to climate change on the other. Clearly, to solve environmental problems—and indeed, to understand human relations in general—it is important to study the psychology of territory and territoriality.

Territory and Territoriality Defined

Personal space is something we carry around with us. A *territory,* on the other hand, is a fixed geographical or architectural location that is controlled or "owned" by a person or by a group of people. *Territoriality* refers to the thoughts and feelings people have about their territories and the behaviors they use to control them (Altman & Chemers 1980; Brown, 1987; Taylor & Brooks, 1980).

Irwin Altman (1975) describes three main kinds of human territories. *Primary territories* are places we feel we have complete control over, such as our homes and private offices. Generally we feel outraged and violated when intruders

Even the homeless establish territories. Is this an example of a primary, secondary, or public territory?

invade such primary territories. *Secondary territories* are shared territories toward which we feel some degree of ownership, some of the time, such as a clubhouse, seats in a classroom, the street in front of our home. For example, you may feel that a particular seat is "your seat" in social psychology class and become annoyed if a classmate sits in this seat. It is highly unlikely, however, that when a statistics class meets in the same room four hours later you will feel entitled to eject the student sitting in "your seat." Finally, *public territories* are areas we can temporarily occupy, but they are nonetheless communal spaces open to anyone on a first come, first served basis. We don't have any special claim on public territories. Examples are areas of a public beach, picnic tables in a public park, and seats at a movie or on a subway.

Subjectively, we feel we "own" primary territories most, secondary territories less so, and public territories least of all. Generally, people enter our primary territories by invitation only. They are freer to come and go in secondary and public territories. We are most likely to fight with someone who invades our primary territory, and less so with people who invade our secondary or public territories. We often personalize and decorate our primary territories, less so secondary territories, and least of all public territories.

Animal versus Human Territoriality

Both animals and people show territoriality. In the case of animals, territoriality is, to a large degree, instinctive (Lorenz, 1966; Wilson, 1975; Wynne-Edwards, 1962). Why do animals establish territories? One reason is to ensure reproduction. Male songbirds, for example, establish territories during the mating and nesting season. This may be adaptive in several ways. It enables birds to breed for strength—only "tough" birds get to reproduce and rear young, because males who successfully establish territories exclude sexual competitors and thus guarantee that their genes and not others' live on. The establishment of territories may also help ensure adequate food for offspring. When they establish territories, animals spread themselves over a range, and thereby avoid overconsumption of resources in limited areas (for example, over hunting of prey species).

Does territoriality serve the same purposes in people as in animals? To some degree, yes. Both people and animals sometimes establish territories to defend themselves against adversaries and to gain resources. Both sometimes fight over territory (although people seem more likely than most animals to *kill* over territory). Both animals and people sometimes mark their territories to keep out intruders. Wolves, for example, urinate on the ground to mark their territories; rabbits mark territories with fecal pellets; and people use a host of marking devices, including fences, signs, and decorations. As we shall see, both animals and people use their territories to enforce social order and to regulate aggression between individuals and groups. And both animals and people sometimes show similar psychological reactions related to their territories—for example, both feel stronger and behave more dominantly when on "home turf."

Despite all these similarities, however, there are some key differences between human and animal territoriality. Perhaps the most noteworthy is the role of cultural

*Territorial markers.
This student shows
that he "owns" this
space by spreading his
books, papers, and
clothing on the table.*

rules in human territoriality (Brown, 1987). Human attitudes toward territories often depend on the symbolic and cultural meanings of places and spaces. For example, how do you feel about your country? Your hometown? Your home? Why do you have strong feelings about these territories? Territoriality in animals seems to be related to basic biological needs (food, reproduction), whereas human territoriality is relatively more related to social motives that are often abstract and symbolic (status, group identity and solidarity, privacy). Animal territories are typically defined only by physical landmarks and chemical markings; human territories are defined by symbolic as well as physical markers and, at even a more abstract level, by complex cultural rules and legal systems. For example, how are the property lines of a house decided? And what defines the boundaries of a state or nation?

Territorial Marking and Defense

As just noted, to display control and ownership of physical places, we often mark our territories with physical objects. We mark primary territories—our rooms, apartments, houses—with personal possessions that have rich emotional and symbolic meaning: photographs of loved ones, valued artwork, souvenirs collected over a lifetime (Brown, 1987). We mark secondary and public territories with more utilitarian objects—for example, a sweater draped over a seat marks a place in a cafeteria, a pile of books marks a place at a library table, and a blanket or towel marks a place on the beach (Becker, 1973; Jason, Reichler, & Rucker, 1981). Touching is a subtle way we sometimes mark places and objects in public places. In restaurants people often touch a newly served plate of food to establish their "ownership," and in video arcades people touch machines to reserve them and keep other users away (Taylor & Brooks, 1980; Truscott, Parmelee, & Werner, 1977; Werner, Brown, & Damron, 1981).

Markers serve both to define territories and to warn others against invading them (Becker, 1973). When alternate space is available, people will usually avoid areas marked with physical objects. For example, when restaurant or cafeteria tables are marked (by the presence of articles of clothing, trays of uneaten food, or books), people will usually choose to sit elsewhere (Sommer, 1969). When space is at a premium, however, people sometimes ignore markers. Personal markers (clothing, notebooks) tend to repel territorial invasions more effectively than impersonal markers (for example, an open newspaper or a stack of books on a library table), and "male" markers (for example, male clothing and personal items) repel invasions more effectively than "female" markers (Haber, 1980; Shaffer & Sadowski, 1975).

Urban street gangs use a unique method of marking their territories: spray-painted graffiti, which typically includes the gang's name. A study of gang territories in Philadelphia showed that the more a gang "owned" a territory, the more frequently and densely it sprayed its graffiti on neighborhood walls (Ley & Cybriwsky, 1974). Furthermore, when rival gangs invaded one another's territory, they announced their intrusions by painting their names in the rival's territory. The invaded gang later retaliated by adding obscenities to the intruders' graffiti.

Territorial markings can make a significant difference in everyday life. For example, they can influence whether or not your house is burglarized. Brown and Altman (1983) studied the territorial markers displayed by over 300 burglarized homes and compared them with nonburglarized homes in the same neighborhoods. Burglarized homes had fewer territorial markers such as fences, walls, and hedges. Interestingly, they also tended to have fewer symbolic markers such as name and address signs.

Territory and Aggression

Individuals sometimes fight to defend their territories, and nations frequently go to war over territory. It is probably not as obvious to you that territories sometimes *reduce* aggression, particularly when they are firm, fixed, and agreed upon. In natural environments, territorial animals tend to fight more when their territories are disputed or in the process of being established (Eibl-Eibesfeldt, 1970; Lorenz, 1966), and studies of people in their natural environments show much the same phenomenon.

The study of Philadelphia street gangs mentioned earlier found that gangs fought with one another more when their territorial boundaries were unclear or unresolved, and less when boundaries were fixed and well established (Ley & Cybriwsky, 1974). Similarly, a study of delinquent boys in a rehabilitation center found that they tended to fight less when their territories were well established, but when new boys arrived in the center and disrupted the status quo, the boys' fighting increased as they worked out new stable territories (Sundstrom & Altman, 1974).

Well-defined territories can also help reduce conflict in highly crowded settings. One study found that when pairs of sailors divided the small rooms they shared into clear territories, they worked together more smoothly, reported less

National territories.
Iraq's invasion of
Kuwait triggered the
1991 Gulf War. This
conflict witnessed
an ominous new
development—
environmental
terrorism—when
Iraq set Kuwait's oil
fields on fire.

To prevent illegal
immigration, U.S.
Army reservists
construct a wall
between Southern
California and
Tijuana, Mexico.

stress, and were better able to tolerate their cramped situation (Altman & Haythorn, 1967; Altman, Taylor, & Wheeler, 1971).

Territory and Performance

Many animals fight off rivals more successfully when they are on their home turf. A chicken, for example, is more likely to peck other chickens when in her home cage, and songbirds will often chase larger birds from their territories and pursue intruders until they get too far from "home base."

People, too, often feel stronger on home ground. This *prior-residence effect* predicts that when on home territory, people will display dominance over visitors. For example, college students feel more relaxed and "in control" when they meet with other students in their own dorm rooms instead of in the other students' rooms (Edney, 1975). Furthermore, college students perform experimental tasks more successfully, negotiate with and persuade others more effectively, and dominate conversations more when in their own rooms and residences (Conroy & Sundstrom 1977; Harris & McAndrew, 1986; Martindale, 1971; Taylor & Lanni, 1981).

Athletes also tend to feel stronger on home territory—that is, they show a *home court advantage*. An analysis of the outcomes of hundreds of professional football, baseball, and hockey games in a single sports season showed that more wins occurred at home than on the road: The percent of total wins that took place at home ranged from 53% for baseball to 64% for hockey (Schwartz & Barsky, 1977). The home court advantage has also been demonstrated in individual sports such as wrestling (McAndrew, 1992). Why does the effect occur? Athletes probably feel more in control when on home territory. They also receive greater support from enthusiastic home crowds.

Does being at home ever work against sports teams? A number of studies show that during championship games, teams may actually show a home court *disadvantage* (Baumeister, 1985; Baumeister & Stenhilber, 1984; Heaton & Sigall, 1989). Perhaps when the pressure to win becomes too intense, the enthusiasm of a home crowd leads athletes to become so aroused that they "choke" under the strain.

☞ ARCHITECTURAL SPACE AND BUILT ENVIRONMENTS

Delegates expecting tropical bliss in Rio de Janeiro at [the] Earth Summit may be in for a shock. Copacabana Beach is still golden, and the boys and girls of Ipanema are still tall and tan. But the ocean is polluted, gangs of thieves roam the sidewalks and *favelas,* or shantytowns, scar the mountainsides near plush hotels.

—*U.S. News and World Report,* June 8, 1992

Like the residents of Rio de Janeiro, most of us live and work in built environments—homes, schools, factories, office buildings. Some of these environments—the plush hotels of Rio de Janeiro, for example—contribute to their residents' happiness and sense of well-being. Others—such as the *favelas* of Rio—do not.

The spaces inside buildings and the arrangement of buildings into larger patterns—neighborhoods, towns, and cities—channel our daily lives in many complex ways. The study of built environments is interesting in its own right, for it helps us understand how we are molded by these environments. In addition, it holds the promise of other important applications. Research on the psychological effects of architecture can help us design and build better offices, classrooms, apartments, and houses. Let's turn to research on the effects of both small-scale architectural environments such as seating arrangements in rooms and large-scale environments such as buildings and neighborhoods.

Space within Buildings

Room designs and furniture arrangements have the power to promote or hinder social interactions. *Sociopetal* environments bring people together and promote interaction by providing comfortable, face-to-face, flexible seating arrangements. In contrast, *sociofugal* environments keep people apart and discourage communication by forcing them into fixed seating arrangements that do not allow easy interaction (Osmond, 1959). An inviting dormitory lounge containing comfortable, movable furniture in small face-to-face clusters is a good example of a sociopetal environment. The seating in a typical church sanctuary or airport waiting area is more likely to be sociofugal—fixed, unmovable, and sometimes uncomfortable furniture arranged so that people are all in one direction or even pointing away from one another.

People often choose different kinds of seating arrangements for different kinds of personal interactions. For example, pairs of people typically choose to sit at two adjacent sides of a table or opposite each other when conversing. They are more likely to sit next to each other on the same side of the table when engaged in a cooperative task, but on opposite sides when competing, and pairs often choose to sit far apart (for example, diagonally across from each other) when working on independent tasks (Sommer, 1969; see Figure 15.5).

When groups interact around rectangular tables, the head of the table seems to be a position of particular strength, and people who sit in this position often talk more, influence others more, are more likely to be seen as leaders, and in fact become leaders (Leavitt, 1951; Strodtbeck & Hook, 1961; see Chapter 13 on situational factors in leadership). More subtly, a kind of gradient of power seems to flow from the head of the table—people who sit closer to the head of the table are judged to have more power and status than people who sit farther away (Malandro, Barker, & Barker, 1989). Don't you automatically assume, for example, that the advisors sitting next to the president at the table "have his ear" more than those sitting farther away?

It probably comes as no surprise to you that there is a relationship between seating patterns in classrooms and students' behavior. In one early study, Griffith (1921) analyzed some 20,000 grades earned by students who were alphabetically assigned seats in very large university lecture halls. He found that students sitting toward the center of the lecture halls tended to receive higher grades than students sitting toward the edges. Studies of smaller classrooms suggest that students sitting toward the front of the class tend to earn higher grades than students sitting farther back (Becker, Sommer, Bee, & Oxley, 1973; Brooks & Rebeta, 1991; Stires, 1980). This tendency is due in part to the fact that abler students often *choose* to sit closer to the front (MacPherson, 1984). It is also due in part to the fact that students sitting near the front of classes tend to interact more with teachers and pay greater attention to teachers and classroom activities (Adams & Biddle, 1970; Levine, O'Neal, Garwood, & McDonald, 1980; Montello, 1988). Perhaps teachers are better able to monitor students toward the front of the class and maintain eye contact with them, and this serves to keep students near the front more alert (Caproni, Levine, O'Neal, McDonald, & Garwood, 1977).

Neighborhoods and Cities

Like small-scale environments such as rooms and buildings, large-scale environments such as housing projects and neighborhoods can have a strong influence on our behavior.

Neighborhoods are regions of cities and towns that are partly defined by geographic boundaries and landmarks (city blocks, churches, rivers), partly by the ethnic, religious, and socioeconomic makeup of residents, and partly by intangible feelings and attitudes, such as a sense of attachment to an area (Holahan & Wandersman, 1987; Tuan, 1974). Neighborhoods vary in the amount of interaction that occurs among their residents, the degree to which residents possess a sense of community and attachment, and the degree to which they interact with outsiders (Warren, 1978). Some neighborhoods, such as the Hasidic Jewish areas of Brooklyn, New York, are extremely cohesive and insular (high interaction among residents, high sense of community, little interaction with outsiders). Other neighborhoods are disorganized almost to the point of disintegration—inner-city slums and Skid Rows, for example, which are characterized by little interaction among residents, little sense of community, and little interaction with the outside world (probably more because of exclusion than by choice).

Residents' satisfaction with their neighborhood is a function of factors such as population and building density, traffic and noise, privacy, degree of similarity with neighbors (for example, shared socioeconomic, ethnic, and educational backgrounds), and access to desired facilities such as parks, schools, hospitals, shopping (Taylor, 1982; Widgery, 1982; Zehner, 1972).

Not surprisingly, many people (at least in North America) aspire to live in a neighborhood of single detached homes (Thorne, Hall, & Munro-Clark, 1982), and city dwellers are often less content with their neighborhoods than suburban or small-town residents (Fischer, 1982). This is due in part to dissatisfactions relating to many of the factors listed above: People in city neighborhoods often must endure high density, traffic, and noise, and they suffer from reduced privacy and access to desired facilities such as parks, good schools, and hospitals. Furthermore, city residents often complain of higher prices, taxes, and crime in their neighborhoods,

PERCENTAGE OF INDIVIDUALS CHOOSING ONE OF SIX SEATING ARRANGEMENTS FOR FOUR KINDS OF SOCIAL INTERACTION				
Seating arrangement	Kind of Social Interaction			
	Conversing	Cooperating	Coacting (working on separate tasks)	Competing
1.	42	19	3	7
2.	46	25	32	41
3.	1	5	43	20
4.	0	0	3	5
5.	11	51	7	8
6.	0	0	13	18
Total	100	100	100	99

FIGURE 15.5 Seating preferences at rectangular tables. *Source:* Sommer (1969).

and they report feeling less safe than their suburban and small town counterparts (Cook, 1988; Fischer, 1982).

Environmental factors such as traffic can have a strong impact on the cohesiveness of urban neighborhoods and social contact among neighbors.

Cabini-Green public housing project in Chicago.

An urban neighborhood in South Boston.

An established residential neighborhood in Brookline, Massachusetts.

An affluent suburban neighborhood in Columbus, Ohio.

One study compared neighbors' interactions on three adjacent San Francisco streets that carried heavy, moderate, or light traffic (about 16,000, 9,000, or 2,000 vehicles per day) (Appleyard & Lintell, 1972). The level of traffic in a given neighborhood was strongly related to residents' reported stress and their degree of interaction with neighbors. For example, residents of the light-traffic neighborhood had about three times as many friends in the neighborhood as did residents of the high-traffic neighborhood. Residents of the high-traffic neighborhood tended to be more withdrawn than residents of the two other neighborhoods, and they made little use of the areas in front of their residences. Not surprisingly, they complained about the negative side effects of the heavy traffic they had to endure: noise, fumes, and dirt.

Another factor that can contribute to residents' dissatisfaction with city neighborhoods is living too close to a store. While people desire convenient access to shopping, they do not like having stores located nearby on their own block (Fleming et al., 1987). Urban residents who live too close to a store are subjected to crowding, traffic congestion, parking hassles, and uncontrollable exposure to numerous strangers. As a result, they experience stress and a perceived loss of control in their lives.

Social networks and the emotional support of neighbors can be as important as physical features in determining residents' satisfaction. People who live in poor and working-class neighborhoods often depend particularly strongly on their neighbors for social support (Fried, 1963; Gans, 1962; Jacobs, 1961; Suttles, 1968; see Chapter 14 for a discussion of social support and health). This support can take many forms: Neighbors lend money and food to one another, watch one another's children, keep an eye on others' residences and property, and exchange neighborhood gossip, including such valuable information as job opportunities. Many established neighborhoods have a rich but invisible social structure that is quite important for residents' happiness and even survival.

Sadly, some "urban renewal" projects have failed to take into account the social structure of neighborhoods. In the 1950s and 1960s, a much-studied urban renewal project in the West End of Boston forced about 10,000 low-income residents to relocate. Although the "renewed" neighborhoods were relatively poor economically, their residents (mostly Italian Americans) had a rich, cohesive network of friends and easy access to many social, religious, and cultural activities. The displaced people of the West End lost not only their physical homes but their friends, their beloved neighborhood, and, indeed, a way of life. After the West End was demolished, many former residents reported returning to their old neighborhoods and walking around with a sense of loss and grief (Fried, 1963); for some, their relocation was so shattering that they experienced deep depression and even physical illness.

Long-term and older residents often report more attachment to their homes and neighborhoods than do short-term, younger residents, and as a result, they are particularly likely to experience distress when forced to relocate (Kasarda & Janowitz, 1974; Norris-Baker & Scheidt, 1990). Sometimes the residents of redeveloped areas such as Boston's West End are left to fend for themselves after being forced from their homes; typically, they find new housing in areas just as poor as their former neighborhood, but without its social support. Sometimes residents relocated by "urban renewal" have the option of moving to public housing.

Early public housing projects are another example of how urban planners sometimes fail to adequately consider the social as well as the physical structure of neighborhoods. The Pruitt-Igoe project in St. Louis provides a notorious model for how *not* to design public housing. Built in 1954 to replace three-story inner-city slum buildings, Pruitt-Igoe consisted of 43 stark high-rise buildings designed to house some 12,000 low-income people. The individual apartments were reasonably pleasant, but the overall design of the complex proved to be a disaster (Yancey, 1971). The buildings contained many hidden isolated areas (stairwells, elevators, hallways), which became settings for vandalism, assaults, and drug dealing. The high-rise structure of the buildings prevented parents from keeping an eye on their children outdoors; they had two options: to keep their children locked in their apartments or to let them "run wild" on the street. Not surprisingly, violent juvenile gangs soon developed at Pruitt-Igoe.

The stark institutional design of Pruitt-Igoe tended to convey to residents the message that they were inferior, "low-class" people, and various cost-cutting measures encouraged the abuse of the facilities. For example, public toilets were not built on the first floors of buildings, and as a result, some residents and visitors relieved themselves in public spaces (elevators, hallways, or stairwells) rather than making the cumbersome and at times dangerous trip to their apartments.

The net result of these many design flaws was that Pruitt-Igoe—intended as a model of compassionate and enlightened public housing—quickly deteriorated into an urban nightmare. Trash was strewn everywhere, buildings smelled of garbage, urine, and feces, and residents feared to leave their apartments because of

The demolition of part of the Pruitt-Igoe housing project in St. Louis in 1972.

assaults, robberies, and rapes. In 1972, less than 20 years after its construction, Pruitt-Igoe was declared an utter failure; the project was abandoned and parts of it were dynamited.

SOCIAL
PSYCHOLOGY
IN EVERYDAY
LIFE

 ### How to Build Successful Public Housing

Social scientists have carefully analyzed failures like Pruitt-Igoe to develop guidelines for building more humane and successful housing projects (Mehrabian, 1976; Newman, 1972; Rohe & Burby, 1988). One recommendation is that buildings not be too high, for crime rates tend to soar in public housing projects when buildings exceed six stories (Newman, 1972).

Many urban planners have noted the importance of creating *defensible spaces* in and around buildings—that is, spaces that can be readily watched and that seem to belong to someone (Newman, 1972; Newman & Franck, 1982; Taylor, Gottfredson, & Brower, 1980, 1984). Established, cohesive neighborhoods often contain many defensible spaces. For example, stoops and sidewalks are places where neighbors congregate, and these public areas are easily watched from windows. In low-rise buildings, parents can keep an eye on their children as they play on the sidewalk. Sharing common space fosters social ties among neighbors; it deters crime and intruders because residents know who's who in their area and recognize strangers.

How can defensible space be built into housing projects? We've already noted one requirement: Buildings should not be too tall. Other design strategies can also help create defensible spaces. When possible, apartments or housing units should be clustered into small suites or groups rather than along long impersonal corridors. Residents in such small clusters are more likely to know one another and take joint responsibility to monitor their common space. Whenever possible, spaces—even those outside of buildings—should appear to belong to somebody. For example, lawns and park areas should be placed so they seem attached to small clusters of buildings or housing units. Massive projects like Pruitt-Igoe tended to have large, detached lawns and parks that were visually isolated from buildings—an open invitation to gangs and criminal activities.

A final recommendation is to eliminate secluded and isolated public areas—for example, parking lots, hallways, and elevators. Horizontal rather than high-rise construction is one sure way to avoid elevators. While hallways and stairways are often unavoidable in housing projects, they can be designed with large windows or with "open air" construction so that their spaces are accessible to public view and surveillance.

A number of studies indicate that defensible spaces in buildings and neighborhoods does help reduce crime (Newman, 1972, 1975; Perkins, Wandersman, Rich, & Taylor, 1993), and this effect seems to be strongest when residents have functioning social networks (Merry, 1981). Research on defensible space shows yet again that both psychological and physical factors are important in the design of successful buildings and neighborhoods.

An impersonal high-rise in the Cabrini-Green public housing project in Chicago.

Defensible space. A resident tends a garden in the Red Hook housing project in Brooklyn.

USING SOCIAL PSYCHOLOGY TO PROTECT THE NATURAL ENVIRONMENT

The broad issues are clear: the developed countries of the North have grown accustomed to life-styles that are consuming a disproportionate share of natural resources and generating the bulk of global pollution. Many of the developing countries of the South, for their part, are consuming irreplaceable global resources—eating the world's seed crop, as it were—to provide for their exploding populations. And both groups have as an object lesson the now bankrupt countries of the East bloc, whose singularly inefficient path to industrialization has produced some of the worst environmental disasters the world has ever seen.

—*Time*, June 1, 1992

We may be the first generation to do irreparable large-scale damage to our natural environment. This is hardly a proud legacy to leave to future generations. As we noted at the start of this chapter, the world currently faces a number of grave environmental problems, including overconsumption of natural resources, pollution of the earth's air, water, and land, and the wholesale destruction of many species and their natural habitats. These problems present the field of social psychology with a dramatic challenge. After all, overconsumption of natural resources, pollution, and destruction of natural habitats are all linked to our attitudes and social behaviors, topics that are at the heart of social psychology. Can social psychology use its special insights about the nature of attitudes and the causes of social behavior to help us behave in ways that protect rather than hurt the environment?

The Challenge of Changing Environmental Behavior

Given that many of us want to protect the environment, why is it so difficult to get us, en masse, to behave in environmentally responsible ways? As you already know from Chapter 6 ("Attitudes and Attitude Change"), people do not always behave consistently with their attitudes, and this seems to be especially true in the case of environmental attitudes and behaviors (Oskamp et al., 1991; Stern & Oskamp, 1987; Tracy & Oskamp, 1983–84). This lack of consistency may be due to the fact that people hold many separate environmental attitudes—attitudes toward recycling, toward driving cars, toward population control—and because these attitudes tend to be isolated from one another, they don't exert a strong effect on our overall environmental actions.

The weakness of the link between environmental attitudes and behavior may also be due to the fact that there are many other kinds of attitudes exerting a strong influence on our environmental behaviors. A study illustrating this point found that homeowners' summer energy use depended more on their attitudes toward comfort than on their attitudes toward conservation (Seligman et al., 1979). Another cause of the discrepancy between environmental attitudes and actions is powerful situational factors that influence our environmental behaviors—for example, peer pressures and group influences.

And yet another reason for the weak relationships among environmental beliefs, attitudes, and actions is that our environmental beliefs and attitudes are often ill defined, and they fail to address how our environmental actions affect us *as individuals*. To make this point more concrete, let's compare environment-related beliefs with health-related beliefs. You'll recall from Chapter 14 that the Health Beliefs Model has helped social psychologists understand what causes people to behave in ways to protect their health. According to this model, there are four main kinds of beliefs that influence our health-related actions: our beliefs about the costs of taking action, our beliefs about the benefits or rewards of taking action, our beliefs about our susceptibility to illness, and our beliefs about the severity of illness. Can a variant of this model—let's call it the "Environmental Beliefs Model"—help social psychologists understand what would cause people to behave in ways that protect the environment?

Let's use our proposed model to look at whether you will set your air conditioner's thermostat higher this summer to save electricity and thereby protect the environment. According to the Environmental Beliefs Model, how you set your thermostat will depend on your beliefs about the costs of taking action (you'll be hot and miserable), your beliefs about the benefits of taking action (you'll lower your electricity bill and help protect the environment), your beliefs about your susceptibility to environmental damage (what *will* happen to you if you consume a lot of electricity, and as a result, energy resources are depleted?) and the severity of the environmental damage (an accelerated "greenhouse effect," world climate change, floods and famine?)

This exercise illustrates a number of points: In deciding whether to engage in behaviors such as smoking or unsafe sexual practices, you are probably fairly clear about the benefits and costs of your actions, your susceptibility to relevant diseases, and their severity should you contract them. But in deciding whether to engage in pro-environment behaviors, you are probably much less certain about the long-term benefits of taking action, your susceptibility to negative outcomes, and their potential severity. The immediate *costs* of taking pro-environmental action are quite clear-cut, however: If you raise the setting on your thermostat this summer, you'll feel immediately hot and miserable. Thus, one reason it may be hard to get people to engage in pro-environmental actions is that they must face immediate costs and discomforts (heat in the summer, cold in the winter, the lack of convenience of driving a car to work) in the pursuit of long-term, broad, and somewhat uncertain goals (conserving resources, protecting the environment, reducing the "greenhouse effect").

You may have noticed another difference between the Health Beliefs Model and our proposed Environmental Beliefs Model: When you engage in health-related behaviors, the consequences of your behavior, whether positive or negative, affect you as an individual. If you smoke cigarettes, for example, you substantially increase your chances of developing lung cancer and heart disease, and if you quit smoking, you substantially reduce your chances. However, when you engage in anti- or pro-environment behaviors, the consequences of your actions often are spread out over many people: You destroy or protect the whole world's resources, you pollute or improve everyone's air, and so on. The consequences of pro- and anti-environment actions seem to be diluted compared with the consequences of many health-related behaviors.

Because the natural environment is a communal resource, there are powerful social psychological factors that influence how we treat it. In Chapter 13 ("Groups") we discussed the Commons Dilemma, which occurs when groups of people use a finite resource that has a fixed rate of replacement (such as forests, electricity, drinkable water). The Commons Dilemma creates a *social trap,* in which the rational pursuit of individual rewards (a nice wood fence, a comfortable home in the summer, a green lawn) sometimes leads to collective ruin (decimated forests, a runaway greenhouse effect, declining water tables). We noted in Chapter 13 that people seem to exploit communal resources more when they act as group members than when they act as individuals, and that larger groups seem to exploit communal resources more than smaller groups. Unfortunately, in real-life Commons Dilemmas (communal use of water, gasoline, and electricity, and the "harvesting" of trees, whales, and fish), people act as members of large groups (cities, companies, nations), and so may be particularly likely to exploit communal resources.

Groups can foster environmentally destructive actions in other ways as well. The anonymity of group settings can contribute to environmentally destructive behaviors when it leads people to feel that they are not personally responsible for their actions and to behave in ways that contradict their attitudes and moral standards (see the discussion of deindividuation in Chapter 13). One study found, for instance, that students eating in a college cafeteria as individuals or in groups of two littered significantly less than students in larger groups (Durdan, Reeder, & Hecht, 1985). Group settings can further contribute to environmentally destructive actions when they lead individuals to feel that they can't make a difference. For example, a person may refuse to recycle with the excuse, "What good will *my* individual recycling efforts do, given the tons and tons of solid waste that are produced in this country every day?"

Even when we wish to behave in environmentally constructive ways, we are tempted not to when we see others get away with their destructive actions. For example, you might say to yourself, "Why should I suffer in a hot house this summer to protect the environment, when everyone else is cool and comfortable?" Conversely, when you see others conserve, you are encouraged to conserve as well.

Our analysis of how beliefs, attitudes, and social settings influence environmental behavior leads to a number of recommendations: To motivate people to act in pro-environmental ways, we need to emphasize immediate and concrete costs and benefits rather than distant and somewhat vague environmental goals. When persuasive messages are used to change people's environmental beliefs, attitudes, and actions, they must focus on concrete outcomes and they must counter people's tendencies to deny individual responsibility for their environmental actions and to hide in the crowd. Because environmental attitudes are only weakly related to relevant behaviors, we must use various proven compliance techniques that rely on situational factors (see Chapter 12) if we are to get people to behave in more environmentally responsible ways.

Let's turn to a recent study in which social psychologists implemented just these kinds of recommendations to promote pro-environmental behavior.

SOCIAL PSYCHOLOGY IN EVERYDAY LIFE

Fostering Home Energy Conservation

Many utility companies provide free home energy audits. At the customer's request, an energy expert visits the customer's home and searches for ways energy is being wasted (for example, through lack of proper insulation and weather stripping). The auditor then makes concrete recommendations for improving energy conservation ("Put an insulating blanket around your water heater, set your hot-water temperature lower, fix the broken flue in your fireplace, and weather-strip your doors and caulk around your windows").

Home energy audits seem as though they should be quite effective. The auditor's instructions are delivered in face-to-face communication (which tends to be more persuasive than written or video messages; see Chapter 6), and the auditor's suggestions are clear and specific. Furthermore, many utility companies provide low-interest and even interest-free loans to people who want to implement these energy-conserving improvements. Despite all these facilitating factors, home energy audit programs are not terribly effective in practice: Only about 20% of the people who request audits end up implementing their

This man conserves energy by installing storm windows. What are the most effective ways to encourage people to make their homes more energy efficient?

recommendations (Aronson, 1990). This result is especially disappointing considering that customers *volunteer* to participate in home energy audits and such customers seem likely to hold pro-conservation attitudes to start with.

In an attempt to improve the effectiveness of its home energy audit program, the Pacific Gas and Electric Company of California sought advice from social psychologists Marti Gonzales, Elliot Aronson, and Mark Costanzo, who devised a three-pronged strategy for increasing homeowners' compliance with auditors' recommendations. The first strategy was to make the consequences of wasting energy more concrete and vivid to homeowners during their energy audits. The second was to frame the consequences of energy wastefulness in terms of immediate costs rather than rewards. And the third strategy was to commit homeowners to behavioral changes through a version of the foot-in-the-door technique (see Chapter 12). A special program was developed to train auditors in the use of these three strategies. Here's how it worked in practice:

Before their training, energy auditors tended to present information to homeowners in a rather dry and statistical fashion. For example, they might point at a door and say, "This needs to be weather-stripped. If you weather-stripped all your doors and caulked around your windows, you could reduce your winter heating bill by at least 15 percent." To make this presentation much more compelling and vivid (strategy #1), Gonzales, Aronson, and Costanzo trained auditors to deliver messages like the following:

> "Look at all the cracks around that door! It may not seem like much to you, but if you were to add up all the cracks around and under each of these doors, you'd have the equivalent of a hole the circumference of a basketball. Suppose someone poked a hole the size of a basketball in your living room wall. Think for a moment about all the heat that you would be *losing* from a hole that size—that's money out the window. You'd want to patch that hole in your wall, wouldn't you? That's exactly what weather stripping does. And that's why I recommend you install weather stripping. . . . And your attic totally lacks insulation. We professionals call that a 'naked' attic. It's as if your home is facing winter not just without an overcoat, but without any clothing at all. You wouldn't let your young kids run around outside in the wintertime without clothes on, would you? It's the same with your attic!" (Aronson, 1990, p. 128)

This pitch also implements the second strategy cited earlier: describing energy waste in terms of *costs* rather than rewards. In Chapter 5 we noted that people tend to perceive costs (losing $5) differently from rewards of equal magnitude (gaining $5). This is one explanation for framing effects, which occur when people's decisions are influenced by the ways decision outcomes are worded. In particular, people seem to respond more to the threat of losses than to the promise of equivalent gains when they make decisions.

Aware of this research, Gonzales, Aronson, and Costanzo instructed auditors to repeatedly emphasize concrete *costs* to homeowners: "Think for a moment of all the heat that you would be *losing* from a hole that size—that's money out the window." The auditors were instructed to compare energy leakage to "having a hole in your pocket," and they made observations like the following: "Until you get the flue fixed, your hard-earned cash is flying right up that chimney." Note that they did *not* say, "You'll *save* money if you follow our recommendation," or "You'll have a good feeling knowing that you're protecting the environment." Rather, they emphasized individual costs in vivid and concrete terms.

To implement their third strategy, gaining a behavioral commitment, Gonzales, Aronson, and Costanzo used a version of the foot-in-the-door technique (see Chapter 12). They instructed auditors to encourage homeowners to do a little "work" of their own during the audit. For example, auditors asked homeowners to climb ladders to inspect insulation, to get on their hands and knees and examine cracks under doors, and to touch their hot water heaters to feel the heat radiating away.

Did these relatively simple persuasion strategies work? Yes. When energy auditors used the three techniques just described, 61% of homeowners proceeded to follow up on auditors' recommendations, whereas only 39% did so when auditors used their usual techniques.

Toward a Healthier Environment

The Gonzales, Aronson, and Costanzo study shows that social psychology can help us devise techniques to get people to behave in more environmentally constructive ways. Still, such techniques can do only part of the job. Our earlier analysis of environmental attitudes and behaviors suggested that immediate and salient costs may often influence environmental behaviors more than attitudes do. If this is true, then economic policy is also a potent factor in influencing pro- and anti-environmental behaviors. For example, if the price of energy increases dramatically, energy consumption will undoubtedly decline.

Other kinds of public policy can also be quite powerful in encouraging pro-environmental behaviors. When cities institute recycling programs that supply residents with two kinds of trash cans—one for garbage and one for recycled materials—and *require* them to sort their waste, they provide strong incentives and cues for residents to recycle. When most of your neighbors recycle, then social pressures are likely to induce *you* to recycle as well. Social psychologists can help city officials design recycling programs that vividly portray the costs of our profligate wastefulness and that behaviorally commit people to recycle, but city officials must establish the program in the first place. Thus, to be effective, social psychologists must work in partnership with policymakers to design programs that help all of us to protect our threatened natural environment.

SOCIAL PSYCHOLOGY AND THE ENVIRONMENT IN PERSPECTIVE

Social psychology and environmental psychology share a major assumption: Our setting has a big impact on our behavior. Social psychologists typically study how the social setting influences our behavior, whereas environmental psychologists focus more on the physical setting. Environmental factors such as seating arrangements and building designs can have a dramatic impact on people's interactions with one another. Social psychologists and environmental psychologists also share an interest in environments composed of other people—for example, crowded settings.

One overriding message of this chapter is that our social environment and behaviors are often inextricably linked with our physical environment. For example, crowding is a function both of the people around us and the physical spaces we inhabit. We often bring social motives to our use of space and territories: We establish personal space to regulate our interactions with others, and we create territories to display our social identities, to defend ourselves against others and regulate aggression, and to maintain privacy. Our seating arrangements are not just for rest and comfort—they also serve to bring us together or keep us apart. Neighborhoods are defined by social ties and relationships as much as by their physical buildings and boundaries.

Social psychology research on the environment emphasizes applied topics, and thus it provides useful information to policymakers. Evidence on the negative effects of crowding can shape public policy on population growth and urbanization, and knowledge about factors that make crowding more and less tolerable can help guide the design of densely populated facilities (such as prisons). Social psychology research on urban renewal projects and public housing projects can help in the development of more humane projects in the future. And finally, research on beliefs and attitudes, group processes, and compliance techniques can help us induce people to behave in ways that protect rather than harm the natural environment.

In a world facing increasingly severe environmental problems, social psychology has an important role to play in studying the complex reciprocal links between our behavior and environments and in helping us to behave in environmentally constructive ways.

KEY POINTS

Crowding

Crowding in Animals

Research on animals shows that crowding can lead to stress, aggression, and disordered reproductive and maternal behaviors.

Crowding in People

Population density refers to the number of people per unit of space in a setting, whereas crowding refers to the negative subjective experience that sometimes results from high density. Social density increases as the number of people in a given space increases. Spatial density increases as the same number of people are placed in a smaller space.

Is Crowding Related to Social Pathology?   Correlational studies show that human crowding is linked to measures of pathology such as crime, delinquency, mental illness, and death rates. However, crowding in real-life settings is confounded with other variables such as poverty and low levels of education, and therefore the cause–effect link between crowding and other variables is unclear.

Chronically Crowded Populations: College Students and Prisoners   Crowded students in long-corridor dorms report more stress and show more social withdrawal than students in short-corridor or suite-style dorms.

Prison studies show that extreme crowding leads to illness complaints, heightened aggression, and higher mortality. In both dorm and prison studies, crowded people do not seem to adapt to crowding over time.

Crowding in Children   Residential crowding is correlated with behavioral and scholastic problems in children living in low-income housing. In laboratory studies, children from crowded residences show symptoms of learned helplessness.

Experiments on the Effects of Crowding   Experiments indicate that short-term crowding can lead to physiological arousal in people. Short-term crowding also interferes with performance, particularly of tasks that require complex thought, and leads to greater aggressiveness, particularly in people with a predisposition to aggressiveness.

Why Does Crowding Have Its Effects?   Crowding is arousing, and this may lead to stress and interfere with the performance of complex tasks. Crowding can produce sensory overload, which can lead to stress and cause people to withdraw from social interaction. Finally, crowding can lead to a loss of control, which is stressful.

Space and Territory

Personal Space

Personal space refers to a preferred space or distance that people maintain between themselves.

Multicultural Perspective: Personal Space in Different Cultures and Subcultures

Anthropologist Edward Hall argued that people in different cultures use personal space differently. Americans tend to divide personal space into four regions: intimate, personal, social, and public distance. The boundary between intimate and personal space occurs at about 18 inches from the body.

Noncontact cultures are those whose members tend to maintain large distances in social interactions, whereas in contact cultures, members maintain smaller distances.

In the United States, whites tend to interact at greater distances than Hispanics. African-Americans tend to interact closer than whites during childhood, but farther than whites in adulthood.

Personal Space and the Regulation of Intimacy   Edward Hall emphasized the use of space to structure social relations and to communicate feelings of intimacy and social status. Social psychologists have noted that distance is one of many nonverbal behaviors people use to regulate their level of arousal and intimacy in interactions with others.

Gender and Personal Space   Men tend to interact at greater distances than women, particularly when they are with other men. Women are more likely than men to vary distance from others as a function of liking, and are more likely to be sensitive to the meanings of distance in side-by-side seating. Men are more sensitive to distance in face-to-face seating. People tend to respect the personal space of men more than that of women.

Territory and Territoriality

Territory and Territoriality Defined   A territory is a fixed geographical or architectural location that is controlled or owned by a person. Territoriality refers to the thoughts and feelings people have about their territories and the behaviors they use to control them.

Primary territories are places we feel we have complete control over. Secondary territories are shared territories toward which we feel some degree of ownership, some of the time. Public territories are areas we can temporarily occupy, but they are communal areas open to anyone on a first come, first served basis.

Animal versus Human Territoriality   Territories can serve biological purposes such as ensuring reproduction and spreading animals out over a range. In humans, they also serve symbolic functions such as displaying status and identity and structuring social relationships.

Territorial Marking and Defense   Territorial markers are physical objects used to indicate the existence and boundaries of a territory and to warn away intruders. Personalized and "male" markers tend to be more effective than impersonal and "female" markers in reserving space.

Territory and Aggression   Both animals and people sometimes fight among themselves over territory. When territories are firmly established and agreed upon, they can help reduce aggression between individuals and groups.

Territory and Performance   Both animals and people show a prior-residence effect—that is, they are more dominant when on home turf. Athletic teams often show a home court advantage—they are more likely to win when at home than when on the road.

Architectural Space and Built Environments

Space within Buildings

Sociopetal environments foster interactions among people, whereas sociofugal environments inhibit such interactions. People choose different seating arrangements for competitive, cooperative, and independent interactions. In classrooms, seating positions can influence grades and classroom performance.

Neighborhoods and Cities

Neighborhoods are areas characterized by geographical landmarks, social composition, and attitudes of attachment. Satisfaction with neighborhoods is a function of many factors such as crowding, privacy, noise, facilities, and perceived safety. In urban neighborhoods, levels of traffic and the presence of nearby stores can have a large impact on neighborhood satisfaction and stress.

Social networks in neighborhoods are important to residents' happiness. The urban renewal of the West End of Boston in the 1950s and 1960s is an example of the unintended destruction of the social structure of a cohesive neighborhood.

The Pruitt-Igoe housing project in St. Louis is a notorious example of how the poor design of a physical environment can create a disastrous social environment.

Social Psychology in Everyday Life: How to Build Successful Public Housing

Successful housing projects make use of defensible space—space that can be readily watched and that seems to belong to someone. Defensible space is created by keeping buildings low, eliminating isolated and nonvisible public areas, and designing lawns and parks so they belong to small groups of housing units.

Using Social Psychology to Protect the Natural Environment

The Challenge of Changing Environmental Behavior

Environmental beliefs, attitudes, and behaviors are often only weakly interrelated. The natural environment is a communal resource that often suffers exploitation because of the Commons Dilemma. In addition, group settings sometimes foster environmentally destructive actions by leading individuals to feel less responsible for their actions and by creating the perception of inequitable sacrifice.

Social Psychology in Everyday Life: Fostering Home Energy Conservation

Home energy auditors can more successfully persuade customers to adopt energy-conserving recommendations when they vividly describe energy waste, emphasize costs rather than rewards, and behaviorally commit customers through application of the foot-in-the-door technique.

KEY TERMS

Behavioral sink: In Calhoun's research on rats, abnormal sexual and social behaviors showed by rats in crowded areas around food and water hoppers.

Contact cultures: According to Edward Hall, cultures in which people interact at close distance and strive for relatively high sensory involvement with one another.

Crowding: The negative subjective experience that sometimes results from being in a setting with high population density.

Defensible space: Space in and around buildings that is easily watched by residents and that appears to belong to someone.

Density: Number of people per unit of space in some setting.

Home court advantage: The tendency for athletes to show more wins at home than when on the road.

Noncontact cultures: According to Edward Hall, cultures in which people interact at large distances and maintain relatively low levels of sensory involvement with one another.

Personal space: The preferred distance or separation people maintain between themselves and others.

Primary territory: In Altman's classification of human territories, a territory that we feel we own and have complete control over.

Prior-residence effect: The tendency for animals and people to feel and act more dominantly when on home territory.

Public territory: In Altman's classification of human territories, a territory that we do not own but rather share with others on a first come, first served basis.

Secondary territory: In Altman's classification of human territories, a shared territory toward which we feel some degree of ownership, some of the time.

Social density: One kind of population density; it increases as more people occupy the same physical space.

Sociofugal environments: Room designs and seating arrangements that inhibit social interaction.

Sociopetal environments: Room designs and seating arrangements that encourage social interaction.

Spatial density: One kind of population density; it increases as the same number of people occupy smaller physical spaces.

Territoriality: Refers to people's thoughts and feelings about their territories and the behaviors they use to control them.

Territory: A fixed geographical or architectural location that is controlled or owned by a person or by a group of people.

SOCIAL PSYCHOLOGY AND THE LAW

Four Los Angeles police officers won acquittals Wednesday in their trial for the beating of black motorist Rodney G. King, igniting renewed outrage over a racially charged case that had triggered a national debate on police brutality.

Hours after the verdicts were announced, angry demonstrators torched buildings, looted stores and assaulted passersby as civic leaders pleaded for calm. Gov. Pete Wilson deployed the National Guard at the request of Mayor Tom Bradley.

Wilson's decision to send in the National Guard came after rioters touched off more than 150 fires, stormed police headquarters and hurled rocks at numerous downtown buildings. Sporadic gunfire flared in the streets, and heavy smoke rising from the fires forced the authorities to reroute landing patterns for aircraft at Los Angeles International Airport.

. . . It was the largest rioting to erupt in Los Angeles since the Watts riots of 1965.

—*Los Angeles Times*, April 30, 1992

Accused Los Angeles police officer Theodore Briseno testifies in court while the video of Rodney King's beating is shown behind him.

Most jury verdicts draw little notice, let alone public outcry. The Rodney King case was different, however. During the months preceding the trial, people throughout the world had repeatedly viewed the case's central piece of evidence: a videotape of Los Angeles police officers violently clubbing King. The trial had strong racial overtones: Rodney King was black; all the police officers who had beaten him were white; and the jury that decided whether the police were guilty of excessive force did not include a single black. When on April 29, 1992, the jury acquitted the four police officers of any wrongdoing against King, the city of Los Angeles exploded in riots that left 44 people dead, some 2,000 injured, and more than a billion dollars' worth of property destroyed.

Despite its devastating aftermath, the trial of the four officers shared many features with scores of other trials, and the questions raised by this incendiary trial raise questions about most other trials as well: Is the criminal justice system fair? Do the courts treat some people more harshly than others? How do juries arrive at their verdicts? Are juries sometimes biased? If so, why? What kinds of evidence are most and least likely to sway juries? Do juries sometimes make mistakes in evaluating evidence? How much impact do lawyers and their questions have on the outcomes of court cases? How much do judges' instructions influence jurors? After conducting hundreds of careful studies, social psychologists have begun to answer questions like these, and in the process, they have uncovered many reliable and, at times, surprising findings about numerous psychological factors that shape the workings of the legal system.

The trial of the Los Angeles policemen provides a real-life example that serves to illustrate such factors, and we will return to it many times in the course of this chapter. Media accounts of the trial generally focused on two main topics: the evidence presented in the trial (the famous videotape, the police officers' testimony, and the fact that Rodney King was not called to testify on his own behalf) and the characteristics of the jurors (nonblack, drawn from a conservative, mostly white suburb of Los Angeles). In our social psychological account of the legal system, we too will focus on questions of evidence and on the selection of juries and how they work. As we shall see, social psychologists have much to say about these topics, and they bring a unique perspective to the study of legal issues that complements the work of legal scholars, criminal justice experts, and law enforcement officials.

EVALUATING EVIDENCE

The jury spent "long and tedious hours" going over evidence in the case, looking at the videotape over and over, sometimes slowing it down so that it could be viewed frame by frame.

—*Los Angeles Times,* April 30, 1992

How many times have *you* seen the infamous videotape of Los Angeles police officers beating Rodney King? How long did it take you to conclude whether the officers were guilty of excessive force? Imagine you were a juror in the police officers' trial. How much weight would you have assigned to the evidence provided by the videotape, and how much to the officers' testimony? Would your decision have been affected by the fact that Rodney King did not testify in his own behalf? All of these questions address evidence and the ways we evaluate it.

The Power of Eyewitness Testimony

"In the main, in the most part," the juror said, "I feel that the officers were quite credible. When they were talking about what actually happened that night, you could see fear and you could see the stress of the whole situation. It had to be a very painful situation, very painful."

—a juror in the police officers' trial, quoted in the *Los Angeles Times,*
April 30, 1992

The Rodney King beating case would seem to be quite open-and-shut. After all, much of the incident was videotaped, and thus the jurors were, in a sense, eyewitnesses themselves to the beating. Videotapes can sometimes be ambiguous, however, and observed events require interpretation. Furthermore, the videotape did not capture the events that led up to the beating. There was powerful eyewitness testimony during the beating trial, and it came from the police officers, not from Rodney King. This testimony may have had a strong impact on the jurors' perceptions of what took place before and during the beating of Rodney King and, ultimately, on their verdicts.

Recent social psychology research delivers a consistent and powerful message: Eyewitness testimony is often extraordinarily convincing to jurors. A study by Elizabeth Loftus (1974) dramatically illustrates this point. Two groups of mock jurors (that is, experimental subjects simulating the role of jurors) had to decide the guilt of a defendant accused of robbing a grocery store and brutally killing the store owner and his granddaughter. The first group heard only circumstantial evidence and was told there were no eyewitnesses to the crime. The second group of jurors heard the same circumstantial evidence *and* eyewitness testimony— a grocery store clerk present during the crime identified the defendant as the robber and murderer. Do you think the eyewitness testimony tipped the balance in favor of a guilty verdict? You are right if you answered yes. Only 18% of the jurors who heard just the circumstantial evidence found the defendant guilty; in contrast, 76% of the jurors who heard the damning eyewitness testimony found him guilty.

While the power of eyewitness testimony in this study may not surprise you, another finding may: People are often swayed by eyewitness testimony even when it has been discredited. To demonstrate this, Loftus presented eyewitness testimony to a third group of mock jurors in her study, testimony that the defense attorney demolished, pointing out that the eyewitness was not wearing his glasses on the day of the crime, and his vision was so poor without glasses that he could not possibly have identified correctly the face of the robber from where he stood. Despite this convincing refutation of the eyewitness testimony, 68% of the jurors still voted to convict the defendant—almost the same number that had voted for conviction after hearing unimpeached testimony. A number of other studies support this finding that even "bad" eyewitness testimony can often be quite persuasive (Whitley, 1987). Eyewitness testimony seems to make a difference in actual as well as in simulated court cases: Research shows that cases that include eyewitness testimony are significantly more likely to result in convictions than cases lacking such evidence (Visher, 1987).

You may be saying to yourself at this point, "Well, certainly jurors don't believe *all* eyewitnesses equally." As we shall see, this is true. But can jurors distinguish "good" from "bad" eyewitnesses, and accurate from inaccurate testimony? Not very well, most studies say. In a particularly realistic experiment, Wells, Lindsay, and Ferguson (1979) staged a "crime" in full view of small groups of students waiting in a room: A woman entered, stole a calculator in plain sight of the onlookers, and then left. The student witnesses were later asked to describe the thief and identify her from a photo lineup, and mock jurors listened to the witnesses' testimony and watched as each witness was cross-examined. Were the jurors swayed by the eyewitness testimony? In general, they believed the eyewitnesses' identifications about 80% of the time—and this was true regardless of whether or not the witness had actually made a correct identification! Studies like this suggest that we often tend to believe eyewitness accounts more than we should.

What Makes an Eyewitness Credible?

There are a number of factors that can influence how much we believe eyewitness testimony. Three factors supported by considerable research are the degree of confidence shown by the eyewitness, the speed and detail of eyewitness testimony, and the eyewitness's age.

Confidence

In general, people believe eyewitnesses who say they are confident and who appear to be confident. One experiment that demonstrated this effect presented a videotaped reenactment of a real trial to 300 undergraduates serving as mock jurors (Cutler, Penrod, & Stuve, 1988). The defendant was accused of robbing a liquor store, and a key piece of evidence in the case was eyewitness testimony provided by the robbery victim, a store clerk. A number of factors that could plausibly affect the jurors' verdicts were varied. Among these were the degree of violence the robber employed, the degree to which the robber was disguised (by wearing or not wearing a knit hat), the length of time that passed before the witness identified the defendant in a lineup (two days versus two weeks), and the eyewitness's reported confidence (she testified she was either 80% or 100% confident). The only factor that had a significant influence on jurors' verdicts was the eyewitness's stated level of confidence. In a replication of this experiment, past and prospective Wisconsin jurors served as subjects rather than college students (Cutler, Penrod, & Dexter, 1990). The results were the same: Only eyewitness confidence was related to jurors' verdicts.

Perhaps jurors attend carefully to an eyewitness's confidence because it actually does provide valid information about the eyewitness's accuracy. The courts have often argued this to be so. Indeed, in the 1972 case of *Neil v. Biggers,* the United States Supreme Court explicitly stated that an eyewitness's expressed level of confidence should be a key factor that determines whether testimony is found to be credible (Kassin & Wrightsman, 1988).

Do social psychology studies support the courts here—is eyewitness confidence in fact a valid indicator of eyewitness accuracy? Not really. Many studies show that eyewitness confidence is at best weakly related to accuracy, and sometimes not at all (Bothwell, Deffenbacher, & Brigham, 1987; Wells & Murray, 1984; Williams, Loftus, & Deffenbacher, 1992). In more than 30 studies on this topic, the correlations between eyewitness confidence and accuracy rarely exceed .25. Thus, people believe eyewitness confidence is related to eyewitness accuracy much more than it actually is.

Speed and Detail of Answers

In some cases, eyewitnesses directly state how confident they feel, and in others, jurors must infer eyewitnesses' degree of confidence from their words and demeanor. How do jurors make these inferences? One cue they use is the speed with which witnesses answer questions or identify suspects. Apparently, many jurors assume that witnesses who respond quickly tend to be more accurate (Kassin, 1985; Smith, Kassin, & Ellsworth, 1989). Unfortunately, jurors are often wrong in this assumption, just as they are wrong in assuming that confidence strongly signals accuracy. Witnesses who provide quick answers are in fact no more accurate than slower responders (Smith et al., 1989). Apparently, some people simply look confident in general and give prompt, assured answers, even when they are wrong (Williams et al., 1992).

Another element that jurors use to infer eyewitnesses' accuracy is the amount of detail provided in the testimony. People often find testimony more credible when it contains lots of specific details (Bell & Loftus, 1988) and when it contains longer rather than shorter answers (Leippe, Manion, & Romanczyk, 1992). Unfortunately, here again the validity of such inferences is not well supported by research findings. Indeed, Wells and Leippe (1981) found some evidence for the opposite: Eyewitnesses who paid attention to and reported small details about the scene of a crime were *less* likely to give accurate testimony about another centrally important piece of information—the face of the criminal!

All in all, jurors frequently seem to use invalid cues when deciding whether to believe eyewitnesses. You may recall that in Chapter 4 we discussed research on how good people are at detecting when others are lying. The general answer was, not very. Those findings complement the ones about jurors: Not only are most people poor detectors of deception, they are not very good at discerning accuracy either.

Eyewitness Age

A third factor that sometimes enters into the credibility of an eyewitness is his or her age. This issue has become very important in recent years as the legal system has grappled with evaluating children's testimony in cases dealing with physical and sexual abuse (DeAngelis, 1989; *Harvard Law Review,* 1985). You might think that children would generally be seen as less credible eyewitnesses than adults. This is sometimes the case (Ross, Dunning, Toglia, & Ceci, 1990). Survey studies indicate that people have more doubts about the accuracy of children's memories than they do about adults'—for example, they think children are more suggestible than adults (Leippe, Brigham, Cousins, & Romanczyk, 1989).

Under certain circumstances, however, children's testimony is perceived to be quite believable. A number of studies indicate that people believe young children who testify that they have been sexually abused more than they believe adolescents and adults who make similar claims (Duggan et al., 1989; Goodman, Bottoms, Herscovici, & Shaver, 1989). Perhaps this is because most of us assume that young children lack the knowledge to fabricate such charges: If they describe the details of sexual abuse, it must be true. The evidence on other kinds of testimony is mixed; sometimes children are seen as less credible than adults, sometimes not. And sometimes children are seen as less capable of intentional deception than adults (Ceci & Bruck, 1993).

In a particularly realistic recent study, groups of young children (5 to 6 years old), older children (9 to 10 years old), and adults were videotaped as they answered questions about a man who had touched them on the arms, head, and face with a

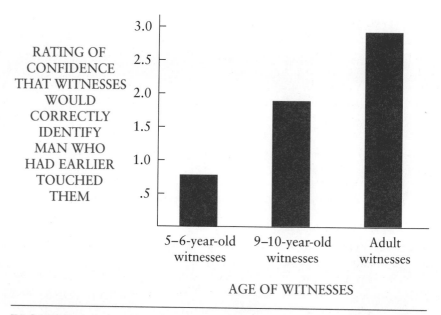

RATING OF
CONFIDENCE
THAT WITNESSES
WOULD
CORRECTLY
IDENTIFY
MAN WHO
HAD EARLIER
TOUCHED
THEM

AGE OF WITNESSES

FIGURE 16.1 Observers' confidence that witnesses of different ages would correctly identify a man who had earlier touched them. *Source:* Leippe, Manion, and Romanczyk (1992).

brushlike instrument earlier in the course of the experiment as part of a bogus skin-sensitivity test. Later, they were also videotaped as they attempted to identify in a photo spread the man who had earlier touched them (Leippe et al., 1992). Groups of college students and parents viewed the videotaped eyewitnesses and rated their accuracy and believability. In general, both college students and parents found 5- to 6-year-olds to be least credible, 9- to 10-year-olds more so, and adults most of all (see Figure 16.1).

Why did subjects perceive the children to be less accurate and credible? One important factor was that their testimony tended to be less coherent and consistent than the adults'. This, however, was probably more a function of the children's communication styles and poorer verbal skills than of their actual level of accuracy.

Eyewitness Testimony in the Rodney King Beating Trial

Let's return at this point to the trial of the Los Angeles police officers. Recall that jurors often accept eyewitness testimony at face value, even when it has been discredited in some cases. The most powerful eyewitness testimony in this trial was provided by the police officers. Furthermore, recall that social psychologists have identified a number of factors that lead jurors to find eyewitness testimony particularly credible. Eyewitnesses who express confidence, appear confident, provide many descriptive details, and are articulate adults are particularly likely to be believed. The police officers testifying in the beating case probably had all these factors working in their favor.

The power of eyewitness testimony. Los Angeles police officer Stacy Koon testifies at the Rodney King beating trial.

As we noted earlier, there was a "missing witness" in the officers' trial: the beating victim, Rodney King. Jurors interviewed after the trial stated that the prosecution's decision not to have King testify on his own behalf may have hurt their case. Perhaps jurors inferred that King had something to hide or that he was not able to justify his actions during the car chase that had preceded his beating by police.

Is it acceptable for jurors to draw inferences about a missing witness? Yes, according to the courts. Over a hundred years ago, in the 1893 case of *Graves* v. *United States*, the Supreme Court established an "empty chair" doctrine, which holds that lawyers may comment on a witness's absence during a trial and ask the jury to draw damaging inferences from it.

Can missing witnesses in fact influence juries' verdicts? The answer seems to be yes—at least in certain circumstances. One recent study found that jurors were particularly likely to draw negative inferences from a missing witness when the witness was central to the case, when the witness could have been readily called to testify, and when attorneys or judges pointed out the negative implications of the witness's absence (Webster, King, & Kassin, 1991). Thus, paradoxically, the absence as well as the presence of eyewitness testimony can have an impact on a jury's decision, and this may have been true in the case of Rodney King.

What Influences the Actual Accuracy of Eyewitnesses?

We have seen the power of eyewitness testimony to sway jurors, and we have identified several factors that determine people's belief in the accuracy of eyewitness testimony. What factors do in fact affect the accuracy of eyewitnesses? Psychological research has pointed to the importance of the degree of arousal eyewitnesses experience when observing events; the time lag between eyewitnesses' observations and their testimony; the questions used to elicit information from eyewitnesses; and the procedures used to obtain visual identifications of suspects, such as photo spreads and lineups. Research on these factors shows yet again that we should maintain healthy skepticism about the accuracy of eyewitness testimony.

Arousal and Eyewitness Accuracy

Laypeople, lawyers, and judges seem to believe that highly aroused people tend to remember events better (Deffenbacher, 1983). After all, don't strong emotions help "burn in" memories? Not always. Arousal may increase the accuracy of our memory up to a point, but high levels of arousal, like those that occur when people witness real crimes and experience extreme levels of fear and distress, can sometimes decrease the accuracy of eyewitnesses' recollections as well (Deffenbacher, 1983; Peters, 1988; Williams et al., 1992).

Two recent studies dramatically illustrate the power of arousing events to undermine the accuracy of memory. In the first, students observed a man either in a highly arousing situation (he entered their class and snatched a woman's purse and then ran out) or in a nonarousing situation (the man merely strolled in front of the class and then exited). In both conditions, the man was visible for seven seconds. Two days later, eyewitnesses were asked to identify the man in a police lineup. Aroused witnesses made correct identifications only 24% of the time, whereas nonaroused witnesses made correct identifications 49% of the time (Bothwell & Hosch, 1987, cited in Williams et al., 1992).

In another realistic study, patients at an immunization clinic were asked to identify in a photo spread the nurse who had given them their shots and a second medical worker who had taken their pulse two minutes after they had received their shots (Peters, 1988). The subjects were clearly more aroused when receiving their shots (average pulse rate of 88 beats per minute) than they were two minutes later (pulse of 71 beats per minute); their memory for the face of the nurse who delivered the shots was significantly worse (41% accurate identifications) than for the person who took their pulse two minutes later (66% accurate identifications). Interestingly, the subjects who showed the most elevated heart rate tended also to show the poorest memory for faces in this study.

The debilitating effect of arousal on memory helps explain the *weapons focus effect* documented in many studies: People often show poorer memory for faces and facts when viewing a weapon or when in the presence of a person carrying a weapon (Kramer, Buckhout, & Eugenio, 1990; Steblay, 1992). Clearly, when people see others pointing guns and brandishing knives, they often feel extremely frightened and aroused, and this arousal may interfere with memory.

A second explanation for the weapons focus effect holds that in the presence of weapons, people often direct much of their attention to the weapons, and as a result, they aren't as aware of other things—the criminal's face, for example (Loftus, Loftus, & Messo, 1987; Tooley, Brigham, Maass, & Bothwell, 1987). This hypothesis finds support in studies showing that witnesses' eyes tend to fixate on

The weapons focus effect. The presence of a weapon strongly captures our attention and thus weakens our memory for other facts.

weapons more than on other stimuli (Loftus et al., 1987). It goes without saying that real-life witnesses to actual crimes are often extremely aroused and they may also be in the presence of real weapons, sometimes pointed at them. Clearly, such conditions could undermine the accuracy of their memories.

Time and Eyewitness Accuracy

It probably comes as no surprise to you that some memories fade with the passage of time. After seeing a face, for example, people forget details quite rapidly—the decay of such memory is very fast at first and then becomes slower over time. Looking at the results of controlled studies, Deffenbacher (1989) estimated that a person's memory for a face typically weakens about 14% during the first five minutes after viewing, and an additional 14% after two days. Clearly, this suggests that eyewitnesses to crimes or accidents should be asked to make facial identifications soon after viewing an event—within a day or so, if possible—to achieve optimal accuracy.

Whereas the memory of an event tends to fade in relation to the amount of time that has passed *after* we witness the event, the memory tends to be more vivid in relation to the amount of time that passes *while* we witness the event. For example, just ten additional seconds spent viewing a face can lead to dramatically higher accuracy when later identifying the face (Shapiro & Penrod, 1986). Research on the impact of exposure time on later memory for facts and faces gives us yet another reason not to accept all eyewitness testimony as automatically true. In real-life crimes and accidents, eyewitnesses often view rapidly changing and complex events only briefly. Much later, they are asked to provide accurate accounts of these events in courts of law.

Misinformation Effects

Eyewitness memory can be distorted yet another way: intentionally, through the use of leading and misleading questions. Loftus and Palmer (1974) showed this in a classic experiment that had subjects watch a film in which two cars collided. Afterward, subjects answered questions about the accident, such as: How fast were the cars going when they collided? The question was worded differently for different groups of subjects. Some were asked how fast the cars were going when they *smashed* each other. Others were asked how fast the cars were going when they *collided with, bumped, hit,* or *contacted* each other. Did the wording make a difference? Yes. The subjects' mean estimate of the cars' speed was 40.8 miles per hour for the most violent wording *(smashed)* versus 30.8 miles per hour for the mildest wording *(contacted).*

In Loftus and Palmer's study, the form of the questions had long-term consequences as well. A week after viewing the filmed car accident, subjects were asked to answer additional questions—did they recall seeing broken glass at the scene of the accident? (In fact, there was no broken glass visible in the filmed accident.) About a third of the subjects who had earlier heard the word *smashed* remembered seeing glass—twice as many as who had earlier heard the word *contacted.* Apparently, the wording used in earlier questions altered subjects' memories!

In a related study, people were led via suggestive questioning to report seeing a barn that wasn't really there. Subjects viewed a film of a car accident that took place on a country road. Afterward, half the subjects were asked, "How fast was the sports car going when it passed the barn while traveling along the country road?" The remaining subjects were asked, "How fast was the sports car going while traveling along the country road?" In fact, there was no barn visible in the film. Later, subjects were asked whether they recalled seeing a barn. Seventeen percent of subjects who had heard the question that referred to a barn recalled seeing it, whereas only 3% of control subjects did (Loftus, 1975). Apparently, when questions about witnessed events incorporate plausible (but untrue) details, people often incorporate these details into their memories of events.

Such misinformation effects have been documented in many different studies (Loftus, 1992), and they are cause for concern in the courtroom because they suggest that police interrogators and lawyers can literally alter eyewitnesses' memories through the use of crafty questions. Misinformation effects are more likely to occur when questions introduce false information in subtle ways and when the passage of time has led the original memory to fade (Loftus, 1992). Children and the very elderly seem to be particularly susceptible to such effects (Ceci & Bruck, 1993; Loftus, Levidow, & Duensing, 1992).

Memory researchers have debated whether suggestive questions literally have the power to alter people's memories or whether, instead, they bias people's answers while the original memories remain intact (Loftus, 1992; McCloskey & Zaragoza, 1985; Smith & Ellsworth, 1987). The debate on this question continues. However, recent evidence suggests that, at least at times, leading or misleading information received by eyewitnesses after viewing events has the power to truly alter memories. For example, even when eyewitnesses are strongly warned that the information they receive after witnessing an event is wrong and that they should discount it and even when they are explicitly asked to recall only exactly what they originally witnessed, misleading post-event information still has the power to alter their memories (Lindsay, 1990).

Problems with Facial Identifications

There is one kind of eyewitness testimony that is crucially important in many legal settings: facial identifications. Eyewitnesses to crimes are often asked to identify suspects from police lineups or photo spreads, and they are often called to testify as sworn witnesses in the courtroom, to point at a defendant and say, "That is the man (or woman) who committed the crime!"

Research on facial identification provides additional evidence that eyewitness testimony can often be inaccurate. In a particularly dramatic study, a staged purse-snatching was videotaped and shown on an evening news program in New York City (Buckhout, 1974). Viewers were then asked to identify the culprit from a six-man lineup. Viewers were informed that the purse-snatcher might not be in the lineup, but in fact he was. Of the more than 2,000 viewers who called in their identifications, only 15% were correct—not much different from what would be expected if viewers were just guessing.

Unfortunately, misidentifications occur in real life as well as in mock TV crimes—sometimes with tragic consequences. Innocent people have been misidentified, apprehended, tried, and convicted simply because they physically resemble the actual criminal. In a case that almost defies imagination, Pittsburgh resident Bob Dillen was arrested 13 times in 1979 and 1980 and accused of committing repeated armed robberies (Kassin & Wrightsman, 1988). Dillen was tried five times solely on the basis of eyewitness evidence, and he was acquitted each time. Finally, during the 13th case, the actual robber was caught, and the authorities learned that Dillen had the singular misfortune to strongly resemble the robber. Dillen went through a personal hell because of facial misidentification, but he was lucky in one sense, for he was repeatedly acquitted.

Lenell Geter was not so lucky. The black engineer, then 26, was convicted in 1982 of the armed robbery of a Kentucky Fried Chicken restaurant based on the testimony of five restaurant employees who mistakenly identified him as the robber from a police lineup. Geter spent more than a year in a Texas prison before his case

Lenell Geter was mistakenly identified by eyewitnesses as a robber, and falsely convicted as a result.

was reopened and his innocence established, largely as a result of media stories and public outrage (Kassin & Wrightsman, 1988).

When are eyewitnesses most likely to misidentify people in lineups and photo spreads? One answer is: when a lineup "suspect" shares some distinctive feature with the witnessed criminal. Comedian Richard Pryor took this principle to comic extremes in a classic *Saturday Night Live* sketch in which he appeared in a police lineup that included a nun, a refrigerator, and a duck. The eyewitness viewing the lineup had earlier remarked that the criminal was a black man, and so, not surprisingly, he picked Pryor out of the lineup. The skit carries a serious message: The authorities who design lineups can stack the deck in favor of certain identifications by manipulating who the "foils," or comparison people, are.

How can lineups be made as fair as possible? Studies suggest that wrong identifications are less likely when "suspects" in lineups or photo spreads are presented to eyewitnesses sequentially rather than simultaneously (Cutler & Penrod, 1988; Lindsay & Wells, 1985; Wells, 1993). Forcing the eyewitness to consider the features of each suspect individually helps avoid the "Richard Pryor" effect of identifications made through gross contrasts with foils. Another way to boost correct identifications is to provide witnesses with neutral instructions that acknowledge the possibility that the criminal may not be in the lineup or photo spread (Cutler & Penrod, 1988). When foils are presented to witnesses making identifications, they should be selected to share features with the witness's *description* of the culprit (Luus & Wells, 1991). Note that the nun, the refrigerator, and the duck would be eliminated from the *Saturday Night Live* lineup using this principle, because they don't share characteristics with the culprit—they aren't men, for one thing!

Finally, when possible, it is useful to offer cues in addition to static poses in lineups. Posture, gait, and voice tone and quality are often important cues that help witnesses identify suspects, and thus if witnesses can view suspects as they move, gesture, and speak, their accuracy may be improved (Cutler & Penrod, 1988).

Many studies show that people tend to be better at facially identifying members of their own race and ethnic group than they are at identifying members of other groups (Brigham, 1986; Shapiro & Penrod, 1986). In one recent study, white, black, and Mexican-American confederates made purchases in 86 convenience stores in El Paso, Texas, and store clerks were later asked to identify these "customers" from photographs (Platz & Hosch, 1988). Clerks were significantly better able to identify customers who belonged to their own racial or ethnic group (see Figure 16.2). Similar findings come from many other studies; the difference in

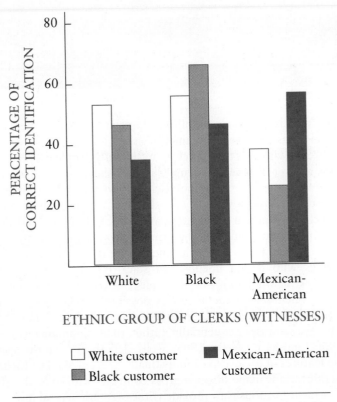

FIGURE 16.2 Accuracy of convenience store clerks identifying customers of various racial and ethnic groups. *Source:* Platz and Hosch (1988).

accuracy between same-race and other-race identifications can sometimes be quite large (Brigham, 1986; Shapiro & Penrod, 1986).

Bringing Eyewitness Research to the Witness Stand

Should social psychologists share their research findings about eyewitness testimony with judges and juries? Psychologists have served as "expert witnesses" in many trials (Williams et al., 1992). Often, their role is to caution jurors about the fallibility of eyewitness testimony and memory by presenting research findings like those you have been reading about in this chapter. (See Summary Table 16.1 below for a succinct review.)

SUMMARY TABLE 16.1 Factors That Influence the Credibility and Actual Accuracy of Eyewitnesses

Factors that Influence Eyewitness Credibility

Confidence. Confident eyewitnesses are judged to be more accurate, but in fact, the relationship between confidence and accuracy is weak.

Speed. Eyewitnesses who answer questions and make identifications quickly are judged to be more credible and accurate, but in fact, speed of response has little relation to accuracy.

Detail. Eyewitnesses who provide many incidental details are judged to be more accurate; however, memory for incidental details may actually be related to *poorer* memory for important facts.

Age. Children are often judged to be less credible witnesses than adults; an exception may be young children who describe details of sexual abuse.

Factors That Influence the Actual Accuracy of Eyewitness Testimony

Arousal. High levels of emotional arousal tend to interfere with observation and undermine subsequent memory.

Presence of weapons. The presence of weapons during an observed event tends to undermine the accuracy of observers' memory for the event.

Passage of time since witnessing event. Memory for events decays over time, quickly at first and then more slowly over time.

Exposure time. The longer a witness has to observe an event, the more accurate his or her memory for the event.

Misinformation effects. Misleading questions or information received after observing events can distort memory for events.

Lineup instructions and procedures. Lineup instructions and procedures can strongly influence the accuracy of "suspect" identification and the chances of misidentification.

Cross-racial and ethnic identification. People tend to be more accurate when facially identifying members of their own racial and ethnic group than when identifying members of other groups.

To determine whether research findings on eyewitness testimony are reliable enough to be cited in courts of law, Kassin, Ellsworth, and Smith (1989) surveyed 63 experts on eyewitness testimony and asked them how well established they believed various findings to be. The experts showed a great deal of consensus. More than 80% agreed that nine findings were strong enough to be presented as established facts in court cases (see Figure 16.3).

The findings in Figure 16.3 are quite reliable, but are they unexpected? This is an especially important question to answer because courts tend to allow expert testimony only when they decide that the experts provide information

	Eyewitness Experts	Laypeople
1. Wording of questions can affect eyewitness testimony.	97%	90%
2. Lineup instructions can affect the accuracy of witnesses' identification of suspects.	95%	68%
3. Eyewitnesses' memory and testimony can be changed by post-event information.	87%	75%
4. An eyewitnesses' confidence is *not* a good indication of his or her accuracy.	87%	49%
5. Preexisting attitudes and expectations can bias eyewitnesses' perception of and memory for events.	87%	89%
6. The less time a witness has to observe an event, the less he or she will remember it.	85%	37%
7. Eyewitnesses sometimes identify as a culprit someone they have seen in another setting.	85%	65%
8. Having an eyewitness identify a single suspect instead of using a full lineup increases the risk of misidentification.	83%	63%
9. The rate of memory loss for an event is greatest right after the event, and then levels off over time.	83%	41%

FIGURE 16.3 Percentage of eyewitness experts and laypeople who believe that findings on nine eyewitness topics are reliable enough to be presented in court. *Source:* Adapted from Kassin, Ellsworth, and Smith (1989); and Kassin and Barndollar (1992).

that goes beyond mere "common sense." Does psychological research on eyewitness testimony tell us more than our common sense already tells us? To answer this question, Kassin and Barndollar (1992) asked 79 laypeople—39 college students and 40 adults at a local shopping mall—to rate how much they believed in the same findings that had been rated by eyewitness experts earlier. The results? Laypeople and experts agreed on some points—for example, both believed quite strongly that high levels of stress can impair the accuracy of eyewitnesses. However, laypeople disagreed with experts on several other points. Compared with experts, for example, laypeople showed significantly less awareness of problems with lineup procedures, the effects of time on memory, and the weak link between eyewitness confidence and eyewitness accuracy (again, see Figure 16.3). Incidentally, of the 79 laypeople participating in this study, 34 were people who had actually been called for jury duty and 9 had actually served as jurors. If their beliefs were typical of those possessed by jurors in general, it seems safe to conclude that many psychological findings on eyewitness testimony are not merely common sense, and psychologists can provide a useful service by presenting their expert knowledge in the courtroom.

TRIAL BY JURY

[The jurors in the Rodney King beating trial] represented all corners of society—a cable splicer, a bank clerk, a retired real estate broker. A phone company technician, a computer analyst, a housekeeper. A retired naval aviator, a park ranger, a trash collector. A program manager, a retired mental health worker, a nurse.

—*Los Angeles Times,* April 30, 1992

The American criminal justice system is built on the right to a trial by jury. Actually, only about 8% of all criminal cases go before a jury. The remainder are either dismissed or settled through plea bargaining (Green, 1985; Hans, 1992; Hans & Vidmar, 1986). Despite their relative infrequency, jury trials hold a special fascination for both laypeople and social scientists. Numerous TV shows, movies, and novels—as well as a huge amount of scientific research—have delved into the workings of juries.

Why? There are several reasons. Jury trials are dramatic by their very nature: They focus on the full range of human passions and offer a spectacle of verbal combat and moral conflict. From a legal perspective, even cases that do not go before a jury are strongly influenced by the *possibility* of a jury trial and by previous juries' decisions. For example, lawyers' plea-bargaining strategies are determined by jury verdicts reached in similar cases (Galanter, 1987). In the United States, criminal cases that are especially significant tend to be tried before juries. Consider the following list: the Rodney King beating trial, the Oliver North/Iran-Contra trial, and the Mike Tyson and William Kennedy Smith rape

A scene from the 1990 movie, "The Bonfire of the Vanities." Courtroom drama and jury trials are a staple of movies and TV shows. The study of courtroom processes has become a staple of social psychology research as well.

trials. Finally, from a social psychology perspective, juries and jury trials provide a kind of real-life laboratory in which researchers can study group decision making, majority and minority influence, and the effects of prejudice and bias on group deliberations.

Clearly, jury trials are fascinating for many reasons. In our discussion, we will focus on three main features of jury trials: jury selection, jury deliberation, and jury reactions to the judge's instructions. Social psychology research has contributed significantly to our understanding of each of these topics. In discussing the social psychology of juries, we shall attempt to answer a number of important questions: Is jury selection fair and unbiased? How do juries arrive at their decisions? Does the size of a jury affect its decisions? How and when are juries biased?

Selecting a Jury

The jurors—none of them black—had been thrown together in their task after a painstaking, monthlong process of jury selection in which 248 other Ventura County residents were eliminated.

—*Los Angeles Times*, April 30, 1992

Because the Rodney King case had received so much publicity and had inflamed so much public passion in Los Angeles, the defense attorneys in the case sought a change of venue (that is, location) for the trial. This was granted, and the trial was moved from Los Angeles to Simi Valley, a small, affluent, largely white suburb west of Los Angeles. Jurors were selected in the usual way: The court compiled lists of eligible jurors (often drawn from lists of registered voters), and then panels of prospective jurors appeared in court to be interviewed by defense and prosecution attorneys—a process known as *voir dire* (pronounced "vwar deer"; literally, "to say the truth," from Old French). Voir dire procedures vary from state to state. Sometimes prospective jurors complete questionnaires; sometimes they are directly questioned by attorneys. Juries are selected within a few minutes in some cases. In the Los Angeles police officers' trial, the process took a month.

Attorneys can typically reject prospective jurors in two different ways (Van Dyke, 1977). If jurors reveal information that clearly shows them to be prejudiced or biased, attorneys may challenge them "for cause." For instance, if a potential juror in the policemen's trial stated that she had seen the videotape of Rodney King's beating many times on television and had already decided the officers were guilty of excessive force, she would likely be challenged by the defense "for cause," and, with the judge's approval, would be dismissed from serving as a juror. Attorneys also can make a limited number of *peremptory challenges*—that is, they can dismiss a set number of jurors without giving a reason. As we shall see, lawyers sometimes base their peremptory challenges on systematic pretrial research. Most of the time, however, they follow their hunches and intuitions.

Can attorneys accurately pick jurors who will favor their clients? To a degree. While attorneys often substantially overestimate their ability to discern the likely verdicts of jurors, savvy lawyers can sometimes select jurors who ultimately do make a difference in the outcome of their case. Not surprisingly, some lawyers seem to be more experienced and successful at picking jurors than others (Bermant, 1977; Zeisel & Diamond, 1978).

Scientific Jury Selection

Today, attorneys need not conduct jury selection solely on the basis of hunches. Social scientists can help them along with a method known as scientific jury selection. This consists of administering surveys to a large sample of residents living in the community jurors are to be drawn from, with the goal of discovering correlations between demographic information (such as age, sex, ethnicity, social class) and attitudes relevant to the particular trial. If, for example, survey research before a rape trial shows that women in the community are more likely than men to find the defendant guilty in this particular case, then the defense attorney might try to choose a jury consisting of as many men as possible.

Scientific jury selection was first used in the early 1970s to defend Vietnam War protesters in the famous "Harrisburg Seven" trial. (The Harrisburg Seven were charged with conspiring to destroy Selective Service records, raid and vandalize government buildings, and kidnap national security advisor Henry Kissinger.) Sociologist Jay Schulman and his colleagues interviewed 252 Harrisburg residents and assessed their demographic characteristics and attitudes relevant to the trial—for example, their attitudes toward the military, the Vietnam War, and anti-war protesters. Using this research, Schulman came up with a profile of the kind of juror who was most likely to be sympathetic to the anti-war protesters on trial: "a female Democrat with no religious preference and a white-collar or a skilled

Is it possible to predict jury verdicts?

"I still say you never can tell which way a jury will go."

blue-collar job" (Schulman, Shaver, Colman, Emrich, & Christie, 1973). The defense lawyers selected a jury based on this profile. The result: The jury split 10 to 2 in favor of acquittal, and the case ended in a mistrial, perhaps due in part to the help of Schulman and his colleagues.

Although scientific jury selection has often proved to be successful (Hans, 1992; Hans & Vidmar, 1982), it has its limits. First, it is only as good as the researchers who practice it, and it remains an art as well as a science. For example, researchers must decide (and sometimes guess) what attitudes and demographic characteristics are most likely to be relevant to their case. Sometimes demographic characteristics simply do not predict jurors' behavior or verdicts very well, and when they do, the relations may be quite idiosyncratic, depending on the specifics of the particular case and the community in which it is tried (Hans, 1992; Hastie, Penrod, & Pennington, 1983). Finally, jury selection—scientific or otherwise—is likely to make the biggest difference in cases that are hard to decide or that involve community standards as well as factual evidence and points of law. It should be reassuring to most of us (who cannot afford scientific jury selection) that jurors generally prove to be more influenced by evidence than by personal attitudes and biases (Kaplan & Miller, 1987; Visher, 1987).

Jury Attitudes and Jury Verdicts

Although jurors' attitudes do not usually overwhelm strong evidence, they can still make a difference in trial outcomes. After jurors in the Rodney King beating trial voted for acquittal, they were accused by many of racial bias against blacks and of excessively pro-police attitudes. Do you think this was so?

More generally, do jurors' racial attitudes sometimes bias juries' decisions? The answer seems to be yes, especially under certain circumstances. For example, white jurors do on average tend to sentence black defendants more harshly than white defendants, and this is particularly true in murder cases (Gross & Mauro, 1989; Sweeney & Haney, 1992). In mock jury studies, racial bias is strongest when the defendant's race is vividly presented (for example, through a photograph or videotape) and when the victim's race is also specified. However, it is important to note that jurors are not necessarily uniformly biased against minorities. Rather, they tend to punish most severely members of out-groups who commit crimes against members of their own group (Sweeney & Haney, 1992).

Of course, the way jury selection works in the United States, this may translate into frequent bias against minority defendants, for minorities are often underrepresented on juries (Fukari, Butler, & Krooth, in press; Silas, 1983), and thus juries (mostly composed of whites) show a tendency to be biased against nonwhites who commit crimes against whites.

Why are American juries often racially unbalanced? Sometimes it is because pools of potential jurors (for example, registered voters) do not represent all racial groups equally. Sometimes the imbalance may result from intentional bias. Attorneys frequently use their peremptory challenges to eliminate jurors of certain racial or ethnic groups when race or ethnicity seems relevant to their case. Although this is technically illegal, in practice it is hard for a judge to determine whether a

The jury in the Rodney King beating trial included no blacks, and its members were drawn from Simi Valley, an affluent suburb of Los Angeles. Did this influence the jury's verdict?

peremptory challenge directed against a particular juror is motivated by racial or other considerations. The Rodney King beating trial provides a much-publicized example of an all-white jury that decided a case with strong racial overtones; although Rodney King was not the defendant in this trial, it is certainly possible that the jury's racial composition increased the likelihood that jurors would be sympathetic to the police officers and unsympathetic to Rodney King.

Racial attitudes are not the only attitudes that can influence jurors' decisions. Authoritarian attitudes, attitudes toward rape, and attitudes toward the death penalty also can have an effect on jurors' decisions and verdicts in relevant cases. You may recall from Chapter 7 that people who score high on authoritarianism tend to be prejudiced, power oriented, and conventional in their sexual, religious, and political attitudes. Highly authoritarian people are typically strongly in favor of "law and order," and as jurors, they would seem more likely to convict accused lawbreakers. Are they in fact? The answer provided by research studies is generally yes (Bray & Noble, 1978; Narby, Cutler, & Moran, 1993).

But in certain kinds of cases, authoritarian jurors are more lenient than their nonauthoritarian peers—such as when the defendant has committed a crime of inappropriate obedience (for example, a soldier who followed an unethical order from a commanding officer; see Chapter 12) or when the defendant is a legitimate authority, like a police officer (Garcia & Griffitt, 1978; Hamilton, 1976). In the Rodney King beating case, do you think a highly authoritarian juror would have been more or less likely to vote to convict the police officers? Research on authoritarianism makes an important point: Personality traits and related attitudes do not always lead jurors to be uniformly more or less likely to convict; rather, their effect depends on the details of the particular case.

Rape trials constitute a specific kind of case in which attitudes frequently play a large role in jurors' verdicts—larger than in many other kinds of cases. Why? One reason is that the evidence in rape trials often boils down to the word of the accuser against the word of the accused, and jurors have to rely on their attitudes to fill in the gaps.

As you may know, victims of rape are often reluctant to bring charges against their attackers because, in addition to the trauma of sexual assault, they must in many cases also face humiliating interrogations about their sexual history and suggestions that they were responsible for their rape (Burgess, 1985; Hilberman, 1976). Rape victims' worst fears are sometimes justified, for research shows that many people do hold attitudes that rape victims often "asked for it." To measure people's attitudes toward rape, Burt (1980) developed a Rape Myths Acceptance Scale that assesses how strongly people subscribe to common false beliefs about rape—for example, that many women unconsciously desire to be raped (see scale items in Figure 16.4). Jurors' degree of endorsement of rape myths does make a difference in their verdicts in mock rape trials: People who tend to believe rape myths are significantly less likely to find rape defendants guilty (Borgida & Brekke, 1985; Field, 1978; Field & Bienen, 1980).

Like authoritarian attitudes and attitudes toward rape, attitudes toward the death penalty have been extensively studied in relation to jury verdicts. Before the

A woman who goes to the home or apartment of a man on their first date implies that she is willing to have sex.

Any female can get raped.

One reason that women falsely report a rape is that they frequently have a need to call attention to themselves.

Any healthy woman can successfully resist a rapist if she really wants to.

When women go around braless or wearing short skirts and tight tops, they are just asking for trouble

In the majority of rapes, the victim is promiscuous or has a bad reputation.

If a girl engages in necking or petting and she lets things get out of hand, it is her own fault if her partner forces sex on her.

Women who get raped while hitchhiking get what they deserve.

A woman who is stuck-up and thinks she is too good to talk to guys on the street deserves to be taught a lesson.

Many women have an unconscious wish to be raped, and may then unconsciously set up a situation in which they are likely to be attacked.

If a woman gets drunk at a party and has intercourse with a man she's just met there, she should be considered "fair game" to other males at the party who want to have sex with her too, whether she wants to or not.

[a]What pecentage of women who report a rape would you say are lying because they are angry and want to get back at the man they accuse?

[a]What percentage of reported rapes would you guess were merely invented by women who discovered they were pregnant and wanted to protect their own reputation?

[b]A person comes to you and claims they were raped. How likely would you be to believe their statement if the person were:

your best friend?

an Indian woman?

a neighborhood woman?

a young boy?

a black woman?

a white woman?

Note: Responses to all items were recorded on a 7-point scale, ranging from "strongly agree" to "strongly disagree," except: items marked [a] used "almost all, about ¾, about half, about ¼, almost none," and items marked [b] used "always, frequently, sometimes, rarely, never."

FIGURE 16.4 Items from the Rape Myths Acceptance Scale. *Source:* Burt (1980).

Supreme Court outlawed the practice in 1968, prosecuting attorneys had the power during voir dire to legally eliminate prospective jurors who expressed *any* reservations (termed "scruples" in legal circles) about sentencing a defendant to death. In the landmark 1968 case of *Witherspoon v. Illinois,* however, the Supreme Court ruled that only jurors who stated that they would not sentence a defendant to death *under any circumstances* could be eliminated. Such anti-death-penalty jurors typically comprise 10% to 15% of the population. The remaining jurors are termed "death-qualified"—that is, they are willing, at least in some circumstances, to vote for the death sentence.

These two groups of jurors clearly differ in their attitudes toward the death penalty. Do they differ in other attitudes as well, and thus does the removal of anti-death-penalty jurors alter the composition of juries? The answer provided by numerous research studies is yes. People who endorse the use of capital punishment differ systematically from opponents of capital punishment in many ways: They are more likely to be male, white, and middle or upper middle class, for example. Furthermore, people who endorse the use of capital punishment tend to be more concerned with crime, more pro-"law and order," more pro-police, and they tend to be more distrusting of defense attorneys and more skeptical about the need to protect defendants' civil rights (Fitzgerald & Ellsworth, 1984; Thompson, Cowan, Ellsworth, & Harrington, 1984).

Do juries composed of death-qualified jurors arrive at verdicts different from those of unselected juries? Here again, the answer is yes. Studies consistently find that death-qualified juries are more likely to vote for conviction, and this holds for actual as well as simulated juries (Cowan, Thompson, & Ellsworth, 1984; Moran & Comfort, 1986). Thus, by permitting lawyers to select only death-qualified jurors in trials, the Supreme Court has permitted a practice that makes juries on average more likely to convict defendants. Summary Table 16.2 presents a brief review of the effects of various attitudes on jurors' decisions.

SUMMARY TABLE 16.2   Juror Attitudes and Jury Behavior

Racial Attitudes—Juries sometimes deliver harsher verdicts and sentences to racial minorities. Racial bias tends to be strongest when in-group jurors hear a case in which an out-group defendant is accused of a crime committed against an in-group victim.

Authoritarian Attitudes—Authoritarian jurors tend to be more conviction-prone and punitive than nonauthoritarian jurors. An exception is when the defendant commits a crime of obedience to authority or when the defendant is an authority figure, such as a police officer.

Attitudes toward Rape—Jurors who endorse rape myths tend to be more lenient toward defendants accused of rape.

Death Penalty Attitudes—Jurors who say they are willing to apply the death sentence in some circumstances tend to be more likely to convict and more punitive than jurors who oppose the death penalty.

Inside the Jury

Count by count, the jurors examined the testimony and tried to reach conclusions. The discussion was emotional but not volatile.

—Los Angeles Times, April 30, 1992

We will never know exactly what took place during the jury deliberations for the Rodney King beating trial. It is illegal in all federal courts and in most state courts to record what goes on in juries. Ironically, the laws prohibiting any violation of the privacy of jury deliberations resulted from a famous social science research project. During the early 1950s, a group of University of Chicago researchers obtained permission from the presiding judge to tape-record the deliberations of five civil juries (Ferguson, 1955). When word of the research leaked out to the press, public outrage was so great that both state and federal laws were soon passed that forbade such recording in the future.

Today researchers generally rely on simulated juries to determine what goes on in actual juries. They also analyze court records, and sometimes interview jurors in actual cases after the case has been decided. What does this research tell us about the inner workings of juries?

A Jury of Peers?

In the United States, a jury consists of 12 people in federal cases and sometimes fewer in state and local cases. In theory, a jury consists of a group of peers who evaluate case evidence and who exchange views with one another in an equal give-and-take. Ideally, the jury trial provides a system of checks and balances. Because juries consist of a number of individuals, they embrace a range of opinions, and the mistakes and biases of any individual juror can thus be corrected or canceled out by other jurors.

That's the theory. Do juries in fact consist of independent individuals who contribute equally to the deliberations? The answer provided by many research studies is a clear no. Jurors usually contribute quite unequally to jury deliberations, and different jurors may exert very different amounts of influence on the jury's final verdict.

In a particularly careful and large-scale study, Hastie, Penrod, and Pennington (1983) presented evidence from a simulated murder trial to a varied group of 800 people assigned to 69 different mock juries. The statements made by each juror were taped and counted. The findings showed that, in general, several of the most talkative members of each jury dominated the conversation, and several of the quietest jurors tended to say almost nothing (see Figure 16.5). This pattern is not unique to juries, by the way. Small-group research has long found that individual participation rates in discussion groups (juries, committees, board meetings) follow exponential curves like those shown in Figure 16.5 (Kadane & Lewis, 1969; Stephan & Mishler, 1952).

Do the most active jurors systematically differ from the least active jurors? Yes. In Hastie, Penrod, and Pennington's (1983) study, jurors who tended to talk

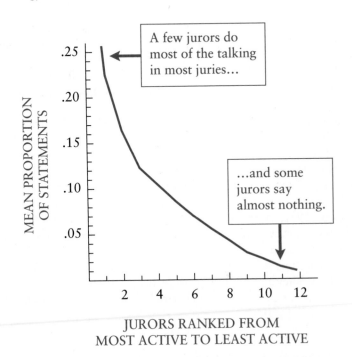

A few jurors do most of the talking in most juries...

...and some jurors say almost nothing.

MEAN PROPORTION OF STATEMENTS

JURORS RANKED FROM
MOST ACTIVE TO LEAST ACTIVE

FIGURE 16.5 Jurors' amount of participation in jury deliberations. *Source:* Adapted from Hastie, Penrod, and Pennington (1983).

more were male, of higher occupational status, and of intermediate age (34–56). Not surprisingly, jury foremen tended to talk a lot during jury deliberations—more than three times as much as the average non-foreman.

The foreman is a particularly influential juror. Who tends to be elected to this position? The word *foreman* is hardly a sexist misnomer. Although juries tend to comprise about equal numbers of men and women, foremen are much more likely to be men than women (Strodtbeck & Mann, 1956), and this pattern holds in recent as well as older research (Kerr, Harmon, & Graves, 1982). (The Rodney King beating trial provides an exception here: The jury elected a forewoman.) Foremen also tend to be better educated and of higher socioeconomic status than non-foremen (Simon, 1967; Strodtbeck, James, & Hawkins, 1957). Finally, jurors who sit at the head of the jury deliberation table are particularly likely to be elected to the position of foreman (Strodtbeck & Hook, 1961).

Although the foreman of the jury talks more than other jurors, he or she is not necessarily the most influential juror in terms of determining the final verdict. Rather, the foreman typically plays largely a procedural role, directing discussion, taking straw votes, and raising points of law (Hastie et al., 1983).

Some jurors are perceived by other members of the jury to be especially persuasive and influential. Such jurors are more likely to be highly educated, of high socioeconomic status, and male (Hastie et al., 1983; Stasser, Kerr, & Bray, 1982). (This list may sound familiar to you by now.) You may recall from Chapter 13 that there are generally two kinds of leaders of small groups: the task-oriented leader, who seeks facts, offers information, and focuses on the job at hand, versus the socioemotional leader, who soothes hurt feelings, mediates disputes, and facilitates harmonious interactions among group members. In juries, men are more likely to be task-oriented leaders, and women socioemotional leaders (Nemeth, Endicott, & Wachtler, 1977).

The Give-and-Take of Jury Deliberations

The first straw vote came at the end of the second day of deliberations, and there were countless straw votes after that.

After all the facts had been reviewed, the only bitter debate revolved around a charge of assault under the color or authority against Powell. On that count, the jury split 8 to 4 and the judge declared a mistrial. The four who voted for conviction believed that Powell should have stopped striking King sooner.

—*Los Angeles Times*, April 30, 1992

Juries are not just static collections of people with varying demographic characteristics, personality traits, and attitudes. They are dynamic groups in which people argue, counterargue, and influence one another in complex ways. Sometimes, jury deliberations lead to unanimous verdicts—which was the case for most of the charges in the Rodney King beating trial. In contrast, some deliberations result in hung juries, with jurors deadlocked in disagreement. In the beating trial, the jury was hung for one charge only—that of "assault under the color of authority" against Officer Powell.

How do juries arrive at their decisions? Like many small groups, juries tend to progress through several definite stages as they proceed with their work (Bales & Strodtbeck, 1951). First, they go through an orientation stage, during which jurors define their task, establish group procedures, and get to know one another. Next, jurors typically move to the nuts and bolts of their task: discussing evidence, arguing, and trying to arrive at a verdict. Often, open conflict occurs during this second stage, with some jurors actively disagreeing with others. Finally, as a group consensus emerges, the jury tries to bring dissenting members into the fold and, if this is accomplished, the group then strives to achieve reconciliation among disagreeing members and factions.

In analyzing the statements of some 800 mock jurors, Hastie, Penrod, and Pennington (1983) found that not only does the emotional tone of discussion change over the course of jury deliberations, the factual content does as well. Juries tend to begin their deliberations discussing the evidence and trying to answer questions such as: What are the facts of the case? Which witnesses were credible and which were not? After reaching consensus on the evidence, the jurors then try to construct a story that explains the evidence.

In other words, it is not sufficient for the jurors simply to agree on the "facts" of the case. They must also agree on what the facts mean. To this end, jurors develop scenarios that explain the motives of the key players in the case, then try to fill in missing gaps in evidence and develop consistent accounts of what actually took place. Evidence, whether strong or weak, becomes more salient to jurors when it can be organized into a cohesive story (Pennington & Hastie, 1992). Jurors in the Rodney King beating trial clearly tried to understand the evidence in human terms. One juror, trying to conceptualize the police officers' behavior, noted, "They're policemen, they're not angels. They're out to do a low-down, dirty job. Would you want your husband doing it, or your son or your father?" (*Los Angeles Times,* May 2, 1992).

Finally, after agreeing on the evidence and constructing a plausible scenario of what took place, jurors turn to issues of law: What are the judge's instructions and what do they mean, what constitutes a "reasonable doubt" (jurors are supposed to convict only when they are sure "beyond a reasonable doubt"), and what are the jury's options in terms of verdicts and sentencing?

Juries generally do arrive at verdicts. Hastie, Penrod, and Pennington (1983) observed that only 4 out of 69 of their mock juries (about 6%) were hung at the end of deliberations. A classic study of actual trials found a remarkably similar figure: 5.6% of trials ended in hung juries when unanimous verdicts were required, and only 3.1% were hung when only a majority was necessary to reach a verdict (Kalven & Zeisel, 1966).

What predicts a jury's verdict? About 90% of the time, juries end up reaching a verdict consistent with the majority's position at the time of the first straw poll. In *The American Jury,* Harry Kalven and Hans Zeisel (1966) offered the following analogy: ". . . the deliberation process might well be likened to what the developer does for an exposed film: It brings out the picture, but the outcome is predetermined . . ." (p. 489).

Given that juries are often split at the first polling, how do they manage so often to reach a consensus? We know many of the answers to this question from Chapter 12 ("Conformity, Compliance, and Obedience") and Chapter 13 ("Groups"). Majorities exert pressure on minorities to conform. Sometimes this pressure takes the form of rational arguments and persuasion (informational social influence), and sometimes it takes the cruder form of direct pressure (normative social influence) that leads minority jurors to cave in even when they do not fully agree (Deutsch & Gerard, 1955). In the words of noted jury researchers Kalven and Zeisel (1966), jury deliberation "is an interesting combination of rational persuasion, sheer social pressure, and the psychological mechanism by which individual perceptions undergo change when exposed to a group discussion" (p. 489).

Although strong, determined, and consistent minority factions can sometimes budge the majority a bit and even bring it over to their side (Moscovici, 1985), in general, the majority wins out in most juries. Juries, like other groups, often undergo group polarization—that is, after deliberation, jurors are likely to become more extreme in their opinions (see Chapter 13). Specifically, juries initially leaning to conviction will be more likely to convict after deliberation, and juries leaning to acquittal will be more likely to acquit after deliberation (Myers & Kaplan, 1976).

In the movie "Twelve Angry Men," a lone holdout in favor of acquittal eventually brought the majority, who favored conviction, to his side. In actual juries, do minorities typically have this much influence on other jurors' decisions?

The polarizing effect of jury deliberations is not as strong toward conviction as it is toward acquittal, however. That is, juries often show a *leniency bias* (MacCoun & Kerr, 1988; Stasser et al., 1982). When a jury is split 6 to 6 at the time of the first polling, the ultimate verdict is likely to be "not guilty." And if the majority favoring conviction at the time of the first polling in a 12-person jury does not exceed 7 or 8, the jury will often end up hung. Thus, a minority of jurors arguing for acquittal tends to be more successful than a minority arguing for conviction.

Perhaps this is because jurors appreciate the gravity of their task, and they would rather err in the direction of letting guilty defendants off than convicting innocent ones. A juror in the Rodney King beating trial expressed just this point: "The law is set up in such a way in our country that sometimes guilty men go free to ensure that innocent men are not locked up unjustly. Some of the people protesting, making comments about the jury, have to realize if they were arrested they would want that same consideration" (*Los Angeles Times*, May 1, 1992).

The Consequences of Small Juries and Less-Than-Unanimous Decision Rules

SOCIAL PSYCHOLOGY IN EVERYDAY LIFE

The United States Supreme Court has ruled that state courts have the right to try cases before juries as small as six people, and they may accept verdicts based on nonunanimous majorities. Do the size of a jury and the nature of its decision rule (unanimous or nonunanimous) make a difference in its verdict? Here is a clear case where social psychology research can give us valuable information about the real-life consequences of group process.

Jury size does not seem to affect relative rates of convictions and acquittals in most juries (Saks, 1977). It can, however, affect whether juries reach a verdict at all: 12-person juries are about twice as likely to end up hung as 6-person juries (Zeisel, 1971). Why is this so? There are two reasons. First, there are likely to be more 1-person dissenting minorities in 6-person than in 12-person juries. As we noted in Chapter 12, single individuals have a harder time resisting pressures to conform in a group than do dissenting factions consisting of more than one (Asch, 1956). Second, large juries are generally more varied and diverse than smaller juries (Saks, 1977). Imagine that a certain minority group (blacks, for example) makes up 10% of the population. Chances are that a 12-person jury will include at least one minority member, whereas 6-person juries are likely *not* to include a minority member. It is often dissenting minority jurors that lead to hung juries, and smaller juries are simply statistically likely to be more homogeneous than larger juries.

The jury's decision rule as well as its size can have a significant impact on its deliberations and decisions. Hastie, Penrod, and Pennington (1983) created three kinds of juries in their study: The first required a unanimous 12-to-0 vote to reach a verdict, whereas the second and third kind required only a 10-to-2 or 8-to-4 majority to reach a verdict. These decision rules made a difference in juries' deliberations and verdicts. Compared with unanimous juries, the majority-rule juries spent less time deliberating before reaching a verdict. Furthermore, jurors in the majority-rule juries tended to quarrel more, and the majorities in these juries adopted "a more forceful, bullying, persuasive style" (Hastie, Penrod, & Pennington, 1983, p. 112). Finally, majority-rule juries were more likely to reach a verdict (less likely to be hung) than unanimous juries, and they showed a tendency to deliver more severe convictions (for example, first-degree murder versus second-degree murder or manslaughter).

Summary Table 16.3 reviews findings we have presented on the effects of jury size, decision rules, and other factors that influence jury deliberations.

Judges and Juries

In fact . . . the outcome of the case may well have been decided when Judge Stanley Weisberg of California Superior Court transferred the case from the city [of Los Angeles] to Simi Valley, an overwhelmingly white, conservative enclave that is the home of the Ronald Reagan Presidential Library.

—*New York Times,* May 1, 1992

Our account of jury trials thus far has ignored a very important person: the judge. Judges play a number of roles during a trial. They ensure that attorneys and witnesses follow proper procedures. They make procedural decisions—for example, granting a change of venue. And judges deliver final instructions and "charges" to the jury. What impact do judges have on trial outcomes, and do juries really understand and follow their instructions?

In analyzing the relationship between judges and jurors, we shall focus on several questions. First, do judges tend to agree with jurors' decisions? Second, do

SUMMARY TABLE 16.3 Factors That Affect Jury Deliberations

Gender and socioeconomic status—Men and jurors of higher socioeconomic status tend to be more likely than women and jurors of lower socioeconomic status to serve as foreman and tend to be highly influential.

Informational and normative social influence—Most juries arrive at verdicts, and the best predictor of the verdict is the majority position at the time of the first polling. The majority brings the minority over to its side through rational information and persuasion and through social pressure. Juries often exhibit *group polarization*—that is, after deliberation, opinions become more extreme.

Leniency bias—Split juries show a stronger tendency to shift toward acquittal than toward conviction.

Jury size—Large (12-person) juries are more likely to end up hung than smaller juries.

Unanimous versus majority-rule juries—Majority-rule juries are less likely to end up hung than unanimous juries. They are also likely to be more punitive and engage in short, combative deliberations.

jurors follow judges' instructions? For example, when judges rule certain pieces of evidence to be "inadmissible," do jurors do what they are told? And when instructed to ignore prejudicial pretrial publicity, do jurors listen? Finally, do judges sometimes exert undue influence on jurors to arrive at a unanimous decision when a jury appears to be deadlocked?

Do Judges Agree with Jurors?

In their classic study of American juries, Kalven and Zeisel (1966) sent questionnaires to 550 judges who presided over 3,576 criminal trials across the nation. The judges were asked to state what they thought the proper verdict should be in each trial. Judges and juries agreed in their verdicts 78% of the time, and when they disagreed, it was generally because the jury voted for acquittal while the judge advocated conviction. (Here again, we see evidence for a leniency bias in juries.)

Why do juries sometimes disagree with judges? It is not simply the case that juries are sometimes biased, whereas judges are generally right. Jurors may define "reasonable doubt" differently from judges. They may not completely understand points of law. Finally, in a process known as "jury nullification," jurors may simply reject the law in particular cases because it violates their personal sense of morality or deeply held community standards. Judges usually tend not to explicitly inform juries of their right to nullify laws, but juries sometimes exercise this right nonetheless.

The trial of 23-year-old Lester Zygmanik provides a dramatic example of jury nullification. Zygmanik, by his own admission, shot his 26-year-old brother in the head with a sawed-off shotgun and killed him. Not surprisingly, he was charged with murder. Given these basic facts, do you think you would have voted to convict Zygmanik if you were a member of the jury that heard his case?

*Judge Stanley
Weisberg presided
over the Rodney King
beating trial.*

Before answering this question too hastily, consider some important additional facts. Lester's brother George had recently been paralyzed from the neck down in a terrible motorcycle accident, and his doctors had told him he would not recover. George was in constant terrible pain, and he continually begged his brother to kill him. Distraught and grief-stricken, Lester finally agreed to his brother's request. Late one night, he came with a gun to the hospital room where his brother lay. The courtroom testimony:

"Now Mr. Zygmanik, you indicated that you hid the gun under your coat?"

"Yes."

"And you said that was because you knew the nurses wouldn't let you walk into your brother's room with a gun?"

"Right."

"Why did you think they wouldn't let you walk in with a gun?"

"Because I had spoken to the doctors there that my brother wanted to die—for them to stop operating on him and cutting him up—and they refused to do that. So, I know they definitely would not let me relieve my brother from his pain."

"You knew it was wrong, didn't you?—to walk in there with a gun?"

"I don't know. At that time, I really wasn't thinking."

"Did you know it was wrong to shoot your brother?"

"At the time, I didn't think about anything but relieving my brother's pain." . . .

"You walked over to your brother's bed? Is that right?"

"Right."

"And he couldn't talk at this point?"

"No."

"Do you recall what you said to him?"

"I asked him if he was in pain. I asked him if the pain was real bad. He nodded, yes. Then I told him I was here to relieve his pain. I asked him if that was all right with him. I believe I told him, 'Don't worry, you won't be in pain any more.' And he nodded, yes."

"And then you shot your brother?"

"Yes." (Mitchell, 1976, pp. 229–230)

Although he freely admitted killing his brother, Lester was acquitted of murder by a New Jersey jury. Despite the clarity of the law, the jury decided that it could not in good conscience convict Lester Zygmanik and chose instead to nullify the law.

Inadmissible Evidence

Jury nullification is rare. Jurors usually try to follow the law and obey the judge's instructions. But is "try" good enough? An interesting case in point is that of inadmissible evidence—trial evidence that the judge rules to be legally impermissible because it biases the case or violates the defendant's rights. We can all recall TV courtroom dramas in which a witness answers an attorney's leading question and the opposing attorney leaps up yelling, "I object." If the judge supports the objection, a damning piece of testimony may be stricken from the record and the jurors instructed to disregard it.

Do jurors in fact obey such an instruction? The answer often seems to be no. One study presented three groups of jurors with different kinds of evidence. The first group read weak circumstantial evidence indicating that the defendant had committed a robbery-murder; the evidence was so weak that no juror in this condition found the defendant guilty. A second group of jurors heard additional evidence: a highly incriminating wiretapped phone call made by the defendant. With this evidence, the conviction rate rose to 26%. A third group of jurors heard the same incriminating wiretapped conversation, but this time the judge ruled that it was inadmissible evidence (for it had been obtained illegally) and that the jurors should disregard it. Did they? No. In fact, the conviction rate was highest for this group: 35% (Sue, Smith, & Caldwell, 1973).

Thus, paradoxically, a judge's instruction to "disregard" evidence can sometimes backfire. Why? When attorneys object to a particular piece of evidence and the judge then rules on its admissibility, the net result may be to focus jurors' attention on the evidence and make it all the more salient. Furthermore, when the judge instructs jurors not to think about certain evidence, they may find it very hard to obey the instruction, even if they want to. It is extraordinarily difficult *not* to think about a specified topic (Wegner & Erber, 1992; Wegner, Schneider, Carter, & White, 1987). For example, try for the next ten seconds *not* to think about Mickey Mouse. Were you successful?

Psychological reactance theory, which argues that people dislike having their freedom restricted (Brehm, 1966; see Chapter 12) provides yet another reason why ruling evidence to be inadmissible may not be effective. When a judge tells a jury *not* to pay attention to a particular piece of evidence, jurors may pay attention just to assert their power and freedom of choice (Wolf & Montgomery, 1977). Finally, jurors may often attend to inadmissible evidence simply because they are trying to do a good and conscientious job. Sometimes evidence is ruled inadmissible because of legal technicalities, not because it is false or unimportant (Wissler & Saks, 1985). If you believed that an "inadmissible" piece of evidence would help you arrive at a just and correct verdict in a case, would you ignore it (even if you could)?

Pretrial Publicity

The problem of pretrial publicity is related to the problems posed by inadmissible evidence. Pretrial publicity provides inappropriate "outside" evidence in a trial, whereas inadmissible evidence comes from "inside" the trial. As you probably know, the Rodney King beating trial suffered from an enormous amount of pretrial publicity. Theoretically, jurors are supposed to base their decisions only on evidence that is presented during the trial, but is this possible in a case like the beating trial?

It is clear that pretrial publicity can sometimes dramatically alter jurors' opinions and verdicts (Constantini & King, 1980–81; Linz & Penrod, 1992). In one study, 120 New York residents eligible for actual jury duty viewed a videotape of a simulated murder trial, but before the trial they read several newspaper clippings about the murder (Padawer-Singer & Barton, 1975). Sometimes these clippings contained information quite damning to the defendant (he had a prior criminal record, and he had confessed to the murder, then recanted), and sometimes the clippings were not prejudicial to the case. Did this pretrial publicity affect the jurors' verdicts? Yes: 78% of the jurors found the defendant guilty after reading the damning articles, but only 55% did when the articles were more neutral. Furthermore, recent studies show that pretrial publicity has the power to influence jurors' attitudes, change their decisions in both criminal and civil cases, and even alter the ways they weigh evidence (Greene & Loftus, 1984; Greene & Wade, 1987; Linz & Penrod, 1992).

Are there ways to reduce the biasing effects of pretrial publicity? We have discussed some already. During voir dire, attorneys can dismiss prospective jurors "for cause" if they have been exposed to potentially prejudicial pretrial publicity. If a trial is slated to take place in a community that has been especially saturated with pretrial publicity, the judge may grant a change of venue. This was the case in the Los Angeles police officers' trial. Sometimes juries are sequestered (separated from the rest of the world), often holed up in a hotel and insulated from press and media

A police spokesperson speaks to reporters before the 1991 William Kennedy Smith rape trial. Can pretrial publicity like this influence juries' decisions?

stories during the course of a trial. And, of course, judges often deliver stern instructions to jurors warning them not to be influenced by pretrial publicity and to base their decisions only on evidence presented during the trial. But as we know from research on inadmissible evidence, such instructions may not be very effective in practice (Kramer, Kerr, & Carroll, 1990). Finally, if all else fails, a verdict biased by pretrial publicity may be appealed and sometimes reversed.

When Judges Pressure Juries: The Dynamite Charge

As we noted earlier, hung juries are relatively rare—they occur in about 6% of criminal trials. Still, hung juries represent a costly failure because the case must often then be retried.

Judges sometimes ask deadlocked jurors to reconsider their positions. Specifically, judges deliver to deadlocked juries a set of instructions known as the dynamite charge—so called because it has the power to "shake up" the jury and get it to reach a verdict. The dynamite charge is known more technically in legal circles as the "Allen charge" because it was first approved by the U.S. Supreme Court in the 1896 case of *Allen v. U.S.* Lawyers have given it many nicknames, including the "shotgun instruction" and the "nitroglycerin charge." What is contained in this explosive set of instructions? The following is a simplified version:

> As you know, the verdict requires a unanimous decision, which has not yet been reached. This verdict must take into account the views of each individual juror, and should not represent the mere acquiescence of an individual to his or her peers. Each of you should examine the question submitted for your consideration with candor and with a proper regard and deference to the opinions of each other. As it is your duty to decide the case if you can conscientiously do so, you should listen, with a disposition to be convinced, to each other's arguments. If most members of the jury are for conviction, a dissenting juror should consider whether his or her doubt is a reasonable one, considering that it made no impression upon the minds of so many other equally honest and intelligent jurors. If, on the other hand, the majority is for acquittal, the minority ought to ask themselves whether they might not reasonably doubt the correctness of a judgment which is not concurred in by the majority. (Kassin, Smith, & Tulloch, 1990, p. 541)

The dynamite charge is controversial because it essentially asks minority holdouts in a deadlocked jury to reconsider their positions, and it tends to place the court and the judge's considerable authority on the side of the jury's majority (American Bar Association, 1968). While some states have restricted its use, the Supreme Court has repeatedly stated that the dynamite charge does not put undue pressure on minority jurors to change their minds and that judges may routinely use it.

Does the dynamite charge work? Legal lore holds that it is extremely effective in breaking jury deadlocks. Recent research concurs. In one study, college students participated in mock juries in which they deliberated by passing notes to one another (Kassin et al., 1990). Some jurors were led to believe that they constituted a one-person minority in deadlocked juries of four people, whereas others believed they were a member of the majority in the deadlocked jury. Independently, half the subjects received the dynamite charge, and half did not.

What were the results? The minority jurors were significantly more likely to capitulate to the majority after receiving the dynamite charge. Furthermore, minority jurors reported feeling more coerced after the dynamite charge was delivered, and in fact, majority jurors did pressure minority jurors more intensely in their written notes after receiving the dynamite charge. Clearly, then, the dynamite charge "works," but at a cost: Hung juries are made to reach a verdict, but they often do so by pressuring minority members to capitulate.

SOCIAL PSYCHOLOGY AND THE LAW IN PERSPECTIVE

The Rodney King story did not end with the trial described in this chapter or the horrible riots in Los Angeles that followed. In 1993, the police officers who had beaten King were tried a second time, this time before a federal jury for violating King's civil rights. The verdict in the second trial was quite different from that in the first: Two officers were found guilty and two officers were acquitted (*Los Angeles Times,* April 18, 1993).

As was the case for the first trial, we can never know for sure why the jury in the second one arrived at its verdict. One thing is clear, however: The different outcomes of the two trials were not simply due to chance. Many of the factors discussed in this chapter undoubtedly played a critical role leading to convictions in the second trial. The eyewitness testimony in the second trial differed dramatically from that in the first. Rodney King *did* testify in his own behalf in the second trial. In addition, the second trial included emotional testimony not present in the first, by Los Angeles police officer Melanie Singer. Singer had witnessed the beating, and she testified that the police officers' violence had been out of control. The second trial took place in Los Angeles, not in Simi Valley, and its jury was racially mixed. And of course, the jury in the second trial knew about the terrible aftermath of the first trial.

Both trials serve as a kind of object lesson about the importance of conducting controlled research on law enforcement practices, courtroom procedures, and jury deliberations. In both beating trials—as in all real-life situations—many different variables were confounded with one another, and thus it is impossible to know for sure "the causes" of the verdicts in each trial. This is exactly why social psychologists analyze data from *many* trials and conduct careful experiments on eyewitness testimony, facial identification, courtroom procedures, and jury deliberations. Such studies provide us with valuable information about the legal system—information that augments the knowledge of legal scholars, criminal justice experts, and law enforcement officials.

Both anecdotal observations about the Rodney King beating trials and the findings of social psychology studies on our legal system remind us of an important point: Witnesses, attorneys, jurors, and judges are people, and as such, they are subject to a host of psychological influences.

Evaluating Evidence

The Power of Eyewitness Testimony

Eyewitness testimony is extremely persuasive to jurors, sometimes even when it has been discredited.

What Makes an Eyewitness Credible?

Eyewitnesses who express confidence and who appear confident are often assumed to be accurate, but in fact, the relation between eyewitness confidence and accuracy is quite weak.

Eyewitnesses who answer questions quickly and who provide numerous details are presumed to be accurate, but these factors prove to be unrelated to accuracy as well.

In general, people assume children are less reliable witnesses than adults. Children's reports of sexual abuse may be one exception to this rule.

Eyewitness Testimony in the Rodney King Beating Trial

Police officers provided the primary eyewitness testimony in the trial. Because officers were generally confident and because eyewitness testimony in general tends to be highly credible, this testimony may have counted heavily in jurors' minds. Jurors may have drawn negative inferences about Rodney King's failure to testify in his own behalf.

What Influences the Actual Accuracy of Eyewitness Testimony?

Extreme emotional arousal can undermine the accuracy of eyewitnesses' memories. The *weapons focus effect* refers to the finding that people who witness events in the presence of a weapon are often highly aroused and focus their attention on the weapon, showing poorer memory for other information as a result.

Eyewitness memory fades over time, quickly at first and then more slowly. People's memory for events is greater with greater exposure time to events.

Leading questions and misleading post-event information can distort people's memory for events.

Lineup procedures have a large effect on people's ability to identify suspects faces accurately. People are frequently better able to facially identify members of their own racial and ethnic groups than members of other groups.

Social Psychology in Everyday Life: Bringing Eyewitness Research to the Witness Stand

Eyewitness experts agree that a number of research findings about eyewitness testimony are well established. Because many of these findings are not intuitively obvious, eyewitness experts often can play a valuable role as expert witnesses in court cases.

Trial by Jury

Selecting a Jury

Trial attorneys select jurors during a pretrial interview known as *voir dire*. During voir dire, attorneys can challenge potential jurors "for cause" or they can make peremptory challenges—that is, without stating a reason.

Scientific jury selection is a method attorneys sometimes use to choose jurors sympathetic to their side. This systematic pretrial research consists of administering surveys to a large sample of residents living in the community jurors are to be drawn from. The goal is to discover correlations between demographic information and attitudes relevant to the particular trial so that jurors with desired attitudes can be selected.

Jurors' level of authoritarianism and their attitudes toward race, rape, and the death penalty can influence their verdicts. Juries may show racial bias, particularly when hearing a case in which a defendant from a racial out-group is accused of committing a crime against a member of the jurors' own racial group. Authoritarian jurors are generally more likely to convict defendants than nonauthoritarian jurors. Jurors who subscribe to rape myths are more likely to be lenient toward defendants in rape trials. And jurors who say they are willing to sentence defendants to death under some circumstances tend to differ in many ways from jurors who oppose the death penalty, and they tend to be more likely to convict defendants.

Inside the Jury

Some jurors, particularly those who are male, of high socioeconomic and occupational status, and of intermediate age, are more likely to participate heavily in juries and thus be more influential. Jury foremen are more likely to be male than female and to have higher socioeconomic status than non-foremen.

Juries typically proceed through definite stages of deliberation. After an orientation stage in which jurors set up procedures and get to know one another, juries progress through a deliberation stage that often entails conflict. In the final stage of deliberation, jurors try to reach agreement and achieve reconciliation. Juries typically progress from considering evidence to constructing stories that account for the evidence and finally, to addressing points of law and sentencing.

Juries generally reach a verdict, even when they start off split. Social psychology concepts such as informational influence, normative social influence, and group polarization help explain how juries reach consensus. Juries often show a leniency bias: When split, they are more likely to move to acquittal than to conviction.

Small juries are less likely to be hung than larger juries. This is due to the greater likelihood of one-person minorities in small juries and the fact that small juries tend to be more homogeneous than larger ones.

Juries that are allowed to reach verdicts with less-than-unanimous majorities are more likely to reach a verdict than juries requiring unanimous verdicts. They are also likely to deliberate less, quarrel more, and deliver more punitive sentences.

Judges and Juries

Judges tend to agree with most juries' verdicts. In a small number of cases, jurors may nullify the law when the law violates their moral principles or deeply held community standards.

Judges sometimes rule evidence to be inadmissible when it unduly biases the case or violates the defendant's rights. However, jurors often attend to inadmissible evidence despite the judge's instructions.

Pretrial publicity has the power to bias jurors' verdicts, and this often occurs despite judges' instructions to disregard such publicity.

Judges sometimes use the dynamite charge to get deadlocked juries to reach a verdict. While this set of instructions is often effective, it may put undue pressure on minority jurors to capitulate to the majority.

KEY TERMS

Authoritarianism: A personality trait characterized by prejudice, submission to authority, and conventional sexual, religious, and political attitudes; in general, people who are high on authoritarianism are more likely to convict defendants than nonauthoritarian people are.

Death-qualified jurors: Jurors who state they are willing, at least in some circumstances, to vote for the death sentence and who are selected to serve on juries for this reason; such jurors are often more likely to convict defendants.

Dynamite charge: More technically known as the "Allen charge"; a set of instructions the judge sometimes delivers to deadlocked juries to get jurors to reconsider their opinions and reach a verdict.

Empty chair doctrine: A legal principle that holds that lawyers may comment on a witness's absence during a trial and ask the jury to draw damaging inferences from it.

Inadmissible evidence: Trial evidence that the judge rules to be legally impermissible because it biases the case or violates the defendant's rights; judges sometimes instruct jurors to disregard inadmissible evidence that has been presented during a trial.

Jury nullification: Occurs when a jury disregards the law in arriving at a verdict because the law violates jurors' personal sense of morality or deeply held community standards.

Leniency bias: The tendency for initially split juries to be more likely to shift toward acquittal than toward conviction.

Misinformation effects: Distortions and alterations that occur in eyewitnesses' memory as a result of leading and misleading questions or exposure to misleading information after the witnessed event.

Peremptory challenge: An attorney's attempt to dismiss a prospective juror during voir dire for no stated reason.

Scientific jury selection: A method of choosing sympathetic jurors through the use of systematic pretrial research; this consists of surveying a large sample of residents living in the community jurors are to be drawn from in order to discover correlations between demographic information and attitudes relevant to the particular trial.

Voir dire: Pretrial interview of prospective jurors by prosecuting and defense attorneys; the purpose of voir dire is to eliminate potentially biased jurors.

Weapons focus effect: The poorer memory for faces and facts people tend to display when viewing a weapon or when in the presence of a person carrying a weapon.

Abelson, R. P. (1972). Are attitudes necessary? In B. T. King & E. McGinnies (Eds.), *Attitudes, conflicts, and social change.* New York: Academic Press.

Abrams, D., Wetherell, M., Cochrane, S., Hogg, M. A., & Turner, J. C. (1990). Knowing what to think by knowing who you are: Self-categorization and the nature of norm formation, conformity, and group polarization. *British Journal of Social Psychology, 29,* 97–119.

Abramson, L. Y., Garbner, J., & Seligman, M. E. P. (1980). Learned helplessness in humans: An attributional analysis. In J. Garbner & M. E. P. Seligman (Eds.), *Human helplessness: Theory and applications.* New York: Academic Press.

Abramson, L. Y., Seligman, M. E. P., & Teasdale, J. D. (1978). Learned helplessness in humans: Critique and reformulation. *Journal of Abnormal Psychology, 87,* 49–74.

Ackerman, N. W., & Jahoda, M. (1950). *Anti-semitism and emotional disorder.* New York: Harper.

Adair, J. G., Dushenko, T. W., & Lindsay, R. C. L. (1985). Ethical regulations and their impact on research practice. *American Psychologist, 40,* 59–72.

Adams, D. (1989). Feminist-based interventions for battering men. In P. L. Caesar & L. K. Hamberger (Eds.), *Treating men who batter: Theory, practice, and programs.* New York: Springer.

Adams, G. R., & Shea, J. A. (1981). Talking and loving: A cross-lagged panel investigation. *Basic and Applied Social Psychology, 2,* 81–88.

Adams, J. S. (1963). Toward an understanding of inequity. *Journal of Abnormal and Social Psychology, 67,* 422–436.

Adams, J. S. (1965). Inequity in social exchange. In L. Berkowitz (Ed.), *Advances in experimental social psychology* (Vol. 2). New York: Academic Press.

Adams, R. S., & Biddle, B. J. (1970). *Realities of teaching: Explorations with videotape.* New York: Holt, Rinehart, & Winston.

Ader, R. (1975). Competitive and noncompetitive rearing and shock-elicited aggression in the rat. *Animal Learning and Behavior, 3,* 337–339.

Adorno, T. W., Frenkel-Brunswick, E., Levinson, D. J., & Sanford, R. N. (1950). *The authoritarian personality.* New York: Harper.

Ahmed, S. M. S. (1979). Invasion of personal space: A study of departure time as affected by sex of intruder and saliency condition. *Perceptual and Motor Skills, 49,* 85–86.

Aiello, J. R. (1987). Human spatial behavior. In D. Stokols & I. Altman (Eds.), *Handbook of environmental psychology* (Vol. 1). New York: Wiley.

Aiello, J. R., & Aiello, T. D. (1974). The development of personal space: Proxemic behavior of children 6 through 16. *Human Ecology, 2*(3), 177–189.

Aiello, J. R., & Cooper, R. E. (1979). Personal space and social affect. Paper presented at the meeting of the Society for Research in Child Development, San Francisco.

Aiello, J. R., & Jones, S. E. (1971). Field study of the proxemic behavior of young school children in three subcultural groups. *Journal of Personality and Social Psychology, 19,* 351–356.

Aiello, J. R., & Jones, S. E. (1979). Proxemic behavior of black and white adolescents of two socioeconomic class levels. Paper presented at the meeting of the Society for Research in Child Development, San Francisco.

Aiello, J. R., Nicosia, G., & Thompson, D. E. (1970). Physiological, social, and behavioral consequences of crowding on children and adolescents. *Child Development, 50,* 195–202.

Aiello, J. R., & Thompson, D. E. (1980). When compensation fails: Mediating effects on sex and locus of control at extended interation distances. *Basic and Applied Social Psychology, 1*(1), 65–82.

Ainsworth, M. D., Blehar, M. C., Waters, E., & Wall, S. (1978). *Patterns of attachment: A psychological study of the strange situation.* Hillsdale, NJ: Erlbaum.

Ajzen, I. (1987). Attitudes, traits, and actions: Dispositional prediction of behavior in personality and social psychology.

In L. Berkowitz (Ed.), *Advances in experimental social psychology* (Vol. 20). San Diego: Academic Press.

Ajzen, I. (1991). The theory of planned behavior. *Organizational Behavior and Human Decision Processes, 50,* 179–211.

Ajzen, I., & Fishbein, M. (1980). *Understanding attitudes and predicting social behavior.* Englewood Cliffs, NJ: Prentice-Hall.

Ajzen, I., & Madden, T. (1986). Prediction of goal-directed behavior: Attitudes, intentions, and perceived behavioral control. *Journal of Experimental Social Psychology, 22,* 453–474.

Albright, L., Kenny, D. A., & Malloy, T. E. (1988). Consensus in personality judgments at zero acquaintance. *Journal of Personality and Social Psychology, 55,* 387–395.

Aldag, R. J., & Fuller, S. R. (1993). Beyond fiasco: A reappraisal of the groupthink phenomenon and a new model of group decision processes. *Psychological Bulletin, 3,* 533–552.

Alden, L., & Cappe, R. (1986). Interpersonal process training for shy clients. In W. H. Jones, J. M. Cheeck, & S. R. Briggs (Eds.), *Shyness: Perspectives on research and treatment.* New York: Plenum.

Allen, H. (1968). Unpublished doctoral dissertation, New York University.

Allen, V. L. (1975). Social support for nonconformity. In L. Berkowitz (Ed.), *Advances in experimental social psychology* (Vol. 8). New York: Academic Press.

Allen, V. L., & Levine, J. M. (1968). Social support, dissent, and conformity. *Sociometry, 31,* 138–149.

Allen, V. L., & Levine, J. M. (1969). Consensus and conformity. *Journal of Experimental Psychology, 5,* 389–399.

Allgeier, A. R., & Byrne, D. (1973). Attraction toward the opposite sex as a determinant of physical proximity. *Journal of Social Psychology, 90,* 213–219.

Alloy, L. B., & Abramson, L. Y. (1979). Judgment of contingency in depressed and nondepressed students: Sadder but wiser? *Journal of Experimental Psychology, General, 108,* 441–485.

Allport, F. (1924). *Social psychology*. Boston: Houghton Mifflin.

Allport, F. H. (1920). The influence of the group upon association and thought. *Journal of Experimental Psychology, 3,* 159–182.

Allport, G. W. (1935). Attitudes. In C. M. Murchison (Ed.), *Handbook of social psychology*. Worcester, MA: Clark University Press.

Allport, G. W. (1937). *Personality: A psychological interpretation*. New York: Holt, Rinehart & Winston.

Allport, G. W. (1950). *The individual and his religion: A psychological interpretation*. New York: Macmillan.

Allport, G. W. (1954). *The nature of prejudice*. Cambridge, MA: Addison-Wesley.

Allport, G. W. (1959). Religion and prejudice. *Crane Review, 2,* 1–10.

Allport, G. W. (1961). *Pattern and growth in personality*. New York: Holt, Rinehart & Winston.

Allport, G. W. (1985). The historical background of social psychology. In G. Lindzey & E. Aronson (Eds.), *Handbook of social psychology* (Vol. 1). New York: Random House.

Allport, G. W., & Odbert, H. S. (1936). Trait-names: A psycho-lexical study. *Psychological Monographs: General and Applied, 47* (1, Whole No. 211).

Allport, G. W., & Postman, L. (1965). *The psychology of rumor*. New York: Russell & Russell. (Originally published 1947.)

Allport, G. W., & Ross, J. M. (1967). Personal religious orientation and prejudice. *Journal of Personality and Social Psychology, 5,* 432–443.

Allred, K. D., & Smith, T. W. (1989). The hardy personality: Cognitive and physiological responses to evaluative threat. *Journal of Personality and Social Psychology, 56,* 257–266.

Altemeyer, B. (1981). *Right-wing authoritarianism*. Winnipeg: University of Manitoba Press.

Altemeyer, B. (1988). *Enemies of freedom: Understanding right-wing authoritarianism*. San Francisco: Jossey-Bass.

Altman, I. (1975). *The environment and social behavior: Privacy, personal space, territory, crowding*. Monterey, CA: Brooks/Cole.

Altman, I., & Chemers, M. M. (1980). *Culture and environment*. Monterey, CA: Brooks/Cole.

Altman, I., & Haythorn, W. W. (1967). The ecology of isolated groups. *Behavioral Science, 12,* 168–182.

Altman, I., & Taylor, D. A. (1973). *Social penetration: The development of interpersonal relationships*. New York: Holt, Rinehart & Winston.

Altman, I., Taylor, D. A., & Wheeler, L. (1971). Ecological aspects of group behavior in social isolation. *Journal of Applied Social Psychology, 1,* 76–100.

Altman, I., Vinsel, A., & Brown, B. A. (1981). Dialectic conceptions in social psychology: An application to social penetration and privacy regulation. In L. Berkowitz (Ed.), *Advances in experimental social psychology* (Vol. 14). New York: Academic Press.

Ambady, N., & Rosenthal, R. (1992). Thin slices of expressive behavior as predictors of interpersonal consequences: A meta-analysis. *Psychological Bulletin, 111,* 256–274.

Ambady, N., & Rosenthal, R. (1993). Half a minute: Predicting teacher evaluations from thin slices of nonverbal behavior and physical attractiveness. *Journal of Personality and Social Psychology, 64,* 431–441.

American Bar Association Project on Minimum Standards for Criminal Justice. (1968). *Standards relating to trial by jury*, Standard 5.4.

American Psychiatric Association. (1987). *Diagnostic and statistical manual of mental disorders* (3rd ed., revised). Washington, DC: Author.

American Psychological Association Ad Hoc Committee on Ethical Standards. (1982). *Ethical principles in the conduct of research with human participants*. Washington, DC: American Psychological Association.

Amir, Y. (1969). Contact hypothesis in ethnic relations. *Psychological Bulletin, 71,* 319–342.

Amir, Y. (1976). The role of intergroup contact in change of prejudice and ethnic relations. In P. Katz (Ed.), *Towards the elimination of racism*. New York: Pergamon Press.

Anastase, A. (1976). *Psychological testing* (4th ed.). New York: Macmillan.

Anderson, C. A. (1983). Abstract and concrete data in the perseverance of social theories: When weak data lead to unshakable beliefs. *Journal of Experimental Social Psychology, 19,* 93–108.

Anderson, C. A. (1987). Temperature and aggression: Effects on quarterly, yearly, and city rates of violent and nonviolent crime. *Journal of Personality and Social Psychology, 52,* 1161–1173.

Anderson, C. A. (1991). How people think about causes: Examination of the typical phenomenal organization of attributions for success and failure. *Social Cognition, 9,* 295–329.

Anderson, C. A., & Anderson, D. C. (1984). Ambient temperature and violent crime: Tests of the linear and curvilinear hypotheses. *Journal of Personality and Social Psychology, 46,* 91–97.

Anderson, C. A., Lepper, M. R., & Ross, L. (1980). Perseverance of social theories: The role of explanation in the persistence of discredited information. *Journal of Personality and Social Psychology, 39,* 1037–1049.

Anderson, C. L. (1981). The effect of a workshop on attitudes of female nursing students toward homosexuality. *Journal of Homosexuality, 7,* 57–69.

Anderson, D., Erwin, N., Flynn, D., Lewis, L., & Erwin, J. (1977). Effects of short-term crowding on aggression in captive groups of pigtail monkeys. *Aggressive Behavior, 3,* 33–46.

Anderson, N. H. (1974). Cognitive algebra: Integration theory applied to social attribution. In L. Berkowitz (Ed.), *Advances in experimental social psychology* (Vol. 7). New York: Academic Press.

Anderson, N. H., & Hubert, S. (1963). Effect of concomitant verbal recall on order effects in personality impression formation. *Journal of Verbal Learning and Verbal Behavior, 2,* 379–391.

Anderson, S. M., & Cole, S. W. (1990). "Do I know you?": The role of significant others in general social perception. *Journal of Personality and Social Psychology, 59,* 384–399.

Andreoli, V., & Worchel, S. (1978). Effects of media, communicator, and position of message on attitude change. *Public Opinion Quarterly, 42,* 59–70.

Antill, J. T. (1983). Sex role complementarity versus similarity in married couples. *Journal of Personality and Social Psychology, 45,* 145–155.

Appleyard, D., & Lintell, M. (1972). The environmental quality of city streets: The resident's viewpoint. *Journal of the American Institute of Planners, 38,* 84–101.

Archer, D., & Gartner, R. (1984). *Violence and crime in cross-national perspective*. New Haven: Yale University Press.

Archer, J., & Lloyd, B. (1985). *Sex and gender*. Cambridge, England: Cambridge University Press.

Argyle, M., & Dean, J. (1965). Eye-contact, distance, and affiliation. *Sociometry, 28,* 289–304.

Arkes, H. R., Boehm, L. E., & Xu, G. (1991). Determinants of judged validity.

Journal of Experimental Social Psychology, 27, 576–605.

Arkin, R. M., & Baumgardner, A. H. (1985). Self-handicapping. In J. H. Harvey & C. Weary (Eds.), *Attribution: Basic issues and applications*. New York: Academic Press.

Aronson, E. (1969). The theory of cognitive dissonance: A current perspective. In L. Berkowitz (Ed.), *Advances in experimental social psychology* (Vol. 4). New York: Academic Press.

Aronson, E. (1978). *The jigsaw classroom*. Beverly Hills, CA: Sage.

Aronson, E. (1990). Applying social psychology to desegregation and energy conservation. *Personality and Social Psychology Bulletin, 16*, 118–132.

Aronson, E., Brewer, M., & Carlsmith, J. M. (1985). Experimentation in social psychology. In G. Lindzey & E. Aronson (Eds.), *Handbook of social psychology* (Vol. 1). New York: Random House.

Aronson, E., & Carlsmith, J. M. (1968). Experimentation in social psychology. In G. Lindzey & E. Aronson (Eds.), *Handbook of social psychology* (Vol. 2) (2nd ed.). Reading, MA: Addison-Wesley.

Aronson, E., & Cope, B. (1968). My enemy's enemy is my friend. *Journal of Personality and Social Psychology, 8*, 8–12.

Aronson, E., Ellsworth, P. C., Carlsmith, J. M., & Gonzales, M. H. (1990). *Methods of research in social psychology* (2nd ed.). New York: McGraw-Hill.

Aronson, E., & Gonzales, M. H. (1990). Alternative social influence processes applied to energy conservation. In J. Edwards, R. S. Tindale, L. Heath, & E. J. Posavac (Eds.), *Social influence processes and prevention*. New York: Plenum.

Aronson, E.. & Mills, J. (1959). The effects of severity of initiation on liking for a group. *Journal of Abnormal and Social Psychology, 59*, 177–181.

Aronson, E., Turner, J. A., & Carlsmith, J. M. (1963). Communicator credibility and communication discrepancy as determinants of opinion change. *Journal of Abnormal and Social Psychology, 67*, 31–36.

Asch, S. E. (1946). Forming impressions of personality. *Journal of Abnormal and Social Psychology, 41*, 258–290.

Asch, S. E. (1951). Effects of group pressure upon the modification and distortion of judgments. In H. Guetzkow (Ed.), *Groups, leadership, and men*. Pittsburgh, Carnegie Press.

Asch, S. E. (1952). *Social psychology*. New York: Prentice-Hall.

Asch, S. E. (1955, November). Opinions and social pressure. *Scientific American, 31–35*.

Asch, S. E. (1956). Studies of independence and conformity: I. A minority of one against a unanimous majority. *Psychological Monographs, 70*, (Whole No. 416).

Ashmore, R. D., & Del Boca, F. K. (1981). Conceptual approaches to stereotypes and stereotyping. In D. L. Hamilton (Ed.), *Cognitive processes in stereotyping and intergroup behavior*. Hillsdale, NJ: Erlbaum.

Ashmore, R. D., Del Boca, F. K., & Wohlers, A. J. (1986). Gender stereotypes. In R. D. Ashmore & F. K. Del Boca (Eds.), *The social psychology of female–male relations*. Orlando, FL: Academic Press.

Ashton, N. L., Shaw, M. E., & Worsham, A. P. (1980). Affective reactions to interpersonal distance by friends and strangers. *Bulletin of the Psychonomic Society, 15*, 306–308.

Attorney General's Commission on Pornography: Final report. (1986). Washington, DC: United States Department of Justice.

Axelrod, R. (1984). *The evolution of cooperation*. New York: Basic Books.

Axelrod, R., & Hamilton, W. D. (1981). The evolution of cooperation. *Science, 211*, 1390–1396.

Azrin, N. H. (1967, May). Pain and aggression. *Psychology Today*, 27–33.

Azrin, N. H., Hutchinson, R. R., & Hake, D. F. (1966). Extinction-induced aggression. *Journal of the Experimental Analysis of Behavior, 9*, 191–204.

Azrin, N. H., Hutchinson, R. R., & McLaughlin, R. (1965). The opportunity for aggression as an operant reinforcer during aversive stimulation. *Journal of the Experimental Analysis of Behavior, 8*, 171–180.

Babad, E. Y., Inbar, J., & Rosenthal, R. (1982). Pygmaleon, Galatea, and the Golem: Investigations of biased and unbiased teachers. *Journal of Educational Psychology, 74*, 459–474.

Bagozzi, R. P. (1978). The construct validity of the affective, behavioral and cognitive components of attitude by analysis of covariance structure. *Multivariate Behavioral Research, 13*, 9–31.

Bain, D. J. G. (1976). Doctor–patient communication in general practice consultations. *Medical Education, 10*, 125–131.

Bakan, D. (1971). *Slaughter of the innocents: A study of the battered child phenomenon*. Boston: Beacon.

Bales, R. F. (1950). *Interaction process analysis: A method for the study of small groups*. Reading, MA: Addison-Wesley.

Bales, R. F. (1958). Task roles and social roles in problem-solving groups. In E. E.

Maccoby, T. M. Newcomb, & E. L. Hartley (Eds.), *Readings in social psychology*. New York: Holt, Rinehart & Winston.

Bales, R. F. (1970). *Personality and interpersonal behavior*. New York: Holt, Rinehart & Winston.

Bales, R. F., & Strodtbeck, F. (1951). Phases in group problem-solving. *Journal of Abnormal and Social Psychology, 46*, 485–495.

Bandura, A. (1965). Influence of model's reinforcement contingencies on the acquisition of imitative responses. *Journal of Personality and Social Psychology, 1*, 589–595.

Bandura, A. (1973). *Aggression: A social learning analysis*. Englewood Cliffs, NJ: Prentice-Hall.

Bandura, A. (1977). *Social learning theory*. Englewood Cliffs, NJ: Prentice-Hall.

Bandura, A. (1986). *Social foundations of thought and action: A social cognitive theory*. Englewood Cliffs, NJ: Prentice-Hall.

Bandura, A., & Huston, A. C. (1961). Identification as a process of incidental learning. *Journal of Abnormal and Social Psychology, 63*, 311–318.

Bandura, A., Ross, D., & Ross, S. A. (1961). Transmission of aggression through imitation of aggressive models. *Journal of Abnormal and Social Psychology, 63*, 575–582.

Bandura, A., Ross, D., & Ross, S. A. (1963a). A comparative test of the status envy, social power and secondary reinforcement theories of identificatory learning. *Journal of Abnormal and Social Psychology, 67*, 527–534.

Bandura, A., Ross, D., & Ross, S. A. (1963b). Vicarious reinforcement and imitative learning. *Journal of Abnormal and Social Psychology, 67*, 601–607.

Baran, S. J., Chase, L. J., & Courtright, J. A. (1979). Television drama as a facilitator of prosocial behavior: "The Waltons." *Journal of Broadcasting, 23(3)*, 277–284.

Bar-Hillel, M., & Fischoff, B. (1981). When do base rates affect predictions? *Journal of Personality and Social Psychology, 41*, 671–680.

Barker, R. G., Dembo, T., & Lewin, K. (1941). Frustration and regression: An experiment with young children. *University of Iowa Studies in Child Welfare, 18(1)*.

Baron, L., & Straus, M. A. (1984). Sexual stratification, pornography, and rape in the United States. In N. M. Malamuth & E. Donnerstein (Eds.), *Pornography and sexual aggression*. Orlando, FL: Academic Press.

Baron, L., & Straus, M. A. (1985). *Legitimate violence, pornography, and sexual inequality as explanations for state and regional differences in rape.* Unpublished manuscript, Yale University, New Haven, CT.

Baron, L., & Straus, M. A. (1986). *Rape and its relation to social disorganization, pornography, and sexual inequality in the United States.* Unpublished, Yale University, New Haven, CT.

Baron, R., & Rodin, J. (1978). Personal control as a mediator of crowding. In A. Baum, J. E. Singer, & S. Valins (Eds.), *Advances in environmental psychology.* Hillsdale, NJ: Erlbaum.

Baron, R. A. (1971). Reducing the influence of an aggressive model: The restraining effects of discrepant modeling cues. *Journal of Personality and Social Psychology, 20,* 240–245.

Baron, R. A. (1972). Reducing the influence of an aggressive model: The restraining effects of peer censure. *Journal of Personality and Social Psychology, 8,* 266–275.

Baron, R. A. (1976). The reduction of human aggression: A field study of the influence of incompatible reactions. *Journal of Applied Social Psychology, 6,* 260–274.

Baron, R. A. (1977). *Human aggression.* New York: Plenum.

Baron, R. A. (1983). The control of human aggression: An optimistic perspective. *Journal of Social and Clinical Psychology, 1,* 97–119.

Baron, R. A., & Bell, P. A. (1975). Aggression and heat: Mediating effects of prior provocation and exposure to an aggressive model. *Journal of Personality and Social Psychology, 31,* 825–832.

Baron, R. A., & Kepner, C. R. (1970). Model's behavior and attraction toward the model as determinants of adult aggressive behavior. *Journal of Personality and Social Psychology, 14,* 335–344.

Baron, R. M. (1988). An ecological framework for establishing a dual-mode theory of social knowledge. In D. Bar-Tal & A. W. Kruglanski (Eds.), *The social psychology of knowledge.* Cambridge, England: Cambridge University Press.

Baron, R. S. (1986). Distraction-conflict theory: Progress and problems. In L. Berkowitz (Ed.), *Advances in experimental social psychology.* Orlando, FL: Academic Press.

Baron, R. S., & Rodin, J. (1978). Perceived control and crowding stress. In A. Baum, J. Singer, & S. Valins (Eds.), *Advances in environmental psychology* (Vol. 1). Hillsdale, NJ: Erlbaum.

Barrera, M., Sandler, I., & Ramsay, T. (1981). Preliminary development of a scale of social support: Studies on college stu-dents. *American Journal of Community Psychology, 9,* 434–447.

Barry, H., Bacon, M. K., & Child, I. L. (1957). A cross-cultural survey of same sex differences in socialization. *Journal of Abnormal and Social Psychology, 55,* 327–332.

Bar-Tal, D. (1976). *Prosocial behavior: Theory and research.* Washington, DC: Hemisphere.

Bartholomew, K., & Horowitz, L. M. (1991). Attachment styles among young adults: a test of a four-category model. *Journal of Personality and Social Psychology, 61,* 226–244.

Basow, S. A. (1986). *Gender stereotypes: Traditions and alternatives* (2nd ed.). Monterey, CA: Brooks/Cole.

Bass, B. M. (1990). *Bass & Stogdill's handbook of leadership: Theory, research and managerial applications* (3rd ed.) New York: Free Press.

Bassoff, E. S., & Glass, G. V. (1982). The relationship between sex roles and mental health: A meta-analysis of twenty-six studies. *Counseling Psychologist, 10,* 105–112.

Batson, C. D. (1987). Prosocial motivation: Is it ever truly altruistic? In L. Berkowitz (Ed.), *Advances in experimental social psychology* (Vol. 20). San Diego: Academic Press.

Batson, C. D. (1990). Good Samaritans—or priests and Levites? Using William James as a guide in the study of prosocial motivation. *Personality and Social Psychology Bulletin, 16,* 758–768.

Batson, C. D., Bolen, M. H., Cross, J. A., & Neuringer-Benefield, H. E. (1986). Where is the altruism in the altruistic personality? *Journal of Personality and Social Psychology, 50,* 212–220.

Batson, C. D., Duncan, B. D., Ackerman, P., Buckley, T., & Birch, K. (1981). Is empathic emotion a source of altruistic motivation? *Journal of Personality and Social Psychology, 40,* 290–302.

Batson, C. D., Dyck, J. L., Brandt, J. R., Batson, J. G., Powell, A. L., McMaster, M. R., & Griffitt, C. (1988). Five studies testing two new egoistic alternatives to the empathy–altruism hypothesis. *Journal of Personality and Social Psychology, 55,* 52–77.

Batson, C. D., & Flory, J. D. (1990). Goal-relevant cognitions associated with helping by individuals high on intrinsic end religion. *Journal of the Scientific Study of Religion, 29,* 346–360.

Batson, C. D., & Gray, R. A. (1981). Religious orientation and helping behavior: Responding to one's own or to the victim's needs? *Journal of Personality and Social Psychology, 40,* 511–520.

Batson, C. D., Jones, C. H., & Cochran, P. J. (1979). Attributional bias in counselors' diagnoses: The effects of resources. *Journal of Applied Social Psychology, 9,* 377–393.

Batson, C. D., Naifeh, S. J., & Pate, S. (1978). Social desirability, religious orientation, and racial prejudice. *Journal for the Scientific Study of Religion, 17,* 31–41.

Batson, C. D., & Oleson, K. C. (1991). Current status of the empathy–altruism hypothesis. In M. S. Clark (Ed.), *Prosocial behavior.* Newbury Park, CA: Sage.

Batson, C. D., Oleson, K. C., Weeks, J. L., Healy, S. P., Reeves, P. J., Jennings, P., & Brown, R. (1989). Religious prosocial motivation: Is it altruistic or egoistic? *Journal of Personality and Social Psychology, 57,* 873–884.

Batson, C. D., & Ventis, W. L. (1982). *The religious experience: A social psychological perspective.* New York: Oxford University Press.

Baum, A., & Davis, G. (1980). Reducing the stress of high-density living: An architectural intervention. *Journal of Personality, 38,* 471–481.

Baum, A., & Greenberg, C. I. (1975). Waiting for a crowd: The behavioral and perceptual effects of anticipated crowding. *Journal of Personality and Social Psychology, 32,* 671–679.

Baum, A., & Paulus, P. (1987). Crowding. In D. Stokols & I. Altman (Eds.), *Handbook of environmental psychology* (Vol. 1). New York: Wiley.

Baum, A., & Valins, S. (1977). *Architecture and social behavior: Psychological studies of social density.* Hillsdale, NJ: Erlbaum.

Baum, A., & Valins, S. (1979). Architectural mediation of residential density and control: Crowding and the regulation of social contact. In L. Berkowitz (Ed.), *Advances in experimental social psychology* (Vol. 12). New York: Academic Press.

Baumeister, R. F. (1985). The championship choke. *Psychology Today, 19*(4), 48–52.

Baumeister, R. F. (Ed.). (1986). *Public self and private self.* New York: Springer-Verlag.

Baumeister, R. F. (1990). Suicide as escape from self. *Psychological Review, 97,* 90–113.

Baumeister, R. F., & Darley, J. M. (1982). Reducing the biasing effects of perpetrator attractiveness in jury simulation. *Personality and Social Psychology Bulletin, 8,* 286–292.

Baumeister, R. F., & Stenhilber, A. (1984). Paradoxical effects of supportive audiences on performance under pressure: The home field disadvantage in sports championships. *Journal of Personality and Social Psychology, 47,* 85–93.

Baumrind, D. (1964). Some thoughts on the ethics of research: After reading Milgram's "Behavioral study of obedience." *American Psychologist, 19,* 421–423.

Bavelas, A., Hastorf, A. H., Gross, A. E., & Kite, W. R. (1965). Experiments on the alteration of group structure. *Journal of Experimental Social Psychology, 1,* 55–70.

Baxter, J. C. (1970). Interpersonal spacing in natural settings. *Sociometry, 33,* 444–456.

Bazerman, M. H., Magliozzi, T., & Neale, M. A. (1985). Integrative bargaining in a competitive market. *Organizational Behavior and Human Decision Processes, 35,* 294–313.

Beaman, A. L., Barnes, P. J., Klentz, B., & McQuirk, B. (1978). Increasing helping rates through information dissemination: Teaching pays. *Personality and Social Psychology Bulletin, 4,* 406–411.

Beaman, A. L., Klentz, B., Diener, E., & Svanum, S. (1979). Objective self-awareness and transgression in children: A field study. *Journal of Personality and Social Psychology, 37,* 1835–1846.

Beck, A. T. (1976). *Cognitive therapy and the emotional disorders.* New York: International Universities Press.

Beck, S. P., Ward-Hull, C. I., & McLear, P. M. (1976). Variables related to women's somatic preferences of the male and female body. *Journal of Personality and Social Psychology, 34,* 1200–1210.

Becker, B. J. (1986). Influence again: Another look at studies of gender differences in social influence. In J. S. Hyde & M. C. Linn (Eds.), *The psychology of gender: Advances through meta-analysis.* Baltimore: Johns Hopkins University Press.

Becker, F. D. (1973). A study of spatial markers. *Journal of Personality and Social Psychology, 26,* 439–445.

Becker, F. D., Sommer, R., Bee, J., & Oxley, B. (1973). College classroom ecology. *Sociometry, 36,* 514–525.

Becker, M. H. (1974). The health belief model and sick role behavior. *Health Education Monographs, 2,* 409–419.

Bedell, J. R., Giordani, B., Amour, J. L., Tavormina, J., & Boll, T. (1977). Life stress and the psychology and medical adjustment of chronically ill children. *Journal of PsychosomaticResearch, 21,* 237–243.

Begam, R. (1977). Voir dire: The attorney's job. *Trial, 13,* 3.

Bell, B. E., & Loftus, E. F. (1988). Degree of detail of eyewitness testimony and mock juror judgements. *Journal of Applied Social Psychology, 18,* 1171–1192.

Bell, P. A. & Baron, R. A. (1976). Aggression and heat: The mediating role of negative affect. *Journal of Applied Social Psychology, 6,* 18–30.

Bell, P. A., Fisher, J. D., Baum, A., & Greene, T. C. (1990). *Environmental psychology.* Fort Worth: Holt, Rinehart and Winston.

Belleza, F. S., & Bower, G. H. (1981). Person stereotypes and memory for people. *Journal of Personality and Social Psychology, 41,* 856–865.

Belmore, S. M. (1987). Determinants of attention during impression formation. *Journal of Experimental Psychology: Learning, Memory and Cognition, 13,* 480–489.

Bem, D. J. (1965). An experimental analysis of self-persuasion. *Journal of Experimental Social Psychology, 1,* 199–218.

Bem, D. J. (1967). Self-perception: An alternative interpretation of cognitive dissonance phenomena. *Psychological Review, 74,* 183–200.

Bem, D. J. (1968). The epistemological status of interpersonal simulations: A reply to Jones, Linder, Kiesler, Zanna, and Brehm. *Journal of Experimental Social Psychology, 4,* 270–274.

Bem, D. J. (1970). *Beliefs, attitudes, and human affairs.* Monterey, CA: Brooks/Cole.

Bem, D. J. (1972). Self-perception theory. In L. Berkowitz (Ed.), *Advances in experimental social psychology* (Vol. 6). New York: Academic Press.

Bem, D. J. (1983). Toward a response-style theory of persons in situations. In M. M. Page (Ed.), *Personality—Current theory and research: Nebraska symposium on motivation 1982.*

Bem, D. J., & Allen, A. (1974). On predicting some of the people some of the time: The search for cross-situational consistencies in behavior. *Psychological Review, 81,* 506–520.

Bem, D. J., Wallach, M. A., & Kogan, N. (1965). Group decision making under risk of aversive consequences. *Journal of Personality and Social Psychology, 1,* 453–460.

Bem, S. L. (1974). The measurement of psychological androgyny. *Journal of Consulting and Clinical Psychology, 42,* 155–162.

Bem, S. L. (1975). Sex role adaptability: One consequence of psychological androgyny. *Journal of Personality and Social Psychology, 31,* 634–643.

Bem, S. L. (1981). Gender schema theory: A cognitive account of sex typing. *Psychological Review, 88,* 354–364.

Bem, S. L., & Lenney, E. (1976). Sex typing and the avoidance of cross-sex behavior. *Journal of Personality and Social Psychology, 33,* 48–54.

Bem, S. L., Martyna, W., & Watson, C. (1976). Sex typing and androgyny: Further explorations of the expressive domain. *Journal of Personality and Social Psychology, 34,* 1016–1023.

Bentler, P. M., & Speckart, G. (1979). Models of attitude–behavior relations. *Psychological Review, 86,* 452–464.

Ben-Veniste, R. (1971). Pornography and sex-crime: The Danish experience. *Technical reports of the committee on obscenity and pornography* (Vol. 8). Washington, DC: U.S. Government Printing Office.

Berelson, B., Lazarsfeld, P. L., & McPhee, W. N. (1954). *Voting.* Chicago: University of Chicago Press.

Bergen, D. J., & Williams, J. E. (1991). Sex stereotypes in the United States revisited: 1972–1988. *Sex Roles, 24,* 413–423.

Berger, C. R. (1980). Power and the family. In M. E. Roloff & G. E. Miller (Eds.), *Persuasion: New directions in theory and research.* Beverly Hills, CA: Sage.

Berglas, S., & Jones, E. E. (1978). Drug choice as a self-handicapping strategy in response to noncontingent success. *Journal of Personality and Social Psychology, 36,* 405–417.

Bergman, J. (1974). Are little girls being harmed by Sesame Street? In J. Staceyu (Ed.), *And Jill came tumbling after: Sexism in American education.* New York: Dell.

Berkman, L. (1985). The relationship of social networks and social support to morbidity and mortality. In S. Cohen & S. L. Syme (Eds.), *Social support and health.* Orlando, FL: Academic Press.

Berkman, L., & Breslow, L. (1983). *Health and ways of living: Findings from the Alameda County study.* New York: Oxford University Press.

Berkman, L., & Syme, S. L. (1979). Social networks, host resistance, and mortality: A nine-year follow-up of Alameda County residents. *American Journal of Epidemiology, 109,* 186–204.

Berkowitz, L. (1965). Some aspects of observed aggression. *Journal of Personality and Social Psychology, 2,* 359–369.

Berkowitz, L. (1968, May). Impulse, aggression, and the gun. *Psychology Today,* 18–22.

Berkowitz, L. (1972). Social norms, feelings and other factors affecting helping behavior and altruism. In L. Berkowitz (Ed.), *Advances in experimental social psychology* (Vol. 6). New York: Academic Press.

Berkowitz, L. (1978). Whatever happened to the frustration–aggression hypothesis? *American Behavioral Scientist, 21,* 691–708.

Berkowitz, L. (1983a). Aversively stimulated aggression: Some parallels and differences in research with animals and humans. *American Psychologist, 38,* 1135–1144.

Berkowitz, L. (1983b). The experience of anger as a parallel process in the display of impulsive, "angry" aggression. In R. G. Geen & E. I. Donnerstein (Eds.), *Aggression: Theoretical and empirical reviews* (Vol. 1). New York: Academic Press.

Berkowitz, L. (1984). Some effects of thoughts on anti- and pro-social influences of media events: A cognitive–neoassociation analysis. *Psychological Bulletin, 95,* 410–427.

Berkowitz, L. (1988). Frustrations, appraisals, and aversively stimulated aggression. *Aggressive Behavior, 14,* 3–11.

Berkowitz, L., Cochran, S., & Embree, M. (1981). Physical pain and the goal of aversively stimulated aggression. *Journal of Personality and Social Psychology, 40,* 687–700.

Berkowitz, L., & Daniels, L. R. (1963). Responsibility and dependency. *Journal of Abnormal and Social Psychology, 66,* 429–436.

Berkowitz, L., & Donnerstein, E. (1982). External validity is more than skin deep: Some answers to criticisms of laboratory experiments (with special reference to research on aggression). *American Psychologist, 37,* 245–257.

Berkowitz, L., & Geen, R. G. (1966). Film violence and the cue properties of available targets. *Journal of Personality and Social Psychology, 3,* 525–530.

Berkowitz, L., & Geen, R. G. (1967). Stimulus qualities of the target of aggression: A further study. *Journal of Personality and Social Psychology, 5,* 364–368.

Berkowitz, L., & LePage, A. (1967). Weapons as aggression-eliciting stimuli. *Journal of Personality and Social Psychology, 7,* 202–207.

Bermant, G. (1977). *Conduct of the voir dire examination: Practices and opinions of federal district judges.* Washington, DC: Federal Judicial Center.

Berry, D. S., & McArthur, L. Z. (1986). Perceiving character in faces: The impact of age-related craniofacial changes in social perception. *Psychological Bulletin, 100,* 3–18.

Berry, D. S., & Zebrowitz-McArthur, L. (1988). What's in a face? Facial maturity and the attribution of legal responsibil-

ity. *Personality and Social Psychology Bulletin, 14,* 23–33.

Berry, G. L. (1980). Television and Afro-Americans: Past legacy and present portrayals. In S. B. Withey & R. P. Abeles (Eds.), *Television and social behavior: Beyond violence and children.* Hillsdale, NJ: Erlbaum.

Berscheid, E. (1983). Emotion. In H. H. Kelley, E. Berscheid, A. Christensen, J. H. Harvey, T. L. Huston, G. Levinger, E. McClintock, L. A. Peplau, & D. R. Petersen (Eds.), *Close relationships.* New York: Freeman.

Berscheid, E. (1985). Interpersonal attraction. In G. Lindzey & E. Aronson (Eds.), *Handbook of social psychology* (Vol. 2). New York: Random House.

Berscheid, E., & Campbell, B. (1981). The changing longevity of heterosexual close relationships: A commentary and forecast. In M. Lerner (Ed.), *The justice motive in times of scarcity and change.* New York: Plenum.

Berscheid, E., Dion, K., & Walster, E. (1971). Physical attractiveness and dating choice: A test of the matching hypothesis. *Journal of Experimental Social Psychology, 7,* 173–189.

Berscheid, E., & Walster, E. (1974a). A little bit about love. In T. L. Huston (Ed.), *Foundations of interpersonal attraction.* New York: Academic Press.

Berscheid, E., & Walster, E. (1974b). Physical attractiveness. In L. Berkowitz (Ed.), *Advances in experimental social psychology.* New York: Academic Press.

Bertenthal, B. I., & Fisher, K. W. (1978). Development of self-recognition in the infant. *Developmental Psychology, 14,* 44–50.

Bertilson, H. S. (1983). Methodology in the study of aggression. In R. G. Geen & E. I. Donnerstein (Eds.), *Aggression: Theoretical and empirical reviews* (Vol. 1). New York: Academic Press.

Bettelheim, B. (1943). Individual and mass behavior in extreme situations. *Journal of Abnormal and Social Psychology, 38,* 417–452.

Bettelheim, B., & Janowitz, M. (1950). *Dynamics of prejudice: A psychological and sociological study of veterans.* New York: Harper & Row.

Bianchi, S. M., Farley, R., & Spain, D. (1982). Racial inequalities in housing: An examination of recent trends. *Demography, 19,* 37–51.

Bickman, L., & Kamzan, N. (1973). The effects of race and need on helping behavior. *Journal of Social Psychology, 98,* 73–77.

Bierly, M. M. (1985). Prejudice toward con-

temporary outgroups as a generalized attitude. *Journal of Applied Social Psychology, 15,* 189–199.

Biernat, M. (1991). Gender stereotypes and the relationship between masculinity and femininity: A developmental analysis. *Journal of personality and social psychology, 61,* 351–365.

Biernat, M., & Wortman, C. B. (1991). Sharing of home responsibilities between professionally employed women and their husbands. *Journal of Personality and Social Psychology, 60,* 844–860.

Billig, M., & Tajfel, H. (1973). Social categorization and similarity in intergroup behavior. *European Journal of Social Psychology, 3,* 27–52.

Black, T. E., & Higbee, K. L. (1973). Effects of power, threat, and sex on exploitation. *Journal of Personality and Social Psychology, 27,* 382–388.

Blanchard, D. C., & Blanchard, R. J. (1986). Punishment and aggression: A critical reexamination. In R. J. Blanchard & D. C. Blanchard (Eds.), *Advances in the study of aggression.* Orlando, FL: Academic Press.

Blanck, P. D., Rosenthal, R., & Cordell, L H. (1985). The appearance of justice: Judges' verbal and nonverbal behavior in criminal jury trials. *Stanford Law Review, 38:89,* 89–164.

Blasi, A. (1980). Bridging moral cognition and moral action: A critical review of the literature. *Psychological Bulletin, 88,* 1–45.

Blass, T. (1991). Understanding behavior in the Milgram obedience experiment: The role of personality, situations, and their interactions. *Journal of Personality and Social Psychology, 60,* 398-413.

Blass, T. (1992). The social psychology of Stanley Milgram. In M. P. Zanna (Ed.), *Advances in experimental social psychology* (Vol. 25). San Diego: Academic Press.

Blau, P. M. (1964). *Exchange and power in social life.* New York: Wiley.

Bleda, P., & Bleda, S. (1978). Effects of sex and smoking on reaction to spatial invasion at a shopping mall. *Journal of Social Psychology, 104,* 311–312.

Bless, H., Bohner, G., Schwarz, N., & Strack, F. (1990). Mood and persuasion: A cognitive response analysis. *Personality and Social Psychology Bulletin, 16,* 331–345.

Block, J. (1971). *Lives through time.* Berkeley, CA: Bancroft.

Block, J., Weiss, D. S., & Thorne, A. (1979). How relevant is a semantic similarity interpretation of personality ratings? *Journal of Personality and Social Psychology, 37,* 1055–1074.

Block, J. H. (1978). Another look at sex differentiation in the socialization behaviors of mothers and daughters. In J. Sherman and F. Denmark (Eds.), *Psychology of women: Future directions of research.* New York: Psychological Dimensions.

Blood, R. O., & Blood, M. (1978). *Marriage* (3rd ed.). New York: Free Press.

Bloom, B. L., White, S. W., & Asher, S. J. (1979). Marital disruption as a stressful life event. In G. Levinger & O. C. Moles (Eds.), *Divorce and separation.* New York: Basic Books.

Bochner, S., & Insko, C. A. (1966). Communicator discrepancy, source credibility, and opinion change. *Journal of Personality and Social Psychology, 4,* 614–621.

Bock, D. C. (1972). Obedience: A response to authority and Christian commitment. Disertation Abstracts International, 33, 3278B–3279B (University Microfilms, No. 72-31, 651).

Bogatz, G. A., & Ball, S. J. (1971). *The second year of Sesame Street: A continuing evaluation.* 2 Vols. Princeton, NJ: Educational Testing Service.

Bohannan, P. (1960). *African homicide and suicide.* New York: Atheneum.

Bollen, K. A., & Phillips, D. P. (1982). Imitative suicides: A national study of the effects of television news stories. *American Sociological Review, 47,* 802–809.

Bond, C. F. Jr. & Titus, L. J. (1983). Social facilitation: A meta-analysis of 241 studies. *Psychological Bulletin, 94,* 265–292.

Bond, M. H. (1986). *The psychology of the Chinese people.* New York: Oxford University Press.

Booraem, C., Flowers, J., Bodner, G., & Satterfield, D. (1977). Personal space variations as a function of criminal behavior. *Psychology Reports, 41,* 1115–1121.

Booth, A., & Welch, S. (1973). The effects of crowding: A cross-national study. Unpublished manuscript, Ministry of State for Urban Affairs, Ottawa, Canada.

Booth, A., & Welch, S. (1974). Crowding and urban crime rates. Paper presented at the annual meeting of the Midwest Sociological Association, Omaha, NE.

Borden, R. J., Bowen, R., & Taylor, S. P. (1971). Shock setting as a function of physical attack and extrinsic reward. *Perceptual and Motor Skills, 33,* 563–568.

Borgatta, E. F., Couch, A. A., & Bales, R. F. (1954). Some findings relevant to the great man theory of leadership. *American Sociological Review, 19,* 755–759.

Borgida, E., & Brekke, N. (1985). Psychological research on rape trials. In A. Burgess (Ed.), *Research handbook on rape and sexual assault.* New York: Garland.

Bornstein, R. F. (1989). Exposure and affect: Overview and meta-analysis of research. *Psychological Bulletin, 102,* 265–289.

Bornstein, R. F., Kale, A. R., & Cornell, K. R. (1990). Boredom as a limiting condition on the mere exposure effect. *Journal of Personality and Social Psychology, 58,* 791–800.

Bossard, J. H. S. (1931). Residential propinquity as a factor in marriage selection. *American Journal of Sociology, 38,* 219–224.

Bothwell, R. K., Deffenbacher, K. A., & Brigham, J. C. (1987). Correlation of eyewitness accuracy and confidence: Optimality hypothesis revisited. *Journal of Applied Psychology, 72,* 691–695.

Boudreau, F. A. (1986). Education. In F. A. Boudreau, R. S. Sennott, & M. Wilson (Eds.), *Sex roles and social patterns.* New York: Praeger.

Bouton, R. A., Gallaher, P. E., Garlinghouse, P. A., Leal, T., Rosenstein, L. D., & Young, R. K. (1989). Demographic variables associated with fear of AIDS and homophobia. *Journal of Applied Social Psychology, 19,* 885–901.

Bowers, K. S. (1973). Situationism in psychology: An analysis and a critique. *Psychological Review, 80,* 307–336.

Bowsher, J. E., & Gerlach, M. J. (1990). Personal control and other determinants of psychological well-being in nursing home elders. *Scholarly Inquiry for Nursing Practice, 4,* 91–102.

Boyanowsky, E. O., & Allen, V. L. (1973). Ingroup norms and self-identity as determinants of discriminatory behavior. *Journal of Personality and Social Psychology, 25,* 408–418.

Boyd, B., & Wandersman, A. (1991). Predicting undergraduate condom use with the Fishbein and Ajzen and the Triandis attitude–behavior models: Implications for public health interventions. *Journal of Applied Social Psychology, 21,* 1810–1830.

Bradbury, T. N., & Fincham, F. D. (1990). Attributions in marriage: Review and critique. *Psychological Bulletin, 107,* 3–33.

Bradbury, T. N., & Fincham, F. D. (1992). Attributions and behavior in marital interaction. *Journal of Personality and Social Psychology, 63,* 613–628.

Bradshaw, J. L. (1969). The information conveyed by varying dimensions of features in human outline faces. *Perception and Psychophysics, 6,* 5–9.

Brady, A. T., & Walker, M. B. (1978). Interpersonal distance as a function of situationally induced anxiety. *British Journal of Social and Clinical Psychology, 17,* 127–133.

Brand, R. J., Rosenman, R. H., Sholtz, R. I., & Friedman, M. (1976). Multivariate prediction of coronary heart disease in the Western Collaborative Group Study compared to the findings of the Framingham Study. *Circulation, 53,* 938–955.

Bray, R. M., Johnson, D., & Chilstrom, J. T. (1982). Social influence by group members with minority opinions: A comparison of Hollander and Moscovici. *Journal of Personality and Social Psychology, 43,* 78–88.

Bray, R. M., & Noble, A. M. (1978). Authoritarianism and decisions of mock juries: Evidence of jury bias and group polarization. *Journal of Personality and Social Psychology, 36,* 1424–1430.

Brehm, J. (1966). *A theory of psychological reactance.* New York: Academic Press.

Brehm, S. S., & Brehm, J. W. (1981). *Psychological reactance.* New York: Academic Press.

Breuer, J., & Freud, S. (1956). *Studies on hysteria.* London: Hogarth Press. (Originally published 1893–1895.)

Brewer, M. B. (1988). A dual process model of impression formation. In T. K. Srull & R. S. Wyer, Jr. (Eds.), *Advances in social cognition* (Vol. 1). Hillsdale, NJ: Erlbaum.

Brewer, M. B., Dull, U., & Lui, L. (1981). Perceptions of the elderly: Stereotypes as prototypes. *Journal of Personality and Social Psychology, 41,* 656–670.

Brewer, M. B., & Kramer, R. K. (1986). Choice behavior in social dilemmas: Effects of social identity, group size, and decision framing. *Journal of Personality and Social Psychology, 50,* 543–549.

Brewer, M. B., & Lui, L. L. (1989). The primacy of age and sex in the structure of person categories. *Social Cognition, 7,* 262–274.

Brewer, M. B., & Silver, M. (1978). Ingroup bias as a function of task characteristics. *European Journal of Social Psychology, 8,* 393–400.

Brickman, P., Becker, L. J., & Castle, S. (1979). Making trust easier and harder through forms of sequential interaction. *Journal of Personality and Social Psychology, 37,* 515–521.

Briggs, S. R., Cheek, J. M., & Jones, W. H. (1986). Introduction. In W. H. Jones, J. M. Cheek, & S. R. Briggs (Eds.), *Shyness: Perspectives on research and treatment.* New York: Plenum.

Briggs, S. R., & Smith, T. G. (1986). The measurement of shyness. In W. H. Jones, J. M. Cheek, & S. R. Briggs (Eds.), *Shyness: Perspectives on research and treatment.* New York: Plenum.

Brigham, J. C. (1971). Ethnic stereotypes. *Psychological Bulletin, 76,* 15–38.

Brigham, J. C. (1986). The influence of race on face recognition. In H. D. Ellis, M. A. Jeeves, F. Newcombe, & A. Young (Eds.), *Aspects of face processing.* Dordrecht, The Netherlands: Martinus Nijhoff.

Brislin, R. W., & Lewis, S. A. (1968). Dating and physical attractiveness: A replication. *Psychological Reports, 22,* 976.

Brockner, J., & Swap, W. C. (1976). Effects of repeated exposure on self-disclosure and interpersonal attraction. *Journal of Personality and Social Psychology, 33,* 531–540.

Brooks, C. I., & Rebeta, J. L. (1991). College classroom ecology: The relation of sex of student to classroom performance and seating preference. *Environment and Behavior, 23,* 305–313.

Broverman, I. K., Vogel, S. R., Broverman, D. M., Clarkson, F. E., & Rosenkrantz, P. S. (1972). Sex-role stereotypes: A current appraisal. *Journal of Social Issues, 28(2),* 59–79.

Brown, B. B. (1987). Territorality. In S. Stokolst & I. Altman (Eds.), *Handbook of environmental psychology* (Vol. 1). New York: Wiley.

Brown, B. B., & Altman, I. (1983). Territoriality, street form, and residential burglary: An environmental analysis. *Journal of Environmental Psychology, 3,* 203–220.

Brown, G. W., & Harris, T. (1978). *Social origins of depression: A study of psychiatric disorder in women.* New York: Free Press.

Brown, J. D., & McGill, K. L. (1989). The cost of good fortune: When positive life events produce negative health consequences. *Journal of Personality and Social Psychology, 57,* 1103–1110.

Brown, P., Keenan, J. M., & Potts, G. R. (1986). The self-reference effect with imagery encoding. *Journal of Personality and Social Psychology, 51,* 897–906.

Brownmiller, S. (1975). *Against our will: Men, women and rape.* New York: Simon & Schuster.

Bryan, J. H. (1972). Why children help: A review. *Journal of Social Issues, 28(3),* 87–104.

Bryan, J. H. (1975). Children's cooperation and helping behaviors. In E. M. Hetherington (Ed.), *Review of child development research* (Vol. 5). Chicago: University of Chicago Press.

Bryan, J. H., & Test, M. J. (1967). Models and helping: Naturalistic studies in aiding behavior. *Journal of Personality and Social Psychology, 6,* 400–407.

Buckhout, R. (1974). Eyewitness testimony. *Scientific American, 321,* 23–31.

Bullough, V. (1976). *Sexual variance in society and history.* New York: Wiley.

Burger, J. M. (1986). Increasing compliance by improving the deal: The that's-not-all technique. *Journal of Personality and Social Psychology, 51,* 277–283.

Burgess, A. (Ed.). (1985). *Research handbook on rape and sexual assault.* New York: Garland.

Burgess, E. W., & Wallin, P. W. (1943). Homogamy in social characteristics. *American Journal of Sociology, 49,* 109–124.

Burgess, E. W., & Wallin, P. (1953). *Engagement and marriage.* Philadelphia: Lippincott.

Burman, B., & Margolin, G. (1992). Analysis of the association between marital relationships and health problems: An interactional perspective. *Psychological Bulletin, 112,* 39–63.

Burnstein, E., & Vinokur, A. (1973). Testing two classes of theories about group-induced shifts in individual choice. *Journal of Experimental Social Psychology, 9,* 123–137.

Burnstein, E., & Vinokur, A. (1977). Persuasive arguments and social comparison as determinants of attitude polarization. *Journal of Experimental Social Psychology, 13,* 315–332.

Burnstein, E., & Worchel, P. (1962). Arbitrariness of frustration and its consequences for aggression in a social setting. *Journal of Personality, 30,* 528–540.

Burt, M. R. (1980). Cultural myths and supports for rape. *Journal of Personality and Social Psychology, 38,* 217–230.

Bushman, B. J., & Cooper, H. M. (1990). Effects of alcohol on human aggression: An integrative research review. *Psychological Bulletin, 107,* 341–354.

Buss, A. H. (1961). *The psychology of aggression.* New York: Wiley.

Buss, A. H. (1966). Instrumentality of aggression, feedback, and frustration as determinants of physical aggression. *Journal of Personality and Social Psychology, 3,* 153–162.

Buss, A. H. (1971). Aggression pays. In J. L. Singer (Ed.), *The control of aggression and violence.* New York: Academic Press.

Buss, D. M. (1985). Human mate selection. *American Scientist, 73,* 47–51.

Buss, D. M. (1987). Sex differences in human mate selection criteria: An evolutionary perspective. In C. Crawford, M. Smith, & D. Krebs (Eds.), *Sociobiology and psychology: Ideas, issues, and application.* Hillsdale, NJ: Erlbaum.

Buss, D. M. (1988). The evolution of human intrasexual competition: Tactics of mate selection. *Journal of Personality and Social Psychology, 54,* 616–628.

Buss, D. M. (1989). Sex differences in human mate preferences: Evolutionary hypothesis. *Behavioral and Brain Sciences, 12,* 1–49.

Buss, D. M., & Barnes, M. (1986). Preferences in human mate selection. *Journal of Personality and Social Psychology, 50,* 559–570.

Buss, D. M., & Craik, K. H. (1980). The frequency concept of disposition: Dominance and prototypically dominant acts. *Journal of Personality, 48,* 379–392.

Buss, D. M., Larsen, R. J., Westen, D., & Semmelroth, J. (1992). Sex differences in jealousy: Evolution, physiology, and psychology. *Psychological Science, 3,* 251–255.

Buss, D. M., & Schmitt, D. P. (1993). Sexual strategies theory: An evolutionary perspective on human mating. *Psychological Review, 100,* 204–232.

Bussey, K., & Bandura, A. (1992). Self-regulatory mechanisms governing gender development. *Child Development, 63,* 1236–1250.

Byeff, P. (1970). *Helping behavior in audio and audio-video conditions.* Senior honors thesis, University of Pennsylvania, Philadelphia.

Byrne, D. (1971). *The attraction paradigm.* New York: Academic Press.

Byrne, D., Baskett, G. D., & Hodges, L. (1971). Behavioral indicators of interpersonal attraction. *Journal of Applied Social Psychology, 1,* 137–149.

Byrne, D., & Clore, G. L. (1970). A reinforcement model of evaluative responses. *Personality: An International Journal, 1,* 102–128.

Byrne, D., Clore, G. L., & Smeaton, G. (1986). The attraction hypothesis: Do similar attitudes affect anything? *Journal of Personality and Social Psychology, 51,* 1167–1170.

Byrne, D., & Kelley, K. (1984). Introduction: Pornography and sex research. In N. M. Malamuth & E. Donnerstein (Eds.), *Pornography and sexual aggression.* Orlando, FL: Academic Press.

Byrne, D., & Nelson, D. (1965). Attraction as a linear proportion of positive reinforcements. *Journal of Personality and Social Psychology, 1,* 659–663.

Byrne, D., Rasche, L., & Kelley, K. (1974). When "I like you" indicates disagreement. *Journal of Research in Personality, 8,* 207–217.

Cacioppo, J. T., Andersen, B. L., Turnquist, D. C., & Petty, R. E. (1986). Psychophysiological comparison processes. In B. L. Andersen (Ed.), *Women with cancer: Psychological perspectives.* New York: Springer-Verlag.

Cacioppo, J. T., Marshall-Goodell, B. S., Tassinary, L. G., & Petty, R. E. (1992). Rudimentary determinants of attitudes: Classical conditioning is more effective when prior knowledge about the attitude stimulus is low than high. *Journal of Experimental Social Psychology, 28,* 207–233.

Cacioppo, J. T., & Petty, R. E. (1979). Effects of message repetition and position on cognitive responses, recall, and persuasion. *Journal of Personality and Social Psychology, 37,* 97–109.

Cacioppo, J. T., & Petty, R. E. (1980). Persuasiveness of commercials is affected by exposure frequency and communicator cogency: A theoretical and empirical analysis. In J. H. Leigh & C. R. Martin (Eds.), *Current issues and research in advertising.* Ann Arbor: University of Michigan Press.

Cacioppo, J. T., & Petty, R. E. (1982). The need for cognition. *Journal of Personality and Social Psychology, 42,* 116–131.

Cacioppo, J. T., & Petty, R. E. (1987). Stalking rudimentary processes of social influence: A psychophysiological approach. In M. P. Zanna, J. M. Olson, & C. P. Herman (Eds.), *Social influence: The Ontario symposium* (Vol. 5). Hillsdale, NJ: Erlbaum.

Cacioppo, J. T., Petty, R. E., & Morris, K. (1983). Effects of need for cognition on message evaluation, recall, and persuasion. *Journal of Personality and Social Psychology, 45,* 805–818.

Cacioppo, J. T., & Tassinary, L. G. (1990). Inferring psychological significance from physiological signals. *American Psychologist, 45,* 16–28.

Caesar, P. L., & Hamberger, L. K. (1989). *Treating men who batter: Theory, practice, and programs.* New York: Springer.

Cagle, L. T. (1973). Interracial housing: A reassessment of the equal-status contact hypothesis. *Sociology and Social Research, 57,* 342–355.

Calder, B. J., & Ross, M. (1973). *Attitudes and behavior.* Morristown, NJ: General Learning Press.

Caldwell, D. F., & O'Reilly, C. A. (1982). Boundary spanning and individual performance: The impact of self-monitoring. *Journal of Applied Psychology, 67,* 124–127.

Calhoun, J. B. (1962). Population density and social pathology. *Scientific American, 206,* 139–148.

Calhoun, J. B. (1970). Space and the strategy of life. *Ekistics, 29,* 425–437.

Calhoun, J. B. (1973). Death squared: The explosive growth and demise of a mouse population. *Proceedings of the Royal Society of Medicine, 66,* 80–88.

Calhoun, L. G., Dawes, A. S., & Lewis, P. M. (1972). Correlates of attitudes toward help-seeking in outpatients. *Journal of Consulting and Clinical Psychology, 38,* 153.

Callaway, M. R., Marriott, R. G., & Esser, J. K. (1985). Effects of dominance on group decision making: Toward a stress-reduction explanation of groupthink. *Journal of Personality and Social Psychology, 49,* 949–952.

Campbell, A. (1981). *The sense of well-being in America.* New York: McGraw-Hill.

Campbell, D. F. (1966). *Revised manual for Strong Vocational Interest Blank.* Stanford, CA: Stanford University Press.

Campbell, D. T. (1967). Stereotypes and the perception of group differences. *American Psychologist, 22,* 817–829.

Campbell, D. T. (1975). On the conflict between biological and social evolution and moral tradition. *American Psychologist, 30,* 1103–1126.

Campbell, D. T. (1983). The two distinct routes beyond kin selection to ultra-sociality: Implications for the humanities and social sciences. In D. L. Bridgeman (Ed.), *The nature of prosocial development.* New York: Academic Press.

Campbell, D. T., & Fiske, D. (1959). Convergent and discriminant validation by the multitrait-multimethod matrix. *Psychological Bulletin, 56,* 81–105.

Campbell, D. T., & Stanley, J. C. (1963). Experimental and quasi-experimental designs for research. In N. L. Gage (Ed.), *Handbook of research in teaching.* Skokie, IL: Rand-McNally.

Campbell, D. T., & Stanley, J. C. (1966). *Experimental and quasi-experimental designs in research.* Skokie, IL: Rand-McNally.

Campbell, J. D. (1986). Similarity and uniqueness: The effects of attribute type, relevance, and individual differences in self-esteem and depression. *Journal of Personality and Social Psychology, 50,* 281–294.

Campbell, J. D., & Fairey, P. J. (1989). Informational and normative routes to conformity: The effect of faction size as a function of norm extremity and attention to stimulus. *Journal of Personality and Social Psychology, 57,* 457–468.

Campos, J. J., Barrett, K. C., Lamb, M. E., Goldsmith, H. H., & Stenberg, C. (1983). Socioemotional development. In M. M. Haith & J. J. Campos (Eds.), *Handbook of child psychology: Vol 2. Infancy and psychobiology.* New York: Wiley.

Cantor, N., & Kihlstrom, J. F. (1987). *Personality and social intelligence.* Englewood Cliffs, NJ: Prentice-Hall.

Capellanus, A. (1969). *The art of courtly love.* J. Parry (Trans.). New York: Norton.

Caplan, N., & Nelson, S. D. (1973). On being useful: The nature and consequences of psychological research on social problems. *American Psychologist, 28,* 199–211.

Caplan, R. D., Robinson, E. A. R., French, J. R. P. Jr., Caldwell, J. R., & Shinn, M. (1976). *Adherence to medical regimens: Pilot experiments in patient education and social support.* University of Michigan Research Center for Group Dynamics, Institute for Social Research, Ann Arbor.

Caproni, V., Levine, D., O'Neal, E., McDonald, P., & Garwood, G. (1977). Seating position, instructor's eye contact availability, and student participation in a small seminar. *Journal of Social Psychology, 103,* 315–316.

Carducci, B. J., Cozby, P. C., & Ward, C. D. (1978). Sexual arousal and interpersonal evaluations. *Journal of Experimental Social Psychology, 14,* 449–457.

Carli, L. L. (1982). *Are women more social and men more task oriented? A meta-analytic review of sex differences in group interaction, reward allocation, coalition formation, and cooperation in the Prisoner's Dilemma Game.* Unpublished manuscript, University of Massachusetts, Amherst.

Carli, L. L., Ganley, R., & Pierce-Otay, A. (1991). Similarity and satisfaction in roommate relationships. *Personality and Social Psychology Bulletin, 17,* 419–426.

Carlsmith, J. M., & Anderson, C. A. (1979). Ambient temperature and the occurrence of collective violence: A new analysis. *Journal of Personality and Social Psychology, 37,* 337–344.

Carlsmith, J. M., Ellsworth, P. C., & Aronson, E. (1976). *Methods of research in social psychology.* Reading, MA: Addison-Wesley.

Carlsmith, J. M., & Gross, A. E. (1969). Some effects of guilt on compliance. *Journal of Personality and Social Psychology, 11,* 232–239.

Carlson, M., Charlin, V., & Miller, N. (1988). Positive mood and helping behavior: A test of six hypotheses. *Journal of Personality and Social Psychology, 55,* 211–229.

Carlson, M., Marcus-Newhall, A., & Miller, N. (1990). Effects of situational aggressive cues: A quantitative review. *Journal of Personality and Social Psychology, 58,* 622–633.

Carlson, M., & Miller, N. (1987). Explanation of the relation between negative mood and helping. *Psychological Bulletin, 102,* 91–108.

Carlson, R., & Brincka, J. (1987). Studies in script theory III: Ideology and political imagination. *Political Psychology, 8,* 563–574.

Carroll, D. (1987, November–December). Humanists versus religiosity in the Boy Scouts. *Humanist,* p. 37.

Carson, R. C., Butcher, J. N., & Coleman, J. C. (1988). *Abnormal psychology and modern life* (8th ed.). Glenview, IL: Scott, Foresman.

Cartwright, D., & Zander, A. (1968). Issues and basic assumptions. In D. Cartwright & A. Zander (Eds.), *Group dynamics: Research and theory* (3rd ed.). New York: Harper & Row.

Carver, C. S. (1975). Physical aggression as a function of objective self-awareness and attitudes toward punishment. *Journal of Experimental Social Psychology, 11,* 510–519.

Carver, C. S. (1989). How should multifaceted personality constructs be tested? Issues illustrated by self-monitoring, attributional style, and hardiness. *Journal of Personality and Social Psychology, 56,* 577–585.

Carver, C. S., DeGregorio, E., & Gillis, R. (1980). Ego-defensive attribution among two categories of observers. *Personality and Social Psychology Bulletin, 6,* 44–50.

Carver, C. S., & Scheier, M. F. (1981). *Attention and self-regulation: A control theory approach to human behavior.* New York: Springer-Verlag.

Caspi, A. (1987). Personality in the life course. *Journal of Personality and Social Psychology, 53,* 1203–1213.

Cassel, J. C. (1976). The contribution of the social environment to host resistance. *American Journal of Epidemiology, 104,* 107–123.

Cattell, R. B. (1965). *The scientific analysis of personality.* Baltimore: Penguin.

Ceci, S. J., & Bruck, M. (1993). Suggestibility of the child witness: A historical review and synthesis. *Psychological Bulletin, 113,* 403-439.

Center for Research on Aggression. (1983). *Prevention and control of aggression.* New York: Pergamon.

Centers for Disease Control. (1980). *Ten leading causes of death in the United States.* Washington, DC: U.S. Government Printing Office.

Centers for Disease Control. (1992, October). *HIV/AIDS Surveillance Report.*

Cerny, J. A., & Polyson, J. (1984). Changing homonegative attitudes. *Journal of Social and Clinical Psychology, 2,* 366–371.

Chaiken, S. (1979). Communicator physical attractiveness and persuasion. *Journal of Personality and Social Psychology, 37,* 1387–1397.

Chaiken, S. (1980). Heuristic versus systematic information processing and the use of source versus message cues in persuasion. *Journal of Personality and Social Psychology, 39,* 752–766.

Chaiken, S. (1987). The heuristic model of persuasion. In M. P. Zanna, J. M. Olson, & C. P. Herman (Eds.), *Social influence: The Ontario symposium* (Vol. 5). Hillsdale, NJ: Erlbaum.

Chaiken, S., & Baldwin, M. W. (1981). Affective–cognitive consistency and the effect of salient behavioral information on the self-perception of attitudes. *Journal of Personality and Social Psychology, 41,* 1–12.

Chaiken, S., & Eagly, A. H. (1976). Communication modality as a determinant of message persuasiveness and message comprehensibility. *Journal of Personality and Social Psychology, 34,* 605–614.

Chaiken, S., & Eagly, A. H. (1983). Communication modality as a determinant of persuasion: The role of communicator salience. *Journal of Personality and Social Psychology, 45,* 241–256.

Chaikin, A. L., Derlega, V. J., & Miller, S. J. (1976). Effects of room environment on self-disclosure in a counseling analogue. *Journal of Counseling Psychology, 23,* 479–481.

Chapman, L. J., & Chapman, J. P. (1967). Genesis of popular but erroneous diagnostic observations. *Journal of Abnormal Psychology, 72,* 193–204.

Chapman, L. J., & Chapman, J. P. (1969). Illusory correlation as an obstacle to the use of valid psychodiagnostic signs. *Journal of Abnormal Psychology, 14,* 271–280.

Chapman, L. J., & Chapman, J. P. (1982). Test results are what you think they are. In D. Kahneman, P. Slovic, & A. Tversky (Eds.), *Judgment under uncertainty: Heuristics and biases.* New York: Cambridge University Press.

Chase, W. G., & Simon, H. A. (1973). Perception and chess. *Cognitive Psychology, 4,* 55–81.

Chasnoff, R. (Ed.). (1978). *Structuring cooperative learning in the classroom: The 1979 handbook.* Minneapolis: Cooperative Network.

Cheek, J. M., & Melchoir, L. A. (1990). Shyness, self-esteem, and self-consciousness. In H. Leitenberg (Ed.), *Handbook of social and evaluation anxiety.* New York: Plenum.

Chen, S. C. (1937). Social modification of the activity of ants on nest-building. *Physiological Zoology, 10,* 420–436.

Choi, P. Y., Parrott, A. C., & Cowan, D. (1990). High-dose anabolic steroids in strength athletes: Effects upon hostility and aggression. *Human Psychopharmacology: Clinical and Experimental, 5,* 349–356.

Christensen, L. (1988). Deception in psychological research: When is its use justified? *Personality and Social Psychology Bulletin, 14,* 664–675.

Christian, J. J. (1963). The pathology of overpopulation. *Military Medicine, 128,* 571–603.

Christian, J. J., & Davis, D. E. (1964). Endocrines, behavior and population. *Science, 146,* 1550–1560.

Christie, R. (1978). Reconsideration: The authoritarian personality. *Human Nature.*

Christie, R. (1991). Authoritarianism and related constructs. In J. P. Robinson, P. R. Shaver, & L. S. Wrightsman (Eds.), *Measures of personality and social psychological attitudes* (Vol. 1 of *Measures of social psychological attitudes*). San Diego: Academic Press.

Christie, R., & Cook, P. (1958). A guide to the published literature relating to the authoritarian personality through 1956. *Journal of Psychology, 45,* 171–199.

Christie, R., & Jahoda, M. (Eds.). (1954). *Studies in the scope and method of "the authoritarian personality."* New York: Free Press.

Church, A. T., & Katigbak, M. S. (1989). Internal, external, and self-report structure of personality in a non-Western culture: An investigation of cross-language and cross-culture generalizability. *Journal of Personality and Social Psychology, 57,* 857–872.

Cialdini, R. B. (1988). *Influence: Science and practice* (2nd ed.). Glenview, IL: Scott, Foresman/Little, Brown.

Cialdini, R. B. (1993). *Influence: Science and practice* (3rd ed.). New York: HarperCollins.

Cialdini, R. B., Borden, R. J., Thorne, A., Walker, M. R., Freeman, S., & Sloan, L. R. (1976). Basking in reflected glory: Three (football) field studies. *Journal of Personality and Social Psychology, 34,* 366–375.

Cialdini, R. B., Cacioppo, J. R., Bassett, R., & Miller, J. A. (1978). Low-ball procedure for producing compliance: Commitment then cost. *Journal of Personality and Social Psychology, 36,* 463–476.

Cialdini, R. B., Darby, B. L., & Vincent, J. E. (1973). Transgression and altruism: A case for hedonism. *Journal of Experimental Social Psychology, 9,* 502–516.

Cialdini, R. B., & Kenrick, D. T. (1976).

Altruism as hedonism: A social developmental perspective on the relationship of negative mood state and helping. *Journal of Personality and Social Psychology, 34,* 907–914.

Cialdini, R. B., Levy, A., Herman, P., Kozlowski, L., & Petty, R. (1976). Elastic shifts of opinion: Determinants of direction and durability. *Journal of Personality and Social Psychology, 34,* 663–672.

Cialdini, R. B., Vincent, J. E., Lewis, S. K., Catalan, J., Wheeler, D., & Darby, B. L. (1975). Reciprocal concessions procedure for inducing compliance: The door-in-the-face technique. *Journal of Personality and Social Psychology, 31,* 206–215.

Cialdini, R. B., Schaller, M., Houlihan, D., Arps, K., Fultz, J., & Beaman, A. L. (1987). Empathy-based helping: Is it selflessly or selfishly motivated? *Journal of Personality and Social Psychology, 52,* 749–758.

Cisin, I. H., Coffin, T. E., Janis, I. L., Klapper, J. T., Mendelsohn, H., Omwake, E., Pinderhughes, C. A., Pool, I., de Sola, Siegel, A. E., Wallace, A. F. C., Watson, A. S., & Wiebe, G. D. (1972). *Television and growing up: The impact of televised violence.* Washington, DC: U.S. Government Printing Office.

Clark, L. A., & Watson, D. (1991). General affective dispositions in physical and psychological health. In C. R. Snyder & D. R. Forsyth (Eds.), *Handbook of social and clinical psychology.* New York: Pergamon.

Clark, L. F., & Woll, S. B. (1981). Stereotype biases: A reconstructive analysis of their role in reconstructive memory. *Journal of Personality and Social Psychology, 41,* 1064–1072.

Clark, M. S., & Mills, J. (1979). Interpersonal attraction in exchange and communal relationships. *Journal of Personality and Social Psychology, 37,* 12–27.

Clark, M. S., Mills, J., & Powell, M. C. (1986). Keeping track of needs in communal and exchange relationships. *Journal of Personality and Social Psychology, 51,* 333–338.

Clark, R. D., & Hatfield, E. (1989). Gender differences in receptivity to sexual offers. *Journal of Psychology and Human Sexuality, 2,* 39–55.

Clary, E. G., & Snyder, M. (1991). A functional analysis of altruism and prosocial behavior: The case of volunteerism. In M. S. Clark (Ed.), *Prosocial behavior.* Newbury Park, CA: Sage.

Clifford, M. M., & Walster, E. (1973). The effect of physical attractiveness on teacher expectation. *Sociology of Education, 46,* 248–258.

Cline, V. B., Croft, R. G., & Courrier, S. (1973). Desensitization of children to television violence. *Journal of Personality and Social Psychology, 27,* 360–365.

Cochran, S. D., Mays, V. M., Ciarletta, J., Caruso, C., & Mallon, D. (1992). Efficacy of the theory of reasoned action in predicting AIDS-related risk reduction among gay men. *Journal of Applied Social Psychology, 22,* 1481–1501.

Cohen, A. (1962). An experiment on small rewards for discrepant compliance and attitude change. In J. W. Brehm & A. R. Cohen (Eds.), *Explorations in cognitive dissonance.* New York: Wiley.

Cohen, A. M., Bennis, W. G., & Wolkon, G. H. (1961). The effects of continued practice on the behavior of problem-solving groups. *Sociometry, 24,* 416–431.

Cohen, B., Waugh, G., & Place, K. (1989). At the movies: An unobtrusive study of arousal-attraction. *Journal of Social Psychology, 29,* 691–693.

Cohen, C. E. (1981). Person categories and social perception: Testing some boundaries of the processing effects of prior knowledge. *Journal of Personality and Social Psychology, 40,* 441–452.

Cohen, C. E., & Ebbesen, E. B. (1979). Observational goals and schema activation: A theoretical framework for behavior perception. *Journal of Experimental Social Psychology, 15,* 305–329.

Cohen, E. G. (1984). The desegregated school: Problems in status, power and interethnic climate. In N. Miller & M. B. Brewer (Eds.), *Groups in contact: The psychology of desegregation.* New York: Academic Press.

Cohen, J. (1977). *Statistical power analysis for the behavioral sciences.* New York: Academic Press.

Cohen, R. (1978). Altruism: Human, cultural, or what? In L. Wispe (Ed.), *Altruism, sympathy, and helping: Psychological and sociological principles.* New York: Academic Press.

Cohen, S., & McKay, G. (1984). Social support, stress, and the buffer hypothesis: A theoretical analysis. In A. Baum, S. E. Taylor, & J. E. Singer (Eds.), *Handbook of psychology and health* (Vol. 4): *Social psychological aspects of health.* Hillsdale, NJ: Erlbaum.

Cohen, S., Mermelstein, R., Kamarck, T., & Hoberman, H. (1984). Measuring the functional components of social support. In I. Sarason (Ed.), *Social support: Theory, research and application.* The Hague, Netherlands: Marine Niijhoff.

Cohen, S., & Syme, S. L. (Eds.). (1985a).

Social support and health. Orlando, FL: Academic Press.

Cohen, S., & Syme, S. L. (1985b). Issues in the study and application of social support. In S. Cohen & S. L. Syme (Eds.), *Social support and health.* Orlando, FL: Academic Press.

Cohen, S., Tyrrell, D. A. J., & Smith, A. P. (1993). Negative life events, perceived stress, negative affect and susceptibility to the common cold. *Journal of Personality and Social Psychology, 64,* 131–140.

Cohen, S., & Williamson, G. M. (1991). Stress and infectious disease in humans. *Psychological Bulletin, 109,* 5–24.

Cohen, S., & Wills, T. A. (1985). Stress, social support, and the buffering hypothesis. *Psychological Bulletin, 98,* 310–357.

Cohen, S. A. (1978). Environmental load and the allocation of attention. In A. Baum, J. E. Singer, & S. Valins (Eds.), *Advances in environmental psychology* (Vol. 1). Hillsdale, NJ: Erlbaum.

Cole, J. R. (1979). *Fair science: Women in the scientific community.* New York: Free Press.

Colligan, M. J., & Murphy, L. R. (1982). A review of mass psychogenic illness in work settings. In M. J. Colligan, J. W. Pennebaker, & L. R. Murphy (Eds.), *Mass psychogenic illness: A social psychological analysis.* Hillsdale, NJ: Erlbaum.

Colligan, M. J., Pennebaker, J. W., & Murphy, L. R. (Eds.). (1982). *Mass psychogenic illness: A social psychological analysis.* Hillsdale, NJ: Erlbaum.

Collins, B. E. (1974). Four components of the Rotter internal–external scale: Belief in a difficult world, a just world, a predictable world, and a politically responsive world. *Journal of Personality and Social Psychology, 29,* 381–391.

Collins, B. E., & Hoyt, M. G. (1972). Personal responsibility for consequences: An integration and extension of the "forced compliance" literature. *Journal of Experimental Social Psychology, 8,* 558–593.

Colvin, C. R., & Funder, D. C. (1991). Predicting personality and behavior: A boundary on the acquaintanceship effect. *Journal of Personality and Social Psychology, 60,* 884–894.

Comstock, G., & Paik, H. (1990). The effects of television violence on aggressive behavior: A meta-analysis. Unpublished report to the National Academy of Sciences Panel on the Understanding and Control of Violent Behavior, Washington, DC.

Conley, J. J. (1985). Longitudinal stability of personality traits: A multitrait–multimethod–multioccasion analysis. *Journal of Personality and Social Psychology, 49,* 1266–1282.

Conner, R. C., & Norriss, K. S. (1982). Are dolphins reciprocal altruists? *American Naturalist, 119,* 358–374.

Conroy, J., & Sundstrom, E. (1977). Territorial dominance in a dyadic conversation as a function of similarity of opinion. *Journal of Personality and Social Psychology, 35,* 570–576.

Constantinople, A. (1973). Masculinity–femininity: An exception to a famous dictum? *Psychological Bulletin, 80,* 389–407.

Cook, C. C. (1988). Components of neighborhood satisfaction: Responses from urban and suburban single-parent women. *Environment and Behavior, 20,* 115–149.

Cook, E. P. (1985). *Psychological androgyny.* New York: Pergamon.

Cook, S. W. (1984). Cooperative interaction in multiethnic contexts. In N. Miller & M. B. Brewer (Eds.), *Groups in contact: The psychology of desegregation.* New York: Academic Press.

Cook, T. D., & Campbell, D. T. (Eds.). (1979). *The design and analysis of quasi-experiments for field settings.* Chicago: Rand McNally.

Cooley, C. H. (1902). *Human nature and the social order.* New York: Scribner.

Cooper, J., & Scher, S. H. (1992). Actions and attitudes: The role of responsibility in persuasion. In T. Brock & S. Shavitt (Eds.), *The psychology of persuasion.* San Francisco: W. H. Freeman.

Cooper, J., & Worchel, S. (1970). Role of undesired consequences in arousing cognitive dissonance. *Journal of Personality and Social Psychology, 16,* 199–206.

Constantini, E., & King, J. (1980–81). The partial juror: Correlates and causes of prejudgment. *Law and Society Review, 15,* 9–40.

Cotton, J. L. (1986). Ambient temperature and violent crime. *Journal of Applied Social Psychology, 16,* 786–801.

Cottrell, N. B., Wack, D. L., Seberak, G. J., & Rittle, R. M. (1968). Social facilitation of dominant responses by the presence of an audience and the mere presence of others. *Journal of Personality and Social Psychology, 9,* 245–250.

Court, J. H. (1984). Sex and violence: A ripple effect. In N. M. Malamuth & E. Donnerstein (Eds.), *Pornography and sexual aggression.* Orlando, FL: Academic Press.

Courtright, J. A. (1978). A laboratory investigation of groupthink. *Communications Monographs, 43,* 229–246.

Cousins, S. (1989). Culture and selfhood in Japan and the U.S. *Journal of Personality and Social Psychology, 56,* 124–131.

Cowan, C. L., Thompson, W. C., & Ellsworth, P. C. (1984). The effects of death qualification on jurors' predisposition to convict and on the quality of deliberation. *Law and Human Behavior, 8,* 53–79.

Cox, V. C., Paulus, P. B., & McCain, G. (1984). Prison crowding research: The relevance for prison housing standards and a general approach regarding crowding phenomena. *American Psychologist, 39,* 1148–1160.

Coyne, J. C., & Bolger, N. (1990). Doing without social support as an explanatory concept. *Journal of Social and Clinical Psychology, 9,* 148–158.

Coyne, J. C., & DeLongis, A. (1986). Going beyond social support: The role of social relationships in adaptation. *Journal of Consulting and Clinical Psychology, 54,* 454–460.

Coyne, J. C., & Gotlieb, I. H. (1983). The role of cognition in depression: A critical appraisal. *Psychological Bulletin, 94,* 472–505.

Cozby, P. C. (1973). Self-disclosure: A literature review. *Psychological Bulletin, 79,* 73–91.

Craig, C. S., & McCann, J. M. (1978). Item nonresponse in mail surveys: Extent and correlates. *Journal of Marketing Research, 15,* 285–289.

Crandall, C. S., Preisler, J. J., & Aussprung, J. (1992). Measuring life event stress in the lives of college students: The Undergraduate Stress Questionnaire. *Journal of Behavioral Medicine, 15,* 627–662.

Crano, W. D., & Brewer, M. B. (1986). *Principles and methods of social research.* Boston: Allyn & Bacon.

Crawford, C., Smith, M., & Krebs, D. (Eds.). (1986). *Sociobiology and psychology: Ideas, issues, and applications.* Hillsdale, NJ: Erlbaum.

Crawford, T. J., & Boyer, R. (1985). Salient consequences, cultural values, and childbearing intentions. *Journal of Applied Social Psychology, 20,* 16–30.

Crocker, J., Cornwell, B., & Major, B. (1993). The stigma of overweight: Affective consequences of attributional ambiguity. *Journal of Personality and Social Psychology, 64,* 60–70.

Crocker, J., & Major, B. (1989). Social stigma and self-esteem: The self-protective properties of stigma. *Psychological Review, 96,* 608–630.

Crocker, J., Voelkl, K., Testa, M., & Major, B. (1991). Social stigma: The affective consequences of attributional ambiguity. *Journal of Personality and Social Psychology, 60,* 218–228.

Crocker, J., & Weber, R. (1983). Cognitive structure and stereotype change. In R. P. Bagozzi & A. M. Tybout (Eds.), *Advances in consumer research* (Vol. 10). Ann Arbor, MI: Association for Consumer Research.

Cromwell, P. F., Marks, A., Olson, J. N., & Avary, D. W. (1991). Group effects on decision-making by burglars. *Psychological Reports, 69,* 579–588.

Cronbach, L. J. (1955). Processes affecting scores on "understanding of others" and "assumed similarity." *Psychological Bulletin, 52,* 177–193.

Cronbach, L. J. (1984). *Essentials of psychological testing.* New York: Harper & Row.

Crow, W. J., & Hammond, K. R. (1957). The generality of accuracy and response in interpersonal perception. *Journal of Abnormal and Social Psychology, 54,* 384–390.

Crutchfield, R. A. (1955). Conformity and character. *American Psychologist, 10,* 191–198.

Cunningham, M. R. (1979). Weather, mood, and helping behavior: Quasi-experiments with the sunshine Samaritan. *Journal of Personality and Social Psychology, 37,* 1947–1956.

Cunningham, M. R. (1986). Measuring the physical in physical attractiveness: Quasi-experiments on the sociobiology of female facial beauty. *Journal of Personality and Social Psychology, 50,* 925–935.

Cunningham, M. R., Barkee, A. P., & Pike, C. L. (1990). What do women want? Facial metric assessment of multiple motives in the perception of male facial physical attractiveness. *Journal of Personality and Social Psychology, 59,* 61–72.

Cunningham, M. R., Steinberg, J., & Greu, R. (1980). Wanting to and having to help: Separate motivation for positive mood and guilt-induced helping. *Journal of Personality and Social Psychology, 38,* 181–192.

Curran, J. P., & Lippold, S. (1975). The effects of physical attractiveness and attitude similarity on attraction in dating dyads. *Journal of Personality, 43,* 528–539.

Curtis, L. (1974). *Criminal violence: National patterns and behavior.* Lexington, MA: Lexington Books.

Curtis, R. C., & Miller, K. (1986). Believing another likes or dislikes you: Behaviors making the beliefs come true. *Journal of Personality and Social Psychology, 51,* 284–290.

Cutler, B. L., & Penrod, S. D. (1988). Improving the reliability of eyewitness identification: Lineup construction and presentation. *Journal of Applied Psychology, 73,* 281–290.

Cutler, B. L., Penrod, S. D., & Dexter, H. R. (1990). Juror sensitivity to eyewitness identification evidence. *Law and Human Behavior, 14,* 185–191.

Cutler, B. L., Penrod, S. D., & Stuve, T. E. (1988). Juror decision making in eyewitness identification cases. *Law and Human Behavior, 12,* 41–55.

Cutrona, C. E. (1990). Stress and social support: In search of optimal matching. *Journal of Social and Clinical Psychology, 9,* 3–14.

Dabbs, J. M. Jr. (1992). Testosterone measures in social and clinical psychology. *Journal of Social and Clinical Psychology, 11,* 302–321.

Dabbs, J. M. Jr., Frady, R. L., Carr, T. S., & Besch, N. F. (1987). Saliva testosterone and criminal violence in young adult prison inmates. *Psychosomatic Medicine, 49,* 174–182.

Dabbs, J. M. Jr. & Morris, R. (1990). Testosterone and antisocial behavior in a large sample of normal men. *Psychological Science, 1,* 209–211.

Dabbs, J. M. Jr. & Stokes, N. A., III. (1975). Beauty is power: The use of space on the sidewalk. *Sociometry, 38*(4), 551–557.

Daly, M., & Wilson, M. (1988). *Homicide.* New York: Aldine DeGruyter.

D'Andrade, R. (1966). Sex differences and cultural institutions. In E. E. Maccoby (Ed.), *The development of sex differences.* Stanford, CA: Stanford University Press.

Danheiser, P. R., & Graziano, W. G. (1982). Self-monitoring and cooperation as a self-presentational strategy. *Journal of Personality and Social Psychology, 42,* 497–505.

Darley, J. M., & Batson, C. D. (1973). From Jerusalem to Jericho: A study of situational and dispositional variables in helping behavior. *Journal of Personality and Social Psychology, 27,* 100–108.

Darley, J. M., & Latané, B. (1968). Bystander intervention in emergencies: Diffusion of responsibility. *Journal of Personality and Social Psychology, 8,* 377–383.

Darley, J. M., Teger, A. I., & Lewis, L. D. (1973). Do groups always inhibit individuals' response to potential emergencies? *Journal of Personality and Social Psychology, 26,* 395–399.

Darwin, C. (1859). *The origin of species.* London: John Murray.

Darwin, C. (1871). *The descent of man.* London: John Murray.

Darwin, C. (1872). *The expression of the emotions in man and animals.* London: John Murray.

Dashiell, J. F. (1930). An experimental analysis of some group effects. *Journal of Abnormal and Social Psychology, 25,* 190–199.

Davies, J. C. (1972). Toward a theory of revolution. In I. K. Feierabend & R. L. Feierabend (Eds.), *Anger, violence, and politics: Theories and research.* Englewood Cliffs, NJ: Prentice-Hall.

Davis, K. E., & Jones, E. E. (1960). Changes in interpersonal perception as a means of reducing cognitive dissonance. *Journal of Abnormal and Social Psychology, 61,* 402–410.

Davis, M. S. (1968). Variations in patients' compliance with doctors' advice: An empirical analysis of patterns of communication. *American Journal of Public Health, 58,* 274–288.

Davitz, J. R. (1952). The effects of previous training on post frustration behavior. *Journal of Abnormal and Social Psychology, 47,* 309–315.

Dawes, R. M. (1976). Shallow psychology. In J. Carroll & J. Payne (Eds.), *Cognition and social behavior.* Hillsdale, NJ: Erlbaum.

Dawes, R. M. (1980). You can't systematize human judgment: Dyslexia. In R. A. Shweder (Ed.), *New directions for methodology of social and behavioral science* (Vol. 4). San Francisco: Jossey-Bass.

Dawes, R. M. (1988). *Rational choice in an uncertain world.* San Diego: Harcourt Brace Jovanovich.

Dawkins, R. (1976). *The selfish gene.* New York: Oxford University Press.

De Angelis, T. (1989, September). Controversy marks child witness meeting. *APA Monitor,* pp. 8–9.

Deaux, K. (1984). From individual differences to social categories: Analysis of a decade's research on gender. *American Psychologist, 39,* 105–116.

Deaux, K. (1985). Sex and gender. In M. R. Rosenzweig & L. W. Porter (Eds.), *Annual Review of Psychology, 36.*

Deaux, K., & Emswiller, T. (1974). Explanation for successful performance on sex-linked tasks: What is skill for the male is luck for the female. *Journal of Personality and Social Psychology, 29,* 80–85.

Deaux, K., & Lewis, L. L. (1983). Assessment of gender stereotypes: Methodology and components. *Psychological Documents, 13,* 25 (Ms. No. 2583).

Deaux, K., & Lewis, L. L. (1984). The structure of gender stereotypes: Interrelationships among components and gender label. *Journal of Personality and Social Psychology, 46,* 991–1004.

Deaux, K., & Major, B. (1987). Putting gender into context: An interactive model of gender-related behavior. *Psychological Review, 94,* 369–389.

de Castro, J. M., & Brewer, E. M. (1992). The amount eaten in meals by humans is a power function of the number of people present. *Physiology and Behavior, 51,* 121–125.

Deci, E. L. (1975). *Intrinsic motivation.* New York: Plenum.

Deci, E. L., & Ryan, R. M. (1980). The empirical exploration of intrinsic motivational processes. In L. Berkowitz (Ed.), *Advances in experimental social psychology* (Vol. 13). New York: Academic Press.

Deci, E. L., & Ryan, R. M. (1985). *Intrinsic motivation and self-determination in human behavior.* New York: Plenum.

Deffenbacher, K. A. (1983). The influence of arousal on reliability of testimony. In S. M. A. Lloyd-Bostock & B. R. Clifford (Eds.), *Evaluating witness evidence.* Chichester, England: Wiley.

Deffenbacher, K. A. (1989). Forensic facial memory: Time is of the essence. In A. W. Young & H. D. Ellis (Eds.), *Handbook of research on face processing.* Amsterdam: Elsevier Science Publishers.

Deikman, A. J. (1990). *The wrong way home: Uncovering the pattern of cult behavior in American society.* Boston: Beacon Press.

DeJong, W. (1979). An examination of the self-perception mediation of the foot-in-the-door effect. *Journal of Personality and Social Psychology, 37,* 2221–2239.

DeJong, W., & Musilli, L. (1982). External pressure to comply: Handicapped versus nonhandicapped requesters and the foot-in-the-door phenomenon. *Personality and Social Psychology Bulletin, 8,* 522–527.

Delbecq, A. L., Van de Ven, A. H., & Gustafson, D. H. (1975). *Group techniques for program planning.* Glenview, IL: Scott, Foresman.

Dellapa, F. (1977). Mediation and the community dispute center. In M. Roy (Ed.), *Battered women: A psycho-sociological study of domestic violence.* New York: Van Nostrand Reinhold.

D'Emilio, J., & Freedman, E. B. (1988). *Intimate matters: A history of sexuality in America.* New York: Harper & Row.

Dengerink, H. A., & Myers, J. D. (1977). The effects of failure and depression on subsequent aggression. *Journal of Personality and Social Psychology, 35,* 88–96.

Dennis, V. C., & Powell, E. R. (1972). Nonverbal communication in across-race dyads. *Proceedings, 80th Annual Convention of the American Psychological Association, 7,* 557–558.

DePaulo, B. (1992). Nonverbal behavior and self-presentation. *Psychological Bulletin, 111*, 203–243.

DePaulo, B. M. (1978). Accepting help from teachers—When the teachers are children. *Human Relations, 31*, 459–474.

DePaulo, B. M., Kenny, D. A., Hoover, C. W., Webb, W., & Oliver, P. V. (1987). Accuracy of person perception: Do people know what kinds of impressions they convey? *Journal of Personality and Social Psychology, 52*, 303–315.

DePaulo, B. M., Lassiter, G. D., & Stone, J. H. (1982). Attentional determinants of success at detecting deception and truth. *Personality and Social Psychology Bulletin, 8*, 273–279.

DePaulo, B. M., & Pfeifer, R. L. (1986). On-the-job experience and skill at detecting deception. *Journal of Applied Social Psychology, 16*, 249–267.

DePaulo, B. M., & Rosenthal, R. (1979). Telling lies. *Journal of Personality and Social Psychology, 37*, 1713–1722.

DePaulo, B. M., Stone, J., & Lassiter, G. D. (1985). Deceiving and detecting deceit. In B. R. Schlenker (Ed.), *The self and social life*. New York: McGraw-Hill.

de Raad, B., & Doddema-Winsemius, M. (1992). Factors in the assortment of human mates: Differential preferences in Germany and the Netherlands. *Personality and Individual Differences, 13*, 103–114.

De Riencourt, A. (1974). *Sex and power in history*. New York: McKay.

Dermer, M., & Pyszczynski, T. A. (1978). Effects of erotica upon men's loving and liking responses for women they love. *Journal of Personality and Social Psychology, 36*, 1302–1309.

Dermer, M., & Thiel, D. L. (1975). When beauty may fail. *Journal of Personality and Social Psychology, 31*, 1168–1176.

Deseran, F. A., & Chung, C. S. (1979). Appearance, role-taking, and reactions to deviance: Some experimental findings. *Social Psychology Quarterly, 42*, 426–430.

Desforges, D. M., Lord, C. G., Ramsey, S. L., Mason, J. A., Van Leeuwen, M. D., West, S. C., & Lepper, M. R. (1991). Effects of structured contact on changing negative attitudes toward stigmatized groups. *Journal of Personality and Social Psychology, 60*, 531–544.

Deutsch, F. M. (1990). Status, sex, and smiling: The effect of role on smiling in men and women. *Personality and Social Psychology Bulletin, 16*, 531–540.

Deutsch, M. (1949). The directions of behavior: A field-theoretical approach to the understanding of inconsistencies. *Journal of Social Issues, 5*, 45.

Deutsch, M. (1968). The effects of cooperation and competition upon group process. In D. Cartwright & A. Zander (Eds.), *Group dynamics: Research and theory* (3rd ed.). New York: Harper & Row.

Deutsch, M. (1973). *The resolution of conflict*. New Haven, CT: Yale University Press.

Deutsch, M., & Collins, M. E. (1951). *Interracial housing: A psychological evaluation of a social experiment*. Minneapolis: University of Minnesota Press.

Deutsch, M., & Gerard, H. B. (1955). A study of normative and informational social influences upon individual judgment. *Journal of Abnormal and Social Psychology, 51*, 629–636.

Devine, P. G. (1989). Stereotypes and prejudice: Their automatic and controlled components. *Journal of Personality and Social Psychology, 56*, 5–18.

Devine, P. G., Monteith, M. J., Zuwerink, J. R., & Elliot, A. J. (1991). Prejudice with and without compunction. *Journal of Personality and Social Psychology, 6*, 817–830.

Dibiase, W., & Hjelle, L. (1968). Body-image stereotypes and body-type preferences among male college students. *Perception and Motor Skills, 27*, 1143–1146.

Dickey, R. V., & Knower, F. H. (1941). A note on some ethnological differences in recognition of simulated expressions of the emotions. *American Journal of Sociology, 47*, 190–193.

Diehl, M., & Stroebe, W. (1987). Productivity loss in brainstorming groups: Toward the solution of a riddle. *Journal of Personality and Social Psychology, 53*, 497–509.

Diehl, M., & Stroebe, W. (1991). Productivity loss in idea-generating groups: Tracking down the blocking effect. *Journal of Personality and Social Psychology, 61*, 392–403.

Diener, E. (1976). Effects of prior destructive behavior, anonymity, and group presence on deindividuation and aggression. *Journal of Personality and Social Psychology, 33*, 497–507.

Diener, E. (1979). Deindividuation, self-awareness, and disinhibition. *Journal of Personality and Social Psychology, 37*, 1160–1171.

Diener, E. (1980). Deindividuation: The absence of self-awareness and self-regulation in group members. In P. B. Paulus (Ed.), *Psychology of group influence*. Hillsdale, NJ: Erlbaum.

Diener, E., Doneen, J., & Endresen, K. (1975). Effects of altered responsibility, cognitive set, and modeling on physical aggressiveness and deindividuation. *Journal of Personality and Social Psychology, 31*, 328–337.

Diener, E., Fraser, S. C., Beaman, A. L., & Kelem, R. T. (1976). Effects of deindividuating variables on stealing by Halloween trick-or-treaters. *Journal of Personality and Social Psychology, 33*, 178–183.

Diener, E., Lusk, R., DeFour, D., & Flax, R. (1980). Deindividuation: Effects of group size, density, number of observers, and group member similarity on self-consciousness and disinhibited behaviors. *Journal of Personality and Social Psychology, 39*, 449–459.

Diener, E., & Wallbom, M. C. (1976). Effects of self-awareness on antinormative behavior. *Journal of Research in Personality, 10*, 107–111.

Digman, J. M. (1990). Personality structure: Emergence of the five-factor model. In M. R. Rosenzweig & L. W. Porter (Eds.), *Annual Review of Psychology, 41*, 417–440.

DiNicola, D. D., & Di Matteo, M. R. (1982). *Achieving patient compliance: The psychology of the medical practitioner's role*. New York: Pergamon.

DiMatteo, M. R. (1985). Physician–patient communication: Promoting a positive health care setting. In J. C. Rosen & L. J. Solomon (Eds.), *Prevention in health psychology*. Hanover, NH: University Press of New England.

DiMatteo, M. R. (1991). *The psychology of health, illness, and medical care: An individual perspective*. Pacific Grove, CA: Brooks/Cole.

DiMatteo, M. R., & Hays, R. (1980). The significance of patients' perceptions of physician conduct: A study of patient satisfaction in a family practice center. *Journal of Community Health, 6*, 18–34.

DiMatteo, M. R., Hays, R., & Prince, L. M. (1986). Relationship of physicians' nonverbal communication skill to patient satisfaction, appointment noncompliance, and physician workload. *Health Psychology, 5*, 581–594.

DiMatteo, M. R., & DiNicola, D. D. (1982). *Achieving patient compliance: The psychology of the medical practitioner's role*. Elmsford, NY: Pergamon.

Dion, K. K., & Berscheid, E. (1972). *Physical attractiveness and social perception of peers in preschool children*. Unpublished manuscript.

Dion, K. K., & Berscheid, E. (1974). Physical attractiveness and peer perception among children. *Sociometry, 37*, 1–12.

Dion, K. K., Berscheid, E., & Walster, E. (1972). What is beautiful is good. *Journal of Personality and Social Psychology, 24,* 285–290.

Dittes, J. E., & Kelley, H. H. (1956). Effects of different conditions of acceptance upon conformity to group norms. *Journal of Abnormal and Social Psychology, 53,* 100–107.

DiVasto, P. V., Kaufman, A., Rosner, L., Jackson, R., Christy, J., Pearson, S., & Burgett, T. (1984). The prevalence of sexually stressful events among females in the general population. *Archives of Sexual Behavior, 13,* 59–67.

Dobash, R. E., & Dobash, R. P. (1977–78). Wives: The appropriate victims of marital violence. *Victimology, 2,* 426–442.

Dodge, K. A. (1991). The structure and function of reactive and proactive aggression. In D. J. Pepler & K. H. Rubin (Eds.), *The development and treatment of childhood aggression.* Hillsdale, NJ: Erlbaum.

Dodge, K. A., Bates, J. E., & Pettit, G. S. (1990). Mechanisms in the cycle of violence. *Science, 250,* 1678–1683.

Doherty, W. J., Schrott, H. G., Metcalf, L., & Iasiello-Vailas, L. (1983). Effects of spouse support and health beliefs on medication adherence. *Journal of Family Practice, 17,* 837–841.

Dohrenwend, B. S., Krasnoff, L., Askenasy, A. R., & Dohrenwend, B. P. (1978). Exemplification of a method for scaling life events: The PERI life events scale. *Journal of Health and Social Behavior, 19,* 205–229.

Dohrenwend, B. S., Krasnoff, L., Askenasy, A. R., & Dohrenwend, B. P. (1982). The psychiatric epidemiology research interview life events scale. In L. Goldberger & S. Breznitz (Eds.), *Handbook of stress: Theoretical and clinical aspects.* New York: Free Press.

Doll, R., & Peto, R. (1981). *The causes of cancer.* New York: Oxford University Press.

Dollard, J., Doob, J., Miller, N., Mowrer, O., & Sears, R. (1939). *Frustration and aggression.* New Haven, CT: Yale University Press.

Dominick, J. R. (1979). The portrayal of women in prime time, 1953–1977. *Sex Roles, 5,* 405–411.

Donnerstein, E. (1980). Aggressive erotica and violence against women. *Journal of Personality and Social Psychology, 39,* 269–277.

Donnerstein, E. (1984). Pornography: Its effect on violence against women. In N. M. Malamuth & E. Donnerstein (Eds.), *Pornography and sexual aggression.* Orlando, FL: Academic Press.

Donnerstein, E., & Berkowitz, L. (1981). Victims' reactions in aggressive erotic films as a factor in violence against women. *Journal of Personality and Social Psychology, 41,* 710–724.

Donnerstein, E., & Donnerstein, M. (1976). Research on the control of interracial aggression. In R. G. Geen & E. C. O'Neal (Eds.), *Perspectives on aggression.* New York: Academic Press.

Donnerstein, E., Donnerstein, M., & Evans, R. (1975). Erotic stimuli and aggression: Facilitation or inhibition. *Journal of Personality and Social Psychology, 32,* 237–244.

Doob, L. W., & Sears, R. R. (1939). Factors determining substitute behavior and the overt expression of aggression. *Journal of Abnormal and Social Psychology, 34,* 293–313.

Dornbusch, S. M., Hastorf, A. H., Richardson, S. A., Muzzy, R. E., & Vreeland, R. S. (1965). The perceiver and the perceived: Their relative influence on categories of interpersonal perception. *Journal of Personality and Social Psychology, 1,* 434–440.

Dorr, A., & Kovaric, P. (1980). Some of the people some of the time—but which people? Televised violence and its effects. In E. L. Palmer & A. Dorr (Eds.), *Children and the faces of television: Teaching, violence, and selling.* New York: Academic Press.

Doty, R. M., Peterson, B. E., & Winter, D. G. (1991). Threat and authoritarianism in the United States, 1978–1987. *Journal of Personality and Social Psychology, 61,* 629–640.

Dovidio, J. F. (1984). Helping behavior and altruism: An empirical and conceptual overview. In L. Berkowitz (Ed.), *Advances in experimental social psychology* (Vol. 17). New York: Academic Press.

Dovidio, J. F., Ellyson, S. L., Keating, C. F., Heltman, K., & Brown, C. E. (1988). The relationship of social power to visual displays of dominance between men and women. *Journal of Personality and Social Psychology, 54,* 233–242.

Dovidio, J. F., Evans, N., & Tyler, R. B. (1986). Racial stereotypes: The contents of their cognitive representations. *Journal of Experimental Social Psychology, 22,* 22–37.

Dovidio, J. F., & Gaertner, S. L. (1991). Changes in the expression of racial prejudice. In H. J. Knopke, R. J. Norrell, & R. W. Rogers (Eds.), *Opening doors: Perspectives in race relations in contemporary America.* Tuscaloosa: University of Alabama Press.

Dovidio, J. F., Piliavin, J. A., Gaertner, S. L., Schroeder, D. A., & Clark, R. D., III (1991). The arousal cost–reward model and the process of intervention: A review of the evidence. In M. S. Clark (Ed.), *Prosocial behavior.* Newbury Park, CA: Sage.

Drachman, D., de Carufel, A., & Insko, C. A. (1978). The extra credit effect in interpersonal attraction. *Journal of Experimental Social Psychology, 14,* 458–465.

Drigotas, S. M., & Rusbult, C. E. (1992). Should I stay or should I go? A dependence model of breakups. *Journal of Personality and Social Psychology, 62,* 62–87.

Dubos, R. (1965). *Man adapting.* New Haven, CT: Yale University Press.

Dudycha, G. J. (1936). An objective study of punctuality in relation to personality and achievement. *Archives of Psychology, 204,* 1–319.

Duggan, L. M., Aubrey, M., Doherty, E., Isquith, P., Levine, M., & Scheiner, J. (1989). The credibility of children as witnesses in a simulated sexual abuse trial. In S. J. Ceci, D. F. Ross, & M. P. Toglia (Eds.), *Perspectives on children's testimony.* New York: Springer-Verlag.

Duncan, B. L. (1976). Differential social perception and attribution of intergroup violence: Testing the lower limits of stereotyping of blacks. *Journal of Personality and Social Psychology, 34,* 590–598.

Durdan, C. A., Reeder, G. D., & Hecht, P. R. (1985). Litter in a university cafeteria: Demographic data and the use of prompts as an intervention strategy. *Environment and Behavior, 17,* 387–404.

Dutton, D. G., & Aron, A. P. (1974). Some evidence for heightened sexual attraction under conditions of high anxiety. *Journal of Personality and Social Psychology, 30,* 510–517.

Duval, S., & Wicklund, R. A. (1972). *A theory of objective self-awareness.* New York: Academic Press.

Dworkin, A. (1987). *Intercourse.* New York: Free Press.

Dymond, R. (1949). A scale for the measurement of empathic ability. *Journal of Consulting Psychology, 13,* 127–133.

Dymond, R. (1950). Personality and empathy. *Journal of Consulting Psychology, 14,* 343–350.

Eagly, A. H. (1978). Sex differences in influenceability. *Psychological Bulletin, 85,* 86–116.

Eagly, A. H. (1987). *Sex differences in social behavior: A social role interpretation.* Hillsdale, NJ: Erlbaum.

Eagly, A. H., Ashmore, R. D., Makhijani, M. G., & Longo, L. C. (1991). What is beautiful is good, but . . . : A meta-analytic review of research on the physical attractiveness stereotype. *Psychological Bulletin, 110,* 109–128.

Eagly, A. H., & Carli, L. L. (1981). Sex of researchers and sex-typed communications as determinants of sex differences in influenceability: A meta-analysis of social influence studies. *Psychological Bulletin, 90,* 1–20.

Eagly, A. H., & Chaiken, S. (1984). Cognitive theories of persuasion. In L. Berkowitz (Ed.), *Advances in experimental social psychology* (Vol. 17). New York: Academic Press.

Eagly, A. H., & Chaiken, S. (1993). *The psychology of attitudes.* Fort Worth: Harcourt Brace Jovanovich.

Eagly, A. H., & Chrvala, C. (1986). Sex differences in conformity: Status and gender-role interpretations. *Psychology of Women Quarterly, 10,* 203–220.

Eagly, A. H., & Crowley, M. (1986). Gender and helping behavior: A meta-analytic review of the social psychological literature. *Psychological Bulletin, 100,* 283–308.

Eagly, A. H., & Johnson, B. T. (1990). Gender and leadership style: A meta-analysis. *Psychological Bulletin, 108,* 233–256.

Eagly, A. H., & Karau, S. J. (1991). Gender and the emergence of leaders: A meta-analysis. *Journal of Personality and Social Psychology, 60,* 685–710.

Eagly, A. H., & Kite, M. E. (1987). Are stereotypes of nationalities applied to both women and men? *Journal of Personality and Social Psychology, 53,* 457–462.

Eagly, A. H., & Mladinic, A. (1989). Gender stereotypes and attitudes toward women and men. *Personality and Social Psychology Bulletin, 15,* 543–558.

Eagly, A. H., Mladinic, A., & Otto, S. (1991). Are women evaluated more favorably than men? An analysis of attitudes, beliefs, and emotions. *Psychology of Women Quarterly, 15,* 203–216.

Eagly, A. H., & Steffen, V. J. (1986a). Gender stereotypes, occupational roles, and beliefs about part-time employees. *Psychology of Women Quarterly, 10,* 252–262.

Eagly, A. H., & Steffen, V. J. (1986b). Gender and aggressive behavior: A meta-analytic review of the social psychological literature. *Psychological Bulletin, 100,* 309–330.

Eagly, A. H., & Warren, R. (1976). Intelligence, comprehension, and opinion change. *Journal of Personality, 44,* 226–242.

Eagly, A. H., & Wood, W. (1991). Explaining sex differences in social behavior: A meta-analytic perspective. *Personality and Social Psychology Bulletin, 17,* 306–315.

Eaton, W. O., & Enns, L. R. (1986). Sex differences in human motor activity level. *Psychological Bulletin, 100,* 19–28.

Eaves, L. J., Eysenck, H. J., & Martin, N. G. (1989). *Genes, culture, and personality: An empirical approach.* London: Academic Press.

Ebbesen, E. G., Duncan, B., & Konecni, V. J. (1975). Effects of content of verbal aggression on future verbal aggression: A field experiment. *Journal of Experimental Social Psychology, 11,* 192–204.

Eccles, J., & Blumenfeld, P. (1985). Classroom experience and student gender: Are there differences and do they matter? In L. C. Wilinson & C. B. Marret (Eds.), *Gender influences in classroom interaction.* Orlando, FL: Academic Press.

Eccles (Parsons), J., Adler, T., & Meece, J. L. (1984). Sex differences in achievement: A test of alternate theories. *Journal of Personality and Social Psychology, 46,* 26–43.

Eder, R. A., Gerlach, S. G., & Perlmutter, M. (1987). In search of children's selves: Development of the specific and general components of the self-concept. *Child Development, 58,* 1044–1050.

Edney, J. H. (1979). The nuts game: A concise commons dilemma analog. *Environmental Psychology and Nonverbal Behavior, 3,* 252–254.

Edney, J. J. (1975). Territoriality and control: A field experiment. *Journal of Personality and Social Psychology, 31,* 1108–1115.

Edwards, D. J. A. (1972). Approaching the unfamiliar: A study of human interaction distances. *Journal of Behavioral Sciences, 1,* 249–250.

Edwards, E. A., & Dean, L. M. (1977). Effects of crowding of mice on humoral antibody formation and protection to lethal antigenic challenge. *Psychosomatic Medicine, 39,* 19–24.

Edwards, V. J., & Spence, J. T. (1987). Gender-related traits, stereotypes, and schemata. *Journal of Personality and Social Psychology, 53,* 146–154.

Efran, M. G. (1974). The effect of physical appearance in the judgment of guilt, interpersonal attraction, and severity of recommended punishment. *Journal of Research in Personality, 8,* 45–54.

Ehrenreich, B., & English, D. (1979). *For her own good: 150 years of experts' advice to women.* Garden City, NY: Anchor/Doubleday.

Eibl-Eibesfeldt, I. (1970). *Ethology: The biology of behavior.* New York: Holt, Rinehart and Winston.

Eibl-Eibesfeldt, I. (1979). *The biology of peace and war: Man, animals, and aggression.* New York: Viking.

Eidelson, R. J. (1980). Interpersonal satisfaction and level of involvement: A curvilinear relationship. *Journal of Personality and Social Psychology, 39,* 460–470.

Einhorn, H. J., & Hogarth, R. M. (1986). Judging probable cause. *Psychological Bulletin, 99,* 3–19.

Einsiedel, E. F. (1988). Uneasy bedfellows: Social science and pornography. *Journal of Communication, 38,* 107–121.

Eisenberg, N. (1992). *The caring child.* Cambridge, MA: Harvard University Press.

Eisenberg-Berg, N. (1979). Relationship of prosocial moral reasoning to altruism, political liberalism, and intelligence. *Developmental Psychology, 15,* 87–89.

Eisenman, R. (1991). Gender and racial prejudice of conservative college women. *Psychological Reports, 68,* 450.

Eisinga, R., Felling, A., & Peters, J. (1990). Religious beliefs, church involvement, and ethnocentrism in the Netherlands. *Journal for the Scientific Study of Religion, 29,* 54–75.

Ekman, P. (1972). Universals and cultural differences in facial expressions of emotion. In J. Cole (Ed.), *Nebraska symposium on motivation* (Vol. 19). Lincoln: University of Nebraska Press.

Ekman, P. (1985). *Telling lies.* New York: Norton.

Ekman, P., Davidson, R. J., & Fiesen, W. V. (1990). The Duchenne smile: Emotional expression and brain physiology. *Journal of Personality and Social Psychology, 58,* 342–353.

Ekman, P., & Friesen, W. V. (1969a). Nonverbal leakage and clues to deception. *Psychiatry, 32,* 88–106.

Ekman, P., & Friesen, W. V. (1969b). The repertoire of nonverbal behavior: Categories, origins, usage, and coding. *Semiotica, 1,* 124–129.

Ekman, P., & Friesen, W. V. (1971). Constants across cultures in the face and emotion. *Journal of Personality and Social Psychology, 17,* 124–129.

Ekman, P., & Friesen, W. V. (1974). Detecting deception from the body or face. *Journal of Personality and Social Psychology, 29,* 288–298.

Ekman, P., & Friesen, W. V. (1975). *Unmasking the face.* Englewood Cliffs, NJ: Prentice-Hall.

Ekman, P., & Friesen, W. V. (1982). Measuring facial movement with the Facial Action Coding System. In P. Ekman (Ed.), *Emotion in the human face.* Cambridge, England: Cambridge University Press.

Ekman, P., Friesen, W. V., & Ancoli, S. (1980). Facial signs of emotional experience. *Journal of Personality and Social Psychology, 39,* 1125–1134.

Ekman, P., Friesen, W. V., & Ellsworth, P. (1972). *Emotion in the human face.* New York: Pergamon.

Ekman, P., Friesen, W. V., & Ellsworth, P. (1982a). What are the similarities and differences in facial behavior across cultures? In P. Ekman (Ed.), *Emotion in the human face* (2nd ed.). Cambridge, England: Cambridge University Press.

Ekman, P., Friesen, W. V., & Ellsworth, P. (1982b). Does the face provide accurate information? In P. Ekman (Ed.), *Emotion in the human face* (2nd ed.). Cambridge, England: Cambridge University Press.

Ekman, P., Friesen, W. V., & O'Sullivan, M. (1988). Smiles when lying. *Journal of Personality and Social Psychology, 54,* 414–420.

Ekman, P., Friesen, W. V., O'Sullivan, M., Chan, A., Diacoyanni-Tarlatzis, I., Heider, K., Krause, R., LeCompte, W. A., Pitcairn, T., Ricci-Bitti, P. E., Scherer, K., Tomita, M., & Tzavaras, A. (1987). Universals and cultural differences in the judgments of facial expressions of emotion. *Journal of Personality and Social Psychology, 53,* 712–717.

Ekman, P., Friesen, W. V., O'Sullivan, M., & Scherer, K. (1980). Relative importance of face, body, and speech in judgments of personality and affect. *Journal of Personality and Social Psychology, 38,* 270–277.

Ekman, P., Friesen, W. V., & Tompkins, S. S. (1971). Facial affect scoring technique (FAST): A first validity study. *Semiotica, 3,* 37–58.

Ekman, P., Hagar, J. C., & Friesen, W. V. (1981). The symmetry of emotion and deliberate facial action. *Psychophysiology, 18,* 101–106.

Ekman, P., & O'Sullivan, M. (1991). Who can catch a liar? *American Psychologist, 46,* 913–920.

Elkin, R. A., & Leippe, M. R. (1986). Physiological arousal, dissonance, and attitude change: Evidence for a dissonance–arousal link and a "don't remind me" effect. *Journal of Personality and Social Psychology, 51,* 55–65.

Elliot, R., & Vasta, R. (1970). The modeling of sharing: Effects associated with vicarious reinforcement, symbolization, age, and generalization. *Journal of Experimental Child Psychology, 10,* 8–15.

Elliott, G. R., & Eisdorfer, C. (Eds.). (1982). *Stress and human health: Analysis and implications of research.* New York: Springer-Verlag.

Ellsworth, P. C., & Carlsmith, J. M. (1968). Effects of eye contact and verbal content on affective response to a dyadic interaction. *Journal of Personality and Social Psychology, 10,* 15–20.

Ellyson, S. L., & Dovidio, J. F. (1985). *Power, performance, and nonverbal behavior.* New York: Springer-Verlag.

Elms, A. C., & Milgram, S. (1966). Personality characteristics associated with obedience and defiance toward authoritive command. *Journal of Experimental Research in Personality, 1,* 282–289.

Emmons, R. A., Diener, E., & Larsen, R. J. (1986). Choice and avoidance of everyday situations and affect congruence: Two models of reciprocal interactionism. *Journal of Personality and Social Psychology, 51,* 815–826.

Endler, N. S. (1981). Persons, situations, and their interactions. In A. I. Rabin (Ed.), *Further explorations in personality.* New York: Wiley.

Endler, N. S. (1983). Interactionism: A personality model, but not yet a theory. In M. M. Page (Ed.), *Personality—Current theory and research: Nebraska symposium on motivation 1982.*

Endler, N. S., & Hunt, J. McV. (1966). Sources of behavioral variance as measured by the S-R inventory of anxiousness. *Psychological Bulletin, 65,* 336–346.

Endler, N. S., & Hunt, J. McV. (1969). Generalizability of contributions from sources of variance in the S-R inventory of anxiousness. *Journal of Personality, 37,* 1–24.

Epstein, C. F. (1988). *Deceptive distinctions: Sex, gender, and the social order.* New Haven, CT: Yale University Press.

Epstein, S. (1973). The self-concept revisited: Or a theory of a theory. *American Psychologist, 28,* 404–416.

Epstein, S. (1979). The stability of behavior: I. On predicting most of the people most of the time. *Journal of Personality and Social Psychology, 37,* 1097–1126.

Epstein, S. (1980). The stability of behavior. II: Implications for psychological research. *American Psychologist, 35,* 790–806.

Epstein, S. (1983). A research paradigm for the study of personality and emotions. In M. M. Page (Ed.), *Personality—Current theory and research: Nebraska symposium on motivation 1982.*

Epstein, S., & O'Brien, E. J. (1985). The person–situation debate in historical and current perspective. *Psychological Bulletin, 98,* 513–537.

Epstein, Y. M. (1982). Crowding, stress, and human behavior. In G. W. Evans (Ed.), *Environmental stress.* New York: Cambridge University Press.

Eron, L. D. (1987). The development of aggressive behavior from the perspective of a developing behaviorism. *American Psychologist, 42,* 435–442.

Eron, L. D., & Huesmann, L. R. (1986). The role of television in the development of prosocial and antisocial behavior. In D. Olweus, J. Block, & M. Radke-Yarrow (Eds.), *Development of antisocial and prosocial behavior: Research, theories, and issues.* Orlando, FL: Academic Press.

Esser, J. K., & Lindoerfer, J. S. (1989). Groupthink and the space shuttle Challenger accident: Toward a quantitative case analysis. *Journal of Behavioral Decision Making, 2,* 167–177.

Evans, G. W. (1978). Design implications of spatial research In J. Aiello (Ed.), *Residential crowding.* New York: Plenum.

Evans, G. W. (1979). Crowding and human performance. *Journal of Applied Social Psychology, 9,* 27–46.

Evans, G. W., & Lepore, S. J. (1992). Conceptual and analytic issues in crowding research. *Journal of Environmental Psychology, 12,* 163–173.

Evans, R. I., Smith, C. K., & Raines, B. E. (1984). Deterring cigarette smoking in adolescents: A psycho-social-behavioral analysis of an intervention strategy. In A. Baum, J. Singer, & S. Taylor (Eds.), *Handbook of psychology and health: Social psychological aspects of health* (Vol. 3). Hillsdale, NJ: Erlbaum.

Exline, R. (1972). Visual interaction: The glances of power and preference. In J. Cole (Ed.), *Nebraska symposium on motivation, 1971.* Lincoln: University of Nebraska Press.

Eysenck, H. J. (1952). *The scientific study of personality.* London: Routledge & Kegan Paul.

Fagot, B. I. (1977). Consequences of moderate cross-gender behavior in pre-school children. *Child Development, 48,* 902–907.

Farina, A., Fischer, E., Sherman, S., Smith, W., Groh, T., & Nermin, P. (1977). Physical attractiveness and mental illness. *Journal of Abnormal Psychology, 86,* 510–517.

Farley, J. U., Lehmann, D. R., & Ryan, M. J. (1981). Generalizing from "imperfect" replication. *Journal of Business, 54,* 597–610.

Farley, R., Schuman, H., Bianchi, S., Colasanto, D., & Hatchett, S. (1978). "Chocolate city, vanilla suburbs": Will the trend toward racially separate communities continue? *Social Science Research, 7,* 319–344.

Fausto-Sterling, A. (1985). *Myths of gender: Biological theories about women and men.* New York: Basic Books.

Fazio, R. H. (1987). Self-perception theory: A current perspective. In M. Zanna, J. M. Olson, & C. P. Herman (Eds.), *Social influence: The Ontario symposium* (Vol. 3). Hillsdale, NJ: Erlbaum.

Fazio, R. H. (1989). On the power and functionality of attitudes: The role of attitude accessibility. In A. R. Pratkanis & A. G. Greenwald (Eds.), *Attitude structure and function.* Hillsdale, NJ: Erlbaum.

Fazio, R. H. (1990). Multiple processes by which attitudes guide behavior: The MODE model as an integrative framework. In M. P. Zanna (Ed.), *Advances in experimental social psychology* (Vol. 23). San Diego: Academic Press.

Fazio, R. H., Chen, J., McDonel, E. C., & Sherman, S. J. (1982). Attitude accessibility, attitude–behavior consistency, and the strength of the object-evaluation association. *Journal of Experimental Social Psychology, 18,* 339–357.

Fazio, R. H., & Zanna, M. P. (1981). Direct experience and attitude–behavior consistency. In L. Berkowitz (Ed.), *Advances in experimental social psychology* (Vol. 14). New York: Academic Press.

Fazio, R. H., Zanna, M. P., & Cooper, J. (1977). Dissonance and self-perception: An integrative view of each theory's proper domain of application. *Journal of Experimental Social Psychology, 13,* 464–479.

Feather, N. T. (1982). *Expectations and actions: Expectancy-value models in psychology.* Hillsdale, NJ: Erlbaum.

Feeney, J. A., & Noller, P. (1990). Attachment style as a predictor of adult romantic relationships. *Journal of Personality and Social Psychology, 58,* 281–291.

Feierabend, I., & Feierabend, R. (1972). Systematic conditions of political aggression: An application of frustration–aggression theory. In I. K. Feierabend, R. L. Feierabend, & T. R. Gurr (Eds.), *Anger, violence, and politics.* Englewood Cliffs, NJ: Prentice-Hall.

Feingold, A. (1988a). Cognitive gender differences are disappearing. *American Psychologist, 43,* 95–103.

Feingold, A. (1988b). Matching for attractiveness in romantic partners and same-sex friends: A meta-analysis and theoretical critique. *Psychological Bulletin, 104,* 226–235.

Feingold, A. (1990). Gender differences in effects of physical attractiveness on romantic attraction: A comparison across five research paradigms. *Journal of Personality and Social Psychology, 59,* 981–993.

Feingold, A. (1991). Sex differences in the effects of similarity and physical attractiveness on opposite-sex attraction. *Basic and Applied Social Psychology, 12,* 357–367.

Feingold, A. (1992a). Gender differences in mate selection preference: A test of the parental investment model. *Psychological Bulletin, 112,* 125–139.

Feingold, A. (1992b). Good-looking people are not what we think. *Psychological Bulletin, 111,* 304–341.

Fellner, C. H., & Marshall, J. R. (1981). Kidney donors revisited. In J. P. Rushton & R. M. Sorrentino (Eds.), *Altruism and helping behavior: Social, personality, and developmental perspectives.* Hillsdale, NJ: Erlbaum.

Fenigstein, A., Scheier, M. R., & Buss, A. H. (1975). Public and private self-consciousness: Assessment and theory. *Journal of Consulting and Clinical Psychology, 43,* 522–527.

Ferguson, C. K., & Kelley, H. H. (1964). Significant factors in overevaluation of own-group's product. *Journal of Abnormal and Social Psychology, 69,* 223–228.

Ferguson, G. (1955). Legal research on trial. *Judicature, 39,* 78–82.

Feshbach, S. (1970). Aggression. In P. H. Mussen (Ed.), *Carmichael's manual of child psychology.* New York: Wiley.

Feshbach, S. (1980). Television advertising and children: Policy issue and alternatives. Paper presented at the annual meeting of the American Psychological Association.

Feshbach, S. (1984). The catharsis hypothesis, aggressive drive, and the reduction of aggression. *Aggressive Behavior, 10,* 91–101.

Festinger, L. (1954). A theory of social comparison processes. *Human Relations, 7,* 117–140.

Festinger, L. (1957). *A theory of cognitive dissonance.* Evanston, IL: Row, Peterson.

Festinger, L., & Carlsmith, J. M. (1959). Cognitive consequences of forced compliance. *Journal of Abnormal and Social Psychology, 58,* 203–210.

Festinger, L., Pepitone, A., & Newcomb, T. (1952). Some consequences of deindividuation in a group. *Journal of Abnormal and Social Psychology, 47,* 382–389.

Festinger, L., Rieken, H. W., & Schachter, S. (1956). *When prophecy fails.* Minneapolis: University of Minnesota Press.

Festinger, L., Schachter, S., & Back, K. (1950). *Social pressures in informal groups: A study of human factors in housing.* New York: Harper & Brothers.

Fiedler, F. E. (1978). Contingency model and the leadership process. In L. Berkowitz (Ed.), *Advances in experimental social psychology.* New York: Academic Press.

Fiedler, F. E. (1993). The leadership situation and the black box in contingency theories. In M. M. Chemers & R. Ayman (Eds.), *Leadership theory and research: Perspectives and directions.* San Diego: Academic Press.

Fiedler, F. E., & Garcia, J. E. (1987). *Leadership: Cognitive resources and performance.* New York: Wiley.

Field, H. S. (1978). Juror background characteristics and attitudes toward rape. *Law and Human Behavior, 2,* 73–93.

Field, H. S., & Bienen, L. B. (1980). Jurors and rape: A study in psychology and law. Lexington, MA: Heath.

Fields, M., & Fields, H. (1973). Marital violence and the criminal process: Neither justice nor peace. *Social Service Review, 47,* 221-240.

Fincham, F. D., & Bradbury, T. N. (Eds.). (1990). *The psychology of marriage: Basic issues and applications.* New York: Guilford.

Fischer, C. S. (1982). *To dwell among friends: Personal networks in town and city.* Chicago: University of Chicago Press.

Fishbein, M. (1963). An investigation of the relationship between beliefs about an object and the attitude towards that object. *Human Relations, 16,* 233–239.

Fishbein, M. (1966). *Sexual behavior and propositional control.* Paper presented at annual meeting of the Psychonomic Society.

Fishbein, M., & Ajzen, I. (1974). Attitudes towards objects as predictors of single and multiple behavioral criteria. *Psychological Review, 81,* 59–74.

Fishbein, M., & Ajzen, I. (1975). *Belief, attitude, intention and behavior: An introduction to theory and research.* Reading, MA: Addison-Wesley.

Fishbein, M., & Ajzen, I. (1980). Predicting and understanding consumer behavior: Attitude–behavior correspondence. In I. Ajzen & M. Fishbein (Eds.), *Understanding attitudes and predicting social behavior.* Englewood Cliffs, NJ: Prentice-Hall.

Fishbein, M., Ajzen, I., & McArdle, J. (1980). Changing the behavior of alcoholics: Effects of persuasive communication. In I. Ajzen & M. Fishbein (Eds.), *Understanding attitudes and predicting social behavior.* Englewood Cliffs, NJ: Prentice-Hall.

Fishbein, M., Chan, D. K-S., O'Reilly, K., Schnell, D., Wood, R., Beeker, C., & Cohn, D. (1992). Attitudinal and normative factors as determinants of gay men's intentions to perform AIDS-related sexual behaviors: A multisite analysis. *Journal of Applied Social Psychology, 22,* 999–1011.

Fishbein, M., Jaccard, J. J., Davidson, A. B., Ajzen, I., & Loken, B. (1980). Predicting and understanding family planning behaviors: Beliefs, attitudes, and intentions. In I. Ajzen & M. Fishbein (Eds.), *Understanding attitudes and predicting social behavior.* Englewood Cliffs, NJ: Prentice-Hall.

Fisher, B. M., & Edwards, J. E. (1988). Consideration and initiating structure and their relationships with leader effectiveness: A meta-analysis. *Best Papers Proceedings, Academy of Management,* Anaheim, CA, 201–205.

Fisher, E. B., & Rost, K. (1986). Smoking cessation: A practical guide for the physician. *Clinics in Chest Medicine, 7,* 551–565.

Fisher, J. D., & Byrne, D. (1975). Too close for comfort: Sex differences in response to invasions of personal space. *Journal of Personality and Social Psychology, 32,* 15–21.

Fisher, J. D., DePaulo, B. M., & Nadler, A. (1981). Extending altruism beyond the altruistic act: The mixed effects of aid on the recipient. In J. P. Rushton & R. M. Sorrentino (Eds.), *Altruism and helping behavior: Social, personality, and developmental perspectives.* Hillsdale, NJ: Erlbaum.

Fisher, J. D., Nadler, A., & Whitcher-Alagner, S. (1982). Recipient reactions to aid. *Psychological Bulletin, 91,* 27–54.

Fiske, A. P. (1991). The cultural relativity of selfish individualism: Anthropological evidence that humans are inherently sociable. In M. S. Clark (Ed.), *Prosocial behavior.* Newbury Park, CA: Sage.

Fiske, S. T. (1993). Social cognition and social perception. In L. Porter and M. R. Rosenzweig (Eds.), *Annual Review of Psychology, 44,* 155–194.

Fiske, S. T., Kinder, D. R., & Larter, W. M. (1983). The novice and expert: Knowledge-based strategies in political cognition. *Journal of Experimental Social Psychology, 19,* 381–400.

Fiske, S. T., & Neuberg, S. L. (1990). A continuum of impression formation from category-based to individuating processes: Influences of information and motivation on attention and interpretation. In M. P. Zanna (Ed.), *Advances in experimental social psychology* (Vol. 23). San Diego: Academic Press.

Fiske, S. T., & Taylor, S. E. (1984). *Social cognition.* Reading, MA: Addison-Wesley.

Fiske, S. T., & Taylor, S. E. (1991). *Social cognition* (2nd ed.). New York: McGraw-Hill.

Fitzgerald, R., & Ellsworth, P. C. (1984). Due process versus crime control: Death qualification and jury attitudes. *Law and Human Behavior, 8,* 31–52.

Flammang, C. J. (1970). *The police and the underprotected child.* Springfield, IL: Charles C. Thomas.

Flay, B. R., Ryan, K. B., Best, J. A., Brown, K. S., Kersell, M. W., d'Avernas, J. R., & Zanna, M. P. (1985). Are social-psychological smoking prevention programs effective? The Waterloo study. *Journal of Behavior Medicine, 8,* 37–59.

Fleishman, E. A. (1973). Twenty years of consideration and structure. In E. A. Fleishman & J. G. Hunt (Eds.), *Current developments in the study of leadership.* Carbondale: Southern Illinois University Press.

Fleming, I., Baum, A., & Weiss, L. (1987). Social density and perceived control as mediators of crowding stress in high-density residential neighborhoods. *Journal of Personality and Social Psychology, 52,* 899–906.

Fletcher, G. J. O. (1983). The analysis of verbal explanations for marital separation: Implications for attribution theory. *Journal of Applied Social Psychology, 13,* 245–258.

Fletcher, G. J. O., Fincham, F. D., Cramer, L., & Heron, N. (1987). The role of attributions in the development of dating relationships. *Journal of Personality and Social Psychology, 53,* 481–489.

Foa, U. G. (1961). Convergences in the analysis of the structure in interpersonal behavior. *Psychological Review, 68,* 341–352.

Ford, J. G., & Graves, J. R. (1977). Differences between Mexican-American and white children in interpersonal distance and social touching. *Perceptual and Motor Skills, 45,* 779–785.

Ford, T. E., & Stangor, C. (1992). The role of diagnosticity in stereotype formation: Perceiving group means and variances. *Journal of Personality and Social Psychology, 63,* 356–367.

Forsterling, F. (1985). Attributional retraining: A review. *Psychological Bulletin, 98,* 495–512.

Forsterling, F. (1989). Models of covariation and attribution: How do they relate to the analogy of analysis of variance? *Journal of Personality and Social Psychology, 57,* 615–625.

Forsyth, D. R. (1983). *An introduction to group dynamics.* Monterey, CA: Brooks/Cole.

Frable, D. E. S., Blackstone, T., & Scherbaum, C. (1990). Marginal and

mindful: Deviants in social interactions. *Journal of Personality and Social Psychology, 59,* 140–149.

Frager, R. (1970). Conformity and anticonformity in Japan. *Journal of Personality and Social Psychology, 15,* 203–210.

Frank, L. K. (1957). Tactile communication. *Genetic Psychology Monographs, 56,* 209–255.

Franklin, B. J. (1975). Need, receipt or denial of aid, and attitudes toward the benefactor. *Journal of Social Psychology, 97,* 261–266.

Fredericks, A. J., & Dossett, D. L. (1983). Attitude–behavior relations: A comparison of the Fishbein-Ajzen and the Bentler-Speckart models. *Journal of Personality and Social Psychology, 45,* 501–512.

Freedman, J., Levy, A., Buchanan, R., & Price, J. (1972). Crowding and human aggressiveness. *Journal of Experimental Social Psychology, 8,* 528–548.

Freedman, J. L. (1975). *Crowding and behavior.* San Francisco: Freeman.

Freedman, J. L. (1992). Television violence and aggression: What psychologists should tell the public. In P. Suedfeld & P. E. Tetlock (Eds.), *Psychology and social policy.* New York: Hemisphere.

Freedman, J. L., Heshka, S., & Levy, A. (1975). Population density and pathology in metropolitan areas. In J. L. Freedman (Ed.), *Crowding and behavior.* San Francisco: Freeman.

Freedman, J. L., Klevansky, S., & Ehrlich, P. I. (1971). The effect of crowding on human task performance. *Journal of Applied Social Psychology, 1,* 7–26.

Freud, S. (1961). *Civilization and its discontents* (J. Strachey, Trans.). New York: Norton. (Original work published 1930)

Fried, M. (1963). Grieving for a lost home. In L. J. Duhl (Ed.), *The urban condition.* New York: Simon & Schuster.

Friedman, H., & Zebrowitz, L. A. (1992). The contribution of typical sex differences in facial maturity to sex role stereotypes. *Personality and Social Psychology Bulletin, 18,* 430–438.

Frieze, I. R., Olson, J. E., & Russell, J. (1991). Attractiveness and income for men and women in management. *Journal of Applied Social Psychology, 21,* 1039–1057.

Fry, A. M., & Willis, F. N. (1971). Invasion of personal space as a function of age of the invader. *Psychological Record, 21,* 385–389.

Fukari, H., Butler, E., & Krooth, R. (in press). Where did Black jurors go? A theoretical synthesis of racial disenfranchisement in the jury system and jury selection. *Journal of Black Studies.*

Funder, D. C. (1991). Global traits: A neo-Allportian approach to personality. *Psychological Science, 2,* 31–39.

Funder, D. C., & Colvin, C. R. (1988). Friends and strangers: Acquaintanceship, agreement, and the accuracy of personality judgment. *Journal of Personality and Social Psychology, 55,* 149–158.

Funder, D. C., & Dobruth, K. (1987). Differences between traits: Properties associated with interjudge agreement. *Journal of Personality and Social Psychology, 52,* 409–418.

Gaebelein, J. W. (1973). Third-party instigation of aggression: An experimental approach. *Journal of Personality and Social Psychology, 27,* 389–395.

Gaertner, S. L., & Dovidio, J. F. (1977). The subtlety of white racism, arousal, and helping behavior. *Journal of Personality and Social Psychology, 35,* 691–707.

Gaertner, S. L., & Dovidio, J. F. (1986). The aversive form of racism. In J. F. Dovidio & S. L. Gaertner (Eds.), *Prejudice, discrimination, and racism.* Orlando, FL: Academic Press.

Gaertner, S. L., Mann, J. A., Dovidio, J. F., Murrell, A. J., & Pomare, M. (1990). How does cooperation reduce intergroup bias? *Journal of Personality and Social Psychology, 59,* 692–704.

Galanter, M. (1987). Jury shadows: Reflections on the civil jury and the "litigation explosion." In *The American Civil Jury,* Roscoe Pound–American Trial Lawyers Foundation.

Galle, O. R., Gove, W. R., & McPherson, J. M. (1972). Population density and pathology: What are the relations for man? *Science, 176,* 23–30.

Gallup, G. (1981a). Percentage of smokers lowest in 37 years. Part One. Abstracted in *Bibliography on smoking and health—1982.* Washington, DC: Superintendent of Documents.

Gallup, G. (1981b). Smoking level declines as more perceive health risk. Abstracted in *Bibliography of smoking and health—1982.* Washington, DC: Superintendent of Documents.

Gallup, G. G. (1977). Self-recognition in primates: A comparative approach to the bidirectional properties of consciousness. *American Psychologist, 32,* 329–338.

Gallup, G. G., & Suarez, S. D. (1986). Self-awareness and the emergence of mind in humans and other primates. In J. Suls & A. G. Greenwald (Eds.), *Psychological perspectives on the self* (Vol. 3). Hillsdale, NJ: Erlbaum.

Gamson, W. A., Fireman, B., & Rytina, S. (1982). *Encounters with unjust authority.* Homewood, IL: Dorsey.

Ganellen, R. J., & Blaney, P. H. (1984). Hardiness and social support as moderators of the effects of life stress. *Journal of Personality and Social Psychology, 47,* 156–163.

Gans, H. J. (1962). *The urban villagers.* New York: Free Press.

Garcia, L. T., & Griffitt, W. (1978). Authoritarianism–situation interactions in the determination of punitiveness: Engaging authoritarian ideology. *Journal of Research in Personality, 12,* 469–478.

Garratt, G. A., Baxter, J. C., & Rozelle, R. M. (1981). Training university police in black-American nonverbal behavior. *Journal of Social Psychology, 113,* 217–229.

Garvey, C. (1977). *Play.* Cambridge, MA: Harvard University Press.

Geen, R. G. (1968). Effects of frustration, attack, and prior training on aggressiveness upon aggressive behavior. *Journal of Personality and Social Psychology, 9,* 316–321.

Geen, R. G. (1979). Effects of being observed on learning following success failure experiences. *Motivation and Emotion, 3,* 355–371.

Geen, R. G. (1989). Alternative conceptions of social facilitation. In P. B. Paulus (Ed.). *Psychology of group influence* (2nd ed.). Hillsdale, NJ: Erlbaum.

Geen, R. G. (1991). Social motivation. *Annual Review of Psychology, 42,* 377–399.

Geen, R. G., & Quanty, M. B. (1977). The catharsis of aggression: An evaluation of a hypothesis. In L. Berkowitz (Ed.), *Advances in experimental social psychology* (Vol. 10). New York: Academic Press.

Geen, R. G., Rokosky, J. J., & Pigg, R. (1972). Awareness of arousal and its relation to aggression. *British Journal of Social and Clinical Psychology, 11,* 115–121.

Geen, R. G., Stonner, D., & Shope, G. L. (1975). The facilitation of aggression by aggression: Evidence against the catharsis hypothesis. *Journal of Personality and Social Psychology, 31,* 721–726.

Gelles, R. J. (1982). Domestic criminal violence. In M. E. Wolfgang & N. A. Weiner (Eds.), *Criminal violence.* Beverly Hills, CA: Sage.

Gelles, R. J., & Cornell, C. P. (1990). *Intimate violence in families* (2nd Ed.). Newbury Park, CA: Sage.

Gelles, R. J., & Straus, M. A. (1979). Violence in the American family. *Journal of Social Issues, 35,* 15–39.

Gentry, C. S. (1987). Social distance regarding male and female homosexuals. *Journal of Social Psychology, 127,* 199–208.

Gerard, H. B. (1983). School desegregation: The social science role. *American Psychologist, 38,* 869–877.

Gerard, H. B., & Mathewson, G. C. (1966). The effects of severity of initiation on liking for a group: A replication. *Journal of Experimental Social Psychology, 2,* 278–287.

Gerbner, G., Gross, L., Signorielli, N., & Morgan, M. (1980). Television violence, victimization, and power. *American Behavioral Scientist, 23,* 705–716.

Gerbner, G., Gross, L., Signorielli, N., & Morgan, M. (1986). *Television's mean world: Violence profile No. 14–15.* Philadelphia: University of Pennsylvania, Annenberg School of Communications.

Gergen, K. J. (1971). *The concept of self.* New York: Holt, Rinehart and Winston.

Gergen, K. J. (1973). Social psychology as history. *Journal of Personality and Social Psychology, 26,* 309–320.

Gergen, K. J. (1978). Experimentation in social psychology: A reappraisal. *European Journal of Social Psychology, 36,* 1344–1360.

Gergen, K. J., & Gergen, M. M. (1971). International assistance from a psychological perspective. In *The yearbook of international affairs* (Vol. 25). London: London Institute of World Affairs.

Gergen, K. J., & Gergen, M. M. (1983). Narratives of the self. In T. R. Sarbin & K. E. Scheive (Eds.), *Studies in social identity.* New York: Praeger.

Gergen, K. J., & Gergen, M. M. (1988). Narrative and the self as relationship. In L. Berkowitz (Ed.), *Advances in experimental social psychology* (Vol. 21). San Diego: Academic Press.

Gergen, K. J., Gergen, M. M., & Barton, W. H. (October, 1973). Deviance in the dark. *Psychology Today,* pp. 129–130.

Gergen, K. J., Gergen, M. M., & Meter, K. (1972). Individual orientations to prosocial behavior. *Journal of Social Issues, 8,* 105–130.

Gesell, A. L., Halverson, H. M., & Amatruda, C. (1940). *The first five years of life: A guide to the study of the preschool child.* New York: Harper.

Gibb, C. A. (1968). Leadership. In G. Lindzey & E. Aronson (Eds.), *Handbook of social psychology* (2nd ed., Vol. 4). Reading, MA: Addison-Wesley.

Gibbons, F. X. (1978). Sexual standards and reactions to pornography: Enhancing behavioral consistency through self-focused attention. *Journal of Personality and Social Psychology, 36,* 976–987.

Gibbons, F. X., & Kassin, S. M. (1987). Information consistency and perceptual set: Overcoming the mental retardation "schema." *Journal of Applied Social Psychology, 17,* 810–827.

Gilbert, D. T. (1991). How mental systems believe. *American Psychologist, 46,* 107–119.

Gilbert, D. T., & Osborne, R. E. (1989). Thinking backward: Some curable and un-curable consequences of cognitive busy-ness. *Journal of Personality and Social Psychology, 57,* 940–949.

Gilbert, D. T., Pelham, B. W., & Krull, D. S. (1988). On cognitive busyness: When person perceivers meet persons perceived. *Journal of Personality and Social Psychology, 54,* 733–740.

Gill, J. J., Price, V. A., Friedman, M., Thoresen, C. E., Powell, L. H., Ulmer, D., Brown, B., & Drews, F. R. (1985). Reduction of type A behavior in healthy middle-aged American military officers. *American Heart Journal, 110,* 503–514.

Gillis, J. S., & Avis, W. E. (1980). The male-taller norm in mate selection. *Personality and Social Psychology Bulletin, 6,* 396–401.

Gilmore, R., & Duck, S. (1980). *The development of social psychology.* London: Academic Press.

Ginosar, Z., & Trope, Y. (1980). The effects of base rates and individuating information on judgments about another person. *Journal of Experimental Social Psychology, 16,* 228–242.

Ginsburg, H. J., Pollman, V. A., Wanson, M. S., & Hope, M. L. (1977). Variation of aggressive interaction as a function of changes in spatial density. *Environmental Psychology and Nonverbal Behavior, 2,* 67–75.

Gintner, G., & Lindskold, S. (1975). Rate of participation and expertise as factors influencing leader choice. *Journal of Personality and Social Psychology, 32,* 1085–1089.

Glass, D. (1964). Changes in liking as a means of reducing cognitive discrepancies between self-esteem and aggression. *Journal of Personality, 32,* 531–549.

Glass, D. C., Ross, D. T., Isecke, W., & Rosenman, R. H. (1982). Relative importance of speech characteristics and content of answers in the assessment of behavior pattern A by the structured interview. *Basic and Applied Social Psychology, 3,* 161–168.

Glass, D. C., & Singer, J. E. (1972). *Urban stress: Experiments on noise and social stressors.* New York: Academic Press.

Glass, G. V., McGraw, B., & Smith, M. L. (1981). Meta-analysis in social research. Beverly Hills, CA: Sage.

Glick, P., Zion, C., & Nelson, C. (1988). What mediates sex discrimination in hiring? *Journal of Personality and Social Psychology, 55,* 178–186.

Goethals, G. P., & Zanna, M. P. (1979). The role of social comparison in choice shifts. *Journal of Personality and Social Psychology, 37,* 1469–1476.

Goffman, E. (1959). *The presentation of self in everyday life.* Garden City, NY: Double-day (Anchor Books).

Goffman, E. (1963). *Stigma: Notes on the management of spoiled identity.* Englewood Cliffs, NJ: Prentice-Hall.

Goffman, E. (1967). *Interaction ritual.* Garden City, NY: Doubleday.

Goldberg, L. R. (1978). Differential attribution of trait-descriptive terms to oneself as compared to well-liked, neutral, and disliked others: A psychometric analysis. *Journal of Personality and Social Psychology, 36,* 1012–1028.

Goldberg, L. R. (1981). Language and individual differences: The search for universals and personality lexicons. In L. Wheeler (Ed.), *Review of personality and social psychology* (Vol. 2). Beverly Hills, CA: Sage.

Goldberg, L. R. (1993). The structure of phenotypic personality traits. *American Psychologist, 48,* 26–34.

Goldberg, P. (1968). Are women prejudicial against women? *Transaction, 5,* 28–30.

Goldman, M., & Fraas, L. A. (1965). The effects of leader selection on group performance. *Sociometry, 28,* 82–88.

Goldmeier, D., & Johnson, A. (1982). Does psychiatric illness affect the recurrence rate of genital herpes? *British Journal of Venereal Diseases, 58,* 40–43.

Goldstein, A. P., Spratfkin, R. P., & Gershaw, N. J. (1976). *Skill training for community living.* New York: Pergamon.

Goldstein, A. P., & Keller, H. R. (1983). Aggression prevention and control: Multi-targeted, multichannel, multiprocess, multidisciplinary. In *Prevention and control of aggression.* New York: Pergamon.

Goldstein, D. (1983). Spouse abuse. In *Prevention and control of aggression.* New York: Pergamon.

Gonzales, M. H., Aronson, E., & Costanzo, M. A. (1988). Using social cognition and persuasion to promote energy conservation: A quasi-experiment. *Journal of Applied Social Psychology, 18,* 1049–1066.

Goodall, J. (1971). *In the shadow of man.* Boston: Houghton Mifflin.

Goodman, G.S., Bottoms, B. L., Herscovici, B. B., & Shaver, P. (1989). Determinants of the child victim's perceived credibility. In S. J. Ceci, D. F. Ross, & M. P. Toglia (Eds.), *Perspectives on children's testimony.* New York: Springer-Verlag.

Gordon, C. (1968). Self-conceptions: Config-

urations of content. In C. Gordon & K. J. Gergen (Eds.), *The self in social interaction* (Vol. 1). New York: Wiley.

Gorn, G. J., & Goldberg, M. E. (1980). Children's responses to repetitive TV commercials. *Journal of Consumer Research, 6,* 421–424.

Gorn, G. J., Goldberg, M. E., & Kanungo, R. N. (1976). The role of educational television in changing the intergroup attitudes of children. *Child Development, 47,* 277–280.

Gorsuch, R. L., & Aleshire, D. (1974). Christian faith and ethnic prejudice: A review and interpretation of research. *Journal for the Scientific Study of Religion, 13,* 281–307.

Gorsuch, R. L., & Key, M. K. (1974). Abnormalities of pregnancy as a function of anxiety and life stress. *Psychosomatic Medicine, 36,* 352.

Gottman, J. M. (1979). *Marital interaction: Experimental investigations.* New York: Academic Press.

Gottman, J. M., & Levenson, R. W. (1992). Marital processes predictive of later dissolution: Behavior, physiology, and health. *Journal of Personality and Social Psychology, 63,* 221–233.

Gough, H. G. (1964). *California Psychological Inventory: Manual.* Palo Alto, CA: Consulting Psychologists Press.

Gouldner, A. W. (1960). The norm of reciprocity: A preliminary statement. *American Sociological Review, 25,* 161–178.

Gourash, N. (1978). Help-seeking: A review of the literature. *American Journal of Community Psychology, 6,* 413–424.

Graesser, A., Woll, S. B., Kowalski, D. J., & Smith, D. A. (1980). Memory for typical and atypical actions in scripted activities. *Journal of Experimental Psychology: Human Learning and Memory, 6,* 503–515.

Graves, N. B., & Graves, T. D. (1983). The cultural context of prosocial development: An ecological model. In D. L. Bridgeman (Ed.), *The nature of prosocial development.* New York: Academic Press.

Graves, S. B. (1980). Psychological effects of black portrayals on television. In S. B. Withey & R. P. Abeles (Eds.), *Television and social behavior: Beyond violence and television.* Hillsdale, NJ: Erlbaum.

Gray, J. D., & Silver, R. C. (1990). Opposite side of the same coin: Former spouses' divergent perspectives in coping with their divorce. *Journal of Personality and Social Psychology, 59,* 1180–1191.

Graziano, W. G., Brothen, T., & Berscheid, E. (1978). Height and attraction: Do men and women see eye-to-eye? *Journal of Personality, 46*, 128–145.

Green, T. A. (1985). *Verdict according to conscience*. Chicago: University of Chicago Press.

Greenberg, J., Pyszczynski, T., & Solomon, S. (1982). The self-serving attributional bias: Beyond self-presentation. *Journal of Experimental Social Psychology, 18*, 56–67.

Greenberg, J., Pyszczynski, T., Solomon, S., Rosenblatt, A., Veeder, M., Kirkland, S., & Lyon, D. (1990). Evidence for terror management theory II: The effects of mortality salience on reactions to those who threaten or bolster the cultural worldview. *Journal of Personality and Social Psychology, 58*, 308–318.

Greenberg, J., & Pyszczynski, T. (1985). The effect of an overheard ethnic slur on evaluations of the target: How to spread a social disease. *Journal of Experimental Social Psychology, 21*, 61–72.

Greene, E., & Loftus, E. F. (1984). What's new in the news? The influence of well-publicized news events on psychological research and courtroom trials. *Basic and Applied Social Psychology, 5*, 211–221.

Greene, E., & Wade, R. (1987). Of private false and public print: General pre-trial publicity and juror decision making. *Applied Cognitive Psychology, 2*, 123–135.

Greenwald, A. G. (1968). Cognitive learning, cognitive responses to persuasion, and attitude change. In A. G. Greenwald, T. C. Brock, & T. M. Ostrom (Eds.), *Psychological foundation of attitudes*. New York: Academic Press.

Greenwald, A. G. (1980). The totalitarian ego: Fabrication and revision of personal history. *American Psychologist, 35*, 602–618.

Greenwald, A. G. (1982). Is anyone in charge? Personalysis versus the principle of personal unity. In J. Suls (Ed.), *Psychological perspective on the self* (Vol. 1). Hillsdale, NJ: Erlbaum.

Greenwald, A. G., & Banaji, M. R. (1989). The self as a memory system: Powerful but ordinary. *Journal of Personality and Social Psychology, 57*, 41–54.

Griffitt, W., & Veitch, R. (1971). Hot and crowded: Influences of population density and temperature on interpersonal affective behavior. *Journal of Personality and Social Psychology, 17*, 92–98.

Griffith, C. R. (1921). A comment upon the psychology of the audience. *Psychological Monographs, 30*, 36–47.

Gross, A. E., & Fleming, I. (1982). Twenty years of deception in social psychology. *Personality and Social Psychology Bulletin, 8*, 107–112.

Gross, A. E., Wallson, B. S., & Piliavin, I. (1979). Reactance attribution, equity and the help recipient. *Journal of Applied Social Psychology, 9*, 297–313.

Gross, S., & Mauro, R. (1989). *Death and discrimination: Racial disparities in capital sentencing*. Boston: Northeastern.

Groth, A. N., & Birnbaum, H. J. (1979). *Men who rape: The psychology of the offender*. New York: Plenum.

Gruder, C. L., Cook, T. D., Hennigan, K. M., Flay, B. R., Alessis, C., & Halamaj, J. (1978). Empirical tests of the absolute sleeper effect predicted from the discounting cue hypothesis. *Journal of Personality and Social Psychology, 36*, 1061–1074.

Guerin, B. (1986). Mere presence effects on humans: A review. *Journal of Personality and Social Psychology, 22*, 38–77.

Gunter, N. C., & Gunter, B. G. (1990). Domestic division of labor among working couples: Does androgyny make a difference? *Psychology of Women Quarterly, 14*, 355–370.

Guttentag, M., & Secord, P. F. (1983). *Too many women? The sex ratio question*. Beverly Hills, CA: Sage.

Haber, G. M. (1980). Territorial invasion in the classroom: Invadee response. *Environment and Behavior, 12*, 17–31.

Haemmerlie, F. M. (1983). Heterosexual anxiety in college females: A biased interaction treatment. *Behavior Modification, 7*, 611–623.

Haemmerlie, F. M., & Montgomery, R. L. (1982). Self-perception theory and unobtrusively biased interactions: A treatment for heterosocial anxiety. *Journal of Consulting Psychology, 29*, 362–370.

Haemmerlie, F. M., & Montgomery, R. L. (1986). Self-perception theory and the treatment of shyness. In W. H. Jones, J. M. Cheek, & S. R. Briggs (Eds.), *Shyness: Perspectives on research and treatment*. New York: Plenum.

Hai, D. M., Khairullah, Z. Y., & Coulmas, N. (1982). Sex and the single armrest: Use of personal space during air travel. *Psychological Reports, 51*, 743–749.

Hall, E. (1984, December). A sense of control. *Psychology Today*, pp. 38–45.

Hall, E. T. (1963). A system for the notation of proxemic behavior. *American Anthropologist, 65*, 1003–1026.

Hall, E. T. (1966). *The hidden dimension*. New York: Doubleday.

Hall, J. A. (1984). *Nonverbal sex differences: Communication accuracy and expressive style*. Baltimore: Johns Hopkins University Press.

Hall, J. A., Roter, D. L., & Rand, C. S. (1981). Communication of affect between patient and physician. *Journal of Health and Social Behavior, 22*, 18–30.

Halleck, S. L. (1971). *The politics of therapy*. New York: Harper.

Hallie, P. P. (1979). *Lest innocent blood be shed*. New York: Harper & Row.

Halpern, D. F. (1992). *Sex difference in cognitive abilities* (2nd ed.). Hillsdale, NJ: Erlbaum.

Halpin, A. W., & Winer, B. J. (1952). *The leadership behavior of the airplane commander*. Columbus: Ohio State University Research Foundation.

Hamaguchi, E. (1985). A contextual model of the Japanese: Toward a methodological innovation in Japan studies. *Journal of Japanese Studies, 11*, 289–321.

Hamill, R., Wilson, T. D., & Nisbett, R. E. (1980). Insensitivity to sample bias: Generalizing from atypical cases. *Journal of Personality and Social Psychology, 39*, 578–589.

Hamilton, D. L. (1981). Stereotyping and intergroup behavior: Some thoughts on the cognitive approach. In D. Hamilton (Ed.), *Cognitive processes in stereotyping and intergroup behavior*. Hillsdale, NJ: Erlbaum.

Hamilton, D. L., & Bishop, G. D. (1976). Attitudinal and behavioral effects of initial integration of white suburban neighborhoods. *Journal of Social Issues, 32*, 47–67.

Hamilton, D. L., Carpenter, S., & Bishop, G. D. (1984). Desegregation of suburban neighborhoods. In N. Miller & M. B. Brewer (Eds.), *Groups in contact: The psychology of desegregation*. New York: Academic Press.

Hamilton, D. L., & Gifford, R. K. (1976). Illusory correlation in interpersonal perception: A cognitive basis of stereotypic judgments. *Journal of Experimental Social Psychology, 12*, 392–407.

Hamilton, H. K., & Rose, M. B. (Eds.). (1982). *Professional guide to diseases*. Springhouse, PA: Springhouse.

Hamilton, V. L. (1976). Individual differences in ascriptions of responsibility, guilt, and appropriate punishment. In G. Bermant, C. Nemeth, & N. Vidmar (Eds.), *Psychology and the law*. Lexington, MA: Heath.

Hamilton, W. D. (1964). The genetical evolution of social behavior. *Journal of Theoretical Biology, 7*, 1–52.

Hanratty, M. A., O'Neil, E., & Sulzer, J. L. (1972). The effect of frustration upon imitation of aggression. *Journal of Personality and Social Psychology, 21*, 30–34.

Hans, V. (1992). Jury decision making. In D. K. Kagehiro & W. S. Laufer (Eds.), *Handbook of psychology and law*. New York: Springer-Verlag.

Hans, V. P., & Vidmar, N. (1982). Jury selection. In R. M. Bray & N. L. Kerr (Eds.), *The psychology of the courtroom*. New York: Academic Press.

Hans, V. P., & Vidmar, N. (1986). *Judging the jury*. New York: Plenum.

Hanseli, S., Sparacino, J., & Ronchi, D. (1982). Physical attractiveness and blood pressure: Sex and age differences. *Personality and Social Psychology Bulletin, 8,* 113–121.

Hansen, C. M., & Hansen, R. D. (1988). Finding the face in the crowd: An anger superiority effect. *Journal of Personality and Social Psychology, 54,* 917–924.

Hardin, G. (1968). The tragedy of the commons. *Science, 162,* 1243–1248.

Harding, J., Proshansky, H., Kutner, B., & Chein, J. (1969). Prejudice and ethnic relations. In G. Lindzey & E. Aronson (Eds.), *Handbook of social psychology* (Vol. 5). Reading, MA: Addison-Wesley.

Hare, P., Borgatta, E. F., & Bales, R. F. (Eds.). (1955). *Small groups: Studies in social interaction*. New York: Knopf.

Hare-Musten, R. T. (1983). An appraisal of the relationship between women and psychotherapy: 80 years after the case of Dora. *American Psychologist, 38,* 593–601.

Hare-Musten, R. T., & Marecek, J. (1988). The meaning of difference: Gender theory, post modernism, and psychology. *American Psychologist, 43,* 455–464.

Harkins, S. G. (1987). Social loafing and social facilitation. *Journal of Personality and Social Psychology, 23,* 1–18.

Harkins, S. G., & Szymanski, K. (1987). Social loafing and social facilitation: New wine in old bottles. In C. Hendrick (Ed.), *Group processes and intergroup relations: Review of personality and social psychology* (Vol. 9). Newbury Park, CA: Sage.

Harlow, H. F. (1932). Social facilitation of feeding in the albino rat. *Journal of Genetic Psychology, 41,* 211–221.

Harries, K. D., & Stadler, S. J. (1988). Heat and violence: New findings from Dallas field data, 1980–1981. *Journal of Applied Social Psychology, 18,* 129–138.

Harrigan, J., Oxman, T., & Rosenthal, R. (1985). Rapport expressed through nonverbal behavior. *Journal of Nonverbal Behavior, 9,* 95–110.

Harris, M. B., Benson, S. M., & Hall, C. L. (1975). The effects of confession on altruism. *Journal of Social Psychology, 96,* 187–192.

Harris, M. J. (1991). Controversy and cumulation: Meta-analysis and research on interpersonal expectancy effects. *Personality and Social Psychology Bulletin, 17,* 316–322.

Harris, P. B., & McAndrew, F. T. (1986). Territoriality and compliance: The influence of gender and location on willingness to sign petitions. *Journal of Social Psychology, 126,* 657–662.

Harrison, W., Thompson, V. D., & Rodgers, J. L. (1985). Robustness and sufficiency of the theory of reasoned action in longitudinal prediction. *Basic and Applied Social Psychology, 6,* 25–40.

Hart, D., & Damon, W. (1986). Developmental trends in self-understanding. *Social Cognition, 4,* 388–407.

Hartmann, H., & Spalter-Roth, R. (1991, February 27). *Improving employment opportunities for women*. Testimony concerning H.R.1 Civil Rights Act of 1991 before the U.S. House of Representatives Committee in Education and Labor.

Hartshorne, H., & May, M. A. (1928). *Studies in the nature of character* (Vol. 1), *Studies in deceit*. New York: Macmillan.

Hartshorne, H., & May, M. A. (1929). *Studies in the nature of character* (Vol. 2), *Studies in service and self-control*. New York: Macmillan.

Hartshorne, H., May, M. A., & Shuttleworth, F. K. (1930). *Studies in the nature of character* (Vol. 3), *Studies in the organization of character*. New York: Macmillan.

Harvey, J. H., & Consalvi, C. (1960). Status and conformity to pressure in informal groups. *Journal of Abnormal and Social Psychology, 60,* 182–187.

Hastie, R. (1981). Schematic principles in human memory. In E. T. Higgins, C. Herman, & M. Zanna (Eds.), *Social cognition: The Ontario symposium on personality and social psychology* (Vol. 1). Hillsdale, NJ: Erlbaum.

Hastie, R., Penrod, S. D., & Pennington, N. (1983). *Inside the jury*. Cambridge, MA: Harvard University Press.

Hatfield, E., & Sprecher, S. (1986). *Mirror, mirror . . . The importance of looks in everyday life*. Albany: State University of New York Press.

Hatfield, E., Traupman, J., & Walster, G. W. (1978). Equity and extramarital sexuality. *Archives of Sexual Behavior, 7,* 127–142.

Hatfield, E., Utne, M. K., & Traupman, J. (1979). Equity theory and intimate relationships. In R. L. Burgess & T. L. Huston (Eds.), *Social exchange in developing relationships*. New York: Academic Press.

Hatfield, E., Walster, G. W., & Berscheid, E.

(1978). *Equity: Theory and research*. Boston: Allyn & Bacon.

Hatfield, E., Walster, G. W., & Traupman, J. (1978). Equity and premarital sex. *Journal of Personality and Social Psychology, 37,* 82–92.

Hathaway, S. R., & McKinley, J. C. (1943). *The Minnesota multiphasic personality inventory*. New York: Psychological Corporation.

Hayashi, C. (1988). *National character of the Japanese*. Tokyo: Statistical Bureau, Japan.

Hayduk, L. A. (1983). Personal space: Where we now stand. *Psychological Bulletin, 94,* 293–335.

Haynes, S. G., Feinleib, M., & Eaker, E. D. (1983). Type A behavior and the ten-year incidence of coronary heart disease in the Framingham heart study. In R. H. Rosenman (Ed.), *Psychosomatic risk factors and coronary heart disease*. Berne, Switzerland: Huber.

Hays, R. B. (1985). A longitudinal study of friendship development. *Journal of Personality and Social Psychology, 48,* 909–924.

Hazan, C., & Shaver, P. (1987). Romantic love conceptualized as an attachment process. *Journal of Personality and Social Psychology, 52,* 511–524.

Hearold, S. (1986). *A synthesis of 1043 effects of television on social behavior*. In G. Comstock (Ed.), *Public communications and behavior* (Vol. 1). New York: Academic Press.

Heatherton, T. F., & Baumeister, R. F. (1991). Binge eating as an escape from self-awareness. *Psychological Bulletin, 110,* 86–108.

Heaton, A. W., & Sigall, H. (1989). The "championship choke" revisited: The role of fear of acquiring a negative identity. *Journal of Applied Social Psychology, 19,* 1019–1033.

Heider, F. (1946). Attitudes and cognitive organization. *Journal of Psychology, 21,* 107–112.

Heider, F. (1958). *The psychology of interpersonal relations*. New York: Wiley.

Heilbrun, A. B. (1976). Measurement of masculine and feminine sex role identities as independent dimensions. *Journal of Consulting and Clinical Psychology, 44,* 183–190.

Heiss, J. (1986). Family roles and behavior. In F. A. Boudreau, R. S. Sennott, & M. Wilson (Eds.), *Sex roles and social patterns*. New York: Praeger.

Helmreich, R. L. (1975). Applied social psychology: The unfulfilled promise. *Per-*

sonality and Social Psychology Bulletin, 1, 548–560.

Helmreich, R. L., & Collins, B. E. (1967). Situational determinants of affiliative preference under stress. *Journal of Personality and Social Psychology, 6,* 79–85.

Hendrick, C., & Hendrick, S. (1986). A theory and method of love. *Journal of Personality and Social Psychology, 50,* 392–402.

Hendrick, C., Hendrick, S., & Adler, N. L. (1988). Romantic relationships: Love, satisfaction, and staying together. *Journal of Personality and Social Psychology, 54,* 980–988.

Hendricks, M., & Bootzin, R. (1976). Race and sex as stimuli for negative affect and physical avoidance. *Journal of Social Psychology, 98,* 111–120.

Henley, N. M. (1977). *Body politics: Power, sex, and nonverbal communication.* Englewood Cliffs, NJ: Prentice-Hall.

Hennigan, K. M., Del Rosario, M. L., Heath, L., Cook, T. D., Wharton, J. D., & Calder, B. J. (1982). Impact of television on crime in the United States: Empirical findings and theoretical implications. *Journal of Personality and Social Psychology, 42,* 461–477.

Henninger, M., & Wyer, R. S. (1976). The recognition and elimination of inconsistencies among syllogistically related beliefs: Some new light on the "Socratic effect." *Journal of Personality and Social Psychology, 34,* 680–693.

Henry, J. P., & Stephens, P. M. (1977). *Stress, health, and the social environment.* New York: Springer-Verlag.

Hepworth, J. T., & West, S. G. (1988). Lynchings and the economy: A time-series reanalysis of Hovland and Sears (1940). *Journal of Personality and Social Psychology, 55,* 239–247.

Herek, G. M. (1984). Beyond "homophobia": A social psychological perspective on attitudes toward lesbians and gay men. *Journal of Homosexuality, 10,* 1–21.

Herek, G. M. (1986). The instrumentality of attitudes: Toward a neofunctional theory. *Journal of Social Issues, 42,* 99–114.

Herek, G. M. (1987a). Can functions be measured? A new perspective on the functional approach to attitudes. *Social Psychology Quarterly, 50,* 285–303.

Herek, G. M. (1987b). Religion and prejudice: A comparison of racial and sexual attitudes. *Personality and Social Psychology Bulletin, 13,* 56–65.

Herek, G. M. (1988). Heterosexuals' attitudes toward lesbians and gay men: Correlates and gender differences. *Journal of Sex Research, 25,* 451–477.

Herek, G. M. (1991). Stigma, prejudice, and violence against lesbians and gay men. In J. C. Gonsiorek & J. D. Weinrich (Eds.), *Homosexuality: Research implications for public policy.* Newbury Park, CA: Sage.

Herek, G. M., & Glunt, E. K. (1988). An epidemic of stigma: Public reaction to AIDS. *American Psychologist, 43,* 886–891.

Hermans, H. J. M., Kempen, H. J. G., & van Loon, R. J. P. (1992). The dialogical self: Beyond individualism and rationalism. *American Psychologist, 47,* 23–33.

Hershorn, M., & Rosenbaum, A. (1985). Children of marital violence: A closer look at the unintended victim. *American Journal of Orthopsychiatry, 55,* 260–266.

Heshka, S., & Nelson, Y. (1972). Interpersonal speaking distance as a function of age, sex, and relationship. *Sociometry, 35,* 491–498.

Heshka, S., & Pylypuk, A. (1975, June). *Human crowding and adrenocortical activity.* Paper presented at the meeting of the Canadian Psychological Association, Quebec, Canada.

Hess, E. H. (1975). *The tell-tale eye.* New York: Van Nostrand.

Hicks, D. J. (1965). Imitation and retention of film-mediated aggressive peer and adult models. *Journal of Personality and Social Psychology, 2,* 97–100.

Hicks, D. J. (1968). Short- and long-term retention of affectively varied modeled behavior. *Psychonomic Science, 11,* 369–370.

Higbee, K. L., Millard, R. J., & Folkman, J. R. (1982). Social psychology research during the 1970s: Predominance of experimentation and college students. *Personality and Social Psychology Bulletin, 8,* 180–183.

Higgins, E. T. (1987). Self-discrepancy: A theory relating self and affect. *Psychological Review, 94,* 319–340.

Higgins, E. T. (1989). Self-discrepancy theory: What patterns of self-beliefs cause people to suffer? In L. Berkowitz (Ed.), *Advances in experimental social psychology* (Vol. 22). San Diego: Academic Press.

Higgins, E. T., & King, G. A. (1981). Accessibility of social constructs: Information-processing consequences of individual and contextual variability. In N. Cantor & J. F. Kihlstrom (Eds.), *Personality, cognition, and social interaction.* Hillsdale, NJ: Erlbaum.

Higgins, E. T., Klein, R., & Strauman, T. (1985). Self-concept discrepancy theory: A psychological model for distinguishing among different aspects of depression and anxiety. *Social Cognition, 3,* 51–76.

Higgins, E. T., Rhodewalt, F., & Zanna, M. P. (1979). Dissonance reduction: Its nature, persistence, and reinstatement. *Journal of Experimental Social Psychology, 5,* 16–34.

Higgins, E. T., Rholes, W. S., & Jones, C. R. (1977). Category accessibility and impression formation. *Journal of Experimental Social Psychology, 13,* 141–154.

Hilberman, E. (1976). Rape: The ultimate violation of the self. *American Journal of Psychiatry, 133,* 436–437.

Hilberman, E. (1980). Overview: The "wife-beater's wife" reconsidered. *American Journal of Psychiatry, 137,* 1336–1346.

Hilgard, E. R. (1980). The trilogy of mind: Cognition, affection, and conation. *Journal of the History of Behavioral Science, 16,* 107–117.

Hill, C., Rubin, Z., & Peplau, L. A. (1976). Breakups before marriage: The end of 103 affairs. *Journal of Social Issues, 32,* 147–167.

Hill, C. H. (1987). Affiliation motivation: People who need people . . . but in different ways. *Journal of Personality and Social Psychology, 52,* 1008–1018.

Hill, G. W. (1982). Group versus individual performance: Are N + 1 heads better than one? *Psychological Bulletin, 91,* 517–539.

Hill, R. (1945). Campus values in mate selection. *Journal of Home Economics, 37.*

Hinken, T. R., & Schriesheim, C. A. (1989). Development and application of new scales to measure the French and Raven (1959) bases of social power. *Journal of Applied Psychology, 74,* 561–567.

Hiroto, D. S., & Seligman, M. E. P. (1975). Generality of learned helplessness in man. *Journal of Personality and Social Psychology, 31,* 311–327.

Hirschel, D., & Hutchison, I. (1992). Female spouse abuse and the police response: The Charlotte, North Carolina, Experiment. *Journal of Criminal Law and Criminology, 83,* 73–119.

Hirt, E. R., Zillman, D., Erickson, G. A., & Kennedy, C. (1992). Costs and benefits of allegiance: Changes in fans' self-ascribed competencies after team victory versus defeat. *Journal of Personality and Social Psychology, 63,* 724–738.

Hitler, A. (1962). *Mein Kampf.* Boston: Houghton Mifflin. (Originally published 1925)

Hoch, S. J. (1987). Perceived consensus and predictive accuracy: The pros and cons of projection. *Journal of Personality and Social Psychology, 53,* 221–234.

Hochschild, A. (1989). *The second shift: Working parents and the revolution at home.* New York: Viking.

Hoelter, J. W. (1983). Factorial invariance and self-esteem: reassessing race and sex difference. *Social Forces, 61,* 834–846.

Hoffman, L. W. (1972). Early childhood experiences and women's achievement motives. *Journal of Social Issues, 28,* 157–176.

Hoffman, M. L. (1976). Empathy, role taking, guilt, and the development of altruistic motives. In T. Lickona (Ed.), *Moral development and behavior.* New York: Holt, Rinehart & Winston.

Hofling, C. K., Brotzman, E., Dalrymple, S., Graves, N., & Pierce, C. (1966). An experimental study of nurse–physician relations. *Journal of Nervous and Mental Disease, 143,* 171–180.

Hogan, R. (1983). A socioanalytic theory of personality. In M. M. Page (Ed.), *Personality—Current theory and research: Nebraska symposium on motivation 1982.*

Hokanson, J. E. (1961). The effects of frustration and anxiety on overt aggression. *Journal of Abnormal and Social Psychology, 62,* 346–351.

Hokanson, J. E., & Burgess, M. M. (1962). The effects of status, type of frustration, and aggression on vascular processes. *Journal of Abnormal and Social Psychology, 65,* 232–237.

Hokanson, J. E., & Shetler, S. (1961). The effect of overt aggression on physiological arousal. *Journal of Abnormal and Social Psychology, 63,* 446–448.

Holahan, C. J., & Wandersman, A. (1987). The community psychology perspective in environmental psychology. In D. Stokols & I. Altman (Eds.), *Handbook of environmental psychology* (Vol. 1).

Hollander, E. P. (1958). Conformity, status, and idiosyncratic credits. *Psychological Review, 65,* 117–127.

Hollander, E. P. (1985). Leadership and power. In G. Lindzey & E. Aronson (Eds.), *Handbook of social psychology* (Vol. 2). New York: Random House.

Hollenbeck, A. R., & Slaby, R. G. (1979). Infant visual and vocal responses to television. *Child Development, 50,* 41–42.

Holloway, S., Tucker, L., & Hornstein, H. A. (1977). The effects of social and nonsocial information on interpersonal behavior of males: The news makes news. *Journal of Personality and Social Psychology, 35,* 514–522.

Holmes, T. H., & Rahe, R. H. (1967). The social readjustment rating scale. *Journal of Psychosomatic Research, 11,* 213–218.

Homans, G. C. (1950). *The human group.* New York: Harcourt, Brace & World.

Homans, G. C. (1961). *Social behavior: Its elementary forms.* New York: Harcourt, Brace & World.

Homans, G. C. (1974). *Social behavior: Its elementary forms* (rev. ed.). New York: Harcourt Brace Jovanovich.

Hope, J. (1990, September–October). Scout's honor: The handbooks tell all. *Mother Earth News,* p. 16.

Horney, K. (1973). On the genesis of the castration complex in women. In J. B. Miller (Ed.), *Psychoanalysis and women.* New York: Brunner/Mazel.

Hornik, J., Zaig, T., & Shadmon, D. (1991). Reducing refusals in telephone surveys on sensitive topics. *Journal of Advertising Research, 31,* 49–56.

Hornstein, H. A. (1975). Social psychology as social intervention. In M. Deutsch & H. A. Hornstein (Eds.), *Applying social psychology: Implication for research, practice, and training.* Hillsdale, NJ: Erlbaum.

Hornstein, H. A., Lakind, E., Frankel, G., & Manne, S. (1975). Effects of knowledge about remote social events on prosocial behavior, social conception, and mood. *Journal of Personality and Social Psychology, 32,* 1038–1046.

Hornstein, H. A.; Masor, H. N., Sole, K., & Heilman, M. (1971). Effects of sentiment and completion of a helping act on observer helping: A case for socially mediated Ziegarnik effects. *Journal of Personality and Social Psychology, 17,* 107–112.

House, J., Robbins, C., & Metzner, H. (1982). The association of social relationships and activities with mortality: Prospective evidence from the Tecumseh community health study. *American Journal of Epidemiology, 116,* 123–140.

House, J. S., & Kahn, R. L. (1985). Measures and concepts of social support. In S. Cohen & S. L. Syme (Eds.), *Social support and health.* Orlando, FL: Academic Press.

Hovland, C. I., Janis, I. L., & Kelley, H. H. (1953). *Communication and persuasion.* New Haven, CT: Yale University Press.

Hovland, C. I., Lumsdaine, A. A., & Sheffield, F. D. (1949). *Studies in social psychology in World War II* (Vol. 3), *Experiments on mass communications.* Princeton, NJ: Princeton University Press.

Hovland, C. I., & Sears, R. R. (1940). Minor studies in aggression: VI. Correlation of lynchings with economic indices. *Journal of Personality, 9,* 301–310.

Hovland, C. I., & Weiss, W. (1951). The influences of source credibility on communication effectiveness. *Public Opinion Quarterly, 15,* 635–650.

Howard, J., & Rothbart, M. (1980). Social categorization and memory for in-group and out-group behavior. *Journal of Personality and Social Psychology, 38,* 301–310.

Hudson, J. W., & Henze, L. F. (1969). Campus values in mate selection: A replication. *Journal of Marriage and the Family, 31,* 772–775.

Hudson, J. W., & Hoyt, L. L. (1981). Personal characteristics important in mate preference among college students. *Social Behavior and Personality, 9,* 93–96.

Huesmann, L. R. (1986). Psychological processes promoting the relation between exposure to media violence and aggressive behavior by the viewer. *Journal of Social Issues, 42,* 125–139.

Huesmann, L. R., Eron, L. D., Berkowitz, L., & Chaffee, S. (1992). The effects of television violence on aggression: A reply to a skeptic. In P. Suedfeld & P. E. Tetlock (Eds.), *Psychology and social policy.* New York: Hemisphere.

Huesmann, L. R., Eron, L. D., Klein, R., Brice, P., & Fischer, P. (1983). Mitigating the imitation of aggressive behaviors by changing children's attitudes about media violence. *Journal of Personality and Social Psychology, 44,* 899–910.

Huesmann, L. R., Eron, L. D., Lefkowitz, M. M., & Walder, L. O. (1984). The stability of aggression over time and generations. *Developmental Psychology, 20,* 1120–1134.

Huesmann, L. R., Lagerspetz, K., & Eron, L. D. (1984). Intervening variables in the TV violence–aggression relations: Evidence from two countries. *Developmental Psychology, 20,* 746–775.

Hull, C. L. (1943). *Principles of behavior.* New York: Appleton-Century-Crofts.

Hull, J. G. (1981). A self-awareness model of the causes and effects of alcohol consumption. *Journal of Abnormal Psychology, 90,* 586–600.

Hull, J. G., Van Treuren, R. R., & Virnelli, S. (1987). Hardiness and health: A critique and alternative approach. *Journal of Personality and Social Psychology, 53,* 518–530.

Hull, J. G., Young, D. Y., & Jouriles, E. (1986). Applications of the self-awareness model of alcohol consumption: Predicting patterns of use and abuse. *Journal of Personality and Social Psychology, 51,* 760–796.

Hunt, M. (1959). *The natural history of love.* New York: Knopf.

Hunt, P. J., & Hillery, J. M. (1973). Social facilitation in a location setting: An examination of the effects over learning trials.

Journal of Personality and Social Psychology, 9, 563–571.

Husband, R. W. (1931). Analysis of methods in human maze learning. *Journal of Genetic Psychology, 39,* 258–277.

Huston, T. L., & Burgess, R. L. (1979). Social exchange in developing relationships: An overview. In R. L. Burgess & T. L. Huston (Eds.), *Social exchange in developing relationships.* New York: Academic Press.

Huston, T. L., & Levinger, G. (1978). Interpersonal attraction and relationships. *Annual Review of Psychology, 29,* 115–156.

Huston, T. L., & Vangelisti, A. L. (1991). Socioemotional behavior and satisfaction in marital relationships: A longitudinal study. *Journal of Personality and Social Psychology, 61,* 721–733.

Hutchinson, R. R. (1972). The environmental causes of aggression. In J. K. Cole & D. D. Jensen (Eds.), *Nebraska symposium on motivation.* Lincoln: University of Nebraska Press.

Hutchinson, R. R. (1983). The pain–aggression relationship and its expression in naturalistic settings. *Aggressive Behavior, 9,* 229–242.

Hutt, C., & Vaizey, M. J. (1966). Differential effects of group density on social behavior. *Nature, 209,* 1371–1372.

Hyde, J. S. (1981). How large are cognitive gender differences? A meta-analysis using 2 and d. *American Psychologist, 36,* 892–901.

Hyde, J. S. (1986). Gender differences in aggression. In J. S. Hyde & M. C. Linn (Eds.), *The psychology of gender: Advances through meta-analysis.* Baltimore: Johns Hopkins University Press.

Hyde, J. S., & Linn, M. C. (1988). Gender differences in verbal ability: A meta-analysis. *Psychological Bulletin, 104,* 53–69.

Hyman, H. H., & Sheatsley, P. B. (1954). "The authoritarian personality"—A methodological critique. In R. Christie & M. Jahoda (Eds.), *Studies in the scope and method of "the authoritarian personality."* New York: Free Press.

Imrich, D., Mullin, C., & Linz, D. (1990). Sexually violent media and criminal justice policy. In R. Surette (Ed.), *The media and criminal justice policy: Recent research and social effects.* Springfield, IL: Charles C. Thomas.

Ingram, R. E., & Smith, T. S. (1984). Depression and internal versus external locus of attention. *Cognitive Therapy and Research, 8,* 139–152.

Insko, C. A. (1965). Verbal reinforcement of attitude. *Journal of Personality and Social Psychology, 21,* 621–623.

Insko, C. A., Drenan, S., Solomon, M. R., Smith, R., & Wade, T. J. (1983). Conformity as a function of the consistency of positive self-evaluation with being liked and being right. *Journal of Experimental Social Psychology, 19,* 341–358.

Insko, C. A., & Schopler, J. (1987). Categorization, competition, and collectivity. In C. Hendrick (Ed.), *Group processes: Review of personality and social psychology* (Vol. 8). Newbury Park, CA: Sage.

Insko, C. A., Smith, R. H., Alicke, M. D., Wade, J., & Taylor, S. (1985). Conformity and group size: The concern with being right and the concern with being liked. *Personality and Social Psychology Bulletin, 11,* 41–50.

Intons-Peterson, M. J. (1988). *Children's concepts of gender.* Norwood, NJ: Ablex.

Intons-Peterson, M. J., & Roskos-Ewoldsen, B. (1989). Mitigating the effects of violent pornography. In S. Gubar & J. Hoff-Wilson (Eds.), *For adult users only.* Bloomington: Indiana University Press.

Intons-Peterson, M. J., Roskos-Ewoldsen, B., Thomas, L., Shirley, M., & Blut, D. (1989). Will educational materials reduce negative effects of exposure to sexual violence? *Journal of Social and Clinical Psychology, 8,* 256–275.

Isen, A. M. (1970). Success, failure, attention and reaction to others: The warm glow of success. *Journal of Personality and Social Psychology, 15,* 294–301.

Isen, A. M. (1987). Positive affect, cognitive processes, and social behavior. In L. Berkowitz (Ed.), *Advances in experimental social psychology* (Vol. 20). San Diego: Academic Press.

Isen, A. M., Clark, M., & Schwartz, M. (1976). Duration of the effect of mood on helping: "Footprints on the sands of time." *Journal of Personality and Social Psychology, 34,* 385–393.

Isen, A. M., Horn, N., & Rosenhan, D. L. (1973). Effects of success and failure on children's generosity. *Journal of Personality and Social Psychology, 27,* 239–247.

Isen, A. M., & Levin, P. F. (1972). Effect of feeling good on helping: Cookies and kindness. *Journal of Personality and Social Psychology, 21,* 384–388.

Isenberg, D. J. (1986). Group polarization: A critical review and meta-analysis. *Journal of Personality and Social Psychology, 50,* 1141–1151.

Isozaki, M. (1984). The effect of discussion on polarization of judgments. *Japanese Psychological Research, 26,* 187–193.

Izard, C. E. (1969). The emotions and emotion constructs in personality and culture research. In R. B. Cattell (Ed.), *Handbook of modern personality theory.* Chicago: Aldine.

Jaccard, J. J. (1974). Predicting social behavior from personality traits. *Journal of Research in Personality, 7,* 358–367.

Jackson, J., & Harkins, S. (1985). Equity in effort: An explanation of the social loafing effects. *Journal of Personality and Social Psychology, 49,* 1119–1206.

Jackson, J., & Williams, K. (1985). Social loafing on difficult tasks: Working collectively can improve performance. *Journal of Personality and Social Psychology, 49,* 937–942.

Jackson, L. A. (1992). *Physical appearance and gender: Sociobiological and sociocultural perspectives.* Albany: State University of New York Press.

Jacobs, J. (1961). *The death and life of great American cities.* New York: Random House.

Jacobs, R. C., & Campbell, D. T. (1961). The perpetuation of an arbitrary tradition through several generations of a laboratory microculture. *Journal of Abnormal and Social Psychology, 62,* 649–658.

Jaffe, D. T., & Kanter, R. M. (1976). Couple strains in communal households: A four-factor model of the separation process. *Journal of Social Issues, 32,* 169–191.

James, W. (1890). *The principles of psychology* (Vols. 1 and 2). New York: Henry Holt.

Jamieson, D. W., Lydon, J. E., & Zanna, M. P. (1987). Attitude and activity preference similarity: Differential bases of interpersonal attraction for low and high self-monitors. *Journal of Personality and Social Psychology, 53,* 1052–1060.

Jamieson, D. W., & Zanna, M. P. (1989). Need for structure in attitude formation and expression. In A. R. Pratkanis & A. G. Greenwald (Eds.), *Attitude structure and function.* Hillsdale, NJ: Erlbaum.

Janis, I. L. (1972). *Victims of groupthink.* Boston: Houghton Mifflin.

Janis, I. L. (1985). Sources of error in strategic decision making. In J. M. Pennings (Ed.), *Organizational strategy and change.* San Francisco: Jossey-Bass.

Janis, I. L., & Feshbach, S. (1953). Effects of fear-arousing communications. *Journal of Abnormal and Social Psychology, 48,* 78–92.

Janis, I. L., Kaye, D., & Kirschner, P. (1965). Facilitating effects of "eating-while-reading" on responsiveness to persuasive communications. *Journal of Personality and Social Psychology, 1,* 181–186.

Janis, I. L., & Rodin, J. (1979). Attribution, control, and decision making: Social psychology and health care. In *Health psychology—A handbook.* San Francisco: Jossey-Bass.

Janz, N. K., & Becker, M. H. (1984). The health belief model: A decade later. *Health Education Quarterly, 11*, 1–47.

Jarvinen, K. A. (1955). Can ward rounds be a danger to patients with myocardial infarction? *British Medical Journal, 1*, 318–320.

Jason, L. A., Reichler, A., & Rucker, W. (1981). Territorial behavior on beaches. *Journal of Social Psychology, 114*, 43–50.

Jemmott, J. B., III, & Magloire, K. (1988). Academic stress, social support, and secretory immunoglobulin A. *Journal of Personality and Social Psychology, 55*, 803–810.

Jenkins, C. D. (1982). Overview: Behavioral perspectives on health risks among the disadvantaged. In D. L. Parron, F. Solomon, & C. D. Jenkins (Eds.), *Behavior, health risks, and social disadvantage*. Washington, DC: Academy Press.

Jennings, D. L., Lepper, M. R., & Ross, L. (1981). Persistence of impressions of personal persuasiveness: Perseverance of erroneous self-assessments outside the debriefing paradigm. *Personality and Social Psychology Bulletin, 7*, 257–263.

Jensen, G. F., White, C. S., & Galliher, J. M. (1982). Ethnic status and adolescent self-evaluations: An extension of research on minority self-esteem. *Social Problems, 30*, 226–239.

Jepson, C., & Chaiken, S. (1986). *The effect of anxiety on the systematic processing of persuasive communications*. Paper presented at the annual meeting of the American Psychological Association, Washington, DC.

Jessop, D. J. (1982). Topic variation in levels of agreement between parents and adolescents. *Public Opinion Quarterly, 46*, 538–559.

John, O. P. (1990). The "Big Five" factor taxonomy: Dimensions of personality in the natural language and in questionnaires. In L. A. Pervin (Ed.) *Handbook of personality: Theory and research*. New York: Guilford.

Johnson, M. A. (1989). Variables associated with friendship in an adult population. *Journal of Social Psychology, 129*, 379–390.

Johnson, R. N. (1972). *Aggression in man and animals*. Philadelphia: Saunders.

Jones, E. E. (1964). *Ingratiation*. New York: Appleton-Century-Crofts.

Jones, E. E. (1979). The rocky road from acts to dispositions. *American Psychologist, 34*, 107–117.

Jones, E. E. (1985). Major developments in social psychology during the past five decades. In G. Lindzey & E. Aronson (Eds.), *Handbook of social psychology* (3rd. ed., Vol. 1). New York: Random House.

Jones, E. E. (1990). *Interpersonal perception*. New York: Freeman.

Jones, E. E., Bell, L., & Aronson, E. (1972). The reciprocation of attraction from similar and dissimilar others. In C. McClintock (Ed.), *Experimental social psychology*. New York: Holt, Rinehart and Winston.

Jones, E. E., & Berglas, S. (1978). Control of attributions about the self through self-handicapping strategies: The appeal of alcohol and the role of under-achievement. *Personality and Social Psychology Bulletin, 4*, 200–206.

Jones, E. E., & Davis, K. E. (1965). From acts to dispositions: The attribution process in person perception. In L. Berkowitz (Ed.), *Advances in experimental social psychology* (Vol. 2). New York: Academic Press.

Jones, E. E., Davis, K. E., & Gergen, K. J. (1961). Role playing variations and their informational value for person perception. *Journal of Abnormal and Social Psychology, 63*, 302–310.

Jones, E. E., Farina, A., Hastorf, A. H., Markus, H., Miller, D. T., & Scott, R. A. (1984). *Social stigma: The psychology of marked relationships*. New York: Freeman.

Jones, E. E., & Gerard, H. B. (1967). *Foundations of social psychology*. New York: Wiley.

Jones, E. E., & Goethals, G. R. (1972). Order effects in impression formation: Attribution context and the nature of the entity. In E. E. Jones, D. E. Kanouse, H. H. Kelley, R. E. Nisbett, S. Valines, & B. Weiner (Eds.), *Attribution: Perceiving the causes of behavior*. Morristown, NJ: General Learning Press.

Jones, E. E., & Harris, V. A. (1967). The attribution of attitudes. *Journal of Experimental Social Psychology, 13*, 1–24.

Jones, E. E., & McGillis, D. (1976). Correspondent inferences and the attribution cube: A comparative reappraisal. In J. H. Harvey, W. J. Ickes, & R. F. Kidd (Eds.), *New directions in attribution research* (Vol. 1). Hillsdale, NJ: Erlbaum.

Jones, E. E., & Nisbett, R. E. (1972). The actor and observer: Divergent perception of the causes of behavior. In E. Jones, D. Kanouse, H. Kelley, R. Nisbett, S. Valins, & B. Weiner (Eds.), *Attribution: Perceiving the causes of behavior*. Morristown, NJ: General Learning Press.

Jones, E. E., & Pittman, T. S. (1982). Toward a general theory of strategic self-presentation. In J. Suls (Ed.), *Psychological perspectives on the self* (Vol. 1). Hillsdale, NJ: Erlbaum.

Jones, E. E., Rock, L., Shaver, K. G., Goethals, G. R., & Ward, L. M. (1968). Pattern of performance and ability attribution: An unexpected primacy effect. *Journal of Personality and Social Psychology, 10*, 317–340.

Jones, E. E., & Sigal, H. (1971). The bogus pipeline: A new paradigm for measuring affect and attitudes. *Psychological Bulletin, 76*, 349–364.

Jones, E. E., & Wortman, C. (1973). *Ingratiation: An attributional approach*. Morristown, NJ: General Learning Press.

Jones, J. M. (1972). *Prejudice and racism*. Reading, MA: Addison-Wesley.

Jones, J. W., & Bogat, G. A. (1978). Air pollution and human aggression. *Psychological Reports, 43*, 721–722.

Jones, S. C. (1973). Self and interpersonal evaluations: Esteem theories vs. consistency theories. *Psychological Bulletin, 79*, 185–199.

Jones, S. E., & Aiello, J. R. (1973). Proxemic behavior of black and white first- third- and fifth-grade children. *Journal of Personality and Social Psychology, 25*, 21–27.

Jones, W. H., & Perlman, D. W. (Eds.). (1991) *Advances in personal relationships* (Vol 3). London: Jessica Kingsley.

Josephs, R. A., Markus, H. R., & Tafarodi, R. W. (1992). Gender and self-esteem. *Journal of Personality and Social Psychology, 63*, 391–402.

Josephson, W. L. (1987). Television violence and children's aggression: Testing the priming, social script, and disinhibition predictions. *Journal of Personality and Social Psychology, 53*, 882–890.

Jourard, S., & Rubin, J. (1968). Self-disclosure and touching: A study of two modes of interpersonal encounter and their inter-relation. *Journal of Humanistic Psychology, 8*, 39–48.

Joy, L. A., Kimball, M. M., & Zabrack, M. L. (1986). Television and children's aggressive behavior. In T. M. Williams (Ed.), *The impact of television: A natural experiment in three communities*. Orlando, FL: Academic Press.

Judd, C. M., Drake, R. A., Downing, J. W., & Krosnick, J. A. (1991). Some dynamic properties of attitude structures: Context-induced response facilitation and polarization. *Journal of Personality and Social Psychology, 60*, 193–202.

Judd, C. M., & Kulik, J. A. (1980). Schematic effects of social attitudes on information processing and recall. *Journal of Personality and Social Psychology, 38*, 569–578.

Judd, C. M., & Park, B. (1993). Definition and assessment of accuracy in social stereotypes. *Psychological Review, 100,* 109–128.

Jussim, L. (1991). Social perception and social reality: A reflection construction model. *Psychological Review, 98,* 54–73.

Justice, A. (1985). Review of the effects of stress on cancer in laboratory animals: Importance of time of stress application and type of tumor. *Psychological Bulletin, 98,* 108–138.

Kadane, J. B., & Lewis, G. H. (1969). The distribution of participation in group discussions. *American Sociological Review, 34,* 710–723.

Kagan, J., & Moss, H. A. (1962). *Birth to maturity.* New York: Wiley.

Kahneman, D., & Tversky, A. (1973). On the psychology of prediction. *Psychological Review, 80,* 237–251.

Kahneman, D., & Tversky, A. (1979). Prospect theory: An analysis of decision under risk. *Econometrica, 47,* 263–291.

Kahneman, D., & Tversky, A. (1984). Choices, values, and frames. *American Psychologist, 39,* 341–350.

Kalven, H., & Zeisel, H. (1966). *The American jury.* Boston: Little, Brown.

Kanfer, F., & Seider, M. L. (1973). Self-control: Factors enhancing tolerance of noxious stimulation. *Journal of Personality and Social Psychology, 25,* 381.

Kanner, A. D., Coyne, J. C., Schaefer, C., & Lazarus, R. S. (1981). Daily hassles and uplifts versus major life events. *Journal of Behavioral Medicine, 4,* 1–39.

Kanouse, D. E., & Hanson, L. R. Jr. (1972). Negativity in evaluations. In E. E. Jones, D. E. Kanouse, H. H. Kelley, R. E. Nisbett, S. Valins, & B. Weiner (Eds.), *Attribution: Perceiving the causes of behavior.* Morristown, NJ: General Learning Press.

Kaplan, H. (1983). A woman's view of DSM-III. *American Psychologist, 38,* 786–792.

Kaplan, M. F., & Miller, C. E. (1987). Group decision making and normative versus informational influence: Effects of type of issue and assigned decision rules. *Journal of Personality and Social Psychology, 53,* 306–313.

Karaz, V. & Perlman, D. (1975). Attribution at the wire: Consistency and outcome finish strong. *Journal of Experimental Social Psychology, 11,* 470–477.

Kardes, F. R., Sanbonmatsu, D. M., Voss, R. T., & Fazio, R. H. (1986). Self-monitoring and attitude accessibility. *Personality and Social Psychology Bulletin, 12,* 468–474.

Karlins, M., Coffman, T. L., & Walters, G. (1969). On the fading of social stereotypes: Studies in three generations of college students. *Journal of Personality and Social Psychology, 13,* 1–16.

Kasarda, J. P., & Janowitz, M. (1974). Community attachment in mass society. *American Sociological Review, 39,* 328–339.

Kasof, J. (1993). Sex bias in the naming of stimulus persons. *Psychological Bulletin, 113,* 140–163.

Kassin, S. M. (1985). Eyewitness identification: Retrospective self-awareness and the accuracy–confidence correlation. *Journal of Personality and Social Psychology, 49,* 878–893.

Kassin, S. M., & Barndollar, K. A. (1992). The psychology of eyewitness testimony: A comparison of experts and prospective jurors. *Journal of Applied Social Psychology, 22,* 1241–1249.

Kassin, S. M., Ellsworth, P. C., & Smith, V. L. (1989). The "general acceptance" of psychological research on eyewitness testimony. *American Psychologist, 44,* 1089–1098.

Kassin, S. M., Smith, V. L., & Tulloch, W. F. (1990). The dynamite charge. *Law and Human Behavior, 14,* 537–550.

Kassin, S. M., & Wrightsman, L. S. (1988). *The American jury on trial: Psychological perspectives.* New York: Hemisphere.

Kastenbaum, R. (1982). Healthy, wealthy, and wise? Health care provision for elderly from a psychological perspective. In G. S. Sanders & J. Suls (Eds.), *Social psychology of health and illness.* Hillsdale, NJ: Erlbaum.

Katsev, R., Edelsack, L., Steinmetz, G., Walker, T., & Wright, R. J. (1978). The effect of reprimanding transgressions on subsequent helping behavior: Two field experiments. *Personality and Social Psychology Bulletin, 4,* 326–329.

Katz, A. M., & Hill, R. (1958). Residential propinquity and family living. *Marriage and Family Living, 20,* 27–34.

Katz, D. (1960). The functional approach to the study of attitudes. *Public Opinion Quarterly, 24,* 163–204.

Katz, D., & Braly, K. W. (1933). Racial stereotypes of 100 college students. *Journal of Abnormal and Social Psychology, 28,* 280–290.

Katz, E., & Lazarsfeld, P. F. (1955). *Personal influence.* Glencoe, IL: Free Press.

Katz, I. (1970). Experimental studies of Negro–white relationships. In L. Berkowitz (Ed.), *Advances in experimental social psychology* (Vol. 5). New York: Academic Press.

Katz, I., & Hass, R. G. (1988). Racial ambiv-

alence and American value conflict: Correlational and priming studies of dual cognitive structures. *Journal of Personality and Social Psychology, 55,* 893–905.

Katz, P. A. (1986). Gender identity: Development and consequences. In R. D. Ashmore & F. K. Del Boca (Eds.), *The social psychology of female–male relationships.* Orlando, FL: Academic Press.

Kaufman, J., & Zigler, E. (1987). Do abused children become abusive parents? *American Journal of Orthopsychiatry, 57,* 186–192.

Keating, C. F. (1985). Human dominance signals: The primate in us. In S. L. Ellyson & J. F. Dovidio (Eds.), *Power, dominance, and nonverbal behavior.* New York: Springer-Verlag.

Keenan, J. M., & Baillet, S. D. (1980). Memory for personally and socially significant events. In R. S. Nickerson (Ed.), *Attention on performance III.* Hillsdale, NJ: Erlbaum.

Keller, H. R., & Erne, D. E. (1983). Child abuse: Toward a comprehensive model. In *Prevention and control of aggression.* New York: Pergamon.

Kelley, H. H. (1967). Attribution theory in social psychology. In D. L. Vine (Ed.), *Nebraska symposium on motivation.* Lincoln: University of Nebraska Press.

Kelley, H. H. (1972). Causal schemata and the attribution process. In E. Jones, D. Kanouse, H. Kelley, R. Nisbett, S. Valins, & B. Weiner (Eds.), *Attribution: Perceiving the causes of behavior.* Morristown, NJ: General Learning Press.

Kelley, H. H., Berscheid, E., Christensen, A., Harvey, J. H., Huston, T. L., Levinger, G., McClintock, E., Peplau, L. A., & Peterson, D. R. (1983). *Close relationships.* New York: Freeman.

Kelly, G. A. (1955). *The psychology of personal constructs* (Vols. 1 and 2). New York: Norton.

Kelman, H. C. (1958). Compliance, identification, and internalization: Three processes of attitude change. *Journal of Conflict Resolution, 2,* 51–60.

Kelman, H. C., & Hamilton, V. L. (1989). *Crimes of obedience: Toward a social psychology of authority and responsibility.* New Haven: Yale University Press.

Keltikangas-Jarvinen, L. (1990). The stability of self-concept during adolescence and early adulthood: A six-year follow-up study. *Journal of General Psychology, 117,* 361–368.

Kemeny, M. E., Solomon, G. F., Morley, J. E., & Herbert, T. L. (1992). Psychoneuroimmunology. In C. B. Nemeroff (Ed.), *Neuroendocrinology.* Boca Raton, FL: CRC Press.

Keniston, K. (1968). *Young radicals: Notes on committed youth*. New York: Harcourt, Brace & World.

Kenny, D. A. (1991). A general model of consensus and accuracy in interpersonal perception. *Psychological Review, 98*, 155–163.

Kenny, D. A., & Albright, L. (1987). Accuracy in interpersonal perception: A social relations analysis. *Psychological Bulletin, 102*, 390–402.

Kenny, D. A., Horner, C., Kashy, D. A., & Chu, L. (1992). Consensus at zero acquaintance: Replication, behavioral cues, and stability. *Journal of Personality and Social Psychology, 62*, 88–97.

Kenny, D. A., & La Voie, L. (1984). The social relations model. In L. Berkowitz (Ed.), *Advances in experimental social psychology* (Vol. 18). Orlando, FL: Academic Press.

Kenrick, D. T., Baumann, D. J., & Cialdini, R. B. (1979). A step in the socialization of altruism as hedonism: Effects of negative mood on children's generosity under public and private conditions. *Journal of Personality and Social Psychology, 37*, 756–768.

Kenrick, D. T., & Cialdini, R. B. (1977). Romantic attraction: Misattribution vs. reinforcement explanations. *Journal of Personality and Social Psychology, 35*, 381–391.

Kenrick, D. T., & Funder, D. C. (1988). Profiting from controversy: Lessons from the person–situation debate. *American Psychologist, 43*, 23–34.

Kenrick, D. T., & Keefe, R. C. (1992). Age preferences in mate reflect sex differences in human reproductive strategies. *Behavioral and Brain Sciences, 15*, 75–133.

Kenrick, D. T., & Stringfield, D. O. (1980). Personality traits and the eye of the beholder: Crossing some traditional philosophical boundaries in the search for consistency in all of the people. *Psychological Review, 87*, 88–104.

Kerckhoff, A. C. (1974). The social context of interpersonal attraction. In T. L. Huston (Ed.), *Foundations of interpersonal attraction*. New York: Academic Press.

Kerckhoff, A. C. (1982). Analyzing a case of mass psychogenic illness. In M. J. Colligan, J. W. Pennebaker, & L. R. Murphy (Eds.), *Mass psychogenic illness: A social psychological analysis*. Hillsdale, NJ: Erlbaum.

Kerckhoff, A. C., & Back, K. W. (1968). *The June bug: A study of hysterical contagion*. New York: Appleton-Century-Crofts.

Kerckhoff, A. C., & Davis, K. E. (1962). Value consensus and need complementarity in mate selection. *American Sociological Review, 27*, 295–303.

Kerr, N. L. (1981). Social transition schemes: Charting the group's road to agreement. *Journal of Personality and Social Psychology, 41*, 684–702.

Kerr, N. L., Harmon, D. L., & Graves, J. K. (1982). Independence of multiple verdicts by jurors and juries. *Journal of Applied Social Psychology, 12*, 12–29.

Kerr, N. L., & MacCoun, R. J. (1985). The effects of jury size and polling method on the process and product of jury deliberation. *Journal of Personality and Social Psychology, 48*, 349–363.

Kerr, S., Schriesheim, C. A., Murphy, C. J., & Stogdill, R. M. (1974). Toward a contingency theory of leadership based upon the consideration and initiating structure literature. *Organizational Behavior and Human Performance, 12*, 62–82.

Kessler, S. J., & McKenna, W. (1978). *Gender: An ethnomethodological approach*. New York: Wiley.

Keys, A., Aravnis, C., Blackburn, H., Van Buchem, F. S. P., Buzina, R., Djordjevic, B. S., Fidanza, F., Kavonen, M. J., Menotti, A., Pudov, V., & Taylor, H. L. (1972). Probability of middle-aged men developing coronary heart disease in 5 years. *Circulation, 45*, 815–828.

Kiecolt-Glaser, J. K., Fisher, L., Ogrocki, P., Stout, J. C., Speicher, C. E., & Glaser, R. (1987). Marital quality, marital disruption, and immune function. *Psychosomatic Medicine, 49*, 13–34.

Kiecolt-Glaser, J. K., & Glaser, R. (1992). Psychoneuroimmunology: Can psychological interventions modulate immunity? *Journal of Consulting and Clinical Psychology, 60*, 1–7.

Kiesler, C. A. (1971). *The psychology of commitments: Experiments linking behavior to belief*. New York: Academic Press.

Kiesler, C. A., & Pallak, M. S. (1976). Arousal properties of dissonance reduction. *Psychological Bulletin, 83*, 1014–1025.

Kihlstrom, J. F., & Cantor, N. (1984). Mental representations of the self. In L. Berkowitz (Ed.), *Advances in experimental social psychology* (Vol. 17). New York: Academic Press.

Kihlstrom, J. F., Cantor, N., Albright, J. S., Chew, B. R., Klein, S. B., & Niedenthal, P. M. (1988). Information processing and the study of self. In L. Berkowitz (Ed.), *Advances in experimental social psychology* (Vol. 21). New York: Academic Press.

Kilham, W., & Mann, L. (1974). Level of destructive obedience as a function of transmitter and executant roles in the Milgram obedience paradigm. *Journal of Personality and Social Psychology, 29*, 696–702.

Kinder, D. R. (1986). The continuing American dilemma: White resistance to racial change 40 years after Myrdal. *Journal of Social Issues, 42*, 151–172.

Kinder, D. R., & Sears, D. O. (1981). Prejudice and politics: Symbolic racism versus racial threats to the good life. *Journal of Personality and Social Psychology, 40*, 414–431.

Kinder, D. R., & Sears, D. O. (1985). White opposition to busing: On conceptualizing and operationalizing group conflict. *Journal of Personality and Social Psychology, 48*, 1141–1147.

Kinsey, A., Pomeroy, W. B., & Martin, C. E. (1948). *Sexual behavior in the human male*. Philadelphia: Saunders.

Kinsey, A., Pomeroy, W. B., Martin, C. E., & Gebhard, P. H. (1953). *Sexual behavior in the human female*. Philadelphia: Saunders.

Kirscht, J. P. (1983). Preventive health behavior: A review of research and issues. *Health Psychology, 2*, 277–301.

Kirscht, J. P., & Dillehay, R. C. (1967). *Dimensions of authoritarianism: A review of research and theory*. Lexington: University of Kentucky Press.

Kite, M. E., & Deaux, K. (1984). Gender belief systems: Homosexuality and the implicit inversion theory. *Psychology of Women Quarterly, 11*, 83–96.

Kite, M. E., & Deaux, K. (1986). Attitudes toward homosexuality: Assessment and behavioral consequences. *Basic and Applied Social Psychology, 7*, 137–162.

Klein, J. G. (1991). Negativity effects in impression formation: A test in the political arena. *Personality and Social Psychology Bulletin, 17*, 412–418.

Klein, R., & Harris, B. (1979). Disruptive effects of disconfirmed expectancies about crowding. *Journal of Personality and Social Psychology, 37*, 769–777.

Klein, S. B., & Loftus, J. (1988). The nature of self-referent encoding: The contributions of elaborative and organizational processes. *Journal of Personality and Social Psychology, 55*, 5–11.

Knight, G. P., & Dubro, A. F. (1984). Cooperative, competitive, and individualistic social values: An individualized regression and clustering approach. *Journal of Personality and Social Psychology, 46*, 98–105.

Kobasa, S. C. (1979). Stressful life events, personality and health: An inquiry into hardiness. *Journal of Personality and Social Psychology, 37*, 1–11.

Kobasa, S. C. (1982). The hardy personality: Toward a social psychology of stress and health. In G. S. Sanders & J. Suls (Eds.), *Social psychology of health and illness*. Hillsdale, NJ: Erlbaum.

Kobasa, S. C., Maddi, S. R., & Kahn, S. (1982). Hardiness and health: A prospective study. *Journal of Personality and Social Psychology, 42,* 168–177.

Kobasa, S. C. O., & Puccetti, M. D. (1983). Personality and social resources in stress resistance. *Journal of Personality and Social Psychology, 45,* 839–850.

Kohlberg, L. (1966). A cognitive-developmental analysis of children's sex role concepts and attitudes. In E. E. Maccoby (Ed.), *The development of sex differences*. Stanford, CA: Stanford University Press.

Kohn, P. M., Lafreniere, K., & Gurevich, M. (1991). Hassles, health, & personality. *Journal of Personality and Social Psychology, 61,* 478–482.

Kohn, P. M., & Macdonald, J. E. (1991). The survey of recent life experiences: A decontaminated Hassles Scale for adults. *Journal of Behavioral Medicine, 15,* 221–236.

Komorita, S. S., & Lapworth, C. W. (1982). Cooperative choice among individuals versus groups in an N-person dilemma situation. *Journal of Personality and Social Psychology, 42,* 487–496.

Koop, C. E. (1987). Report of the surgeon general's workshop on pornography and public health. *American Psychologist, 42,* 944–945.

Kornhauser, A., Sheppard, H. L., & Mayer, A. J. (1956). *When labor votes*. New York: University Books.

Korte, C. (1981). Constraints on helping in an urban environment. In J. P. Rushton & R. M. Sorrentino (Eds.), *Altruism and helping behavior: Social, personality, and developmental perspectives*. Hillsdale, NJ: Erlbaum.

Krail, K., & Leventhal, G. (1976). The sex variable in the intrusion of personal space. *Sociometry, 39,* 170–173.

Kramer, G. P., Kerr, N. L., & Carroll, J. S. (1990). Pretrial publicity, judicial remedies, and jury bias. *Law and Human Behavior, 14,* 409–437.

Kramer, T. H., Buckhout, R., & Eugenio, P. (1990). Weapon focus, arousal, and eyewitness memory. *Law and Human Behavior, 14,* 167–184.

Krantz, D. S., Arabian, J. M., Davia, J. E., & Parker, J. S. (1982). Type A behavior and coronary artery bypass surgery: Intraoperative blood pressure and perioperative complications. *Psychosomatic Medicine, 44,* 273–284.

Kraus, S. (1962). *The great debates: Background, perspective, effects*. Bloomington: Indiana University Press.

Kraut, R. E. (1980). Humans as lie-detectors: Some second thoughts. *Journal of Communication, 30,* 209–216.

Kraut, R. E., & Poe, D. (1980). Behavioral roots of person perception: The deception judgments of customs inspectors and laymen. *Journal of Personality and Social Psychology, 39,* 784–798.

Kravitz, D. A., & Martin, B. (1986). Ringelmann rediscovered: The original article. *Journal of Personality and Social Psychology, 50,* 936–941.

Krebs, D. L. (1970). Altruism—An examination of the concept and a review of the literature. *Psychological Bulletin, 73,* 258–302.

Krebs, D. L. (1978). A cognitive-developmental approach to altruism. In L. Wispe (Ed.), *Altruism, sympathy, and helping: Psychological and sociological principles*. New York: Academic Press.

Krebs, D., & Adinolfi, A. A. (1975). Physical attractiveness, social relations, and personality style. *Journal of Personality and Social Psychology, 31,* 245–253.

Krebs, D. L., & Miller, D. T. (1985). Altruism and aggression. In G. Lindzey & E. Aronson (Eds.), *Handbook of social psychology* (Vol. 2, 3rd ed.). New York: Random House.

Krebs, D. L., & Rosenwald, A. (1977). Moral reasoning and moral behavior in conventional adults. *Merrill-Palmer Quarterly of Behavior Development, 23,* 77–88.

Krebs, D. L., & Sturrup, B. (1974). Role-taking ability and altruistic behavior in elementary school children. *Personality and Social Psychology Bulletin, 1,* 401–407.

Krementz, J. (1989). *How it feels to fight for your life*. Boston: Little, Brown.

Krosnick, J. A. (1988). The role of attitude importance in social evaluation: A study of political preferences, presidential candidate evaluations, and voting behavior. *Journal of Personality and Social Psychology, 55,* 196–210.

Krosnick, J. A. (1989). Attitude importance and attitude accessibility. *Personality and Social Psychology Bulletin, 15,* 297–308.

Krosnick, J. A., Betz, A. L., Jussim, L. J., Lynn, A. R., & Stephens, L. (1992). Subliminal conditioning of attitudes. *Personality and Social Psychology Bulletin, 18,* 152–162.

Kruglanski, A. W. (1970). Attributing trustworthiness in supervisor–worker relations. *Journal of Experimental Social Psychology, 6,* 214–232.

Kruglanski, A. W. (1989). The psychology of being "right": The problem of accuracy in social perception and cognition. *Psychological Bulletin, 106,* 395–409.

Kruglanski, A. W., & Freund, T. (1983). The freezing and unfreezing of lay inferences: Effects of impressional primacy, ethnic stereotyping, and numerical anchoring. *Journal of Experimental Social Psychology, 19,* 448–468.

Kruglanski, A. W., Hamel, I. Z., Maides, S. A., & Schwartz, J. M. (1978). Attribution theory as a special case of lay epistemology. In J. H. Harvey, W. Ickes, & R. F. Kidd (Eds.), *New directions in attribution research* (Vol. 2). Hillsdale, NJ: Erlbaum.

Kulik, J. A., & Brown, R. (1979). Frustration, attribution of blame, and aggression. *Journal of Experimental Social Psychology, 15,* 183–194.

Kulik, J. A., & Mahler, H. I. M. (1989). Social support and recovery from surgery. *Health Psychology, 8,* 221–238.

Kunkel, L. E., & Temple, L. L. (1992). Attitudes towards AIDS and homosexuality: Gender, marital status, and religion. *Journal of Applied Social Psychology, 22,* 1030–1040.

Kurdek, L. A., & Schmitt, J. P. (1986). Interaction of sex role self-concept with relationship quality and relationship beliefs in married, heterosexual cohabiting, gay, and lesbian couples. *Journal of Personality and Social Psychology, 51,* 365–370.

Kutchinsky, B. (1973). Eroticism without censorship. *International Journal of Criminology and Penology, 1,* 217–225.

Lagerspetz, K. (1964). Studies of the aggressive behavior of mice. *Annales Academiae Scientiarum Fennicae*, Series B, *131,* 1–131.

Lake, R. W. (1981). *The new suburbanites: Race and housing in the suburbs*. New Brunswick, NJ: Center for Urban Policy Research.

Lamm, H., & Trommsdorff, G. (1973). Group versus individual performance on tasks requiring ideational proficiency (brainstorming): A review. *European Journal of Social Psychology, 3,* 361–388.

Lance, L. M. (1987). The effects of interaction with gay persons on attitudes toward homosexuality. *Human Relations, 40,* 329–336.

Landis, C. (1924). Studies of emotional reactions: II. General behavior and facial expression. *Journal of Comparative Psychology, 4,* 447–509.

Landis, C. (1929). The interpretation of facial expression in emotion. *Journal of General Psychology, 2,* 59–72.

Landy, D., & Sigall, H. (1974). Beauty is talent: Task evaluation as a function of the performer's physical attractiveness. *Journal of Personality and Social Psychology, 29*, 299–304.

Langer, E. (1981). Old age: An artifact? In S. Kiesler & J. McGaugh (Eds.), *Biology, behavior, and aging.* New York: Academic Press.

Langer, E., & Rodin, J. (1976). The effects of choice and enhanced personal responsibility for the aged: A field experiment in an institutional setting. *Journal of Personality and Social Psychology, 34*, 191–198.

Langer, E. J. (1978). Rethinking the role of thought in social interaction. In J. H. Harvey, W. J. Ickes, & R. F. Kidd (Eds.), *New directions in attribution research* (Vol. 2). Hillsdale, NJ: Erlbaum.

Langer, E. J., & Abelson, R. P. (1974). A patient by any other name: Clinical group differences in labeling bias. *Journal of Consulting and Clinical Psychology, 42*, 4–9.

Langhorne, M. C., & Secord, P. F. (1955). Variations in marital needs with age, sex, marital status, and regional composition. *Journal of Social Psychology, 41*, 19–37.

Langley, R., & Levy, R. C. (1977). *Wife beating: The silent crisis.* New York: Dutton.

Langlois, J. H., & Roggman, L. A. (1990). Attractive faces are only average. *Psychological Science, 1*, 115–121.

Langlois, J. H., Roggman, L. A., & Rieser-Danner, L. A. (1990). Infants' differential social responses to attractive and unattractive faces. *Developmental Psychology, 26*, 153–159.

LaPiere, R. T. (1934). Attitudes vs. actions. *Social Forces, 13*, 230–237.

LaPiere, R. T. (1936). Type-rationalization of group antipathy. *Social Forces, 15*, 232–237.

Larsen, K. M., & Smith, C. K. (1981). Assessment of nonverbal communication in the patient–physician interview. *Journal of Family Practice, 12*, 481–488.

Lasswell, H. D. (1948). The structure and function of communication in society. In L. Bryson (Ed.), *Communication of ideas.* New York: Harper.

Latané, B. (1970). Field studies in altruistic compliance. *Representative Research in Social Psychology, 1*, 49–61.

Latané, B. (1981). The psychology of social impact. *American Psychologist, 36*, 343–356.

Latané, B., & Darley, J. M. (1968). Group inhibition of bystander intervention.

Journal of Personality and Social Psychology, 10, 215–221.

Latané, B., & Darley, J. M. (1970). *The unresponsive bystander: Why doesn't he help?* New York: Appleton-Century-Crofts.

Latané, B., Nida, S. A., & Wilson, D. W. (1981). The effects of group size on helping behavior. In J. P. Rushton & R. M. Sorrentino (Eds.), *Altruism and helping behavior: Social, personality, and developmental perspectives.* Hillsdale, NJ: Erlbaum.

Latané, B., Williams, K., & Harkins, S. (1979). Many hands make light the work: The causes and consequences of social loafing. *Journal of Personality and Social Psychology, 37*, 822–832.

Latané, B., & Wolf, S. (1981). The social impact of majorities and minorities. *Psychological Review, 88*, 438–453.

LaTorre, R. A., & Wendenbury, K. (1983). Psychological characteristics of bisexual, heterosexual, and homosexual women. *Journal of Homosexuality, 9*, 87–97.

Laudenslager, M. L., Ryan, S. M., Drugan, R. C., Hyson, R. L., & Maier, S. F. (1983). Coping and immunosuppression: Inescapable but not escapable shock suppresses lymphocyte proliferation. *Science, 221*, 568–570.

Laumann, E. O. (1969). Friends of urban men: An assessment of accuracy in reporting their socioeconomic attributes, mutual choice, and attitude development. *Sociometry, 32*, 54–69.

Layden, M. A. (1982). Attributional therapy. In C. Anataki & C. Brewin (Eds.), *Attributions and psychological change: Applications of attributional theories to clinical and educational practice.* London: Academic Press.

Lazarus, R. S., DeLongis, A., Folkman, S., & Gruen, R. (1985). Stress and adaptational outcomes: The problem of confounded measures. *American Psychologist, 40*, 770–779.

Lazarus, R. S., & Folkman, S. (1984). *Stress, appraisal, and coping.* New York: Springer-Verlag.

Leary, M. R., & Kowalski, R. M. (1990). Impression management: A literature review and two-component model. *Psychological Bulletin, 107*, 34–47.

Leary, T. (1957). *Interpersonal diagnosis of personality.* New York: Ronald Press.

Leavitt, H. J. (1951). Some effects of certain communications patterns on group performance. *Journal of Abnormal and Social Psychology, 46*, 38–50.

Le Bon, G. (1896). *The crowd: A study of the popular mind.* New York: Macmillan.

Lederer, L. (1980). *Take back the night: Women on pornography.* New York: Morrow.

Lederer, W. J., & Jackson, D. D. (1968). *The mirages of marriage.* New York: Norton.

Lee, A. M. (1946). The press in control of intergroup tensions. *Annals of the American Academy of Political and Social Science, 244*, 144–151.

Lee, J. A. (1973). *The colors of love: An exploration of the ways of loving.* Don Mills, Ontario: New Press.

Lefcourt, H. M. (1984). *Research with the locus of control construct* (Vol. 3): *Extensions and limitations.* New York: Academic Press.

Lefcourt, H. M., & Davidson-Katz, K. (1991). Locus of control and health. In C. R. Snyder & D. R. Forsyth (Eds.), *Handbook of social and clinical psychology.* New York: Pergamon.

Lefkowitz, M. M., Eron, L. D., Walder, L. O., & Huesmann, L. R. (1972). Television violence and child aggression: A followup study. In G. A. Comstack and E. A. Rubinstein (Eds.), *Television and social behavior* (Vol. 3): *Television and adolescent aggressiveness.* Washington, DC: U.S. Government Printing Office.

Leifer, A. D., & Roberts, D. F. (1972). Children's response to television violence. In J. P. Murray, E. A. Rubinstein, & G. A. Comstock (Eds.), *Television and social behavior* (Vol. 2): *Television and social learning.* Washington, DC: U.S. Government Printing Office.

Leippe, M. R., Brigham, J. C., Cousins, C., & Romanczyk, A. (1989). The opinions and practices of criminal attorneys regarding child eyewitnesses. In S. J. Ceci, D. F. Ross, & M. P. Toglia (Eds.), *Perspectives on children's testimony.* New York: Springer-Verlag.

Leippe, M. R., Manion, A. P., & Romanczyk, A. (1992). Eyewitness persuasion: How and how well do fact finders judge the accuracy of adults' and children's memory reports? *Journal of Personality and Social Psychology, 63*, 181–197.

Lepore, S. J., Evans, G. W., & Schneider, M. L. (1991). Dynamic role of social support in the link between chronic stress and psychological distress. *Journal of Personality and Social Psychology, 61*, 899–909.

Lepper, M. R., & Greene, D. (Eds.). (1978). *The hidden costs of rewards: New perspectives in the psychology of human motivation.* Hillsdale, NJ: Erlbaum.

Lepper, M. R., Greene, D., & Nisbett, R. E. (1973). Undermining children's intrinsic interest with external rewards: A test of the overjustification hypothesis. *Journal of Personality and Social Psychology, 28,* 129–137.

Lerman, L. G. (1992). The decontextualization of domestic violence. *Journal of Criminal Law and Criminology, 83,* 217–240.

Lerner, M. J. (1980). *The belief in a just world: A fundamental delusion.* New York: Plenum.

Lerner, M. J., & Meindl, J. R. (1981). Justice and altruism. In J. P. Rushton & R. M. Sorrentino (Eds.), *Altruism and helping behavior: Social, personality and developmental perspectives.* Hillsdale, NJ: Erlbaum.

Lerner, M. J., & Miller, D. T. (1978). Just world research and the attribution process: Looking back and ahead. *Psychological Bulletin, 85,* 1030–1051.

Levenson, H., Burford, B., Bonno, B., & Davis, L. (1975). Are women still prejudicial against women? *Journal of Psychology, 59,* 67–71.

Leventhal, H., & Cleary, P. D. (1980). The smoking problem: A review of the research and theory in behavioral risk modification. *Psychological Bulletin, 88,* 370–405.

Leventhal, H. (1970). Findings and theory in the study of fear communication. In L. Berkowitz (Ed.), *Advances in experimental social psychology* (Vol. 5). New York: Academic Press.

Levin, I. P., Schnittjer, S. K., & Thee, S. L. (1988). Information framing effects in social and personal decisions. *Journal of Experimental Social Psychology, 24,* 520–529.

Levin, J., & Levin, W. C. (1980). *Ageism: Prejudice and discrimination against the elderly.* Belmont, CA: Wadsworth.

Levine, D., O'Neal, E., Garwood, S. G., & McDonald, P. (1980). Classroom ecology: The effects of seating position on grades and participation. *Personality and Social Psychology Bulletin, 6,* 409–416.

Levinger, G. (1976). A social psychological perspective on marital dissolution. *Journal of Social Issues, 32,* 21–47.

Levinger, G. (1980). Toward the analysis of close relationships. *Journal of Experimental Social Psychology, 16,* 510–544.

Levinger, G. (1983). Development and change. In H. H. Kelley, E. Berscheid, A. Christensen, J. H. Harvey, T. L. Huston, G. Levinger, E. McClintock, L. A. Peplau, & D. R. Peterson (Eds.), *Close relationships.* New York: Freeman.

Levinger, G., & Snoek, J. D. (1972). *Attraction in relationships: A new look at interpersonal attraction.* New York: General Learning Press.

Levy, L., & Herzog, A. N. (1974). Effects of population density and crowding on health and social adaptation in the Netherlands. *Journal of Health and Social Behavior, 15,* 228–240.

Lewin, K. (1935). *A dynamic theory of personality.* New York: McGraw-Hill.

Lewin, K. (1936). *Principles of topological psychology.* New York: McGraw-Hill.

Lewin, K. (1948). *Resolving social conflicts: Selected papers on group dynamics.* New York: Harper.

Lewinsohn, P. M., Hoberman, H., Teri, L., & Hautziner, M. (1985). An integrative theory of depression. In S. Reiss & R. Bootzin (Eds.), *Theoretical issues in behavior therapy.* New York: Academic Press.

Lewis, M. (1986). Origins of self-knowledge and individual differences in early self-recognition. In J. Suls & A. G. Greenwald (Eds.), *Psychological perspectives on the self* (Vol. 3). Hillsdale, NJ: Erlbaum.

Lewis, M., & Brooks, H. (1978). Self-knowledge and emotional development. In M. Lewis & L. Rosenblum (Eds.), *The development of affect.* New York: Plenum.

Ley, D., & Cybriwsky, R. (1974). Urban graffiti as territorial markers. *Annals of the Association of American Geographers, 64,* 491–505.

Leyens, J. P., & Parke, R. D. (1975). Aggressive slides can induce a weapons effect. *European Journal of Social Psychology, 5,* 229–236.

Lieberknecht, K. (1978). Helping the battered wife. *American Journal of Nursing, 4,* 654–656.

Liebert, R. M., & Baron, R. A. (1972). Some immediate effects of televised violence on children's behavior. *Developmental Psychology, 6,* 469–475.

Liebert, R. M., & Spiegler, M. D. (1987). *Personality: Strategies and issues.* Chicago: Dorsey.

Liebert, R. M., & Sprafkin, J. (1988). *The early window: Effects of television on children and youth* (3rd ed.). New York: Pergamon.

Life (1993, February). Scenes from a marriage, pp. 29–39.

Ligett, J. C. (1974). *The human face.* New York: Stein & Day.

Likert, R. (1932). A technique for the measurement of attitudes. *Archives of Psychology,* No. 140.

Linder, D. E., Cooper, J., & Jones, E. E. (1967). Decision freedom as a determinant of the role of incentive magnitude in attitude change. *Journal of Personality and Social Psychology, 6,* 245–254.

Lindsay, D. S. (1990). Misleading suggestions can impair eyewitnesses' ability to remember event details. *Journal of Experimental Psychology: Learning, Memory, and Cognition, 16,* 1077–1083.

Lindsay, R. C. L., & Wells, G. L. (1985). Improving eyewitness identifications from lineups: Simultaneous versus sequential lineup presentations. *Journal of Applied Psychology, 70,* 556–564.

Lingle, J. H., Geva, N., Ostrom, T. M., Leippe, M. R., & Baumgardner, M. H. (1979). Thematic effects of person judgments on impression organization. *Journal of Personality and Social Psychology, 37,* 674–687.

Lingle, J. H., & Ostrom, T. M. (1979). Retrieval selectivity on memory-based judgments. *Journal of Personality and Social Psychology, 37,* 180–194.

Linton, M. (1978). Real world memory after six years: An in vivo study of very long term memory. In M. Gruenberg, P. Morris, & R. Sykes (Eds.), *Practical aspects of memory.* New York: Academic Press.

Linville, P. W. (1982a). The complexity–extremity effect and age-based stereotyping. *Journal of Personality and Social Psychology, 42,* 193–211.

Linville, P. W. (1982b). Affective consequences of complexity regarding the self and others. In M. S. Clark & S. T. Fiske (Eds.), *Affect and cognition: The 17th annual Carnegie symposium on cognition.* Hillsdale, NJ: Erlbaum.

Linville, P. W. (1985). Self-complexity and affective extremity: Don't put all of your eggs in one cognitive basket. *Social Cognition, 3,* 94–120.

Linville, P. W. (1987). Self-complexity as a cognitive buffer against stress-related illness and depression. *Journal of Personality and Social Psychology, 52,* 663–676.

Linville, P. W., & Jones, E. E. (1980). Polarized appraisals of out-group members. *Journal of Personality and Social Psychology, 38,* 689–703.

Linville, R. (1982). Consequences of complexity regarding the self and others. In M. S. Clark & S. T. Fiske (Eds.), *Affect and cognition: The 17th annual Carnegie symposium on cognition.* Hillsdale, NJ: Erlbaum.

Linz, D., Arluk, I., & Donnerstein, E. (1990). Mitigating the negative effects of sexually violent mass media through pre-exposure briefings. *Communications Research, 17,* 641–674.

Linz, D., & Donnerstein, E. (1988). The methods and merits of pornography research. *Journal of Communication, 38,* 180–192.

Linz, D., Donnerstein, E., & Penrod, S. (1987). The findings and recommendations of the attorney general's commission on pornography: Do the psychological "facts" fit the political fury? *American Psychologist, 42,* 946–953.

Linz, D., & Penrod, S. (1992). Exploring the first and sixth amendments: Pretrial publicity and jury decision making. In D. K. Kagehiro & W. S. Laufer (Eds.), *Handbook of psychology and law*. New York: Springer-Verlag.

Linz, D., Wilson, B. J., & Donnerstein, E. (1992). Sexual violence in the mass media: Legal situations, warnings, and mitigation through education. *Journal of Social Issues, 48,* 145–171.

Lipe, M. G. (1991). Counterfactual reasoning as a framework for attribution theories. *Psychological Bulletin, 109,* 456–471.

Lippa, R. (1976). Expressive control and the leakage of dispositional introversion–extraversion during role-played teaching. *Journal of Personality, 44,* 541–559.

Lippa, R. (1978). Expressive control, expressive consistency, and the correspondence between expressive behavior and personality. *Journal of Personality, 46,* 438–461.

Lippa, R. (1983). Expressive behavior. In L. Wheeler & P. Shaver (Eds.), *Review of personality and social psychology*. Beverly Hills, CA: Sage.

Lippa, R. (1991). Some psychometric characteristics of gender diagnosticity measures: Reliability, validity, consistency across domains, and relationship to the Big Five. *Journal of Personality and Social Psychology, 61,* 1000–1011.

Lippa, R., & Connelly, S. (1990). Gender diagnosticity: A new Bayesian approach to gender-related individual differences. *Journal of Personality and Social Psychology, 59,* 1051–1065.

Lippmann, W. (1922). *Public opinion*. New York: Harcourt, Brace.

Lips, H. M. (1993). *Sex and gender: An introduction* (2nd ed.). Mountain View, CA: Mayfield.

Little, K. B. (1968). Cultural variations in social schemata. *Journal of Personality and Social Psychology, 10,* 1–7.

Lively, W. J., & Bromly, D. B. (1973). *Person perception in childhood and adolescence*. New York: Wiley.

Locksley, A., Borgida, E., Brekke, N., & Hepburn, C. (1980). Sex stereotypes and social judgment. *Journal of Personality and Social Psychology, 39,* 821–831.

Locksley, A., Ortiz, V., & Hepburn, C. (1980). Social categorization and discriminatory behavior: Extinguishing the minimal inter-

group discrimination effect. *Journal of Personality and Social Psychology, 39,* 773–783.

Loftus, E. F. (1974, December). Reconstructing memory: The incredible eyewitness. *Psychology Today,* pp. 117–119.

Loftus, E. F. (1975). Leading questions and the eyewitness report. *Cognitive Psychology, 7,* 560–572.

Loftus, E. F. (1992). When a lie becomes memory's truth: Memory distortion after exposure to misinformation. *Current Directions in Psychological Science, 1,* 121–123.

Loftus, E. F., Levidow, B., & Duensing, S. (1992). Who remembers best? Individual differences in memory for events that occurred in a science museum. *Applied Cognitive Psychology, 6,* 93–107.

Loftus, E. F., Loftus, G. R., & Messo, J. (1987). Some facts about "weapon focus." *Law and Human Behavior, 11,* 55–62.

Loftus, E. F., & Palmer, J. C. (1974). Reconstruction of automobile destruction: An example of the interaction between language and memory. *Journal of Verbal Learning and Verbal Behavior, 13,* 585–589.

London, H., & Nisbett, R. (1974). Elements of Schachter's cognitive theory of emotional states. In H. London & R. E. Nisbett (Eds.), *Thought and feeling*. Chicago: Aldine.

London, P. (1970). The rescuers: Motivational hypotheses about Christians who saved Jews from the Nazis. In J. Macaulay & L. Berkowitz (Eds.), *Altruism and helping behavior*. New York: Academic Press.

Long, G. T., Selby, J. W., & Calhoun, L. G. (1980). Effects of situational stress and sex on interpersonal distance preference. *Journal of Psychology, 105,* 231–237.

Loo, C., & Kennelly, D. (1979). Social density: Its effects on behaviors and perceptions of preschoolers. *Environmental Psychology and Nonverbal Behavior, 3,* 131–146.

Lord, C. G. (1980). Schemas and images as memory aids: Two modes of processing social information. *Journal of Personality and Social Psychology, 38,* 257–269.

Lord, C. G., Lepper, M. R., & Mackie, D. (1984). Attitude prototypes as determinants of attitude–behavior consistency. *Journal of Personality and Social Psychology, 46,* 1254–1266.

Lord, C. G., Ross, L., & Lepper, M. R. (1979). Biased assimilation and attitude polarization: The effects of prior theories on subsequently considered evidence. *Journal of Personality and Social Psychology, 37,* 2098–2109.

Lore, R. K., & Schultz, L. A. (1993). Control of human aggression: A comparative perspective. *American Psychologist, 48,* 16–25.

Lorenz, K. (1966). *On aggression*. New York: Harcourt, Brace & World.

Los Angeles Times. (1991, February 14). Women in the Gulf force, p. A7.

Los Angeles Times. (1991, September 4). 1989 Santa Monica illness that struck 247 called mass hysteria, p. B1.

Los Angeles Times. (1991, November 18). Cub Scouts, twins at odds over God, p. A3.

Los Angeles Times. (1991, November 21). Twins, 10, testify in suit against Scouts, p. A39.

Los Angeles Times. (1992, April 30). All 4 in King beating acquitted, p. A1.

Los Angeles Times. (1992, May 1). Beaten driver a searing image of mob cruelty, p. A1.

Los Angeles Times. (1992, May 1). Jurors rattled by aftermath; Defend verdicts, p. A1.

Los Angeles Times. (1992, May 2). What swayed the jury? p. A1.

Los Angeles Times. (1993, April 18). 2 officers guilty, 2 acquitted: Guarded calm follows verdicts in King case, p. A1.

Lott, A., & Lott, B. (1961). Group cohesiveness, communication level, and conformity. *Journal of Abnormal and Social Psychology, 62,* 408–412.

Lott, A., & Lott, B. (1968). A learning theory approach to interpersonal attitudes. In A. G. Greenwald, T. C. Brock, & T. M. Ostrom (Eds.), *Psychological foundations of attitudes*. New York: Academic Press.

Lott, A., & Lott, B. (1974). The role of reward in the formation of positive interpersonal attitudes. In T. L. Huston (Ed.), *Foundations of interpersonal attraction*. New York: Academic Press.

Lott, B., & Lott, A. (1985). Learning theory in contemporary social psychology. In G. Lindzey and E. Aronson (Eds.), *Handbook of social psychology* (Vol. 1). New York: Random House.

Lubinski, D., & Benbrow, C. P. (1992). Gender differences in abilities and preferences among the gifted: Implications for the math–science pipeline. *Current Directions in Psychological Science, 1,* 61–66.

Lubinski, D., & Humphreys, L. G. (1990). A broadly based analysis of mathematical giftedness. *Intelligence, 19,* 327–355.

Luce, R. D., & Raiffa, H. (1957). *Games and decisions*. New York: Wiley.

Luchins, A. S. (1957). Primacy–recency in impression formation. In C. Hovland (Ed.),

The order of presentation in persuasion. New Haven, CT: Yale University Press.

Lumsdaine, A. A., & Janis, I. L. (1953). Resistance to "counterpropaganda" produced by one-sided and two-sided "propaganda" presentation. *Public Opinion Quarterly, 17,* 311–318.

Lunneborg, P. W. (1972). Dimensionality of MF. *Journal of Clinical Psychology, 28,* 313–317.

Luus, C. A. E., & Wells, G. L. (1991). Eyewitness identification and the selection of distractors for lineups. *Law and Human Behavior, 15,* 43–57.

Lyon, E. (1986). The economics of gender. In F. A. Boudreau, R. S. Sennott, & M. Wilson (Eds.), *Sex roles and social patterns.* New York: Praeger.

Lyons, V. (Ed.). (1980). *Structuring cooperative learning in the classroom: The 1980 handbook.* Minneapolis, MN: Cooperative Network.

Maass, A., & Clark, R. D., III. (1982). *Minority influence theory: Is it applicable only to majorities?* Paper presented at the 33rd Congress of the German Psychological Association, Mainz, West Germany.

Maass, A., & Clark, R. D., III. (1983). Internalization versus compliance: Differential processes underlying minority influence and conformity. *European Journal of Social Psychology, 13,* 45–55.

Maass, A., & Clark, R. D., III. (1984). Hidden impact of minorities: Fifteen years of minority influence research. *Psychological Bulletin, 95,* 428–450.

Maass, A., Clark, R. D., III, & Haverhorn, G. (1982). The effects of differential ascribed category membership and norms on minority influence. *European Journal of Social Psychology, 12,* 89–104.

Maass, A., West, S. G., & Cialdini, R. B. (1987). Minority influence and conversion. In C. Hendrick (Ed.), *Group processes: Review of personality and social psychology* (Vol. 8). Newbury Park, CA: Sage.

Maccoby, E. E. (1966). Sex differences in intellectual functioning. In E. E. Maccoby (Ed.), *The development of sex differences.* Stanford, CA: Stanford University Press.

Maccoby, E. E., & Jacklin, C. N. (1974). *The psychology of sex differences.* Stanford, CA: Stanford University Press.

Maccoby, E. E., & Jacklin, C. N. (1980). Sex differences in aggression. A rejoinder and reprise. *Child Development, 51,* 954–980.

MacCoun, R. J., & Kerr, N. L. (1988). Asymmetric influence in mock jury deliberations: Jurors' bias for leniency. *Journal of Personality and Social Psychology, 54,* 21–33.

Mace, K. C. (1972). The "over-bluff" shoplifter: Who gets caught? *Journal of Forensic Psychology, 4,* 26–30.

MacEvoy, B., Lambert, W. W., Karlberg, P., Karlberg, J., Klackenberg-Larsson, I., & Klackenberg, G. (1988). Early affective antecedents of adult Type A behavior. *Journal of Personality and Social Psychology, 54,* 108–116.

Mackie, D. M. (1986). Social identification effects in group polarization. *Journal of Personality and Social Psychology, 50,* 720–728.

Mackie, D. M. (1987). Systematic and nonsystematic processing of majority and minority persuasive communications. *Journal of Personality and Social Psychology, 53,* 41–52.

Mackie, D. M., & Worth, L. T. (1989). Cognitive deficits and the mediation of positive affect in persuasion. *Journal of Personality and Social Psychology, 57,* 27–40.

MacPherson, J. C. (1984). Environments and interaction in row-and-column classrooms. *Environment and Behavior, 16,* 481–502.

Maddi, S. R. (1976). *Personality theories: A comparative analysis* (3rd ed.). Chicago: Dorsey.

Maddi, S. R., Bartone, P. T., & Puccetti, M. C. (1987). Stressful events are indeed a factor in physical illness: Reply to Schroeder & Costa (1984). *Journal of Personality and Social Psychology, 52,* 833–843.

Maddux, J. E., & Rogers, R. W. (1983). Protection motivation and self-efficacy: A revised theory of fear appeals and attitude change. *Journal of Experimental Social Psychology, 19,* 469–479.

Mahl, G. F. (1968). Gestures and body movements in interviews. In J. M. Shlien (Ed.), *Research in psychotherapy.* Washington, DC: American Psychological Association.

Maier, N. R., & Thurber, J. A. (1968). Accuracy of judgments of deception when an interview is watched, heard, and read. *Personal Psychology, 21,* 23–30.

Major, B. (1980). Information acquisition and attribution processes. *Journal of Personality and Social Psychology, 39,* 1010–1024.

Major, B., & Konar, E. (1984). An investigation of sex differences in pay expectations and their possible causes. *Academy of Management Journal, 27,* 777–792.

Malamuth, N. M. (1981). Rape fantasies as a function of exposure to violent sexual stimuli. *Archives of Sexual Behavior, 10,* 33–47.

Malamuth, N. M. (1984). Aggression against women: Cultural and individual causes. In N. M. Malamuth & E. Donnerstein (Eds.),

Pornography and sexual aggression. Orlando, FL: Academic Press.

Malamuth, N. M., & Check, J. V. P. (1981). The effects of media exposure on acceptance of violence against women: A field experiment. *Journal of Research in Personality, 15,* 436–446.

Malamuth, N. M., & Check, J. V. P. (1985). The effects of aggressive pornography on beliefs in rape myths: Individual differences. *Journal of Research in Personality, 19,* 299–320.

Malamuth, N. M., Check, J. V. P., & Briere, J. (1986). Sexual arousal to aggression: Ideological, aggressive, and sexual correlates. *Journal of Personality and Social Psychology, 50,* 330–340.

Malandro, A. W., Barker, L., & Barker, D. A. (1989). *Nonverbal communication* (2nd ed.). New York: Random House.

Malof, M., & Lott, A. J. (1962). Ethnocentrism and the acceptance of Negro support in a group pressure situation. *Journal of Abnormal and Social Psychology, 65,* 254–258.

Mandler, G. (1975). *Mind and emotion.* New York: Wiley.

Mann, J. H. (1959). The relationship between cognitive, affective, and behavioral aspects of racial prejudice. *Journal of Social Psychology, 49,* 223–228.

Mann, R. D. (1959). A review of the relationships between personality and performance in small groups. *Psychological Bulletin, 56,* 241–270.

Mann, V. A., Sasanuma, S., Sakuma, N., & Masaki, S. (1990). Sex differences in cognitive abilities: A cross-cultural perspective. *Neuropsychologia, 28,* 1063–1077.

Mantell, D. M. (1971). The potential for violence in Germany. *Journal of Social Issues, 27,* 101–112.

Manton, K. G., & Myers, G. C. (1977). The structure of urban mortality: A methodological study of Hanover, Germany (Pt. 2). *International Journal of Epidemiology, 6,* 213–223.

Marks, G., & Miller, N. (1987). Ten years of research on the false-consensus effect: An empirical and theoretical review. *Psychological Bulletin, 102,* 72–90.

Marks, G., Richardson, J. L., Graham, J. W., & Levine, A. (1986). The role of health locus of control beliefs and expectations of treament efficacy in adjustment to cancer. *Journal of Personality and Social Psychology, 51,* 443–450.

Markus, H. (1977). Self-schemas and processing information about the self. *Journal of Personality and Social Psychology, 35,* 63–78.

Markus, H. (1978). The effect of mere presence on social facilitation: An unobtrusive test. *Journal of Experimental Social Psychology, 14,* 389–397.

Markus, H., Crane, M., Bernstein, S., & Siladi, M. (1982). Self-schemas and gender. *Journal of Personality and Social Psychology, 42,* 38–50.

Markus, H. R., & Kitayama, S. (1991). Culture and the self: Implications for cognition, emotion, and motivation. *Psychological Review, 98,* 224–253.

Markus, H., & Nurius, P. (1986). Possible selves. *American Psychologist, 41,* 954–969.

Markus, H., & Sentis, K. (1982). The self in social information processing. In J. Suls (Ed.), *Social psychological perspectives on the self.* Hillsdale, NJ: Erlbaum.

Markus, H., & Smith, J. (1981). The influence of self-schemata on the perception of others. In N. Cantor & J. Kihlstrom (Eds.), *Personality, cognition, and social interaction.* Hillsdale, NJ: Erlbaum.

Markus, H., Smith, J., & Moreland, R. L. (1985). Role of the self-concept in the perception of others. *Journal of Personality and Social Psychology, 49,* 1494–1512.

Markus, H. R., & Wurf, E. (1987). The dynamic self-concept: A social psychological perspective. *Annual Review of Psychology, 38,* 299–337.

Markus, H., & Zajonc, R. B. (1985). The cognitive perspective in social psychology. In G. Lindzey & E. Aronson (Eds.), *Handbook of social psychology* (Vol. 1). New York: Random House.

Marsh, H. W., & Byrne, B. M. (1991). Differentiated additive androgyny model: Relations between masculinity, femininity, and multiple dimensions of self-concept. *Journal of Personality and Social Psychology, 61,* 811–828.

Marshall, G., & Zimbardo, P. G. (1979). Affective consequences of inadequately explained physiological arousal. *Journal of Personality and Social Psychology, 37,* 970–988.

Martin, C. L. (1987). A ratio measure of sex stereotyping. *Journal of Personality and Social Psychology, 52,* 489–499.

Martin, D. (1982). Wife beating: A product of sociosexual development. In M. Kirkpatrick (Ed.), *Women's sexual experience: Explorations of the dark content.* New York: Plenum.

Martindale, D. A. (1971). Territorial dominance behavior in dyadic verbal interaction. *Proceedings of the 79th annual convention of the American Psychological Association, 6,* 305–306.

Martinek, T. J. (1981). Physical attractiveness: Effects on teacher expectations and dyadic interactions in elementary age children. *Journal of Sports Psychology, 3,* 196–205.

Maslach, C. (1979). Negative emotional biasing of unexplained arousal. *Journal of Personality and Social Psychology, 37,* 953–969.

Masserman, J. H., Wechkin, S., & Terris, W. (1964). Altruistic behavior in rhesus monkeys. *American Journal of Psychiatry, 121,* 584–585.

Matthews, K. A. (1982). Psychological perspectives on the type A behavior pattern. *Psychological Bulletin, 91,* 293–323.

Matthews, K. A. (1988). Coronary heart disease and type A behaviors: Update on and alternative to Booth-Kewley and Friedman (1987) quantitative review. *Psychological Bulletin, 104,* 373–380.

Matthews, K. A., Krantz, D. S., Dembroski, T. M., & MacDougall, J. A. (1982). The unique and common variance in the structured interview and the Jenkins activity survey measures of the type A behavior pattern. *Journal of Personality and Social Psychology, 42,* 303–313.

Maynard-Smith, J. (1974). The theory of games and the evolution of animal conflict. *Journal of Theoretical Biology, 47,* 209–221.

Mazur, A. (1983). Physiology, dominance and aggression in humans. In *Prevention and control of aggression.* New York: Pergamon.

McAlister, A., Perry, C., Killen, J., Slinkard, L. A., & Maccoby, N. (1980). Pilot study of smoking, alcohol and drug abuse prevention. *American Journal of Public Health, 70,* 719–721.

McAndrew, F. T. (1992). The home advantage also operates in individual sports: A study of high school wrestlers. Paper presented at the meeting of the Eastern Psychological Association, Philadelphia.

McArthur, L. Z. (1972). The how and the what of why: Some determinants and consequences of causal attribution. *Journal of Personality and Social Psychology, 22,* 171–193.

McArthur, L. Z. (1982). Judging a book by its cover: A cognitive analysis of the relationship between physical appearance and stereotyping. In A. Hustorf, & A. Isen (Eds.), *Cognitive social psychology.* New York: Elsevier North-Holland.

McArthur, L. Z., & Baron, R. M. (1983). Toward an ecological theory of social perception. *Psychological Review, 90,* 215–247.

McArthur, L. Z., & Berry, D. S. (1987). Cross-cultural agreement in perceptions of babyfaced adults. *Journal of Cross-Cultural Psychology, 18,* 165–192.

McCain, G., Cox, V. C., & Paulus, P. B. (1976). The relationship between illness complaints and degree of crowding in a prison environment. *Environment and Behavior, 8,* 283–290.

McCallum, D. M., Harring, K., Gilmore, J. P., Insko, C. A., & Thibaut, J. (1985). Competition and cooperation between groups and between individuals. *Journal of Experimental Social Psychology, 21,* 301–320.

McCarthy, S. J. (1980). Pornography, rape and the cult of the macho. *Humanist, 56,* 11–20.

McCauley, C. (1989). The nature of social influence in groupthink: Compliance and internalization. *Journal of Personality and Social Psychology, 57,* 250–260.

McCauley, C., & Stitt, C. L. (1978). An individual and quantitative measure of stereotypes. *Journal of Personality and Social Psychology, 36,* 929–940.

McCauley, C., Stitt, C. L., & Segal, M. (1980). Stereotyping: From prejudice to prediction. *Psychological Bulletin, 87,* 195–208.

McClanahan, K. K., Gold, J. A., Lenney, E., Ryckman, R. M., & Kulberg, G. E. (1990). Infatuation and attraction to a dissimilar other: Why is love blind? *Journal of Social Psychology, 130,* 433–445.

McClelland, D. C., & Apicella, F. S. (1945). A functional classification of verbal reactions to experimentally induced failure. *Journal of Abnormal and Social Psychology, 46,* 376–390.

McClintock, C. G., & Liebrand, W. B. (1988). Role of interdependence structure, individual value orientation, and another's strategy in social decision making: A transformational analysis. *Journal of Personality and Social Psychology, 55,* 396–409.

McClintock, C. G., & Van Avermaet, E. (1982). Social values and rules of fairness: A theoretical perspective. In V. J. Derlega & J. Grzelak (Eds.), *Cooperation and helping behavior: Theories and research.* New York: Academic Press.

McCloskey, M. E., & Glucksberg, S. (1978). Natural categories: Well-defined or fuzzy sets? *Memory and Cognition, 6,* 462–472.

McCloskey, M., & Zaragoza, M. (1985). Misleading postevent information and memory for events: Arguments and evidence against memory impairment hypotheses. *Journal of Experimental Psychology: General, 114,* 1–16.

McConahay, J. B. (1986). Modern racism, ambivalence, and the modern racism scale. In J. F. Dovidio & S. L. Gaertner (Eds.), *Prejudice, discrimination, and racism.* Orlando, FL: Academic Press.

McCoy, S. B., Gibbons, F. X., Reist, J., Gerrard, M., Luus, C. A. E., & Sufka, A. V. W. (1992). Perceptions of smoking risk as a function of smoking status. *Journal of Behavioral Medicine, 15,* 469–487.

McCrae, R. R., & Costa, P. T. Jr. (1985). Updating Norman's "adequate taxonomy": Intelligence and personality dimensions in natural language and in questionnaires. *Journal of Personality and Social Psychology, 49,* 710–721.

McCrae, R. R., & Costa, P. T. Jr. (1987). Validation of the five-factor model of personality across instruments and observers. *Journal of Personality and Social Psychology, 52,* 81–90.

McCullum, D. M., Harring, K., Gilmore, R., Drenan, S., Chase, J. P., Insko, D., & Thibaut, J. (1985). Competition and cooperation between groups and between individuals. *Journal of Experimental Social Psychology, 21* 301–320.

McDavid, J. W., & Sistrunk, F. (1964). Personality correlates of two kinds of conformity behavior. *Journal of Personality, 32,* 421–435.

McFarland, S. G. (1989). Religious orientation and the targets of discrimination. *Journal for the Scientific Study of Religion, 28,* 324–336.

McFarland, S. G., Ageyev, V. S., & Abalakina-Paap, M. A. (1992). Authoritarianism in the former Soviet Union. *Journal of Personality and Social Psychology, 63,* 1004–1010.

McGuire, W. J. (1960). A syllogistic analysis of cognitive relationships. In M. J. Rosenburg & C. I. Hovland (Eds.), *Attitude organization and change.* New Haven, CT: Yale University Press.

McGuire, W. J. (1964). Inducing resistance to persuasion: Some contemporary approaches. In L. Berkowitz (Ed.), *Advances in experimental social psychology* (Vol. 1). New York: Academic Press.

McGuire, W. J. (1968a). Personality and susceptibility to social influence. In E. F. Borgatta & W. W. Lambert (Eds.), *Handbook of personality theory and research.* Chicago: Rand-McNally.

McGuire, W. J. (1968b). Personality and attitude change: An information-processing theory. In A. G. Greenwald, T. C. Brock, & T. M. Ostrom (Eds.), *Psychological foundations of attitudes.* New York: Academic Press.

McGuire, W. J. (1981). The probabilogical model of cognitive structure. In R. E. Petty, T. M. Ostrom, & T. C. Brock (Eds.), *Cognitive responses in persuasion.* Hillsdale, NJ: Erlbaum.

McGuire, W. J. (1985). Attitudes and attitude change. In G. Lindzey & E. Aronson (Eds.), *Handbook of social psychology* (Vol. 2). New York: Random House.

McGuire, W. J., & McGuire, C. V. (1982). Significant others in self-space: Sex differences and developmental trends in the social self. In J. Suls (Ed.), *Psychological perspectives on the self.* Hillsdale, NJ: Erlbaum.

McGuire, W. J., & McGuire, C. V. (1988). Content and process in the experience of self. In L. Berkowitz (Ed.), *Advances in experimental social psychology* (Vol. 21). San Diego: Academic Press.

McGuire, W. J., McGuire, C. V., Child, P., & Fujioka, T. (1978). Salience of ethnicity in the spontaneous self-concept as a function of one's ethnic distinctiveness in the social environment. *Journal of Personality and Social Pscyhology, 36,* 511–520.

McGuire, W. J., & Padawer-Singer, A. (1976). Trait salience in the spontaneous self-concept. *Journal of Personality and Social Psychology, 33,* 743–754.

McGuire, W. J., & Papageorgis, D. (1961). The relative efficacy of various types of prior belief-defense in producing immunity against persuasion. *Journal of Abnormal and Social Psychology, 62,* 327–337.

McKillip, J., & Riedel, S. L. (1983). External validity of matching on physical attractiveness for same and opposite sex couples. *Journal of Applied Social Psychology, 13,* 328–337.

McLeod, J. M., Atkin, C. K., & Chaffee, S. H. (1972a). Adolescents, parents, and television use: Adolescent self-report measures from Maryland and Wisconsin samples. In G. A. Comstock & E. A. Rubinstein (Eds.), *Television and social behavior* (Vol. III), *Television and adolescent aggressiveness.* Washington, DC: U.S. Government Printing Office.

McLeod, J. M., Atkin, C. K., & Chaffee, S. H. (1972b). Adolescents, parents, and television use: Self-report and other-report measures from the Wisconsin sample. In G. A. Comstock & E. A. Rubinstein (Eds.), *Television and social behavior* (Vol. III), *Television and adolescent aggressiveness.* Washington, DC: U.S. Government Printing Office.

McMillen, D. L. (1971). Transgression, self-image, and compliant behavior. *Journal of Personality and Social Psychology, 20,* 176–179.

McMillen, D. L., Sander, D. V., & Solomon, G. S. (1977). Self-esteem, attentiveness, and helping behavior. *Personality and Social Psychology Bulletin, 3,* 257–261.

McNemar, Q. (1946). Opinion–attitude methodology. *Psychological Bulletin, 43,* 289–374.

McTavish, D. G. (1971). Perceptions of old people: A review of research, methodologies and findings. *Gerontologist, 11,* 90–102.

Mead, G. H. (1934). *Mind, self, and society.* Chicago: University of Chicago Press.

Mead, M. (1935). *Sex and temperament.* New York: Morrow.

Medcof, J. W. (1990). PEAT: An integrative model of attribution processes. In M. P. Zanna (Ed.), *Advances in experimental social psychology* (Vol. 23). San Diego: Academic Press.

Mediating effects on sex and locus of control at extended interaction distances. *Basic and Applied Social Psychology, 1*(1), 65–82.

Mednick, S. A., Brennan, P., & Kandel, E. (1988). Predisposition to violence. *Aggressive Behavior, 14,* 25–33.

Meehl, P. E. (1954). *Clinical vs. statistical prediction: A theoretical analysis and a review of the evidence.* Minneapolis: University of Minnesota Press.

Mehrabian, A. (1976). *Public places and private spaces.* New York: Basic Books.

Mehrabian, A., & Wiener, M. (1967). Decoding of inconsistent communication. *Journal of Personality and Social Psychology, 6,* 108–114.

Meindl, J. R., & Lerner, M. J. (1985). Exacerbation of extreme responses to an outgroup. *Journal of Personality and Social Psychology, 47,* 71–84.

Mellen, S. L. W. (1981). *The evolution of love.* San Francisco: Freeman.

Mentzer, S. J., & Snyder, M. L. (1982). The doctor and the patient: A psychological perspective. In G. S. Sanders & G. Suls (Eds.), *Social psychology of health and illness.* Hillsdale, NJ: Erlbaum.

Merry, S.E. (1981). Defensible space undefended: Social factors in crime control through environmental design. *Urban Affairs Quarterly, 16,* 397–422.

Merton, R. K. (1948). The self-fulfilling prophecy. *Antioch Review, 8,* 193–210.

Merton, R. K. (1957). *Social theory and social structure.* Glencoe, IL: Free Press.

Merton, R. K., & Kitt, A. A. (1950). Contributions to the theory of reference group behavior. In R. K. Merton & P. F. Lazarsfeld (Eds.), *Continuities in social research: Studies in the scope and method of the American soldier.* Glencoe, IL: Free Press.

Messick, D. M., Wilke, H., Brewer, M. B., Krammer, R. M., Zemke, P. E., & Lui, L. (1983). Individual adaptations and structural change as solutions to social dilemmas. *Journal of Personality and Social Psychology, 44,* 294–309.

Meyer, P. (1970, February). If Hitler asked

you to electrocute a stranger, would you? . . . What if Mr. Milgram asked you? *Esquire*, pp. 72–73.

Milberg, S., & Clark, M. S. (1988). Moods and compliance. *British Journal of Social Psychology, 27*, 79–90.

Milgram, S. (1963). Behavioral study of obedience. *Journal of Abnormal and Social Psychology, 67*, 371–378.

Milgram, S. (1964). Issues in the study of obedience: A reply to Baumrind. *American Psychologist, 19*, 848–852.

Milgram, S. (1970). The experience of living in cities. *Science, 167*, 1461–1468.

Milgram, S. (1974). *Obedience to authority: An experimental view*. New York: Harper & Row.

Miller, A. G. (1986). *The obedience experiments: A case study of controversy in social science*. New York: Praeger.

Miller, D. T. (1978). What constitutes a self-serving attributional bias? A reply to Bradley. *Journal of Personality and Social Psychology, 36*, 1211–1223.

Miller, D. T., & McFarland, C. (1987). Pluralistic ignorance: When similarity is interpreted as dissimilarity. *Journal of Personality and Social Psychology, 53*, 298–305.

Miller, D. T., & Ross, M. (1975). Self-serving biases in the attribution of causality: Fact or fiction? *Psychological Bulletin, 82*, 213–225.

Miller, G. A., Galanter, E., & Pribram, K. H. (1960). *Plans and the structure of behavior*. New York: Holt, Rinehart and Winston.

Miller, G. I. Jr. (1992). *Living in the environment*. Belmont, CA: Wadsworth.

Miller, H. L., & Rivenbark, W. H., III. (1970). Sexual differences in physical attractiveness as a determinant of heterosexual liking. *Psychological Reports, 27*, 701–702.

Miller, J. G., Bersoff, D. M., & Harwood, R. L. (1990). Perceptions of social responsibilities in India and in the United States: Moral imperatives or personal decisions. *Journal of Personality and Social Psychology, 58*, 33–47.

Miller, N., & Brewer, M. B. (1984). The social psychology of desegregation: An introduction. In N. Miller & M. B. Brewer (Eds.), *Groups in contact: The psychology of desegregation*. New York: Academic Press.

Miller, N. E., & Bugelski, R. (1948). The influence of frustrations imposed by the ingroup on attitude expressed toward out-group. *Journal of Psychology, 25*, 437–442.

Miller, N. E., & Dollard, J. (1941). *Social learning and imitation*. New Haven, CT: Yale University Press.

Miller, R. L. (1990). Beyond contact theory: The impact of community affluence on integration efforts in five suburban high schools. *Youth and Society, 22*, 12–34.

Miller, T. Q., Turner, C. W., Tindale, R. S., Posavac, E. J., & Dugoni, B. L. (1991). Reasons for the trend toward null findings in research on Type A behavior. *Psychological Bulletin, 110*, 469–485.

Millman, M. (1980). *Such a pretty face: Being fat in America*. New York: Norton.

Mills, J., & Clark, M. S. (1982). Communal and exchange relationships. In L. Wheeler (Ed.), *Review of personality and social psychology* (Vol. 3). Beverly Hills, CA: Sage.

Milton, C. (1972). *Women in policing*. Washington, DC: Police Foundation.

Mischel, W. (1966). A social learning view of sex differences. In E. E. Maccoby (Ed.), *The development of sex differences*. Stanford, CA: Stanford University Press.

Mischel, W. (1968). *Personality and assessment*. New York: Wiley.

Mischel, W. (1970). Sex-typing and socialization. In P. H. Mussen (Ed.), *Carmichael's manual of child psychology* (Vol. 2). New York: Wiley.

Mischel, W. (1973). Toward a cognitive social learning reconceptualization of personality. *Psychological Review, 80*, 252–283.

Mischel, W. (1977). The interaction of person and situation. In D. Magnusson & N. S. Endler (Eds.), *Personality at the crossroads: Current issues in interactional psychology*. Hillsdale, NJ: Erlbaum.

Mischel, W. (1982). *A cognitive–social learning approach to assessment*. New York: Guilford.

Mischel, W., Ebbesen, E. B., & Zeiss, A. R. (1973). Selective attention to the self: Situational and dispositional determinants. *Journal of Personality and Social Psychology, 27*, 129–142.

Mischel, W., & Grusec, J. (1966). Determinants of the rehearsal and transmission of neutral and aversive behavior. *Journal of Personality and Social Psychology, 3*, 197–205.

Mischel, W., & Peake, P. K. (1982). Beyond *déjà vu* in the search for cross-situational consistency. *Psychological Review, 89*, 730–755.

Mischel, W., & Peake, P. K. (1983). Analyzing the construction of consistency in personality. In M. M. Page (Ed.), *Personality—Current theory and research: Nebraska symposium on motivation 1982*.

Mitchell, P. (1976). *Act of love: The killing of George Zygmanik*. New York: Knopf.

Mixon, D. (1989). *Obedience and civilization*. London: Pluto.

Money, J., & Ehrhardt, A. A. (1972). *Man and woman, boy and girl*. Baltimore: Johns Hopkins University Press.

Monroe, S. M., & Steiner, S. C. (1986). Social support and psychopathology: Interrelationships with preexisting disorder, stress, and personality. *Journal of Abnormal Psychology, 95*, 29–39.

Monson, T. C., Helsey, J. W., & Chernick, L. (1981). Specifying when personality can and cannot predict behavior: An alternative to abandoning the attempt to predict single-act criteria. *Journal of Personality and Social Psychology, 43*, 385–399.

Montagu, A. (1976). *The nature of human aggression*. New York: Oxford University Press.

Montano, D., & Adamopoulos, J. (1984). The perception of crowding in interpersonal situations: Affective and behavioral responses. *Environment and Behavior, 16*, 643–666.

Montello, D. R. (1988). Classroom seating location and its effect on course achievement, participation, and attitudes. *Journal of Environmental Psychology, 8*, 149–157.

Montemayor, R., & Eisen, M. (1977). The development of self-conceptions from childhood to adolescence. *Developmental Psychology, 13*, 314–319.

Montepare, J. M., & Vega, C. (1988). Women's vocal reactions to intimate and casual male friends. *Personality and Social Psychology Bulletin, 14*, 103–113.

Montepare, J. M., & Zebrowitz-McArthur, L. (1989). Children's perceptions of baby-faced adults. *Perceptual and Motor Skills, 69*, 467–472.

Montgomery, B. M. (1988). Quality communication in personal relationships. In S. W. Duck (Ed.), *Handbook of personal relationships*. Chichester, England: Wiley.

Mook, D. G. (1983). In defense of external invalidity. *American Psychologist, 38*, 379–387.

Moore, B. S. Underwood, B., & Rosenhan, D. L. (1973). Affect and altruism. *Developmental Psychology, 8*, 99–104.

Moorhead, G., Ference, R., & Neck, C. P. (1991). Group decision fiascoes continue: Space shuttle Challenger and a revised groupthink framework. *Human Relations, 44*, 539–550.

Moran, G., & Comfort, C. (1986). Neither "tentative" nor "fragmentary": Verdict preference of impaneled felony jurors as a function of attitude toward capital punishment. *Journal of Applied Psychology, 71*, 146–155.

Mori, D., Chaiken, S., & Pliner, P. (1987). "Eating lightly" and the self-presentation of femininity. *Journal of Personality and Social Psychology, 53*, 693–702.

Moriarity, D., & McCabe, A. E. (1977). Studies of television and youth sport. In *Ontario Royal Commission on Violence in the Communications Industry report* (Vol. 5): *Learning from the media.* (Research Reports.) Toronto: Queen's Printer for Ontario.

Moriarity, T. (1975). Crime, commitment and the responsive bystander: Two field experiments. *Journal of Personality and Social Psychology, 31,* 370–376.

Morin, S. F. (1988). AIDS: The challenge to psychology. *American Psychologist, 43,* 838–842.

Morse, S. J., & Gergen, J. J. (1971). Material aid and social attraction. *Journal of Applied Social Psychology, 2,,* 34–46.

Moscovici, S. (1976). *Social influence and social change.* London: Academic Press.

Moscovici, S. (1980). Toward a theory of conversion behavior. In L. Berkowitz (Ed.), *Advances in experimental social psychology* (Vol. 13). New York: Academic Press.

Moscovici, S. (1985). Social influence and conformity. In G. Lindzey & E. Aronson (Eds.), *Handbook of social psychology* (Vol. 2). New York: Random House.

Moscovici, S., Lage, E., & Naffrechoux, M. (1969). Influence of a consistent minority on the response of a majority in a color perception task. *Sociometry, 32,* 365–379.

Moscovici, S., & Personnaz, B. (1980). Studies in social influence: V. Minority influence and conversion behavior in a perceptual task. *Journal of Experimental Social Psychology, 16,* 270–282.

Moscovici, S., & Zavalloni, M. (1969). The group as a polarizer of attitudes. *Journal of Personality and Social Psychology, 12,* 125–135.

Moyer, K. E. (1976). *The psychology of aggression.* New York: Harper & Row.

Mugny, G. (1975). Negotiations, image of other and the process of minority influence. *European Journal of Social Psychology, 5,* 204–229.

Mugny, G. (1982). *The power of minorities.* London: Academic Press.

Mulder, M., & Stemerding, A. (1963). Threat, attraction to group, and need for strong leadership. *Human Relations, 16,* 317–334.

Mullen, B., Atkins, J. L., Champion, D. S., Edwards, C., Hardy, D., Story, J. E., & Vanderklok, M. (1985). The false consensus effect: A meta-analysis of 115 hypothesis tests. *Journal of Experimental Social Psychology, 21,* 262–283.

Mullen, B., Johnson, C., & Salas, E. (1991). Productivity loss in brainstorming groups: A meta-analytic integration. *Basic and Applied Social Psychology, 12,* 3–23.

Murphy, G., & Likert, R. (1938). *Public opinion and the individual: A psychological study of student attitudes on public questions, with a retest five years later.* New York: Harper.

Murray, D. M., Johnson, C. A., Luepker, R. V., & Mittelmark, M. B. (1984). The prevention of cigarette smoking in children: A comparison of four strategies. *Journal of Applied Social Psychology, 14,* 274–288.

Murray, H. A. (1933). The effect of fear upon estimates of the maliciousness of other personalities. *Journal of Social Psychology, 4,* 310–329.

Murray, H. A. (1962). *Explorations in personality.* New York: Science Editions.

Murray, J. B. (1980). *Television and youth: 25 years of research and controversy.* Boys Town, NE: Boys Town Center for the Study of Youth Development.

Murstein, B. I. (1970). Stimulus–value–role: A theory of marital choice. *Journal of Marriage and Family, 32,* 465–481.

Murstein, B. I. (1974). *Love, sex, and marriage through the ages.* New York: Springer.

Murstein, B. I. (1976). *Who will marry whom? Theories and research in marital choice.* New York: Springer.

Mussen, P., & Eisenberg-Berg, N. (1977). *Roots of caring, sharing, and helping: The development of prosocial behavior in children.* San Francisco: Freeman.

Myers, A. M., & Gonda, G. (1982). Utility of the masculinity–femininity construct: Comparison of traditional and androgyny approaches. *Journal of Personality and Social Psychology, 43,* 514–522.

Myers, D. (1982). Polarizing effects of social interaction. In H. Brandstatter, J. H. Davis, & Z. Stocker-Kriechgauer (Eds.), *Group decision making.* London: Academic Press.

Myers, D. G., & Bishop, G. D. (1970). Discussion effects on racial attitudes. *Science, 169,* 778–779.

Myers, D. G., & Kaplan, M. F. (1976). Group-induced polarization in simulated juries. *Personality and Social Psychology Bulletin, 2,* 63–66.

Myers, D. G., & Lamm, H. (1976). The group polarization phenomenon. *Psychological Bulletin, 83,* 602–627.

Myers, M. (1979). Rule departures and making law: Juries and their verdicts. *Law and Society Review, 13,* 781–797.

Myerscough, R., & Taylor, S. (1985). The effects of marihuana on physical aggression. *Journal of Personality and Social Psychology, 49,* 1541–1546.

Nadler, A. (1986). Help seeking as a cultural phenomenon: Differences between city and kibbutz dwellers. *Journal of Personality and Social Psychology, 51,* 976–982.

Nahemow, L., & Lawton, M. P. (1975). Similarity and propinquity in friendship formation. *Journal of Personality and Social Psychology, 32,* 205–213.

Napoleon, T., Chassin, L., & Young, R. D. (1980). A replication and extension of physical attractiveness and mental illness. *Journal of Abnormal Psychology, 89,* 250–253.

Narby, D. J., Cutler, B. L., & Moran, G. (1993). A meta-analysis of the association between authoritarianism and jurors' perceptions of defendant culpability. *Journal of Applied Psychology, 78,* 34–42.

National Commission on the Causes and Prevention of Violence. (1969). *Commission statement on violence in television entertainment programs.*

Nemeth, C. (1986). Differential contributions of majority and minority influence. *Psychological Review, 93,* 23–32.

Nemeth, C., Endicott, J., & Wachtler, J. (1977). From the '50's to the '70's: Women in jury deliberations. *Sociometry, 39,* 292–304.

Nemeth, C., Swedlund, M., & Kanki, B. (1974). Patterning of the minority's responses and their influence on the majority. *European Journal of Social Psychology, 4,* 53–64.

Nemeth, C., & Wachtler, J. (1973). Consistency and modification of judgment. *Journal of Experimental Social Psychology, 9,* 65–79.

Nemeth, C., & Wachtler, J. (1974). Creating the perceptions of consistency and confidence: A necessary condition for minority influence. *Sociometry, 37,* 529–540.

Nemeth, C. J. (1992). Minority dissent as a stimulant to group performance. In S. Worchel, W. Wood, & J. A. Simpson (Eds.), *Group process and productivity.* Newbury Park, CA: Sage.

Newberger, E., & Bourne, R. (1985). *Unhappy families: Clinical and research perspectives on family violence.* Littleton, MA: PSG.

Newcomb, M. D. (1990). Social support and personal characteristics: A developmental and interactional perspective. *Journal of Social and Clinical Psychology, 9,* 54–68.

Newcomb, T. M. (1929). Consistency of certain extrovert-introvert behavior patterns in 51 problem boys. New York: Columbia University Teachers College, Bureau of Publication.

Newcomb, T. M. (1943). *Personality and social change.* New York: Dryden.

Newcomb, T. M. (1951). Social psychological theory. In J. H. Roher & M. Sherif (Eds.), *Social psychology at the crossroads.* New York: Harper.

Newcomb, T. M. (1953). An approach to the study of communicative acts. *Psychological Review, 60,* 393–404.

Newcomb, T. M. (1961). *The acquaintance process.* New York: Holt, Rinehart and Winston.

Newcomb, T. M. (1963). Persistence and regression of changed attitudes: A long-range study. *Journal of Social Issues, 19,* 3–14.

Newman, O. (1972). *Defensible space: Crime prevention through urban design.* New York: Macmillan.

Newman, O. (1975). Reactions to the defensible space study and some further findings. *International Journal of Mental Health, 4,* 48–70.

Newman, O., & Franck, K. A. (1982). The effects of building size on personal crime and fear of crime. *Population and Environment, 5,* 203–220.

Newsweek. (1981, August 10). A fairy tale come true, pp. 40–46.

Newsweek. (1984, February 27). Suing over a scarlet letter, p. 46.

Newsweek. (1987, June 13). The divorce game: Slippery numbers, p. 55.

Newsweek. (1987, August 10). Gunplay on the freeway, p. 18.

Newsweek. (1987, November 23). How to protect abused children, pp. 70–71.

Newsweek. (1991, November 4). David Duke: A nightmare scenario, p. 33.

Newsweek. (1991, November 18). The real David Duke: Nazi, Klansman, governor?, pp. 24–27.

Newsweek. (1992, January 13). Breaking the divorce cycle, pp. 48–53.

Newsweek. (1992, April 27). Europe's new right, pp. 32–34.

Newsweek. (1992, June 1). Earth at the summit, pp. 20–22.

Newsweek. (1992, November 2). Talking with Madonna: The unbridled truth, pp. 102–103.

Newsweek. (1992, December 21). Throne out, pp. 68–73.

Newton, D. (1974). Dispositional inferences from effects of actions: Effects chosen and effects forgone. *Journal of Experimental Social Psychology, 10,* 489–496.

New York Times (1991, July 21) Should women be sent into combat? p. E3.

New York Times (1991, November 9) Smoking rate declines to 28%, survey says, p. 10.

New York Times (1992, May 1) Switching case to white suburb may have decided outcome, p. A10.

New York Times (1992, October 18). Women's progress stalled? It just isn't so. Business Section.

Nieva, V. F., & Guteck, B. A. (1981). Sex effects in evaluation. *Academy of Management Review, 5,* 267–276.

Nisbett, R. E., Caputo, C., Legant, P., & Marecek, J. (1973). Behavior as seen by the actor and as seen by the observer. *Journal of Personality and Social Psychology, 27,* 154–164.

Nisbett, R. E., & Ross, L. (1980). *Human inference: Strategies and shortcomings of social judgment.* Englewood Cliffs, NJ: Prentice-Hall.

Nisbett, R. E., & Schachter, S. (1966). Cognitive manipulation of pain. *Journal of Experimental Social Psychology, 2,* 227–236.

Nisbett, R. E., Zuckier, H., & Lemley, R. E. (1981). The dilution effect: Nondiagnostic information weakens the implications of diagnostic information. *Cognitive Psychology, 13,* 248–277.

Nissen, H. W., & Crawford, M. P. (1936). A preliminary study of food-sharing behavior in young chimpanzees. *Journal of Comparative Psychology, 22,* 383–419.

Norman, W. T. (1963). Toward an adequate taxonomy of personality attributes: Replicated factor structure in peer nomination personality ratings. *Journal of Abnormal and Social Psychology, 66,* 574–583.

Norris-Baker, C., & Scheidt, R. J. (1990). Place attachment among older residents of a "ghost town": A transactional approach. In R. I. Selby, K. H. Anthony, J. Choi, & B. Orland (Eds.), *Coming of age.* Oklahoma City: Environmental Design Research Assocation.

Nunes, E. V., Frank, K. A., & Kornfeld, D. S. (1987). Psychological treatment for the Type A behavior pattern and for coronary heart disease: A meta-analysis of the literature. *Psychosomatic Medicine, 48,* 159–173.

Oakes, P. J., & Turner, J. C. (1980). Social categorization and intergroup behavior: Does minimal intergroup discrimination make social identity more positive? *European Journal of Social Psychology, 10,* 295–301.

O'Grady, K. E. (1982). Sex, physical attractiveness, and perceived risk for mental illness. *Journal of Personality and Social Psychology, 43,* 1064–1071.

Ohbuchi, K., & Kambara, T. (1985). Attacker's intent and awareness of outcome, im-pression management, and retaliation. *Journal of Experimental Social Psychology, 21,* 321–330.

O'Heron, C. A., & Orlofsky, J. L. (1990). Stereotypic and nonstereotypic sex role trait and behavior orientations, gender identity and psychological adjustment. *Journal of Personality and Social Psychology, 58,* 134–143.

Okun, L. (1986). *Women abuse.* Albany: State University of New York Press.

Olian, J. D. Schwab, D., & Haberfeld, Y. (1988). The impact of applicant gender compared to qualifications on hiring recommendations: A meta-analysis of experimental studies. *Organizational Behavior and Human Decision Processes, 41,* 180–195.

Oliner, S. P., & Oliner, J. M. (1988). *The altruistic personality: Rescuers of Jews in Nazi Europe.* New York: Free Press.

Olson, J. M. (1988). Misattribution, preparatory information, and speech anxiety. *Journal of Personality and Social Psychology, 54,* 758–767.

Olson, J. M., & Zanna, M. P. (1993). Attitudes and attitude change. In L. W. Porter & M. R. Rosenzweiz (Eds.), *Annual Review of Psychology, 44,* 117–154.

Olweus, D. (1979). Stability of aggressive reaction patterns in males: A review. *Psychological Bulletin, 86,* 852–876.

Olweus, D. (1980). Familial and temperamental determinants of aggressive behavior in adolescent boys: A causal analysis. *Developmental Psychology, 16,* 644–666.

Olweus, D. (1986). Aggression and hormones: Behavioral relationships with testosterone and adrenaline. In D. Olweus, J. Block, & M. Radke-Yarrow (Eds.), *Development of antisocial and prosocial behaviors: Research, theories, and issues.* Orlando, FL: Academic Press.

Olweus, D. (1991). Bully/victim problems among schoolchildren: Basic facts and effects of a school-based intervention program. In D. J. Pepler & K. H. Rubin (Eds.), *The development and treatment of childhood aggression.* Hillsdale, NJ: Erlbaum.

Orne, M. (1962). On the social psychology of the psychology experiment. *American Psychologist, 17,* 776–783.

Osborn, A. F. (1957). *Applied imagination.* New York: Scribner.

Osborne, R. T., Noble, C. E., & Wey, N. J. (Eds.). (1978). *Human variation: Biopsychology of age, race, and sex.* New York: Academic Press.

Osgood, C. E., Luria, Z., Jeans, R. E., & Smith, S. W. (1976). The three faces of

Evelyn: A case report. *Journal of Abnormal Psychology, 85,* 249–270.

Osgood, C. E., Suci, G., & Tannenbaum, P. H. (1957). *The measurement of meaning.* Urbana: University of Illinois Press.

Osgood, C. E., & Tannenbaum, P. H. (1955). The principle of congruity in the prediction of attitude change. *Psychological Review, 62,* 42–55.

Oskamp, S. (1977). *Attitudes and opinions.* Englewood Cliffs, NJ: Prentice-Hall.

Oskamp, S. (Ed.). (1988). *Television as a social issue. Applied social psychology annual* (Vol. 8). Newbury Park, CA: Sage.

Oskamp, S., Harrington, M. J., Edwards, T. C. Sherwood, D. L., Okuda, S. M., & Swanson, D. C. (1991). Factors influencing household recycling behavior. *Environment and Behavior, 23,* 494–519.

Osmond, H. (1959). The relationship between architect and psychiatrist. In C. Goshen (Ed.), *Psychiatric architecture.* Washington, DC: American Psychiatric Association.

Ostrom, T. M. (1989). Interdependence of attitude theory and measurement. In A. R. Pratkanis & A. G. Greenwald (Eds.), *Attitude structure and function.* Hillsdale, NJ: Erlbaum.

Padawer-Singer, A., & Barton, A. H. (1975). The impact of pretrial publicity on jurors' verdicts. In R. J. Simon (Ed.), *The jury system in America: A critical overview.* Beverly Hills, CA: Sage.

Pagan, G., & Aiello, J. R. (1982). Development of personal space among Puerto Ricans. *Journal of Nonverbal Behavior, 7* (2), 59–68.

Page, M. M. (1969). Social psychology of a classical conditioning of attitudes experiment. *Journal of Personality and Social Psychology, 11,* 177–186.

Page, M. M. (1971). Postexperimental assessment of awareness in attitude conditioning. *Educational and Psychological Measurement, 31,* 891–906.

Page, M. M. (1974). Demand characteristics and the classical conditioning of attitudes experiment. *Journal of Personality and Social Psychology, 30,* 468–476.

Page, M., & Scheidt, R. (1971). The elusive weapons effect: Demand awareness evaluation and slightly sophisticated subjects. *Journal of Personality and Social Psychology, 20,* 304–318.

Paicheler, G. (1976). Norms and attitude change: I. Polarization and styles of behavior. *European Journal of Social Psychology, 6,* 405–427.

Paicheler, G. (1977). Norms and attitude change: II. The phenomenon of bipolarization. *European Journal of Social Psychology, 7,* 5–14.

Pallak, M., & Pittman, T. S. (1972). General motivational effects of dissonance arousal. *Journal of Personality and Social Psychology, 21,* 349–358.

Pallak, M. S., Cook, D. A. & Sullivan, J. J. (1980). Commitment and energy conservation. In L. Bickman (Ed.), *Applied social psychology annual* (Vol. 1). Beverly Hills, CA: Sage.

Pallak, S. R., Murroni, E., & Koch, J. (1983). Communicator attractiveness and expertise, emotional versus rational appeals, and persuasion. *Social Cognition, 2,* 122–141.

Park, B. (1986). A method for studying the development of impressions of real people. *Journal of Personality and Social Psychology, 51,* 907–917.

Park, B., & Judd, C. M. (1989). Agreement in initial impressions: Differences due to perceivers, trait dimensions, and target behaviors. *Journal of Personality and Social Psychology, 56,* 493–505.

Park, B., & Rothbart, M. (1982). Perception of out-group homogeneity and levels of social categorization: Memory for the subordinate attributes of in-group and out-group members. *Journal of Personality and Social Psychology, 42,* 1051–1068.

Park, B., Ryan, C. S., & Judd, C. M. (1992). Role of meaningful subgroups in explaining differences in perceived variability for in-group and out-groups. *Journal of Personality and Social Psychology, 63,* 553–567.

Parke, R. D., Berkowitz, L., Leyens, J. P., West, S. G., & Sebastian, J. (1977). Some effects of violent and nonviolent movies on the behavior of juvenile delinquents. In L. Berkowitz (Ed.), *Advances in experimental social psychology* (Vol. 10). New York: Academic Press.

Parkinson, M. G. (1979). Language behavior and courtroom success. Paper presented at British Psychological Society meeting, University of Bristol, England.

Partridge, C., & Johnston, M. (1989). Perceived control of recovery from physical disability: Measurement and prediction. *British Journal of Clinical Psychology, 28,* 53–59.

Passini, F. T., & Norman, W. T. (1966). A universal conception of personality structure? *Journal of Personality and Social Psychology, 4,* 44–49.

Patterson, A. H. (1974). Hostility catharsis: A naturalistic quasi-experiment. Paper presented at the annual meeting of the American Psychological Association.

Patterson, G. R. (1983). *Coercive family process: A social learning approach* (Vol. 3). Eugene, OR: Castalia.

Patterson, G. R., Littman, R. A., & Bricker,

W. (1967). Assertive behavior in children: A step toward a theory of aggression. *Monographs for the Society for Research in Child Development, 32(5)* (Serial No. 113).

Patterson, M. L. (1975). Personal space: Time to burst the bubble? *Man–Environment Systems, 5(2),* 67.

Patterson, M. L. (1984). Nonverbal exchange: Past, present, and future. *Journal of Nonverbal Behavior, 8(4),* 350–359.

Patterson, M. L., Mullens, S., & Romano, J. (1971). Compensatory reactions to spatial intrusion. *Sociometry, 34(1),* 114–121.

Paulus, P. B. (1980). Crowding. In P. B. Paulus (Ed.), *Psychology of group influence.* Hillsdale, NJ: Erlbaum.

Paulus, P. B. (1988). *Prison crowding: A psychological perspective.* New York: Springer-Verlag.

Paulus, P. B., Annis, A. B., Seta, J. J. Schkade, J. K., & Matthews, R. W. (1976). Crowding does affect task performance. *Journal of Personality and Social Psychology, 34,* 248–253.

Paulus, P. B., Dzindolet, M. T., Poletes, G., & Camacho, L. M. (1993). Perception of performance in group brainstorming: The illusion of group productivity. *Personality and Social Psychology Bulletin, 19,* 78–89.

Paulus, P. B., McCain, G., & Cox, V. C. (1978). Death rates, psychiatric commitment, blood pressure, and perceived crowding as a function of institutional crowding. *Environment Psychology and Nonverbal Behavior, 3,* 107–116.

Paulus, P. B., McCain, G., & Cox, V. (1981). Prison standards: Some pertinent data on crowding. *Federal Probation, 15,* 48–54.

Paunonen, S. V. (1989). Consensus in personality judgments: Moderating effects of target–rater acquaintanceship and behavior observability. *Journal of Personality and Social Psychology, 56,* 823–833.

Paunonen, S. V., Jackson, D. N., Trzebinski, J., & Forsterling, F. (1992). Personality structure across cultures: A multimethod evaluation. *Journal of Personality and Social Psychology, 62,* 447–456.

Payne, T. J., Connor, J. M., & Colletti, G. (1987). Gender-based schematic processing: An empirical investigation and reevaluation. *Journal of Personality and Social Psychology, 52,* 937–945.

Peabody, D. (1968). Group judgments in the Philippines: Evaluative and descriptive aspects. *Journal of Personality and Social Psychology, 12,* 296–300.

Pederson, F. A. (1991). Secular trends in human sex ratios: Their influence on individual and family behavior. *Human Nature, 2,* 271–291.

Pence, E. (1989). Batterer programs: Shifting from community collusion to community confrontation. In P. L. Caesar & L. K. Hamberger (Eds.), *Treating men who batter: Theory, practice, and programs.* New York: Springer.

Pennebacker, J. W. (1984). Accuracy of symptom perception. In A. Baum, S. E. Taylor, and J. E. Singer (Eds.), *Handbook of psychology and health* (Vol. IV): *Social psychological aspects of health.* Hillsdale, NJ: Erlbaum.

Penner, L. A., Dertke, M. C., & Achenbach, C. J. (1973). The "flash" system: A field study of altruism. *Journal of Applied Social Psychology, 3,* 362–370.

Pennington, N., & Hastie, R. (1992). Explaining the evidence: Tests of the story model for juror decision making. *Journal of Personality and Social Psychology, 62,* 189–206.

Pepinsky, P. N., Hemphill, J. K., & Shevitz, R. N. (1958). Attempts to lead, group productivity, and morale under conditions of acceptance and rejection. *Journal of Abnormal and Social Psychology, 57,* 47–54.

Pepler, D. J., & Rubin, K. H. (Eds.). (1991). *The development and treatment of childhood aggression.* Hillsdale, NJ: Erlbaum.

Percival, L., & Quinkert, K. (1987). Anthropometric factors. In M. A. Baker (Ed.), *Sex differences in human performance.* Chichester, England: Wiley.

Perdue, C. W., & Gurtman, M. B. (1990). Evidence for the automaticity of ageism. *Journal of Experimental Social Psychology, 26,* 199–216.

Perkins, D. D., Wandersman, A., Rich, R. C., & Taylor, R. B. (1993). The physical environment of street crime: Defensible space, territoriality and incivilities. *Journal of Environmental Psychology, 13,* 29–49.

Pessin, J., & Husband, R. W. (1933). Effects of social stimulation on human maze learning. *Journal of Abnormal and Social Psychology, 28,* 148–154.

Peters, D. P. (1988). Eyewitness memory and arousal in a natural setting. In M. M. Gruneberg, P. E. Morris, & R. N. Sykes (Eds.), *Practical aspects of memory: Current research and issues:* (Vol. 1) *Memory in everyday life.* Chichester, England: Wiley.

Peters, L. H., Hartke, D. D., & Pohlmann, J. R. (1985). Fiedler's contingency theory of leadership: An application of the meta-analysis procedures of Schmidt and Hunter. *Psychological Bulletin, 97,* 274–285.

Peterson, C., & Bossio, L. M. (1991). *Health and optimism.* New York: Free Press.

Peterson, C., Seligman, M. E., & Vaillant, G. E. (1988). Pessimistic explanatory style is a risk factor for physical illness: A thirty-five year longitudinal study. *Journal of Personality and Social Psychology, 55,* 23–27.

Peterson, D. R. (1968). *The clinical study of social behavior.* New York: Appleton-Century-Crofts.

Pettigrew, T. (1961). Social psychology and desegregation research. *American Psychologist, 16,* 105–112.

Pettigrew, T. F. (1958). Personality and socio-cultural factors in intergroup attitudes: A cross-national comparison. *Journal of Conflict Resolution, 2,* 29–42.

Pettigrew, T. F. (1979). The ultimate attribution error: Extending Allport's cognitive analysis of prejudice. *Personality and Social Psychology Bulletin, 5,* 461–476.

Pettigrew, T. F. (1980). Prejudice. In *Harvard encyclopedia of American ethnic groups.* Cambridge, MA: Harvard University Press.

Petty, R. E., & Cacioppo, J. T. (1977). Effects of forewarning of persuasive intent and involvement on cognitive responses and persuasion. *Personality and Social Psychology Bulletin, 5,* 173–176.

Petty, R. E., & Cacioppo, J. T. (1981). *Attitudes and persuasion: Classic and contemporary approaches.* Dubuque, IA: Brown.

Petty, R. E., & Cacioppo, J. T. (1984). The effects of involvement on responses to argument quantity and quality: Central and peripheral routes to persuasion. *Journal of Personality and Social Psychology, 46,* 69–81.

Petty, R. E., & Cacioppo, J. T. (1986). *Communication and persuasion: Central and peripheral routes to attitude change.* New York: Springer-Verlag.

Petty, R. E., Cacioppo, J. T., & Heesacker, M. (1981). The use of rhetorical questions in persuasion: A cognitive response analysis. *Journal of Personality and Social Psychology, 40,* 432–440.

Petty, R. E., Cacioppo, J. T., & Schumann, D. (1983). Central and peripheral routes to advertising effectiveness: The moderating role of involvement. *Journal of Consumer Research, 10,* 134–148.

Petty, R. E., & Krosnick, J. A. (1992). *Attitude strength: Antecedents and consequences.* Hillsdale, NJ: Erlbaum.

Pfau, M., & Burgoon, M. (1988). Inoculation in political campaign communication. *Human Communication Research, 15,* 91–111.

Phares, E. J. (1976). *Locus of control in personality.* Morristown, NJ: General Learning Press.

Pheterson, G. I., Kiesler, S. B. & Goldberg, P. A. (1971). Evaluation of the performances of women as a function of their sex, achievement, and personal history. *Journal of Personality and Social Psychology, 19,* 114–118.

Phillips, D. P. (1979). Suicide, motor vehicle fatalities, and the mass media: Evidence toward a theory of suggestion. *American Journal of Sociology, 84,* 1150–1174.

Phillips, D. P. (1983). The impact of mass media violence on U. S. homicides. *American Sociological Review, 48,* 560–568.

Phillips, D., & Carstensen, L. (1990). The effect of suicide stories on various demographic groups 1968–1985. In R. Surette (Ed.), *The media and criminal justice policy: Recent research and social effects.* Springfield, IL: Charles C. Thomas.

Piaget, J. (1966). *Judgment and reasoning in the child.* Totowa, NJ: Littlefield, Adams. (Originally published 1924.)

Piliavin, J. A., Dovidio, J. F., Gaertner, S. L., & Clark, R. D. (1981). *Emergency intervention.* New York: Academic Press.

Piliavin, J. A., & Piliavin, I. M. (1972). The effect of blood on reactions to a victim. *Journal of Personality and Social Psychology, 23,* 253–261.

Piliavin, J. A., Piliavin, I. M., & Trudell, B. (1974). *Incidental arousal, helping, and diffusion of responsibility.* Unpublished study, University of Wisconsin, Madison.

Piliavin, I. M., Rodin, J., & Piliavin, J. A. (1969). Good Samaritanism: An underground phenomenon? *Journal of Personality and Social Psychology, 13,* 289–299.

Pitcher, E. G., & Schultz, L. H. (1983). *Boys and girls at play: The development of sex roles.* New York: Praeger.

Platz, S. J., & Hosch, H. M. (1988). Cross-racial/ethnic eyewitness identification: A field study. *Journal of Applied Social Psychology, 18,* 972–984.

Pleck, J. (1979). Men's family work: Three perspectives and some new data. *Family Coordinator, 28,* 481–488.

Pliner, P., Chaiken, S., & Flett, G. L. (1990). Gender differences in concern with body weight and physical appearance over the life span. *Personality and Social Psychology Bulletin, 16,* 263–273.

Plomin, R., & Daniels, D. (1986). Genetics and shyness. In W. H. Jones, J. M. Cheek, & S. R. Briggs (Eds.), *Shyness: Perspectives on research and treatment.* New York: Plenum.

Poppleton, P. K., & Pilkington, G. W. (1964). A comparison of four methods of scoring an attitude scale in relation to its reliability and validity. *British Journal of Social and Clinical Psychology, 3,* 36–39.

Porier, G. W., & Lott, A. J. (1967). Galvanic skin responses and prejudice. *Journal of*

Personality and Social Psychology, 5, 253–259.

Porter, A. M. W. (1969). Drug defaulting in a general practice. *British Medical Journal, 1,* 218–222.

Powell, S. R., & Juhnke, R. G. (1983). Statistical models of implicit personality theory: A comparison. *Journal of Personality and Social Psychology, 44,* 911–922.

Pratkanis, A. R., Breckler, S. J., & Greenwald, A. G. (Eds.). (1989). *Attitude structure and function.* Hillsdale, NJ: Erlbaum.

Pratkanis, A. R., & Greenwald, A. G. (1989). A sociocognitive model of attitude structure and function. In L. Berkowitz (Ed.), *Advances in experimental social psychology* (Vol. 22). San Diego, CA: Academic Press.

Pratkanis, A. R., Greenwald, A. G., Leippe, M. R., & Baumgardner, M. H. (1988). In search of reliable persuasion effects: III. The sleeper effect is dead. Long live the sleeper effect. *Journal of Personality and Social Psychology, 54,* 203–218.

Pratto, F., & John, O. (1991). Automatic vigilance: The attention-grabbing power of negative social information. *Journal of Personality and Social Psychology, 61,* 380–391.

Prentice-Dunn, S., & Rogers, R. W. (1980). Effects of deindividuating situation cues and aggressive models on subjective deindividuation and aggression. *Journal of Personality and Social Psychology, 39,* 104–113.

Priest, R. F., & Sawyer, J. (1967). Proximity and peership: Bases of balance in interpersonal attraction. *American Journal of Sociology, 72,* 633–649.

Pryor, J. B., Gibbons, F. X., Wicklund, R. A., Fazio, R. A., & Hood, R. (1977). Self-focused attention and self-report validity. *Journal of Personality, 45,* 513–527.

Pyszczynski, T. (1982). Cognitive strategies for coping with uncertain outcomes. *Journal of Research in Personality, 16,* 386–399.

Pyszczynski, T., & Greenberg, J. (1985). Depression and preference for self-focusing stimuli following success and failure. *Journal of Personality and Social Psychology, 49,* 1066–1075.

Pyszczynski, T., & Greenberg, J. (1987). Self-regulatory perseveration and the depressive self-focusing style: A self-awareness theory of reactive depression. *Psychological Bulletin, 102,* 122–138.

Pyszczynski, T., Hamilton, J. C., Herring, F. H., & Greenberg, J. (1989). Depression, self-focused attention, and negative memory bias. *Journal of Personality and Social Psychology, 57,* 351–357.

Quanty, M. B. (1976). Aggression catharsis: Experimental investigations and implications. In R. G. Geen & E. C. O'Neal (Eds.), *Perspectives on aggression.* New York: Academic Press.

Quinn, R. P. (1978). *Physical deviance and occupational mistreatment: The short, the fat, and the ugly.* Master's thesis, University of Michigan Survey Research Center, Ann Arbor.

Rabkin, J. G., & Struening, E. L. (1976). Life events, stress, and illness. *Science, 194,* 1013–1020.

Radecki, T. (1990). *National Coalition against Television Violence Newsletter, 11.*

Ragland, D. R., & Brand, R. J. (1988). Type A behavior and mortality from coronary heart disease. *New England Journal of Medicine, 318,* 65–69.

Rahe, R. H. (1984). Developments in life change measurement: Subjective life change unit scaling. In B. S. Dohrenwend & B. P. Dohrenwend (Eds.), *Stressful life events and their contexts.* New Brunswick, NJ: Rutgers University Press.

Rahe, R. H., & Lind, E. (1971). Psychosocial factors and sudden cardiac death: A pilot study. *Journal of Psychosomatic Research, 15,* 19–24.

Ramirez, J., Bryant, J., & Zillman, D. (1983). Effects of erotica on retaliatory behavior as a function of level of prior provocation. *Journal of Personality and Social Psychology, 43,* 971–978.

Ramsoy, N. R. (1966). Assortative mating and the structure of cities. *American Journal of Sociology, 31,* 773–786.

Rapoport, A. (1960). *Fights, games, and debates.* Ann Arbor: University of Michigan Press.

Rapaport, K., & Burkhart, B. R. (1984). Personality and attitudinal characteristics of sexually coercive college males. *Journal of Abnormal Psychology, 93,* 216–221.

Rasinski, K. A., Crocker, J., & Hastie, R. (1985). Antoher look at sex stereotypes and social judgments. An analysis of the social perceiver's use of subjective probabilities. *Journal of Personality and Social Psychology, 49,* 317–326.

Razran, G. H. S. (1938). Conditioning away social bias by the luncheon technique. *Psychological Bulletin, 35,* 693.

Razran, G. H. S. (1940). Conditioned response changes in rating and appraising sociopolitical slogans. *Psychological Bulletin, 37,* 481.

Regan, D. R., Williams, M., & Sparling, S. (1972). Voluntary expiation of guilt: A field experiment. *Journal of Personality and Social Psychology, 24,* 42–45.

Regan, D. T. (1971). Effects of a favor and

liking on compliance. *Journal of Experimental Social Psychology, 7,* 627–639.

Reid, D., & Ware, E. E. (1974). Multidimensionality of internal versus external control: Addition of a third dimension and non-distinction of self versus others. *Canadian Journal of Behavioral Science, 6,* 131–142.

Reid, D. W., & Ziegler, M. (1981). The desired control measure and adjustment among the elderly. In H. M. Lefcourt (Ed.), *Research with the locus of control* (Vol. 1). New York: Academic Press.

Reinisch, J. M., Rosenblum, L. A., & Sanders, S. A. (Eds.). (1987). *Masculinity/femininity: Basic perspectives.* New York: Oxford University Press.

Reisenzein, R. (1983). The Schachter theory of emotion: Two decades later. *Psychological Bulletin, 94,* 239–264.

Reiss, A. J. Jr. & Roth, J. A. (Eds.). (1993). *Understanding and preventing violence.* Washington, DC: National Academy Press.

Report of the Presidential Commission on the space shuttle Challenger accident. (1986). Washington, DC.

Report of the Commission on Obscenity and Pornography. (1970). Washington, DC: U.S. Government Printing Office.

Reychler, L. (1979). The effectiveness of a pacifist strategy in conflict resolution. *Journal of Conflict Resolution, 23,* 228–260.

Rheingold, H., & Cook, K. (1975). The contents of boys' and girls' rooms as an index of parents' behavior. *Child Development, 4,* 459–463.

Rhodes, N., & Wood, W. (1992). Self-esteem and intelligence affect influenceability: The mediating role of message reception. *Psychological Bulletin, 111,* 156–171.

Rhodewalt, F., & Smith, T. W. (1991). Current issues in type A behavior, coronary proneness, and coronary heart disease. In C. R. Snyder & D. R. Forsyth (Eds.), *Handbook of social and clinical psychology.* New York: Pergamon.

Rhodewalt, F., & Smith, T. W. (1991). Type A behavior, coronary proneness, and coronary heart disease: Current issues for research and intervention. In C. R. Snyder & D. F. Forsyth (Eds.), *Handbook of social and clinical psychology: The health perspective.* New York: Pergamon.

Rhodewalt, F., & Zone, J. B. (1989). Appraisal of life change, depression, and illness in hardy and nonhardy women. *Journal of Personality and Social Psychology, 56,* 81–88.

Richards, M. H., Gitelson, I. B., Petersen, A. C., & Hurtig, A. L. (1990). Adolescent personality in girls and boys: The role of mothers and fathers. *Psychology of Women Quarterly, 15,* 65–81.

Ridley, M., & Dawkins, R. (1981). The natural selection of altruism. In J. P. Rushton & R. M. Sorrentino (Eds.), *Altruism and helping behavior: Social, personality, and developmental perspectives*. Hillsdale, NJ: Erlbaum.

Riggio, R. E., Lippa, R., & Salinas, C. (1990). The display of personality in expressive movement. *Journal of Research in Personality, 24*, 16–31.

Ringelmann, M. (1913). Research on animate sources of power: The world of man. *Annales de l'institut national agronomique*, 2e série—tome XII, 1–40.

Robinson, D. (1973, July 15). Ten noted doctors answer ten tough questions. *Parade*.

Rodin J. (1976). Density, perceived choice, and response to controllable and uncontrollable outcomes. *Journal of Experimental Social Psychology, 12*, 564–578.

Rodin, J. (1985). The application of social psychology. In G. Lindzey and E. Aronson (Eds.), *Handbook of social psychology* (3rd ed., Vol. 2). New York: Random House.

Rodin, J., & Baum, A. (1978). Crowding and helplessness: Potential consequences of density and loss of control. In A. Baum & Y. M. Epstein (Eds.), *Human response to crowding*. Hillsdale, NJ: Erlbaum.

Rodin, J., & Langer, E. (1977). Long-term effect of a control-relevant intervention. *Journal of Personality and Social Psychology, 35*, 897–902.

Rodin, J., & Salovey, P. (1989). Health psychology. In M. R. Rosenzweig & L. W. Porter (Eds.), *Annual Review of Psychology, 40*, 533–579.

Rodin, M., Price, J., Sanchez, F., & McElligot, S. (1989). Derogation, exclusion, and unfair treatment of persons with social flaws: Controllability of stigma and the attribution of prejudice. *Personality and Social Psychology Bulletin, 15*, 439–451.

Rofe, Y. (1984). Stress and affiliation: Activity theory. *Psychological Review, 91*, 235–250.

Rogers, R. W. (1975). A protection motivation theory of fear appeals and attitude change. *Journal of Psychology, 91*, 93–114.

Rogers, R. W. (1983). Cognitive and physiological processes in fear appeals and attitude change: A revised theory of protection motivation. In J. Cacioppo & R. Petty (Eds.), *Social psychophysiology*. New York: Guilford.

Rogers, R. W. (1984). Changing health-related attitudes and behavior: The role of preventive health psychology. In J. H. Harvey, J. E. Maddux, R. P. McGlynne, & C. D. Stottenberg (Eds.), *Social perception in clinical and counseling psychology* (Vol. 2). Lubbock: Texas Tech University Press.

Rogers, R. W., & Mewborn, R. (1976). Fear appeals and attitude change: Effects of a threat's noxiousness, probability of occurrence, and the efficiency of coping response. *Journal of Personality and Social Psychology, 34*, 54–61.

Rogers, T. B., Kuiper, N. A., & Kirker, W. S. (1977). Self-reference and the encoding of personal information. *Journal of Personality and Social Psychology, 35*, 677–688.

Rogot, E. (1974). Smoking and mortality among U.S. veterans. *Journal of Chronic Diseases, 27*, 189–203.

Rohe, W. M., & Burby, R. J. (1988). Fear of crime in public housing. *Environment and Behavior, 20*, 700–720.

Rohe, W., & Patterson, A. H. (1974). *The effects of varied levels of resources and density on behavior in a day care center*. Paper presented by the Environmental Design Research Association, Milwaukee, WI.

Rohrer, J. H., Baron, S. H., Hoffman, E. L., & Swander, D. V. (1954). The stability of autokinetic judgments. *Journal of Abnormal and Social Psychology, 49*, 595–597.

Rokeach, M. (1956). Political and religious dogmatism: An alternative to the authoritarian personality. *Psychological Monographs, 70(18)* (Whole No. 425).

Rokeach, M. (1960). *The open and closed mind*. New York: Basic Books.

Rokeach, M. (1968). *Beliefs, attitudes, and values: A theory of organization and change*. San Francisco: Jossey-Bass.

Ronis, D. L., Yates, J. F., & Kirscht, J. P. (1989). Attitudes, decisions, and habits as determinants of repeated behavior. In A. R. Pratkanis & A. G. Greenwald (Eds.), *Attitude structure and function*. Hillsdale, NJ: Erlbaum.

Rook, K. S. (1990). Parallels in the study of social support and social strain. *Journal of Social and Clinical Psychology, 9*, 118–132.

Roper Organization. (1974). *The Virginia Slims opinion poll* (Vol. 3). New York: Author.

Rosegrant, T. J., & McCroskey, J. C. (1975). The effects of race and sex on proxemic behavior in an interview setting. *Southern Speech Communication Journal, 40* (Summer), 408–420.

Rosenbaum, M. E. (1980). Cooperation and competition. In P. B. Paulus (Ed.), *The psychology of group influence*. Hillsdale, NJ: Erlbaum.

Rosenbaum, M. E. (1986). The repulsion hypothesis: On the nondevelopment of relationships. *Journal of Personality and Social Psychology, 51*, 1156–1166.

Rosenberg, L. A. (1961). Group size, prior experience, and conformity. *Journal of Abnormal and Social Psychology, 63*, 436–437.

Rosenburg, S., Nelson, C., & Vivekanathan, P. S. (1968). A multidimensional approach to the structure of personality impressions. *Journal of Personality and Social Psychology, 9*, 283–294.

Rosenkrantz, P., Vogel, S., Bee, H., Broverman, I., & Broverman, D. M. (1968). Sex-role stereotypes and self-concepts in college students. *Journal of Consulting and Clinical Psychology, 32*, 286–295.

Rosenman, R. H., Brand, R. J., Sholtz, R. I., & Friedman, M. (1976). Multivariate prediction of coronary heart disease during 8.5 year follow-up in the Western Collaborative Group Study. *American Journal of Cardiology, 37*, 903–910.

Rosenstock, I. M. (1966). Why people use health services. *Millbank Memorial Fund Quarterly, 44*, 94–127.

Rosenstock, I. M. (1974). Historical origins of the health belief model. *Health Education Monographs, 2*, 328–335.

Rosenstock, I. M. (1988). Enhancing patient compliance with health recommendations. *Journal of Pediatric Health Care, 2*, 67–72.

Rosenthal, R. (1966). *Experimenter effects in behavioral research*. New York: Appleton-Century-Crofts.

Rosenthal, R. (1984). *Meta-analytic procedures for social research*. Beverly Hills, CA: Sage.

Rosenthal, R., & Fode, K. L. (1963). Three experiments in experimenter bias. *Psychological Reports, 12*, 491–511.

Rosenthal, R., Hall, J. A., DiMatteo, M. R., Rogers, P. L., & Archer, D. (1979). *Sensitivity to nonverbal communication: The PONS test*. Baltimore: Johns Hopkins University Press.

Rosenthal, R., & Jacobson, L. (1968). *Pygmalion in the classroom: Teacher expectation and pupils' intellectual development*. New York: Holt, Rinehart and Winston.

Rosenthal, R., & Rubin, D. D. (1982). Further meta-analytic procedures for assessing cognitive gender differences. *Journal of Educational Psychology, 74*, 708–712.

Ross, D. F., Dunning, D., Toglia, M. P., & Ceci, S. J. (1990). The child in the eyes of the jury: Assessing mock jurors' perceptions of the child witness. *Law and Human Behavior, 14*, 5–23.

Ross, L. (1977). The intuitive psychologist and his shortcomings: Distortions in the attribution process. In L. Berkowitz (Ed.), *Advances in experimental social psychology* (Vol. 10). New York: Academic Press.

Ross, L., Amabile, T. M., & Steinmetz, J. L. (1977). Social roles, social control, and biases in social perception processes. *Journal of Personality and Social Psychology, 35*, 485–494.

Ross, L., Greene, D., & House, P. (1977). The "false consensus effect": An egocentric bias in social perception and attribution processes. *Journal of Experimental Social Psychology, 13*, 279–301.

Ross, L., & Nisbett, R. E. (1992). *The person and the situation: Perspectives of social psychology.* New York: McGraw-Hill.

Ross, L. D., & Anderson, C. A. (1982). Shortcomings in the attributions process: On the origins and maintenance of erroneous social assessments. In D. Kahneman, P. Slovic, & A. Tversky (Eds.), *Judgment under uncertainty: Heuristics and biases.* New York: Cambridge University Press.

Ross, L. D., Lepper, M. R., & Hubbard, M. (1975). Perseverance in self-perception and social perception: Biased attributional processes in the debriefing paradigm. *Journal of Personality and Social Psychology, 32*, 880–892.

Ross, M., & Fletcher, G. J. O. (1985). Attribution and social perception. In G. Lindzey & E. Aronson (Eds.), *Handbook of social psychology* (Vol. 11). New York: Random House.

Rothaus, P., & Worchel, P. (1964). Ego-support communication, catharsis, and hostility. *Journal of Personality, 32*, 296–312.

Rothbart, M. (1981). Memory processes and social beliefs. In D. L. Hamilton (Ed.), *Cognitive processes in stereotyping and intergroup behavior.* Hillsdale, NJ: Erlbaum.

Rothbart, M., Fulero, S., Jensen, C., Howard, J., & Birrell, P. (1978). From individual to group impressions: Availability heuristics in stereotype formation. *Journal of Experimental Social Psychology, 14*, 237–255.

Rotter, J. B. (1966). Generalized expectancies for internal versus external control of reinforcement. *Psychological Monographs, 80* (Whole No. 609).

Rotter, J. B. (1975). Some problems and misconceptions related to the construct of internal versus external control of reinforcement. *Journal of Consulting and Clinical Psychology, 40*, 313–321.

Rotton, J., Barry, T., Frey, J., & Soler, E. (1978). Air pollution and interpersonal attraction. *Journal of Applied Social Psychology, 8*, 57–71.

Rotton, J., & Frey, J. (1985). Air pollution, weather, and violent crimes: Concomitant time-series analysis of archival data. *Journal of Personality and Social Psychology, 49*, 1207–1220.

Roy, M. (1977). *Battered women: A psycho-sociological study of domestic violence.* New York: Van Nostrand Reinhold.

Roy, P. (Ed.). (1982). *Structuring cooperative learning in the classroom: The 1982 handbook.* Minneapolis, MN: Interaction Books.

Ruback, R. B., & Carr, T. S. (1984). Crowding in a women's prison: Attitudinal and behavior effects. *Journal of Applied Social Psychology, 14*, 57–68.

Rubin, J. Z., & Brown, B. R. (1975). *The social psychology of bargaining and negotiation.* New York: Academic Press.

Rubin, J. Z., Provenzano, F. J., & Luria, Z. (1974). The eye of the beholder: Parents' views on the sex of newborns. *American Journal of Orthopsychiatry, 44*, 512–519.

Rubin, Z. (1970). Measurement of romantic love. *Journal of Personality and Social Psychology, 16*, 265–273.

Rubin, Z. (1973). *Liking and loving: An invitation to social psychology.* New York: Holt, Rinehart and Winston.

Rubin, Z. (1974). From liking to loving: Patterns of attraction in dating relationships. In T. L. Huston (Ed.), *Foundations of interpersonal attraction.* New York: Academic Press.

Rubin, Z., Peplau, L. A., & Hill, C. T. (1981). Loving and leaving: Sex differences in romantic attachments. *Sex roles, 7*, 821–835.

Ruble, D. N., & Feldman, N. S. (1976). Order of consensus, distinctiveness, and consistency information and causal attribution. *Journal of Personality and Social Psychology, 34*, 930–937.

Ruble, T. L. (1983). Sex stereotypes: Issues of change in the 1970s. *Sex Roles, 9*, 397–402.

Rusbult, C. E. (1980). Commitment and satisfaction in romantic associations: A test of the investment model. *Journal of Experimental Social Psychology, 16*, 172–186.

Rusbult, C. E. (1983). A longitudinal test of the investment model: The development (and deterioration) of satisfaction and commitment in heterosexual involvements. *Journal of Personality and Social Psychology, 45*, 101–117.

Rusbult, C. E., Johnson, D. J., & Morrow, G. D. (1986). Impact of couple patterns on problem solving in distress and nondistress in dating relationships. *Journal of Personality and Social Psychology, 50*, 744–753.

Rusbult, C. E., Verette, J., Whitney, G. A., Slovik, L. F., & Lipkus, I. (1991). Accommodation processes in close relationships: Theory and preliminary empirical evidence. *Journal of Personality and Social Psychology, 60*, 53–78.

Rusbult, C. E., & Zembrodt, I. M. (1983). Response to dissatisfaction in romantic involvements: A multidimensional scaling analysis. *Journal of Experimental Social Psychology, 19*, 274–293.

Rushton, J. P. (1980). *Altruism, socialization, and society.* Englewood Cliffs, NJ: Prentice-Hall.

Rushton, J. P. (1981a). Television as a socializer. In J. P. Rushton & R. M. Sorrentino (Eds.), *Altruism and helping behavior: Social, personality, and developmental perspectives.* Hillsdale, NJ: Erlbaum.

Rushton, J. P. (1981b). The altruistic personality. In J. P. Rushton & R. M. Sorrentino (Eds.), *Altruism and helping behavior: Social, personality, and developmental perspectives.* Hillsdale, NJ: Erlbaum.

Rushton, J. P. (1988). Epigenic rules in moral development: Distal-proximal approaches to altruism and aggression. *Aggressive Behavior, 14*, 35–50.

Rushton, J. P., Fulker, D. W., Neale, M. C., Nias, D. K. B., & Eysenck, H. J. (1986). Altruism and aggression: The heritability of individual differences. *Journal of Personality and Social Psychology, 50*, 1192–1198.

Rushton, J. P., & Owen, D. (1975). Immediate and delayed effects of TV modeling and preaching on children's generosity. *British Journal of Social and Clinical Psychology, 14*, 309–310.

Rushton, J. P., & Sorrentino, R. M. (1981). Altruism and helping behavior: An historical perspective. In J. P. Rushton & R. M. Sorrentino (Eds.), *Altruism and helping behavior: Social, personality, and developmental perspectives.* Hillsdale, NJ: Erlbaum.

Rutkowski, G. K., Gruder, C. L., & Romer, D. (1983). Group cohesiveness, social norms, and bystander intervention. *Journal of Personality and Social Psychology, 44*, 545–552.

Ryan, E. D. (1970). The cathartic effect of vigorous motor activity on aggressive behavior. *Research Quarterly, 41*, 542–551.

Sadalla, E. K., Kenrick, D. T., & Vershure, B. (1987). Dominance and heterosexual attraction. *Journal of Personality and Social Psychology, 52*, 730–738.

Sadker, M., & Sadker, D. (1982). *Sex equity handbook for schools.* New York: Longman.

Saegert, S. (1978). High-density environments: The personal and social consequences. In A. Baum, & Y. M. Epstein (Eds.), *Human responses to crowding.* Hillsdale, NJ: Erlbaum.

Saegert, S. (1982). Environment and children's mental health: Residential density and low income children. In A. Baum &

J. E. Singer (Eds.), *Handbook of psychology and health* (Vol. 2). Hillsdale, NJ: Erlbaum.

Saegert, S., Swap, W., & Zajonc, R. B. (1973). Exposure, context, and interpersonal attraction. *Journal of Personality and Social Psychology, 25,* 234–242.

Sagar, H. A., & Schofield, J. W. (1980). Racial and behavioral cues in black and white children's perceptions of ambiguously aggressive cues. *Journal of Personality and Social Psychology, 39,* 590–598.

Saks, M. J. (1977). *Jury verdicts.* Lexington, MA: Lexington Books.

Sakurai, M. M. (1975). Small group cohesiveness and detrimental conformity. *Sociometry, 38,* 340–357.

Salovey, P., Mayer, J. D., & Rosenhan, D. L. (1991). Mood and helping: Mood as a motivator of helping and as a regulator of mood. In M. S. Clark (Ed.), *Prosocial behavior.* Newbury Park, CA: Sage.

Samora, J., Saunders, L., & Larson, R. F. (1961). Medical vocabulary knowledge among hospital patients. *Journal of Health and Social Behavior, 2,* 83–89.

Sampson, E. E. (1977). Psychology and the American ideal. *Journal of Personality and Social Psychology, 35,* 767–782.

Samuelson, C. D., Messick, D. M., Rutte, C. G., & Wilke, H. (1984). Individual and structural solutions to resource dilemmas in two cultures. *Journal of Personality and Social Psychology, 47,* 94–104.

Sanders, G. S., & J. Suls (Eds.). (1982). *Social psychology of health and illness.* Hillsdale, NJ: Erlbaum.

Sanders, G. S., & Baron, R. S. (1977). Is social comparison irrelevant for producing choice shifts? *Journal of Experimental Social Psychology, 13,* 303–314.

Sandler, B. R., & Hall, R. M. (1982). *The classroom climate: A chilly one for women?* Association for American Colleges, Project on the Status and Education of Women. Washington, DC.

Sandler, B. R., & Hall, R. M. (1986). *The campus climate revisited: Chilly for women faculty, administrators, and graduate students.* Association for American Colleges, Project on the Status and Education of Women. Washington, DC.

Sanna, L. J. (1992). Self-efficacy theory: Implications for social facilitation and social loafing. *Journal of Personality and Social Psychology, 62,* 774–786.

Sanna, L. J., & Shotland, R. L. (1990). Valence of anticipated evaluation and social facilitation. *Journal of Experimental Social Psychology, 26,* 82–92.

Sarason, I. G., Johnson, J. H., & Siegel, J. M. (1978). Assessing the impact of life changes: Development of the life experiences survey. *Journal of Consulting and Clinical Psychology, 46,* 932–946.

Sarason, I. G., Levine, H. M., Basham, R. B., & Sarason, B. R. (1983). Assessing social support: The social support questionnaire. *Journal of Personality and Social Psychology, 14,* 127–139.

Sarason, I. G., & Sarason, B. R. (1984). Life changes, moderators of stress, and health. In A. Baum, S. E. Taylor, & J. E. Singer (Eds.), *Handbook of psychology and health* (Vol. 4): *Social psychological aspects of health.* Hillsdale, NJ: Erlbaum.

Sarnoff, I., & Zimbardo, P. G. (1961). Anxiety, fear and social affiliation. *Journal of Abnormal and Social Psychology, 62,* 356–363.

Schachter, S. (1951). Deviation, rejection, and communication. *Journal of Abnormal and Social Psychology, 46,* 190–207.

Schachter, S. (1959). *The psychology of affiliation.* Stanford, CA: Stanford University Press.

Schachter, S., & Singer, J. (1962). Cognitive, social and physiological determinants of emotional state. *Psychological Review, 69,* 379–399.

Schafer, R. B., & Keith, P. M. (1990). Matching by weight in married couples: A life cycle perspective. *Journal of Social Psychology, 130,* 657–664.

Scheier, M. F., Buss, A. H., & Buss, D. M. (1978). Self-consciousness, self-reports of aggressiveness, and aggression. *Journal of Research in Personality, 12,* 133–140.

Scheier, M. F., & Carver, C. (1977). Self-focused attention and the experience of emotion: Attraction, repulsion, elation and depression. *Journal of Personality and Social Psychology, 35,* 625–636.

Scheier, M. F., & Carver, C. S. (1985). Optimism, coping, and health: Assessment and implications of generalized outcome expectancies. *Health Psychology, 4,* 219–247.

Scheier, M. F., & Carver, C. S. (1992). Effects of optimism on psychological and physical well-being: Theoretical overview and empirical update. *Cognitive Therapy and Research, 16,* 201–228.

Scheier, M. F., & Carver, C. S. (1993). On the power of positive thinking: The benefits of being optimistic. *Current Directions in Psychological Science, 2,* 26–30.

Scheier, M. F., Carver, C. S., & Gibbons, F. X. (1979). Self-directed attention, awareness of bodily states, and suggestibility. *Journal of Personality and Social Psychology, 37,* 1576–1588.

Scheier, M. F., Carver, C. S., & Gibbons, F. X. (1981). Self-focused attention and reactions to fear. *Journal of Research in Personality, 15,* 1–15.

Scheier, M. F., Weintraub, J. K., & Carver, C. S. (1986). Coping with stress: Divergent strategies of optimists and pessimists. *Journal of Personality and Social Psychology, 51,* 1257–1264.

Schein, E. H. (1956). The Chinese indoctrination program for prisoners of war: A study of attempted "brainwashing." *Psychiatry, 19,* 149–172.

Scher, S. J., & Cooper, J. (1989). Motivational basis of dissonance: The singular route of behavior consequences. *Journal of Personality and Social Psychology, 56,* 899–906.

Schlenker, B. R. (1980). *Impression management: The self-concept, social identity, and interpersonal relations.* Monterey, CA: Brooks/Cole.

Schlenker, B. R. (1985). *The self and social life.* New York: McGraw-Hill.

Schmidt, D. E., & Keating, J. P. (1979). Human crowding and personal control: An integration of the research. *Psychological Bulletin, 86,* 680–700.

Schmied, L. A., & Lawler, K. A. (1986). Hardiness, type A behavior, and the stress–illness relation in working women. *Journal of Personality and Social Psychology, 51,* 1218–1223.

Schmitt, B. H., Gilovich, T., Goore, N., & Joseph, L. (1986). Mere exposure and social facilitation: One more time. *Journal of Experimental Social Psychology, 22,* 242–248.

Schmitt, J. P. (1983). Focus of attention in the treatment of depression. *Psychotherapy: Theory, Research, and Practice, 20,* 457–463.

Schmitt, R. C. (1966). Density, health, and social disorganization. *American Institute of Planners Journal, 32,* 38–40.

Schnare, A. B. (1980). Trends in residential segregation by race: 1960–1970. *Journal of Urban Economics, 7,* 293–301.

Schneider, D. J., Hastorf, A., & Ellsworth, P. C. (1979). *Person perception* (2nd ed.). Reading, MA; Addison-Wesley.

Schoell, W. F., & Guiltinan, J. P. (1992). *Marketing: Contemporary concepts and practices.* Boston: Allyn & Bacon.

Scholing, A., & Emmelkamp, P. M. G. (1990). Social phobia: Nature and treatment. In H. Leitenberg (Ed.), *Handbook of social and evaluation anxiety.* New York: Plenum.

Schradle, S. B., & Dougher, M. J. (1985). Social support as a mediator of stress: Theoretical and empirical issues. *Clinical Psychology Review, 5,* 641–661.

Schucker, B., & Jacobs, D. R. (1977). Assessment of behavior pattern A by voice characteristics. *Psychosomatic Medicine, 39,* 219–228.

Schul, Y., & Burnstein, E. (1985). The informational basis of social judgments: Using past impression rather than the trait description in forming a new impression. *Journal of Experimental Social Psychology, 21,* 421–439.

Schulman, J., Shaver, P., Colman, R., Emrich, B., & Christie, R. (1973, May). Recipe for a jury. *Psychology Today,* pp. 37–44, 77–84.

Schulz, R. (1976). Effects of control and predictability on the physical well-being of the institutionalized aged. *Journal of Personality and Social Psychology, 33,* 563–573.

Schulz, R., & Aderman, D. (1973). Effect of residential change on the temporal distance of death of terminal cancer patients. *Omega: Journal of Death and Dying, 4,* 157–162.

Schulz, R., & Hanusa, B. H. (1978). Long-term effects of control and predictability enhancing interventions: Findings and ethical issues. *Journal of Personality and Social Psychology 36,* 1194–1201.

Schuman, H., & Johnson, M. P. (1976). Attitudes and behavior. *Annual Review of Sociology, 2,* 161–207.

Schumann, D. W., Petty, R. E., & Clemons, D. S. (1990). Predicting the effectiveness of different strategies of advertising variation: A test of the repetition–variation hypothesis. *Journal of Consumer Research, 17,* 192–202.

Schutz, W. C. (1958). *FIRO: A three-dimensional theory of interpersonal behavior.* New York: Rinehart.

Schwartz, B. (1978). *Psychology of learning and behavior.* New York: Norton.

Schwartz, B., & Barsky, S. F. (1977). The home court advantage. *Social Forces, 55,* 641–661.

Schwarz, N., Bless, H., Bizman, A., & Bohner, G. (1991). Mood and persuasion: Affective states influence the processing of persuasive communications. In M. P. Zanna (Ed.), *Advances in experimental social psychology* (Vol. 24). San Diego, CA: Academic Press.

Schwarzer, R., & Leppin, A. (1991). Social support and health: A theoretical and empirical overview. *Journal of Social and Personal Relationships, 8,* 99–127.

Schwarzwald, J., Bizman, A., & Raz, M. (1983). The foot-in-the-door paradigm: Effects of second request size on donation probability and donor generosity. *Personality and Social Psychology Bulletin, 9,* 443–450.

Scott, J. E., & Schwalm, L. A. (1988a). Pornography and rape rates by state. In J. E. Scott & T. Hirschi (Eds.), *Controversial is-*

sues in crime and justice. Beverly Hills, CA: Sage.

Scott, J. E., & Schwalm, L. A. (1988b). Rape rates and the circulation rates of adult magazines. *Journal of Sex Research, 24,* 241–250.

Scott, J. P. (1973). Hostility and aggression. In B. Wolman (Ed.), *Handbook of general psychology.* Englewood Cliffs, NJ: Prentice-Hall.

Sears, D. O. (1975). Political socialization. In F. I. Greensteing & N. W. Polsby (Eds.), *Handbook of political science* (Vol. 2). Reading, MA: Addison-Wesley.

Sears, D. O. (1986). College sophomores in the laboratory: Influences of a narrow data base on social psychology's view of human nature. *Journal of Personality and Social Psychology, 5,* 515–530.

Sears, D. O., Lau, R. R., Tyler, T. R., & Allen, H. M. Jr. (1980). Self-interest vs. symbolic politics in policy attitudes and presidential voting. *American Political Science Review, 74,* 670–684.

Sears, R. R. (1970). Relation of early socialization experiences to self-concepts and gender in middle childhood. *Child Development, 41,* 267–289.

Sears, R. R., Maccoby, E. E., & Levin, H. (1957). *Patterns of child rearing.* Evanston, IL: Row, Peterson.

Secord, P. F., Dukes, W. F., & Bevan, W. (1954). Personalities in face: I. An experiment in social perceiving. *Genetic Psychology Monographs, 49,* 231–279.

Segal, M. W. (1974). Alphabet and attraction: An unobtrusive measure of the effect of propinquity in a field study. *Journal of Personality and Social Psychology, 30,* 654–657.

Segall, A., & Roberts, L. W. (1980). A comparative analysis of physician estimates and levels of medical knowledge among patients. *Sociology of Health and Illness, 2,* 317–334.

Seligman, C., Kriss, M., Darley, J. M., Fazio, R. H., Becker, L. J., & Pryor, J. B. (1979). Predicting summer energy consumption from homeowners' attitudes. *Journal of Applied Social Psychology, 9,* 70–90.

Seligman, M. E. P. (1975). *Helplessness.* San Francisco: Freeman.

Selye, H. (1956). *The stress of life.* New York: McGraw-Hill.

Selye, H. (1976). *Stress in health and disease.* Reading, MA: Butterworths.

Sergios, P.A., & Cody, J. (1985). Physical attractiveness and social assertiveness skills in male homosexual dating behavior and partner selection. *Journal of Social Psychology, 125,* 505–514.

Severy, L., Forsyth, D., & Wagner, P. O. (1979). A multimethod assessment of personal space development in female and

male, black and white, children. *Journal of Nonverbal Behavior, 4,* 68–86.

Shaffer, D. R., & Sadowski, C. (1975). This table is mine: Respect for marked barroom tables as a function of gender of spatial marker and desirability of locale. *Sociometry, 38,* 408–419.

Shanab, M. E., & Yahya, K. A. (1977). A behavioral study of obedience in children. *Journal of Personality and Social Psychology, 35,* 530–536.

Shapiro, P. N., & Penrod, S. (1986). Meta-analysis of facial identification studies. *Psychological Bulletin, 100,* 139–156.

Sharpe, D., Adair, J. G., & Roese, N. J. (1992). Twenty years of deception research: A decline in subjects' trust? *Personality and Social Psychology Bulletin, 5,* 585–590.

Shavitt, S. (1989). Operationalizing functional theories of attitude. In A. R. Pratkanis & A. G. Greenwald (Eds.), *Attitude structure and function.* Hillsdale, NJ: Erlbaum.

Shavitt, S. (1990). The role of attitude objects in attitude functions. *Journal of Experimental Social Psychology, 26,* 124–148.

Shaw, M. E., & Costanzo, P. R. (1970). Theories of social psychology. New York: McGraw-Hill.

Shaw, M. E., Rothschild, G. H., & Strickland, J. F. (1957). Decision processes in communication nets. *Journal of Abnormal and Social Psychology, 54,* 323–330.

Sheridan, C. L., & King, R. G. (1972). Obedience to authority with an authentic victim. *Proceedings of the American Psychological Association,* 165–166.

Sherif, M. (1935). A study of some social factors in perception. *Archives of Psychology, 27,* 1–60.

Sherif, M. (1966). *Group conflict and cooperation: Their social psychology.* London: Routledge & Kegan Paul.

Sherif, M., Harvey, O. J., White, B. J., Hood, W. R., & Sherif, C. W. (1961). *Intergroup conflict and cooperation: The Robbers Cave experiment.* Norman: University of Oklahoma Book Exchange.

Sherif, M., & Sherif, C. W. (1953). *Groups in harmony and tension: An integration of studies on intergroup relations.* New York: Octagon Books.

Sherman, L. W. (1992). Introduction: The influence of criminology on criminal law: Evaluating arrests for misdemeanor domestic violence. *Journal of Criminal Law and Criminology, 83,* 1–45.

Sherman, L. W., & Berk, R. A. (1984). The specific deterrent effects of arrest on domestic assault. *American Sociological Review, 49,* 261–272.

Sherman, L. W., Schmidt, J. D., Rogan, D. P.,

Smith, D. A., Gartin, P. R., Cohn, E. G., Collins, D. J., & Bacich, A. R. (1992). The variable effects of arrest on criminal careers: The Milwaukee domestic violence experiment. *Journal of Criminal Law and Criminology, 83,* 137–169.

Sherman, S. J. (1980). On the self-erasing nature of errors of prediction. *Journal of Personality and Social Psychology, 39,* 211–221.

Sherman, S. J., Judd, C. M., & Park, B. (1989). Social cognition. In M. R. Rosenzweig & L. W. Porter (Eds.), *Annual review of psychology* (Vol. 40). Palo Alto, CA: Annual Reviews.

Sherrod, D. R. (1974). Crowding, perceived control and behavioral aftereffects. *Journal of Applied Social Psychology, 4,* 171–186.

Sherrod, D. R., & Cohen, S. (1979). Density, personal control and design. In A. Baum, & J. R. Aiello (Eds.), *Residential crowding and design.* New York: Plenum.

Sherrod, D. R., Hage, J. M., Halpern, P. L., & Moore, B. S. (1977). Effects of personal causation and perceived control on responses to an aversive environment: The more control the better. *Journal of Experimental Social Psychology, 13,* 14–27.

Sherwood, R. J. (1983). Compliance behavior of hemodialysis patients and the role of the family. *Family Systems Medicine, 1,* 60–72.

Shields, S. A. (1975). Functionalism, Darwinism, and the psychology of women: A study in social myth. *American Psychologist, 30,* 739–754.

Shils, E. A. (1954). Authoritarianism: "Right" and "left." In R. Christie & M. Jahoda (Eds.), *Studies in the scope and method of "the authoritarian personality."* New York: Free Press of Glencoe.

Shotland, R. L., & Straw, M. K. (1976). Bystander response to an assault: When a man attacks a woman. *Journal of Personality and Social Psychology, 34,* 990–999.

Shumaker, S. A., & Hill, D. R. (1991). Gender differences in social support and physical health. *Health Psychology, 10,* 102–111.

Shupe, A., Stacey, A., & Hazlewood, L. R. (1987). *Violent men, violent couples: The dynamics of domestic violence.* Lexington, MA: Lexington Books.

Shure, G. H., Meeker, R. J., & Hansford, E. A. (1965). The effectiveness of pacifist strategies in bargaining games. *Journal of Conflict Resolution, 9,* 106–117.

Shweder, R. A. (1982). Fact and artifact in trait perception: The systematic distortion hypothesis. In B. A. Maher (Ed.), *Progress in experimental personality research* (Vol. 11). New York: Academic Press.

Siem, F. M., & Spence, J. T. (1986). Gender-related traits and helping behavior. *Journal of Personality and Social Psychology, 51,* 615–621.

Sigall, H., & Ostrove, N. (1975). Beautiful but dangerous: Effects of offender attractiveness and nature of the crime on juridic judgment. *Journal of Personality and Social Psychology, 31,* 410–414.

Sigall, H., & Page, R. (1971). Current stereotypes: A little fading, a little faking. *Journal of Personality and Social Psychology, 18,* 247–255.

Sigelman, C. K., Berry, C. J., & Wiles, K. A. (1984). Violence in college students' dating relationships. *Journal of Applied Social Psychology, 5,* 530–548.

Sigler, R. T. (1989). *Domestic violence in context: An assessment of community attitudes.* Lexington, MA: Lexington Books.

Signorella, M. L., & Jamison, W. (1986). Masculinity, femininity, androgyny, and cognitive performance: A meta-analysis. *Psychological Bulletin, 100,* 207–228.

Silas, F. (1983). A jury of one's peers: Peremptory challenges of minorities raises fairness issues. *American Bar Association Journal, 69,* 1607–1610.

Silveira, J. (1972). Thoughts on the politics of touch. *Women's Press, 1,* 13.

Silverman, I. (1971, September). Physical attractiveness. *Sexual Behavior,* pp. 22–25.

Silverman, L. J., Rivera, A. N., & Tedeschi, J. T. (1979). Transgression–compliance: Guilt, negative affect, or impression management? *Journal of Social Psychology, 108,* 57–62.

Simon, R. J. (1967). *The jury and the defense of insanity.* Boston: Little, Brown.

Simpson, G. E., & Yinger, J. M. (1985). *Racial and cultural minorities: An analysis of prejudice and discrimination.* New York: Plenum.

Simpson, J. A. (1987). The dissolution of romantic relationships: Factors involved in relationship stability and emotional distress. *Journal of Personality and Social Psychology, 53,* 683–692.

Simpson, J. A. (1990). Influence of attachment styles on romantic relationships. *Journal of Personality and Social Psychology, 59,* 971–980.

Singer, J. E., Lundberg, V., & Frankenhaeuser, M. (1978). Stress on trains: A study of urban commuting. In A. Baum, J. E. Singer, & S. Valins (Eds.), *Advances in environmental psychology* (Vol. 1). Hillsdale, NJ: Erlbaum.

Singh, B. R. (1991). Teaching methods for reducing prejudice and enhancing academic achievement for all children. *Educational Studies, 17,* 157–171.

Sistrunk, F., & McDavid, J. W. (1971). Sex variables in conformity behavior. *Journal of Personality and Social Psychology, 17,* 200–207.

Skinner, B. F. (1938). *The behavior of organisms.* New York: Appleton-Century.

Skinner, B. F. (1953). *Science and human behavior.* New York: Macmillan.

Skowronski, J. J., & Carlston, D. E. (1987). Social judgment and social memory: The role of cue diagnosticity in negativity, positivity, and extremity biases. *Journal of Personality and Social Psychology, 52,* 689–699.

Skrypnek, B. J., & Snyder, M. (1982). On the self-perpetuating nature of stereotypes about women and men. *Journal of Experimental Social Psychology, 18,* 277–291.

Slovic, P., Fischoff, B., & Lichtenstein, S. (1977). Behavioral decision theory. *Annual Review of Psychology, 28,* 1–39.

Smith, B. L., Lasswell, H. D., & Casey, R. D. (1946). *Propaganda, communication, and public opinion.* Princeton, NJ: Princeton University Press.

Smith, G. F., & Dorfman, D. D. (1975). The effect of stimulus uncertainty on the relationship between frequency of exposure and liking. *Journal of Personality and Social Psychology, 31,* 150–155.

Smith, M. B., Bruner, J. S., & White, R. W. (1956). *Opinions and personality.* New York: Wiley.

Smith, T. W., Ingram, R. E., & Roth, D. L. (1985). Self-focused attention and depression: Self-evaluation, affect, and life stress. *Motivation and Emotion, 9,* 323–331.

Smith, T. W., Pope, M. K., Rhodewalt, F., & Poulton, J. L. (1989). Optimism, neuroticism, coping, and symptom reports: An alternative interpretation of the Life Orientation Test. *Journal of Personality and Social Psychology, 56,* 640–648.

Smith, V. L., & Ellsworth, P.C. (1987). The social psychology of eyewitness accuracy: Misleading questions and communicator expertise. *Journal of Applied Psychology, 72,* 294–300.

Smith, V. L., Kassin, S. M., & Ellsworth, P. C. (1989). Eyewitness accuracy and confidence: Within- versus between-subjects correlations. *Journal of Applied Psychology, 74,* 356–359.

Sniderman, P. M., Brody, R. A, & Tetlock, P. E. (1991). *Reasoning and choice: Explorations in political psychology.* New York: Cambridge University Press.

Sniderman, P. M., & Hagen, M. (1985). *Race and inequality.* New York: Chatham House.

Sniderman, P. M., & Tetlock, P. E. (1986). Symbolic racism: Problems of motive attribution in political analysis. *Journal of Social Issues, 42,* 129–150.

Snow, M. E., Jacklin, C. N., & Maccoby, E. E. (1983). Sex-of-child differences in father–child interaction at one year of age. *Child Development, 54,* 227–232.

Snyder, M. (1974). The self-monitoring of expressive behavior. *Journal of Personality and Social Psychology, 30,* 526–537.

Snyder, M. (1979). Self-monitoring processes. In L. Berkowitz (Ed.), *Advances in experimental social psychology* (Vol. 12). New York: Academic Press.

Snyder, M. (1981). On the self-perpetuating nature of social stereotypes. In D. L. Hamilton (Ed.), *Cognitive processes in stereotyping and intergroup behavior.* Hillsdale, NJ: Erlbaum.

Snyder, M. (1982). When believing means doing: Creating links between attitudes and behavior. In M. P. Zanna, E. T. Higgins, & C. P. Herman (Eds.), *Consistency in social behavior* (Vol. 2). Hillsdale, NJ: Erlbaum.

Snyder, M. (1987). *Public appearances/Private realities.* New York: Freeman.

Snyder, M. (1992). Motivational foundations of behavioral confirmation. In M. P. Zanna (Ed.), *Advances in experimental social psychology* (Vol. 25). San Diego: Academic Press.

Snyder, M. (1993). Basic research and practical problems: The promise of a "functional" personality and social psychology. *Personality and Social Psychology Bulletin, 19,* 251–264.

Snyder, M., Berscheid, E., & Glick, P. (1985). Focusing on the exterior and the interior: Two investigations of the initiation of personal relationships. *Journal of Personality and Social Psychology, 48,* 1427–1439.

Snyder, M., Berscheid, E., & Matwychuk, A. (1988). Orientations toward personnel selection: Differential reliance on appearance and personality. *Journal of Personality and Social Psychology, 54,* 972–979.

Snyder, M., & Campbell, B. H. (1980). Testing hypotheses about other people: The role of the hypothesis. *Personality and Social Psychology Bulletin, 6,* 421–426.

Snyder, M., & DeBono, K.G. (1985). Appeals to images and claims about quality: Understanding the psychology of advertising. *Journal of Personality and Social Psychology, 49,* 586–597.

Snyder, M., & DeBono, K. G. (1987). A functional approach to attitudes and persuasion. In M. P. Zanna, J. M. Olson, & C. P. Herman (Eds.), *Social influence: The Ontario symposium* (Vol. 5). Hillsdale, NJ: Erlbaum.

Snyder, M., & DeBono, K. G. (1989). Understanding the functions of attitudes: Lessons from personality and social behavior. In A. R. Pratkanis & A. G. Greenwald (Eds.), *Attitude structure and function.* Hillsdale, NJ: Erlbaum.

Snyder, M., & Gangestad, S. (1982). Choosing social situations: Two investigations of self-monitoring processes. *Journal of Personality and Social Psychology, 43,* 123–135.

Snyder, M., Gangestad, S., & Simpson, J. A. (1983). Choosing friends as activity partners: The role of self-monitoring. *Journal of Personality and Social Psychology, 45,* 1061–1072.

Snyder, M., & Haugen, J. A. (1990). *Why does behavioral confirmation occur? A functional perspective.* Paper presented at the annual meeting of the American Psychological Association, Boston.

Snyder, M., & Ickes, W. (1985). Personality and social behavior. In G. Lindzey & E. Aronson (Eds.), *Handbook of social psychology* (3rd ed.). New York: Random House.

Snyder, M., & Monson, T. C. (1975). Persons, situations, and the control of social behavior. *Journal of Personality and Social Psychology, 32,* 637–644.

Snyder, M., & Omoto, A. M. (1992a). Volunteerism and society's response to the HIV epidemic. *Current Directions in Psychological Science, 1,* 113–115.

Snyder, M., & Omoto, A. M. (1992b). Who helps and why? The psychology of AIDS volunteerism. In S. Spacapan & S. Oskamp (Eds.), *Helping and being helped: Naturalistic studies.* Newbury Park, CA: Sage.

Snyder, M., & Simpson, J. A. (1984). Self-monitoring and dating relationships. *Journal of Personality and Social Psychology, 47,* 1281–1291.

Snyder, M., & Swann, W. B. Jr. (1976). When actions reflect attitudes: The politics of impression management. *Journal of Personality and Social Psychology, 34,* 1034–1042.

Snyder, M., & Swann, W. B. (1978). Hypothesis-testing processes in social interaction. *Journal of Personality and Social Psychology, 36,* 1202–1212.

Snyder, M., & Tanke, E. D. (1976). Behavior and attitude: Some people are more consistent than others. *Journal of Personality and Social Psychology, 44,* 510–517.

Snyder, M., Tanke, E. D., & Berscheid, E. (1977). Social perception and interpersonal behavior: On the self-fulfilling nature of social stereotypes. *Journal of Personality and Social Psychology, 35,* 656–666.

Snyder, M., & Uranowitz, S. W. (1978). Reconstructing the past: Some cognitive consequences of person perception. *Journal of Personality and Social Psychology, 36,* 941–950.

Social indicators of equality for minorities and women (1978). A report of the United States Commission on Civil Rights.

Solomon, H., Solomon, L. Z., Arnone, M. M., Maur, B. J., Reda, R. M., & Rother, E. O. (1981). Anonymity and helping. *Journal of Social Psychology, 113,* 37–43.

Solomon, R. L., & Corbit, J. D. (1974). An opponent-process theory of motivation: I. Temporal dynamics of affect. *Psychological Review, 81,* 119–145.

Sommer, R. (1969). *Personal space: The behavioral basis of design.* Englewood Cliffs, NJ: Prentice-Hall.

Sorrentino, R. M., & Field, N. (1986). Emergent leadership over time: The functional value of positive motivation. *Journal of Personality and Social Psychology, 50,* 1091–1099.

Spence, J. T., Deaux, K., & Helmreich, R. L. (1985). Sex roles in contemporary American society. In G. Lindzey & E. Aronson (Eds.), *Handbook of social psychology* (Vol. 2). New York: Random House.

Spence, J. T., & Helmreich, R. L. (1978). *Masculinity and femininity: The psychological dimensions, correlates, and antecedents.* Austin: University of Texas Press.

Spence, J. T., & Helmreich, R. L. (1980). Masculine instrumentality and feminine expressiveness: Their relationships with sex role attitudes and behaviors. *Psychology of Women Quarterly, 5,* 147–163.

Spence, J. T., Helmreich, R. L., & Stapp, J. (1974). The Personal Attributes Questionnaire: A measure of sex role stereotypes and masculinity–femininity. *JSAS Catalog of Selected Documents in Psychology, 4,* 43. (MS No. 617.)

Spence, J. T., & Sawin, L. L. (1985). Images of masculinity and femininity: A reconceptualization. In V. E. O'Leary, R. K. Unger, & B. S. Wallston (Eds.), *Women, gender, and social psychology.* Hillsdale, NJ: Erlbaum.

Sperber, B. M., Fishbein, M., & Ajzen, I. (1980). Predicting and understanding women's occupational orientations: Factors underlying choice intentions. In I. Ajzen & M. Fishbein (Eds.), *Understanding attitudes and predicting social behavior.* Englewood Cliffs, NJ: Prentice-Hall.

Spivey, C. B., & Prentice-Dunn, S. (1990). Assessing the directionality of deindividuation: Effects of deindividuation, modeling, and private self-consciousness on aggressive and prosocial responses. *Basic and Applied Social Psychology, 11,* 387–403.

Sprafkin, J. N., Liebert, R. M., & Poulos, R. W. (1975). Effects of a prosocial televised example on children's helping. *Jour-*

nal of Experimental Child Psychology, *20,* 119–126.

Squire, R. W. (1990). A model of empathetic understanding, and adherence to treatment regimens in practitioner–patient relationships. *Social Science and Medicine, 30,* 325–339.

Sroufe, A. L. (1978). Attachment and the roots of human competence. *Human Nature, 1(10),* 50–57.

Staats, A. W., & Staats, C. K. (1958). Attitudes established by classical conditioning. *Journal of Abnormal and Social Psychology, 57,* 37–40.

Stake, J. E. (1992). Gender differences and similarities in self-concept within everyday life contexts. *Psychology of Women Quarterly, 16,* 349–363.

Stangor, C., Lynch, L., Duan, C., & Glass, B. (1992). Categorization of individuals on the basis of multiple social features. *Journal of Personality and Social Psychology, 62,* 207–218.

Stangor, C., & McMillan, D. (1992). Memory for expectancy-congruent and expectancy-incongruent information: A review of the social and social developmental literature. *Psychological Bulletin, 111,* 42–61.

Stangor, C., & Ruble, D. N. (1989). Strength of expectancies and memory for social information: What we remember depends on how much we know. *Journal of Experimental Social Psychology, 25,* 18–35.

Stangor, C., Sullivan, L. A., & Ford, T. E. (1991). Affective and cognitive determinants of prejudice. *Social Cognition, 9,* 359–380.

Stanley, J. C., & Benbrow, C. P. (1982). Huge sex ratios at upper end. *American Psychologist, 37,* 972.

Stapp, J., & Fulcher, R. (1981). The employment of APA members. *American Psychologist, 36,* 1263–1314.

Stark, E., & Flitcraft, A. (1987). Violence among intimates: An epidemiological review. In V. B. Van Hasselt, R. L. Morrison, A. S. Bellack, & M. Hersen (Eds.), *Handbook of family violence.* New York: Plenum.

Stasser, G. (1992). Pooling of unshared information during group discussions. In W. Worchel, W. Wood, & J. A. Simpson (Eds.), *Group processes and productivity.* Newbury Park, CA: Sage.

Stasser, G., Kerr, N. L., & Bray, R. N. (1982). The social psychology of jury deliberation: Structure, process, and product. In R. M. Bray & N. L. Kerr (Eds.), *The psychology of the courtroom.* New York: Academic Press.

Staub, E. (1970). The effect of focusing responsibility on children in their attempts

to help. *Developmental Psychology, 2,* 152–154.

Staub, E. (1974). Helping a distressed person: Social, personality, and stimulus determinants. In L. Berkowitz (Ed.), *Advances in experimental social psychology* (Vol. 7). New York: Academic Press.

Staub, E. (1975). To rear a prosocial child: Reasoning, learning by doing, and learning by teaching others. In D. Palma & J. Folly (Eds.), *Moral development: Current theory and research.* Hillsdale, NJ: Erlbaum.

Staub, E. (1979). *Positive social behavior and morality* (Vol. 2): *Socialization and development.* New York: Academic Press.

Staw, B. M., & Ross, J. (1987). Behavior in escalating situations: Antecedents, prototypes, and solutions. *Research in Organizational Behavior, 9,* 39–78.

Steblay, N. M. (1992). A meta-analytic review of the weapon focus effect. *Law and Human Behavior, 16,* 413–424.

Steele, B. (1975). *Working with abusive parents.* Washington, DC: Department of Health, Education and Welfare, Office of Human Development, National Center on Child Abuse.

Steele, C. M. (1988). The psychology of self-affirmation: Sustaining the integrity of the self. In L. Berkowitz (Ed.), *Advances in experimental social psychology* (Vol. 21). San Diego: Academic Press.

Steele, C. M., & Liu, T. J. (1983). Dissonance processes as self-affirmation. *Journal of Personality and Social Psychology, 45,* 5–19.

Steffensmeier, D. J., & Terry, R. M. (1973). Deviance and respectability: An observational study of reactions to shoplifting. *Social Forces, 51,* 417–426.

Stein, A. H., & Bailey, M. N. (1973). The socialization of achievement orientation in females. *Psychological Bulletin, 80,* 345–366.

Stein, R. T., & Heller, T. (1979). An empirical analysis of the correlations between leadership, status and participation rates reported in the literature. *Journal of Personality and Social Psychology, 37,* 1993–2002.

Steinberg, C. (1985). *TV facts.* New York: Facts on File Publications.

Steiner, I. D. (1972). *Group process and productivity.* New York: Academic Press.

Steiner, I. D. (1976). Task-performing groups. In J. W. Thibaut, J. T. Spence, & R. C. Carson (Eds.), *Contemporary topics in social psychology.* Morristown, NJ: General Learning Press.

Steinmetz, S. K. (1980). Women and violence: Victims and perpetrators. *American Journal of Psychotherapy, 3,* 334–349.

Stephan, F. F., & Mishler, E. G. (1952). The distribution of participation in small groups: An exponential approximation. *American Sociological Review, 17,* 598–608.

Stephan, W. (1991). School desegregation: Short-term and long-term effects. In: H. H. Knopke, R. J. Norrell, & R. W. Rogers (Eds.), *Opening doors: Perspectives on race relations in contemporary America.* Tuscaloosa: University of Alabama Press.

Stephan, W. G., Berscheid, E., & Walster, E. (1971). Sexual arousal and heterosexual perception. *Journal of Personality and Social Psychology, 20,* 93–101.

Stern, G. S., McCants, T. R., & Pettine, P. W. (1982). Stress and illness: Controllable and uncontrollable life events' relative contributions. *Personality and Social Psychology Bulletin, 8,* 140–145.

Stern, P. C., & Oskamp, S. (1987). Managing scarce environmental resources. In D. Stokols & I. Altman (Eds.), *Handbook of environmental psychology* (Vol. 2). New York: Wiley.

Sternberg, R. (1986). A triangular theory of love. *Psychological Review, 93,* 119–135.

Sternberg, R. J., & Grajek, S. (1984). The nature of love. *Journal of Personality and Social Psychology, 47,* 312–329.

Sternglanz, S. H., & Serbin, L. A. (1974). Sex role stereotyping in children's TV programs. *Developmental Psychology, 10,* 710–715.

Steuer, F. B., Applefield, J. M., & Smith, R. (1971). Televised aggression and the interpersonal aggression of preschool children. *Journal of Experimental Child Psychology, 11,* 442–447.

Stevens, S. (1971, November 28). The "rat packs" of New York. *New York Times.*

Stevenson-Hinde, J., Hinde, R. A., & Simpson, A. E. (1986). Behavior at home and friendly or hostile behavior in preschool. In D. Olweus, J. Block, & M. Radke-Yarrow (Eds.), *Development of antisocial and prosocial behavior: Research, theories, and issues.* Orlando, FL: Academic Press.

Stewart, J. E., II. (1980). Defendant's attractiveness as a factor in the outcome of criminal trials: An observational study. *Journal of Applied Social Psychology, 10,* 348–361.

Stires, L. (1980). The effect of classroom seating location on student grades and attitudes: Environment for self-selection? *Environment and Behavior, 12,* 241–254.

Stoeckle, J. D., Zola, I. K., & Davidson, G. E. (1963). On going to see the doctor: The contributions of the patient to the decision to seek medical aid. *Journal of Chronic Diseases, 16,* 975–989.

Stogdill, R. M. (1974). *Handbook of leadership.* New York: Free Press.

Stokols, D. (1972). On the distinction between density and crowding: Some implications for future research. *Psychological Review, 79,* 275–277.

Stokols, D., Rall, M., Pinner, B., & Schopler, J. (1973). Physical, social, and personal determinants of the perception of crowding. *Environment and Behavior, 5,* 87–115.

Stoner, J. A. F. (1961). *A comparison of individual and group decisions involving risk.* Unpublished master's thesis, Massachusetts Institute of Technology, Cambridge, MA.

Storms, M. D. (1973). Videotape and the attribution process: Reversing actors' and observers' points of view. *Journal of Personality and Social Psychology, 27,* 165–175.

Strauman, T. J., & Higgins, E. T. (1987). Automatic activation of self-discrepancies and emotional syndromes: When cognitive structures influence affect. *Journal of Personality and Social Psychology, 53,* 1004–1014.

Straus, M. A. (1974). Leveling, civility, and violence in the family. *Journal of Marriage and the Family, 36,* 12–29.

Straus, M. A. (1980). The marriage license as a hitting license: Evidence from popular culture, law and social science. In M. Straus & G. Hotaling (Eds.). *The social causes of husband–wife violence.* Minneapolis: University of Minnesota Press.

Straus, M. A., Gelles, R. J., & Steinmetz, S. K. (1980). *Behind closed doors: Violence in the American family.* Garden City, NY: Anchor Books.

Straus, M. A., & Hotaling, G. T. (Eds.), (1980). *The social causes of husband–wife violence.* Minneapolis: University of Minnesota Press.

Strayer, F. F., Wareing, S., & Rushton, J. P. (1979). Social constraints on naturally occurring preschool altruism. *Ethology and Sociobiology, 1,* 3–11.

Strickland, B. R. (1989). Internal–external control expectancies: From contingency to creativity. *American Psychologist, 44,* 1–12.

Strickland, L. H. (1958). Surveillance and trust. *Journal of Personality, 26,* 200–215.

Strodtbeck, F. L., James, R. M., & Hawkins, C. (1957). Social status in jury deliberations. *American Sociological Review, 22,* 713–718.

Strodtbeck, F. L., & Hook, L. H. (1961). The social dimensions of a twelve-man jury table. *Sociometry, 24,* 397–415.

Strodtbeck, F. L., James, R. M., & Hawkins, C. (1958). Social status in jury deliberations. In E. E. Maccoby, T. M. Newcomb, & E. L. Hartley (Eds.), *Readings in social psychology* (3rd ed.). New York: Holt.

Strodtbeck, F. L., & Mann, R. D. (1956). Sex role differentiation in jury deliberations. *Sociometry, 19,* 3–11.

Stroebe, W., Diehl, M., & Abakoumkih, G. (1992). The illusion of group effectivity. *Personality and Social Psychology Bulletin, 18,* 643–650.

Stroebe, W., Insko, C. A., Thompson, V. D., & Layton, B. D. (1971). Effects of physical attractiveness, attitude similarity, and sex on various aspects of interpersonal attraction. *Journal of Personality and Social Psychology, 18,* 79–91.

Strong, E. K. (1943). *Vocational interests of men and women.* Stanford, CA: Stanford University Press.

Strube, M. J., & Garcia, J. E. (1981). A meta-analytic investigation of Fiedler's contingency model of leadership effectiveness. *Psychological Bulletin, 90,* 307–321.

Student note. (1985). The testimony of child victims in sex abuse prosecutions. *Harvard Law Review, 98,* 806–827.

Sue, S., Smith, R. E., & Caldwell, C. (1973). Effects of inadmissible evidence on the decisions of simulated jurors: A moral dilemma. *Journal of Applied Social Psychology, 3,* 345–353.

Suls, J., & Greenwald, A. G. (Eds.). (1986). *Psychological perspectives on the self* (Vol. 3). Hillsdale, NJ: Erlbaum.

Suls, J. M., & Miller, R. L. (Eds.). (1977). *Social comparison processes: Theoretical and empirical perspectives.* Washington, DC: Halsted-Wiley.

Suls, J., & Mullen, B. (1981). Life events, perceived control and illness: The role of uncertainty. *Journal of Human Stress, 7,* 30–34.

Suls, J., & Wills, T. A. (Eds.). (1991). *Social comparison: Contemporary theory and research.* Hillsdale, NJ: Erlbaum.

Sundstrom, E. (1975). An experimental study of crowding: Effects of room size, intrusion, and goal-blocking on nonverbal behaviors, self-disclosure, and self-reported stress. *Journal of Personality and Social Psychology, 32,* 645–654.

Sundstrom, E., & Altman, I. (1974). Field study of territorial behavior and dominance. *Journal of Personality and Social Psychology, 30,* 115–124.

Sundstrom, E., & Altman, I. (1976). Interpersonal relationships and personal space: Research review and theoretical model. *Human Ecology, 4,* 47–67.

Surette, R. (1990). Estimating the magnitude and mechanisms of copycat crime. In R. Surette (Ed.), *The media and criminal justice policy: Recent research and social effects.* Springfield, IL: Charles C. Thomas.

Sutherland, E. H., & Cressey, D. R. (1966). *Principles of criminology* (7th ed.). Philadelphia: Lippincott.

Suttles, G. D. (1968). *The social order of the slum: Ethnicity and territory in the inner city.* Chicago: University of Chicago Press.

Sutton, S., Marsh, A., & Matheson, J. (1990). Microanalysis of smokers' beliefs about the consequences of quitting: Results from a large population sample. *Journal of Applied Social Psychology, 20,* 1847–1862.

Svarstad, B. L. (1976). Physician–patient communication and patient conformity with medical advice. In D. Mechanic (Ed.), *The growth of bureaucratic medicine: An inquiry into the dynamics of patient behavior and the organization of medical care.* New York: Wiley.

Swann, W. B. (1984). Quest for accuracy in person perception: A matter of pragmatics. *Psychological Bulletin, 91,* 457–477.

Swann, W. B. Jr. & Read, S. J. (1981). Self-verification processes: How we sustain our self-conceptions. *Journal of Experimental Social Psychology, 17,* 351–372.

Swap, W. C. (1977). Interpersonal attraction and repeated exposure to rewarders and punishers. *Personality and Social Psychology Bulletin, 3,* 248–251.

Sweeney, L. T., & Haney, C. (1992). The influence of race on sentencing: A metaanalytic review of experimental studies. *Behavioral Sciences and the Law, 10,* 179–195.

Sweeney, J. (1973). An experimental investigation of the free rider problem. *Social Science Research, 2,* 277–292.

Sweet, W. H., Ervin, F., & Mark, V. H. (1969). The relationship of violent behavior to focal cerebral disease. In S. Garattini & E. B. Sigg (Eds.), *Aggressive behavior.* New York: Wiley.

Swim, J., Borgida, E., Maruyama, G., & Myers, D. G. (1989). Joan McKay versus John McKay: Do gender stereotypes bias evaluations? *Psychological Bulletin, 105,* 409–429.

Symons, D. (1979). *The evolution of human sexuality.* New York: Oxford University Press.

Szymanski, D., & Harkins, S. G. (1987). Social loafing and self-evaluation with a social standard. *Journal of Personality and Social Psychology, 5,* 871–897.

Taft, R. (1955). The ability to judge people. *Psychological Bulletin, 52,* 1–23.

Tajfel, H. (Ed.). (1978). *Differentiation between social groups.* New York: Academic Press.

Tajfel, H. (1981). *Human groups and social categories.* Cambridge, England: Cambridge University Press.

Tajfel, H. (1982). *Social identity and intergroup relations*. Cambridge, England: Cambridge University Press.

Tajfel, H., Billig, M. G., Bundy, R. P., & Flament, C. (1971). Social categorization and intergroup behavior. *European Journal of Social Psychology, 1*, 149–178.

Tajfel, H., & Turner, J. C. (1979). An integrative theory of social conflict. In W. Austin & S. Worchel (Eds.), *The social psychology of intergroup relations*. Monterey, CA: Brooks/Cole.

Tanford, S., & Penrod, S. (1984). Social influence model: A formal integration of research on majority and minority influence processes. *Psychological Bulletin, 95*, 189–225.

Tausig, H. L. (1982). Measuring life events. *Journal of Health and Social Behavior, 23*, 52–64.

Tavris, C., & Wade, C. (1984). *The longest war: Sex differences in perspective*. New York: Harcourt Brace Jovanovich.

Taylor, D. G., Sheatsley, P. B., & Greeley, A. M. (1978, June). Attitudes toward racial integration. *Scientific American, 238*, (6), 42–49.

Taylor, D. W., Berry, P. C., & Block, C. H. (1958). Does group participation when using brainstorming facilitate or inhibit creative thinking? *Administrative Science Quarterly, 3*, 23–47.

Taylor, J. A. (1953). A personality scale of manifest anxiety. *Journal of Abnormal and Social Psychology, 48*, 285–290.

Taylor, M. C., & Hall, J. A. (1982). Psychological androgyny: Theories, methods, and conclusions. *Psychological Bulletin, 92*, 347–366.

Taylor, R. B. (1982). *Environmental stress*. New York: Cambridge University Press.

Taylor, R. B., & Brooks, D. K. (1980). Temporary territories?: Responses to intrusions in a public setting. *Population and Environment, 3*, 135–143.

Taylor, R. B., De Soto, C. B., & Lieb, R. (1979). Sharing secrets: Disclosure and discretion in dyads and triads. *Journal of Personality and Social Psychology, 37*, 1196–1203.

Taylor, R. B., Gottfredson, S. D., & Brower, S. (1980). The defensibility of defensible space: Synthetic framework for future research. In T. Hirshi & M. Gottfredson (Eds.), *Understanding crime*. Beverly Hills, CA: Sage.

Taylor, R. B., Gottfredson, S., & Brower, S. (1984). Understanding block crime and fear. *Journal of Research in Crime and Delinquency, 21*, 303–331.

Taylor, R. B., & Lanni, J. C. (1981). Territorial dominance: The influence of the resi-

dent advantage in triadic decision making. *Journal of Personality and Social Psychology, 41*, 909–915.

Taylor, S. E. (1979). Hospital patient behavior: Reactance, helplessness, or control? *Journal of Social Issues, 35*, 156–184.

Taylor, S. E. (1981b). The interface of cognitive and social psychology. In J. Harvey (Ed.), *Cognition, social behavior, and the environment*. Hillsdale, NJ: Erlbaum.

Taylor, S. E. (1990). Health psychology: The science and the field. *American Psychologist, 45*, 40–50.

Taylor, S. E., & Brown, J. D. (1988). Illusion and well-being: A social psychological perspective on mental health. *Psychological Bulletin, 103*, 193–210.

Taylor, S. E., & Fiske, S. T. (1978). Salience, attention, and attribution: Top of the head phenomena. In L. Berkowitz (Ed.), *Advances in experimental social psychology* (Vol. 11). New York: Academic Press.

Taylor, S. E., & Fiske, S. T. (1975). Point of view and perception of causality. *Journal of Personality and Social Psychology, 32* 439–445.

Taylor, S. E., Lichtman, R. R., & Wood, J. V. (1984). Attributions, beliefs about control, and adjustment to breast cancer. *Journal of Personality and Social Psychology, 46*, 489–502.

Taylor, S. E., & Lobel, M. (1989). Social comparison activity under threat: Downward evaluation and upward contacts. *Psychological Review, 96*, 569–575.

Taylor, S. E., & Thompson, S. C. (1982). Stalking the elusive "vividness effect." *Psychological Review, 89*, 155–181.

Taylor, S. P. (1986). The regulation of aggressive behavior. In R. J. Blanchard & D. C. Blanchard (Eds.), *Advances in the study of aggression*. Orlando, FL: Academic Press.

Tedeschi, J. T., Schlenker, B. R., & Bonoma, T. V. (1971). Cognitive dissonance: Private ratiocination or public spectacle? *American Psychologist, 26*, 685–695.

Tennis, G. H., & Dabbs, J. M. Jr. (1976). Race, setting, and actor–target differences in personal space. *Social Behavior and Personality, 4*, 49–55.

Terman, L. M., & Miles, C. C. (1936). *Sex and personality: Studies in masculinity and femininity*. New York: Russell & Russell.

Tesser, A. (1986). Some effects of self-evaluation maintenance on cognition and action. In R. M. Sorrentino & E. T. Higgins (Eds.), *The handbook of motivation and cognition: Foundations of social behavior*. New York: Guilford.

Tesser, A. (1993). The importance of heritability in psychological research: The case

of attitudes. *Psychological Review, 100*, 129–142.

Tesser, A., & Brodie, M. (1971). A note on the evaluation of a computer date. *Psychonomic Science, 23*, 300.

Tesser, A., Campbell, J., & Smith, M. (1984). Friendship choice and performance: Self-evaluation maintenance in children. *Journal of Personality and Social Psychology, 46*, 561–574.

Tesser, A., & Moore, J. (1986). Convergence of public and private aspects of self. In R. F. Baumeister (Ed.), *Public self and private self*. New York: Springer-Verlag.

Tesser, A., & Rosen, S. (1975). The reluctance to transmit bad news. In L. Berkowitz (Ed.), *Advances in experimental social psychology* (Vol. 8). New York: Academic Press.

Tessler, R. C., & Schwartz, S. H. (1972). Help seeking, self-esteem, and achievement motivation: An attributional analysis. *Journal of Personality and Social Psychology, 21*, 318–326.

Tetlock, P. E., & Boettger, R. (1989). Accountability: A social magnifier of the dilution effect. *Journal of Personality and Social Psychology, 57*, 388–398.

't Hart, P. (1990). *Groupthink in government: A study of small groups and policy failure*. Amsterdam: Swets & Zeitlinger.

Thibaut, J. W., & Kelley, H. H. (1959). *The social psychology of groups*. New York: Wiley.

Thibaut, J. W., & Rieken, W. H. (1955). Some determinants and consequences of the perception of social causality. *Journal of Personality, 24*, 114–133.

Thomas, J. R., & French, K. E. (1985). Gender differences across age in motor performance: A meta-analysis. *Psychological Bulletin, 98*, 260–282.

Thomas, M. H. (1982). Physiological arousal, exposure to a relatively lengthy aggressive film, and aggressive behavior. *Journal of Research in Personality, 16*, 72–81.

Thompson, D. J., & Baxter, J. C. (1973). Interpersonal spacing in two-person cross-cultural interactions. *Man–Environment Systems, 3*, 115–117.

Thompson, W. C., Cowan, C. L., Ellsworth, P. C., & Harrington, J. C. (1984). Death penalty attitudes and conviction proneness: The translation of attitudes into verdicts. *Law and Human Behavior, 8*, 95–113.

Thoreau, H. D. (1840, June 27). *The writings of Henry David Thoreau, Journal I, 1837–1846*. Boston: Houghton Mifflin.

Thorne, R., Hall, R., & Munro-Clark, M. (1982). Attitudes toward detached houses, terraces, and apartments: Some current pressures towards less preferred but more accessible alternatives. In P. Bart, A. Chen, & G. Francescato (Eds.), *Knowledge for design: Proceedings of the 13th Environmental Design Research Association Conference* (pp. 435–448). Washington, DC: Environmental Design Research.

Thurstone, L. L. (1928). Attitudes can be measured. *American Journal of Sociology, 33,* 529–554.

Thurstone, L. L., & Chave, E. J. (1929). *The measurement of attitude.* Chicago: University of Chicago Press.

Tice, D. M., & Baumeister, R. F. (1985). Masculinity inhibits helping in emergencies: Personality does predict the bystander effect. *Journal of Personality and Social Psychology, 49,* 420–428.

Time. (1981, March 9). Prince Charles picks a bride, pp. 66–67.

Time. (1984, March 26). Marian and the elders, p. 70.

Time. (1986, March 10). "A serious deficiency": The Rogers commission faults NASA's "flawed" decision making process, pp. 38–42.

Time. (1986, March 24). Painful legacies of a lost mission, pp. 28–29.

Time. (1986, June 9). Fixing NASA, pp. 14–25.

Time. (1988, October 31). "They lied to us": Unsafe, aging U.S. weapons plants are stirring fear and disillusion, pp. 60–65.

Time. (1992, June 1). Summit to save the earth, pp. 40–58.

Time. (1992, November 30). Separate lives, pp. 52–58.

Time. (1993, January 18). 'Til death do us part, pp. 38–45.

Time. (1993, March 15). More harm than good, pp. 40–45.

Tipton, R. M., & Browning, S. (1972). The influence of age and obesity on helping behavior. *British Journal of Social and Clinical Psychology, 11,* 404–406.

Toch, H., & Lizotte, A. J. (1992). Research and policy: The case of gun control. In P. Suedfeld & P. E. Tetlock (Eds.), *Psychology and social policy.* New York: Hemisphere.

Tocqueville, A. de (1856). *The old regime and the French Revolution.* New York: Harper Brothers. (The Stuart Gilbert translation, Garden City, NY: Doubleday, 1955).

Tompkins, S. S. (1965). The psychology of being right—and left. *Transaction, 3,* 23–27.

Tompkins, S. S. (1987). Script theory. In J. Aronoff, A. I. Rubin, & R. A. Zucker (Eds.), *The emergence of personality.* New York: Springer.

Tooby, J., & Cosmides, L. (1990). On the universality of human nature and the uniqueness of the individual: The role of genetics and adaptation. *Journal of Personality, 58,* 17–68.

Tooley, V., Brigham, J. C, Maass, A., & Bothwell, R. K. (1987). Facial recognition: Weapon effect and attentional focus. *Journal of Applied Social Psychology, 17,* 845–849.

Torrance, E. P. (1955). Some consequences of power differences on decision making in permanent and temporary three-man groups. In A. P. Hare, E. F. Gorgotta, & R. F. Bales (Eds.), *Small groups: Studies in social interaction.* New York: Knopf.

Touhey, J. C. (1974). Effects of additional women professionals in ratings of occupational prestige and desirability. *Journal of Personality and Social Psychology, 29,* 86–89.

Tracy, A. P., & Oskamp. S. (1983–1984). Relationships among ecologically responsible behaviors. *Journal of Environmental Systems, 13,* 115–126.

Trafimow, D., Triandis, H. C., & Goto, S. G. (1991). Some tests of the distinction between the private self and the collective self. *Journal of Personality and Social Psychology, 60,* 649–655.

Travis, L. E. (1925). The effect of a small audience upon eye–hand coordination. *Journal of Abnormal and Social Psychology, 20,* 142–146.

Triandis, H. C. (1977). *Interpersonal behavior.* Monterey, CA: Brooks/Cole.

Triandis, H. C. (1978). Some universals of social behavior. *Personality and Social Psychology Bulletin, 4,* 1–16.

Triandis, H. C. (1989). The self and social behavior in different cultures. *Psychological Review, 96,* 506–520.

Triplett, N. (1897). The dynamogenic factors in pacemaking and competition. *American Journal of Psychology, 9,* 507–533.

Trivers, R. L. (1971). The evolution of reciprocal altruism. *Quarterly Review of Biology, 46,* 35–57.

Trivers, R. L. (1972). Parental investment and sexual selection. In B. Campbell (Ed.), *Sexual selection and the descent of man.* Chicago: Aldine.

Trivers, R. L. (1983). The evolution of cooperation. In D. L. Bridgeman (Ed.), *The nature of prosocial development.* New York: Academic Press.

Truscott, J. C., Parmelee, P., & Werner, C. (1977). Plate touching in restaurants: Preliminary observations of a food-related marking behavior in humans. *Personality and Social Psychology Bulletin, 3,* 425–428.

Tuan, Y. (1974). *Topophilia: A study in environmental perception, attitude, and values.* Englewood Cliffs, NJ: Prentice-Hall.

Tunnell, G. (1980). Intraindividual consistency in personality assessment: The effects of self-monitoring. *Journal of Personality, 48,* 220–232.

Turnbull, C. M. (1972). *The mountain people.* New York: Simon & Schuster.

Turner, C. W., & Layton, J. F. (1976). Verbal imagery and connotation as memory-induced mediators of aggressive behavior. *Journal of Personality and Social Psychology, 33,* 755–763.

Turner, C. W., & Leyens, J. P. (1992). The weapons effect revisited: The effects of firearms on aggressive behavior. In P. Suedfeld & P. E. Tetlock (Eds.), *Psychology and social policy.* New York: Hemisphere.

Turner, J. C. (1978). Social categorization and social discrimination in the minimal group situation. In H. Tajfel (Ed.), *Differentiaton between social groups.* London: Academic Press.

Turner, J. C., Hogg, M. A., Oakes, P. J., Reicher, S. D., & Wetherell, M. S. (1987). *Rediscovering the social Group: A self-categorization theory.* Oxford, England: Basil Blackwell.

Turner, M. E., Pratkanis, A. R., Probasco, P., & Leve, C. (1992). Threat, cohesion, and group effectiveness: Testing a social identity maintenance perspective in groupthink. *Journal of Personality and Social Psychology, 63,* 781–796.

Turner, R. J. (1981). Social support as a contingency in psychological well-being. *Journal of Personality and Social Psychology, 22,* 357–367.

Tversky, A., & Kahneman, D. (1973). Availability: A heuristic for judging frequency and probability. *Cognitive Psychology, 5,* 207–232.

Tversky, A., & Kahneman, D. (1974). Judgment under uncertainty: Heuristics and biases. *Science, 185,* 1124–1131.

Tversky, A., & Kahneman, D. (1981). The framing of decisions and the psychology of choice. *Science, 211,* 453–458.

Tversky, A., & Kahneman, D. (1982). Judgments of and by representativeness. In D. Kahneman, P. Slovic, & A. Tversky (Eds.), *Judgment under uncertainty: Heuristics and biases.* New York: Cambridge University Press.

TV Guide. (1992, August 22–28). Violence on TV, pp. 9–23.

Tyler, T. R., & Lind, A. (1992). A relational model of authority in groups. In M. Zanna (Ed.), *Advances in experimental social psychology* (Vol. 25). San Diego: Academic Press.

Ulrich, R., & Azrin, N. H. (1962). Reflexive fighting in response to aversive stimulation. *Journal of the Experimental Analysis of Behavior, 5,* 511–520.

Ulrich, R. E., Johnson, M., Richardson, J., & Wolff, P. (1963). The operant conditioning of fighting behavior in rats. *Psychological Record, 13,* 465–470.

Ulschak, P. L., Nathanson, L., & Gillan, P. G. (1981). *Small group problem solving.* Reading, MA: Addison-Wesley.

Underwood, B., & Moore, B. (1982). Perspective-taking and altruism. *Psychological Bulletin, 91,* 143–173.

Unger, R. K. (1979). Toward a redefinition of sex and gender. *American Psychologist, 34,* 1085–1094.

Unger, R. K. (Ed.). (1989). *Representations: Social constructions of gender.* Amityville, NY: Baywood.

United Nations: Demographic Yearbook. (1986). New York: United Nations.

U.S. Department of Education. (1992). *Digest of Educational Statistics, 1992.* Washington, DC: U.S. Government Printing Office.

U.S. Department of Health and Human Services. (1981). The health consequences of smoking: The changing cigarette: A report of the Surgeon General. Washington, DC: Public Health Service.

U.S. Department of Health and Human Services. (1984). *Annual summary of births, deaths, marriages, and divorces: United States, 1983.* (DHHS Publication No. PHS 84-1120). Washington, DC: U.S. Government Printing Office.

U.S. Department of Health and Human Services. (1989). *Reducing the health consequences of smoking. 25 years of progress: A report of the Surgeon General.* (Publication No. PHS89-8411). Rockville, MD: author.

U.S. Department of Labor, Women's Bureau. (1983). *Times of change: 1983 handbook on women workers.*

U. S. News & World Report. (1992, June 8). The Rio Summit: The poverty tour, p. 14.

Vallacher, R. R., & Wegner, D. M. (1989). Levels of personal agency: Individual variation in action identification. *Journal of Personality and Social Psychology, 57,* 660–671.

Vandell, D., & Fishbein, L. (1989). *Equitable treatment of girls and boys in the classroom.* American Association of Women Issue Brief. Washington, DC.

Vandenberg, S. G. (1972). Assortative mating, or who marries whom? *Behavior Genetics, 2,* 127–158.

Van den Putte, B. (1991). *20 years of the theory of reasoned action of Fishbein and Ajzen: A meta-analysis.* Unpublished manuscript, University of Amsterdam, The Netherlands.

Van Der Pligt, J., & Eiser, J. R. (1983). Actors' and observers' attributions, self-serving bias, and positivity. *European Journal of Social Psychology, 13,* 95–104.

Van Dyke, J. (1977). *Jury selection procedures.* Cambridge, MA: Ballinger.

Van Valey, T. L., Roof, W. C., & Wilcox, J. E. (1977). Trends in residential segregation: 1960–1970. *American Journal of Sociology, 82,* 826–844.

Vaughan, D. (1986). *Uncoupling.* New York: Vintage Books.

Veitch, R., DeWood, R., & Bosko, K. (1977). Radio news broadcasts: Their effect on interpersonal helping. *Sociometry, 40,* 383–386.

Vernon, P. E. (1964). *Personality assessment: A critical survey.* New York: Wiley.

Visher, C. A. (1987). Juror decision making: The importance of evidence. *Law and Human Behavior, 11,* 1–17.

Wadden, T. A., Foster, G. D., Brownell, K. D., & Finley, E. (1984). Self-concept in obese and normal-weight children. *Journal of Consulting and Clinical Psychology, 52,* 1104–1105.

Waitzkin, H. (1984). Doctor–patient communication: Clinical implications of social scientific research. *Journal of the American Medical Association, 252,* 81–101.

Waitzkin, H. (1985). Information giving in medical care. *Journal of Health and Social Behavior, 26,* 81–101.

Waitzkin, H., & Stoeckle, J. D. (1976). Information control and the micropolitics of health care: Summary of an ongoing research project. *Social Science and Medicine, 10,* 263–276.

Walker, K. E., & Woods, M. E. (1976). *Time use: A measure of household production of goods and services.* Washington, DC: American Home Economics Association.

Wall Street Journal. (1991, September 13). Survey of students shows tobacco use is not falling.

Wall Street Journal. (1992, February 20). Why activists fume at anti-smoking ads, p. B9.

Wall Street Journal. (1992, March 13). Study says teen-agers' smoking habits seem to be linked to heavy advertising, p. B8.

Wallace, J., & Sadalla, E. (1966). Behavioral consequences of transgressions: II. The effects of social recognition. *Journal of Experimental Research in Personality, 1,* 187–194.

Wallach, M. A., Kogan, N., & Bem, D. J. (1962). Group influence on individual risk taking. *Journal of Abnormal and Social Psychology, 65,* 75–86.

Waller, W. (1930, 1967). *The old love and the new: Divorce and readjustment.* Carbondale: Southern Illinois University Press.

Wallston, B. S., Alagna, S. W., DeVellis, B. M., & DeVellis, R. F. (1983). Social support and physical health. *Health Psychology, 2,* 367–391.

Wallston, K. A., & Wallston, B. S. (1982). Who is responsible for your health? The construct of health locus of control. In G. S. Sanders & J. Suls (Eds.), *Social psychology of health and illness.* Hillsdale, NJ: Erlbaum.

Wallston, K. A., Wallston, B.S., & DeVellis, R. (1978). Development of the multidimensional health locus of control (MHLC) scales. *Health Education Monographs, 6,* 161–170.

Wallston, B. S., Wallston, K. A., Kaplan, G. D., & Maides, S. A. (1976). Development and validation of the health locus of control (HLC) scale. *Journal of Consulting and Clinical Psychology, 44,* 580–585.

Walster, E. (1965). The effect of self-esteem on romantic liking. *Journal of Experimental Social Psychology, 1,* 184–197.

Walster, E., Aronson, E. Abrahams, D., & Rottman, L. (1966). Importance of physical attractiveness in dating behavior. *Journal of Personality and Social Psychology, 4,* 508–516.

Walster, E., & Berscheid, E. (1971, June). Adrenaline makes the heart grow fonder. *Psychology Today,* pp. 46–50.

Walster, E., & Walster, G. W. (1978). *A new look at love.* Reading, MA: Addison-Wesley.

Walster, E., Walster, G. W., & Berscheid, E. (1978). *Equity: Theory and research.* Boston: Allyn & Bacon.

Walters, R. H., & Brown, M. (1963). Studies of reinforcement of aggression: III. Transfer of responses to an interpersonal situation. *Child Development, 34,* 536–571.

Wann, D. L., & Branscombe, N. R. (1990). Person perception when aggressive or nonaggressive sports are primed. *Aggressive Behavior, 16,* 27–32.

Wardle, M. G., Gloss, M. R., & Gloss, D. S., III. (1987). Response differences. In M. A. Baker (Ed.), *Sex differences in human performance.* Chichester, England: Wiley.

Warren, D. I. (1978). Exploration in neighborhood differentiation. *Sociological Quarterly, 19,* 310–331.

Washington Post. (1991, November 19). Fatal attraction: Teenagers and tobacco, Health Section.

Washington Post. (1992, September 22). They're on board the ships, but it's still a man's world, p. B1.

Watson, D. (1982). The actor and the observer: How are their perceptions of causality divergent? *Psychological Bulletin, 92,* 682–700.

Watson, D., & Pennebaker, J. W. (1989). Health complaints, stress, and distress: Exploring the central role of negative affectivity. *Psychological Review, 96,* 234–254.

Watson, O. M. (1970). *Proxemic behavior: A cross-cultural study.* The Hague: Mouton.

Watson, O. M., & Graves, T. D. (1966). Quantitative research in proxemic behavior. *American Anthropologist, 68,* 971–985.

Watson, R. I. Jr. (1973). Investigation into deindividuation using a cross-cultural survey technique. *Journal of Personality and Social Psychology, 25,* 342–345.

Webb, E. J., Campbell, D. T., Schwartz, R. D., Sechrest, L., & Grove, J. (1981). *Nonreactive measures in the social sciences.* Boston: Houghton Mifflin.

Weber, R., & Crocker, J. (1983). Cognitive processes in the revision of stereotypic beliefs. *Journal of Personality and Social Psychology, 45,* 961–977.

Webster, T. M., King, H. N., & Kassin, S. M. (1991). Voices from an empty chair: The missing witness inference and the jury. *Law and Human Behavior, 15,* 31–42.

Weed, J. A. (1980). National estimates of marriage dissolution and survival. *Vital and Health Statistics,* series 3, no. 19.

Wegner, D. M., & Erber, R. (1992). The hyperaccessibility of suppressed thoughts. *Journal of Personality and Social Psychology, 63,* 903–912.

Wegner, D. M., Schneider, D. J., Carter, S. R., & White, T. L. (1987). Paradoxical effects of thought suppression. *Journal of Personality and Social Psychology, 53,* 5–13.

Wegner, D. M., & Vallacher, R. R. (Eds.). (1980). *The self in social psychology.* New York: Oxford University Press.

Wegner, D. M., & Vallacher, R. R. (1986). Action identification. In R. M. Sorrentino & E. T. Higgins (Eds.), *Handbook of motivation and cognition: Foundations of social behavior.* New York: Guilford.

Weigel, C., Wertlieb, D., & Feldstein, M. (1989). Perceptions of control, competence, and contingency as influences on the stress–behavior symptom relation in school-age children. *Journal of Personality and Social Psychology, 56,* 456–464.

Weigel, R., Wiser, P., & Cook, S. (1975). The impact of cooperative learning experiences on cross-ethnic relations and attitudes. *Journal of Social Issues, 31,* 219–243.

Weigel, R. H., & Howes, P. W. (1985). Conceptions of racial prejudice: Symbolic racism revisited. *Journal of Social Issues, 41,* 124–132.

Weiner, B. (1985). "Spontaneous" causal thinking. *Psychological Bulletin, 97,* 74–84.

Weiner, B., Frieze, I., Kukla, A., Reed, L., Rest, S., & Rosenbaum, R. M. (1972). Perceiving the causes of success and failure. In E. Jones, D. Kanouse, H. Kelley, R. Nisbett, S. Valins, & B. Weiner (Eds.), *Attribution: Perceiving the causes of behavior.* Morristown, NJ: General Learning Press.

Weiner, H. (1977). *Psychobiology and human disease.* New York: American Elsevier.

Weiss, R. S. (1975). *Marital separation.* New York: Basic Books.

Wells, G. L. (1993). What do we know about eyewitness identification? *American Psychologist, 48,* 553–571.

Wells, G. L., & Gavanski, I. (1989). Mental simulation of causality. *Journal of Personality and Social Psychology, 56,* 161–169.

Wells, G. L., & Leippe, M. R. (1981). How do triers of fact infer the accuracy of eyewitness identification? Memory for peripheral detail can be misleading. *Journal of Applied Psychology, 66,* 440–448.

Wells, G. L., Lindsay, R. C. L., & Ferguson, T. J. (1979). Accuracy, confidence, and juror perceptions in eyewitness identification. *Journal of Applied Psychology, 64,* 440–448.

Wells, G. L., & Murray, D. M. (1984). Eyewitness confidence. In G. L. Wells & E. F. Loftus (Eds.), *Eyewitness testimony: Psychological perspectives.* New York: Cambridge University Press.

Werner, C. M., Brown, B. B., & Damron, G. (1981). Territorial marking in the game arcade. *Journal of Personality and Social Psychology, 41,* 1094–1104.

West, S. G., Gunn, S. P., & Chernicky, P. (1975). Ubiquitous Watergate: An attributional analysis. *Journal of Personality and Social Psychology, 32,* 55–65.

Weyant, J. M. (1978). Effects of mood states, costs, and benefits on helping. *Journal of Personality and Social Psychology, 36,* 1169–1176.

Wheeler, L. (1966). Toward a theory of behavioral contagion. *Psychological Review, 73,* 179–192.

Wheeler, L., & Caggiula, A. R. (1966). The contagion of aggression. *Journal of Experimental Social Psychology, 2,* 1–10.

White, G. L., Fishbein, S., & Rutsein, J. (1981). Passionate love and the misattribution of arousal. *Journal of Personality and Social Psychology, 41,* 56–62.

White, G. L., & Knight, T. D. (1984). Misattribution of arousal and attraction: Effects of salience of explanations for arousal. *Journal of Experimental Social Psychology, 20,* 55–64.

White, J. D., & Carlston, D. E. (1983). Consequences of schemata for attention, impressions, and recall in complex social interactions. *Journal of Personality and Social Psychology, 45,* 538–549.

White, L. A. (1979). Erotica and aggression: The influence of sexual arousal, positive affect, and negative affect on aggressive behavior. *Journal of Personality and Social Psychology, 37,* 591–601.

White, T. H. (1961). *The making of the president, 1960.* New York: Atheneum.

Whiting, J. W. M., & Whiting, B. B. (1973). Altruistic and egoistic behavior in six cultures. In L. Nader & T. Maretzki (Eds.), *Cultural illness and health.* Washington, DC: American Anthropological Association.

Whitley, B. E. Jr. (1987). The effects of discredited eyewitness testimony: A meta-analysis. *Journal of Social Psychology, 127,* 209–214.

Whitley, B. E. Jr., McHugh, M. C., & Frieze, I. H. (1986). Assessing the theoretical models of sex differences in causal attribution. In J. S. Hyde & M. C. Linn (Eds.), *The psychology of gender: Advances through meta-analysis.* Baltimore: Johns Hopkins University Press.

Whyte, W. H. (1943). *Street corner society.* Chicago: University of Chicago Press.

Whyte, W. H. (1956). *The organization man.* New York: Simon & Schuster.

Wicker, A. W. (1969). Attitudes vs. action: The relation of verbal and overt behavioral responses to attitude objects. *Journal of Social Issues, 25(4),* 41–78.

Wicklund, R. A. (1982). How society uses self-awareness. In J. Suls (Ed.), *Psychological perspectives on the self* (Vol. 1). Hillsdale, NJ: Erlbaum.

Widgery, R. N. (1982). Satisfaction with the quality of urban life: A predictive model. *American Journal of Community Psychology, 10,* 37–48.

Widiger, T. A., & Frances, A. (1985). Axis II personality disorders: Diagnostic and treatment issues. *Hospital and Community Psychiatry, 36,* 619–627.

Widiger, T. A., & Settle, S. A. (1987). Broverman et al. revisited: An artificial sex bias. *Journal of Personality and Social Psychology, 53,* 463–469.

Widom, C. S. (1989). Does violence beget violence? A critical examination of the literature. *Psychological Bulletin, 106,* 3–28.

Wiebe, D. J. (1991). Hardiness and stress moderation: A test of proposed mechanisms. *Journal of Personality and Social Psychology, 60,* 89–99.

Wiebe, D. J., & Williams, P. G. (1992). Hardiness and health: A social psychophysiological perspective on stress and adaptation. *Journal of Social and Clinical Psychology, 11,* 238–262.

Wiener, N. (1948). *Cybernetics: Control and communication in the animal and the machine.* Cambridge, MA: MIT Press.

Wilcox, B. L. (1987). Pornography, social science, and politics: When research and ideology collide. *American Psychologist, 42,* 941–943.

Wilder, D. A. (1977). Perception of groups, size of opposition, and social influence. *Journal of Experimental Social Psychology, 13,* 253–268.

Wilder, D. A. (1984). Intergroup contact: The typical member and the exception to the rule. *Journal of Experimental Social Psychology, 20,* 177–194.

Wilke, H., & Lanzetta J. T. (1970). The obligation to help: The effects of amount of prior help on subsequent helping behavior. *Journal of Experimental Social Psychology, 6,* 488–493.

Williams, B. (1979). *Report of the committee on obscenity and film censorship.* London: Her Majesty's Stationery Office.

Williams, J. E., & Best, D. L. (1982). *Measuring sex stereotypes: A thirty-nation study.* Beverly Hills, CA: Sage.

Williams, J. E., & Best, D. L. (1990). *Sex and psyche: Gender and self viewed cross-culturally.* Newbury Park, CA: Sage.

Williams, K. D., & Karau, S. J. (1991). Social loafing and social comparison: The effects of expectation of co-worker performance. *Journal of Personality and Social Psychology, 61,* 570–581.

Williams, K. D., Loftus, E. F., & Deffenbacher, K. A. (1992). Eyewitness evidence and testimony. In D. K. Kagehiro & W. S. Laufer (Eds.), *Handbook of psychology and law.* New York: Springer-Verlag.

Williams, P. G., Wiebe, D. J., & Smith, T. W. (1992). Coping processes as mediators of the relationship between hardiness and health. *Journal of Behavioral Medicine, 15,* 237–255.

Willis, R. H. (1965). Conformity, independence, and anticonformity. *Human Relations, 18,* 373–388.

Willis, R. H., & Levine, J. M. (1976). Interpersonal influence and conformity. In B. Seidenberg & A. Snadowski (Eds.), *Social psychology: An introduction.* New York: Free Press.

Wills, T. A. (1981). Downward comparison principles in social psychology. *Psychological Bulletin, 90,* 245–271.

Wills, T. A. (1991). Similarity and self-esteem in downward comparison. In J. Suls & T. A. Wills (Eds.), *Social comparison: Contemporary theory and research.* Hillsdale, NJ: Erlbaum.

Wilson, E. O. (1975). *Sociobiology: The new synthesis.* Cambridge: Harvard University Press.

Wilson, E. O. (1978). *On human nature.* Cambridge, MA: Harvard University Press.

Wilson, F. D., & Taeuber, K. E. (1978). Residential and school desegregation: Some tests of the association. In F. D. Bean & W. P. Frisbie (Eds.), *The demography of racial and ethnic groups.* New York: Academic Press.

Wilson, G. (1977). Introversion/extraversion. In T. Blass (Ed.), *Personality variables in social behavior.* Hillsdale, NJ: Erlbaum.

Wilson, T. D., Dunn, D. S., Kraft, D., & Lisle, D. J. (1989). Introspection, attitude change, and attitude–behavior consistency: The disruptive effects of explaining why we feel the way we do. In L. Berkowitz (Ed.), *Advances in experimental social psychology* (Vol. 22). San Diego: Academic Press.

Wilson, T. D., Hull, J. B., & Johnson, J. (1981). Awareness and self-perception: Verbal reports on internal states. *Journal of Personality and Social Psychology, 40,* 53–71.

Wilson, T. D., & Linville, P. W. (1982). Improving the academic performance of college freshmen: Attribution therapy revisited. *Journal of Personality and Social Psychology, 42,* 367–376.

Wilson, T. D., & Linville, P. W. (1985). Improving the performance of college freshmen with attributional techniques. *Journal of Personality and Social Psychology, 49,* 287–293.

Wilson, W., & Miller, H. (1968). Repetition, order of presentation, and timing of arguments as determinants of opinion change. *Journal of Personality and Social Psychology, 9,* 184–188.

Wimer, S., & Kelley, H. H. (1982). An investigation of the dimensions of causal attribution. *Journal of Personality and Social Psychology, 43,* 1129–1162.

Winch, R. (1958). *Mate-selection: A study of complementary needs.* New York: Harper.

Wish, M., Deutsch, M., & Kaplan, S. J. (1976). Perceived dimensions of interpersonal relations. *Journal of Personality and Social Psychology, 33,* 409–420.

Wishner, J. (1960). Reanalysis of "impression of personality." *Psychological Review, 67,* 96–112.

Wissler, R. L., & Saks, M. J. (1985). On the inefficacy of limiting instructions: When jurors use prior conviction evidence to decide on guilt. *Law and Human Behavior, 9,* 37–48.

Wolf, S., & Montgomery, D. A. (1977). Effects of inadmissible evidence and level of judicial admonishment to disregard on the judgments of mock jurors. *Journal of Applied Social Personality, 7,* 205–219.

Wolinski, F. D. (1978). Assessing the effects of predisposing, enabling, and illness–morbidity characteristics on health service utilization. *Journal of Health and Social Behavior, 19,* 384–396.

Wood, J. V., Taylor, S. E., & Lichtman, R. R. (1985). Social comparison in adjustment to breast cancer. *Journal of Personality and Social Psychology, 49,* 1169–1183.

Wood, W. (1987). Meta-analytic review of sex differences in group performance. *Psychological Bulletin, 102,* 53–71.

Wood, W., Wong, F. Y., & Cachere, J. G. (1991). Effects of media violence on viewers' aggression in unconstrained social interaction. *Psychological Bulletin, 109,* 371–383.

Woods, P. J., & Burns, J. (1984). Type A behavior and illness in general. *Journal of Behavioral Medicine, 7,* 411–415.

Woods, P. J., Morgan, B. T., Day, B. W., Jefferson, W., & Harris, C. (1984). Findings on a relationship between type A behavior and headaches. *Journal of Behavioral Medicine, 7,* 277–286.

Worchel, S. (1992). Beyond a commodity theory analysis of censorship: When abundance and personalism enhance scarcity effects. *Basic and Applied Social Psychology, 13,* 79–93.

World Almanac. (1988). New York: Pharos Books.

World Almanac. (1992). New York: World Almanac.

Worringham, D. J., & Messick, D. M. (1983). Social facilitation of running: An unobtrusive study. *Journal of Social Psychology, 121,* 23–29.

Wright, J. C., & Dawson, V. L. (1988). Person perception and the bounded rationality of social judgment. *Journal of Personality and Social Psychology, 55,* 780–794.

Wright, J. C., & Mischel, W. (1987). A conditional approach to dispositional constructs: The local predictability of social behavior. *Journal of Personality and Social Psychology, 53,* 1159–1177.

Writers' War Board (1945). *How writers perpetuate stereotypes.* New York: author.

Wyer, R. S., & Srull, T. K. (1980). The processing of social stimulus information: A conceptual integration. In R. Hastie, T. M. Ostrom, E. B. Ebbesen, R. S. Wyer, D. Hamilton, & D. E. Carlston (Eds.), *The cognitive basis of social perception.* Hillsdale, NJ: Erlbaum.

Wyer, R. S., Srull, T. K., & Gordon, S. E. (1984). The effects of predicting a person's behavior on subsequent trait judgments. *Journal of Experimental Social Psychology, 20,* 29–46.

Wylie, R. (1979). *The self-concept* (Vol. 2): *Theory and research on selected topics.* Lincoln: University of Nebraska Press.

Wynne-Edwards, V. C. (1962). *Animal dispersion in relation to social behavior.* Edinburgh-London: Oliver and Boyd.

Yancey, W. L. (1971). Architecture, interaction, and social control: The case of a large-scale public housing project. *Environment and Behavior, 3,* 3–21.

Yang, N., & Linz, D. (1990). Movie ratings and the content of adult videos: The sex–violence ratio. *Journal of Communication, 40,* 28–42.

Yarrow, M. R., Scott, P. M., & Waxler, C. Z. (1973). Learning concern for others. *Developmental Psychology, 8,* 240–260.

Yinon, Y., Sharon, I., Gonen, Y., & Adam, R. (1982). Escape from responsibility and help in emergencies among persons alone or within groups. *European Journal of Social Psychology, 12,* 301–305.

Young, W. R. (1977, February). There's a girl on the tracks! *Reader's Digest,* pp. 91–95.

Yu, E. S. H. (1974). Achievement motive, familism, and *hsiao:* A replication of McClelland-Winterbottom studies. *Dissertation Abstracts International, 35,* 593A. (University Microfilms No. 74-14, 942).

Zajonc, R. B. (1965). Social facilitation. *Science, 149,* 269–274.

Zajonc, R. B. (1968). Attitudinal effects of mere exposure. *Journal of Personality and Social Psychology,* Monograph Supplement 9, 1–27.

Zajonc, R. B. (1980). Compresence. In P. B. Paulus (Ed.), *Psychology of group influence.* Hillsdale, NJ: Erlbaum.

Zajonc, R. B., Heingartner, A., & Herman, E. M. (1969). Social enhancement and impairment of performance in the cockroach. *Journal of Personality and Social Psychology, 13,* 83–92.

Zajonc, R.B., Shaver, P., Tavris, C., & Kreveld, D. V. (1972). Exposure, satiation, and stimulus discriminability. *Journal of Personality and Social Psychology, 21,* 270–280.

Zanna, M. P., & Hamilton, D. L. (1972). Attribute dimension and patterns of trait inferences. *Psychonomic Science, 27,* 353–354.

Zanna, M. P., & Hamilton, D. L. (1977). Further evidence for meaning change in impression formation. *Journal of Experimental Social Psychology, 13,* 224–238.

Zanna, M. P., & Pack, S. J. (1975). On the self-fulfilling nature of apparent sex differences in behavior. Journal of Experimental Social Psychology, 11, 583–591.

Zanna, M. P., Kiesler, C. A., & Pilkonis, P. A. (1970). Positive and negative attitudinal affect established by classical conditioning. *Journal of Personality and Social Psychology, 13,* 224–238.

Zdep, S. M., & Oakes, W. I. (1967). Reinforcement of leadership behavior in group discussion. *Journal of Experimental Social Psychology, 3,* 310–320.

Zebrowitz, L. A. (1990). *Social perception.* Pacific Grove, CA: Brooks/Cole.

Zebrowitz, L. A., Brownlow, S., & Olson, K. (1992). Baby talk to the babyfaced. *Journal of Nonverbal Behavior, 16,* 143–158.

Zebrowitz-McArthur, L. (1988). Person perception in cross-cultural perspective. In M. H. Bond (Ed.), *The cross-cultural challenge to social psychology.* Newbury Park, CA: Sage.

Zegans, L. S. (1982). Stress and the development of somatic disorders. In L. Goldberger & S. Breznitz (Eds.), *Handbook of stress: Theoretical and clinical aspects.* New York: Free Press.

Zehner, R. B. (1972). Neighborhood and community satisfaction: A report on new towns and less planned suburbs. In J. F. Wohlwill & D. H. Carson (Eds.), *Environment and the social sciences: Perspectives and applications.* Washington, DC: American Psychological Association.

Zeisel, H. (1971). . . . And then there was none: The diminution of the federal jury. *University of Chicago Law Review, 38,* 710–724.

Zeisel, H., & Diamond, S. (1978). The effect of peremptory challenges on jury and verdict: An experiment in a federal district court. *Stanford Law Review, 30,* 491–531.

Zellinger, D. A., Fromkin, H. L., Speller, D. E., & Kohm, C. A. (1974). *A commodity theory analysis of the effects of age restrictions on pornographic materials* (Paper No. 400). Lafayette, IN: Purdue University Institute for Research in the Behavioral, Economic, and Management Sciences.

Zillman, D. (1971). Excitation transfer in communication-mediated aggressive behavior. *Journal of Experimental Social Psychology, 7,* 417–434.

Zillman, D. (1979). *Hostility and aggression.* Hillsdale, NJ: Erlbaum.

Zillman, D. (1983). Arousal and aggression. In R. G. Geen & E. Donnerstein (Eds.), *Aggression: Theoretical and empirical reviews.* New York: Academic Press.

Zillman, D. (1988). Cognition–excitation interdependencies in aggressive behavior. *Aggressive Behavior, 14,* 51–64.

Zillman, D., & Bryant, J. (1974). Effect of residual excitation on the emotional response to provocation and delayed aggressive behavior. *Journal of Personality and Social Psychology, 30,* 782–791.

Zillman, D., Hoyt, J. L., & Day, K. D. (1974). Strength and duration of aggressive, violent, and erotic communications on subsequent behavior. *Communication Research, 1,* 286–306.

Zillman, D., Johnson, R. C., & Day, K.D. (1974). Attribution of apparent arousal and proficiency of recovery from sympathetic activation affecting activation transfer to aggressive behavior. *Journal of Experimental Social Psychology, 10,* 503–515.

Zimbardo, P. G. (1970). The human choice: individuation, reason, and order versus deindividuation, impulse, and chaos. In W. J. Arnold & D. Levine (Eds.), *Nebraska symposium on motivation, 1969.* Lincoln: University of Nebraska Press.

Zimbardo, P. G. (1972, April). Psychology of imprisonment. *Transaction/Society,* pp. 4–8.

Zimbardo, P. G. (1977). *Shyness: What it is and what to do about it.* Reading, MA: Addison-Wesley.

Zimbardo, P. G. (1986). The Stanford Shyness Project. In W. H. Jones, J. M. Cheek, & S. R. Briggs (Eds.), *Shyness: Perspectives on research and treatment.* New York: Plenum.

Zimbardo, P. G., Weisenberg, M., Firestone, I., & Levy, B. (1965). Communicator effectiveness in producing public conformity and private attitude change. *Journal of Personality, 33,* 233–255.

Zirkel, S., & Cantor, N. (1990). Personal construal of life tasks: Those who struggle for independence. *Journal of Personality and Social Psychology, 58,* 172–185.

Zuckerman, M. (1978). Actions and occurrences in Kelley's cube. *Journal of Personality and Social Psychology, 36,* 647–656.

Zuckerman, M., Bernieri, F., Koestner, R., & Rosenthal, R. (1989). To predict some of the people some of the time: In search of moderators. *Journal of Personality and Social Psychology, 57,* 279–293.

Zuckerman, M., DePaulo, B. M., & Rosenthal, R. (1981). Verbal and nonverbal communication in deception. In L. Berkowitz (Ed.), *Advances in experimental social psychology* (Vol. 14). New York: Academic Press.

Zuckerman, M., Koestner, R., DeBoy, T., Garcia, T., Maresca, B. C., & Sartoris, J. M. (1988). To predict some of the people some of the time: A reexamination of the moderator variable approach in personality theory. *Journal of Personality and Social Psychology, 54,* 1006–1019.

Zuckier, H. (1982). The role of the correlation and the dispersion of predictor variables in the use of nondiagnostic information. *Journal of Personality and Social Psychology, 43,* 1163–1175.

AUTHOR INDEX

SUBJECT INDEX

References to figures, tables, photographs, and illustrations are printed in italic type

CREDITS

Chapter 1: 1: Excerpt from *Time,* March 15, 1993. Copyright 1993 Time Inc. Reprinted by permission. **Chapter 3: 70:** Figure 3.1 adapted from O. P. John, "The Big Five Factor Taxonomy: Dimensions of Personality in the Natural Language and in Questionnaire," in L. A. Pervin (Ed.), *Handbook of Personality: Theory and Research,* 80. Copyright 1990 by The Guilford Press. Adapted by permission; **91:** Figure 3.6 from "Culture and the Self: Some Implications for Cognition, Emotion, and Motivation," by H. R. Markus, and S. Kitayama, 1991, *Psychological Review, 98,* 224-253. Copyright © 1991 by the American Psychological Association. Reprinted by permission of the author; **98:** Figure 3.10 adapted from "Public and Private Self-Consciousness: Assessment and Theory," by A. Fenigstein, M. R. Scheier, & A. H. Buss, 1975, *Journal of Consulting and Clinical Psychology, 43,* 522-527. Copyright 1975 by the American Psychological Association. Reprinted by permission of the author. **Chapter 4: 115:** Excerpt from *Newsweek,* October 21, 1991. © 1991, Newsweek, Inc. All rights reserved. Reprinted by permission; **137:** Figure 4.2 from "A Multidimensional Approach to the Structure of Personality Impressions," by S. Rosenburg, C. Nelson, and P. S. Vivekanathan, 1968, *Journal of Personality and Social Psychology, 9,* 283-294. Copyright 1968 by the American Psychological Association. Reprinted by permission of the author. **Chapter 5: 157:** The excerpt is reprinted courtesy of SPORTS ILLUSTRATED from the November 18, 1991 issue. Copyright © 1991, Time Inc. "Like One of the Family," by Leigh Montville. All Rights Reserved; **175:** Figure 5.5 adapted from "Point of View and Perception of Causality," by S. Taylor and Fiske, 1975, *Journal of Personality and Social Psychology, 32,* 439-445. Copyright 1975 by the American Psychological Association. Used with permission of Shelley Taylor; **185:** Figure 5.8 from *The Psychology of Rumor* by Gordon W. Allport and Leo Postman, copyright 1947 and renewed 1975 by Holt, Rinehart and Winston, Inc, reprinted by permission of the publisher. **Chapter 6: 210** (top excerpt), **213, 220, 225, 229:** Excerpts from *Mein Kampf* by Adolph HItler, translated by Ralph Manheim. Copyright 1943 and copyright © renewed 1971 by Houghton Mifflin Company. Reprinted by permission of Houghton Mifflin Company; **210:** Middle excerpt from *Newsweek,* November 18, 1991. © 1991, Newsweek, Inc. All rights reserved. Reprinted by permission; **210:** Bottom excerpt from *Newsweek,* April 27, 1992. © 1992, Newsweek, Inc. All rights reserved. Reprinted by permission; **216:** Figure 6.1 from "Can Functions be Measured? A New Perspective on the Functional Approach to Attitudes," by Gregory M. Herek, 1987, *Social Psychology Quarterly, 50,* 285-303. Copyright 1987 by American Sociological Association. Reprinted by permission; **217:** Excerpt from *Newsweek,* November 18, 1991. © 1991, Newsweek, Inc. All rights reserved. Reprinted by permission; **218:** Figure 6.2 adapted from "Attitudes toward Homosexuality: Assessment and Behavioral Consequences," by M. E. Kite and K. Deaux, 1986, *Basic and Applied Social Psychology, 7,* 137-162. Copyright 1986 by Lawrence Erlbaum Associates, Inc. Reprinted by permission; **225:** Excerpt from *Newsweek,* November 18, 1991. © 1991, Newsweek, Inc. All rights reserved. Reprinted by permission; **238:** Excerpt from *Newsweek,* April 27, 1992. © 1992, Newsweek, Inc. All rights reserved. Reprinted by permission; **239:** Excerpt from *Newsweek,* November 18, 1991. © 1991, Newsweek, Inc. All rights reserved. Reprinted by permission; **240:** Excerpt from *Newsweek,* November 18, 1991. © 1991, Newsweek, Inc. All rights reserved. Reprinted by permission; **242:** Excerpt from *Newsweek,* November 18, 1991. © 1991, Newsweek, Inc. All rights reserved. Reprinted by permission; **244:** Excerpt from *Newsweek,* November 4, 1991. © 1991, Newsweek, Inc. All rights reserved. Reprinted by permission; **246:** Figure 6.7 adapted from "The Need for Cognition," by J. T. Cacioppo and R. E. Petty, 1982, *Journal of Personality and Social Psychology, 42,* 116-131. Copyright 1982 by the American Psychological Association. Adapted by permission of John Cacioppo; **246:** Excerpt from *Newsweek,* November 18, 1991. © 1991, Newsweek, Inc. All rights reserved.

TO THE OWNER OF THIS BOOK

I hope that you have found *Introduction to Social Psychology, Second Edition,* useful. To improve this book in a later edition, would you take the time to complete this sheet and return it? Future students, Richard Lippa, and Brooks/Cole thank you for your help.

School and address: _____

Department: _____

Instructor's name: _____

_____

1. What I like most about this book is: _____

_____

2. What I like least about this book is: _____

_____

3. My general reaction to this book is: _____

_____

4. My reaction to the opening cases and how they were woven into the chapters was:

_____

_____

5. Were the figures, tables, and photographs "just right," "too much," or would more of them have made the concepts clearer? _____

_____

6. In the space below, or on a separate sheet of paper, please write specific suggestions for improving this book and anything else you'd care to share about your experience in using it.

_____

_____

_____

_____

_____

_____

Optional:

Your name: _____ Date: _____

May Brooks/Cole quote you, either in promotion for *Introduction to Social Psychology, Second Edition*, or in future publishing ventures?

Yes: _____ No: _____

Sincerely,

Richard Lippa

FOLD HERE

NO POSTAGE
NECESSARY
IF MAILED
IN THE
UNITED STATES

BUSINESS REPLY MAIL
FIRST CLASS   PERMIT NO. 358   PACIFIC GROVE, CA

POSTAGE WILL BE PAID BY ADDRESSEE

ATT: *Richard Lippa*

Brooks/Cole Publishing Company
511 Forest Lodge Road
Pacific Grove, California 93950-9968

FOLD HERE